LEGAL
MEDICINE

LEGAL MEDICINE

American College of Legal Medicine Textbook Committee

S. Sandy Sanbar, M.D., Ph.D., J.D., F.C.L.M.
Editor
Chairman (1984 to 2004),
Past President, ACLM (1989 to 1990)

Marvin H. Firestone, M.D., J.D., F.C.L.M.
Deputy Editor
Past President, ACLM (1993 to 1994)

Fillmore Buckner, M.D., J.D., F.C.L.M.
Past President, ACLM (2001 to 2002)

Allan Gibofsky, M.D., J.D., F.A.C.P., F.C.L.M.
Past President, ACLM (1994 to 1995)

Theodore R. LeBlang, J.D., F.C.L.M.
President, ACLM (2004 to 2005)

Jack W. Snyder, M.D., J.D., M.F.S., M.P.H., Ph.D., F.C.L.M.
Past President, ACLM (2000 to 2001)

Cyril H. Wecht, M.D., J.D., F.C.L.M.
Past President, ACLM (1969 to 1972)

Miles J. Zaremski, J.D., F.C.L.M.
Past President, ACLM (2002 to 2003)

Sixth Edition

American
College of
Legal
Medicine

 Mosby

An Affiliate of Elsevier

An Affiliate of Elsevier

The Curtis Center
Independence Square West
Philadelphia, Pennsylvania 19106

LEGAL MEDICINE, SIXTH EDITION   ISBN 0-323-02398-3
Copyright © 2004, Mosby, Inc. All rights reserved.

No part of this publication may be reproduced or transmitted in any form or by any means, electronic or
mechanical, including photocopying, recording, or any information storage and retrieval system, without
permission in writing from the publisher. Permissions may be sought directly from Elsevier's Health
Sciences Rights Department in Philadelphia, PA, USA: phone: (+1) 215 238 7869, fax: (+1) 215 238 2239,
e-mail: healthpermissions@elsevier.com. You may also complete your request on-line via the Elsevier Science
homepage (http://www.elsevier.com), by selecting 'Customer Support' and then 'Obtaining Permissions'.

NOTICE

Pharmacology is an ever-changing field. Standard safety precautions must be followed, but as new
research and clinical experience broaden our knowledge, changes in treatment and drug therapy may
become necessary or appropriate. Readers are advised to check the most current product information
provided by the manufacturer of each drug to be administered to verify the recommended dose, the method
and duration of administration, and contraindications. It is the responsibility of the licensed prescriber,
relying on experience and knowledge of the patient, to determine dosages and the best treatment for each
individual patient. Neither the publisher nor the editor assumes any liability for any injury and/or damage
to persons or property arising from this publication.

Previous editions copyrighted 1988, 1991, 1995, 1998, 2001.

Library of Congress Cataloging-in-Publication Data

Legal medicine/American College of Legal Medicine Textbook Committee, S. Sandy
    Sanbar . . . [et al.]—6th ed.
       p.   cm.
"American College of Legal Medicine."
    ISBN 0-323-02398-3
       1. Medical laws and legislation—United States.   I. Sanbar, Shafeek S.   II. American
College of Legal Medicine.

KF3821.L44   2004
344.7304′1—dc22   2003065177

Acquisitions Editor: Thomas H. Moore
Developmental Editor: Alison Nastasi
Project Manager: Daniel Clipner

Printed in the United States of America
Last digit is the print number: 9   8   7   6   5   4   3   2   1

Contributors

W
32.5
AA1
L47
2004

$148.50

4-2-04

53076290

STEPHANIE L. ANDERSON, M.D., J.D.
Research Assistant Professor,
Department of Pediatrics,
Bioethics Program,
University of Miami School of Medicine,
Miami, Florida
Chapter 23: The Human Genome Project

GEORGE J. ANNAS, J.D., M.P.H.
Edward R. Utley Professor and Chair,
Department of Health Law, Bioethics and Human Rights,
School of Public Health,
Boston University,
Boston, Massachusetts
*Chapter 1: Legal Medicine: Historical Roots and Current
   Status*
Appendix 1-3: Introduction to Health Law
Appendix 1-4: Human Rights and Health
Chapter 64: Legal Aspects of Bioterrorism

RICHARD R. BALSAMO, M.D., J.D., F.C.L.M.
Corporate Medical Director, Unicare;
Vice President, WellPoint Health Networks,
Chicago, Illinois
Chapter 17: Risk Management

ELLEN BARKER, M.S.N., R.N., A.P.N., C.N.R.N.,
C.L.C.P., A.B.D.A.
President, Neuroscience Nursing Consultants,
Greenville, Delaware
Chapter 26: Life Care Planning: Ethical and Legal Issues

JOSEPH A. BARRETTE, B.S., J.D.
College of Law,
Syracuse University,
Syracuse, New York
Chapter 11: Complementary and Alternative Medicine

W. EUGENE BASANTA, B.A., J.D., LL.M.
Professor, School of Law,
Southern Illinois University,
Carbondale, Illinois
Appendix 1-2: M.D./J.D. Dual Degree Program

SCOTT D. BATTERMAN, Ph.D.
Forensic Engineering Consultant,
Cherry Hill, New Jersey
Chapter 66: Forensic Engineering

STEVEN C. BATTERMAN, Ph.D.
Professor Emeritus,
University of Pennsylvania;
Forensic Engineering Consultant,
Cherry Hill, New Jersey
Chapter 66: Forensic Engineering

LOUIS E. BAXTER, Sr., M.D., F.A.S.A.M.
Assistant Clinical Professor of Medicine,
University of Medicine and Dentistry New Jersey,
Newark, New Jersey;
Executive Medical Director,
Medical Society of New Jersey,
Lawrenceville, New Jersey
Chapter 10: Health Care Professional Impairment

ROY G. BERAN, M.D., F.R.A.C.P., F.R.C.P.,
F.R.A.C.G.P., F.A.C.L.M., B.Leg.S., M.H.L.
Conjoint Associate Professor of Medicine,
South Western Sydney Clinical School,
University of New South Wales;
Visiting Consultant Neurologist,
Liverpool Hospital,
Sydney, Australia;
Principal of Strategic Health Evaluators (SHE),
Chatswood, Sydney, Australia;
President of the Australian College of
   Legal Medicine
Chapter 74: Privacy
Chapter 75: Drivers and the Law

STEVEN B. BISBING, Psy.D., J.D., F.C.L.M.
Private Practice,
Clinical and Forensic Psychology,
Mental Health Consultation and Analysis, Inc.,
Takoma Park, Maryland
Chapter 4: Competency and Capacity: A Primer

MAX DOUGLAS BROWN, J.D.
Associate Professor, College of Health Sciences;
Associate Professor (Conjoint Appointment),
Rush University College of Medicine;
Vice President and General Counsel,
Office of Legal Affairs,
Rush University Medical Center,
Chicago, Illinois
Chapter 17: Risk Management

FILLMORE BUCKNER, M.D., J.D., F.C.L.M.
Clinical Professor,
Department of Obstetrics and Gynecology,
University of Washington School of Medicine,
Seattle, Washington
Chapter 32: Medical Records
Chapter 33: Electronic Records
*Chapter 38: Electronic Mail Communication with
Patients*
Chapter 39: Telemedicine

JOHN R. CARLISLE, M.D., LL.B., F.C.L.M.
College of Physicians and Surgeons of Ontario,
Toronto, Ontario, Canada
Chapter 20: Ethics and Bioethics

DAVID P. CLUCHEY, M.A., J.D.
Associate Dean and Professor of Law,
University of Maine Law School,
Portland, Maine
Chapter 5: Antitrust

MIKE COOPER, M.D.
Cardiology Fellow,
Ohio State University,
Columbus, Ohio
*Chapter 60: Competitive Athletes: Cardiovascular
Preparticipation Screening*

KEVIN J. DALTON, D.F.M.S., LL.M., Ph.D.,
F.R.C.O.G., F.C.L.M.
Obstetrics and Gynaecology, and Legal Medicine,
Addenbrooke's Hospital,
University of Cambridge,
Cambridge, England
*Chapter 73: Physician Licensing and Disciplining
in England and Europe*

EDWARD DAVID, M.D., J.D., F.C.L.M.
Deputy Chief Medical Examiner,
State of Maine,
Bangor, Maine
Chapter 5: Antitrust

L. JEAN DUNEGAN, M.D., J.D., F.C.L.M.
Diplomate, American Board of Surgery;
Director, Ann Arbor Pain Consultants,
Ann Arbor, Michigan;
Director, Hillsdale Pain Center,
Hillsdale, Michigan;
Author, *The Handbook of Pain Management,*
www.a2pain.com
Chapter 58: Pain Management

JAMES A. FILKINS, M.D., J.D., Ph.D., F.C.L.M.
Assistant Corporation Counsel,
Department of Law,
City of Chicago;
Former Deputy Medical Examiner,
Cook County, Illinois
Chapter 49: Criminalization of Medical Negligence

MARVIN H. FIRESTONE, M.D., J.D., F.C.L.M.
President, Northern California Psychiatric Society;
Distinguished Life Fellow of the American Psychiatric
Association;
Former Hirsh Professor of Legal Medicine and Ethics,
George Washington University,
Washington, D.C.;
Faculty and Lecturer, Psychiatric Residency Programs,
Stanford University Hospital and San Mateo County
Medical Center;
Past President, ACLM;
San Mateo, California
Chapter 3: Agency
*Chapter 8: Medical Staff Peer Review in the
Credentialing and Privileging of Physicians*
Chapter 68: Psychiatric Patients and Forensic Psychiatry

SAL FISCINA, M.D., J.D., F.C.L.M.
Adjunct Professor of Law,
Georgetown University Law Center;
Lecturer, Columbia University College of Physicians and
Surgeons;
Chairman, American Board of Legal Medicine
Rockville, Maryland
*Chapter 35: Liability of Health Care Entities for
Negligent Care*
Glossary: Selected Health Care and Legal Terminology

GERALD F. FLETCHER, M.D.
Professor of Medicine,
Division of Cardiology,
Mayo Clinic,
Jacksonville, Florida
*Chapter 60: Competitive Athletes: Cardiovascular
Preparticipation Screening*

FREDERICK W. FOCHTMAN, Ph.D., D.A.B.T.,
D.A.B.F.T.
Director and Chief Toxicologist,
Forensic Science Laboratory Division,
Allegheny County Coroner's Office;
Director, Forensic Science and Law Program,
Bayer School of Natural and Environmental Sciences,
Duquesne University,
Pittsburgh, Pennsylvania
Chapter 67: Forensic Toxicology

DANIEL J. GAMINO, J.D.
Attorney at Law,
US Supreme Court—Admitted,
Oklahoma Supreme Court—Admitted,
Oklahoma City, Oklahoma
Chapter 7: Medical Practice: Education and Licensure

ALLAN GIBOFSKY, M.D., J.D., F.A.C.P., F.C.L.M.
Professor of Medicine and Public Health,
Weill Medical College of Cornell University;
Attending Physician,
The New York Presbyterian Hospital;
Attending Rheumatologist,
The Hospital for Special Surgery;
Adjunct Professor of Law,
Fordham University School of Law,
New York, New York
Chapter 6 : Alternative Dispute Resolution

JUDITH A. GIC, R.N., J.D.
Private Practice,
West Hartford, Connecticut
Chapter 47: Nursing and the Law

LEONARD H. GLANTZ, J.D.
Associate Dean and Professor of Health Law,
Boston University School of Public Health,
Boston, Massachusetts
Appendix 1-3: Introduction to Health Law

JAY A. GOLD, M.D., J.D., M.P.H., F.C.L.M.
Senior Vice President,
MetaStar, Inc.,
Madison, Wisconsin
Chapter 63: Public Health Law

RICHARD S. GOODMAN, M.D., J.D., F.A.A.O.S., F.C.L.M.
Adjunct Attending, Department of Orthopedics,
Long Island Jewish/North Shore Hospitals,
New Hyde Park, New York;
Courtesy Staff, Department of Orthopedics,
St. Catherine's of Sienna,
Smithtown, New York
Chapter 59: Sports Medicine

MARK GREENWOOD, D.O., J.D., F.C.L.M.
Fellow, Emergency Medical Services,
University of Chicago,
Chicago, Illinois;
Flight Physician,
Aero Med at Spectrum Health,
Grand Rapids, Michigan
Chapter 9: Physician Profile Databases

MICHAEL A. GRODIN, M.D.
Professor of Health Law, Socio-Medical Sciences,
Community Medicine and Psychiatry,
Boston University Schools of Public Health and Medicine;
Medical Ethicist,
Boston Medical Center,
Boston, Massachusetts
*Chapter 1: Legal Medicine: Historical Roots
and Current Status*
Appendix 1-3: Introduction to Health Law
Appendix 1-4: Human Rights and Health

E. LYLE GROSS, M.D.
Medical Director, Worker Injury Rehabilitation,
Consult Service,
Impairment/Disability Assessment Unit,
Physical Medicine and Rehabilitation,
Mayo Clinic,
Rochester, Minnesota
Chapter 61: Impairment, Disability, and Work Issues

SPENCER A. HALL, M.D., J.D., F.C.L.M.
Lincoln, New Mexico
*Chapter 44: Legal Issues of Prehospital Emergency
Medical Systems*

NEAL H. HASKELL, Ph.D.
Professor of Forensic Entomology,
Department of Biology,
St. Joseph's College,
Rensselaer, Indiana
Chapter 70: Forensic Entomology

CHARLES G. HESS, M.S., M.D.
Clinical Instructor of Pediatrics,
Department of Pediatrics,
Baylor College of Medicine;
Former Chairman of Pediatric Section,
Department of Pediatrics,
Heights Hospital;
Former Chairman of Pediatric Section,
Department of Pediatrics,
Memorial-Hermann Northwest Hospital;
Active Staff, Department of Pediatrics,
Texas Children's Hospital,
Houston, Texas
Chapter 14: Physician as an Employer

FREDDIE ANN HOFFMAN, M.D.
HeteroGeneity, LLC,
Washington, D.C.
*Chapter 15: Health Professionals and the Regulated
Industry: The Laws and Regulations Enforced by
the U.S. Food and Drug Administration*

EDWARD E. HOLLOWELL, J.D., F.C.L.M.
Hollowell, Mitchell, Peacock & Von Hagen, P.A.,
Raleigh, North Carolina;
Chapter 13: Coproviders and Institutional Practice

MATTHEW L. HOWARD, M.D., J.D., F.C.L.M.
Staff Physician,
Kaiser Permanente Medical Center,
Santa Rosa, California;
Sole Practice Law,
Ukiah, California;
Associate Clinical Professor of Otolaryngology,
University of California,
San Francisco Medical School,
San Francisco, California
Chapter 30: Physician-Patient Relationship

JAMES R. HUBLER, M.D., J.D., F.C.L.M.,
F.A.C.E.P., F.A.A.E.M.
Clinical Assistant Professor of Surgery,
Department of Emergency Medicine,
University of Illinois College of Medicine at Peoria;
EMS Medical Director,
Central Illinois Center for Emergency Medicine,
OSF St. Francis Hospital,
Peoria, Illinois
*Chapter 16: Health Insurance and Professional Liability
    Insurance*

JAMES C. JOHNSTON, M.D., J.D., F.C.L.M.
Consultant Neurologist and Attorney,
Private Practice,
San Antonio, Texas;
Director of Neurology Services,
Legal Medicine Consultants, Inc.,
Eugene, Oregon
Chapter 46: Liability of Neurologists

MICHAEL KAMINSKI, M.L.I.S.
Assistant Librarian/Public Services,
Trinity University,
San Antonio, Texas
Chapter 9: Physician Profile Databases

MARSHALL B. KAPP, J.D., M.P.H., F.C.L.M.
Office of Geriatric Medicine and Gerontology,
Wright State University School of Medicine,
Dayton, Ohio;
Dr. Arthur W. Grayson Distinguished Visiting Professor
    of Law and Medicine at Southern Illinois University
    School of Law,
Carbondale, Illinois
Chapter 54: Geriatric Patients

EUGENE LINWOOD KASTELBERG, Jr., M.D.
Law Student,
University of Richmond,
Richmond, Virginia
Chapter 52: Children as Patients

AARON SETH KESSELHEIM, M.D., J.D., F.C.L.M.
Department of Medicine,
Division of Internal Medicine,
Brigham and Women's Hospital,
Boston, Massachusetts
Chapter 18: Patents, Intellectual Property, and Licenses

RAYMUND C. KING, M.D., J.D., F.C.L.M.
Healthcare Litigation Attorney,
Cowles & Thompson, P.C.,
Dallas, Texas
Chapter 39: Telemedicine
Chapter 42: Liability of Otolaryngologists

GARY LANE, M.D
Consultant, Assistant Professor of Medicine,
Department of Cardiovascular Diseases,
Mayo Clinic;
Director of Catheterization Lab/Chairman of Cardiology,
Department of Cardiology,
St. Luke's Hospital,
Jacksonville, Florida
*Chapter 60: Competitive Athletes: Cardiovascular
    Preparticipation Screening*

CAROLYN S. LANGER, M.D., J.D., M.P.H.
Instructor in Occupational Medicine,
Occupational Health Program,
Harvard School of Public Health,
Boston, Massachusetts
Chapter 62: Occupational Health Law

THEODORE R. LeBLANG, J.D., F.C.L.M.
Professor and Chair,
Department of Medical Humanities,
Southern Illinois University School of Medicine
Springfield, Illinois
Appendix 1-1: Program of Law and Medicine
Appendix 1-2: M.D./J.D. Dual Degree Program
*Chapter 31: Informed Consent to Medical and Surgical
    Treatment*

BRADFORD H. LEE, M.D., J.D., M.B.A., F.A.C.E.P.,
F.C.L.M.
Seymour Johnson Air Force Base,
Goldsboro, North Carolina
Chapter 51: Countersuits by Health Care Providers

HENRY C. LEE, Ph.D.
Distinguished Professor,
Forensic Science Department,
University of New Haven,
West Haven, Connecticut;
Chief Emeritus,
Department of Public Safety,
Division of Scientific Services,
Meriden, Connecticut
Chapter 69: Criminalistics

MICHAEL S. LEHV, M.D., J.D., F.C.L.M.
Adjunct Professor,
Capital University Law School,
Columbus, Ohio
Chapter 37: Medical Product Liability

JEFFREY L. LENOW, M.D., J.D., F.C.L.M.,
F.A.A.F.P
Associate Professor,
Department of Family Medicine,
Jefferson Medical College of Thomas Jefferson University,
Philadelphia, Pennsylvania
Chapter 24: Fetal Interests

JOAN LICHTMAN, M.A., M.S.P.A., C.I.T.T., C.P.A.
Health Care Services Systems®,
Philadelphia, Pennsylvania, and Montreal, Quebec
Chapter 21: Access to Medical Care

ELLEN L. LUEPKE, J.D., LL.M.
Attorney,
Barnes & Thornburg,
Chicago, Illinois
Chapter 12: Practice Organizations and Joint Ventures

WENDY K. MARINER, J.D., LL.M., M.P.H.
Professor of Health Law,
Boston University School of Public Health;
Professor of Law,
Boston University School of Law,
Professor of Socio-Medical Sciences and Community
   Medicine,
Boston University School of Medicine,
Boston, Massachusetts
Appendix 1-3: Introduction to Health Law

JOSEPH P. McMENAMIN, M.D., J.D., F.C.L.M.
Attorney, Partner, Litigation,
McGuireWoods, LLP,
Richmond, Virginia
Chapter 52: Children as Patients

ELAINE M. PAGLIARO, M.S., J.D.
Adjunct Professor,
Departments of Graduate Nursing/Criminal Justice/
   School of Law,
Quinnipiac University,
Hamden, Connecticut;
Adjunct Faculty,
Department of Chemistry,
St. Joseph College,
West Hartford, Connecticut;
Assistant Director,
Division of Scientific Services,
Forensic Science Laboratory,
Connecticut Department of Public Safety,
Middletown, Connecticut
Chapter 69: Criminalistics

TIMOTHY E. PATERICK, M.D., J.D., M.B.A., F.C.L.M.
Professor of Medicine,
Division of Cardiology,
Mayo Clinic,
Jacksonville, Florida
*Chapter 60: Competitive Athletes: Cardiovascular
   Preparticipation Screening*

HOWARD A. PETH, Jr., M.D., J.D., F.C.L.M.
Assistant Professor,
Department of Emergency Medicine,
University of Missouri School of Medicine,
Columbia, Missouri
Chapter 45: Professional Liability in Emergency Medicine

JOSEPH D. PIORKOWSKI, Jr., D.O., J.D., M.P.H.,
F.C.P.M., F.C.L.M.
Adjunct Professor,
Georgetown University Law Center;
Partner, Shook, Hardy & Bacon, LLP,
Washington, D.C.
Chapter 34: Medical Testimony and the Expert Witness

MICHAEL M. RASKIN, M.D., M.S., J.D., M.P.H.,
M.A., F.C.L.M.
Clinical Associate Professor of Radiology,
University of Miami School of Medicine;
Neuroradiologist,
University Medical Center,
Tamarac, Florida
Chapter 43: Liability of Radiologists

PETER H. RHEINSTEIN, M.D., J.D., M.S., F.C.L.M.
Senior Vice President for Medical and Clinical Affairs,
Cell Works Inc.,
Baltimore, Maryland
*Chapter 15: Health Professionals and the Regulated
   Industry: The Laws and Regulations Enforced by
   the U.S. Food and Drug Administration*

BEN A. RICH, J.D., Ph.D.
Associate Professor of Bioethics,
University of California,
Davis School of Medicine,
Sacramento, California
Chapter 27: The Process of Dying

KAREN S. RIEGER, B.A., J.D.
Crowe & Dunlevy,
Oklahoma City, Oklahoma
*Chapter 19: Federal Health Information Privacy
   Requirements*

STEPHANIE RIFKINSON-MANN, M.D., J.D.,
F.C.L.M.
Pediatric Neurosurgery,
Mount Kisco, New York
Chapter 2: Health Care Provider Contracts

ARNOLD J. ROSOFF, J.D., F.C.L.M.
Professor of Legal Studies and Health Care Systems,
The Wharton School;
Senior Fellow,
The Leonard Davis Institute of Health Economics,
University of Pennsylvania,
Philadelphia, Pennsylvania
Chapter 31: Informed Consent to Medical and Surgical Treatment

MIKE A. ROYAL, M.D., J.D., F.C.L.M.
Clinical Adjunct Professor,
Department of Medicine and Anesthesiology/Pain Management,
Oklahoma University College of Medicine,
Pain Evaluation and Treatment Center,
Tulsa, Oklahoma
Chapter 57: Patients with HIV Infection and AIDS

MARK E. RUST, J.D.
Office Managing Partner,
Barnes & Thornburg,
Chicago, Illinois
Chapter 12: Practice Organizations and Joint Ventures

S. SANDY SANBAR, M.D., Ph.D., J.D., F.C.L.M.
President, Royal Oaks Cardiovascular Clinic, Inc.,
Oklahoma City, Oklahoma;
Law of Medicine, Attorney at Law,
Oklahoma City, Oklahoma;
Cardiology Consultant,
The Ringrose Clinic, Inc.,
Guthrie, Oklahoma;
Clinical Sub-Investigator,
The Oklahoma Hypertension and Cardiovascular Center,
Oklahoma City, Oklahoma
Chapter 1: Legal Medicine: Historical Roots and Current Status
Chapter 7: Medical Practice: Education and Licensure
Chapter 28: Physician-Assisted Suicide

MICHAEL F. SAULINO, M.D., Ph.D.
Assistant Professor,
Department of Rehabilitation Medicine,
Thomas Jefferson University,
Philadelphia, Pennsylvania
Chapter 26: Life Care Planning: Ethical and Legal Issues

BRUCE H. SEIDBERG, D.D.S., M.Sc.D., J.D., D.A.B.E., F.A.C.D., F.P.F.A., F.A.A.H.D., F.C.L.M.
Private Dental (Endodontic) Practice,
Syracuse and Liverpool, New York;
Dental-Legal Consultant,
Lecturer, Risk Management Skills and Legal Aspects of Dentistry;
Former Associate Professor,
SUNY School of Dentistry,
Buffalo, New York;
Chief of Dentistry, Crouse Hospital, and Senior Attending Dentist and Former Director,
General Dental Residency,
St. Joseph's Hospital Health Center,
Syracuse, New York
Chapter 48: Dental Litigation: Triad of Concerns

†JANET B. SEIFERT, J.D.
Glossary: Selected Health Care and Legal Terminology

STUART G. SELKIN, M.D., J.D., F.A.C.S., F.C.L.M.
Consultant, Private Practice,
Melville, New York;
Chairman of the Board of Directors,
Long Island Medicine, Ethics, and Law Society, Inc.,
Melville, New York
Chapter 28: Physician-Assisted Suicide

MARK F. SELTZER, J.D.
Attorney at Law,
Philadelphia, Pennsylvania
Chapter 10: Health Care Professional Impairment

PHILIP A. SHELTON, P.A., M.D., J.D., F.C.L.M.
Assistant Clinical Professor of Ophthalmology,
University of Connecticut School of Medicine;
Lecturer in Ophthalmology,
Tufts University School of Medicine,
Boston, Massachusetts
Chapter 41: Liability of Ophthalmologists

MELVIN A. SHIFFMAN, M.D., J.D., F.C.L.M.
Chief of Surgery,
Surgery Department,
Tustin Hospital and Medical Center,
Tustin, California
Chapter 55: Oncology Patients

---

†Deceased.

MICHAEL A. SHIFLET, J.D.
Attorney,
Frasier, Frasier and Hickman, LLP,
Tulsa, Oklahoma
Chapter 57: Patients with HIV Infection and AIDS

JENNIFER L. SMITH, J.D.
Hollowell, Mitchell, Peacock & Von Hagen, P.A.,
Raleigh, North Carolina
Chapter 13: Coproviders and Institutional Practice

JACK W. SNYDER, M.D., J.D., M.F.S., M.P.H.,
Ph.D., F.C.L.M.
National Library of Medicine
Bethesda, Maryland
Chapter 53: Domestic Violence Patients

MICHAEL N. SOBEL, D.M.D., D-A.B.F.O.
Clinical Associate Professor,
Department of Dental Public Health,
University of Pittsburgh School of Dental Medicine;
Consultant in Forensic Sciences,
Departments of Dental Medicine and Surgery,
University of Pittsburgh Medical Center;
Consultant in Forensic Sciences,
Child Advocacy Center,
Children's Hospital of Pittsburgh;
Chief Forensic Odontologist,
Allegheny County Coroner's Office
Pittsburgh, Pennsylvania
Chapter 71: Forensic Odontology

KATRICE TAYLOR, B.A.
Law Student,
University of Richmond School of Law,
Richmond, Virginia
Chapter 52: Children as Patients

ROBERT TURBOW, M.D., J.D., F.C.L.M.
Staff Neonatologist,
Department of Pediatrics,
Phoenix Children's Hospital;
Staff Neonatologist,
Department of Pediatrics,
Good Samaritan Hospital,
Phoenix, Arizona;
Chief Executive Officer,
PatientPatents, Inc.,
San Luis Obispo, California
Chapter 40: Legal Issues in Newborn Intensive Care

STAN TWARDY, J.D., LL.M.
Twardy Law Office,
Oklahoma City, Oklahoma
Chapter 50: Crimes by Health Care Providers

CLARK WATTS, M.D., J.D., F.C.L.M
Attending Physician,
Department of Neurosurgery,
Southwest Methodist Hospital,
San Antonio, Texas;
Adjunct Professor of Law,
University of Texas School of Law,
Austin, Texas
Chapter 56: Brain-Injured Patients

JAY WEAVER, J.D., E.M.T.-P
Attorney, Private Practice;
Paramedic, Boston Public Health Commission;
Adjunct Faculty, Northeastern University,
Boston, Massachusetts
*Chapter 16: Health Insurance and Professional Liability
Insurance*

CYRIL H. WECHT, M.D., J.D., F.C.L.M.
Clinical Professor,
Department of Pathology,
University of Pittsburgh School of Medicine;
Adjunct Professor,
School of Law,
Duquesne University;
Coroner of Allegheny County;
Clinical Professor,
Department of Pathology,
University of Pittsburgh School of Dentistry;
Adjunct Professor,
Department of Epidemiology,
Graduate School of Public Health,
University of Pittsburgh,
Pittsburgh, Pennsylvania
*Chapter 1: Legal Medicine: Historical Roots and Current
Status*
Chapter 22: Research and Experimentation
Chapter 65: Forensic Pathology
*Chapter 72: Utilization of Forensic Science in the
Civil and Criminal Justice Systems: Forensic Use of
Medical Information*

CHRISTOPHER WHITE, M.D., J.D., F.C.L.M.
Combined Program Resident Physician,
Cross Appointments in the Departments of Family
    Medicine and Psychiatry,
University of Cincinnati,
Cincinnati, Ohio
*Chapter 31: Informed Consent to Medical and Surgical
    Treatment*

MILES J. ZAREMSKI, J.D., F.C.L.M.
Immediate Past President, American College of Legal
    Medicine;
Chair, Standing Committee on Medical Professional Liability,
American Bar Association;
Lecturer in Health Law,
University of Chicago and Case Western Reserve
    University Law Schools (2000–2003);
Assistant Professor (Adjunct),
Department of Family Medicine,
Finch University/Chicago Medical School;
Partner, Kaminsky & Rubinstein,
Lincolnwood/Chicago, Illinois
Chapter 36: Liability of Managed Care Organizations

Preface

The American College of Legal Medicine (ACLM) is the foremost, established organization in the United States concerned with medical jurisprudence and forensic medicine. The ACLM, founded in 1955, has devoted itself to addressing problems that exist at the interface of law and medicine. The ACLM serves as a natural focal point for those professionals interested in the study and advancement of legal medicine. The ACLM is composed of health care and legal professionals whose diverse education, training, and experience enable the College to promote interdisciplinary cooperation and an understanding of issues where law and medicine converge. Indeed, the ACLM is a professional community of physicians, attorneys, dentists, allied health professionals, administrators, scientists, and others with a sustained interest in medical legal affairs.

The central mission of the ACLM is education in legal medicine. Through its medico-legal resources, the ACLM educates and assists health care and legal professionals, advances the administration of justice, influences health policy and improves health care, promotes research and scholarship, and facilitates peer group interaction.

The sixth edition of this text by the ACLM adheres to the objective that the more knowledge that can be available concerning the relevant legal concepts, principles, and rules, the more effective an individual can become as a medical or legal practitioner. This text has been updated and substantially expanded from 50 chapters in the fifth edition to 75 chapters in the current edition. Among the new chapters included in this text are physician profile databases, health care professional impairment, complementary and alternative medicine, patents, intellectual property and licenses, HIPAA privacy rules, access to medical care, the Human Genome Project, ethical and legal issues of life care planning, electronic records, legal issues of neonates, several liability issues of health care specialists, criminalization of medical malpractice, legal aspects of bioterrorism, a markedly expanded section on forensic science and medicine, and chapters from international contributors from England and Australia dealing with physician licensing and disciplining in England and Europe, privacy, and drivers and the law.

As with the previous editions, this text attempts to highlight those areas of professional endeavor in a health care institution that constitute potential pitfalls and problems of a legal nature. The field of legal medicine is extremely broad and far-reaching, with new developments of a significant nature occurring constantly. The text is structured to explore and illustrate the legal implications of medical practice and the special legal issues attendant on organized health and medical care. The text is an excellent resource for all health care providers and attorneys. The text is also ideally suited for use to teach a course in legal medicine at medical and law schools.

On behalf of the ACLM and its membership, it is my honor and privilege to extend our deep appreciation, thanks, and gratitude to all the authors and contributors of the textbook chapters, the deputy editor, and the members of the Textbook Editorial Committee. Their contributions represent true labors of love to the ACLM and a monumental work in the field of legal medicine.

Finally, special thanks are expressed to all the staff of Elsevier, especially Alison Nastasi, Thom Moore, and Daniel Clipner, for their tremendous help and contribution to the text.

S. Sandy Sanbar, M.D., Ph.D., J.D., F.C.L.M.
Chairman, ACLM Textbook Committee
Editor

Contents

I

Legal Medicine and Health Law Education

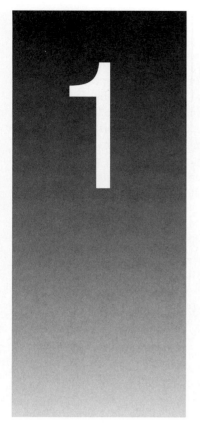

Legal Medicine: Historical Roots and Current Status

S. SANDY SANBAR, M.D., Ph.D., J.D., F.C.L.M.
GEORGE J. ANNAS, J.D., M.P.H.
MICHAEL A. GRODIN, M.D.
CYRIL H. WECHT, M.D., J.D., F.C.L.M.

LEGAL MEDICINE
LEGAL MEDICINE IN AMERICA
THE AMERICAN COLLEGE OF LEGAL MEDICINE
THE AMERICAN SOCIETY OF LAW, MEDICINE, AND ETHICS
HEALTH LAW IN LAW SCHOOLS
HEALTH LAW CONTENT
M.D./J.D. DEGREES
HEALTH LAW AND BIOETHICS IN MEDICAL SCHOOLS
HEALTH LAW AND MEDICAL ETHICS
CONTINUING EDUCATION
HUMAN RIGHTS AND HEALTH
CONCLUSION

Law and medicine are separate professions, and attorneys and physicians often see their professions in conflict. There are, however, more similarities than differences between the two professions. And there are areas of mutual concern and overlap that demand the application of both legal and medical knowledge for the good of society. These areas have historically been united under the broader term of *health law*. This chapter introduces readers to a field that has been known by at least three different names by reviewing some historical highlights in its development and explaining how it is approached in legal, medical, and continuing professional education. What emerges is a field in evolution that has moved from almost exclusive concern with forensic pathology and psychiatry in country-specific settings to now encompass the bioethics, organization, and management of health care delivery and the growing global movement toward human rights in health.

LEGAL MEDICINE

The roots of legal medicine can be traced back to the sixteenth century in Italy and the late eighteenth century in Britain. Published treatises generated from Italy and Britain guided the development of legal medicine in Germany, France, and the United States. *Médecine légale*, or legal medicine, is a French term that first appeared during the late eighteenth and early nineteenth centuries.[1] The French legal medicine subject was broad and included medical evidentiary matters and medical areas of legal significance, for example, the criminally insane and the rehabilitation of criminals.

Harvard University established a separate professorship in legal medicine in 1877. In 1942 Dr. Alan R. Moritz, then the occupant of that professorship, defined legal medicine as

the application of medical knowledge to the needs of justice. Although by definition this would appear to be a broad and scientifically heterogeneous field, the practice of legal medicine is concerned chiefly with what might be most adequately described as forensic pathology.[2]

In 1975 another prominent Harvard professor of legal medicine, Dr. William J. Curran, who founded the Law-Medicine Institute at Boston University Law School in 1955 (now the Health Law Department of Boston University School of Public Health), defined the term *legal medicine* as

the specialty areas of medicine concerned with relations with substantive law and with legal institutions. Clinical medical areas, such as the treatment of offenders and trauma medicine related to law, would be included herein.[3]

The introduction of the term *medical jurisprudence* in America was the result of developments in Britain. In 1788 Dr. Samuel Farr of Britain published the *Elements of*

3

Medical Jurisprudence. Until that time, the British did not systematically study or teach legal or forensic medicine, and no comprehensive British work on the subject was available.[4]

In 1789 Dr. Andrew Duncan was appointed professor of the Institutes of Medicine at the University of Edinburgh, and he began to give lectures in medical jurisprudence and public hygiene.[5] Duncan was the first in Britain to provide systemic instruction in legal medicine. He used the term *medical jurisprudence* to encompass both "medical police and juridical medicine." Dr. James S. Stringham of New York, who was at Edinburgh earning his medical degree in 1799, brought the term with him to America.

In 1804 Stringham defined medical jurisprudence as "that science which applies the principles and practice of the different branches of medicine to the elucidation of doubtful questions in courts of justice."[6] In 1975 Curran argued that the unfortunate title of "medical jurisprudence should at long last be relegated to the lexicographer's scrap heap. It was incorrectly applied to the medical side of the field in the first place. It is now either inappropriate or too pretentious a term for the legal aspects of the subject."[7] More recently the term *health law* has gained wide acceptance and is used in textbook and course titles in most law schools and law firms to denote the field, as well as in some medical schools and almost all schools of public health.

LEGAL MEDICINE IN AMERICA

Numerous excellent articles on the history of legal medicine have been published in the medical and legal professional journals, some of which are referred to in this chapter. Five extensive and authoritative references of articles on the general history of legal medicine are those by Gilbert H. Stewart (1910),[8] Sir Sydney Smith (1954),[9] Chester R. Burns (1977),[10] William J. Curran (1980),[11] and James C. Mohr (1993).[12] Some of these publications also include discussions of the history of medical ethics. This chapter focuses on the history of legal medicine and the early legal medicine scholars in America.

In the United States, legal medicine started to develop at the beginning of the nineteenth century. Stringham studied medicine first in his native city of New York and subsequently at Edinburgh, Great Britain, where he graduated with the doctor of medicine degree in 1799. In 1804 Stringham instituted a course of lectures in legal medicine at Columbia College of Physicians and Surgeons in New York. He was the first systematic teacher of legal medicine in America. In 1813 he was appointed professor of medical jurisprudence at the College of Physicians and Surgeons, a post he held until his death in 1817.

Dr. Benjamin Rush is credited with emphasizing the significance of the relationship between law and medicine in the early 1800s. As the nation's first surgeon general and a signatory of the Declaration of Independence, Rush established American legal medicine with his published lecture "On the Study of Medical Jurisprudence," which he delivered to medical students at the University of Pennsylvania, Philadelphia, in 1811.[13] The lecture dealt with homicide, mental disease, and capital punishment.

The work of Stringham and Rush inspired the teaching of medical jurisprudence in other American medical schools. Among the early teachers were Dr. Charles Caldwell in Philadelphia and Dr. Walter Channing at Harvard. In 1819 Dr. Thomas Cooper, a legal officer of distinction and president of the College of South Carolina, published *Tracts on Medical Jurisprudence*. This volume contained almost all available literature written in English on legal medicine.

In 1815 Dr. T. Romeyn Beck was appointed lecturer on medical jurisprudence at Western Medical College, New York State. In 1823 Beck published the *Elements of Medical-Jurisprudence*, which defined the field of legal medicine for about half a century of American medical practice. Beck's two volumes included impressive topics, such as rape, impotence and sterility, pregnancy and delivery, infanticide and abortion, legitimacy, presumption of survivorship, identity, mental alienation, wounds, poisons, persons found dead, and feigned and disqualifying diseases.

In 1838 Isaac Ray published *A Treatise on Medical Jurisprudence of Insanity*. In 1855, the year that Beck died, Francis Wharton, an attorney, and Dr. Moreton Stille, a physician, collaborated to publish *A Treatise on Medical Jurisprudence*. In 1860 Dr. John J. Elwell, a physician and an attorney, published a book entitled *A Medico-Legal Treatise on Malpractice, Medical Evidence, and Insanity Comprising the Elements of Medical Jurisprudence*, which highlighted the issue of malpractice in the medical jurisprudence literature. Elwell's book presented excerpts from contemporary cases for the purpose of teaching physicians what to expect from malpractice litigation. Dr. John Odronaux, also a physician and an attorney, published *Jurisprudence of Medicine* in 1867 and *Judicial Aspects of Insanity* in 1878. In 1894 Randolph A. Witthaus and Tracy C. Becker published *Medical Jurisprudence, Forensic Medicine and Toxicology*.

For medical students and physicians, medical jurisprudence assumed the position of central importance in U.S. schools of medicine throughout most of the 1800s. During the course of the nineteenth century, the institutions, laws, and judicial decisions in America reflected the increasing influence of sound medicolegal principles, especially those pertaining to mental disease and criminal lunacy.

After the Civil War, however, things changed drastically; legal medicine became temporarily dormant. American Professor and Dean Stanford Emerson Chaille expressed his view of the deplorable condition of medical jurisprudence in the United States. Chaille demonstrated how the teaching of medical jurisprudence had deteriorated by noting that in some medical colleges the course had been dropped altogether, in others it had been attached to some other subject, and in many colleges the teaching of medical students was entrusted to an attorney with no formal training in the medical field.[14]

Even in the early twentieth century the teaching of medical jurisprudence was relegated to a position as an occasional subject taught outside the mainstream. However, by the middle of the twentieth century, legal medicine underwent a renaissance, as evidenced by the establishment of the American College of Legal Medicine (ACLM), the founding of the Law-Medicine Institute at Boston University, and the rekindling of contemporary interest in a vast array of legal medicine issues, medical ethics, physician and patient rights, and business and professional aspects of medical practice.

In 1867 the Medico-Legal Society was organized in New York. It was the first society in the world to be organized for the purpose of promoting the principles that an attorney could not be fully equipped for the prosecution or the defense of an individual indicted for homicide without some knowledge of anatomy and pathology and that no physician or surgeon could be a satisfactory expert witness without some knowledge of the law.[15]

THE AMERICAN COLLEGE OF LEGAL MEDICINE

In 1955, recognizing the growing impact of legislation, regulations, and court decisions on patient care and the general effect of litigation and legal medicine on modern society, a group of physicians and surgeons, some of whom were educated in the law, organized what would later become the ACLM. The college was incorporated on September 23, 1960, by nine doctors of medicine, three of whom were attorneys. Of the 36 physicians who were designated "founding fellows," 10 had earned law degrees.

The ACLM is the oldest and most prestigious U.S. organization devoted to problems at the interface of medicine and law. Its membership is made up of professionals in medicine, osteopathy, and allied sciences, including dentistry, nursing, pharmacy, podiatry, psychology, and law. The ACLM has published a scholarly journal, the *Journal of Legal Medicine*, since 1973. In 1988 the ACLM also published the first edition of this textbook, *Legal Medicine*; subsequent editions were published in 1991, 1995, and 1998.

THE AMERICAN SOCIETY OF LAW, MEDICINE, AND ETHICS

In 1972 a physician and two attorneys founded the American Society of Law and Medicine (Ethics was added in 1992; ASLME) as a successor organization to the Massachusetts Society of Examining Physicians. Its founding president was cardiologist Dr. Elliot Sagall, who also cotaught the law and medicine course at Boston College Law School with George J. Annas, an attorney. The organ-

ization quickly became the largest medicolegal organization in the world dedicated to continuing education, as well as the publisher of the two leading medicolegal journals, the *Journal of Law, Medicine, and Ethics* and the *American Journal of Law and Medicine*; the latter is published as a law review at Boston University Law School. The ASLME also has sponsored international meetings in locations around the world in an effort to bring physicians, attorneys, ethicists, and others interested in health law together.

HEALTH LAW IN LAW SCHOOLS

From World War II until the late 1960s, the field of legal medicine was defined by law school courses that were almost exclusively concerned with issues of forensic psychiatry and pathology and were properly considered advanced courses in criminal law. In the late 1960s some law and medicine courses began concentrating on broader medicolegal issues faced in the courtroom, including disability evaluation and medical malpractice. These courses were properly considered either advanced tort or trial practice courses.

In the 1970s the concerns of at least some law and medicine courses expanded to include public policy, including issues of access to health care and the quality of that care. At the same time, advances in medical technology created new legal issues to explore—from brain death and organ donation to abortion and in vitro fertilization. These issues were increasingly incorporated into law and medicine courses, which were themselves becoming known by the broader term of *health law*.

Teachers of health law in law schools and medical schools, together with health law teachers in schools of public health and schools of management, began meeting on a regular basis in 1976 when the first national health law teachers' meeting took place at Boston University under the auspices of the law school's Center for Law and Health Sciences (the successor organization to the Law-Medicine Institute).[16] The purpose was to help define the expanding field and develop necessary teaching materials. In 1987 the American Association of Law Schools sponsored its first teaching workshop on health law.[17] Although this narrower group only recently convened, its program and proceedings offer useful insight into the current state of health law in law schools. As the organizers of the workshop saw it, law and medicine (fields primarily concerned with medical malpractice, forensic medicine, and psychiatric commitment) had become subdivisions of the new field of health law.[18] Health law itself has three additional subdivisions: economics of health care delivery, public policy and health care regulation, and bioethics. These three subdivisions are actually three different approaches to the same subject matter—the health care industry.[19] Health law is applied law, much the way medical ethics is applied ethics.

Health law should be studied by all law students for at least the following five reasons:

1. No other applied legal field can match the "magnitude, complexity, and universality of health care."[20]
2. Health law introduces attorneys to the problems confronted by members of another great profession in the United States, medicine.
3. Changes in medicine directly affect what humans can do and how humans think about humanity itself (and therefore what rights and obligations humans should have).
4. As issues of public health and safety capture center stage in American culture, the prudent use of law to protect health and safety assumes a role of central importance.
5. Issues of social justice and resource allocation are presented more compellingly in the medical care context than in any other.[21]

Other reasons could be added to this list, of course. Health care accounts for almost 15% of the gross national product, and cost increases continue out of control. Most importantly, constitutional law questions now focus on medical issues, such as abortion, the right to die, and free speech in the physician-patient relationship. Legal jobs in health care exist in a wide variety of settings, including local, state, and federal regulatory agencies; private health care facilities; health maintenance or managed care organizations and insurance companies; and law firms, to name just the major employers. Furthermore, a factor that is perhaps more important to most who teach health law, there is no more intrinsically fascinating area of law than law applied to the health care field. Entire courses in law schools have been based on a single medical development, such as organ transplantation, and a single specialized medical activity, such as human experimentation.

Health law provides a uniquely critical and intrinsically fascinating field to which to apply law, as well as a field that can be fruitfully approached from a wide variety of perspectives. Rand Rosenblatt, for example, has suggested that health law can be approached from the traditional law and medicine avenue and from three more modern perspectives: a law and economics approach, a social justice approach, and a bioethics approach. A fourth approach is a public health approach, and a fifth approach of course tries to integrate (or at least expose) all of these approaches.[22] Each approach deserves comment.

Law and economics have provided many law school teachers with an overarching approach to all legal problems. To oversimplify, the basic viewpoint from which health law is approached is that private property regimes presumptively serve to maximize social welfare; in a many-seller market, goods are available at marginal costs; private contracts should be enforced; relationships among noncontracting parties must be governed by explicit legal rule; and

income distribution is and should be primarily a function of productive capabilities. Even some of its harshest critics concede that the law and economics movement "provides the most coherent and intelligible realization of the liberal social theoretical agenda."[23]

A different approach to health law is taken by the critical legal studies (CLS) approach. Like the law and economics rubric, the CLS rubric is used here as oversimplified shorthand for a course that is approached from an ideological perspective that dominates the discussion. Unlike the law and economics school with its market model, CLS has no single, coherent set of principles to apply to any given industry. Nonetheless, those who describe CLS as a "social justice" approach imply that it is concerned with questioning the assumptions of capitalism (or at least looking "critically" at those assumptions).[24] Such an approach to the health law industry does not ignore how society got where it is and does not assume that traditional race, class, and gender power relationships are proper or deserve to be privileged and given presumptive validity.

Adherents of the law and economics and the CLS schools are at home with theoretical and macroeconomics levels but not with medical ethics. When it comes to dealing with the real problems of real physicians and patients, they each have much less to say. Perhaps that is why members of both of these politically hostile camps agree (mistakenly, the authors think) that issues of medical decision-making, such as autonomy and the physician-patient relationship (the natural focus of a medical school course), should be relegated to a separate course called *bioethics*.

The fourth approach, the public health approach, has yet to receive much attention in law schools and is currently used primarily in schools of public health.[25] Nonetheless, as issues of public health, such as teen pregnancy, drug abuse, drunk driving, smoking, acquired immunodeficiency syndrome (AIDS), nuclear energy, the quality of the environment, and worker health and safety, continue to dominate the news and public policy development, such courses will naturally find a home in the law school. When this happens, the pioneering work that has been done in the school of public health context will find a ready home in the development of courses that take a public health approach, including the issues of social justice and resource allocation.[26]

HEALTH LAW CONTENT

Regardless of the teaching approach taken, the available teaching material is especially rich. As the health care delivery system rapidly changes, it provides a real-world laboratory for examining the influences of law—from the courtroom (e.g., medical malpractice and termination of treatment) and constitutional litigation (e.g., the right of privacy) to legislation (e.g., various proposals for Medicare reform and national health insurance) and regulations (e.g., the Food and Drug Administration, the revised drug safety rules, and state rules regarding licensing of physicians and facilities). New medical technologies present new legal challenges that are so intrinsically fascinating that they routinely appear on the front pages of newspapers and news magazines and have no trouble holding the attention of law students.

The cases of Karen Ann Quinlan, Nancy Cruzan, and Mary Beth Whitehead are only a few examples of health law dramas played out in the courts. *Roe v. Wade,* the premier health law case, continues to be contested and contracted; and the right of privacy, so central to medicine and the physician-patient relationship, continues to play the key role in the politics of judicial appointments. Issues of organ transplants and implants, including the case of Barney Clark, also present particularly compelling case studies that naturally lead to broader policy discussions. Public health issues, including the use of drugs, alcohol, and tobacco; food consumption; the quality of the environment; the need for exercise; and the use of seat belts and motorcycle helmets, are of direct importance to the day-to-day lives of students. And, perhaps as important, health law permits direct study of (and possibly joint courses with) the other major profession in the United States, medicine. Relationships between the two professions have become increasingly adversarial, and increased knowledge may help restore more reasonable and socially constructive relationships. Finally, the advice attorneys give their clients in the health law field often has a direct impact on the lives and the manner of deaths of real people. Professional responsibility has an immediacy in this legal field that is lacking in most others.[27]

When no medical courses are offered in law school, unfortunately, self-education is the method used by attorneys involved in legal-medicine cases. Aside from the lack of time to prepare for medical case issues and acquire a medicolegal background, the foremost obstacle for an attorney is the move from the inductive reasoning of law to the deductive logic of the basic sciences. An additional problem is the diversity of medical knowledge required. A legal case may involve questions of anatomy, embryology, physiology, biochemistry, pharmacology, and pathology in a myriad of medical specialties and subspecialties. Attorneys, however desirous they may be of acquiring some medical training, lack the underlying basic science courses to support effective self-education.

Formal education is essential if the attorney is to be effective in evaluating medical evidence, both friendly and adversarial. An attorney who specializes in health law must possess a specific knowledge of pertinent medical services and specialties required in any particular case situation. Undertaking a medical issues case in spite of a lack of such knowledge could constitute legal malpractice.

M.D./J.D. DEGREES

In an effort to bridge the gap between law and medicine, some attorneys enroll in medical school or in dual-degree M.D./J.D. programs. The number of medical school courses extraneous to a legal practice specializing in medicine also discourages attorneys from a formal medical education.

In 1993 Harry Jonas, Sylvia Etzel, and Barbara Barzansky noted that students can earn combined doctor of medicine and doctor of jurisprudence (M.D./J.D.) degrees in only 9 out of 125 degree-granting U.S. medical schools fully accredited by the Liaison Committee on Medical Education (LCME).[28] Presently, there are 15 such programs. In contrast, students can earn combined doctor of medicine and doctor of philosophy (M.D./Ph.D.) degrees in 113 of the 125 U.S. medical schools. The majority of individuals who currently have M.D./J.D. degrees, however, earned their doctorate degrees separately, with most of them earning the M.D. first.

In 1985 Eugene Schneller and Terry Weiner published their findings regarding individuals who earned M.D./J.D. dual degrees and noted that cross-professional education in law and medicine remains a relatively rare phenomenon in the United States.[29] They concluded that "without the development of institutionalized career lines and the acceptance of cross-disciplinary approaches to problem solving, M.D./J.D.s must negotiate their jobs and job descriptions within an occupational structure that rewards disciplinary efforts. The marginal status of the interprofessional specialist persists in the decade of the 1980s."[30] A combined M.D./J.D. program is probably not the most effective way to teach medical concepts to law students, and it is doubtful that many students are willing to pursue such a long period of training. Moreover, there is more than enough to learn in either field.

These reasons probably explain the increasingly popular movement toward providing a health law concentration in many law schools and offering joint J.D./M.P.H. degree programs (such as those at Boston University and Georgetown University) for students interested in health law. Practicing attorneys need a working knowledge of the health care industry but do not need to know most of the material taught in medical schools. A well-developed health law program designed to fit into the law school curriculum can prepare an attorney to handle medical issues competently. Existing programs, such as health law concentrations at Boston University, Georgetown, Case-Western, St. Louis University, and Loyola of Chicago, are still few in number.

HEALTH LAW AND BIOETHICS IN MEDICAL SCHOOLS

Health law and medical ethics education is critical to the practice of both medicine and public health. Many health law dilemmas raise serious ethical concerns, and many ethical issues similarly raise serious legal questions. Medical ethics education and health law education are intimately intertwined, and the disciplines must be taught together in medical schools so that the student can learn about the cross-fertilization of the two.[31] Ethical principles, such as autonomy, beneficence, and justice, are intimately intertwined in legal analysis. Medical students should understand the similarities and differences in the ways medicine and law frame questions, address problems, and approach moral quandaries, as well as the various resources available to analyze these problems.

Medical students and physicians should learn that it is as problematic to never follow the law as it is to always mechanically follow what they consider to be the letter of the law. Physicians who do not understand how the law works often practice inappropriate defensive medicine, thinking that they are following the law or looking only to the law and the question of legal liability to decide what is "right." Most importantly a lack of a minimal understanding of the law can lead to inappropriate and misguided treatment of patients.

Medical ethics education dates back to the time of Hippocrates. The Hippocratic schools and Hippocratic ethics attempted to establish moral guidelines for the practicing physician. Throughout most of history, medical ethics was taught through apprenticeship in an attempt to inculcate values. The idea was to model the knowledge, skill, and behavior of seasoned physicians as part of a professionalization process. Before the 1970s such role modeling or mentorship was the primary method of teaching medical ethics. In the early 1970s, however, specific courses began to be taught in medical schools. These courses focused on the content, theory, and philosophy of medicine. In 1972 only 4% of medical schools had formal, separate, required courses for teaching medical ethics. By 1989 that number had risen to 34%, and close to three-quarters of medical schools covered medical ethics within other required courses.[32] It wasn't until the late 1980s, however, that residency programs began providing separate education in medical ethics as well.

HEALTH LAW AND MEDICAL ETHICS

Several key elements have been proved necessary for a successful health law and medical ethics program. First, health law and medical ethics must be prominent within the curriculum, substantiating their importance. Ethics education should be relevant, rigorously taught, and horizontally and longitudinally integrated into the curriculum from the classroom through the clinical clerkships. It must be seen as part of and integral to the practice of medicine. It must be taught over time, space, departments, and courses. As such, interdisciplinary teaching is almost an imperative.

For ethics education to be successful there must be specific learning objectives. Those objectives must be content and method focused. Some objectives of health law and medical ethics education are to sensitize students to the value and nature of medical practice, to supply them with methods to identify and describe legal and ethical dilemmas, and to give them formal, procedural, and substantive methodologies for resolving such dilemmas. Ultimately the goal is to graduate medical students who are committed to being physicians with high moral character and an understanding of the law and to practicing moral medicine.

The goals of health law and medical ethics should be to increase legal knowledge and provide skills in ethical analysis, as well as to educate students about tolerance and diversity of ethical opinions. Case-based analysis should draw on the student's experience. Courses must teach the history of law and medical ethics and its use and abuse in areas such as human experimentation, consent to treatment, euthanasia, and rationing. Students should also be familiar with important legal cases that deal with informed consent, abortion, and refusal of treatment. Ethical behavior still must be learned through role modeling that continues through the clinical years, fostering collaboration between nurses, administrators, and attorneys and ultimately adding a broader humanistic approach to improve interactive skills.

Basic curriculum goals have been identified. Seven skills that medical students should master by the end of health law and ethics education are as follows:

1. The ability to identify the legal and moral aspects of medical practice.
2. The ability to obtain a valid informed consent or a valid refusal of treatment.
3. Knowledge of how to proceed if a patient is only partially competent or incompetent to consent to or refuse treatment.
4. Knowledge of how to proceed if a patient refuses treatment.
5. The ability to decide when it is legally and morally justified to withhold information from a patient.
6. The ability to decide when it is morally justified to breach confidentiality.
7. Knowledge of the legal and moral aspects of care of patients with a poor prognosis, including patients who are terminally ill.[33]

There is a consensus that teaching should focus on standard principles of biomedical ethics, such as autonomy, justice, and beneficence, as well as on broader, more complex notions, such as feminist, virtue-based, Marxist, casuistic, and narrative critiques.[34] There have been several suggested specific curricular content goals. Although law students need to learn many facts related to medicine, medical students primarily need to learn only how to think about legal and moral issues in their practice.

The health law and bioethics curriculum at the Boston University School of Medicine is one of the oldest and most extensive in the country. The curriculum begins in the first year, when an integrated 20-hour health law and medical ethics course is a requirement for all students. The course is taught by health attorneys and uses both lecture and seminar formats. The primary topics covered are a basic introduction to the legal system and bioethics, patients rights and informed consent, medical malpractice, confidentiality and privacy, reproduction and the law, death and organ transplantation, terminal illness and right to refuse treatment, human experimentation, medical student responsibilities, and the regulation of medical practice (Appendix 1-3).

The Boston University School of Medicine's health law and bioethics curriculum is integrated into other courses taken during the second year of medical school, such as drug law and research ethics in pharmacology and abortion in reproductive endocrinology. The clinical years also offer health law and bioethics faculty the opportunity to do general faculty inservice teaching, deliver formal grand rounds, participate in case conferences, consult to medical education (such as in the intensive care unit or a human immunodeficiency virus [HIV] clinic), and assist in creating policies. Specific health law and bioethics case studies have been developed for use in the third- and fourth-year clerkships and in the integrated problems seminar required of all students.

CONTINUING EDUCATION

Postgraduate medicolegal education should be an integral part of every specialty training program throughout each year of residency and fellowship. This can usually be accomplished with relative academic ease because the physicians (for the most part) are physically present in the hospital complex and can be convened at appropriate times. Moreover, because most residency training programs are located in large medical centers, there are often full- or part-time attorneys available at the center itself or within the close surrounding community who could be called on to give lectures and spearhead discussions on a variety of medicolegal subjects. In addition, staff physicians (hospital-employed and private practitioners), hospital administrative personnel, and other health care professionals can participate in these educational sessions.

Although much useful medicolegal information can be imparted to medical school students, many of these topics assume greater significance and critical importance to graduate physicians as they pursue their chosen careers in more focalized fashion. Broad philosophical concepts and generalized references then begin to have more immediate and identifiable applications to the actual daily practices of their designated specialties. This keener awareness of what is expected of them from the judicial system should be capitalized on to the fullest extent possible.

Regularly scheduled discussions of an informal nature should be augmented by more formal presentations given by experts on specific subjects. From time to time, visiting academicians and outstanding medical and legal practitioners are available in the community. They should be contacted in advance and invited to meet with staff and resident physicians to share their knowledge and experiences.

More formally structured programs should be implemented for appropriate specialties (forensic pathology instruction at the coroner's or medical examiner's office; forensic psychiatry at prisons, detention centers, and community mental health facilities; forensic aspects of orthopedic surgery and physical medicine at large trauma and rehabilitation centers, etc.).

Continuing medicolegal education for fully trained practicing physicians should be encouraged and facilitated by local medical and bar associations, specialty societies, and medical and law schools. Luncheons and dinner meetings with special speakers can be appropriate and pleasant forums in which to provide mandatory continuing medical education credits. Pharmaceutical companies, private foundations, insurance companies, large law firms, and some governmental agencies can be ethically solicited to sponsor such events. Many communities have annual interprofessional medicolegal meetings that can be used as vehicles to disseminate traditional information (e.g., preparing the treating physician for expert testimony) and newer concepts (e.g., physician-assisted suicide).

In 1982 the American Board of Legal Medicine was established to administer examinations to individuals with both legal and medical degrees. Since then, this Board has certified approximately 250 M.D./J.D.s in legal medicine. These examinations are given annually. Other specialty groups that may have some relevance to M.D./J.D.s are the American College of Physician Executives and the American College of Quality Assurance.

Although a law degree is not a prerequisite, formal legal training can be of great value to forensic pathologists seeking certification in that subspecialty by the American Board of Pathology and quite similarly to forensic psychiatrists seeking certification in their subspecialty by the American Board of Psychiatry.

HUMAN RIGHTS AND HEALTH

By the middle of the 1990s it was recognized that health law and medical ethics could constructively be combined in the growing area of international human rights, especially in the area of "human rights in health." The fiftieth anniversary of the Nuremberg physicians' trial, in which physicians and attorneys worked together to bring some of the Nazi physicians to justice, was observed in 1996.[35] The anniversary spurred the International Association of Bioethics to devote major portions of its biannual meeting to discussing health and human rights and an international commemoration meeting at the U.S. Holocaust Memorial Museum in late

1996. It also led to the foundation of Global Lawyers and Physicians (GLP), a new international organization devoted to bringing attorneys and physicians together to promote human rights in health around the world. GLP works with existing physician and attorney groups, such as Physicians for Human Rights and the Lawyers' Committee for Human Rights, toward realizing this goal.[36] There are a growing number of health and human rights courses, seminars, and student groups at schools of law, medicine, and public health (Appendix 1-4). A new course textbook focusing on the inextricable link between health and human rights also was recently published.[37]

CONCLUSION

As global interdependence grows and the metaphor of the global village approaches at least informational reality, the need for interdisciplinary study and real-world cooperation has taken on new meaning. Perhaps nowhere have both the need and opportunities for professional cooperation expanded as dramatically as in the field that was historically known as *legal medicine*. Physicians and attorneys must work together to both shape and respond to the new global realities in which country- and culture-based practices and laws are increasingly shaped by international events and the recognition of the impact of human rights on health. These exciting and challenging times demand both intensive health law and ethics education in medical and law schools, as well as constructive cooperation between the legal and medical professions in addressing the health-related problems of the world.

ENDNOTES

1. William J. Curran, *Titles in the Medicolegal Field: A Proposal for Reform*, 1 Am. J.L. Med. 1-11 (1975).
2. Alan R. Moritz, *The Need of Forensic Pathology for Academic Sponsorship*, 33 Arch. Pathology 382-386 (1942).
3. *Supra* note 1.
4. Sir Sidney Smith, *The History and Development of Legal Medicine*, in *Legal Medicine*, 1-19 (R.B.H. Gradwohi ed., C.V. Mosby Co., St Louis 1954).
5. *Id.*
6. Gilbert H. Stewart, *Legal Medicine*, 1-6 (Bobbs-Merrill Co., Indianapolis 1910).
7. *Supra* note 1.
8. *Supra* note 6.
9. *Supra* note 4.
10. Chester R. Burns, *Legacies in Law and Medicine* (Science History Publications, Canton 1977).
11. William J. Curran, *History and Development*, in *Modern Legal Medicine, Psychiatry, and Forensic Science*, 1-26 (William J. Curran et al. eds., F.A. Davis Co., Philadelphia 1980).
12. James C. Mohr, *Doctors and the Law: Medical Jurisprudence in the Nineteenth Century America* (Oxford University Press, New York 1993).
13. Benjamin Rush, *Introductory Lectures upon the Institutes and Practices of Medicine*, 363 (Bradford and Innskeep, Philadelphia 1811). *See* Curran, *supra* note 1.
14. *Id.*
15. *Id.*
16. George Annas chaired the first National Health Law Teachers conference, which was sponsored by Boston University's Center for Law and Health Sciences. Since 1976 the Health Law Teacher's Meeting has been held a dozen times, biannually until 1985 and annually since.
17. *Teaching Health Law: A Symposium*, 38 J. Legal Educ. 485-576 (1988).
18. 5. Law, *Teaching Health Law: A Symposium: Introduction*, 38 J. Legal Educ. 485, 486 (1988). The basic text for the standard law and medicine course is William J. Curran et al., *Law, Medicine and Forensic Science* (4th ed., Little, Brown and Company, Boston 1991).
19. R. Rosenblatt, *Conceptualizing Health Law for Teaching Purposes: The Social Justice Perspective*, 38 J. Legal Educ. 489 (1988).
20. C. Havighurst, *Health Care as a Laboratory for the Study of Law and Policy*, 38 J. Legal Educ. 499 (1988).
21. George J. Annas, *Health Law at the Turn of the Century: From White Dwarf to Red Giant*, 2 Comm. L. Rev. 551 (1989).
22. Standard texts include B. Furrow et al., *Health Law* (2d ed., West Publishing Co., St Paul, Minn. 1994) and *American Health Law* (Little, Brown and Company, Boston 1990).
23. M. Kelman, *A Guide to Critical Legal Studies*, 186 (Harvard University Press, Cambridge, Mass. 1987).
24. *Id.*
25. K. Wing, *The Law and the Public's Health* (6th ed., Health Administration Press, Ann Arbor, Mich. 2003).
26. Ten years ago one of us (George J. Annas) proposed devoting the entire last semester of law school to health law for all students. It is no secret to most law students and faculty that the final semester of the third year is often a lost semester. It is also no secret that law school curriculum is becoming increasingly detached from the real world, attorneys are becoming increasingly alienated from their work, and their fellow citizens are becoming increasingly alienated from them. *See, e.g.*, D. Bok, *A Flawed System of Law Practice and Teaching*, 33 J. Legal Educ. 570 (1983). *See also* H. Wellington, *Challenges to Legal Education: The "Two Cultures" Phenomenon*, 37 J. Legal Educ. 327 (1987) and J. White, *Doctrine in a Vacuum: Reflections on What a Law School Ought (and Ought Not) To Be*, 36 J. Legal Educ. 155 (1986). As already stressed, health law is applied law, and providing students with the opportunity to apply what they have learned in law school to a particular field of human endeavor gives them an opportunity to synthesize their knowledge and approach the world in an encompassing rather than a reductive mode. As Dean George Schatzki of the University of Connecticut Law School stressed in opening a 1989 health law symposium: "Law is concerned with making the world a better place to live in." (From *Welcoming Remarks, Conference on Law and Medicine: Unresolved Issues for the 1990s*, University of Connecticut School of Law, March 29, 1989.) When Dean Robert Clark of Harvard Law School was asked what he considered the "leading issues in the study of law today" he listed "health care regulations" first (March 31 *New York Times* B6 [1989]). Dean Schatzki went on to list the four areas that are central to individuals' lives but are seldom dealt with in law school—family, work, recreation, and health. Health law is the only field that can cover all of these areas and thus play a key role in humanizing the law school curriculum and encouraging attorneys and law students to get involved in and help solve critical human problems.
27. There are a variety of curriculum options. One would be to have all students take a basic overview course on health law in the fall of the third year, with special emphasis on developing an understanding of the health care industry itself. The second semester would then consist of three or four courses, each approaching the industry from a different perspective (such as law and economics, social justice, bioethics, technology, public health, environmental law, occupational health and safety law, and law and medicine). Students would then participate in a writing seminar, a clinical project, or both, preferably with one or

more medical students. Health law presents an opportunity to apply law and its rules and procedures to the most intrinsically fascinating and substantively influential industry in the United States. As the subject matter of health law—the fields of medicine, public health, and bioethics—continues to expand, so does the field of health law itself. Of course, once the health care system is under control, the final semester could concentrate on other real-world problems, such as the criminal justice system, education, energy, transportation, and the environment.

28. Harry S. Jonas et al., *Educational Programs in U.S. Medical Schools,* 270 J.A.M.A. 1061-1068 (1993).

29. Eugene S. Schneller & Terry S. Weiner, *The M.D./J.D. Revisited: A Sociological Analysis of Cross-Educated Professionals in the Decade of the 1980s,* 6 J. Legal Med. 337-359 (1985).

30. *Id.*

31. B. Blechner et al., *The Jay Healey Technique: Teaching Law and Ethics to Medical and Dental Students,* 20 Am. J. Law Med. 439 (1994).

32. S. Miles et al., *Medical Ethics Education: Coming of Age,* 64 Academic Medicine 705-714 (1989).

33. C.M. Culver et al., *Special Report: Basic Curricular Goals in Medical Ethics,* 312(4) New Engl. J. Med. 253-255 (1985).

34. M.A. Grodin ed., *Meta Medical Ethics: The Philosophical Foundations of Bioethics* (Kluwer Academic Press, Norwell, Mass. 1995).

35. M.A. Grodin & George J. Annas, *Legacies of Nuremberg: Medical Ethics and Human Rights,* 276 J.A.M.A. 1682 (1996).

36. George J. Annas & Michael A. Grodin eds., *The Nazi Doctors and the Nuremberg Code: Human Rights in Human Experimentation* (Oxford University Press, New York 1992).

37. Jonathan Mann, Sofia Gruskin, Michael A. Grodin, & George J. Annas eds., *Health and Human Rights* (Routledge, New York 1999).

APPENDIX 1-1   Program of Law and Medicine

SOUTHERN ILLINOIS UNIVERSITY SCHOOL OF MEDICINE
THEODORE R. LeBLANG, J.D., F.C.L.M. (PROGRAM DIRECTOR)

PROGRAM OVERVIEW

The Department of Medical Humanities offers a curriculum designed to provide students with core knowledge in the humanities, emphasizing application of the content and methodologies of humanities disciplines to the practice of medicine. Substantive areas of teaching emphasis include ethics, health policy, law, medical history, philosophy, and psychosocial care. Department faculty provide educational experiences for undergraduate medical students during Years One and Two. During Year Three, the Department delivers a two-week curricular segment, entitled "The Physician-Patient Relationship." This two-week segment forms part of the School's Doctoring curriculum. Also during Year Three, the Department delivers multiple integrated learning experiences, or "modules," that form part of the Clinical Clerkships. During Year Four, a second two-week curricular segment is delivered, which is entitled "Society, Law, and Health Care: The Physician's Role." This segment also forms part of the Doctoring curriculum. Additionally, numerous electives are offered during Year Four for students enrolled in the M.D. and M.D./J.D. dual degree programs.

The program of law and medicine, which began in the mid-1970s, is an academic program in the Department of Medical Humanities. Although teaching activity in the program is integrated throughout the four-year curriculum, required instruction in legal medicine is concentrated during Years Three and Four.

In Year Three, the two-week Medical Humanities curricular segment focuses on the physician-patient relationship. Significant issues in law and medicine are considered as part of learning experiences focusing on confidentiality and privacy, informed consent, standards of care (malpractice), withholding and withdrawing life-sustaining treatment,

assisted death, and organ donation. Teaching methodologies include lectures, panel discussions, case conferences, tutor group activities, and simulated patient interactions. Throughout the segment, teaching emphasis is placed on strengthening the physician-patient relationship.

In Year Four, the two-week Medical Humanities curricular segment comprises the following content areas: (1) the physician's role in the administration of justice; and (2) the physician's role in society, with emphasis on current changes in health care delivery. During the first part of the segment, students are exposed to an overview of the judicial process and the manner in which physicians serve as expert witnesses in civil and criminal trial proceedings. Systems of medicolegal investigation also are discussed, with emphasis on forensic pathology.

Students further explore issues involving regulation of medical expert testimony in the courts. Finally, a mock trial is staged, permitting students to observe the trial process in a courtroom setting. During the second part of the segment, students examine various important issues relating to health care in the United States. These issues include the following: access to and availability of health care; the economics, financing, and cost of health care; responsibility and accountability of physicians; assessing quality in health care; access to care for rural and underserved populations; and clinical, ethical, legal, and policy issues in managed care.

Educational activities in the program of law and medicine are based on prescribed learning objectives that convey to each student relevant faculty expectations. Learning objectives are contained in modules, which are the basic learning components of the curriculum. Modules are self-contained curriculum units, wherein faculty designate specific learning objectives, required and recommended learning activities, and the criteria for successful completion.

Presentation of legal medicine modules during Year 3 (the clinical clerkship year) familiarizes students with important legal principles at a time when these principles are particularly relevant to their clinical activities. Within the two-week Medical Humanities curricular segment, as previously described, approximately 50% of learning modules focus entirely, or in part, on issues arising at the interface of law and medicine. In addition to the modules that form part of this curricular segment, numerous additional modules focus on issues that are uniquely relevant to the medical specialties of internal medicine, obstetrics and gynecology, pediatrics, and psychiatry. These modules are integrated directly into the respective clinical clerkships.

In the internal Medicine Clerkship, a multidisciplinary module on domestic violence focuses on clinical, legal, and psychosocial considerations relating primarily to partner abuse. In the Obstetrics and Gynecology Clerkship, a learning module focuses on the legal aspects of abortion. In the Pediatrics Clerkship, a learning module focuses on the legal aspects of child abuse and neglect. And in the Psychiatry Clerkship, a learning module focuses on issues involving the following topics: civil commitment and patients' rights after involuntary hospitalization; concepts of insanity, competency, and testamentary capacity; confidentiality and privacy within the psychiatrist-patient relationship; and psychiatric malpractice, with emphasis on potential areas of liability, including the failure to warn third parties of a patient's dangerous propensities. Thus throughout the clinical clerkship segment of the undergraduate curriculum, students participate in numerous required learning modules addressing important issues in legal medicine.

During Year Four, law and medicine teaching is included in the second two-week Medical Humanities curricular segment. Additionally, a diverse selection of electives is offered to students in the M.D. program who wish to further their knowledge in areas of legal medicine. Included among these electives are the following: AIDS: Law and Ethics; Health Policy Issues for the 21st Century—eHealth, Public Health, and Beyond; Law and Bioethics; Legal and Policy Issues in Aging; Legal and Ethical Issues in Organ and Tissue Donation and Transplantation; Negotiation and Dispute Resolution in Health Care; and Studies in Law and Medicine.

CURRICULUM DETAIL

Titles and descriptions of the various required and elective learning experiences that form part of the program of law and medicine are detailed in the following sections.

Year One

Confidentiality: legal and ethical issues. As soon as medical students begin their studies, they face legal and ethical questions about protecting patient confidentiality and privacy. These questions will persist throughout their professional lives in one form or another. The purpose of this module is to give students a legal and ethical framework for thinking about whether to protect or breach confidentiality and privacy. The module focuses on dilemmas that participants face as students.

Year Two

Introduction to family violence. With increasing frequency, physicians are confronted with problems of family violence in the context of patient care. Accordingly, students should be familiar with the basic clinical, legal, ethical, and psychosocial issues that may arise in treating victims of child abuse, partner abuse, or elder abuse. This multidisciplinary learning experience provides students an opportunity to explore these issues in the context of lectures and small group, case-based discussions.

Year Three

Two-week Medical Humanities (doctoring) curricular segment

Legal perspectives on the physician-patient relationship: overview of sources of law. Various societal expectations pertaining to the clinical practice of medicine have been codified in law. Predominantly this codification takes the form of state and federal legislation, as well as applicable regulations of state and federal agencies. Common law principles, which are articulated by state and federal courts, also constitute an important source of law in this regard.

It is the purpose of this module to provide students with an overview of the sources and types of law that bear upon the physician-patient relationship. Certain illustrative Illinois statutes have been selected for discussion. In varying ways, each of these legislative enactments has an impact on the practice of medicine and the physician-patient relationship. Consideration of these statutes provides an excellent foundation for evaluating legal issues that arise in the context of clinical practice.

Standard of care: legal rights and responsibilities in the physician-patient relationship. The physician-patient relationship has at its core a set of rights and responsibilities attributable both to the physician and to the patient. These rights and duties establish the broad parameters of the relationship and are affected in various ways by established common law doctrines and pertinent statutory enactments. These bodies of law delineate the nature and scope of such concepts as medical malpractice, informed consent, physician-patient privilege, and privacy and confidentiality.

Because of the significance of these legal concepts in the context of the physician-patient relationship, it is essential to develop awareness of the specific meaning and applicability of these concepts and the legal bases on which they are founded. It is the purpose of this module to discuss the common law and statutory bases of medical malpractice against the background of specific clinical case illustrations in which medical malpractice may have occurred. Emphasis is placed on consideration of the standard of care in the context of health care delivery and the physician-patient relationship.

Informed consent in the physician-patient relationship. Within the physician-patient relationship there is a set of legal rights and responsibilities applicable to both physician and patient. These rights and responsibilities provide a framework for consideration of the doctrine of informed consent. Under this legal doctrine, physicians are obligated to disclose to patients the nature of a proposed medical treatment or procedure, the anticipated benefits and material risks thereof, and any reasonably available alternatives. This disclosure obligation is evaluated based on application of principles of negligence and medical malpractice law, with emphasis on the standard of care.

It is the purpose of this module to discuss common law and statutory foundations for the legal doctrine of informed consent against the background of specific case illustrations that demonstrate applicability of this doctrine in clinical situations. Historical evolution of the informed consent doctrine also is traced with emphasis on medical ethics.

Confidentiality and privacy: ethical and legal considerations. Confidentiality within the physician-patient relationship facilitates full, frank, and candid disclosure of medical information from patient to treating physician. This is intended to permit the physician to reach an appropriate diagnosis and achieve a satisfactory clinical outcome. Because of the personal nature of confidential patient information, in most situations physicians are ethically and legally obligated to protect such information from improper disclosure. Moreover, a statutory privilege exists to ensure that, as a general rule, physicians are not required to disclose confidential information in certain courtroom situations.

It is the purpose of this module to discuss the common law and statutory predicates of the legal doctrines of confidentiality and privacy against the background of specific case illustrations that demonstrate applicability of these principles in clinical situations. Related ethical and philosophical considerations also are addressed.

Legal, ethical, and psychosocial aspects of withholding or withdrawing treatment. Some physicians believe that they have an obligation to prolong life without regard to its quality or other considerations. CPR and ICU technologies have made it possible to prolong life in individuals who have little or no prospect of improving. Death is kept at bay as if death were always undesirable and the physician's enemy. As a result, patients have sometimes been forced to endure a prolonged process of dying or to live what they or others judge to be a meaningless existence.

The ethical, legal, and psychosocial issues associated with these behaviors are complex. The purpose of this module is to familiarize students with a variety of issues, including the following: Do physicians really have an obligation to prolong life under all circumstances? Is withholding or withdrawing life support killing? If it is proper to withhold or withdraw care in some circumstances, then who makes this decision? What criteria should be used to decide when medical care should be withheld or withdrawn? What mechanisms exist to insure that the previously expressed desires of incompetent patients, with respect to withholding or withdrawing life-sustaining treatment, may be acted on by health care providers?

Case studies in withholding or withdrawing treatment. This module focuses on the practical clinical problems associated with managing cases of terminal illness. In particular, the module explores the professional attitudes and beliefs that contribute to difficulties surrounding terminal illness involving communicating and decision-making with patients, their surrogates, and other health professionals.

Assisted death: legal and ethical issues. The growing controversy over whether physicians should assist patients in dying raises difficult ethical and legal questions. The purpose of this module is to help students understand the concepts that are used to make ethical distinctions among the "options of last resort" practiced in the United States, how those distinctions are imbedded in law, and how the law in turn shapes the options available to terminally ill patients and their physicians.

Organ donation. During the last 40 years the science of organ transplantation has advanced rapidly. Concomitant advances in medical procedures and medical technology have rapidly increased the number of patients who are medically eligible to receive donated organs as well. In an effort to respond positively to this demand, state and federal laws have changed repeatedly. Each change and proposal for change has raised questions about the rights and responsibilities of individuals, their families, physicians, and other health care professionals in supplying organs for potential recipients.

Physicians, because of their close relationships with patients, are sometimes looked to as a source of information about organ donation. They also manage dying patients who will be organ donors. As such, they need to understand legal and ethical frameworks for organ donation.

Internal Medicine Clerkship (multidisciplinary learning module)

Domestic violence: interdisciplinary workshop. Medical Humanities faculty participate with Department of Internal Medicine faculty in the context of a domestic violence workshop, focusing primarily on spousal abuse. Clinical, legal, social, and psychosocial issues are explored in lectures, small group discussions, and simulated patient examinations that are observed and critiqued by faculty.

Obstetrics and Gynecology Clerkship (integrated learning module)

Legal aspects of abortion. Illinois statutes regarding abortion, as well as U.S. constitutional law, have undergone considerable change in response to the social, philosophical, cultural, religious, and political issues that relate to abortion. The changes have become increasingly significant, and in the absence of a constitutional amendment, the relevant decisions of the U.S. Supreme Court, on their face and through resulting state statutes, affect the parameters of the physician-patient relationship.

It is the purpose of this module to familiarize students with certain important Supreme Court decisions relating to abortion. It is also the purpose of this module to acquaint students with relevant Illinois laws that relate to abortion and to trace the development of these laws.

Pediatrics Clerkship (integrated learning module)

Legal aspects of child abuse and neglect. Although children have been victims of maltreatment throughout history, child abuse has become a major concern for our society. As a result of the rapidly increasing numbers of abused and neglected children, there is a significant likelihood that the practicing physician will be confronted with such children in a variety of contexts.

It is the purpose of this module to familiarize physicians with their statutory rights and responsibilities in the context of providing care and treatment to abused and neglected children. This module focuses on the Illinois Abused and Neglected Child Reporting Act. Emphasis also is placed on significant provisions of the Illinois Juvenile Court Act that pertain to cases of child abuse and neglect. In this regard, the role of the physician as a participant in juvenile court proceedings and how the physician can effectively carry out this role are examined and discussed. Finally, this module addresses the issue of civil liability, which may result from a physician's failure to report instances of child abuse and neglect.

Psychiatry Clerkship (integrated learning module)

Psychiatry and law. The impact of law on clinical psychiatry has become increasingly apparent. Judicial decisions, state and federal legislation, and administrative regulatory schemes affect day-to-day clinical decision-making across a broad range of psychiatric settings and patient populations.

It is the purpose of this module to familiarize the student with significant statutory and common law developments at the state and federal levels that impact the nature and delivery of psychiatric patient care. Primary emphasis is placed on legal issues that involve hospitalization of mentally ill patients, patients' rights, confidentiality and privilege, psychiatric negligence, insanity, and fitness to stand trial.

Year Four

Two-week Medical Humanities (doctoring) curricular segment

Overview of the judicial process. Because of the significant potential for physician involvement in litigation either as a witness on behalf of a patient, an expert witness, or a party to a lawsuit, it is important for the physician to possess a general knowledge of the judicial process. The purpose of this module is to provide a broad overview of the judicial process with emphasis on pretrial, trial, and post-trial procedures. This module also addresses the appellate court process and its relationship to trial court activities. Federal and state court activities and litigation also are compared.

The physician as expert witness. Throughout the course of an active medical practice, a physician is likely to become involved as an expert witness during the course of civil or criminal litigation. In the capacity of a medical expert, the physician may be asked to give testimony regarding the nature and cause of injuries suffered as a consequence of an automobile accident or employment-related mishap. The physician expert also may be called on to testify regarding the standard of care in a medical malpractice case or regarding medical facts that bear directly upon a criminal prosecution charging homicide or sexual assault.

In any of these situations it is important that the physician be aware of the precise role played by the medical expert and the manner in which the medical expert's responsibilities may best be fulfilled. The purpose of this module is to examine the physician's role as a medical expert witness in civil and criminal proceedings, placing focus on pretrial and trial involvement.

Forensic medicine: medical-legal investigation. Forensic medicine, broadly defined, has to do with an interaction between medicine and law and more specifically relates to medical problems that result in subsequent legal procedures. Forensic pathology is that branch of forensic medicine that involves the examination of deaths generally falling into the following categories: (1) physical injury; (2) chemical injury; and (3) unexpected "natural" death. The forensic pathologist is expected to aid in determining the cause of death, the mechanisms of death, and the manner of death.

Forensic pathology is conducted within the framework of a specific system created by state or local laws. The systems currently operating within the United States are the coroner's system and the medical examiner's system. Medical-legal investigation includes the circumstances of death, the postmortem examination, and a variety of laboratory procedures, including toxicology and trace analysis. Investigation of the circumstances of death is carried out by various law enforcement agencies along with representatives of the coroner's or medical examiner's offices. The postmortem examination is generally carried out by a pathologist; however, in some instances practicing physicians perform postmortem examinations. Laboratory procedures may be performed in the pathologist's laboratory (usually a hospital laboratory), a state toxicology laboratory, and the so-called crime laboratory.

In Illinois, there are three systems for handling medical-legal investigation. In Cook County, a medical examiner's system is responsible for all branches of the medical-legal investigation. A large number of remaining counties use the classic coroner's system. On the basis of the Illinois constitution, some more thinly populated counties eliminate the coroner, and the county board appoints a "death investigator." The death investigator may be the local sheriff, a physician in the community, or some other citizen in the community.

The physician as expert witness—regulating the medical expert. Physicians make ideal expert witnesses: they are well-educated, well-respected members of society with superior knowledge of complex scientific issues. A physician expert witness who can present to the jury an articulate, plausible opinion as to why a particular chain of events led to a particular result can be a primary reason why a jury will come to a particular decision.

While most physician experts perform their roles admirably, there are concerns that some others, through inaccuracies or misrepresentations in their testimony, are contributing to the ever-rising costs of health care services and malpractice insurance, damaging the public's confidence in the medical profession, and occasionally leading to the destruction of personal and professional reputations.

This module explores what is being done to ensure that the physician who appears as an expert witness is a responsible participant in the administration of justice, as well as a practitioner who is promoting sound medicine.

Mock trial. The opportunity for the medical student to integrate substantive and procedural legal knowledge in the context of a clinical courtroom proceeding is an essential adjunct to a full and complete law and medicine learning experience. It is the purpose of this module to stage a mock trial presentation that offers a realistic forum for consideration of substantive and procedural law.

To ensure maximum reality, the mock trial takes place in the Circuit Court of Illinois, Seventh Judicial Circuit. The landmark Illinois case of *Darling v. Charleston Memorial Hospital* is reenacted in an abridged fashion with emphasis on demonstrating the major aspects of a complete civil trial.

Introduction to the United States health care system. As a result of economic overhaul of the health care delivery system in the United States, it is important that students be provided with an overview of the United States health care system. Strengths and inadequacies of the current system are considered. Various modules incorporate certain legal issues in evaluating health care delivery from the perspectives of cost, quality, and access. These include the following: Introduction to the United States Health Care System; Financing Health Care; Managed Care—Physician and Hospital Services; Clinical Decision Making and Quality of Care—Con-

temporary Challenges; Access to Health Care—EMTALA; Mental Health Care: Cost, Quality, and Access; and Health Care Access and Availability for Vulnerable Populations.

Electives

AIDS: law and ethics. The purpose of this elective is to enable students to understand and think critically about the ethical and legal questions surrounding the AIDS epidemic. Those issues include but are not limited to testing, screening, reporting, partner notification, quarantine, and drug development. Students engage in research that results in an oral presentation and written research paper.

Health policy issues for the 21st century—eHealth, public health, and beyond. The health care delivery landscape of the twenty-first century looks drastically different from that of a generation ago, and the regulators and legislators who oversee physicians and other service providers must promptly recognize the new terrain and find ways both to allow for continued innovation and to effectively address new public protection concerns as they arise.

In this elective, students examine the following issues: the use of the internet and computers in medicine; the law of public health, including responses to bioterrorism and issues concerning vaccination of children and the general public; and patients' rights, which may include discussions of managed care regulation, the uninsured, privacy and confidentiality in medicine, and direct-to-consumer advertising of pharmaceuticals and health services. A wide array of resources are used to help students scrutinize the legal, political, ethical, practical, and medical challenges arising within each of these subject areas. Students are afforded the option of examining health policy areas of personal interest in place of one or more of the above-listed topics. In addition, students are required to make an oral presentation on a related subject of their choice.

Law and bioethics. Students read and discuss significant legal cases on issues such as reproductive technologies, assisted suicide, organ transplantation, the right to refuse treatment, human subjects research, the definition of death, confidentiality, and informed consent. A two-page written analysis of a question related to a case is required for each session.

Legal and policy issues in aging. In the year 2011, the first members of the 76-million-strong baby boomer generation will turn 65. This will have enormous economic, social, and political consequences, and put even greater strain on the country's already unstable health care delivery system. This elective is designed to enable students to develop an understanding of policy and legal issues concerning the care and treatment of America's aged population. Issues addressed may include the role of managed care in Medicare and Medicaid, the impact of changes in use of home health, assisted living, and nursing home services, proposed and recently adopted changes to the Medicare system, and special circumstances affecting the rural elderly. During the course of the elective, students engage in research that results in an oral presentation and written research paper. Students also are responsible for completing assigned readings and participation in small group discussion.

Legal and ethical issues in organ and tissue donation and transplantation. The purpose of this elective is to enable students to understand and think critically about the legal and ethical issues related to organ and tissue donation and transplantation. Topics include the following: gift vs. market paradigms; use of anencephalic fetuses, prisoners, minors, and non-heart-beating cadavers as sources of organs and tissue; rationing of scarce, life-saving medical resources; and cost-effectiveness analysis of transplantation. The Uniform Anatomical Gift Act, the End-Stage Renal Disease Amendments to the Social Security Act, the National Organ Transplant Act, statutory and proposed definitions of brain death, routine inquiry, and required request, and other statutes and proposals are analyzed.

Negotiation and dispute resolution in health care. Negotiation occurs daily at all levels of the health care industry—from discussing treatment options with patients and insurance companies to resolving intra-office conflicts to engineering multi-billion-dollar hospital mergers. Knowing how to effectively negotiate solutions to problems and disagreements is critical to a physician's ability to practice successfully in today's complex health care environment. This elective is designed to enable medical students to learn negotiation and dispute resolution techniques that can be used in medical and nonmedical settings. Students enrolled in this elective study the various forms of dispute resolution available outside the courtroom setting. Through assigned readings and role-playing exercises, students learn techniques that will enable them to resolve conflicts by identifying and building upon mutual interests.

Studies in law and medicine. This elective enables students to develop the ability to analyze medical decisions from a legal viewpoint. It involves review of case law relating to health care delivery, the physician-patient relationship, and the physician's role in the administration of justice. The elective emphasizes a sophisticated analysis of national case law and a comparison of issues raised in previous medical humanities rotations.

Students attend lectures and seminars provided by various faculty, including attorneys from state agencies and professional organizations, representing the interests of health care providers. Students also examine medical-legal issues that are of specific interest to them.

APPENDIX 1-2   M.D./J.D. Dual Degree Program

SOUTHERN ILLINOIS UNIVERSITY SCHOOLS OF MEDICINE AND LAW
THEODORE R. LeBLANG, J.D., F.C.L.M. (PROGRAM DIRECTOR, SCHOOL OF MEDICINE)
W. EUGENE BASANTA, B.A., J.D., LL.M. (PROGRAM DIRECTOR, SCHOOL OF LAW)

PROGRAM OVERVIEW

Recognizing the heightened level of interaction between the professions of law and medicine in today's society, Southern Illinois University Schools of Medicine and Law offer an M.D./J.D. dual degree program to accommodate the increasing number of individuals seeking a carefully structured interdisciplinary education. The dual degree program is designed to lead to the concurrent award of degrees in law and medicine at the completion of a six-year program involving academic and clinical study.

CURRICULUM DESIGN AND PROGRAM CONTENT

The SIU program requires students to spend their first year at the School of Law in Carbondale, where they complete 31 credit hours of prescribed first-year course work. Students then enroll in the law school summer session and complete 6 credit hours of advanced course work, as well as a 1-hour legal research course offered during the summer intersession.

During the second academic year, students continue as full-time law students in Carbondale, completing an additional 32 credit hours of course work with concentration in health law. Enrollment in a second summer session is required, during which students complete 6 credit hours of course work. This session may include legal research and clinical experience at state or federal agencies or private not-for-profit organizations involved in health policy development, regulation of public health, or the activities of the medical profession.

Students spend their third academic year enrolled as first-year students in the School of Medicine at Carbondale, where they complete all requirements of Year One of the medical school curriculum. Students then move to Springfield, where they continue as full-time medical students, completing Years Two and Three of the curriculum.

During Year Four of medical school, students are required to take a specially designed set of law, medicine, and health policy electives lasting 14 weeks full-time. In completing degree requirements for both the M.D. and J.D. degrees, this 14-week elective sequence fulfills 14 credit hours of course work required for attainment of the

J.D. degree and 14 weeks of elective course work required for attainment of the M.D. degree.

M.D./J.D. ELECTIVE SEQUENCE

Eighteen weeks of electives are available to M.D./J.D. program students, from which they must select and participate in at least 14 weeks full-time. Descriptions of these electives are detailed here.

Forensic psychiatry subinternship

This elective provides a focused clinical experience in forensic psychiatry that builds on and enhances the basic clinical experience provided in the psychiatry clerkship. Emphasis is placed on clinical interaction with forensic patients and inpatients who have been involuntarily hospitalized under the provisions of the Illinois Mental Health and Developmental Disabilities Code. Students act as subinterns at the Chester Mental Health Center (Chester).

Supervision is provided by designated attending forensic psychiatrists at Chester and consists of daily oral review of diagnosis, treatment, and management plans and individual supervisory sessions reviewing all aspects of patient care, with emphasis on forensic considerations and medical-legal interventions.

Activities and experiences include daily rounds, psychiatric evaluation and management of assigned patients, daily written progress notes and orders, and preparation of forensic reports based on psychiatric assessments of patients involved in criminal proceedings regarding their sanity and fitness to stand trial. Students also participate in treatment interventions with medical-legal ramifications, such as involuntary treatment, restraint, and seclusion.

Health policy formulation: the legislative and regulatory processes in Illinois

This elective is designed to enable students to develop an understanding of health policy formulation in Illinois; emphasis is on the nature and scope of both the legislative and regulatory processes. Students are involved in reviewing proposed legislation and regulations having an impact on the development of health policy and the practice of medicine in Illinois. Students interact with the Illinois General Assembly with an objective of obtaining insights into the legislative process. In situations where interest groups are attempting to influence legislation affecting health policy, students interact with members of these groups to explore and evaluate their views.

Learning experiences also include interaction with regulatory personnel at state agencies having jurisdiction over medical practice, health care delivery, public health, and health welfare programs. Students are afforded the opportunity to evaluate proposed regulations and to examine the assessment by the Joint Committee on Administrative Rules.

During the elective, students undertake sophisticated analysis of proposed health laws and regulations. Students also attend seminars, lectures, and tutorials with state agency regulatory personnel, general assembly members and staff, and teaching faculty. In addition, students are responsible for completing assigned readings describing the legislative and regulatory processes in Illinois.

History of medical jurisprudence in American medical education

This elective provides students with an overview of the development of medical jurisprudence as a special area for scholarly inquiry. Emphasis is placed on the early history of medical jurisprudence teaching in nineteenth-century U.S. medical schools, but important European influences are also explored. Students trace the evolution of medical jurisprudence as a subject of study in medical schools from its era of central importance in the early 1800s to the resurgence of interest in law and medicine in contemporary curricula.

In exploring the history of medical jurisprudence, students pay particular attention to classic areas of medicolegal overlap, including medicine's role in assisting with legal definitions of paternity and insanity. The role of physicians as expert witnesses is discussed, and the history of toxicology as a forensic tool is explored. Attention also is paid to the development of a number of related legal issues as they have informed the curricula of American medical schools, particularly the emergence of malpractice as the central concern of medicolegal study.

Hospital and health care organizations: current legal issues

This elective is intended to provide students with an overview of legal issues that bear upon the structure, organization, and operation of health care organizations. By attending seminars, students will gain insights into predominant aspects of the administration, management, and operation of health systems and associations. Additional learning activities focus on legal issues that form part of the policy agenda of the Illinois Hospital and Health Systems Association.

Issues in mental disability law

This elective provides the student with an opportunity to undertake in-depth scholarly study of some of the critical legal issues involving persons with mental disabilities.

There is a general overview of mental disability law and a review of some of the major cases affecting mental health services. The elective focuses on the following three issues: (1) the role of the psychiatrist in the implementation of the death penalty, such as participation in the insanity defense, competency to stand trial, and testimony concerning fitness to be executed; (2) the effect of the major "patient's rights" lawsuits on the quality of state mental health services, the impact of landmark court decisions on improving institutional conditions, and Supreme Court case law that sets a standard for violation of constitutional rights in institutions; and (3) the development and implementation of the right to refuse psychotropic medication in Illinois and other states, with emphasis on major cases defining such a right and studies on the impact of such a right on the delivery of mental health services.

Each issue is examined with emphasis on the interaction between law and psychiatry. Death penalty cases involve a potential moral dilemma of a psychiatrist asked to perform an evaluation and thereby become part of a legal process he or she may find objectionable. The institutional quality cases reflect the effect of law on public policy both on the state bureaucracy and the daily treatment and living conditions of the patients. The right to refuse cases are the paradigm of a conflict between the "medical model" and the "rights model" in mental health service delivery.

Medical-legal investigation: advanced studies in forensic pathology

This elective provides students with an in-depth understanding of the systems for medical-legal investigation. The role of forensic pathology in the context of medical-legal investigation is carefully explored. Student learning activities and experiences may include participation in and attendance at activities such as coroner's inquests, crime scene and laboratory investigations, postmortem examinations, criminal trial proceedings, and off-site visits to facilities that support medical-legal investigations (e.g., polygraph testing facilities and toxicology laboratories) or facilities where investigations may occur (e.g., investigations of death in prisons, jails, and mental health facilities).

During the course of the elective, students are responsible for completing various assigned readings focusing on topics in forensic pathology, maintaining a daily record of activities, and preparing a 1-hour formal oral presentation using photographs, graphics, and an annotated bibliography.

Regulation of the medical profession: current legal and policy issues

This elective provides students with the opportunity to examine some of the key policy and legal issues confronted by state medical licensing boards in the context of regulating the medical profession. The role of the professional regulatory board in the context of the modern health care delivery system will be examined in depth. Discussion will focus on issues such as the role of licensing boards in managed care, prescribing practices and privileges, the impact of technology on physician oversight, and the changing supervisory role of physicians over allied health professionals. A seminar/tutorial teaching format is used, with emphasis on student research and class discussion.

Studies in medical-legal aspects of obstetrics and gynecology

This elective is intended to provide students with an overview of medical-legal issues that have arisen in the context of clinical obstetrics and gynecology, with additional consideration of relevant research-related medical-legal issues. A seminar and tutorial teaching format is used, with emphasis on student research and group discussion.

Students are expected to read and evaluate assigned cases, focusing on important constitutional and common law issues involving such topics as abortion, maternal-fetal conflict, artificial human reproduction, the rights of newborns (including anencephalic infants), and other assigned topics. Relevant statutory law also is considered and discussed. Student activities include attendance at lectures, participation in interactive seminar discussions, and oral presentation of assigned research.

APPENDIX 1-3   Introduction to Health Law

BOSTON UNIVERSITY SCHOOL OF MEDICINE
GEORGE J. ANNAS, J.D., M.P.H.
LEONARD H. GLANTZ, J.D.
WENDY K. MARINER, J.D., LL.M., M.P.H.
MICHAEL A. GRODIN, M.D.

Course	Learning objectives	Required readings	Lecture outline
Introduction to the American legal system	1. Explain the basic legal system and its purposes 2. Distinguish various types of laws and their applications to medicine 3. Read and analyze judicial opinions related to medicine	1. Wind, *The Law and the Legal System*, "Introduction" (pp. 4-15) 2. "Reading a Legal Case" (2 pages) 3. Massachusetts laws on physician licensure 4. The "Student Doctor" and "A Wary Patient" 5. *Legacies of Nuremberg*	I. Role and function of the law II. "Kinds" of law III. Application of various kinds of law IV. Judge-made law (including how a case is heard and appealed)

Medical malpractice litigation	1. Understand the basic concepts of negligence law and how these apply to physicians 2. Understand what is meant by "standard of care" and how it is established 3. Understand the liability of health care institutions 4. Understand the obligation of institutions to provide emergency care	1. *Darling v. Charleston Hospital* 2. *Helling v. Carey* 3. *Wilmington General Hospital v. Manlove* 4. Massachusetts Good Samaritan Statute 5. Massachusetts regulation on provision of medical services in emergencies 6. Annas, *Rights of Patients*, Chapters IV and XIV	I. The elements of negligence II. The concepts of the "reasonable person" and burden of proof III. The role of the "expert witness" IV. The difference between harm and negligence V. The legal liability of institutions: corporate and vicarious liability VI. The legal obligation to render emergency care
Informed consent	1. Understand the concepts underlying the theory of informed consent 2. Understand the difference between battery and negligence 3. Understand the difference between informed consent and informed consent forms	1. *Cobbs v. Grant* 2. "Neglected Aspects of Informed Consent," letter to the editor 3. *Truman v. Thomas* 4. *Informed Consent, Cancer and Truth in Prognosis* 5. Massachusetts statute on HTLV testing 6. Consent form for anti-HIV test 7. *Rights of Patients*, Chapters VI and VII	I. The legal concept of battery II. Consent and implied consent III. The creation of the legal theory of informed consent and its purpose IV. The application of informed consent in different contexts V. The purpose of consent forms VI. Defenses
Confidentiality and privacy	1. Distinguish privacy, confidentiality, and privilege 2. Explain elements of a lawsuit alleging breach of confidentiality 3. Determine when it is reasonable to breach confidentiality to protect others	1. *Rights of Patients*, Chapters X and XI 2. *Home v. Patton* 3. *Berthiaume v. Pratt* 4. *Tarasoff v. Regents of University of California* 5. Massachusetts general laws on medical records and confidentiality	I. The nature of the dilemma (the role of confidentiality and its rationale) II. *Home v. Patton* III. *Berthiaume v. Pratt* IV. *Tarasoff v. Regents of University of California* V. Conclusion
Reproduction and the law	1. Acquire a basic understanding of how the U.S. Constitution limits state power and protects individual rights 2. Understand the constitutional "right of privacy" 3. Understand how courts balance individual rights and state power 4. Understand the nature and limits of the constitutional right of privacy as it pertains to reproductive decisions	1. *Roe v. Wade* 2. *Planned Parenthood v. Danforth* 3. *Summary of U.S. Supreme Court Decisions on Abortion* 4. Mariner, *The Supreme Court, Abortion, and the Jurisprudence of Class* 5. *Rights of Patients*, Chapter VIII	I. Constitutional limitations on state actions II. Early right of privacy cases and contraception III. *Roe v. Wade* and the rights of physicians IV. The application of *Roe* in subsequent cases V. *Planned Parenthood v. Casey* and the future of abortion litigation
Death and organ transplantation	1. Define death 2. Determine when organ donation is appropriate 3. Distinguish the dead from the dying 4. Define competence (to consent to and to refuse treatment)	1. *Rights of Patients*, Chapters IX and XIII 2. "A Definition of Irreversible Coma," *JAMA* 3. *Notes on Brain Death and Organ Harvesting* 4. *Lane v. Candura* 5. *Matter of Quinlan* 6. "The Promised End: Constitutional Aspects of Physician-Assisted Suicide"	I. Definition of death (brain and respiration criteria) II. Relationship of brain death to organ transplantation III. Consent mechanisms for organ donation IV. Competence to consent to (and refuse) medical interventions (*Candura*) V. The persistent vegetative state as an example of dying (*Quinlan*) VI. Refusing treatment v. suicide prevention

Continued

Course	Learning objectives	Required readings	Lecture outline

Treatment of the dying	1. Distinguish various types of advance directives, especially living wills and health care proxies
	2. Recognize the barriers to patient autonomy near death
	3. Distinguish between refusing treatment and physician-assisted suicide
		1. *Rights of Patients*, Chapter XII
		2. Annas, "Nancy Cruzan and the Right to Die," *N Engl J Med*
		3. Massachusetts Health Care Proxy Form
		4. SUPPORT, "A Controlled Trial to Improve Care for Seriously Ill Hospitalized Patients," *JAMA*
		5. The Oregon Death with Dignity Act
			I. Patient rights at the end of life
			II. Documenting patient directives
			  A. The living will
			  B. The health care proxy (including the Massachusetts model)
			III. The SUPPORT study and its lessons
			IV. Physician-assisted suicide
			  A. What it is (and is not)
			  B. Why now
			V. Conclusion

HTLV, Human T cell leukemia/lymphoma virus; *HIV*, human immunodeficiency virus.

APPENDIX 1-4   Human Rights and Health

BOSTON UNIVERSITY SCHOOL OF PUBLIC HEALTH
MICHAEL A. GRODIN, M.D.
GEORGE J. ANNAS, J.D., M.P.H.

COURSE DESCRIPTION

Human health is closely linked to the realization of human rights. Preventable illness, infant mortality, and premature death, for example, are closely tied to violation of human rights. This course explores the relationship between human rights and health by examining relevant international declarations in historical context, exploring the meaning of "human rights" and "health," and analyzing specific case studies that illuminate the problems, prospects, and potential methods of promoting health by promoting human rights on the national and international levels.

Goals and objectives

By the end of this course the student will:
1. Understand the relationship between human rights and health.
2. Be familiar with the Universal Declaration of Human Rights and the International Conventions on Human Rights.
3. Understand the history, role, and function of non-governmental organizations (NGOs) in addressing human rights problems.
4. Be able to determine when human rights have been violated, and be able to suggest strategies to protect and promote human rights.

Students

This course will be of special interest to the non-U.S. students (who are exempt from the introductory U.S.-focused Health Law courses) as well as U.S. students interested in international health, international law, and human rights.

Course texts

- Wiesel, E. *Night* (New York: Bantam, 1982) ISBN 0553272535 (pbk.)
- Steiner, H.J. & Alston, P. *International Human Rights in Context: Law, Politics, Morals*, 2d ed. (New York: Oxford University Press, 1996) ISBN 0-19-829849-8 (pbk.)
- Mann, J., Gruskin, S., Grodin, M. & Annas, G. *Health and Human Rights: A Reader* (New York: Routledge, 1999) ISBN 0-415-92102-3 (pbk.)

Requirements

A 20-page research paper (80% of final grade) addressing a specific problem in the area of human rights and health. The topic, outline, and bibliography must be submitted and discussed with faculty prior to writing the final paper. The paper will be written in two parts.

Part I:
- define the nature, scope and context of a human rights and health problem;
- describe the impediments to addressing the problem.

Part II:
- prepare a detailed proposed policy agenda for problem resolution which includes identifying foes and allies, funding considerations, implementation strategies, and mechanisms for review of plan efficacy.

Students will also give a brief oral presentation of their proposals to the class (10% of final grade). Class participation, preparation of the readings, and quizzes will also be considered in the final grade (10% of final grade).

COURSE OUTLINE

Preassignment

Wiesel

- Entire book

Reader (Pp. 281-335)

- The Nuremberg Doctors' Trial
- Medicine and Human Rights: Reflections on the Fiftieth Anniversary of the Doctors' Trial
- Questing for Grails: Duplicity, Betrayal, and Self-Deception in Postmodern Medical Research

Class One: Health and Human Rights in the Shadow of the Holocaust; Introduction to Health and Human Rights; the Link Between Health Status, Vulnerability and Rights

Steiner & Alston

- Pp. 1-17—Introduction to Human Rights Issues and Discourse (Global Snapshots)
- Skim pp. 18-55—Introduction to Human Rights Issues and Discourse (From Death Row to Execution: The Global Framework for Contemporary Human Rights Discourse)

Reader (Pp. 1-71)

- Introduction
- Human Rights and Public Health
- The Impact of Health Policies and Programs on Human Rights

Class Two: Human Rights Instruments and Documents: The International Bill of Human Rights

Steiner & Alston

- Pp. 56-135—Up to Nuremberg: Background to the Human Rights Movement
- Pp. 1365-1401—Charter of the United Nations; Universal Declaration of Human Rights; International Covenant on Civil and Political Rights; Protocols to the International Covenant on Civil and Political Rights; International Covenant on Economic, Social, and Cultural Rights

Reader (Pp. 480-481)

- List of documents

Class Three: Mechanisms of Enforcement and Reporting

Steiner & Alston

- Pp. 137-158, 180-186, 220-222, 224-236—Civil and Political Rights

- Pp. 237-319—Economic and Social Rights
- Pp. 592-604, 612-615, 619-623, 641-643, 694-698—Intergovernmental Enforcement of Human Right Norms: The United Nations System
- Pp. 1192-1198—The International Criminal Court

Class Four: Human Rights in Public Health Practice—Universality vs. Cultural and Ethical Relativism (Case Study: Female Genital Mutilation, Family Planning)

Steiner & Alston

- Pp. 323-324, 341 (note), 366-368—Rights, Duties, and Cultural Relativism
- Pp. 403-428—Conflicting Traditions and Rights: Illustrations

Reader (Pp. 336-372)

- Irreversible Error: The Power and Prejudice of Female Genital Mutilation

Class Five: Non-Governmental Organizations, Epidemiology Case Study: Amnesty International, Physicians for Human Rights, Global Lawyers and Physicians

Steiner & Alston

- Pp. 936-955, 965-967, 976-983—Civil Society: Human Rights NGOs and Other Groups

Reader (Pp. 397-438)

- How to Proceed from Concept to Action

Class Six: AIDS and TB Policy and Research and Its Relation to Human Rights—Discrimination, Immigration, and Stigmatization (Case Study: AIDS in Africa—Treatment and/or Prevention)

Steiner & Alston

- Pp. 705-714—Treaty Organizations: The ICCPR Human Rights Committee
- Pp. 814-835—Regional Arrangements (Cases)
- Pp. 987-1005—Interpretation of International and National Systems: Internal Protection of Human Rights by States

Reader (Pp. 202-226, 373-394)

- Interrelationship Between Gender Relations and the HIV/AIDS Epidemic: Some Possible Considerations for Policies and Programs
- Human Rights and AIDS: The Future of the Pandemic
- Human Rights and Maternal-Fetal HIV Transmission Prevention Trials in Africa
- Human Rights and Human Genomic Variation Research

UN Millennium Statement

Class Seven: Human Rights in Extremis, Humanitarian Law, Geneva Convention— Physician Involvement in Human Rights Violations—Armed Conflict and Torture (Case Study: Boston Center for Refugee Health and Human Rights) (Part One of paper due)

Reader (Pp. 75-112)

- Health Impacts Resulting from Violations of Human Rights

Handouts—Boston Center for Refugee Health and Human Rights

Class Eight: International Criminal Court and Criminal Tribunals for the Former Yugoslavia and Rwanda

Steiner & Alston

- Pp. 1131-1195—Massive Human Rights Tragedies: Prosecutions and Truth Commissions

Class Nine: Economics and Human Rights— Development, Economic Social and Cultural Rights, Sanctions, Multinational Corporations, World Bank, IMP, Structural Adjustment, Debt Relief

Steiner & Alston

- Pp. 1306-1361—Globalization, Development, and Human Rights
- Pp. 1079-1081—Craig Scott, Multinational Enterprises and Emergent Jurisprudence on Violations of Economic, Social, and Cultural Rights
- Pp. 1109-1115—Case Study: Most Favored Nation Treatment and the People's Republic of China

Class Ten: Families, Women, and Children and Human Rights—Problems of Gender Discrimination, Empowerment of Women, Children and Population Control, CRC, CEDAW, Cairo, Beijing

Steiner & Alston

- Pp. 158-224—Women's Rights and CEDAW
- Pp. 511-533—Children
- Pp. 972-976—NGOs in the United Nations Setting
- Pp. 1402-1419—Convention on the Elimination of All Forms of Discrimination Against Women

Reader (Pp. 253-280)

- Gender, Health, and Human Rights
- Health, Human Rights, and Lesbian Existence

Class Eleven: Oral Presentations and Discussion of Individual Papers

Class Twelve: Right to Health—General Comment 14, Iowa Declaration on the Right to Health

Readings to be handed out in class

Class Thirteen: Future of Health and Human Rights, Human Rights Advocacy; Lobbying; Use of the Media

Reader (Pp. 439-450)

- Medicine and Public Health, Ethics and Human Rights

Class Fourteen: Course Review (final paper due)

PAPER TOPIC AREAS IN HUMAN RIGHTS AND HEALTH

General topic areas

Sexual rights and health in [country or region]
Refugees and internally displaced people in [country]
Mental health and human rights in [country]
Environment, health, and human rights [focusing on specific environmental problem]
Universalism and cultural relativism [in specific context]
HIV/AIDS: new frontiers in prevention
Health professionals and the legacy of Nuremberg: where should we go from here?
Complex humanitarian emergencies: lessons from past failures (e.g. Somalia)
Homelessness: is it a human rights issue?
Women's health and human rights in [country]
Child labor: necessary evil for economic development?

Paper topics from past years

Truthtelling and patients' rights in Japan: the case of HIV
Child prostitution in Brazil
Rape as a war crime in Bosnia
Persecution of Coptic Christians in Egypt
Palestinian human rights in the West Bank
Economic sanctions in South Africa
Needle exchange program in Anchorage, Alaska
Group consent human genome diversity project
Child soldiers: the role of children in armed conflict
Trafficking: sale of women/children into forced prostitution in Thailand—effects on health
Corporal punishment in U.S. schools
Mandatory HIV testing of infants and women's rights
Dowry-related crimes in India
Canadian Red Cross tainted blood scandal
The Ogoni situation in Nigeria

HIV vaccine in developing countries

Routine episiotomy as violation of women's human rights

TB in developing countries in a context of human rights and health

Human rights: a new basis for public health?

Guatemalan human rights abuses: the 1996 Peace Accord

Environmental protection and disease prevention

Physicians' role in torture in Turkey

Human rights violation in orphanages in China

Capital punishment in U.S. death row inmates: human rights violations

Torture and the medical profession in Chile

Female genital mutilation in Egypt

Enforcing the Biological Weapons Convention

Environmental degradation as a human rights violation

HIV clinical trials in Africa

Involuntary sterilization

Women, reproductive rights, and pregnancy discrimination in Mexico

Disability rights in China

Effectiveness of the Truth Commission and human rights in El Salvador

Human rights of the elderly: a new convention on human rights

The media campaign to abolish the death penalty

Native American land claims

Embargos including food and medicine as a political weapon

Human rights and China's orphan policy

Genocide and unaccompanied children in Rwanda

Chernobyl: environmental contamination from nuclear power plants

The Taliban's rule over women

Human rights: political asylum seekers and victims of torture

The problem of early marriage within a health and human rights framework

HIV/AIDS vaccine clinical trials

Human rights of the mentally ill

Health Care Provider Contracts

STEPHANIE RIFKINSON-MANN, M.D., J.D., F.C.L.M.

MANAGED HEALTH CARE GOALS: EFFECT ON CONTRACTING HEALTH CARE
   PROVIDERS
CONTRACTING AND REIMBURSEMENT: CHANGES IN HEALTH CARE CONTRACTING
HEALTH CARE PROVIDER CONTRACTS
CONTRACT ANALYSIS
CONCLUSION

Physicians once labored under gentlemen's agreements to provide medical care to their patients on an individual basis. These agreements were promises inferred from acts or conduct, a contract implied in fact.[1] With the advent of the modern health care industry, safeguarding the exchange of medical services in that competitive market has become a priority. Contracts, a set of promises for the breach of which the law gives a remedy,[2] are the indispensable instrument by which this safeguard is accomplished, especially as cost-containment measures become a prerogative.

The right to contract in a free enterprise system is based upon common law, and is constitutionally guaranteed under the Due Process Clause of the Fourteenth Amendment.[3] Contract is a private issue between individuals who are bound to their promises once manifestations of mutual assent have been made.[4] A person is presumed to understand the contract that he or she has made, and is supposed to protect his or her own interests.[5] This assumes that the bargaining parties are on an equal footing socially, economically, and possibly educationally.

Mass markets, including health care markets, beget mass contracts. The general terms in these contracts have become standardized for convenience by "managed care organizations" (MCOs). An MCO is a reimbursement system within a health care framework combined into a single entity responsible for integrating and coordinating the financing and delivery of services that traditionally were divided between physicians and patients.[6] Two examples of MCOs are "health maintenance organizations" (HMOs) and "preferred provider organizations" (PPOs). HMOs provide health care directly through their own employed or contracted providers. HMOs share the risks of providing health care with the providers through fixed reimbursement fees and withholds or bonuses based on expense of treatment prescribed and utilization experience. PPOs consist of groups of providers who agree to provide care to patient populations for discounted fee-for-service rates. Patients who go "out of plan" to providers who do not participate in a health care plan ("nonpreferred providers") pay increased fees for their healthcare, and are therefore steered to preferred "participating providers" so as to contain costs.

Uniformity of contract terms enhances the calculation of risks for health care companies, thereby eliminating uncertainties and reducing costs, so MCOs offer standard "boilerplate" mass contracts.[7] This situation may make it difficult for the physician to shop around for better terms, primarily because there may be no better opportunity available.[8] These contracts result in the MCO being in a stronger bargaining position than the physician to whom the contract is offered. For this reason, it is imperative that the physician understand the details of the contract that he or she is offered before agreeing to it, since the long-term consequences of signing onto a particular health care plan may not be those that he or she envisioned.

Patients enrolled in the MCO may encompass a substantial proportion of the population in an area where a particular physician works. If the physician is not enrolled as a provider in that MCO, he or she may not have access to that patient population. He or she may be obligated to move from that area to find medical work elsewhere, or, if he or she cannot move, he or she may be forced to accept whatever terms the MCO offers in order to integrate those patients into his or her practice. He or she may even submit to changes in contract terms that might be communicated to him or to her at a later date, if the prospective agreement appears to be one he or she decides to pursue. Such issues mandate that physicians be cautious about the agreements they enter into with a health care entity.

This chapter outlines the concerns that the physician should have in contracting with a health care company. The following section briefly outlines the historical events giving rise to the development of health care reform and the goals of managed care. Next, contracting issues of importance for the individual health care provider are reviewed and the ways in which contract conditions may affect compensation[9] for physician services are discussed. Finally, details of health care contracts that the physician should be aware of before signing any agreement with a managed care company are reviewed.

MANAGED HEALTH CARE GOALS: EFFECT ON CONTRACTING HEALTH CARE PROVIDERS

Prepaid group practices date back to 1910, when the Western Clinic in Tacoma, Washington was developed.[10] Managed care, a process by which parties responsible for paying for health care services (such as employers) buy a program of health care benefits from a company for a preset fee or premium, evolved as a response to skyrocketing health care costs.[11]

With traditional indemnity plans, patients had no incentive to choose "economically efficient providers" who considered the financial impact of their medical decision-making. Costs were of no consequence to the patient because a third party (such as the employer) was footing his or her health care bill.[12] Physicians did not need to control the number of medical services rendered since under the cost-based payment systems, reimbursements for services were based on "customary, usual and reasonable" charges and payment was guaranteed. This resulted in overutilization of medical technology, highly specialized physicians and support staff, in-hospital care, and surgical procedures, with minimal control exercised upon the volume of services billed.[13] Physician consultations and fees increased.

Managed care developed as a response to spiraling costs by emphasizing preventive health measures. The organizations maintain tight control over health care delivery systems by offering financial incentives and management controls to deter patients from unnecessarily consulting physicians and to prevent health care providers from overutilizing health care services through different methods. These include quality assurance controls that assure "appropriate" care. Primary care physician gatekeepers are employed to regulate the use of specialty and other services.[14] Utilization management is applied, and consists of a procedural review performed by nurses, physicians, or special companies that evaluates the "medical necessity" of services for which claims are made (although there is no consensus as to the meaning of the term "medical necessity").[15] Concurrent and prospective review of health care provisions and expenditures is conducted. "Concurrent review," often called "pre-certification" or "pre-authorization" of services, is an analysis of treatment costs at the time treatment is administered to determine whether or not the costs will be covered by the health care plan. "Prospec-

tive review" analyzes potential costs of treatment before treatment is rendered to determine whether or not a health care plan ultimately will "cover" or pay for that service.[16]

Today's MCO is based upon a series of contracts among different entities, merging medical care with health insurance, selling health care from the managed care plan's providers to enrollees who purchase this combined product for a prenegotiated fee.[17] The MCO's cost-containment measures require that members obtain their health care from a restricted list of designated providers as a condition of coverage. The company sells a package of specific benefits to the buyer, including medical services to enrolled members through a network of providers participating in the plan. To keep patient enrollees' fees low and therefore attractive, the MCO negotiates lower compensation rates with physicians who participate in the plan.

The participating providers function as independent contractors under written contractual or employment agreements, and their selection as participating providers is controlled by the MCO.[18] The participating provider acts like an independent contractor, a person who, in the pursuit of any independent business, undertakes to do a specific piece of work for another person or entity, using his or her own means and methods without submitting himself or herself to their control in respect to the details of the business. The will of the employer is represented by the result of the work and not the means by which it was accomplished.[19] In the case of an MCO, the work accomplished is delivery of health care services. The methodology by which health care is supplied presumably is under the control of the physician. The significance of being considered an independent contractor for the physician is that he or she can be held liable for the manner in which he or she carries out their work. An added consequence for the physician of being considered an independent contractor is that his or her participation is considered terminable at the will of the MCO. Most jurisdictions in fact view MCO provider agreements as contracts between independent parties, although some courts describe them as employment relationships.[20]

MCOs offer financial incentives to health care providers whose practice styles are less costly. A common component of some MCO agreements is the "withhold," whereby the health care plan retains a portion of the provider's reimbursement as a reserve to cover unexpected expenses. If utilization of services does not exceed projections, and if plan costs are within the MCO's budget, some or all of the withhold is returned to the physician. A variation on this withhold is the "variant-risk withhold" system in which a physician who does an above-average job of managing health care utilization receives the full withhold in addition to a bonus payment. Both systems encourage the provider to implement fewer services. More money remains in the pool of funds withheld initially, thereby assuring the efficient provider a larger withhold at the end of the term.[21]

Only those physicians willing to comply with the plan's cost-cutting goals by accepting decreased reimbursements for their services are included in the restricted group of providers. There are strict physician credentialing requirements, including financial analyses of physicians' practice patterns in an effort to identify physicians who use health services more efficiently and less expensively through a process called "physician profiling."[22] Whereas traditional health insurance provided incentives for physicians to provide as much care as possible, managed care now forces the physician to reconcile his or her medical decisions with cost-containment policies. The physician must understand, therefore, that his or her own compensation may be diminished by providing medically indicated treatments that may be costly to the MCO. If a physician does not fit the profile the MCO seeks, he or she may not be included on the preferred provider list for that company. If he or she has already signed a contract with termination clauses (giving either party the right to terminate the agreement without cause),[23] and flexible terms that change with time, and his or her practice patterns are not economically efficient from the MCO's perspective, his or her contract may be terminated without any explanation.

The financial incentive for the physician to accept lower compensation rates from the MCO stems from one of two options. The physician might make a profit because of the increased volume of work he or she gets when more patients are referred to them because they are on the MCO preferred provider list. Alternatively, the physician might feel obligated to participate in a given health care plan because many of his or her patients become enrolled in that plan and he or she might otherwise lose a significant portion of their practice.[24] Two of every three privately insured Americans are now enrolled in managed care plans.[25] Physicians whose patients have joined these managed care plans stand to lose a significant portion of their practice unless they are enrolled as participating providers. The physician has to be cognizant of this implicit threat to his or her medical practice.

CONTRACTING AND REIMBURSEMENT: CHANGES IN HEALTH CARE CONTRACTING

Physician income has decreased in recent years, largely due to managed health care.[26] Health care providers find themselves selling their services through managed care organizations, which have the sophistication and incentive to bargain with them for low prices.[27] Physicians must apply to be included in health care plans as "preferred" providers, a term defined as a physician participating in an agreement with an MCO, directly or through an intermediary, to provide covered services to members. Participation in managed care provider networks is not automatic; however, the threat implicit in these agreements is that, if the physician

does not offer a discount acceptable to the plan, the plan will shift its enrollees to another provider.[28]

Contracting with MCOs may result in loss of professional independence for the physician since his or her medical judgment may be directed by HMO payment decisions, especially denials of payment.[29] This can have a detrimental impact on reimbursement to the physician for services provided, since the MCO is in a position to enforce its cost-containment decisions under the guise of quality assurance by penalizing a provider or terminating a provider's participation with the plan without explaining why, by simply not credentialing them, or by "deselecting" them from their provider plans.[30]

There are several critical contract issues of concern for most physicians. These include professional liability and indemnity clauses, contract language by which the physician indemnifies the health care plan. Such contract terms may subject him or her to litigation risks for actions of other physicians or policies of the plan that directly affect how he or she is allowed to manage the patient's care. Since malpractice does not protect the physician who indemnifies, he or she may be assuming an uninsured risk.[31] Regarding the scope of services covered, unless specifically stated in the agreement, the physician should assume that he or she is obligated to perform all services relevant to his or her specialty, though experimental protocols and unusually complex, subspecialized procedures are excluded. In addition, he or she needs be aware that the MCO may not allow the physician to arrange coverage for his or her practice with other physicians unless they are also contracted with the plan.[32] Term renewal, exclusivity of contract, and termination of contracts should all be of concern to the contracting physician. Health care contracts typically provide for automatic renewal at the end of period, which usually is one year; however, they may not provide for renegotiation of the terms of the agreement. The contract that the physician signs should not be assignable to any other party without the physician's prior written approval. The health care plan may contract exclusively with a physician or physician group, which may have significant potential for the physician. However, any agreement by a physician to contract exclusively with only one health care plan calls for his or her giving up the right to participate in other managed care business. This could be detrimental for the physician's practice.[33] Termination clauses must be negotiated up front, and should specify termination both with and without cause.[34] Gag rules, which do not allow physicians to discuss treatment options not covered by the managed care plan, are rarely used, but should be watched for.[35]

Mode of compensation for services provided must be clearly delineated and understood. The payment structure of the contract is the most important provision for both the provider and the managed health care plan. Managed care contracts generally involve one of two arrangements. The plan offers either modified fee-for-service for specialists, where the provider is reimbursed for each service provided,[36] or capitation fees for primary care physicians, a fixed payment to a physician to cover a specified set of services, regardless of the actual number of services provided to each patient. Fixed or capitated payments are based on actuarial data; medical service utilization date; size, age, and gender of the patient population served; geography; and the type of medical service provided. If patient costs exceed the capitation amount, the physician must absorb these additional costs. If costs are below the capitation, the physician may keep the additional money.[37]

Managed care plans often will select physicians who care for healthy populations unlikely to require costly medical attention.[38] Since managed care emphasizes improved disease management, MCOs encourage primary care fields such as pediatrics, internal medicine, and family practice in which preventive care may be implemented.[39] Doctors generally are considered cost-effective if they perform fewer procedures, hospitalize fewer HMO subscriber patients, order fewer diagnostic tests, write drug prescriptions in an effort to avoid hospitalization, and minimize referrals to more costly specialists.[40]

Managed care contracts can demand that providers partly subsidize their state-funded benefits plans. Specialists often are asked to assume a portion of the economic responsibility of caring for certain populations[41] by furnishing services on a discounted fee-for-service basis like network doctors or those in a capitated agreement with an MCO, an arrangement some physicians may not be able to afford. Despite this, managed care plans continue to make increasing demands upon health care professionals to improve health care delivery by doing so more efficiently and cheaply, and health care provider contracts play an important role in this effort.[42]

HEALTH CARE PROVIDER CONTRACTS

In the health care industry, the physician signs a standardized contract with an MCO, expecting to receive reasonable payment for his or her services.[43] These standardized contracts share characteristics of boilerplate contracts seen in ordinary consumer transactions, such as life insurance policies, loan agreements, and residential leases, in which the contracting parties occupy substantially unequal bargaining positions and the weaker party may be forced to adhere to the terms in the other's printed form.[44] The physician contemplating such a contract must be aware of the issues that arise in standardized contracts offered by health care organizations that often are in the stronger bargaining position.

Signing a standard health care contract

While the law presumably prevents unfair surprise and oppression, it may not always relieve the physician from the effect of a bad bargain.[45] A physician may not understand contract terms. Unfair surprise and unconscionability may result if the MCO drafting the contract includes a term, knowing that the term does not accord with the physician's expectations, or that it may include unintelligible legal language.[46] Contract provisions may deprive the physician of the benefits of the contract or leave him or her with no remedy if the MCO does not perform as he or she expects. Contract provisions such as exculpatory[47] and termination clauses[48] may be treated by the courts as a matter of public policy, community common sense seen as one's palpable duty to one's fellow,[49] rather than being seen as reasons to invalidate a contract merely on the grounds of fairness.

In health care contracts, the product offered is participation in the health care plan. The MCO exercises control in the health care market by directing individual patients to preferred provider physicians who abide by the plan's contract terms.[50] If a nonparticipating physician's patients enroll in a particular managed care plan, the physician stands to lose that patient base unless he or she also enrolls in the same plan.[51] Despite this risk, some courts have found that a "take it or leave it" contract may not necessarily be unconscionable if there is no disparity of bargaining power between the parties negotiating the contract.[52]

Ability to negotiate terms

Dominance in market control places the MCO in a stronger bargaining position than the physician. MCOs have the resources, experience, and political power to negotiate freely[53] while the physician may not be able to negotiate terms in the contract due to disparities in bargaining power or because the MCO refuses to negotiate.[54] Unilateral terms favoring the MCO may result.[55] In past situations where health care providers tried to unite to form groups in order to enhance bargaining position so as to negotiate with MCOs, courts found that their actions restricted trade and were illegal.[56]

MCO contracts may be unfair because they shift most of the financial risks and legal liabilities of managing health care onto the physician while also imposing restrictions on the care the physician provides. MCO cost-containment methods that discourage referrals to specialty providers may force primary physicians to perform procedures they are not trained for or accustomed to doing, thereby increasing liability risks. MCOs, however, save money if the primary care gatekeeper performs a specialty procedure, because the gatekeeper receives the same reimbursement regardless of what procedures he or she performs based upon capitation rates, while the specialists would be paid according to the procedure performed.[57]

Health care organizations may decide to implement decreased reimbursement rates for particular procedures to discourage their implementation by medical providers unwilling to undertake liability risks without further compensation. However, physicians still may be liable for the consequences of medical decisions shaped by cost-effective concerns of the MCO. Physicians who adhere to contracts with "hold harmless" clauses are vulnerable to malpractice claims arising from MCO denials of medical care to patients.[58] If a physician loses a malpractice case, the payment made on his or her behalf as part of the settlement may be permanently documented in the National Practitioner Data Bank.[59] This data currently is accessible to licensure boards, hospitals, and other entities. Although the general public does not have access to this information, there have been several proposals to allow increased access, most recently in Massachusetts and New York.[60]

MCOs seek to enlist physicians to establish networks of providers in certain areas. Once an MCO establishes a critical market share by signing physicians onto its provider list, it can terminate any of those physicians at any time without cause, by virtue of the termination clause in its contract. Often this termination is based upon a review of the costs physicians incur in delivering health care, with the costlier physician terminated by the MCO as part of its cost-containment policy. This evaluation of physician productivity may exclude concerns for medical justification for the care rendered and may disregard complexity of care and time spent by the physician in rendering it.

Since most MCO plans are predicated upon preventive health care measures, those physicians who cannot abide by the MCO's cost-containment measures can be terminated, especially if those measures include restrictions on delivery of costlier health care (even in situations where physicians have no control, such as medical emergencies). Forcing physicians to accept decreased reimbursement rates delineates a financial policy that is based upon MCO business data and not upon the health care needs of the patient, which the physician should be aware of. Termination clauses may provide one of the strongest incentives for a physician to restrict medical treatment, which under other circumstances might have been prescribed freely and appropriately.

Most MCO agreements allow the MCO to terminate the agreement "for cause," including loss of medical licenses, hospital privileges, board or DEA certifications, or malpractice coverage, including other issues such as breach of contract provisions, misconduct, or anything that reflects poorly on the MCO.[61] In addition to terminations for cause, most provider contracts include the right to terminate the contract "without cause" without any "good faith" requirements.[62] The termination may pertain to the MCO only, to the physician, or to both the MCO and the physician; however, the MCO's right to terminate a physician "without cause" has been upheld by the courts.[63]

Freedom of contract is intertwined with competition in free-enterprise capitalism. Without impartial arbitration and appeals processes, physicians alone bear the burden of proving that they might be unfairly terminated in conjunction with the standardized contracts they adhere to. For this reason, the physician must insist upon a fair appeals process to resolve disputes between the physician and the health care entity with which he or she contracts.

CONTRACT ANALYSIS

Physician agreements must be reviewed carefully to see how contract conditions affect compensation for physician services. The ability of the physician to modify reimbursement amounts or contract requirements is key. In most contracts, managed care plans retain complete control over reimbursement rates, payment adjustments, and determination of the medical necessity of all services provided prior to forwarding payment to the enrolled provider. Some contracts call for physician payments that consist of a percentage of the premium dollars collected from insured population groups. These contract terms shift risks onto the provider, much like capitation does.[64] Physician incomes are safer when specific dollar amounts are paid for procedures or services.

The physician's compensation for services is usually made in accordance with a current MCO "reasonable" fee schedule, which the MCO can unilaterally adjust as it sees fit. The MCO can determine at any time whether it considers a service "medically necessary" and also can determine what criteria it will implement in order to reimburse the provider for his or her service, having maintained the final authority to do so. Requirements for provision of services generally stipulate that the physician provider is obligated to care for any member enrolled in the plan. The health care provider is required to accept whatever reimbursement rate the MCO designates as appropriate,[65] including care for state-subsidized health care recipients enrolled in the MCO, whose care is paid for at rates lower than those noted in the MCO fee schedule.

Managed care plans do not offer any financial assistance to the physician toward obligatory malpractice insurance. Since the MCO views the physician as an independent contractor rather than an employee, it is the physician's obligation to obtain malpractice insurance.[66] Health care contracts require that the physician purchase and maintain his or her own malpractice insurance policy at their own expense. "Hold harmless" clauses stipulate that the physician solely is liable for any treatment decisions he or she makes, whether or not the decisions are made in accordance with MCO requirements or guidelines, leaving the MCO free of potential liability.[67] In effect, the physician pays for malpractice insurance coverage for the MCO as well as for himself or herself, a detail that physicians should be aware of.

Fee schedules, usually listed in an exhibit according to CPT codes,[68] must be reviewed carefully. Often information concerning reimbursement and fee schedules does not appear in the main text of the contract, but is referenced or mentioned at some point in the contract.[69] Any documentation incorporated by reference is an integral part of the contract, which the physician must be aware of. Plans receiving state funds offer lower reimbursement fees for services rendered to certain populations. These fees range from 30% to 75% of private market prices, the upper range going to less expensive primary care services such as pediatrics and family practice.[70] For those providers participating in plans that include "underprivileged" populations that are insured through state-provided funds, the provider's obligation to serve those populations at significantly reduced fees may not have been what he or she originally agreed to but may be included in fee schedules adhered to by the health care plan. Rates of reimbursement also vary from state to state and between specialties. The most costly care is the least reimbursed, such as surgical and medical subspecialties, which may not cover the physician's expenses in maintaining a medical practice.[71] Since the MCO retains complete control over all contract terms, the physician is obligated to submit to the MCO's conditions, including the significantly diminished reimbursement rates for certain state-funded patient insurance groups.

CONCLUSION

In view of spiraling health care costs, managed care cannot be ignored to the detriment of overall health care. The health care provider must understand that the meaning of freedom to contract has changed with the type of contract and with the degree of monopoly enjoyed by the author of the standardized agreement. Freedom to contract implies that the law will not interfere with the exercise of contract, for which reason the physician must be cognizant of his or her rights and must be aware of the consequences that may arise once he or she signs onto a particular health care plan.

Given the anxiety of medical practitioners and patients concerning the affordability of medical care, it is notable that physicians often have not been advised legally before entering into a contract with a managed care entity. The important issue of whether or not freedom of contract exists in MCO contracts depends upon the physician's knowledge of the various loopholes often found in the language with which the contract is crafted. For this reason, physicians should avail themselves of legal counsel before signing a contract with a health care company.

ENDNOTES

1. Restatement (Second) of Contracts §4.
2. Restatement (Second) of Contracts: Contract Defined §1.
3. *Allgeyer v. Louisiana*, 165 U.S. 578 (1897) (holding a state law unconstitutional for depriving a person of the right to make contracts protected by the Due Process Clause).
4. *See generally* Restatement (Second) of Contracts, Chapter 3: Formation of Contracts—Mutual Assent.
5. *Ray v. William G. Eurice & Bros., Inc.*, 201 Md. 115, 93 A. 2d. 272 (1952) (holding that one signing a contract is assumed to have the capacity to understand it, assuming no fraud, duress, or mutual mistake). *See also* Williston, *Contracts* (Rev. Ed.) §1577 (1936).
6. *See* Barry R. Furrow et al., *Health Law: Cases, Materials and Problems* 799 (1997) [hereinafter "Furrow, *Health Law*"].

7. *See* Friedrich Kessler, *Contracts of Adhesion—Some Thoughts About Freedom of Contract*, 43 Columbia L. Rev. 629, 631–32 (1943).
8. *Id.* at 632.
9. "Compensation" refers to reimbursement or payment for services rendered.
10. *See* John A. Kusske, *Managed Care—the Growth of Cost Containment and the Impact on Neurosurgical Practice*, in *Neurosurgery in Transition: The Socioeconomic Transformation of Neurological Surgery* 3, 6 (James R. Bean ed., 1998) [hereinafter "Kusske, *Managed Care*"].
11. *See* Rand E. Rosenblatt, *Law and the American Health Care System* 551-52 (1997). *See also* Barry R. Furrow et al., *The Law of Health Care Organization and Finance* 325 (1991) [hereinafter "Furrow, *Finance*"]; The Business Council of New York State, Inc., *Inside the Business Council* [hereinafter "BCNYS"], *Managing with Care*, at §2 (June 1998). The enactment of Medicare and Medicaid coincided with a dramatic escalation in national health care spending. *See* Kenneth W. Wing, *American Health Policy in the 1980s*, 36 Case W.L. Rev. 608, 620 (1986). *See also* BCNYS, *supra*, at §1.
12. *See* Mark A. Hall & Ira Mark Ellman, *Health Care Law and Ethics in a Nutshell* 8-13 (1990).
13. E.H. Morreim, *Cost Containment and the Standard of Medical Care*, 75 Calif. L. Rev. 1719 (1987). *See* Rosenblatt, *supra* note 11, at 18.
14. *See Corcoran v. United HealthCare, Inc.*, 965 F. 2d 1321 (5th Cir. 1992), *cert. denied*, 506 U.S. 1033. *See also* Daniel R. Sullivan & Perry Oxley, *Managed Care Organizations*, in *The Physician's Perspective on Health Law* 355 (Howard H. Kaufman & Jeff L. Lewin, eds. 1997).
15. "Medical necessity" has been defined as "efficacious and safe" (*Dallis v. Aetna Life Ins. Co.*, 574 F. Supp. 547 (N.D.Ga. 1983), *aff'd*, 768 F. 2d 1303 (11th Cir. 1985)); "appropriate" and "consistent with community medical standards" (*Hughes v. Blue Cross of Northern Cal.*, 263 Cal. Rptr. 850 (Cal. Ct. App. 1989)); or an issue to be decided by a jury because of the ambiguity of the term (*Siegal v. Health Care Service Corp.*, 401 N.E. 2d 1037 (Ill. App. Ct. 1980)).
16. *See Managed Care Handbook for Neurological Surgeons* 73-74 (John A. Kusske et al., eds., 1994).
17. *See* Rosenblatt, *supra* note 11, at 547-48.
18. *See Murphy v. American Home Products Corporation*, 58 N.Y. 2d 293, 300, 461 N.Y.S. 2d 232, 448 N.E. 2d 86 (1983) (where employment is for an indefinite term, it is presumed to be a hiring at will which may be freely terminated by either party at any time for any reason or even for no reason at all).
19. *Black's Law Dictionary* 326 (6th ed. 1990).
20. *See* Bryan A. Liang, *Deselection under Harper v. Healthsource: A Blow for Maintaining the Physician-Patient Relationship in the Era of Managed Care*, 72 Notre Dame L. Rev. 799, 853 (1997).
21. It is possible that the withhold may be construed as a "bribe" and subject to criminal penalties. *See* Kusske, *Handbook*, *supra* note 16, at 103.
22. *See* Rosenblatt, *supra* note 11, at 560.
23. *See id.* at 513, 517. *See also* John P. Little, *Managed Care Contracts of Adhesion: Terminating the Doctor-Patient Relationship and Endangering Patient Health*, 49 Rutgers L. Rev. 1397, 1446, 1456 (1997).
24. Joseph A. Snoe, *Selected Managed Care Provider Issues*, in *American Health Care Delivery Systems* 456, 456 (1998). *See* Note, *The Impact of Medicaid Managed Care on the Uninsured*, 110 Harv. L. Rev. 731, 754 [hereinafter *Medicaid Managed Care*]; *see also* Little, *supra* note 23, at 1397.
25. *See Kartell v. Blue Shield of Massachusetts, Inc.*, 749 F. 2d 922 (1st Cir. 1984), *cert. denied*, 471 U.S. 1029 (1985) (finding that because of the large number of subscribers, doctors are under "heavy economic pressure" to take them as patients and to agree to Blue Shield's system for charging the cost of their care).
26. Milt Freudenheim, *Doctors' Incomes Fall as Managed Care Grows*, N.Y. Times, Nov. 17, 1995, at A1.

27. *See* Furrow, *Health Law*, *supra* note 6, at 735.

28. *See Medicaid Managed Care*, *supra* note 24, at 754; *see also* Little, *supra* note 23, at 1422.

29. *See Wickline v. State of California*, 239 Cal. Rptr. 661, 810 (Cal. App. 1986), *petition for review dismissed*, 741 P. 2d 613 (Cal. 1987) (holding that a physician is still liable for negligence even if he or she complies with an MCO decision to deny care that he or she believes is medically necessary). Implicit in this decision is the theory that the physician has a nondelegable fiduciary duty to do what is in his or her patient's best interest.

30. *See* Sullivan, *supra* note 14, at 355; *see also* Rosenblatt, *supra* note 11, at 1002-11; Kusske, *Handbook*, *supra* note 16, at 26; *Medicaid Managed Care*, *supra* note 24, at 1629. *See also Harper v. Healthsource New Hampshire, Inc.*, 674 A. 2d 962 (N.H. 1996) (holding that a termination without cause provision in the contract was legal).

31. *See Wickline v. State of California*, 239 Cal. Rptr. 810 (Cal. App. 1986), *petition for review dismissed*, 741 P. 2d 613 (Cal. 1987) (holding that while third party payers of health care services can be held legally accountable when medically inappropriate decisions result from implementation of cost containment, the treating physician remains legally responsible for quality of care).

32. *See* Kusske, *Handbook*, *supra* note 16, at 94, 99.

33. *See id.* at 91, 93, 96-99.

34. Termination with or without cause is the right of either party; however, a health care plan may offer termination clauses that are not equally fair to both parties. Such unfair wording might appear as follows: "This Agreement may be terminated a) by MCO at any time with or without cause upon thirty (30) days written notice; and b) by Physician at any time with or without cause upon ninety (90) days advance written notice." Such a provision allows the plan to dispense quickly with a physician, disrupting his or her cash flow abruptly as opposed to the plan's far longer (90-day) allowance to adjust to the change, although the physician still has obligations post termination for continuity of care of panel member patients until transition of their care to another provider.

35. An example of such wording might be as follows: "Physician agrees not to make any communication or take any action which undermines the confidence of enrollees." *See also* Paul Gray, *Gagging the Doctors: Critics Charge That Some HMO's Require Physicians to Withhold Vital Information from Their Patients*, Time, Jan. 8, 1996.

36. A variation is the "discounted fee-for-service," a straight discount on charges or a discount based on volume or a sliding scale. Other variations on fee-for-service include global, flat, or case rates. The "flat rate" is a single fee paid for a procedure regardless of how much time and effort the physician expends providing service. A "global fee" is a flat rate encompassing more than a single type of service, such as postoperative care and follow-up office visits that are included in a single surgical reimbursement fee. "Case rates" are single reimbursements that combine both institutional and professional charges into one lump sum. Surgical subspecialties most commonly use a relative value scale, such as the resource-based relative value scale (RBRVS) or a fee allowance schedule, where each procedure is assigned a relative value, which is then multiplied by a conversion factor so as to arrive at a payment. In a fee allowance schedule, the fees are explicitly defined in the contract. *See* Kusske, *Managed Care*, *supra* note 10, at 23. Linda O. Prager, *Fee-for-Service Plans Tops Among Doctors in Most Markets*, Amer. Med. News, Oct. 12, 1998, at 15.

37. *See* Douglas Hastings et al., *Fundamentals of Health Law* 269 (1995). *See also* Rosenblatt, *supra* note 11, at 563. *See* Peter R. Kongstevedt, *The Essentials of Managed Care* 77-78 (1995).

38. *See* Rosenblatt, *supra* note 11, at 553.

39. *See* Polly Miller, *Doctors' Incomes: Who's Up, Who's Down*, Med. Economics, Oct. 1998, at 45.

40. *See* Rosenblatt, *supra* note 11, at 563. *See also* Snoe, *supra* note 24, at 457; Little, *supra* note 23, at 1412.

41. Typical wording for such contract conditions might be exemplified by the following provision: "Member Physician authorizes MCO to withhold from any fees payable to the Member Physician such amounts as are deemed necessary by MCO to allow Member Physician to share the risk of costs and utilization in the state-funded Health Benefit Plan."

42. *See Medicaid Managed Care*, *supra* note 24, at 754. Costs for emergency care for one patient can total up to the entire amount received for caring for a patient group on a capitated basis. *See* Howard Kim, *Medi-Cal Tells Physicians to Shape Up*, Amer. Med. News, Aug. 24/31, 1998, at 5.

43. Legally, "reasonable" is synonymous with "fair, proper, just, moderate, suitable under the circumstances." *Black's Law Dictionary* 1265 (6th ed. 1990). In health care contracts, "reasonable" is determined by the MCO, not by the physician. Typical wording for such contract terms specifies that the physician's compensation for services is to be made in accordance with the current MCO "reasonable" fee schedule. The definition of "reasonable" usually is not provided in the contract, something the physician should be aware of.

44. *See Wheeler v. St. Joseph Hospital*, 63 Cal. App. 3d 345 (1977). *See also* Marvin Chirelstein, *Concepts and Case Analysis in the Law of Contracts* 68 (2d ed. 1993).

45. *See* Gordon D. Schaber & Claude D. Rohwer, *Contracts* 229 (3d ed. 1990). A contract, or a clause in a contract, is "unconscionable" if it is so grossly unfair to one of the parties because of the stronger bargaining powers of the other party. It suggests that no person in their senses, not under any delusion, would make such a contract, and which no fair and honest person would accept. *Black's Law Dictionary* 1525 (6th ed. 1990). *See* U.C.C.: Unconscionable Contract or Clause §2-302; Restatement (Second) of Contracts §208.

46. This is "procedural unconscionability," since including such a term without calling it to the other party's attention involves unfair bargaining in the negotiating procedure. *See* U.C.C.: Comment §2-303.

47. Exculpatory clauses are "hold harmless" clauses by which the physician indemnifies the health care plan, thereby exposing himself or herself to the risk of liability for acts beyond his or her control, including actions of other physicians or MCO policies that directly affect the manner in which the physician is allowed to manage the case. *See* Kusske, *Managed Care*, *supra* note 16, at 97-98.

48. *See Sabetay v. Sterling Drug, Inc.*, 69 N.Y. 2d 329, 514 N.Y.S. 2d 209, 506 N.E. 2d 919 (1987) (holding that termination by either party for any reason or for no reason at all does not imply an obligation on the part of an employer to deal in good faith with an employee at will).

49. *Black's Law Dictionary* 1231 (6th ed., 1990).

50. See *Patel v. Healthplus, Inc.*, 684 A. 2d 904, 909 (finding that because the MCO had bulk buying power, it was able to direct enrollees to seek care from its preferred providers).

51. In 1994, a New York pediatric practice noted a 40% decline in the number of patients coming to the group's office after several local employers enrolled their employees in an HMO. The physician group applied to the HMO to join its physician roster, but was declined. *See* Elisabeth Rosenthal, *Doctors Slow to Join H.M.O.s Now Often Find Doors Shut*, N.Y. Times, June 25, 1994, at A1.

52. *Clinic Masters, Inc. v. District Court*, 556 P. 2d 473, 475-76 (1976).

53. Robin Toner, *Harry and Louise Were Right, Sort of*, N.Y. Times, Nov. 24, 1996, at D1.

54. *See Ambroze, M.D., P.C. v. Aetna Health Plans of N.Y., Inc.*, No. 95 CIV. 6631 (DLC), 1996 WL 282069, at 3 (S.D.N.Y. May 28, 1996).

55. *See Shell Oil Co. v. Marinello*, 307 A. 2d 598, 601 (1973).

56. *See* Robert Kuttner, *Physician-Operated Networks and the New Antitrust Guidelines*, 336 N. Eng. J. Med. 386 (1997).

57. *See* Kusske, *Managed Care*, *supra* note 10, at 23. *See also* Rosenblatt, *supra* note 11, at 563; Hastings, *supra* note 37, at 269.

58. *See* Lawrence A. Cunningham & Arthur J. Jacobson, *Corbin on Contracts* §559F, at 358; §559H, at 362 (1993 & Supp. 1997); *see also* Kusske, *Managed Care*, *supra* note 10, at 97-98.

59. The Data Bank was established by the Health and Human Services Department under the umbrella of the Health Care Quality Improvement Act of 1986 ("HCQIA"), 42 U.S.C. §11152.

60. *See* Furrow, *Health Law, supra* note 6, at 86; *see also* Linda O. Prager, *Online Disciplinary Reports Likely for N.Y. Physicians*, 43(14) Amer. Med. News 11 (April 10, 2000).

61. *See* Snoe, *supra* note 24, at 459.

62. Good faith encompasses an honest belief, the lack of malice, and the absence of design to defraud or to seek an unconscionable advantage. *Black's Law Dictionary* 693 (6th ed. 1990).

63. *See* Little, *supra* note 23, at 1145.

64. *See* Kusske, *Handbook, supra* note 16, at 100.

65. *See Maltz v. Aetna Plan of N.Y.*, 114 F. 3d 9, 10 (2d Cir. 1997).

66. Typical wording for this type of contract condition may appear as: "Physician shall provide and maintain malpractice insurance subject to the approval of MCO, and shall not be less than $1,000,000 per claim and $3,000,000 per year;" or "Physician at his sole expense shall procure and maintain policies of general and professional liability and other insurance as is necessary to insure him and his employees against any claim for damages arising by reason of personal injuries or death occasioned directly or indirectly in connection with the performance of services hereunder in connection with this agreement."

67. *See Howard v. Sasson*, Civil Action No. 95–0068, 1995 WL 581960 (E.D.Pa., Oct. 3, 1995) (holding that ERISA preemption of claims against health care providers does not exist without allegations that the organization refused to pay for or authorize treatment).

68. *See* American Medical Association, *Physicians' Current Procedural Terminology* (1997) ["CPT"].

69. Typical wording appears as phrases such as "incorporated by reference and attached as Exhibit X," or "as set forth in Section Y and incorporated by reference."

70. *See* Rosenblatt, *supra* note 11, at 418.

71. *See* BCNY, *supra* note 11, at §2. *See also* Stephanie Rifkinson-Mann, *The Impact of Managed Care Payer Contracts on the Subspecialty Medical Provider: Policy Implications That Impact on the Care of Disabled Children*, 27(6) Fordham Urban L.J. 1943 (2000).

Agency

MARVIN H. FIRESTONE, M.D., J.D., F.C.L.M.

THE LAW OF AGENCY
PARTIES AND THE RELATIONSHIP
RIGHTS AND DUTIES BETWEEN PRINCIPAL AND AGENT
LIABILITIES OF PARTIES BASED IN TORT

THE LAW OF AGENCY

An agency is a consensual relationship between two persons whereby one person (the agent) is given a varying degree of authority to act for and on behalf of another (the principal). The *Restatement of the Law of Agency* defines the relationship as follows:

Agency is a fiduciary relationship that results from the manifestation of consent by one person to another that the other shall act on his behalf and subject to his control and consent by the other so to act.[1]

The liabilities, duties, benefits, and remedies attained through the agency relationship develop from both tort and contract law. Most agency relationships are formed by agreement, so that the usual defenses to the formation of a contract will, if successful, also negate the existence of an agency. However, other agencies arise as a result of the status of the parties or by operation of law and must be analyzed under other legal principles.

PARTIES AND THE RELATIONSHIP

The parties

To form an agency, the parties involved must have legal capacity. The power to act through another depends on the capacity of the principal to do the act himself or herself. For example, contracts entered into by a minor or an insane person are considered "voidable," that is, cancelable by or on behalf of the minor or insane party. Consequently the appointment of an agent by a minor or an insane person and any contracts resulting thereby are likewise voidable.

The author gratefully acknowledges work previously contributed by Robert Schur, J.D.

Capacity to be an agent is somewhat different from capacity required for contract formation or the execution of a will. An adult principal can appoint a minor agent. The fact that the agency agreement itself may be voidable does not in and of itself disqualify the agent from making a contract binding on the principal. An adult acting on behalf of a minor who could not make a binding contract directly may create such obligations, but they will be enforceable as against the adult agent rather than as against the minor principal.

Types of agencies, agents, and principals

Agencies may be classified in different ways. The relationship may be one of actual agency, in which valid authority, express or implied, has been given by the principal to the agent to act on the principal's behalf. An example of this is the retaining of a real estate broker to represent a seller in a particular transaction. Often, actual agencies are defined and created by the use of a written agency agreement (in this example, the listing contract).

An ostensible (or "apparent") agency arises when, in the absence of an actual agency, the conduct of the principal induces others to reasonably infer that an agency exists.[2] Most often an ostensible agency arises when the scope of an actual agency is exceeded by the agent, causing a third party to assume that the agent has authority where he or she does not. For example, P may appoint A to act on his or her behalf to sell a parcel of land to any buyer who qualifies and is willing to pay the asking price. A, in negotiating with buyer B, is unable to make a sale of the property in question but offers to sell another parcel, also owned by P, which is more to B's liking. By appointing A as his or her agent to sell one property, P may have created a reasonable assumption that A can act on his or her behalf to sell any property that P owns. If P fails to take reasonable precautions to limit the scope of A's actual authority, the resulting contract to sell the second property may be enforced in B's favor. This so-called agency by estoppel exists when a person by his or her conduct clothes another with indicia of authority by which a third party inferred that an agency relationship existed and relied on that inference when dealing with the agent.[3] The conduct of the principal leading to the creation of such an agency may be intentional or merely negligent, and the inference must be reasonable.[4] It is not a true agency because the consent element is lacking, but on equitable grounds the law prohibits the principal from denying the existence of the agency so as to cause harm to the party who acted in reliance.

An agent may act on behalf of a principal whose existence and identity have not been revealed to a third party. The "undisclosed principal" is bound by contracts forged by the agent with a third party despite the secrecy of the agency relationship, but unlike an actual agent the agent of an undisclosed principal is also bound. An agent who acts on behalf of a principal whose existence (but not identity) has been revealed to the third party serves a "partially disclosed" principal, rendering both the principal and the agent contractually liable to the third party. Some cases have held that, once the third party learns the identity of the principal, he or she must make an election as to whether the agent or the principal will be held responsible for the contractual obligations.

Agents are also commonly classified as *general* or *special*.[5] A general agent is authorized to transact all business or at least all business of a particular kind at a particular locale for its principal. A special agent is authorized to act for the principal only in a particular transaction. A subagent is appointed by an agent, with the express or implied consent of the principal, to assist the agent in the conduct of its agency duties. This subagent is the agent of the agent, and because the agent has the authority to make such an appointment, the subagent also has authority to bind the principal. Moreover, the subagent is in a fiduciary relationship with both the agent and the principal.

One common characterization of agency is the "master-servant" relationship. A "servant" generally has limited authority, such as performing physical or ministerial tasks assigned by the "master." The master has the right to direct what is to be done, as well as how it is to be done. In most cases it is doubtful whether a servant could enter into a contract that would bind the principal without the presence of some expression of intent that the servant be clothed with such authority. So, in carrying out his duties, a delivery clerk is certainly the agent of the grocer, but no one would assume that he has authority to purchase a new truck on the grocer's behalf. On the other hand, the clerk's negligent handling of the old truck, causing accidental injury, will be imputed to his master based on the existence of the agency relationship under the doctrine of *respondeat superior* ("let the master answer").

The master-servant relationship is distinguished from that of the independent contractor. Like the servant, the independent contractor is hired to perform a specific task. However, the master or principal exercises less control over the performance of the act, allowing the agent to determine the means and methods of carrying out the purpose of the agency. Independent contractors commonly fall into a professional category. As such, this concept is important for the medical practitioner. The physician practicing medicine encounters numerous situations in which the status of being an independent contractor effects legal rights, duties, and liabilities. For example, a physician usually is considered an independent contractor to the hospital or other facility where he or she treats patients even if the hospital has the right to determine which patients the physician treats, where and when he or she treats them, and what equipment or facilities will be made available for such treatment. The hospital, it is claimed, neither controls the manner in which physicians apply their skills and knowledge to the patients' care nor assumes responsibility for errors in their judgment or technique.

An agency exists when individuals form partnerships, corporations, or any combination thereof. A general partner acts as agent for the partnership and for all the other general partners, with regard to partnership business. A corporate officer acts as agent for the corporation. A corporation or partnership may act as agent for an individual.

Formation of the agency

An agency may be formed by an oral or written contract.[6] An agency also may result by implication from the circumstances (an "implied" agency). However, unlike an ordinary contract, in which consideration is required for formation, an agency may be gratuitous (lacking in any promise of compensation for the agent). Such a gratuitous agency does not effect the validity of contracts formed by the agent for the benefit of the principal.

Ratification is an affirmance by the principal of an unauthorized act of an agent, or purported agent, after the fact. Ratification relates back in time to the commission of the act, thus binding the principal just as if the agency had been authorized at the time.[7]

Termination of the agency

An agency, once created, continues until terminated. Termination may occur in a number of ways. The time of termination may be specified in the agency agreement itself, where the relationship terminates as of a stated time. In the absence of a specified time, the agency is deemed terminable at will, and a reasonable time limitation may be implied from the facts and circumstances.

The agency agreement also may specify that the relationship is to terminate on the occurrence of a particular event or may be terminated by a material change in the circumstances underlying the agency agreement. Destruction of the subject matter of the authority, insolvency or bankruptcy of the agent or the principal, a drastic change in pertinent business conditions, and changes to the law that substantially affect the purposes of the agency may terminate the agency. A breach of the agent's fiduciary duty may effectively terminate the agency. When either the agent or the principal unilaterally acts to terminate the agency, the principal is best advised to take reasonable steps to notify potential third parties that the agent no longer holds authority to bind the principal.

Finally, an agency may be terminated by operation of law, such as upon the death of either the agent or the principal or the loss of either party's legal or mental capacity. Where a partnership or corporation holds the position of agent or principal, dissolution of the partnership or corporation effects a termination.

RIGHTS AND DUTIES BETWEEN PRINCIPAL AND AGENT

Duties imposed on the agent

The law of agency attaches certain duties of performance to the agent. First, the agent is responsible to the principal as a fiduciary.[8] A fiduciary duty arises out of a relationship of trust and confidence. Fiduciary duties define many common agency relationships, including those of trustee and beneficiary, corporate directors and shareholders, attorney and client, and employee and employer. Breach of one's fiduciary duty often results in legal sanctions for the party at fault.

The agent owes the principal the utmost in loyalty and good faith. Therefore an agent must act only in the interests of the principal and not in the interests of himself, herself, or another. Thus an agent may not represent the principal in any transaction in which the agent has a personal or financial interest. To do so would be a conflict of interest.[9] This duty prevents an agent from competing with the principal concerning the subject matter of the agency. Moreover, an agent may not use information obtained during the course of the agency for his or her own benefit or retain a secret profit gained in the course of the agency; all profits belong to the principal. The principal's legal remedies include the right to demand an accounting and the right to force the agent to disgorge profits.

The fiduciary duty also requires an agent to use reasonable efforts to notify the principal of developments or information reasonably calculated to be relevant to the affairs of the agency.[10] Knowledge of the agent is expected to include all information gained during the conduct of transactions for the principal, as well as information that (by the exercise of reasonable inquiry) the agent should have attained. Moreover, knowledge of facts material to the agency gained through transactions unrelated to the agency also may be imputed to the principal if this knowledge was present in the mind of the agent and used to the advantage of the principal during the agency. However, the agent is not required

to notify his or her principal of facts gained while dealing for another principal (provided those facts were not acquired for the benefit of the first principal). With certain exceptions, knowledge gained by the agent after the termination of the relationship is not imputed to the principal unless it was gained from a third party who previously dealt with the agent during the pendency of the agency and who had no knowledge of the termination (there being an apparent authority). Moreover, the imputed knowledge of the principal is constructive knowledge and not actual; a principal cannot, for example, be held liable for a crime for which actual knowledge is an essential requirement, solely on the basis of imputed or constructive knowledge.

Violation of the fiduciary duty may be both a breach of contract (agency) and a tort (fraud).[11] Thus an injured principal has a choice of remedies. The agent may be held accountable for all damages proximately suffered by his or her principal. In tort situations in which malice or bad faith is proved, punitive damages also may be awarded. When the agent is found to have gained personally from the breach, the principal may void any transactions made with third parties that emanate from the violation of the fiduciary duty. For property held by the agent in violation of the fiduciary duty, the law may impose a constructive trust on the property for its transfer to the principal.

The agency relationship imparts other duties on the agent as well. One is the duty to perform. This duty requires the agent to act for the principal only as authorized and to obey all reasonable instructions and directions. The agent also must act with reasonable care, diligence, and skill in the completion of tasks.

Duties imposed on the principal

The principal also is subject to certain duties in the agency relationship. For example, the agent is owed reasonable compensation (unless of course it is a gratuitous agency) for services in the conduct of the agency. Furthermore, the agent is due indemnification from its principal for all reasonable expenses and losses incurred by the agent during discharge of authorized duties.[12]

A principal also owes the agent the duty of cooperation. To this end a principal must assist and provide to the agent any and all known information that is relevant to the conduct of the agency. More important, this duty prohibits the principal from interfering in a way that would hinder or prevent performance by the agent. Consider the example of the physicians' group practice that contracts with a search firm to find a qualified ophthalmologist and the contract with the search firm is one of an exclusive agency. Furthermore, the search firm will be paid a finder's fee in the amount of a percentage of the hired specialist's compensation package. Later, certain members of the group, while at a medical seminar, locate and hire an ophthalmologist for the group. Under these circumstances, most courts would find for the search firm and award damages for the lost profits it would have made if it had located the new specialist. Such remedy is likely to be specified in the firm's contract as well.

If the principal breaches the contract of agency, the agent's remedies lie in an action in contract. Therefore most of the remedies available to a contracting party are likewise available to the agent. In addition, the agent may have the right to claim a retaining lien against the property of his or her principal that is in the lawful possession of the agent, as well as any other liens provided by law. Such liens usually extend also to a subagent as to property lawfully in the subagent's possession, but only to the extent of the primary agent's rights in the property. Further remedies available to an agent include the rights to withhold performance, claim a setoff in any action brought by the principal, or demand an accounting by the principal. However, because the agency relationship is consensual in nature, there is generally no right by either the agent or the principal to the remedy of specific performance of the agency contract.

Powers vested in the agent

The power vested in an agent, if any, is to be strictly construed. As such, an agent is deemed to possess those powers that were expressly given or are reasonably required for the agent to perform his or her duties. Powers inherent in the agency, such as the power to sell land for a realty agency, are included.

In cases in which authority is present, an agent may provide warranties. Such warranties may be express or implied. A most important warranty of the implied type is the warrant of authority. An agent is deemed to impliedly warrant that he or she has the authority to act on behalf of the principal.

An agent is deemed to hold all powers that a reasonable third party would believe he or she holds. This principle is known as *inherent agency power* and holds true even if the principal expressly denied the agent such a power. The rationale behind this policy is the protection of innocent third parties. An example of such a power is the agent's power to make representations concerning the subject matter of the agency.

LIABILITIES OF PARTIES BASED IN TORT

Liability of the principal for the agent's acts

One who commits a tort is usually held liable to those harmed. This rule is true for an agent acting within the scope of his or her agency, and a principal may be held liable to third persons for the torts committed by the agent. This principle is called the doctrine of *respondeat superior*. *Respondeat superior* (Latin meaning, "let the master answer") is simply one form of vicarious liability. This doctrine developed in early common law when the servant was

treated as property of the master. Because the master was deemed to have absolute control over the acts of the servant, the master might properly be held to answer for those acts, both rightful and wrongful. The basis for a finding of vicarious liability against the principal is based upon whether the servant's act or omission occurred in the course and scope of employment of the agent. The tortious act must have been committed while the agent was engaged in work of the type that he or she was appointed to perform for the principal.

Today this doctrine has been retained in the law on the rationale of at least two theories. The first is based on the premise that, because the employer has the right of control and termination of the employee, the threat of holding the employer liable will cause the employer to act more prudently in the selection, guidance, and supervision of employees. Moreover, it is the employer who profits from the acts of the employee. This rationale justifies placing the ultimate responsibility for the safety of others on the principal.

The second theory holds that public policy requires that an injured third person be afforded the most effective relief available. This doctrine assumes that the employer is generally wealthier than the employee and therefore more likely to be able to pay damages. First-year law students learn this as the "deep pocket" theory of recovery. In modern times probably nothing has encouraged our litigious society more than this doctrine. Plaintiffs seeking large recoveries have little chance of doing so against a mere employee. But the huge coffers of business, professional, and government treasuries or their insurance companies lie for the taking. A plaintiff may seek recovery against the principal, the agent, or both, when injured.

Respondeat superior imposes on the principal a "strict liability" (i.e., liability without fault on the part of the principal), and it attaches notwithstanding the principal's due care in the selection of the agent or employee and in the subsequent supervision thereof. Such liability is both joint and several with that of the agent or employee. Of course, the plaintiff is not entitled to a double recovery. Recovery against either defendant bars recovery against the other.[13] When the principal is found to be vicariously liable, he or she is usually entitled to seek indemnification against the agent or employee for damages paid to the victorious third party.

Hospital as principal of the physician

Increasingly, plaintiffs injured by malpractice are bringing actions against both the negligent physician and the hospital where care was provided. Several legal theories support such a suit, including direct negligence in the operation of the hospital and insufficient supervision of residents who are employees of the institution. All jurisdictions hold that there is hospital liability for the negligent acts of a physician employed by the hospital. Thus, under the doctrine of *respondeat superior*, the hospital may be liable for the acts or omissions of a physician in training but not for those of an attending physician because the latter is an independent contractor not subject to such control.[14]

In addition, if there is a showing that the professional in question is an employee rather than an independent contractor, the act in question must be shown to have occurred within the scope of employment. Among other requirements, to meet this showing, the act must be reasonably foreseeable by the employer.[15] When supervision and control are provided by a hospital or an attending physician over a resident, the suit will likely turn on the degree of control available. Presumably the more senior the resident, the less control may be exercised by the hospital and its employees. Nurses and other providers who are employed by the hospital or who answer to administrators are almost always considered agents for purposes of imputing liability. However, when the provider is beyond the control of the institution in performing his or her duties, employment alone may not sustain a charge of liability against the hospital.[16]

An important exception to the doctrine of *respondeat superior* is known as the *fellow servant rule*. This rule holds that a principal is not liable for injury done to one employee by another employee of the same principal in the same general enterprise. The rationale behind this doctrine is that a person who accepts appointment by a given principal assumes any risk that he or she might be injured by another appointed by the same principal and that he or she is in at least as good a position as the principal to discover such risks and protect himself or herself from them. These are poor justifications for such a rule, and the courts are not in favor of it, seeking generally to avoid its application. Today there are many exceptions to the applicability of the fellow servant rule (e.g., where the plaintiff seeks recovery based on the employer's negligence in hiring a fellow employee or where the plaintiff is injured by a superior employee who is acting within his or her authority in supervision of an inferior employee).

ENDNOTES

1. Restatement (Second) of the Law, Agency, §1, American Law Institute (1957).
2. *See* Restatement, Agency §267.
3. *See* Restatement, Agency §8B. The result is an agency created by operation of law. Such an agency also may be created by statute, such as where the law of state A directs that an out-of-state corporation doing business in state A automatically appoints the Secretary of State as its agent for service of process within state A.
4. There are some exceptions to this relation back doctrine, namely (1) where the principal, on the date of ratification or the date of the unauthorized act, lacked the capacity to do so; (2) where to do so would now be illegal; or (3) most important, where to do so would prejudice innocent third persons who have acquired rights in the transaction during the interim period.
5. *See* Restatement, Agency §3.
6. Agency agreements made orally may be invalidated by the state's statute of frauds, whereby certain contracts are required to be in writing to be enforceable. Many states have enacted what generically may be called *equal dignity laws* providing that when the statute of frauds requires an agreement be made in writing the agent's authority also must be in writing. A written agency agreement is often in the form of a "power of attorney" appointing the agent as the principal's attorney-in-fact for a specific purpose (or in general to conduct the principal's business).
7. *Adamski v. Taco General Hospital*, 579 P. 2d 970, at 978 (Wash. App. 1978). Note that the term *reasonable* connotes an objective rather than a subjective standard. The proper test is what a reasonable person under the circumstances would believe.
8. *See* Restatement, Agency §13.
9. Full disclosure of the conflict and written authority to act despite the conflict may relieve the agent from liability for breach of the agency agreement; however, this entails some risk for the agent, whose position as a fiduciary is not defeated by the disclosure.
10. *See* Restatement, Agency §11, 381. The effect of this rule is that notice of all matters coming to the agent is imputed to the principal. Thus, as to third persons who dealt with the agent, the principal is deemed to know or have constructive knowledge of all that the agent should have told him or her. It would then seem useless for a principal to instruct his or her agent with the admonition, "I don't want to know of it!" *See also* Restatement, Agency §272.
11. *See* Restatement, Agency §399.
12. The scope of this right is usually defined by contract. Absent this, the courts will indemnify the agent where it is just to do so, considering the nature of the relationship, the transaction entered into, and the costs and losses involved. Note that there is no right of indemnification for unauthorized acts. Furthermore, there is likewise no right for costs and losses incurred for the commission of illegal acts.
13. Note that where the plaintiff entertains a suit against only the agent and is denied recovery by the court, this action will generally operate to release the principal as well because there can be no vicarious liability without primary liability. Still, the principal may be sued for his or her own negligence, such as in the hiring or supervision of the agent or employee.
14. *See, e.g., Kirk v. Michael Reese Hosp.*, 513 N.E. 2d 387 (Ill. 1987); *Gregg v. National Medical Health Care*, 699 P. 2d 925 (Ariz. App. 1985). *See also* Chapter 14 below for discussion of other theories of liability of health care entities besides *respondeat superior*.
15. *Fock v. U.S.*, 597 F. Supp. 1325 (D.C. Kan. 1982).
16. *Foster v. Englewood Hospital Association*, 19 Ill. App. 3d 1055, 313 N.E. 2d 255 (1974).

4

Competency and Capacity: A Primer

STEVEN B. BISBING, Psy.D., J.D., F.C.L.M.

COMPETENCY IN GENERAL
THE LAW IN GENERAL
COMMON COMPETENCY AREAS

COMPETENCY IN GENERAL

In American society there are few aspects of human endeavor that are not affected in some way by the law. Generally, for someone to "lawfully" engage in some endeavor and be held accountable for his or her actions he or she must be *competent*. Essentially, "legal" competency refers to "having sufficient ability . . . possessing the natural or legal qualifications [to engage in something as recognized by law]."[1] This definition is deliberately vague because the term *competency* refers to a broad concept that encompasses many different situations and legal issues. As a consequence the definition, requirements, and application of the term can vary greatly, depending on the act or issue in question. Regardless of the circumstance, however, the law seeks to underscore a basic assumption: only acts of a relatively rational person are to be afforded recognition by the public. In doing so the law attempts to reaffirm the autonomy of the individual and the general integrity and value of society.

Generally, competency refers to some minimal mental, cognitive, or behavioral trait, ability, or capability required to perform a particular legally recognized act or to assume some legally recognized role. Appendix 4-1 identifies a sample of different situations in which competency is typically an essential component. The term *capacity*, which is frequently interchanged with and mistaken for the word *competency*, refers to an individual's actual ability to understand, appreciate, and form a relatively rational intention with regard to some act.

Appendix 4-2 identifies several human acts for which capacity is legally defined for the purpose of determining whether a person's actions can be legally recognized as competent. As a distinction, the term *incompetent* is applied to an individual whose actions fail a legal test of capacity. When such a designation is made, the individual is considered by law to be mentally incapable of performing a particular legally recognized act (e.g., executing a will or making medical decisions) or assuming a particular legally recognized role (e.g., serving as a guardian or participating in a trial).

Several important distinctions about competency must be clarified. First, the adjudication of incompetence is subject or task specific. In other words, the fact that a person is adjudicated incompetent to execute a will, for example, does not automatically render him or her incompetent to do other things, such as consent to treatment or testify as a witness. Accordingly, determinations of competency should be made on a case-by-case basis with regard to a person's present mental capacity and the specific legal right or act that he or she wishes or is asked to exercise. Second, a finding of incompetency does not translate into and should not be interpreted as a finding of mental illness. The threshold question in any civil or criminal competency inquiry is the ability to understand and engage in whatever legal requirements are defined for a given act (e.g., make a contract, stand trial, or marry). A person may be actively delusional, mentally retarded, or deaf and mute yet still meet the legal specifications associated with certain competency tests. Third, legal incompetency is not synonymous with the need for psychiatric treatment. The fact that a patient is or is not competent has no bearing on his or her need for treatment nor does such a finding necessarily equate with finding an individual dangerous to self or others. Fourth, incompetency and insanity are two entirely distinct concepts, although they are commonly confused with one another. In addition to different legal requirements for their determination, they are viewed from opposite temporal contexts. Legal competency reflects an individual's present capacity to engage in an act at the time of an evaluation. Legal insanity and questions regarding criminal responsibility refer to a person's ability, mental state, or both at the time of the offense. Insanity is therefore a historical perspective.

THE LAW IN GENERAL

Generally the law recognizes only those decisions or choices that have been made by a competent individual. The reason for this is that the law seeks to protect the incompetent from the effects of his or her actions and from being taken advantage of because of his or her lack of capacity. Persons over the age of majority, which is now 18 years,[2] are presumed to be competent.[3] However, this presumption can be rebutted based on evidence of an individual's incapacity.[4]

The issue of competency, whether in a civil or criminal context, is commonly raised in cases involving two classes of parties—minors and persons appearing to be mentally impaired. In many situations minors are not considered legally competent and therefore require the consent of a parent or designated guardian. There are, of course, exceptions to this general rule, such as minors who are considered emancipated[5] or mature[6] and some cases of medical need[7] or emergency.[8]

The mentally impaired individual presents a slightly different problem in terms of competency. Lack of capacity or incompetency cannot be presumed based on either treatment for mental illness[9] or institutionalization.[10] Moreover, evidence of significant mental illness, such as acute psychosis or chronic schizophrenia, does not in and of itself render a person incompetent in any particular area or in all areas of functioning. Instead, such a condition should trigger an assessment to determine whether a person is incapable of making a particular kind of decision or performing a particular type of task as defined or required by law. When there is a question about a person's mental status with regard to the capacity to engage in some legal act, one commentator suggests that two questions be addressed:[11]

1. Is there evidence of mental illness or deficiency (e.g., alcohol induced, age related, organic, etc.)?
2. If so, does this condition prevent the person from satisfying the relevant legal test or criterion for competency?

Thus although it is not always obvious from the legal tests themselves (Appendix 4-2), there is typically a threshold condition of cognitive or mental illness or deficiency that serves as a qualifying consideration. However, such conditions, no matter how seemingly severe, should not trigger reflexive examinations intended to "confirm" a premeditated finding of incompetency. Respect for individual autonomy[12] demands that individuals be allowed to make decisions of which they are capable, even if they are seriously mentally ill. As a rule, therefore, a patient or person with a history of mental illness generally must be judicially declared incompetent before he or she loses the legal power to do what adults who are not mentally ill have the legal right or power to do.

COMMON COMPETENCY AREAS

Civil law

Consent to medical treatment. One of the most controversial and vexing areas of potential substitute decision-making concerns the medical treatment of individuals whose competency is in question. The doctrine of informed consent, as described in the following section, was developed to address this issue. Historically, concern about patient decision-making has centered around two essential but sometimes conflicting purposes—individual autonomy and rational decision-making.[13] As one commentator aptly summarized, the interest in protecting autonomy in treatment-related decision-making is not merely a matter of the value that is placed on liberty or freedom for its own sake. Protection of autonomy also serves to humanize the physician-patient relationship and to restore the balance of authority between the physician and the patient on whose body or mind the proposed treatment would intrude.[14]

THE DOCTRINE OF INFORMED CONSENT. Under the doctrine of informed consent, health care providers have a legal duty to abide by the treatment decisions made by their patients unless a compelling state interest exists. The term *informed consent* is a legal principle in medical jurisprudence that generally holds that a physician must disclose to a patient sufficient information to enable the patient to make an "informed" decision about a proposed treatment or procedure.[15]

For a patient's consent to be considered informed, it must adequately address three essential elements—information, competency, and voluntariness. In general the patient must be given enough information to make a truly knowing decision, and that decision (consent) must be made voluntarily by a person who is legally competent. Each of these requirements must be met, or any consent given will not be considered informed or legally valid.

COMPETENT MEDICAL DECISION-MAKING. Only a competent person is legally recognized as being able to give informed consent. For health care providers working with patients who are sometimes of questionable competence because of mental illness, narcotic abuse, or alcoholism, this issue can be particularly important. The law presumes that an adult is competent unless he or she has been either judicially determined incompetent or incapacitated by a medical condition or emergency. The mere fact that a person is being treated for a mental illness[16] or is institutionalized[17] does not automatically render him or her incompetent. However, in addition to instances in which a patient's competency is manifestly suspect (i.e., he or she is acutely psychotic), there are several other circumstances in which competency considerations may be raised. First, and likely the most common, a patient of uncertain competency may refuse clearly necessary treatment; such a decision is especially questionable if the explanation for the refusal is illogical or indicates poor comprehension of the treatment information provided. Second, a physician may seek a consultation regarding the ability of a patient who is to undergo a significant medical procedure but is of questionable competency to give informed consent. This consideration may have more to do with protecting the physician against possible liability than with respect for patient liberty and autonomy. Third, a competency evaluation may be sought for a patient who has been legally found to be incompetent in one context (e.g., testamentary capacity) but "appears" to be competent in another context (e.g., giving informed consent to pursue a circumscribed course of treatment, such as drug therapy). Again, this practice may be motivated more by defensive medicine than deference to patient rights.

Notwithstanding the reasons that a person's competency to make medical decisions is questioned, the manner in which such a determination should be made is rarely described in the law and is not universally understood and practiced in the various health care professions. Instead, the treating provider (theoretically) is left to engage in a thoughtful analysis of the existing circumstances and arrive at a reasonable determination. From a legal perspective, the term *competency* is narrowly defined in terms of cognitive capacity.[18] Because there are no set criteria for determining a patient's competence, some commentators have likened "the search for a single test of competency to a search for a Holy Grail."[19] Regardless of the lack of a standard, health care providers should ensure that at a minimum the patient is capable of the following:[20]

1. Understanding the particular treatment being offered.[21]
2. Making a discernible decision, one way or another, regarding the treatment being offered.[22]
3. Communicating, verbally or nonverbally, that decision.[23]

To assist with what can be a daunting determination for some health care providers to make on behalf of some patients and under some circumstances, asking the following straightforward questions can help in the assessment of a patient's capacity: What is the patient's primary health problem at this time? What intervention was recommended? If the recommended intervention is implemented, what is likely to occur? If the recommended intervention is not pursued, what is likely to happen? What is the basis of the patient's decision to accept or refuse the recommended intervention?[24]

Mentally ill patients who have been determined to lack the requisite competency to make a treatment decision, except usually in an emergency,[25] will have an authorized representative or guardian appointed to make medical decisions on their behalf.[26]

Capacity to contract. To execute any business transaction between two parties, the law recognizes that each party must have sufficient capacity to give free and relatively knowing consent to enter into an agreement or contract. Minors and the mentally incompetent historically have been recognized as being incapable of executing a legally recognized transaction because of their presumed lack of the requisite cognitive capacity.

This presumption can be traced back as far as Roman law, which held that "an insane person cannot contract any business whatever because he does not know what he is doing." Similarly the common law of contracts in England required that two persons who wished to enter into a business agreement had to reach a "meeting of the minds." If one of the parties lacked the necessary mental capability to reach such a meeting, the law would not recognize the contract.

In *Dexter v. Hall* the U.S. Supreme Court commented on the effect that mental illness could have on the legality of a contract:

[T]he fundamental idea of a contract is that it requires the assent of two minds. But a lunatic, or person non compos mentis ("not of sound mind"), has nothing which the law recognizes as a mind, and it would seem, therefore, upon principle, that he cannot make a contract which may have efficacy as such.[27]

As noted in the introduction, evidence of mental illness is not "per se" evidence of incompetency. Therefore for the "lunatic" in *Dexter* to legally be considered incapable of executing a contract, he or she would have to demonstrate a present inability to meet the applicable standards for doing so as defined by law.[28]

The lack of capacity to contract may be total or partial. In cases of total incapacity a person is unable to enter into any contractual obligation, and any attempt to do so would be considered void. For instance, a person whose property is under the supervision of a legal guardian as a result of a legal adjudication of incompetence is considered "totally lacking contractual capacity." Capacity to contract also may be partial, as is generally the case with minors, the mentally ill, and persons whose cognitive faculties have been impaired by drugs, alcohol, or medication.[29] The extent of the ability of such persons to legally contract depends on the nature of the transaction and the surrounding circumstances.

The interests of commerce underlie the basic values associated with requirements of competency in contracts. When the incapacity or mental unsoundness of one of the parties affects a contract, two contrary public policies come into play. From a business perspective there is a fundamental view that the security of the transaction should be upheld to promote the development of commerce and ensure that the reasonable expectations of the parties are met. However, there is a countervailing public policy grounded in notions of morality and fairness that states that persons who are unable to appreciate the consequences of their actions should not be held accountable for them.

At one time the law regarding contracts entered into by persons lacking capacity held that such contracts were void.[30] However, the overwhelming weight of modern authority is that such contracts are merely voidable at the incompetent person's election.[31] One exception to this rule is the party who is so mentally disabled that he or she has been adjudicated mentally incompetent and a guardian of the property had been appointed before a given transaction was entered into. In many states a contract made under such circumstances would be considered void.[32]

Generally, mental incapacity rising to the level of incompetency to contract is said to exist where a "party does not understand the nature and consequences of his acts at the time of the transaction."[33] This rather broad and flexible definition often leads to the implicit conclusion that, if the contract is fair and beneficial to the individual alleged to be incompetent, he or she was (would be considered) "sane"; otherwise the tendency is to find him or her incompetent.[34] The more contemporary view uses a cognitive test ("ability to understand") and may conclude that the contract is voidable if the party "by reason of mental illness or defect . . . is unable to act in a reasonable manner in relation to the transaction and the other party has reason to know of this condition."[35] This approach allows the incompetent person to disaffirm an agreement or contract that he or she might be capable of understanding but because of some infirmity was without power to resist entering into.[36]

Cases involving challenges to a party's competency typically involve one of two scenarios. In the first scenario there is evidence of a mental condition that impairs a person's cognitive ability (the ability to understand the nature and consequences of the proposed transaction). In the second scenario the evidence indicates that there are mental conditions that impair a party's motivation or ability to act rationally. When a party to a contract lacks cognitive capacity, the contract is voidable without regard to whether the other person knew or had reason to know of the mental impairment. However, when one party has impaired motivational control, the contract is usually held to be voidable only if the other party knew or had reason to know of the mental condition (e.g., alcohol or narcotics intoxication).[37]

Finally, there are two situations—restitution and necessity—in which the incompetency of a party may not necessarily void the provisions of an agreement. Sometimes a contract may be executed and its conditions performed before the issue of competency is raised. A person seeking to avoid a contract has the burden of proving why it should be voided.

Generally, if one party is incompetent and the contract is still to be executed[38] or if the contract is based on grossly inadequate provisions,[39] rescission or cancellation will be granted. If, however, the other party had no reason to know of the mental infirmity and the contract is not otherwise unfair, the right to void the agreement may be lost to the extent that the contract has already been executed.[40] In the latter situation, at the least the incompetent party would have the responsibility to place the other party in the status quo ante (or place he was in before the contract).

In such situations, mental incompetents, like minors, cannot void a contract in which "necessities of life" have been provided.[41] Whether a good or service is considered a necessity is a matter for the jury, but certainly food, shelter, and clothing qualify. Other provisions, such as medical assistance, legal services, and transportation, usually are evaluated based on the party's situation at the time of the contract.

Wills and testamentary capacity. A second area of business activity in which competency is a significant legal factor is the execution of a will. As with contracting, the competency to execute a will is not a matter of general competency but rather is related to specific legal requirements associated with formulating a will. For example, if the individual writing the will, or "testator," is judged to be without the requisite competency (referred to as *testamentary capacity*) at the time of writing the will, the will would not be admitted to "probate" and would not be judged legally valid. If this occurs, the will's terms or provisions have no legal effect. In these situations the distribution of the testator's estate is guided by any valid will that exists. If no other will is available, the rules of "intestate secession" (which favor the immediate family and relatives) are applied. If no immediate family is available, the estate can "escheat" (or revert) to the state.

The conveyance of property through some form of testamentary process has a long and colorful history. Before the sixteenth century there was no law recognizing the written conveyance of real property to third parties. Typically, property rights were passed from one person to another or from one family member (e.g., father) to another (e.g., eldest son) in the form of an oral agreement or understanding. Public declaration or formal written representation of this change of ownership was uncommon and generally had no legal effect even if executed. The basic integrity and good faith of the two parties involved provided the basis of any exchange of property. If a person died without settling his estate, personal or real, his personal possessions were considered to be "up for grabs" and the local authorities, acting in the name of the king or crown, typically seized his real property. In 1540 the first English Statute of Wills was passed.[42] This statute and its later amendments authorized wills of land, provided that they were in writing. No other formality was required.

Today the law recognizes that a person may dispose of his or her property in any way he or she sees fit as long as it does not violate state law. However, for a will to be considered valid, it, like a contract, must be executed knowingly and voluntarily. Challenges to the validity of a will frequently concern whether the testator had sufficient testamentary capacity when making the will or was free from any undue influences (i.e., the will was voluntarily made).

Any person wishing to execute a legally binding will must possess, among other things, testamentary capacity. Analogous to the fundamental criminal law concept of mental competency, testamentary capacity involves an individual having a certain level of understanding of what he or she is doing in disposing of his or her property. There are no hard and fast rules or requisite elements that define testamentary capacity. However, the majority of jurisdictions in the United States require some variations of the elements articulated in the early English case, *Banks v. Goodfellow*.[43] In *Banks* the court fashioned the following five-part test:

To make a valid will one must be of sound mind though he need not possess superior or even average mentality. One is of sound mind for testamentary purposes only when he can understand and carry in his mind in a general way:
1. The nature and extent of his property,
2. The persons who are the natural objects of his bounty, and
3. The disposition which he is making of his property.

He also must be capable of:
4. Appreciating these elements in relation to each other, and
5. Forming an orderly desire as to the disposition of his property.

If a will is challenged on the basis that the testator lacked the requisite capacity, a probate judge will generally inquire the following: Was the testator aware that he or she was making a will? Was he able to assess and appraise the amount and value of the property? Was he aware of his legal heirs? Finally, was there some organized or rational scheme to the distribution of the property?

In assessing each of these or similar criteria a probate judge will entertain any evidence by the challengers that indicates a contrary finding of fitness. As with all questions involving adults and issues of competency, a testator is presumed to possess the requisite capacity. Therefore the burden is on the challenger to prove that at the time the will was made the testator lacked the requisite capacity.

In determining whether testamentary capacity exists under the standards already articulated, the law does not require a high degree of capacity or extensive knowledge. As with many tests of competency, only a minimum level of functioning is required. For example, in *In re Estate of Fish*,[44] a New York appellate court held that a testator "did not need to know the precise size of estate" to be considered competent.

Similar to other areas of competency, the presence of an apparent disability, infirmity, or mental dysfunction, such as mental illness, alcoholism, or narcotics addiction,[45] does not automatically invalidate an individual's testamentary capacity. Although these conditions can cloud or impair a person's ability to think and reason, the extent of any adverse effect is variable and therefore must be assessed. Moreover, even a person who is or appears to be significantly impaired should not be presumed to lack testamentary capacity. For example, if the will is written during a "lucid interval," it can be deemed valid.[46] Similarly, evidence of personality quirks, abnormalities in perception, idiosyncrasies, or forgetfulness in and of themselves generally are not sufficient to support a claim of testamentary incapacity.

Guardianship. Guardianship can be defined as the delegation by the state of authority over an individual's person or estate to another party. Historically the state or sovereign possessed the power and authority to safeguard the estate of incompetent persons.[47] This traditional role still reflects the purpose of guardianship today. In some states there are separate provisions for the appointment of a "guardian of one's person" (for health care decision-making) and a "guardian of one's estate" (who has the authority to, for example, make contracts to sell one's property).[48] This latter type of guardian is frequently referred to as a *conservator*, although this designation is not uniformly used throughout the United States. Further distinctions found in some jurisdictions are general (plenary) and specific guardianships.[49] As the name implies, the latter type of guardian is restricted to exercising decisions about a particular subject. For instance, the specific guardian may be authorized to make decisions about major or emergency medical procedures while the disabled person retains the freedom to make decisions about all other medical matters. General guardians, in contrast, have total control over the disabled individual's person, estate, or both.[50]

DETERMINATION OF NEED. A guardian is necessary only when there is some question as to whether the individual is de facto (actually) incompetent. An interesting aspect of the guardianship proceeding is its relatively flexible and relaxed atmosphere. In most states any interested person can petition to have someone declared incompetent and subject to guardianship.[51] Often there is no requirement of a specific allegation in the petition, and notice to the respondent is limited to the fact that a hearing will be held.[52] At the hearing itself the respondent frequently has no right to counsel[53] or trial by jury.[54] In some jurisdictions the respondent is rarely present.[55] If counsel is appointed, he or she is often designated as a guardian ad litem and is free to act in what he or she believes is in the respondent's best interest.[56] Moreover, if the respondent is determined to be in need of a guardian, he or she usually bears the burden of challenging that issue at a later time if he or she is no longer in need of a guardian.[57] At a later hearing, such a person is placed in the awkward position of persuading the court that the situation has changed and he or she is now competent. This hearing is required even though the respondent has had no opportunity to manage his or her own affairs, which would be compelling evidence that competency has been restored and a guardian is no longer needed.

The informality and procedural permissiveness that define a guardianship proceeding are matched by the vagueness of the standards by which the need for a guardian is determined. For a general guardianship, most jurisdictions simply require evidence of deficient mental status (e.g., mental illness or senility) and incapacity to "care for oneself or one's estate."[58] Standards for specific guardianship are not much better than are those for general guardianship in providing concrete requirements or descriptions. Despite this lack of rigor in definition, some state courts require considerable evidence of incompetency and incapacity before they will order guardianship.[59] Other courts are less stringent in their scrutiny of the facts.[60]

SELECTION. Anyone can petition the court to become a guardian over the person or estate of another. A diversity of parties may be appointed, ranging from family members and relatives to government agencies and law enforcement authorities.[61] As a rule, the selection of one guardian over another is more likely than not a matter of policy or law.

ROLE. After appointment, the guardian is generally charged with the responsibility to safeguard an incompetent individual's interests pursuant to one of two decision-making models. In one model an objective test is employed. This test guides the guardian by framing his or her responsibilities in terms of the following question: What action will most effectively serve and protect the incompetent individual's best interests? The second, subjective, model uses a form of "substituted judgment." In this model the guardian asks to assume the role of the ward and should "act as he or she thinks the ward would have acted, if the ward had been competent."[62] In situations in which there is no relevant history or reliable information from which to hypothesize how a ward might have acted if competent, a guardian is usually left with no alternative but to employ a form of "best interests" test.[63] Under these circumstances it is likely that the guardian will objectively evaluate as much relevant information as is available and then determine a course of action that best serves the ward's interests.

Competency to testify. Competency to give testimony has generally been defined as follows: "[I]n the law of evidence, the presence of those characteristics, or the absence of those disabilities, which render a witness legally fit and qualified to give testimony in a court of justice."[64] The determination of whether a witness is competent to provide testimony[65] rests solely within the sound discretion of the trial court.[66] The test typically is composed of the following four separate inquiries:[67]

1. Whether, at the time of the event in question, the witness had the capacity "to observe intelligently."
2. Whether at the time of the trial the witness possessed the capacity to recollect that event.
3. Whether the witness had the "capacity mentally to understand the nature of the questions put and to form and communicate intelligent answers."
4. Whether the witness had "a sense of moral responsibility, of the duty to make the narration correspond to the recollection and knowledge (i.e., to speak the truth as he sees it)."

Often there are no statutorily defined requirements or standards for evaluating the competency of a witness to provide testimony. Instead, the courts (i.e., judges) apply traditional common law principles in making this determination.[68] Therefore there is no single, fixed standard of competency to be applied "across the board" to all witnesses.

Because perceptions and memories of events can vary widely and are prone to distortion and impairment by any witness, courts are especially vigilant to question any potential testimony that may be misleading. This concern is commonly raised with regard to the individual whose memory or perception of reality appears suspect because of developmental immaturity or mental or cognitive impairment. Thus in litigation, especially a criminal trial, the issue of competency to testify often arises if the prospective witness is a child, is mentally retarded, or is psychiatrically impaired (e.g., psychotic).

CHILDREN. Child witnesses present special challenges for the law. As observed by one court:

Not only does it pose problems in terms of the child's appreciation of the need to tell the truth with precision and accuracy, but the trauma attendant upon testimony in open court—subject to examination and cross-examination—before the unfamiliar faces of jurors, lawyers and judges may be particularly terrifying to a young child.[69]

In general there is a rebuttable presumption that children are not legally competent to testify. However, the age at which this presumption is rebuttable varies across jurisdictions. Notwithstanding this threshold there is no precise age that determines competence to testify.[70] The trial court has wide discretion in determining competence and selecting the method for arriving at that determination.[71] Competence of a minor will generally "depend on the capacity and intelligence of the child, his appreciation of the difference between truth and falsehood, as well as his duty to tell the truth."[72] To allow the testimony of a child, the court must determine that the child (1) possesses the intellect to differentiate truth and falsity and to appreciate the duty to tell the truth and (2) can recall the events in question.[73]

MENTALLY HANDICAPPED AND DISABLED INDIVIDUALS. Prospective witnesses who are intellectually handicapped, mentally ill, or mentally disabled as a result of drug or alcohol abuse may potentially testify, provided the court is satisfied that they are capable. For example, the determination of testimonial capacity of a witness who is intellectually limited or has learning difficulties generally proceeds in the same manner as the determination of testimonial capacity of a child witness. Expert testimony may be useful or required.[74]

When a witness is a known abuser of alcohol or illicit drugs, the court's determination is guided by whether the witness (1) was under the influence at the time of the events about which he or she will testify, (2) is under the influence while testifying, or (3) is mentally disabled as a result of long-term substance abuse. Because of the potentially technical nature of these questions, their assessment must be thorough,[75] and competency hearings rely on a variety of evidence, including the examination of medical records, lay and expert testimony, and the results of mental and physical examinations.[76]

A mentally ill person may be a competent witness.[77] As in the case of the substance-impaired witness, the court may conduct the usual examination of relevant evidence, such as the review of medical records, expert testimony, and the results of mental examinations, in making a determination.[78]

Criminal law

It is generally accepted in Western jurisprudence that incompetent individuals should not be permitted to proceed with a trial.[79] Conviction of an accused person while he or she is legally incompetent deprives him or her of liberty without due process of law.[80] Effective representation of a defendant with mental problems is a difficult task, demanding special skill and care in dealing with the defendant, as well as knowledge of a complicated body of statutory and case law. Consequently, every criminal attorney, judge, or other officer of the court must be alert to the possibility that a defendant's mental state—at the present time, at the time of the alleged offense, or both—may be relevant to the handling of his defense.

Standards and assessment of competency to stand trial. The legal standard for assessing pretrial competency is well established by the landmark case *Dusky v. United States*.[81] Throughout his or her involvement with the trial process, the defendant must have "sufficient present ability to consult with his attorney with a reasonable degree of rational understanding (and have) a rational as well as factual understanding of the proceedings against him."[82] These standards are general legal conclusions, and the precise meanings are deliberately ambiguous. The *Dusky* language suggests several fundamental elements. First, competency reflects a defendant's present ability to consult with counsel and to understand the proceedings. Second, the test of competency applies to the defendant's capacity rather than motivation or willingness* to relate to the attorney and understand the proceedings. Third, the criterion that the defendant must have a "reasonable" degree of understanding implies that the test for competency in a given case is flexible. As with other tests of capacity, "perfect" or complete understanding on the part of the defendant is not required.[83] Fourth, the court's focus on the defendant's "factual" and "rational" understanding suggests an emphasis on cognitive functioning. This final consideration reiterates the fact that evidence of a mental illness or the need for psychiatric treatment is not an automatic indicator of incompetency.[84] These factors are relevant only insofar as they affect or represent a sufficient impairment in the defendant's ability to meet the legal test of competency.

Numerous commentators have sought to identify specific reality-based factors that could be used in assessing the general standards established in *Dusky*.[85] These efforts typically focus on two areas—the defendant's comprehension

---

*There is presently no single "test" that is given to a defendant and yields a valid finding of competency or incompetency.

of the criminal process, including the role of participants (e.g., attorneys, judge, and jury) in the process, and the defendant's ability to function in that process, primarily through consultation with defense counsel. For instance, one court noted that a defendant would be determined competent to stand trial if the following were found:

- The defendant possesses the "mental capacity to appreciate his presence in relation to time, place, and things."[86]
- The defendant has "sufficient elementary mental processes to apprehend (i.e., to seize and grasp with what mind he has) that he is in a court of justice, charged with a criminal offense."
- The defendant understands that there is a judge on the bench.
- The defendant "understands that a prosecutor is present who will try to convict him of a criminal charge."
- The defendant "understands that a lawyer will undertake to defend him against that charge."
- The defendant understands that "he is expected to tell his lawyer the circumstances, to the best of his mental ability (whether colored or not by mental aberration), the facts surrounding him at the time and place where the law violation is alleged to have been committed."
- The defendant understands that there will be a jury present to determine guilt or innocence.
- The defendant "has memory sufficient to relate those things in his own personal manner."[87]

The degree of a defendant's impairment in one specific area of functioning does not automatically equate with incompetency. The ultimate determination of incompetency is solely for the court to decide.[88] Moreover the impairment must be considered in the context of the particular case or proceeding.

[O]ne or another of the items will not be equal nor is it intended to be. Neither will the weight assigned to a given item by the court in reaching a finding on competency for a particular defendant necessarily apply to the next defendant. Considerations of the weight to be assigned a given item in the case of a particular defendant goes [sic] beyond the scope of what should be expected of the examining clinician. The task for the clinician is the providing of objective data, the import of which is the responsibility of the Court.[89]

Controversy exists regarding the general scope of the term *competency to stand trial* and its practical application in today's criminal justice system. Some commentators have suggested that the concept is overly broad, inadequate, and misleading in its current use.[90] For example, some defendants may be required to testify, decide whether to plead insanity, or make choices about plea options and plea bargains. Depending on the nature of the decision to be made, some commentators have argued that a given defendant may be competent to make certain decisions but not others. Although this analysis may be clinically valid and more realistic, it does not square with the present legal precedents on this issue. In a recent Supreme Court case, *Godinez v. Moran*, the majority held that the standard for the various types of competency (e.g., competency to plea, to waive counsel, and to stand trial) should be considered the same.[91]

While the decision to plead guilty is undeniably a profound one, it is no more complicated than the sum total of decisions that a defendant may be called upon to make during the course of a trial. . . . Nor do we think that a defendant who waives his right to the assistance to counsel must be more competent than the defendant who does not, since there is not reason to believe that the decision to waive counsel requires an appreciably higher level of mental functioning than the decision to waive other constitutional rights.[92]

Judicial evaluation. The judicial determination of competency must be an informed one.[93] Accordingly the court has broad discretion in both hearing a motion for a competency examination[94] and weighing evidence in making a final determination.[95] Because a careful evaluation of the accused's mental condition is required,[96] a hospital report that he or she is mentally competent to stand trial is not binding on the court,[97] especially if there is no supporting information or reasons regarding that conclusion.[98] The law often requires that a report or certificate be issued by a qualified mental health professional (e.g., psychiatrist), establishing that a person is competent to stand trial before the court.[99] This certificate does not preclude the expert testimony of a psychologist,[100] though less weight may be given to his or her testimony.[101] The determination of competency does not rest exclusively or primarily on the opinion of experts.[102] For instance, the U.S. Court of Appeals for the District of Columbia Circuit has stated that it would be useful for trial judges to question both the defendant and defense counsel about the ability of the accused to consult with his or her attorney because the attorney's own first-hand evaluation may be just as valuable as an expert's opinion.[103]

There are a number of checklists and psychometric tests designed to assist the clinician in assessing a person's competency to stand trial.[104] One of the more commonly used instruments is the Competency to Stand Trial Instrument (CSTI) designed by the Laboratory of Community Psychiatry.[105] The CSTI involves the consideration of 13 functions "related to what is required of a defendant in criminal proceedings in order that he may adequately cope with and protect himself in such proceedings."[106] The purpose of the CSTI is to standardize, objectify, and qualify relevant criteria for the determination of an individual's competency to stand trial. The presentation of these functions was written so it would be useful and acceptable to both the legal and medical professions. The 13 functions to be assessed include, among other factors:

- Appraisal of available legal defenses.
- Unmanageable behavior.

- Quality of relating to attorney and planning of legal strategy.
- Understanding of court procedure.
- Appreciation of charges and nature of possible penalties.
- Capacity to disclose to attorney available pertinent facts surrounding the offense.

All "competency-related" assessment instruments are essentially structured formats for interviewing the defendant. Generally a competency evaluation can be performed within the context of an outpatient interview. Actual psychological testing is not likely to be a cost-effective means of gathering relevant information, nor is it any more capable of directly answering the requisite competency questions.

Special considerations: the amnestic defendant. At face value, the defendant who has no memory of the criminal act of which he or she is accused appears to be incompetent on the grounds that the amnesia prevents reasonable consultation with counsel in preparing a defense.[1] However, as a general rule a claim of amnesia is not grounds for a finding of incompetency per se.[107] This rule is largely borne out of judicial mistrust of the authenticity of such claims. However, while generally rejecting outright such claims as an automatic determinant of incompetency, courts have labored to establish guidelines in determining the competency of the defendant claiming amnesia. Probably the most thoughtful analysis of this issue is found in *Wilson v. United States*.[108] In *Wilson* the defendant had no memory regarding the time of the alleged robbery because he suffered from permanent retrograde amnesia. This impairment was caused by injuries he suffered in an automobile accident that occurred as the police were pursuing him after the offense. The court concluded that the competency issue should be tested in accordance with the following criteria:

1. The extent to which the amnesia affected the defendant's ability to consult with and assist his attorney.
2. The extent to which the amnesia affected the defendant's ability to testify on his own behalf.
3. The extent to which the evidence could be extrinsically reconstructed in view of the defendant's amnesia. (Such evidence would include evidence relating to the crime itself, as well as any reasonably possible alibi.)
4. The extent to which the government assisted the defendant and his counsel in that reconstruction.
5. The strength of the prosecution's case. (Most important here is whether the government's case is such as to negate all reasonable hypotheses of innocence. If there is any substantial possibility that the accused could, but for his amnesia, establish an alibi or other defense, it should be presumed that he would have been able to do so.)
6. Any other factors and circumstances that would indicate whether or not the defendant had a fair trial.

For the clinician faced with a defendant claiming severe memory problems, the first objective is to determine whether the claim of amnesia is valid. If the claim is valid, the "customary" competency examination may proceed because all other functions associated with competency (e.g., communicating with counsel and understanding the legal proceedings) may be unaffected. Moreover, the amnestic defendant may be able to assist the defense by identifying and assessing other evidence depicting his or her conduct at the time of the crime.

Raising the competency issue. The competency of a defendant may be raised at any stage in the proceedings up until the time of sentencing.[109] However, prima facie evidence must be presented to support a request for a competency examination, particularly when the request comes on the eve of or the day of trial.[110]

Although questions regarding competency are usually raised by the defense attorney,[111] the court and the prosecutor have an obligation to ensure that a defendant whose competency is in question is not permitted to proceed with the trial until competency issues are resolved.[112]

ENDNOTES

1. *Black's Law Dictionary* 257 (7th ed., West Group, St. Paul, Minn. 1999).
2. *See e.g.*, Department of Health and Human Services, *The Legal Status of Adolescents 1980* 41 (DHHS, Washington, D.C. 1981).
3. *See e.g.*, *Meek v. City of Loveland*, 276 P. 30 (Colo. 1929).
4. *See e.g.*, *Scaria v. St. Paul Fire & Marine Insurance*, 227 N.W. 2d 647 (Wis. 1975).
5. J.T. Smith, *Medical Malpractice: Psychiatric Care* 178-179 (Shepard's/McGraw-Hill, Colorado Springs, Colo. 1986)
6. *See e.g.*, *Gulf Southern Railroad Co. v. Sullivan*, 119 So. 501 (Miss. 1929).
7. *See e.g.*, *Planned Parenthood v. Danforth*, 428 U.S. 52, 74 (1975) (abortion); Ill. Rev. Stat. ch. 91 1/2, para 3-501(a) (1983) (mental health counseling).
8. *See e.g.*, *Jehovah's Witnesses v. King County Hospital*, 278 F. Supp. 488 (W.D. Wash. 1967).
9. *See e.g.*, *Wilson v. Lehmann*, 379 S.W. 2d 478, 479 (Ky. Ct. App. 1964).
10. *See e.g.*, *Rennie v. Klein*, 462 F. Supp. 1131 (D. N.J. 1978).
11. H. Weihofen, *The Definition of Mental Illness*, 21 Ohio St. L. J. 1 (1960).
12. *See e.g.*, *Schloendorff v. New York Hospital*, 105 N.E. 92 (N.Y. 1914).
13. *See e.g.*, M.B. Stauss, *Familiar Medical Quotations* 157 (Little, Brown, Boston 1968) (quoting a 1649 Massachusetts Bay colony law that forbade physicians, midwives, and others from acting on mentally competent patients without their consent). Although the concept of informed consent has deep roots in the centuries-old individual liberty movement, its actual development as a legal doctrine did not occur until the 1960s. *See e.g.*, *Salgo v. Leland Stanford Jr. Univ. Bd. of Trustees*, 317 P. 2d 170 (Cal. Dist. Ct. App. 1957); *Natanson v. Kline*, 350 P. 2d 1093, *rehg. den.* 354 P. 2d 670 (Kan. 1960).
14. J. Katz, *The Silent World of Doctor and Patient* 59-80 (Free Press, New York 1984).
15. *Supra* note 1, at 701.
16. *Supra* note 9.
17. *Supra* note 10.
18. *See e.g.*, *Yahn v. Folse*, 639 So. 2d 261 (La. App. 1993). (An 82-year-old illiterate and hard of hearing woman was sufficiently alert [cognitively] and communicative to give valid consent to a medical procedure.)
19. Meisel, Roth & Lidz, *Tests of Competency to Consent to Treatment*, 134 Am. J. Psychiatry 279, 283 (1977).
20. *See also* Appelbaum & Grisso, *Assessing Patients' Capacities to Consent to Treatment*, 319 N. Engl. J. Med. 1635-1638 (1988) (proposing four different standards for assessing competency to consent to treatment).
21. Meisel, Roth & Lidz, *Toward a Model of the Legal Doctrine of Informed Consent*, 134 Am. J. Psychiatry 285 (1977).
22. M. Perlin, *Mental Disability Law: Civil and Criminal*, vol. 3, 80 (Michie Co., Charlottesville, Va. 1989).
23. *Supra* note 21, at 287 citing 139 Am. Law Rep. 1370 (1942); *but see Lipscomb v. Memorial Hospital*, 733 F. 2d 332, 335-36 (4th Cir. 1984).
24. P.A. Singer & M. Siegler, *Elective Use of Life-Sustaining Treatments in Internal Medicine*, in *Advances in Internal Medicine* 66 (G.H. Stollerman, ed., Year Book Medical Publishers, Chicago 1991).
25. *See e.g.*, *Frasier v. Department of Health and Human Resources*, 500 So. 2d 858, 864 (La. Ct. App. 1986).
26. *See e.g.*, *Aponte v. United States*, 582 F. Supp. 555, 566-69 (D.P.R. 1984).
27. *Dexter v. Hall*, 82 U.S. 15 (1872).
28. *See generally* J. Calamari & J. Perillo, *The Law of Contracts* 305-330 (4th ed. St. Paul, Minn., West Group, 1998) (capacity of parties).
29. *See e.g.*, Sharpe, *Medication as a Threat to Testamentary Capacity*, 35 N.C.L. Rev. 380 (1957).
30. *See e.g.*, *Hovey v. Hobson*, 53 Me. 451 (1866).
31. *See* 2 Williston, *Contracts* §§249-252.
32. Restatement (Second) Contracts, §13.
33. *See e.g.*, *Cundick v. Broadbent*, 383 F. 2d 157 (10th Cir. 1967), *cert. den.* 390 U.S. 948 (1968); *see also* Guttmacher & Weihofen, *Mental Incompetency*, 36 Minn. L. Rev. 179 (1952).
34. *See e.g.*, Green, *Proof of Mental Incompetency and the Unexpressed Major Premise*, 53 Yale L. J. 271 (1944); Green, *The Operative Effect of Mental Incompetency on Agreements and Wills*, 21 Tex. L. Rev. 554 (1943).
35. Restatement (Second) Contracts, §15.
36. *See e.g.*, Danzig, *The Capability Problem in Contract Law*, 148-204 (Foundation Press, Mineola, N.Y. 1978); *but see* Hardisty, *Mental Illness: A Legal Fiction*, 48 Wash. L. Rev. 735 (1975).
37. *See generally* McCoid, *Intoxication and its Effect upon Civil Responsibility*, 42 Iowa L. Rev. (1956); 2 Williston, *Contracts* §§258-263.
38. *See e.g.*, *Cundell v. Haswell*, 51 A. 426 (R.I. 1902).
39. *See e.g.*, *Alexander v. Haskins*, 68 Iowa 73, 25 N.W. 935 (1885).
40. *See e.g.*, Restatement (Second) Contracts, §15(2).
41. *See e.g.*, *Coffee v. Owens' Admiralty*, 216 Ky. 142 (1926).
42. E. Clark, L. Lusky & A. Murphy, *Gratuitous Transfers*, 372 (3d ed., West Publishing, St. Paul, Minn. 1985).
43. *Banks v. Goodfellow*, 5 Q.B. 549 (1870).
44. *In re Estate of Fish*, 522 N.Y.S. 2d 970 (App. Div. 1987).
45. 79 Am. Jur. 2d *Wills* §§77-101.
46. *See generally* 18 Am. Jur. P.O.F. 2d *Mentally Disordered Testator's Execution of Will During Lucid Interval* §1 (1979).
47. *See generally* Regan, *Protective Services for the Elderly: Commitment, Guardianship, and Alternatives*, 13 Wm. & Mary L. Rev. 569, 570-573 (1972).
48. B. Sales, D.M. Powell & R. Van Duizend, *Disabled Persons and the Law: State Legislative Issues* 461 (Plenum Press, New York 1982).
49. *Id.* at 462.
50. *Id.* at 461-462.
51. *Id.* at 463.
52. *Supra* note 47, at 605.
53. *Supra* note 48, at 463. (As of 1988, 10 states provide no statutory right to counsel.)
54. *Id.* (As of 1988, 22 states provide the respondent with the right to jury.)
55. *Id.* (As of 1988, only 38 states guarantee the right to be present and that right is often waivable with only a physician's certificate stating that the respondent is unable to attend.)
56. *Supra* note 48, at 463.

57. *Id*. at 464.

58. *Id*. at 469-474.

59. *See e.g., Plummer v. Early*, 190 Cal. Rptr. 578 (Ct. App. 1983). (Evidence that schizophrenic respondent was dirty, disheveled, and incontinent and spent the majority of his time in the backyard of his home was insufficient to warrant conservatorship or guardianship of person.)

60. *See e.g., In re Oltmer*, 336 N.W. 2d 560 (Neb. 1983).

61. *See generally* Hodgson, *Guardianship of Mentally Retarded Persons: Three Approaches to a Long Neglected Problem*, 37 Alb. L. Rev. 407 (1973).

62. *See e.g., In re Roe III*, 421 N.E. 2d 40 (Mass. 1981); *Rogers v. Commissioner of Mental Health*, 458 N.E. 2d 308 (Mass. 1983).

63. *See generally* Melton & Scott, *Evaluations of Mentally Retarded Persons for Sterilization: Contributions and Limits of Psychological Consultation*, 15 Prof. Psychol. Res. Prac. 34, 35-36 (1984).

64. *Supra* note 1, at 257.

65. Competency issues are frequently raised about a number of aspects of a witness's or defendant's conduct or litigation procedures (e.g., waive right to silence, counsel, or jury; stand trial; be sentenced; serve a sentence; and be executed).

66. *See generally Wheeler v. United States*, 159 U.S. 523, 524-525 (1895); *United States v. Benn*, 476 F. 2d 1201 (D.C. Cir. 1972); *In re B.D.T.*, 435 A. 2d 378, 379 (D.C. 1981).

67. J. Wigmore, *Evidence*, §478 (Chadbourn rev. 1979).

68. The four-part test enunciated by Wigmore would be a typical example of a common law rule or guiding principle.

69. *U.S. v. Comer*, 421 F. 2d 1149, 1152 n.3 (D.C. Cir. 1970).

70. *See e.g., Galindo v. U.S.*, 630 A. 2d 202 (D.C. 1993) (3-year-old found competent); *Wheeler v. U.S.*, 159 U.S. 523, 524 (D.C. Cir. 1895) (5-year-old found competent).

71. *U.S. v. Schoefield*, 465 F. 2d 560, 562 (D.C. Cir. 1972), *cert. den.* 409 U.S. 881 (1972).

72. *Id*.

73. *See e.g., Johnson v. U.S.*, 364 A. 2d 1198, 1202 (D.C. 1976); *In re A.H.B.*, 491 A. 2d 490, 492 (D.C. 1985).

74. *See e.g., U.S. v. Benn*, 476 F. 2d 1127, 1130-31 (D.C. Cir. 1972).

75. *U.S. v. Crosby*, 462 F. 2d 1201, 1203 (D.C. Cir. 1972).

76. *See e.g., U.S. v. Heinlein*, 490 F. 2d 725, 730 (D.C. Cir. 1973); *U.S. v. Butler*, 481 F. 2d 531, 533 (D.C. Cir. 1973).

77. *See e.g., In re Penn*, 443 F. 2d 663, 666 (D.C. Cir. 1970).

78. *See generally Vereen v. U.S.*, 587 A. 2d 456 (D.C. App. 1991), *Collins v. U.S.*, 491 A. 2d 480, 484 (D.C. App. 1985), *cert. den.* 475 U.S. 1124 (1986).

79. *See generally* W. Blackstone, *Commentaries on the Laws of England* (9th ed., Clarendon Press, Oxford 1773); *see also Frith's Case*, 22 How. St. Tr. 307 (1790).

80. *See e.g., Pate v. Robinson*, 383 U.S. 375, 378 (1966).

81. *Dusky v. United States*, 362 U.S. 402 (1960) (established the threshold test for determining a defendant's competency to stand trial).

82. *Id*. This standard also is applied to juvenile proceedings; *see e.g., In re W.A.F.*, 573 A. 2d 1264, 1267 (D.C. 1990).

83. The threshold for being found competent to stand trial is generally believed to be low; *see generally Incompetency to Stand Trial*, 81 Harv. L. Rev. 454, 457-458 (1967).

84. Typically, evidence of a mental disease, condition, or defect is associated with the question of incompetence. However, a defendant may be adjudged incompetent to stand trial even if he or she lacks a mental disorder as defined by current mental health diagnostic standards, such as the American Psychiatric Association's *Diagnostic and Statistical Manual of Mental Disorders*, Fourth Edition (DSM-IV); *see generally Wilson v. U.S.*, 391 F. 2d 460, 463 (D.C. Cir. 1968).

85. *See e.g.,* T. Grisso, *Competency to Stand Trial: Evaluations* 97-106 (Professional Resource Exchange, Sarasota, Fla. 1988). (See Appendix C: List of Defendant's Abilities and Trial Demands for Use in Pretrial Competency Evaluations and Appendix D: Information about Competency Evaluation Instruments.)

86. Competency is not met by a defendant's mere understanding or the fact that he or she has "orientation to time and place and [has] some recollection of events." *Supra* note 81.

87. *Weiter v. Settle*, 193 F. Supp. 318, 321-22 (W.D. Mo. 1961).

88. *United States v. David*, 511 F. 2d 355 (D.C. Cir. 1975).

89. *Id*. at 99-100.

90. *See e.g.*, Roesch & Golding, *Defining and Assessing Competency to Stand Trial*, in *Handbook of Forensic Psychology* 378-394 (Weiner I.B. & Hess A.K., eds., J. Wiley, New York 1987).

91. *Godinez v. Moran*, 113 S.Ct. 2680 (1993).

92. *Id*. at 2686; *but see id.* at 2691-2694 (J. Blackmon, dissenting). (The "majority's analysis is contrary to both common sense and long-standing case law"; competency cannot be considered in a vacuum, separate from its specific legal context; "competency for one purpose does not necessarily translate to competency for another purpose," noting that prior Supreme Court cases have "required competency evaluations to be specifically tailored to the context and purpose of the proceeding.")

93. *See Blunt v. U.S.*, 389 F. 2d 545 (D.C. Cir. 1967).

94. *Bennett v. United States*, 400 A. 2d 322 (D.C. App. 1979).

95. 18 U.S.C. §4241 (federal statute authorizing a psychiatric or psychological examination of a defendant on the issue of competency to stand trial and presentation of a report to the court).

96. *Supra* note 93.

97. *See e.g., Wider v. United States*, 348 F. 2d 358 (D.C. Cir. 1965).

98. *See e.g., Holloway v. United States*, 343 F. 2d 265 (D.C. Cir. 1964).

99. *See e.g., Bennett v. United States*, 400 A. 2d 322 (D.C. App. 1979). (If neither party objects, the court, without conducting a hearing, may enter an order adjudicating the defendant to be competent based on the certification of the examining psychiatrist.)

100. *See e.g., Jenkins v. United States*, 307 F. 2d 637, 643 (D.C. Cir. 1962).

101. *See e.g., Blunt v. United States*, 389 F. 2d 545 (D.C. Cir. 1957). (The lack of a general medical background may affect the weight given to a psychologist's testimony in a competency hearing.)

102. By analogy, testimony by lay witnesses as to their observations and opinions of the defendant's mental condition is admissible in support of the insanity defense. *Carter v. United States*, 252 F. 2d 608, 618 (D.C. Cir. 1957).

103. *United States v. David*, 511 F. 2d 355 (D.C. Cir. 1975).

104. *See generally* T. Grisso, *Competency to Stand Trial Evaluations: A Manual for Practice* 101-105 (Professional Resource Exchange, Sarasota, Fla. 1988).

105. *Competency to Stand Trial and Mental Illness*, a monograph sponsored by the Center for Studies of Crime and Delinquency, National Institute of Mental Health, DHEW Pub. No. (HSM) 73-9105 (1973) (out of print).

106. *Id*.

107. *See generally* 46 A.L.R. 3d 544 (1972).

108. *Wilson v. United States*, 391 F. 2d 460, 463 (D.C. Cir. 1968).

109. *In Leach v. United States*, 334 F. 2d 945 (D.C. Cir. 1964). (A sentence was set aside and remanded with directions when a district court judge failed to consider evidence presented to him about the psychological unfitness of the individual he was sentencing. The appellate court specifically cited the lower court's failure to make any disposition of the prisoner's repeated request for a mental examination before sentencing. The appellate court noted that the trial court had psychiatric services at its disposal and this was precisely the situation in which to employ them.)

110. *See e.g., Thorne v. United States*, 471 A. 2d 247 (D.C. 1983).

111. An affidavit by defense counsel stating that he or she has serious doubts about the defendant's mental capacity to assist him or her intelligently is sufficient to require the granting of a motion for a mental examination. *Cannady v. United States*, 351 F. 2d 817 (D.C. Cir. 1965).

112. *See e.g., Winn v. United States*, 270 F. 2d 326 (D.C. Cir. 1959), *cert. den.* 365 U.S. 848 (1961).

113. *See e.g., In re Guardianship of Pamela*, 519 N.E. 2d 1335 (Mass. Sup. Jud. Ct. 1988).

114. *See e.g., McAlister v. Deatheridge*, 523 So. 2d 387 (Ala. 1988).

115. *See e.g., Daughton v. Parson*, 423 N.W. 2d 894 (Iowa Ct. App. 1988) (transfer of property set aside where the grantor did not have sufficient mental capacity to execute the deed).

116. *See e.g.*, Annas & Densburger, *Competence to Refuse Medical Treatment: Autonomy vs. Paternalism*, 15 U. Toledo L. Rev. 561 (1984).

117. *See e.g., Weldon v. Long Island College Hospital*, 535 N.Y.S. 2d 949 (Sup. Ct. 1988).

118. *See e.g., Pace v. Pace*, 513 N.E. 2d 1357 (Ohio Ct. App. 1986).

119. *See e.g., Manhattan State Citizen's Group, Inc. v. Bass*, 524 F. Supp. 1270 (S.D. N.Y. 1981).

120. 42 U.S.C. §423(d)(1)(A) (1983 and Cumm. Supp. 1985 *et seq.*); *see also* 20 C.F.R. §404.1520-404.1574 (1983).

121. *In re Conservatorship Estate of Moehlenpah*, 763 S.W. 2d 249 (Mo. Ct. App. 1988).

122. *See e.g.,* D.C. Code §16-904 (d)(1)-(5) (grounds for annulment of marriage, including "insanity" at the time of marriage).

123. *See e.g., In re Marriage of Steffan*, 423 N.W. 2d 729 (Minn. Ct. App. 1988) (divorce decree binding where the wife's mental condition did not interfere with her comprehension).

124. *See e.g., In re Jason Y*, 744 P. 2d 181 (N.M. Ct. App. 1987).

125. *See e.g., In re J.O.L. II*, 409 A. 2d 1073 (D.C. 1979). (Defining factors used in the District of Columbia delineate whether an adoption by a petitioning party is in the "best interests of the child." Among these factors is the mental state of the petitioning party. Clearly, if the petitioner were incompetent, placement would not be in a child's best interests.)

126. *Dusky v. United Sates*, 362 U.S. 402 (1960).

127. *Drope v. Missouri*, 420 U.S. 162 (1975); *Pate v. Robinson*, 383 U.S. 375 (1966).

128. A defendant who has been found "competent" is not necessarily capable of making intelligent decisions on all issues, for example, the decision to waive an insanity defense. *Frendak v. United States*, 408 A. 2d 364, 379 (D.C. App. 1979).

129. *See e.g., Lyles v. U.S.*, 254 F. 2d 725 (D.C. Cir. 1975).

130. *See e.g., Nebraska v. Tully*, 413 N.W. 2d 910 (Neb. 1987) (defendant's confession and guilty plea held to be "knowingly, intelligently, and voluntarily made" despite IQ of 81 and diagnosis of mild mental retardation).

131. *See e.g., Faretta v. California*, 422 U.S. 806 (1975).

132. *See e.g.*, Note, *Mental Aberration and Postconviction Sanctions*, 15 Suffolk Univ. L. Rev. 1219 (1981); *State v. Hehman*, 520 P. 2d 507 (Ariz. 1974); *Commonwealth v. Robinson*, 431 A. 2d 901 (Pa. 1981).

133. *See e.g., In re Hews*, 741 P. 2d 983 (Wash. 1987).

134. *North Carolina v. Alford*, 400 U.S. 25 (1970).

135. *See e.g., Jurney v. Arkansas*, 766 S.W. 2d 1 (Ark. 1989).

136. *See e.g., Ford v. Wainwright*, 477 U.S. 399 (1986); Note, *The Eighth Amendment and the Execution of the Presently Incompetent*, 32 Stan. L. Rev. 765 (1980).

137. *See e.g., United States v. Thornton*, 498 F. 2d 749 (D.C. Cir. 1974); *Bethea v. United States*, 365 A. 2d 64 (D.C. App. 1976).

138. *See e.g., Fuller v. Texas*, 737 S.W. 2d 113 (Tex. Ct. App. 1987).

SUGGESTED READINGS

General

S. Brakal, J. Parry & B. Weiner, eds., *The Mentally Disabled and the Law* (3d ed., American Bar Foundation, Chicago 1985).

T. Grisso, *Evaluating Competencies: Forensic Assessments and Instruments* (Plenum Press, New York 1986).

G.B. Melton, J. Petrila, N.G. Poythress & C. Slobogin, *Psychological Evaluations for the Courts* (2d ed., Guilford Press, New York, 1997).

R. Reisner & C. Slobogin, *Law and the Mental Health System: Civil and Criminal Aspects* (2d ed., West Publishing, St. Paul, Minn. 1990).

Competency to stand trial

T. Grisso, *Competency to Stand Trial Evaluations: A Manual for Practice* (PAR Inc., Sarasota, Fla. 1988).

M. Perlin, *Mental Disability Law: Civil and Criminal* (3 volumes) (Michie Publishing, Charlottesville, Va. 1989).

Public Defender Service, *Criminal Practice Institute Trial Manual* (PDS, Washington, D.C. 1996).

Children and juveniles

S.J. Ceci & M. Bruck, *Jeopardy in the Courtroom: A Scientific Analysis of Children's Testimony* (American Psychological Association, Washington, D.C. 1995).

T. Grisso, *Juveniles' Waiver of Rights: Legal and Psychological Competence* (Plenum Press, New York 1981).

Consent to research

Berg, *Legal and Ethical Complexities of Consent with Cognitively Impaired Research Subjects: Proposed Guidelines*, 24 J.L. Med. & Ethics 18 (1996).

Guardianship

J. Parry, *Incompetency, Guardianship, and Restoration*, in *The Mentally Disabled and the Law* (S. Brakal, J. Parry & B. Weiner eds., American Bar Foundation, Chicago 1985).

Parry & Hulme, *Guardianship Monitoring and Enforcement Nationwide*, 15 Ment. & Phys. Disability L. Rptr. 304 (May/June 1991).

Treatment decision-making

B. Winick, ed., *A Critical Examination of the MacArthur Treatment Competence Study: Methodological Issues, Legal Implications, and Future Directions*, 2 Psychol., Pub. Policy & L. 3-181 (1996).

American Bar Association, *The Right to Refuse Antipsychotic Medication* (American Bar Association, Washington, D.C. 1986).

B. Corsino, *Informed Consent: Policy and Practice* (Virginia National Center for Clinical Ethics, White River Junction, Va. 1996).

Redding, *Children's Competence to Provide Informed Consent for Mental Health Treatment*, 50 Wash. & Lee L. Rev. 695 (1993).

APPENDIX 4-1   **Some Areas of Law in Which Competency is an Issue**

CIVIL LAW

- Guardianship (care for one's self and property)[113]
- Contract[114]
- Make a will[115]
- Consent to treatment[116]

- Authorize disclosure of medical records
- Sue[117] or be sued[118]
- Testify in court
- Vote[119]
- Obtain a driver's license

- Act in public or professional capacity
- Receive benefits (e.g., Social Security)[120]
- Retain private counsel[121]

FAMILY LAW

- Marry[122]
- Divorce[123]
- Terminate parental relations with a child[124]
- Adopt[125]

CRIMINAL LAW

- Stand trial[126]
- Assume responsibility for a criminal act

- Raise the question of competency and order an examination[127]
- Waive the insanity defense[128]
- Make a distinction between insanity and competency[129]
- Make a confession[130]
- Waive the right to counsel[131]
- Be sentenced[132]
- Make a plea[133]
- Plead guilty[134]
- Provide testimony in court[135]
- Be executed[136]
- Entertain premeditation or "specific intent" of a crime[137]
- Consent to sexual intercourse[138]

APPENDIX 4-2   **Some General Tests of Competency**

Relevant act	General legal test regarding competency
Make a will	Understand the nature and object of the will, one's holdings, and natural objects of one's bounty
Make a contract	Understand the nature and effect of the proposed agreement or transaction
Marry	Understand the nature of the marital relationship and the rights, duties, and obligations it creates
Drive	Understand the pertinent laws of the state with regard to licensure; refrain from driving in a dangerous manner
Testify in court	Be capable of observing, remembering, and communicating about events in question; understand the nature of an oath
Be responsible for a criminal act	Possess sufficient capacity (cognitive) to understand and appreciate the criminality of one's acts and conform one's conduct to the requirements of the law
Stand trial	Possess sufficient capacity to rationally and factually understand the nature of the proceedings and be able to assist and consult with legal counsel
Make a confession	Possess sufficient capacity to make a knowing and intelligent waiver of certain constitutional rights and a knowing and voluntary confession
Be executed for a criminal act	Possess sufficient capacity to rationally and factually understand the nature of the trial proceedings and purpose of punishment
Consent to treatment	Possess sufficient mental capacity to understand the particular treatment choice being proposed and any relevant adverse effects associated with it

The specific and applicable language of these and other tests of capacity is generally defined by state or federal statute or administrative regulation. Their interpretation and practical usage are typically defined in case law, scholarly treatises, and commentaries.

5 Antitrust

DAVID P. CLUCHEY, M.A., J.D.
EDWARD DAVID, M.D., J.D., F.C.L.M.

HISTORY AND INTRODUCTION

The principal objective of antitrust laws is the prohibition of practices that interfere with free competition in the marketplace. Business enterprises are expected to compete on the basis of price, quality, and service. The underlying assumption of the antitrust laws is that "the unrestrained interaction of competitive forces will yield the best allocation of our economic resources, the lowest price, the highest quality, and the [greatest consumer satisfaction.]"[1]

The U.S. economy underwent far-reaching and significant change after the Civil War. Technological development and rapid industrialization led to the emergence of a complex economic system. The laissez-faire policy of government during this time led to the amassing of vast economic power by individuals and certain large firms. Often this power was used to destroy smaller rivals with the goal of achieving and maintaining market control.

The public response to this economic system was colored by the changing social conditions of urbanization and immigration. Many felt that business firms should not be permitted to accumulate such wealth and exercise such great control over economic conditions. Discontent was particularly prominent among farmers and laborers. The specific targets of their outrage were the giant combinations that came to be called trusts. Chief among these was Standard Oil, apparently the first to use the trust device as a vehicle for merging numerous enterprises into a cohesive entity.[2] Various other trusts followed. The trust device was largely replaced after the turn of the century by the holding company, but the name *trust* remained.[3]

The last two decades of the nineteenth century saw the legal authorities in some states moving to break up business trusts. By 1890, 14 states had constitutional provisions prohibiting monopolies, and 13 had antitrust statutes.[4] These statutes commonly outlawed any contract, agreement, or combination to fix a common price. They also prohibited activity that tended to limit the quantity of a product sold or manufactured. Although some success was realized, the state constitutional provisions and statutes were for the most part ineffective in controlling or breaking up the large business combinations of the day.[5] This failure was due in part to the limit of each state's jurisdiction. The business enterprise could reincorporate in another state or otherwise change its practices to avoid specific restrictions. This perception of business's abuse of power led to public demand that Congress deal with trusts on a national basis.[6]

The congressional response to public outrage about monopoly and predatory business practices was the Sherman Antitrust Act of 1890. Because of opposition to the trusts from both political parties, passage of the Sherman Act took several years. Senator Sherman's proposals were strenuously attacked despite the nearly unanimous desire to enact antitrust legislation. The debates focused on the limits of the commerce power as the constitutional basis for such legislation and the definition of common law restrictions on monopolies and predatory business practices.

The Sherman Act as finally enacted has been described as being "as good an antitrust law as the Congress of 1890 could have devised."[7] It was a compromise that restated common law principles prohibiting restraints of trade and monopolization. However, the Sherman Act went beyond common law in several respects. Unlike common law prohibitions that were entirely civil in nature, the Sherman Act provided for criminal prosecution and penalties.[8] The Sherman Act also expressly provided the United States the authority to bring civil actions to enjoin violations of the act and authorized private citizens damaged by violations to seek injunctive relief and treble damages. The nationwide effect of the act and access to the federal courts resolved the most serious problems of limited jurisdiction under state law.

Indifference and failure characterized early antitrust policy under the Sherman Act.[9] The drafters of the Sherman Act had intended to curb both the power and monopolistic abuses of the great trusts. It had been assumed that the Sherman Act would be self-enforcing because the business community would follow its prohibitions. Assumptions of voluntary compliance proved incorrect. The Trans-Missouri Freight Association case was the government's first major antitrust victory.[10] The Supreme Court overturned a lower court determination that the prohibitions of the Sherman Act did not apply to price-fixing agreements between members of a railroad association. This decision was quickly followed by successful prosecutions in *United States v. Joint Traffic Association* and *United States v. Addyston Pipe & Steel Co.*[11,12] Overall, however, results were not impressive, and one senator was able to compile a list of 628 trusts formed between 1898 and 1908.[13]

After the enactment of the Sherman Act, there was substantial concern about its general language. In 1911 the Supreme Court decided the Standard Oil case.[14] In *Standard Oil* the court interpreted Section 1 of the Sherman Act as a prohibition on "unreasonable restraints of trade" and left to the courts the task of applying this "rule of reason."[15] Some concluded that the ambiguity of the statutory language and the new rule of reason gave excessive discretion to the courts. A movement for explicit prohibition of practices inimical to free competition gained momentum, and in 1914 Congress passed the Clayton Act.[16]

In 1914 Congress also passed the Federal Trade Commission (FTC) Act.[17] The FTC was modeled on the Interstate Commerce Commission, and it was anticipated that the commission would notify businesses of conduct that violated the FTC Act by issuing cease-and-desist orders without initial penalty. The FTC Act was another attempt to alleviate the uncertainty caused by the general language of the Sherman Act. The language of these three basic antitrust laws has been changed little since 1914.[18]

Before 1975, it generally was believed that the antitrust laws did not apply to the health care industry. In 1975, however, the Supreme Court held in *Goldfarb v. Virginia State Bar* that "learned professions" were not exempt from the antitrust laws.[19] Consequently the court has applied the antitrust laws to the activities of both individual health care providers and institutional health care providers, finding that the provision of medical service, as a "trade or commerce," is within the scope of the antitrust laws.[20,21] Especially since the 1980s, with the health care industry undergoing substantial restructuring in response to pressure to reduce costs and governmental regulatory changes, the industry has experienced an increasing number of antitrust actions.[22]

CONDUCT VIOLATIONS

Section 1 of the Sherman Act prohibits combinations, contracts, and conspiracies in restraint of trade among the states or with foreign nations.[23] To violate this section, an individual must engage in some type of concerted action that restrains trade in interstate commerce or with foreign countries. One of the issues concerning this concerted action requirement is whether joint action by two subsidiaries of the same parent corporation can lead to antitrust liability. In *Copperweld Corp. v. Independent Tube Corp.*, the Supreme Court held that a parent corporation and its wholly owned subsidiary are legally incapable of conspiring in violation of Section 1 of the Sherman Act.[24] Further extending the court's reasoning in *Copperweld* that an agreement between two subdivisions of a single corporation was not likely to be anticompetitive, courts have generally determined that two subsidiaries wholly owned by the same parent corporation are legally incapable of conspiring with one another for purposes of the Sherman Act.[25,26] Similarly, when an acute care hospital was alleged to conspire with its corporate affiliate, the court found no concerted action under the Sherman Act.[27] The same reasoning has been applied in concluding that a hospital and its medical staff— a creature of the hospital—do not engage in concerted action for the purposes of the antitrust laws.[28]

The interstate commerce requirement is a prerequisite to the jurisdiction of the federal courts over alleged antitrust violations. The conduct in question must have an appreciable impact on interstate commerce.[29]

In the health care field the Supreme Court has found that a particular hospital was not strictly a local, intrastate business because of the impact that it exerted on the purchases of drugs and supplies from out-of-state sources, as well as the revenues derived from out-of-state insurance companies.[30] Denial of staff privileges may satisfy an "effects" test by showing that commerce in the form of medical insurance from out-of-state sources, supplies from out-of-state sources, and interstate patients using a hospital was affected.[31] On the other hand, a number of courts have not found the interstate commerce requirement satisfied in cases involving denial of hospital privileges.[32] Almost all business can be found to have some connection with interstate commerce. This connection, no matter how tenuous, may serve to bring the conduct of a health care provider within the scope of the relevant antitrust statutes. Note, however, that the Clayton Act requires that the prescribed activity be in commerce. This requirement limits jurisdiction to persons or activities within the flow of interstate commerce, and incidental effects on interstate transactions are insufficient to confer jurisdiction.[33] This provides little solace to potential defendants because the Sherman Act provisions are broad enough to reach most anticompetitive conduct prohibited by the Clayton Act.

Rule of reason

Section 1 of the Sherman Act prohibits restraints of trade but contains no explicit limiting language. In interpreting this language, the courts initially struggled with the question of whether Congress intended to prohibit all restraints of trade. In 1911 the Supreme Court decided *Standard Oil Co. of New Jersey v. United States*, which held that Section 1 of the Sherman Act was intended to prohibit only unreasonable restraints of trade.[34] What constitutes an unreasonable restraint of trade remains somewhat ambiguous, but since *Standard Oil*, the general approach to allegations of illegal restraints of trade has been to evaluate the alleged restraints under the rule of reason. The rule of reason requires a court applying Section 1 of the Sherman Act to evaluate whether a restraint of trade is an unreasonable restraint on competition. If it is found to be unreasonable, it is in violation of the statute. The rule of reason was described by Justice Brandeis in *Chicago Board of Trade v. United States* as follows:

Every agreement concerning trade, every regulation of trade, restrains. To bind, to restrain, is of their very essence. The true test of legality is whether the restraint imposed is such as merely regulates and perhaps thereby promotes competition or whether it is such as may suppress or even destroy competition. To determine that question the court must ordinarily consider the restraint as applied; the nature of the restraint and its effect, actual or probable. The history of the restraint, the evil believed to exist, the reason for adopting the particular remedy, the purpose or end sought to be attained are all relevant facts.[35]

Substantial debate has revolved around what courts may consider in evaluating the reasonableness of a restraint. The current view is that courts are limited to considering impacts on competition and may not consider social policy or some worthy purpose allegedly furthered by the restraint. In the application of antitrust principles to the conduct of health care providers, this issue is confronted when a restraint is defended on the grounds that it advances quality of care, access to care, or some other laudable public purpose.

A good example of the Supreme Court's approach to this issue is found in the discussion of the ban on competitive bidding by professional engineers considered by the court in *National Society of Professional Engineers v. United States*.[36] The society defended the ban as a means of minimizing the risk that competition would produce inferior engineering work, thereby endangering public safety. Noting that the Sherman Act does not require competitive bidding but prohibits unreasonable restraints on competition, the court pointed out that:

Petitioners' ban on competitive bidding prevents all customers from making the price comparisons in the initial selection of an engineer, and imposes the Society's view of the costs and benefits of competition on the entire marketplace. It is this restraint that must be justified under the Rule of Reason, and petitioner's attempt to do so on the basis of the potential threat that competition poses to the public safety and the ethics of its profession is nothing less than a frontal assault on the basic policy of the Sherman Act.[37]

Despite this rather strong statement about the scope of the rule of reason, some lower courts have been willing to consider issues other than the impact on competition in applying the rule of reason in cases involving the health care industry. In *Wilk v. American Medical Association, Inc.* the Court of Appeals for the Seventh Circuit indicated that it would allow a jury to consider issues of patient care in evaluating a prohibition on dealing with chiropractors as a restraint on trade under the rule of reason.[38] The court held that once the plaintiffs had established that the defendants' conduct had restricted competition, the burden shifted to the defendants to show that they had a genuine and objectively reasonable concern for patient care, that this concern had motivated the conduct in question, and that the concern would not have been satisfied with a less restrictive alternative.[39] The court was careful to distinguish this approach from a general consideration of the public interest served by the restraint, which would have put its approach in direct conflict with the Supreme Court decisions noted earlier.[40]

In *Hospital Building Co. v. Trustees of Rex Hospital* the Court of Appeals for the Fourth Circuit used a narrow rule of reason to permit a nonprofit hospital to defend against charges of market allocation and a concerted refusal to deal on the grounds that the planning activities in which the hospital participated were undertaken in good faith and their actual and intended effects were contemplated by federal health planning legislation.[41] This special rule of reason was described by the court as follows:

Because on this view the relevant federal health care legislation is in limited derogation of the normal operation of the antitrust laws, we further think that the burden of proof to show reasonableness of challenged planning and activities under this special rule of reason should be allocated as an affirmative defense to defendants seeking on this ground to avoid antitrust liability. On this basis a claimant, such as plaintiff here, makes out a prima facie case by showing acts that, but for the health care planning legislation, would constitute a per se violation of § 1 under traditional antitrust principles. This establishes liability for appropriate damages unless the defendants then persuade the trier of fact by a preponderance of the evidence that their planning activities had the purpose (and effect if plaintiff proves anticompetitive effects) only of avoiding a needless duplication of health care resources under the objective standard of need above defined.[42]

It remains to be seen whether the Supreme Court will be willing to accept considerations of patient care in rule-of-reason analysis in the health care industry.[43] In *FTC v. Indiana*

Federation of Dentists the court rejected the patient care argument when the restraint did not produce any procompetitive benefits.[44] The court, however, left open the possibility that if concerns for the quality of patient care lead to the adoption of restraints that have procompetitive effects, the patient care concerns may be considered to balance against the anticompetitive effects of the restraints.[45]

Rule-of-reason analysis, even if limited to issues of competition, can be extremely complex, and the burden of litigating a rule of reason case is substantial. This factor was recognized by the courts, and a presumption of unreasonableness was established quite early for certain specific categories of anticompetitive conduct.[46] This presumption is known as the per se rule.[47]

Per se rule

In contrast to the rule of reason, the courts will apply a per se rule of illegality to practices that generally have been shown to have anticompetitive effects on competition. These practices are presumed to be illegal without inquiry into specific anticompetitive effects.

There are certain agreements or practices which because of their pernicious effect on competition and lack of any redeeming virtue are conclusively presumed to be unreasonable and therefore illegal without elaborate inquiry as to the precise harm they have caused. . . . Among the practices which courts have deemed to be per se unlawful are price-fixing . . . ; division of markets . . . ; group boycotts . . . ; and tying arrangements.[48]

Because application of the per se rule forecloses an in-depth analysis of the alleged restraint and its market effect and risks, sweeping potentially procompetitive activity within a categorical condemnation, the Supreme Court has cautioned that "[i]t is only after considerable experience with certain business relationships that courts classify them as per se violations of the Sherman Act."[49] Therefore when the case involves a professional association or an industry in which certain restraints on competition may be essential to its product, the Supreme Court has declined to invoke the per se rule, even though it is apparent on their face that the restraints in question will increase price or constitute a refusal to deal.[50,51] Instead the court undertakes a "quick-look" analysis under the rule of reason to ascertain the likelihood of anticompetitive effects, reasoning that an observer with even a rudimentary understanding of economics could conclude that the restraints would have an anticompetitive effect on customers and markets.[52]

The use of such a "quick-look" analysis, however, is not unlimited. In a recent case, *California Dental Association v. FTC*, the Supreme Court stated that, where the anticompetitive effects of given restraints are comparably obvious, the rule of reason demands a more thorough inquiry into the consequences of those restraints than the quick-look

analysis.[53] In this case, California Dental Association (CDA), a voluntary nonprofit association of local dental societies, required its dentist members to refrain from advertising falsely or misleadingly under its Code of Ethics.[54] To help members comply with the code, CDA issued a number of advisory opinions and disclosure rules, which cautioned that price advertising must be based on verifiable data substantiating any comparison or statement of relativity and suggested that quality advertising is likely to be false or misleading because it cannot be measured or verified. The FTC brought action against CDA for unreasonably restricting truthful, nondeceptive discount or quality advertising in violation of Section 5 of the FTC Act.[55] The Court of Appeals for the Ninth Circuit found the restrictions on across-the-board discount advertising to be a naked restraint on price competition and the nonprice advertising restrictions to be a form of output limitation. Accordingly the court held that these restrictions were sufficiently anticompetitive on their face to constitute unreasonable restraints of trade under a quick-look analysis.[56] The Supreme Court, however, found that the obvious anticompetitive effect that triggers the quick-look analysis had not been proved with respect to both the restraints on discount advertising and the restraints on nonprice advertising. According to the court, even assuming that the CDA disclosure rules essentially bar advertisement of across-the-board discounts, it does not obviously follow that such a ban would have anticompetitive effects. As a matter of economics, it is possible that "any costs to competition associated with the elimination of across-the-board advertising will be outweighed by gains to consumer information (and hence competition) created by discount advertising that is exact, accurate, and easily verifiable (at least by regulators)."[57]

In a similar vein the court found that restricting quality or patient comfort advertising may have a procompetitive effect by preventing false or misleading claims that distort the market. Based on the foregoing analysis, the court held that an extended examination of the possible factual underpinnings should be conducted so as to determine whether the advertising restraints violate the relevant antitrust law. Although the court did not elaborate on the scope of such an extended examination, its aversion to the quick-look analysis in *California Dental Association* may signal the court's inclination to adopt a heightened rule-of-reason analysis when the restraints in question arise in a professional context.[58]

Specific violations

Price-fixing. The courts have found certain types of conduct to have so pernicious an effect on competition and to be so lacking in any redeeming virtue that they are accorded per se illegal status.[59] One such type of conduct is price-fixing. As the Supreme Court noted in *United States v. Trenton Potteries Co.*, "the aim and result of every price-fixing agreement, if effective, is the elimination of one form of competition."[60] The economic power to fix a price reflects control of a market. It does not matter whether or not the fixing of prices is exercised in a reasonable or unreasonable manner. An agreement that creates such power "may well be held to be ... unreasonable ... without the necessity of minute inquiry whether a particular price is reasonable or unreasonable ... and without placing on the government ... the burden of ascertaining ... whether it has become unreasonable through the mere variation of economic conditions."[61]

The agreement to fix prices need not be formal. The agreement itself can be demonstrated by circumstantial evidence.[62] An agreement that tampers with price (whether it raises, lowers, or stabilizes prices) is a per se violation.[63] Even agreements that affect price indirectly often are prohibited.[64] Once a practice is characterized as price-fixing, it is per se illegal. Making that characterization, however, can be difficult.

The leading price-fixing decision in the health care field is *Arizona v. Maricopa County Medical Society*.[65] There the Supreme Court applied the per se rule to an agreement among physicians to set maximum fees pursuant to a foundation program established by the county society. Approximately 70% of the physicians in Maricopa County were involved in the Maricopa plan. These physicians agreed not to charge more than the maximum agreed price for specified services and agreed with insurance companies to provide care to insured patients on that basis. The society defended the foundation plan on the grounds that it fixed only maximum prices, that it was an agreement among members of a profession, that it had procompetitive justifications, and that the courts should further investigate the health care industry before applying a per se rule to the conduct of health care providers. The majority in *Maricopa* rejected each of these arguments and held that the setting of maximum prices constituted per se illegal price-fixing.[66] The majority was unwilling to assign any weight to the unique characteristics of the market for physician services or to the plan's purported cost-containment purposes.[67]

Reimbursement policies of health insurance companies have been challenged as illegal price-fixing agreements.[68] Courts have shown interest in such claims when evidence of provider control over reimbursement rates may exist.[69] When the evidence shows unilateral action with an effect on prices, courts have not been receptive to claims of price-fixing.[70]

Agreements or approaches resulting in the stabilization of prices generally are considered per se violations. Relative value scales have been challenged as price-fixing mechanisms because they allegedly tend to standardize charges for professional services. The FTC entered into multiple consent orders barring the use of relative value scales in the late 1970s.[71]

The critical issue of rising health care costs has led the purchasers of health care services to take various actions in an effort to stabilize or reduce their costs. Individual action rarely poses antitrust concerns. Collective action, including the joint buying of services through preferred provider organizations (PPOs), however, may trigger antitrust price-fixing concerns.[72] An agreement among buyers not to compete on price in the purchase of goods or services is just as much unlawful price-fixing as is a similar agreement among sellers not to compete on price.[73]

However, joint purchasing of health care can be procompetitive by allowing individual purchasers to share information and develop skills in negotiating and contracting collectively with health care providers.[74] Therefore, absent significant market power, such joint purchasing programs should be able to pass muster under the Sherman Act. When joint purchasers possess some market power, the purpose of the joint purchase must be scrutinized more closely and the probable procompetitive effects of the arrangement must be weighed against possible anticompetitive harm.[75]

By the same token, hospitals can typically purchase supplies and services jointly without antitrust concerns. The Supreme Court has implicitly sanctioned wholesale purchasing cooperatives as arrangements seemingly designed to increase economic efficiency and render markets more rather than less competitive.[76] The Department of Justice (DOJ) and the FTC, in the 1996 Statements of Antitrust Enforcement Policy in Health Care (Health Care Statements), also emphasize that most joint purchasing arrangements among hospitals or other health care providers increase efficiencies and do not raise antitrust concerns.[77] The Statements provide a safety zone for any joint purchasing arrangement among hospitals and other health care providers if (1) the purchases account for less than 35% of the total sales of the purchased product or service in the relevant market and (2) the cost of the products and services purchased jointly accounts for less than 20% of the total revenues from all products or services sold by each competing participant in the joint purchasing arrangement. Beyond the safety zone, the law is not clear. Some suggest that the procompetitive effect inherent in joint purchasing arrangements dictates that a flexible per se standard should be applied.[78] Under this standard, horizontal pricing agreements among joint purchasers would be per se unlawful unless the purchasers could make an argument that the joint purchasing resulted in productive efficiencies and these efficiencies could be achieved only through an agreement designed to force prices below competitive levels.[79] Whether the courts will accept such a standard is difficult to predict.

Some large purchasers of health care services have sought to lower costs by insisting that health care providers include a so-called most favored nation clause in the agreement for the purchase of services. The purpose of such clauses is to ensure that the purchaser receives the lowest price given to any other purchaser. Although, in the usual case the antitrust law would support efforts to lower prices, when the purchaser has market power, a most favored nation clause could bring the price-cutting process to a halt because any additional price cut would have to be shared with the large purchaser.[80]

The development of new vehicles for the delivery of health care services has led to creative approaches to limiting prices paid for those services. This action in turn has sometimes resulted in allegations of price-fixing being put forward by private parties. In one such instance the Eleventh Circuit upheld a conclusion that there was no price-fixing involved in the negotiation of a reimbursement schedule by a PPO, in which the payers decided the maximum amount they were willing to pay providers for medical services and the providers decided whether they were willing to accept the limitation on reimbursement.[81]

Physicians seeking to avoid price-fixing problems should not agree with competing physicians on any term of price, quantity, or quality. Agreement on fee schedules and relative value scales is prohibited.[82] Although there may be exceptions to this relatively simple statement, the purported exceptions should be carefully examined with the assistance of competent and experienced antitrust counsel.

Tying and exclusive dealing. Tying may be defined as the sale or lease of a product or service conditioned on the buyer taking a second product or service. Tying arrangements may be attacked as unreasonable restraints of trade under Section 1 of the Sherman Act.[83] Anticompetitive tying arrangements are specifically prohibited by Section 3 of the Clayton Act and are deemed illegal under Section 5 of the FTC Act.[84,85] The Clayton Act is rarely encountered in suits against physicians and other health care providers because it applies only to the sales of commodities.[86]

The legal standard employed in evaluating tying arrangements may be viewed as a modified per se rule. This standard was discussed by the Supreme Court in the health care context in *Jefferson Parish Hospital District No. 2 v. Hyde*.[87] In *Jefferson Parish* the East Jefferson Hospital had entered into an exclusive agreement with Roux and Associates for the provision of anesthesiology services at the hospital. Dr. Edwin Hyde, a board-certified anesthesiologist, had applied for admission to the hospital's medical staff, and because of the exclusive contract the hospital's board had denied his application. Hyde sued the hospital and others, alleging that East Jefferson Hospital had engaged in tying by mandating that any person using services of the hospital requiring anesthesia also use the services of anesthesiologists employed by Roux and Associates. In *Jefferson Parish* the Supreme Court described an illegal tying agreement as follows: "[T]he essential characteristic of an invalid tying arrangement lies in the seller's exploitation of its control over the tying product to force the buyer into the purchase of a tied product that the buyer either did not want at all, or might have preferred to purchase elsewhere on different terms."[88] The court concluded that tying should be subject to per se condemnation when the probability of anticompetitive forcing is high.[89]

In general, to invoke the per se rule against a tying arrangement, the plaintiff must establish the existence of two separate products. In addition, the plaintiff must show that the party accused of tying has sufficient market power in the tying product to force acceptance of an unwanted tied product and that it has used that power to tie the products.[90]

In applying this analysis to the facts of *Jefferson Parish* the court concluded that East Jefferson Hospital had no significant power in the market for hospital services—the alleged tying product.[91] Absent this condition, the court was unwilling to apply the per se rule against the arrangement. In evaluating the arrangement under the rule of reason, the court concluded that there was insufficient evidence in the record to support a finding that the arrangement unreasonably restrained competition.[92]

Before the court's decision in *Jefferson Parish* there was substantial debate about whether inpatient hospital care could be divided into a number of different products for purposes of a tying analysis. In *Jefferson Parish* the court had no difficulty determining that the evidence amply supported the treatment of anesthesiology services as a separate product for purposes of the tying analysis.[93] The mere fact that services, such as anesthesia and surgery, are functionally linked does not foreclose treating the services as separate products.[94] This determination depends on a realistic appraisal of whether the products are distinct in the view of the purchasers and whether there is a distinct demand for each product.[95]

The utility of *Jefferson Parish* in evaluating the antitrust risks in other factual contexts is limited. The decision in the case turned entirely on an analysis of the market power of East Jefferson Hospital with regard to in-patient services. The court has, however, once again made it clear that no special consideration will be given to the fact that an alleged antitrust violation occurs in a health care context.[96]

Illegal tying issues also may arise when a health maintenance organization (HMO) conditions membership in the HMO network of medical prescription providers on a pharmacy's agreement to give its third-party administrator business to a subsidiary of the HMO. In *Brokerage Concepts, Inc. v. U.S. Healthcare, Inc.*, U.S. Healthcare refused to approve the application of a small Pennsylvania pharmacy chain for participation in its medical prescription network until it transferred its third-party administrator business to Corporate Health Administrators, a U.S. Healthcare subsidiary.[97] The Third Circuit Court of Appeals found no illegal tying, reasoning that U.S. Healthcare did not exercise appreciable market power in a properly defined tying market and that the alleged tying posed no harm to competition in the market for the tied product.[98]

An exclusive dealing arrangement involves an agreement by one party to buy particular products exclusively from another party. This arrangement has the effect of foreclosing to competitors of the seller the opportunity to compete for the purchases of buyers who are parties to exclusive dealing agreements. Exclusive dealing arrangements have been challenged under Section 1 of the Sherman Act, Section 3 of the Clayton Act, and Section 5 of the FTC Act.[99–101] Generally, exclusive dealing is regarded as a vertical restraint, which is evaluated under the rule of reason.[102] In evaluating exclusive dealing arrangements under Section 3 of the Clayton Act, the Supreme Court has found a violation where the arrangement foreclosed competition in a substantial share of the line of commerce affected.[103] In a more recent case the court used the same test but conducted a rigorous structural analysis and considered a number of unique characteristics of the market in concluding that a substantial share of the market was not foreclosed by the arrangement.[104]

Exclusive dealing agreements are common in the health care industry. A typical example is a contract between a physician or a group of physicians and a hospital to provide exclusive services to that hospital in a particular medical specialty, such as pathology, radiology, anesthesiology, or emergency medicine. In *Jefferson Parish* the arrangement between Roux and Associates and East Jefferson Hospital is properly characterized as an exclusive dealing arrangement. The court did not find sufficient evidence of anticompetitive impact on competition among anesthesiologists as a result of the arrangement to find it unreasonable and noted that Hyde did not undertake to prove unreasonable foreclosure of the market for anesthesiological services.[105] Nevertheless, Justice O'Connor, representing the view of four justices, noted:

Exclusive dealing is an unreasonable restraint on trade only when a significant fraction of buyers or sellers are frozen out of a market by the exclusive deal. . . . When the sellers of services are numerous and mobile, and the number of buyers is large, exclusive dealing arrangements of narrow scope pose no threat of adverse economic consequences. To the contrary, they may be substantially pro-competitive by ensuring stable markets and encouraging long-term, mutually advantageous business relationships.[106]

In evaluating the facts of *Jefferson Parish* as exclusive dealing, Justice O'Connor readily concluded that there was no potential for an unreasonable impact on competition as a result of the arrangement between Roux and Associates and the hospital.[107]

Before the decision in *Jefferson Parish*, a number of lower courts had upheld exclusive dealing arrangements between physicians and hospitals. *Harron v. United Hospital Center, Inc.* dealt with a radiologist's suit brought after he lost an exclusive contract because of a hospital merger.[108] The merged entity had contracted with a second physician to operate its radiology department. The Fourth Circuit Court of Appeals upheld the right of the new hospital to contract on an exclusive basis with another physician, stating that it was "frivolous to urge that the employment of a single physician to operate the radiology department of a hospital invokes the Sherman Act."[109]

The exclusion of an anesthesiologist from a hospital because that hospital had awarded an exclusive contract to the physician group with which the plaintiff had formerly been associated was the focus of concern in *Dos Santos v. Columbus-Cuneo-Cabrini Medical Center*.[110] The plaintiff anesthesiologist sued the hospital and the anesthesiology group under Sections 1 and 2 of the Sherman Act and under the Illinois Antitrust Act. The Seventh Circuit Court of Appeals vacated a preliminary injunction against the exclusive arrangement and remanded the case back to the District Court, noting that in its opinion the District Court had improperly limited the relevant geographic market solely to the hospital from which the plaintiff was excluded. The Court of Appeals suggested, "should the instant case proceed to trial, the district court should reconsider on the basis of more complete evidence its preliminary finding regarding the relevant market."[111] The court also suggested that the District Court "reexamine the basis of its conclusion that there is no effective competition among hospitals."[112] Although the Court of Appeals disposed of the case on a finding that the plaintiff had not satisfied other necessary prerequisites for the issuance of a preliminary injunction, it also expressed doubt that the plaintiff would succeed on the merits.[113]

Allegations of exclusive dealing also have been brought against a variety of exclusive contracting arrangements in the managed care context. In *U.S. Healthcare, Inc. v. Healthsource, Inc.*, Healthsource, a New Hampshire HMO, offered its panel physicians greater compensation if they agreed to a clause that precluded them from serving as participating physicians for any other HMO plan.[114] The First Circuit Court of Appeals held that the exclusive clause in question did not constitute an illegal restraint on competition. Absent a compelling showing of foreclosure of substantial dimension, the court saw no need to pursue any further inquiry into Healthsource's motive, the balance between harms and benefits, or the possible existence and relevance of any less restrictive means of achieving the benefits. It emphasized that proof of substantial foreclosure and "of probable immediate and future effects" in the market are the essential basis for an attack on an exclusivity clause.[115]

An exclusive dealing allegation is unlikely to prevail absent a convincing showing that a substantial portion of a rigorously defined relevant market is foreclosed by the arrangement. It also may be assumed that a court will consider seriously and weigh in the balance of a rule-of-reason analysis any legitimate procompetitive aspects of the arrangement.[116]

Concerted refusals to deal (boycotts). A concerted refusal to deal occurs when a group of competitors or a competitor and others through collective action exclude or otherwise interfere with the legitimate business activities of one or more other competitors. Courts use the terms *boycott* and *concerted refusal to deal* interchangeably when referring to the exclusion of a competitor by collective action. Boycotts involve concerted action and are challenged under Section 1 of the Sherman Act.[117] In general, boycotts have been held to be per se violations of the antitrust laws.[118] More recently, however, the Supreme Court has taken a more flexible approach, insisting that the potential for anticompetitive impact be established before the per se rule will be applied.[119]

In *Northwest Wholesale Stationers, Inc. v. Pacific Stationery and Printing Co.* the Supreme Court concluded that the exclusion of a retail office supply store from a nonprofit cooperative buying association was not a per se violation of the antitrust laws. The court noted that the per se rule generally has been applied in those cases where "the boycott . . . cut off access to a supply, facility, or market necessary to enable the boycotted firm to compete, . . . and frequently the boycotting firms possessed a dominant position in the relevant market."[120] The court held that:

A plaintiff seeking application of the per se rule must present a threshold case that the challenged activity falls into a category likely to have predominantly anticompetitive effects. . . . When the plaintiff challenges expulsion from a joint buying cooperative, some showing must be made that the cooperative possesses market power or unique access to a business element necessary for effective competition.[121]

Because such showing had not been made in *Northwest Stationers*, the court remanded the case for a review of the rule-of-reason analysis undertaken by the District Court.

Although myriad opportunities exist within the health care arena for boycott activity, the issue has arisen most commonly in cases involving the refusal of medical staff privileges at a hospital. Existing members of a medical staff, who would be in direct competition with an applicant for staff privileges, often have significant influence, if not control, over the determination of whether or not to grant privileges. In some circumstances a denial of privileges may constitute an effective bar to competition (e.g., denial of privileges to a new physician at the only hospital in a community). The privileges issue is complicated by the fact that the training, professional competence, and need for a new physician may be relevant and legitimate issues for the hospital considering an application for privileges, and physicians currently active in the applicant's specialty will have substantial expertise and information to contribute regarding these questions.

The lower courts that have examined boycott allegations in the context of disputes over privileges have adopted a variety of approaches. In *Weiss v. York Hospital* the Court of Appeals for the Third Circuit concluded that the conduct of members of a hospital medical staff in opposing the granting of hospital privileges to a class of osteopathic physicians was the equivalent of a concerted refusal to

deal.[122] Ultimately the court determined that the per se rule should be applied to this conduct.[123] It suggested, however, that rule-of-reason analysis would be appropriate if questions of professional competence or unprofessional conduct were at issue or the exclusion was otherwise based on public service or ethical norms.[124]

In *Wilk v. American Medical Association, Inc.* the plaintiff chiropractor sued a number of medical organizations under the Sherman Act for an alleged conspiracy to induce individual medical physicians and hospitals to refuse to deal with the plaintiff and other chiropractors.[125] Although the trial court instructed the jury on the per se rule, the Court of Appeals for the Seventh Circuit concluded that in the context of these facts "the nature and extent of [the] anticompetitive effect are too uncertain to be amenable to per se treatment."[126] Moreover, the court determined that the existence of substantial evidence of a patient care motive for the conduct of the organizations made application of the per se rule inappropriate.[127] Other courts have adopted a similar approach.[128]

In *Patrick v. Burget* the U.S. Supreme Court reinstated a treble damages verdict in excess of $2 million against three Oregon physicians because of their participation in a peer review process that recommended that the plaintiff surgeon's hospital privileges be revoked.[129] Although the reason given for revocation was substandard care, the evidence strongly supported the conclusion that the true motivation was anticompetitive bias. Although there is some protection for peer review activities under the state action exemption and the Health Care Quality Improvement Act of 1986, peer review activity stemming from anticompetitive motivation that results in the denial or revocation of hospital privileges may be held to be illegal group boycott activity.[130,131]

In addition, the issue of concerted refusal to deal has been raised when a PPO denied a physician's application for provider membership. In *Levine v. Central Florida Medical Affiliates, Inc.* the plaintiff internist sought physician provider membership with Healthchoice, a PPO in which physicians agreed to accept no more than a maximum allowable fee for services rendered to plan enrollees in exchange for a potentially higher volume of patients. Healthchoice denied Levine's request on the ground that it did not need any more internists in his geographic area.[132] The Court of Appeals for the Eleventh Circuit determined that the per se rule was not warranted in analyzing the alleged boycott because the plaintiff failed to prove that Healthchoice had market power and because selective contracting may be a method through which Healthchoice limited its provider panels in an effort to achieve quality and cost-containment goals, thereby enhancing its ability to compete against other networks.[133] Applying a rule-of-reason analysis, the court found that Levine's illegal boycott claim could not succeed because he failed to define the relevant product and geographic markets and failed to prove that Healthchoice had sufficient market power to affect competition.[134] The Levine court's decision and in particular its unwillingness to adopt a per se analysis indicate that, absent necessary market power, a multiprovider network, such as a PPO, would have ample leeway in selecting its preferred providers without incurring antitrust liability.[135]

Market allocation. Another type of conduct that raises serious questions of restraint of trade is market allocation. Competitors, by agreeing to divide geographic markets or customers, can achieve the benefits of monopoly as to their exclusive market share. In general the Supreme Court has regarded market allocation agreements among competitors as per se illegal under Section 1 of the Sherman Act.[136] There are, however, substantial questions of characterization that qualify that statement. For example, territorial or customer restraints that are insisted on by a party operating at a different level of production, such as restraints imposed by a manufacturer on wholesalers, will be evaluated under the rule of reason.[137] There may be a substantial question whether the market allocation scheme is the primary objective of an agreement among competitors or merely ancillary to an otherwise legitimate joint venture. If the latter is the case, the court may well evaluate the entire venture under the rule of reason.[138]

Market allocation agreements among hospitals or physicians could take the form of agreements on geographic placement of institutions or offices. This type of arrangement could be characterized as a geographic market division. Agreements allocating the provision of certain services exclusively to particular hospitals or physicians would be another approach to market division. Evaluation of such agreements is likely to raise complex questions of motivation and anticompetitive effect. For example, some such arrangements may be dictated or at least approved by a state agency under applicable health planning statutes. The significance of such approval by a state agency is discussed in the section on defenses. Joint ventures among hospitals generally have not been challenged by federal antitrust enforcement agencies.[139]

Market allocation issues also arise in the context of managed care. In *Blue Cross & Blue Shield United of Wisconsin v. Marshfield Clinic*, the Court of Appeals for the Seventh Circuit affirmed a jury verdict upholding the plaintiff's market allocation claim under Section 1 of the Sherman Act.[140] The evidence in this case showed that Marshfield Clinic and North Central Health Protection Plan (North Central), an HMO, established "free flow" arrangements that allowed the physicians of North Central, a subsidiary of Marshfield Clinic, to refer patients to each other without getting each HMO's approval. The plan of the physician who rendered the service would bill the other plan for its cost. As part of the arrangements, the parties involved purposely chose not to place in writing clear descriptions of their respective service areas so as to minimize any risks of antitrust violations, but their understanding was to discourage the physician providers of one plan from establishing practices in the service area of the other plan. Based on these findings, the Court of Appeals for the Seventh Circuit upheld the jury's determination that the defendants had engaged in a market allocation.[141]

Monopolization. Section 2 of the Sherman Act prohibits monopolization, attempts to monopolize, and conspiracies to monopolize.[142] Section 2, by its terms, does not prohibit monopoly. The antitrust laws promote competition. As a result of competition a successful competitor may achieve a monopoly in a particular market. To declare such a result illegal seems unfair and illogical.[143]

The Supreme Court has suggested that a monopolization offense has two elements: "(1) the possession of monopoly power in the relevant market and (2) the willful acquisition or maintenance of that power as distinguished from growth or development as a consequence of a superior product, business acumen, or historic accident."[144]

Determination of the existence of the first element may be complicated. Monopoly power has been defined by the courts as the "power to control prices or exclude competition."[145] Although the Supreme Court has suggested that monopoly power may be inferred from a predominant share of the relevant market, substantial question remains as to what constitutes a "predominant share" and how the "relevant market" should be defined.[146,147] Over time, the calculation of market share and the definition of the relevant market have become much more sophisticated.[148]

The second element of monopolization—the willful acquisition or maintenance of monopoly power—may be similarly elusive. In *United States v. Aluminum Co. of America* the court suggested that by embracing new opportunities and anticipating the need for new capacity Alcoa had monopolized the market for aluminum ingot.[149] More recently the courts appear to require something more than behavior motivated by legitimate business purposes to support a charge of monopolization.[150]

The offense of attempt to monopolize generally requires the proof of three elements: (1) specific intent to control prices or to exclude competitors, (2) predatory conduct directed to accomplishing this purpose, and (3) a dangerous probability of success.[151] Precise definition of conduct that satisfies these elements has proven to be controversial.[152]

In a recent example of an attempted monopolization case in the health care field, *Delaware Health Care, Inc. v. MCD Holding Co.*, Delaware Health Care (DHC), a provider of home care, brought an antitrust action against MCD Foundation and its subsidiaries, asserting that before the formation of Infusion Services of Delaware (ISD), a subsidiary of MCD Foundation, discharge planners of MCD's subsidiary hospitals recommended home care providers to patients on an informal rotating basis.[153] When ISD was formed, however, this informal rotation process was dismantled, and the defendant hospitals issued a directive to channel patients only to ISD. In addition, ISD was given exclusive access to patients in defendant hospitals' rooms to solicit business. As a result, ISD quickly gained a substantial share of the home infusion therapy market in the county where DHC and 13 other home care providers operated. DHC alleged two specific methods by which defendants had attempted monopolization. First, MCD Foundation "leveraged" its monopoly in the hospital market to extend its monopoly into the home health care market. Second, defendant hospitals denied DHC access to an "essential facility," the home care patients already discharged or about to be discharged from the defendant hospitals, and those patients' records. In response, MCD Foundation and the other defendants moved for summary judgment.[154]

With respect to the "leveraging" claim, the District Court for the District of Delaware started by analyzing the defendants' monopoly power in the "upstream" hospital market. Without monopoly power in the hospital market, there could be no illegal leveraging of the downstream home care market. Because the parties agreed that the relevant upstream product market was inpatient hospital services, the court turned its attention to the determination of the proper geographic market, noting that "[t]he geographic market must be broad enough that consumers would be unable to switch to alternative sellers in sufficient numbers to defeat an exercise of market power."[155] Rejecting the defendants' argument that DHC failed to define the relevant market according to the "standard methodology" of the DOJ Merger Guidelines by considering the crucial forward-looking component that asks what patients would do in the event of a price increase, the court found that the Elzinga-Hogarty (E-H) test analyzing the flow of consumers in and out of the proposed market may be proper because a reasonable juror could conclude that consumers of health care would not choose to leave their local hospital market as a result of a price increase.[156] Moreover, the court held that MCD Foundation and its subsidiary hospitals' 62% share of the market, together with other evidence, could prove that the defendants possessed monopoly power in the particular geographic market. However, to succeed on the leveraging claim, DHC also had to prove that the use of the defendants' monopoly power in inpatient hospital services had resulted in "actual or threatened" monopoly power in the home infusion therapy market. It was this element that the court held DHC had failed to establish. According to the court, the information that 75.9% of ISD's patients are residents of the county does not by itself define the county as the geographic market. To define that market, DHC must consider all home infusion therapy services produced in the county. Moreover, the court opined that the home therapy market could not be properly analyzed using the E-H test. The prong of the E-H test that measures the percentage of the goods or services produced outside the market that were purchased by consumers within the market does not aid the analysis of the geographic market because the home care services are always produced in the consumer's residence. Consequently the court granted the defendants' motion for summary judgment on the illegal leveraging claim.[157]

With respect to the "essential facility" claim, the court found that, even accepting DHC's alleged inability to gain referrals for the defendant hospitals' patients as true, other sources of business for DHC existed in a sufficient amount that the patient discharge and referral process at defendant hospitals could not be considered an "essential facility." Given the availability of these other sources of business within DHC's service area, the access to the defendant hospitals' patient discharge process could not be deemed vital to DHC's competitive viability, and the denial of such access would not necessarily inflict a severe handicap that threatened to eliminate competition in the market. Accordingly the court held that DHC's evidence was insufficient to survive summary judgment on its essential facility claim.[158]

In the context of health care the most common instance of alleged monopolization is the situation in which a hospital with monopoly power is acting to maintain that power and to avoid competition.[159] Similarly an association of all or most physicians of a given specialty in a relevant market could support a finding of monopoly power in support of an allegation of monopolization.[160] In particular contexts an HMO, PPO, or other provider organization could face monopolization allegations.

Mergers. Mergers between business entities are generally evaluated under Section 7 of the Clayton Act.[161] Section 7 prohibits mergers in which the effect may be "substantially to lessen competition, or to tend to create a monopoly" in an activity "affecting commerce in any section of the country."[162] The purpose of Section 7 is to reach incipient problems of monopoly, and hence the rather broad language noted previously.

Section 7 applies to the acquisition of stock or assets of any person by any other person. It is clear that the term *person* includes corporations and unincorporated business enterprises and that the section applies to partial acquisitions of assets.[163,164] Section 7 may apply to joint ventures, as well as to more complete integration of business resources.[165]

The determination of whether an acquisition or merger substantially lessens competition or tends to create a monopoly has generated enormous controversy. In applying Section 7, the Supreme Court has engaged in increasingly rigorous structural analyses of the effect of the transaction on competition.[166] This trend also has been true of merger analysis undertaken by the FTC.[167]

The merger guidelines issued by the DOJ in 1968 and substantially revised in 1982, 1984, and 1992 have been exceptionally useful and influential in advancing the analysis of the competitive effect of mergers. The merger guidelines provide a structured approach to defining relevant product and geographic markets.[168,169] The merger guidelines use the Herfindahl-Hirschman index to measure market concentration and provide an outline of enforcement policy for different levels of and increases in market concentration.[170]

Merger cases brought in the health care context generally have involved for-profit hospitals.[171] Hospitals represent one of the largest economic entities engaged in the provision of health care services, and the expansionary activities of for-profit hospital chains have elicited the interest of antitrust enforcement authorities. Whether the developing merger activities of other types of health care providers will elicit the same interest remains to be seen.

When a merger involves nonprofit hospitals, the initial dispute may concern the threshold issue of whether the FTC has authority to challenge the merger under Section 7 of the Clayton Act.[172] Section 7 provides in relevant part: "[N]o person subject to the jurisdiction of the Federal Trade Commission shall acquire the whole or any part of the assets of any other person . . . where in any line of commerce . . . in any section of the country, the effect of such acquisition may be substantially to lessen competition."[173]

Some courts have held that to determine those persons "subject to the jurisdiction of the Federal Trade Commission" a court must turn to the FTC Act, which excludes nonprofit institutions from the jurisdiction of the FTC.[174] Other courts and the government, however, have taken the view that the FTC's jurisdiction to enforce the Clayton Act is determined by Section 11 of the same act, which provides no exemption for nonprofit hospitals.[175]

The Statements of Antitrust Enforcement Policy in Health Care, revised and reissued by the DOJ and the FTC in 1996, address the issue of mergers among hospitals.[176] Statement 1 provides a safety zone for mergers "between two general acute care hospitals where one of the hospitals (1) has an average of fewer than 100 licensed beds over the three most recent years, and (2) has an average daily inpatient census of fewer than 40 patients over the three most recent years," and the hospital has been in operation for longer than 5 years.[177] The DOJ and FTC recognize that a hospital qualified for safety zone protection is often the only hospital in a relevant market and is unlikely to achieve the efficiencies that larger hospitals enjoy. A merger involving such a hospital is unlikely to have a substantial anticompetitive effect.[178]

Outside of the safety zone, hospital mergers are evaluated under the 1992 Merger Guidelines. The Statements do recognize that "[m]ost hospital mergers and acquisitions do not present competitive concerns."[179] This statement suggests that the government enforcement agencies might take a less strict approach in analyzing hospital mergers than mergers in other industries. For example, approximately 229 hospital mergers occurred between 1987 and 1991, and the federal antitrust enforcement authorities investigated only 27 and challenged only 5.[180]

ENFORCEMENT

The federal antitrust laws are enforced by the DOJ, the FTC, and private persons. In addition, state attorneys general have authority under Section 4C of the Clayton Act to bring federal antitrust actions as parens patriae on behalf of the citizens of the state.[181] They also enforce antitrust laws enacted by their state legislatures.

On the federal level, the Antitrust Division of the DOJ is responsible for enforcing the Sherman Act and the Clayton Act through either civil or criminal prosecutions. The FTC is mainly charged with the enforcement of the FTC Act and has concurrent jurisdiction with the Antitrust Division over some sections of the Clayton Act.

Any person or entity that has been injured by conduct in violation of the antitrust laws may bring a lawsuit under Section 4 of the Clayton Act for treble damages, costs of suit, and attorney's fees. To maintain such a private antitrust cause of action, a plaintiff must demonstrate (1) that it has suffered an injury (2) to business or property by (3) the violation of an antitrust law.[182] Over the years, the Supreme Court has required that the injury suffered by a private party be an "antitrust injury." That is, the injury suffered by a private person must be a type of injury that "the antitrust laws were intended to prevent and that flows from that which makes the defendants' acts unlawful."[183] Only after establishing an "antitrust injury" may a plaintiff proceed to the liability and damage issues in a private lawsuit.

DEFENSES

State action exemption

There are a number of defenses or exemptions from liability under the antitrust laws. Although some of these exemptions are the result of action by Congress creating a specific statutory exception to the application of the antitrust laws, perhaps the most important—the state action exemption—was created by judicial decision.

The state action exemption is grounded on the principle of federalism. A state may choose to displace competition in the provision of certain goods or services within its borders and to replace market control with state regulation. As long as this action by the state qualifies under the state action exemption, private parties are protected from liability under the federal antitrust laws for acting in compliance with this state mandate.

The state action exemption was initially articulated by the Supreme Court in *Parker v. Brown*.[184] At issue in *Parker* was whether a raisin marketing program that had the effect of restricting production and maintaining prices but was created by state legislation was in violation of federal antitrust laws. In refusing to rule against the state program, the Supreme Court noted:

We find nothing in the language of the Sherman Act or in its history which suggests that its purpose was to restrain a state or its officers or agents from activities directed by its legislature. In a dual system of government in which under the Constitution, the states are sovereign, save only as Congress may constitutionally subtract from their authority, an unexpressed purpose to nullify a state's control over its officers and agents is not lightly to be attributed to Congress.[185]

In a number of cases decided since *Parker v. Brown*, the Supreme Court has elaborated on the state action exemption.[186] In *California Liquor Dealers v. Midcal Aluminum Inc.* the Supreme Court suggested a two-pronged test for determining whether a state regulatory scheme is exempted from the federal antitrust laws.[187] First, the restraint must be clearly articulated and affirmatively expressed as state policy.[188] Second, the anticompetitive conduct must be actively supervised by the state.[189]

Most recently the Supreme Court has reaffirmed the two-prong Midcal test as the appropriate analytical approach for evaluating anticompetitive conduct by private parties acting pursuant to state statute.[190] The court also has made clear that the second prong of the Midcal test is not applicable to municipalities.[191]

The state action exemption has been raised as a defense by defendants in a variety of health care–related antitrust suits. A number of state statutes have been suggested as a basis for the state action exemption, including state certificate of need statutes, state statutes mandating physician peer review, and state authorization of municipal- and county-owned hospitals to grant or deny physician privileges.[192–194] The lower courts have engaged in substantial debate as to whether a state statute constitutes a clearly articulated and affirmatively expressed state policy to displace competition and whether there is adequate state supervision to satisfy the Midcal test.

In several cases in which municipalities have been sued for allegedly anticompetitive conduct in contracting for ambulance services, the lower courts have applied only the first prong of the Midcal test.[195] Requiring an explicit state policy to displace competition, these courts successfully anticipated the Supreme Court's decision in *Town of Hallie v. City of Eau Claire*, holding that the second requirement of *Midcal*—active state supervision—was not required when a municipality was following an expressed state policy.[196] Liability of municipalities and other political subdivisions for damages under the antitrust laws has now been clarified by statute.[197]

The Supreme Court has recently clarified the active supervision prong of the state action exemption. The clarification was made in the 1992 case *FTC v. Ticor Insurance Co.*[198] In the Ticor decision the court described state action immunity as "disfavored" and explained that active supervision means more than endowing a state agency with the duty to regulate.[199]

Explicit and implied exemption

Of course the antitrust statutes are subject to any limits and exemptions that Congress chooses to place on them. Over the years, Congress has enacted a number of specific exemptions for labor organizations, the business of insurance (to the extent regulated by state law), agricultural cooperatives, fishery associations, joint newspaper operating agreements, intrabrand territorial restrictions on franchisees of soft drink companies, joint small business programs for research and development, agreements between businesses necessary for the national defense, and joint exporting companies.[200–208]

Partially in response to the decision in *Patrick v. Burget*, Congress enacted the Health Care Quality Improvement Act of 1986.[209,210] This statute provides a general immunity from damages under the antitrust laws for physicians engaging in professional peer review.[211] In addition, any person providing information to a professional review body regarding the competence or professional conduct of a physician is given immunity from damages under state or federal law.[212,213] In the event that a suit is brought against a person engaging in professional peer review and is unsuccessful, the statute imposes liability on the person bringing the suit for the costs of suit, including a reasonable attorney's fee, if the claim of the person bringing suit was frivolous, unreasonable, without foundation, or in bad faith.[214]

In addition to the exemptions noted, there are express exemptions to aspects of the antitrust laws in the statutes establishing federal regulatory schemes for particular industries. These exemptions are generally specific and limited in scope.[215]

A more difficult question is generated when Congress has not enacted a specific statutory exemption to the antitrust laws but has entrusted authority over certain matters in an industry to a regulatory agency. The question becomes whether Congress has by implication created an exemption from the antitrust laws. In general, implied exemptions from the antitrust laws are disfavored by the courts and are found only when there is a clear conflict between the antitrust laws and other federal statutes.[216]

In the context of health care the Supreme Court has refused to find an implied exemption from the antitrust laws in federal health planning legislation.[217] In *National Gerimedical Hospital*, Blue Cross defended against a charge of anticompetitive conspiracy as a result of denying a hospital participating status by arguing that it was acting pursuant to the local Health System Agency (HSA) plan and furthering the purposes of the National Health Planning and Resources Development Act (NHPRDA) of 1974.[218]

The Supreme Court concluded that in light of the strict approach taken in evaluating the claims of implied exemption to the antitrust laws, Blue Cross would remain subject to the antitrust laws in this case. The court was not persuaded that there was a clear repugnancy between the NHPRDA and the antitrust laws, at least not on the facts of this case.[219] The court left open the possibility that an implied exemption from the antitrust laws might be found in other factual contexts in the health care industry, specifically for activities necessary to make the federal health planning legislation work.[220]

Noerr-Pennington doctrine

The courts have created an exemption from the antitrust laws for conduct by private parties intended to influence governmental action by the legislative, judicial, or executive branches. This exemption is known as the *Noerr-Pennington doctrine*, drawing its name from two U.S. Supreme Court cases wherein the court discussed the defense.[221] The underlying purpose of the Noerr-Pennington doctrine is to protect the right of citizens to petition government and to ensure that government's access to information about the desires of citizens remains unimpaired by the threat of liability under the antitrust laws.[222] Although the Noerr-Pennington doctrine is available to protect persons genuinely undertaking to influence governmental action, it is not available where the conduct is "a mere sham to cover what is actually nothing more than an attempt to interfere directly with the business relationships of a competitor."[223]

Appeals to certificate of need agencies and to physician licensing boards are types of conduct that may be subject to Noerr-Pennington protection unless subject to the sham exception just noted.[224] Hospital peer review committees have not been recognized as governmental agencies for purposes of the Noerr-Pennington doctrine.[225] Unilateral or joint action that does not take the form of an appeal to a governmental decision-maker is not accorded protection under Noerr-Pennington.[226]

ROBINSON-PATMAN ACT

In light of the recent practice of physicians dispensing medications and the joint venture movement, the Robinson-Patman Act is pertinent.[227] The act prohibits vendors from selling and customers from buying supplies at discriminatorily low prices (i.e., prices not generally available to other customers). The statute forbids price discrimination by vendors among their purchasers so as to lessen competition. However, an amendment to the Non-Profit Institutions Act exempts nonprofit hospitals but only on supplies purchased for the facility's "own use."[228] The exemption allows nonprofit purchasers to receive discounts on supplies for their own use. Customarily, nonprofit hospitals have paid less for drugs than the corner pharmacy, with the buyer and seller being protected by the statutory exemption.

In *Abbott Laboratories v. Portland Retail Druggists Association*, "for their own use" was interpreted as applying to hospital purchases of drugs dispensed for admitted patients, emergency department clientele, patients about to be discharged, some patients receiving outpatient treatment, and for personal use of employees, students, and physicians but not for walk-in customers.[229] "Own use" also has been defined as referring to treatment of hospital emergency department patients, patients receiving outpatient treatment on hospital premises, and immediate take-home use by discharged patients. These hospitals also may resell products to the medical staff for the personal use of physicians and their dependants. Although the potential liability in damages for defendants in antitrust actions should not be taken lightly, in the health care field it appears that these suits are more likely to be pursued as a threat to alter the defendants' conduct than with the expectation of recovering a judgment. Thus far, recoveries have been uncommon among reported cases.

RECENT DEVELOPMENTS IN ANTITRUST AND HEALTH CARE REFORM

In recognition of the substantial structural change occurring in the health care industry in recent years, the DOJ and the FTC issued Statements of Antitrust Enforcement Policy in Health Policy, regarding mergers and joint activities in the health care arena.[230] The first of these statements was issued on September 15, 1993. These statements were expanded and revised in September 1994 and further revised and reissued in August 1996. The most recent version of the statements addresses the following nine specific topics:

1. Hospital mergers.
2. Hospital joint ventures involving expensive medical equipment.
3. Hospital joint ventures involving specialized clinical or other expensive health care services.
4. Providers' collaboration to provide non-fee–related information to purchasers of health care services.
5. Providers' collaboration to provide fee-related information to purchasers of health care services.
6. Provider exchanges of price and cost information.
7. Joint purchasing arrangements among health care providers.
8. Physician network joint ventures.
9. Multiprovider networks.

The statements issued by the federal antitrust enforcement agencies include antitrust safety zones in seven of the nine areas discussed. Conduct will not be challenged absent extraordinary circumstances when it falls within one of these zones. Analytical principles and illustrations are included for activity falling outside of the safety zones. The statements also commit the agencies to an expedited review process on antitrust issues in health care. The agencies will respond to requests for an opinion on enforcement intentions within 90 days after all necessary information is received regarding matters addressed in the statements, except nonsafety zone merger requests and requests regarding multiprovider networks. The agencies will respond within 120 days to requests on all other nonmerger health care matters.

Several of the statements of antitrust enforcement policy rely on a four-step rule-of-reason analysis for health care joint ventures that fall outside the safety zones defined by the agencies. The first step in this process is to define the relevant market. Typically, doing so involves the identification of the service being produced by the joint venture. The second step is to evaluate the competitive effects of the venture. This step begins with an examination of the structure of the relevant market and continues with an analysis of whether the joint venture restricts competitive activity among health care providers participating in the venture. In the event that it is determined that the venture has anticompetitive effects, it will be necessary to undertake the third step in the process and evaluate the impact of procompetitive efficiencies likely to be generated by the venture. This step includes the balancing of procompetitive efficiencies against the anticompetitive effects of the venture. Any venture in which the anticompetitive effects predominate will not survive this step of the analysis. The fourth step is the evaluation of collateral agreements that are likely to restrict competition to ensure that these collateral agreements are reasonably necessary to achieve the procompetitive efficiencies to be generated by the venture. This description of the rule-of-reason analytical approach reflects a refinement of judicial approaches and is likely to be drawn on by judges and attorneys faced with making such an analysis.

The statements of antitrust enforcement policy are an extraordinary and unprecedented effort by antitrust enforcement agencies to provide guidance to participants in the health care industry. The statements were motivated by the uncertainty generated by the antitrust laws at a time of fundamental change in the health care industry. Consolidations, mergers, and restructuring continue in the health care industry, driven primarily by market forces. These changes in the health care industry will generate significant antitrust questions for many years to come.

ENDNOTES

1. *Northern Pacific Railway v. United States*, 356 U.S. 1, 4-5 (1958).
2. Standard Oil adopted the trust format in 1879, and this action was followed by the rapid development of trusts in other industries. The trust as a vehicle for combining economic power commonly involved a trust agreement among the shareholders of the corporations involved. This agreement gave control over the stock in the corporations to the trustees, in return for which the shareholders received trust certificates evidencing their interest in the property controlled by the trust.
3. *See generally* E. Kinter, *Federal Antitrust Law* (1980).
4. *Id.* at 130.
5. *Id.* at 128, 130.
6. *See generally* E. Letwin, *Law and Economic Policy in America*, 53-99 (1965); Kinter, *supra* at 125-129.
7. Letwin, *supra* at 95.
8. Initially a violation of the act was a misdemeanor punishable by a fine of up to $5000 and by imprisonment of up to 1 year. The maximum fine was increased in 1955. In 1974 a violation of the act was made a felony, and penalties were substantially increased. A corporation may now be fined up to $10 million and any other person, $350,000. The maximum term of imprisonment is now 3 years. The Sherman Act is codified at 15 U.S.C. §§1-7.
9. *See generally* Letwin, *supra* at 106-142.
10. *United States v. Trans-Missouri Freight Association*, 166 U.S. 290 (1897).
11. *United States v. Joint Traffic Association*, 171 U.S. 505 (1898).
12. *United States v. Addyston Pipe & Steel Co.*, 175 U.S. 211 (1899).
13. 51 Cong. Rec. 14218 21 (1914).
14. *Standard Oil Co. of New Jersey v. United States*, 221 U.S. 1 (1911).
15. *Id.* at 138.
16. Act of October 15, 1914, ch. 322, 38 Stat. 730, 15 U.S.C. §§12-27. The Clayton Act deals specifically with tying, exclusive dealing, price discrimination, and mergers.
17. Act of September 26, 1914, ch. 11, 38 Stat. 717, 15 U.S.C. §§41-51.
18. The most significant change was the amendment of the law of price discrimination by the Robinson-Patman Act in 1936. Act of June 19, 1936, ch. 592, 49 Stat. 1526.
19. *Goldfarb v. Virginia State Bar*, 421 U.S. 73 (1975).
20. *E.g., Summit Health, Ltd. v. Pinhas*, 500 U.S. 322 (1991).
21. *E.g., Hospital Building Co. v. Trustees of Rex Hospital*, 425 U.S. 738 (1976)
22. *See* Phillip A. Proger, *Application of the Sherman Act to Health Care: New Developments and New Directions*, 59 Antitrust L.J. 173 (1990).
23. 15 U.S.C. §1.
24. *Copperweld Corp. v. Independent Tube Corp.*, 467 U.S. 752 (1984).
25. *Id.* at 772.
26. *See, e.g., Directory Sales Management Corp. v. Ohio Bell Tel. Co.*, 883 F. 2d 606, 611 (6th Cir. 1987); *Hood v. Tenneco Texas Life Ins. Co.*, 739 F. 2d 1012, 1015 (5th Cir. 1984). *But see In re Ray Dobbins Lincoln-Mercury v. Ford Motor Co.*, 671 F. Supp. 1525, 1544 (W.D. Va. 1984) (*Copperweld* does not apply to an allegation of conspiracy between two subsidiaries of the same parent corporation), *affir'd on other issues in an unpublished opinion*, 813 F. 2d 402 (4th Cir. 1985).
27. *Advanced Health-Care Serv. v. Radford Community Hosp.* 910 F. 2d 139, 143, 146 (4th Cir. 1990).
28. *See Weiss*, 745 F. 2d at 814-817, *cert. denied*, 470 U.S. 1060 (1985); *Feldman v. Jackson Memorial Hospital*, 571 F. Supp. 1000 (S.D. Fla. 1983), *aff'd*, 752 F. 2d 647 (11th Cir. 1985); *Cooper v. Forsyth County Hospital Authority*, 604 F. Supp. 685 (M.D. N.C. 1985). *But see Nurse Midwifery Associates v. Hibbett*, 918 F. 2d 605 (1990), *cert. denied*, 112 S.Ct. 406 (1991). It is, of course, clear that a medical staff is composed of individual physicians, and the conduct of physicians within a medical staff or as individual competitors in the market for physician services is not protected by the *Copperweld* doctrine. *See* discussion of this point in *Weiss*, 745 F. 2d at 815-816; *see also Nurse Midwifery Associates*, 918 F. 2d 605 (1990), *cert. denied*, 112 S.Ct. 406 (1991).
29. *See Summit Health, Ltd. v. Pinhas*, 500 U.S. 322 (1991); *McLain v. Real Estate Board of New Orleans*, 444 U.S. 232 (1980).
30. *Hospital Building Co.*, 425 U.S. 738, 744 (1976).
31. *Summit Health*, 500 U.S. 322 (1991); *Everhart v. Jane C. Stormont Hospital and Training School for Nurses*, 1982-1 Trade Cas. (CCH) 164, 703 (D. Kan. 1982).
32. *See, e.g., Cardio-Medical Associates v. Crozer-Chester Medical Center*, 536 F. Supp. 1065, 1073-1074 (E.D. Penn. 1982), *rev'd*, 721 F. 2d 68 (3d Cir. 1983); *Riggall v. Washington County Medical Society*, 249 F. 2d 266, 269 (8th Cir. 1957), *cert. denied*, 55 U.S. 954 (1958); *Nankin Hospital v. Michigan Hospital Service*, 361 F. Supp. 1199, 1210 (E.D. Mich. 1973).
33. *See Gulf Oil Corp. v. Coff Paving Co.*, 419 U.S. 186, 194 (1974).

34. *Standard Oil*, 221 U.S. 1 (1911).

35. *Chicago Board of Trade v. United States*, 246 U.S. 231, 238 (1918).

36. *National Society of Professional Engineers v. United States*, 435 U.S. 679 (1978).

37. *Id.* at 695. *See also Fashion Originator's Guild of America v. Federal Trade Commission*, 312 U.S. 457 (1941).

38. *Wilk v. American Medical Ass'n, Inc.*, 719 F. 2d 207, 227 (7th Cir. 1983), *cert. denied*, 467 U.S. 1210 (1984).

39. *Id.* at 227.

40. *Id.* at 226.

41. *Hospital Building Co.*, 691 F. 2d 678, 685 (4th Cir. 1982), *cert. denied*, 464 U.S. 890 (1983).

42. *Id.* at 686.

43. *See Arizona v. Maricopa County Medical Society*, 457 U.S. 332 (1982) (health care industry entitled to no unique treatment).

44. *FTC v. Indiana Federation of Dentists*, 476 U.S. 447, 459 (1986).

45. *See id.* at 464.

46. The development of this presumption in the area of price-fixing began with *United States v. Joint Traffic Ass'n*, 171 U.S. 505, 568 (1897), continued in *United States v. Trenton Potteries Co.*, 273 U.S. 392, 397 (1927), and reached its high point in *United States v. Socony-Vacuum Oil Co.*, 310 U.S. 150, 221-223, 224 n. 59 (1940).

47. The term *per se* was first used in *Socony-Vacuum*, 310 U.S. at 223.

48. *Northern Pacific Railway*, 356 U.S. at 5.

49. *United States v. Topco*, 405 U.S. 596, 607-07 (1972).

50. *See National Society of Professional Engineers*, 435 U.S. 679 (1978); *Indiana Federation of Dentists*, 476 U.S. at 458.

51. *See NCAA v. Board of Regents*, 468 U.S. 85, 100 (1984).

52. *California Dental Association v. FTC*, 526 U.S. 756, 770 (1999).

53. *See id.* at 770-778.

54. *Id.* at 760.

55. 15 U.S.C.S. 45.

56. *California Dental Association*, 526 U.S. at 763.

57. *Id.* at 775.

58. The court in *California Dental Association* seemed to suggest that a detailed market analysis might not be necessary in that case. It was, however, not entirely clear how extensive the examination needed to be to satisfy the rule-of-reason analysis. As the court stated, "[T]here is generally no categorical line to be drawn between restraints that give rise to an intuitively obvious inference of anticompetitive effect and those that call for more detailed treatment. What is required, rather, is an enquiry meet for the case, looking to the circumstances, details, and logic of a restraint." *Id.* at 780-781.

59. *Northern Pacific Railway*, 356 U.S. 1 (1958).

60. *Trenton Potteries Co.*, 273 U.S. at 397.

61. *Id.* at 397-398.

62. *Eastern States Lumber Association v. United States*, 234 U.S. 600, 612 (1914).

63. *Socony-Vacuum*, 310 U.S. at 221.

64. *But see Broadcast Music Inc. v. Columbia Broadcasting System, Inc.*, 441 U.S. 1, 23 (1979).

65. *Maricopa County Medical Society*, 457 U.S. 332 (1982).

66. *Id.* at 357.

67. *Id.* at 351. *Maricopa* was decided by a vote of four to three, two justices not participating. The dissent criticized the failure of the majority to recognize the uniqueness of the market for medical services. *Id.* at 366 n. 13.

68. *See, e.g., Glen Eden Hospital v. Blue Cross & Blue Shield of Michigan*, 740 F. 2d 423 (6th Cir. 1984).

69. *Id.* at 430.

70. *See, e.g., Kartell v. Blue Shield of Massachusetts, Inc.*, 749 F. 2d 922 (1st Cir. 1984).

71. The American College of Radiology, 3 Trade Reg. Rep. (CCH) 121, 236; Minnesota State Medical Association, 3 Trade Reg. Rep. (CCH) 121, 293; the American College of Obstetricians and Gynecologists, 3 Trade Reg. Rep. (CCH) 121, 171; the American Academy of Orthopedic Surgeons, 3 Trade Reg. Rep. (CCH) 121, 171.

72. *See* Clark C. Havighurst, *Antitrust Issues in the Joint Purchasing of Health Care*, Utah L. Rev. 409, 417 (1995).

73. *Mandeville Island Farms, Inc. v. American Crystal Sugar Co.*, 334 U.S. 219, 235 (1948).

74. Havighurst, *supra*, at 422.

75. *Id.* at 428

76. *Northwest Wholesale Stationers, Inc. v. Pacific Stationery and Printing Co.*, 472 U.S. 284, 295 (1985) (quoting from *Broadcast Music*, 441 U.S. at 20).

77. *Department of Justice and Federal Trade Commission Statements of Antitrust Enforcement Policy in Health Care*, 1996-4 Trade Reg. Rep. (CCH), s. 13,153.

78. *See* Roger D. Blair & Jeffrey L. Harrison, *Cooperative Buying, Monopoly, Power, and Antitrust Policy*, 86 Nw. U. L. Rev. 331, 366 (1992).

79. *Id.* at 366-367.

80. *Cf. Blue Cross & Blue Shield United of Wisconsin v. Marshfield Clinic*, 65 F. 3d 1406,1415 (7th Cir. 1995), *cert. denied*, 516 U.S. 1184 (1996).

81. *Levine v. Central Florida Medical Affiliates, Inc.*, 72 F. 3d 1538, 1548 (11th Cir. 1996).

82. *See* "Remarks of Charles F. Rule Before the Interim Meeting of the American Medical Association House of Delegates," Dallas, Texas, December 6, 1988.

83. 15 U.S.C. §1.

84. 15 U.S.C. §14.

85. 15 U.S.C. §45.

86. 15 U.S.C. §14.

87. *Jefferson Parish Hospital District No. 2 v. Hyde*, 466 U.S. 2 (1984).

88. *Id.* at 12.

89. *Id.* at 15-16.

90. *Id.* at 17. Justice O'Connor, in an opinion concurring with the judgment in *Jefferson Parish*, which three other justices joined, suggests three prerequisites to an illegal tie: (1) The seller must have power in the tying product market; (2) there must be a substantial threat that the seller will acquire market power in the tied product; and (3) there must be a coherent economic basis for treating the tied products as distinct products. *Id.* at 1571. She also rejected per se treatment of tying arrangements even if these conditions are met. *Id.* at 37-40.

91. *Id.* at 26-27.

92. *Id.* at 29.

93. *Id.* at 21.

94. *Id.* at 22-24.

95. *Id.* at 23.

96. *Id.* at 25-26, n. 42 (citing *Maricopa County Medical Society*, 457 U.S. 332 [1982]); *National Gerimedical Hospital v. Blue Cross*, 452 U.S. 378 (1981); *American Medical Ass'n v. United States*, 317 U.S. 519 (1943).

97. *Brokerage Concepts, Inc. v. U.S. Healthcare, Inc.*, 140 F. 3d 494, 501 (3d Cir. 1998).

98. *Id.* at 519.

99. 5 U.S.C. §1.

100. 15 U.S.C. §14.

101. 15 U.S.C. §45.

102. *Continental T.V., Inc., v. GTE Sylvania, Inc.*, 433 U.S. 36 (1977). *See also Jefferson Parish Hospital*, 466 U.S. at 45 (J. O'Connor, concurring).

103. *Standard Oil Co. v. United States*, 337 U.S. 293, 314 (1949).

104. *Tampa Electric Co. v. Nashville Coal Co.*, 365 U.S. 320 (1961).

105. *Jefferson Parish Hospital*, 466 U.S. at 30 n. 51 (1984).

106. *Id.* at 45 (J. O'Connor, concurring).

107. *Id.*

108. *Harron v. United Hospital Center, Inc.*, 522 F. 2d 1133 (4th Cir. 1975), *cert. denied*, 424 U.S. 916 (1976).

109. *Id.* at 1134.

110. *Dos Santos v. Columbus-Cuneo-Cabrini Medical Center*, 684 F. 2d 1346 (7th Cir. 1982).

111. *Id.* at 1354.

112. *Id.* at 1355.

113. *Id.* at 1352.

114. *U.S. Healthcare, Inc. v. Healthsource, Inc.*, 986 F. 2d 589, 592 (1st Cir. 1993).

115. *Id.* at 596-597.

116. *See, e.g., Jefferson Parish Hospital*, 466 U.S. at 45 (J. O'Connor, concurring); *U.S. Healthcare, Inc. v. Healthsource, Inc.*, 986 F. 2d 589 (1st Cir. 1993).

117. 15 U.S.C. §1. Section 1, by its terms, requires some contract, combination, or conspiracy for a violation of the section to occur. Unilateral action by a businessman has long been recognized as legitimate conduct unrestrained by the antitrust laws. *United States v. Colgate Co.*, 250 U.S. 300 (1919). One significant exception to this proposition would be unilateral action, which could be characterized as monopolization or as an attempt to monopolize.

118. *See Klor's, Inc. v. Broadway-Hale Stores, Inc.* 359 U.S. 207 (1959); *United States v. General Motors Corp.*, 384 U.S. 127 (1966).

119. *Northwest Wholesale Stationers*, 472 U.S. 284 (1985).

120. *Id.* at 294 (citations omitted).

121. *Id.* at 2621.

122. *Weiss v. York Hospital*, 745 F. 2d 786, 818 (3d Cir. 1984), *cert. denied*, 470 U.S. 1060 (1985).

123. *Id.* at 820.

124. *Id.* at 820. The court drew on language from *Arizona v. Maricopa County Medical Society*, 457 U.S. 332, 348-349 (1982), recognizing some limited vitality for a learned profession's exemption from the operation of the antitrust laws.

125. *Wilk*, 719 F. 2d 207 (7th Cir. 1983), *cert. denied*, 467 U.S. 1210 (1984).

126. *Id.* at 221.

127. *Id.* at 221. *See* discussion of the rule-of-reason approach in *Wilk* at 182.

128. *See, e.g., Pontious v. Children's Hospital*, 552 F. Supp. 1352 (W.D. Pa. 1982); *Chiropractic Cooperative Association of Michigan v. American Medical Ass'n.*, 617 F. Supp. 264 (E.D. Mich. 1985).

129. *Patrick*, 486 U.S. 94 (1988).

130. *See* discussion at 174-175.

131. 42 U.S.C. §§11101-11152. This statute was, in part, in response to the verdict in the trial court in *Patrick v. Burget.*

132. *Levine v. Central Florida Medical Affiliates, Inc.*, 72 F. 3d 1538, 1542-1543 (11th Cir. 1996).

133. *Id.* at 1550.

134. *Id.* at 1552.

135. *See, e.g., Doctor's Hospital v. Southeast Medical Alliance*, 123 F. 3d 301 (5th Cir. 1997). In this case a PPO controlled by local hospitals terminated the defendant hospital's membership, and accepted a rival hospital in the area as a new member instead. The court applied the rule of reason and found insufficient evidence of injury, noting that the plaintiff was affiliated with several other PPOs in the area and that the plaintiff failed to show that its exclusion from the defendant PPO would lead to increased prices under managed care plans, diminished consumer choice, or had an impact on its long-term ability to compete. 15 U.S.C. §1.

136. *United States v. Topco Associates, Inc.*, 405 U.S. 596 (1972).

137. *Continental T.V. v. G.T.E. Sylvania*, 433 U.S. 36 (1977).

138. *Cf. Broadcast Music*, 441 U.S. 1 (1979).

139. *See, e.g., Department of Justice and Federal Trade Commission Statements of Antitrust Enforcement Policy in Health Care*, 1996-4 Trade Reg. Rep. (CCH), s. 13,153.

140. *Blue Cross & Blue Shield United of Wisconsin v. Marshfield Clinic*, 65 F. 3d 1406, 1416 (7th Cir. 1995).

141. *Id.*

142. 15 U.S.C.A. §2.

143. *United States v. Aluminum Co. of America*, 148 F. 2d 416, 430 (2d Cir. 1945) ("The successful competitor, having been urged to compete, must not be turned upon when he wins.")

144. *United States v. Grinnell Corp.*, 384 U.S. 563, 571 (1966).

145. *United States v. duPont & Co.*, 351 U.S. 377, 391 (1956); *accord Grinnell Corp.*, 384 U.S. at 571.

146. *Grinnell Corp.*, 384 U.S. at 571.

147. In *Aluminum Co. of America*, 148 F. 2d at 424, Judge Learned Hand noted that "The percentage we have already mentioned—over 90—results only if we both include all 'Alcoa's' production and exclude 'secondary.' That percentage is enough to constitute a monopoly; it is doubtful whether 60% or 64% would be enough; and certainly 33% is not."

148. *See* in this regard the revised merger guidelines issued by the United States Department of Justice in 1992; §2.1 Product Market Definition; §2.3 Geographic Market Definition; §2.4 Calculating Market Shares.

149. *Aluminum Co. of America*, 148 F. 2d at 431.

150. *Aspen Skiing Co. v. Aspen Highlands Skiing Co.*, 472 U.S. 585, 603-605 (1985); *Berkey Photo Inc. v. Eastman Kodak Co.*, 603 F. 2d 263, 274 (2d Cir. 1979), *cert. denied*, 444 U.S. 1093 (1980).

151. *See William Inglis & Sons v. ITT Continental Baking Co.*, 668 F. 2d 1014, 1027 (9th Cir. 1981), *cert. denied*, 459 U.S. 825 (1982).

152. *See, e.g.,* Cartensen, *Reflections on Hay, Clark and the Relationship of Economic Analysis to Rules of Antitrust Law*, 83 Wis. L. Rev. 953 (1983); Cooper, *Attempts and Monopolization: A Mildly Expansionary Answer to the Prophylactic Riddle of Section Two*, 72 Mich. L. Rev. 373 (1974).

153. *Delaware Health Care, Inc. v. MCD Holding Co.*, 957 F. Supp. 535 (D. Del. 1997), *aff'd*, 141 F. 3d 1153 (3d Cir. 1998).

154. *See id.* at 538-539.

155. *Id.* at 541 (citation omitted).

156. *Id.* at 541-543.

157. *Id.* at 544-546.

158. *Id.* at 547-548.

159. *See, e.g., Weiss*, 745 F. 2d at 825, *cert. denied*, 470 U.S. 1060 (1985) (§2 violation reversed because no showing of willful conduct on part of hospital); *Robinson v. Magovern*, 621 F.Supp. at 887 (30% market share does not constitute monopoly power).

160. Allegations of monopolization, *inter alia*, by the attorney general of the State of Maine against an association of anesthesiologists in Portland, Maine, resulted in a consent decree restricting the practices of that association. *State of Maine v. Anesthesia Professional Ass'n*, Maine Superior Court, Consent Decree, June 12, 1984. In *Bhan v. NME Hospitals, Inc.*, 772 F. 2d 1467 (9th Cir. 1985) a nurse anesthetist alleged violations of §§1 and 2 of the Sherman Act by anesthesiologists and a hospital acting in combination to deny access to the hospital to nurse anesthetists.

161. 15 U.S.C. §18. The FTC may review a merger pursuant to 15 U.S.C. §45, which incorporates the provisions of Section 7. *Stanley Works v. FTC*, 469 F. 2d 498, 499 n. 2 (2d Cir. 1972), *cert. denied*, 412 U.S. 28 (1973).

162. 15 U.S.C. §18.

163. 15 U.S.C. §12. In regard to asset acquisitions, the acquiring party must be subject to the jurisdiction of the FTC. For discussion of this point, *see* Miles and Philip, *Hospitals Caught in the Antitrust Net: An Overview*, 24 Duquesne L. Rev. 489, 664 (1985), *and see FTC v. University Health Inc.*, 938 F. 2d 1206 (11th Cir. 1991) and *U.S. v. Rockford Memorial Hospital*, 898 F. 2d 1278 (7th Cir. 1990).

164. 5 U.S.C. §18.

165. *United States v. Penn-Olin Chemical Co.*, 378 U.S. 158 (1964).

166. *Cf. United States v. Von's Grocery Co.*, 384 U.S. 270 (1966), with *United States v. General Dynamics Corp.*, 415 U.S. 486 (1974) and *United States v. Marine Bancorporation*, 418 U.S. 602 (1974).

167. *See, e.g., Hospital Corporation of America*, 3 Trade Reg. Rep. (CCH) 122, 301 (FTC Oct. 25, 1985); *American Medical International*, 3 Trade Reg. Rep. (CCH) 122, 170 (FTC July 2, 1984).

168. 1992 Merger Guidelines, §2.1.

169. *Id.* at §2.3.

170. The Herfindahl-Hirschman index (HHI) is the sum of the squares of the individual market shares of all the firms judged to be appropriately included in the market. An HHI of below 1000 in a postmerger market generally is considered unconcentrated, whereas an HHI above 1800 generally is considered highly concentrated. An HHI between 1000 and 1800 will be reviewed with emphasis on the increase in the HHI caused by the merger and other factors. This statement is a summary explanation of the process followed under the Merger Guidelines and reference to the Merger Guidelines is strongly recommended.

171. *See Hospital Corporation of America v. FTC*, 807 F. 2d 1381 (7th Cir. 1986), *cert. denied*, 481 U.S. 1038 (1987); *American Medical International*, 3 Trade Reg. Rep. (CCH) 122,170 (FTC July 2, 1984); *United States v. Hospital Affiliates International, Inc.*, 1980-1981 Trade Cases (CCH) 163, 721 (E.D. La. 1980); *American Medicorp, Inc. v. Humana, Inc.*, 445 F. Supp. 589 (E.D. Pa. 1977).

172. *See, e.g., FTC v. Freeman Hospital*, 69 F. 3d 260 (8th Cir. 1995).

173. 15 U.S.C. §18.

174. *See, e.g., United States v. Carilion Health Service, Inc.*, 707 F. Supp. 840 (W.D. Va. 1988), *aff'd without opinion*, 892 F. 2d 1042 (4th Cir. 1989).

175. *See, e.g., FTC v. University Health, Inc.*, 938 F. 2d 1206, 1214-1215 (11th Cir. 1991); *United States v. Rockford Memorial Corp.*, 898 F. 2d 1278 (7th Cir. 1990), *cert. denied*, 498 U.S. 920 (1990).

176. 4 Trade Reg. Rep. (CCH) s. 13,153, Statement 1.

177. *Id.*

178. *Id.*

179. *Id.*

180. *See* Statement of Charles A. James, Acting Assistant Attorney General, Antitrust Division, to the Joint Economic Committee of the House-Senate Subcommittee on Investment, Jobs and Prices, June 24, 1992.

181. 15 U.S.C. §15c.

182. *See Brunswick Corp. v. Pueblo Bowl-O-Mat, Inc.*, 429 U.S. 477 (1977).

183. *Id.* at 489.

184. *Parker v. Brown*, 317 U.S. 341 (1943).

185. *Id.* at 350.

186. *See, e.g., Goldfarb v. Virginia State Bar*, 421 U.S. 773 (1975); *Cantor v. Detroit Edison Co.*, 428 U.S. 579 (1976); *Bates v. State Bar of Arizona*, 433 U.S. 350 (1977).

187. *California Liquor Dealers v. Midcal Aluminum Inc.*, 445 U.S. 97 (1980).

188. *Id.* at 105.

189. *Id.*

190. *See Patrick v. Burget*, 486 U.S. 94 (1988); *see also Southern Motor Carriers Rate Conference v. United States*, 471 U.S. 48 (1985). In *Southern Motor Carriers* the court rejected the contention that to gain the benefit of the state action exemption the anticompetitive conduct of the private party must be compelled by the state statute.

191. *Town of Hallie v. City of Eau Claire*, 471 U.S. 34 (1985).

192. *See, e.g., State of North Carolina ex rel. Edmisten v. P.I.A. Asheville, Inc.*, 740 F. 2d 274 (4th Cir. 1984), *cert. denied*, 469 U.S. 1070 (1985).

193. *See, e.g., Marrese v. Interequal, Inc.*, 748 F. 2d 373 (7th Cir. 1984), *cert. denied*, 472 U.S. 1027 (1985); *Quinn v. Kent General Hospital, Inc.*, 617 F. Supp. 1226 (D.C. Del. 1985).

194. *See, e.g., Coastal Neuro-Psychiatric Associates v. Onslow County Hospital Authority*, 607 F. Supp. 49 (D.C.N.C. 1985).

195. *Springs Ambulance Service v. City of Rancho Mirage*, 745 F. 2d 1270 (9th Cir. 1984); *Gold Cross Ambulance and Transfer v. City of Kansas City*, 705 F. 2d 1005 (8th Cir. 1983), *cert. denied*, 469 U.S. 538 (1985). Both cases involved exclusive contracts for the provision of ambulance services to the citizens of the municipalities.

196. *Town of Hallie*, 471 U.S. at 47.

197. Local Government Antitrust Act of 1984, Pub. L. 98-544, October 24, 1984, 15 U.S.C. §§34-36.

198. 112 S.Ct. 2169 (1992).

199. *Id.* at 2178.

200. 15 U.S.C. §17.

201. 15 U.S.C. §§1011-1015 (McCarran-Ferguson Act). *See Union Life Insurance Co. v. Pireno*, 458 U.S. 119 (1982); *Group Life & Health Ins. Co. v. Royal Drug Co.*, 440 U.S. 205 (1979); *St. Paul Fire & Marine Ins. Co. v. Barry*, 438 U.S. 531 (1978).

202. 15 U.S.C. §17; 7 U.S.C. §§291-292 (Capper-Volstead Act).

203. 15 U.S.C. §521 (The Fisheries Cooperative Marketing Act).

204. 15 U.S.C. §§1801-1804 (The Newspaper Preservation Act).

205. 15 U.S.C. §§3501-3503 (The Soft Drink Interbrand Competition Act of 1980).

206. 15 U.S.C. §638(d)(1), (2).

207. 15 U.S.C. §§640, 2158.

208. 15 U.S.C. §§62, 4001-4021 (Webb-Pomerene Act, Export Trading Company Act of 1982).

209. *Patrick*, 486 U.S. 94 (1988).

210. 42 U.S.C. §§11101-11152.

211. The professional review action must meet the standards set forth in 42 U.S.C. §11112(a). This immunity may be lost if a health care entity fails to report information as required by the statute. 42 U.S.C. §11111(b).

212. Professional review body is defined at 42 U.S.C. §11151(11). It includes a health care entity conducting professional review and any committee of a health care entity or of a medical staff of such an entity conducting such review when assisting the governing body of the institution.

213. Immunity is not provided if the information is false and the person providing it knew it was false. 42 U.S.C. §11111(a)(2).

214. 42 U.S.C. §11113.

215. *See, e.g.*, The Reed-Bullwinkle Act, 49 U.S.C. §10706 (joint rate filings with ICC by carriers); the Shipping Act of 1916, 46 U.S.C. §§813a, 814 (rate agreements between maritime carriers).

216. *See, e.g., United States v. National Association of Securities Dealers*, 422 U.S. 694 (1975); *United States v. Philadelphia National Bank*, 374 U.S. 321 (1963); *Silver v. New York Stock Exchange*, 373 U.S. 341 (1963).

217. *See National Gerimedical Hospital v. Blue Cross*, 452 U.S. 378 (1981).

218. 42 U.S.C. §3001 (National Health Planning and Development Act of 1974).

219. 452 U.S. at 391.

220. *Id.* at 393 n. 18.

221. *Eastern Railroad Presidents Conference v. Noerr Motor Freight, Inc.*, 365 U.S. 127 (1961); *United Mine Workers v. Pennington*, 381 U.S. 657 (1965).

222. *Noerr Motor Freight*, 365 U.S. at 137.

223. *Id.* at 144; *see also Professional Real Estate Investors Inc. v. Columbia Pictures Industries, Inc.*, 113 S.Ct. 1920 (1993); *City of Columbia v. Omni Outdoor Advertising, Inc.*, 111 S.Ct. 1344 (1991); *California Motor Transport Co. v. Trucking Unlimited*, 404 U.S. 508, 513 (1972).

224. *See, e.g., Hospital Building Co.*, 692 F. 2d at 687-688; *Feminist Women's Health Center v. Mohammad*, 586 F. 2d 530, 442-447 (5th Cir. 1978).

225. *Feminist Women's Health Center*, 586 F. 2d at 454.

226. *Virginia Academy of Clinical Psychologists v. Blue Shield of Virginia*, 624 F. 2d 476, 482 (4th Cir. 1980), *cert. denied*, 450 U.S. 916 (1981).

227. Robinson-Patman Antidiscrimination Act, ch. 592, §1-4, 49 Stat. 1526, 15 U.S.C. 13, 13a, 13b, 21a, 13c (1936).

228. Non-Profit Institutions Act, ch. 283, 52 Stat. 446, 15 U.S.C. 13c (1938).

229. *Abbott Laboratories v. Portland Retail Druggists Ass'n*, 425 U.S. 1 (1976).

230. 1996-4 Trade Reg. Rep. (CCH), §13,153. In the 1996 revised statements the agencies elaborated on their discussion in two critical areas—physician and multiprovider networks.

Alternative Dispute Resolution

ALLAN GIBOFSKY, M.D., J.D., F.A.C.P., F.C.L.M.

MEDIATION
ARBITRATION
HYBRID METHODS
OTHER FORMS OF ALTERNATIVE DISPUTE RESOLUTION
ALTERNATIVE DISPUTE RESOLUTION AND MEDICAL MALPRACTICE CLAIMS
ALTERNATIVE DISPUTE RESOLUTION AND OTHER MEDICAL DISPUTES
CONCLUSION

Disputes are as common in health care as in other industries and social circumstances that involve differing interests. However, resolving medical disputes using the formal process of litigation is time-consuming and expensive and may not suit the parties' needs. Thus, beyond formal adjudication, other alternatives may provide better opportunities to effectuate a resolution that is acceptable to the parties.

The alternative dispute resolution (ADR) movement has recognized the limitations of formal adjudication and has employed other mechanisms through which conflicts may be resolved. ADR methods, in combination with formal adjudication, offer a broad range of tools to address the concomitantly broad array of conflicts that may arise in health care.

Generally the binding or nonbinding nature of any ADR process is based on contract. The terms of the agreement dictate whether and which specific ADR process must be followed in an effort to resolve a dispute and whether the assessment is simply advisory or is legally binding on both parties.

This chapter reviews some of the main ADR methods and indicates the types of circumstances that appear to be most beneficial for each method's use. In addition, the controversial subject of ADR application to malpractice claims is discussed. Finally, application of ADR methods to nonmalpractice, modern health care disputes is illustrated through the presentation and review of several case scenarios.

MEDIATION

Mediation is a process by which a neutral third party assists disputing parties in negotiating a resolution. The mediator merely assists the parties; he or she has no formal power to impose any outcome on them. Usually the mediator does not evaluate the legal rights of either party and merely acts as a facilitator for communication between the parties. The parties generally select the mediator. The process usually is informal, with no set rules except those imposed by the parties or the mediator in an effort to further productive communications (e.g., no interruptions when one party is speaking).

Mediation is a voluntary process entered into by the parties in an effort to resolve their dispute. Generally, enforceability of these mediated resolutions is a function of private contract law; any agreement to mediate, as well as an agreement to abide by the mediated decision, is enforceable according to the terms of the contract.

The major advantages of mediation include the private nature of the process and the confidentiality of its results; the process focuses on improving communication between the parties so that interests, goals, and needs of each are identified and communicated to the other. This dynamic leads to the identification of common interests and hence to a mutually acceptable resolution of the conflict for the parties. This process also gives the parties an opportunity to express emotion (in or outside the presence of the other party), shifts the focus of the conflict from past to future, allows the disclosure of interests important to the individual parties that each is reluctant to disclose to the other, and permits the parties to provide new information that may be helpful in resolving the dispute.

ARBITRATION

Arbitration is a formalized system of dispute resolution in which parties provide proofs and arguments to a neutral third party who has the power to impose a binding decision on the parties. A common variation incorporates the use of multiple arbitrators (e.g., one is selected by each party and the chosen arbitrators choose a third). Arbitration is similar to formal adjudication except that the parties are allowed

Member, Textbook Editorial Committee, edited this chapter, which was authored by Bryan A. Liang, M.D., Ph.D., J.D., in the 5th edition. This chapter is dedicated to the memory of James B. Boskey, Esq., Professor of Law, Seton Hall University School of Law.

only limited pretrial discovery if any, the hearing is less formal, and the rules of evidence are not as rigidly applied in an arbitration proceeding.

Arbitration has been mandated by law for certain conflicts, such as labor disputes, and is used voluntarily by parties to resolve private disputes. When private parties agree to use arbitration, they must address a certain number of issues to ensure that the process will be useful. For example, the parties must decide on a method for selection of the arbitrator or arbitrators; stipulate who will pay for these services; set an objective standard by which the arbitrator or arbitrators will assess the conflict and claims of the parties (e.g., the law, trade or industry customs, or some combination); and specify the procedural rules that the arbitrator or arbitrators will follow. Unless otherwise indicated in the terms for arbitration, arbitration does not allow for pretrial discovery. Arbitration is most frequently used as a final, binding procedure.

There are several major advantages that may result from using arbitration. For example, arbitration allows the parties to draw upon arbitrators with specialized expertise relating directly to the conflict, the arbitrated decision is final, the dispute proceedings and the decision itself are private, the procedural rules are determined by the parties, and the cost for resolving the dispute is relatively low (in terms of time and money) as compared with formal adjudication. Of course, whether these advantages are realized depends on the specific conflict, the parties, and the arbitrator or arbitrators involved. There is a strong public policy in favor of arbitration, and state and federal law makes agreements to arbitrate specifically enforceable.[1]

Unlike formal adjudication, once an arbitration decision has been made, there is no default mechanism through which the decision is enforced. However, the arbitration decision may be judicially confirmed by bringing the decision to court; failure to abide by the arbitration decision at that point constitutes contempt of court. Both the Federal Arbitration Act and the Uniform Arbitration Act give courts jurisdiction to confirm (or refuse to confirm) an arbitration decision.

Arbitration also may be part of an official state-sanctioned process. In these situations the government mandates that the parties go through arbitration before formal adjudication. Generally this "court-annexed arbitration" is provided by state law and may require that a certain class of cases (e.g., automobile torts) or a certain monetary amount be at issue.[2] Some states, however, exclude certain types of claims from arbitration, such as those involving personal injury, tort, and/or insurance contracts.[3]

HYBRID METHODS

Med-arb

"Med-arb" is a combination of mediation and arbitration. In this ADR process the parties agree to mediate their dispute first, using a neutral third party as a mediator. If mediation does not result in an agreement or settlement, then the mediator changes roles and becomes an arbitrator with the power to issue a final and binding decision with regard to the dispute. The primary advantage of using this hybrid method is its potential efficiency: the same neutral third party is used in both mediation and arbitration so that there is no need to educate him or her regarding the facts of the dispute and interests of the parties. However, a significant disadvantage of med-arb is that the parties may not substantively participate in the mediation stage because sensitive disclosures may be used against them if and when the neutral evaluator assumes the role of an arbitrator.

An alternative to this standard med-arb is med-arb that results in only an advisory arbitration decision. This process attempts to mitigate the identified problems with med-arb involving binding arbitration. Because the mediator has no binding power to arbitrate a final decision, the parties have an increased incentive to substantively use mediation to resolve their dispute. It also serves to allow the mediator as an advisory arbitrator to merely indicate what he or she believes the ultimate result would be at arbitration. However, the clear disadvantage of this process is its potential length; an extra step of binding arbitration may be required.

Mini-trial

The mini-trial is an evaluative process most often used for business and commercial disputes. Attorneys representing each party make summary presentations to a panel composed of a neutral advisor and high level executives from each party who have the power to accept a settlement. After the presentations, the executives try to settle the dispute through negotiation. If negotiation fails to result in a settlement, the neutral advisor provides an assessment as to what he or she considers to be the probable outcome of the dispute. Major beneficial characteristics of a mini-trial are that the process is voluntary and confidential; the parties agree to follow certain protocols or procedures; before the mini-trial, the parties agree to informally exchange important documents, provide summaries of witness testimony, and provide short statements regarding the dispute (and often provide that this information is confidential and inadmissible in any future proceeding); and a neutral third party who has expertise in the subject matter (e.g., a former judge) is chosen by consent of the parties (this neutral party may take a passive role in the process or be more active, such as taking on the role of a mediator).

Summary jury trial

The summary jury trial is an evaluative process similar to a mini-trial, but it differs in several important ways. These differences stem from the goal of the process—determining what a jury might decide in the case. Hence, instead of a third-party neutral and corporate executives, a judge and an advisory jury drawn from the jury pool are used. Jurors are not told that their role is advisory until after they give their verdict. Attorneys for each side make summary presentations as in the mini-trial; however, the presentations usually are based on information that has been the subject of discovery and would be admissible at trial. Once the advisory jury has announced its decision, jury members answer questions regarding the verdict and their assessment and reaction to particular evidence and arguments. The attorneys and their respective executive representatives then attend a mandatory conference to discuss settlement. If no settlement occurs, the advisory jury verdict is not admissible in future final adjudication procedures.

A summary jury trial requires significant time and resources because it is similar to formal adjudication. This method is thus most useful when the dispute is unique or novel, when circumstances preclude an easy prediction of what a jury would decide, and when such unpredictability is what is preventing settlement.

OTHER FORMS OF ALTERNATIVE DISPUTE RESOLUTION

Early neutral evaluation

Early neutral evaluation is usually a court-annexed process that requires the parties to have their dispute assessed by an experienced third-party neutral evaluator on the basis of short presentations by both parties. It is thus a rights-based procedure like arbitration and formal adjudication. Usually the third-party neutral is a volunteer attorney chosen by the court. Once the presentations are made, the parties negotiate in an effort to settle the dispute. If the parties do not settle, the neutral evaluator assists them in simplifying and clarifying the case so that it will be more amenable to formal adjudication.

Private judging

With the advent and growth of ADR, a significant private market has emerged to render adjudicative services and decisions. Private judging (also known as *rent-a-judge*) is a reflection of this growth. Many of these participants are retired judges who provide informal adjudication or engage in other ADR processes. These private judges are paid by the parties involved and may be empowered by state statute to enter final judgments that have precedential value and are appealable to appellate courts, as are rulings made in formal adjudication.[4] California, Florida, and Texas have statutory provisions that require referral of certain court cases to private ADR providers paid for by the parties.[5]

"Rights-based" mediation

Generally, traditional mediation (also known as interest-based mediation) focuses on creating a mutually acceptable solution to resolve disputes and does not involve an evaluation of the legal strengths and weaknesses of each party's case. However, in rights-based mediation there is a focus on the legal rights of the parties, and thus the process is more akin to evaluative processes, such as early neutral evaluation.

Screening panels

Screening panels usually are involved in state-mandated pretrial assessments of medical malpractice cases. Plaintiffs, before submitting their medical malpractice claims for trial, are required to have their case assessed by a special panel; this panel usually is composed of physicians or other medical professionals, attorneys, and laypersons. The panel hears the plaintiff's case and may issue a nonbinding opinion. Usually, either party can bring the case to court, regardless of the panel's assessment. Some states allow the panel's findings to be introduced as evidence in the court adjudication. Difficulties center around the administrative burdens these panels represent and the associated delays; furthermore, assessments may be made too early in the process, before discovery has been accomplished.

Settlement conference

In another form of ADR known as the *settlement conference* or *voluntary settlement conference*, a judge, a set of attorneys, or a "settlement master" (i.e., an independent party who assesses such conflicts) reads briefs and materials and hears presentations from both sides of a dispute, and then actively seeks to craft a settlement for the parties. As opposed to mediation, where the intermediary is merely a facilitator, in a settlement conference the intermediary is an active participant in the process. Often, after reading the submitted documents and hearing each side, the intermediary may caucus with each party independently and move between the parties in an effort to fashion a settlement. Courts use settlement conferences before formal adjudication to encourage parties to settle cases before they go to trial. Indeed, some courts will not set a case for trial unless a settlement conference has been held.

ALTERNATIVE DISPUTE RESOLUTION AND MEDICAL MALPRACTICE CLAIMS

Although a wide variety of medical disputes are amenable to ADR methods, one type of conflict that has drawn significant attention to the use of ADR (specifically, arbitration) is the medical malpractice dispute. Those in favor of using ADR methods to resolve malpractice claims cite the associated reduction in cost, the involvement of a more informed decision-maker, the reduction in emotional trauma that results from formal adjudication, the ability for plaintiffs with "minor" injuries to have their claims heard, and the reduction in frivolous malpractice cases. State law often dictates how these contractual agreements must appear and the conditions under which they are valid,[6] subject to federal law.[7]

The difficulty with applying ADR to medical malpractice disputes is primarily twofold. First, any voluntary process requires participation by all parties and their attorneys. However, the parties may believe that a trial by jury will increase their chance of success. Defendants may be reluctant to participate because they will be reported to the National Practitioner Data Bank if any amount is paid to end the dispute. Second, malpractice cases involve complex issues of fact, and full and adequate assessment will most likely require extensive time and effort. Summary processes therefore do not easily lend themselves to malpractice disputes. Mandatory, binding arbitration could address the voluntary party and attorney participation problem, as well as provide for appropriate technical expertise; however, it too is limited by the summary nature of the assessment.

Although arbitration has its limitations, many institutional health care providers and managed care organizations (MCOs) now use mandatory arbitration in their contractual agreements with patients to resolve any patient care disputes. Broad-scale use of binding arbitration was pioneered by Kaiser-Permanente in California and has spread rapidly throughout the United States as managed care has become the predominant mode of medical care delivery. Patients' challenges to mandatory arbitration clauses generally have been rejected by the courts.[8] Significantly the Federal Arbitration Act,[9] as well as state laws in at least 40 states, provides a basis for enforcing these provisions.[10] However, because of the potential advantages for "repeat players," such as MCOs, these entities must meet specific legal requirements regarding their use of arbitrators and their participation in arbitration.

Because of the controversy surrounding the use of binding arbitration in malpractice disputes, the largest arbitration association in the United States, the American Arbitration Association (AAA), participates in the arbitration of medical malpractice disputes under mandatory binding arbitration clauses in managed care contracts only in limited circumstances. AAA participates in these arbitration proceedings only if the patient asks for arbitration or if the patient agrees to such a method for dispute resolution after the dispute arises.[11] With regard to the use of ADR in medical malpractice disputes, AAA, in conjunction with the American Medical Association and the American Bar Association, has drafted policy guidelines. These guidelines specify the following:[12]

- ADR can and should be used to resolve disputes over health care coverage and access arising out of the relationship between patients and private health plans and MCOs.
- ADR can and should be used to resolve disputes over health care coverage and access arising out of the relationship between health care providers and private health plans and MCOs.
- In disputes involving patients, binding forms of dispute resolution should be used only when the parties agreed to do so after the dispute arose.

- Due process protections should be afforded to all participants in the ADR process.
- Review of managed health care decisions through ADR complements the concept of internal review of determinations made by private MCOs.

It is not yet clear how or whether these policy guidelines will substantively affect the use of arbitration in malpractice disputes because of the significant number of non-AAA arbitrators available and the standard nature of these clauses in patient care contracts.

ALTERNATIVE DISPUTE RESOLUTION AND OTHER MEDICAL DISPUTES

Aside from the controversial use of ADR in medical malpractice conflicts, a large number of potential disputes in the health care arena are amenable to ADR processes. Because health care has become increasingly commercialized, ADR processes can address commercial disputes between facilities and those between facilities and medical providers in the same way that other commercial disputes are addressed. However, the provider's reputation, the health of a party, and the emotional concerns intimately related to illness, disease, and treatment make disputes in the health care arena unique. Some circumstances, such as end-of-life situations, simply are not well suited to ADR or formal adjudication. However, by assessing each party's needs and goals in the context of the specific social and medical circumstances, as well as their underlying incentives, an appropriate dispute resolution strategy can usually be ascertained.

Examples of voluntary applications of ADR to several modern medical disputes outside the malpractice context follow.[12] These examples illustrate the process of choosing a particular ADR method but are not definitive statements on health law or policy.

Example 1: an interfacility dispute

Background. In the current health care climate, cost control has been a predominant consideration in the allocation of medical resources. As a result, federal, state, and local governments have used various strategies to minimize health care costs. One strategy has been to limit potential demand for expensive diagnostic technology by limiting the availability of such technology through requiring state-level approval before this type of asset can be purchased. However, if a health care facility can demonstrate to the state authority that there is sufficient patient need, there is no overlap between this form of capital investment and services derived therefrom, and there is available money to purchase and support the equipment, the facility may be granted a so-called certificate of need (CON), which is a permit that allows the facility to acquire such equipment. Such a grant is valuable because of the highly exclusive nature of the grant and the concomitant income arising therefrom.

Case scenario. In a local city, St. Francis Hospital has merged with Johnson City Hospital. Each hospital has been under pressure to expand services and improve reimbursements obtained from their patients' insurance. Both are located in the same urban area but in different neighborhoods. St. Francis is a nonprofit, private facility that caters primarily to middle-class patients in its neighborhood. Johnson City Hospital is a nonprofit, private, inner-city facility established during the forgone days of prosperity in its community. Its current clientele consists of poor, disenfranchised patients who primarily are Medicaid program participants or are uninsured. Johnson City Hospital is a teaching hospital for the prestigious Physicians and Surgeons Medical School (P & S), which is located in the city. It is thus staffed with outstanding resident physicians (house staff) who supplement the hospital's retained attending physicians.

St. Francis and Johnson City merged just over 1 year ago. Subsequent to the merger, the hospital applied for and obtained a CON for a new magnetic resonance imaging (MRI) machine that would significantly enhance physicians' ability to diagnose disorders in emergency and other clinical situations. The hospital was granted the CON on the basis of Johnson City's locale (health care resources there are limited) and St. Francis' fiscal soundness, which would allow purchase and maintenance of the machinery.

The current dispute is over where to locate the MRI machine. Johnson City contends that the machine should be located at its facility because CON approval was based on its patients' medical needs. St. Francis' position is that the machine could not have been purchased without its funds, and thus the machine should be located at St. Francis. The state authority has expressed no opinion on the matter. There is vague talk of legal action by the parties. How can this dispute be settled?

From an ADR standpoint, before the methodology can be chosen, the goals of the parties must be ascertained. From Johnson City's point of view, the MRI machine should be located on its site primarily for financial reasons. Reimbursement for MRI procedures is relatively high compared with operational costs, and Johnson City has lost significant revenues by not having such services available. In addition, if Johnson City had the MRI machine, P & S would likely send more of its house staff to Johnson City. This action would reduce certain staff costs because P & S pays the salary of the house staff, and an increase in the number of house staff would reduce the need to employ other health care providers. Finally, Johnson City's patient population would be better served by having advanced diagnostic equipment, such as an MRI machine, available on site. When Johnson City physicians refer patients elsewhere for an MRI procedure, the patients often do not follow through with the referral to obtain the scan.

St. Francis has similar goals. It also wants to take advantage of the high reimbursement rate for MRI services. However, it also wishes to use the MRI machine as a marketing tool. The marketing department envisions hosting an event and running advertisements using the phrase "St. Francis and the Twenty-First Century: Bringing Advanced Health Care to the Community."

Alternative dispute resolution assessment. The continuing relationship between St. Francis and Johnson City mitigates against the desirability of formal adjudication. The nature of the dispute (not involving novel legal issues or the desire to establish precedent) also makes formal adjudication inappropriate.

Arbitration is a possibility. Advantages include involvement of an arbiter who has expertise in the area, thus ensuring that technical arguments can be made, and who can issue a final decision. Additional advantages include confidentiality, relatively low cost, and rapid resolution, as compared with formal adjudication. Most likely, both parties would find all of these characteristics agreeable. However, arbiters' decisions usually are based on objective standards because arbitration is a rights-based procedure. In this case there is no clear-cut, single objective standard: the CON application apparently does not decide the issue: the state authority has expressed no opinion; the law does not seem to apply; and a rights-based process may sully the future relationship between the parties. Furthermore, the possibility of either party withdrawing its support (Johnson City's patient base and St. Francis' money) would likely preclude acquisition of the MRI machine. Finally, arbitration does not fare well as compared with other ADR methods in terms of relative cost, speed, and ability to improve the parties' relationship by focusing on their joint interests. Thus there appear to be some significant disadvantages in using arbitration to settle this dispute.

Mediation provides potential for clarifying communication and allowing for a creative resolution of the dispute without the necessity of revisting the divergent motivation for the CON application. The mediator also can take into account the possible internal pressures from the marketing department at St. Francis. Because the mediation process can focus on the future of the relationship and the joint interests of the parties, it can provide a foundation for building consensus between the hospitals. As well, because these parties are relatively new partners, a creative solution could spur additional, innovative joint ventures while simultaneously providing for and integrating into the process a communications pattern that takes into account the important allocative decisions that affect an organizational entity with separate and distinct sites. Furthermore, an evaluative course of action, providing both parties with the opportunity for reflection and feedback, could be integrated into the process for each joint project so that important lessons are learned from each effort. These lessons of course could and should be applied to future projects. Thus mediation has many advantages in this situation.

Within this purview, it appears that evaluative hybrid methods would be inappropriate. For example, a summary jury trial which is best for disputes involving a disparate view of the facts and the law by opposing parties, would be inappropriate because the parties do not disagree on the governing law. In addition, early neutral evaluation has similar limitations.

Thus in this interfacility dispute a mediation process might be proposed by appropriate representatives from the two hospitals. The mediation process fits best with the underlying sources of the dispute and addresses these issues from the perspective of an ongoing relationship with much promise for the future. It allows for the application of creative, mutually beneficial solutions. Because both parties have a strong incentive to come to the bargaining (or mediation) table (the valuable property interest that they jointly own, or the CON), the likelihood for a successfully mediated settlement is enhanced. Mediation also could provide for retrospective analysis of the conflict, which can teach important lessons to be applied in the future.

Although it meets some of the needs to clarify past miscommunications, arbitration does not look to the parties' future relationship. Moreover, it requires some relatively objective standard for dispute resolution that is not available. Finally, law-based processes (evaluative hybrids), as well as formal adjudication, seems inapplicable in this type of case because of the ambiguity of applicable legal rules.

Example 2: an intrafacility conflict—exclusive contracts and provider termination

Background. To procure necessary health care services, it is extremely common for health care facilities to contract for these services either with a single physician or with physician groups as independent contractors. This contractual arrangement thus allows the health care facility to offer 24-hour physician services in the particular specialty and avoids the necessity and the expense of providing health, retirement, and other benefits to these individuals.

In this regard, hospitals use an exclusive contract for hospital-based physician services. Hospitals typically contract with physicians for a specified time with the stipulation that, if given the amount of notice specified in the agreement, either the hospital or independent contractor physician may terminate the contract without cause.

Thus these contracts are double-edged swords. On the one hand, within the period for which the exclusive contract is applicable, the physician or physician group has the right and the power to charge for all physician services in the specialty, to the exclusion of other, nonexclusive contract physicians. On the other hand, the hospital has the power to terminate the relationship for any or no reason at all after giving the requisite notice as indicated in the contract.

Case scenario. Drake Hospital is a relatively large (450-bed) community hospital located in an affluent suburb. It serves primarily middle- to upper-class patients in the area and offers all of the major medical specialty services. Virtually none of the patients who come to Drake receive Medicaid benefits. Those who receive care from the hospital uniformly report satisfaction with its services. Patients generally find the new physical building, available parking, and courteous staff quite pleasing. The cafeteria is modern, and its food is delicious. Private physicians enjoy the facility's amiable atmosphere, delicious food, and private patient population.

Dr. Smith is a board-certified radiologist at Drake. After graduating from P & S and doing his residency training there, Dr. Smith entered private practice at Drake. Dr. Smith has worked at the hospital for the past 21 years under an exclusive contractual arrangement. Under the terms of the contract, Drake pays Dr. Smith a small salary; this salary is supplemented by charges to the hospital and referred patients' third-party insurers for rendered radiology services (as is normal practice). Dr. Smith also sees several of his own patients who come to Drake for specific radiologic procedures. For example, he performs and interprets chest x-ray films for a patient who was diagnosed several years ago with Hodgkin's disease and underwent curative radiation therapy but requires annual radiologic films to check for any recurrence. There have never been any allegations regarding the quality of care provided by Dr. Smith. Two years ago, Dr. Smith was awarded Drake Hospital's community service award for distinguished and long-term service to the hospital and its patients.

One month ago, Dr. Smith was in the radiology department reading room interpreting some MRI scans when a hospital administrator entered the room. The administrator asked to speak with Dr. Smith in private. When both were in Dr. Smith's office, the administrator told Dr. Smith: "As you know, in about 3 months your contract is up for renewal. We on the board have been happy with the work you've done, but we are not going to renew your contract. We just think it's time for some new blood."

After the administrator left, Dr. Smith sat alone and thought: "Why is this happening? This place is more than a workplace for me; this can't be happening. What can an older physician do for money? This shouldn't be happening; they don't have the right to sully my reputation. Should I contact an attorney? I'm going to challenge this somehow." Dr. Smith then finished up the MRI readings for the day and left for home.

Alternative dispute resolution assessment. The goals of the parties in this situation are not entirely clear. The hospital board wants to terminate Dr. Smith, and it appears that this action is well within its contractual and legal rights. A question is raised regarding why the board wants to terminate Dr. Smith, particularly in light of his service to the facility and the fact that they are happy with his work.

From Dr. Smith's perspective, termination results in the prospect of unemployment. Furthermore, concerns regarding reputation are evident. It is clear that Dr. Smith would like to stay at Drake if possible. He apparently has significant emotional ties to the hospital. However, it is also clear that Dr. Smith is contemplating legal action.

Because the goals of the hospital administration are unclear or unexpressed, there may be a lack of good communication between the parties. Perhaps the administrator was uncomfortable explaining to Dr. Smith that the board felt he was getting too old to maintain the rigors of a full-time practice. Or, although happy with Dr. Smith's services, the hospital board may have been offered a lower-cost contract by another radiologist or radiology group. Thus a method of dispute resolution that addresses this communication problem would be best.

From this assessment, mediation most likely would be an appropriate choice. The nature of the dispute seems to require the exchange of more information or the disclosure of new information. The parties must learn more about their respective interests. Given the apparent difficulty in communication, mediation may provide a sensitive and reasonable forum in which the dispute can be resolved.

Dr. Smith, however, appears to have conflicting goals that affect the choice of forum. On the one hand, Dr. Smith wishes to keep his radiology position at the hospital. Thus a continuing relationship is desired. However, it also appears that Dr. Smith has strong feelings that termination would be inappropriate. Furthermore, there is a concern that his reputation will suffer.

In contract disputes involving physicians, this potential effect on reputation is an important concern. There are few other professions to which this concept applies so broadly and to such a great degree. For Dr. Smith, reputation relates to patients, as well as to other physicians. If other physicians attempt to refer patients to Dr. Smith and he is required to inform them that he no longer has privileges at Drake, then there may be some implication of questionable competence or poor quality of care. Furthermore, if Dr. Smith attempts to find other work, the same reputational problems may arise. Although Dr. Smith sees some private patients at the hospital, the majority of his income is derived from hospital practice and referrals from other physicians. Accordingly, reputation becomes a significant concern to Dr. Smith as he considers actions involving (and possibly against) the hospital.

Thus, on one hand, a clearer understanding of the issues (the "why is this happening" factor), the desire to continue as the radiologist at the hospital, and the emotional ties might point toward a mediation approach. On the other hand, Dr. Smith's desire to maintain his reputation in the community (and with respect to other potential employers) would favor some other form of dispute resolution.

In this case a combination of mediation and arbitration might be optimal. Perhaps a mediation-advisory arbitration rather than a mediation-binding arbitration would be best because the latter form has some significant disadvantages as applied to this situation. First, there is a high probability that the hospital board members would not want to be completely candid when discussing their decision to renew Dr. Smith's contract if they knew that there could be a binding decision later. Thus the mediator would have relatively little information with which to work when attempting to help the parties craft a jointly creative and beneficial solution. Furthermore, because subsequent arbitration may focus on whether one party is "right" (hence changing the dynamic so as to divert the dispute resolution process away from interest-based solutions to the conflict), the parties may be less likely to try to resolve the problem at the mediation stage. Indeed, the parties may make a significant effort to convince the mediator that one or the other is deserving of a favorable decision.

The hospital most likely would not wish to enter into a binding process and risk losing when it is in a favorable legal position. Nevertheless, the hospital may wish to enter into an ADR procedure to avoid the legal costs of formal adjudication and eschew negative publicity. Moreover, certain "emotional" considerations may induce Drake administrators to treat Dr. Smith in a fair manner.

Mediation-advisory arbitration could address the disadvantages of mediation-binding arbitration. First, advisory arbitration is just that, only advisory. Advisory arbitration would preserve the creative solution emphasis and restore the mediation dynamic to the process rather than focus on a determination of who is "right." Perhaps the mediator could open the lines of communication between the parties, allowing the parties to participate actively in the dispute resolution process. If mediation fails, an advisory position (an evaluative process) could give Dr. Smith and Drake an objective assessment regarding the conflict and the outcome should the matter proceed to formal adjudication.

This process also could serve Dr. Smith's need to address his reputational concern; the settlement or possibly an acceptable advisory opinion could expressly state that the hospital's actions regarding Dr. Smith were not based on any quality of care concerns, or similar language to that effect. This statement would allow Dr. Smith to seek employment with other providers and show that a neutral third party had found (and the hospital had stated) that no quality of care issues triggered his change in status at the hospital.

However, a possible disadvantage of mediation-advisory arbitration is the potential length of the process. With both mediation and advisory arbitration, time may be spent on adjudicatory arbitration or formal court activity in addition to the extra step of advisory arbitration. However, empirical data suggest that there is a significant possibility that the dispute could be resolved without resorting to formal adjudication.

Thus, in this physician termination scenario, mediation-advisory arbitration appears to be appropriate. Pure evaluative procedures, such as summary jury trial and early neutral evaluation, could be helpful if there were a different view of the legal rights of the parties. In this case the hospital has the authority to terminate Dr. Smith's contract. Arbitration, although possibly favorable to the hospital, would not serve Dr. Smith's interest-based concerns and, as a single method, would be inappropriate.

CONCLUSION

Disputes regarding medical care delivery are common. Many of these disputes can be addressed and resolved using ADR methods in combination with formal adjudication. An understanding of the various ADR methods, their strengths and weaknesses, their legal status, and the interests and goals of each party can usually but not always bring about an effective resolution to the dispute in the health care context.

ENDNOTES

1. *See, e.g.*, Federal Arbitration Act, 9 U.S.C.A. §§2 *et seq.*; *see also* Administrative Dispute Resolution Act, 5 U.S.C.A. §§5581-5593, Ariz. Rev. Stat. Ann. §§12-1501 to 12-1518 (West 1994); Ark. Code Ann. §§16-108-201 to 16-108-224 (Mich. 1995); Del. Code Ann. tit. 10 §§5701-5725 (1996); Fla. Stat. ch. 682.01-682.22 (1990); Idaho Code §§7-901 to 7-922 (1990); Iowa Code Ann. §§679A.1-679A.19 (1987); Kan. Stat. Ann. §§5-401 to 5-422 (1995); Ky. Rev. Stat. Ann. §§4417.145-417.240 (Michie 1996); Minn. Stat. §§572.08-572.30 (1996); Mont. Code Ann. §§27-5-111 to 27-5-324 (1996); Nev. Rev. Stat. §§38.015-38.360 (1995); N.J. Stat. Ann. §§2A:23A-1 to 2A:23A-19 (West 1996); Ohio Rev. Code Ann. §§2711.01 to 2711.16 (West 1992); Pa. Cons. Stat. §§7301-7320 (1982); R.I. Gen. Laws §§10-3-1 to 10-3-21 (1996); S.D. Codified Laws §§21-25A-1 to 21-5A-38 (Michie 1996); Tenn. Code Ann. §§29-5-301 to 29-5-320 (1996); Utah Code Ann. §§78-31a-1 to 78-31a-20 (1996); Vt. Stat. Ann. tit. 12, §§5651-5681 (1996); Wyo. Stat. Ann §§1-36-101 to 1-36-119 (Michie 1986).
2. *See, e.g.*, Cal. Health & Safety Code §1373.19 (indicating that single arbitrator may assess claims for health services claims up to $200,000); Hawaii Arb. Rules, Rule 8 (Michie 1995) (monetary claims for amounts less than $150,000 must go to court-annexed arbitration except under certain circumstances).
3. *See, e.g.*, Ark. Code Ann. §16-108-201(b) (Michie 1997); Kan. Stat. Ann. §5-401(c) (1997); Mont. Code Ann. §27-5-114 (2) (1997); S.C. Code Ann. §15-48-10 (1998); Tex. Civ. Prac. Code Ann. §171.001 (1997).
4. *See Assami v. Assami*, 872 P. 2d 1190 (Cal. 1994); *Estate of Kent*, 57P. 2d 901 (Cal. 1936); *Solorzano v. Sup. Ct.*, 22 Cal. Rptr. 2d 401 (Cal. 1993).
5. *See, e.g.*, Tex. Alcoholic Beverage Code §102.77 (parties must pay for arbitration costs); Fla. Stats. Ann. §44.103; Fla. Alt. Disp. Res. §718.1255 (mandating voluntary mediation and mandatory nonbinding arbitration).
6. *See, e.g.*, Cal. Civ. Pro. §1295 (describing wording, font, and color of enforceable medical malpractice arbitration agreement) subject to federal law.
7. *See, e.g., Perry v. Thomas*, 482 U.S. 483 (1987) (state laws that are unique to arbitration agreements are preempted by federal law governing arbitration).
8. *See, e.g., Coon v. Nicola*, 21 Cal. Rptr. 2d 846 (Cal. Ct. App. 1993); *Buraczynski v. Eyring*, 919 S.W. 2d 314 (Tenn. 1996); *Broemmer v.*

Otto, 821 P. 2d 204 (Ariz. 1991); *Wilson v. Kaiser Found. Hosps.* 190 Cal. Rptr 649 (Cal. Ct. App. 1983); *Dinong v. Kaiser Found. Hosp.*, 162 Cal. Rptr. 606 (Cal. Ct. App. 1980); *Madden v. Kaiser Found. Hosps.*, 131 Cal. Rptr. 882 (Cal. 1976) (all upholding use of ADR); *but see Colorado Permanente Med. Group v. Evans*, 926 P. 2d 1218 (Colo. 1996); *Saika v. Gold*, 56 Cal. Rptr. 2d 922 (Cal. Ct. App. 1996); *Beynon v. Garden Grove Med. Group*, 161 Cal. Rptr. 146 (Cal. Ct. App. 1980); *but see Rosenfield v. Sup. Ct.*, 143 Cal. App. 3d 198 (Cal. 1983); *Graham v. Scissor-Tail, Inc.*, 28 Cal. 3d 807 (Cal. 1990); *Cheng-Canindin v. Renaissance Hotel Assocs.*, 50 Cal. App. 4th 676 (Cal. Ct. App. 1996).
9. 9 U.S.C.A. §2.
10. P.I. Carter, *Binding Arbitration in Malpractice Disputes: The Right Prescription for HMO Patients?*, 18 Hamline Journal of Public Law and Policy 423-451 (1997).
11. G.H. Friedman, *AAA, ABA and AMA Issue Joint Resolution: Recommendations for Health Care Dispute Resolution*, 15 Med. Mal. L. Strategy 1 (1998).
12. B.A. Liang, *Understanding and Applying Alternative Dispute Resolution Methods in Modern Medical Conflicts*, 19 J. Legal Med. 397-430 (1998).

INTERNET REFERENCES

Alternative Dispute Resolution Resources
http://adrr.com

American Arbitration Association
http://www.adr.org

American Bar Association Section of Dispute Resolution
http://www.abanet.org/dispute

Chartered Institute of Arbitrators
http://www.arbitrators.org

Conflict Research Consortium
http://www.colorado.edu/conflict

CPR Institute for Dispute Resolution
http://www.cpradr.org

Georgetown University ADR resources page
http://www.ll.georgetown.edu/lr/rs/adr.html

Guide to Alternate Dispute Resolution
http://hg.org/adr.html

Institute for Conflict Analysis and Resolution
http://web.gmu.edu/departments/ICAR/

Law Forum: Alternative Dispute Resolution
http://www.lawforum.net/services/alternative.htm

Mediation Information and Resource Center
http://www.mediate.com

Program on Negotiation at Harvard Law School
http://www.pon.harvard.edu

Self-Administered ADR: Its Advantages and How it Works
http://www.cpradr.org/selfadm.htm

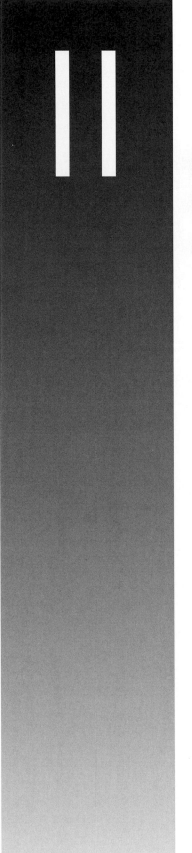

Medical Licensure, Credentialing, Privileging, and Profiling

7

Medical Practice: Education and Licensure

S. SANDY SANBAR, M.D., Ph.D., J.D., F.C.L.M.
DANIEL J. GAMINO, J.D.

THE "RIGHT" TO BE A PHYSICIAN
MEDICAL SCHOOL ADMISSION CRITERIA
MEDICAL SCHOOL RETENTION AND GRADUATION
MEDICAL LICENSURE
CONCLUSION

Medical education—from admission to medical school to completion of postgraduate training—occurs in a definite legal framework. Both the student and the state enjoy certain legal rights and duties.

State licensure to practice medicine and surgery is also basic. The requirements for licensure and the ways in which that medical licensure may be lost or curtailed are many.

More than 400 years ago Shakespeare observed, "Oh, how full of briers is this working-day world."[1] This observation is still true for medicine today. This chapter points out the briers.

THE "RIGHT" TO BE A PHYSICIAN

There is no vested property or constitutional right to attend medical school. However, acceptance to a medical school class may not be based on any violation of the applicant's general civil rights nor may requirements be arbitrary or capricious. A medical school may not employ quotas but may employ some affirmative action in selecting students. The relationship of the medical student and the school is an enforceable contractual one. Some courts have held that a student admitted to medical school has a "liberty right or interest" mandating procedural due process necessary for administrative problems and substantive due process for disciplinary situations. The general rule is one of fair play in making rules regarding information, discipline, and punishment.

MEDICAL SCHOOL ADMISSION CRITERIA

Each medical school, public or private, can establish its own admission standards. The admission criteria must be uniformly applied to each candidate. The primary area of legal interest in medical school admissions is that of affirmative action admissions programs, which make race, gen-

der, or ethnic origin a factor of greater or lesser degree in the acceptance decision.

Early medical school admission cases focused on a variety of legal theories. The courts have allowed the return of entrance application fees under a theory of false pretenses when the standards used for admission were not in keeping with those advertised in the medical school's bulletin.[2] Professional schools have been ordered to award degrees to students who were denied admission or retention on an arbitrary or unreasonable basis.[3]

Judicial review

Judicial review of the medical school admissions process on constitutional equal protection grounds requires the existence of "state action" sufficient to trigger the provisions of the applicable constitutional provision or federal statute. In *Cannon v. University of Chicago* a female student's suit under the federal gender and age discrimination statutes was denied as failing to state a cause of action due to a failure to prove the existence of state action.[4]

In a decision foreshadowing the *Bakke* decision, the Court of Appeals of New York held that a strict scrutiny standard of review applied to racial reverse discrimination in medical school admissions. The New York court did not discuss less restrictive alternatives available to the university because the cessation of the minority admissions program still would not have entitled the plaintiff to a place in the incoming class.[5]

The Bakke decision

The seminal court decision involving medical school admission requirements is that of *University of California Regents v. Bakke*.[6] In that case Mr. Bakke was denied admission to the University of California, Davis Medical School because

medical school. This approach is typical in educational contract cases. However, it is at variance from the more traditional viewpoint that a contract should be construed strictly with respect to the person drafting the contract, in this case the medical school.[20]

Handicapped students

The ADA, originally enacted by Congress in 1990, is changing how medical schools and all other schools approach handicapped students.[21] This act requires medical schools to make "reasonable accommodations" for students with certain physical and mental disabilities. Dyslexia, narcolepsy, drug and alcohol dependency, and mental disorders all fall within the scope of disabilities and certain protections of the law, along with the more traditional physical handicaps.[22] Little case law has as yet developed.

Substance and content of medical school education

Increasingly the demands to include new information in the medical school curriculum (e.g., courses on acquired immunodeficiency syndrome [AIDS]) have produced a problem of serious dimensions in medical school class scheduling. The phenomenon can be seen both within the medical school educational process and the process of health care law instruction within the legal community.[23]

The AIDS crisis exemplifies the difficulty of providing education and maintaining medical ethics within the medical school process. The medical student is presented with the dilemma when assigned to a rotation that requires treatment of AIDS patients. AIDS demonstrates the potential for new requirements of specific substantive courses within medical school education by state law, a step that would be historically unique within the medical school process.[24]

Substance of content requirements also has been increasingly dictated in a variety of other areas, on both a voluntary and an involuntary basis.[25] These trends point to the tendency toward further standardization of the medical school education process.

House officers

A medical school graduate is required to complete at least one year of postgraduate training or residency, usually in a hospital. Many then go on to advanced training programs, further residency training, and fellowships certified by a variety of organizations.

In the past, house officers were considered employees and were subject to the whim of the hospital administration. California case law, noting the impact of the arbitrary cancellation of a house officer's contract on his or her career, imposed the requirement of a due process hearing, with all its protections.[26]

Clinical training programs raise potential questions in the area of medical malpractice. There is considerable divergence among jurisdictions on the standard of care for residents in the academic medical context. Although *Rusk v. Akron General Hospital* represents the position that a special standard of care is applicable for residents within the clinical context, more recent cases suggest that the standard of care to be applied should be the standard of a general physician or the standard of the specialty in which the resident is being trained.[27–29] Although there appear to be no reported cases covering the standard of care for medical students, the medical student, intern, or resident must be aware that he or she could be held to the standard of care applicable to the attending physician supervising his or her education and clinical process.[30]

In addition, the team-teaching approach presents informed consent issues. Consent is specific to the individual physician. Thus consent given by the patient to allow the attending physician to engage in a procedure does not automatically grant consent for the procedure to be performed by proxy (e.g., by a resident or intern), even if the procedure is done at the attending physician's or senior resident's request.[31] In the academic medical context several possibilities for liability arise that do not normally arise within the private practice setting. The attending physician and student must be aware of the potential for liability, take steps to ensure proper consent on the part of the patients, and maintain the highest possible standards of care.[32]

MEDICAL LICENSURE

Theory and requirements

Power of the state. To exclude any incompetent practitioners, the state may require that professionals obtain a license to practice medicine and to perform surgery. The practice of medicine is viewed as a privilege granted by the state licensure board.[33] The state has a right to continue to evaluate a physician's professional practice. "The right of a physician to toil in his profession . . . with all its sanctity and safeguards is not absolute. It must yield to the paramount right of government to protect the public health by any rational means."[34]

Licensing statutes are justified under a state's sovereign power to protect the health and welfare of its citizens. Medical practice acts create and define the composition of a state medical board, define the requirements for licensure, and vest the board with the authority to license candidates. The state medical board is mandated to regulate the practice of medicine in the public interest and to advance the medical profession. Establishing and vigilantly enforcing standards of conduct to ensure the competence and the scruples of physicians are the responsibilities of the board. This stewardship is viewed by courts as an entrustment by the state and is subject to judicial review.

Licensure statutes were originally designed to exclude the untutored, unskilled, and incompetent from the practice of medicine by certifying a minimally acceptable qualification of training, knowledge, and competence after evaluating and certifying submitted credentials. In a landmark case in 1898 the U.S. Supreme Court stated that licensure powers could be extended beyond credentialing to include standards of behavior and ethics. The case held that, in a physician, "character is as important a qualification as knowledge."[35] Sanctions may include denial of license, revocation of license, suspension of license, probation, oral or written reprimands, imposition of monetary fines, and censuring.

The authority of the courts to oversee the licensing of physicians also is mandated by statute. The courts, however, seldom intercede until the physician has completely exhausted his or her administrative remedies, unless the licensing board has acted wholly outside of its jurisdiction. At the conclusion of the administrative proceedings, the courts typically intervene only when the physician successfully argues that the licensing board violated the physician's constitutional rights, acted outside of its jurisdiction, or failed to follow its own rules and regulations.

Types of licensure. Virtually all state medical licenses are unlimited (i.e., unrestricted to any particular branch of medicine or surgery). Thus the holder of a medical license may take routine histories and do physical examinations or perform specialized neurosurgery under the same license.

Some states have a restricted license for postgraduate training, such as residency. Other states issue limited or special licenses governed by specified restrictions.[36] In some cases the credentialing process is delegated de facto to the supervising institution. Physicians in state hospitals or correctional facilities sometimes hold licenses restricted to such institutional use. Again, the respective state legislature, medical board, or both, sets forth the specific types of licensure available in that state.

Obtaining a license. As a necessary function of its duty to protect the public interest, a state board may require physicians and related practitioners to demonstrate a certain degree of skill and learning. It may also include conditions of licensure bearing a direct, substantial, and reasonable relationship to the practice of medicine, such as a statutorily specified amount of malpractice insurance coverage, before the licensee may practice medicine. In exercising its licensing authority the state has the inherent power to determine precisely the qualifications the applicant must possess. It may investigate educational credentials, professional competence, and moral character. The applicant bears the burden to prove his or her fulfillment of all requirements for licensure.

U.S. citizenship was once required for medical licensure, but that requirement was struck down by the U.S. Supreme Court in 1973 as unconstitutional discrimination. Another barrier to licensure was a residency requirement of a specific number of months. That requirement also was struck down as discrimination that only furthered the parochial interest of state physicians. Closely related to residency restrictions is reciprocity licensure. A state is not required to license a physician merely because he or she holds a license in another state; otherwise the state would be obligated to automatically grant a license to everyone who holds a license in every other state. Thus reciprocity is neither constitutionally discriminatory nor an infringement on a physician's rights and privilege of practice. Most states also have established a minimum age of 21 years for licensure.

Invariably, "good moral character" is required for licensure. A typical reason for denying a license on that ground is a prior criminal conviction, even if the crime on which the conviction was based has no obvious connection with the practice of medicine. Such candidates must be prepared to demonstrate total rehabilitation. The nature of the offense is a material consideration. For example, a licensing board should be prepared to differentiate between a trespass conviction arising out of a 1970s antiwar demonstration and the offense of grand larceny.

State requirements of educational achievement for licensure vary but have generally been upheld. Educational requirements cannot be arbitrary and must be rationally related to competence. Requirements of preprofessional education and professional education from "accredited schools" have been held reasonable and valid.[37] Experience requirements of postgraduate education are likewise considered to be rational, reasonable, and valid. If an individual's experience has provided comparable or superior education but licensure required a diploma, it has been held that the diploma requirement was not capricious or arbitrary and did not deprive one of a constitutional right of due process or equal protection.[38] Requiring malpractice insurance, a recent mandate in at least one state (Idaho), was upheld as reasonable because it bears a rational relationship to the welfare of citizens.

Supervision and disciplinary sanctions

Grounds for discipline. Until a few years ago, licensure sanctions against physicians resulting from inadequate patient care were few and far between, in large part because of the reluctance of physicians to report or take action against colleagues. In particular, physicians feared that their colleagues who were reported would sue them for libel, slander, or restraint of trade. In addition, the boards were nearly impotent, having more restricted investigative abilities and less sanctioning authority than they enjoy today.

Recently, however, courts have held hospitals and physicians liable for failure to "ferret out" bad physicians. Legislatures have given administrative agencies new power and have granted immunity to honorable informants and their authorized listeners. Licensing boards no longer have to wait for a formal report or complaint; they may now begin an inquiry and proceedings on their own initiative.

Grounds for discipline of the medical licensee are generally set forth in statute as "unprofessional conduct"[39] or violation of the Medical Practice Act.

The least precise ground for disciplinary action is the allegation of unprofessional, immoral, dishonorable, or gross misconduct.[40–44] Such concepts are difficult to define. It is manifestly impossible to categorize all of the acts subject to discipline. Such unspecific and vague standards are enforceable because there is a common professional understanding of what the public interest requires. Precise definitions made by the state medical boards are usually left intact, but on occasion the courts reverse them and impose their own definitions. As long as a board bases its finding of unprofessional conduct or gross misconduct on expert testimony (on the record) as to the proper standard of care, the board should be upheld.

Discipline on grounds of incompetence is also somewhat vague and difficult to define. Incompetence is not established by rare and isolated instances of inadequate performance; rather, repeated defects in the exercise of everyday skills are the gist of such complaints. In rare cases a single act of gross negligence is so wanton that it sufficiently demonstrates incompetence.

Fraud and deceit in the practice of medicine are grounds for discipline; most often fraud or deceit is alleged when a physician bills a third party (Medicare or an insurance company) for work he or she did not perform. Fraud or deceit in nonprofessional activities is an offense more often in the nature of moral turpitude or immoral conduct.

A felony conviction empowers the board in most states to revoke a license.[45] In some states, revocation cannot occur until all appeals have been exhausted. Misconduct in another state also may be grounds for revocation. Fraudulently obtaining a license or aiding and assisting an unlicensed practitioner in the practice of medicine also are grounds for revocation.

Medical boards have become increasingly active in dealing with physicians who practice while impaired by alcohol or controlled substances. Some states track these physicians through the traditional disciplinary route. Other states have formally established diversion recovery programs that give physicians an opportunity to avoid formal disciplinary proceedings if they quickly agree to comprehensive treatment, supervision of their medical practice, and random testing.

Defenses to disciplinary charges. One of the most common practitioner defenses is that due process of law was denied by the board's commingling of investigative and adjudicatory functions within the same administrative agency. Courts have generally rejected this argument, stating that, absent a showing of bias, there was not sufficient risk of prejudice to taint the decision.[46]

Occasionally, disciplinary proceedings are brought years after the alleged improper conduct of the physician, most often because of the initial unwillingness of witnesses to come forward or because of the lengthy processes in state and federal courts. Generally a defense of inordinate delay in prosecution for an alleged offense from the too distant past, though valid in criminal and civil judicial proceedings, has been considered an invalid defense in administrative disciplinary proceedings.[47] However, some states specifically include a statute of limitations. Whether or not he or she practices in one of the few states with a statute of limitations on medical board disciplinary proceedings, the physician can defend by asserting the "equitable doctrine of laches." This doctrine protects defendants in cases of an unexcused delay in bringing a disciplinary procedure that is inequitably prejudicial to the defendant.

Entrapment is a defense that asserts that law enforcement agents coerced, tricked, induced, or persuaded the defendant physician to commit an offense that would not have been committed if not for the agents' conduct. Entrapment may be a valid defense, but in a few cases the defense has been rejected as being limited to criminal proceedings.[48]

Evidence gained by unlawful search and seizure may sometimes be suppressed and may constitute a successful defense. Courts typically explore the policies underlying the exclusionary rule before automatically applying it to professional licensure proceedings.[49] However, this evidence is not always subject to the usual prohibition because of the necessity of strict supervision in certain highly regulated business activities (e.g., firearms or narcotics).[50]

Double jeopardy (the risk of double punishment for a single offense), alleged in instances of multiple license revocations, has been held an invalid defense. In addition, a board may impose discipline even when the physician has prevailed in a related criminal proceeding and the principle of double jeopardy does not apply.[51]

A defense of recovery from an impairment (with or without monitoring from an impaired physician committee) or assertion of the right to resume practice after voluntary surrender of license is not in and of itself a defense in sanction proceedings. Typical board considerations when recovery is alleged include establishing that the impairment was the cause of misconduct, that the subject has indeed recovered, that the recovery has arrested the threat to public health and safety, and that relapse is unlikely.

Presentation by a convicted felon of a "certificate of rehabilitation" under a "Rehabilitated Convicted Offenders Act" is not a dispositive defense. Proof of a degree of rehabilitation does not preclude a license authority from disqualifying applicants.[52]

A jurisdictional challenge based on voluntary surrender of (or failure to renew) a license depends on whether the physician retains any remaining rights to revive the license. Furthermore, the state can assert an interest in going forward with its proof at a time when evidence and witnesses' memories are fresh.[53]

R.P. Reeves has described the defense of winning by "intimidation."[54] Such defenses include "tying up" board members or assistant attorneys general and staff with repeated requests for continuances, voluminous discovery requests, subpoenas for spurious documents or witnesses, floods of character witnesses, applications for stays, and collateral attacks in federal court.

Finally, physicians facing disciplinary charges have tried to bring federal civil rights actions under 42 U.S.C. §1983. Because boards are sitting in both their prosecutorial and quasi-judicial capacities when carrying out disciplinary functions, board members and their staffs are usually granted absolute immunity from such suits.[55] Physicians who bring such suits also may be ordered to pay the attorney fees of their successful opponents.

Disciplinary proceedings after formal charges are filed.
The license to practice medicine and surgery is a right substantive enough to warrant compliance with all the requirements of due process (i.e., proper notice of charges, notice of the hearing before a properly constituted tribunal, the right to cross-examine and produce witnesses, and the right to a full consideration and fair determination based on the facts).[56]

Proper notice need not be exact and formal, but it must be sufficient to permit a full opportunity to prepare an adequate defense.[57] Hearings, which are usually required by statute to be public, are typically held before a hearing officer or, because of financial constraints, the board en banc without a hearing officer. The structure of the hearings is controlled by statute or agency rules. Some boards employ a hearing officer who reviews the records of the investigative officers and makes findings of fact, conclusions of law, and recommendations. Other boards employ a hearing officer to sit only as a judge who rules on motions and the admissibility of evidentiary documents while the board sits as a jury. Other board cases are tried by a subcommittee of the entire board, and the subcommittee then reports its findings and recommendations to the board en banc.

In whatever process is devised under state law, full opportunity must be given to challenge the testimony of adverse witnesses and other evidence in a proceeding before the full board.[58] The right to appear with counsel is uniform. During the pendency of the formal adjudicatory hearing, the board, as the decision-maker, must be sufficiently separated from its own investigative agents so that it may be free from bias and prejudice.[59]

The rules of evidence in a board hearing are not identical to courthouse rules of evidence. Hearsay testimony, both written and oral, is commonly admissible as long as it goes to prove an issue and sustain a finding. The evidence must be substantive. Whether the evidence must be sufficient to establish a "preponderance," a "clear preponderance," "clear and satisfactory proof," or "clear and convincing proof" varies by state.[60]

The final decision, rendered by a hearing officer or a board en banc, must adopt specific findings of fact, which is a concise and explicit statement of the events supporting the decision. It also must contain conclusions of law in a form that permits judicial review. Appeals to the judicial process generally are limited to reviews, not retrials. Stays pending further appeal are within the discretion of the court.[61] Courts are sometimes prohibited by statute from granting such stays, but even then a court can intervene with a stay if the physician successfully asserts that he or she is likely to prevail on a procedural due process claim. When a board has determined its sanction, courts are generally reluctant to interfere unless persuaded that there has been a clear abuse of discretion.

Discovery. Efforts to determine the nature and extent of witnesses against a defendant physician before the time of hearing are termed *discovery*. The administrative law process does not normally offer opportunity for full use of normal pretrial discovery. Depositions, interrogatories, requests to produce, requests for admission, and inspection of site usually may not be used to determine the strength and intensity of the state board's case.

Recusal of board members. Generally, state administrative law provides a mechanism to request the recusal of any board member who "cannot accord a fair and impartial hearing or consideration."[62] Usually that request must be accompanied by an affidavit and must be promptly filed upon discovery of the alleged disqualification, stating with particularity the grounds on which it is claimed that a fair and impartial hearing cannot be accorded. This threshold issue must be determined quickly by the board.

This pretrial remedy must be exercised with care. An unsuccessful or frivolous attempt to disqualify a board member may ignite other board members' passions against the defendant physician. Historically this remedy is rarely sought in the administrative law process and is rarely granted. There is a strong presumption that the administrative tribunal is unbiased.[63] However, if evaluation of the case and the board's process indicates substantial grounds that make recusal necessary, it should be strongly considered.

Attorney fees. Some states' statutes provide that, when an administrative proceeding is brought without reasonable basis or is frivolous, the board may become liable for the licensee's attorney fees.[64] This statute is powerful. Under the proper circumstances it can be an "equalizer" to help the defendant physician retain his or her rights. Making aggressive demands for attorney fees and putting the agency on notice may give a defendant physician leverage in settlement negotiations or may result in the dismissal of charges.

Sanctions. All state boards have laws authorizing sanctions, some more detailed than others.[65] License revocation is the most severe sanction available because its term is indefinite, usually "forever placing the offender beyond the pale."[66] Other sanctions include suspension, probation, written or oral reprimand, censure, curtailment of professional activities, oral or written competency exam, community service, re-education, and monetary fines.

Restoration of a revoked license requires a petition and review process that could take years to complete. If the cause was physician impairment and if a board so chooses, a surrendered license may be restored without protracted and formalized procedures if and when demonstrated recovery can be established. Suspension of a license is similar to a revocation, except that it is for a limited period of time.

Probation is a formalized sanction in which a formal surveillance procedure is initiated. Terms and conditions of probation must be set forth in the board order. Systematic and periodic reviews are implemented, typically for years, especially when related to mental illness or substance abuse/dependence, because relapse remains a valid concern years later.[67]

Reprimand (a formal and sharp rebuke of record) and censure (a judgment of fault and blame of record) are intended to induce a mending of ways. They are lenient sanctions when other sanctions are deemed too severe. In practice, such actions are more effective as a means of defining minimal acceptable levels of conduct than as a means of disciplinary enforcement. Licenses may be restricted to prohibit writing any prescriptions, to prohibit writing Schedule II controlled drugs, to limit hospital practice, or to limit all practice beyond supervised positions in state hospitals or teaching centers. In the past, restricted licensure has been used to provide supervision of the wayward, but this practice has fallen from favor because of an insufficient emphasis on the rehabilitation of restricted physicians.

Sanctions are generally imposed only after the physician has received notice and an opportunity to be heard in the adversary proceeding, with witnesses, cross-examination, and the like as set forth earlier. However, if a board determines that there is an imminent and material danger to patients or public health, safety, and welfare, a summary suspension, and later hearing, can be imposed. However, the physician is entitled to a prompt, postsuspension hearing that concludes without appreciable delay.[68] Summary suspension is the single exception to the rule that sanctions are imposed only after a full hearing.

Sanctions to protect the public are the primary responsibility of the medical board. Public opinion has become increasingly critical of the paucity of revocations, inadequate supervision, and investigative impotence.[69] A perception persists that professional compassion for a colleague can sacrifice public protection and that some sanctions are inconsistent, lenient, and seemingly ineffective. Contributing factors to the inadequacy of the boards include court-issued stay orders, injunctions, appeals, new trials granted on technical grounds, inadequate financing, and resistance by defense attorneys, hospital administrators, and district attorneys.

National collectors of disciplinary data. Three national clearinghouses currently collect disciplinary data on physicians. These data are retained and made available to other boards in states where a physician may hold a license, principally in response to reports of physicians "jumping jurisdictions" after disciplinary action is taken in one state of licensure.

The Federation of State Medical Boards in Fort Worth, Texas, has maintained a national clearinghouse on physician discipline for several years.[70] The federation collects information about disciplinary actions taken by the 65 member jurisdictions and then transmits a summary of those actions to each of the other jurisdictions on a monthly basis. State medical boards can then contact a sister state and obtain details of disciplinary action taken against a physician who is also licensed in their state.

A part of the 1986 Health Care Quality Improvement Act (Pub. L. 99–660) established the National Practitioner Data Bank.[71] Like many federal projects, the data bank was initially slow to receive adequate funding and slow to get under way. The legislation included a requirement that hospitals must query the data bank at least every 2 years about all physicians on their staff. Medical boards and certain others also may query the data bank. Federal law requires medical boards and hospital staffs that impose a curtailment on a license of more than 30 days to report that incident to the data bank.

The third national clearinghouse will be under the Health Insurance Portability and Accountability Act (HIPAA) (see Chapter 19).

Appeals. Judicial review of an administrative decision usually is limited to determining whether the administrative agency acted arbitrarily, capriciously, or fraudulently; whether the order was substantially supported by the evidence presented; or whether the administrative agency's actions were within the scope of its legal authority as created by the statute. Although courts review a decision of law made by the administrative agency, decisions regarding the credibility of evidence and witnesses ordinarily are a matter for the administrative agency itself and are overturned only if they are clearly contrary to the weight of the evidence. Courts seldom intervene to substitute their judgment in determining a sanction or an assessment of mitigating circumstances.

Although there is no fundamental right to appeal an administrative decision, virtually all jurisdictions grant appeal by state statute. Licensees have fought any limitation of the appeals process by arguing that such limits would compromise access to the judicial process and limit board accountability.

Typically, courts restrict appeals to the appeals process specified by statute. This restriction could result in denying judicial access until the board has had a rehearing or the petitioner has exhausted all other administrative remedies. Some statutes typically limit judicial appeals to those approved by the board, known as *by leave appeals*, as opposed to those allowed by right. Courts typically limit their scope of review to the issues of law. Rarely, however, courts have granted a new trial as part of the appeals process, as if no administrative proceeding had occurred.

As a practical matter, some state courts may choose to review cases however they like, accepting limits that suit their convenience or needs. On one hand, they may choose to protect a licensee from administrative arbitrariness with strict scrutiny.[72] On the other hand, they may choose to accept virtually all board findings with routine affirmance.

Restoration of a license. Restoration of a license after revocation or suspension is a matter of serious concern for the public, the profession, and the physician. The odds of restoration are against the physician. And the physician clearly bears the burden of proof to demonstrate that there has been a substantial change of conditions in his or her qualifications, practice methods, or both since the discipline was originally imposed. The process of reinstatement has no due process entitlements, supposedly because reinstatement fights are not substantive enough property rights to warrant such protection.[73]

A surrendered license cannot be used to avoid a restoration process and consequent hearing and sanction. Licenses so surrendered are deemed final. In suspension, as compared with revocation, resumption of practice is automatic. There also is an early automatic reinstatement for a licensee who has failed to pay a routine renewal fee.

In the restoration process, a petition must be submitted (usually after at least one year) to initiate a preliminary investigative process. The investigation might involve an interview of the petitioner, review of character references, and contacts with other law enforcement agencies. The board might take steps to ensure that those providing character references are fully familiar with the facts the board found that led to the initial loss of license. Board concern focuses on rehabilitation and maintenance of skills, and it always keeps the public interest in mind. If a restoration petition is denied, reconsideration, future resubmission, or court challenges are available as alternative appeals. A court appeal of a denied reinstatement petition has virtually no chance of success because the decision is left to the board's discretion. A board may require a minimum waiting period before resubmission of a reinstatement petition.

CONCLUSION

Physicians and the medical services they provide greatly affect public health, safety, and welfare. Because of that impact and the historically high-profile nature of the medical profession, state government has the authority to regulate medical education and to erect a medical licensure process. The state also exercises a continuing jurisdiction over the professional activities of licensed physicians and may impose sanctions thereon. Currently the pendulum of public opinion is swinging to favor more oversight and accountability of physicians, rather than less.

ENDNOTES

1. Shakespeare, *As You Like It*, Act 1, Scene 3.
2. *Steinberg v. Chicago Medical School*, 354 N.E. 2d 586 (Ill. App. 1976).
3. *DeMarco v. Chicago Medical School*, 352 N.E. 2d 356 (Ill. App. 1976); *In re Florida Board of bar Examiners*, 339 So. 2d 637 (Fla. 1970).
4. *Cannon v. University of Chicago*, 559 F. 2d 1063 (7th Cir. 1977).
5. *Alevy v. Down State Medical Center* 384 N.Y.S. 2d 82 (1976).
6. *University of California Regents v. Bakke*, 438 U.S. 265 (1978).
7. *Craig v. Boren*, 429 U.S. 190 (1976).
8. Smith, *A Third Rate Case Shouldn't Make Hard Law*, Jurisdoctor 31 (Feb. 1978).
9. *DeFunis v. Odegoard*, 416 U.S. 312, 94 S.Ct. 1704, 40 L.Ed. 2d 164 (1974).
10. *DeFunis v. Odegoard*, 529 P. 2d 438 (Wash. 1974).
11. Pub. L. 101-336, 104 Stat. 327 (codified at 42 U.S.C. §121 01 *et seq.*). An excellent discussion of the ADA is found at Jones, *Overview and Essential Requirements of the Americans with Disabilities Act*, 64 Temple L. R. 471 (Summer 1991).
12. 42 U.S.C. §12181.
13. As examples, *see Kaltenberger v. Ohio College of Podiatric Medicine*, 162 F. 3d 432 (6th Cir. 1998); and *El Kouni v. Trustees of Boston University*, 169 F. Supp. 211 (D. Mass. 2001).
14. *Board of Curators of the University of Missouri v. Horowitz*, 96 S.Ct. 948 (1978).
15. *Sanders v. Ajir*, 555 F. Supp. 240 (W.D. Wis. 1983).
16. *Ross v. Pennsylvania State University*, 445 F. Supp. 147 (M.D. Penn. 1978).
17. *Goss v. Lopez*, 95 S.Ct. 729 (1975).
18. *Matthews v. Eldridge*, 424 U.S. 319 (1976).
19. *Ewing v. Board of Regents University of Michigan*, 742 F. 2d 913 (6th Cir. 1984), *cert. granted* 53 U.S.L.W. 3687 (U.S. Mar. 25, 1985).
20. *Lions v. Salva Regina College*, 568 F. 2d 200 (1st Cir. 1977).
21. 42 U.S.C. §12101 *et seq.*
22. S. Rep. No. 116, 101st Cong., 1st Sess. 22 (1989); H.R. Rep. No. 485, 101st Cong., 2d Sess. 56 (1990).
23. *Teaching Health Law, A Symposium*, 38 J. Legal Educ. 489-497, 505-509, 545-554, 567-576 (Dec. 1988).
24. J.W. Burnside, *AIDS and Medical Education*, 10 J. Legal Med. 19 (Nov. 1, 1989).
25. Allen R. Felhous & Robert D. Miller, *Health Law and Mental Health Law Courses in U.S. Medical Schools*, 15 Bull. Am. Acad. Psychiatric Law 319 (Dec. 1987).
26. *Enehiol v. Winkler*, 20 Cal. 3d 267, 142 Cal. Rptr. 418, 572 P. 2d 32 (1977).
27. *Rusk v. Akron General Hospital*, 84 Ohio App. 2d 292, 171 N.E. 2d 378 (1987).
28. *McBride v. United States*, 462 F. 2d 72 (9th Cir. 1972).
29. *Pratt v. Stein*, 298 Pa. Super. 92, 444 A. 2d 674 (1982).
30. Ben A. Rich, *Malpractice Issues in the Academic Medical Center*, 36 Del. Law J. 641-646 (Dec. 1987).
31. *Id.* at 652.
32. Harold I. Hirsch, *The Evils of Admitting Private Patients to Hospitals with Teaching Programs: A View from Outside the Ivory Tower*, 16 Legal Aspects Med. Prac. (Nov. 1988).
33. *See, e.g.*, 59 O.S. 2001, §620.
34. *Lawrence v. Board of Registration in Medicine*, 239 Mass. 424, 428, 132 N.E. 174 (1921).
35. *Hawke v. New York*, 170 U.S. 189, 194 (1898).
36. *See, e.g.*, 59 O.S. 2001, §493.4.
37. *Dent v. West Virginia*, 129 U.S. 114, 123 (1888).
38. *In re Hansen*, 275 N.W. 2d 700 (Minn. 1978).
39. *See, e.g.*, 59 O.S. 2001, §509.

40. This includes false or deceptive advertising. Many states have specific statutes and regulations providing for discipline on this ground.

41. *Brun v. Lazell*, 172 Md. 314, 191 A. 240 (1937) (revocation of license to practice dentistry based on guilty plea to criminal charges of indecent exposure).

42. *Raymond v. Board of Registration in Medicine*, 387 Mass. 708, 443 N.E. 2d 391-394 (1982) (where the board disciplined a physician upon his conviction for possession of unregistered submachine guns the court held that "lack of good moral character and conduct that undermines public confidence in the integrity of the medical profession are grounds for discipline").

43. *Urick v. Comm. Board of Osteopath Examination*, 43 Pa. Commonw. 248, 402 A. 2d 290 (1979) (court upheld licensure revocation for committing a crime of moral turpitude where the physician was convicted of conspiracy to use the mails to defraud and conspiracy to unlawfully distribute and possess Schedule II controlled substances).

44. *Lawrence v. Board of Registration in Medicine*, 239 Mass. 424, 428, 430, 132 N.E. 174 (1921) (gross misconduct in the practice of medicine is not too indefinite as a ground for discipline).

45. Includes felonies clearly unrelated to the practice of medicine, such as income tax evasion.

46. *Withrow v. Larkin*, 421 U.S. 35 (1975).

47. Note that a statute of limitations defense was not valid to block admission into evidence in a licensure proceeding, a felony conviction more than 3 years old was admissible, even where that state required that legal actions be commenced within 3 years. *Colorado State Board of Medical Examiners v. Jorganson*, 198 Colo. 275, 599 P. 2d 869 (1979).

48. *See generally* R.P. Reaves, *The Law of Professional Licensing and Certification*, 255-257 (1st ed. 1984).

49. *See, e.g., Emslie v. State Bar of California*, 11 Cal. 3d 210, 520 P. 2d 991, 1000 (1974) (rule not applied to attorney disciplinary action); *Elder v. Board of Medical Examiners*, 241 Cal. App. 2d 246, 50 Cal. Rptr. 304 (1966), *cert. denied* 385 U.S. 101 (1967) (rule applied in disciplinary action against physician).

50. *United States v. Biswell*, 406 U.S. 311 (1972).

51. *Arthurs v. Board of Registration in Medicine*, 383 Mass. 299, 418 N.E. 2d 1236 (1981).

52. *Hyland v. Kehayas*, 157 N.J. Super. 258, 384 A. 2d 902 (1978).

53. *See Cross v. Colo. State Bar of Dental Examiners*, 37 Colo. App. 504, 508, 552 P. 2d 38 (1976) ("It is logical and sensible that where such grave charges of . . . unprofessional or dishonorable conduct are alleged, the Board has the right to preserve (any) evidence . . . of these charges otherwise witnesses may disappear and the passage of time itself may well dim or even eradicate the memory of the witnesses and thus preclude the construction of an adequate record.")

54. R.P. Reeves, *The Law of Professional Licensing and Certification*, 258 (1st ed. 1984). But such tactics may lead to assessment of attorney fees or costs in some states, 12 O.S. 2001, §941B and 75 O.S. 2001, §318D.

55. *See, e.g., Horowitz v. State Board of Medical Examiners of Colorado*, 822 F. 2d 1508 (10th Cir.) (members of state medical board absolutely immune for actions in connection with suspension of podiatrist's licensure), *cert. denied* 484 U.S. 964 (1987); *Vakas v. Rodriquez*, P. 2d 1293 (10th Cir.), *cert. denied* 469 U.S. 981 (1984); *see Batz v. Economou*, 438 U.S. 478, 508-517 (1978).

56. *Johnson v. Board of Governors of Registered Dentists of the State of Oklahoma*, 913 P. 2d 1339 (Okla. 1996).

57. *Bloch v. Ambach*, 528 N.Y.S. 2d 204 (N.Y. App. Div. 1988).

58. *Physicians and Surgeons*, 61 Am. Jur. 2d. §105 (1981).

59. *Morrissey v. Brewer*, 408 U.S. 471, 92 S.Ct. 2593, 33 L.Ed. 2d 494 (1972).

60. *See, e.g., Johnson v. Board of Governors of Registered Dentists, supra.*

61. *See, e.g.,* 75 O.S. 2001, §319.

62. *See, e.g.,* 75 O.S. 1991, §316.

63. *Schneider v. McClure*, 456 U.S. 188, 102 S.Ct. 1665, 72 L.Ed. 2d (1982); *National Labor Relations Board v. Ohio New & Rebuilt Parts, Inc.*, 760 F. 2d 1443 (6th Cir.), *cert. denied* 474 U.S. 1020 (1980).

64. *See, e.g.,* 12 O.S. 2001, §941B, and 75 O.S. 2001, §318.

65. *See, e.g.,* 59 O.S. 2001, §509.1.

66. Derbyshire, *Offenders and Offenses*, 19 Hosp. Prac. 981 (1984).

67. Shore, *The Impaired Physician, Four Years After*, J.A.M.A. 248:3127 (1982).

68. *See Barry v. Barchi*, 443 U.S. 55, 66 (1979); *Ampueto v. Department of Professional Regulation*, 410 So. 2d 213 (Fla. D.C. App. 1982) (6-month delay in postsuspension hearing found unreasonable).

69. *See* 18 Hosp. Prac. 251 (1983) (10-year saga of a license revocation).

70. Federation of State Medical Boards, 2630 West Freeway, Suite 138, Fort Worth, TX 76102-7199.

71. Codified at 42 U.S.C. §11101 *et seq.*

72. R.P. Reeves, *supra* note 48, at 276.

73. *Hicks v. Georgia State Board of Pharmacy*, 553 F. Supp. 314 (Ga. 1982), citing *Meachum v. Fano*, 427 U.S. 215, 228 (1976).

8 Medical Staff Peer Review in the Credentialing and Privileging of Physicians

MARVIN H. FIRESTONE, M.D., J.D., F.C.L.M.

MEDICAL STAFF PEER REVIEW
CREDENTIALING
PRIVILEGING
PROCTORING
DUE PROCESS
PHYSICIAN RIGHTS UNDER MANAGED CARE
APPLICATION OF DUE PROCESS PRINCIPLES
CONFIDENTIALITY AND PEER REVIEW PRIVILEGE
PEER REVIEW CORRECTIVE ACTION: AN UNFAIR PROCESS?

MEDICAL STAFF PEER REVIEW

The purpose of credentialing medical staff is to maintain quality patient care. This is an ongoing process during which the physician's training, skill, experience, and clinical competence are evaluated to ensure that the privileges granted match the physician's expertise.[1] The application of "corporate liability" concepts to hospital malpractice lawsuits after the landmark case of *Darling v. Charleston Community Memorial Hospital*[2] led to more aggressive physician peer review because hospitals could no longer deny responsibility for acts and omissions by their staff physicians. To encourage more aggressive peer review by the medical staffs, many states have enacted immunity statutes to protect hospitals' peer review committees.[3] In addition, federal law related to Medicare and Medicaid programs mandate some form of peer review if hospitals are to be compensated for services.[4] Therefore federal and state laws, regulations, and case law all emphasize a hospital's duty to monitor patient care and serve as the impetus for credentialing. The Joint Committee on Accreditation of Healthcare Organizations (JCAHO) also requires its member hospitals to have a credentialing process in place for accreditation and hold the hospital's governing board ultimately responsible for peer review by its medical staff.[5]

The Health Care Quality Improvement Act (HCQIA) of 1986 grants health care entities and peer review committees immunity from liability for credentialing and privileging activities as long as due process is afforded the affected physician. The HCQIA also established the National Practitioner Data Bank (NPDB), an information clearinghouse regarding licensure actions, malpractice payments, and final adverse actions taken by hospitals and other health care entities that restrict physicians' practice privileges for more than 30 days. Hospitals and other health care entities must also query the NPDB when credentialing physicians for appointment and reappointment to the medical staff.

CREDENTIALING

Case law regarding credentialing generally supports the premise that a hospital could be held liable for a patient injured by a staff physician because the hospital should have known of the physician's poor performance or incompetence and failed to investigate or take reasonable corrective action. After the *Darling* case, the Wisconsin Supreme Court ruled in *Johnson v. Misericordia Community Hospital*[6] that the hospital had a duty to properly credential physicians on its staff even when the physician falsified his or her application for privileges. Similarly, in *Elam v. College Park Hospital*,[7] the court held that the hospital may be responsible for the conduct of its physicians under the doctrine of corporate negligence. These cases underscore the need for ongoing peer review to maintain quality care.

All credentialing criteria must be clearly stated in the medical staff bylaws and communicated to members of the medical staff and new applicants. Any changes adopted by

The author gratefully acknowledges work previously contributed by Robert Schur, J.D.

the medical staff must be approved by the hospital's governing body. The medical staff bylaws should clearly identify the mechanisms and procedures to be used in the credentialing processes for appointment and reappointment. Standards for the evaluation and verification of applicant information, the delineation of privileges, and the procedures for appealing adverse decisions should also be clearly documented in the bylaws or rules and regulations of the medical staff. Applicants should not be asked for information related to gender, nationality, race, creed, sexual orientation, age, religion, ethnic origin, or any other data that can be viewed as having a discriminatory purpose. Likewise, provisions of the Americans with Disabilities Act (ADA) protect rehabilitated drug or alcohol abusers; therefore information requested of applicants should address *current* alcohol or drug abuse that has not been rehabilitated.

PRIVILEGING

The objective of the privileging decisions should be the delineation of the specific diagnostic and therapeutic procedures, whether medical or surgical, that may be performed in the hospital and the types of clinical situations to be managed by the physician. The JCAHO requires that privileges be granted before any care is provided to patients, noting that temporary privileges must be time limited. Physicians working in outpatient facilities owned or managed by JCAHO-approved health care entities are also subject to the credentialing and privileging process.

PROCTORING

For all new applicants for privileges (or additional privileges) and for physicians who may be returning to practice after a significant absence, proctoring is usually required for a time to ensure that the physician is competent to perform the procedures for which privileges are requested. Appropriate proctors should be selected and can include members of the medical staff who are noncompetitors, when possible, and senior active staff who have privileges in the same area of practice. The number of cases or length of proctoring and the method of proctoring (such as direct observation or prospective and retrospective review of cases) should be determined and communicated to the applicant in writing. The form of the proctor's report should be standardized and submitted to the department chair for periodic review. The physician being proctored should be apprised of his or her progress, including observed strengths and weaknesses, and should be given copies of any written evaluations submitted to the department chair. Final recommendations of the proctor should then be reviewed by the department chair and forwarded to the credentialing committee for final recommendation to the medical executive committee. Privileges approved by this committee should be formally granted by the governing board.

DUE PROCESS

In the context of medical staff peer review in credentialing and privileging, *due process* refers to the fair and consistent treatment of physicians who first apply for privileges or who reapply for privileges that were involuntarily restricted, suspended, or revoked. Clearly written due process procedures must be established, understood, and properly implemented by the hospital because physicians have legal rights to protect their careers. In government-owned hospitals, these rights may be found under the due process provisions of the United States and in state constitutions, but in privately operated hospitals, constitutional rights may not apply.[8]

Cases in which the power of the medical staff was abused for discriminatory or other improper motives have led some states' courts and legislatures to gradually extend legal protections to physicians whose staff privileges are attacked. Since the 1950s, the trend has been toward upholding the physician's right to fully practice his or her profession, a right that has in some states been considered "fundamental" for purposes of extending constitutional protections.[9] This view mandates fair procedures in disciplinary actions for medical staff.[10] Fair procedure includes, at a minimum, adequate notice of the charges on which the action is based and the opportunity to present evidence on one's own behalf to an unbiased decision-maker.[11] However, other protections usually found in civil and criminal actions, such as the right to cross-examine adverse witnesses and the right to be represented by counsel, have generally not been accorded in disciplinary hearings.

State laws provide for the right to legally challenge a decision restricting or terminating medical staff privileges, but judicial review may be limited by numerous factors, including the requirement that one must fully exhaust all available administrative remedies before seeking redress in the courts. Courts have traditionally shown a great deal of deference to the decisions of administrative bodies such as hospital boards and committees, even when due process may have been lacking at the administrative level, and are loathe to interfere in what is viewed as the exclusive bailiwick of hospitals and physicians.

Although many states have begun to address these issues, there is wide variance in the extent to which physicians' rights to practice in the hospital can be protected under the law. Most states, however, have done nothing to address similar problems created by managed care organizations, medical societies, and other entities that perform peer review and credentialing functions but that are not necessarily required by law to have an organized and independent medical staff.

PHYSICIAN RIGHTS UNDER MANAGED CARE

In California, the law applying to hospitals extends by statute to state medical societies, but only recently have the courts begun to extend the same protections in cases involving private insurers, health maintenance organizations, and managed care payors.[12] These cases hold that entities controlling "important economic interests" may not arbitrarily deprive a physician of privileges or contract rights without providing a fair hearing procedure, even if existing law requires that the action be reported to the state medical board or to the NPDB.[13]

In the seminal *Delta Dental* case, the court determined that the managed care organization had a duty to accord its member dentists the right to common law fair procedure in a dispute over a reduction in the payment rates because the plan was "the largest dental health plan in California, covering over 8 million individuals."[14] Thus the court apparently viewed the importance of the defendant's market power in general, rather than its impact on the plaintiff's business in particular, as controlling.

In the *Ambrosino* case that followed *Delta Dental*, the plaintiff podiatrist was terminated from participation in a managed care plan on the basis of "a short-term chemical dependency problem" that he claimed did not render him impaired to practice.[15] The plan refused to grant him a hearing because under its contract, any history of substance abuse was considered grounds for termination. The court first cited *Delta Dental* for the proposition that "[t]he common law right to fair procedures has recently been held to extend to health care providers' membership in provider networks such as that operated by defendant because managed care providers control substantial economic interests."[16] Then in determining that the *Delta Dental* criteria had been met, the court noted that approximately 15% of the plaintiff's patients were insured by defendant and concluded that therefore the plaintiff "had a common law right to fair procedures, including the right not to be expelled from membership for reasons which are arbitrary, capricious and/or contrary to public policy," notwithstanding the termination-at-will clause in the participation contract.[17]

These two cases were hailed by many as opening a new era in the law relating to managed care and physicians' rights. However, there was ample support for the *Ambrosino* decision in long-standing California case law, including the 1974 *Ascherman* case.[18] The true significance of the *Delta Dental* case seems to be that the common law right to fair procedure was accorded there despite the fact that no issue of the plaintiff's competence, fitness, or quality of care was raised; the decision to reduce payments under the plan was purely economic. The retroactive nature of the action, and consequently its effect on previously "vested" rights, also seems to have been an important factor. The California Supreme Court has recently extended the fair procedure doctrine to cases of "economic credentialing," wherein a hospital or managed care entity terminates participation on a physician plan for purely business reasons without according the affected physicians notice or a fair

hearing.[19] Whether the courts will be willing to extend this doctrine to hospital privilege cases is uncertain.

APPLICATION OF DUE PROCESS PRINCIPLES

Due process requires that the right to practice medicine not be infringed on in an arbitrary or capricious manner.[20] The critical question concerns what procedures will suffice to satisfy due process requirements. Unfortunately there is no one answer to this query; due process varies according to the facts and circumstances of each case and according to the law of each jurisdiction where it is applied. The Supreme Court has stated that:

> Due process is flexible and calls for such procedural protections as the particular situation demands. Consideration of what procedures due process may require under any given set of circumstances must begin with a determination of the precise nature of the government function involved as well as of the private interest that has been affected by governmental action.[20]

The nature and extent of the private interest involved are necessarily fact-based determinations based in most cases on the application of state law.

A flexible formula suggests that the type of hearing afforded may vary from case to case. Clearly, however, due process requires "some form of hearing" before an individual may be deprived of a protected interest.[21] Furthermore, it is generally accepted that "in a highly technical occupation (like the practice of medicine), the members of the profession should have the power to set their own standards. Due process requires that the evaluations of whether one gets along and meets the standards not be made in bad faith or arbitrarily and capriciously."[22] On the other hand, there is no constitutional requirement that physicians be given a formal adversarial hearing, nor even that the decision-makers be completely uninvolved in the underlying matter.[23] "The common law requirement of a fair procedure does not compel formal proceedings with all the embellishment of a court trial, nor adherence to a single mode of due process. It may be satisfied by any one of a variety of procedures which afford a fair opportunity for an applicant to present his position."[24] Under the HCQIA, peer review participants are immune from civil liability in connection with the peer review action if the affected physician is given a fair procedure under the terms outlined in the statute.[25]

Various elements constitute "fair procedure" or "due process" under the law, depending on the particular jurisdiction's legislative and judicial history of providing protection in this area. California offers what is probably the most comprehensive legislative scheme protecting the medical staff privileges of physicians (and similar property interests), as well as judicial interpretation and application of the law. For example, in California, the required hearing procedures include an unbiased hearing officer; an unbiased trier of fact, whether composed of a panel of peers or an arbitrator (or arbitrators); notice of the nature of the proposed action, the right to a hearing, and the time in which to request a hearing; notice of the reasons for the proposed action and of the fact that the action will be reported when final; and the right to inspect and copy documents to be used in support of the adverse action and to learn the identity of witnesses to be called by the representatives of the medical staff.[26] The precise methods to be followed may vary according to the rules and regulations of the institution.

Although medical staff bylaws vary from one institution to the next, most are similar in providing for an initial investigation by a credentials committee or similar body, during which the physician generally has few (if any) procedural rights but may be required to appear and answer questions in the matter; a hearing, including the basic elements previously discussed; and an appeal to the governing board of the hospital, medical society, or other institution. Medical societies have promulgated model medical staff bylaws prescribing procedures for each of these steps, and these models are generally geared toward ensuring a fair procedure for the physician whose privileges are under review.[27] Model bylaws are an excellent resource for attorneys and administrators involved in drafting and updating bylaws in any jurisdiction.

The final element of due process in adverse actions affecting staff privileges is that of judicial review. This right also varies considerably from one jurisdiction to another, again depending on each state's interpretation of *due process*, the property or liberty rights recognized, and the extent to which the courts have been willing to intervene in what have traditionally been considered private, or semipublic, concerns. Nevertheless, the majority of jurisdictions now recognize the right to obtain redress in the courts when due process is not provided by the institution with respect to medical staff privileges. Judicial review may be limited to a review of the written record of proceedings held by the peer review body or may encompass a full evidentiary hearing de novo, although the latter may be available only under limited circumstances.

CONFIDENTIALITY AND PEER REVIEW PRIVILEGE

Generally, records of peer review actions and proceedings are exempted from discovery and evidentiary use in civil actions. This may be expressed as an "immunity" from discovery, as an evidentiary "peer review privilege," or both. Exceptions may be found in cases in which a plaintiff has made a bona fide, prima facie case against the hospital for negligently credentialing the physician or in which the litigation concerns the physician's rights against the institution (as opposed to a malpractice claim). Some courts have upheld the protection against discovery in such actions, and some have not. There is also an open question as to whether, and in what circumstances, a peer review participant otherwise entitled to claim a privilege may waive it by voluntarily disclosing the records or

facts pertaining to the peer review action; at least one court has held that a participant in the peer review process who may not be compelled to testify to the "privileged" matters may nevertheless do so of his own free will.[28]

Confidentiality may be ensured by means other than the law. Medical staff bylaws often require members involved in peer review proceedings to hold confidential all information and records relating to the proceedings or otherwise be subjected themselves to disciplinary action. The authors are unaware of any case challenging such a provision. However, it is important to keep in mind that in some states the bylaws may be considered a binding contract, whereas in others the courts have not adopted that view.

Numerous instances continue to exist in which a physician's medical staff privileges may be revoked or withdrawn and due process protections cannot be invoked, such as when a hospital acts for purely business or economic reasons or some other cause that does not relate to the quality of care practiced by the physician or his or her fitness to practice. For example, courts have held that a hospital may close its staff or a particular service, such as radiology or anesthesiology, or award an exclusive contract to one physician or group while excluding all others (including those already on staff). Although such actions have occasionally been challenged on both due process and antitrust theories, these cases have failed to produce decisions limiting the hospital's discretion to make such decisions, even when the resulting effects on individual physicians are harmful or seemingly anticompetitive.[29]

PEER REVIEW CORRECTIVE ACTION: AN UNFAIR PROCESS?

Most physicians must carry hospital staff privileges in one or more facilities. The medical staff is self-policing and is independent of the hospital.[30] Its functions include reviewing the care provided by its physician members to patients and acting as a liaison between the hospital administration and individual physicians. As a peer review body, the medical staff is responsible for shielding patients from incompetent or unstable physicians; at the same time, by controlling physicians' access to both the patients and the facilities, the medical staff wields considerable power over physicians, and when that power is abused, the physician's professional reputation, standing, and license to practice may be disrupted and damaged.

Despite a growing trend toward protecting physicians' fundamental rights and interests in medical staff privileges, medical staffs continue to operate independently, without strict controls, when determining which physicians are granted credentials and which physicians should lose their credentials. At every stage of the disciplinary process, the affected physician is at a disadvantage. The disciplinary hearing under medical staff bylaws is like a malpractice action against the affected physician with one's own colleagues acting as witnesses, prosecutors, and judges. Dozens of charges involving the care of numerous patients may be leveled at one time. If the physician loses, he or she will probably have no insurance coverage against either the costs of defense or the economic impact on his or her medical practice.

There is little opportunity to obtain discovery of evidence before it is presented. The chairman of the medical executive committee usually selects the jury panel members and hearing officer (sometimes subject to the physician's challenges for bias, which may be overruled). There may be use of hearsay evidence, including medical opinions of experts who cannot be compelled to appear and be cross-examined. Frequently, the physician is denied the assistance of counsel in the hearing room and must represent himself or herself or depend on a medical colleague to act in a representative capacity. Other procedural protections, such as the right to subpoena witnesses or documents, are usually lacking, and witnesses in a peer review hearing may enjoy absolute immunity from civil suits for slander or malicious injury, even if their testimony is false.[31] The hospital and medical staff members are also immune from suit under federal law unless it is proved that they acted in bad faith when taking the peer review action.[32]

An adverse outcome for the physician may destroy his or her career. Actions adversely affecting medical staff privileges must be reported by the hospital to the state medical board, as well as the NPDB and the Healthcare Integrity and Protection Data Bank, nationwide data bases accessible to hospitals and managed care organizations.[33] The state Medical Board may then commence an investigation, finding the physician an easy target because damning evidence has already been compiled in the medical staff hearing. Although the state medical board may decide not to prosecute, in almost all cases it can do nothing to aid the physician to clear his or her name, regain staff privileges, or obtain redress for the economic, professional, and emotional injuries sustained. The physician's reputation and career may be ruined, and his or her legal recourse is extremely limited. Although physicians have sued for deprivation of hospital staff privileges on any number of legal theories, including breach of contract, various tort theories, and antitrust, these suits are difficult, costly, and rarely successful.

Although the objective of peer review is to ensure the quality of care and retention of competence of medical staff, peer review functions as performed by physician staff members who are uncompensated for their efforts retain the risk of being sued by the affected physician despite immunity statutes. In addition, peer review immunity may not necessarily be extended if a federal claim, such as antitrust or unlawful discrimination, is proved.

Clearly, there is a continuing need for improvement in the credentialing and peer review processes. Extension of procedural due process principles to all facets of peer review must be accomplished with due respect to the reali-

ties of the health care environment and marketplace. Although credentialing and peer review remain as important functions of the organized medical staff, the courts and legislatures are increasingly involved in the process. Physicians and hospitals alike should continuously assess their peer review processes in light of the evolution of the law.

ENDNOTES

1. *See generally* F.A. Rozovsky, L.E. Rozovsky & L.M. Harpster, *Medical Staff Credentialing: A Practical Guide* (American Medical Association, Chicago, 1994).
2. *Darling v. Charleston Community Memorial Hospital*, 211 N.E. 2d 253, 260 (1965).
3. *See* Hammock, *The Antitrust Laws and the Medical Peer Review Process*, 9 J. Contemp. Health Law Policy 419 (1993).
4. Blum, *Medical Peer Review*, 38 J. Legal Educ. 525 at 531 (1988).
5. ECRI, *Medical Staff Credentialing*, in *Healthcare Risk Control. Risk Analysis: Medical Staff I*, Volume 3 (ECRI, Plymouth Meeting, Penn. Reissued January 1996).
6. *Johnson v. Misericordia Community Hospital*, 301 N.W. 2d 156 (Wis. 1981).
7. *Elam v. College Park Hospital*, 132 Cal. App. 3d 332, 183 Cal. Rptr. 2d 156 (1982).
8. Most states' laws still distinguish between public and private hospitals in determining whether, or to what extent, a physician is entitled to due process in respect to the termination or restriction of medical staff privileges. Others have largely eliminated this distinction, either by finding "state action" in the hospital's acceptance of federal funds, such as Hill-Burton Act payments, or by focusing on the quasipublic character of a hospital's business. *See, e.g., Ascherman v. San Francisco Medical Society*, 114 Cal. Rptr. 681 (Cal. App. 1974); *Silver v. Castle Memorial Hospital*, 497 P. 2d 564 (Hawaii 1972) (*cert. denied*, 409 U.S. 1048, *reh'g denied* 409 U.S. 1131); *Peterson v. Tucson General Hospital, Inc.*, 559 P. 2d 186 (Ariz. Ct. App. 1976). In California the courts have expressly held that a common law doctrine of "common law fair procedure" exists and requires the same elements of fair procedure as would be required under a due process analysis. *Applebaum v. Board of Directors of Barton Memorial Hospital*, 104 Cal. App. 3d 648, 163 Cal. Rptr. 831 (1980).
9. *See, e.g., Ascherman v. San Francisco Medical Society, supra* note 8.
10. California's statutory scheme governing procedures in medical staff privileges disciplinary hearings may be found in Cal. Bus. Prof. Code, §§809, *et seq.*
11. *Applebaum, supra* note 8.
12. *Potvin v. Met Life Insurance*, 22 Cal. 4th 1060, 997 P. 2d 1153, 95 Cal. Rptr. 2d 496 (2000); *Delta Dental Plan of California v. Banasky*, 33 Cal. Rptr. 2d 381 (Cal. App. 1994); *Ambrosino v. Metropolitan Life Insurance Company*, 899 F. Supp. 438 (N.D. Cal. 1995); *Hallis & Nopoletano v. CIGNA Health Care of Connecticut, Inc.* (1996), 680 A. 2d 127, *cert. denied*, 137 L.Ed. 2d 308; *Paul J. Harper, MD v. Healthsource New Hampshire, Inc.*, 674 A. 2d 962 (1995).
13. *Supra* note 9.
14. *Ibid.* note 12, 33 Cal. Rptr. 381, 385.
15. *Ibid.* note 12, 899 F. Supp. 438, 440.
16. *Id.* note 12, 899 F. Supp. 445.
17. *Id.*
18. *Ibid.* note 12.
19. *Potvin v. Metropolitan Life Insurance Company*, 22 Cal. 4th 1060, 997 P. 2d 1153, 95 Cal. Rptr. 2d 496 (2000), reaffirms *Ambrosino* by stating that the key issue in determining whether a payor entity must accord a fair procedure hearing to its members is the defendant's ability to control significant economic interests, following *Ascherman* and other existing case law.

20. *Anton v. San Antonio Community Hospital*, 19 Cal. 3d 802, 823, 567 P. 2d 1162, 140 Cal. Rptr. 442 (1977); *see also Anton v. San Antonio Community Hospital*, 132 Cal. App. 3d 638, 183 Cal. Rptr. 423 (1982).

21. *Mathews v. Eldridge*, 424 U.S. 319, 335 96 S.Ct. 893, 963, 47 L.Ed. 2d 68 (1975).

22. *Stretten v. Wadsworth Veterans Hospital*, 537 F. 2d 361, 369, n.18 (9th Cir. 1976).

23. *Arnett v. Kennedy*, 416 U.S. 134, 94 S.Ct. 1633, 40 L.Ed. 2d 15.

24. *Pinsker v. Pacific Coast Society of Orthodontists*, 12 Cal. 3d 541, 555, 526 P. 2d 253, 116 Cal. Rptr. 245 (1974). *See also Tiholiz v. Northridge Hospital Foundation*, 151 Cal. App. 3d 1197, 11203, 199 Cal. Rptr. 338 (1984) (procedures must ensure physician is "treated fairly"); *Cipriotti v. Board of Directors*, 147 Cal. App. 3d 144, 152, 196 Cal. Rptr. 367 (1983) (procedural protections are designed to give the physician "an opportunity to confront the witnesses and evidence against him and to present his defense").

25. 42 U.S.C. §11112(b).

26. Cal. Bus. Prof. Code §809, *et seq.*

27. *See, e.g.*, California Medical Association Model Medical Staff Bylaws.

28. *See, e.g., West Covina Hospital v. Superior Court (Tyus)*, 226 Cal. Rptr. 132 (1986), a California Supreme Court decision narrowly holding that the state's evidence code prohibition against discovery of peer review proceedings was no bar to a participant's *voluntary* testimony (i.e., that the privilege to protect such information could be waived).

29. *See, e.g., Jefferson Parish v. Hyde*, 466 U.S. 2 (1984); *Eszpeleta v. Sisters of Mercy Health Corp.*, 800 F. 2d 119 (7th Circ. 1986); *Beard v. Parkview Hosp.*, 912 F. 2d 138 (6th Cir. 1990); *Capital Imaging Associates v. Mohawk Valley Medical Assn*, 791 F. Supp 956 (N.D.N.Y. 1992); *Anne Arundel Gen. Hosp. v. O'Brien*, 432 A. 2d 483 (Md. App. 1981); *Holt v. Good Samaritan Hosp.*, 590 N.E. 2d 1318 (Ohio App. 1990); *Caine v. Hardy*, 943 F. 2d 1406 (5th Cir. 1991).

30. The Joint Commission on Accreditation of Healthcare Organizations is one source of the requirement that medical staffs be self-governing. State laws also may require that the hospital not only recognize but also require independent governance of its professional staff. *See, e.g.*, 22 Cal. Code Regs. §70701.

31. California provides such an absolute immunity to witnesses in a peer review proceeding (Cal. Civil Code §47(b)) and a qualified immunity to all participants who act without malice in the reasonable belief that the action is warranted by the facts (Cal. Civil Code §43.7). Federal law extends essentially the same protections under the Health Care Quality Improvement Act, 42 U.S.C. §11111, *et seq.*

32. Immunity is provided under the "safe harbor" provisions of the federal Health Care Quality Improvement Act of 1986 (42 U.S.C. §11111, *et seq.*) when the peer review body observes certain minimal standards for fair procedure and acts in good faith for the purpose of furthering quality health care. 42 U.S.C. §11112(a).

33. The NPDB was created by the Health Care Quality Improvement Act of 1986 (*supra* note 8). Hospitals and other entities responsible for credentialing physicians are required not only to report to the NPDB when taking peer review actions, 42 U.S.C. §11132, but also to query the NPDB when granting or renewing a physician's privileges, 42 U.S.C. §11135. The Healthcare Integrity and Protection Data Bank was recently established under the provisions of the Health Insurance Portability and Accountability Act of 1996, 45 C.F.R. §61.1.

9

Physician Profile Databases

MARK GREENWOOD, D.O., J.D., F.C.L.M.
MICHAEL KAMINSKI, M.L.I.S.

GROUPING OF DATABASES
CATEGORIES OF INFORMATION
CONSUMER-ACCESSED DATABASES
PUBLISHING MALPRACTICE INFORMATION
RELIABILITY OF MALPRACTICE INFORMATION
EMERGING TYPES OF INFORMATION
UNINTENDED CONSEQUENCES

Databases that compile information on physicians and other health care providers have been in existence for some time. The first of these databases reflected the interest that the federal and state governments had in fulfilling their role in maintaining public health. Hospitals and other employers also maintained an interest in assuring physician accountability, with emphasis on clinical competence and economic efficiency. Increasingly, consumers too are demanding physician and health care facility accountability—a reflection of the fact that an individual's health, and the health of his or her family, are among an individual's greatest concerns. It is against this backdrop of government, employer, and consumer interests that various factors have combined to allow consumer access to physician databases. The most controversial information provided by databases is physician malpractice history, information concerning adverse events, and patient-physician relationships.

GROUPING OF DATABASES

When grouping databases, a number of methods can be used. They can be grouped according to the entity that creates the database, according to the entity that has access to it, or according to the entities that maintain the highest interest in the operation of the database. The latter of these provides the most insight into the database itself and is the method chosen by these authors.

State and federal government interest

The interest of state and federal governments in health care databases has traditionally focused on limiting inappropriate prescribing and dispensing of narcotics, and in reducing

An earlier version of this chapter appeared in the Journal of Legal Medicine [Mark J. Greenwood, *The Physician Profile Database: Publishing Malpractice Information on the Internet*, 21 J. Legal Med. 477 (2000)].

the incidence of fraud and abuse in the Medicare/Medicaid and other federal and state insurance programs. That these interests are ongoing is evidenced by the continuing existence of the Drug Enforcement Administration's Controlled Substances Data Base, and the more recent development of the Healthcare Integrity and Protection Data Bank (HIPDB). HIPDB contents include final adverse actions such as both civil judgments and federal and state criminal convictions that are related to the delivery of a health care item or service. Increasingly, governments have been creating databases designed to improve the quality—as well as to limit the costs—of medical care.

Employer interest

The marked growth in physician and health care provider databases reflects not only an increase in government demand for physician and other health care professional accountability, but an increase in demand on the part of employers for accountability as well. The interest of employers, including hospitals, clinics, managed care organizations, and other provider networks, largely mirrors that of the federal and state governments: compiling and maintaining access to information on individual health care providers' clinical performance, and the provider's licensing, disciplinary and malpractice history.

Consumer interest

A number of factors have combined to increase consumers' access to physician database information:

- The existence of databases maintained by the government, especially state governments.
- Regarding disciplinary action taken against licensed professionals.

- The high incidence of fraud in government-sponsored health insurance on the part of physicians, hospitals, and health-related equipment suppliers, which has resulted in the creation of antifraud databases such as the HIPDB.
- The rise of managed care organizations and other like-minded health provider entities whose orientation is on making a profit, which has resulted in their use of commercial databases to profile physicians and other health care providers as a means to this end.
- The frustration on the part of the government and consumers regarding the perceived lack of discipline meted out by state disciplinary boards.
- The perception among those in government and on the part of consumers that there is a national crisis of medical malpractice.
- The consumer's access to the capabilities of the Internet.
- The emerging patient safety and error reduction movement.

The end result is that information that was once restricted to use by federal and state governments, and health care provider entities such as hospitals and clinics, increasingly has been put into the hands of the consumer (see Tables 9-1 and 9-2).

CATEGORIES OF INFORMATION

Clinical performance data

A physician's clinical performance, that is, clinical outcomes and economic efficiency, is determined by collecting information on clinical encounter and billing claim data specific to individual providers. Indicators of clinical performance are arrived at through a process of "profiling." The purpose of provider profiling is to collect data in order

TABLE 9-1 Consumer-Accessed Databases

Demographic, complementary, and related information

American Medical Association (http://www.ama.assn.org)
American Board of Medical Specialties
    (http://certifieddoctor.org.verify)
Cigna Health Care Company (http://www.cigna.com)
Medicine Online (http://www.medicineonline.com)
MyDoctor.com (http://www.mydoctor.com)
Wellpoint Health Networks (http://www.wellpoint.com)

Clinical performance

Best Doctors (http://www.bestdoctors.com)

Disciplinary and/or malpractice history

Association of State Medical Board Executive Directors—
    Administrators in Medicine (AIM)
    (http://www.docboard.org/docfinder)
Consumer Info Central (a fee is required) (http://www.
    ConsumerInfoCentral.com)
Federation of State Medical Boards (a fee is required)
    (http://www.docinfo.org)
HealthGrades (http://www.healthgrades.com)
HealthScope (http://www.healthscope.org)
WebMD (http://www.webmd.com)

TABLE 9-2 Consumer-Accessed, State-Sponsored Databases

Alaska, Alabama, Arizona, Arkansas, California, Colorado, Connecticut, Florida, Georgia, Idaho, Illinois, Indiana, Iowa, Kansas, Kentucky, Louisiana, Maine, Maryland, Massachusetts, Michigan, Minnesota, Missouri, Nebraska, New Jersey, New Mexico, New York, North Carolina, North Dakota, Ohio, Oklahoma, Oregon, Rhode Island, Pennsylvania, South Carolina, Tennessee, Texas, Utah, Vermont, Virginia, West Virginia, Wisconsin, and Wyoming.

to compare individual physicians with others practicing in a particular hospital or region. Profiling databases are used to gather information concerning quality assurance, utilization review, and assessment of physician performance. These data often include physician information relating to mortality, complications, morbidity, drug use variances, blood utilization, infection control, and the like.

The data may then be merged with routine practice data such as number of hospital admissions, lengths of patient stay, and numbers of external reviews. Computer analysis is then used to identify variations in a particular physician's performance, based on application of various clinical and economic thresholds. By adjusting for differences in physician case mix and patient severity, employers and other entities may make valid comparisons of resource use, costs, and medical outcomes by physician, network, business unit, and employer.

The purpose in releasing these profiles to the public was to allow consumers to better understand those characteristics of individual patients that adversely affect outcomes; to improve the results of treatment of disease; to improve the provision of health care; and to provide information to consumers to allow them to make better-informed decisions when selecting a physician.

A consumer's having access to information regarding clinical competence, although helpful, has limited value. For example, data concerning a physician's outcomes for selected surgical or other procedures are too specific and are of value only to those consumers with both the need for such a procedure and in a position to select among a group of physicians that perform it.

Licensing and disciplinary history data

The second category of data compiled includes information relating to licensing status and disciplinary actions taken by state medical boards or other entities. Because of the

---

BOX 9-1. MEDICAL-LEGAL PEARL

Federal regulations for unique "National Provider Identifiers," required by the simplification provisions of the Health Insurance Portability and Accountability Act (HIPAA), will make it easier to access information related to individual physicians across organizations and websites.

government's role as *parens patriae*, some of the first professional databases that were created by states were those that collected information on professionals who had been sanctioned by state licensing boards.

Theoretically this information has always been available to consumers as this is generally considered public information. However, as a practical matter this information, until recently, has been far from the reach of consumers. In order to locate information on individual professionals, the consumer was required either to contact the regulatory office directly, or to locate those mostly obscure state professional publications that chose to report the names of the professionals who were sanctioned.

A number of state medical boards or departments of health through their websites are increasingly providing licensing and disciplinary information to the public free of charge. Both state and private organizations have begun to incorporate a wide variety of health-related information, along with licensing and disciplinary data, on websites available to consumers without charge.

Data concerning licensing and disciplinary history, although they may allow consumers to discover those among the profession that most would consider the "least desirable," have limited value because this information is relevant to only those few professionals who have had licensing problems or have been disciplined. They provide no information on the large majority of providers of the health care services.

Malpractice history data

The third, and most controversial, category of information collected is that related to a physician's malpractice history. Reacting to what Congress described as a nationwide rise in medical malpractice, and a need to improve the quality of medical care, the National Practitioner Data Bank (NPDB) was created as part of the Health Care Quality Improvement Act (HCQIA) of 1986. This database became operational in 1990. The purpose of the NPDB is to remedy the perceived nationwide crisis in medical malpractice by collecting information relating to the professional competency of physicians and other health care professionals. Information, such as malpractice payments and disciplinary actions against providers by state licensing boards and adverse actions by health care entities, such as occurs through the peer review process, must be reported to the data bank. Hospitals are then required to query the data bank before granting clinical privileges.

The NPDB was unique in that it did not restrict the database information to use by government entities, as had been the case with previous databases. Rather, it not only allowed, but required, that hospitals and other health care entities access this information. For other health care provider entities, access is allowed, but not required. Although one purpose of the database was to improve the quality of health care, it is important to note that consumers have not been allowed access to the NPDB. Whether this should occur has been the subject of Congressional debate. However, beginning primarily in 1996 in Massachusetts, and since then in an increasing number of other states, consumers have been allowed access to other databases that compile information on malpractice.

CONSUMER-ACCESSED DATABASES

Databases that provide information to consumers generally are sponsored by government bodies (e.g., state medical boards), self-regulatory agencies (e.g., medical societies), and private organizations (e.g., consumer advocacy groups). For the latter of these, information reported may be culled from various sources including state medical boards, insurance companies, government agencies, including the courts, from physician self-reporting, and, more recently, from reports on individual physicians made by consumers themselves.

For any database, and particularly those accessed by consumers, there are a number of concerns, both operational and informational. Operational concerns relate to cost of operating the database, the format in which the information is presented, and the method by which it is accessed: phone, fax, letter, or by the Internet. Informational concerns relate to the extent that the data are:

- Complete (is the information missing important data fields?).
- Current (information that is not up-to-date limits the value of the database).
- Accurate (was the information independently verified?).
- Unbiased (is the source of the information the physician or a public interest group?).
- Meaningful and relevant (does the goal in providing the information achieve its purpose?).

Information disseminated

Demographic information. Information relating to a physician's demographics is the most neutral of the information provided to consumers. This information includes the address of the physician's practice location, the name of the school the physician attended, graduate education, any specialty board certifications that are held, the availability of translating services that are provided at the practice location, and whether the physician participates in the Medicaid program.

Complementary information. Reporting of complementary information provides a means for the physician to balance any negative information reported with information that reflects more positively. In what may be described as a concession to physicians, in many databases physicians are allowed to include such information as appointments to medical school faculties, responsibilities for graduate medical education, publications in peer-reviewed medical literature, and professional or community service activities and awards.

Disciplinary information. Reporting disciplinary information provides to the consumer what is potentially the most damaging to physicians. This information is culled from various sources including the criminal courts, the state medical board, and hospital disciplinary bodies. As to criminal matters, information may include descriptions of any criminal convictions for felonies and serious misdemeanors, as well as descriptions of any charges to which the physician pleads *nolo contendere* or where sufficient facts of guilt were found. As to state medical board disciplinary actions, information may include descriptions of any state's final board disciplinary actions. Finally, as to hospital disciplinary matters, there may be disseminated descriptions of revocation or involuntary restriction of hospital privileges for reasons related to competence or character, and descriptions of the restriction of privileges at a hospital in lieu of or in settlement of a pending disciplinary case related to competence and character in any hospital.

PUBLISHING MALPRACTICE INFORMATION

In addition to demographic, complementary, and disciplinary information, consumers are increasingly allowed access to malpractice information. Publication of this information presents a number of concerns relating to competing interests of public versus provider, and involves issues of accessibility, format, and context of the information.

Competing interests

The issues that arise in regard to the creation and operation of any database, but become more acute in relation to consumer-accessed databases, include:

1. On whom is information to be collected.
2. Who is to have access to the information.
3. What information is to be collected.
4. For what purpose is the information to be used.

As it is recognized that consumers have a legitimate right to data on health care providers, the competing interests involved in the health care provider database do not come down to the consumer's right to access versus the provider's right of privacy, but rather, the consumer's right to access versus the provider's right to control the extent and manner in which the provider information is to be disseminated.

Accessibility

Those entities that maintain websites will either provide consumers with malpractice information on individual physicians directly on the site, or will instruct consumers in how to obtain this information in another way. For example, and perhaps most onerous, some states require consumers to make direct requests for malpractice information on an individual physician by telephone or in writing to the appropriate state agency. In these instances consumers generally are then sent a summary report listing the amount of payment

---

> **BOX 9-2. MEDICAL-LEGAL PEARL**
>
> The Administrators in Medicine (AIM) Docfinder website is maintained by the Association of State Medical Board Executive Directors and provides the most important Internet portal to physician profile databases operated by individual states: http://www.docboard.org/docfinder.

and a brief description of the injury. But increasingly, the trend is for states to provide malpractice history information on individual physicians as part of the website itself. In those states, for consumers with access to the Internet and the ability to locate the appropriate website, this represents a convenient source of physician malpractice information.

Format

Consumers are provided with malpractice information on individual physicians in one of three ways.

Graduated categories. Dissemination according to graduated categories: below, at, and above average. This allows for comparing an individual licensee's medical malpractice judgment awards and settlements to the experience of other physicians within the same specialty.

Payment amounts. Dissemination in raw form according to actual payment amounts.

Expanded malpractice information. Dissemination of *pending* malpractice claims to the public. In some states, potential plaintiffs in a medical malpractice suit must notify potential defendants, as well as the state department of health, of their intention. This information may be made available to the public. Medical groups object to the release of this information to consumers by the state agency because it involves allegations of malpractice for which probable cause has not been determined. The medical groups' concern is that release of unfounded accusations would unfairly identify physicians who may be threatened with frivolous and unfounded lawsuits.

Context

Part of the publication of malpractice information involves the placing of that information in context. Consequently, consumers are advised of a number of factors, many of which overlap:

1. An individual physician's malpractice information should be compared to the experience of other physicians who perform procedures and treat patients with a similar degree of risk.
2. Physicians treating certain patients and performing certain procedures are more likely to be the subject of litigation than others.

BOX 9-3. **MEDICAL-LEGAL PEARL**

Settlement of a claim may occur for a variety of reasons which do not necessarily reflect negatively on the professional competence or conduct of the physician. A payment in settlement of a medical malpractice action or claim should not be construed as creating a presumption that medical malpractice has occurred. The Standard Settlement Disclaimer.

---

3. The number of years a physician has been practicing may impact the data.
4. Paid malpractice claims may involve incidents that took place years before the payment was made.
5. Treating high-risk patients may affect a physician's malpractice history.
6. Malpractice cases may be settled for reasons other than liability and cases may be settled without the physician's consent.

Information regarding settlements is believed to be the most easily misunderstood by consumers and so is often accompanied by a disclaimer.

RELIABILITY OF MALPRACTICE INFORMATION

Although for almost any database there are concerns for accuracy, scope, and cost, other concerns are particularly apparent. For example, the issue of database reliability—the degree to which the database is able to fulfill the purpose for which it was created—is particularly important. Because the purpose of the consumer-accessed physician profile database is to provide information to consumers regarding individual physicians to allow consumers to determine at least the worst, if not the best, among the group, the question becomes whether the information provided to consumers actually allows this determination.

By knowing that a particular physician has been disciplined by a licensing board or has been convicted of a crime, consumers could, perhaps fairly reliably, conclude that the physician is among the worst of those in the profession. By knowing that a physician is board certified and has a number of awards, honors, and publications, consumers could, perhaps fairly reliably, conclude that the individual is among the best of the professional group. But reporting only this information does not allow more informed selection of those who are neither among the worst nor best, that is, those who are somewhere in between. Consequently, the strength of the database that reports a physician's malpractice history is in its presumably giving the consumer the opportunity to choose the most, and to avoid the least, competent among a group of *average* physicians, for these, by chance alone, are the ones most likely to be providing services to the consumer. The weakness of these databases is that consumers may not be able to determine the average physician's competence reliably.

Perception of malpractice

The central issue regarding a physician's adverse malpractice judgment is consumer perception of the degree to which a past adverse judgment is predictive of future lack of ability necessary to provide quality patient care. Do consumers perceive that an instance of malpractice, even when it conforms to its proper definition, that is, "negligence," under tort law (as opposed to "negligence" as determined by a sympathetic jury or in settlement of a "frivolous" claim) equates with lack of quality? In other words, to what extent do consumers perceive that a physician who has a history of making a legitimate mistake should be avoided?

In weighing the value of malpractice information as a possible indicator of lack of quality, consumers are likely to get mixed messages. Both messages will be received indirectly as consumers are not likely to have personal experience with physicians whom they know to have a malpractice history. On the one hand, consumers in some states may get physician profile information that goes to great lengths when reporting malpractice information to put a physician's malpractice history in the best light. In other words, consumers will be provided with contextual information that downplays the significance of claims. On the other hand, some consumer advocacy groups will provide consumers with health-related information that puts malpractice information in the worst light. For example, instead of providing information regarding the extent and nature of malpractice claims as it relates to the average physician, that is, a physician with malpractice history that includes a settlement or two, some consumer groups discuss malpractice claims as on par with such conduct as traditionally requiring discipline by a medical board—conduct such as substance abuse, gross negligence, and others.

Many studies strongly suggest that quality of care is not a major determinant of whether a patient initiates a malpractice claim, but studies do show that a history of malpractice claims is, in fact, indicative of a physician's interpersonal skills. Consequently, consumers may be encouraged to consider more heavily a primary care physician's malpractice history, because of the relative importance of the interpersonal aspects of the physician-patient relationship, such as communication skills and rapport. Conversely, they may be encouraged to consider less heavily a surgeon's malpractice history, and the malpractice history of other specialists who perform invasive procedures, because of the relative importance of technical skill, which is less predictive by claim history.

BOX 9-4. **MEDICAL-LEGAL PEARL**

The value that consumers place on having access to malpractice information depends upon their perception of how a history of malpractice claims is predictive of future lack of ability to provide quality medical care. Consumers will face the most difficulty in choosing whether to receive care from a physician who has a single, perhaps remote-in-time, adverse medical negligence judgment, but who has otherwise good qualifications.

EMERGING TYPES OF INFORMATION

The type and volume of information contained in databases, including those accessible to consumers, continues both to increase and to reflect the general focus of information contained in previous databases: quality and competence of the physician.

Adverse events information

To assure the highest quality of care requires a commitment to identify, analyze, and to some extent report adverse medical events. Examples of databases that compile information on adverse medical events include the Joint Commission on Accreditation of Healthcare Organizations (JCAHO) Sentinel Event Program and the New York Patient Occurrence Reporting and Tracking System (NYPORTS) (http://www.rapiddevelopers.com/nyports). Examples of national reporting systems of adverse events related to medications and medical products are the Federal Drug Administration's "Safety Information and Adverse Event Reporting Program" (http://fda.gov/medwatch), and the MedMARx (http://www.medmarx.com) databases.

Although data collection of adverse events has been in existence for some time, newer developments allow for hospitals and other health care facilities both to obtain feedback on their own patterns of reporting and to compare them with other facilities. Use of Internet-based systems allow for data entry, and may allow for limited reporting to consumers of results of aggregate analysis of data. An important limitation in the value of adverse event reporting systems is that reporting may be voluntary and, if required, may still be subject to underreporting. Evidence of institutional underreporting may be based on wide regional variations and low hospital reporting rates.

The general rule in adverse event reporting systems is that data regarding specific events be nonidentifiable, i.e., no patient or physician names are used. Disclosure of such information may be prevented under law. In the case of NYPORTS, for example, New York State Public Health Law prevents disclosure of incident reports under the Freedom of Information Law.

There is a narrow exception to the rule that consumers are prevented from obtaining information about specific adverse events. Medicare beneficiaries who file written complaints are required to be informed of whether their care met professionally recognized standards of care and of the final disposition of the complaint. This may include being informed of any actions that are taken against the physician or hospital. This information could presumably be used in lawsuits and other action against physicians and health facilities.

Patient-physician relational information

Databases that rely on patient ratings of the physician and facility quality are among the newest sources of information available to consumers. The value of these databases is severely limited, not only because they rely exclusively on the subjective perception of individual patients, but also by the limited number of participants in patient satisfaction or experience surveys and the exceedingly few physicians who are included in the database.

UNINTENDED CONSEQUENCES

Compiling a broad range of information on physicians, particularly their malpractice history, may have harmful consequences beyond simply providing to consumers unreliable data.

Access to physicians

When the physician database reports malpractice information to allow the consumer to select the best among a group of physicians, the effect may be to actually limit the consumer's ability to gain access to those physicians. In knowing that data will be recorded and disseminated, even the best physicians may be discouraged from performing those services that may carry higher risks of being sued. For example, physicians may be discouraged from taking high-risk patients or performing highly technical procedures for fear that their record will be tarnished if there is a bad outcome. As a result, consumers who most need those physicians whose practices involve stretching the limits of what the profession and technology have to offer will be deprived of this benefit. Another result may be a "chilling effect" on research into new therapies and procedures.

Defense costs

When physicians know that an adverse legal or disciplinary board finding will not only be recorded, but disseminated to state and federal governments, employers, third-party payors, and especially to consumers, they may be less willing to settle a case, in hopes of having the case dismissed or getting a favorable judgment at trial or on appeal. This will result in increased burdens on the legal system, as well as to hospital and state disciplinary boards, in the form of increased time and resources spent on attorneys preparing cases, experts preparing to provide opinions and testifying, judges and disciplinary board members reviewing and hearing cases, and by others involved in the legal and disciplinary process.

Use by attorneys

Regardless of the database, information may be obtained for use in ways that were not intended. That this occurs is the result of database information having a value in addition to that which allows the goal of the database to be fulfilled. Those whose interest in the physician profiling database lies apart from its intended use may include both plaintiff and defense attorneys.

Plaintiff attorneys. The plaintiff attorney's interest in these data may be the result of its value in allowing an attorney to decide whether to pursue a case against a particular physician, preparing for a case already taken, and, possibly, using the information as evidence of a physician's lack of character or competence.

Defense attorneys. Database information has the potential of being used by database subjects as a shield in defending a negligence claim. For example, a plaintiff's case against a physician may be weakened if the physician can show that, by having access to database information—information suggesting that the physician is a provider of inferior services—the plaintiff assumed the risk in seeking his or her services. This is similar to the way in which hospitals, and other health care entities, are legally presumed to have knowledge, through the National Practitioner Data Bank, of disciplinary and medical negligence data regarding any health care professional whom they employ.

Peer reporting

At least some of what would appear in a physician profile, such as licensing and disciplinary information, may be generated by the physician's peers—whether one's partner, colleague, or co-worker—or by those in agencies responsible for administering and investigating consumer or other complaints. Having information on a physician's licensing and disciplinary actions available to consumers may sufficiently raise the stakes so that a physician's peers and others are reluctant to make reports and investigate incidents of possible substandard care or inappropriate behavior.

Consumer privacy

As more information concerning the health care system is obtained, its value in improving clinical treatment, providing for more informed patient choice of health care provider, and providing for advances in health research and public health surveillance is enhanced. The value of data used for profiling a physician is particularly enhanced, for example, as a way to measure the physician's ability to efficiently and economically provide a service, when it is placed in the context of an aggregate of individual clinical encounters. However, data on these clinical encounters often are tied with information on individual patients, thereby raising concerns for patient privacy.

GENERAL REFERENCES

United States General Accounting Office, *National Practitioner Data Bank: Major Improvements Are Needed to Enhance Data Bank's Reliability*, GAO-01-130, Nov. 2000 (provides an overview of the NPDB and discusses its limitations).

Federation of State Medical Boards, *Report of the Special Committee on Physician Profiling*, 2000 (http://www.fsmb.org) (a lengthy document that provides a detailed review of recommended physician profile components).

E.M. Stone, J. Heinold, L.M. Ewing & S.C. Schoenbaum, *Program on Health Care Quality Improvement: Accessing Physician Information on the Internet* (New York: The Common Wealth Fund, 2002) (describes the nature and types of profiling data and provides a comprehensive and detailed list of regional and nationwide databases).

National Organization for State Medical and Osteopathic Board Executive Directors in the United States, *DocProfiles* (http://www. docprofiles. addr.com) (provides information on physician profiles and components of profile laws in the United States).

S. Greenfield, S.H. Kaplan, R. Kahn, et al., *Profiling Care Provided by Different Groups of Physicians: Effects of Patient Case-Mix (Bias) and Physician-Level Clustering on Quality Assessment Results*, 136 Ann. Intern. Med. 111-121 (2002) (provides examples of the difficulty in using clinical data sets to assess physician performance quality).

G. Gillespie, *Medical Errors Reporting and Prevention: Weathering the Storm Ahead*, Health Data Management 60-61 (Feb. 2001) (describes the basis for the growing interest in reporting systems, and provides examples of existing systems).

Center for Medicare and Medicaid Services, *Peer Review Organization Manual, Part 5: Beneficiary Complaint Review* (http://www.cms. hhs.gov/manuals/19_pro/pr05.asp) (describes the procedure by which information about specific adverse events is provided to Medicare beneficiaries).

Health Care Professional Impairment

LOUIS E. BAXTER, Sr., M.D, F.A.S.A.M.
MARK F. SELTZER, J.D.

HEALTH CARE PROFESSIONAL IMPAIRMENT
PHYSICIAN RIGHTS
REGULATORY ISSUES: PUBLIC PROTECTION
HEALTH CARE PROFESSIONAL DISABILITY INSURANCE
CONCLUSION

HEALTH CARE PROFESSIONAL IMPAIRMENT

The impaired health care professional has become the focal point of many recent legal proceedings. The problem of practitioner impairment was resurrected in 1999 when the National Institute of Medicine published a report entitled *Medical Errors*. The report stated that each year nearly 100,000 patient deaths were a result of mistakes made by medical personnel. The question of health care professional impairment was raised. Accordingly, it is important that these health care providers are identified and whenever possible treated.

With the advent of the Joint Commission on Accreditation of Health Organization's mandate of January 1, 2001, that requires each hospital in America to create and develop a physician impairment committee, it is expected that more physician impairment will be identified and the potential for legal difficulties will increase. The impaired health care provider may face legal difficulties that may arise from hospital staff suspensions and disciplinary actions by a state licensing authority. Disciplinary action will trigger a report from the state licensing authority to the National Practitioner Data Bank. Such a report, as required by law, may lead to disqualification from health maintenance organizations and federally funded insurance plans. Once the impaired health care professional is able to receive treatment for the impairing illness and is able to begin to recover, these potential legal problems will need to be addressed.

Historical

Since the publication of *The Sick Physician* by the American Medical Association's Council on Mental Health in 1973, Americans have acknowledged and become more aware of health care professional impairment. The *Sick Physician* report suggested that health care professionals (physicians were the focus at that time) suffered from diseases of impairment, primarily drug and alcohol dependence. More recently, recognition of psychiatric illnesses as conditions of impairment have occurred.

The report also recommended that committee be formed to help identify, treat, and advocate for these impaired professionals. Finally, the report recommended that legislation be developed to allow these individuals to receive treatment rather than punishment for their medical illnesses. Before *The Sick Physician* these practitioners were thought to be "bad" people, without disability, who deserved to be punished. The modern view is that impaired professionals are people with disabling conditions, who have rights and protection under the law, and deserve treatment for their illness.

Diseases of impairment

Health care professionals suffer from the various diseases of impairment at rates similar to the general public. The major diseases of impairment (as defined in the *Diagnostic Statistical Manual IV—DSM-IV*) include alcohol use disorders, drug use disorders, psychiatric disorders, behavioral disorders, metabolic disorders, and psychosexual boundary issue disorders. Any of these disorders at any time can cause or provide impairment.

Metabolic disorders such as diabetes mellitus or thyroid disease or cardiovascular disorders like atherosclerosis and arrhythmia can also be impairing conditions. Physical conditions, such as carpal tunnel syndrome or ulnar nerve entrapment, can impair a surgeon's ability to perform and, as such, can become diseases of impairment as well.

The authors gratefully acknowledge Robert Conroy, J.D., and Gregory Rokosz, D.O., J.D., for their help and contribution to this chapter.

More and more practitioners are working longer and are becoming subject to the impairing affects of old age. Impaired memory and cognition are becoming issues in medical practice today. The changing medical economy is affecting physicians both young and old. The rising cost of medical liability insurance is forcing many clinicians to modify or otherwise tailor their practices. Some are opting out of medical practice. There is also the mounting stress of other litigation and practice pressures. Medical practice stress is an impairing condition in some instances.

Treatment and monitoring

The most important step in addressing health care professional impairment is making an accurate diagnosis. Once the diagnosis is made the individual needs to be referred to the appropriate level of care. The American Society of Addiction Medicine Patient Placement Criteria—2 were developed to insure that persons with diseases of impairment are matched to the level of care that would give the best treatment outcome. The levels of care range from traditional weekly outpatient individual counseling to long-term residential therapy, an intensive daily experience that may go on for many months. Some individuals have cooccurring disorders and need specialized treatment to effectively address their needs.

After these individuals have undergone the primary treatment for their impairing disorder, they require ongoing monitoring to assure their continued wellness and compliance with the treatment plan that has been developed for their care. In some instances, the monitoring is required as a condition of licensure. The monitoring serves two purposes. It allows the therapist to measure the effectiveness of the treatment plan and it provides documentation of ongoing wellness.

Advocacy

Health care professionals who have been diagnosed and have undergone treatment for their illness often find themselves in need of an advocate. Sometimes there may be licensing board issues that need to be addressed. Some states have mandatory reporting requirements that can result in a temporary loss of license until the licensee is able to demonstrate that he or she is no longer impaired. Most states have a physicians assistance program that can help to coordinate the necessary activities on the physician's behalf. Unfortunately, the same is not true for many of the other health care practitioners such as nurses, pharmacists, dentists, licensed social workers, psychologists, and others.

Recovering health care professionals may need an advocate to assist with facilitating their relicensure, return to hospital staffs, employment with medical groups, and reenrollment in insurance plan provider panels. Advocacy has also been required in some instances to help recovering practitioners to obtain medical liability and personal health insurance.

PHYSICIAN RIGHTS

Physicians have legal rights that are well defined and protected by state and federal law. Physicians as patients also enjoy the same rights as nonphysician patients. When health care providers become ill with diseases of impairment, some of these rights are called into question by the possible need to protect the public.

Health care professional's rights as a patient

The physician-patient relationship has existed since the Code of Hammurabi. The Hippocratic oath also seems to codify rules of a physician-patient relationship that admonishes to "first do no harm."

Once an impaired health care professional enters into treatment with another provider or agency, the rules and regulations of the physician-patient relationship apply. Under such conditions physician-patient confidentiality applies, as well. The health care professional undergoing treatment should have the same confidence that the non-health care professional has that his or her medical records will be protected. This sanctity is recognized by the American Medical Association, the Principles of Medical Ethics, and is provided for by some state medical societies (e.g., New York). The information contained in the records of some of these health care providers is further protected by Title 42 CFR Part 2 and requires a special authorization for release of that information pertaining to drug and alcohol treatment. There are special federal rules that deal with the confidentiality of information concerning patients treated for or referred for treatment of alcoholism or drug abuse. These rules apply to any facility receiving federal funds for any purpose, including Medicare or Medicaid reimbursement. The regulations preempt any state law that purports to authorize disclosures contrary to the regulations, but states are permitted to impose tighter confidentiality requirements.

Some states have a "duty to report" impaired health care professionals clause in the rules and regulations for licensure. The confidentiality of a patient's records is waived in situations where the patient may be a threat to him or herself or others. There are many other important issues of ownership and access, privileged communication, testimonial disclosures, approved disclosures, and limitations of disclosure that are discussed thoroughly elsewhere in this volume.

Health care professionals' rights as a licensee

Once an individual obtains a medical license to practice in a state, he or she must maintain it. Medical licenses are subject to sanctioning for a number of reasons. These include acts that are usually associated with diseases of impairment, such as failure to cooperate with a board investigation, sexual advances toward patients, false or inaccurate patient records, loss of hospital privileges, diverting controlled substances, and unprofessional conduct.

Licenses have been removed for active alcohol and drug dependence. Restoration of a license can occur if the licensee can provide evidence that he or she has sufficiently recovered from their disease of impairment. The restoration of a license hinges upon multiple factors including concern for the public safety and welfare, as well as the welfare of the medical profession.

In situations where a license is suspended, it is assumed that at some point it will be restored. Health care providers who have license suspension as a result of an impairing condition can request to have the license reinstated if they can demonstrate recovery from that impairing condition.

Health care providers as employees

The American with Disabilities Act of 1990 provides protection for those with disabilities, which include those individuals in recovery from alcoholism and drug abuse. This act extends the protection of the 1973 Rehabilitation Act which prohibits discrimination on the basis of a handicap by federal agencies, or any program or activity that receives federal funds, and provides great protections for those recovering health care providers who are also employees of hospitals and other health provider groups. There may also be other federal, state, and/or local statutes and rules that protect the health care provider's rights as an employee. For example, New Jersey has the Law Against Discrimination and New York City has an Administrative Code that provides protection for employees.

REGULATORY ISSUES: PUBLIC PROTECTION

The paramount concern and function of the state licensing agencies is to protect the public safety and welfare by continuing to evaluate a practitioner's professional practice. Medical practice acts create and define the composition of state licensure agencies, define the requirements for licensure, and vest the agency with powers to manage its charge.

The public is best protected by a mechanism to identify and remove unsafe practitioners from practice. The Medical Practice Act in most states allows for confidential reporting of suspected practitioners and provides a mechanism for treatment. This encourages colleague and self-reporting. Self-reporting of impairment is greater in states that have confidential reporting system than in states that do not. There are more legal questions that may need to be answered in light of the new HIPPA regulations, and the "public right-to-know" legislation regarding the information about recovering health care professional treatment and disciplinary records.

HEALTH CARE PROFESSIONAL DISABILITY INSURANCE

Disability insurance can be an extremely important component of the recovery process. The receipt of these benefits allows the provider to focus seriously on the recovery process. It is important to understand the policy provisions and the issues that are likely to arise when the claim is filed. Being aware of these issues beforehand increases the likelihood that the claim will be honored and maintained.

Policy provisions: individual disability income policies

Total disability. Most policies issued to physicians are "own occupation" policies. The definition of total disability is usually defined as the inability to perform the material and substantial duties of the physician's own occupation. The physician must be under the care of a physician other than him or herself.

Residual disability. Residual (partial) disability is usually defined as the inability to perform one or more of the material and substantial duties of one's own occupation or the ability to perform all of the duties but for less time than prior to the disability and a loss of income. Once again, there is a physician's care requirement.

Preexisting condition. A preexisting condition is a "medical condition or impairment" that was not disclosed in the application for issuance of the insurance and was not excluded by name, but which will be excluded from coverage by the company.

Incontestability clause. Generally, an insurance company cannot contest a disability policy after it has been in effect for 2 years. However, the company's right to contest after 2 years is subject to the language in the incontestability clause in the policy. There are two types of incontestability clause. In the first type, the company cannot contest the statements in the application after the policy has been in effect for 2 years. Some policies exclude periods of disability from the 2 years. In the second type, the company can contest the policy if the application contains "fraudulent misstatements."

Policy provisions: group policies (long-term disability)

Generally, group policies are subject to the Employee Retirement Security Act that sets up the administrative procedure used in the claims process. These cases are usually reviewed by an "arbitrary and capricious" standard. There are important differences in the policy provisions.

Coverage. While it is assumed that the professional has coverage in an individual policy, the provider must satisfy the coverage provision in a group policy in order to receive benefits.

Preexisting conditions. Preexisting conditions are usually limited to those medical conditions or impairments that existed 3 months prior to the effective date of the coverage and as a result of which disabled the provider within 12 months after the effective date.

Total disability. It is common that the "own occupation" definition of total disability is limited to a specific benefit period. After that limited time period, it is again common for the definition of total disability to change to a definition of "any occupation." In addition, there may be a requirement for a loss of income from that of the predisability income.

Mental illness and/or drug and alcohol limitation. Group policies often contain a provision or provisions limiting the benefit period for 2 years for claims involving mental illness or drug and alcohol addiction.

Legal issues/defenses

Preexisting condition. A preexisting condition is a nondisclosed medical condition or impairment that existed prior to the issuance of the policy. These conditions will be excluded from the policy. This may work in concert with the incontestability clause.

Incontestability clause. Also, as stated, the critical issue is whether or not the incontestability clause contains the "fraudulent misstatement" language. The second parties in with the preexisting condition clause.

Own occupation. Own occupation, for total or residual disabilities, is the specialty or specialties that the provider practiced at the onset of the disability. The provider is insured for the inability to practice his or her specialty, not medicine in general. It is also possible that the provider, depending upon his material and substantial duties and specialty, may be totally disabled even though he can perform some of his former duties.

Appropriate care. The second part of the definition of total or residual disability requires physician's care. If that language requires care that is "appropriate" for the condition causing the disability, the provider must establish that the care received rises to the level of being appropriate under the circumstances.

Legal disability. A "legal disability" is the loss of the ability to work in the provider's own occupation as a result of an intentional act, as opposed to a disabling condition. Common legal disabilities are the loss of a license to practice medicine or imprisonment.

Risk of relapse. Probably the most crucial issue to the "impaired practitioner" with a disability claim as a result of an addiction is the risk of relapse. This issue will almost invariably be raised by the disability insurance carrier as a defense to payment of ongoing benefits. The insurance carriers, as well as the courts, do accept the disease model of addiction. However, it is often difficult to determine whether the "impaired provider," who is in recovery and has achieved remission and stability, is disabled as a result of an addiction.

Key points

Listed below are five key points to be remembered when considering a disability insurance claim.

Dual-purpose medical professionals. You must choose medical professionals who are competent, capable of providing appropriate care, well credentialed, and have experience treating the disabling condition. They must also be willing to participate in the claims process.

Know the policy. The contractual requirements of the policy must be satisfied in order to obligate the company to pay the benefits. The policies are fact specific and not only differ between companies but also from year to year within the same company.

Know the issues. Many of the important issues or defenses have been reviewed that may arise in the course of a claim. It is important to recognize when these issues will be raised, to anticipate their application, and to prepare for these circumstances in advance.

Know your own occupation. It is important that your treating doctors are fully acquainted with the specific duties you are required to perform in your specialty.

Disability equation. The recovering provider and the treating provider need to establish the restrictions and the limitations that exist as a result of the disabling condition and how those restrictions prevent the recovering provider from performing the material and substantial duties of the occupation. These opinions must be medically based.

CONCLUSION

Health care professionals are not immune to diseases of impairment. In fact, the incidence of impairment is at least equal to the incidence seen in the general public. When providers become ill, they risk significant legal exposure and their rights as patients become blurred because they also have practice standards and ethical obligations that they must meet as health care providers, by law.

The receipt of disability insurance benefits enables the recovering provider to focus fully on recovery without added worries about financial instability. It is very important that the disability policy and the procedures are fully understood. Attaining knowledge and understanding of the process is invaluable.

Health care providers have rights and these rights as patients and practitioners need to be honored and defended.

REFERENCES

American Medical Association Council on Mental Health, *The Sick Physician* (1973).

Federal Privacy Act, 5 U.S.C. §552(a) (1974), M.D.-Patient Confidentiality.

Firestone, *"Shh! Patient Privacy and Confidentiality in a Lawsuit"; Physician Privilege v. Discovery*, 13 Legal Aspects Med. Practice 1-3 (Feb. 1985).

Hicks v. Georgia State Board of Pharmacy, 553 F. Supp. 314 (Ga. 1982), citing *Meachum v. Fano*, 427 U.S. 215, 228 (1976).

Baxter, Center for Substance Abuse Treatment, *Healthcare Professional Impairment Task Force Report* (2002).

American Medical Association Council on Mental Illness, *The Sick Physician: Impairment by Psychiatric Disorder Including Alcoholism and Drug Dependence*, 233 J.A.M.A. 684-687 (1973).

P. Reeve, *Physicians at Risk: Some Epidemiologic Considerations of Alcoholism, Drug Abuse and Suicide*, 26 J. Occup. Med. 503-508 (1984).

J.N. Robins, et al., *Lifetime Prevalence of Specific Psychiatric Disorders in 3 Cities*, 41 Arch. Gen. Psychiatry 949-958 (1984).

G.D. Talbott, *Treating Impaired Physicians: Fourteen Keys to Success*, 113 V.A. Med. 95-99 (1986).

Business Aspects
of Medical Practice

Complementary and Alternative Medicine

JOSEPH A. BARRETTE, B.S., J.D.

INTRODUCTION: RECOGNITION OF COMPLEMENTARY AND ALTERNATIVE MEDICINE (CAM) BY THE BIOMEDICAL COMMUNITY

The attention of the entire health care industry was captured by two surveys published in the *New England Journal of Medicine* and the *Journal of the American Medical Association*.[1] The American Medical Association (AMA) recognized the need for medical schools to respond to the demand for alternative health care.[2] Approximately 60% of U.S. medical schools offer courses in CAM. 80% of medical students and 70% of family physicians want training in CAM therapies. Nearly 60% of conventional physicians have either made referrals or are willing to refer their patients to CAM practitioners. CAM special interest groups have been formed by the Group on Educational Affairs of the Association of American Medical Colleges, the Society of Teachers of Family Medicine, and the American Public Health Association.[3]

Physicians have integrated CAM therapies into their practices by either performing the therapy themselves or referring their patients to CAM practitioners. Physicians who have or may be interested in integrating CAM therapies into their conventional medical practices are concerned about malpractice liability and exposure to disciplinary action for unprofessional conduct.

DISCIPLINARY PROCEDURES

The Fourteenth Amendment of the U.S. Constitution provides that no state shall "deprive any person of life, liberty, or property, without due process of law." A license to practice medicine is a valuable property right. It is subject to regulation under states' police power, but may only be denied or withdrawn under procedures consistent with constitutional due process.[4] Physicians who integrate CAM therapies into their practices are peculiarly subject to potentially unfair disciplinary medical procedures.

Typically, state medical boards are required to investigate every complaint they receive.[5] However, medical boards may not be limited to investigating a single complaint but have the discretion to comprehensively investigate all aspects of a physician's practice.[6]

After receipt of a complaint, medical boards will request patient and related records. The physician must comply with this request or may be charged with failure to cooperate.[7] This charge may result in the suspension of the physician's license. In order to obtain the physician's records, medical boards may also resort to either statutory authority, which permits a comprehensive medical review (CMR),[8] or serve upon the targeted physician a subpoena duces tecum. A subpoena duces tecum is a command to a witness to produce at the hearing documents that he has in his possession. Because "no agency of government may conduct an unlimited and general inquisition into the affairs of persons within its jurisdiction solely on the prospect of possible violations of law being discovered,"[9] some courts have required that medical boards demonstrate a justifiable basis for a good faith investigation of professional misconduct.[10] A targeted physician may challenge the reasonableness of either a CMR or a subpoena duces tecum.[11]

A physician who is the subject of a medical misconduct charge is entitled to a peer review disciplinary process.[12] The issue presented for CAM physicians is whether the review will be by physicians who are their peers. That is, will physicians who are familiar with CAM clinical practices constructively participate at any stage during the disciplinary process? There are several stages in the disciplinary process when other CAM physicians could constructively participate: during the investigation, as members of the hearing committee, or as members of an administrative review board that reviews the hearing committee's decision.

Some courts have held that CAM physicians are not entitled to have members of the hearing committee or administrative review board to "be practitioners of the same specialty as the physician under review, much less that they be adherents to the same philosophy of medicine."[13] If the effectiveness of a CAM therapy is either the basis of a complaint of misconduct or of general concern to medical boards, it seems appropriate to encourage the constructive participation of CAM physicians in the peer review process.

PARTICULAR CAM PRACTICES

In most of the reported cases, the physicians were subjected to having their licenses being revoked or suspended even though the patients were not harmed and did not file a complaint to the medical board. The cases can broadly be divided into several types of CAM therapies: homeopathy, nutrition, ozone and nutrition, and chelation.

Homeopathy

Metzler v. N.Y. State Board of Professional Medical Conduct involved a New York physician's request to a court to review a determination by the Administrative Review Board for Professional Conduct (ARB) which revoked the physician's medical license.[14] The ARB sustained the Hearing Committee's findings that the physician did "not practice orthodox or allopathic medicine but practices homeopathy."[15] The physician argued that the standard of care was only applicable to allopathic medicine and not homeopathy.

Dr. Guess was a licensed physician practicing family medicine in North Carolina. Dr. Guess integrated homeopathy into his practice only as a treatment of last resort. The State Board of Medical Examiners (Board) revoked his license based exclusively upon the fact that he integrated homeopathy into his medical practice. The Board and the court concluded that the practice of homeopathy "departs from and does not conform to the standards of acceptable and prevailing medical practice in this State."[16]

Both the *Metzler* and the *Guess* courts failed to define what may be "acceptable and prevailing medical practice."

Nutritional therapy

In *Gonzalez v. N.Y. State Department of Health*, the physician treated mostly patients with advanced and incurable cancer.[17]

Each patient had either exhausted or rejected conventional medical care. The Office of Professional Medical Conduct (OPMC) charged the physician with incompetence and negligence. The court held that despite patient consent, the physician was required to comply with the "usual standard of care."

Ozone and nutrition

The physician in *Atkins v. Guest* treated cancer patients with a combination of ozone therapy and nutritional supplements.[18] A complaint was filed by an emergency room physician after Dr. Atkins sent his patient to the hospital following an ozone treatment. The patient was released with no apparent side effects or injuries. Dr. Atkins moved to quash a subpoena duces tecum by the OPMC and asserted that he could not be legally found negligent or incompetent. The court denied the motion and left the determination of negligence or incompetence to the New York State Board for Professional Conduct.[19]

Chelation

In *State Board of Medical Examiners of Florida v. Rogers*, the physician was ordered by the County Medical Association to discontinue the treatment of chelation for arteriosclerosis.[20] An administrative complaint was lodged against the physician for unprofessional conduct. The Florida courts held that the State Board of Medical Examiners unreasonably interfered with Dr. Rogers' right to practice medicine. The Florida Supreme Court concluded that the Medical Board's decision was not reasonably related to the protection of the public health and welfare because of a lack of evidence that chelation therapy was harmful. The court also noted that Dr. Rogers fully informed his patients about the experimental nature of chelation, including the possibility of no improvement.

UNPROFESSIONAL CONDUCT STANDARD

Professional medical cases frequently turn on standard of care issues.[21] The courts and most medical boards apply the standard that a physician's conduct must conform to acceptable medical practices.[22] This standard of care is essentially equivalent to the standard applied by the courts in medical malpractice cases. However, an important difference "is that it is generally not required that the state medical board establish that the questioned medical care caused injury."[23] Nor is there a requirement that the medical care created a risk of patient injury.[24] However, state statutory medical disciplinary schemes are directed toward protecting the health and safety of patients and the state's citizens. "The common thread running through each of these reasons [the delineated acts of professional misconduct] for revocation of a license is the threat or potential for harm to patients and the public."[25]

When the applicable standard of care is the prevailing and accepted medical practices, CAM physicians are particularly vulnerable to misconduct charges based upon negligence and/or incompetence. This is due to the fact that when physicians offer CAM therapies, they are by definition deviating from conventionally accepted medical standards.[26]

If physicians who offer CAM are charged with misconduct in a jurisdiction that applies the prevailing and accepted medical practice standard, they should consider a defense based upon "two schools of thought"[27] or a reasonableness standard.[28] This will be discussed later in this chapter.

In some jurisdictions, a patient's consent to CAM therapy does not relieve the physician from the conventional medical standard within the context of medical disciplinary proceedings. In other jurisdictions the consideration will be whether there has been patient harm or the risk thereof. Because of the heightened risk of license revocation by physicians who practice CAM, some states have enacted legislation specifically intended to protect the right of physicians to offer CAM and the right of patients to choose their own medical care.

MEDICAL FREEDOM ACTS

In twelve states, physicians who integrate CAM into their practices are safeguarded by health freedom laws that are designed to protect them from discriminatory discipline while facilitating patient access to CAM therapies.[29] Several states specifically permit physicians to offer EDTA chelation[30] and some states license homeopathic physicians.[31]

These state laws require patient injury or risk thereof and/or require the medical board to demonstrate that the CAM therapy being integrated is unsafe or inefficacious. For example, in response to the *In re Guess* case, North Carolina amended its disciplinary medical provisions to provide that "the Board shall not revoke the license of . . . a person solely because of that person's practice of a therapy that is experimental, nontraditional, or that departs from acceptable and prevailing medical practices unless, by competent evidence, the Board can establish that the treatment has a safety risk greater than the prevailing treatment or that the treatment is generally not effective."[32] Alaska requires that the medical board "may not base a finding of professional incompetence solely on the basis that a licensee's practice is unconventional or experimental in the absence of demonstrable physical harm to a patient."[33]

However, despite the intent of these health freedom laws, physicians are cautioned to continue to comply with conventional medical practices such as testing, patient monitoring, and record-keeping. In addition, physicians are advised to continue with conventional medical practices in cases that the philosophy of the CAM therapy may be inconsistent with the biomedical paradigm, such as homeopathy or acupuncture. In some of the jurisdictions that have Medical Freedom Acts, physicians' unprofessional conduct is not based upon practicing CAM but failing to maintain "minimum standards of acceptable medical practice."[34] For

example, the minimum standard from which Dr. Gonzalez deviated included the failure to perform an adequate physical examination, perform sufficient follow-up monitoring, and maintain adequate records.[35] CAM physicians are held "to the same standard of care to which all physicians . . . are held . . . [t]here are no different standards for licensed physicians based on their philosophy, religion or personal approach to their calling."[36]

Some of the Medical Freedom Acts specifically inform CAM physicians of the required minimum standards of acceptable medical practice. For example, Louisiana and Texas require, *inter alia*, a detailed patient evaluation prior to offering a CAM therapy, a medical diagnosis, a treatment plan, periodic patient reviews, complete and accurate record-keeping, and informed consent.[37]

Physicians should inform themselves of (1) whether the state within which they practice has a Medical Freedom Act, and (2) whether there are required minimum standards of acceptable medical practice. In states that do not delineate the minimum standards or do not have a Medical Freedom Act, it would be prudent for physicians to comply with the accepted and prevailing medical practice.

MEDICAL MALPRACTICE

Standard of care

Generally, the legal standard for medical malpractice liability is whether a particular therapy deviated from accepted medical practice in the community and if that therapy resulted in patient injury. The standard duty of care is the same for all physicians regardless of whether they practice conventional or nonconventional therapies.[38] "[I]t would seem that no practitioner of alternative medicine could prevail on such a [standard] as the reference to the term 'nonconventional' may well necessitate a finding that the doctor who practices such medicine deviates from 'accepted' medical standards."[39] However, there are several defenses that may result in either a total or partial bar to recovery in a medical malpractice claim: assumption of risk based upon a patient's informed consent; the respectable minority or two schools of thought doctrine; and covenant not to sue.

Defenses

Assumption of risk. Patients have the right to determine what shall be done to their own bodies.[40] This includes the right of patients "to make [an] informed decision to go outside currently approved medical methods in search of an unconventional treatment."[41] Physicians' failure to obtain informed consent for the use of a CAM therapy may give rise to an independent malpractice claim.[42] Either the reasonable medical practitioner or the prudent patient standard determines what constitutes adequate information.[43] Informed consent may be written or orally obtained. The question is whether the patient knowingly accepted all of the risks inherent in the offered therapy. In *Schneider v. Revici*, the physician treated cancer patients with nontoxic, noninvasive methods that were not recognized by the medical community. The patient signed a detailed consent form. After 14 months of treatment, the cancer spread and the patient sued. The court held that a patient may expressly "assume the risk of medical malpractice and thereby dissolve the physician's duty to treat a patient according to the medical community standards."[44] An expressed assumption of risk would be a total bar to recovery in a malpractice claim.

In *Boyle v. Revici*, the patient did not sign a consent form. However, at the trial upon a malpractice claim the physician submitted evidence that the patient consciously and with knowledge of the risk decided to forgo conventional cancer treatment and instead sought the physician's nonconventional medical care. The Court held that "[a]bsent a statutory requirement that express assumption of risk requires a writing . . . a jury should decide whether a plaintiff has knowingly accepted all of the risks of a defendant's negligence."[45] Therefore, a defense may be based upon an implied assumption of risk.

The physician in *Charell v. Gonzalez* used hair analysis and nonconventional therapies to diagnose and treat cancer patients. A patient's cancer metastasized and eventually caused blindness and severe back problems. The patient brought a malpractice action based upon the physician's departure from good and accepted medical practice, as well as a cause of action for the physician's failure to obtain informed consent. The jury found that the patient impliedly assumed the risk of injury and apportioned 51% of the responsibility to the physician and 49% of the responsibility to the patient. The court held that "even though [the physician] had not given appropriate information regarding the risks of his procedure . . . it was within the province of the jury, based upon the evidence, . . . that [the patient] independently obtained sufficient information . . . to conclude that there was an implied assumption of risk."[46] The evidence showed that the patient was well educated, and that she, her husband, and her daughter did a significant amount of investigation regarding the physician's nonconventional treatment.

Respectable minority or two schools of thought doctrine.
The respectable minority is also referred to as the two schools of thought doctrine. The test to determine whether a physician's treatment falls under the respectable minority doctrine is unclear. The two tests applied by most jurisdictions that have adopted the respectable minority doctrine are either (1) the treatment is advocated by a considerable number of physicians, or (2) the treatment is what a reasonable and prudent doctor would have done under the same or similar circumstances.

In the Arizona case of *Leech v. Bralliar*, the federal district court considered the appropriateness of prolotherapy

treatment for a whiplash injury to the neck.[47] The court found that prolotherapy "was recognized as an appropriate method of therapy by a small minority of physicians in the United States."[48] The Court stated that "[t]his minority of physicians has not been shown to be other than respectable physicians."[49] The respectable minority consisted of only 65 physicians throughout the United States. The court also noted that the therapy had not been generally accepted by the medical profession.

The plaintiff in *Hood v. Phillips* claimed that the physician was negligent in the choice of a surgical technique.[50] The Texas Supreme Court reviewed the various respectable minority tests and rejected the notion that the tests are to be based solely upon numbers because it conveyed to the jury that "the standard for malpractice is to be determined by a poll of the medical profession."[51] The Court held that "[a] physician who undertakes a mode or form of treatment which a reasonable and prudent member of the medical profession would undertake under the same or similar circumstances shall not be subject to liability for harm caused thereby to the patient." The Court added that "this standard should be applied whether the mode or form of treatment is experimental, outmoded, or rejected."[52]

Finally, in *Jones v. Chidester* the Pennsylvania Supreme Court held that the applicable standard to avoid malpractice liability is whether a physician "followed a course of treatment advocated by a considerable number of recognized and respected professionals. . . ."[53] The court reasoned that this hybrid test integrates both the quantitative and qualitative standards applied by the other jurisdictions. Because the contours of the respectable minority or two schools of thought doctrine are "too fluid and imprecise," some have opined that it does not provide a workable test for an alternative standard of care in CAM malpractice cases.[54] However, as CAM therapies become more recognized and accepted by the general medical community, the standard of care will shift to include those CAM therapies.[55]

Covenant not to sue. In *Colton v. New York Hospital*, plaintiffs sued for medical malpractice related to an experimental kidney transplant from one brother to another.[56] The operation was successful but the recipient brother soon died as a result of a preexisting liver ailment. The donor brother experienced life-threatening complications resulting in physical disabilities. The brothers signed an explicit and detailed form labeled " . . . Consent to Kidney Transplant, And Covenant Not To Sue Upon, And Release of All Claims." The defendants argued that the document was a complete bar to recovery. The plaintiffs claimed that to the extent the instrument sought to relieve defendants from their own negligence it was void as against public policy. The court held that "an experimental procedure which . . . may ordinarily be in and of itself a departure from customary and accepted practice (and thus possibly actionable as malpractice) even if performed in a non-negligent manner, may be rendered unactionable by a covenant not to sue."[57] While a covenant not to sue may permissibly embrace negligence that is based upon a deviation from accepted medical practice, it must be strictly construed against the party asserting it and must be clear and unequivocal. In *Colton*, the covenant not to sue did not specifically enumerate negligence or malpractice.

In *Schneider v. Revici*, the court reviewed the application of a covenant not to sue to CAM.[58] The court recognized the efficacy of a covenant not to sue in the context of medical treatment. However, the court contrasted the form in the *Schneider* case with that in the *Colton* case and found that it was not labeled a covenant not to sue and that it was not clear and unequivocal. Therefore, the facts did not support the defense being submitted to the jury.

Many courts have held that it is against public policy for medical negligence to be the subject of a preinjury release.[59] However, with proper informed consent, patients may consent to experimental medical care that might otherwise not be generally accepted by the medical community.[60] The distinction made by the *Vodopest* court as contrasted with the *Colton* court is that the parties may covenant to exempt the physician from liability for patient injuries that are the consequences of the nonnegligent, proper performance of the experimental procedure.

MALPRACTICE LIABILITY MANAGEMENT STRATEGY

Cohen and Eisenberg suggest the following steps to minimize potential malpractice liability:[61]

1. Determine the clinical risk level by reviewing existing medical literature to assess the evidence for safety and efficacy of a given CAM therapy.
2. Document the literature supporting the therapeutic choice.
3. Provide adequate informed consent by engaging in a clear discussion of the risks and benefits of using the CAM therapy.
4. If feasible, obtain the patient's express, written agreement to use the CAM treatment.
5. Continue to monitor the patient conventionally.

MALPRACTICE LIABILITY FOR CAM REFERRAL

There are no reported cases that consider physicians' malpractice liability for the failure to refer a patient to a CAM practitioner. However, as CAM therapies are proven to be efficacious, physicians may have a duty to refer patients to CAM practitioners.[62] Physicians may be exposed to malpractice liability for either the negligent or vicarious referral of patients to a CAM practitioner. Although there are no reported cases for either situation, courts may extend the legal theories applied to conventional medicine cases.

A cause of action for negligent referral may be based upon the theory that the patient suffered a loss of chance of recovery.[63] If a CAM referral "delays, decreases, or eliminates the opportunity for the patient to receive"[64] more appropriate and necessary health care from another provider, the referring physician may be liable.[65] Negligent referral may also arise in situations where the physician knows or has reason to know that either the provider is incompetent or the CAM therapy is ineffective or dangerous.[66]

Vicarious liability has been recognized when there has been joint employment, a concert of action, some control of the course of one by the other, or agency.[67] The general rule is "that the mere referral of a patient by one physician to another, without more, does not render the referring doctor vicariously liable for the negligence of the treating physician."[68] However, courts have held physicians liable when they have exercised supervisory responsibility or control over other health care providers including other physicians.[69] The referring physician must act in good faith, with reasonable care in the selection of the CAM provider and without knowledge of the CAM provider's incompetence or lack of skill.[70] The CAM provider should also be properly credentialed and in good standing. Physicians who work closely with CAM practitioners, such as in an integrative health clinic, may be considered to have engaged in a joint undertaking or to have acted in concert.[71] Therefore, any harm to the patient as a result of the CAM therapy could be vicariously imputed to the physician.

Cohen and Eisenberg recommend the following referral liability management strategies:[72]

1. Closely monitor the clinical risk level.
2. Document the literature supporting the decision to refer.
3. Provide adequate informed consent of the risk and benefits of the CAM therapy.
4. Document the discussion of the patient's decision to visit a CAM provider.
5. Continue to monitor the patient conventionally.
6. Inquire about the CAM provider's competence.

Physicians who integrate CAM therapies into their medical practice may take consolation in the fact that there are substantially fewer malpractice claims against CAM practitioners.[73] In addition, claims of patient injury were considerably less severe with CAM practitioners as compared to claims against conventional physicians.[74] Also, patients who are likely to use CAM therapies are more educated, knowledgeable, and tend to use the therapies for less serious illnesses.[75]

CONCLUSION

Integrating the use of CAM therapies into a medical practice increases a physician's risk for license suspension or revocation. Currently, medical boards require physicians to practice consistent with accepted and prevailing medical standards. Although misconduct charges may be based upon the physician's practice of CAM, the charges typically tend to allege a failure to perform adequate patient evaluation, testing, monitoring, and record-keeping. Therefore, it is recommended that physicians who use CAM therapies continue to comply with all of the conventional medical practices. Many states have enacted legislation that provides some protection for physicians who practice CAM. The Medical Freedom Acts of most states delineate the minimum standards of acceptable medical practice that physicians must maintain prior to and contemporaneous with the use of CAM.

Patients file fewer complaints against CAM practitioners than they do against conventional physicians. Therefore, physicians who practice CAM are at low risk for malpractice claims against them. However, malpractice claims have been brought by terminally ill patients who have exhausted conventional medicine and underwent CAM treatments that proved to be unsuccessful. To adequately defend against a malpractice claim, physicians should obtain from the patient a detailed written consent that thoroughly explains the risks and benefits of the CAM therapy. It is recommended that physicians continue to provide conventional medical care or advise their patients to continue to consult their primary care physician.

There is low risk of physicians' liability for medical malpractice or referral to CAM practitioners. However, physicians would be wise to consider the malpractice liability and the referral liability management strategies outlined above.

ENDNOTES

1. David M. Eisenberg et al., *Unconventional Medicine in the United States: Prevalence, Costs, and Patterns of Use*, 328 New. Eng. J. Med. 246 (1993) (the survey was conducted in 1990); David M. Eisenberg et al., *Trends in Alternative Medicine in the United States, 1990-1997*, 280 J.A.M.A. 1569 (1998).

2. Miriam S. Wetzel et al., *Courses Involving CAM at U.S. Medical Schools*, 280 J.A.M.A. 784, 784 (1998).

3. *Id.*

4. *Doe v. Axelrod*, 123 A.D. 2d 21, 26 (1st Dept. 1986). *See also Keney v. Derbyshire*, 718 F. 2d 352, 354-355 (C.A.N.M. 1983).

5. *See, e.g.*, N.Y. Pub. Health Law §230(10)(a)(i) (1991).

6. *Alter v. New York Dept. of Health, State Bd. for Prof'l Conduct*, 145 Misc. 2d 393, 395-396 (N.Y. Sup. Ct. 1989).

7. N.Y. Pub. Health Law §230(10)(a)(iv) (1991).

8. *Id.*

9. *A'Hearn v. Comm. on Unlawful Practice of Law of N.Y. Lawyers' Ass'n*, 23 N.Y. 2d 916, 918 (1969). *See also Levin v. Murawski*, 59 N.Y. 2d 35, 41 (1983).

10. *Murawski*, 59 N.Y. 2d at 41. *See also Matter of BU 91-04-1356A*, 186 A.D. 2d 1054 (4th Dept. 1992).

11. *Murawski*, 59 N.Y. 2d at 35. *See also, e.g.*, N.Y. Pub. Health Law §230(10)(o) (1991) for challenges to a CMR.

12. *See* Cal. Bus. & Prof. Code §805 (1991); N.Y. Pub. Health Law §230 (1994).

13. *Metzler v. N.Y. Bd. for Prof'l Med. Conduct*, 203 A.D. 2d 617, 619 (3d Dept. 1994).

14. *Id.* at 617.

15. *Id.*

16. *In re Guess*, 393 S.E. 2d 833, 835 (N.C. 1990).

17. *Gonzalez v. N.Y. Dept. of Health*, 232 A.D. 2d 886 (3d Dept. 1996).

18. *Atkins v. Guest*, 158 Misc. 2d 426 (N.Y. Sup. Ct. 1993).

19. *Id.* at 431.

20. *State Bd. of Med. Examiners of Fla. v. Rogers*, 387 So. 2d 937, 937 (Fla. 1980).

21. Glenn E. Bradford & David G. Meyers, *The Legal and Regulatory Climate in the State of Missouri for Complementary and Alternative Medicine: Honest Disagreement Among Competent Physicians or Medical McCarthyism?*, 70 U.M.K.C. Law Rev. 55, 58 (2001).

22. The standard may be statutorily defined as in *In re Guess*, 393 S.E. 2d 833. Or it may be judicially defined as in *Metzler*, 203 A.D. 2d 617.

23. Bradford & Meyers, *supra* note 21, at 102 n.26.

24. *In re Guess*, 393 S.E. 2d at 838. *See also Metzler*, 203 A.D. 2d 617, and *Gonzalez*, 232 A.D. 2d 886.

25. *Guess*, 393 S.E. 2d at 840-841.

26. Michael H. Cohen, *Holistic Health Care: Including Alternative and Complementary Medicine In Insurance and Regulatory Schemes*, 38 Ariz. L. Rev. 83, 109 (1996).

27. Mary S. Newbold, *Medical Malpractice Law—Pennsylvania's "Two Schools of Thought" Doctrine Revisited: Definition and Application Clarified—Underlying Goal Thwarted—Jones v. Chidester*, 610 A. 2d 964 (Pa. 1992), 66 Temp. L. Rev. 613, 613 (1993).

28. Barbara D. Goldberg, *As Alternative Treatments Increase, So May Malpractice Claims*, 16(7) Med. Malpractice Law & Strategy 1 (1999).

29. *See, e.g.*, Alaska Stat. §08.64.326(a)(8)(A) (1990); Colo. Rev. Stat. §12-36-117 (1997); Fla. Stat. ch. 456.41 (2001); Ga. Code Ann. §43-34-42.1 (1997); Mass. Gen. Laws Ann. ch. 112, §7 (1901); N.Y. Educ. Law §6527(4) (1994) and N.Y. Pub. Health Law §230(1), 230(10)(a) (1994); N.C. Gen. Stat. §90-14(a)(6) (1993); Ohio Rev. Code Ann. §4731.227 (2000); Okla. Stat. tit. 59, §§492(F), 493.1(M), and 509.10(2) (1994); Or. Rev. Stat. §677.190(1) (1995); 22 Tex. Admin. Code §200.1-200.3 (1998); Wash. Rev. Code Ann. §18.130.180(4) (1991).

30. *See* South Dakota Professions and Occupations Statute, S.D. Codified Laws §36-4-29 (1993); Louisiana 1999 La. Acts R.S. 37:1285.3, 40:678 and La. Rev. Stat. tit. 40(4)(II-B) (1999).

31. Arizona, Connecticut, and Nevada license homeopathic practice for physicians already licensed in any state.

32. N.C. Gen. Stat. §90-14(a)(6) (1993).

33. Alaska Stat. §08.64.326(a)(8)(A) (1990).

34. *Metzler*, 203 A.D. 2d at 618.

35. *Gonzalez*, 232 A.D. 2d at 887.

36. *Metzler*, at 618-619.

37. La. Reg. tit. 46, §7103-7107 (2001) (Professional and Occupational Standards, Chapter 41, Integrative and Complementary Medicine); 22 Tex. Admin. Code §200.1-200.3 (1998).

38. *Gray v. Gonzalez*, 290 A.D. 2d 292, 292 (1st Dept. 2002).

39. *Charell v. Gonzalez*, 173 Misc. 2d 227, 227 (N.Y. Sup. Ct. 1997).

40. *Schloendorff v. Soc'y of the N.Y. Hosp.*, 211 N.Y. 125, 126 (1914).

41. *Schneider v. Revici*, 817 F. 2d 987 (2d Cir. 1987).

42. Edward Ernst & Michael H. Cohen, *Informed Consent in Complementary and Alternative Medicine*, 161 Arch. Intern. Med. 2288 (2001).

43. Hunter L. Prillaman, *A Physician's Duty to Inform of Newly Developed Therapy*, J. Contemp. Health Law and Policy 43, 45 (1990).

44. *Schneider*, 817 F. 2d at 995.

45. *Boyle v. Revici*, 961 F. 2d 1060, 1063 (2d Cir. 1992).

46. *Charell*, 173 Misc. 2d at 233.

47. *Leech v. Bralliar*, 275 F. Supp. 897 (D.C. Ariz. 1967).

48. *Id.* at 899.

49. *Id.*

50. *Hood v. Phillips*, 554 S.W. 2d 160 (Tex. Sup. Ct. 1977).

51. *Id.* at 165.

52. *Id.*

53. *Jones v. Chidester*, 610 A. 2d 964, 969 (Pa. Sup. Ct. 1992).

54. Michael H. Cohen, *Complementary and Alternative Medicine: Legal Boundaries and Regulatory Perspectives* 58 (1998).

55. *Id.*

56. *Colton v. New York Hospital*, 98 Misc. 2d 957 (1979).
57. *Id*. at 970.
58. *Schneider v. Revici*, 817 F. 2d 987, 993 (2d Cir. 1987).
59. *Vodopest v. MacGregor*, 913 P. 2d 779, 789 (Wash. 1996).
60. *Id*.
61. Michael H. Cohen & David M. Eisenberg, *Potential Physician Malpractice Liability Associated with Complementary and Integrative Medical Therapies*, 136 Ann. Intern. Med. 596, 599 (2002).
62. *Id*. at 597. *See also* Cohen, *supra* note 54, at 59.
63. *Delaney v. Cade*, 873 P. 2d 175 (Kan. 1994).
64. David M. Studdert et al., *Medical Malpractice Implications of Alternative Medicine*, 280 J.A.M.A. 1610, 1612 (1998).
65. *Delaney*, 873 P. 2d at 182.
66. Cohen & Eisenberg, *supra* note 61, at 600.
67. *Reed v. Bascon*, 530 N.E. 2d 417 (Ill. 1988).
68. *Datiz v. Shoob*, 71 N.Y. 2d 867 (1988).
69. *Harris v. Miller*, 438 S.E. 2d 731 (N.C. 1994) (nurse); *Reed*, 530 N.E. 2d 417 (Ill. 1998) (physician).
70. *Jennings v. Burgess*, 917 S.W. 2d 790 (Tex. 1996).
71. Cohen & Eisenberg, *supra* note 61, at 600.
72. *Id*. at 601.
73. Studdert et al., *supra* note 64, at 1610.
74. *Id*.
75. David M. Eisenberg et al., *Unconventional Medicine in the United States: Prevalence, Costs, and Patterns of Use*, 328 New. Eng. J. Med. 246, 251 (1993).

Practice Organizations and Joint Ventures

MARK E. RUST, J.D.
ELLEN L. LUEPKE, J.D., LL.M.

Throughout much of the twentieth century, fee-for-service solo practice characterized the medical delivery system in the United States.[1] At the dawn of the twenty-first century, this type of medical practice had diminished in importance, replaced primarily by health care delivery systems that emphasize large, physician contracting groups or the "vertical integration" of physicians, hospitals, other health facilities, and related health care providers.[2] Managed care, the dominant method for financing and delivering care, is largely driving this change, prompted by technological advances, the glut of specialist physicians, and health care costs, which soared through the 1970s and 1980s but seemed to subside in the mid-1990s coincident with high managed care penetration.[3] Meanwhile, increased educational debt and an inability to participate adequately in managed care on an equitable basis have made it more difficult for the individual practitioner to enter or maintain the solo practice.

In the 1970s and 1980s the insurance industry responded to employer demands for manageable health benefit costs by developing new products and introducing methods of controlling costs for services covered under conventional insurance plans. These included discounted fee-for-service organizations, such as preferred provider organizations (PPOs), and payer devices, such as prospective payment, concurrent review, and second opinions. The 1990s saw an explosion in managed care as delivered through health maintenance organizations (HMOs), particularly in response to the Health Security Act proposed by President Clinton in 1993.[4] Federal and state governments acted to limit their financial liability under Medicare and Medicaid by limiting fee increases and increasing utilization and quality assurance reviews. In response to these forces,

physicians are organizing, along with other providers, in arrangements designed to help profitably deliver high-tech, quality health care at funding levels now forcefully controlled by government and employers.

To participate in these new arrangements, physicians have restructured the way they practice. In addition to using partnerships, sharing arrangements, group practices, and multiple specialty groups, physicians are developing joint venture contracting arrangements, joining physician-hospital organizations, or forming practice management companies. Grouping physicians in large practices, whether fully integrated for all practice purposes or in joint ventures for some limited purposes, often leads to economies of scale not achieved by a solo practice. Technology has permitted the development of out-patient surgery, imaging, lithotripsy, mammography, laser, and walk-in medical centers. Joint ventures between those who have the ability and willingness to fund such facilities and those who know how to manage them have played a key role. Physicians have banded together and invested in various types of out-patient centers, although such activity has been sharply circumscribed by federal legislation in the 1990s, limiting the types of investments referring physicians can make in such ventures.[5] The resulting physician practice arrangements are designed to maximize delivery and price efficiency in the managed care environment.

PRACTICE ORGANIZATIONS AMONG PHYSICIANS

The physician may be an owner, shareholder, employee, or independent contractor of a practice. The form such practice takes is designed to accommodate physician and business needs.

Solo practice, sole proprietor

The simplest form of physician practice, although increasingly rare, is the solo practitioner, sole proprietor form.

Advantages. The physician is free to establish professional relationships as necessary to create a practice environment.

Disadvantages. As with any other proprietorship, the owner is personally responsible for the liabilities of the business on a personal level. This includes liability for local, state, and federal medical regulations (e.g., occupancy and use, medical licensing, tax, provider reimbursement requirements), as well as all regulations controlling a regular business. The legal disadvantage of the sole proprietorship is the personal liability of the owner for business losses, debt, and negligence. The practical disadvantage to the sole proprietorship form is the difficulties inherent in coverage and participating with any degree of control in sophisticated managed care contracting arrangements.

Sharing arrangements

Sharing arrangements are associations between two or more physicians in which they share office space, equipment, and possibly employees. They may also share coverage of hospital and office patients on a rotating basis or when one or the other is not available.

Advantages. Sharing arrangements permit shared overhead expenses, allowing the participants to attain economies not available in a solo practice. Depending on the arrangement, it may permit shared capital expenditures and relative savings in rent, salaries, fixed costs such as utilities, and assured coverage. A sharing arrangement can exist between solo practitioners who are incorporated or unincorporated. The physicians involved may be partners in ventures that provide services to their individual practices, such as real estate and computer equipment. It has much of the advantages of solo practice while diluting the disadvantages.

Disadvantages. The practices may become so interlocked that to the general public the physicians are regarded as partners and not as solo practitioners. Legally, this means expanded liability for what may be deemed a de facto partnership. Failure to maintain separate employees, records, and billing may be introduced as evidence that there was no separation of medical practices. Liability may not only be extended from one practice to another for day-to-day business dealings but also in the event of medical negligence.[6] In addition, poor planning of the arrangement at its inception, as well as the lack of a clear and comprehensive agreement, will lead to trouble. The ground rules of the sharing arrangement must be established at the time of its creation and be reflected in a contract. Purchases (if jointly made), employee benefits (if shared), lease responsibilities, and other aspects of the arrangement must be defined.

Any employee sharing arrangement may lead to complex benefit plan questions. For example, it may not be possible for one physician with a generous retirement plan to share an employee with a second physician, when neither the second physician nor the employee has any retirement plan benefits.

Partnership

As defined in the Uniform Partnership Act now adopted in various forms by 49 states, a partnership is an association for two or more persons to carry on, as co-owners, a business for profit.[7] The "partner" may be a legal entity such as a corporation. A partnership is contractual in nature but is regulated and controlled by the partnership statute of a given state. Being contractual, the parties may structure the relationship to suit their specific needs. The partnership agreement should spell out the relative duties and obligations of the partners. The agreement should cover the right to manage, operate, and share profits and losses.

Partners have several fundamental rights unless specifically otherwise stated in the agreement: (1) equal participation in the management of the partnership business and (2) majority voting rules. Other than in a limited partnership, or by agreement of the parties, profits and losses are shared equally and, theoretically, no partner can draw a salary. Salary is, in reality, profit.

If not created for a specific period, any partner can terminate a partnership at any time. The death of a partner terminates the partnership unless arrangements have been made to carry on the business in surviving partners' names. Loss of a partner can be chaotic to the business, and the partnership agreement should foresee this eventuality.

Advantages. A partnership provides the device for sharing overhead, arranging formally among the partners to share comprehensively all aspects of their business, and pooling capital. Other advantages include equal management, control, and shared profits.

Disadvantages. The tax consequences, rights and obligations, and liability of a partnership should be assessed before its formation. Being a partner in a general partnership carries certain rights but also creates obligations and liabilities. A general partner is personally responsible for the actions of his or her partners if those acts were made within the scope of partnership business. This extends to professional negligence, as well as commitments for equipment and loans. The partners are also personally responsible for business losses. For these reasons, it is important to determine the reliability of potential partners before entering this type of business arrangement.[8]

Corporation

Unlike a partnership, which can be maintained even without a formal agreement or filing, a corporation is strictly a creation of statute. It is an entity with a defined business purpose that comes into being only after a formal filing. It is created by one or more individuals pursuant to statute to act as the legal representative of those individuals who contribute to its formation or become shareholders in the entity. Most states allow the formation of a *professional corporation*. This subspecies of corporation permits a licensed professional to form a corporation to engage in the business of practicing medicine in those states that would otherwise forbid such practices by regular business corporations. The definition of a professional or description of who can incorporate this type of business is contained within the appropriate state statute.[9] Professionals who incorporate generally form professional corporations, which may also be designated as *professional associations* or *service corporations* (SCs). One or more physicians can form professional corporations.

The major difference between a corporation and a partnership is the degree to which a participant may suffer personal liability for the acts of colleagues. A partner has unlimited personal liability for all partnership losses whether he or she individually incurred them or not. In a corporation, losses are limited to the extent of investment; only rarely can personal assets be touched. A professional corporation is equally liable for the acts of its physician employees in the event of medical negligence, just as any company is liable for the acts of its employees. For this reason, professional liability policies are written in the name of the individual physician with supplemental coverage for the corporation. Thus in the event of a suit for medical negligence, both physician and corporate assets may be at risk if the award or settlement exceeds insurance policy limits, but not the personal assets of fellow physician shareholders.

The physicians should explore asset management at the time of corporate inception. A shareholder is not responsible for the ordinary business losses of a corporation, and a corporation may be dissolved when liability exceeds assets without prejudice to its shareholders. Tax treatment is another major difference between a partnership and a corporation. Partnership profits and losses accrue to the personal tax returns of partners, but, unless a corporation elects Subchapter S status (now available[10] to corporations with fewer than 75 shareholders who have only one class of stock), the corporation will pay a tax on profits before distribution of dividends. Those professional corporations usually define all net revenue as salary paid out by the corporation, not profit, to avoid this result on a normal yearly basis.

The corporate form does not offer all the technical "loophole" protections that it is often thought to offer. At one time, corporations could deposit a greater percentage of salary into a pension plan than could an individual. This anomaly was rectified by the Tax Reform Act of 1986. Separate corporations cannot be maintained and controlled by physician owners that would have the effect of cutting off rank-and-file employees from the employee benefits, such as the pension plan, enjoyed by the physician owners.[11]

Advantages. Limited personal liability, possible benefit plans, certain tax breaks, and continuity in the event of the death of a shareholder are some advantages of incorporation. The practice is also more saleable if it possesses a corporate name and life outside its existing individual physician founder.

Disadvantages. Forming a corporation involves double taxation and significant difficulties in a tax-advantaged sale of the physician practice (unless the corporation has elected Subchapter S status) and in the maintenance of the corporate entity (e.g., minute books, records, attorney fees).

Limited liability company

Starting in 1994, physicians in many states had the opportunity of forming their practice as a limited liability company (LLC). LLCs are recognized in virtually every state, but not all states recognize the right of an LLC to perform medical services.

The LLC was specifically designed to take advantage of the type of tax treatment available to partnerships (where profits and losses flow directly through to the owners) while providing the type of liability shelter that is typically identified only with corporations. This type of entity, by the late 1990s, was rapidly becoming the entity of choice for physician joint ventures formed for the purpose of managed care contracting.

Advantages. The LLC offers the advantage of a single level of tax at the owner level with the highest degree of protection from liability for the acts of fellow owners. Further these taxation benefits can be obtained, unlike in the S corporation, regardless of the number of owners or classes of ownership.

Disadvantages. Case law is not well developed with respect to LLC disputes. LLC formation is more involved, and the governance mechanism is less familiar to most physicians. Costs are generally higher for the maintenance of an LLC than for a corporation. Also, if an LLC decides for business purposes to retain capital in a particular year instead of distributing it to the owners, the owners will still be credited with the receipt of such monies and will be taxed accordingly.

Independent contractor

A physician may choose to provide services as an independent contractor to an individual physician, a professional corporation, health care institution, urgent care center, or any other practice setting available. This is a contractual relationship in which the physician generally has no equity interest. The services may be provided on a continuous or temporary basis.

Advantages. No commitment to office space or overhead mobility, a fixed work schedule, and fixed income on an hourly, daily, or weekly basis are some of the advantages of being an independent contractor.

Disadvantages. The independent contractor may be expendable, may be uninsured, and has no permanency to his or her practice situation. The relationship is strictly a matter of contract between the parties, so lack of a written agreement clarifying the parties' intention is a serious mistake. The issue of medical negligence insurance should also be examined carefully. The agreement should specify who will provide and pay for the insurance. Generally, if one is engaged as an independent contractor by a *locum tenens* agency, malpractice insurance will be provided. If an independent contractor appears to operate in a manner more often associated with employees, the Internal Revenue Service (IRS) may characterize the physician as an employee, triggering a series of negative tax consequences for both parties. A series of common-law tests are available to make this determination.[12]

Employee

Increasingly, physicians are starting or remaining in practice as the employee of an institution, another physician, medical group, or other practice setting. The key part of this relationship is the contract between the parties, which should address salary and benefits, incentives, liability insurance (and prior acts or "tail" coverage), termination, requirements for hospital privileges, and restrictive or noncompete covenants.

Advantages. The employment relationship is often strengthened by rights spelled out in a contract. A contract is a written expression of the agreement between two parties. Both independent contractors and employee physicians are sometimes faced with the same problem. Because they lack an equity position in the practice, clinic, office, or other health institution, such physicians may have a difficult time negotiating language sufficient to protect their position in the community, as well as liability and income. Such physicians must understand, however, that the contract is the ultimate definition of the working relationship between the parties and that generally, oral understandings not expressed in the contract's "four corners" will not be taken into account. Before starting a long-term relationship, an employee can test the good faith of his or her employer by seeking clarification of a number of issues. The contract should at a minimum specify responsibility for insurance coverage, tail insurances, and termination. The individual employee's objective should be to protect himself or herself from termination, just or unjust, without malpractice tail insurance coverage.

The written agreement may also include a noncompete clause or restrictive covenant, which restricts a departing physician from seeing patients he or she previously saw through the employer. The validity of these covenants varies with the jurisdiction. From the employed physician's viewpoint, if inclusion can be avoided, it should be omitted, although from the employer's viewpoint, it may be a non-negotiable part of the deal. For an employed physician, if inclusion cannot be avoided, it should be limited as to when it will apply, and a cash buyout formula should be defined in the agreement.

MANAGED HEALTH CARE

Provider services were traditionally delivered to the health care consumer on a direct fee-for-service basis. Even physicians who were hospital based or employed generally billed the consumer directly. With the advent of the federal government as payer through Medicare, for patients 65 and over, and with the expansion of third-party insurance coverage to employees as part of a negotiated pension and benefit package, the traditional financial relationship of provider and patient evolved.

For many decades, from the 1930s and 1940s through the 1970s, insurance simply paid the lion's share of the physician's charge directly to the physician on a claim assigned to him by the patient, and the patient paid the remainder. By the late 1970s and 1980s, however, government and employers stepped in to create an alternative system, one where they could manage the product to reduce costs rather than allowing consumers to choose and pay directly for services. The pervasiveness of these alternative delivery methods, spurred largely by the payers and, most significantly, HMOs, PPOs, and their progeny, gradually eroded the ability of the physician to control what was paid for his or her services and where those services were performed. It even changed, in many cases, whether the patient could continue to see his or her own physician. What used to be called "alternate and managed health care delivery systems," because it was the alternative to the standard indemnity approach, has become the standard itself and today is simply known as "managed health care."

The dominant forms of managed health care are HMOs and PPOs. These organizations introduced prepayment and negotiated fees for service as an alternative to traditional fee for service. The HMO is generally a prepaid plan whereby primary care providers are paid on a monthly capitated basis for each enrollee, who in turn pays a relatively nominal coinsurance payment for medical service. The PPO is a provider group, traditionally assembled by an insurance company but today increasingly organized by physicians or entrepreneurs, that provides services on a discounted basis to the consumer.[13]

Health maintenance organizations

The term *health maintenance organization* was first coined by Dr. Paul Ellwood in the mid-1960s.[14] The Nixon administration pushed federal legislation and financing during the late 1960s and early 1970s, which enabled HMOs to gain a national foothold.[15] National membership in HMOs has grown to approximately one quarter of the population.[16]

An HMO is an integrated health care delivery system that combines the traditional financial risk of a health insurer with the hospital and physician service delivery responsibilities of a provider network. The HMO presumes it can contain costs by limiting hospitalizations, specialty referrals, and procedures and shifting some financial risk to the provider. It sells insurance coverage to consumers on a premium basis and attempts to create a provider network that is both competent and cost conscious. The goal in assuming the financial risk is the delivery of quality health care to the enrolled consumer at a controlled and predictable price. To do so, the HMO usually contracts with providers on a per capita basis for primary care and a discounted basis for diagnostic and specialty referrals. To enforce the system, many plans use a "gatekeeper" concept in which the primary care provider determines whether specialty or diagnostic referral is needed. Consumer self-referral is generally excluded from coverage.

HMOs generally structure themselves on one of five models for delivery of physician services: staff, independent practice association (IPA), group, network, and mixed.

Staff model. HMO-owned clinics staffed by physician employees are known as staff model HMOs. Such models are increasingly rare. Cost savings in this model are achieved by fixed provider costs and HMO ownership of hospitals and ancillary service centers. Control of these cost centers increases profitability for the plan as a whole by decreasing referred, in-patient, emergency department, and diagnostic costs.

Independent practice association. This model has two categories. In the first category the IPA may consist of providers, such as primary care and specialist physicians, assembled as a provider group by the plan, who contract individually or by group to provide services. These services may be paid on a fee-for-service or discounted basis but increasingly are paid on a per capita, or capitation, basis. In *capitation* the provider is paid on a per member, per month basis in advance of delivering care. The IPA in this case consists of a physician panel that is assembled by the HMO.

The second category, provider-created IPAs, represent and negotiate contracts for the group as a whole with HMOs. The IPA is composed of individual practitioners and group practices. Physician-controlled HMOs and IPAs raise significant issues under antitrust law. These providers may substantially control the market, as reflected by their large market share. Even when such groups are small, they may have been seen as an illegitimate joint venture of physicians that attempts collectively to set a fee-for-service price for its physicians without benefit of any form of clinical integration; this is a criminal violation of the antitrust laws (see later section on joint ventures).

Group model. In this model an HMO contracts for services with independent practice groups; the basis for the contract may be either discounted fees or capitation in exchange for exclusivity. Hospitals, diagnostic centers, surgicenters, and urgent care centers may be arranged on a

similar basis for services not provided by the group. Although price fixing within an independent group is not possible and therefore not an issue, size can be, particularly where the HMO is primarily controlled by its relationship with a single group.

Network (primary care) model. In this form, primary care providers are assembled in a network that serves as the provider panel. The primary care physicians serve as gatekeepers paid on a capitation basis who limit referrals to hospitals, specialists, and diagnostic centers. The HMO sometimes contracts for specialty services, and sometimes transfers "full medical risk" for medical service delivery to the group, which in turn subcontracts with specialists. Less commonly, the HMO may contract through such a group for "full risk," including hospital services, and the group will subcontract for both specialist and hospital services.

Mixed models. The mixed model may be any combination of the preceding systems. This system is more complex to assemble, but it may allow an HMO to tailor services to a specific market need.

HMOs employ various methods to control costs. The first method limits covered services for enrollees to a specific provider network. The second method requires a copayment, which is usually nominal. The third method limits services to the primary care physicians, the so-called gatekeepers who determine whether specialty referral and diagnostic testing are necessary. The HMO contract with patients or "subscribers" denies these individuals the right of self-referral. Additionally, the contract between the HMO and providers tends to put the providers at financial risk for overutilization of services. These services may be diagnostic tests, specialty referrals, or hospitalizations. In some cases the contract creates a holdback amount of about 10% to 20% of the capitation, discounted, or fee-for-service rate. Often the HMO will also create a pool or budgeted account for diagnostic testing and hospitalizations. If the primary care physician has a low referral or utilization rate at the end of each quarter or year, the HMO may share a portion of savings from this budgeted account in a bonus to the provider.

Preferred provider organizations

PPOs evolved as another form of managed health care. An HMO is considered an integrated managed health care system in that it assumes risk for patient care. It integrates the financial aspects of an insurance company and the health delivery dimension of a provider network. In contrast, the PPO deals only with health care delivery; it is not an insurance company. This permits the PPO to escape most of the state, federal, and insurance regulations that apply to an HMO. The PPO contracts with physicians who deliver services on a discounted basis. The employer or administrator of the PPO is able to offer financial incentives to enrollees in the form of lower health care costs. The physicians, in turn, agree to abide by the utilization and quality assurance controls implemented by the PPO. The beneficiary is responsible for a deductible and coinsurance fee for services rendered. If the beneficiary sees a physician or obtains a service outside the panel, financial disincentives are imposed in the form of higher deductibles and coinsurance payment.

Non–hospital-based facilities

As coverage plans evolved and facilities providing care morphed from the one-dimensional world of the hospital to the multidimensional world of urgent care centers (walk-in medical centers), ambulatory surgical centers, diagnostic imaging centers, and freestanding laboratories, opportunities for physicians to be employees, independent contractors, or investors have increased. The advantage of being an investor, where not prohibited by law, is that the return on equity is related to the investment and thus generates passive income. An employee owner shares in profit in the facility as an investor, while also earning income on a fee-for-service or salary basis as a professional who provides services.

The issue of ownership and self-referral, however, is a problem for the health care industry, especially for the provider. The temptations for overutilization and overcharging are great. A physician-run laboratory is utilized about 30% to 40% more than a commercial non–provider-owned entity.[17] As a result, a number of states[18] have passed laws that prohibit referrals by a physician to a facility in which he or she has an interest, variously defined narrowly as an "ownership" interest or broadly as any "financial" interest (sweeping in debt, rentals, indirect ownership by relatives, and the like).

Most significantly, federal law now circumscribes a large variety of the types of ventures referring physicians may participate in as owners or, indeed, on any basis. The 1992 federal ban on physician referrals to clinical laboratories in which the referring physician has a financial interest outside their own office (*Stark I*) was expanded in 1994 to prohibit referrals for 12 designated health care services, including hospital in-patient and out-patient services, diagnostic services, and physical therapy (*Stark II*).[19] For the definition of what constitutes a "referral" and what constitutes a "financial interest" in such arrangements, Congress chose the broadest language possible.[20] As a result, Stark I and Stark II cast a large number of previously legal physician-related ventures into either clear illegality or the shadows of legal uncertainty. Before participating in any of these ventures, legal counsel intimately familiar with physician practices and the subtleties of the federal anti–self-referral ban must be consulted.

Legal considerations

PPOs and HMOs, as well as entities formed for the operation of a facility that provides an alternative to hospital-based care, have diverse ownership structures. They range from large, publicly held corporations to small, physician/investor-owned companies. To understand why these structures are chosen, it is essential to understand three related areas of law: the law of joint ventures, the antitrust law, and the general regulatory controls on the delivery and corporate practice of medicine.

JOINT VENTURES

Changing patterns of health care utilization and reimbursement, along with increasing competitive pressures, have led to declining revenues and market share for both physicians and institutions. In an attempt to compensate for these declines in both patient and cash flow, physicians, hospitals, and other types of health care providers have joined forces to prevent or reverse such losses through joint ventures. In recent years the joint venture has become a common method to capitalize on new opportunities in the health care market. Hospitals and physicians may need one another to form HMOs, PPOs, physician hospital organizations (PHOs), and other associations that compete with commercial models. Hospitals often need physicians to be partners in out-patient ventures, including out-patient diagnostic facilities (e.g., magnetic resonance imaging [MRI] centers, mammography centers, other imaging services), urgent care centers, freestanding surgicenters, and freestanding rehabilitation centers, although the federal and state anti–self-referral laws have severely curtailed the numbers and types of such ventures. Because these types of ventures primarily need capital for construction and equipment, they could be built by hospitals, alone, without the joint ventures cooperation of physicians. However, the need for active physician participation in and commitment to providing services in the evolving health care delivery system often forces hospitals to reach out to physicians as partners.

Joint ventures among physicians, health care providers, institutions, and businesspersons are a growing phenomenon. The legality of these ventures depends on federal and state policies that regulate referral relationships and commercial competition generally. Each venture requires that both federal and state law be researched as to the venture's legality. Unfortunately, no clear law can be found and applied. Rather, extrapolations and analogies may have to be drawn from vague or loosely related statutes and cases. Ultimately, the joint venture may be forced to proceed on the basis of a series of educated guesses. A syndicated real estate venture might be legitimate, whereas a physician-owned MRI center may not, even though the venture involves the same two parties. Variations in state law make it extremely difficult to apply one type of experience to another state without adequate research into that jurisdiction's laws and regulations.

Rather than giving specific legal advice, which is impossible without reviewing all the facts of a particular venture, this section provides a primer for the creation of a joint venture.

Definition and characteristics

A joint venture is an association of two or more persons or entities that combine their resources to carry out a business enterprise for profit. This suggests creation of a new entity having managerial, financial, and productive capacity to enter or serve a new market. The agreement between the parties may establish a completely new entity or utilize pre-existing entities to serve new markets or provide a new product. Creation of a completely new venture having independent management, facilities, and autonomy is generally advisable to avoid unnecessary legal and tax complications. The degree of independence enjoyed by the joint venture from either party is important in determining whether the enterprise is a bona fide business. The bona fides of the business are important in determining the existence of fraud, individual liability, or corporate liability.

Joint ventures are created to meet hospital, physician, and business goals. Their main purpose may not be solely for capital formation. The reason why two parties may joint venture together, when these two parties have a referral relationship, is always subject to close scrutiny under the federal anti-kickback law, a criminal statute.

In addition to raising capital, hospitals may develop relationships with physicians, insurance companies, and others (1) to develop "new profit centers" within the hospital or in an out-patient setting; (2) to create alternative delivery systems to satisfy third-party payers; (3) to increase and enhance market penetration of the physicians and hospital; (4) to alter hospital-patient mix, limit debt financing, and increase community support for the hospital; and (5) to cement the relationship with physicians and other providers who support the institution. This list could be extended, but the goal is increased profitability by controlling costs, penetrating the patient care market on both an in-patient and out-patient basis, and securing the support of the local community and health providers.

Physician goals for entering joint venture agreements with one another or with hospitals include (1) entering new service areas, (2) creating out-patient facilities, (3) increasing or maintaining market share, (4) controlling costs, (5) sharing financial risk, and (6) participating in investment opportunities and acquiring capital management and marketing skills that might otherwise be more expensive to acquire. Joint ventures also allow physicians to invest and profit in areas that might otherwise be closed to them.

Joint venture permutations include physician-physician, physician-hospital, and realtor-physician. They range from life retirement centers to physician-owned laboratories and surgicenters. Because these ventures have increased in such numbers, the federal government, mostly through regulation of Medicaid and Medicare, has had the effect of limiting the access of physician referrers to certain investment

vehicles. Increased capital requirements created by new equipment and treatment modalities have forced providers and institutions to reassess their relationship.

The six basic legal models for establishing joint ventures are (1) contract, (2) corporate (the traditional choice), (3) partnership (limited and general), (4) LLC (the form most often used in recent years because of its tax flexibility), (5) franchise, and (6) venture capital.

Contract model

The contract model is simplest, because the entire joint venture is contained within the four corners of a contract between the parties.[21] This could involve a service agreement lease, for example, in which physicians lease land from a hospital for the construction of a building that they then lease back to the hospital. In that example, the hospital does not have to contribute capital, and the builders have a leased building with a guaranteed rate of return. No separate legal entity would be formed. Instead, the relationship is defined by the contract itself and is negotiated on the relative power of the joint venture partners.

The advantages to this form of joint venture are that it is simple to organize and understand, and it requires no new corporations or infrastructure. The contractual relationship is between preexisting entities. The disadvantage is that the contractual relationship creates new liabilities for the parties while lacking the near-permanence and additional protection that grow from the creation of an entity.

Corporate model

This model requires a corporate entity to be formed by the joint venturers, who will become shareholders. The joint venturers may be physicians, hospitals, or other investors. Individuals, corporations, or partnerships may own shares. Ownership need not be limited to physicians or hospitals.

The corporation acts through its board of directors. These joint ventures begin with a preincorporation agreement establishing terms of participation. The board has the day-to-day authority to run the business and set policy. The preincorporation agreement might describe the business plan, but it would not be incorporated into the bylaws of the corporation.

The corporation model results in a distinct legal entity that may expand on its own without further joint venturer participation or increased risk. The corporation will protect the investors from legal responsibility that exceeds their capital investment. The disadvantage to the corporation form, unless formed as a nonprofit organization, is that it is generally subject to double taxation. In addition, compliance with state and federal securities laws may be necessary before capitalization, increasing start-up costs.

General partnership model

A general partnership is the association of two or more entities or persons who act as co-owners of a for-profit business. Profits and losses are equally shared unless otherwise agreed in the partnership agreement. The partnership agreement states the rights and duties of the partners. The partnership agreement specifies any arrangement the partners may wish to institute. The partnership is subject to the specific statutes of the state in which it is created.

The advantages of the partnership are single taxation and joint ownership and management. The major disadvantage is that each general partner is legally obligated to third parties for 100% of the losses, debts, and liability of the business as a whole.

Limited partnership model

A limited partnership consists of at least one general partner with unlimited liability who is responsible for the management of the business. There can be one or more limited partner investors who have equity ownership with a liability potential limited to the amount of their investment, but who are not involved in the management.

The advantages are similar to a general partnership; however, limited partners are not responsible for losses in excess of their contributions. General partners in a limited partnership may be incorporated, thus limiting liability to their corporate assets. Limited partners gain security and limit their losses but are barred from exerting day-to-day control over the business. Management participation of a limited partner may expose them to the liability of the general partner.

Limited liability company

The LLC is the preferred choice for joint ventures among physicians, often seen in the development of physician networks formed for managed care contracting purposes.[22] An LLC protects participants from liability, just as a corporation does, but allows all revenues and expenses associated with the enterprise to be treated, from a tax perspective, as though the entity is a partnership.[23] Thus an LLC is usually regarded as closer to a partnership than a corporation.

This tax advantage is important. Particularly in an evolving health care market, where consolidation is rampant and where the likelihood of the LLC being subsumed or acquired by another entity is high, negative tax consequences from such sales must be anticipated.

Within an LLC, physicians may retain earnings, declare profits (and losses), or reap the benefits of sales proceeds without the double-taxation penalty. They may also create different classes of ownership interests and avoid any limitation on the size of membership. Further, a network of physicians could preserve its option of offering memberships to individual physician participants, as opposed to their professional corporations, without fear of exposing these personal participants to the liabilities of the entity.

An LLC may also be the choice of physicians and hospitals that co-venture certain projects, and this leads to one disadvantage when physicians venture with hospitals exempt from federal taxation. From a business perspective, there may be good reasons to retain LLC earnings in the venture for new costs or infrastructure. To a tax-exempt organization, there is no impact. To the tax-paying physician, however, those retained monies are deemed income on which tax is owed, even though the physician never actually received a distribution. This is the subject of ongoing tension in such ventures.

Venture capital model

The most common venture capital approach to joint venturing among physicians, hospitals, and commercial interests currently may be found in management services organizations (MSOs), generally associated with hospitals but sometimes privately held, and physician practice management companies (PPMCs), usually associated with commercial investors or publicly traded companies. In both cases the management company purchases the assets of a physician's practice, including furniture, fixtures and equipment, and accounts receivable. It also purchases the obligation of the physician group and its individual physicians not to practice elsewhere in competition with the venture. A physician's professional corporation remains intact, possessing only its employment relationships with its physician shareholders and physician employees, and their ongoing relationships and contracts to provide medical services. The management company then contracts with the professional corporation on a long-term basis (usually 20 to 40 years) to manage the professional corporation in exchange for some percentage of revenues, usually calculated in a specific formula designed to comply with state corporate practice of medicine and fee-splitting rules.

Because the management company does not practice medicine but solely maintains assets and purchases accounts receivable from the professional corporation on a regular basis through its management agreement, it is largely free of a wide range of state and federal regulations that might otherwise apply to a medical practice limiting opportunities for investor participation. As a result, everyone from hospitals to commercial financial houses to Wall Street may participate as a joint venture with physicians in their effort to become a larger and more sophisticated player in the evolving health care marketplace.

Financing considerations

State and federal interest in the nature of joint ventures and referral patterns may affect the type of venture and finance arrangements selected by the joint ventures. Stark I, Stark II,[24] and evolving tax law (particularly where a venture with a tax-exempt entity is concerned) have subjected physician joint venture to increasing governmental review. Arrangements where physicians "self-refer" to a service or facility where they have a financial interest are suspect. As a result, these laws may play a role in the way in which a venture is financed.

Conventional debt financing. Debt financing takes the form of a loan payable in a specific term, a revolving line of credit, or a demand line of credit. In general, a loan involves a set amount, for a certain term with a specified rate of interest. It may be for interest only with a balloon payment or amortized over a set time. The interest may be specified or may vary according to a specified formula (e.g., prime rate).

Bonds. Tax-exempt bonds issued by a state or a political subdivision of a state may be exempted from federal taxation. They generally are not tax-free in the state issued unless the state waives the right to tax the bonds. At least 75% of the bonds issued by the state or a political subdivision must be used in a tax-exempt trade or business, as specified in Section 501-C-3 of the IRS code.

Industrial development bonds are bonds issued to create nonexempt businesses, which are defined as entities with more than 25% of the proceeds used to finance nonexempt businesses. Tax-exempt status is determined on a case-by-case basis.

Public and private equity and debt offering. Securities registration statements for a public offering must be filed, and the requirements are time-consuming and costly. Exemptions to the filing and disclosure requirements include insurers of securities, incorporators of businesses, and all offers of sales in which 80% of the sales, proceeds, revenues, and assets remain in one state for the first 6 months. Resales must be made within the same state 9 months after the sale. The aggregate offering price must be less than $1.5 million, and the Securities and Exchange Commission (SEC) must clear the offering 10 days before the offer of sale.

Qualified private equity offerings are exempted from requirements to file a security statement. The requirements to qualify for the exemption are precise and statutorily mandated. The dollar amount must be less than $500,000, regardless of the number of investors. Alternatively, the offering can be for less than $5 million to 35 or fewer unaccredited investors and an unlimited number of accredited investors. An accredited investor must have a net worth exceeding $2 million or a net income in excess of $200,000 for the last 2 years. In some states an offering limited to less than 50 or 35 investors, depending on the state, may be exempt under state blue-sky laws.

Venture capital. Venture capitalists are risk-takers who gamble that a gain will be achieved by private or public sale of a newly established business. Venture capitalists only recently entered the physician segment of the health care industry in significant numbers, largely as a result of development of PPMCs. Previously, venture capitalists have assisted in starting up ambulatory health care companies in the 1980s. In return for their capital, they often assume a large degree of control and a preferred percentage of profits.

Equipment lease financing. Equipment may be acquired for the purpose of leasing to a health care facility or medical practice. The facility may be a hospital, ambulatory care center, or physician's office or clinic. The advantages may be accelerated depreciation, guaranteed rent, and capital conservation for the lessee.

The terms of the lease financial arrangements, maintenance agreements, sublease, replacement, or acquisition by the lessee are all subject to negotiation as part of the contract, but may be subject to fair market value limitations when executed between referring parties.

ANTITRUST CONSIDERATIONS

Antitrust law distinguishes between impediments to competition that are "horizontal" (i.e., between competitors) and those that are "vertical" (i.e., impede competition because a product has been tied up through a relationship between the various players that produce the product's components, such as the primary care physicians, specialists, and hospitals that, together, produce the in-patient hospital product). This section focuses primarily on horizontal issues, which most often arise in the development of the new physician organizations that are responding to the evolution in managed care.

The key distinction between types of physician organizations pivots on the degree to which the organizations are "integrated" on the one end of the spectrum or "nonintegrated" on the other end, with degrees of integration or "partial integration" in between. A medical clinic that is a single professional corporation with multiple specialty physicians as employees is fully integrated. On the other end of the spectrum, an IPA that engages only in fee-for-service contracts and does not attempt to build any sort of joint clinical data operation is completely nonintegrated. Network joint ventures that negotiate fees with clinical integration; network joint ventures that negotiate risk-based contracts, such as capitation; PPMCs that manage a variety of professional corporations; and PPMCs that manage a single professional corporation provide increasingly greater, but not full, integration along the integration scale.

The key elements in determining the degree of integration are the extent to which previously separate organizations have combined their assets and the extent to which the previously separate organizations will combine their liabilities in the future. Certain specific attributes of integration may be important, such as the degree to which the parties share defined liabilities (e.g., risk under a capitation contract) or the degree to which the parties share defined assets, which may grow or evaporate depending on their collective performance (e.g., fee withholds under contracts performed by the group). Also important are the degree to which the participants in the combination have invested their own capital and the degree to which the venture participants intend to create new efficiencies through clinical integration (i.e., tracking information on all participants and using that information to reduce utilization, reduce costs, and increase profits or revenues to venture participants).

No horizontal entity can negotiate contracts on behalf of its members without first achieving the degree of integration required to avoid triggering the antitrust laws. Section 1 of the Sherman Antitrust Act prohibits contracts, combinations, or conspiracy in restraint of trade.[25] Physicians who are independent actors and who collectively negotiate for fees are engaged in a *per se violation* of Section 1, meaning that no further argument regarding the rationale for such behavior will be entertained by a court that is considering either the criminal or civil penalties for such behavior. These principles exclude traditional IPA fee-for-service agreements from collective negotiation.[26] Approaches have been developed to allow individual IPA members to opt into or out of such agreements, which are generally referred to as *messenger model* devices.[27]

However, physician joint ventures such as IPAs and networks that seek to negotiate non–fee-based contracts (capitation, global arrangements, substantial withholds), or such ventures that have sufficient clinical integration and desire to negotiate fee-based contracts, will not be subject to per se treatment but rather will be permitted to collectively negotiate such contracts if such collective negotiations are reasonable under the economic circumstances. This important development arose from the joint statements of the U.S. Department of Justice and the Federal Trade Commission (FTC) issued in August 1996.[28] The most significant and subtle development in those joint statements is the groundbreaking acknowledgment by the enforcement agencies that even fee-based contracts can be jointly negotiated by a physician group if the group is legitimate in its desire to integrate clinically and is not a sham group simply designed to maintain or increase utilization and prices. Finally, when all physicians are contained in a single, fully integrated group, there can be no fee negotiation difficulty under the antitrust laws. The group is a single actor, and violations of Section 1 can occur only when two or more parties or entities combine or conspire to violate it.

Even fully integrated groups, however, could violate the antitrust laws if they are large enough to exert market power. For example, physician mergers in which "all the doctors in town" are involved might be prohibited if their effect "may be substantially to lessen competition or tend to create a monopoly" under another important antitrust law, the Clayton Act.[29] Even joint ventures, such as physician networks, are subject to this prohibition. As a result, the FTC and the Justice Department identified market shares of physicians that, in joint ventures, will never create a cause for concern. If physicians formed groups that include a larger percentage of physicians than those identified in the joint statements (30% of the physicians in a particular specialty in nonexclusive groups), a "rule of reason" analysis

would have to be conducted to determine whether such a venture was lawful.

Because of the imprecise nature of determining when a group has "market power," the group's "percentage of market share" is used as a rough rule of thumb for whether the group will have market power. This is a presumption that may, and should in the case of physicians, be rebutted. Commentators have consistently pointed out that market share is only one factor requiring consideration when determining market power.[30] Enforcement agencies have extensively refined their view of market percentages as an indicator of possible anticompetitive effects.

Enforcement agencies have stated that exclusive physician networks consisting of 20% or fewer of the physicians in each specialty with active hospital staff privileges who practice in the relevant geographic market and share substantial financial risk, or nonexclusive physician networks consisting of no more than 30% of such physicians, will not, absent extraordinary circumstances, be challenged by the agencies. To show that they do not believe networks should be limited to 30% of physicians, however, they have issued a series of advisory opinions and business review letters that have "blessed" networks with significantly greater than 30% market share.[31] As an important limit to the agencies' willingness to bless sizeable networks, they are particularly reluctant to bless networks where they believe that it is difficult, if not impossible, for competitors to enter the market.[32]

REGULATORY AND RELATED CONSIDERATIONS

Joint ventures and medical delivery arrangement are affected by a wide variety of regulations. This section focuses on those unique to medicine.

Licensure

Joint ventures may be organized between physicians and hospitals or by physicians alone. Freestanding urgent care centers or surgicenters may be organized and run solely by and for the benefit of the physicians who provide services, or they may be open to physician and nonphysician investors. These permutations may be determined by state licensing requirements.

A hospital-run facility may fall under the general licensing and certificate-of-need regulations (if any) of the particular state; each state's statutes must be reviewed. In most states freestanding surgicenters, HMOs, and diagnostic facilities are highly regulated, whereas an urgent care center may be treated as a physician's office, with little or no regulation imposed.

Regardless of the specific state regulations that regulate these centers, generally accepted legal precepts will apply. Each facility must be able to deliver the type and quality of services it advertises. The appropriate staff, equipment, and ancillary support services must be provided to maintain acceptable standards of care. Failure to maintain these standards opens the door to litigation not only with the physicians and entity but also with the investors.

The Joint Commission on Accreditation of Healthcare Organizations (JCAHO) has approved standards applicable to freestanding urgent care centers. Its *Accreditation Manual*, generally updated yearly, contains these standards. The National Association of Freestanding Emergency Centers has established the Accreditation Association for Ambulatory Care. This voluntary association provides an *Accreditation Handbook* that should be used as a guide to the establishment and management of freestanding urgent care centers. Standards are suggested concerning medical records, patient rights, and services provided by the facility.

Insurance regulations

Joint ventures may create insurance companies. Since the advent of HMOs, physicians, hospitals, and other joint venturers have joined forces, in many combinations, to provide health insurance plans to consumers. The HMO was the first and probably the most popular method of uniting physicians. By accepting the economic burden of the patients, the HMO falls under the jurisdiction of both federal HMO and state insurance regulations, and PPOs may also fall under the purview of the state insurance statutes. Regulation of PPOs is generally much less onerous than that applicable to HMOs and other types of insurance companies.

Although an HMO must comply with federal HMO legislation if it intends to become "federally qualified," state law generally controls HMOs and PPOs. These laws impose reserve requirements, regulatory approval of the text of policies, reinsurance, and frequent and regular reporting to state agencies. The joint ventures may be unable to sell the product even if the business is in compliance with all regulations. As investors, the physicians and other providers have to maintain an arm's-length relationship to avoid any questions of price fixing. The plan itself, whatever the product mix, may be compelled to offer certain types of benefit packages and may not be allowed to exclude or rate insured clients.

Tort liability for the enterprise

There is a growing trend in the United States to hold organizations independently responsible for their acts. The concept of corporate negligence has begun to permeate the medical arena. As a result, PPOs, HMOs, hospitals, and other entities (e.g., laboratory services, urgent care centers, diagnostic centers) are potentially liable for negligence, regardless of provider affiliation.[33]

Additionally, there is the potential for employers and the insurance network to be liable, because patients in prepaid plans are forced to select physicians from the panel chosen by the plan and indirectly by the purchaser of the insurance.[34] This expanded liability imposes on the joint venturers an obligation to follow through with credentialing, peer review, quality assurance, and risk management where required.

A further component of the problem is the limitation of care provided. The HMO and PPO tend to try to limit referrals and laboratory testing. Under the guidelines established by the joint venture, this may indicate a breach in the standard of care. As physicians, hospitals, health care providers, and venture capitalists enter the health care arena, their liability exposure mushrooms. In considering a joint venture with diversified services, the investor should explore the potential for personal liability. One way to limit loss exposure is to institute risk management programs. Florida was one of the first states to initiate mandatory risk management as a component of health delivery systems.[35]

The integration of internal utilization review, quality assurance, and risk management programs may decrease potential loss exposure. The Health Care Quality Insurance Act of 1986 created a national data bank for reporting physicians and providing data to certain organizations to credential physicians.[36] Failure to properly credential an individual could open the way for civil litigation based on failure to report or failure to query the data bank for information.[37]

Fraud, abuse, and ethical considerations

Medicare has prohibited the solicitation, receipt, or payment of any fee directly, indirectly, overtly, or covertly for the referral of a Medicare or Medicaid beneficiary for a covered item of service, whether it be for goods, services, facilities, or other benefits.[38] The advent of physician-owned ventures has opened an area of potential abuse.

The Judicial Council of the American Medical Association has ruled that physicians can engage in commercial ventures, but they should be aware of potential conflicts of interest. If the physician's commercial interest conflicts with patient care, alternative arrangements should be made.[39]

Stark I/II is designed to deal with the issue of physician self-referral. It reverses the burden of the fraud and abuse statutes, which require the government to prove illegal intent to refer or receive referrals for remuneration. Instead, it prohibits all referrals between financially interested parties unless they meet narrow exceptions, and it requires the physician to prove an exception has been met.

Legislation enacted in 1987 allows the inspector general of the Department of Health and Human Services (DHHS) to exclude a person from Medicare participation if he or she engages in a prohibited remuneration scheme. The act also required the secretary of DHHS to promulgate "safe harbor" regulations, which give physicians comfort that their referral relationships are legal. Legislation enacted in 1996 extends the reach of federal law into fraudulent health care billing in the commercial sector, making such activities a federal crime.[40] The growing use of "Qui Tam" actions, or whistle-blower lawsuits, has generated a new growth industry in litigation involving schemes for overbilling.[41]

In addition to the federal statutory prohibition on "fraud and abuse," the careful planner of health care ventures must also consider the statutory and common-law prohibitions on fraud that might be applied to any industry. Schemes to "kick back" money to a referrer of services or to seek payment without providing service outside the Medicare payment system might constitute fraud under a state statute.[42]

Corporate practice of medicine

Corporations are generally prohibited from practicing medicine.[43] The standards established by a facility or other type of venture must reflect standards promulgated by health care providers and not by the partnership, corporation, or any other type of entity. The goal is to provide quality care while avoiding interference with the provider-physician relationship. The JCAHO and state, federal, and voluntary accrediting agencies strive to maintain provider control over standards of care.

Joint ventures may create managed health care entities, diagnostic facilities, treatment centers, or other types of health care delivery mechanisms. In each of these cases the role of the nonprovider manager and investor should be kept separate from the care delivered. To avoid pitfalls, the organization should structure the relationship of the providers, specify the type of facility, and delineate the responsibilities of the nonprovider managers and owners.

Ethical considerations

The medical literature, legislative subcommittees, insurance carriers, and the public all question the entrepreneurial aspects of joint ventures among physicians, hospitals, diagnostic facilities, and treatment centers. The suspicion is that a system of self-referral will lead to overutilization with concomitant increases in health care costs.

The ethical and legal issue of fee-for-service medicine for patients at facilities owned by the referring physicians alone or in conjunction with another institution has been raised as a result of increasing health care costs.

CONCLUSION

Increasing market competition and capital requirements have brought together different combinations of providers, hospitals, and business persons; however, their interests are not always the same.

The formation of a joint venture can subject investors to antitrust investigation, private litigation, state and federal enforcement activity, and increased exposure to negligence, both medical and corporate. In addition, investors may have ethical conflicts within their investor groups.

Increasing governmental intrusion affects the methods used to create a joint venture, with regard to both legal requirements and capital contributions. Nevertheless, the promotion of integrated services, the exploitation of new markets, and the provision of new and valuable services for the health care consumer present exciting challenges for physicians and hospitals.

ENDNOTES

1. P. Starr, *The Social Transformation of American Medicine* (Basic Books, New York 1982).
2. Hermann et al., *Integrated Delivery Systems in a Changing Healthcare Environment: New Legal Challenges*, Monograph No. 1 (Forum on Healthcare Law of the American Bar Association, Nov. 1994).
3. Levit et al., *Health Care Spending in 1994*, 15 Health Affairs 130-144 (Summer 1996).
4. Health Security Act, H.R. 3600/S1757, Report No. 773, *Medicare and Medicaid Guide* (Commerce Clearing House, Chicago 1993).
5. 42 U.S.C. 1395nn.
6. *Insiga v. LaBella*, 14 Fla. L. Weekly 214 (Apr. 21, 1989).
7. Uniform Partnership Act, Am. Jur. 2D.
8. Uniform Partnership Act §18.
9. Fla. Stat. §607, Professional Service Corporations 766.101, 1988 (Florida); 805 ILCS 15/1 *et seq.* (Illinois).
10. Pursuant to the Small Business Administration Act of 1996, the number of eligible shareholders has increased from 35 to 75. In addition, certain charitable and other organizations can now be S corporation shareholders (the law used to limit shareholders to individuals only).
11. Internal Revenue Code, §414M.
12. Internal Revenue Code, §530, as modified by the Small Business Job Protection Act of 1996; *Riverbend Country Club v. Patterson*, 399 S.W. 2d 382 (Tex. Civ. App. 1965). The IRS, under its Audit Guidelines for agents, has also set forth a checklist of 20.
13. For a comprehensive listing of such organizations, see *Health Network and Alliance Sourcebook* (Faulkner & Gray, Inc., New York, http:\www.FaulknerGray.com\healthcare).
14. *The Flowering of Managed Care*, Med. Economics (March 1990).
15. *Supra* note 1.
16. Pear, *Congress Weighs More Regulation of Managed Care*, New York Times 1 (March 10, 1997).
17. Mitchell et al., *New Evidence of the Prevalence and Scope of Physician Joint Ventures*, 268 J.A.M.A. 80 (1992).
18. For a detailed listing of current state law relating to physician self-referral prohibitions, *see* Mayo, *State Illegal Remuneration and Self-Referral Laws*, NHLA Monograph Series (National Health Lawyers Association, Washington, D.C. 1997).
19. Omnibus Budget Reconciliation Act of 1993, Pub. L. No. 103-66, 107 Stat. 312 (1993). The designated services are physical therapy services; occupational therapy services; radiology, including magnetic resonance imaging, computed tomography scans, and ultrasound services; radiation therapy services and supplies; durable medical equipment and supplies; parenteral and enteral nutrients, equipment, and supplies; orthotic and prosthetic devices; home health services and supplies; out-patient prescription drugs; and in-patient and out-patient hospital services.
20. "Referral" is defined as, in the case of an item or service for which payment may be made under Part B of Medicare, the request by a physician for the item or service, including a consultation by another physician and any test or procedure ordered by, or to be performed by, that other physician (or someone under his or her supervision). Additionally, *the request or establishment of a plan of care* by a physician that includes the provision of a designated health service constitutes a referral, 42 U.S.C. §1395nn(h)(5)(A)(B). (Emphasis added.)
21. Rosenfeld, *Joint Venture Organizational Models*, Twelve Topics in Healthcare Financing 38-44 (Winter 1985).

22. Rust, *Advice for the Doctor: the Formation of Single Specialty Networks,* 42 Practical Lawyer (Oct. 1996).

23. The authority for treating limited liability companies as partnerships for tax purposes comes from U.S. Treasury regulations that state that the classification of an entity as a partnership or an association taxable as a corporation depends on whether the entity has more corporate characteristics than noncorporate characteristics. The four relevant corporate characteristics are (1) continuity of life, (2) centralization of management, (3) limited liability, and (4) free transferability of interests. To be taxable as a "partnership," an entity must lack at least two of the four factors. *See Philip G. Larson,* 66 T.C. 159 (1976); *George Zuckman,* 524 F. 2d 729 (Ct. Cl. 1975).

24. Racketeer Influenced and Corrupt Organizations Act, 18 U.S.C. 1961.

25. 15 U.S.C. §1.

26. *Arizona v. Maricopa County Medical Society,* 457 U.S. 332 (1982).

27. *United States of America v. Healthcare Partners, Inc., Danbury Area IPA, Inc., and Danbury Health Systems,* Civil Action No. 395-CV-01945 RNC, Sept. 1995 (definition of messenger model in final judgment action against independent physician association).

28. United States Department of Justice, Federal Trade Commission, *Statement of Antitrust Enforcement Policy and Healthcare* (Aug. 1996).

29. 15 U.S.C. §12-27.

30. Landes & Posner, *Market Power in Antitrust Cases,* 94 Harv. L. Rev. 937 (1981).

31. Letter from Ann K. Bingaman, Department of Justice, to J.F. Fischer (Jan. 1996) ("substantially more" than 30% of several specialties in a number of local markets, including more than 50% in one specialty); letter from Ann K. Bingaman to M.J. Fields (Dec. 1995) (44% of board-certified dermatologists); letter from Ann K. Bingaman to D. Hartzog (Oct. 1994) (up to 50% of chiropractors).

32. Department of Justice Business Review letter to Ted R. Callister (March 1996) finding that the Orange Los Angeles Medical Group, Inc. (ORLA) operating with in excess of 30% of the anesthesiologists in the defined market, may be challenged by the Department of Justice.

33. *Darling v. Charleston Memorial Hospital,* 211 N.E. 2d 253 (1966); *Pedrosa v. Bryant,* 677 P. 2d 166 (1984).

34. *Harrell v. Total Healthcare, Inc.,* 781 S.W. 2d 58 (1989). Court stated that an IPA model HMO owed a duty to its participants to investigate the competence of its panel members and to exclude physicians who pose a "foreseeable risk of harm."

35. Fla. Stat. 766.110, 395.041, 641.55, 624.501.

36. Pub. L. 99-660 (Nov. 1986); 42 U.S.C. 11101 *et seq.*

37. 42 U.S.C. 11135 Section 425(b).

38. 42 U.S.C. 1320a-7(b)(b).

39. *Report of the Judicial Council of the American Medical Association,* J.A.M.A. 2425 (Dec. 1984).

40. Health Insurance Portability and Accountability Act of 1996, Pub. L. 104-191, 110 Stat. 1936 (1996). Subtitle E, Section 241 adds: "Federal health care offense" defining a new federal health care offense in the criminal code to mean a violation of, or conspiracy to violate, a number of provisions in the federal criminal code if the violation or conspiracy relates to a "health care benefit program."

41. Relief includes injunctive actions and the seizure of assets, 18 U.S.C. §1345(a)(1), (2).

42. *Supra* note 22.

43. Chase-Lubitz, *The Corporate Practice of Medicine Doctrine: an Anachronism in the Modern Healthcare Industry,* 40 Vanderbilt Law Rev. 445 (1987); *Berlin v. Sarah Bush Lincoln Health Center,* 279 Ill. App. 3d 447 (1996).

Coproviders and Institutional Practice

EDWARD E. HOLLOWELL, J.D., F.C.L.M.
JENNIFER L. SMITH, J.D.

COPROVIDERS
INSTITUTIONAL PRACTICE

COPROVIDERS

Physicians do not practice alone. That fact is unalterable in our complex medical care system. Physicians depend on the expertise and competence of technicians, nurses, nurse practitioners, physician assistants, paramedics, administrators, nurse's aides, orderlies, medical records personnel, and even maintenance and repair staff, just to name a few. In addition, it is important to recognize that the relationships of coproviders are necessarily bilateral. The competence of the individuals working together is additive rather than independent. It is obvious that the observations and efforts of all those who provide care for a patient affect the outcome; as a result the legal interdependence of coproviders is unavoidable. The more complex that health care becomes and the more technical the capabilities of health care providers, the greater the interdependence of coproviders. Further, when coproviders work together smoothly and professionally, it is evident to the patient; this instills trust and facilitates communication, which, in turn, tends to minimize malpractice and malpractice claims. It is often feeling or perception that something was wrong that influences a patient to seek an attorney and file a claim. Good teamwork catches errors before untoward results occur. It also creates the perception in the patient that he or she is receiving competent, efficient, and high-quality health care.

The definition of coproviders in the context of the health care system can be greatly expanded. For example, the competence of the line worker involved in the manufacturing process of a piece of medical equipment could, in the most extreme assessment of the nature of "coproviders," affect the performance of nurses and physicians who use that particular piece of equipment.

The authors gratefully acknowledge the past contributions of John Dale Dunn, M.D., F.C.L.M.; James B. Couch, M.D., J.D., F.C.L.M.; Marvin Firestone, M.D., J.D., F.C.L.M.; Gary N. Hagerman, LL.B., F.C.L.M.; and William Goebert, Jr., M.D., J.D., F.C.L.M.

The first part of this chapter focuses on the health care providers who are directly involved with the patient and who have some form of professional licensure or responsibility for patient care. These providers include physicians, nurses, nurse practitioners, physician assistants, dentists, podiatrists, licensed psychologists, vocational nurses, registered technicians, and other personnel who work in the health care system and directly affect the provision of care to the patient. In addition, the nature of relationships that create coexisting responsibilities and duties among these providers is discussed.

The second part of the chapter explores legal aspects concerning the hospital, the institution in which these health care providers work together. It focuses primarily on the hospital's legal relationship to its patients and to the physicians who serve on its staff and committees.

State licensure

Licensed professionals are obligated not only to act within the authority and parameters set out by their own licensure act, but also, in most states, are required to report other professionals if they know that those professionals are acting in violation of the licensure acts. For example, state laws require that physicians report the incompetence of another physician if his or her act has the potential to harm a patient. Physicians are also required to report the incompetence or impairment of a nurse or any other health care provider. In this respect, licensure creates a public duty that, at times, can override the natural instinct not to be a "tattletale."

Once a physician has been reported to his or her licensing board, the board will meet with the physician if it believes the problem can be remedied informally. The licensing board may even ask the physician to voluntarily surrender his or her license if it is necessary to protect the public. Whether the license is surrendered or not, the physician can be diverted to a supportive program if he or she acknowledges the existence of a problem. If the physician refuses to acknowledge the problem, the board can formally charge the physician with violating the state's licensing act and order the physician's appearance before it at a formal hearing. In some states, under some conditions, the board may suspend the physician's license or impose less severe limitations on his or her practice privileges if doing so is deemed to be in the public's interest.

At such a hearing, the board usually receives evidence and testimony. It then makes findings of fact and forms conclusions of law as to the charges and appropriate action or sanction. Most states permit a sanctioned physician to request a stay of the sanction and to bring an appeal of the board's decision before a court of law. Of course, if the board finds insufficient proof (usually according to a preponderance of the credible evidence) in the facts to support an order or sanction, the matter is dismissed and, if necessary, the license and privileges are restored.

Practice in a health care institution

Apart from the responsibility created by state licensure laws to report professional impairment, incompetence, or other acts in violation of licensing laws, institutional environments may create an additional burden and duty for professionals: monitoring the competence and performance of coproviders with whom they work. The interdependence of professionals within a particular institutional environment is best exemplified by the hospital, but it exists in other health care settings such as nursing homes, mental health institutions, and outpatient settings. Obvious examples would be the responsibilities of the medical staff to the institution to monitor the quality of health care in the hospital as outlined by state licensure laws, voluntary accreditation standards, and common sense, as well as the common law.

In many cases, institutions, which normally depend on the quality of the peer review conducted by their medical staffs, have been found liable for failure to discover or for choosing to ignore an individual health care provider's incompetence where that individual is practicing within that institution.[1] This well-established common-law rule receives additional support as a reasonable interpretation of the Standards of Accreditation of the Joint Commission on Accreditation of Healthcare Organizations (JCAHO), which are voluntary. In addition, the common law reflects the interpretation of state licensure laws requiring effective quality assurance programs in hospitals, medical association standards, and medical society standards. Further, the institutional duty to provide quality care ultimately rests with the hospital's governing body.

Thus, health care providers find themselves obligated and responsible for the competence and quality of their peers' performance and for discovering and preventing the incompetence or impairment of professionals at other levels— either above or below their own—from harming the public or an individual patient. Thus, nurses are obligated to report an impaired, incompetent, or otherwise deficient physician; but they would also be required to report a technician who fails to function at an acceptable level.

Peer review

Quality assurance programs in hospitals depend on the process of peer review because coproviders with the same professional training are the best judges of the competence and capabilities of their peers and colleagues. The quality assurance process is described best in terms of problem solving and the promotion of desired levels of patient care. Although it is easy to talk in generalities about the importance of quality, the actual process of quality assurance is difficult in the health care setting. However, the duty to provide good and effective peer review is clear.

Quality assurance programs. All health care institutions, health care provider groups, health maintenance organizations (HMOs) and managed care programs, and others directly or indirectly responsible for patient care necessarily deal with the developing field of quality assurance (QA) in health care. Small area analysis, comparison of health care practices, and widespread inconsistencies in approaches to various disease processes and surgical problems have created great concern and even governmental intervention in attempts to standardize approaches to health care problems. The unfortunate by-product of this concern and resulting standardization is that it is difficult to be certain of the relative benefits of the various approaches to problems. It is clear that many management approaches are effective, and diversity in health care should not be discarded for a theoretical and unproven cost or quality benefit. In medicine as well as in other "arts," there are many ways to "skin a cat."

The *Journal of the American Medical Association* has published a column on clinical decision-making with the specific objective of studying the problems of variation in clinical approaches to medical problems.[2]

In QA programs, it is important to eliminate deviations below and outside of acceptable medical practice, particularly those deviations that put patients at risk. Therefore the JCAHO, medical societies, medical professional organizations, and others are actively involved in attempting to establish standards for practice. The American Medical Association has also studied standards in cooperation with Rand Corporation, and 20 medical specialty societies have published some form of standards.

Standards of care. Quality assurance, peer review, and coprovider relationships are dependent on the personal perceptions of those providing the care together, regarding what are considered to be appropriate standards of care. Unfortunately, the legal system and professional liability litigation in particular have confused how such standards are considered and applied in a way not easily explained. This can cause "defensive medicine."

This does not mean that it is impossible to reconcile institutional practice with understanding these standards.

What is necessary is the acknowledgment that quality assurance and risk management must work in tandem, with each complementing the other to ensure that medical care is provided which meets the patient's needs and interests. An understanding of those needs is the first step. The legal system defines the duty a health care provider owes to the patient in terms of what is in the patient's interest:

1. To use his or her best judgment in care and treatment.
2. To exercise reasonable care and diligence in the application of his or her knowledge and skills.
3. To act in compliance with the standard of health care required by law.[3]

Thus, risk management and quality assurance programs must be used to constantly educate the institution's staff regarding how to fulfill these duties during the day-to-day provision of health care.

Normative versus actual standards of care. Elsewhere in this text, the issues regarding standards of care are defined more completely. However, it is important to recognize that, generally, courts define a standard of care in terms of that degree of skill and expertise normally possessed and exercised by a reasonable and prudent practitioner with the same level of training in the same or similar circumstances. What this means in a courtroom can become quite different from what the health care provider contemplates while treating the patient. Too often, medical testimony presented in a courtroom deals with issues as they relate to "normative" standards rather than "actual" standards. In reality, physicians hope to perform at one level but actually perform at another level. For example, John Holbrook, M.D. (personal communication), an emergency physician interested in risk management in Massachusetts, reviewed more than 100,000 emergency department records and found that fewer than 5% of patients treated at the emergency department for a headache actually received a funduscopic examination. Whether this would be an actual standard that is acceptable is subject to debate, but it cannot be ignored as a reality. In a courtroom, the normative standard is described for the benefit of the judge or jury as expected performance recited by a "medical expert" adequately and sometimes superlatively qualified to discuss a particular area of professional expertise. It may not be an actual standard but rather a "normative" standard defined as the degree of skill and expertise that we strive to achieve rather than actually achieve as average prudent practitioners. Of course, states can and often do define who is a "medical expert" and what, generally, is the defined standard of care, for application in the courtroom.

In the quality assurance setting, it is important for those involved in the definitions of standards and practices to recognize the difficulties of defining appropriate standards of care and evaluating coproviders. Within those parameters, it is still possible to define unacceptable deviance and deal with it appropriately as part of the peer review mechanism.

However, difficulty can arise, especially in evaluating coproviders, when disparity exists among researchers, instructors, and various schools and institutions that train the coproviders. Such disparities need to be considered in both individual evaluations and coprovider training. Such continuing training can be a useful tool for establishing the "normative" standard an institution adheres to, in order to avoid any conflicts and unnecessary disputes over adherence. It is possible that a significant number of investigations and staff disciplinary actions arise not from actual lack of knowledge or personal dedication to high quality of care, but from differences in training among coproviders.

Normally quality assurance programs are described in terms of the "controlled loop" process of identification of a problem, discussion, and evaluation resulting in proposed action, real action, and then reevaluation to determine whether the problem has been properly managed. Every professional organization that assumes responsibility for patient care, including hospital medical staffs, managed care organizations, and medical practice groups, must establish a quality assurance program. Without such a program, these patient care organizations will not be able to efficiently monitor the health care their coproviders provide.

There has been an increasing interest in and use of guidelines for comparing actual performance with the applicable standard of care. Some institutions prepare internal guidelines for the most commonly encountered or performed conditions or situations, basing them on academic research. Other institutions make use of external sources, such as the National Guideline Clearinghouse (NGC). The NGC maintains a comprehensive database of evidence-based clinical practice guidelines and related documents produced by the Agency for Healthcare Research and Quality (AHRQ). It works with the American Medical Association and the American Association of Health Plans. Its stated mission is to provide physicians, nurses, and other health professionals with a source of objective, detailed information on clinical practice guidelines. By doing so, it is promoting the dissemination, implementation, and use of such guidelines. The NGC's database is available on the Internet at http://www.guideline.gov/.

Disciplinary activities in peer review. Practicing with coproviders necessarily results in disciplinary peer review actions when unacceptable and incurable deviance is identified. It is important for those involved in peer review and quality assurance matters that have a direct impact on an individual practitioner to be aware of the concept of due process and the laws of the state and nation that govern disciplinary and peer review activities in the health care setting. The Health Care Quality Improvement Act of 1986[4] is a federal statute that provides guidance for establishment of due process within peer review through specific requirement:

1. The subject physician must be notified of an organization's intent to bring disciplinary action.

2. The subject physician must have an opportunity to respond, request a hearing if he or she desires, and prepare a defense.

3. The subject physician must have adequate notice of the nature of the charges.

4. The subject physician must receive the right to advice and counsel of the physician's choice, including an attorney, in any hearing conducted as part of peer review.

5. The subject physician must receive a fair hearing with an impartial panel of noncompeting peers for consideration of the proposed action to be taken.

6. The subject physician must be given an opportunity to examine the evidence against him or her, prepare a defense, cross-examine witnesses, and present arguments in his or her favor.

7. A written opinion must be provided by the hearing panel if disciplinary action is recommended, along with the written decision of the health care governing body or final arbitrator.

The importance of these guidelines lies in the statutory establishment of bilateral protection. The organization that is conducting peer review and following these guidelines ultimately derives as much benefit from them as the physician who is at risk. If a physician who has been disciplined under a peer review proceeding decides to sue individuals who participated in the process or the institution for having imposed the discipline, and if the defendants can show that the disciplinary action was undertaken in the "reasonable belief" that it was for the furtherance of good health care and with no malice or inappropriate motivations, this federal law provides "qualified immunity" from the civil claim. Further, if the defendants prove that the sanctioned physician's suit was brought inappropriately, they can collect damages for defense expenses and court costs. The federal law provides this remedy to encourage physicians to participate in peer review. However, failure to conduct peer review can create potential liability under the common-law theories described earlier.

Supervisory liability

Physicians supervise nurses, technicians, assistants, paramedics, and, at times, other physicians. This supervision can be direct, but it is often done by telephone, radio, or written communication. Generally, a physician's responsibility and potential liability for such injuries and mistakes resulting from the care given under such supervision are directly proportional to the degree of control held over the coproviders' actions and the supervisor's knowledge of such actions.

Physicians who are supervising their own employees bear special responsibilities because direct vicarious liability exists for any employees' negligent actions. Likewise, where a state's laws grant special status to nurse practitioners and physician's assistants, authorizing expanded delegated duties, such laws generally require that physicians formally report to the state the supervisory relationship's existence. Further, such reports or applications for approval often formally create delegated standard orders and other protocols to provide for proper guidelines. In addition, many states have established definite limits on the nature of the supervision that might be provided. For example, most states require the supervising physician to be physically available to the nurse practitioner or physician's assistant for consultation and assistance. However, in many states these coproviders can act, within their standing orders, in a relatively liberal manner, sometimes even using signed prescription pads. Some state medical practice acts provide that a physician can delegate any responsibility to a properly trained person; thus the basic issue in determining vicarious liability can center on the physician's judgment of that coprovider's qualifications. Of course, one would not expect to find a physician delegating performance of a neurosurgical procedure to a physician's assistant; it is far more common to find less critical responsibilities delegated to the coprovider, such as when a nurse harvests veins for cardiovascular surgeons.

Vicarious liability is that liability arising from an employer-employee relationship. Employee physicians, nurses, technicians, and others can create liability for their employer through their negligence, if such negligence causes an injury. One should also be aware of the "borrowed servant" doctrine; a physician using employees of another to carry out the borrower's activities can be held liable for the "borrowed" employee's negligence. One's liability when borrowing another's "servant" is proportional to the amount of control one exercised. For example, in the health care setting, the "captain of the ship" theory at one time was used to resolve the issue of liability for the acts of nurses and others in the operating room. However, the courts have recognized that surgeons do not directly control the administrative duties of others in the operating room. Scrub technicians, circulating nurses, anesthesiologists, and others are working there, although they must defer to the judgment and authority of the surgeon on the case. Obviously, they have separate and independent duties and responsibilities proportional to their professional competence. It is therefore unreasonable to make the surgeon liable for an improper sponge, needle, or instrument count, just as it would be inappropriate for a surgeon to be responsible for the conduct of an anesthesiologist who fails to properly intubate the patient. If the problem comes to the surgeon's attention and he or she fails to act in the patient's interest, liability increases proportionately, but the primary responsibility still lies with that person who acts independently regardless of the level of professional expertise and who has separate and independent ministerial duties and authority.

Radio control and prehospital care

An interesting and important area of medical care involving delegation of medical practice to a remote person is the use of radio control for prehospital care. Separate and independent duties and responsibilities are created for licensed prehospital care personnel. In addition, it is important to recognize that prehospital care services are required by law to have a medical director who establishes proper medical care/prehospital care protocols and monitors the competence of the prehospital care personnel through a functioning quality assurance program.

The physician who directs or controls the paramedic at the scene has the same liability as a physician who would direct or control a nurse and has ultimate responsibility for the patient. In the case of radio control, the physician has a responsibility proportional to his or her knowledge of the situation, recognizing that the physician is dependent on the eyes, ears, and observational skills of the paramedic or emergency medical technician (EMT).

Appropriate prehospital care protocols still vary widely throughout the United States. Variations easily result from the diverse qualifications of persons working in prehospital care settings, from personal opinions of medical directors, and from different state laws. State law specifically designates levels of skill in terms of basic care providers, special skill care providers, and full paramedic level providers. National and state registry and licensure are a part of the definition of these various levels of skill. The control of prehospital care personnel is similar to the type of remote control that exists when patients are in the hospital and nurses are used as observers reporting to physicians the condition of a patient and then carrying out appropriate therapeutic and diagnostic orders.

Ultimately, the health care professional who delegates responsibilities to others or controls others by providing care directly and in person or remotely by phone or radio, is still responsible to act in a professional manner and within acceptable standards of care. A professional duty to monitor the coprovider's professional competence and ability, above or below one's level of licensure or professional skill, is a controlling factor and a legal principle that must be accepted by all professionals. In the institutional setting, coproviders are codependent and coresponsible. Even though direct responsibility may not exist, indirect responsibility for general considerations of quality assurance requires vigilance and appropriate action when problems and an incompetent coprovider are identified.

Independent contractors

Whether a health care provider is an independent contractor is a question implicating labor, employment, and tax law, as well as a consideration that affects professional liability. If a person works as an employee, the employer's vicarious liability is direct, but if that person is an independent contractor, the liability would be in proportion to the amount of control exercised. For example, many physicians function as independent contractors in various settings, but they exercise independent judgment over their professional practice. The independent contractor concept is one that properly suits a professional role because professionals are licensed as individuals and are responsible for making personal professional decisions about patient care. However, hospitals, health care facilities, and professional individuals are still responsible for monitoring the competence of the independent practitioner.

Ostensible agency

In most states, certain independent contractor relationships have been found to be ineffective to deflect liability from the party contracting for the services. For example, in a hospital situation, an independent physician contractor may be the only one available to the patient; therefore the hospital may automatically be considered to be vicariously liable through ostensible agency. It has used the agent physician for carrying out some of its institutional responsibilities.[5] When the patient has no way of knowing that the physician is not an employee or when the hospital uses the physician just as the hospital would use an employee, many states accept the concept that the hospital is therefore vicariously liable for the physician's actions. This area has not been as well defined outside the hospital-based physician situation, because other members of the medical staff are more independent. The concept generally has widespread support in the case of hospital-based physicians when patients come to a hospital and have no choice as to which physician to pick.[6]

Independent contractors working within a hospital setting or in a medical group are still subject to the same basic peer review and quality assurance controls, and therefore the institution or the professional organization can be considered liable if it fails to properly conduct the following: (1) proper credentialing and application; (2) adequate peer review and quality assurance review; (3) monitoring of physicians for ongoing appropriateness of care, continued education if indicated, and proper recertification, relicensure, and other matters related to ongoing practice requirements; and (4) proper corrective and disciplinary action when a physician performs inappropriately or below the standard of care.

Under the common law propounded by most states, the hospital may be considered liable for poor peer review. This liability of a health care institution as outlined in the common law has been extended to the medical staff when the medical staff knows that a physician has become incompetent and fails to take corrective action.[7]

Consultants and referring physicians

A consultant and the referring physician share responsibility for the patient's care based on their respective proportion of knowledge and control and the foreseeability for potential harm. For example, if the general practitioner refers the patient to a neurosurgeon for a neurosurgical problem, then his or her responsibility for the case decreases in proportion to his or her knowledge of the problem, control over the care given the patient, and actions taken in response to any problems identified. Failure to choose an appropriate consultant can occasionally create liability for the referring physician, particularly if the choice of consultant is based not on the competence of the consultant, but on other financial or personal relationships. If the consultant is known to be incompetent and it can be proven that the referring physician used that consultant anyway, then liability would revert to the referring physician.

Substitutes and sharing on-call time can create some liability if one chooses a substitute who is incompetent. This would generally depend on the facts and circumstances. For example, if a physician going on vacation is not careful in his or her choice of a competent substitute, the patient could easily consider this as failure to take proper care in choosing a substitute. In the case of sharing call with another physician, the responsibility is less because the other physician is independent. However, if a physician using shared call knows that another physician sharing call is incompetent or impaired, he or she exposes the patients in his or her practice to that physician and would be considered liable in proportion to his or her knowledge of the incompetence or impairment of the call-sharing physician.

Nursing and other technical practices in the hospital

State nurse practice acts are the laws that define the proper scope of nursing practice. These laws and hospital protocols and procedures control the scope of nurses' professional activities. The physician is not responsible for designing protocols and policies, although the medical staff is generally responsible for the quality of care in the hospital.[8] In the case of a hospital setting or other health care institutional setting, the administration generally includes nursing administration and therefore sets policy for the nursing practices within that institution. The medical staff provides oversight for the governing body on the quality of care provided in the institution, but depends on the nursing administration to develop policies and protocols for nursing care. The physician would be responsible for incompetence or impairment of a nurse or an inappropriate nursing action.

The physician should either intervene to prevent harm to the patient or deterioration of the patient's condition or report the events so that actions can be taken by the health care institution. Failure to do so, to ensure that the professional staff of the hospital is functioning in a way that provides quality patient care, could result in liability for the physician. The same responsibilities exist for nurses toward other nurses or technicians and for technicians with regard to other professional personnel in the hospital.

Professionals within a hospital or health care institutional setting assume liability in proportion to their knowledge of the problem and their ability to effect change. Within the institution, following protocol and procedure for registering complaints and attempting to provide for corrective action satisfy the responsibilities of the individual. The failure of the institution to act after being informed will create a separate institutional liability.

State medical practice acts and nurse practice acts as well as federal law[9] provide immunity for people who report in good faith the incompetence, impairment, or inappropriate practice of another professional.

Conclusion

The health care environment requires cooperation and teamwork. Physicians are dependent on many other health care professionals in a health care institution to ensure good patient care. These interdependencies are unavoidable and are increasing in magnitude and complexity; therefore it is important to understand that, generally, the team members' potential liability and legal responsibility are easy to analyze. The degree of duty and responsibility is in proportion to the amount of control and knowledge of the potential for foreseeable harm. The health care professional is obligated to take actions to protect the interests of patients, who are innocent parties in the health care environment. A failure to act in the interest of good patient care or in the protection of the public welfare creates liability. Apart from concern about becoming a codefendant because of a failure to discipline or supervise, health care professionals should consider the fact that there are many different ways to fail the patient, including allowing another to harm the patient. The public responsibility of licensed health care professionals is the "brother's keeper" responsibility. Health care institutions, on the other hand, have a separate and independent corporate responsibility to ensure quality of care within their organizations. Failure to require proper credentials, inappropriate hiring practices, and failure to develop proper quality assurance and peer review within the institution place the governing body and the institution at great risk if patient harm results from that failure.

INSTITUTIONAL PRACTICE

Historical origins

Hospitals evolved in this country during the eighteenth, nineteenth, and early twentieth centuries along the lines of the European (particularly the British) model as charitable institutions and, in some cases, as almshouses for the poor. Because of this focus, many hospitals were affiliated with or originated from various religious orders. To foster and support these institutions, the law developed the doctrine of charitable immunity to protect hospitals from legal liability.[10] The cases recognizing this doctrine represented a natural outgrowth of their community's origins and the interest in providing services primarily to the downtrodden in society.

It was not until the 1870s, when university teaching hospitals and municipal hospitals began to appear, that secular institutions began to flourish. Despite this shift away from religious affiliations, hospitals continued to enjoy insulation from legal liability, retaining charitable immunity, primarily because of their origins.

Evolution of functional hospital organization and management (1914 to 1984). Early in the twentieth century, hospital organizations began to evolve into bipartite and tripartite institutions. The leading case to perpetuate this separation was *Schloendorff v. New York Hospital*, a New York Court of Appeals decision issued in 1914.[11] The administrative staff was regarded as the governing body responsible for the overall administration of the hospital, while the medical staff was in charge of rendering patient care. The artificial separation was promulgated in the courts by their erecting a distinction between the "purely ministerial acts" performed by the hospital administration and the medical acts performed by members of the hospital medical staff:

It is true, I think, of nurses, as of physicians, that in treating a patient, they are not acting as servants of the hospital. But nurses are employed to carry out the orders of the physicians, to whose authority they are subject. . . . If there are duties performed by nurses foreign to their duties in carrying out the physician's orders, and having relationship to the administrative conduct of the hospital, the fact is not established by the record.[12]

This medical/ministerial dichotomy continued after *Schloendorff*, although the functional distinction between hospital administration and medical staffs became increasingly blurred. The forces behind this blurring were the increasing use of professional management and business practices, and the increasing professionalism of hospital-employed ancillary health care providers. Physicians are expected to understand, appreciate, and direct multifaceted teams, which often specialize within their own fields in very complex procedures, such as organ transplantation or treatment of specific communicable diseases. Thus, the difference between medical and administrative acts is often decided based on all of the surrounding circumstances, making for limited consistency and predictability. For example, it was held that administering the right blood by transfusion to the wrong patient was a "ministerial act" in *Necolaff v. Genesee Hosp.*,[13] while administering the wrong blood to the right patient was a "medical act" in *Berg v. N.Y. Society for the Relief of the Ruptured and Crippled*.[14]

This distinction was finally abrogated in 1957, in *Bing v. Thunig*.[15] The New York Court of Appeals overturned *Schloendorff*. Since *Bing*, both regulatory and common law in the health care field have evolved to reflect the interrelationships and interdependencies of the hospital and its medical staff. The JCAHO guidelines also reinforce this corporate relationship.[16] This view of the medical staff as an integral component of the hospital corporation has been confirmed in the decision of *Johnson v. Misericordia County Hospital*.[17] The antitrust case of *Weiss v. York Hospital*[18] may have muddied the water somewhat by referring to the medical staff as being independent to the extent that it may be the "sole decision maker." Nevertheless, in terms of more practical economic realities, for both hospitals and their medical staffs to survive and, perhaps, thrive in the increasingly competitive health care marketplace, each must emphasize its common directives and capitalize on them in forming new partnerships. To paraphrase Benjamin Franklin, we must hang together or, surely, we shall hang separately.

Evolution of the legal responsibilities for quality assurance in the hospital

THE MOVEMENT AWAY FROM CAPTAIN OF THE SHIP DOCTRINE. The evolution of the legal responsibilities for quality assurance within the hospital paralleled to a great extent the organizational changes throughout this period. A major development in establishing the legal view that the hospital is more than just a physician's workshop, but with independent responsibilities of its own, arose from the decision of *Tonsic v. Wagner*.[19] In that decision, the Supreme Court of Pennsylvania overturned their "captain of the ship" holding (from *McConnell v. Williams*, in which a hospital might escape liability for the negligent acts of employees temporarily under the direction of independently contracting physicians): "But such an employee can be temporarily detached, in whole or in part, from the hospital's general control."[20] Thus the *Tonsic* decision firmly established the principle that a hospital should be held liable for the negligent act of any of its employees even if under the supervision of a nonemployee at the time.

THE EXTENSION OF HOSPITAL LIABILITY TO THE ACTS OF INDEPENDENT CONTRACTORS: APPARENT AGENCY. The doctrine of apparent agency has substantially contributed to the demise of the hospital's independent contractor defense. One of the most important judicial pronouncements of this doctrine came again from the Superior Court of Pennsylvania in the case of *Capan v. Divine Providence Hosp.*[21] First, the hospital's changing role creates a likelihood that patients will look to the institution rather than the individual physician for care. Thus patients commonly enter the hospital seeking a wide range of hospital services rather than personal treatment by a particular physician. This is especially true for patients who have no family practitioner. It would be absurd to require such a patient to be familiar with the law of respondeat superior, meaning the patient would have to ask each health care provider whether he or she is an employee of the hospital or an independent contractor. Similarly, it would be unfair to allow this secret limitation on liability contained in a physician's contract with the hospital to bind the unknowing patient.

Liability of hospitals and medical staff physicians

Hospital admissions.

NONEMERGENCY. In general, a hospital has no duty to admit a patient. However, it must not discriminate because of race, color, gender, religion, or nationality. Under limited circumstances, based on statutory (governmental hospitals), contractual (subscribes to an HMO or other similar arrangement), or common-law principles (injury caused by the hospital), the hospital may have a duty to admit. In hospitals engaged in clinical research mandated by the government, the institution is usually allowed discretion to refuse admission, even if the patient may meet criteria for admission. A teaching hospital, however, may not admit a patient contingent on the patient's participation in the teaching program. Otherwise, the patient's constitutional right of privacy would be invaded.

Even if a patient otherwise has a right to be admitted, if there is no medical necessity or if the hospital does not possess the services needed, the hospital need not admit the nonemergency patient.[22] The principle of no duty to admit reflects judicial restraint in dictating how a hospital should allocate scarce medical resources. Although many of the cases supporting this common-law principle date back to the turn of the last century, the majority of the courts continue to apply this doctrine today.[23]

Special circumstances may exist that obligate a hospital under common-law doctrines to admit a patient if a prior relationship existed between the hospital and patient or where the hospital was the cause of patient injury (i.e., has placed the person in a position of peril). Such circumstances exist if the original injury or complication of treatment occurred as the result of the hospital's acts or omissions or the hospital begins to provide care to the patient. The hospital may be liable for abandonment if admission is denied under such circumstances.

EMERGENCY. The national trend of the law is to impose liability on hospitals for refusal to treat emergencies or if negligent care is provided in their emergency departments. Theories supporting such liability include the following: (1) reliance, (2) agency (respondeat superior), (3) apparent authority ("holding" self out), (4) corporate negligence, and (5) nondelegable duty. These theories are discussed next.

Reliance theory. If the patient relies on a hospital's well-established custom to render aid in an emergency situation, then the hospital may be found liable for refusing to provide the necessary care or for providing negligent care. In *Wilmington General Hosp. v. Manlove,*[24] the hospital was found liable under this theory. A child needing emergency care was not admitted to the hospital after the child's private pediatrician could not be reached to approve the admission. In *Stanturf v. Sipes,*[25] the hospital was held liable when the administrator refused to approve the admission because of the patient's inability to pay. The court stated:

> The members of the public . . . had reason to rely on the [hospital], and . . . that plaintiff's condition was caused to be worsened by the delay resulting from the futile efforts to obtain treatment from the . . . [hospital].[26]

Agency theory. If the emergency department personnel who deviate from the applicable standard of care and cause harm to the plaintiff are considered "servants" of the hospital, then the hospital is vicariously liable under the doctrine of respondeat superior. A servant is defined as "a person employed to perform services in the affairs of another and who with respect to the physical conduct in the performance of the service is subject to the other's control or right to control."[27] Other than house staff, staff physicians are usually considered "independent contractors" rather than "servants." Courts must determine that an agency relationship exists based on an analysis of the facts of the case before holding a hospital liable under this theory.[28]

In *Thomas v. Corso,*[29] the hospital was found liable when the emergency room nurse failed to contact the on-call physician. *Citizens Hosp. Ass'n. v. Schoulin*[30] is a similar case. The claim was based on nursing negligence in failing to report all the patient's symptoms to the on-call physician, failing to conduct a proper examination, and failing to follow the physician's directions. The court found the hospital liable under respondeat superior.

Apparent authority. A hospital may be found vicariously liable for an emergency room physician's negligence even if the physician is considered an independent contractor. The facts would have to establish apparent authority (also referred to as "ostensible agency" or "agency by estoppel"). This theory of liability exists because the hospital is "holding itself out." The hospital will be found liable when it permits or encourages patients to believe that independent contractor physicians are the hospital's authorized agents. The "holding out" must come from the hospital, not the physician.

The landmark case on which this theory is based is *Gizzi v. Texaco, Inc.*[31] In *Gizzi,* Texaco was held liable for its representations to the public, "You can trust your car to the man who wears the star." This advertisement was sufficient to support the jury's finding against Texaco for the apparent authority it vested in an independent contractor/dealer. The contractor had sold a used car in which the brakes failed, injuring the purchaser. Texaco did not profit from the sale but was aware that the dealer was engaged in this collateral activity.

Corporate negligence. The doctrine of corporate negligence asserts that there exists an independent duty of the hospital for the medical care rendered in its institution. Like the apparent agency theory, it holds the hospital liable for an independent contractor/physician's negligence. However, a corporate negligence claim is based on the hospital's independent negligence in allowing an incompetent physician to practice on its premise.

Nondelegable duty. The main reason for employers to use independent contractors is to "farm out" services that may be of benefit to the employers but that they may not be willing or able to provide themselves. They also may wish to avoid legal liability for such services. The immunity from liability may be misused or abused. The independent contractor immunity is therefore riddled with exceptions.[32]

For public policy reasons, certain duties delegated to an independent contractor have been determined not to confer immunity on the employer. These exceptions have been termed nondelegable duties. They usually represent situations wherein the employer's duty is important, urgent, or imperative. Employers who have such responsibilities cannot avoid liability by delegating those responsibilities to an independent contractor.

In *Marek v. Professional Health Services, Inc.*,[33] the health service was held liable even though it entrusted the reading of a patient's chest x-ray film to a competent independent contractor/radiologist. The theory of liability was that reading the film was a nondelegable duty.

In another case, the Alaska Supreme Court ruled that the defendant hospital was vicariously liable for negligence in its emergency department.[34] Such a duty "may be imposed by statute, by contract, by franchise or by charter, or by common law."[35] As discussed in this landmark case, the hospital had a nondelegable duty to provide nonnegligent care in its emergency department, based on its state license as a general acute care hospital, JCAHO standards, and its own bylaws.

Statutory bases for hospital liability for emergency room care. Negligence through the provision of substandard care is not the only source of liability. In the last three decades, the law has made denial of emergency care grounds for liability. In *Guerro v. Copper Queen Hosp.*,[36] a privately owned hospital operated only for employees of one company was held liable for refusing treatment to an illegal alien who sought care. The Arizona Supreme Court reasoned that the state licensing statute precluded the hospital from denying emergency care to a patient.

A federal law, the Emergency Medical Treatment and Active Labor Act, commonly referred to as EMTALA or the *antidumping statute*, is contained in the miscellaneous provisions of the Budget Reconciliation Act (COBRA) of the Ninety-ninth Congress.[37] This statute is a codification of common law theories of liability and emergency department duties. It applies to all hospitals that participate in Medicare and other government medical assistance programs created by the Social Security Act.

The law has had a significant impact on emergency medical care in hospitals. It has improved the plaintiff's chances of recovering damages from hospitals because it eliminates the requirement of proving some of the elements of medical negligence. It governs hospitals with an emergency department wherein a patient with an emergency medical condition or a woman in active labor seeks medical care. If such a patient is "transferred" from the health care facility to another facility or is discharged, the patient may recover damages for "personal harm" if the condition worsens during or after such transfer or discharge. The patient must prove only that the condition was not "stabilized" at the time of transfer and that the condition deteriorated because of the transfer. To avoid liability, the attending physician or other medical personnel at the hospital must sign a certification that, based upon the information available at the time, the medical benefits reasonably expected from the provision of appropriate medical treatment at another facility outweigh the "increased risks" of transfer.

In addition to the certification requirement, the transfer must also be an "appropriate transfer." Although the signed certification is a simple enough procedure for the hospital to incorporate within its medical record forms, the requirements that will satisfy the transfer include all the following: (1) the receiving facility ... has available space and qualified personnel ... has agreed to accept transfer ... and to provide appropriate medical treatment; (2) the transferring hospital provides ... appropriate medical records of examination and treatment; (3) transfer is effected through qualified personnel and transportation equipment; and (4) such other requirements as the Secretary [of Health and Human Services] may find necessary.

Presumably the physician or other medical personnel who transfer the patient have the requisite knowledge of the staffing and competence of the receiving facility and have sought agreement for acceptance by the receiving facility before transfer. These requirements seem applicable whether the receiving facility is an outpatient clinic, nursing home, day care program, or a more intensive treatment center.

Although the physician must be acting as an employee or under contract with the hospital and the hospital must be a participating Medicare provider for the penalty provisions of this law to apply, these are not required for recovery of damages under state law. In addition, the hospital will be liable for damages under this statute or state law whether or not the involved physician is considered an independent contractor under state law.

This federal law seems to preempt state law that "directly conflicts with any of its requirements." It further provides for federal jurisdiction and allows the injured individual to obtain "such equitable relief as is appropriate," giving the federal court discretion to award damages it considers to be warranted. Legal action may be brought up to 2 years after the violation.

A patient who suffers "personal harm" resulting from violation of provisions of this law will be entitled to those damages allowed under the state's substantive law of personal injury and wrongful death statutes. In addition to these damages, penalties of up to $50,000 per violation against the hospital and the involved physician alike are applicable to provider hospitals and their employed or contracted physicians. The hospital receiving the transferred patient is also indemnified against any financial losses by the transferring hospital if the transferring hospital has violated the statute.

Clearly, hospitals are no longer to be considered the "physician's workshop." Thus the modern hospital is an integrated center for delivery of health care services, possessing in-house staff and independent contractor/physicians with an array of staff privileges. The hospital can farm out professional services; however, based on public policy and other legal considerations, the trend of the law is to hold the hospital liable for harm resulting from negligence in handling admissions and transfers of patients in its emergency department. As hospitals have become more profitable and business oriented, the adversarial relationship and the law governing hospitals, patients, and physicians have changed. Although there is no duty for nonemergency admissions by hospitals, under emergency circumstances, the trend of the law is for hospital liability if the patient is harmed as a result of denial of admission or improper care.

Corporate liability of hospitals. No doctrine exemplifies the notion of a hospital as a corporate entity with subsidiary components functioning interdependently to deliver a health care product better than the judicially pronounced theory holding a hospital corporately liable for the quality of care delivered by its medical staff. Under this doctrine, it does not matter whether the staff members are employees or purely independent contractors. Under corporate liability, the hospital may be held directly liable for its own negligence in ensuring the quality of health care delivered within its walls.

This doctrine of direct corporate liability of hospitals is traceable to the famous case of *Darling v. Charleston Memorial Hospital*.[38] In the *Darling* case, a patient was admitted for treatment of a broken leg through the emergency room of a private, nonprofit hospital, and was attended by a hospital staff physician who was rotating on emergency duty. The attending physician was not skilled in orthopedic work, and a cast was improperly applied so that circulation to the leg was blocked. Although the patient subsequently complained about the leg, and the nurses involved in his care observed the discoloration of his toes, nothing was done. When he was finally examined by another physician, the leg required amputation. The court's decision against the hospital could have been based on a finding of apparent agency on the grounds that the plaintiff had no reason to think that the hospital's attending physician was not employed by the hospital. However, the court went further in holding the hospital itself directly liable for breaching its own duty of care to the patient in failing to "require consultation" with a member of the hospital surgical staff skilled in such treatment or to review the treatment rendered to the plaintiff, and to require consultants to be called in as needed.

The court recognized the hospital's own central role in the overall treatment of the patient, thereby requiring the hospital itself to become directly involved in the health care delivery process. Hospitals could be held directly liable for their own corporate negligence in providing health care services. Before this case, the corporate duties of hospitals were limited to three areas, unrelated to direct patient care:

1. The duty of reasonable care in the maintenance and use of equipment.
2. The availability of equipment and services.
3. The duty of reasonable care in the selection and retention of employees.

Since *Darling* and its progeny, hospitals must be much more mindful of their selection and retention of staff physicians.[39-43]

Medical staff credentialing

Evolution of the basic hospital-physician relationship. The rights, duties, and protections afforded to the hospital and its medical staff have traditionally been analyzed by reference to the quality and quantity of the delivery of patient care. The law recognizes that the hospital's governing body must assess the qualifications of physicians who request admission to the hospital staff and must monitor the quality of medical care delivered to hospital patients.

The hospital is generally protected under the law when its decision whether to appoint or reappoint is based on considerations related to the quality of medical care rendered within the hospital or to a physician's professional conduct. Such considerations may involve an assessment of the physician's technical and clinical competence, as well as other relevant factors, such as his or her ability to cooperate with co-workers and support staff.

Although the hospital governing body has the duty to ensure the quality of patient care in the hospital, it has neither the expertise nor the proximity to specific situations to monitor adequately the actual delivery of medical services. Accordingly, the typical hospital governing body delegates much of its quality assurance responsibilities to the medical staff, and the governing body retains the ultimate monitoring or oversight responsibility. The medical staff organization usually uses its committee structure to provide the actual quality assurance mechanism by which the institution's quality of care may be maintained. This structure is formalized through the hospital and medical staff's bylaws, rules and regulations, standards of performance, and procedures for peer review.

The professional and economic significance of hospital staff privileges. The hospital, with its special care facilities and interaction of experts and trained professionals, has been the major centralized provider of medical services in the United States for over a century. However, more and more treatment procedures are becoming decentralized with the establishment of ambulatory surgery centers, less invasive treatments, and home health care. However, it remains true that a physician who is denied access to a hospital facility may be severely hampered in his or her practice. Gaining and retaining clinical privileges in at least one hospital has become practically essential for most physicians to practice medicine.

Still, staff privileges are just that—privileges. There is no fundamental or constitutional right to practice at a particular hospital.[44] In some jurisdictions, however, the procurement of a valid license may create a right to appointment in the absence of actual incompetence.[45] The current revolution in health care financing and competition is adding yet another layer of complexity to this decision-making process. As physicians seek to attain or retain clinical privileges, hospitals and medical staffs are becoming more selective with respect to whom they grant clinical privileges. In some cases, as part of long-term strategic planning, whole departments of clinical services may be eliminated or curtailed substantially because of economics, an adverse reimbursement climate, and patient population needs. All of these developments have brought the dilemma of hospital corporate liability versus physician staff privileges disputes into bold relief. These issues are discussed in more detail later in this chapter. The remainder of this part deals with the various types of staff privileges available, the process involved in obtaining and retaining them, and the protections, theories of liability, and remedies available in the denial, deferral, limitation, or withdrawal of these staff privileges.

Nature and type of staff membership

Active medical staff. In most hospitals the active medical staff consists of practitioners who meet certain basic educational, training, and background experience requirements. Typically, they are either board certified or board eligible in their area of specialty. They may regularly admit patients to the hospital, or are otherwise involved in the care of hospital patients, or participate in a teaching or research program of the hospital. They are normally required to actively participate in the staff's patient care audit and quality assurance activities. It is not unusual for active staff members to be required to provide care within their area of specialty to those "unassigned" patients who are admitted through the emergency room. Each active medical staff member retains responsibility within his or her area of professional competence (as prescribed by clinical privilege delineation determinations) for the daily care and supervision of each patient in the hospital for whom he or she provides services.

Consulting staff. Typically the consulting staff consists of practitioners who are members of the active staff of another hospital where they actively participate in the patient care audit and other quality assurance activities, who are of recognized professional ability in a specialized field, and who are not members of another category of the medical staff. Consulting staff members cannot admit patients and their clinical privileges are limited to their particular area of expertise.

Courtesy staff. The courtesy staff consists of practitioners who admit a limited number of patients per year and who are members of another hospital's active medical staff where they actively participate in patient care audit and other quality assurance activities.

Affiliate staff. The affiliate staff group consists of practitioners who are not active but have a long-standing relationship with the hospital. Typically, these practitioners may not admit patients or be eligible to hold office or vote in general staff and special meetings.

Outpatient staff. The outpatient staff consists of practitioners who are regularly engaged in the care of outpatients on behalf of the hospital or in a program sponsored by or associated with the hospital, who do not wish to assume all the responsibilities incumbent on active staff membership. Each outpatient staff member retains responsibility within his or her area of professional competence for the daily care and supervision of patients under his or her care while actively participating in the patient care audit or other quality assurance activities required of the staff.

Honorary or emeritus staff. Members of the honorary or emeritus staff are practitioners who are not active in the hospital but are being honored for their outstanding accomplishments or reputation. These members may also be former members of the active staff who have retained and may retain admitting and clinical privileges to the extent recommended by the medical board and board of directors.

House staff. Members of the house staff group are either fully licensed physicians or physicians who have received appropriate certification from the state medical board authorizing them to enter postgraduate study in a particular hospital. They may admit patients within the specialty department to which they are assigned with the approval of an active staff member in that department who is responsible for the care of that patient, and they may exercise clinical privileges as established within the residency training program.

Allied health professional staff. Allied health professionals represent a group of nonphysician coproviders, including podiatrists, nurses, psychologists, and so forth, who may provide specified patient care services under the supervision or direction of a physician member of the medical staff. They may write orders to the extent established in the rules of the staff and department to which they are assigned, but not beyond the scope of their licenses, certificates, or other legal credentials. The 1990 JCAHO Accreditation Manual for Hospitals accommodates the entry of these nonphysician providers into the hospital's health care delivery system.

Staff application and renewal

The public/private hospital distinction. Constitutional and statutory protections typically have imposed more restrictions on public hospitals in the area of staff privileges decisions. Increasingly, however, acts of formerly private hospitals have come under a level of scrutiny similar to that for public hospitals.

The two most common theories of medical staff guarantees advanced by physicians have been (1) that the hospital has a fiduciary relationship with the public because of its tax-exempt status, as well as its health and charitable activities, and (2) that by virtue of the hospital's receipt of certain public monies (e.g., Hill-Burton funds), its acts amount to "state action." Such hospital acts were therefore claimed to be subject to the Fifth and Fourteenth Amendments to the Constitution, requiring due process of law for the benefit of persons otherwise being deprived of life, liberty, or property rights. This justification finds its specific application to the physician appointment and reappointment process through the analysis of staff privileges as a necessary means of guaranteeing the liberty right of practicing one's profession.

Delegation of credentialing decisions to the medical staff. The governing body of the hospital (although ultimately responsible for the quality of care delivered) delegates to the medical staff the decision-making process for physician credentialing. The medical staff ordinarily then delegates these specific functions to a select credentials or peer review committee to make these determinations. Initial appellate decision-making authority for these determinations is usually passed to a medical executive committee. The composition of this committee is variable, but it usually consists of clinical department and division chiefs or service and section heads, as well as medical and hospital administrative personnel.

The process. A current or aspiring member to a medical staff submits a completed application including proof of medical education, licensure, board eligibility or certification, supporting materials including recommendations concerning current clinical competence and ethical practice, recent (5 years) ongoing as well as adverse claim experience, and a completed privileges delineation request form to the secretary of the medical staff or the hospital administrator. After this, the physician may be interviewed by the department chair who prepares a written report and recommendation concerning staff appointment and clinical privileges, which is then transmitted to the credentials committee.

After initial processing, the application for past record is reviewed by the credentials committee. The credentials committee then transmits to the medical executive committee (sometimes known as the medical board) a written report and recommendation as to staff appointment, category, department, and clinical privileges delineation, including special conditions.

The medical executive committee then forwards to the executive director for transmittal to the board of directors a written report and recommendation for clinical privileges to be granted with any special conditions to be attached to the appointment. Physicians receiving adverse determinations may follow an appellate procedure roughly paralleling the foregoing process.

Considerations for acceptance or rejection

The following represent general criteria considered in the staff privileges decision-making process:

1. Education, training, background, and experience.
2. Need in the department.
3. Ability to work with others.
4. Ability to meet eligibility or other requirements specified in bylaws.
5. Freedom from conflict of interest.
6. Utilization of hospital experience facilities.
7. Maintenance of professional liability insurance.
8. Willingness to make a full-time commitment to the institution.
9. Whether the hospital is the physician's primary inpatient facility.
10. Status of medical record-keeping and risk management experience.
11. Freedom from false or misleading information.
12. Current clinical competence, ethical practice, and health status.
13. A willingness to comply with bylaws and regulations.
14. Continuing medical education as required.
15. Evidence of previous or current action taken in licensure or privilege matters.

Several of the preceding criteria might carry potential antitrust implications if applied to deny or limit clinical privileges in some contexts. Curtailment, based on these criteria, should specify with considerable particularity why privileges were denied, deferred, or limited.

Legal protections available to the physician

Hospital and medical staff bylaws. It is well settled under the law that hospitals acting through their medical staffs must comply with their own internal procedural rules (i.e., bylaws). Failure to do so, at the very least, will invite judicial review. On finding a significant failure, a court could nullify the whole process and require the hospital to review the physician's qualifications again in accordance with all internal policies, procedures, and bylaws. Examples of particular procedural rules that should appear in bylaws include (but are not limited to) the following:

1. Adequate notice to the physician of the adverse decision.
2. Making available a fair hearing process for aggrieved physicians.
3. Communicating adequately to physicians the factors governing the credentialing decision.
4. Allocating properly the burden of proof during the hearings.

Contract theory of medical staff bylaws. In Pennsylvania and some other states, the medical staff bylaws may be viewed as part of a contractual relationship between the hospital and members of its medical staff, so that modifications may only be made pursuant to amendment procedures established in the bylaws themselves. In Pennsylvania, as well as other states adopting this approach, it may be considered a breach of contract for a hospital to violate procedural protections afforded under its medical staff bylaws in the physician credentialing process.

There may have been an inadequate number of court decisions to make it clear whether any such breach would make available to aggrieved physicians the whole panoply of common-law contractual remedies. It is also unclear whether this contractual analogy may apply to the situation of an applicant who is not yet a member of the medical staff.

Protection from economic harm. There may be some protection from tortious interference with a physician's ability to practice his or her profession. In many jurisdictions (e.g., New Jersey), this has been recognized as a valid claim under tort law. In general the intent to deny privileges without legal justification is sufficient to permit this type of claim to go forward in litigation. In addition, interference with trade or business may be alleged as a violation of the federal or state constitution, if the hospital is considered to be a public institution as discussed earlier. If two or more individual staff members or other persons conspire to deny privileges wrongfully, then a "restraint of trade" claim may also be possible (i.e., a Sherman Act Section 1 violation as discussed later in the antitrust subsection). In addition to possible claims under federal antitrust laws, some state courts (notably New Jersey) also permit these suits.

Protection from defamation. Physicians involved in the credentialing process are usually seen to be protected from defamation, or "the holding of a person up to ridicule, in a respectable and considerable part of the community." Typically, the hospital and medical staff may have several defenses available to claims by physicians that they have been defamed during the credentialing process.

First, no liability from defamation will attach to the hospital or its staff if the allegedly defamatory statements are true. Second, the physician applicant consents to the making of these statements by voluntarily going through the credentialing process. Third, public policy requires that persons who are asked to give statements to assist in the credentialing process should be protected by the law for such statements to guarantee that they are given without fear of reprisal and to ensure that the best possible decisions are made to ensure patient safety and welfare. In most contexts, this is a qualified privilege. In the absence of malice, this privilege applies to physicians and others involved in the credentialing decision—physicians, in making comments, must make them in a proper setting for statements to be protected.

Due process protection. In the case of hospitals owned or controlled by public agencies or private hospitals acting under the color of state law by having a fiduciary relationship with the public, substantive and due process safeguards may become available to physicians seeking to attain or retain staff privileges.

Substantive due process requires that the reasons behind the denial of a physician's staff privileges must be rational and not arbitrary or capricious. Claims based on an alleged violation of substantive due process may involve, for example, challenges to per se rules imposed by the hospital, such as minimum educational requirements (beyond those required for licensure) or board certification in a clinical specialty.

Procedural due process requires that the physician receive adequate safeguards concerning the process itself in determining whether he or she should be granted staff privileges at a particular hospital. A significant number of federal court decisions have held that denial of privileges by a private health care provider is not sufficiently regulated or controlled by the state to invoke federal jurisdiction.[46,47] However, it is now becoming clear that regardless of whether the hospital concerned is public or private, a physician has a federally protected right to due process.[48,49] These procedural safeguards may include (but are not limited to) the following:

1. Notification of the adverse determination.[50]
2. If the physician requests a hearing, written notice of the charges with sufficient specificity to give the physician adequate notice of the reason for an adverse ruling.[51]
3. Adequate time to prepare a defense.[52]
4. Opportunity for prehearing discovery.[53]
5. A hearing panel composed of impartial, fair-minded physicians.[54]
6. Appearance before the decision-making panel.
7. Assistance of legal counsel during the hearing.
8. Cross-examination of witnesses.
9. Presentation of witnesses and evidence in defense.[55]
10. Transcript of panel hearing available for review before appellate hearing.[56]
11. Written decision from the panel for judicial review.

Employment practices discrimination. A newer theory that physicians might be able to assert comes under the umbrella of employment practices discrimination. Although this cause of action historically arose in occupations other than medicine, it may be available, at least, to employed physicians. Another type of action might become available to physicians who have lost or failed to obtain staff privileges as a result of their having made prior written or oral statements critical of peers or of the policies of the hospital at which they have lost privileges. A relevant court decision in this connection is *Novosel v. Nationwide Insurance Co.*[57] There, the federal appeals court in Philadelphia upheld an employee's right to sue his employer where he may have been wrongfully discharged for having asserted a right protected by an important public policy, namely, freedom of speech and political association.

Antitrust safeguards. Approximately 26% of this country's physicians are involved in exclusive contracts with hospitals. These contracts with providers such as radiologists, pathologists, anesthesiologists, and sometimes cardiologists or emergency physicians have become the subject of Sherman Act antitrust challenges in recent years. To invoke a violation of Section 1 of this act, a plaintiff must assert the following:

1. That the parties against whom the antitrust action is brought have agreed among or between themselves (i.e., conspired) to engage in activities that restrain trade.
2. That the effect of this conspiracy is to restrain trade and is anticompetitive in nature.
3. That these anticompetitive practices affect consumer choice of services in a relevant market population covered by the agreement or conspiracy.
4. That these anticompetitive practices have a substantial and adverse impact on interstate commerce.

Aggrieved parties have also alleged violation of Section 2 of the Sherman Antitrust Act. Section 2 prohibits the willful acquisition or maintenance of monopoly power in a relevant geographic market within which the provider of services operates, and as a practical matter to which the purchaser of those services may turn for these services. Acquiring or maintaining the power to control market prices and exclude competition in such an area could amount to a Section 2 violation involving monopolistic practice. Section 2 violations do not require a conspiratorial agreement. Assuming that federal jurisdiction may be established by showing that anticompetitive practices have a substantial adverse impact on interstate commerce, an analysis of the merits of an antitrust claim in a credentialing case may proceed.[58] In the most famous recent case analyzing the merits of an antitrust claim concerning the staff privileges of an unsuccessful applicant to a closed medical staff of anesthesiologists, the U.S. Supreme Court held that this type of exclusive contract did not violate Section 1 of the Sherman Antitrust Act.[59]

The theory of liability was that, through the vehicle of this exclusive contract, consumer choice was limited because the anesthetic services of the hospital were illegally tied to its surgical services (i.e., if you went to a hospital to undergo surgery, then you had to accept the exclusive panel of anesthesiologists). The Supreme Court, however, held that there was no shortage of other hospitals with comparable services in the New Orleans area from which patient/consumers could choose other surgeons and anesthesiologists for their operations.

Justice O'Connor and three other justices concurred in the result, but stated that this type of practice should have been sustained because it was justified by matters of medical and administrative efficiency (i.e., it satisfied rules of reason while not constituting an illegal practice according to federal antitrust laws). This decision (although not finding an antitrust violation) may be most significant to the health care industry by confirming that relationships among hospitals, physicians, and their patients are subject to the same antitrust principles that apply to others involved in commercial activities.

The decision may also be just as notable for what it does not say. For example, exclusive contracts in areas with only one hospital near state borders, which involve services with independent markets, may well violate Section 1 of the Sherman Act. Clearly, now that the courts regard health care as a commercial activity, the range of antitrust violations may well increase depending on the specific facts and circumstances in each case.

In 1984 the Third Circuit United States Court of Appeals reconfirmed the applicability of traditional commercial analysis to the activities of hospitals and their medical staffs in excluding certain groups from staff membership.

In *Weiss v. York Hospital,*[60] Dr. Malcom Weiss had filed a Sherman Act antitrust action as a member of a group (osteopathic physicians) who had been excluded from membership on the hospital's medical staff. The lower court had found that this group boycott by York Hospital and its medical staff violated Sections 1 and 2 of the Sherman Act. The Third Circuit Court of Appeals in Philadelphia, while reversing the Section 2 violation finding, concurred with the lower court that this practice violated Section 1 of the Sherman Act. The appellate court found that regardless of whether or not the medical staff was acting as an agent or independently of the hospital in this practice, there was a conspiracy among individual staff physicians to exclude osteopathic physicians.

This case confirmed that whether or not the medical staff is an entity separate from the hospital, individual physicians compete with each other and thus may conspire to limit competition in violation of Section 1 of the Sherman Act. With the dramatically increasing numbers of M.D.s, D.O.s, D.D.S.s, D.P.M.s, D.C.s, M.S.N.s, P.A.s, and other health care professionals, the impact that this case should have on future efforts by M.D.s to boycott certain non-M.D. groups cannot be overstated.

physicians from staff membership were for anticompetitive or other reasons not directly related to improving the overall quality of care.

The *Patrick* decision established constraints on physician peer review, the reasons for excluding physicians from medical staffs, and the procedures used in achieving this. Following *Patrick,* physicians may not be excluded primarily for economic, as opposed to quality of care, considerations. Moreover, to escape federal antitrust liability, the peer review must allow physicians undergoing evaluation full fair hearing protection to ensure adequate procedural due process. Medical staff physicians and their hospitals can use a number of approaches to limit their federal antitrust liability. Specifically, some of these include (but are not limited to) the following:

1. Rewrite medical staff bylaws to ensure that all requisite procedural due process safeguards protecting the evaluated physician are in place and are enforced fairly;
2. Have each medical staff peer review member establish his or her freedom from economic conflicts of interest before making recommendations that could adversely affect the staff privileges of another potentially competing physician;
3. Have physician peer reviewers subject their own requests for continuing staff membership and clinical privileges to review bodies constituted by professionals not sitting on the same committees or departments that are chaired by the physician being evaluated to avoid possible claims of undue influence; and
4. Have, as chairs of credentialing committees and other sensitive medical care review committees, salaried physician executives who are not dependent on referrals from physicians being evaluated.

As instructed by the U.S. Supreme Court, if physician peer reviewers are still not satisfied with the protections afforded by the *Patrick* decision, then they may look to Congress—specifically to the protections from federal antitrust immunity following from compliance with the Health Care Quality Improvement Act of 1986.[62]

The Health Care Quality Improvement Act of 1986. In an attempt to minimize the problem of unqualified physicians hopping from state to state and to improve the process of physician credentialing in general, Congress, on November 14, 1986, passed the Health Care Quality Improvement Act. This act, in conjunction with the Medicare and Medicaid Patient Protection Act of 1987 and the Social Security Amendments of 1987, created a National Practitioner Data Bank which will collect, store, and release information on the nation's 6 million health care practitioners, including the following:

1. The details of any professional liability actions filed against them following the implementation of the bank;
2. The circumstances behind any licensure restrictions;

3. Whether they have had their staff or clinical privileges restricted for a period of more than 30 days at any hospital or other health care entity; and
4. The facts behind any professional society membership loss or restriction.

Hospitals and other health care entities must access this information concerning all physicians and nonphysician health care practitioners whenever these persons are subject to credentialing or recredentialing. Failure to do so will result in the hospital or health care entity losing the act's limited federal antitrust immunity provisions. In any corporate liability or similar action it will be presumed that the hospital or other health care entity has knowledge of these practitioners' credentials (or relative lack thereof).

The hospital must also routinely (every 2 years) request information from the clearinghouse concerning all licensed health care practitioners with medical staff membership or clinical privileges at the hospital.

The act allows the Secretary of Health and Human Services to disclose clearinghouse information affecting a particular physician or health care practitioner, to that person. Procedures would also be established for disputing the accuracy of such information. The act enables parties involved in medical malpractice actions, including plaintiffs' attorneys, to obtain access to information held by the clearinghouse.

Risk management principles

One area in which risk management is particularly necessary involves exclusive contracts between hospitals and physicians. Exclusive contracts are usually permissible; however, they must have rational reasons to support their existence. Legitimate reasons for exclusive contracts include (but are not limited to) the following:

1. Controlling the efficient administration of a specific type of medical service;
2. Limiting the department's size to cope with bed limitations and the hospital's overall mission;
3. Maintaining the economics of hospital operations;
4. Optimizing the effective use of personnel and technologies by having such controlled by only one physician group;
5. Promoting uniform teaching and research methodologies; and
6. Limiting the utilization of certain technological equipment to those most qualified.

When negotiating exclusive contracts, it is usually unwise to specify too narrowly in the contract language the reasons for entering into the exclusive arrangement. Overspecification might restrict the hospital's maneuverability in the event that the exclusive contract is challenged on specific antitrust grounds. The exclusive contract should delineate reasons for its existence, but it is better to frame these reasons in general terms, such as those specified in the previous paragraph. Similarly, it is better to specify several reasons for the exclusive arrangement rather than merely one reason. Some attorneys believe it may be best simply to use broad language supporting the hospital's goal of optimal medical care within the limitations of the facilities and resources available.

Hospitals and their staff physicians have become more economically interdependent than ever. Both must be continually conscious of how their present health care practice styles may economically affect their ability to continue to provide high-quality care in the future. A hospital's ability to compete effectively will soon be related directly to its ability to influence the economic aspects of its physicians' medical practice styles. Similarly, a physician's ability to compete effectively will soon depend on his or her ability to gain ready access to the extensive resources of at least one economically viable hospital with state-of-the-art technology and high-quality personnel.

Hospitals have a legal right and duty to maximize the quality of care provided on the one hand, but they also must afford certain safeguards to physicians in the appointment and reappointment process. The key to minimizing litigation is to strike a delicate balance between the private rights of physicians to practice medicine and the public rights of patients to reasonable medical care.

Hospitals (and physicians) face unprecedented economic pressures to compete effectively in a buyer's market. Exclusive arrangements between hospitals and physicians in an attempt to insulate themselves from this free market competition may subject them to the risk of treble damages arising from Sherman Act Section 1 or 2 violations. These arrangements must be reasonable in light of the practices of comparable institutions, local market conditions, and the medical as opposed to the economic motivations behind such agreements.

The practice of medicine in America is in the midst of an unprecedented economic transformation. This metamorphosis will carry into the next century. The traditional providers, including inpatient hospitals and fee-for-service private practitioners, must take the lead to respond to this changing environment. These providers have the unique skills and resources that permit them to compete effectively with virtually any new alternative health care delivery system, without compromising the quality of care or the integrity of the medical profession.

Hospital privileges and due process*

Because of the increasing number of practicing physicians[63] and expanding theories of liability against hospitals based on the granting of privileges[64] or the failure to restrict or revoke privileges,[65] there are now a significant number of judicial decisions dealing with the entire privileging process. What follows is a discussion on the legal issues involved with special emphasis on the due process

*From Hagerman, 13 L.A.M.P. 51 (July 1985).

rights that must be accorded to a physician when his or her privileges are denied, reduced, or revoked.

The nature of a physician's interest in hospital privileges. As mentioned, the great majority of physicians need hospital facilities for the pursuit of their profession.[66] Although a physician does not have a constitutional right to practice medicine in a hospital,[67] obtaining a medical degree and a license to practice medicine does give the physician a property interest that is given certain constitutional protection. In *Anton v. San Antonio Community Hospital,*[68] the court described this interest as follows: "The essential nature of a qualified physician's right to use the facilities of the hospital is a property interest which directly relates to the pursuit of his livelihood."[69] The court in *Unterhiner v. Desert Hospital District of Palm Springs*[70] stated: "A doctor who has been licensed by the state to practice medicine has a vested right to practice his profession and it cannot be said that there are no elements of a right to be admitted to a hospital."[71] Because the states and their subdivisions are prohibited by the United States Constitution from depriving any person of property without due process of law,[72] a hospital must afford a physician substantive and procedural due process when it acts with regard to his or her hospital privileges.[73]

PRIVATE VERSUS PUBLIC HOSPITALS. Numerous decisions have dealt with the distinction between private and public hospitals.[74] When a public hospital is involved there is no question that the hospital is acting as an agency of the state.[75] In cases involving a private hospital, there usually must be a finding that the hospital's actions constituted state action or were done under color of state law.[76] This requirement of state action has been found where the hospital receives substantial federal or state funds,[77] licensing by the state,[78] or even contributions from the public during the hospital's annual fund drive.[79] Some courts have chosen to focus on the responsibilities of the hospital rather than the rights of the physicians and have held that a private hospital occupies a fiduciary trust relationship between itself, the medical staff, and the public, and the actions of the hospital are, therefore, subject to judicial review.[80] In cases involving judicial review of hospital decisions regarding privileges, California has done away with the distinction between private and public hospitals altogether.[81]

A significant number of federal court decisions hold that denial of privileges by a private health care provider is not sufficiently regulated or controlled by the state to invoke federal jurisdiction.[82] Nevertheless, it is becoming clear that regardless of whether the hospital concerned is public or private, a physician has a federally protected right to due process[83] and the right to be free from arbitrary action on the part of a hospital.[84]

INITIAL PRIVILEGES VERSUS EXISTING PRIVILEGES. The majority of decided cases dealing with hospital privileges involve a physician whose previously granted privileges are revoked or reduced.[85] Some cases, however, deal with the physician's rights on initial application for privileges.[86] It has been pointed out that a physician who has had privileges has more of a "vested interest than one who is newly applying."[87] In California, the extent and nature of judicial review depend on whether the decision of the hospital involved an initial application or existing privileges. In cases involving existing privileges, the court is to make an independent judgment review in determining whether the decision of the hospital is supported by the weight of the evidence. In cases involving new applications, the court is to make a substantial evidence review to determine whether the decision of the hospital is supported by substantial evidence in light of the whole record.[88] Even though a physician applying for new privileges may have less of a vested interest than one who has already been granted privileges, the physician must be afforded due process that is adequate to safeguard the physician's interest in pursuing his or her profession, and the hospital cannot act arbitrarily or discriminatorily with regard to his or her application.[89]

The physician's due process rights in hospital proceedings. Hospital proceedings that affect a physician's privileges usually occur on four different levels. At the first level there may be a complaint brought against a physician who already has privileges by a patient, another physician, the administrator of the hospital, or the board of directors.[90] At the second level a committee of the hospital, usually the credentials committee when a new application for privileges is involved, or the executive committee of the medical staff where existing privileges are involved, conducts an inquiry into whether the subject physician's privileges should be granted, denied, restricted, or revoked. No reported cases have been found that give the physician any due process rights at these two levels. Once a decision has been made by a committee or other authority within the hospital that may adversely affect the physician's present or requested privileges, the physician should be given the following due process rights.

NOTIFICATION OF THE ADVERSE RECOMMENDATION. Once an adverse recommendation has been made that will result in denial, revocation, or restriction of a physician's privileges, the physician must be notified and informed of his or her right to request a hearing before a panel established to review his or her privileges or application for privileges.[91]

WRITTEN NOTICE OF THE CHARGES. If the physician requests a hearing, then he or she must be given written notice of the charges that will be presented against him or her at the hearing.[92] The charges must be sufficiently specific to give the physician adequate notice of the nature of the charges.[93] A few courts have noted with apparent approval the practice of providing the physician with the hospital chart numbers of those cases that substantiate the charges against him or her.[94] Although this may be sufficient in view of the reasonable assumption that the physician can read his or her own charts, one court has said that the charges must state "in reasonable fullness the nature of the criticism in each case."[95]

ADEQUATE TIME TO PREPARE A DEFENSE. After the physician has been advised of the charges, he or she must be given adequate time to prepare a defense.[96] The time interval between notification and the hearing date will necessarily vary somewhat according to the circumstances and the extent and complexity of the charges that the physician must defend against.

PREHEARING DISCOVERY. The physician or the physician's attorney sometimes wishes to conduct discovery before the hearing before the panel. Courts have reached different decisions on this issue depending on the nature of the discovery sought. In *Garrow v. Elizabeth General Hospital,*[97] the court held that the information that was relied on in making the adverse recommendation should be made available to the physician before the hearing so as to enable the physician to make adequate preparations for a defense. Similarly, in *Suckle v. Madison General Hospital,*[98] the court held that the physician had a right to access all relevant hospital and medical records during the period in which he was preparing a response to the charges. In cases where the discovery sought is more formal in nature, however, it has not been allowed.[99] This is in keeping with the often made statement that, in hospital due process proceedings, the physician is "not entitled to a full blown judicial trial."[100] In *Woodbury v. McKinnon,*[101] the physician involved was not allowed to conduct discovery by means of depositions and interrogatories to obtain evidence to support his contention that other members of the medical staff were not as good as he was.

A HEARING PANEL COMPOSED OF IMPARTIAL, FAIR-MINDED PHYSICIANS. The panel charged with the responsibility of giving the physician his or her due process hearing must be composed of physicians who are impartial and fair-minded.[102] If any physician on the panel actively participated in the investigation of the subject physician or made the original adverse recommendation, then he or she will be subject to challenge on the grounds of bias or lack of impartiality.[103] In other words, if the functions of investigator, prosecutor, and judge are being carried out by the same person, then a fair hearing will be presumed to be unavailable and actual bias need not be shown.[104] Courts have recognized, however, that prior involvement by a hearing panel member on some other level will not disqualify that person from sitting on the panel if the involvement was not substantial and did not bring about the adverse recommendation under review.[105] The following additional factors have been identified as having a high probability of destroying impartiality: (1) the panel member has a direct pecuniary interest in the outcome; (2) the member has been personally involved in a dispute with the subject physician or has been the target of his criticism; or (3) the panel member is embroiled in other matters involving the physician whose rights he or she is determining.[106] As stated in *Applebaum v. Board of Directors*: "Biased decision makers are constitutionally impermissible and even the probability of unfairness is to be avoided."[107] If the hospital is a small one and the matter has been particularly vitriolic and disruptive, then consideration should be given to having physicians from outside the immediate hospital area sit on the hearing panel. It has been said, however, that the physician under review is "not entitled to a panel made up of outsiders or of physicians who had never heard of the case and who knew nothing about the facts of it or what they supposed the facts to be."[108]

In some instances the physician or his or her attorney has sought to *voir dire* the panel members to discover any bias or lack of impartiality. In *Duffield v. Charleston Area Medical Center, Inc.,*[109] the subject physician asked for and received permission to examine all members of the panel before the hearing began. The trial court in *Hackethal v. California Medical Association and San Bernardino County Medical Society*[110] concluded that the subject physician's *voir dire* of the panel members was unduly restricted, and this was found to be a denial of procedural due process. Because a physician has a vital interest in having a fair and impartial panel, it appears that he or she should have a reasonable opportunity to question the panel regarding any matters that may affect their objectivity or lack thereof.

APPEARANCE BEFORE THE PANEL. The right to personally appear before the decision-making panel and be heard has been held to be essential.[111] As stated in *Grannis v. Ordean*: "The fundamental requisite of due process of law is the opportunity to be heard."[112] The opportunity to speak on one's behalf must also be given at a time when it will be effective. As the court said in *Lew v. Kona Hospital,* "The fundamental requirement of due process is the opportunity to be heard at a meaningful time and in a meaningful manner."[113] Thus, in a case where all the proceedings leading up to a letter of termination of privileges were done in secret and without any opportunity to be heard, it was found that the physician had not received due process and his privileges were reinstated.[114]

ASSISTANCE OF LEGAL COUNSEL DURING HEARING. To date only one jurisdiction has recognized the right of a physician to be assisted by legal counsel in a hospital due process hearing. In *Garrow v. Elizabeth General Hospital,*[115] the Supreme Court of New Jersey examined the issue and found that in view of the physician's substantial interest in such proceedings, the ability of an attorney to marshal the evidence, counter adverse testimony, and present argument on the physician's behalf tipped the balance in favor of allowing the physician the right to an attorney at mandated hospital hearings.[116] The court also pointed out that the attorney would be subject to the control of the person in charge of the hearings.[117] A few courts have held that it should be within the discretion of the hearing panel as to whether legal counsel may attend the hearing and actively participate.[118] Other courts have noted the participation of counsel for the physician without indicating whether the allowance of counsel in such proceedings is required in order to satisfy due process.[119]

CROSS-EXAMINATION OF WITNESSES. Although some courts have held that a physician is not constitutionally entitled to cross-examine witnesses who testify against him or her at the hearing,[120] the better rule clearly appears to be that a physician does have the right to confront and cross-examine any witnesses who appear and testify against him or her.[121] Due process means fair procedure,[122] and to allow a witness to testify against the physician without being subject to cross-examination would certainly seem to violate the rules of fair play.

PRESENTATION OF WITNESSES AND EVIDENCE IN DEFENSE. The right of a physician to present witnesses and evidence in his or her own behalf has been clearly recognized.[123] This is an integral part of fundamental fairness that has been equated with procedural due process.[124]

TRANSCRIPT OF PANEL HEARING. It is advisable to have an accurate record made of the due process hearing so that any objections raised by the subject physician can be reviewed in a hospital appellate review of the panel's decision.[125] In addition, without an accurate record, it may be difficult for a court to determine whether the physician was accorded due process at the hearing.

WRITTEN DECISION FROM PANEL. The decision of the panel should be written so that it can provide a record for hospital and judicial review.[126] A copy should be given to the physician.[127] In reaching its decision, the panel must not rely on *ex parte* communications that were not made known to the physician in question, and the decision must be based on evidence that was presented at the hearing and to which the physician had an opportunity to respond.[128] The decision of the panel should be based on substantial evidence.[129]

The fourth level of hospital proceedings concerning a physician's privileges is appellate review of the decision of the hearing panel and a final decision by the governing authority. Hospital bylaws normally provide a mechanism whereby the physician can obtain review of the panel decision by an appellate review committee.[130] The physician is usually allowed to submit a written statement of his or her position to the committee, but the right to make an oral statement is within the discretion of the appellate review body.[131] New or additional evidence not raised during the due process hearing or otherwise reflected in the record will be allowed to be introduced at the appellate review level only under unusual circumstances.[132] After the appellate review committee issues its decision, the final decision must be made by the highest governing authority of the hospital. The final hospital decision is transmitted to the physician concerned, and the hospital proceedings are then complete.[133]

The scope of judicial review of hospital decisions. It is now well established that courts have jurisdiction to review hospital decisions that adversely affect a physician's privileges.[134] In addition to jurisdiction based on alleged violations of rights guaranteed by the Fifth and Fourteenth Amendments, federal courts often find jurisdiction under 42 U.S.C. §1983[135] in conjunction with 28 U.S.C. §1343(3).[136] However, the extent of judicial review in such cases is limited.[137] If the court finds that the physician was afforded due process in the hospital proceedings[138] and the hospital neither violated its bylaws[139] nor acted in an arbitrary or capricious manner,[140] the decision of the hospital will be upheld. This limited review is necessitated by the court's lack of medical expertise, as was pointed out in *Laje v. R.E. Thomason General Hospital*:

Judicial intervention must be limited to an assessment of those factors which are within the court's expertise to review. For this reason, our cases have gone no further than to require that the procedures employed by the hospital are fair, that the standards set by the hospital are reasonable, and that they have been applied without arbitrariness and capriciousness.[141]

It has also been said that "the decision of a hospital's governing body concerning the granting of hospital privileges is to be accorded great deference."[142] Therefore once the court has determined that the decision of the hospital is "supported by substantial evidence and was made using proper criteria, after a satisfactory hearing, on a rational basis, and without irrelevant, discriminatory and arbitrary influences, the work of the court comes to an end."[143]

Conclusion. In light of current judicial concepts of due process, it appears that the distinction between public and private hospitals will continue to lose viability where physicians' hospital privileges are concerned. It is also expected that more jurisdictions will follow New Jersey in allowing the physician to be represented by counsel at the due process hearing. Because the panel hearing is by far the most important proceeding for the physician, this seems both sensible and fair.

Although a physician applying for privileges may be seen as having less of a vested interest than one who has previously enjoyed them, it is apparent that both are equally entitled to due process. In every case, the hospital must be guided by fundamental fairness; keep in mind the words of the U.S. Supreme Court in *Hannah v. Larche*: "Due process is an elusive concept. Its exact boundaries are undefinable, and its content varies according to specific factual contexts."[144]

Hospital-required malpractice insurance*

The increased number of suits against health care providers, the increased number of health care providers in each suit, and the increased amount of awards and settle-

---

*From Goebert, 13 L.A.M.P. 1 (Nov. 1985).

ments have created unrest, tension, and distrust between hospitals and their medical staff. Physicians have a decerebrate posturing response to being named in a malpractice suit. They have a lesser "knee-jerk" response when having to pay malpractice insurance premiums. Hospitals are developing the same responses because of escalating malpractice premiums and claims. Their corporate assets are being threatened, their costs continue to escalate, and the inevitable government regulation that results has added to their problems. When the hospital requires insurance for staff privileges, the effect is similar to adding sodium to water. The resulting explosion not only damages the hospital and its medical staff, but also involves the legal community, the state and federal legislature, and ultimately, as always, the public.

The National Association of Insurance Companies' 1975 to 1978 study showed that more than 70% of paid claims are a result of physician activity occurring in the hospital.[145] Hospitals have increasing legal "corporate responsibility" for physician activities. The trustees of hospitals have "fiduciary responsibility" to maintain corporate assets. Joint and several liability makes hospitals the "deep pocket" for uninsured or poorly insured physician staff members.

Physicians have not only patient care requirements, but also hospital-related functions such as teaching, emergency care, emergency coverage, and committee functioning, especially in credentialing and policy-making. The line between physician patient care activity and hospital patient care activity becomes more and more indistinct. Hospitals and their physician staff look to each other for support, but once sued, look to each other for money. This is a major problem that is frequently solved by hospitals paying more than their fair share to the injured patient.

Is mandatory fiscal responsibility as a requirement for staff privileges a viable answer? In some states, hospitals require this, and in other states, the requirement is linked with licensure. We shall discuss what happens with the two approaches. In the mid-1970s in response to the "malpractice crisis," Alaska, Hawaii, Idaho, Kansas, Kentucky, North Dakota, and Pennsylvania all required physicians to carry professional liability insurance as a condition of obtaining and maintaining licensure. In Hawaii, the Hawaii Medical Association sought to enjoin the state from enforcing the malpractice insurance requirement against them by a preliminary injunction.[146] This suit was dismissed but the licensing board did not enforce the requirement, so the next year Hawaii legislatively deleted it. Also, Alaska repealed the requirement in 1978.[147] Now individual hospitals are reacting by requiring financial responsibility as a condition for staff privileges.

Kentucky and North Dakota ruled the requirement unconstitutional. Kentucky found the statute a violation of due process.[148] The legislature had arbitrarily imposed and restricted the practice of medicine, mainly because all health care providers were being considered inherently negligent or financially irresponsible. There had not been a legislative finding that such was the case. On the other hand, in North Dakota the State Supreme Court found all statutory malpractice changes unconstitutional.[149] When addressing the mandatory insurance provision, the court specifically withheld a final decision but did have serious doubts as to the constitutionality of requiring malpractice insurance for all physicians without regard to their ability to pay when the law was silent on the effect of some physicians' inability to pay the premiums.

On the other hand, Pennsylvania, Idaho, and Kansas courts ruled in favor of the law. Pennsylvania stated that there existed a rational relationship between requiring insurance and the public interest in ensuring compensability.[150] There is no unconstitutional denial of equal protection nor a prohibition against pursuing one's occupation. The Idaho Supreme Court remanded the malpractice statutes back to the lower courts for further investigation, but they had no problem stating that protection to patients who may be injured as a result of medical malpractice is in the public welfare and compulsory insurance is constitutional.[151] The Kansas Supreme Court also found its statute constitutional.

These cases are important because they give the legal arguments both pro and con for allowing a state to specifically regulate the medical profession by requiring insurance. They address the right to engage in a lawful occupation, the police power of the state, and substantive due process of individuals guaranteed by the constitution. Some courts required only a rational reason for the legislature to require insurance. Other states require a more serious constitutional scrutiny than the rational basis analysis, because the regulation is not truly related to competence and places some burden on the individual's right to engage in a lawful profession. Close scrutiny will balance the respective interest of both the physician and the public.[152]

Can hospitals require malpractice insurance as a condition of privileges? Yes, but in the absence of a statute, state hospitals would have the same type of scrutiny placed on them as state statutes had in the preceding paragraphs. In an earlier case, a California hospital that required malpractice insurance as a condition of admission was challenged successfully. The rule was arbitrary and not related to the state's regulation of physicians.[153] Following this case, the California legislature passed a law allowing hospitals to require malpractice insurance, and this was found constitutional.[154] In 1977, a survey of U.S. community hospitals showed that out of 4478 hospitals, 26.4% required physicians to have a minimum amount of malpractice insurance.[155]

When private hospitals require malpractice insurance for staff privileges, physicians present a number of arguments.[156] First is "state action" because the private hospital is receiving either state or federal funds; therefore the court has jurisdiction to determine whether an impermissible imposition infringed on constitutional rights or the physicians' civil rights.[157] The physicians will allege a breach of contract action because hospital privileges were given for a longer length of time. The hospital is taking away privileges without showing that the physician is unqualified or unskilled. Many of the physicians have been members of hospital committees and have been on the teaching staffs of universities, and all have state licensure. Some arguments show a violation of the antitrust provisions of the Sherman Act if any of the deciding physicians involved with denying privileges are in competition with the physician being restricted.[158]

A number of cases have addressed the question of a hospital acting under the color of state law. These have found that the specific activity complained of by the physician being denied privileges must be related to the way that the state is acting on the private hospital. There must be a nexus between state action and denial of privileges. These cases show that the granting of funds from Hill-Burton monies, Medicaid, Medicare payments, training of residents from state institutional programs, use of tax-free bonds, hospital licensure and inspection by the state, and reporting of privileges revocations to a state board all are state actions or federal actions; but none have a required nexus. The restricted physician must show that those state actions have something to do with a denial of privileges when the physician does not have insurance.[159–161] The due process hearings required in civil rights actions under U.S.C. §1983 have not been upheld, but state courts have said that hospitals need to show or need to give due process to physicians before a revocation of privileges.[162] The test in these cases is whether a hospital acts arbitrarily and capriciously or denies the physician due process. Physicians have also argued that they are unable to afford the insurance, that they do not have a big enough practice, or that they have an indigent patient population in their practice and therefore the public will suffer.[163–165]

Hospitals argue, on the other hand, that this is not arbitrary and capricious. It is rational policy supported by good fiscal management and preservation of the hospital resources.[166] The requirement is not excessively burdensome and can be met by providing insurance or fiscal responsibility. The hospital must be able to show that it has done everything necessary to obtain facts supporting the policy. Meetings with concerned individuals, a review by the medical staff executive committee, surveys of the physicians, letters to other hospitals and to insurance people finding out the costs and alternatives, and attempts at legislative tort reform are all things that would be helpful to a hospital initiating these actions.

The courts have supported and allowed the hospitals to initiate such action. Florida,[167] Arizona,[168] Louisiana,[169] and Indiana[170] have all heard arguments both pro and con and ruled in favor of the hospital and against the restricted physician as long as procedural due process and prior notice was afforded the physician. Physicians scream, but the courts have not listened.[171,172]

Courts have addressed the California legislative policy of allowing a hospital to require malpractice insurance and they have stated that the interests of society served by such insurance requirements are not so arbitrary that it would be considered unreasonable. The amount of insurance established by the hospital and the requirement that the insurance company must be admitted to do business in California were reasonable.[173]

The final argument in favor of this policy is that the real reason for such a policy is the requirement that the hospital pay its fair share of liability and the physician pay his or her fair share of liability. In *Holmes*, the situation is summarized as follows:

> We cannot ignore the realities of modern procedural practice. If a patient is injured while in the hospital regardless of who is at fault, the hospital will almost always be joined as a codefendant. Despite the outcome of such an action, the hospital must expend valuable financial resources in its own defense, and will, if innocent of wrongdoing, be more likely to recover its expenses from the tortfeasor physician if that physician is insured. If, indeed, some conscientious lawyer decides not to include the hospital in an action where the finger of negligence points directly and solely to the doctor, we can be certain it will only be because the physician does indeed have malpractice insurance.[174]

The hospital has the right to take reasonable measures to protect itself and the patient it serves. We cannot say, as a matter of law, that the hospital board's attention to its medical staff's malpractice insurance is unlawful, arbitrary, or capricious. As a practical matter, we cannot say it is irrational or unreasonable. In *Pollack*, the court states:

> We find the plaintiff (physician) has no liberty or property interest sufficient to invoke the due process requirements of the Fourteenth Amendment. While the right to practice an occupation is a liberty interest protected by the Fourteenth Amendment, . . . plaintiff is not precluded from exercising that right by the insurance requirements in order to continue his membership on the hospital staff. . . . Requiring its staff physicians to carry insurance and to submit proof to the hospital of that fact is surely a reasonable exercise of financial responsibility on the part of the hospital.[175]

Basically, the hospital has three alternatives regarding malpractice insurance:

1. To use the information regarding the physician's malpractice as one of the criteria to decide on appointment or reappointment;
2. To require malpractice coverage as a condition of appointment or reappointment; or
3. To take no policy position.

The first two of these alternatives are legally permitted. The last does not solve the problem. The hospital can avoid much internal stress by recognizing that this problem is a shared or joint problem with the medical staff. The hospital should involve the staff in trying to solve the problem as alternatives can be searched for and harmony fostered.

ENDNOTES

1. *Darling v. Charleston Community Hosp.*, 200 N.E. 2d 149 (Ill. Sup. Ct. 1965); *Elam v. College Park Hosp.*, 183 Cal. Rptr. 156 (1982); *Corletto v. Shore Memorial Hosp.*, 350 A. 2d 534 (N.J. Sup. Ct. 1975).
2. D. M. Eddy, *Clinical Decision Making: From Theory to Practice— The Challenge*, 1 J.A.M.A. 287-290 (1990).
3. *See*, e.g., *Wall v. Stout*, 310 N.C. 184, 192, 311 S.E. 2d 571 (1984); also see *Physicians, Surgeons, Etc.*, 61 Am. Jur. 2d §167, 298-299 (1981).
4. Pub. L. 99-660, part IV; 42 U.S.C. §11111 *et seq.*
5. *Brownsville Medical Center v. Garcia*, 704 S.W. 2d 68 (Tex. App. Corpus Christi 1985).
6. *Smith v. Baptist Memorial Hosp. System*, 720 S.W. 2d 618 (Tex. App. San Antonio 1986, writ ref. n.r.e.).
7. *Corletto, supra* note 1.
8. Joint Commission on Accreditation of Healthcare Organizations, *Accreditation Manual for Hospitals*, Standard M.S. 6 *et seq.* (JCAHO, Chicago 1990).
9. *Supra* note 4.
10. *McDonald v. Massachusetts General Hosp.*, 120 Mass. 432, 21 A. 529 (1876).
11. *Schloendorff v. New York Hosp.*, 211 N.Y. 125, 105 N.E. 92 (1914).
12. *Id.* at 132 and 194.
13. *Necolaff v. Genessee Hosp.*, 296 N.Y.S. 936, 73 N.E. 2d 117 (1947).
14. *Berg v. N.Y. Society for the Relief of the Ruptured and Crippled*, 154 N.Y.S. 455, 456 (1956).
15. *Bing v. Thunig*, 2 N.Y. 2d 656, 143 N.E. 2d 3 (1957). But see *Weiss v. Rubin*, 9 N.Y. 2d 230, 173 N.E. 2d 791 (1961), in which the Court of Appeals found that the surgeon had a duty to inquire into details of how the hospital performed its duty (providing blood for transfusion) as part of his duty of reasonable care. Justice Van Voorhis' dissent called for strict application of *Bing*.
16. Cf. generally, *supra* note 8, at Medical Staff Section.
17. *Johnson v. Misericordia County Hosp.*, 99 Wis. 2d 708, 301 N.W. 2d 156 (1981), *aff'd*, 99 Wis. 2d 78, 301 N.W. 2d 156 (1981). The Wisconsin Supreme Court also held that a hospital has a legal duty to its patients to exercise reasonable care in selecting its medical staff and in granting privileges but, in *Humana Medical Corp. v. Peyer*, 456 N.W. 2d 355 (1990), declined to find or establish an ancillary duty requiring a hospital to disclose credentialing information to a third party.
18. *Weiss v. York Hosp.*, 745 F. 2d 786 (1984).
19. *Tonsic v. Wagner*, 329 A. 2d 497 (Pa. 1974).
20. *McConnell v. Williams*, 361 Pa. 355, 65 A. 2d 243 (1949). But see J. Jones' dissent, in *Yorston v. Pennell*, 153 A. 2d 255 (1959), which would have circumscribed application of this rule to matters only within the directing physician's responsibility.
21. *Capan v. Divine Providence Hosp.*, 410 A. 2d 1282 (Pa. Super. Ct. 1979).
22. *People v. Flushing Hosp. and Medical Center*, 471 N.Y.S. 2d 745 (N.Y. Cir. Ct. 1983), where the hospital was charged with a misdemeanor when it refused emergency care because the hospital was full; *People ex rel. M.B.*, 312 N.W. 2d 714 (S.D. 1981), where the South Dakota Supreme Court ruled that a lower court exceeded its jurisdiction by ordering an admission when no space was available; *contra, see Pierce County Office of Involuntary Commitment v. Western State Hosp.*, 97 Wash. 2d 264, 644 P. 2d 131 (1982), where the

Washington Supreme Court interpreted a state mental health statute to require admission of all patients who sought treatment at the hospital, despite a lack of space.

23. *See*, e.g., *Fabian v. Matzko*, 236 Pa. Super. 267, 344 A. 2d 569 (1975).

24. *Wilmington General Hosp. v. Manlove*, 54 Del. 15, 174 A. 2d 135 (1961).

25. *Stanturf v. Sipes*, 447 S.W. 2d 558 (Mo. 1969).

26. *Id.* 4475.W. 2d, at 562.

27. Restatement (Second) of Agency §220 (1958).

28. *See*, e.g., *Smith v. St. Francis Hosp.*, 676 P. 2d 279 (Okla. App. 1983). However, Oklahoma's Supreme Court extended this reasoning, applying the patient's perception of whether the hospital merely served as the physician's work site, to avoid finding respondeat superior was applicable. *See Weldon v. Seminole Muni. Hospital*, 709 P. 2d 1058 (Okla. 1985).

29. *Thomas v. Corso*, 265 Md. 84, 288 A. 2d 379 (1972).

30. *Citizens Hosp. Ass'n. v. Schoulin*, 48 Ala. App. 101, 262 So. 2d 303 (1972).

31. *Gizzi v. Texaco, Inc.*, 437 F. 2d 308 (3d Cir. 1971).

32. See F. Harper, F. James, Jr., & O. Gray, Law of Torts 26.11, 60-94 (2d ed. 1986) for a discussion of the immunity rule and its exception.

33. *Marek v. Professional Health Services, Inc.*, 179 N.J. Super. 433, 437 A. 2d 538 (1981).

34. *Jackson v. Power*, 743 P. 2d 1376 (Alaska 1987). In a comparison case, *Harding v. Sisters of Providence*, no. 371 (Alaska, Oct. 16, 1987), liability was extended to an independent contractor/radiologist's negligence on the basis of a nondelegable duty owed by the hospital to its patients. Distinguished: *Miltiron v. Franke*, 793 P. 2d 824 (1990).

35. W. Prosser & W. Keeton, Law of Torts §71 at 511-512 (5th ed. 1984).

36. *Guerro v. Copper Queen Hosp.*, 112 Ariz. 104, 537 P. 2d 1329 (1975). *Thompson v. Sun City Community Hospital*, 688 P. 2d 647 (1983).

37. 42 U.S.C. §1395dd (Apr. 7, 1986).

38. *Darling v. Charleston Memorial Hosp.*, 33 Ill. 2d 326, 211 N.E. 2d 253 (1965); *cert. denied* 383 U.S. 946 (1966). Distinguish this situation from that in *Weldon, supra* note 28, wherein the patient's care "was never within the discretion of the hospital."

39. *Fiorentino v. Wagner*, 227 N.E. 2d 296 (1967).

40. *Moore v. Board of Trustees of Carson City Hosp.*, 495 P. 2d 605 (Nev. 1972).

41. *Mitchell City Hosp. Authority v. Joiner*, 229 Ga. 140, 109 S.E. 2d 413 (1972). *Butler v. South Fenton Med. Center*, 215 Ga. App. 809, 452 S.E. 2d 768 (1994).

42. *Purcell v. Zimbleman*, 18 Ariz. App. 75, 500 P. 2d 335 (1972).

43. *Corletto v. Shore Memorial Hospital*, 138 N.J. Super. 302, 350 A. 2d 534 (1975).

44. *Hayman v. Galveston*, 273 U.S. 414, 47 S.Ct. 363 (1927).

45. *Porter Memorial Hosp. v. Harvy*, 279 N.E. 2d 583 (1972).

46. *Lubin v. Crittenden Hosp. Ass'n.*, 713 F. 2d 414 (8th Cir. 1983).

47. *Cardiomedical Assoc. v. Crozier-Chester Med. Ctr.*, 536 F. Supp. 1065 (E.D. Pa. 1982).

48. *Northeast Georgia Radiological Assoc. v. Tidwell*, 670 F. 2d 507 (5th Cir. 1982). In *Bellam v. Clayton County Hospital*, the U.S. District Court limited this principle to instances in which the privilege was terminated or withdrawn, declining to apply it where a privilege was just restricted. But see *Bloom v. Hennepin County*, 783 F. Supp. 418 (D. Minn. 1992), in which the court determined that there was no right to due process arising out of revocation of privileges when the plaintiff held the privileges pursuant to the bylaws and a contract with the hospital, which was terminated.

49. *Klinge v. Lutheran Charities Ass'n. of St. Louis*, 523 F. 2d 56 (8th Cir. 1975).

50. *Silver v. Castle Memorial Hosp.*, 53 Haw. 475, 497 P. 2d 564, *cert. denied* 409 U.S. 1048 (1972).

51. *Christhilf v. Annapolis Emergency Hosp. Ass'n., Inc.*, 496 F. 2d 174 (4th Cir. 1974).

52. *Id.*

53. *Garrow v. Elizabeth General Hosp.*, 79 N.J. 549, 401 A. 2d 533 (1979).

54. *Supra* note 49, at 60.

55. *Branch v. Hempstead County Memorial Hosp.*, 539 F. Supp. 908 (W.D. Ark. 1982).

56. California Medical Association-California Hospital Association, Uniform Code of Hearing and Appeal Procedures §3(e).

57. *Novosel v. Nationwide Insurance Co.*, 721 F. 2d 894 (1983).

58. *Cardiomedical Association, Ltd. v. Crozier-Chester Med. Ctr.*, 721 F. 2d 68 (1983).

59. *Jefferson Parish Hosp. District No. 2 v. Hyde, M.D.*, 466 U.S. 2 (1984).

60. *Supra* note 18.

61. *Patrick v. Burget*, 486 U.S. 94 (1988).

62. Health Care Quality Improvement Act of 1986 (Pub. L. 99-660, as amended by Pub. L. 100-93 and 100-177).

63. Tarlov, *Special Report, Shattuck Lecture: The Increasing Supply of Physicians—The Changing Structure of the Health-Services System and the Future Practice of Medicine*, 308 N. Engl. J. Med. 1235 (1983).

64. *Supra* note 17; Annot. 51 A.L.R. 3d 981 (1973).

65. *Supra* note 42; *Elam v. College Park Hosp.*, 132 Cal. App. 3d 332, 183 Cal. Rptr. 156, *modified*, 133 Cal. App. 3d 94 (1982).

66. *See Falcone v. Middlesex County Medical Society*, 34 N.J. 582, 170 A. 2d 791 (1961).

67. *Supra* note 44; *Sosa v. Bd. of Managers of Val Verde Memorial Hosp.*, 437 F. 2d 173 (5th Cir. 1971).

68. *Anton v. San Antonio Comm. Hosp.*, 19 Cal. 3d 802, 140 Cal. Rptr. 442, 567 P. 2d 1162 (1977).

69. *Id.* at 814, 140 Cal. Rptr. at 454, 567 P. 2d at 1174.

70. *Unterthiner v. Desert Hosp. Dist. of Palm Springs*, 33 Cal. 3d 285, 188 Cal. Rptr. 590, 656 P. 2d 554 (1983).

71. *Id.* at 297, 188 Cal. Rptr. at 598, 656 P. 2d at 562.

72. U.S. Constitution, amend. V, XIV.

73. *Supra* notes 49 and 51; *Woodbury v. McKinnon*, 447 F. 2d 839 (5th Cir. 1971).

74. *See*, e.g., *supra* note 50 and cases cited therein; *The Physician's Right to Hospital Staff Membership: The Public-Private Dichotomy*, 485 Wash. U.L.Q. (1966).

75. *Foster v. Mobile County Hosp. Bd.*, 398 F. 2d 227 (5th Cir. 1938).

76. *See*, e.g., *Suckle v. Madison Gen. Hosp.*, 362 F. Supp. 1196 (W.D. Wis. 1973), *aff'd*, 499 F. 2d 1364 (7th Cir. 1974).

77. *Supra* note 51.

78. *Schlein v. Milford Hosp.*, 423 F. Supp. 541 (D. Conn. 1976). The Second Circuit United States Court of Appeals declined to adopt this case because it applies to the reasoning that clinical privileges do not create property interests. *See Greenwood v. New York*, 163 F. 3d 119 (2d Cir. 1998).

79. *Sussman v. Overlook Hosp. Ass'n.*, 231 A. 2d 389, 95 N.J. Super. 418 (1967).

80. *Supra* notes 50 and 53; *Greisman v. Newcomb Hosp.*, 40 N.J. 389, 192 A. 2d 817 (1963).

81. *Supra* note 68; *Ascherman v. St. Francis Memorial Hosp.*, 45 Cal. App. 3d 507, 119 Cal. Rptr. 507 (1975).

82. *Supra* notes 46 and 47, and cases cited therein.

83. *Supra* notes 48 and 49.

84. *Citta v. Delaware Valley Hosp.*, 313 F.Supp. 301 (E.D. Pa. 1970); *Avol v. Hawthorne Comm. Hosp. Inc.*, 135 Cal. App. 3d 101, 184 Cal. Rptr. 914 (1982); *Kelly v. St. Vincent Hosp.*, 102 N.M. 201, 692 P. 2d 1350 (1984).

85. *See generally*, Comment, *Hospital Medical Staff Privileges: Recent Developments in Procedural Due Process Requirements*, 12 Willamette L.J. 137 (1975).

86. *Sosa, supra* note 67; *supra* notes 70, 75, 78, and 79.

87. *Supra* note 70.

88. *Supra* notes 68 and 70.

89. *Supra* notes 70, 75, 78, and 79.

90. *Avol*, *supra* note 84.

91. *Supra* note 50; *see* JCAHO, *Accreditation Manual for Hospitals*, Standards for Medical Staff, standard III, 104 (JCAHO, Chicago 1995); California Medical Association-California Hospital Association, *Uniform Code of Hearing and Appeal Procedures*, 32 (1972).

92. *Supra* notes 51 and 53.

93. *Supra* notes 50 and 76. However, specificity that amounts to pleading of evidence is not constitutionally required. *Truly v. Madison Gen. Hosp.*, 673 F. 2d 763 (5th Cir. 1982).

94. *Supra* note 73; *Branch v. Hempstead County Memorial Hosp.*, 539 F. Supp. 908 (W.D. Ark. 1982); *supra* note 68.

95. *Woodbury*, *supra* note 73, at 1211.

96. *Supra* note 51; *Miller v. Eisenhower Med. Ctr.*, 27 Cal. 3d 614, 166 Cal. Rptr. 826, 614 P. 2d 258 (1980); *supra* note 50.

97. *Supra* note 53.

98. *Supra* note 76.

99. *Woodbury*, *supra* note 73; *Hackethal v. California Med. Ass'n. and San Bernardino County Medical Society*, 138 Cal. App. 3d 435, 187, Cal. Rptr. 811 (1982).

100. *Supra* note 49, at 60.

101. *Woodbury*, *supra* note 73.

102. *Supra* note 49; *Citta*, *supra* note 84; *Hackethal*, *supra* note 99; *Applebaum v. Board of Directors*, 104 Cal. App. 3d 648, 163 Cal. Rptr. 831 (1980).

103. *See*, e.g., *Applebaum*, *supra* note 102.

104. *Citta*, *supra* note 84.

105. *Duffield v. Charleston Area Med. Ctr., Inc.*, 503 F. 2d 512 (4th Cir. 1974); *Hoberman v. Lock Haven Hosp.*, 377 F. Supp. 1178 (M.D. Pa. 1974).

106. *Hackethal*, *supra* note 99; *Applebaum*, *supra* note 102.

107. *Applebaum*, *supra* note 102, at 104 Ca. App. 3d at 657, 163 Cal. Rptr., at 840.

108. *Supra* note 49, at 63.

109. *Duffield*, *supra* note 105.

110. *Hackethal*, *supra* note 99.

111. *Supra* note 51; *Poe v. Charlotte Memorial Hosp., Inc.*, 374 F. Supp. 1302 (W.D. N.C. 1974).

112. *Grannis v. Ordean*, 234 U.S. 385, 394, 34 S.Ct. 779, 783, 58 L.Ed. 1363, 1369 (1914).

113. *Lew v. Kona Hosp.*, 754 F. 2d 1420 at 1424 (9th Cir. 1985).

114. *Poe*, *supra* note 111.

115. *Supra* note 53.

116. *Id.*

117. *Id.*

118. *Supra* notes 50 and 68.

119. *Laje v. R.E. Thomason Gen. Hosp.*, 564 F. 2d 1159 (5th Cir. 1977); *Citta*, *supra* note 84; *Miller*, *supra* note 96.

120. *Woodbury*, *supra* note 73; *Kaplan v. Carney*, 404 F. Supp. 161 (E.D. Mo. 1975); *supra* note 79; in *Woodbury* and *Kaplan* no witnesses testified.

121. *Supra* notes 50, 51, and 55; *Poe*, *supra* note 111; *Hackethal*, *supra* note 99.

122. *Poe*, *supra* note 111.

123. *Supra* notes 50 and 55; *Hackethal*, *supra* note 99.

124. *Supra* note 53.

125. Section 3(e) of the California Medical Association-California Hospital Association *Uniform Code of Hearing and Appeal Procedures* provides: "Record of Hearing. The judicial review committee may maintain a record of the hearing by one of the following methods: a shorthand reporter present to make a record of the hearing, a recording, or minutes of the proceedings. The cost of such shorthand reporter shall be borne by the party requesting same."

126. *Supra* note 50.

127. *See supra* note 49, at 60.

128. *Duffield*, *supra* note 105; *Suckle*, *supra* note 93; *supra* note 50.

129. *Storrs v. Lutheran Hosp. & Homes Society of America*, 661 P. 2d 632 (Alaska 1983); *see Laje*, *supra* note 119; *Sosa*, *supra* note 86; *Kaplan*, *supra* note 120.

130. *See* Hershey & Purtell, Medical Staff Bylaws. Art. XVI (1985).

131. *Id.* at §16.6-2.

132. *Id.* at §16.6-5.

133. *See generally*, *supra* note 49.

134. *See*, e.g., *supra* notes 50, 51, and 53.

135. "Every person who, under color of any statute, ordinance, regulation, custom, or usage, of any state or territory, subjects, or causes to be subjected, any citizen of the United States or other person within the jurisdiction thereof to the deprivation of any rights, privileges, or immunities secured by the Constitution and laws, shall be liable to the party injured in an action at law, suit in equity, or other proper proceeding for redress."

136. *See*, e.g., *Daly v. Sprague*, 675 F. 2d 716 (5th Cir. 1982).

137. *Supra* notes 49, 50, and 113.

138. *See*, e.g., *Woodbury*, *supra* note 73.

139. *See*, e.g., *supra* note 48; *In re Murphy v. St. Agnes Hosp.*, 484 N.Y.S. 2d 40 (App. Div. 1985); however, failure to strictly comply with the bylaws will not be fatal if due process is given. *Kaplan*, *supra* note 120; *Avol*, *supra* note 84.

140. *See*, e.g., *supra* note 75.

141. *Laje*, *supra* note 119, at 1162.

142. *Id.*; *see* Hollowell, *Decisions about Hospital Staff Privileges: A Case for Judicial Deference*, 11 Law Med. and Health Care 118 (1983).

143. *Woodbury*, *supra* note 73, at 846.

144. *Hannah v. Larche*, 363 U.S. 420, 442, 80 S. Ct. 1502, 1514, 4 L. Ed. 2d 1307, 1321 (1960).

145. Bulletin of the American College of Surgeons (Mar. 1982).

146. *Hawaii Medical Ass'n. v. State of Hawaii*, No. 49777 (Hawaii, 1st Cir. Feb. 4, 1977): Haw. Rev. Stat. §§4538, 67136 (1976); Haw. Rev. Stat. §§4538 (1977).

147. Alaska Stat. §§08.64.215a (1976); repealed 1978 Alaska Sess. Laws §§40 ch. 177.

148. *McGuffy v. Hall*, 557 S.W. 2d 401 (Ky. 1977).

149. *Arenson v. Olson*, 270 N.W. 2d 125 (N.D. 1977).

150. *McCoy v. Commonwealth Board of Medical Education and Licensure*, 37 Pa. Comwlth. 530, 391 A. 2d 723.

151. *Jones v. State Board of Medicine*, 97 Idaho 859, *cert. denied* (1976).

152. These constitutional issues are thoroughly discussed in Muranaka, *Compulsory Medical Malpractice Insurance Statutes: An Approach in Determining Constitutionally*, 12 U.S.F.L. Rev. 599 (Summer 1978).

153. *Rosner v. Peninsula Hospital District*, 224 Cal. App. 2d 115 (1964).

154. *Wilklerson v. Madera Community Hosp.*, 192 Cal. Rptr. 593 (Cal. App. 1983).

155. Unpublished results prepared by D.L. Matthews, Projects Director, American Hospital Association Hospital Data Center, in Association with Andrew J. Korsak and Ross Mullner.

156. Propriety of Hospitals' Conditioning Physicians' Staff Privileges on his Carrying Professional Liability or Malpractice Insurance, 7 A.L.R. 4th 1238 (1981).

157. Action of Private Hospital as State Action under 42 U.S.C.S. §§1983 or Fourteenth Amendment, 42 A.L.R. Fed. 463.

158. *Watkins v. Mercy Hosp. Medical Center*, 520 F. 2d 894 (9th Cir. 1975).

159. *Pollack v. Methodist Hosp.*, 392 F. Supp. 393 (E.D. La. 1975).

160. *Kavka v. Edgewater Hosp., Inc.*, 586 F. 2d 59, *cert. denied* (7th Cir. 1978. reported sub nom, *Musso v. Suriano*).

161. *Asherman v. Presbyterian Hosp. of Pacific Medical Center, Inc.*, 507 F. 2d 1103 (9th Cir. 1974).

162. *Supra* note 50; *Silver v. Queen's Hosp.*, 63 Haw. 430, 629 P. 2d 1116 (1981).

163. Laird, *Requiring Liability Insurance Is Unfair*, Am. Med. News 20 (Apr. 24, 1981).

164. Lufton, *Hospital Privileges Revoked: Malpractice Insurance Ruling Awaited*, Am. Med. News (Sept. 4, 1981).

165. *Hospital Privileges, Restraint of Trade, and Professional Liability*, 10 Neurosurgery 285 (1982).

166. *Sosa, supra* note 67.

167. *Maxie v. Martin Memorial Hosp. Ass'n., Inc.*, No. 82330Ca (Fla. Cir. Ct. May 24, 1983).

168. *Holmes v. Maricopa*, 473 P. 2d 477 (Ariz. 1977).

169. *Supra* note 159.

170. *Renforth v. Fayette Memorial Hosp. Ass'n., Inc.*, 383 N.E. 2d 368 (Ind. Ct. App. 1978).

171. Doudera, *Can or Should a Hospital Require Its Medical Staff to Obtain Malpractice Insurance*, 6 Med. Legal News 16 (Summer 1978).

172. *Professional Liability Insurance as a Requirement for Medical Staff Privileges*, 10 Neurosurgery 788 (1982); *Professional Liability Insurance as a Condition for Staff Membership*, 80 J. Med. Soc. N.J. 334 (May 1983).

173. *Supra* note 154.

174. *Holmes v. Hoemaku Hosp.*, 573 P. 2d 477 (Ariz. 1977).

175. *Supra* note 159.

GENERAL REFERENCES

J. Couch & N. Caesar, *Physician Staff Privileges Disputes: A Risk Management Guide for Hospitals and Medical Staffs*, 81 Philadelphia Med. (Sept. 1985).

J. Couch & N. Caesar, *Cooperation Between Hospitals and Physicians for Better Cost Effective Medical Care Delivery: The Health Care Joint Venture*, 81 Philadelphia Med. (Oct. 1985).

J. Couch, N. Caesar, & W. Steigman, *The Legal and Economic Significance of Hospital Medical Staff Appointments and Exclusions*, 81 Philadelphia Med. (Feb. 1984).

J. Couch, N. Caesar, & W. Steigman, *The Effect of Some Recent Antitrust Decisions Regarding Hospital Medical Staff Privileges*, 81 Philadelphia Med. (June 1985).

C.D. Creech, *The Medical Review Committee Privilege: A Jurisdictional Survey*, 67 N.C.L. Rev. 179 (Nov. 1988).

Furrow, *The Changing Role of the Law in Promoting Quality in Health Care: From Sanctioning Outlaws to Managing Outcomes*, 26 Hous. L. Rev. 147 (1989).

Gnessin, *Liability in the Managed Care Setting*, in *Practicing Law Institute Handbook Series: Managed Health Care in 1988—Legal and Operational Issues*, 471 PLI/Comm 405 (Sept. 1, 1988).

Hall, *Institutional Control of Physician Behavior: Legal Barriers to Health Care Cost Containment*, 137 Pa. L. Rev. 431 (1988).

Harvard Law Review Association, *Antitrust-State Action-Private Parties Immune from Liability When Acting in an Official Capacity: Sandcrest Outpatient Services v. Cumberland County Hospital System*, 853 F. 2d 1139 (4th Cir. 1988), 102 Harv. L. Rev. 1080 (Mar. 1989).

E. Hollowell, *The Medical Staff: An Integral Part of the Hospital or a Legal Entity Separate from the Hospital?* Presented at the Twenty-fifth Annual International Conference on Legal Medicine, New Orleans, La. (May 1985).

Joy, *The Health Care Quality Improvement Act of 1986: A Proposal for Interpretation of Its Protection*, 20 St. Mary's L.J. 955 (Oct. 1, 1989).

Rosenberg, *Independent Practice Associations: Moving Toward an Integrated Medical Group Model*, 471 PLI/Comm 197.

A. Southwick, *Hospital Liability: Two Theories Have Been Merged*, 4 J. Legal Med. 1 (1983).

Physician as an Employer

CHARLES G. HESS, M.S., M.D.

HAZARD COMMUNICATION STANDARD
AMERICANS WITH DISABILITIES ACT
BLOOD-BORNE PATHOGENS STANDARD
CLINICAL LABORATORY IMPROVEMENT AMENDMENTS
HEALTH INSURANCE PORTABILITY AND ACCOUNTABILITY ACT

Federal laws passed in the United States since 1980 have profoundly affected the practice of medicine. The government's control over the practice of medicine reached new heights with the passage of the Health Insurance Portability and Accountability Act (HIPAA) in 1996. Any hopes some of its rules might be withdrawn were dashed by the (George W.) Bush administration on April 14, 2001, when the Department of Health and Human Services (DHHS) made the standard effective. This chapter deals with the legal responsibilities of the physician-employer, in his or her role as the head of a medical practice.

HAZARD COMMUNICATION STANDARD

Some of the almost 600,000 chemical products in the United States pose serious problems for exposed employees. In 1983 the Occupational Safety and Health Administration (OSHA) issued a regulation called *hazard communication* that applied to employers in the manufacturing sector. Under the Hazard Communication Standard (HCS), the employee is required to be informed of the contents of the law, the hazardous properties of chemicals encountered in the workplace, and measures (such as safe handling procedures) needed to protect employees from these chemicals. The law was expanded in 1988 to include employers in the nonmanufacturing sector such as the physician-employer; thus HCS became the first regulation to concern itself specifically with the health and safety of medical employees.

Under the general duty clause of this law, the physician-employer "shall furnish a place of employment which is free from recognized hazards that are causing or are likely to cause death or serious physical harm to his or her employees." The physician is required to post the Job Safety and Health Protection Poster (OSHA Form 2203) in the office or clinic. New for 2002 are updated Forms 300 (Log of Work-Related Injuries and Illnesses), 301 (Injury and Illness Incident Report), and 300A (Summary of Work-Related Injuries and Illnesses). After January 1, 2003, work-related hearing losses and musculoskeletal disorders will have to be reported.

Hazard communication plan

Under HCS, each physician-employer who has one or more employees exposed to a hazard is required to develop a written program to protect those individuals. The hazard communication plan (HCP) must outline those health and safety policies and procedures placed into effect by the employer to protect his or her workers.

Hazardous chemicals. A complete inventory must be taken once a year of all products in the office or clinic. The HCS requires that all chemicals imported, produced, or used in a workplace undergo a "hazard determination." This evaluation, which may be delegated to an employee, should include not only medical supplies (such as isopropyl alcohol and bleach), but also office supplies (such as correction fluid and copier toner). OSHA considers products to be hazardous when a hazardous chemical makes up 1% or more of the product or a carcinogen makes up 0.1% or more of the product. There are essentially two ways to determine whether a product is considered hazardous. One way involves writing the product's manufacturer or distributor for a material safety data sheet (MSDS); the other involves comparing chemicals in office products with those on lists prepared or recommended by OSHA.

Most consumer products containing hazardous chemicals that are used in the office are cleansing agents. Medications that are dispensed by a pharmacist to a physician for direct administration to a patient are exempt. Drugs in sold form (pills or tablets) are also considered exempt, as well as most injectables and other medications used in office settings.

Material safety data sheets. A material safety data sheet is an informational sheet furnished by a product's manufacturer to the user in order to identify the hazardous characteristics of the product. Every hazardous product must have a MSDS, provided by the manufacturer or distributor on written request. In 1986 OSHA developed Form 174 to provide a universal form that would meet the HCS requirements; use of the form is not mandatory, but OSHA requires all the information on the form.

Once a year, requests should be made for MSDSs on all hazardous products that have been changed or are new to the office. Such sheets should be kept for 5 years. MSDSs may be kept on a computer disk or microfiche as long as there are "no barriers to employee access." Under the present rule, drug package inserts cannot be accepted in lieu of MSDSs for "less than solid" drugs (creams, ointments, liquids, and injectables). Drug samples, if not used in the office, do not require MSDSs.

Hazard labels. After MSDSs are obtained, if not "rated," they have to be rated in order to create hazard labels. Under HCS, the practice is required to label, tag, or mark hazardous chemicals in the office or clinic. The purpose of the label is to serve as an "immediate warning" and as a "reminder of more detailed information" in the MSDS. Instead of labeling specific containers, OSHA permits the posting of proper information on the front or back sides of cabinet doors where hazardous materials are stored. The label must show the identity of its hazardous chemical or chemicals and any appropriate hazard warnings. There is no single labeling system recommended by OSHA. The widely used label is an adaptation of one developed by the National Fire Protection Agency (NFPA 704 Standard). The NFPA label is a diamond-shaped, color-coded label, with a different color for each represented hazard.

Training program. HCS requires employers to provide a training program for all employees exposed to hazards in the routine performance of their duties. As with training programs under other standards, employees must be trained at scheduled staff meetings, with each session documented on a training log.

AMERICANS WITH DISABILITIES ACT

In 1990 the Americans with Disabilities Act (ADA) was passed to prevent unfair discrimination against disabled persons with visual, hearing, and other physical and mental impairments. This law prohibits discrimination on the basis of disability and protects qualified applicants, employees, and the general public who have disabilities from discrimination in all aspects of employment and public access to services and facilities. All sorts of disabilities are covered, including persons with cancer, human immunodeficiency syndrome (HIV), blindness, deafness, attention deficit disorder (ADD), learning disabilities, mental retardation, and mental illness. Individuals who are former drug or alcohol abusers are also covered under ADA. The law requires the physician to place a poster in his or her office describing the provisions of ADA.

As a five-part regulation, ADA requires several different aspects of compliance. Only Titles I and III, however, are applicable to medical practices.

Title I

The original law prohibited job discrimination in offices with 25 or more employees after July 26, 1992. The present law, however, exempts only those employers with fewer than 15 employees. Under Title I, the employer must use the same employment standards in all hiring, paying, training, promoting, and firing decisions. Neither the physician-employer nor any of his or her office staff may engage in any illegal job-recruiting or job-interviewing practices. For example, during a job interview, the employer cannot inquire about a history of disability, illness, absenteeism, or workers' compensation benefits. The employer cannot ask the applicant about the presence of a disability but can ask about the applicant's ability to perform certain tasks. Also, a physical examination cannot be performed until an offer of employment has been made. Although the applicant can be excluded for his or her inability to perform "essential" tasks, the applicant cannot be excluded for an inability to perform "marginal" tasks. If a disabled person applying for a job is judged to be the best-qualified applicant (without consideration of the applicant's disability), ADA requires the employer to hire that individual. Also, a physician-employer cannot decide against hiring a disabled person because employment of that individual would require "reasonable accommodation," that is, "one that does not cause significant difficulty or expense in relation to the employer's operations, financial resources or facilities." Additional stipulations in this section require employers to make certain accommodations for disabled persons already employed.

Title III

Under Title III, the physician is responsible for making his or her practice accessible to persons with disabilities. As of January 26, 1992, persons owning, leasing, or operating places of public accommodation must reasonably alter their policies, procedures, and practices to promote equal opportunities for all individuals. All existing health care facilities must make their common use areas "accessible" if removal of structural barriers is "readily achievable," that is, "easily accomplished and able to be executed without much difficulty or expense."

Access

Accessibility guidelines for new construction and alteration of the existing structures have been developed for ADA. For example, an adequate number of "accessible" parking spaces should be provided—at least one accessible space for every 25 parking spaces. Furthermore, one of every eight accessible parking spaces must be van-accessible and so marked. Total compliance is required only for new construction and alterations. Tax incentives are available for the removal of architectural barriers.

Auxiliary services

The ADA requires the physician to provide (and pay) for those auxiliary aids and services necessary to ensure effective communication with individuals "unless an undue burden or fundamental alteration of services would result." In some cases, office policies and procedures may have to be altered. For example, an office or clinic may need to allow the entry of guide dogs for blind patients. With regard to auxiliary aids, the needs of the patient must be considered in deciding whether to use a notepad, Brailled materials, other formats (e.g., audiotape), or an interpreter.

Does the physician have to hire a sign-language interpreter? The area of concern to most physicians is how to deal with hearing-impaired patients. The answer to the question is "maybe." Although the intent of the law is to require appropriate auxiliary aids and services "when necessary," the service must not cause "significant difficulty or expense." The law does not impose on a physician the requirement that primary consideration be given to a disabled person's requests. In most cases, an interpreter should not be needed if a patient can read questions and write answers. Another alternative to the use of a notepad is a computer terminal on which the physician and patient can exchange typewritten messages. The Justice Department cites situations in which it believes the services of an interpreter are needed. One example is when a hearing-impaired person needs to undergo major surgery; other areas besides health include financial, legal, and personal matters. The end result, however, is that "in those situations requiring an interpreter, the public accommodation (such as a physician's office or clinic) must secure the services of a qualified interpreter, unless an undue burden would result."

BLOOD-BORNE PATHOGENS STANDARD

The second federal law to concern itself with the safety of medical employees was the Blood-Borne Pathogens Standard (BBP) of 1991, by OSHA. The intent of this law is to reduce exposure in the health care workplace to all blood-borne pathogens, particularly the hepatitis B virus (HBV) and HIV. Hepatitis B virus infection is considered the major infectious blood-borne occupational hazard to health care workers; the Centers for Disease Control and Prevention (CDC) estimate that about one million Americans are infected with the virus; as of September 1, 1993, CDC had logged nearly 400,000 AIDS cases, with about 200,000 deaths. OSHA has reported that at least 46 workers were apparently infected with HIV through occupational exposure to blood or other potentially infectious materials at their work sites.

Exposure control plan

Any employer having at least one employee with occupational exposure is required to have a written exposure control plan (ECP). The stated purpose of the plan is to eliminate or minimize occupational exposure to blood and other potentially infectious materials. The employer is required to make a copy of this plan available to all employees and any OSHA representative. It must be reviewed and updated at least once a year.

Exposure determination

Each employer who has one or more employees with occupational exposure is required to perform an exposure determination. The exposure determination list consists of the following:

1. A list of job titles in which all employees have occupational exposure.
2. A list of job titles in which some employees have occupational exposure.
3. A list of all tasks (or groups of closely related tasks and procedures) that identify certain employees within a job classification where some, but not all, employees have occupational exposure.

Exposure incident

The ECP must also explain how the employer will evaluate the circumstances surrounding exposure incidents. This evaluation should include the circumstances of the incident, synopsis of present controls, and evaluation of present "failures." Additionally, medical practices with more than 10 employees are now required to keep a log that describes all sharps-related injuries, detailing how, when, and where injuries occurred and what device was involved.

Exposure control

BBP was drafted so that employees will be protected by performance-oriented standards. The specific provisions of the ECP are an effort to make clear "what is necessary" to protect employees. It is the responsibility of the physician-employer to limit worker exposure through implementation of the following categories of control:

1. Universal precautions.
2. Workplace controls.
3. Personal protective equipment.
4. Housekeeping policies.
5. Hazard communication policies.
6. Hepatitis B program.
7. Training program.

Universal precautions. OSHA's method for reducing exposure to blood-borne pathogens is based on the adoption of universal precautions as the foundation for a plan of infection control. Under BBP, workers are required to exercise universal precautions to prevent contact with blood or other potentially infectious materials.

Workplace controls. Workplace controls are of two types: engineering controls and work practice controls. Engineering controls reduce employee exposure by either removing the worker from the hazard or removing the hazard itself. Examples of engineering controls are sharps containers, biosafety cabinets, and self-sheathing needles. Work practice controls reduce employee exposure by altering the manner in which a procedure is performed. The employer is required to incorporate the following work practice controls into the ECP:

1. *Washing hands*: Employers are required to provide hand-washing facilities that are readily accessible to employees.
2. *Handling blood*: Mouth pipetting or suctioning of blood or other potentially infectious materials is prohibited.
3. *Handling equipment*: Equipment used for diagnosis or treatment must be examined before servicing or shipping and must be decontaminated unless the employer can demonstrate that decontamination of such equipment is not feasible.
4. *Handling personal items*: Employees must not keep food or drink either in refrigerators, freezers, or cabinets, or on shelves, countertops, or benchtops where blood or other potentially infectious materials are present.
5. *Handling sharps*: Employees must not bend, break, or shear contaminated needles and other contaminated sharps. Contaminated needles and other contaminated sharps cannot be recapped or removed unless it can be demonstrated that no alternative is feasible or that such action is required by a specific medical procedure.

With the passage of the Needlestick Safety and Prevention Act, which became effective in April 2001, medical practices have to consider safer needle devices as part of the reevaluation of appropriate engineering controls during the annual review of the ECP. The physician-employer, together with frontline employees who actually handle the sharps, must choose, evaluate, and implement such safety-engineered devices. Such "good faith" efforts to determine if any of the newer devices is applicable to the practice must be documented.

Personal protective equipment. When engineering and work practice controls are insufficient to eliminate exposure, personal protective equipment (PPE) must be used "to prevent or minimize the entry of materials into the worker's body." BBP states that "when there is occupational exposure, the employer shall provide, at no cost to the employee, appropriate personal protective equipment such as, but not limited to, gloves, gowns, lab coats, face shields or masks and eye protection, and mouthpieces, resuscitation bags, pocket masks, or other ventilation devices." OSHA places the responsibility of protecting employees directly on the employer. The employer must not only provide appropriate PPE, but also make sure that it is used "when necessary."

Housekeeping policies. BBP requires employers to keep workplaces "in a clean and sanitary condition." Under housekeeping policies, the employer is required to schedule, and then to implement, a written agenda for cleaning and decontaminating the office, including the following:

1. Cleaning of surfaces.
2. Cleaning of equipment.
3. Cleaning of linens.
4. Discarding of regulated waste.

Hazard communication policies. BBP requires the use of hazard communication through labels or signs to ensure that employees receive adequate warning in order to eliminate or minimize their exposure to blood-borne pathogens. Such labels are to be affixed to refrigerators and freezers containing blood or other potentially infectious material, as well as other containers used to store, transport, or ship blood or other potentially infectious materials. Red bags or red containers may be substituted for labels.

Hepatitis B program. The employer is required to make the hepatitis B vaccine available to all employees who have occupational exposure. Ordinarily, the hepatitis B vaccination series has to be offered within 10 working days of the initial assignment at no cost to the employee. Those who decline to accept the vaccination must sign a statement to that effect. For those who have had an exposure incident, the employer is also required to obtain a postexposure evaluation and a medical follow-up examination. After an exposure incident, the employer is required to provide the employee with the following information:

1. The route and circumstances of exposure.
2. The name of the source individual (unless impossible).
3. The results of the source individual's blood test, if available.

The employer is required to furnish the employee with a copy of the evaluating physician's written opinion within 15 days of receipt of his or her report. As part of the medical follow-up examination, the employee is entitled to prophylactic medications (if recommended by the U.S. Public Health Service), counseling sessions, and medical evaluation of postexposure illnesses. Medical records for each employee with regard to hepatitis B vaccination and occupational exposure must be kept for the duration of employment plus 30 years.

Training program. Training about the hazards associated with blood and other potentially infectious material must be provided by the employer to all employees with occupational exposure. The employer is required to keep training records for all employees with occupational exposure for 3 years from the date on which the training occurred. The same rules that apply to medical records also apply to training records.

CLINICAL LABORATORY IMPROVEMENT AMENDMENTS

The Clinical Laboratory Improvement Amendments (CLIA) were passed in 1988 to ensure the accuracy of laboratory tests performed on human specimens. Most of the regulations became effective on September 1, 1992. The physician is no longer able to perform tests on patients in his or her office without legal permission from the federal government.

Certification

This law requires all laboratories, including physician office laboratories (POLs), to obtain one of five certificates: a registration certificate, a certificate of waiver, a certificate of provider-performed microscopy, a certificate of compliance, or a certificate of accreditation. Even if only one test is performed (and even if no charge is made for that test), the Health Care Financing Administration (HCFA) requires the physician-employer to obtain a certificate. Once an application is received, HCFA may issue a registration certificate, together with a CLIA number (for requests for laboratory testing reimbursement made to Medicare or Medicaid third-party payers after January 1, 1994).

A registration certificate permits a laboratory to continue operations for 2 years or until a determination of compliance can be made, whichever is shorter. The certificate of accreditation can be issued by the Commission of Office Laboratory Assessment (COLA) to those laboratories (including POLs) desiring an alternative to federal inspections under CLIA. Also, a laboratory in a state with a federally approved licensure program may choose to receive a state license in place of a CLIA certificate, provided it complies with the regulations of that state.

Categories of tests

Present laboratory tests, numbering about 10,000, have been classified according to the degree of difficulty in the performance of the test. This ranking initially resulted in a three-tier organization of tests into categories called *waived, moderate complexity,* and *high complexity,* to which a fourth category (now called provider-performed microscopy) was added in February 1993. Depending on its certification, a laboratory can perform tests in one or all four categories.

A laboratory that limits itself to performing waived tests is essentially exempt (except for manufacturers' instructions) from CLIA requirements. Procedures classified under provider-performed microscopy must be performed by either the physician or a health care provider, in conjunction with an examination of the patient in the office. Laboratories performing waived and provider-performed microscopy tests are not subject to routine inspections, but are subject to random compliance and complaint investigations.

Nonwaived tests

Those laboratories performing provider-performed microscopy, moderate-complexity tests, and high-complexity tests must fulfill certain requirements for personnel standards, patient test management, quality control, proficiency testing, and quality assurance.

Personnel standards. Each laboratory performing non-waived tests must meet certain personnel standards (PS), which are tied to the complexity of the testing process. The rules, which differ for moderate-complexity testing and high-complexity testing, list detailed personnel responsibilities and qualifications; qualifications are based on formal education, laboratory experience, and/or laboratory training. Laboratories performing tests in the moderate-complexity category must employ a laboratory director, technical consultant, clinical consultant, and testing personnel. Laboratories performing tests in the high-complexity category must employ a laboratory director, technical supervisor, clinical consultant, general supervisor, and testing personnel.

Patient test management. Each laboratory performing nonwaived tests is required to have in place a system ensuring the correct performance of the entire testing process, beginning with the preparation of the patient and ending with the distribution of test results. Patient test management (PTM) consists of two parts: (1) written policies and (2) documentation (to verify the former). The regulations require written policies for the following:

1. Preparing patients.
2. Processing (collecting, preparing, identifying, storing, transporting, and discarding) specimens.
3. Reporting results.

With regard to test results, normal or reference ranges must be available, but they do not have to be printed on reports. The laboratory is also required to develop a written policy (or protocol) to follow when a life-threatening or "panic" value occurs. The protocol demands that the individual ordering the test or the individual responsible for utilizing the test results be notified immediately when any test result indicates an immediate danger to a person's life.

With the second part of PTM, three documents are required: the test requisition, the test record (patient log), and the test report, all of which must be retained for a minimum of 2 years. Tests can be performed only on the oral, written, or electronic order of an "authorized" person. That authorized person will usually be the physician (or another state-authorized individual). The authorized person must sign written requests; oral orders are permitted as long as written orders are obtained within 30 days. The "three R's" of PTM allow a laboratory to track and positively identify patient specimens as they move through the complete testing process. Specific information must be contained in these three documents to comply with the law.

Quality control. Manufacturers of instruments, kits, and test systems usually provide guidelines for quality control (QC) of their products. One kind of internal QC procedure involves the use of QC samples; these samples, similar to patient specimens, have known test results. QC samples, when run at the same time as patient specimens, can provide the operator with a "within run" check to confirm test results. Each laboratory performing nonwaived tests is required to develop and follow written QC procedures that monitor the quality of the analytic testing process of each test method. Of the two sections on QC, one contains general requirements, and the other contains special requirements for specialties or subspecialties.

Laboratories using uncleared tests must follow the full QC rules. Full QC rules are also required for all tests of moderate complexity that have been cleared but have been modified or developed in-house and for all tests of high complexity.

Proficiency testing. One way of making sure a particular laboratory's performance is in line with that of other laboratories performing the same analysis involves the testing of unknown samples from an outside source. Just as QC samples provide a type of internal QC, proficiency testing (PT) offers a kind of external QC. Each laboratory performing tests of moderate or high complexity must enroll in an approved PT program for all specialties or subspecialties in which it desires to be certified. The PT provider must be either a private, non-profit organization or a federal or state entity.

Once the laboratory has been enrolled, the PT provider will send samples to its subscriber three times a year; each shipment includes five samples for that "event." The samples, whose values are not known, are run along with the laboratory's regular workload of patient specimens. It is unlawful to send portions of PT samples to other laboratories for "comparison" studies. The final results are sent to the PT provider, together with an attestation form signed by both the operator and the laboratory director. For most tests, the minimum passing score is 80%. Any laboratory failing two consecutive or two out of three testing events will be subject to sanctions (including cancellation for that specialty, subspecialty, or test).

Quality assurance. Every laboratory performing non-waived tests must implement and follow written policies and procedures for a quality assurance (QA) program designed to monitor and evaluate the quality of the total testing process. CLIA is the first standard to require a QA program as part of the law. It is the responsibility of the employer, as laboratory director, to ensure the accuracy of test results and the adequacy of laboratory services. In a POL, laboratory testing may be done by two workers or one worker and the director; in all cases, all members should make up the QA committee. The QA committee is responsible for making sure that "quality" evaluations take place and that corrective actions take place whenever problems are identified; to reach this goal, the seven key elements to be addressed are:

1. Procedure manual.
2. Personnel standards.
3. Patient test management.
4. Quality control.
5. Proficiency testing.
6. Complaint investigations.
7. Quality assurance review.

HEALTH INSURANCE PORTABILITY AND ACCOUNTABILITY ACT

The Health Insurance Portability and Accountability Act (HIPAA) of 1996 was passed into law on August 21, 1996. The original purpose of this law was to make health care insurance "portable," so that an individual's insurance could be passed from one employer to another employer. Because of additions to help fight fraud and abuse, ensure the security of medical records, protect the privacy of a patients' confidential health information, and a worthwhile goal to replace paper transactions with electronic transactions, the HIPAA Standard has become one of the most widespread and complicated regulations ever passed. After April 14, 2003, HIPAA will launch a whole new era of medical care. The way medicine is practiced will forever be changed. As we enter the electronic age of medicine, it is the responsibility of the physician-employer to make sure his employees conduct themselves in a manner that supports the provisions of this ambitious standard. Two of the rules that fall under the part of HIPAA known as the Administrative Simplification Act presently concern us: the Transactions Rule and the Privacy Rule.

Transactions Rule

Transactions standards. If a medical office currently processes financial and administrative transactions electronically, either itself or through a vendor who transmits them to a health plan electronically (billing service or clearinghouse), that office falls under the Transactions Rule. This rule does not affect paper transactions. At present, there are 437 different formats for online processing of health claims. Under HIPAA, the Department of Health and Human Services (DHHS) is required to establish national standards for health care transactions and code sets. The intent of this piece of HIPAA is to have a single standard claim form, replacing electronic versions of the HCFA 1500 and UB 92. The original compliance deadline was October 16, 2002; however, a one-year extension was granted to those practices filing the CMS Model Compliance Plan.

Each transaction standard has specific format and content requirements in order to be processed by health plans and clearinghouses. The Transactions Rule specifies standards for the following eight transactions:

ASC X12N 837	Health Claims or Encounter Information
ASC X12N 835	Payments and Remittances
ASC X12N 837	Coordination of Benefits (COB)
ASC X12N 276/277	Health Care Claim Status
ASC X12N 834	Enrollment and Disenrollment
ASC X12N 270/271	Eligibility Verifications
ASC X12N 820	Health Plan Premium Payments
ASC X12N 278	Precertifications and Referral Authorizations

Code sets. The Transactions Rule also requires the use of national code sets. Use of the current versions of the medical code sets ICD-9-CM, CPT-4, and HCPS is required. Other standard code sets (such as zip codes) are also required. Local codes will be eliminated.

Options. The first step toward compliance with the Transactions Rule is the physician's consideration of his options:

- Comply with both content and format requirements:
    Send the HIPAA-compliant transactions directly to health plans
- Comply with both content and format requirements:
    Send some HIPAA-compliant transactions directly to health plans
    Send other HIPAA-compliant transactions to clearinghouses
- Comply only with content requirements:
    Send nonstandard formats to a clearinghouse (to format) and then the HIPAA-compliant transactions to a health plan
- Comply only with content requirements and use direct data entry (DDE) to send nonstandard formats to health plans accepting DDE.

Transactions officer. Before the medical practice begins the enormous task of software reprogramming, the physician needs to employ or appoint a "transactions officer." It is this individual who will help the physician bring the office into compliance. The transactions officer is responsible for inventorying present transactions, assembling vendor data, discovering data gaps, and finally ensuring the new computer system is HIPAA-compliant.

INVENTORYING DUTIES. The transactions officer must prepare inventory lists, matching transactions with all vendors (their billing products), clearinghouses, and health plans.

DATA-ASSEMBLING DUTIES. After completing the inventory lists, the transactions officer must communicate orally or in writing with the practice's vendors, clearinghouses, and health plans to discover their plans and timetables for becoming compliant. Relevant information should be recorded in the inventory lists.

DATA-DISCOVERING DUTIES. Since there are new data elements required by the "837 Professional Claim," the practice must have a way to "capture" these elements. The upgraded system should allow for this capability.

MANAGING DUTIES. After assemblying all the information concerning the readiness of the practice's vendors, clearinghouses, and health plans, the physician, with the help of the transactions officer, must make final decisions on specific strategies for compliance. Ideally, the software should permit the office to conduct all the transaction types directly with health plans. At the least, the practice should be able to supply the content for transactions to a clearinghouse. The office will have to choose one of three possible solutions:

- Upgrade the present billing software.
- Submit claims to a clearinghouse.

- Purchase a new computer system with HIPAA-compliant billing software.

After the installation of upgraded or new software (and the entering of additional data elements), the transactions officer should begin training employees. Once the training has been completed, the practice's vendor should be able to supply test data that will put the system through all possible transaction scenarios. Finally, employees should do computer-to-computer testing to ensure that the office's computer system can transmit information from the office through any clearinghouse and on to any health plan.

Privacy Rule

The Privacy Rule basically controls what is called protected health information (PHI). PHI is individually identifiable health information that is held or released by a practice regardless of how it is communicated (oral, paper, or electronic). The entire Privacy Rule was created to make sure that a patient's PHI is not used or disclosed to those individuals or parties that do not need to know such information.

Uses and disclosures. The physician's first order of business is to determine what uses and disclosures of PHI by office staff are legally granted by the Privacy Rule. Confidential health information is "used" when it is examined, analyzed, utilized, or otherwise shared inside the medical office. This information is "disclosed" when it is accessed, transferred, released, or otherwise shared outside the medical office. With one exception ("opt out" opportunities), disclosures are usually considered to be of three types: permitted, required, or authorized.

PERMITTED DISCLOSURES. Permitted disclosures are routine disclosures made for "treatment, payment, and health care operations" (TPO) purposes. Examples here are disclosures for prescriptions, coordination of benefits, and quality assurance.

REQUIRED DISCLOSURES. Required disclosures are disclosures the physician makes for the sake of public safety or order ("the public good"). Examples here are disclosures for child abuse or neglect or subpoenas.

AUTHORIZED DISCLOSURES. Authorized disclosures are those "allowed" by the patient; these disclosures require a written authorization from the patient. An example here would be psychotherapy notes. (Psychiatrists must obtain authorizations to release a patient's mental health records.) With some exceptions, authorizations are also required for preemployment or preinsurance physicals, marketing activities, fund-raising activities, and research activities. Authorizations can be revoked at any time.

"OPT OUT" OPPORTUNITIES. "Opt out" opportunities involve situations where the patient is given an opportunity to verbally agree or object with regard to disclosure of his or her PHI.

Minimum necessary rule. In general, the Privacy Rule requires medical practices to take reasonable steps to limit use of disclosure of PHI to the *minimum necessary* to achieve an intended purpose. This rule does not apply to uses or disclosures made to the patient, another provider (for treatment purposes), or governmental authorities.

Privacy officer. The physician's second order of business is the employment or appointment of a privacy officer, upon whose shoulder falls the burden of the Privacy Rule. It is this individual who will help the physician bring the office into compliance. The privacy officer oversees all ongoing activities related to maintaining the privacy of PHI consistent with state law. It is his or her duty to report to the physician-employer the status of the office's compliance efforts. Specific responsibilities of the privacy officer have been subdivided into managing, safeguarding, documenting, training, and sanctioning duties.

MANAGING DUTIES. With regard to patient rights, the privacy officer must develop a protocol for addressing patient requests; he or she must also develop a protocol for responding to patient appeals for denials or requests. Another managerial task is the identification of all business associates (BAs). The privacy officer may be called upon to negotiate or help negotiate BA contracts.

SAFEGUARDING DUTIES. The privacy officer must put in place appropriate safeguards to protect the privacy of PHI. Safeguards are classified as administrative, physical, and technical. Examples of administrative safeguards are lowering of voices for any conversations involving PHI, facing computer screens toward the user and away from patients, and calling patients to examining rooms by their first name only or last name only. Common examples of physical safeguards are locks on cabinets or doors, bars on windows or doors, and alarm systems. Examples of technical (electronic) safeguards are passwords, tokens, fingerprint scans, and encryption.

DOCUMENTING DUTIES. The privacy officer must first prepare the "Notice of Privacy Practices." After posting this notice in the office, the privacy officer should next turn his or her attention to the development of the office's "Privacy Policies and Procedures," which he or she will coauthor with the physician. Once this major task has been accomplished, implementation of the policies and procedures should follow. It is also this officer's responsibility to develop or select appropriate documents, such as "Patient Request" forms, "Acknowledgement" forms, "Patient Authorization" forms, and "Business Associate" contracts. When such documents are ready for disposal, it is the privacy officer's responsibility to see that documents containing PHI are shredded or deidentfied.

TRAINING DUTIES. The privacy officer is also responsible for implementing a training program for all members of the workforce. The privacy officer will train all existing employees before April 14, 2003, and all new employees after April 14, 2003. Employees whose tasks are affected by changes in the Privacy Rule will be retrained. All training must be documented.

SANCTIONING DUTIES. The privacy officer's final responsibility is the development of a protocol for identifying, investigating, documenting, and finalizing all privacy incidents and sanctions. The privacy officer will help the physician make decisions with regard to employee infractions. Specific sanctions must be recorded in that employee's personnel file.

Notice of Privacy Practices. The "Notice of Privacy Practices" is a kind of "reverse" informed consent. As of April 14, 2003, any physician who has a direct-treatment relationship (DTR) with an individual has to provide that individual with a "Notice of Privacy Practices" no later than the date of first service delivery after the compliance date. Furthermore, the medical practice must provide a copy of the current notice to anyone who asks for it (whether a patient or not). The notice must explain:

- How PHI may be used or disclosed by the practice.
- The patient's privacy rights as to PHI.
- The practice's obligations as to PHI.

The final Privacy Rule only requires the physician who has a direct-treatment relationship with a patient to make a "good faith" effort to obtain a patient's written "acknowledgment" that he or she has received the "Notice of Privacy Practices." The patient cannot be "made" to sign such a statement. Additionally, the patient can file a complaint against the practice for alleged violations of privacy policies. The person who receives these complaints is the privacy officer; the "Notice of Privacy Practices" must contain the name and telephone number of this individual, together with an explanation as to how to file a complaint. The privacy officer must document all complaints, recording the final disposition of each complaint. The unsatisfied patient must be informed that he or she has the right to file a complaint with the Secretary of the DHHS.

Patient rights. Under HIPAA, the patient has the following rights:

1. The right to receive a copy of the practice's "Notice of Privacy Practices."
2. The right to request a restriction on uses and disclosures.
3. The right to request receipt of confidential communications by alternative means or at alternative locations.
4. The right to request access to inspect and copy the medical record.
5. The right to request an amendment to the medical record.
6. The right to request an accounting of disclosures.

With the exception of the first "right," note that these rights are all followed by the phrase "to request." The practice does not have to grant all requests; as with any law, there are exceptions to the rules. However, if the physician agrees to a request, any violation of the request is a violation of the privacy regulations.

The patient's right to request an amendment should demand particular attention from the physician. If the amendment is granted, it must be linked to the disputed portion of the PHI in the medical record. Under some circumstances, the physician can deny the request to amend. If this happens, the patient can place a statement of disagreement in the record. The physician can also counter with a rebuttal, a copy of which must be given to the patient.

The office can require these requests to be written requests. Each of these requests has a time limit for the physician's response. If the request is refused, the physician must give the reason for denial. In some cases the patient may be able to appeal the denial, asking for a review.

Legal issues. There are many legal issues other than those of civil and criminal penalties for violations of the HIPAA Standard.

BUSINESS ASSOCIATES. New to the delivery of medical care is the term "business associate" (BA). Basically, a BA is an individual or company with whom the physician shares confidential information. Excluded from the definition of BAs are office staff, physicians, financial institutions, and health care organizations. BAs must enter into written contracts to protect any PHI received.

A BA may also be a BA of another entity; in this case, the other entity is also bound by the provisions of the contract with the medical practice. The practice has the right to terminate the contract if the BA violates any of the provisions of the contract. Also, if a physician knows of a material breach of the BA's obligations, that physician must take "reasonable steps" to end the violation or cure the breach. If termination is not feasible, the physician must report the BA to the DHHS.

PERSONAL REPRESENTATIVES. A personal representative is the legal representative of the patient; for all intents and purposes the personal representative is the patient. This individual has the authority to act on behalf of the patient in making decisions involving medical care. There are different rules for adults and emancipated minors, unemancipated minors, and decedents.

STATE LAWS. As a rule of thumb, if a state's laws are stricter (or offer greater protection or privacy rights) than HIPAA's regulations, then the state's law, in most circumstances, will apply; on the other hand, if HIPAA's regulations are stricter (or offer greater protection or privacy rights) than the state's laws, the HIPAA's regulations will apply.

SELECTED REFERENCES

A. McLaughlin & J. Pendergrass, *Hazard Communication: A Compliance Kit* A-1 (U.S. Government Printing Office, Washington, D.C. 1988).

L. Traverse, *The Generator's Guide to Hazardous Materials/Waste Management* 119 (Van Nostrand Reinhold, New York 1991).

Program notes, Eagle Associates seminar, presented by Joseph Suchocki (Apr. 1990).

J. Suchocki et al., *The Safety Resource Guide for OSHA Compliance,* 12 (Eagle Associates, Ann Arbor, Mich. 1990).

Hazard Communication Changes, Am. Prac. Adv. 116 (1994).

The Illusive Material Safety Data Sheet, Am. Prac. Adv. 120 (1993).

Alert for Material Safety Data Sheets, Am. Prac. Adv. 77 (1993).

Questions and Answers, Am. Prac. Adv. 10 (1992).

The Americans with Disabilities Act of 1990, Am. Prac. Adv. 43 (1995).

Reviewing the Americans with Disabilities Act, Am. Prac. Adv. 43 (1995).

The Americans with Disabilities Act of 1990, Am. Prac. Adv. 47 (1992).

What Every Doctor Needs to Know (Americans with Disabilities Act) [information sheet] (American Medical Association 1990).

H. Barton, *Physicians Discover Maze of Regulations under ADA,* 88(11) Tex. Med. 55 (1992).

S. Dunn, *Needle Safety Laws Loom on the Horizon,* Physicians Marketplace 44 (1999).

Occupational Exposure to Bloodborne Pathogens (summary), 29 C.F.R. Part 1910.1030 at 64124.

CLIA 1988 Compliance (information sheet) 4 (American Proficiency Institute 1993).

Patient Test Management System Trilogy, Am. Pract. Adv. 61 (1992).

Regulations for Implementing Clinical Laboratory Improvement Amendments of 1988: A Summary, 267 J.A.M.A. 1731 (1992).

C. Hess, *Office Compliance Manual* 91 (All-Med Press, Houston 1995).

Family Leave Law, Am. Pract. Adv. 7 (1993).

Practice Growth Means Revisiting Personnel Issues, Am. Med. News 18 (Jul 17, 1995).

J. Starke, *Tuberculosis: What the Pediatrician Really Needs to Know (and Do),* program notes, Infectious Diseases in Children Symposium (Nov. 1996).

Updating Your TB Control Plan, Am. Pract. Adv. 123 (1995).

Inside Training: TB Infection Control Plan—Part I, Am. Pract. Adv. 201 (1996).

Tuberculosis and Airborne Guidelines, Am. Pract. Adv. 138-140 (1994).

Health Insurance Portability and Accountability Act of 1996: A Tempered Victory, 24 J. Law, Med. & Ethics 381 (1996).

A New Health Insurance Law Enacted, Am. Pract. Adv. 34 (1997).

15

Health Professionals and the Regulated Industry: The Laws and Regulations Enforced by the U.S. Food and Drug Administration

FREDDIE ANN HOFFMAN, M.D.
PETER H. RHEINSTEIN, M.D., J.D., M.S., F.C.L.M.

HISTORICAL PERSPECTIVE
GENERAL CONSIDERATIONS FOR REGULATED PRODUCTS
DRUGS FOR HUMAN USE
BIOLOGICS
FOODS
COSMETICS
ANIMAL PRODUCTS
MEDICAL DEVICES
REPORTING PROBLEMS: ADVERSE EVENTS AND PRODUCT QUALITY ISSUES
FDA'S ROLE IN THE "PRACTICE OF MEDICINE"

No textbook in legal medicine would be complete without a discussion of the regulation of health care products for the U.S. marketplace and the role of the U.S. Food and Drug Administration (FDA). The U.S. market is almost unique. Unlike foreign markets, the range of products available to the consumer and the practicing health professional is based on marketability and competitiveness rather than on preselection by a national governmental body. With the advent of managed care, this marketplace is changing. Although many federal agencies have an impact on the regulation of products sold in the United States (Fig. 15-1), the FDA is the main agency responsible for foods, drugs, biologics, medical devices (including energy-emitting products such as cathode ray tubes and microwave ovens), and cosmetics. Approximately one out of every four dollars spent in the United States is under the FDA's jurisdiction. Although foods represent the largest category of consumer purchases, the FDA spends almost twice as much in the regulation of drugs and biologics. This chapter provides an overview of the current laws and regulations governing the manufacture, packaging, import and export, and approval of products for the U.S. marketplace. Also discussed are the requirements for the development of new products and the responsibilities of clinical investigators, manufacturers, and health professionals in the use of both investigational and approved products, as well as for products for which approval is not required.

HISTORICAL PERSPECTIVE

Most food and drug regulation is an outgrowth of consumer concern with the safety of products. Table 15-1 provides a brief overview of the major legislation affecting U.S. food and drug regulation. Federal legislation dates back to the Drug Importation Act of 1848 requiring U.S. Customs inspection to bar entry of foreign adulterated drugs. It was not until the twentieth century, however, that federal regulatory authority became fully established. Regulation of the purity and safety of serums, vaccines, and similar products used to prevent or treat diseases in humans was initiated by the 1902 Biologics Control Act. Growing concerns over the unsanitary conditions in meat-packing plants, the use of poisonous preservatives and dyes in foods, and exaggerated claims for unproven and dangerous patent medicines sparked debate over the regulation of foods and drugs. On June 30, 1906, both the first comprehensive Food and Drugs Act and the Meat Inspection Act were signed into law. The new law prohibited the interstate commerce of misbranded and adulterated foods, drinks, and drugs; required disclosure of drug ingredients on the label; and introduced new controls over the manufacturing and processing of foods.

The Food and Drug Administration was formally established as an agency in 1930. By this time many had tried and failed to revise the now outdated 1906 statute. It would

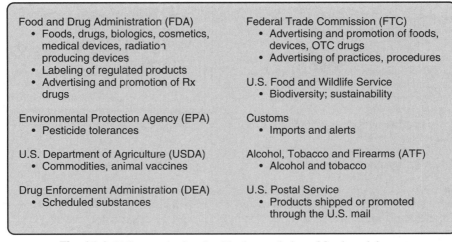

Fig. 15-1. U.S. agencies involved in the regulation of foods and drugs.

TABLE 15-1 Food and drug regulation: key U.S. legislation

1848	**Drug Importation Act** requires U.S. Customs Service inspection to stop entry of adulterated drugs from overseas.
1902	**Biologics Control Act (Virus, Serum, and Toxins Act)** ensures purity and safety of serums, vaccines, and similar products used to prevent or treat diseases in humans.
1906	**Food and Drugs Act** prohibits interstate commerce in misbranded and adulterated foods, drinks, and drugs. **Meat Inspection Act** is passed by Congress on the same day, June 30. Both signed by President Theodore Roosevelt.
1911	Supreme Court rules in *U.S. v. Johnson* that the 1906 Food and Drugs Act does not prohibit false therapeutic claims—only false and misleading statements about the ingredients or identity of a drug.
1912	**Sherley Amendment** addresses *U.S. v. Johnson* rule by prohibiting the labeling of medicines with false therapeutic claims intended to defraud the purchaser, a standard difficult to prove.
1927	**Food, Drug, and Insecticide Administration** established.
1930	Agency renamed as **Food and Drug Administration (FDA).**
1933	Introduction of first Senate bill to launch a five-year legislative battle to update the obsolete **Foods and Drugs Act 1906**.
1937	**Elixir of Sulfanilamide**, containing the poisonous solvent diethylene glycol, kills 107 persons, many of whom are children, dramatizing the need to establish drug safety before marketing and to enact the pending food and drug law.
1938	**Federal Food, Drug, and Cosmetic (FDC) Act** contains new provisions: extends control to cosmetics and therapeutic devices; requires new drugs to be shown safe before marketing, starting a new system of drug regulation; eliminates the Sherley Amendment requirement to prove intent to defraud in drug misbranding cases; provides safe tolerances to be set for unavoiable poisonous substances; authorizes factory inspections; adds the remedy of court injunctions to the previous penalties of seizures and prosecutions. **Wheeler-Lea Act** charges the **Federal Trade Commission** with overseeing advertising of FDA-regulated products, except prescription drugs.
1941	**Insulin Amendment** requires FDA to test and certify purity and potency of this life-saving drug for diabetes.
1943	*U.S. v. Dotterweich*: Supreme Court rules that responsible officials of a corporation, as well as the corporation itself, may be prosecuted for violations. It need not be proven that the officials intended, or even knew of, the violations.
1944	**Public Health Service Act** covers a broad spectrum of health concerns, including regulation of biological products and control of communicable diseases.
1945	**Penicillin Amendment** requires FDA testing and certification of safety and effectiveness of all penicillin products. Later amendments extended this requirement to all antibiotics. Repealed in 1983.
1951	**Durham-Humphrey Amendment** defines the kinds of drugs that cannot be safely used without medical supervision and restricts their sale to prescription by a licensed practitioner.
1958	**Food Additives Amendment** requires manufacturers of new food additives to establish safety. The Delaney proviso prohibits the approval of any food additive shown to induce cancer in humans or animals. FDA publishes in the Federal Register the first list of nearly 200 substances, those substances **Generally Recognized As Safe (GRAS).**
1960	**Color Additive Amendment** enacted, requiring manufacturers to establish the safety of color additives in foods, drugs, and cosmetics. The Delaney proviso prohibits the approval of any color additive shown to induce cancer in humans or animals.
1962	**Kefauver-Harris Drug Amendments** ensure drug efficacy and greater drug safety following thalidomide disaster. Drug manufacturers now required to prove to FDA the effectiveness of therapeutic products prior to sale. Exempts from the Delaney proviso animal drugs and animal feed additives shown to induce cancer but which leave no detectable levels of residue in the human food supply.
1966	FDA contracts with the National Academy of Sciences/National Research Council to evaluate the **effectiveness of 4000 drugs** approved on the basis of safety alone between 1938 and 1962.
1968	FDA placed in the Public Health Service. FDA forms the **Drug Efficacy Study Implementation (DESI)** to implement recommendations of the National Academy of Sciences investigation of effectiveness of drugs first marketed between 1938 and 1962. **Radiation Control for Health and Safety Act** protects consumers against unnecessary exposure to radiation from electronic products

TABLE 15-1 Food and drug regulation: key U.S. legislation—(*contd.*)

1970	*Upjohn v. Finch*: Court of Appeals upholds enforcement of the 1962 drug effectiveness amendments by ruling that commercial success alone does not constitute substantial evidence of drug safety and efficacy.
1972	**Over-the-counter drug review** starts to enhance the safety, effectiveness, and appropriate labeling of drugs sold without prescription. **Regulation of biologics**, including serums, vaccines, and blood products, is transferred from NIH to FDA.
1976	**Medical Device Amendments** ensure safety and effectiveness of medical devices, including diagnostic products. Manufacturers required to register with FDA and follow quality control procedures. Some products must have premarket approval by FDA; others must meet performance standards before marketing. **Vitamins and Minerals Amendments** ("Proxmire Amendments") stop FDA from establishing standards limiting potency of vitamins and minerals in food supplements or regulating them as drugs based solely on potency.
1980	**Infant Formula Act** establishes special FDA controls to ensure necessary nutritional content and safety.
1982	**Tamper-Resistant Packaging Regulations** issued by FDA to prevent poisonings such as deaths from cyanide placed in Tylenol capsules.
1983	**Orphan Drug Act** allows FDA to promote research and marketing of drugs needed for treating rare diseases, which have little commercial value. **Federal Anti Tampering Act** makes it a crime to tamper with packaged consumer products.
1984	**Drug Price Competition and Patent Term Restoration Act** (Hatch-Waxman) expedites marketing of generic drugs, while providing that brand-name companies can apply for up to 5 years additional patent protection for the new medicines, to make up for time lost while their products were going through FDA's approval process.
1986	**National Childhood Vaccine Injury Act** requires patient information on vaccines, gives FDA authority to recall biologics, and authorizes civil penalties.
1988	**Food and Drug Administration Act** officially establishes FDA as an agency of the Department of Health and Human Services with a Commissioner of Food and Drugs appointed by the President with the advice and consent of the Senate, and broadly spells out the responsibilities of the Secretary and the Commissioner for research, enforcement, education, and information. **Prescription Drug Marketing Act** bans the diversion of prescription drugs from legitimate commercial channels; requires drug wholesalers to be licensed by the states; restricts reimportation from other countries; and bans sale, trade, or purchase of drug samples, and traffic or counterfeiting of redeemable drug coupons.
1990	**Nutrition Labeling and Education Act** requires all packaged foods to bear nutrition labeling and all health claims for foods to be consistent with terms defined by the Secretary of Health and Human Services. **Safe Medical Devices Act** authorizes FDA to order device product recalls; requires facilities to report incidents where a medical device may have caused or contributed to a serious adverse event; requires manufacturers to conduct postmarket surveillance on permanently implanted devices whose failure might cause serious harm or death, and to establish methods for tracing and locating patients depending on such devices.
1991	Regulations published to **Accelerate the review of drugs** for life-threatening diseases.
1992	**Generic Drug Enforcement Act** imposes debarment and other penalties for illegal acts involving abbreviated drug applications. **Prescription Drug User Fee Act** requires drug and biologics manufacturers to pay fees for product applications and supplements, and other services. The act also requires FDA to use these funds to hire more reviewers to assess applications.
1994	**Dietary Supplement Health and Education Act** establishes specific labeling requirements, provides a regulatory framework, and authorizes FDA to promulgate good manufacturing practice regulations for dietary supplements. This act defines "dietary supplements" and "dietary ingredients" and classifies them as food. The act also establishes a commission to recommend how to regulate claims.
1997	**Food and Drug Administration Modernization Act** reauthorizes the Prescription Drug User Fee Act of 1992 and mandates the most wide-ranging reforms in agency practices since 1938. Provisions include measures to accelerate review of devices, regulate advertising of unapproved uses of approved drugs and devices, and regulate health claims for foods.

Adapted from *FDA Backgrounder* BG99-4. Updated Aug. 5, 2002.

take a major disaster—the death of 107 people, mostly children, after ingestion of an "elixir of sulfanilamide" containing a poisonous solvent (ethylene glycol)—to reform the act resulting in the passage of the Federal Food, Drug, and Cosmetic Act (FDCA) (21 United States Code [U.S.C.] 321 to 394). Enacted in 1938, the FDCA continues to be the cornerstone for food and drug regulations in the United States. The FDCA encompassed new and important provisions, the most monumental of which was the requirement that new drugs be shown to be safe before marketing, marking a new direction in drug regulation. In the ensuing years, the FDA was given expanded responsibilities. In 1951, what became known as the Durham-Humphrey Act established criteria for distinguishing prescription and over-the-counter (OTC) drugs.

Following the thalidomide disaster in the early 1960s, in which pregnant women took a sleep-inducing drug approved in Europe and subsequently gave birth to infants with the severe birth defect, phocomelia, the U.S. Congress passed significant amendments to the FDCA, called the Kefauver-Harris Act. This new legislation now required that drugs not only be proven safe before marketing, but also effective for the intended use.

Over the last 30 years, Congress has continued to expand the FDA's regulatory responsibilities, necessitating frequent reorganization. The 1966 Fair Packaging and Labeling Act (15 U.S.C. Sections 1451-1461) required that all consumer products in interstate commerce be honestly and informatively labeled, bearing a legible, prominent statement of net quantity of contents in terms of weight, measure, or numerical count. The 1968 Radiation Control for Health and Safety Act expanded the federal government's regulatory role, protecting consumers against unnecessary exposure to radiation from electronic products, and in 1971 the Bureau of Radiological

Health was transferred from the old Nuclear Regulatory Commission to the FDA. In 1972, sections of the Public Health Service (PHS) Act of 1944, addressing biologics for human use (42 U.S.C. 262 to 263), mammography (42 U.S.C. 263b), and control of communicable diseases (42 U.S.C. 264), were also brought under the FDA's purview.

The mission of the FDA is to enforce laws enacted by the U.S. Congress and to establish and enforce regulations to protect the health, safety, and pocketbook of the consumer.[1] In general, the FDCA is intended to assure the consumer that foods are pure and wholesome, safe to eat, and produced under sanitary conditions; that drugs and devices are safe and effective for their intended uses; that cosmetics are safe and made from appropriate ingredients; and that all labeling and packaging are truthful, informative, and not deceptive. Today the FDA is organized into five major regulatory centers: the Center for Biologics Evaluation and Research, the Center for Drug Evaluation and Research, the Center for Devices and Radiological Health, the Center for Food Safety and Applied Nutrition, and the Center for Veterinary Medicine.

GENERAL CONSIDERATIONS FOR REGULATED PRODUCTS

Premarket testing and approval

Prior to marketing, new drugs, biological drugs, and certain devices (including their labeling) must be approved for safety and effectiveness. Substances added to food must be approved as safe, "generally recognized as safe," or "prior sanctioned." Premarketing clearances are based on scientific data provided by manufacturers, subject to review and acceptance by government scientists for scope and adequacy. The type and extent of premarket testing required for a particular product depends on how it is categorized and what kinds of claims are made about the product by those with a vested interest in it. Testing may include physical and chemical studies, nonclinical laboratory studies, animal tests, and clinical trials on humans.

Current "good practices" [cGxP] regulations

The importance of the laboratory, animal toxicological, and clinical data derived from premarketing testing demands that these studies be conducted according to sound scientific protocols and procedures. For products under the FDA's jurisdiction, regulations describing the requirements needed for manufacturing and developing are delineated. The requirements include: Good Laboratory Practices (GLP); Good Manufacturing Practices (GMP); and Good Clinical Practices (GCP). Together the requirements are abbreviated, current GxP. These regulations are codified in Title 21, Code of Federal Regulations. **Good Laboratory Practices** (GLPs) (21 CFR Part 58) address nonclinical laboratory research. For each product category the FDA has published a set of current **Good Manufacturing Practices** (GMPs). GMPs emphasize written records documenting compliance within process

controls for every step of the production process. In order to meet GMPs, manufacturing procedures must be validated. Validation documents that the manufacturing processes, the systems, and other procedures will consistently and reproducibly produce the product to prescribed specifications and attributes. GMPs also stipulate adequate training of personnel, maintenance requirements for buildings, facilities, equipment, reliable and secure computerized operations, as well as the avoidance of errors to ensure sanitation. The GMP requirements for drugs and biologics are far more rigorous than those for foods. Within the foods categories, different types of foods may have different GMP requirements.

Manufacturers, clinical investigators, and clinical trial monitors are expected to know their responsibilities for the clinical evaluation of products. These responsibilities, called current **Good Clinical Practices**, can be found in the regulations, "General Responsibilities of Investigators" (21 CFR Sections 312, Subpart D, and 812, Subparts E and G). GCPs address selection and qualifications of the clinical investigators and the documentation of the commitment of the investigator to supervise and to assume responsibility for those involved in the clinical studies. The cGCP requirements stipulate that a scientifically sound clinical protocol must be followed, control be maintained over the disposition of all test articles, appropriate human subject protection assurances are in place, and the monitoring and reporting of clinical and adverse events (see below).

Enforcement actions against clinical investigators

Two enforcement tools—*debarment* and *disqualification*—are used by the FDA to protect the integrity of the product approval process. Sponsors or investigators convicted of criminal actions or who are found to have engaged in activities to undermine the drug approval process can be prevented from obtaining or participating in subsequent drug approvals or from providing any services to a drug product applicant. This procedure is called *debarment* and extends to persons working for applicants of human, animal, and biological drug products. Submission of false data to secure approval is a criminal violation of the laws that prohibit giving false information to the government. The FDA is authorized to conduct debarment procedures under the Generic Drug Enforcement Act of 1992 (FDCA Sections 306 to 308), which includes fines ranging up to a million dollars. Clinical investigators conducting studies of investigational drugs, biologics, or devices and who violate FDA regulations can be *disqualified* through informal hearings conducted by the FDA (21 CFR Part 16). Disqualification prevents the investigator from receiving investigational products. Product sponsors must certify that they have not used the services of a disqualified individual or debarred individual or firm in any capacity in connection with a marketing application. The FDA publishes the names of investigators and corporations that have been disqualified, disbarred, or who have signed consent agreements, along with information about their reinstatement.[2,3]

Adulteration and misbranding

The FDCA prohibits the import, sale, or distribution of adulterated or misbranded products in the United States. *Adulterated* products are those that are defective, unsafe, filthy, or produced under unsanitary conditions (Sections 402, 501, 601, codified at 21 U.S.C. 342, 351, 361). A product is *misbranded* if it includes statements, designs, or pictures in labeling that are false or misleading, as well as the failure of the manufacturer to provide required information in labeling (Sections 403, 502, 602, codified at 21 U.S.C. 343, 352, 362). Products required to undergo premarketing approval by the FDA cannot be distributed without such approval, as described above (see Section 704 (21 U.S.C. 374)). Definitions of these terms are included in the law itself and have been interpreted by hundreds of court decisions.

Product recall and reporting systems

Under the FDCA, the FDA has the authority to remove violative products from the market. Removal or the *recall* of products is one of the main means by which the FDA fulfills its mandate of consumer protection. Products failing to meet GMPs or labeling requirements, or those that are defective, are candidates for recall. Voluntary recall is the quickest way for product removal from the market and may be initiated by the manufacturer or shipper of the product, or at the request of the FDA. Recall actions undertaken by industry are reported weekly in the FDA Enforcement Report. Product recalls fall into three categories. Class I designation signifies an imminent health hazard, for which the consequences may be serious illness or death (e.g., incorrect dose, contamination with a pathogenic organism). For a Class I recall, the FDA may order the recall, or the notification to product users, or both. Class II recalls are designated when a product may cause temporary or reversible adverse health consequences, or where the probability of serious consequences is remote (e.g., potency assay does not meet specifications). A Class III recall is designated when it is unlikely that the product will produce adverse health consequences. Class III recalls are often administrative in nature (e.g., label printing errors) and may have little or no impact on the product's use. For medical device recalls, manufacturers are required to notify health professionals by issuing a Medical Device Notification at the FDA's request and to report to the FDA actions undertaken to remove or correct violative devices in commerce. Voluntary Safety Alerts can also be issued.

Although cooperation in a recall may make court proceedings unnecessary to remove the product from the market, it does not relieve a person or firm from possible civil or criminal liability for violations. The FDA prefers, when possible, to promote compliance by other means than going to court. The FDA has the authority to observe conditions or practices of a manufacturer, and during inspections when conditions are noted that may result in violations, a written report (FDA Form 483) of the observations is left with management. By correcting these conditions or practices promptly, manufacturers may bring their operations into compliance. FDA inspectors will also report any voluntary corrective action they witness during an inspection, or that management may bring to their attention. Copies of these reports are available to the public through the FDA's Freedom of Information office.

Product seizures

The FDA's authority includes the right to seize products. Seizure is a civil court action against goods to remove them from the channels of commerce. After seizure, the goods may not be altered, used, or moved, except by permission of the court. The owner or claimant of the seized merchandise is usually given about 30 days by the court to decide on a course of action. The claimant may do nothing, in which case the goods will be disposed of by the court; decide to contest the government's charges by filing a claim and answering the charges, and the case will be scheduled for trial; or consent to condemnation of the goods, while requesting permission of the court to bring the goods into compliance with the law. To bring the goods into compliance, the owner of the goods is required to provide a bond (money deposit) to assure the court that the orders will be carried out and must pay for FDA supervision of any compliance procedure.

Federal Anti Tampering Act

The Federal Anti Tampering Act (Pub. L. 98-127), signed into law in 1983, amends Title 18 of the U.S. Code to establish graduated penalties for tampering with intent to cause injury or death. The penalties range from a maximum of $25,000 and 10 years imprisonment in the case of an attempt to tamper to a maximum of $100,000 and life imprisonment in a case where death results from the tampering. The law also establishes penalties for tampering with or mislabeling consumer products with intent to injure a business; for knowingly communicating false information that a consumer product has been tainted and if such tainting had occurred, would create a risk of death or bodily injury; and for threatening and conspiracy to tamper with a consumer product. *Consumer product* is defined as including any articles subject to the FDCA, and the FDA is designated as having authority to investigate violations.

Drug and device listing and establishment registration

Under Section 510 of the FDCA (21 U.S.C. 360; also see 21 CFR 207), listing is required for all drugs, biologics (including blood products), device products, veterinary drugs, and medicated premixed animal feeds. The authority to require registration and listing of blood banks is from the PHS Act (see 21 CFR 607.20-607.21). The FDA uses the

National Drug Code numbering system in assigning a number. Registration of establishments is also required. "Establishments" include facilities to manufacture, process, repackage, or otherwise change the container, wrapper, or labeling of a product, and the law applies to both bulk and finished dosage forms, as well as products for export. Failure to register and list is a violation of the law at Section 301(p). Devices for human use proposed for commercial distribution must undergo not only registration, but also premarket notification (Section 510(k), codified at 21 U.S.C. 360(k)) of the FDA at least 90 days before beginning such distribution (21 CFR 807), unless specifically exempted by regulation (Section 514, codified at 21 U.S.C. 360d). This allows the FDA to determine if premarket approval is necessary.

Orphan products: regulation and promotion of products for rare diseases and conditions

To encourage the development of products for rare conditions and diseases that would not ordinarily be commercially viable for a company, Congress passed the Orphan Drug Act (Pub. L. 97-414, 96 Stat. 2049) in 1983, which amended the FDCA to provide manufacturers with economic incentives. In order to meet the definition of an "orphan product," the condition must affect fewer than 200,000 persons in the United States annually, or more than 200,000 persons in the United States and for which there is no reasonable expectation that the development cost will be recovered in the domestic sales of the product. On application by the sponsor, such products may qualify for an "Orphan Drug Designation." Orphan designation of a product does not in any way alter the standard regulatory requirements for marketing approval. However, it does permit tax credits (26 U.S.C. 44H) for clinical research undertaken by a sponsor to generate required data and the granting of exclusive approval for 7 years for a designated drug or biological product. More recently the FDA has also included regulations for devices, called Humanitarian Use Devices (HUDs), for use in conditions affecting less than 4000 persons annually in the U.S. (see 21 CFR 814 Subpart H).[4]

DRUGS FOR HUMAN USE

The United States regulates products by their intended use. *Intended use* is derived from the explicit and implicit claims made in the product's labeling, and in the product's advertisements or promotional activities. The FDCA defines drugs as "articles intended for use in the diagnosis, cure, mitigation, treatment, or prevention of disease in man or other animals" and "articles (other than food) intended to affect the structure or any function of the body of man or other animals" (FDCA Section 201(g), codified at 21 U.S.C. 321(g)). Thus, even products that are not being currently sold as drugs, including conventional foods, dietary supplements, and cosmetics, are subject to the drug requirements

of the law, if therapeutic or prevention claims are made, as illustrated in Fig. 15-2.

Official drugs

The FDCA recognizes as official drugs those products identified in the following official compendia: the United States Pharmacopeia (USP), the Homeopathic Pharmacopeia of the United States (HPUS), and the National Formulary (NF) (see FDCA Section 201(j)). USP monographs provide standards, specifications, and methods of analysis for approximately 3200 drugs, and the NF monographs contain standards for an additional 250 pharmaceutical materials. All drugs named in the compendia are required by the FDCA to meet the standards of strength, quality, or purity set forth in such compendia and must be packaged and labeled in the manner prescribed by the official compendia. If a drug differs from or falls outside the limits specified in an official compendium, the nature and extent of its difference from such standard must be plainly stated on the label (Section 501(b), codified at 21 U.S.C. 351(b)).[5]

A drug not recognized in an official compendium is adulterated if its strength differs from or its purity or quality falls below that which it purports to have or is represented to possess (Section 501(c), codified at 21 U.S.C. 351(c)). For example, any drug intended for use by injection and any ophthalmic ointment or solution must be sterile; if such a product is contaminated with microorganisms, it is adulterated. Also, a drug is adulterated under the FDCA if any substance has been mixed with it so as to reduce the quality or strength of the product or to constitute a substitute of the product (Section 501(d), codified at 21 U.S.C. 351(d)).

Prescription and nonprescription (over-the-counter) drugs

Up until the Prescription Drug Act of 1951 (also called "Durham-Humphrey"), drugs were generally available to the public. The 1951 amendments required that those drugs that cannot be used safely without professional supervision be dispensed only by prescription because they are habit-forming, toxic, or have too great a potential for harmful effects, or are for medical conditions that cannot be readily self-diagnosed. In addition, if a product cannot be self-administered by the consumer (e.g., intravenous), or if a product cannot be labeled with instructions for use that are reasonably understood by a consumer, it must be dispensed by prescription. Prescription drugs may be dispensed only by or on the prescription of a licensed health practitioner and must bear the statement: "Rx Only" (Section 503(b)(4), added in 1951 by Pub. L. 65-648, codified at 21 U.S.C. 353(b)(4)). The definition of a *licensed practitioner* is a matter of state law and varies from state to state.

A drug is to be made available without a prescription if, by following the labeling, consumers can use it safely and effectively without professional guidance. Nonprescription or

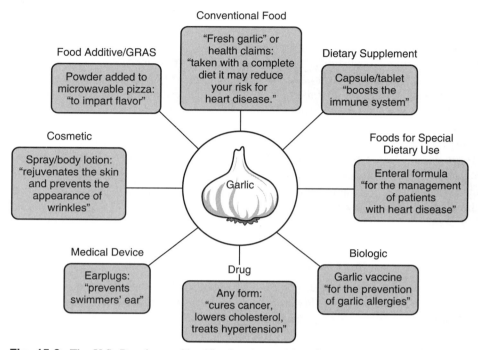

Fig. 15-2. The U.S. Regulatory Classification (e.g., claims for garlic products). (Courtesy Freddie Ann Hoffman, M.D., and Thomas Garvey IV, J.D.)

"over-the-counter" (OTC) drugs sold directly to consumers are indicated for conditions that are self-limiting and can also be recognized and treated successfully by consumers without professional monitoring. Standards for safety, effectiveness, and labeling for OTC products are described in 21 CFR 330.10(a)(4). With the passage of the Kefauver-Harris Amendments in 1962, documentation of not only a drug's safety but also its efficacy was required for the drug to continue to be marketed in the United States. FDA responded to the mandate by initiating the Drug Efficacy Study Implementation (DESI) program, which reviewed the evidence for safety and efficacy of drugs marketed for the first time between 1938 and 1962. Drugs, such as digitalis, morphine, and phenobarbital, marketed prior to the 1938 FDCA were exempt from review. In 1966, the FDA commissioned expert panels to determine whether sufficient information supported the criterion of "substantial evidence" of effectiveness, as required by the new law. DESI evaluated over 3000 separate products and over 16,000 therapeutic claims. As an outgrowth of the DESI review, the process of the Abbreviated New Drug Application (ANDA) was established. ANDAs were accepted for reviewed products that required changes in existing labeling to be in compliance. In September 1981 final regulatory action had been taken on 90% of all DESI products. By 1984, final action had been completed on 3443 products; of these, 2225 were found to be effective, 1051 were found not effective, and 167 were pending.

The Drug Price Competition and Patent Term Restoration (Hatch-Waxman) Act of 1984 was a compromise between the brand-name and generic drug industries. The brand-name industry received patent term restoration equal to half the time spent in clinical trials plus all the time that the FDA spent reviewing the New Drug Application. The restoration was limited to a maximum of 5 years and the length of a patent after restoration to 14 years. Innovators also received 5 years of nonpatent exclusivity for a new chemical entity and 3 years of exclusivity for a new indication or dosage form. Generic manufacturers were relieved from the requirement of reproving the safety and efficacy of the active ingredient, but required to show with a degree of statistical precision that their products delivered the same active ingredient to the bloodstream or site of action to the same extent and at the same rate as the innovator products. The current issue of FDA's "List of Approved Drug Products with Therapeutic Equivalence Evaluations" has details and can be downloaded from the FDA website.

In May 1972, the FDA applied the principle of a retrospective review to OTC drugs. The structure for this OTC review needed to be different from that of the prescription drug review, mainly because of the more than 300,000 available OTC products. FDA developed an OTC drug monograph process. At the time the FDA identified more than 80 therapeutic classes and about a thousand active ingredients. For each therapeutic class, ingredients were classified as: Category I, Generally Recognized As Safe and Effective ("GRAS" & "GRAE"); Category II, not GRAS/E; or Category III, insufficient data available to permit classification. The OTC drug monograph is a three-phase rule-making process. It begins with an Advance Notice of Proposed Rulemaking (ANPR) based on advisory panel recommendations, followed by a Proposed Rule (PR) (tentative final monograph). A Final Rule (final monograph) taking into account all available information and data for each therapeutic class of drugs is then published in the CFR. To organize its workload, the FDA originally allowed only those ingredients marketed in the United States for a *material time and extent* to be eligible for the monograph process. On January 23, 2002, however, the FDA expanded the monograph process to include ingredients with foreign marketing experience. For each therapeutic drug class (e.g., expectorants, internal analgesics) the OTC monograph delineates acceptable ingredients, dose ranges, formulations, routes, schedules, ingredient combinations, and labeling claims that may appear on OTC drug products. Nonconforming OTC drug products must undergo the new drug review process, as described below.

New drugs

The 1962 amendments to the FDCA defined a "new" drug as any article marketed after 1938 intended to diagnose, treat, prevent, mitigate, or cure a disease or condition that is not generally recognized as safe or effective (GRAS/E) under the conditions prescribed, recommended, or suggested in the labeling (Section 201(p), codified at 21 U.S.C. 321(p)). Thus, a new drug would require premarket approval by the FDA for safety and efficacy. The FDA reviewed the marketing applications, called a New Drug Application (NDA) (21 CFR 314) submitted by the drug's sponsor (usually, but not always, its manufacturer), containing acceptable scientific data from tests to evaluate its safety, and *substantial evidence* of effectiveness for the conditions for which the drug is to be offered (Section 505, codified at 21 U.S.C. 355). *Substantial evidence* is defined as "evidence consisting of *adequate and well controlled investigations*, including clinical investigations, by experts qualified by scientific training and experience to evaluate the effectiveness of the drug involved, on the basis of which it could fairly and responsibly be concluded by such experts that the drug will have the effect it purports or is represented to have under the conditions of use prescribed, recommended, or suggested in the labeling or proposed labeling thereof" (Section 505(d)). After the FDA approves a drug, the drug's formula, manufacturing process, labeling, packaging, dosage, and methods of testing generally may not be altered or modified from those stated in the NDA, without the approval of a supplemental application (21 CFR 314.70). Although drugs that are not "new" drugs are exempt from the new drug premarketing procedure, they must comply with all other drug requirements, including registration, labeling, and manufacturing practices.

Most prescription drugs are new drugs. In some cases, prescription drugs may be "switched" from prescription to OTC status ("Rx to OTC switch") through a supplemental NDA. To justify the sale of the product directly to the consumer, the information submitted in the application must support the dose, route, indication, and safety of the drug for nonprescription use. To augment the FDA's resources and to reduce the time to approval of new drugs, in 1992 Congress passed the Prescription Drug User Fee Act (PDUFA; Pub. L. 102-571, Title I). This law authorizes the FDA to collect "user fees" for the filing and review of certain applications for approval of human drug and biological products, and for establishments where the products are made. User fees are not applicable to generic or monographed drugs, whole blood and blood components used for transfusion, some large volume parenterals, allergenic extract products, in vitro diagnostic biological products, and certain drugs derived from bovine blood. Under some specific conditions, the FDA may waive, reduce, or delay payment of the fees.

Investigational drugs

In order to market a new drug, the sponsor must demonstrate the drug's clinical safety and efficacy for the intended indication. The development of a new drug usually proceeds in an orderly fashion from discovery, through preclinical studies (in vitro and animal studies), clinical studies, to the filing of the NDA (Fig. 15-3). During this process the new drug is considered to be an *investigational new drug* (Section 505(i), codified at 21 U.S.C. 355(i)). An Investigational New Drug (IND) application must be filed with the FDA before an investigational new drug may be distributed across state lines or imported for human trials (21 CFR 50 and 312). A product under an IND may not be promoted or advertised for the indications being studied prior to approval under an NDA (21 CFR 312). The clinical evaluation is usually conducted in stages or *phases*. Phase I studies are the initial studies in humans; safety is the main study objective. Phase II studies address safety and efficacy and pharmacokinetics and pharmacodynamics. Although not described in regulation, Phase III trials are large, well-controlled studies. Often these are pivotal studies to confirm the results for submission in the NDA. Postmarketing, or Phase IV studies, may be required by the FDA to elucidate the safety of the product in broader populations or may be carried out by the sponsor to establish a new indication or promotional claim.

The design of the clinical protocol should be supported by information already known about the product. This includes information about the pharmacology, toxicity, and effects observed in preclinical studies, as well as any previous human use that supports the safety of the dose, route, and schedule. Protocols must contain essential elements, which include objectives, a description of the study population, subject selection criteria, product information, monitoring plan, end point determination, and analyses to be performed. The protocol must also be accompanied by an informed consent form that meets the requirements set out in 21 CFR 50.20 and 50.25. The FDA is continually evaluating the risk to benefit ratio in permitting trials to proceed and in approving drugs for

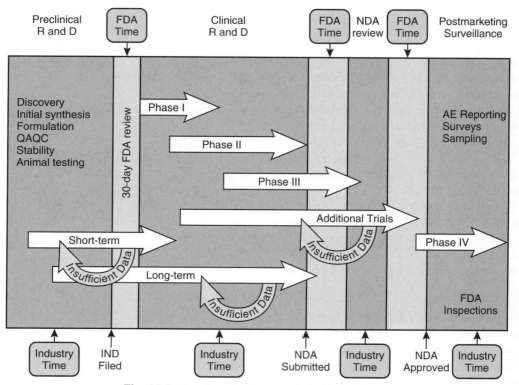

Fig. 15-3. New drug development in the United States.

the U.S. market. The FDA publishes *Guidance* documents on the design and conduct of preclinical and clinical drug development, as well as on other parts of the development process.

Accelerated approvals and expanded access to investigational products

New drugs, antibiotics, and biologics (discussed later) for the treatment of serious or life-threatening illnesses may be developed under expedited procedures (see Subpart E of the regulations 21 CFR 312.80 to 312.88).[6,7] When the following four criteria exist, a Treatment IND can be filed permitting use by a wider population of promising agents when the product: (1) is intended to treat serious or immediately life-threatening disease; (2) there is no comparable or satisfactory alternative drug or other therapy; (3) is already under investigation in a controlled (Phase II or III) clinical trial or all clinical trials have been completed; and (4) marketing approval is being actively pursued (21 CFR 312.34).[8] Treatment INDs have been filed for treatments of the human immunodeficiency virus and other serious conditions.

The label and "labeling" of drugs

The FDCA defines label to mean the written, printed, or graphic matter on the immediate container (Section 201(k), codified at 21 U.S.C. 321(k)) and the outer carton or wrapper of the package. Labeling includes all labels and other written, printed, or graphic matter accompanying the product.

The word *accompanying* is interpreted very broadly; therefore labeling may include material that does not physically accompany the product, if it serves to identify the article, tell its uses, give directions, and so on. How a drug is labeled is determined by its classification, that is, whether it is an investigational drug, a new drug, a prescription-only drug, or an OTC drug. Each of these has special labeling requirements.

The label itself must bear identifying information, such as the dosage strength and the quantity of content, active ingredients, expiration date, name and quantity or proportions of any habit-forming substance with appropriate statements (e.g., "Warning: May be habit forming," as stated in Section 502(d), codified at 21 U.S.C. 352(d)). An important provision states that a drug is misbranded if its labeling is false or misleading in any particular (Section 502(a), codified at 21 U.S.C. 352(a)). Prescription drugs must be labeled "Rx Only." The package insert should contain the following sections: description, clinical pharmacology, indications and usage, contraindications, warnings, precautions, adverse reactions, drug abuse and dependence, overdosing (where applicable), dosage and administration, and how supplied (21 CFR 201.50 through 201.57). For OTC preparations, the principal display panel must bear similar information, as required under 21 CFR 201.61 to 201.62. Additionally, most OTC drug products are required to have tamper-evident packaging and labeling (21 CFR 211.132). Drugs that are dispensed by a licensed practitioner are exempted from the need to use the labeling required in the manufacturer's package if the dispensed products have the pharmacist's label containing the legally required elements, such as the names and addresses of the prescriber and patient, directions for use, and so on (Section 503(b)(2), codified at 21 U.S.C. 353(b)(2)). In addition to the requirements listed, a drug must not imitate another drug or be offered for sale under the name of another drug (Sections 301(I) and 502(I)(2)).

Advertisements for prescription drugs

Whereas advertisements for OTC drugs are regulated by the Federal Trade Commission, advertisements for drugs sold by prescription are regulated by the FDA (Section 502(n), codified at 21 U.S.C. 352(n)).[9] Until the late 1970s, such advertising was directed exclusively to health professionals, although there is no prohibition on advertisements to consumers. The first prescription drug advertised to consumers was a pneumonia vaccine intended for healthy elderly persons who may not be seeing a health professional regularly. In recent years, direct-to-consumer advertisements for prescription drugs have become increasingly common. The regulations for prescription drug advertisements are specific in the kinds of information that is necessary to be included (21 CFR 202). These regulations apply regardless of whether the advertisement is directed to health professionals or consumers. Dissemination of prescription drug advertisements that are not in compliance with the regulations constitutes misbranding. Advertisements may be submitted to the FDA for comment before publication. A drug can be advertised only for those conditions for which the FDA has approved an NDA or an appropriate supplement. These conditions are listed in the approved package insert. By including the term *Physicians' Desk Reference* (PDR) in the definition of labeling, FDA regulations (21 CFR Section 202.1) require that, if a manufacturer chooses to list a product in the PDR, the listing must be in the same words as the package insert. Testimonials of users constitute misbranding if they give the impression that a preparation is effective for a condition for which it could not otherwise be promoted.

Statements by sales representatives

The objective intent of the persons legally responsible for the labeling of drugs is determined by their expressions or may be shown by the circumstances surrounding distribution of a product. For example, the objective intent may be shown by labeling claims, advertising matter, or oral or written statements by such persons or their representatives. The circumstances may show that the article is misbranded because such persons or their representatives know that the drug is offered for a purpose for which it is neither labeled nor advertised (21 CFR Section 201.128). Health professionals wishing to report questionable promotional activities can call FDA's toll-free hotline (888 INFO-FDA or 888-4630-332).

Homeopathic drugs

Homeopathy is a system of medicine popularized in the 1700s by Samuel Hahnemann in Germany. Based on a "Law of Similars", it contends that "like treats like." For example, a substance that produces symptoms—such as ipecac, which produces nausea and vomiting at pharmacological concentrations—would be expected to treat these same conditions, when administered in smaller concentrations in a homeopathic preparation. In stark contrast to the science of modern pharmacology, a major tenet of homeopathy is the premise that the more dilute a substance is, the more potent it can be in treating symptoms. Traditionally homeopathic drugs are prepared by taking a starting substance through a prescribed series of dilutions and "succussions" (shakings), also termed "potentization," often ending up with such an infinitesimal amount of starting substance as to contain statistically less than one molecule of active drug substance in the final vial. The 1938 FDCA (Copeland Act, after Royall Copeland, a U.S. Senator and homeopathic physician from New York) specifically allows for homeopathic drugs by the law's recognition of the Homeopathic Pharmacopeia of the United States as an official compendium (see above). Therefore, any product labeled as "homeopathic" must, by definition, be a "drug," including products that might otherwise be regulated as biologics or foods. By policy the FDA has deferred regulation of homeopathic drugs, mostly due to their dilute nature and historical lack of safety concerns. However, the agency has not relinquished its authority to require homeopathic drugs to be reviewed as "new" drugs. Thus, homeopathic drugs do not bear the FDA imprimatur of approval for either safety or efficacy, nor do they undergo any formal FDA review process. They must, however, meet all other drug requirements, including GMP and labeling requirements.

BIOLOGICS

Section 351(a) of the Public Health Service (PHS) Act (42 U.S.C. 262) defines a biologic as " . . . any virus, therapeutic serum, toxin, antitoxin, vaccine, blood, blood component or derivative, allergenic product, or analogous product . . . applicable to the prevention, treatment, or cure of diseases or injuries of man. . . . " Biologics include such vitally important products as polio and measles vaccines, diphtheria and tetanus toxoids, and skin test substances, as well as whole blood and blood components for transfusion. The newer biotech products, such as monoclonal antibodies, cytokines, growth factors, and genetically engineered products, are also regulated as biologics or jointly as "biologic drugs." In September 2002, the FDA announced that regulation of these biologic drugs would be moved from CDER to CBER and integrated with the review of conventional therapeutic agents. Biologics differ from drugs in their legislative history and regulatory approach. The 1902 Virus, Serum, and Toxins Act was enacted following the deaths of 12 children who received improperly prepared diphtheria antitoxin. The comprehensive PHS Act of 1944 amended and updated the regulations for human biologics. Under the PHS Act biologics can also be legally defined as drugs (therapeutics) or devices (e.g., test kits to release blood products for human use) and are subject to all of the adulteration, misbranding, and registration provisions of the FDCA.

Similar to drugs, the development of biologics also requires the filing of an IND application, which is reviewed by the FDA Center for Biologics Evaluation and Research. Because biologics are often derived from living organisms, including human tissues and viruses, they are by nature potentially dangerous if improperly prepared or tested. The regulation of biologics necessarily stresses the demonstration of potency, sterility, purity, and identity (see 21 CFR Part 610). Manufacturing of biologics differs greatly from most single chemical entity drugs products. Biologics consistency and reproducibility are addressed through lot specifications and the control of lot-to-lot variation through strict manufacturing process controls. In addition, such products must undergo a "general safety" test, which is conducted in animals to determine if there is an unsafe batch (Section 610.11). Close surveillance of biologics production, batch-to-batch testing, and research toward improving the quality of biologics are activities conducted by the FDA Center for Biologics Evaluation and Research (CBER), and the development of standards for these products and proper control procedures are backed by the center's research program. CBER also has jurisdiction over banked human tissue intended for transplantation.[10]

Batch samples and lot release protocols

Similar to NDA approvals for drugs, the PHS Act requires biologics have an approved Biologics Licensing Application (BLA) prior to entering into interstate commerce, or for import or export (21 CFR Parts 600 through 680 and Part 211). Before a licensed biological product is released for commercial sale or use, specified materials must be submitted to and cleared by CBER. These materials include a sample of the product and detailed records of the product's specifications and batch-to-batch consistency. The FDA supplies standard reference preparations for potency tests of certain licensed products, such as antitoxins, bacterial and viral vaccines, and skin tests. Manufacturers are required to obtain and use these preparations in their testing of licensed products.

Blood banks

Interstate shipment of blood and blood components requires the issuance of U.S. product and establishment licenses, in accordance with the PHS Act. A licensed blood bank must comply with appropriate federal standards in preparing and testing the products being shipped. In accordance with FDA regulations (21 CFR 607.20 and 607.21), every blood bank collecting units of blood must register with the FDA within 5 days after commencing operations and must submit a list of blood products prepared. All blood banks must operate in compliance with the FDA's current GMP regulations for blood and blood components (21 CFR 606) and are by law subject to FDA inspection once every 2 years. As with other products, blood and blood components must undergo registration and product listing.

FOODS

Foods are defined as (1) articles used for food or drink for humans or other animals, (2) chewing gum, and (3) articles used for components of any such article (FDCA, Section 201(f), codified at 21 U.S.C. 321(f)). Foods are regulated by the Center for Food Safety and Applied Nutrition and include products classified as conventional foods, food additives, spices, dietary supplements, and foods for special dietary use. Except for cooking wine, and beverages with less than 7% alcohol content which are solely within the jurisdiction of the FDA, beer, wine, liquor, liqueur, and other alcoholic beverages are specifically subject to laws enforced by the Bureau of Alcohol, Tobacco and Firearms (BATF) of the U.S. Treasury Department.

In contrast to the more stringent drug GMPs, food GMPs focus on sanitation. A food is considered adulterated, and therefore illegal, if it contains harmful substances that are either added, or occur naturally, that may render it injurious to health; if it has been prepared, packed, or held under unsanitary conditions; or if any part of it is unfit for consumption (see Section 402(a), codified at 21 U.S.C. 342(a)). Raw agricultural products are illegal if they contain residues of pesticides not authorized by, or in excess of, tolerances established by regulations of the Environmental Protection Agency (Section 402(a)(2)(b) and Section 408).

Labeling

The Nutrition Labeling and Education Act (NLEA) of 1990 (Pub. L. 101-535, 104 Stat. 2353) has led to significant changes in the food labeling regulations. The NLEA addresses three primary areas: the nutrition label, nutrient content claims, and health claims. The regulations specify the nutrition information that must be on the label and the format in which it is to be presented (Fig. 15-4). The regulations further specify the display of which nutrients are required and their order. In addition to these mandatory nutrients, manufacturers may voluntarily choose to include other information, such as other vitamins and minerals for which Recommended Daily Intakes (RDIs) have been established. In addition to nutrients, the NLEA requires standards to define serving sizes (21 CFR 101.12). Nutrient content claims are those that describe the amount of a nutrient in the food (such as "sodium free" or "low fat") and are defined by FDA regulation (21 CFR 101.13). The food label is shown in Fig. 15-4.

Infant formulas and foods for patient populations (e.g., diabetics) are categorized as foods for special dietary use. In 1980 Congress passed the Infant Formula Act (Pub. L.

94-1190), which establishes nutrient requirements.(Section 201(z)) and provides the FDA authority to establish GMPs and requirements for nutrient quantity, nutrient quality control, and record-keeping, and for reporting and recalling infant formulas that pose a potential hazard to health.

Dietary Supplement Health and Education Act of 1994

The Dietary Supplement Health and Education Act (DSHEA) (Pub. L. 103-417, 108 Stat. 4325) of 1994 amended the FDCA to establish a new category of foods. A dietary supplement is a product (other than tobacco) that is intended to supplement the diet. It can be composed of a vitamin, mineral, herb or other botanical, amino acid, dietary substance or concentrate, metabolite, constituent, extract, or combination of these ingredients, and includes drugs and biologics, if marketed as a dietary supplement of food prior to approval. Under DSHEA a dietary supplement is adulterated if it or one of its ingredients presents "a significant or unreasonable risk of illness or injury" when used as directed on the label or under normal conditions of use. A dietary supplement that contains a new dietary ingredient (i.e., an ingredient not marketed for dietary supplement use in the United States before October 15, 1994) must demonstrate that there is adequate information to provide reasonable assurance that the ingredient will not present a significant or unreasonable risk of illness or injury in a New Dietary Ingredient (NDI) notification which is submitted to the FDA at least 75 days prior to marketing the dietary supplement. Unlike the confidential filing of an IND, the NDI notification is in the public domain. The Secretary of the Department of Health and Human Services (DHHS) may also declare that a dietary supplement or dietary ingredient poses an imminent hazard to public health or safety. However, as with any other foods, it is a manufacturer's responsibility to ensure that its products are safe and properly labeled before marketing. The agency is in the process of promulgating regulations for dietary supplements, including GMPs, which will revise 21 CFR 101.36. As part of the provisions of the DSHEA, retail outlets may display educational materials about the health-related benefits of the dietary supplement or its ingredients. These materials, which can include articles, book chapters, scientific abstracts, or other third-party publications, cannot be false or misleading, cannot promote a specific brand of supplement, and must be displayed with other similar materials to present a balanced view. The literature must be displayed separately from the dietary supplements themselves and may not have other information attached, such as product promotional literature.

Dietary supplement claims

Under the new legislation, dietary supplements may make four types of claims: health claims, nutrient content claims, structure or function claims, and claims of well-being. *Health claims* must be preapproved by the FDA and describe a relationship between a food substance and a disease or health-related condition (e.g. "Healthful diets with adequate folate may reduce a woman's risk of having a child with a brain or spinal cord birth defect"). Once approved, any food product that meets the criteria to bear the claim may do so without further review or approval by the FDA. Claims of *nutritional support* are statements about classical nutrient deficiency diseases (a product containing sufficient vitamin C to prevent scurvy) are permissible as long as such statements disclose the prevalence of the disease in the United States. DSHEA also authorizes manufacturers to describe the role of a nutrient or dietary ingredient intended to affect a structure or function in humans (e.g., "calcium builds strong bones," "fiber maintains bowel regularity," "antioxidants maintain cell integrity"), or on general *well-being* ("ginseng makes you feel more energetic"). To support these claims manufacturers must have substantiation that the statements are truthful and not misleading. In addition, the product label must bear the statement: "This statement has not been evaluated by the Food and Drug Administration. This product is not intended to diagnose, treat, cure, or prevent any disease." Unlike health claims, nutritional support statements, structure or function claims, and claims of well-being are not subject to FDA preapproval, although the agency must receive notification of the claims no later than 30 days after a product that bears the claim is first marketed. Similar to other foods, dietary supplement products must bear ingredient labeling. If a supplement is covered by specifications in an official compendium and is represented as conforming, it is misbranded if it fails to conform to those specifications. If not covered by a compendium, a dietary supplement must be the product identified on the label and have the strength it is represented as having. Nutrition labeling is also required.

Foods for special dietary uses and foods used as drugs

Foods for special dietary uses (FSDU) are another category under the food section of the law (FDCA Section 411(c)(3), codified at 21 U.S.C. 350(c)(3)). FSDU may supply a special dietary need that exists because of a physical, physiological, pathological, or other condition, including but not limited to the conditions of disease, convalescence, pregnancy, lactation, infancy, allergic hypersensitivity to food, underweight, overweight, or the need to control the intake of sodium. An example might be the foods used in phenylketonuria diets. When a FSDU, or for that matter any food or dietary supplement, is labeled, advertised, or promoted with claims of disease prevention, treatment, mitigation, cure, or diagnosis, the FDA regards these claims as *drug claims*. Such products must comply with the drug provisions of the FDCA, unless the claim is a *health claim* authorized by regulation. Also, if a food ingredient is recognized in an *official compendium*, such as the USP,

The new food label will carry an up-to-date, easier-to-use nutrition information guide, to be required on almost all packaged foods (compared to about 60 percent of products up till now). The guide will serve as a key to help in planning a healthy diet.*

Serving sizes are now more consistent across product lines, are stated in both household and metric measures, and reflect the amounts people actually eat.

The **list of nutrients** covers those most important to the health of today's consumers, most of whom need to worry about getting too much of certain nutrients (fat, for example), rather than too few vitamins or minerals, as in the past.

The label of larger packages may now tell the number of calories per gram of fat, carbohydrate, and protein.

Nutrition Facts

Serving Size 1 cup (228g)
Servings Per Container 2

Amount Per Serving

Calories 260   Calories from Fat 120

	% Daily Value*
Total Fat 13g	**20%**
Saturated Fat 5g	**25%**
Cholesterol 30mg	**10%**
Sodium 660mg	**28%**
Total Carbohydrate 31g	**10%**
Dietary Fiber 0g	**0%**
Sugars 5g	
Protein 5g	

Vitamin A 4%	•	Vitamin C 2%
Calcium 15%	•	Iron 4%

* Percent Daily Values are based on a 2,000 calorie diet. Your daily values may be higher or lower depending on your calorie needs:

	Calories:	2,000	2,500
Total Fat	Less than	65g	80g
Sat Fat	Less than	20g	25g
Cholesterol	Less than	300mg	300mg
Sodium	Less than	2,400mg	2,400mg
Total Carbohydrate		300g	375g
Dietary Fiber		25g	30g

Calories per gram:
Fat 9 • Carbohydrate 4 • Protein 4

New title signals that the label contains the newly required information.

Calories from fat are now shown on the label to help consumers meet dietary guidelines that recommend people get no more than 30 percent of the calories in their overall diet from fat.

% Daily Value shows how a food fits into the overall daily diet.

Daily Values are also something new. Some are maximums, as with fat (65 grams or less); others are minimums, as with carbohydrate (300 grams or more). The daily values for a 2,000- and 2,500-calorie diet must be listed on the label of larger packages.

* This label is only a sample. Exact specifications are in the final rules.
Source: Food and Drug Administration, 1994

Fig. 15-4. The food label at a glance. (From DHHS, FDA, *Focus on Food Labeling: Read the Label, Set a Healthy Table.* An FDA Consumer Special Report. May 1993, DHHS Publication No. 93-2262.)

the product is considered to be both a drug and a food (see later discussion) and may be an ingredient of products that fall into both of these regulatory categories. For example, calcium is an ingredient that is marketed not only as a dietary supplement, but also is included under the OTC drug monograph as a stomach antiacid.

COSMETICS

Cosmetics, like foods, are under the jurisdiction of the FDA Center for Food Safety and Applied Nutrition (CFSAN). U.S.-marketed cosmetics must comply with the FDCA, as well as the Fair Packaging and Labeling Act, and the regulations issued under the authority of these laws (21 CFR

Parts 700 to 740). FDCA defines cosmetics as *articles intended to be applied to the human body for cleansing, beautifying, promoting attractiveness, or altering the appearance without affecting the body's structure or functions.* Included in this definition are products such as skin creams, lotions, perfumes, lipsticks, fingernail polishes, eye and facial makeup preparations, shampoos, permanent waves, hair colors, toothpastes, deodorants, and any ingredient intended for use as a component of a cosmetic product. Soap products consisting primarily of an alkali salt of fatty acid and making no label claim other than cleansing of the human body are not considered cosmetics under the law.

With the exception of color additives and a few prohibited ingredients, cosmetic manufacturers may, on their own responsibility, use essentially any raw material as a cosmetic ingredient and market the product without prior FDA approval. Cosmetic manufacturers are not required to test their products for safety; however, the FDA strongly urges cosmetic manufacturers to conduct appropriate safety testing of their products. There is no mandatory registration for cosmetic products. Although firms may voluntarily make available safety data or other information before a product is marketed, voluntary registration and assignment of a registration number by the agency do not confer approval of a firm, raw material, or product by the FDA (21 CFR Parts 710, 720, and 730).

Cosmetic labeling and cosmetic drugs

Cosmetics distributed domestically must comply with labeling regulations under the FDCA and the Fair Packaging and Labeling Act (21 CFR Parts 701 and 740). Some cosmetics must bear label warnings or cautions prescribed by regulation (21 CFR 740). Declaration of ingredients is only required for cosmetics produced or distributed for retail sale to consumers for their personal care (21 CFR 701.3). Some cosmetics are also intended to treat or prevent disease, or affect the structure or function of the human body. Examples include fluoride toothpastes, sun-tanning preparations intended to protect against sunburn, antiperspirants that are also deodorants, and antidandruff shampoos. These products are regulated as cosmetic drugs, and must comply with both drug and cosmetic provisions of the law. Cosmetics that are also drugs must first identify the active drug ingredient(s) before listing the cosmetic ingredients (21 CFR 701.3(d)).

ANIMAL PRODUCTS

The FDA regulates drugs, devices, feeds, pet foods, and the color and food additives intended for animals under the FDCA. In contrast, animal biologics (e.g., vaccines) are regulated under the Animal Virus, Serum, and Toxins Act (AVSTA) of 1913 (21 U.S.C Sections 151 et seq.), which has been subsequently amended. The AVSTA is under the authority of the Veterinary Biologics Staff of the Animal and Plant Health Inspection Service (APHIS) of the U.S.

Department of Agriculture. Many of the requirements for veterinary products are similar to those for the comparable human products. To protect the national food supply, the FDCA requires the approval of applications for use of new animal drugs in the manufacture of animal feeds. Products administered or used by food-producing animals are evaluated for not only their effect on the animal, but also for their residues in food tissues, such as meat, milk, and eggs. As with human products, a "new animal drug" may not be marketed or imported for commercial marketing unless it has been approved as safe and effective in the United States.

Pesticidal drugs

Depending on the claims made, animal products that are pesticidal preparations, such as rodenticides, fungicides, and insecticides, may be subject both to the FDCA and the Federal Insecticide, Fungicide and Rodenticide Act (7 U.S.C, Sections 136 et seq.), administered by the Pesticide Registration Division of the Environmental Protection Agency. A Memorandum of Understanding between the two agencies specifies which agency will process petitions for products subject to dual jurisdiction. Petitions may be submitted to either agency and will be referred, if necessary.

MEDICAL DEVICES

The FDCA defines a medical device as any health care product that does not achieve its principal intended purposes by chemical action in or on the body or by being metabolized. FDA regulates several thousand medical device products, from simple articles such as tongue depressors and heating pads to in vitro test kits, contraceptive devices, anesthesia machines, and heart valves. In 1968 the Radiation Control for Health and Safety Act was enacted to protect the public from unnecessary exposure to radiation from electronic products (Sections 531 to 542). Thus, electronic products and radiation control are also under the FDA's purview (21 CFR Parts 1000 to 1050). The Medical Device Amendments of 1976 revised and extended the device requirements of the 1938 FDCA, resulting in significant new authority to ensure safe and effective devices. Later the Safe Medical Devices Act (SMDA) of 1990 and the Medical Device Amendments of 1992 enhanced premarket and postmarket controls and provided for additional regulatory authority.

Based on the 1976 amendments, devices fall into three regulatory classes. Class I devices (e.g., tongue blades) are subject to "general controls" that apply to all devices. General controls include the registration of manufacturers, record-keeping requirements, labeling requirements, and compliance with GMP regulations. Class II devices (e.g., catheters) are subject to "special controls" where general controls are insufficient to ensure safety and effectiveness, and for which enough information exists to develop special controls to provide such assurance, including performance standards, postmarket surveillance, patient registries, guidelines, recommendations, and other appropriate actions. Class III devices include those devices that are life-supporting or life-sustaining (e.g., implants, anesthesia equipment), where special controls are necessary to provide adequate assurance of the safety and efficacy. Similar to new drugs, Class III devices must undergo premarket approval through the filing of an Investigational Device Exemption (IDE) application and a Premarketing Application (PMA). Such devices must have FDA approval for safety and effectiveness before they can be marketed, unless the FDA determines that premarket approval is unnecessary. FDA can require premarket approval of Class I or II devices, if general controls are insufficient to ensure safety and effectiveness and insufficient information is available to establish special controls. Regulations on classification of devices are in 21 CFR 860 and in Parts 862 through 892. All manufacturers are required to give premarket notification (Section 510(k)) giving the FDA 90 days to determine whether or not the device is "substantially equivalent" to a pre-amendment device. For a complete review of the regulations, see 21 CFR Part 860 through 892.

Investigational devices

Class III and, in some cases, Class II devices may require clinical studies for marketing. While studies are ongoing to determine their safety and effectiveness, the devices are considered *investigational devices* (Section 520(g)). Similar to the drug and biologics regulations, sponsors who wish to conduct these investigations can be granted exemptions from certain requirements of the FDCA, by filing an IDE application 21 CFR 812 (general) and 813 (intraocular lenses). Unlike the drug regulations, if a study is reviewed and found to be of nonsignificant risk to the subjects by an Institutional Review Board, the trial may be conducted without filing an IDE. However, the FDA may later require an IDE to be filed if the manufacturer must submit a Premarketing Application (PMA). Consultation with the agency staff is recommended.

Custom devices

Custom medical devices ordered by health professionals to conform to their own special needs or to those of their patients (e.g., certain dental devices and specially designed orthopedic footwear) are considered *custom devices* and are exempt from registration and otherwise applicable performance standards or premarket approval requirements (Section 520(b)). The exemption applies only to devices not generally available to or used by other health professionals. Custom devices are not exempt from other provisions of the FDCA and regulations.

REPORTING PROBLEMS: ADVERSE EVENTS AND PRODUCT QUALITY ISSUES

An *adverse drug experience* is defined by the regulations (21 CFR 310.305(b)(2)) as ". . . any adverse event associated with the use of a drug in humans, whether or not considered drug related." This includes adverse events occurring in the course of the use of a drug product in professional practice; as a result of an overdose, whether accidental or intentional; as a result of abuse or recreational use; from withdrawal; and as any reaction that occurs because of a failure to produce an expected pharmacological or biological action. Adverse effects can range from mild side effects to severe reactions, including death. Adverse experiences that result in death, hospitalization, or permanent disability are always considered serious. Cancer, congenital anomalies, and overdose are adverse drug experiences that are also considered serious. Events may be predictable or unpredictable. Predictable events are most often expected extensions of an individual product's known properties and are responsible for the majority of events encountered. Unpredictable events, however, include idiosyncratic reactions, immunological or allergic reactions, and carcinogenic or teratogenic events. Unlike predictable events, these events are usually not associated with the known pharmacological activity of the product. They seem to be more a function of patient susceptibility than the intrinsic toxicity of the drug. They are rarely avoidable and are generally independent of dose, route, or schedule of administration. Unpredictable events are often among the most serious and potentially life-threatening of all adverse events and are the major cause of important drug-induced disease.

The reporting of adverse events may lead to the discovery of new uses. The phocomelia (limb reduction defects) seen in children whose mothers took thalidomide during the early stages of pregnancy is now thought to be due to inhibition of the formation of new blood vessels. Because of this activity, this same drug is now undergoing clinical trials as an anticancer agent. Excessive hair growth seen in clinical trials of minoxidil tablets (Loniten) for the treatment of hypertension led to development of topical minoxidil (Rogaine) for the treatment of baldness.

Although reporting by health professionals remains voluntary, product sponsors are required to keep the FDA informed regarding any developments that may affect the safety and effectiveness of their products, whether under clinical study or after FDA approval for marketing. (See FDCA, Sections 505(i), (j), and (k), and 21 CFR 310.303, 310.304, 310.305, 312.32, and 314.) Adverse events that occur during clinical studies are to be reported to the FDA, as specified in the regulations for Investigational New Drugs for drugs and biologics or Investigational Device Exemption for devices. For products already marketed, adverse events should be reported to the FDA through MedWATCH. The MedWATCH form (FDA form 3500) allows for the reporting of all FDA-regulated products. In addition, the Vaccine Adverse Event Reporting System (VAERS) program was established by the National Childhood Vaccine Injury Act of 1986.[11] The FDA jointly manages the VAERS program, a joint surveillance program for human vaccine products, with the Centers for Disease Control and Prevention, located in Atlanta, Georgia. The CDC focuses on collective reports, attempting to detect unusual epidemiological trends and associations. The FDA reviews individual reports, assessing whether a reported event is adequately reflected in product labeling, including directions for use. The FDA also closely monitors reporting trends for individual vaccine manufacturers and vaccine lots, which may lead to manufacturing improvements, or in some cases where necessary, the recall of the product from the market. Adverse events can be reported on the FDA website (www.fda.gov), by telephone (1-800-FDA-1088), modem (1-800-FDA-7737), or fax (1-800-FDA-0178). VAERS forms may be obtained by calling 1-800-822-7967.

Drug and Device Quality Reporting System

FDA's Drug Quality Reporting System (DQRS) is a voluntary system to monitor the quality of drugs and devices. Reportable problems include improper labeling, defects, performance failures, poor packaging, and incomplete or confusing instructions. Problems may be reported at the agency's toll-free hotline (888 INFO-FDA or 888-4630-332).

FDA'S ROLE IN THE "PRACTICE OF MEDICINE"

Although the FDA regulates most products used in the practice of the healing arts (e.g., medicine, dentistry, acupuncture), nevertheless, it does not directly regulate the practitioners themselves. Where applicable, the approvals and licensing of health professionals are left to the jurisdiction of the states (see Chapter 7). In addition, the FDA does not regulate procedures, techniques, or lifestyle interventions, such as diet or exercise, or surgical procedures. Procedures such as bone marrow transplantation are considered *technologies* that are evaluated by both federal and private organizations. Such *technology assessments* can have a major impact on whether insurance carriers or health management organizations will allow or reimburse for the procedures.

Unlabeled uses of FDA-approved products

Although the FDCA prohibits a manufacturer or distributor from promoting an approved drug or device or unapproved use for an approved product, the FDCA does not prohibit the manner of use by a health professional in the direct management of patients. Once a product has been approved for marketing, a practitioner may prescribe the drug for *unapproved* or, more accurately, *unlabeled* uses, which may be appropriate under certain circumstances and may in fact reflect approaches that have been extensively reported in the medical literature.[12] Indeed, valid new uses for marketed products are often first discovered by innovative approaches taken by health professionals, which are later confirmed by well-controlled clinical trials. Before the product's label may be revised to include new indications, the substantiating data

must be submitted to the FDA for review and approval. This process takes time, and without the cooperation of the manufacturer whose product is involved, it may never occur. For this reason, accepted medical practice often includes unlabeled uses that are not reflected in the product's current labeling. The FDA has taken a similar stance with respect to medical devices. For veterinary practice, two new laws have amended the FDCA, expanding the ability of veterinarians to prescribe unlabeled uses for animals. The Animal Medicinal Drug Use Clarification Act of 1994 allows veterinarians to prescribe extralabel use of not only veterinary drugs, but also approved human drugs for animals under specific circumstances. The Animal Drug Availability Act of 1996 allows the FDA to modify its current definition of "substantial effectiveness" and supports flexible labeling, by broadening the drug approval process to extrapolate information to "minor" species—those animals that are too few in number to allow cost recovery from the development of indications for these species.

Product resales and samples

Section 503 of the FDCA (codified at 21 U.S.C. 353), as amended by the Prescription Drug Marketing Act, prohibits the sale, purchase, or trade of prescription drug samples and drug coupons. A drug sample is a unit of a prescription drug that is not intended to be sold, but is intended to promote the sale of the drug product. A coupon is a form that may be redeemed at no—or reduced—cost for a prescription drug. The law also prohibits resale of prescription drugs purchased by hospitals or other health care entities, or donated or supplied at reduced cost to charitable organizations. Exceptions for group purchasing organizations, nonprofit affiliates, and entities under common control are provided in the FDCA. Additional exceptions provide for medical emergencies and for dispensing of drugs pursuant to a prescription. Under Section 503 a manufacturer or distributor is also permitted to distribute drug samples to a licensed practitioner or pharmacy of a health care entity by mail or by other means on written request.

Industry-supported continuing medical education

Scientific and educational activities on FDA-regulated products directed at health care professionals that are performed by or on behalf of the companies that market the products have traditionally been viewed by the FDA as subject to regulation under the labeling and advertising provisions of the FDCA. On November 27, 1992, the FDA published a draft policy statement (57 F.R. 56412)[13] to distinguish between those activities supported by companies that are otherwise independent from the promotional influence of the supporting company and those that are not. On October 8, 1996, the FDA finalized this statement (61 F.R. 52800-52801), identifying 12 factors that the agency will consider in determining whether a manufacturer through its support of scientific and educational activities evidenced a "new use" of its drugs or devices. This statement was further clarified in another FDA statement issued on March 16, 2000 (65 F.R. 14286-14288). The final policy statement was the product of extensive consultation with scientific and health care professionals, regulated industry, consumer groups, and other government agencies. This policy, which speaks to FDA-regulated companies that support continuing medical education (CME), reflects documents issued by the Accreditation Council for Continuing Medical Education speaking to accredited providers, the Association of American Medical Colleges speaking to CME faculty members, and the American Medical Association speaking to physicians. Representatives of these organizations, academia, industry, and CME providers meet regularly as the National Task Force for CME Provider/Industry Collaboration hosted by the American Medical Association.

Alternative or complementary medical practices

Although the FDA has no legal or regulatory definition for complementary or alternative medicine (CAM), it does regulate medical products used in such practices, particularly when claims of diagnostic or therapeutic intent are made. As in the conventional practice of medicine, the FDA does not regulate the use of massage, light or music therapy, meditation, or prayer per se. However, when any product is used and promoted for the purpose of diagnosing, preventing, treating, curing, or mitigating human or animal illness, by definition in the FDCA it becomes a drug or device. The FDA does not comment on the source or historical controversies that may surround a use of a particular product, and many useful and well-accepted approved drugs and devices were derived from unusual and unexpected sources. Since 1992, when Congress appropriated funding to the National Institutes of Health (NIH) to establish an Office of Complementary and Alternative Medicine (now the National Center for Complementary and Alternative Medicine), there has been a marked increase in research conducted into the uses and roles of previously unaccepted interventions. As the result of the increased interest in clinical investigation with such products, the FDA has provided guidances to the industry regarding the evaluation of some product categories. One such guidance is the "Draft Guidance for Industry on the Development of Botanical Drugs" (August 10, 2000). FDA has also responded to the public's concerns to examine not only the uses, but also the potential harmful effects, of CAM products.

Importation of products for personal use

Consumers may receive prescription drugs only through a licensed practitioner or, on his or her order, by a registered pharmacist. Under certain limited circumstances, a limited supply of drugs may be shipped directly to a consumer, for personal use only from a foreign source, in accordance with the personal importation guidance policy. Importation is generally permitted for those products representing a supply for 3 months or less of therapy and that are personally carried, shipped by a personal noncommercial representative of the consignee, or shipped from a foreign medical facility where a person has undergone treatment. FDA personnel do not routinely inspect mail or personal baggage. U.S. Customs brings items to the FDA's attention and the U.S. Postal Service may also become involved. Generally denied entries are large shipments of which the quantity suggests commercial distribution and small shipments solicited by traditional mail order promotions.[14]

ENDNOTES

1. DHHS, PHS, FDA, *Requirements of Laws and Regulations Enforced by the U.S. Food and Drug Administration*. DHHS Publication No. (FDA) 89-1115 (Revised 1997).
2. S.L. Nightingale & G. Bagley, *FDA Sanctions for Practitioners for Violations of Clinical Trial Regulations and Other Misconduct*, 81(1) Federation Bulletin 7-13 (1994).
3. DHHS, FDA, *21 CFR Part 812. Investigational Device Exemptions; Disqualification of Clinical Investigators, final rule*, 62(50) Federal Register 12087-12096 (Friday, March 14, 1997).
4. DHHS, FDA, *21 CFR Parts 20 and 814. Medical Devices; Humanitarian Use Devices, final rule*, 61(124) Federal Register 33232-33248 (Wednesday, June 26, 1996).
5. The Committee of Revision of the United States Pharmacopeial Convention, Inc., *USP 24 The United States Pharmacopeia NF 19 the National Formulary* (The United States Pharmacopeial Convention, Inc., Rockville, MD 2000).
6. DHHS, FDA, *21 CFR Parts 312 and 314. Investigational New Drug, Antibiotic, and Biological Drug Product Regulations; Procedures for Drugs Intended to Treat Life-Threatening and Severely Debilitating Illnesses, interim rule*, 53(204) Federal Register 41516-41524, Part VI (Friday, October 21, 1988).
7. DHHS, FDA, *CFR Parts 314.500, 314.560, and 601.40-46. New Drug, Antibiotic, and Biological Drug Product Regulations, accelerated approval final rule*, 57(239) Federal Register 58942-58960, Part VIII (Friday, December 11, 1992).
8. DHHS, FDA, *21 CFR Part 312. Investigational New Drug, Antibiotic, and Biological Drug Product Regulations, treatment use and sale final rule*, 52(99) Federal Register 19466-19477, Part IV (Friday, May 22, 1987).
9. DHHS, *Office of the Inspector General, Prescription Drug Advertisements in Medical Journals*, OEI 01-90-00482 (June 1992).
10. DHHS, FDA, *21 CFR Parts 16 and 1270. Human Tissue Intended for Transplantation, final rule*, 62(145) Federal Register 40429-40447 (Tuesday, July 29, 1997).
11. I.B. Stehlin, *How FDA Works to Ensure Vaccine Safety*, 29(10) FDA Consumer Magazine 6-10 (1995).
12. FDA, *Use of Approved Drugs for Unlabeled Indications*, 12(1) FDA Drug Bulletin 4-5 (1982).
13. DHHS, FDA, *Draft Policy Statement on Industry Supported Scientific and Educational Activities, Notice*, Federal Register 56412-56414 (Friday, November 27, 1992).
14. FDA, Chapter 9-71 Coverage of Personal Importations, FDA Regulatory Procedures Manual, Part 9, Import Procedures (1988).

16 Health Insurance and Professional Liability Insurance

JAMES R. HUBLER, M.D., J.D., F.C.L.M., F.A.C.E.P., F.A.A.E.M.
JAY WEAVER, J.D., E.M.T.-P

HEALTH INSURANCE
MEDICAL MALPRACTICE INSURANCE
FORMATION OF THE INSURANCE CONTRACT
INTERPRETATION OF INSURANCE CONTRACTS
FRAUD
INSURANCE REGULATION
NATIONAL PRACTITIONER DATA BANK
INSURANCE ACCOUNTING

Insurance is a form of contract under which one party protects another from risk of loss in exchange for the payment of a fee, or "premium." The insurer, in turn, pools these premiums into a coverage fund that compensates any member of the group who suffers a defined loss. The goal of this process is to minimize risk to the individual by distributing the burden of loss over a large number of contributors.

Today, insurance may be purchased to guard against virtually any risk. Life insurance, disability insurance, and casualty insurance all are widely available and purchased. This chapter will focus on the types of insurance that have had the greatest impact on the practice of medicine in this country: health insurance, which indemnifies patients for medical expenses, and medical malpractice insurance, which indemnifies health care providers against claims of professional negligence. Both have been subjects of intense legislative debate in recent years, and both promise to generate complex legal issues in the future.

HEALTH INSURANCE

Unlike other industrialized nations, the United States does not provide its citizens with comprehensive health care. As recently as the 1930s, Americans paid all of their health expenses out of pocket. Then came the Great Depression, which prompted doctors and hospitals to establish Blue Cross and Blue Shield plans—nonprofit

The authors gratefully acknowledge the previous contributions of James G. Zimmerly, M.D., J.D., F.C.L.M., M.P.H., L.L.D. (Hon.), Richard F. Gibbs, M.D., J.D., L.L.D., F.C.L.M., Richard Moore, Jr., J.D., C.P.C.U., and Erica Cohen, J.D.

arrangements that financed health care for those who otherwise could not afford it. During this same period, commercial insurance companies made health coverage available to the public. Today, Americans rely primarily on employment-related group insurance for their health coverage, while specific populations benefit from government-financed health programs such as Medicare and Medicaid.[1]

Private health insurance exists today in many forms. *Indemnity* coverage reimburses the policyholder for out-of-pocket medical expenses deemed "usual and customary." These policies are unique in that they typically impose no limitations on the selection of a health care provider. *Service-benefit plans*, in contrast, require the insured to select from a pool of participating health care facilities and practitioners. These plans reimburse health care providers directly and fully for services rendered. To prevent excessive service use, many service-benefit plans require co-payments or deductables.[2]

Health maintenance organizations (HMOs) represent an increasingly common alternative to the traditional health insurance policy. Members of these organizations receive care through a network of contracted providers who are compensated by the HMO on a fixed or per capita basis, without regard to services actually rendered. Hybrid plans, such as preferred provider organizations (PPOs), combine various characteristics of the service-benefit plan and the HMO. Participants may choose from a list of contracted providers, or they may seek care from an independent provider outside of the system. Reimbursement is often limited, however, if the participant selects the latter option.

In the 1990s, HMO coverage and other forms of managed care surpassed fee-for-service insurance as the predominant mode of health care financing in this country. Outraged by media reports of "drive-through" deliveries, nonreimbursed mammographies, and deaths caused by delays in treatment approval, the public soon demanded increased coverage and access to care. Legislators responded to these concerns by proposing managed care regulation in Congress and in every state. Today, health insurance of all kinds is regulated by a vast array of federal and state laws, including the Employee Retirement Income Security Act of 1974 (ERISA),[3] the Health Maintenance Act,[4] the Consolidated Omnibus Budget Reconciliation Act of 1985 (COBRA),[5] and the Health Insurance Portability and Accountability Act of 1996 (HIPAA).[6]

MEDICAL MALPRACTICE INSURANCE

Medical malpractice insurance indemnifies health care providers against claims of professional negligence. Available from commercial insurance companies and joint underwriting associations, this type of coverage is required under the laws of many states as a condition of professional practice. Rates tend to vary by specialty, geographic region, and the complexity of the procedures to be covered. The amount to be paid on each claim is often limited, as is the amount to be paid in aggregate during the term of the policy.

Medical malpractice insurance has become a subject of great controversy in recent years.[7] Escalating premiums, brought about by increasingly frequent litigation against health care providers, have been passed along to the public in the form of higher fees. At the same time, physicians have taken to the practice of "defensive medicine," ordering tests and procedures of dubious value in an effort to "cover all bases" and avoid malpractice claims entirely. Together, these phenomena have produced skyrocketing health care costs, higher health insurance premiums, and diminished access to care.[8]

Efforts to alleviate this "malpractice crisis" have met with varying degrees of success. Beginning in the 1970s, insurance companies generally abandoned "occurrence-based" policies, which covered malpractice committed at any time during the policy period, in favor of "claims-made" policies, which cover only those acts and omissions for which claims are filed during the term of the policy. This change has reduced malpractice premiums, but in some cases it has left practitioners uninsured for claims filed after the expiration of their malpractice policies.

State legislatures, too, have taken measures to rectify the problem. More than forty states have shortened their statutes of limitations on malpractice actions in an effort to limit the number of claims. Some states, including Massachusetts and Maryland, utilize pretrial screening panels to weed out frivolous claims. A successful, yet controversial,

solution to the malpractice crisis entails the statutory capping of punitive damages. According to one study, shortened statutes of limitations, combined with statutory caps on awards, have reduced amounts paid to plaintiffs by nearly 40%.[9] However, some states have dismissed award caps as unconstitutional.[10]

In the past, patients initiated malpractice claims only against those who had actually rendered the care. Recently, however, courts have extended malpractice liability to HMOs and other managed care organizations. In *Petrovich v. Share Health Plan of Illinois*, for example, the Illinois Supreme Court held that an HMO may incur vicarious liability for the malpractice of an independent-contractor physician under the doctrines of apparent and implied authority. The physician in that case had declined to order magnetic resonance imaging and computerized tomography on a patient later found to have oral carcinoma, since he believed that the HMO would not pay for the tests.[11] Similarly, in *Pappas v. Asbel*, the Pennsylvania Supreme Court held that a patient who sustained permanent quadriplegia from an epidural abscess could sue his HMO for negligently delaying his transfer to a facility where specialized neurosurgical intervention was available.[12] Other jurisdictions have allowed patients to sue managed care organizations for breaches of fiduciary duty—as, for example, where savings from denials of treatment were passed along to a physician-administrator in the form of a bonus.[13]

Managed care organizations have begun to protect themselves from vicarious liability claims by insisting that physicians agree to indemnify them for negligence claims brought against the physician. Under such an agreement, the physician may incur liability for the full amount of the claim, as well as for attorneys' fees and expenses. The physician also may forfeit the right to seek contribution from the managed care organization on a cross-claim.[14] In order to avoid substantial out-of-pocket losses, practitioners must ensure that their insurance policies do not limit or exclude contractual liability coverage.

FORMATION OF THE INSURANCE CONTRACT

Insurance coverage begins with the execution of a contract between the insurer and the insured. Like all contracts, this requires a lawful object, genuine assent of competent parties, and payment of sufficient consideration.

In a typical insurance transaction, the party seeking insurance contacts a broker or agent, who in turn procures coverage from an insurance company or underwriting association. A broker usually works for the consumer, while an agent generally represents the insurer. This distinction can be an important one, because the power of these intermediaries to bind the insurer can vary drastically.[15]

Insurers sometimes authorize agents to issue "binders," or short-term guarantees of coverage, pending the execution of the complete policy. As a general rule, however, the submission of a completed application to the insurer constitutes only an offer to purchase insurance. Coverage does not begin until the insurer receives the application, reviews it, and agrees to indemnify the applicant. Even so, the majority of courts now hold that an insurer is liable under an insurance contract when it has failed to act on an application within a reasonable time.

INTERPRETATION OF INSURANCE CONTRACTS

The language of a written contract defines the obligations of the parties. Conditions, limitations, and exceptions typically are negotiated by both sides and incorporated into the contract document. When litigation arises over one party's failure to perform, the wording of the agreement often determines the outcome.

Insurance policies differ from most contracts, however, in that they are adhesion contracts. Drafted by the insurer and submitted to the potential client on a "take it or leave it" basis, they place the insurer in a superior bargaining position by eliminating the client's opportunity to negotiate. Policyholders often do not understand terminology used by the insurer, or, indeed, they may agree to the coverage without reading the contract at all. Group policies are not adhesion contracts, but courts traditionally have treated them as such.[16]

To compensate for this inequity in bargaining power, the courts have adopted a rule of construction under which ambiguities in policy language are construed against the insurer.[17] Justified by the principles of waiver and estoppel, this rule is intended to protect the reasonable expectations of the policyholder—including the expectation that medical treatment generally will be covered. Accordingly, insurers often find themselves indemnifying policyholders as a result of contractual provisions that easily could be interpreted as creating no such obligation.[18] In *Ponder v. Blue Cross of Southern California*, for example, the California Court of Appeal allowed a patient to recover for treatment of temporomandibular joint syndrome despite language in the insurance certificate that explicitly excluded this syndrome from coverage. The court reasoned that the insurer had disappointed the expectations of the policyholder by failing to make the exclusion "plain" and "conspicuous."[19]

Much of the litigation arising from health insurance contracts revolves around eligibility for coverage. Courts often must decide whether the language of a policy obligates the insurer to indemnify a particular individual for a specific condition. The principal issue in many insurance disputes, then, is the scope of coverage intended by the parties at the time of contract formation.

In recent years, insurers have begun to include in their policies blanket exclusions for "experimental" or "medically unnecessary" services. These exclusions are meant to limit liability for expensive, and at times unproven, technology.

When a blanket exclusion provides the sole basis for denial of payment, the court generally will compel indemnification as long as the patient's physician has deemed the services necessary, even where the scientific community has not universally validated the service in question.[20] Courts are much more likely to uphold a denial of payment where the excluded treatments are enumerated in the policy, or where the method of determining medical necessity is clearly spelled out.[21]

Other types of exclusion clauses may appear in policies as well. Claims-made policies generally contain retroactive exclusion clauses, for example, which hold the insurer harmless for any incident that occurred before the date on which the insured first took out a policy with the company. This provision has no impact on new practitioners who take out their first malpractice policy with no preexisting claims to cover. Nor will it affect a practitioner who switches from an occurrence-based policy to any other policy, since the occurrence-based policy will cover claims made even after the policy expires. A gap can occur, however, when a claims-made policy terminates for any reason, because the former policy will not cover claims made after its effective period, and the latter policy will not cover incidents that occurred before it became effective.[22] Practitioners can avoid this kind of problem by purchasing a "reporting endorsement" from the issuer of the former policy. These endorsements amend claims-made policies to cover all incidents that occurred during the term of the policy, regardless of the date on which they are reported. Effectively, these endorsements convert claims-made policies into occurrence-based policies.

Some insurance policies also deny coverage where the insured had knowledge of a claim but failed to report it during the policy period. Insurers utilize such clauses to avoid assuming known risks. Some courts have interpreted such clauses strictly, while others have been accused of converting claims-made policies into occurrence-based ones by finding the insurer liable on the basis of "excusable delay" by the insured.[23]

Parties to all contracts, including insurance contracts, must adhere to a covenant of good faith and fair dealing.[24] In the past, courts treated a breach of this covenant as a breach of contract. Recovery therefore was limited to the amount specified in the policy. During the past quarter-century, however, a number of jurisdictions have held that a breach of good faith during insurance transactions can give rise to tort actions as well.[25] This is especially true in the context of liability insurance, where the insurer's interest in defending against a third-party claim often conflicts with the interest of the policyholder in settling the claim below the policy limit.

Communale v. Traders and General Insurance Company illustrates this principle. There, the insurer wrongfully refused to defend a liability action brought by a third party against the policyholder, and then refused an offer of settlement within the policy limits. The California Supreme Court held the insurer liable for the full amount of a third-party claim—including the portion that exceeded the policy limits—because of the insurer's bad faith in handling the claim.[26]

Policyholders owe insurers a duty of good faith as well, albeit a somewhat less stringent one. As the California Supreme Court noted in *Commercial Union Assurance Co. v. Safeway Stores, Inc.*, "We have no quarrel with the proposition that a duty of good faith and fair dealing in an insurance policy is a two-way street running from the insured to his insurer as well as vice versa. However, what that duty embraces is dependent upon the nature of the bargain struck between the insurer and the insured and the legitimate expectations of the parties which arise from the contract."[27] Under this rationale, a policyholder might incur tort liability to his insurer, where, for example, the insured's refusal to cooperate in an investigation results in the unnecessary payment of a claim.

At times, the doctrines of election, waiver, and estoppel can alter rights established by the written contract. Election is a choice between available rights that extinguishes the right not chosen. A policyholder may have a contractual right to receive disability benefits in a lump sum, for example, or in annual payments, or in the form of an annuity. Under the doctrine of election, a policyholder who has elected one of these methods of payment loses the right to demand a different method where a changing economic climate renders the original choice undesirable.[28]

A waiver is an intentional relinquishment of a known right.[29] Waivers may be written into the insurance contract, or their existence may be inferred from circumstances.[30] One type of waiver common to insurance policies is a "waiver of premium" that suspends the insurer's right to collect premium payments for a specified period of time—as, for example, where the policyholder becomes disabled and cannot work. Insurers typically offer this type of waiver to policyholders in exchange for slightly increased premiums during the life of the policy.[31] Once granted, an express waiver can be rescinded only by mutual agreement of the parties. Even a letter of notification does not restore the right previously waived.

Estoppel, in the context of insurance law, is a representation of fact, which, when relied upon by another party, renders any subsequent denial of obligation based on that representation unfair. The party claiming estoppel must show that the representation pertained to a material fact; that the reliance was reasonable; and that detriment resulted.[32] Thus, an insurer that erroneously names a party as an additional insured in an insurance certificate is estopped from denying coverage to that party.[33] Similarly, an insurer is estopped from denying coverage for nonpayment of premiums when it fails to send the insured a cancellation notice, after having done so on previous occasions.[34]

Insurers sometimes guard against estoppel-based obligations through the use of reservation-of-rights notices and nonwaiver agreements. The reservation-of-rights notice informs the policyholder that the insured intends to conduct an investigation for the purpose of determining coverage eligibility, and that the insurer's activities do not necessarily represent a defense against a third-party claim or a waiver of any future rights to deny coverage. This notification may prevent the insured from claiming that he relied on the insurer to defend against the claim, and that the insurer is therefore estopped from denying coverage. Because it is a unilateral action, however, a reservation-of-rights notice is not always effective. To be fully protected, the insurer may incorporate a nonwaiver agreement into the insurance contract. This agreement indicates that neither party will waive its rights under the policy as a result of an investigation or initial defense of the action until the extent of coverage has been determined.

FRAUD

Fraud renders an insurance contract voidable. In the context of an insurance contract, fraud exists where one party knowingly misrepresents a material fact with intent to deceive or with reckless indifference to the truth, thereby causing reliance and injury.[35] A material fact, in turn, is one that induces the other party to enter the contract. False statements of opinion generally do not constitute fraud.[36]

In the past, insurers often used their clients' misrepresentations to their advantage. The insurer would collect premiums over a long period of time, then deny a claim on the basis of some earlier misrepresentation by the insured.[37] State legislatures responded to the resulting widespread public suspicion of the insurance industry by requiring insurance contracts to include an "incontestability clause," under which the parties agree that the validity of the contract cannot be challenged after a specified period. These clauses do not bar all validity contests, of course. To the contrary, courts often permit insurers to challenge claims for nonpayment of premiums, or where the eligibility of the insured or the occurrence of a covered event is questioned, notwithstanding the existence of an incontestability clause.[38] These clauses originated in life insurance contracts. Today, however, many states require them by law to appear in health insurance policies as well.[39]

Most courts have held that insurance applicants retain a duty to disclose changes in material facts discovered prior to the onset of coverage. The courts generally agree, however, that this obligation ceases once the policy takes effect.

INSURANCE REGULATION

Prior to World War II, the courts did not treat insurance sales as transactions in commerce. As a result, the insurance industry enjoyed immunity from federal antitrust laws.[40]

Insurers worked in conjunction with rating bureaus to gather actuarial data and to establish uniform rates and policies.

A 1944 Supreme Court decision, *South-Eastern Underwriters Association v. U.S.*, temporarily disrupted this practice. In *South-Eastern*, the Court expanded the definition of commerce and held that insurance transactions were subject to federal regulation.[41] Congress recognized that state regulation of the insurance industry already was firmly established, however, and less than a year later, the McCarron-Ferguson Act effectively returned control to the states, subject to the limited applicability of federal antitrust laws.[42]

Today, state governments grant charters to insurance companies and license their agents, establish standards for the content and filing of policy forms, regulate marketing and claims practices, and investigate consumer complaints within the industry. States also strive to protect the solvency of insurers by imposing controls on insurers' financial reserves and investments—a role that is especially important given the aleatory nature of the insurance contract. In so doing, the state may prevent policyholders who pay premiums for many years from being disappointed by insurers that cannot meet their financial obligations upon the filing of a claim.

Many states dictate the premiums charged by property-casualty insurers. Rates for health and liability insurance, in contrast, are typically regulated only indirectly, through the application of Unfair Trade Practice Acts and requirements that policy forms be approved by the state insurance commissioner. The goal of this regulation is to strike a balance between affordability and availability. When malpractice premiums climb too high, physicians tend to migrate to other states, or to abandon the relevant area of practice altogether. This can lead to a shortage of specialists within the region.[43] Similarly, when health insurance premiums rise to a critical level, patients on fixed incomes may be left without access to health care. On the other hand, if premiums drop too low, the insurer risks insolvency, and it may elect to stop issuing certain kinds of insurance altogether. This, in turn, may leave practitioners without liability insurance, and patients without health insurance.

Despite these efforts, insolvencies sometimes do occur. To protect policyholders, states have established guarantee funds to ensure that claims will be paid even after insolvency. All states currently have property-casualty guarantee funds, and many states have created life and health funds as well. Through these funds, the rest of the insurance industry shoulders the burden of the insolvent company to ensure indemnification.

State legislatures have imposed thousands of mandates upon insurers and health plans that are unrelated to premium rates.[44] *Mandated provider laws* require insurers to pay specified practitioners if they would pay a medical doctor for the same service. *Mandated coverage laws* limit insurers' ability to cancel or refuse to renew policies.

Mandated benefit laws require payment for certain types of claims and, with regard to health insurance, payment for certain conditions. Some states have bolstered their mandated benefit laws through antidiscrimination statutes. Toward this end, insurance commissioners in New York and Massachusetts attempted to ban the use of HIV tests in determining insurability, but courts in both states subsequently invalidated the regulations.[45]

Most states have retained authority to oversee rate classification systems, which require policyholders with similar risks to pay the same premiums.[46] An emerging controversy in this area involves classification based on genetic characteristics.[47] Now that genetic markers make it possible to predict medical problems even before birth, insurers argue that they should be able to factor this information into risk classification. To ignore such predictors, they say, would be unfair to policyholders with favorable genetic characteristics, whose premiums will be inflated by the claims of those with poor genes. Consumer, disability, and privacy advocates, on the other hand, feel that insurers should not penalize afflicted individuals for conditions over which they have no control. Allowing genetic information to be used in such a way, they suggest, will result in more frequent insurance denials and increased dependence on public health insurance programs.

Federal statutes, too, have affected insurance in the health care setting. Congress passed the Employee Retirement Income Security Act of 1974 (ERISA) in response to fraud and mismanagement of employee pension funds. Because it governs employee welfare benefit plans, however, ERISA also covers employer-provided health insurance.[48] Congress intended ERISA as a regulatory statute, but its effects on health insurance have been principally deregulatory. By preempting state law, it precludes many actions that once could be brought in state courts. Excluded by ERISA, for example, are common law bad faith claims against ERISA-qualified health plans,[49] actions to compel referral to a specialist,[50] and actions to compel payment for a particular type of treatment[51] or condition.[52] The courts have distinguished between "quantity of benefits" issues and "quality of benefits" issues, however, and most jurisdictions have held that issues pertaining to the caliber of insurer-provided care are properly addressed by the states.[53] Moreover, ERISA establishes universal requirements regarding claims procedures,[54] determination review,[55] fiduciary obligations,[56] and disclosure of benefits to plan participants.[57]

The Comprehensive Omnibus Reconciliation Act of 1985 (COBRA) amended ERISA to mandate the continuation of group insurance for those who otherwise would lose such coverage as a result of layoffs, loss of dependent status, or other changes.[58] Applicable to entities that sponsor a group health plan and employ 20 or more persons on an average day, COBRA protects "qualified beneficiaries" whose insurance lapses because of a "qualifying event."

Qualifying beneficiaries include employees and their spouses and dependent children who were covered under the terminated insurance as of the day before the qualifying event, as well as children born or adopted during the continuation period.[59] Qualifying events for employees include reduction of hours and termination of employment for reasons other than gross misconduct.[60] Qualifying events for dependents include loss of coverage due to death of the employee, termination of the employee, or reduction in hours; loss of coverage due to divorce or legal separation from a covered employee; loss of coverage due to eligibility of the employee for Medicare; and loss of coverage due to changing status as a dependent of the covered employee.[61] Filing for bankruptcy can serve as a qualifying event where the covered employee has retired.[62] The duration of continuation coverage under COBRA ranges from 18 months to 36 months, depending on the qualifying beneficiary and event.[63] COBRA beneficiaries are entitled to the same health insurance coverage as regular plan participants,[64] and when the continuation period expires, the beneficiary may enroll in any conversion health plan that would have been available within the previous 180 days.[65]

The Health Insurance Portability and Accountability Act of 1996 (HIPAA) represents an effort by Congress to reduce health care fraud, simplify health care financing, establish more favorable tax treatment for medical savings accounts, and improve the portability and continuity of health insurance.[66] It limits the use of preexisting conditions clauses,[67] prohibits discrimination by insurers against individuals with regard to group health plan enrollment eligibility and premiums,[68] and limits the ability of insurers to deny coverage to small employers[69] and previously insured individuals.[70] HIPAA preempts state law, except where the state legislation affords equal or greater protection to the insured. Enacted along with HIPAA was one statute requiring group health plans to cover hospitalization for specified minimum periods in the event of childbirth,[71] and another that prohibits health plans from restricting annual or lifetime mental health benefits to a greater extent than physical health benefits.[72]

Another federal regulation, the Health Maintenance Act, governs HMOs. Amended several times since its adoption in 1973, this statute imposes a wide array of medical and organizational duties on qualified plans. Qualified plans obligations include providing health services "with reasonable promptness"; reimbursing members for emergency treatment obtained outside of the plan; accepting Medicaid beneficiaries; and taking precautions against insolvency.[73] HMO regulations of various types also have been enacted by every state.

NATIONAL PRACTITIONER DATA BANK

Since 1990 the medical and dental boards of the states have been required to report to the National Practitioner Data Bank certain disciplinary actions taken against the professionals they license. Professional societies, too, must report certain adverse actions taken against their members,[74] while insurers must report all malpractice payments.[75] The U.S. Department of Health and Human Services makes this information available to state licensure boards and certain health care entities to facilitate the tracking of professionals who are disciplined in one state, then seek licensure in another. Health care facilities must query the Data Bank at least every two years regarding each member of their staff.[76]

Created by Congress as part of the Health Care Quality Improvement Act of 1986, the Data Bank immediately became the subject of controversy. The Department of Health and Human Services requires state licensure boards to report all revocations, suspensions, censures, reprimands, probations, and license surrenders, as well as revisions to such actions, including reinstatements.[77] Denials of initial applications and fines unaccompanied by licensing restrictions need not be reported, however.[78] This has caused some observers to speculate that state licensing boards are tailoring penalties so as to avoid the reporting requirement.[79]

Controversial, too, has been the Data Bank's role in the issue of closure. In the past, settlement provided physicians with peace of mind over malpractice claims. Now, though, with practitioners precluded by law from contesting the merits of any claim mentioned within the Data Bank, malpractice settlements become a permanent part of the practitioner's record. And while insurers do not have access to information contained within the Data Bank, some physicians have claimed that they have been required to produce their own Data Bank records as a condition of coverage.[80] If true, this means that an insurer's decision to settle a malpractice claim—which may have more to do with finances than the actual wrongdoing of the defendant practitioner—will leave a permanent scar on the practitioner's record, which in turn can affect the ability of the practitioner to obtain malpractice insurance in the future. Unfortunately, most policies allow the insurance carrier to make settlements without the consent of the insured physician. In addition, insurance carriers are unwilling to relinquish control of their ability to induce settlement.

INSURANCE ACCOUNTING

Insurers must provide accurate financial information to a number of interested parties, including the state insurance commissions that have jurisdiction over their activities. The National Association of Insurance Commissioners has assisted insurers in this role by establishing uniform accounting standards for use by insurers when filing statements with government entities. Unlike other businesses, insurers often do not become aware of revenues and losses until many years after the relevant accounting period has closed. This is especially true with regard to "long-tail" lines of insurance, such as medical malpractice insurance. By the time a patient detects a problem, files a claim, and litigates it to completion, 25 years may have elapsed since the policy terminated. Insurance accounting therefore requires unique practices.

The most important of these practices entails the creation of loss reserves. To ensure that sufficient assets will be available to pay future claims, the insurer must estimate those claims as accurately as possible. Insurers often base their reserves on average claim values, or on the typical ratio between premiums and losses for a particular type of claim. Where a type of claim tends to be large and relatively infrequent, however, an insurer generally will include in its loss reserve an estimate of the amount necessary to ultimately settle each claim. Because of their size, medical malpractice claims usually rate this type of individualized attention.

When establishing loss reserves, insurers must consider not only known losses, but also losses that are incurred and not reported. Fewer than 10% of all medical malpractice claims are reported during the policy year in which they occur, and almost none of these claims result in final payment during that period. To avoid understating its financial position, an insurer often will employ the services of an actuary, who can analyze past reporting trends to determine the percentage of claims likely to be filed after the close of a particular policy year. The insurer then can add this amount to estimated known losses to create a more realistic loss reserve.

ENDNOTES

1. Congressional Research Service, *Health Insurance and the Uninsured: Background Data and Analyses* (1988).
2. *Id.*
3. 29 U.S.C.A. §§1001-1461.
4. 42 U.S.C.A. §§300e to 300e-17.
5. 29 U.S.C.A. §§1161-1168.
6. Pub. L. 104-191 (codified as amended in scattered sections of 29 U.S.C.A.).
7. Josh Goldstein, *S.J. Medical Leaders Huddle over Malpractice Insurance*, Philadelphia Inquirer, Nov. 23, 2002, at C1.
8. *The Insurance Crisis: Now Everyone Is in a Risky Business*, Business Week, March 10, 1986, at 88.
9. *See* Frank A. Sloan et al., *Effects of Tort Reforms on the Value of Closed Medical Malpractice Claims: A Microanalysis*, 14 J. Health Pol., Pol., & Law 663 (1989).
10. *See, e.g., Lakin v. Senco Prod., Inc.*, 987 P. 2d 463 (Ore. 1999) (holding that caps violate plaintiffs' right to jury trial); *Smith v. Schulte*, 671 So. 2d 1334 (Ala. 1995) (equal protection violation); *Knowles v. U.S.*, 544 N.W. 2d 183 (S.D. 1996) (substantive due process violation).
11. *Petrovich v. Share Health Plan of Illinois, Inc.*, 719 N.E. 2d 756 (Ill. 1999). *But see Jones v. U.S. Healthcare*, 723 N.Y.S. 2d 478 (N.Y. App. Div. 2001) (vicarious liability held not to exist where insurance document expressly described defendant HMO's physicians as "independent contractors").
12. *Pappas v. Asbel*, No. 98 E.D. App. Dkt. 1996 (Pa. Apr. 3, 2001).
13. *Herdrich v. Pegram*, 154 F. 3d 362 (7th Cir. 1998).
14. *See Dunn v. Praiss*, 656 A. 2d 413 (N.J. 1995).
15. *County Forest Prod., Inc. v. Green Mountain Agency, Inc.*, 758 A. 2d 59 (Me. 2000).
16. *McLaughlin v. Connecticut Gen. Life Ins. Co.*, 565 F.Supp. 434 (N.D. Cal. 1983).
17. Robert E. Keeton, *Insurance Law Rights at Variance with Policy Provisions*, 83 Harv. L. Rev. 961 (1971).
18. *Providence Hosp. v. Morrell*, 427 N.W. 2d 531 (Mich. 1988).
19. *Ponder v. Blue Cross of Southern California*, 193 Cal. Rptr. 632 (Cal. Ct. App. 1983).
20. *See* Mark A. Hall & Gerard F. Anderson, *Health Insurers' Assessment of Medical Necessity*, 140 U. Pa. L. Rev. 1637 (1992).
21. *Stock v. SHARE*, 18 F. 3d 1419 (8th Cir. 1994).
22. *See Gereboff v. Home Indemnity Co.*, 383 A. 2d 1024 (R.I. 1978).
23. *Stine v. Continental Cas. Co.*, 315 N.W. 2d 887 (Mich. Ct. App. 1982).
24. *Communale v. Traders & Gen. Ins. Co.*, 328 P. 2d 198 (Cal. 1958).
25. *See Frazier v. Metropolitan Life Ins. Co.*, 214 Cal. Rptr. 883 (Cal. Ct. App. 1983).
26. *Communale, supra* note 24.
27. *Commercial Union Assurance Co. v. Safeway Stores, Inc.*, 610 P. 2d 1038 (Ca. 1980).
28. *See Biggus v. Ford Motor Credit Co.*, 613 A. 2d 986 (Md. App. 1992).
29. *Wadia Enterprises, Inc. v. Hirschfeld*, 618 A. 2d 506 (Conn. 1992).
30. *Novella v. Hartford Accident & Indem. Co.*, 316 A. 2d 394 (Conn. 1972).
31. *See Protective Life Ins. Co. v. Sullivan*, 682 N.E. 2d 624 (Mass. 1997).
32. *Grimberg v. Marth*, 659 A. 2d. 1287 (Md. App. 1985).
33. *Lenox Realty, Inc. v. Excelsior Ins. Co.*, 679 N.Y.S. 749 (N.Y. App. Div. 1998).
34. *Minnick v. State Farm. Mut. Auto Ins. Co.*, 174 A. 2d 706 (Del. 1961).
35. *Zimmerman v. Continental Cas. Co.*, 150 N.W. 2d 268 (Neb. 1967).
36. *Vackiner v. Mutual of Omaha Ins. Co.*, 137 N.W. 2d 859 (Neb. 1965).
37. *Powell v. Mut. Life Ins. Co. of N.Y.*, 144 Ill. 825 (Ill. 1924).
38. *Crawford v. Equitable Life Assurance Soc'y of United States*, 305 N.E. 2d 144 (Ill. 1973).
39. *See, e.g.*, Mass. Gen. Laws ch. 175, §108 (2002).
40. *Paul v. Virginia*, 75 U.S. (8 Wall.) 168 (1868).
41. *South-Eastern Underwriters Ass'n. v. U.S.*, 322 U.S. 533 (1944), *reh'g denied*, 323 U.S. 811 (1944).
42. McCarron-Ferguson Act, 15 U.S.C. §1011.
43. Goldstein, *supra* note 7.
44. *More Mandates on Their Minds*, 17 Bus. & Health 20 (1999).
45. *Health Ins. Ass'n of America v. Corcoran*, 551 N.Y.S. 2d 615 (N.Y. App. Div. 1990); *Life Ins. Ass'n of Mass. v. Comm'r of Ins.*, 530 N.E. 2d 168 (Mass. 1988).
46. *See, e.g., Colonial Life Ins. Co. of America v. Curiale*, 617 N.Y.S. 2d 377 (N.Y. App. Div. 1994).
47. Barbara Berry, *The Human Genome Project and the End of Insurance*, 7 U. Fla. J. L & Public Pol'y 205 (1996).
48. 29 U.S.C.A. §§1003(a), 1002(1).
49. *Pilot Life Ins. Co. v. Dedeaux*, 481 U.S. 41 (1987).
50. *Pell v. Shmokler*, 1997 WL 83743 (E.D. Pa. 1997).
51. *Parrino v. FHP, Inc.*, 146 F. 3d 699 (9th Cir. 1998) (claim for denial of proton beam therapy for brain tumor held precluded).
52. *Brandon v. Aetna Servs., Inc.*, 46 F.Supp. 2d 110 (D.C. Conn. 1999) (claim against plan administrator who refused to pay for treatment of anxiety disorder held preempted).
53. *Dukes v. U.S. Healthcare, Inc.*, 57 F. 3d 350 (3d Cir. 1995).
54. 29 C.F.R. §2560.503-1.
55. 29 U.S.C.A., §1132(a)(3).
56. 29 U.S.C.A. §1104.
57. 29 C.F.R. §2520.102-2 to -4.
58. 29 U.S.C.A. §§1161-68.
59. 29 U.S.C.A. §1167(3); 42 U.S.C.A. §300bb-8(3).
60. 29 U.S.C.A. §1163(2); 42 U.S.C.A. §300bb-3(2).
61. 29 U.S.C.A. §1163; 42 U.S.C.A. §300bb-3.

62. 29 U.S.C.A. §§1163(3)(C); 1163(6).

63. 29 U.S.C.A. §1162(2)(A)(ii); 42 U.S.C.A. §§300bb-2(2)(A)(ii).

64. 29 U.S.C.A. §1162(1); 42 U.S.C.A. §300bb-2(1),

65. 29 U.S.C.A. §1162(5); 42 U.S.C.A. §300bb-2(5).

66. 29 U.S.C.A. §§1181-82; 42 U.S.C.A. §300gg-41.

67. 29 U.S.C.A. §§1181(a)(1), 300gg(a)(1).

68. 29 U.S.C.A. §1182(a), (b).

69. 42 U.S.C.A. §§300gg-11(a).

70. 42 U.S.C.A. §§300gg-41(a), (b).

71. 42 U.S.C.A. §1185a.

72. 42 U.S.C.A. §1185a(a).

73. 42 U.S.C. §§300e to 300e-17.

74. 42 U.S.C.A. §11132.

75. 45 C.F.R. §60.7.

76. 42 U.S.C.A. §11135(a).

77. 45 C.F.R. §60.8.

78. Department of Health and Human Services, *National Practitioner Data Bank Guidebook Supplement* (August 1992).

79. Fitzhugh Mullan et al., *The National Practitioner Data Bank: Report from the First Year*, 268 J.A.M.A. 73 (1992).

80. Brian McCormick, *Debate on Data Bank Reveals Physicians' Frustrations*, 34 Am. Med. News 5(1) (July 8, 1991).

Risk Management

RICHARD R. BALSAMO, M.D., J.D., F.C.L.M.
MAX DOUGLAS BROWN, J.D.

ORIGIN AND SCOPE
RISK IDENTIFICATION
RISK PRIORITIZATION
RISK CONTROL
RECENT DEVELOPMENT: USE OF ALTERNATIVE DISPUTE RESOLUTION
RISK PREVENTION
RISK FINANCING
EXTERNAL REQUIREMENTS
CONCLUSION

ORIGIN AND SCOPE

Risk management programs began in the 1970s as a response to increasing numbers of medical malpractice claims of hospitals, and they have since been adopted by other types of health care organizations. Risk management is the process of protecting an organization's financial assets against losses from legal liability. It is defined by the Joint Commission on Accreditation of Healthcare Organizations (JCAHO) as "clinical and administrative activities that [health care organizations] undertake to identify, evaluate, and reduce the risk of injury and loss to patients, personnel, visitors, and [the organization] itself."[1]

Comprehensive risk management is both reactive in its response to events that have already occurred and proactive in its prevention of further occurrences. The primary responsibilities of a comprehensive risk management program are identification of legal risk, prioritization of identified risk, determination of proper organizational response to risk, management of recognized risk cases with the goal of minimizing loss (risk control), establishment of effective risk prevention, and maintenance of adequate risk financing. Risk management in a health care organization requires knowledge of the law and of the legal process, an understanding of clinical medicine, and familiarity with the organization's administrative structure and operational realities.

The full scope of risk management encompasses all organizational activity—operational and clinical—because liability may originate in either area. This purview includes proper building maintenance and food preparation as well as adverse outcomes of medical care and accurate medical record keeping. This chapter, however, focuses on risk management as it relates to the medical care that is provided by a

health care organization, called *"clinical" risk management.* Clinical risk management requires close cooperation between the legal department and the clinical administrators responsible for quality assessment and improvement and for clinical functional units (e.g., a hospital patient care unit, a medical office, or the physical therapy department).

Risk management is usually the prime responsibility of either a risk management department or the legal department, which in carrying out this function typically establishes a close working relationship with the clinical administrative staff. Nevertheless, important risk management functions, such as risk identification, clinical case review, and clinical risk prevention, are the direct responsibility of the clinical staff. Many organizations employ specialized staff, commonly called *risk managers*, who often have training and experience in a clinical field, such as nursing, to work with the legal staff and take day-to-day responsibility for some specified risk management functions, such as the management of recognized risk cases (risk control) and the coordination of overall risk management activity. In this chapter the term *risk administrators* refers to those individuals in an organization with formal, organization-wide risk management responsibility, most notably the legal staff and risk managers. In the context of clinical duties, the term's meaning incorporates clinical administrators such as the director of quality assessment and improvement (quality management) and the chief medical staff officer.

Role

The escalating frequency of litigation and the decreasing affordability of liability insurance have generated the demand for increased sophistication in the identification, control, prevention, and financing of medical risk. For example, the trust fund of a self-insured hospital represents a sizable and important asset of that hospital. A highly synergistic commonality of purpose exists between financial management and risk management. A risk administrator seeks to manage what is substantially a financial risk—the loss of financial assets. This loss occurs through the payment of claims for damages and expenses arising from untoward events that become potentially compensable through judgments or settlements and that may erode the hospital's assets and increase the cost of providing health care.[2]

Although the basic purpose of a risk management program is to minimize the cost of loss, there is a tendency to evaluate a risk management program solely from a financial standpoint with regard to current cases and claims. Most administrators of successful risk management programs agree that such a "bottom line" view misses the overriding purpose of a clinical risk management program. Risk management in a health care institutional setting should be considered first and foremost a means of improving and maintaining quality patient care—the cornerstone of risk prevention.[3]

In pursuing this goal, risk administrators must have a close, trusting relationship with the clinical administrators who have direct responsibility for many risk management functions. Effective risk management depends on their active participation. Moreover, formal organizational quality assessment and improvement functions should be operationally linked to the risk management program. This linkage should include the exchange of all relevant information and the sharing of formal risk management responsibilities to maximize the understanding of all risk management issues, specific cases, and organizational data. Nonclinical risk administrators must have quick, thorough, and reliable access to medical consultation about clinical issues, specific cases, and organization performance data. The proper relationship avoids duplication of effort, the potential for misunderstanding between the clinical and legal staffs, and the potential to work at cross-purposes in carrying out specific risk management functions.

Risk administrators and quality managers in turn must be operationally linked to and influential in the overall management of the organization. For example, tragic consequences can befall the health maintenance organization (HMO) whose risk and quality administrators' efforts to reverse increasing risk exposure resulting from poor after-hours access to care are ignored and defeated by a financially driven, organization-wide effort to reduce emergency room use.

Despite the necessity of a close working relationship, risk management and quality management are not ideally combined in one department. Risk management is an extension of the legal responsibilities of an organization. Thus an attorney ultimately should direct risk management activity.

Fulfillment of quality management responsibilities requires detailed medical knowledge and the trust, respect, and attention of the medical staff. Thus quality management activity is best led and directed by a physician.

An effective risk management program begins with its system for identifying the specific events likely to result in loss and the general clinical areas of risk exposure. This system should be predicated on a current, thorough understanding of the varied sources of legal risk faced by a health care organization. Risk management then proceeds to risk prioritization, risk control, risk prevention, and risk financing.

Sources of legal risk: new developments and recent trends

Detailed discussion of the varied sources of legal risk that confront health care providers is covered elsewhere in this text and is beyond the scope of this chapter. However, it may be useful here to point out some recent data and trends that indicate the developing legal risks that are especially problematic for health care providers.[4]

The legal risk most commonly associated with the health care organization is medical malpractice. One of the more recent reports to provide detailed data on the clinical and operational sources of malpractice risk is that provided by St. Paul Fire and Marine Insurance Company in its 1999 year-end report. In this report, St. Paul offered its policyholders an analysis of claims of physicians and surgeons for the period between July 1997 and June 1999. Appendixes 17-1 through 17-3 demonstrate, respectively, St. Paul's findings as to the top 10 malpractice allegations by average cost, the top 10 malpractice allegations by frequency, and all malpractice allegations by location.

The growing use of clinical practice guidelines may develop as a cause of increased medical malpractice risk.[5] When followed, practice guidelines are widely viewed as means to improve the quality and appropriateness of care and as shields against liability. Unquestionably they provide great benefits to the extent that they improve the quality and efficiency of care. Unfortunately, they also have the potential to stultify and codify the practice of medicine by establishing innumerable sets of microstandards useful to plaintiffs in proving a departure from the standard of care. In the absence of legal protection accompanying their adoption, fear of deviating from guidelines and the difficulty of remembering their many details may bedevil physicians in years to come.

Another developing contributor to medical malpractice risk is the sometimes inordinate deference given to the principle of patient control over treatment choices. Obstetrical care may be the most problematic area. Today, many patients demand home deliveries, impose restrictions on care given to infants, and even refuse cesarean sections, all of which may pose a grave danger to an infant's health and increase the likelihood of an adverse outcome. Courts have generally been tolerant of patients' asserting their right to pick and choose how obstetrical care will be provided. At the same time, this attitude causes great unease among risk administrators, who note that the single most costly source of risk to a health care organization is birth-related infant trauma, which usually can be avoided by cesarean section. In the absence of reasonable limitations on patient choices, it is fully expected that childbirth-related trauma and other adverse outcomes stemming from increasing patient control over care will grow even more costly to both physicians and their health care organizations.

Failure to obtain informed consent is another important source of risk. It may give rise to an intentional tort or may be a secondary count in a medical malpractice action. States are divided in their approach to determining what information must be provided to patients to enable them to decide whether to accept the risks of proposed treatment. Some states require the disclosure of information that a reasonable physician would disclose to that patient, whereas others require the disclosure of information that a reasonable patient would feel was material to his or her decision of whether to accept the risks of treatment. As more clinical outcomes performance data become available, those data may play an increasingly important role in determining the content of disclosure. Risk administrators must be aware of and educate their physicians about the need to meet the legal standard of disclosure, particularly if their organizations are located in states applying the "reasonable patient" standard. For example, a patient preparing to undergo heart bypass surgery at a hospital that is a high mortality outlier for this surgery might expect such information to be disclosed when the risks of surgery are discussed. In a cogent essay, physicians Topol and Califf argue for more extensive disclosure to patients of institution- and physician-specific outcomes data. Using coronary artery bypass surgery as an example, they suggest the following:

In the future, an ideal approach would be to shift "full disclosure" to inform patients. On the consent forms that patients sign before the procedure, the cardiologist and cardiac surgeon could include their actual risk and success rates, when appropriate, for the past several years, the cumulative number of procedures the physician has done, and the site's overall rate of complications for the procedure. This up-front disclosure to patients would be revolutionary because it is rarely practiced today. Without furnishing such data up front, we are not truly providing informed consent.[6]

Within the context of a patient's right to consent to or refuse treatment, an important question is whether care or treatment may be withheld or withdrawn from certain patients. The law in this area remains in a rather formative stage and varies from jurisdiction to jurisdiction. Generally speaking, care may be withheld if such care or treatment would be futile or would only delay the certainty of death. Withdrawal of care that has already been initiated is more

problematic. In the absence of death, reliance may be given to living wills and durable powers of attorney for health care that under certain circumstances allow for care to be withdrawn. One or the other of these two types of advance directives is recognized by most states. In addition, some states have enacted health care surrogacy acts, which permit individuals other than the patient (usually the next of kin) in the absence of an advance directive to consent to or refuse medical care on behalf of a patient who lacks decisional capacity and may be terminally ill, in a persistent vegetative state, or suffering from an incurable or irreversible condition that will ultimately cause death. On the condition that they follow in detail the requirements set forth, these acts generally provide immunity from suit for health care providers who withdraw care from patients. In the absence of the death of a patient and in the absence of an executed advance directive, withdrawal of care may still be permissible on the order of a court of competent jurisdiction. Although resorting to courts may be costly and time-consuming and may generate media exposure, recourse to a court of law in an area that has not been previously clarified in a particular jurisdiction will provide the greatest amount of protection to the hospital, patient, family members, and other health care providers.

Another developing area of medical care–associated risk is maintenance of confidentiality. Examination of state law reveals an array of privacy protections, frequently with gaps and areas of uncertainty. Often, paper records are presumed, so the status of electronic data is unclear. Consequently a developing area of risk is the release of electronic, patient-level data to government regulators, business coalitions, insurers, and quality monitoring projects. A health care organization's marketing, information systems, and quality management staff may be insufficiently aware of confidentiality issues and therefore may release data with patient identifiers, such as name, address, and social security number, linked with personal information, such as diagnoses and procedures. All staff should be educated about the importance of maintaining patient confidentiality and should ensure that any electronic patient information released from their organization without specific patient consent is stripped of externally recognizable unique patient identifiers and is allowable under law.

Increasingly, health care institutions will be held accountable for the actions of providers on their staffs through the expansion of the corporate negligence theory, in which institutions have been held to have duties to properly maintain their facilities, to have available the necessary equipment, to hire, supervise, and retain competent and adequate provider staff, and to develop and implement policies and procedures that promote quality care. More recently, many courts have enhanced the corporate responsibility of health care institutions through the use of agency theory and a more expansive concept of corporate negligence, incorporating the duty to protect patients from medical staff negligence through the assumption of more control over the quality of care delivered within its facility and the duty to properly credential medical staff members.[7] The federal Health Care Quality Improvement Act of 1986 extended the corporate responsibility of health care organizations by requiring them to make reports to and check with the National Practitioner Data Bank maintained by the Department of Health and Human Services. Failure to check the data bank may subject an organization to the burden of being constructively informed of (i.e., deemed to have knowledge of) the information it would have received had it done so, with this information being admissible in medical malpractice actions.

Finally, important developing sources of medical liability risk for both managed care insurers and managed care providers are found in the areas of utilization review, benefit determination, and capitation reimbursement. The line between insuring care and directing care is rapidly evaporating. Insurers have exerted leverage through a variety of maneuvers, such as requiring second opinions, denying claims, and canceling provider agreements. In the trade-off of discounted fees for patient referrals, the best interests of patients may not always be given sufficient consideration. It is likely that this will be an area of increasing controversy between patients and health care organizations. Although verdicts against managed care organizations (MCOs) may serve as a wake-up call to insurers (e.g., *Fox v. Health Net of California*), hospitals and physicians have no immunity from being equally culpable if medical decisions are made on financial grounds.[8] Risk administrators of MCOs should be vigilant in searching for inappropriate financial incentives to limit benefit coverage and utilization of services.

RISK IDENTIFICATION

Importance of early risk identification

Risk of financial loss through legal liability presents itself to an organization in one of two ways. It can appear in the form of an individual patient event that, on inspection, carries with it a significant risk of liability. The actions that may result in liability in a specific case could be unique to that case or could be part of a general pattern of problem care or activity that can be referred to as *risk exposure*. Risk exposure can be identified even in the absence of a specific risk case related to it because a pattern of activity may be "risky" in terms of liability even though no specific patient injury related to that activity has yet occurred. The earliest recognition of both types of risk is crucial to a health care organization and as such is a fundamental risk management activity.[9]

The benefit of early risk detection is that it enables risk administrators to conduct the earliest possible investigation of any identified risk cases and to intervene against risk exposure with prevention strategies before any, or at least

further, risk cases develop. Successful risk management departments do not wait to be sued before undertaking an investigation of a case and establishing a defense or settlement posture. Within a 2-year time (the period for most statutes of limitations pertaining to medical malpractice), valuable testimony and evidence about a risk case may be lost. All health care organizations should have a set of methods in place to obtain the earliest possible notice or warning of a specific risk case or risk exposure. Quick recognition of a risk case can enable attorneys and risk managers to record the facts of the case when the events are fresh in the minds of the participants and to counsel members of the organization on how to respond to the event. A particular opportunity exists to ensure that the organization delivers subsequent care and administrative services in an expedited and satisfactory way to minimize any patient and family anger over the incident. With proper methods in place, a risk management program should have knowledge of most risk cases long before service of process is made. More sophisticated risk management programs should have notice of 75% or more of the incidents that eventually result in lawsuits filed against the organization.

Methods

Most health care organizations use a variety of means to identify risk cases and risk exposure. In reactive case identification an organization assesses for risk in cases identified external to the organization as being problematic. In proactive case identification an organization initiates the identification of cases that are more likely than others to contain risk. Finally, in data-based performance monitoring an organization moves beyond the individual case as the basis of risk identification and focuses on performance monitoring as the means to uncover risk exposure. Risk administrators should use each of these three general approaches in their identification of risk cases and risk exposure. These approaches are complementary, for risk detected by one may be entirely missed by the others. Risk management programs that rely on only one or two of the approaches run the great danger of failing to recognize all identifiable risk cases and areas of risk exposure. However, some methods within each approach are more likely than others to detect risk, so risk administrators with limited resources should select those methods that are most cost-effective in their organizations. Once a case has been identified as a risk case it is managed according to the principles discussed in later sections on risk prioritization and risk control.

External case identification

Legal actions. The easiest and most instinctive approach to the identification of risk is the assessment of clinical events that come to an organization's attention in the ordinary conduct of its business. The clearest example of this is a lawsuit. Every organization is compelled to assess and respond to legal actions against it. Such an assessment usually entails a careful examination of the specific circumstances of the clinical case, including a peer review of the medical record. By definition, a lawsuit establishes a case as a risk case because even if an organization feels that the likelihood of loss from liability is small, the cost of preparing for litigation and the cost of the litigation itself amount to a significant financial loss even without the finding of liability.

Medical record requests. The review of medical records requested by attorneys is another method by which risk can be identified. The fact that an attorney is requesting the records indicates that the case is involved in some legal activity, and some organizations routinely review all such cases. However, reviewing all attorney-requested records, no matter how natural it may seem as a response, can be problematic. First, medical records may be requested for reasons other than suspicion of wrongdoing by providers or institution (e.g., disputes involving payment of claims or worker's compensation). In the absence of knowledge about the reason for the record request, detailed review of every requested record can be an unfocused activity that may produce a low yield of findings and hence may not be cost-effective. At the same time, a cursory review of requested records might produce reliable identification of those cases deserving more detailed review.

Patient complaints. Review of patient complaints is a good way to detect cases with risk and poor quality. Many organizations have a formalized mechanism for handling patient complaints. Often, descriptive statistics of patient complaints are generated routinely, such as a monthly compilation of all complaints by type, clinical/administrative area, and involved providers. A focused review of complaints that on their face suggest risk or poor quality can be a reasonably productive undertaking when attempting to discover problematic cases.

Billing disputes. Often, patients refuse to pay bills because they believe that the care received was substandard and therefore not deserving of payment. As a result, like patient complaints, review of billing disputes is an excellent method of identifying risk and quality deficiencies. However, the cost-effectiveness of reviewing billing disputes is compromised because some patients make accusations of poor quality simply to justify their refusal to pay for care. Even reviewing the records of only those billing disputes in which there is an accusation of poor quality would result in the review of many cases in which the accusation was knowingly unfounded. Detailed clinical review of all cases resulting in a billing dispute should probably be reserved for cases involving either large sums of money or significant accusations of substandard quality.

Internal case identification

Occurrence (incident) reporting. Rather than wait for a legal action, a record request, a patient complaint, or a billing dispute to initiate the process of risk identification, most organizations ask their staff to notify the risk management or legal department whenever an untoward or unusual incident occurs. This process is often referred to as *occurrence reporting*. Often a special form, commonly referred to as an *incident report form*, is provided for this purpose. This form indicates the minimum, specific information that must be provided about the incident (Appendix 17-4 is an example). Although the information contained in incident reports is commonly protected from legal discovery by state law, some institutions request that reports of patient harm resulting from medical misdiagnoses, therapies, and procedures be reported verbally rather than in writing.

Incident reporting can be useful in identifying areas of risk exposure. Its usefulness as a method of identifying specific risk cases is limited, however, by a number of factors. The reliability of incident reporting can be compromised by the clinical staff's failure to appreciate a risk case or an area of risk exposure, uncertainty about what events to report, fear of getting involved, ignorance of how to file a report, and apathy. Risk administrators must recognize these barriers to reliable incident reporting and take active steps to eliminate them. Risk administrators should work hard to establish a trusting relationship with all physicians, who often see incident reporting as a nursing function and are wary of admitting the occurrence of adverse clinical outcomes. Physicians should be continually reassured that their communications will be held in the strictest confidence and that their statements will be protected from legal discovery. Physicians should be allowed to report incidents verbally, which should make reporting easier and somewhat alleviate their fear of reporting.

Progressive organizations actively cultivate a network of risk-sensitive and risk-educated clinical and administrative staff to facilitate incident reporting—a matrix of what can be called *risk management champions*. This effort is especially directed at having risk management champions in important areas of patient care and patient interaction. The theory underlying this matrix approach to information gathering is that within an organizational infrastructure (departments, units, sections, and ancillary services) there are certain essential intersections through which potential plaintiffs are likely to pass. Important intersections include a hospital's surgical recovery room, emergency room, intensive care unit, and patient relations department. In addition, the utilization management department, given its expanding role both in hospitals and in MCOs and the detailed data bases used, can be one of the best and most reliable sources of information about potential risk cases. Furthermore, the clinical departments of radiology and perhaps even more importantly pathology often are recipients of crucial information that medical malfeasance has occurred. Progressive risk administrators aggressively solicit and maintain a network of risk management champions located in important areas of patient contact.

A refinement of incident reporting is specified occurrence reporting. With this method, risk administrators specify a set of events that must be reported by staff. This approach takes incident reporting a step further to educate the staff about what specific events must be reported. Staffs are nonetheless still encouraged to report any unspecified event or possible area of risk exposure. Specified occurrences can be significant adverse outcomes of medical care (such as significant postoperative complications), accidents or mishaps in the provision of ancillary medical services (such as needle stick injuries), and non–medical-care-related accidents that occur in the institution (such as slip and fall injuries). Many of the specified occurrences are organization-specific based on the particular risk exposure history.

Random medical record review. Random medical record review was one of the first proactive approaches taken to uncover problem cases. It consisted of unfocused peer review of randomly selected medical records and for a time was a widespread "quality assurance" activity. However, because of its low yield of positive findings, it has now fallen into disfavor as a method of case identification in quality management. It never found use in risk management because the less frequent occurrence of risk, compared with quality deficiency, made this method cost-ineffective for risk identification. Nevertheless a program of random medical record review by providers can be beneficial in educating them about the wide variety of practice styles and approaches present among the staff and over time may lead to a group consensus on the identity of relatively weak performers.

Occurrence screening. In an effort to avoid the potential unreliability of occurrence reporting, many risk administrators identify groups of cases for screening review without depending on reporting from the staff. This method identifies groups of cases in which the yield of detailed review is likely to be higher than with routine review of cases identified through incident reporting (or its variant of specified occurrence reporting). The criteria used to identify cases for review are event based (e.g., all emergency room deaths) and can be specified as the result of a known institutional area of concern about clinical quality or risk (e.g., all coronary care unit deaths from cardiac dysrhythmias). The event that flags a case for review can on its face represent a quality problem (e.g., all medication errors), which may or may not create risk depending on the specific facts of the case, or can be nonspecific (generic). The latter events are generic in the sense that they are not particular to a certain type of case or a certain field of medical practice. Commonly used generic screening events, often called *generic indicators*, include unexpected in-patient death, unplanned postoperative return to the operating room during the same admission, and unplanned postdischarge readmission to the hospital within a specified time period (such as 14 days). The occurrence of a generic event does not imply a quality deficiency or the presence of risk in that case. That is, the fact that a patient recently discharged from the hospital needed to be readmitted within 14 days of discharge does not imply a quality or risk problem. Each case identified by a generic occurrence indicator must be carefully reviewed to determine whether any quality deficiency or risk is present.

Occurrence screening has found wider use in quality management than in risk management, where the approach to case evaluation is still based primarily on external case identification and occurrence reporting. Even in quality management, though, occurrence screening has met with mixed results as a method for uncovering quality deficiencies. Most cases that meet a criterion are not found by detailed peer review to have a quality deficiency, leading many to conclude that the expense involved in identifying the cases and then having them all reviewed by busy professionals is not justified by the relatively low yield of findings. The growing consensus is that most cases with quality problems and risk are not detected by the widely used generic screening criteria, and that of the cases that do meet screening criteria, after careful and time-consuming review most do not contain risk or a quality deficiency.

Case evaluation

Once a case has been identified as a possible risk case through one of the methods just discussed, the medical record is reviewed clinically. A physician who is an experienced reviewer of cases and who has an understanding of the potential sources of liability should first review the case. This physician should recognize the need to be completely objective in assessing for quality of care deficiencies, a risk event, and risk exposure. This physician may have a formal administrative role in the organization, such as the medical director overseeing the quality management activity. If the care is squarely within the field of the experienced physician reviewer, that review may be the only one necessary, especially if the physician finds no arguable evidence of quality deficiency or risk. In any cases of doubt the physician reviewer should refer the case to another physician for a second review. Risk administrators should realize that complex cases often involve care in more than one clinical field. Therefore it is imperative that all aspects of the patient's care be carefully reviewed. This may require a review by an internist or pediatrician (general or subspecialized) of surgical cases because all surgical cases involve at least some "medical" care.

Evaluation of clinical care by peer review usually includes determination of any culpability of the involved providers and institution. The results of case review can help assess the risk in that specific case, as well as identify organizational risk exposure or substandard providers. Unfortunately, peer case review as a method of identification of risk and quality deficiency is compromised by the understandable reluctance of clinicians conducting the review to criticize the care provided by colleagues with whom they may practice and socialize. This reluctance is magnified by the frequent defensive posture of clinicians regarding clinical care in general and the widespread fear that an adverse assessment will create interpersonal conflicts and be returned in kind when the roles of reviewer and reviewee are reversed in a future case. Moreover, clinicians often differ in the issues that they think are of paramount importance in a specific type of clinical case, which occasionally results in multiple reviewers of the same case focusing on different events and different aspects of care.[10] These factors create a bias against the recognition of poor quality and risk. This bias may be less problematic in a provider's assessment of system deficiencies, as opposed to provider-related deficiencies, but still could be considerable. Risk administrators must recognize the potential for this bias in provider assessments of individual cases and take decided action to minimize it. Initial review by a trained reviewer and the subsequent use of multiple reviewers can reduce the effects of this bias.

Many experienced risk administrators and clinical managers have had the experience of seeing two physicians come to dramatically different conclusions after reviewing the same case record.[11] Sometimes this discordance stems from a genuine disagreement over the proper clinical care for a specific problem. Occasionally, however, in complex cases two physicians (or other clinical providers) may focus on entirely different sequences of care and come to different conclusions about the case in question. Informed only that a suit has been filed by the family of a hospital patient who died unexpectedly as a result of postoperative sepsis, one reviewer may concentrate on postoperative wound care, whereas another may direct most attention to the question of whether the proper prophylactic antibiotics were given.

A second problem with peer review is that, even when practitioners agree on the specific care to be examined, they may not agree on the appropriate standard of care against which to judge the actual care provided. Indeed, some reviewers have difficulty articulating a standard of care at all and may appear to regard all but the most egregious care as acceptable.

A third problem with peer review is that often it is not thorough. Many practitioners, especially physicians, feel overwhelmed by the time demands of clinical practice and are unwilling to devote much energy to ancillary responsibilities like peer review. Moreover, physicians in particular are often hostile toward the legal process and may have a tendency to diminish the legitimacy of clinical issues identified through it. At times, physicians charged with conducting a case review only cursorily review the record, skimming physician notes and ignoring nonphysician notes all together. (Nonphysician notes are often of crucial importance in understanding the care in a case.) Laboratory data, radiology reports, and pathology data may receive only brief attention.

Risk administrators can use a number of approaches to increase the usefulness and reliability of peer review. One approach is to cultivate a network of willing, fair, and thorough case reviewers on which to rely. Risk administrators should continually reinforce the need for thoroughness and fairness in the evaluation of care by peers. Risk administrators should foster the development of this group with informal training and should demonstrate appreciation for the reviewers' efforts.

Another approach is to adopt a structured, explicit method of case review. Structured, explicit case review is designed to reduce the unreliability of case review through explicit identification of questionably problematic sequences of related care and the corresponding standards of care. Case review begins with a "foundation review" by an experienced case reviewer, preferably with a background in quality and risk management, who identifies the major processes of care and any issues associated with them. For each issue identified a written form is prepared that asks subsequent reviewers to explicitly state in writing the standard of care for all aspects of related care in which a problem was spotted and to assess the care against that standard. Reviewers can be asked to reference applicable published or organizational practice guidelines. Reviewers are given space to identify and comment on issues not identified during the foundation review.

A final technique is to ask more than one reviewer to perform a structured, explicit review. As stated earlier, it is often useful to have reviewers of different specialties assess a case, particularly if it is a surgical one.

Routine structured, explicit peer review of all cases identified as possible risk cases is too costly and is unnecessary. Although they are an important and indispensable source of information, most cases identified either internally or externally, with the exception of lawsuits, ultimately are not found to contain either risk or a quality deficiency. Therefore an experienced reviewer who can create a structured, explicit case review form if necessary should screen all identified cases first. Structured, explicit case review should be reserved for those cases that appear on initial screening review to have resulted in a serious adverse outcome and a measurable risk of liability.

Strengths and limitations of case identification methods

Although all case identification methods can reveal cases with a risk of loss, some are more useful than others in identifying cases with probable losses. For example, informal studies by hospitals indicate that incident reports are generally poor predictors of lawsuits, which perhaps is not surprising given the large number that are filed in organizations with aggressive risk management programs. However, incident reports remain useful sources of information that can reveal potential risk cases and areas of risk exposure. On the other hand, attorneys' requests for medical records, patient complaints, and billing disputes are factors associated with a higher probability that a lawsuit will follow.

However, case-by-case evaluation does not provide the entire picture of organization-wide clinical risk exposure and quality of care. It paints a picture only of those cases that were identified and is not a complete sample of all cases with risk, risk exposure, and quality problems. In particular, cases that result in a patient complaint are a biased sample of patients from which to make inferences about overall organizational clinical risk because not all patients are equally likely to register a complaint given the same care. Inferences about the general state of clinical risk exposure and quality of care should not be made solely from a review of cases flagged through external identification methods and by occurrence reporting.

Despite various strengths and limitations, all of the aforementioned methods for case identification should be used by a health care organization. Because no method is perfect, a case overlooked by one method may be detected by another. The use of a wide variety of case-specific risk identification methods can be enhanced but not replaced as a method of identifying risk exposure by data-based performance monitoring.

Data-based performance monitoring

Data-based performance monitoring is a method for assessing organizational quality of care and risk exposure that has developed recently and is growing in importance. It is a method for identifying areas of quality deficiency and risk exposure as opposed to specific risk cases. Its premise is that an indispensable way to assess organization-wide clinical risk exposure and quality of care is to monitor everyday activity, which has the benefit of avoiding the reporting bias encountered with many of the already discussed methods of risk identification. Data derived from continuous monitoring are used to either identify quality deficiencies and risk exposure or monitor an organization's response to corrective action taken to remedy previously identified quality and risk problems.

The initial purpose of data-based performance monitoring was the assessment of quality of care. Interinstitutional public release of data-based assessments of clinical performance began in earnest with the Health Care Financing Administration's report on hospital mortality rates in the care of selected Medicare patients. Subsequently, various projects have begun ongoing compilation and reporting of comparative hospital performance. Some are sponsored by state agencies and some by voluntary coalitions. Private comparative data are also available. A primary goal of these programs is to stimulate internal quality improvement through comparative performance assessments. Many organizations also gather clinical outcomes data internally and compare their results with published benchmarks or information obtained from outside data bases.

Risk administrators should be aware of all comparative performance data available on their organizations. Proper interpretation of comparative performance data requires a working familiarity with the strengths and limitations of clinical outcomes monitoring and provider performance profiling.[12,13]

Heretofore, analysis of clinical outcomes data has been the province of clinical quality management staff, in no small part because of its substantial clinical and statistical content. However, comparative clinical outcomes data should be of great interest to risk administrators because they may point out areas of substandard hospital performance and consequently risk exposure. Hospitals with high adverse outcome rates (e.g., mortality) in specific areas of care should aggressively analyze their processes of care in an effort to reduce the rate of adverse outcomes to the lowest achievable levels. High adverse outcomes in specific clinical areas may indicate unusually high-risk exposure in those areas. Although performance data aggregated over hundreds and thousands of cases do not give information about a specific case, a pattern of persistently high severity-adjusted adverse outcomes in a specific clinical area may signal a deficiency in the quality of care, which may have already and could in the future lead to liability in specific cases. For example, a hospital with a high surgical mortality rate, after adjustment for the severity of illness of its patients before surgery, may have clinical problems that result in greater risk exposure than hospitals with lower rates. Comparative performance data afford risk administrators an excellent means of risk identification.

Performance data have a second important use. They are indispensable as a tool used inside an organization to continually assess its success in eliminating areas of known risk exposure. This process entails the design and continual measurement of risk indicators and is discussed later in the section on risk prevention.

RISK PRIORITIZATION

Risk administrators must prioritize identified risks to expend organizational resources in the most cost-effective way. Organizations usually have limited resources of personnel time and attention. Most risk administrators concentrate risk prevention efforts on events that are infrequent but of great consequence, on the one hand, and events that are of lesser import but of frequent occurrence.

A rare event of relatively minor consequence often can be handled directly without assembling a quality improvement team. Sometimes the source of risk exposure is suggested by a pattern of events or by data, and the challenge is first to discover the source of the problem. At times the cause of risk exposure is obvious, such as a physician office's failure to have all routine screening mammogram reports reviewed by a physician or nurse, and so preventive efforts can be focused immediately on faulty clinical or operational processes. The intensity of administrative risk prevention efforts should be tailored to the complexity of each individual risk. Clinical problems will usually require a multidisciplinary team, including physicians, with familiarity in all involved clinical and operational areas.

Risk prioritization is important in both assessing the proper response to a recognized risk case (risk control) and in allocating resources for risk prevention. For example, medication errors frequently occur in hospitals. These errors generally include delays in providing patients with pre-scribed doses of medicine. Identification of such delays is most frequently accomplished through incident reports but also may be identified through occurrence screening, ran-dom medical record review, or patient complaints. The total number of medication delays may then be divided between those delays that actually injured patients and those that had the potential to injure patients. Obviously, risk management personnel must give immediate attention to an error that has resulted in an injury to a patient. In determining the proper response to a medication delay, risk administrators should seek to answer the following questions: Did the error result in an injury to the patient? How significant was the injury? Was the injury of a temporary nature or of a more perma-nent nature? Has it compromised the care of the patient? Will the adverse effect on the patient extend beyond the cur-rent hospitalization? What was the reason for the delay? Was the delay the result of an individual error or a larger institutional problem? Is this an error that has occurred before, on a particular unit, or during a specific shift? Did a specific health care provider cause the error?

The differences between iatrogenic and custodial injuries serve as an illustration of the kind of considerations important in risk prioritization. The distinction between iatrogenic and custodial injuries is relevant when assessing these two types of injuries in terms of frequency and severity—the two major considerations in prioritizing the organization's response to specific risks. Frequency refers to how often the type of injury occurs, and severity refers to how likely it is that the type of injury will result in financial loss. Custodial injuries are esti-mated to account for as much as 75% to 85% of all patient injuries in hospitals and ambulatory care areas. However, measured in terms of financial loss, custodial injuries account for less than 25% of aggregate losses. Iatrogenic injuries, on the other hand, although less frequent than custodial injuries, account for approximately 75% to 85% of hospital losses.[14] The lesson to be learned from the distribution of risk between iatrogenic and custodial injuries is not that a concentrated effort should be directed only toward the prevention or man-agement of iatrogenic claims; hospital risk management pro-grams obviously must address both types of injuries. The lesson, rather, is that their relative risks must be carefully evaluated to achieve a balanced approach in preventing and managing both types of injuries.

Identification of major risks

What risks should be considered major risks? For most organizations a list of major risks can be found in their reporting requirements under excess liability policies. For hospitals, such mandatory reporting is typically required in the event of the following injuries to a patient: unexpected death; brain damage; neurological deficit, nerve damage, or paralysis; loss of limb; or failure to diagnose a condition that results in a continuous course of treatment. In addition to the aforementioned events, a catch-all provision is often included that requires reporting of any claim or medical incident the value of which is equivalent to a certain per-centage (e.g., 50%) of the self-insured retention limits. This list is not exhaustive, but if a hospital risk management pro-gram is constrained because of financial or staffing limita-tions, it can serve as a priority list that fulfills most needs.

Key specific risks

Risk management programs of large health care organiza-tions may find it necessary to use a more detailed list of key specific risks. Such a list may be compiled based on the indi-vidual experience of that organization. Using a hospital as an example, a typical list includes the following major headings: medication error, patient fall, equipment related, security related, blood related, surgery related, anesthesia related, food related, patient induced, policy related, radiology related, medical record related, laboratory related, intra-venous line related, newborn related, maternal related, and physician related. Box 17-1 contains a representative sample of subcategories for each of the aforementioned key specific risks. The categorization of risks associated with a specific hospital will, of course, vary depending on the risk experi-ence of that hospital.

RISK CONTROL

Risk control is the process of managing a recognized risk case to minimize the potential for loss. Most risk adminis-trators find their time primarily directed toward risk control, rather than risk prevention, for an obvious reason: A lawsuit represents an actual loss. Even if successfully defended, a lawsuit will result in expenditures for its defense, primarily in terms of fees for legal counsel and expert witnesses. Tan-gentially there also may be an increase in insurance premi-ums or in the organization's deductible. Consequently, risk administrators find a greater part of their time allocated to risk control than to risk prevention.

Completing the initial investigation

On identification of a risk case an initial investigation is undertaken. This investigation has two purposes—the early assessment of probability and value of loss and the identifica-tion of relevant sources of information. The essential steps necessary to complete these objectives are (1) review of the medical record; (2) interview of the potential defendants for whom the organization provides insurance coverage; (3) iden-tification, cataloging, and collection of physical evidence that may be relevant and could otherwise be lost or misplaced (e.g., monitor tracings, temporary logs, and policy and proce-dures); (4) identification of witnesses who may have informa-tion concerning the incident and who might have to be interviewed at a later time because of time constraints; and

BOX 17-1 OPERATIONAL SUBCATEGORIES OF KEY HOSPITAL RISKS

Medication error

Adverse reaction
Wrong route
Wrong patient
Pharmacy error
Medication not given
Wrong medication given
Medication duplicated
Medication not ordered
Medication not given at correct time
Transcription error
Medication given despite hold order
Wrong dosage

Patient falls

Caused by a liquid or substance on floor
Fall from bed (siderails up? siderails down? position of siderails unknown?)
Fall in bathroom
Fall in room
Fall outside of room
Fall off table or equipment
Fall in elevator
Fall from crutches or walker
Fall outside of building
Fall from chair or wheelchair
Near fall with assistance

Equipment related

Failure of life support or monitor
Equipment missing or unavailable
Injury related to medical device

Security related

Personal property damage
Personal property disappeared
Injury resulting from conduct of another patient

Blood related

Wrong blood
Transfusion reaction
Delay in transfusion

Surgery related

Incorrect sponge count
Incorrect surgical instrument count
Surgical instrument broken
Loss of pathology specimen
Unplanned return to surgery
Removal of retained foreign body
Unplanned return after readmission

Anesthesia related

Respiratory distress reaction
Related to intubation or related to extubation

Food related

Poisoning
Foreign body
Improper diet
NPO order violated
Burns from foods or liquids

Patient induced

Attempted suicide
Self-mutilation
Refusal to consent to treatment
Returned late from approved pass
Discharge against medical advice
In possession of drugs, alcohol, or weapon

Policy related

Procedural error
Violation of physician order
Performance of wrong procedure
Autopsy signed with no autopsy performed

Laboratory related

Transport delay
Identification problem
Loss or damage of laboratory specimen
Incorrect reading

Intravenous line related

Infiltration

Wrong solution
Contaminated or expired solution
Line disconnected
Incorrect timing
Pump malfunction
Incorrect rate
Central line complication

Newborn related

Apgar scores of less than 3 at 1 minute
Apgar scores of less than 7 at 7 minutes
Skull fracture
Resuscitation
Transfer from in-house nursery to special-care nursery
Meconium aspiration

Maternal related

Maternal injury from obstetrical treatment
Blood loss

Physician related

Failure to diagnose
Unexpected death
Brain damage resulting from treatment
Neurological deficit or nerve injury resulting from treatment
Injury relating to resident supervision
Adverse reaction
Delay in response

Radiology related

Reaction to contrast dye
Unmonitored cardiac or respiratory arrest
Disappearance of films

Medical records related

Orders not charted
Consent not signed
Disappearance of record

(5) collection of medical bills. This five-step initial investigation is not intended to serve as an extensive investigation or to replace the more thorough investigation conducted upon service of process. It is only a preliminary action to determine the essential facts of the case and to identify which personnel have personal information about the incident.

With this information in hand, risk managers and attorneys select and prioritize those incidents that warrant further investigation. This process fulfills the essential risk control functions of gathering and assessing information about potential losses and prioritizing time and efforts toward investigation of probable losses.

Predicting the potential plaintiff

An important part of identifying those risk cases likely to result in loss is predicting which patients will bring a lawsuit. As varied as plaintiffs may be, many of them share certain common characteristics. The following factors often determine which patients are most likely to sue a health care organization.

Poor or unexpected results. The most reliable identifying characteristic of the potential plaintiff is that he or she has suffered an unsatisfactory outcome as a result of or despite medical care. The outcome may be direct harm (e.g., a postsurgical complication) or a result that, although not harmful per se, is less than that expected after the care (e.g., unsatisfactory outcome of cosmetic surgery). A poor or unexpected result from medical care does not mean, of course, that any medical malfeasance has occurred.

Seriousness of injury. Another characteristic of the potential plaintiff is that the injury sustained is permanent and serious, involving death, disability, or disfigurement. Disability may be manifested in various ways; at a minimum, it usually must be sufficient to have resulted in lost wages. The economics of pursuing a legal claim and the impact of medical malpractice reforms have served to impose a modicum of self-regulation and limitation on medical malpractice claims, reducing claims for minor injury and claims that might be frivolous.

Weak physician-patient relationship. A third trait of the potential plaintiff is the absence of a strong relationship with his or her physician. The single greatest deterrent to litigation remains a strong physician-patient relationship rich with positive interactions and communication. A recent study analyzing the demographics and risk of malpractice concludes that a physician's gender, specialty, and age affect the risk of a suit. Of note, male physicians were three times as likely to be in a high claims group as female physicians. The investigators surmised that female physicians may interact more effectively with patients than their male colleagues.[15]

Uncertain financial future. Many plaintiffs are individuals who face an uncertain financial future. They are often unable to withstand the financial burden of medical expenses attendant with a poor or unexpected result. Therefore potential plaintiffs are frequently unemployed, underemployed, recently retired, single or recently divorced, or students.

Strong support group. The last trait frequently found among potential plaintiffs is the presence of a strong support group, especially if there are family members who are directly or indirectly associated with medicine or law. As socially acceptable as litigation may be in the United States, persevering through the process of selecting an attorney and initiating legal action still requires a certain degree of motivation and strength, which can be buttressed by supportive family and friends.

In preparing themselves to initiate a lawsuit, potential plaintiffs commonly use similar phrases, with which most risk managers quickly become familiar. Many potential plaintiffs, instead of making a direct threat to sue, often use expressions such as "I want to make sure that this never happens to another patient," "I want to teach you a lesson," and "I am not interested in the money, it's the principle."

Conducting investigations

In conducting investigations, risk administrators need to be aware of legally imposed limits and restrictions. For example, some courts have ruled that risk administrators may not interview subsequent caregivers of an injured patient. Some courts have extended this theory to prohibit discussions even with members of a hospital's house staff and nursing staff. The rationale is that such ex parte discussions violate the sanctity of the physician-patient relationship and are prohibited under physician-patient privilege statutes.[16] A second rationale offered is that a physician has a fiduciary duty to refrain from assisting his or her patient's adversary.

Although the aforementioned rationales may be persuasive regarding subsequent providers who care for the patient and are not used by the health care organization, application of a rule that bars an organization from interviewing employees creates a number of practical problems. Such a restriction would prevent the organization from being able to respond to a complaint, develop litigation strategy, provide accurate or complete responses to discovery requests, prepare employees adequately for depositions or trial, depose experts adequately, and prepare the best presentation at trial.

Of equal concern to an attorney is the protection of investigative reports and interviews from disclosure. There are two avenues by which such protection may be ensured. A recognized principle is that such information constitutes "work product." The work product principle protects an attorney's representation of his or her client's interest and requires that good cause be shown before a court will allow discovery of an attorney's preparation of the client's case. Generally, work product includes information prepared by an attorney or his or her representative (e.g., a risk manager) in anticipation of litigation. Such information includes personal knowledge and legal theories, as well as statements of witnesses. This principle, though, does not necessarily protect information about the location of such information and the names and addresses of witnesses. In applying this principle to the protection of reports and interviews made by attorneys and risk managers, care should be taken to follow the general rules of the work product principle. Disclosure of such information to a third party may result in loss of ability to assert the principle to defeat discovery requests by the other party. If information is gathered by nonattorney risk administrators, the information should be forwarded to the attorney, sometimes with the inclusion of a statement that it is being sent to assist the attorney in contemplated litigation.

A second means of protecting such information from discovery by the other party may be available under state statutes that prohibit disclosure of information used internally to improve patient care or to reduce morbidity and mortality. Precise adherence to the rules set forth in a statute usually is critical to protect the information from disclosure. Some statutes may address only hospitals and have not been updated to incorporate HMOs. Generally, information is protected when used and discussed within recognized health care organization committees for quality improvement purposes.

Notifying insurance carriers

Risk administrators have the responsibility to properly notify an insurance carrier of a claim or possible claim that exposes its coverage. Reference to the exact wording of the insurance policy, of course, is critical as to the necessary timing and scope of notification. Generally, the notice requirement is phrased in one of two ways: A policy may require that the insured give the carrier "immediate notice of a lawsuit" or may require notice "when it appears that an occurrence is likely to involve indemnity" under the policy. The second type of notice language can be particularly problematic for a health care organization because it is vulnerable to a subjective interpretation as to when an occurrence is "likely to involve indemnity." The phrase may be interpreted from both an objective and a subjective standard. The controlling rule in insurance law is that if the language of an insurance policy is ambiguous or otherwise susceptible to more than one reasonable interpretation, it is to be construed in favor of the insured. Notwithstanding this rule, insureds may wish to be cautious and provide notification at the earliest possible moment that it appears a carrier's insurance policy may be exposed.

Selecting defense counsel

The skills expected of a litigator are likely to be different from those of a corporate attorney. Of course, competency, truthfulness, honesty, and responsiveness are important traits in both, as well as the ability to communicate effectively with the client. On the other hand, a certain aggressiveness that might be expected of a litigator might be inappropriate in a corporate attorney. Undoubtedly, one of the greatest assets of a litigator is that he or she possesses the capabilities to take a case to trial, advocate the position of the defendant(s), and, of course, obtain a favorable verdict.

As with the selection of any other consultants, in selecting defense counsel a health care organization would do well to keep in mind the following:

1. Selection should not be made solely on the basis of price.
2. Expectations should be made clear to the defense counsel from the outset.
3. A new defense counsel, regardless of his or her reputation, should always be started on a small project or a single case to ensure that a positive working relationship will result.

4. The defense counsel should be allowed reasonable professional latitude to do his or her best job, although giving defense counsel freedom of action does not eliminate the organization's responsibility to monitor defense counsel's progress.
5. The results achieved by defense counsel should be fairly evaluated because both the organization and defense counsel deserve honest feedback from each other.

Assisting defense counsel

A medical malpractice action may be costly to an organization, but it can be extraordinarily disturbing to a health care provider named as a defendant. Generally speaking, physicians and nurses are unaccustomed to the confrontation and adversity that characterize the litigation process. They may be frightened and intimidated by the procedures that may appear to them to be geared more toward proving them culpable than determining what actually happened.

In the discovery or fact-finding stage of the litigation proceeding, risk administrators have a dual role. Both roles reduce the cost of use of outside litigation counsel and the possibility of loss to an adverse verdict or disadvantageous settlement. Risk administrators should assist outside defense counsel in discovery. This task may be easy or difficult, depending on the thoroughness with which the initial investigation was conducted. Equally important, risk administrators should help guide the defendant through the litigation process.

Clarification of expectations. The first step in assisting legal counsel is to express the expectations of the organization's risk administrators about how defense counsel will handle the claim. Expectations are best clarified in advance and with a single attorney charged with managing the case. It is important that direction be given to defense counsel in the following five areas: assignment of file, initial review, conduct of discovery, conduct of trial, and arrangement for billing.

If the relationship involves multiple claims, the defense firm and risk administrator should mutually designate an attorney who will have overall responsibility for supervising the various cases referred to that firm. If because of a conflict or another reason the defense firm to which a case has been sent is unable to represent the organization, this fact should be communicated immediately to the organization by telephone and the file should be returned promptly. As to the assignment of a case to a particular attorney, some organizations defer to the supervising attorney at the defense firm. Conversely, some risk administrators prefer matching particular cases to the skills, styles, or personalities of particular attorneys and will retain the right to make the selection. An assignment letter should include the name of the risk administrator working on the file. If a defense attorney other than the one selected to handle the case works on the case, this fact should be communicated to the organization.

As soon as possible after a claim is assigned to a defense firm, the primary defense attorney should send an acknowledgment, as well as his or her assessment of the case, to the risk administrator. This review should include a summary of the pertinent facts revealed to date, a review of medical records, a recitation of the issues presented in the complaint, a mention of areas that will require additional research and investigation, and, if there is sufficient information available, a statement of opinion as to liability, verdict potential, and settlement value.

Any motions filed on behalf of the organization should be limited to meaningful issues and receive prior approval from the risk administrator. Any requests by the defense attorney to interview employees of the organization or to retain outside experts should also receive prior approval from the risk administrator. The risk administrator should obtain a status report from the defense attorney at least twice a year.

Defense attorney requests for approval of travel expenditures should be made in writing and should include the purpose of the trip; the travel destination; the time period required to complete the work; the exact means and the cost of travel; the specific identification, location, and cost of lodgings; and the cost of car rental, if required. In any event reimbursement should always be supported by receipts. The billing cycle also should be clearly understood, and the hourly fees of all defense attorneys working on the case should be provided in writing. Changes in those fees should not be made without the approval of the risk administrator. To enable evaluation of the charge, the bill should provide details of the legal services rendered, including (1) the date of service, (2) a clear description of the service rendered, (3) the actual time expended, and (4) the identity of the attorney who rendered the service. Charges for review of files should be kept at a minimum, and interoffice conferences between attorneys of the defense firm should be discouraged or prohibited. Finally, the defense firm should be informed of which legal expenses will not be reimbursed. Such items might include interoffice conferences, time spent filing papers with the court, secretarial time, copying charges, and unsupported charges for travel.

Distribution of responsibilities. The manner in which the risk administrator and the primary defense attorney share responsibilities during discovery should be clear to both. The risk administrator should help compile answers to interrogatories, if he or she is not entirely responsible for their completion. It is cost-effective for risk administrators to undertake as much of this task as possible. Similarly, risk administrators should be responsible for the production of documents, such as medical records, billing statements, policy and procedure manuals, incident reports, photographs, laboratory reports, logs, scheduling reports, and other physical evidence.

In most risk management programs, risk administrators automatically assume primary responsibility for drafting answers and producing documents. However, they are probably not as involved as they should be in preparing witnesses for depositions. This task is too often left to defense counsel. As with drafting answers to interrogatories and producing documents, witness preparation should be a shared responsibility between defense counsel and the risk administrator.

A common complaint of deponents is that they have not been adequately prepared. Unfortunately, at times defense counsel may not have or may not take the time to prepare each witness adequately. To avoid this situation, risk administrators should be trained and ready to prepare witnesses. The two important aspects of this preparation are to provide the general rules of demeanor and conduct of a witness in a deposition and to review in detail the care and treatment rendered by the deponent, relying in particular on office or hospital records.

Some organizations have shown prospective deponents videotapes of staged depositions. Such tapes are commercially available. In addition, various articles and monographs have been written on the subject. In their excellent book, *Preventing Malpractice: The Co-Active Solution*, Dr. Thomas Leaman and attorney James Saxton provide 10 rules for deposition preparation (Box 17-2).[17] Although the rules are directed to physicians, they are equally applicable to other health care providers or for that matter to any person who is required to give a deposition.

RECENT DEVELOPMENT: USE OF ALTERNATIVE DISPUTE RESOLUTION

Alternative dispute resolution has been used successfully in a variety of settings to bring people to agreement. Now, physicians and hospitals are adapting these same methods of reconciling differences to medical malpractice cases to avoid the hassle and expense associated with trial preparation. The two forms of alternative dispute resolution with which most people are familiar are mediation and arbitration. Mediation is the process whereby a neutral third party assists parties in a dispute to reach a voluntary settlement of their differences. In arbitration a neutral third party hears the evidence and arguments of each party and then renders a final and generally binding decision.

Rush-Presbyterian-St. Luke's Medical Center in Chicago has developed an interesting model for the use of mediation in medical malpractice litigation. In 1995 it began the first hospital-based mediation program in Illinois and one of the first in the country in response to the excessive costs, adversarial nature, and unpredictable outcomes associated with jury trials in Cook County. The program was created in an effort to resolve disputes in a rational and reasoned manner and as an alternative to trials by juries, which are susceptible to emotional appeals.

One of the unique features of the Rush model is the use of co-mediators. These individuals are drawn from the ranks of the most prominent and active trial attorneys from

BOX 17-2 TEN RULES FOR THE PHYSICIAN'S DEPOSITION

1. The physician must know the records intimately—office records, hospital charts, any statements by other health care professionals, medical literature, and alternative treatments.

2. The physician must listen to the question carefully and respond only when he or she understands it completely. If the physician does not understand it, then the attorney must be asked to rephrase it. Never help to rephrase it or suggest a more appropriate question.

3. The physician should respond thoroughly, but directly and to the point, and not tell stories, ramble, digress, or volunteer information. On certain topics one may need to be more comprehensive if appropriate to the theme of the defense.

4. The physician should use the medical record. If the record is in order, it can be the best defense tool. For example, the plaintiff's attorney may describe the client's level of pain and suffering. If the physician's records do not confirm this, the chart can be used to demonstrate it.

5. The theatrics of the plaintiff's attorney should be disregarded. Sometimes the attorney will act surprised and shocked by a response, use body language, or repeat certain phrases in an attempt to irritate the defendant. Such theatrics are intended to make the physician uncomfortable and unsure of the response.

   At times the plaintiff and defense attorneys may resort to arguing with each other. It is important for the physician not to misinterpret the defense attorney's anger to mean that something has gone wrong or that there is a problem with the responses. Such battles may be a technique for the defense attorney to maintain control of the deposition. If such tactics are to be used, they should be discussed with the physician before the deposition. Their use should also be minimal; professional courtesy is an important part of legal ethics.

6. The physician should be consistent. If the physician does not give the desired response to a question from the plaintiff's attorney, the attorney may ask the question over and over, each time phrasing it a bit differently, looking for an inconsistent response. The physician should remember that the plaintiff's attorney has been working on these questions for weeks before the deposition. The physician's failure to give the anticipated response can be devastating; the attorney will work hard to get the needed response or at least neutralize the damage from an unfavorable, unanticipated response.

7. The physician should wait for the next question after finishing a response. Often the plaintiff's attorney will pause, using body language to urge the physician to say more. The physician should not try to fill the void, but should simply wait patiently for the next question.

8. The physician should be extremely cautious in responding to leading questions, such as "Is it a fair statement . . . ," "Let me summarize your testimony as follows . . . ," and "Doctor, just so I understand what you are saying. . . ." Statements like these mean the plaintiff's attorney is about to reinterpret the physician's testimony. Usually there is a slight twist to that interpretation, which the attorney is hoping to have affirmed. The physician should remember that fairness has nothing to do with this process; the interpretation may not correctly reflect what was said. The physician should agree only with those statements with which he or she is comfortable. If the physician disagrees, then he or she must simply say so, and repeat the previous response.

9. The physician should be careful of conversation during breaks. Although inappropriate, the plaintiff's attorney may try to engage the physician in conversation. This could have an impact on the case. A deposition is not the time for social niceties. Breaks should be used to relax and regain composure. One must be on guard from arrival at the deposition until departure.

10. The physician should be courteous, professional, firm, and credible. Demeanor should be professional and serious, for a physician's professional ability has been challenged. As such, a deposition is neither the time nor the place for chitchat and humor. However, under no circumstances should a physician be offensive, insulting, or argumentative.

From T. Leaman & J. Saxton, *Preventing Malpractice: The Co-Active Solution* 68-70 (Plenum, New York 1993).

both the plaintiff and defense bar. They undergo mediation training offered by the medical center in association with local law schools. As an indication of the fairness and neutrality of that training, the Rush program allows the plaintiff to pick both of the mediators. Plaintiffs agree to mediation when it is offered largely because they can see the benefits of a fast, less expensive resolution.

The mediation process begins with both parties voluntarily agreeing to participate in the program. Premediation submissions, including a statement of the facts, description of the injury, claim of special damages, and past and future expenses, are exchanged. A neutral location is selected in which the mediation will take place. To once again enhance the neutrality of the process, the mediation proceedings generally are held in a location away from the hospital.

The experiment in the use of alternative dispute resolution by Rush-Presbyterian-St. Luke's Medical Center in the first 4 years has been positive. An average of 12 cases have been submitted to the Rush program each year, with close to 90% of the cases being resolved, many on the same day of the mediation. The operational costs of the mediations have been nominal and, in the event a lawsuit has been resolved, there have been substantial savings through the elimination of additional defense costs.[18]

RISK PREVENTION

Effective risk prevention depends on the reliable recognition of risk exposure, determination of its causes, implementation of corrective action, and continual monitoring of risk indicators to determine if risk exposure resolves. This process requires close and active cooperation of risk administrators and clinical managers.

Assessing risk exposure

Risk exposure is identified either by examination of the facts of an individual case, which could reveal a continuing source of liability risk, or from examination of data, which can be trend data of a particular risk indicator or clinical performance data. Once risk exposure is identified, quantitative measures, or indicators, reflective of that exposure should be developed to enable risk administrators to determine the presence of similar risk in other areas of the organization and to be used as a measuring stick to gauge the success of interventional efforts. Literally hundreds of indicators can be measured, so risk administrators must identify a manageable number that will yield the required information.

Indicators are usually rates of selected events, such as hospital falls, medication errors, and adverse clinical outcomes. They may be measured in targeted areas or throughout the entire organization. Data for indicators can be obtained from a wide variety of sources in an organization. Unique data bases are often found in claims and billing (whose data bases typically contain patient encounter data consisting of at least ICD-9-CM codes, visit status, care delivered, and patient disposition), utilization management (often a rich source of data), the pharmacy, medical staff offices (including the credentialing data base), the patient relations department (which might have a detailed data base of patient complaints and corrective actions), and quality management (which should have all available clinical performance data). The risk administrator should have in his or her own department data on lawsuits, risk cases, incident reports, and specified occurrence reports and screening.

As an example, if a hospital risk administrator identifies falls by patients, staff, and visitors as a source of risk exposure, he or she might determine that much of the problem relates to travel on floors that are wet from cleaning. Further analysis may lead to the identification of a number of interventions that would serve to minimize or eliminate travel on wet floors. Interventions might include using large yellow plastic warning signs placed six feet apart around the wet area, confining routine floor cleaning to evenings (after visiting hours), and cleaning no more than 50% of the width of a walkway at one time. Appropriate indicators for monitoring risk exposure could include the monthly rates of a series of measurements based on routine, random walk-around inspections, such as the percentage of just-mopped floors without proper warning signs, the percentage of floors actually cleaned during visiting hours, and the percentage of floor cleanings in which more than half the hallway was mopped. These three represent "process" indicators that reflect the success in executing the interventions. Of course, if the hypothesis that these three interventions will be effective in reducing the rate of falls is wrong, then successful implementation of the interventions will have no effect on the rate of falls. Therefore it is crucial to include measurement of an "outcome" indicator that will provide information about whether the problem was ameliorated by the interventions. A useful outcome indicator would be the monthly number of falls by patients, staff, and visitors. Outcome indicators, as opposed to process indicators, should be reflective of the level of risk exposure and thus should be the measure of success of any risk prevention effort.

Clinical quality indicators are often but not always risk indicators. Clinical risk indicators are limited to those aspects of medical care that present risk. Quality management, however, encompasses the improvement of medical care that is not considered to present any legal risk. For example, a hospital with the lowest rate of surgical complications in town may seek to lower it even further through an aggressive quality improvement project. If no risk exposure in that area had been identified, the indicators developed to monitor surgical complications would be clinical quality indicators but not clinical risk indicators. Similarly, not all risk indicators are clinical quality indicators. An institution may identify risk exposure because of the failure of its medical staff to consistently obtain proper written informed consent before certain procedures, as required by the staff bylaws. The indicator of percentage of procedures with written informed consent forms completed beforehand would be useful to assess risk in this situation. However, failure of the physician to obtain written informed consent to a procedure is a legal rather than a medical issue, so an indicator of this failure would be an indicator of legal risk but not of clinical quality.

Risk indicators should be valid reflections of the clinical or operational activity they are intended to measure. They should be free from measurement bias, and each measured event should be reliably observed. Poorly crafted risk indicators prevent the accurate recognition of risk exposure and the understanding of its causes and doom to failure many risk avoidance efforts.

Defining performance expectations

The next step in risk reduction is to establish for each indicator a target level that will be used as the measure of success in risk reduction. For example, a project to reduce medication errors could establish a target of a 50% reduction in errors over 3 months, and a rate in subsequent months of no higher than 10 incidents per month throughout the organization. These targets are the standards against which the success of the project should be measured, and if the indicator target rate is not met, further corrective action is warranted. Many risk reduction and quality improvement projects ultimately fail despite initial promise because of inadequate long-term monitoring of the risk exposure and the lack of a predetermined commitment to further action if expected results are not achieved.

Monitoring the results of action is so important that the necessary indicators and their expected values over time should be established before any action is taken. The measuring sticks (the indicators) and the criteria for success (the expected values) should be established before taking action so that the determination of whether an intervention is successful will not be biased by the personal stakes acquired by staff in the development and implementation of the corrective action plan.

In particularly troublesome areas, performance expectations can be formalized and reinforced through operational protocols and clinical practice guidelines. These guides are written formal expressions of courses of action expected in defined circumstances. Classic examples are nursing protocols for initiating blood transfusions and physician practice guidelines for pacemaker insertion. Care must be taken, however, to avoid the interpreting of clinical practice guidelines as strictly defined standards of care. Nevertheless, protocols and guidelines, when properly and carefully designed, can be an effective way of standardizing selected features of operations and clinical care and reducing risk exposure. Adherence to them can be measured through indicators.

Taking specific action to reduce risk

Risk prevention depends on the accurate identification of those clinical and operational processes in need of corrective efforts. In their efforts to diagnose the causes of risk exposure, risk administrators should adopt a structured problem-solving technique predicated on an organized approach to identifying all of the clinical and operational processes that affect the clinical area with risk exposure. This approach may include the construction of process flow diagrams and cause-and-effect diagrams. Input should be obtained from staff with daily working knowledge of each relevant clinical and operational process.

Once an operational or clinical process has been identified as a problem, corrective interventions should be crafted, and each step necessary for their successful implementation should be detailed in a written "corrective action" plan. The plan's formulation should be made with multidisciplinary input, and specific responsibilities and times for completion of each task should be specified. Successful implementation of a corrective action plan will

often depend on widespread, continual staff education and committed involvement of managers in all relevant clinical and operational departments.

Adopting general risk avoidance strategies

Risk administrators should develop a general risk avoidance plan that includes organization-specific strategies. Two universally important components deserve specific mention. The first is to provide regular general risk management education to all staff. This program need not go into detail about legal principles but should keep all staff—clinical and nonclinical—aware of the constant need to avoid risk and report it whenever discovered. This education is particularly important for physicians, given the greater risk exposure encountered in their work. Periodic (e.g., annual) seminars should review the essentials of risk prevention in clinical practice, stressing the crucial elements of good communication and proper medical record keeping. The presentation of recent organizational and comparative trend data on risk indicators can be an effective tool to stimulate physician interest and maintain attention.

A second important component of a risk avoidance plan is to strengthen the medical staff credentialing criteria and procedures. Criteria for good standing should be far beyond mere possession of current licensure and malpractice insurance. Data on quality of care, risk cases, patient complaints, and particularly the clinical outcomes of the physician's care (e.g., surgical mortality and complication rates) should play a role. It is becoming increasingly perilous for health care organizations to ignore such data in their credentialing process. In their review of the impact of performance data on medical practice, physicians Topol and Califf comment that:

The problem of too many physicians [doing procedures, many of whom perform too few each year to achieve competency,] is compounded by the lack of adequate training for many, who too frequently derive their "training" by attendance at a demonstration course. Careful consideration should be given to the criteria for privileges of individual physicians. Low-volume physicians whose patients have poor outcomes should be prohibited from doing procedures. The minimum number of cases per year should be strictly enforced. [For example,] the Joint American College of Cardiology and American Heart Association Task Force recommends that cardiac surgeons do at least 100 bypass operations per year, but in a review of the data now available in New York and Pennsylvania, more than one third of cardiac surgeons did not meet this criterion. Volume is not the only issue; guidelines are necessary for the actions that should be triggered when indicators of poor-quality medicine are evident. Indeed, availability of outcome data would likely alter the behavior of low-volume or poor-outcome practitioners. However, if these measures are unsuccessful, strategies ranging from admonitory communication to frank termination of procedural privileges could be used.[19]

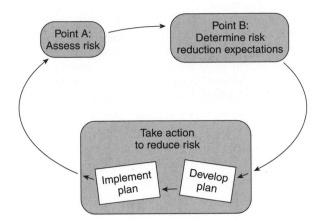

Fig. 17-1. Cycle of continuous risk reduction.

Continually reassessing risk exposure: the cycle of continuous risk reduction

Risk reduction is a continuous cyclical process (Fig. 17-1). The first step of the cycle is the assessment of risk, which includes the identification of risk exposure and its measurement through risk indicators. In doing this step, an organization is determining its degree of exposure to a certain risk, which is referred to as point A in the diagram. The second step is the creation of expectations of where the level of risk exposure should fall to over time; in this step the organization determines its risk reduction goal (referred to as point B). The third and final step is taking action to reduce the risk exposure, that is, to reduce risk exposure from point A to point B. This step requires the development of a corrective action plan and its successful implementation. Once action is taken, the steps of the cycle are repeated as necessary. Risk exposure is reassessed to gauge the success of the intervention and the need for further action. If risk reduction expectations are not met, they are revised as appropriate and further action is taken. Failure to monitor known risk exposure, especially once improvement begins, can allow attention and resources to be diverted to other projects and lead to the ultimate failure of an initially successful intervention.

RISK FINANCING

A health care organization finances the risk of loss from liability in one of two ways. It may retain the risk, or it may seek to shift or transfer the risk.[20]

Retaining risk

The use of internal funds to pay losses is referred to as *loss retention* or *retaining risk*. Under this arrangement, a health care organization may either fund or not fund the cumulative value of the risks retained. Of course, the more fiscally responsible approach is to fund the losses in a self-insur-

ance program by which a trust fund is established and the organization makes annual contributions according to actuarial studies as to the estimated value of losses retained. A self-insurance program is most appropriate when a hospital (1) wishes to achieve an advantageous cash flow, (2) has the capacity to satisfy actuarial funding requirements, (3) possesses the sophistication to set appropriate reserves, (4) is able to maintain a reasonably low level of self-retention or deductible, and (5) finds it otherwise impossible or impractical to transfer the risk.

On occasion an organization that has a fully funded self-insurance program, nevertheless, may elect to assume a risk for a type of loss not covered under the self-insurance program if insurance for such a risk is either unavailable or the price is prohibitive. The organization, despite accepting responsibility for it, may neglect to fund it. In the event a loss does materialize, the organization would have to fund it from general operating funds. An alternative is to fund a loss reserve or consider alternative approaches to self-insurance.

Self-insurance programs pose some inherent problems for the institution. Pressures to achieve short-term financial objectives can jeopardize long-term financial viability of the self-insurance program. For example, some institutions limit the funding of a self-insurance fund to actual lawsuits as opposed to probable claims. This approach eventually could result in an inadequate surplus in the trust fund. A similar tendency is for organizations to accept coverage of losses in cases in which the losses are less clear or more unpredictable. Such losses would more prudently be either transferred or covered under a commercial insurance policy. Yet another disadvantage of a self-insurance program is the inability to counteract pressures by excess carriers to increase the self-insured retention limits.[21]

Other insurance arrangements might serve as alternatives to developing a self-insured retention program. These arrangements include insurance purchasing groups, risk retention groups, and offshore captive insurance companies.[22] However, these alternative structures may be more expensive and time-consuming to implement and operate than a self-insured trust and may be more applicable to a multihospital system or a physician hospital organization as opposed to a single hospital entity.

Transferring risk

For most organizations the transfer of risk in whole or in part takes place in one of three ways. Most commonly, risk is transferred to a commercial insurance company under a primary or excess policy. A second approach is to share risk by requiring physicians who are members of the medical staff or network to maintain minimum levels of insurance. These two approaches are commonplace and do not require further elaboration.

The third approach is also fairly common but has been the subject of misunderstanding and misuse. It attempts to shift liability by use of an indemnification or "hold harmless" agreement in a contract. Such a provision allows one party to transfer the legal liability to another contracting party and is frequently insisted on by vendors, insurers, and managed care programs. Health care organizations should not unwittingly accept such provisions. First of all, many malpractice insurance policies expressly exclude such transfers of liability so that the acceptance of the liability of another may be an uninsured loss. In addition, such provisions are typically worded in an overly broad fashion. An even worse alternative is a mutual indemnification clause. Neither should be accepted by an organization. A one-way agreement unfairly shifts liability to the hospital, whereas mutual indemnification ensures that both parties will become entangled in the question of liability.

When faced with an indemnification provision, an organization's legal counsel should endeavor to have it deleted, should not accept a mutual indemnification, and may suggest the following alternative wording:

It is understood and agreed that neither of the parties to this agreement shall be liable for any negligent or wrongful act chargeable to the other and that this agreement shall not be construed as seeking to either enlarge or diminish any obligation or duty owed by one party against the other or against third parties. In the event of a claim for any wrongful or negligent act, each party shall bear the cost of its own defense.

EXTERNAL REQUIREMENTS

The environment within which a health care organization's risk management program operates is a fabric of loosely connected laws, regulations, and accreditation requirements. Voluntary accreditation is available from a number of organizations, including the JCAHO and the National Committee for Quality Assurance (NCQA). This environment continues to be one of constant change, with, for example, revisions to some accreditation requirements released annually. Risk administrators must vigilantly monitor the ever-changing external regulatory environment and ensure organizational compliance with all risk management–related requirements.

CONCLUSION

Health care organizations are dynamic entities in which programs, personnel, priorities, and external requirements are in a constant state of flux. As a result, legal risks often can assume a fluid state. A successful approach to the prevention of injuries caused by a certain set of circumstances may ultimately fail when those circumstances change. The benefits of a fall prevention program successfully instituted in a geriatric unit might be undermined by a reduction in nursing staff, expansion of the unit, change in patient mix, or physical reconfiguration of the unit. When that happens, new solutions and alternative approaches will be required. Risk management programs must be modifiable, adapting to changing patterns and trends. Risk administrators must realize that problems once solved may reappear and require new solutions, sometimes repeatedly. Constant vigilance through monitoring is essential. Effective risk management requires continual attention to the ever-changing organizational realities and legal milieu.

ENDNOTES

1. Joint Commission on Accreditation of Healthcare Organizations, *Accreditation Manual for Hospitals* 262 (JCAHO 1992).
2. G. Troyer & S. Salman, *Handbook of Healthcare Risk Management* 81 (Aspen Systems, Germantown, Md. 1986).
3. B.L. Brown, *Risk Management for Hospitals: A Practical Approach* 2 (Aspen Systems, Germantown, Md. 1979).
4. M. Holoweiko, *What Are Your Greatest Malpractice Risks?*, Medical Economics 144 (1992).
5. E. Hirshfeld, *Should Practice Parameters Be the Standard of Care in Malpractice Litigation?*, 266 J.A.M.A. 2886–2891 (1991).
6. E. Topol & R. Califf, *Scorecard Cardiovascular Medicine: Its Impact and Future Directions*, 120 Ann. Intern. Med. 68 (1994).
7. *See* A. Southwick, *The Law of Hospital and Health Care Administration* 554–578 (2d ed., Health Administration Press, Ann Arbor, Mich. 1988) for a more detailed discussion of corporate negligence.
8. *Fox v. Health Net of California*, Calif. Super. Ct. (Riverside), No. 219692 (1993).
9. L. Harpster & M. Veach eds., *Risk Management Handbook for Health Care Facilities* 255 (American Hospital Publishing, Chicago 1990).
10. H. Rubin et al., *Watching the Doctor-Watchers: How Well Do Peer Review Organization Methods Detect Hospital Care Quality Problems?*, 267 J.A.M.A. 2349-2354 (1992).
11. A. Localio et al., *Identifying Adverse Events Caused by Medical Care: Degree of Physician Agreement in a Retrospective Chart Review*, 125 Ann. Intern. Med. 457-464 (1996).
12. R. Balsamo & M. Pine, *Twelve Questions to Ask about Your Outcomes Monitoring System*, 20 Physician Executive 13-16, 22-25 (1994).
13. R. Balsamo & M. Pine, *Important Considerations in Using Indicators to Profile Providers*, 21 Physician Executive 38-45 (1995).
14. J. Orlikoff, *Preventing Malpractice: The Board's Role in Risk Management*, Trustee 9 (1991).
15. M. Tragin et al, *Physician Demographics and Risk of Medical Malpractice*, 93 Am. J. Med. 541 (1992).
16. *Petrillo v. Syntex Laboratories, Inc.*, 148 Ill. App. 3d 581, 499 N.E. 2d 952 (1st Dist. 1986).
17. T. Leaman & J. Saxton, *Preventing Malpractice: The Co-Active Solution* 68–70 (Plenum, New York 1993).
18. M. Brown, *Rush Hospital's Medical Malpractice Mediation Program: An ADR Success Story*, 86 Illinois Bar Journal 432 (1998).
19. Topol & Califf, *supra* note 6.
20. A. Sielicki, *Current Philosophy of Risk Management*, Top. in Health Care Financing 6 (Spring 1983).
21. J. Hamman, J. Ziegenfuss, & J. Williamson eds., *Risk Management Trends and Applications* 73 (American Board of Quality Assurance and Utilization Review Physicians, Sarasota, Fla. 1988).
22. B. Youngberg, *Essentials of Hospital Risk Management* 145-147 (Aspen Publishers, Rockville, Md. 1990).

APPENDIX 17-1   Top 10 Allegations by Average Cost*

1998 Rank	1999 Rank	Allegation	Claims (no.)	Average cost
1	1	Improper treatment—Birth-related	309	$260,300
6	2	Failure to diagnose—Hemorrhage	91	$221,900
9	3	Failure to diagnose—Abdominal problems/other	91	$167,600
2	4	Failure to diagnose—Myocardial infarction	150	$166,100
3	5	Surgery—Postoperative death	109	$160,800
5	6	Failure to diagnose—Cancer	379	$149,500
8	7	Failure to diagnose—Pregnancy problems	75	$147,100
+	8	Surgery—Unnecessary	64	$141,400
4	9	Failure to diagnose—Circulatory problem	170	$128,600
7	10	Failure to diagnose—Infection	232	$125,900

From St. Paul Fire and Marine Insurance Co. (1999).
*Table did not appear in 1998 Allegations Review.

APPENDIX 17-2   Top 10 Allegations by Frequency

1998 Rank	1999 Rank	Allegation	Claims (no.)	Average cost
1	1	Surgery—Postoperative complications	901	$85,800
2	2	Failure to diagnose—Cancer	379	$149,500
5	3	Improper treatment—Insufficient therapy	364	$64,000
3	4	Improper treatment—Birth-related	309	$260,300
4	5	Surgery—Inadvertent act	265	$107,000
6	6	Improper treatment—During examination	240	$51,000
8	7	Failure to diagnose—Infection	232	$125,900
9	8	Improper treatment—Drug side effect	221	$89,200
7	9	Failure to diagnose—Fracture/dislocation	189	$54,100
10	10	Improper treatment—Infection	178	$101,200

From St. Paul Fire and Marine Insurance Co. (1999).

APPENDIX 17-3   All Allegations by Location

Location	Claims (no.)
Hospital	
Emergency department	846
Labor/delivery/nursery	363
Other	298
Outpatient surgery	200
Patient care area	643
Surgery	1517
SUBTOTAL	3867
Office	
Physician office/clinic	2446
Other	217
Surgicenter	20
SUBTOTAL	2683
TOTAL	6550

From St. Paul Fire and Marine Insurance Co. (1999).

APPENDIX 17-4 **Unusual Incident Report**

THIS IS AN INTERNAL QUALITY CONTROL DOCUMENT
DO NOT PLACE IN PATIENT RECORD

I. NAMEPLATE

I. _____ PATIENT _____ VISITOR _____ OTHER (check one)

Date of incident: _____ Time of incident: _____ A.M. _____

P.M. _____

Location of incident: _____
(Unit/Area)

If NO addressograph, print   Attending physician:_____

name, DOB, unit, patient number;   Witness: _____ Phone no.: _____

if visitor, give address.   Witness: _____ Phone no.: _____

II. TYPE OF INCIDENT: (check at least one)

_____ Reaction to contrast/dye
Type:_____
_____ Wrong blood given
_____ Unexpected return to the operating room
Brain damage that could be the result of
treatment or medical intervention
_____ Neurological deficit, nerve injury or
paralysis that could be the result of
treatment or medical intervention
_____ Unexpected patient death
_____ Inaccurate needle or sponge count
_____ Unplanned hospital admission subsequent
to outpatient surgery procedure

_____ Informed consent form not signed or inaccurate
_____ Total or partial loss of limb or the use of limb
_____ Needle stick to patient or visitor
_____ Burns from food, liquid, or mechanical equipment
_____ Central line complication/problem resulting
in patient injury
_____ Intubation/extubation injury
_____ Damage to or disappearance of personal property
_____ I.V. infiltration (provide detail in Section III)
_____ Fall (provide detail in Section III)
_____ Medication error (provide detail in Section III)
_____ OTHER (provide detail in Section III)
_____ Serious illness or injury (including death) to patient that might have
been caused by medical device* (see Section IV)

III. INCIDENT FACTS/DATA: (should be consistent with what is written in the medical record)

_____
_____
_____
_____
_____

IV. PRODUCT IDENTIFICATION: (this information is required by the FDA through The Safe Medical Device
Act of 1990 if the Medical Device has caused serious illness or injury [including death] to patient)
List all products/devices connected to the patient at the time of the incident:

Product/Device name	Lot #/Expiration date	Serial #	Manufacturer
1. _____	_____	_____	_____
2. _____	_____	_____	_____
3. _____	_____	_____	_____
4. _____	_____	_____	_____
5. _____	_____	_____	_____
6. _____	_____	_____	_____

Disposable items *should not be discarded* until cleared by Risk Management.
Location of medical device/product: _____

V. Preparer's signature: _____ Date: _____ Time: _____ A.M. _____

P.M. _____

Title: _____

Unit Leader's Signature: _____ Date: _____ Unit: _____

Routing instructions: 1. Submit original to Office of Risk Management (ORM).
2. Original must be received by the ORM within 24 hours of incident.
3. For Patient Care Units, carbon to be maintained by Quality Improvement Coordinating Committee Chairperson.
4. For Ancillary Units, carbon to be maintained by Ancillary Care Evaluation Committee Chairperson.
SERIOUS INCIDENTS—CALL OFFICE OF RISK MANAGEMENT DIRECTLY
THIS FORM MAY NOT BE DUPLICATED

FORM/n0325 Rev. 2/92

FOR OFFICE USE ONLY

From Rush-Presbyterian-St. Luke's Medical Center, Chicago, 1997.

Patents, Intellectual Property, and Licenses

AARON SETH KESSELHEIM, M.D., J.D., F.C.L.M.

PATENTS
OTHER FORMS OF INTELLECTUAL PROPERTY
OWNERSHIP AND LICENSING

Got a great idea? The field of health care is driven by innovation, and the source of most of that innovation is from health care professionals themselves. It seems like each week a remarkable advance in medical progress hits the market in the form of a new medical device, drug, or biopharmaceutical. The physicians, researchers, nurses, and technicians who work daily to improve patient health are in the best position to evaluate inefficiencies in the system and develop novel solutions. Intellectual property refers to the legal rights that apply to the tangible manifestations of human creativity, and all inventors need to be aware of what intellectual property rights they are eligible for and how best to protect those rights.

This chapter surveys options for health care professionals who want to develop their research or ideas into new inventions. The first section describes patents, a powerful form of protection for inventions. The second section examines other types of intellectual property, including trade secrets, copyrights, and trademarks. Finally, the third section looks at how to take these intellectual property rights to the market through licensing and other development options.

PATENTS

Health care professionals, medical research companies, and universities have used patented innovations to change the practice of medicine. The process of giving anesthesia, for example, was patented in 1844 and the Bayer Company patented aspirin in 1900.[1] Getting a patent, however, is not simple. The multistep process takes an average of 2 years to complete and can cost up to $10,000.[2] Medical practitioners interested in patenting their innovations must understand what a patent is and the basics of applying for patents before they begin the arduous process of pursuing this form of intellectual property protection.

What is a patent?

A patent is a legal monopoly over a particular invention, granted by the federal government through the Patent and Trademark Office (PTO). The Patent Act was promulgated under constitutional authority to "promote the progress of science and the useful arts"[3] and dates back to 1790. Notably, patents do not give inventors any affirmative rights; rather, they give patent owners the right to "exclude others from making, using, offering to sell, or selling in the United States" the invention claimed in the patent.[4] The monopoly lasts for 20 years from the date the inventor officially applies for the patent.

A patent is classically thought of as a quid pro quo.[5] On the one hand, the government provides a monopoly—which might otherwise be illegal—for a limited time. The patent encourages inventors to risk the cost and time to develop their ideas, because it gives them a competition-free period in which to market a successful invention. On the other hand, the patent document becomes part of the public domain and can help inspire other inventions.

Why apply for a patent? Patents are not required to market inventions, but once a nonpatented item is put on public display, any rival company can copy and sell it with impunity. Thus, patents can defend against encroachment on an inventor's idea. Patents can also be used as an offensive strategy to grab a segment of a market and force others to execute agreements, such as licenses, with the inventor.

Three types of patents exist. Utility patents cover any "process, machine, manufacture, or composition of matter"[6] and can therefore be used for new medical equipment, drugs, or computer programs. Design patents shield the aesthetic qualities of items such as lamps, clothing, and furniture. The third kind of patent is reserved for plants.

Requirements for patentability

Subject matter and usefulness limitations. To qualify for a utility patent, inventors must be able to classify their inventions under one of the four statutory subcategories listed in the Act—that is, a process, machine, manufacture, or composition of matter. In reality, the threshold for meeting this statutory requirement is very low. In *Diamond v. Chakrabarty*, the Supreme Court ruled that a bacterial plasmid was patentable because it was man-made, noting that "anything under the sun made by man" falls under one of the categories.[7] Examples of impermissible subject matter include laws of nature (e.g., cardiac output = heart rate $\times$ stroke volume), material found unadulterated in nature (e.g., the bark of a tree), and physical phenomena (e.g., lightning). Obviously, this leaves a great deal of subject matter available for the potential inventor.

Another low-threshold statutory limitation is that of usefulness. Inventions, to be patentable, must be useful,[8] but just so long as the applicant postulates any reasonable use, it will be taken as presumptively correct[9] and the requirement will be satisfied. Usefulness remains an issue mostly when attempting to patent so-called "incredible" inventions, like perpetual motion machines, and new chemical compounds where utility might not be immediately apparent.

Novelty and anticipation. Another requirement for patentability is that the invention be "novel," which is akin to saying that one cannot get a patent for reinventing the wheel. If the invention is substantially the same as a previous invention that is either in existence or described in a patent application or other publication (which, together, is called the "prior art"), it is ineligible for patenting.[10] Detailed regulations in the Patent Act define "prior art."[11] Practically speaking, to ensure compliance with the novelty limitation, inventors should look for any devices, publications, or patent applications that anticipate their proposed inventions and thus make the patent application unsupportable. As with the subject matter limitation, "novelty" is interpreted broadly; to be excluded, every single aspect of the new invention must also be found in a piece of prior art.

Notably, pending patent applications anticipate proposed inventions. The United States, however, grants patents to the first inventor to conceive of an idea, even if that person files the patent application second. Inventors, therefore, should take rigorous steps to document the conception dates of their ideas by writing down brainstorms, having a witness attest to the date, and keeping all further development work in a signed and dated log book. As long as the inventor does not "abandon, suppress, or conceal"[12] his or her invention after this point on the way to developing a prototype or getting a patent, the evidence can prove the date of conception and defeat an earlier-filed patent application that otherwise would anticipate the invention.

Nonobviousness. The final major statutory requirement for patentability is that the proposed invention must be nonobvious in light of the prior art. If "novelty" was the only standard, then any small change to a prior invention would render it patentable. Obviousness ensures that small changes are not accorded patents, so that each patent adds to the progress of science and the useful arts. According to the Patent Act, the proper way to evaluate what is obvious is from the point of view of a "person of ordinary skill in the art,"[13] that is, the field to which the invention relates.

Obviousness is one of the least predictable aspects of patent law, so patent cases often turn on this issue. Courts are supposed to place themselves in the era when the invention was made, but one problem is that what may seem obvious in hindsight was not obvious at that time. Another issue is how broadly or narrowly to define the field in which the "person of ordinary skill in the art" is deemed to encompass. A third issue is how much to weigh so-called "objective indicia of non-obviousness,"[14] such as commercial success of the invention and long-felt need for the particular invention in the field.

For example, in *Cardiac Pacemakers v. St. Jude Medical*, the court had to decide whether the invention of an externally programmable implantable cardiac defibrillator was obvious.[15] In the "prior art" were programmable external defibrillators and the existence of implantable pacemakers that could be externally modulated. Was it obvious to a person of ordinary skill in the art to apply the technology from pacemakers to the defibrillators? The court thought not, finding no evidence in the record of any suggestion to combine those pieces of prior art.

The basic principle behind nonobviousness is that trivial variations in known inventions will not support a patent. Rather, some level of ingenuity is needed.

Applying for a patent

The patent document. Putting together a patent application and submitting it to the PTO for approval is the next step. Applicants can proceed by themselves ("pro se") or can hire a patent attorney or agent, a legal representative (who may or may not be a lawyer) with a technical background and a special certification from the PTO. The process can be lengthy and expensive, involving much back-and-forth communication with the PTO and multiple processing fees. Moreover, deadlines emerge at each step that, if missed, can render a patent application void. Given these pitfalls, inventors with the means to do so are strongly encouraged to seek out a patent attorney or agent.

The patent document traditionally includes a number of different sections, such as an abstract, a summary, and drawings, but the most important part of the application is the claim. The claim is the meat of the patent and defines the limits of the patent holder's intellectual property right. Despite what may be written elsewhere in the patent document, inventors must officially "claim" a particular feature to get patent protection over it.

The Patent Act requires four other significant formalities to complete the patent document.[16] The first is a written description of the invention, telling readers what the invention is and notifying people that the inventor understands what he or she is trying to patent. The second is an enablement requirement, which means that the patent document must "[e]nable any person skilled in the art . . . to make and use invention."[17] This helps fulfill the inventor's contribution to the patent quid pro quo—in exchange for a limited-term monopoly, the inventor must fully reveal to the public how to make and use the invention.

The third requirement is that inventors disclose the "best mode" (if they have contemplated one) available for making their inventions work. For example, a patent for an ultrasonic-assisted liposuction device was invalidated in part because a jury found that the patentees had determined, but did not disclose in the patent document, the device's "preferred frequency stabilizing circuit."[18] Fourth, patent claims must be definite, meaning that inventors must "particularly point out and distinctly claim"[19] their invention. Using comparative terms like "substantially" or "approximately" jeopardizes a patent's validity if they make the claims too vague for a person of ordinary skill in the art to understand the nature of the invention.

The examination process. Completed patent documents go to the PTO for evaluation, along with a fee and an oath attesting to the fact that the inventor is correctly named and that the inventor has disclosed any knowledge of prior art that may impact its patentability. The PTO classifies the invention based on the subject matter of its claims and sends it to an examination group, or "art unit." These groups are composed of patent examiners, PTO employees who have expertise in the general subject matter of their unit. One particular examiner assumes responsibility for the patent.

The examiner then checks the application for technical accuracy and examines the claims by comparing them to the prior art. This begins what can be a long process of communications and responses between the patent examiner and the applicant in which the examiner may require multiple alterations or rewording of claims to make them patentable. Applicants can invoke appeals and resubmissions to argue their cases further. The process can take months to years, depending on how back-logged the particular art unit is and how many changes are needed.

Special patenting issues for health care professionals

Though the patenting process is the same for a new mechanical heart or a skateboard, there remain a few special considerations for health care professionals who pursue patents, including a special exception to the patent law, the desire of many medical practitioners to seek publication of new results, and the ethics of medical patenting in general.

Medical process patents. In 1993, controversy arose when an Arizona ophthalmologist patented a "no-stitch" incision process for cataract surgery, and then sued a Vermont ophthalmologist for infringing the patent by using the procedure on his patients.[20] This was the first known occurrence of a lawsuit being used to enforce a patent for a medical process.[21] Commentators worried that such process patents would threaten patient access to new procedures, increase health care costs through licensing prices, and hinder the advance of medical knowledge.[22]

In 1996, Congress amended the Patent Act, depriving patentees of remedies for patents on surgical or medical procedures not involving a new drug or device.[23] While medical and surgical methods are patentable, the patent cannot be enforced against a health care practitioner utilizing the procedure. If any step of a medical process involves using a patented device, however, the health care professional still infringes the device patent. As a result, pure medical or surgical methods, such as the Heimlich maneuver or carotid artery massage to lower heart rate, are not worth patenting, no matter how novel or nonobvious they might be.

Publication and use of patentable inventions. Many health care professionals look to publish their research results and new ideas in the medical literature in order to disseminate the information among colleagues and gain professional respect. They also seek to put their inventions into practice as soon as possible, to advance patient care or test their effectiveness. There is no reason to restrain these practices, but if the health care professional also wants to seek a patent, a few principles should be understood.

First, according to the Patent Act, an inventor's own dissemination or publication will not serve as prior art to impact patentability unless it occurred more than a year before the patent application, or a less formal and less expensive version called a "provisional" patent application, was filed.[24] This so-called "statutory bar" is inflexible and can result in complete surrender of patent rights. According to the Federal Circuit, in determining what acts will invoke the bar, "the touchstone is public accessibility."[25] Submission to a journal for consideration of publication does not start the clock, but placing a single copy in a remote public depository in Alaska does. Health care professionals, therefore, should not necessarily feel constrained in publishing their inventive ideas. Rather, they should mark all prepublication copies as "classified" to restrict dissemination, and ultimately be cognizant of the publication date.

Any public use of an invention begins the one-year grace period for patent application submission as well. Experimental uses intended to perfect an invention, however, are not considered public uses. Thus, if health care professionals want to test their inventions before determining whether to pursue patents, they should take extra care to receive no payments, sign confidentiality agreements with all users, maintain written research progress notes, and ensure that they have complete control over the parameters of the test. These and other factors will help show that the use was experimental and does not invoke the statutory bar.

The ethics of medical patenting. Some have argued against pursuing health care patents because of the potential barriers it places to the dissemination of ideas and innovations. The AMA Code of Ethics in the 1950s claimed patenting medical devices was unethical.[26] Concerns include an increase in health care costs due to higher research costs from the legal and administrative expenditures in the patenting process, and a drive away from basic science research toward more profit-seeking motives.[27] Some argue that competing patents can slow scientific research because of all the licensing arrangements and permissions that would be needed to undertake meaningful research projects.[28]

Currently, however, while the AMA considers medical process patents unethical, it permits the patenting of drugs and devices.[29] Other commentators note that patenting ideas can help bring more advances into the public arena by providing future economic incentives for initial research and development costs.[30] Also, they provide for full disclosures of discoveries in the patent document, whereas otherwise inventors might keep them secret. It is an ethical decision for health care practitioners to make for themselves.

OTHER FORMS OF INTELLECTUAL PROPERTY

Patents are not the only form of intellectual property protection available; trade secrets, copyrights, and trademarks provide different kinds of protections. Health care professionals can utilize these legal creations in many aspects of their practices as well.

Trade secrets

A trade secret is a piece of information whose economic value derives from it being kept confidential. Many corporations have trade secrets, including, for example, the ingredients in Coca-Cola syrup. The classified information is protected by state law—unlike the act of Congress that created patents—so the definition of a trade secret varies from state to state. Most states agree, however, that the company must have invested time and money in developing the information, the information must be valuable to the conduct of the business, and the company must make a constant, vigilant effort to keep the information secret.[31]

Trade secrets also differ from patents in that statutory requirements like "novelty" and "non-obviousness" are not required. Any confidential, economically valuable piece of information can be considered a trade secret. Moreover, there is no 20-year time limit—a trade secret stays enforceable as long as the information remains a secret.

On the other hand, in many ways, patent protection is more secure than trade secret protection. The vitality of the trade secret depends on the vigilance used in guarding it, and any public pronouncements make the secret moot. If an enterprising customer deduces the secret information on his or her own, then the intellectual property protection is lost as well. A patented item is protected no matter how simple it may be for other people to construct.

Trade secrets are perfect for discrete pieces of knowledge that can easily be kept confidential or, like a recipe for Coca-Cola syrup, are unpatentable. Yet it is important to keep in mind that some trade secrets may be eligible for patenting, which can provide more substantive intellectual property protection.

Copyright

A copyright, like a patent, is a statutory entity. According to the Copyright Act, a copyright attaches to an "original work of authorship fixed in any tangible medium of expression."[32] Copyrights give the authors "exclusive rights" to profit from their work by copying, performing, publicly displaying, or producing derivative works from it.[33]

The two key aspects for copyright eligibility are originality and fixation in tangible form.[34] The Supreme Court ruled that to be original, a work must be independently created and possess "some minimal degree of creativity."[35] Copyrights and patents, which have their own requirement of novelty, therefore serve the similar purpose of helping encourage the production of original, creative works by attaching government-sponsored monopoly rights to them.

The primary difference between copyrights and patents is in what they protect. Utility patents cover technological innovations in their entirety, such that any item that matches the claims of a particular patent (or is an obvious variation thereof), no matter what it looks like, infringes the patent. A copyright, on the other hand, protects a specific individual expression of an idea.[36] Moreover, only true copying of the expression is protected, so two parties who, for example, separately draw similar maps of the same region can both copyright their own maps.[37]

Other differences are also important. Whereas patents last for 20 years, copyrights (for works created on or after January 1, 1978) last for the life of the author plus 70 years.[38] Unlike patents, a copyright immediately affixes to any tangible expression, so one need not engage in an application process. In fact, since March 1989, official notice does not even have to be placed on the item as a condition of copyrighting.[39]

Health care professionals who write textbooks, develop patient education videos, or publish journal articles should be aware that copyright protection vests in those works. Copyrights, like patents, can be exploited by licensing, assigning, or selling them. Moreover, health care professionals should be careful that they do not unintentionally infringe others' copyrights. For example, in *American Geophysical Union v. Texaco*, the Second Circuit found that the "institutional, systematic, archival multiplication of copies" of articles from scientific journals for its researchers violated the journals' copyrights.[40]

Trademark

A third important form of intellectual property is the trademark, a distinctive entity used to identify goods that a person or business intends "to use in commerce . . . to identify and distinguish his or her goods . . . from those manufactured or sold by others."[41] Trademarks can attach to anything distinctive—a word or phrase, a symbol, packaging, or any combination thereof. Trademarks protect the name of the business and prevent unscrupulous businessmen from deceiving customers by attempting to capitalize on someone else's success.

Trademark protection occurs on the federal level,[42] but like trade secrets, state laws and common law also protect trademarks.[43] As a result, one can either register a trademark through the official process with the PTO, or can acquire common law trademark protection over time simply by employing his or her mark in commerce. Trademarks can last indefinitely, as long as the mark remains in commercial use.

As with patents and copyrights, trademarks protect the business-related activities of health care professionals. For example, pharmaceutical companies register trademarks in their medication names, and Blue Cross/Blue Shield has a well-known health care services trademark. So, in developing a business to sell a patented item, be sure to register your trademark to protect your distinctive line from copycat products in the future.

OWNERSHIP AND LICENSING

Issuing a patent is just the beginning. This section examines patents as pieces of intellectual property, first by discussing the issue of who owns the patent and then by examining what can be done with it, including basic principles of patent licensing and marketing.

Ownership of the invention

According to the Patent Act, patents have "the attributes of personal property"[44] and so can be transferred, assigned in wills, and even mortgaged. The inventor named in the patent application becomes the original owner. If two or more inventors are listed, each is a joint owner of the patent, and each can make, use, or sell the patented invention without the consent of the other coinventors.[45] Such "freedom to exploit" the patent includes the ability to "license to others to exploit the patent"[46] as well, so a manufacturer can receive an exclusive license to produce a patented item from any of the joint owners, and the contract will bind them all.

Inventor/owners have three major options regarding what they can do with their patents. They can assign their patent rights to third parties, they can grant licenses under their patents, or they can pursue the development and marketing of their inventions by themselves.

Assigning patent rights

Patents are freely assignable, so inventors can directly convey their entire patent rights to a third party. The assignment is legally binding only if the assignment is in writing and then recorded in the PTO within 3 months.[47] In the case of joint inventors, each can assign his or her own patents rights, but all joint owners must agree to assign the full patent to a third party.

Under certain circumstances, inventors have a legal duty to assign their ownership rights in a patent. Courts will uphold premade express agreements to assign patent rights, as long as the agreements meet the standard requirements of any basic contract. In addition, there is a long-standing common law principle that people hired to perform specific inventive tasks must assign any forthcoming patent rights to their employer, even in the absence of an agreement.[48]

Outside of this one narrow case, however, dividing up patent assignment rights in the employer/employee context is more complicated. The default rule is that employees own the rights to their inventions, even if it is made on an employer's facility, during working hours, or with an employer's materials.[49] No generalized obligation to assign patent rights exists for employees. Rather, under these circumstances, the employer automatically receives a "shop right," a nonexclusive and nontransferable license to use the particular invention for free during the lifetime of the patent.

Savvy employers should therefore include an invention assignment clause in their employees' contracts, because courts are reluctant to imply such an agreement. For example, such a clause might require employees to disclose all inventive activity and to assign their inventions' "right, title, and interest."[50] This requirement ensures that employees do not steal employers' time, materials, or ideas for individual profit.

Yet limits on employee assignment provisions prevent employers from laying claim too broadly on employee inventive activity. Courts often insist that employee obligatory assignment clauses be reasonable in breadth and time, restricted to inventions relevant to the employer's business and made during the term of employment (or some reasonable duration of time thereafter). Some states have codified these principles into invention assignment statutes. California law states that employers cannot require employees to "assign that which is solely the product of the employee's time and effort outside of the employment assignment."[51]

Health care employers should establish a reasonable and predefined patent rights assignment policy—and health care employees should analyze the particulars of their employment contract. For example, Cedars-Sinai Hospital in Los Angeles requires all employees to sign an invention disclosure statement giving the hospital the rights to all employee inventions, but the clause specifically excludes intellectual property developed on employees' own time without the use of hospital equipment, unless it relates to hospital business or results from work performed by hospital researchers.[52] Employees, for their part, should define their job responsibilities and expectations, segregate their inventive activity, using their own supplies and time, and always act in good faith regarding their employers' intellectual property.[53]

Licensing patent rights

The entity that gains control of the patent rights must then decide what to do with them. One option is to develop, perfect, and sell the item individually. This alternative can maximize profits and control. The entrepreneur should contact designers to commission prototypes, contract with factories to engage in mass production, and work with retailers to move the product to the public. This approach, however, also has the most risk. Some estimate the average cost of perfecting a product and marketing it to be $250,000.[54] Moreover, busy health care professionals often cannot commit the requisite free time and leg work this strategy entails.

A more feasible means for health professionals to develop their inventions, then, is to work with an established production company that can provide the start-up capital and other resources. The patent holder can establish this relationship by signing a license with the company, a contract agreeing that the patent holder will not sue the company for infringing its patent rights when it subsequently develops the invention. Licenses can be exclusive, so that the licensee is guaranteed that no other company will be granted the same rights, or nonexclusive.

Determining when to pursue a licensing agreement is an important issue. A basic principle of licensing transactions is that the further established the intellectual property, the better one's bargaining position is with potential licensees.[55] Some entrepreneurs go further and develop a working prototype of their idea that they can use in pitch meetings with potential licensing partners.[56] The goal of improving bargaining position, however, must be weighed in each entrepreneur's mind against the incremental cost of taking each step along the way.

The first phase for patent holders interested in licensing their patent rights is to find a suitable licensing partner. For health care professionals, this can involve soliciting representatives from companies presenting similar products at national meetings or direct contact via phone or mail with companies' marketing directors or vice-presidents of research and development. Do not reveal too much information at this early stage, or else the company can use the idea to develop a similar item that does not infringe the patent; only the product specifically outlined in the patent,

not the general idea behind it, is protected. It is more prudent to sign a nondisclosure agreement with licensees before meeting with them. This document should outline that any disclosures will be held confidential, in return giving the potential licensee a fixed amount of time to decide whether it wants to license the invention.

In executing the license, the patent holder must consider a number of important contractual points. The most obvious is how much the rights to develop the invention cost. This normally involves an up-front licensing fee and a royalty, either a fixed sum per unit sold or a percentage of net sales. The average royalty rate for nonexclusive licenses is less than 5%, while exclusive licenses can command up to 15%.[57] Royalties can also be graduated, to either increase or decrease after the licensee reaches a certain sales volume.

Yet other contractual points should not be overlooked. The inventor can use the license contract to encourage the licensee to market the product better by setting a minimum royalty payment or early termination. The license should cover who owns future intellectual property rights in the invention, such as improvements made to the technology either by the inventor or the licensee. The inventor can contract with the licensee to provide technical assistance for proper development if the invention is complicated. The inventor can even contract to review the licensee's accounting practices or advertising practices to have confidence in the royalty payments and assure the quality of the item once it is mass-produced. Some intellectual property textbooks have examples of template license agreements that cover these points and more.[58]

Entrepreneurs need to consider carefully every eventuality that may arise in the licensee/licensor relationship and outline a basic agreement in the license contract. Many companies will have standard licensing agreements that they have developed, but entrepreneurs can negotiate points to reflect their predilections. Health care professionals who are not skilled in contract negotiations should consider working with an intellectual property attorney to help them understand and fashion an appropriate contract in this regard.

ENDNOTES

1. Chris J. Katopis, *Patients v. Patents? Policy Implications of Recent Patent Legislation*, 71 St. John's L. Rev. 329, 348 (1997).
2. Susan M. Skewes, *Got a Bright Idea? Patent It*, 62 R.N. 44-46 (1999).
3. U.S. Const. art. I, §8, cl. 8.
4. 35 U.S.C. §101.
5. Frank P. Porcelli & John A. Dragseth, *Patents: A Historical Perspective* 195 (2002).
6. 35 U.S.C. §101.
7. 447 U.S. 303, 309 (1980).
8. 35 U.S.C. §101.
9. *In re Brana*, 51 F. 3d 1560 (Fed. Cir. 1995).
10. Porcelli & Dragseth, *supra* note 5, at 48.
11. 35 U.S.C. §102.
12. 35 U.S.C. §102(g).

13. 35 U.S.C. §103.

14. *Stratoflex, Inc. v. Aeroquip Corp.*, 713 F. 2d 1530, 1538 (Fed. Cir. 1983).

15. 2002 U.S. Dist. LEXIS 4000, at *78 (S.D. Ind. 2002).

16. 35 U.S.C. §112.

17. 35 U.S.C. §112 ¶1.

18. *Mentor H/S, Inc. v. Medical Device Alliance Inc.*, 244 F. 3d 1365, 1371 (Fed. Cir. 2001).

19. 35 U.S.C. §112 ¶2.

20. *Pallin v. Singer*, No. 593CV202 (D. Vt. filed July 6, 1993).

21. *Medical Procedure Patent Claims Are Invalidated in Consent Judgment*, 51 Patent, Trademark & Copyright J. (April 11, 1996).

22. Katopis, *supra* note 1, at 335.

23. 35 U.S.C. §287(c).

24. 35 U.S.C. §102(b).

25. *In re Hall*, 781 F. 2d 897, 898-99 (Fed. Cir. 1986).

26. Katopis, *supra* note 1, at 354.

27. Samuel Packer, *Ethics and Medical Patents*, 177 Arch. Ophthal. 824-26 (1999).

28. Michael A. Heller & Rebecca S. Eisenberg, *Can Patents Deter Innovation? The Anticommons in Biomedical Research*, 280 Science 698-701 (1998).

29. American Medical Association, Council on Ethical and Judicial Affairs, *Ethical Issues in the Patenting of Medical Procedures*, 53 Food Drug L. J. 341 (1998).

30. Coe A. Bloomberg et al., *Patenting Medical Technology*, 317 New Engl. J. Med. 565-67 (1987).

31. Iver P. Cooper, *Biotechnology and the Law* §11.0 (West Group 2001).

32. 17 U.S.C. §102.

33. 17 U.S.C. §106.

34. Robert A. Gorman & Jane C. Ginsburg, *Copyright: Cases and Materials*, 5th ed., 75 (Lexis Law Press 1999).

35. *Feist Publications v. Rural Telephone Service Co.*, 499 U.S. 340 (1991).

36. *Mazer v. Stein*, 37 U.S. 201 (1954).

37. *Fred Fisher Inc. v. Dillingham*, 298 F. 145, 151 (S.D.N.Y. 1924).

38. 17 U.S.C. §302(a).

39. Berne Convention Implementation Act of 1988.

40. 60 F. 3d 913 (2nd Cir. 1994).

41. 15 U.S.C. §1127 (1994 & Supp. V 1999).

42. Lanham Act of 1946, Federal Trademark Dilution Act of 1996.

43. Mass. Gen. Laws Ann. ch. 110B, 12 (West 1996).

44. 35 U.S.C. §261.

45. 35 U.S.C. §262.

46. *Ethicon Inc. v. United States Surgical Corp.*, 135 F. 3d 1456, 1468 (Fed. Cir. 1998).

47. Or prior to a future claimant of assignment rights, whichever comes last. 35 U.S.C. §261.

48. *Standard Parts v. Peck*, 264 U.S. 52 (1924)

49. Cooper, *supra* note 31, at §7.01[2][a].

50. Arthur H. Seidel, *Counseling the Potential Patent Applicant*, 30 Practical Lawyer 63-72 (1984).

51. H. Clarke Anawalt, *Idea in the Workplace: Planning for Protection* 44 (Carolina Academic Press 1988).

52. Bloomberg, *supra* note 30, at 567.

53. Anawalt, *supra* note 51, at 80.

54. Neil Chesanow, *Who Wants to Be a Millionaire Inventor?*, 78 Med. Econ. 145-52 (2001).

55. Cooper, *supra* note 31, at §7.02[1].

56. George C. Christoudias, *The Making of an Instrument: From Concept to Market*, 2 J. Soc. Laparoendoscopic Surg. 301-07 (1998).

57. Cooper, *supra* note 31, at §7.02[5][a].

58. Robert C. Dorr & Christopher H. Munch, *Protecting Trade Secrets, Patents, Copyrights, and Trademarks*, 3rd ed., §4.18e (Aspen Law & Business 2000).

Federal Health Information Privacy Requirements

KAREN S. RIEGER, B.A., J.D.

FEDERAL HEALTH INFORMATION PRIVACY REGULATIONS
STATE HEALTH INFORMATION PRIVACY LAWS
CONCLUSION

The public's assurance of privacy in health care information must be preserved so that patients remain willing to communicate sensitive personal information to their health care providers. Failure to address privacy concerns undermines public confidence in the health care system. Protection of confidential medical information may encourage individuals to seek treatment and seek it earlier. Maintaining confidentiality of health information bolsters the health care system while reducing liability risks to the providers charged with protecting the private information they receive. Federal law and state laws have requirements regarding access to, and protection of, health care information, as summarized below.

FEDERAL HEALTH INFORMATION PRIVACY REGULATIONS

On December 28, 2002, the Department of Health and Human Services released the final version of the federal health information privacy regulations, which were implemented in conjunction with the Health Insurance Portability and Accountability Act of 1996 ("HIPAA"), Public Law 104-191.[1] Amendments to the privacy regulations were published in the *Federal Register* on August 14, 2002.[2] These regulations are located in the Code of Federal Regulations at 45 C.F.R. Parts 160 and 164. The regulations are referenced in this chapter as the HIPAA Privacy Regulations. In most cases, compliance with the HIPAA Privacy Regulations was required on or before April 14, 2003.

The purposes of the HIPAA Privacy Regulations are to (1) provide consumers access to their health information and control inappropriate uses of their information; (2) improve the quality of health care by restoring trust in consumers; and (3) improve the efficiency and effectiveness of health care delivery by creating a national framework for the use and disclosure of sensitive health care information.[3]

Covered entities

The HIPAA Privacy Regulations apply to health information created or maintained by "Covered Entities," which are defined to include (1) health plans, (2) health care clearinghouses, and (3) health care providers who transmit any health information in electronic form in connection with a transaction covered by the HIPAA Privacy Regulations.[4] The HIPAA Privacy Regulations protect individually identifiable health information that is created or received by a health care provider, health plan, employer, or health care clearinghouse and that relates to the past, present, or future physical or mental health of a person, the provision of health care to a person, and/or the payment for health care.[5] Such protected health information is referenced in this chapter as "PHI."

Use and disclosure for treatment, payment, and health care operations

Under the HIPAA Privacy Regulations, a Covered Entity may use or disclose a patient's PHI without obtaining patient consent or an authorization for purposes of treatment, payment, and health care operations.[6] "Treatment" under the regulations includes the provision, coordination, or management of health care and related services by one or more health care providers, including coordination of care between a provider and a third party; consultation between health care providers relating to a patient; or the referral of a patient for health care from one health care provider to another.[7] The use for "payment" purposes includes a broad range of activities, including determination of insurance coverage and/or eligibility for coverage; billing and collection activities; and utilization review activities.[8] "Health care operations" is defined in the HIPAA Privacy Regulations to include such things as business and financial planning; peer review and quality assurance activities; conducting or arranging for accounting, legal, and other professional services; and business management and administrative activities.[9]

Written authorization requirements

For uses and disclosures of PHI *other than* for treatment, payment, and health care operations, the Covered Entity must obtain the patient's written authorization unless otherwise permitted or required by law.[10] The HIPAA Privacy Regulations set forth specific requirements for this written authorization form. In particular, the form must be written in plain language and is required to include the following:

- Who can disclose the PHI subject to the authorization.
- The exact information authorized to be disclosed.
- The purpose of the disclosure.
- The right of the patient to revoke the authorization, and the effect of a revocation.
- The name or class of persons to whom the covered entity is authorized to release the PHI.
- An expiration date or event.
- Whether the Covered Entity will receive any compensation/remuneration in connection with the PHI authorized to be released.
- A statement that the PHI authorized for disclosure may be redisclosed by the recipient and not protected.
- The signature of the patient or his or her legally recognized personal representative.[11]

In addition to the elements of an authorization required under the HIPAA Privacy Regulations, applicable state law may require an authorization to include additional information.[12]

Notice of privacy practices

The HIPAA Privacy Regulations also require health care providers, on the first encounter with the patient following August 14, 2003, to provide patients with a written notice of the provider's privacy policies and to make a good faith effort to obtain written acknowledgment of the patient's receipt of the notice. A health plan was required to provide this notice by April 14, 2003, unless it qualifies as a small health plan, which have another year to comply.[13]

If a Covered Entity is not able to obtain a written acknowledgment of the patient's receipt of the notice, it should document in its records the reasons such acknowledgment could not be obtained.[14] The notice of privacy practices is required to include a number of specific disclosures.[15]

Business associate requirements

Although the HIPAA Privacy Regulations cover only the Covered Entities mentioned above, the regulations expand protections by requiring that Covered Entities obtain written assurances from their "business associates" that the business associate will appropriately safeguard the individual's PHI.[16] Business associates are individuals or entities, other than members of the Covered Entity's workforce, that receive, create, or have access to PHI and perform a function or service

on behalf of the Covered Entity.[17] The business associate agreement also must include provisions such as the following: restrictions on how the business associate may use or disclose the PHI; a promise to protect the information; an obligation to return or destroy the information at the end of the contract; and assurances to make the information available to the Covered Entity for compliance purposes.[18] The commentary to the August 14, 2002 amendments to the HIPAA Privacy Regulations contains some sample language for business associate agreements.[19] However, Covered Entities should consult with their legal counsel before using such language, to be certain that the agreements are drafted in a manner that complies with applicable state law.

Certain permitted/required uses and disclosures

The general rule under the HIPAA Privacy Regulations is that a Covered Entity may not use or disclose an individual's PHI without the individual's written authorization (1) except for treatment, payment or health care operations, or (2) unless otherwise permitted or required by the HIPAA Privacy Regulations or other laws or regulations. However, unrestricted access and/or disclosure of PHI may be necessary for certain purposes such as protecting the public health, reducing health care fraud, and improving the quality of treatment of patients. In these instances, obtaining an authorization may hinder a health care provider's ability to adequately protect and promote public health. Therefore, in certain limited circumstances, a health care provider may disclose PHI without the patient's consent, authorization, or providing the patient the opportunity to agree or object. This includes but is not limited to the following:

- Reporting abuse or neglect of children and vulnerable adults.
- Reporting criminally inflicted injuries.
- Certain limited disclosures to law enforcement officials.
- Disclosures to appropriate health authorities conducting public health surveillance, public health investigations, public health interventions, and regulatory oversight.
- Disclosures for purposes of the Medicaid program.
- Reports of certain deaths to the medical examiner.
- Disclosures to funeral directors and for cadaveric organ, eye, or tissue donations.
- Disclosures under workers' compensation laws.[20]

Disclosures in facility directories

In addition to the exceptions above, a Covered Entity may include certain patient information in a facility directory (i.e., the patient's name, location within the facility, and one-word condition, such as fair, critical, serious, or death), disclose it to members of the clergy, or disclose it to family or close friends of the patient who ask for the patient by name without patient authorization. The Covered Entity must give the patient the opportunity to object or agree to these disclosures. The objection may be oral or in writing.[21]

Research requirements

As noted above, a health care provider may use a patient's PHI in the course of treatment, payment, and health care operations without obtaining an authorization. However, because most research activities fall outside of these areas, specific patient authorization is generally necessary for use or disclosure of PHI for research purposes unless an exception applies. The HIPAA Privacy Regulations do permit providers to use or disclose research information using data that has been stripped of its identifiers, known as "de-identified health information." De-identified health information is health information that does not identify the patient and in which there is no reasonable basis to believe that the health information can be used to identify the patient. Because de-identified health information has been stripped of all identifiers, it is not subject to authorization requirements.[22]

Limited data set use

A "limited data set" is an additional disclosure method applicable to research. A limited data set is PHI that does not directly identify the patient, but which contains certain potentially identifying information. A limited data set may be used or disclosed by a provider without patient consent or authorization only for the purposes of research, public health, or health care operations, and is subject to certain restrictions. Limited data sets have the same identifiers removed as de-identified data sets with three exceptions. Limited data sets may include identifiers such as birth date, dates of hospital admissions and discharges, and an individual's residence by city, county, state, and five-digit zip code. Recipients of PHI contained in limited data sets must enter into a data use agreement with the provider before receiving the limited data set. Certain other limited exceptions permit disclosure of a patient's PHI without consent or authorization in certain limited circumstances.[23]

Specific patient rights

In addition to placing restrictions on a Covered Entity's ability to use or disclose PHI, the HIPAA Privacy Regulations also provide patients with certain rights regarding their PHI. These include the following:

Access to PHI. Generally, a patient has the right to access, inspect, and obtain a copy of his or her PHI upon request. This does not include psychotherapy notes, records compiled by a Covered Entity in reasonable anticipation of, or for use in, a civil, criminal, or administrative proceeding, or information subject to law that prohibits access to such information. There also are some limited circumstances under which a patient or his or her personal representative can be denied access to the patient's PHI if a licensed

health care professional believes such access would endanger the patient or another person.[24]

Amendment of PHI. A patient has the right to request the Covered Entity to amend the patient's PHI for as long as the information is maintained by the Covered Entity. The Covered Entity may deny the request for an amendment if the patient asks to amend information that: (1) was not created by the Covered Entity, unless the person or entity that created the information is no longer available to make the amendment; (2) is not part of the medical health information kept by the Covered Entity; or (3) is not part of the information which a patient is permitted to inspect and copy by law. Further, a Covered Entity may deny a request for amendment if it believes the information is accurate and complete. If the Covered Entity declines to make a requested amendment to a patient's PHI, the patient is permitted to submit a written statement regarding the amendment that was requested. This statement must be included with the patient's medical record and released as part of the record.[25]

Accounting of disclosures. Patients have a right to request a list of certain disclosures the Covered Entity has made of their PHI. This right does not include disclosures made for treatment, payment, and health care operations; disclosures for certain law enforcement activities; disclosures of directory information and/or disclosures to family members or friends involved in the patient's care; disclosures pursuant to an authorization; or disclosures to the individuals themselves.[26]

Restrictions. A Covered Entity must permit a patient to request certain restrictions on the use and disclosure of his or her PHI. The Covered Entity is not obligated to agree to such requested restrictions. However, if it does agree to a restriction, it may not use or disclose PHI in violation of the restriction.[27]

Communications by alternative means. A Covered Entity must permit patients to request to receive communication of PHI by alternative means or at alternative locations. The Covered Entity must accommodate any reasonable requests and may not require an explanation.

Minimum necessary rule

A key requirement of the HIPAA Privacy Regulations is that a Covered Entity must make reasonable efforts to limit protected health information used and/or disclosed to the minimum necessary to accomplish the intended purpose of the use, disclosure, or request.[28] For example, if a consulting physician needs to review only a specific portion of the patient's medical record, only that portion should be disclosed. Further, members of a Covered Entity's workforce should only access and use the portions of a patient's PHI that such person needs to perform his or her job functions. The Department of Health and Human Services has indicated that the use of reasonable safeguards will be acceptable to meet this requirement. For example, patient files should be maintained in locked file cabinets when they are not needed for treatment, payment, or health care operational purposes, and should not be left unattended on desks and in other locations where the patient's PHI could be inadvertently seen. On the other hand, the regulators have made clear that the "reasonable necessary" requirement will still permit the use of patient sign-in sheets, surgery scheduling boards, and other common practices of health care professionals that might result in the disclosure of a minimal amount of PHI.[29]

Penalties for noncompliance

A number of penalties may be imposed on Covered Entities that violate the HIPAA Privacy Regulations. In particular, a civil penalty of $100 per violation, not to exceed $25,000 per person per calendar year, may be imposed. In addition, the following criminal penalties can be imposed for egregious violations:

- Up to $50,000 and/or 1 year in prison for knowingly misusing PHI.
- Up to $100,000 and/or 5 years in prison for using PHI under false pretenses.
- Up to $250,000 and/or 10 years in prison for inappropriately using PHI for "commercial advantage."[30]

The HIPAA Privacy Regulations do not give an individual patient the right to sue a Covered Entity for noncompliance. Thus, only the government may seek to enforce these regulations.

STATE HEALTH INFORMATION PRIVACY LAWS

The HIPAA Privacy Regulations were adopted, in part, to create a uniform, national system for the use and disclosure of medical records and other PHI. These regulations provide that they will preempt, or take precedence over, any state laws that are contrary to the provisions of the HIPAA Privacy Regulations. A state law is considered contrary if (1) it is not possible to comply with both, or (2) the state law is an obstacle to accomplishing and executing the purposes and objectives of the HIPAA Privacy Regulations.[31] However, there are some situations, or exceptions, in which a state law will not be preempted, and will continue to apply. The exceptions applicable to health care providers are described below.

First, state laws that provide for the reporting of disease or injury, child abuse, birth and death statistics, and/or the conduct of public surveillance, investigation, or intervention in order to promote public health, will not be preempted by the HIPAA Privacy Regulations.

Second, the Secretary of the Department of Health and Human Services, upon a written request from a state governor, may request an exception for a specific state law in order to (1) prevent fraud and abuse; (2) ensure appropriate state regulation of insurance and health plans; (3) provide

for state reporting on health care delivery or costs; or (4) to serve a compelling need related to public health, safety, welfare, etc. To date, no such exception has been requested by any governor.

Finally, and perhaps most importantly, the HIPAA Privacy Regulations do not preempt state laws that are more "stringent" than the requirements of the HIPAA Privacy Regulations. A state law is more stringent if (1) it is more restrictive on use and disclosure of PHI; (2) it permits greater rights of access or amendment by a patient to his or her PHI; (3) it provides the patient more information about the use, disclosure, rights, and/or remedies relating to his or her PHI; (4) in connection with a state law dealing with the required form, substance, or need for express legal permission to release, the state law narrows the scope or duration of permitted releases of the patient's PHI, increases privacy protections, or reduces coercive effects regarding release; (5) it requires retention or reporting of more detailed information and/or for a longer duration; and (6) it provides greater privacy protection to the patient regarding his or her PHI.

Many states have physician/patient privilege laws that, subject to a number of exceptions, allow the patient to prevent the disclosure of the patient's health information without the patient's specific consent.[32] Courts have recognized a health care provider's obligation to invoke a privilege on the patient's behalf, to the extent protected information is requested from the provider.[33] A physician/patient privilege law generally permits a patient to prevent the disclosure of his or her health information that was disclosed to a health care provider for purposes of diagnosis and/or treatment. Courts have not recognized the privilege in connection with disclosures made for other purposes. For example, in the case of *Tarrant County Hospital District v. Hughes*,[34] a hospital was required to release the names of blood donors whose blood was infused into a patient who contracted AIDS. The court found that this information was not provided for diagnosis and/or treatment of the blood donors.

As noted above, the HIPAA Privacy Regulations do not require patient consent in order for the patient's physician or other health care provider to release and use the patient's PHI for treatment, payment, and/or health care operations. However, because state physician/patient privilege laws may provide greater protection for a patient's PHI when the patient has not waived the privilege, such laws will not be preempted by the HIPAA Privacy Regulations. In addition to the physician/patient privilege statute, many states have other professional privilege laws that also provide more protection for a patient's PHI, and will not be preempted. These include patient/social worker privilege laws; patient/psychologist privilege laws; patient/licensed professional counselor privilege laws; and licensed marital and family therapist privilege laws.

Further, many states have laws that contain some very restrictive requirements regarding the use and disclosure of a patient's PHI that may contain communicable disease information,[35] and records containing mental health information and/or substance abuse information.[36]

CONCLUSION

It is important for all health care providers to understand their obligations under both the HIPAA Privacy Regulations and any applicable state health information privacy laws and regulations. This chapter should be viewed as a starting point in identifying key health information privacy requirements, and directing such professionals to more detailed information regarding these legal issues. A health care provider should consult with any attorney licensed in his or her state to obtain specific advice regarding the health information privacy requirements applicable in that particular state.

ENDNOTES

1. 65 Federal Register 82462.
2. 67 Federal Register 53182.
3. *Id.*
4. 45 C.F.R. §160.103.
5. 45 C.F.R. §160.103.
6. Because of ambiguities regarding consent requirements imposed by a state, however, it may nonetheless be necessary in some instances for a Covered Entity to obtain patient consent.
7. 45 C.F.R. §164.501.
8. 45 C.F.R. §164.501.
9. 45 C.F.R. §164.501.
10. For example, an individual's authorization is required for fundraising activities, except for limited activities involving only demographic information and date of service, and for marketing activities, except for certain face-to-face encounters and promotional gifts of nominal value.
11. 45 C.F.R. §164.508.
12. For example, Oklahoma law requires that the following language be included in order for an authorization to be valid: "The information authorized for release may include records which may indicate the presence of a communicable or venereal disease which may include, but are not limited to, diseases such as hepatitis, syphilis, gonorrhea and the human immunodeficiency virus, also known as acquired immune deficiency syndrome (AIDS)."
13. 45 C.F.R. §164.520.
14. 45 C.F.R. §164.520(c)(2)(ii).
15. 45 C.F.R. §164.520.
16. 45 C.F.R. §164.504(e).
17. 45 C.F.R. §160.103.
18. 45 C.F.R. §164.504(e).
19. 67 Federal Register 53264.
20. 45 C.F.R. §164.512.
21. 45 C.F.R. §164.510.
22. 45 C.F.R. §164.514.
23. 45 C.F.R. §164.514.
24. 45 C.F.R. §164.524.
25. 45 C.F.R. §164.526.
26. 45 C.F.R. §164.528.
27. 45 C.F.R. §164.522(a).
28. 45 C.F.R. §164.502.
29. *See, e.g.*, OCR HIPAA Privacy Guidance, December 3, 2002.
30. 42 U.S.C. §1320d-5, 42 U.S.C. §1320d-6.
31. 45 C.F.R. §160.201 *et seq.*
32. *See, e.g.*, 12 Okla. Stat. §2503.
33. *Hospital Corporation of America v. Superior Court of Pima County*, 755 P. 2d 1198 (Ariz. App. 1988); *Parkson v. Central Du Page Hospital*, 435 N.E. 2d 140 (Ill. App. 1982).
34. 734 S.W. 2d 675 (Tex. App. 1987).
35. *See, e.g.*, 63 Okla. Stat. §1-502.2.
36. *See, e.g.*, 43 A Okla. Stat. §1-109.

IV

Medical Legal and Ethical Encounters

Ethics and Bioethics

JOHN R. CARLISLE, M.D., LL.B., F.C.L.M.

TRUTH TELLING
THE PRINCIPLES OF BIOMEDICAL ETHICS
AUTONOMY
BENEFICENCE (AND ITS COUNTERPART, NONMALFEASANCE)
JUSTICE

It may seem strange to some that there is a chapter touching on bioethics in a textbook of legal medicine. Many physician readers might think that the practice of law has little to do with ethics, and the legal readers might be forgiven for failing to perceive much effect of ethical discourse in contemporary medical practice. Both these viewpoints are unfair, and it is consistent with the role and mission of the American College of Legal Medicine (ACLM) to show how ethical discourse has a significant influence on the interface between law and medicine.

Both law and medicine, when practiced at their best, seek to do what is right and good, and ethics helps both disciplines better define and ultimately achieve that objective. The contemporary construction of bioethics was first well formulated in the United States in the mid-1970s by the statement of the four principles of bioethics elucidated by Beauchamp and Childress.[1] These principles, which are intended to guide the resolution of all ethical dilemmas in biomedicine, have become at once the mantra of ethicists and the generally accepted guiding principles for all bioethical discourse. They are as follows:

1. Autonomy of the person
2. Beneficence
3. Nonmalfeasance (which some see as an element of beneficence)
4. Justice

With these goals to guide personal morality, directing as it does all aspects of professional behavior, the performance of physicians, attorneys, and medicolegal specialists will generally tend toward the good and urge others to do so as well.

There is considerable need for ethical thought in the twenty-first century as the practice of both medicine and law tends more and more to regard commercial concerns as an appropriate if not a principal concern. As a result, professionals training for practice in these fields should certainly be given a basis for understanding ethical issues and generating ethical discourse in their medical and law schools so that an effective balance between commercial concerns and moral principles may suffuse medicolegal problem solving. It has been widely argued that the resurgent feeling of need for ethical evaluation has resulted from the rapid progression of medical technologies in various fields, making it technically possible to do so many things that previously were not considered because they could not be done. The thesis is that because we can do so many more things, we are ever more impelled to ask ourselves whether we ought to do those things. Although clearly those issues have been involved in the needed resurgence of ethical discourse, in the twenty-first century different and perhaps even more profound changes appeared in our society and in the way we delivered health and legal services. These changes have worked even more strongly to bring ethical issues into relevance. Certainly many of the issues posed by the exponential growth of "managed care" involve intense ethical concerns and have prompted a resurgence of interest in the subject.

In addition the rise in general levels of education and the broad sweeping prominence of concepts of autonomy have driven the idea of benevolent paternalism, which in the past had been a large part of the ethos of both law and medicine, into the background. The desire, in fact the demand, of patients, families, and clients to understand all of the alternatives and to make meaningful choices whether or not they are considered wise by professional advisors has forced physicians and attorneys to think in ever more ethically oriented terms about what they tell people, what they counsel them about, the alternatives they put to them, and the way in which they interact with patients' choices. As with any change, there is some resistance within the professions, but many believe that overall these changes in attitude will be a great advantage to the professions, their patients and clients, and society in general.

Ever more physicians and attorneys will need to concern themselves as much with what ought to be as with what could be, and it is hoped that, together with colleagues in other interested disciplines, they will be equipped to engage in an ethical discourse that will effectively inform and guide those deliberations.

In recognition of the increasing importance of ethical guidance in medical and medicolegal practice, many organizations interested in those fields publish codes of ethics and ethical opinions designed to assist professionals in considering bioethical issues. Guidance is offered by the American Medical Association's Ethical Code and supplanted by the published opinions of the Council on Judicial and Ethical Affairs. The Canadian Medical Association has promulgated a new Code of Ethics following up on a several-year study by its Committee on Ethics. Ethical codes in medicine and law contain constant principles but are ever changing in response to rapid and important changes in their environment. The Canadian Medical Association code, revised only several years ago, is about to undergo another update to meet rapidly changing circumstances of practice to which it must respond.

These general guidelines are supplanted by ethical codes provided by a number of medical, medicolegal, and legal societies. The ACLM recently adopted its own Code of Ethics for medicolegal practice, which it is hoped will be of assistance at the interface of law and medicine. In addition there are international codes, such as the Declaration of Geneva, the International Code of Medical Ethics, the Declaration of Tokyo, the Declaration of Oslo, and the Declaration of Helsinki. In their latest revised editions, many of the codes provide additional guidance to supplement traditional medical texts, such as the Oath of Hippocrates. A number of governmental agencies and research funding bodies also have devised and made available ethical guidelines that will be helpful.

TRUTH TELLING

As previously indicated, there is much in the obligation between a physician and patient that is like the fiduciary relationship with which attorneys are familiar. The imbalance of power between the physician and the patient dictates that society must hold the physician to owe the highest duty of fidelity, honesty, and lack of self-interest to his or her patient. The physician must tell the patient the truth, the whole truth, and nothing but the truth and must act at all times in the best interests of the patient, forsaking any personal interest that conflicts with that of the patient. He or she must not deal secretly with others who are contrary in interest to the patient and must at any time reasonably account to the patient for his or her activity on their behalf. Physicians' duties related to confidentiality and conflict of interest arise from this fiduciary relationship.

What then should be the obligation of the physician when he or she knows that a serious mistake has been made in the patient's treatment? One might think that it would be the clear obligation of the physician to disclose any error

made, to assist the patient as much as possible to recover from that error, and to seek any recompense to which he or she might be entitled. Indeed most learned professions, including the law, recognize such obligations in their ethical codes and guidelines. It is interesting and somewhat regrettable, however, that the medical profession by and large does not recognize this obligation and certainly does not in the large part practice as if it were recognized. The culture of blaming, which is part of medical training; the litigious nature of the medicolegal field; and physicians' abhorrence of the idea that they could be responsible through simple human error for adverse outcomes suffered by patients make physicians reluctant to discuss errors and certainly reluctant to disclose them. The recently published study from the Institute of Medicine, edited by Linda Kohn, Janet Corrigan, and Molla Donaldson,[2] discusses this phenomenon at length and points out how far the medical profession has to go in recognizing and dealing with error and in prescribing and fostering open communications with patients and their families when error occurs.

Generally it is the burden of learned professions to spend time and considerable effort assisting patients in understanding complex and unfamiliar concepts (e.g., during the process of obtaining informed consent and directions for action). As physicians continually improve their skills and attitudes in this aspect of their practices, it would serve them well to consider how those same skills might be applicable to honest communication with patients and families when adverse outcomes occur. If physicians truly believe themselves to be obligated to act as advocates for their patients in the health care system and if the profession wishes to retain the good reputation for honesty and skill and the public trust that it thereby enjoys, this issue should certainly be on the front burner of professional discussion in the next few years. Without pointing any fingers from a professional corner that is far from entirely blameless, attorneys and ethicists may be able to help in this consideration and should make every effort to do so.

Telling the truth surely must be one of the principal hallmarks of all professional callings, particularly in the field of legal medicine. All trainees in that field should recognize this fact and should work through the complicated discussions that surround this seemingly simple concept. Competence to deal with such issues should be seen as a prerequisite for entering independent professional practice.

The fiduciary nature of the relationship between physician and patient represents that fundamental trust that is the essence of the interaction between physicians and the community. It is the basic reason that people trust physicians. Much in the rest of this book describes the legal result of the outrage people exhibit when they feel that their trust has been betrayed, and this backlash serves as evidence of a basic public expectation that physicians will honor that ethical trust. In an era when so many influences and so much money seek to draw the physician's loyalty to agendas other than those of the patient, there is a growing need for frank discussion among physicians, attorneys, and social policy-makers as to what these expectations are and should be.

For physicians, the trust between them and their patients is fundamental to patients seeking care and to their compliance during the provision of care. For the medical profession, the meeting of those public expectations when moves are afoot to divide physicians' loyalties in the health care system is essential, and to that end, considerable public discussion and ethical discourse must happen.

An example of emerging policies favouring honesty and disclosure can be found in the website of the University of Toronto Joint Centre for Bioethics and the Sunnybrook & Women's College Health Sciences Centre, one of the largest university hospitals in Canada (www.utoronto.ca/jcb/resources/admin-manual_disclosure&errors/htm).

THE PRINCIPLES OF BIOMEDICAL ETHICS

The basic principles set out and elucidated in ethical codes serve to guide decision-making. They are often individually imprecise or indecisive and may even be in conflict, and thus ethical discourse serves to analyze and determine the best approach to the good in individual cases and factual situations. The study of ethics thus involves the development of facility in ethical discourse, mostly through the study of worked case examples rather than as a general philosophical discussion. It is perhaps for this reason that bioethical analysis has become so helpful and popular in the medicolegal context, mirroring in its methods as it does, the way in which the substantive elements of the medical and legal disciplines are generally analyzed.

The classic sources of medical ethics were in the continental line of humanist philosophy, which had as its goal to seek rules capable of universality. Modern examples of this line of thought are the Declarations of the World Medical Association and the World Health Organization, arising from the Universal Declaration of Human Rights of 1948. This set of fundamental principles is rooted in an analysis of the evils of World War II and is declared to be of fundamental and universal applicability. The principles are equality among human beings, protection of individual liberties, respect for the dignity of all persons, and privacy. The more modern formulation of fundamental principles has been largely adopted for bioethical discourse and considers *autonomy, beneficence, nonmalfeasance*, and *justice*, although many would consider *nonmalfeasance* a part of *beneficence* and some would add *compassion*.

AUTONOMY

The word *autonomy* is derived from the Greek *auto nomos*, or self-rule, and involves in essence the idea of individual free choice or what citizens of Western democracies often call *freedom* or *liberty*. In the bioethical sense the concept

is that physicians and attorneys have an obligation to respect the free choice of the patient or client and more than that to facilitate in every reasonably possible way the making of such a free choice by each client or patient. In medical terms the concept is that the patient should control what happens to him or her in a medical sense by the exercise of free will and free choice. As early as 1914, Justice Cordozo pronounced the most famous and lasting statement of this principle when he wrote, "Every human being of adult years and sound mind has a right to determine what shall be done with his own body."[3]

Western societies have put a high value on free choice and liberty, and thus respect for even foolish or eccentric decisions is ultimately required because of the perception that the sort of society that does not require respect for autonomy is profoundly unacceptable. In practical terms, relating to medical encounters, a patient is often not in a position without the assistance of the physician to marshal enough information about the choice to be made that his or her unassisted preference could be considered genuinely autonomous. Thus for physicians and patients the concept of autonomy resolves itself into the patient's right to receive information sufficient to allow a reasonable person to make an intelligent decision and the patient's right to make a decision as to whether to accept or refuse the recommended medical treatment. From this practical interpretation of the importance of autonomy arise our legal rules relating to informed consent and what has come to be called *informed refusal*. This is but one example of how law takes ethical discourse and makes it into a practical requirement for everyone involved. An understanding of the ethical analysis of autonomy makes it easier to understand why informed consent is required and easier to enter into a legal debate about what the elements of that consent should be and how the law should characterize and implement the requirement.

Law is mostly about limits on autonomy, for clearly autonomy is limited. Whereas each individual should be free to make autonomous decisions about issues that affect only his or her own rights and interests, there must be limits on purely autonomous decision-making when the rights and interests of others are affected. To use a popular phrase, "Your rights end where my nose begins." Many of the issues that arise from "hard times" in medicine and the need to consider prioritizing and rationing available medical services are about the proper limits on autonomous decision-making, and this is discussed in the following section.

Wishes

In medicine, encounters between physicians and patients in which treatment recommendations would ordinarily be made often occur in circumstances in which the patient is not, at the time of treatment, able to express his or her wishes or exercise the right of autonomy. Increasingly in today's society, patients are able to foresee that there may be a time later in life when they are in a situation in which they wish to influence the decisions about their care but are unable to articulate their wishes at the time. Contemporary thought dictates that if wishes were previously expressed and are known to those recommending treatment, the previously expressed wishes ought to be respected as the best available indicator of the patient's autonomous choice. Previous wishes also must be interpreted carefully, and an attempt should be made to understand how those wishes might apply to current circumstances that significantly differ from what the patient might have been contemplating when the previous wishes were expressed.

Various types of formal advance directives have become popular and are now part of most health care settings. Many forms of living wills or advance directives are available, and many jurisdictions have dealt in statute with the way in which such documents should be used and interpreted. There does not seem to be any ethical reason that a person should not be able to contemplate at one point in his or her life circumstances he or she believes may occur later and exercise autonomous choice regarding responses to those circumstances at an earlier time. Equally there does not seem to be any obvious reason why physicians should not respect choices made at an earlier time provided there is no reasonable ground to believe that they have changed in the interval.

Many early living wills were quite simple and did not give much detail about the patient's wishes. Physicians often had difficulty interpreting these simple directives, and this limited their utility in facilitating the autonomy expressed. A patient's statement that he or she "did not wish to be kept alive artificially" did not provide much practical guidance to physicians treating the patient in a later critical illness. Did the patient mean that he or she did not want cardiopulmonary resuscitation but did want other supportive treatments? Did the patient mean that he or she did not want only any supportive treatments or any treatment at all? Did the patient mean that he or she did not wish to be kept alive by artificial means only when suffering from a predictably terminal illness for which no reasonable treatment is available, or did the patient mean that he or she did not wish to be given a brief, although admittedly artificial, form of treatment that would quickly bring an acute episode under control? In the last few years, all of these questions have resulted in much more well-thought-out forms of advance directives that ask patients more detailed questions about their preferences and give much more helpful guidance to physicians. A number of bioethical institutes have issued such documents, which seem to be both helpful and in high demand.*

---

*See, for example, www.utoronto.ca/jcb/_biodisclaimer/living_will.htm.

In the event of the apparent need for acute intervention to save life or limb, the default condition, at least in the bioethics of the Western world, has been generally accepted as being in favor of lifesaving treatment. The majority of ethical discourse suggests that it is reasonable to presume that most people wish to be saved at least from acute danger. This presumption must be interpreted carefully, however, against the zeal of the physician to provide care that he or she knows may be curative but may have been prohibited. The physician, whose personal feelings may strongly dictate in favor of treatment, must not be allowed to cavalierly ignore the principle of patient autonomy. A recent Canadian case illustrates this principle.[4]

A 57-year-old woman was brought unconscious to the emergency room. She had suffered significant injuries, including a head injury and multiple lacerations of her upper body, face, and scalp, in a severe motor vehicle accident. The attending physician conscientiously believed that the patient would die from exsanguination quite shortly and that he must administer a blood transfusion to save her life. In searching the patient's belongings, nurses found a card in her wallet stating that she was a Jehovah's Witness and would never wish to receive blood products or transfusions. Although this card was signed, places provided for a date and for a witness's signature were blank. The attending physician knew about the card and administered the transfusion anyway. The patient recovered and sued, alleging battery. The court found that the transfusion had been necessary from a medical standpoint and that it had saved the patient's life. The court also found that the physician was fully aware that this treatment was against the patient's wishes and contravened her direction. The physician was found to have committed battery, and damages were awarded in the amount of $20,000. The court held that, where the patient's refusal was based on religious grounds, it would not apply a test of reasonableness to them. The court held that it could not and would not absolve the physician from his responsibility to respect the patient's autonomous choice by finding the patient's religious convictions to be unreasonable.

Substitute decision-makers

The principle of autonomy should not be considered to be restricted to the patient's own choice whether personally expressed or expressed by advance directive. The patient may appoint a substitute decision-maker to serve in the event of his or her incapability, and in many jurisdictions statute law provides for decisions to be made on behalf of the patient by others. The decisions made by substitutes are to be treated in all respects as if the patient made them personally. Most of the laws recognize that the substitute decision-maker is in as much need of information from the physician as the patient would be if making the decision and require disclosure of such information. Most such statutes provide that if the physician is persuaded that the substitute decision-maker is not acting in the best interest of the patient or is not acting in accordance with the best knowledge available of the patient's actual wishes, he or she may seek the guidance of a court when practical.

Although it is clear that the principle of autonomy should be respected as a fundamental principle of medical ethics, it is equally clear that respect for that principle does not mean that the patient's wishes must be accepted and complied with in every case. Medical ethics does not require physicians to accede to patient choices that are illegal, illicit, or self-destructive. For example, patient demands to illegally prescribe drugs or to assist the patient in self-destruction or self-destructive activity may properly be resisted. It is more difficult to analyze the physician's proper response to a patient's choice that is unhealthy or foolish but falls short of impropriety. It is nevertheless clear that freedom of choice includes the freedom to make foolish choices, even choices that may be quite harmful or destructive, and these freedoms are not limited to choices in medical care but extend to lifestyle choices, such as the use of drugs, alcohol, tobacco, and other unhealthy lifestyles.

Of particular concern is the patient's request that the physician end his or her life or assist him or her in doing so. In most jurisdictions it is not a criminal offense to commit suicide, but in some jurisdictions it is an offense to assist or counsel another person to commit suicide. The principle of autonomy, as we have discussed, should not be interpreted as a requirement to always do what the patient wants, but at the same time the physician is dedicated to making the patient better if possible or making the patient feel as much better as possible, and classic texts dictate against the taking of life or the doing of harm.

Good palliative care often requires extreme measures to relieve pain and suffering, using powerful drugs that also may shorten the patient's life. This double effect has come to be accepted as a proper approach both ethically and legally in most jurisdictions, and treatment designed to reduce the suffering of a patient of a reasonable character is not interpreted by most as the doing of harm even though it may be reasonably foreseen to shorten the patient's life.

Positive actions taken by the physician to end or shorten the patient's life are criminal in most jurisdictions and are seen as sufficiently significant breaches of the principle of nonmalfeasance that many feel they cannot be justified by claims of respect for a patient's autonomous decision to die. In several European countries tentative steps have been taken to relax the legal rules surrounding euthanasia, and there is a fierce discussion in the ethical community and an equally fierce political and legal dispute in North America regarding the proper response to this situation. The proper ethical principle to apply and the societal determination of the conflict of principles between respect for autonomy and nonmalfeasance are yet to be resolved in most jurisdictions and will continue to be the subjects of intense ethical discourse and litigation for some years to come.

This debate will indeed be exacerbated by the fact that patients with serious life-ending illnesses survive longer because of the efficacy of their treatments, and their states of reduced function and thus reduced ability to exercise their autonomous choice create problems. As patients' ability to express their choice is reduced by their illness, it often becomes more and more difficult to determine whether their expressed wishes are their genuine choice or whether their apparent capability to make choices is illusory.

Refused autonomy

Sometimes patients, particularly those with long-term, chronic illnesses that have made them dependent in many ways, do not wish to make choices and do not wish to have information about their illness. The state of dependency extends to the patient's stated desire to simply depend on the physician to provide treatment in his or her best interest (in a maternalistic way) rather than be told all of the facts on which choices might be based. The principle of autonomy requires respect for patient wishes and decisions but should not be interpreted as requiring patients to make those decisions if they do not want to make them.

Ethical issues that arise from the principle of autonomy

A number of ethical issues in law and medicine are not directly part of the principle of autonomy but arise from it. Prominent among these are privacy, confidentiality, and its limits; the duty to warn; and the physician-patient relationship as a fiduciary obligation.

Privacy and confidentiality. Most authors include considerations of privacy and confidentiality in the discussion of the principle of autonomy because privacy is viewed as a principle closely related to autonomy. The right of self-determination or self-rule, particularly in today's society, in many ways revolves around the right to keep to oneself intimate information and thought. Dissemination of a person's most closely held secrets and thoughts robs the individual in many cases of the ability to exert self-determination and violates the self of the individual in a way that destroys autonomy. In both medicine and law the ancient texts require the maintenance of patients' or clients' secrets to the exclusion of all others, and almost every licensing and self-governing authority in both professions enforces strict rules to ensure the maintenance of patient or client confidences.

This principle is generally thought to be more than just an ethical precept; it is indeed a practical necessity for the practice of the profession. The attorney cannot effectively represent a client who out of fear of disclosure fails to tell the attorney every relevant detail about the matter, and similarly the physician must obtain from the patient a history, including every relevant detail no matter how embarrassing it may be or how much it might subject the patient to public odium if disclosed. For these reasons, patients and clients clearly must know that the ethics of the profession prohibit the practitioner from disclosing any information obtained through the physician-patient or attorney-client relationship. Only in this way will the patient or client be encouraged to be forthcoming, and only in this way will optimal services be delivered.

In contemporary society there is so much health information electronically shuttled around the world in computer banks for the purpose of billing, quality management, statistical analysis, and research it perhaps is not surprising that there have been a number of notable incidents in which privacy has not been accorded the value that it once was, and the confidentiality interests of the patient or client have been violated or ignored. A large Royal Commission Inquiry in Ontario, Canada, several years ago revealed widespread abuses of patient confidentiality by attorneys, insurance companies, and government agencies, and similar improprieties have been disclosed from time to time all over the Western world. Given the devastating effects that inappropriate disclosures may have on patients and given the ever-increasing spread of this information by electronic means, it perhaps is not surprising that there has been a resurgence of interest in the confidentiality of health information, and a number of jurisdictions have attempted various legislative means of ensuring privacy through regulations. From the point of view of the physician and attorney, the privacy rights of the patient as part of the ethical principle of autonomy should be viewed as extremely important and, wherever possible, should be highly respected. Rules requiring the maintenance of patient and client confidentiality should be carefully respected and should be broken only for a good reason or when required by law.

Of course, some overriding public interests will require breaches of confidentiality on the established principle that autonomy always has its limits and that in appropriate circumstances the autonomy of the individual must yield to the higher interests of the public and the state.

Most professional rules provide that confidentiality may be breached when such breach is required by law; mandatory reporting laws related to infectious disease, unfit drivers, unfit commercial pilots, and gunshot and grievous wounds are proper legal and ethical justifications for breach of confidentiality.

In both the United States and Canada a plethora of new laws and regulations regarding privacy and confidentially of health information has recently been introduced in response to public concerns about health information in the information age. Implementation of regulations often made without much input from clinicians may pose a number of serious problems as ethical principles come into conflict with hard practicalities in the delivery of health services.

The duty to warn. Of particular interest are situations in which the autonomy and confidentiality interests of a patient or client conflict with the personal safety interests of another person. When a patient indicates to an attorney, therapist, or physician that he or she intends to kill or seriously harm another person, it is often difficult to balance these interests. On the one hand, attorneys and physicians know that normal people often casually make statements of that kind without any real intent of carrying them out. They also are aware of a number of widely reported and tragic circumstances in which patients or clients who made such threats, which were not reported, went on to carry them out at the cost of the life of the threatened person. Because the prediction of general dangerousness is so difficult and may be impossible, it will often be extremely problematic for the practitioner to determine any reasonable basis on which to make a prediction as to when such threats might be carried out and when they might safely be treated as merely part of a normal, if strained, professional interview.

In many jurisdictions the law now requires that practitioners err on the side of safety by imposing a duty to warn individuals who are the subject of such threats in breach of confidentiality even if it does not seem likely that the threats will be carried out. This erring on the side of prevention of harm is favored by most ethicists as a sound decision, erring toward the achievement of the good. The literature now discloses reasonably good consensus as to warning signs suggesting that such threats are more likely to be carried out. Such warning signs are a definite and an immediate plan to take action, the apparent means to take action, a recent acquisition of the named weapon, availability of the victim to the perpetrator, and the description of a detailed plan of attack. If such signs are present, the knowledge that an actual attack is more likely will further ethically justify warning the putative victim.

The physician-patient or attorney-client relationship as a fiduciary relationship. The ethical requirement to respect autonomy of the patient as the principal pillar of bioethics causes consideration of the nature of that relationship. This is one of the areas where the professions of law and medicine have somewhat divergent views as to the implications of the ethical principle for the relationship of the professional with the patient or client.

In the legal profession, most codes of ethics of the bar and most legal licensing statutes establish clearly that the attorney-client relationship is a fiduciary relationship of utmost trust and fidelity and requires complete disclosure, utmost honesty, and utmost fidelity. For example, most bar codes strictly require the attorney to inform the client if any mistake, error, or misconduct occurs and to advise the client to obtain independent counsel. In most bar rules the records and papers pertaining to a transaction, when properly paid for, belong to the client and must be delivered forthwith, and in the attorney-client relationship everything that passes between the attorney and his or her client must be strictly accounted for and a full accounting must be delivered at any time it is demanded.

In contrast, the relationship between the physician and patient is not viewed by most medical societies and licensing authorities as so clearly of a fiduciary nature. Although the physician is expected to do his or her best for the patient and to see himself or herself at all times as principally obligated to the patient, many ordinary features of a fiduciary relationship are not accorded as much importance. The ownership and delivery of medical records are not nearly so clear, and there is no recognized obligation on the part of the physician in most jurisdictions to inform the patient of any error or misconduct or to suggest the obtaining of an independent and alternate caregiver. The concept of therapeutic privilege, which allows the physician the privilege in some circumstances to withhold the truth from the patient on the basis of his or her opinion that the truth might hurt the patient psychologically or make him or her resort to rash action such as refusing treatment, still seems to have some currency in sectors of the medical profession. There also continues to be some legitimacy accorded the idea that the use of placebos and other therapeutic fibs is necessary for cure in some situations. All of this speaks interestingly of the somewhat different approach to the incidents of autonomy in the two professions.

BENEFICENCE (AND ITS COUNTERPART, NONMALFEASANCE)

Beneficence is the duty to do good, be caring, and to help and support on all occasions. Nonmalfeasance is the duty to endeavor to do no harm, and both concepts certainly date at least from the time of the Hippocratic oath in which the physicians swore, "I will follow that system of regimen which according to my ability and judgment I consider for the benefit of my patients and abstain from whatever is deleterious and mischievous."[5]

Every medical student is taught that the first precept of medicine is to do no harm and that secondarily everything should be done to benefit the patient and to be supportive, caring, and helpful whenever possible. The physician is meant to relieve suffering, produce beneficial outcomes wherever possible, avoid bad outcomes, and enhance the patient's quality of life if possible. This concept is connected with the concept of autonomy, which directs that the physician do what the patient wishes whenever possible and most often that will be to relieve the patient's suffering

and provide a cure. Doing no harm is a value inculcated in all physicians, but some have considerable difficulty recognizing when unreasonable persistence in treatment that is designed to do good in the face of a clinical situation in which further treatment is useless because it cannot alter the ultimate and inevitable outcome is not beneficent and may be malfeasant.

Although it is true that there are often great difficulties in determining in medical terms when a treatment passes from the therapeutic to the futile, it will often be a function of patient autonomy to make that decision with the best information the practitioner can provide. In any event the principle of nonmalfeasance requires that the physician be alert to circumstances in which futility may supervene beneficent attempts at a cure, and unreasonable persistence in treatment stops being beneficent and starts constituting malfeasance.

JUSTICE

The fourth principle of bioethics is justice, and in simple terms justice can be thought of as fair play or at the very least freedom from unfair discrimination. As resources to provide health care become more constrained, problems related to the principle of justice will become more important in the ethical discourse of biomedicine. It is likely in the future that the discussion of this fourth principle will assume an ever-greater predominance in the discourse and may approach the prominence heretofore accorded to autonomy.

In many ways the issues that flow from the principle of justice may be seen as the antithesis of those that flow from autonomy. Justice deals with the fair distribution of the system, with whether patients get what they reasonably may consider their due from the health care system, and with the definition of what is a fair distribution of the resources that are available. If autonomy dictates that the patient's interest is always foremost and what is best for the patient should be first in the physician's mind, the principle of justice dictates that the physician must have concern for the fair distribution of the system's resources and for ensuring that they are not distributed in a way that depends on inappropriate discrimination.

A common formulation designed to distribute services fairly is that patients should exercise their autonomy to receive such services as they desire provided that the system can and will provide only those services that are judged to be medically necessary. Of course, many years of experience in health administration and health insurance administration demonstrate that determining what is medically necessary is the most difficult and problematic determination that must be made within those systems. What is really needed? Are treatments that are designed to make the patient better necessary, and are those that are designed to make the patient feel better unnecessary? How would it be reasonably determined whether a treatment designed to make a patient get better has a sufficient and reasonable likelihood of doing so that the resources of the system should be directed to it in preference to meeting some other patient's needs or demands? To what extent may treatment be denied to patients because there is no scientific evidence that it will make them better in the face of their persistent and apparently honest assertion that the receipt of the treatment makes them feel better?

Are some patients entitled to a greater share of the system's resources because of their station in life or contributions to society? Are highly intelligent contributors to science worth more than poorly educated workers? Are wealthy persons who have made huge contributions to the public welfare to be given preference over the poor? Is it legitimate to consider a patient less entitled to system resources if he or she suffers from a disease to which his or her own behavior, such as substance abuse or smoking, has avoidably contributed? Is a patient's entitlement to health care cumulative over a lifetime? Does there come a point where the patient has used so much of the resources of the system that he or she is not entitled to any more until the needs of others have been satisfied?

In determining whether to allocate resources to the patient it may be legitimate to consider the likely benefit to the patient and to increase the allocation of resources to those who are more likely to benefit or whose quality of life is likely to be improved. Is it legitimate to increase the allocation of resources where the duration of the benefit is likely to be greater rather than lesser or where the patient's condition is more urgent than that of a competing patient? Are some treatments, although likely to be successful and very beneficial, simply so resource intensive that they should not be given because they just consume too much of the available pie for the benefit of one individual? Box 20-1 shows the opinion of the Council on Ethical and Judicial Affairs of the American Medical Association with respect to some of these issues.[6]

How should the independent practitioner allocate his or her time as a resource between the many patients who will assert demands for care? Is it inevitable that physicians will give more time and effort to patients they like or whose disease is treatable than to those who are obnoxious or whose condition is intractable?

Can a physician properly participate in organizations for the delivery of care that insert questionable incentives into the physician's attempts to do justice to his or her patients? Is it appropriate for a physician to participate in a managed care plan that provides a large percentage of his or her yearly remuneration as a bonus, which the physician receives only if he or she meets a goal to restrain service delivery, meaning he or she will have to work hard not to give care and not to refer patients? Is it appropriate for a physician to practice within a scheme that forbids him or her to discuss with the patient alternatives for care that are not offered by the patient's benefit plan? Should society permit or prohibit those sorts of schemes? If it is not possible to achieve optimal justice in every patient encounter, ethical discourse suggests that at the very least inappropriate discrimination must not be tolerated.

All professional practitioners understand that their practice must be as free as possible from inappropriate discrimination and bias, and certainly all are aware of the inappropriateness of discrimination based on race, religion, national origin, gender, sexual orientation, or political opinion. However, there is considerable literature to suggest that the practice of medicine, perhaps without intention, has contained a good deal of bias on some, if not all those grounds, in particular on the basis of age, race, and gender.

Numerous variance studies done in a number of jurisdictions demonstrate that there appear to be variations in relation to access to care between patients of different ages, genders, and racial origins for no reason that appears to be grounded in science or medicine. It must be presumed that many subtle factors that are hard to identify often combine to produce such discrimination. Clearly, in the name of the justice principle, bioethics requires each practitioner to search his or her practice and all practice protocols in which he or she is involved for the subtle influence of prejudice and discrimination and to eliminate it whenever and wherever possible. Of course it is sometimes extremely difficult for practitioners to perceive these differences or to even be aware of the possibility of their existence. Thus it will be the role of the bioethicist and bioethics committees to assist practitioners in identifying elements of their practices or programs in which infractions of the justice principle may exist. This use of the ethical discourse ought not to be seen as a search for "bad apples" or rule infractions but as a necessary assistance to practitioners, groups, and health institutions in eliminating these most subtle but important infractions of the justice principle.

At the same time there are a few circumstances where scientific principles properly discriminate between age

---

BOX 20-1. ACCEPTABLE CRITERIA FOR RESOURCE ALLOCATION AMONG PATIENTS

Likelihood of benefit to the patient
Improvement in the patient's quality of life
Duration of benefit
Urgency of the patient's condition
Amount of resources required for successful treatment

groups, gender groups, and races on the basis of demonstrable real differences between them. Considerable study will often be required to distinguish between situations of subtle discrimination and situations in which scientific and medical considerations dictate an appropriate discrimination between persons and groups with regard to access to, or the nature of, treatment offered.

Limitations of space have permitted only a brief outline of the basic principles of bioethics in a medicolegal context. It is hoped that this chapter and the way in which ethical discourse presents an opportunity to reflect in a different way on the medicolegal dilemmas evident elsewhere in this book may stimulate the interest of the reader in further exploring ethics as a medicolegal tool.

ENDNOTES

1. T.L. Beauchamp & J.F. Childress, *Principles of Bio-Medical Ethics* (Oxford University Press, London 1979).
2. Community on Quality of Health Care in America, Institute of Medicine, *To Err Is Human: Building a Safer Health System* (Linda Kohn, Janet Corrigan, & Molla Donaldson eds., National Academy Press, Washington, D.C. 2000).
3. *Schoendorf v. Society of New York Hospital*, 1914, 105 N.E. 92 (N.Y.C.A.).
4. *Malette v. Shulman*, 63O. R. 2d, 243, 72O. R. 2d, 417 (O.C.A.).
5. Mason & McCall-Smith, *Oath of Hippocrates*, in *Law and Medical Ethics* 251 (Butterworths, London 1983).
6. AMA Council on Ethical and Judicial Affairs, *Ethical Considerations in the Allocation of Organs and Other Scarce Medical Resources Among Patients*, 155 Arch. Intern. Med. 401 (1995).

21 Access to Medical Care

JOAN LICHTMAN, M.A., M.S.P.A., C.I.T.T., C.P.A.

ACCESS
AVAILABILITY
STANDARDS
CONCLUSION

Until very late in the twentieth century, access to medical care was decided solely by "doctors' orders." The doubling of the world's population, the severe constraints due to scarce nonrecyclable resources, and increasingly sophisticated and expensive technology, are three major factors permanently altering the means of delivering medical care. For the purposes of this chapter, "medical care" refers to the allopathic practice of diagnosis and treatment in the United States, and "health care" includes both "medical care" and preventative medicine. Decision-making is a complex set of mechanisms that permit, or prevent, delivery of medical care. "Doctors' orders" are but a necessary signpost on the journey from resource allocation to result—an often rocky road between life and death.

Access to medical care, today, is set by one's having a means to pay for care. Our nation has tens of thousands of insurance policies, both public and private. Each insurance policy constitutes its own medical care delivery system. These policies essentially divide the population by insurance coverage type, since patients' care is covered only by one policy at a time.

Availability of care depends on limited resources. All tens of thousands of systems vie for the same limited set. Inefficiencies of matching patients' medical need with their ability to pay for care waste our scarce, nonrecyclable, nonrenewable resources. The resulting quantity and quality of actually delivered care leaves patients' medical needs unmet. Untreated disease, caused by improper, insufficient, or no care, constitutes systemic malpractice. "Malpractice avoidance" is a primary motivator in medical decision-making.

Defined as a deviation from the standard of care, malpractice astronomically drives up the costs of care, in order to prevent or avoid adverse consequences of ineffective or absent treatment. Were medical care delivered timely, efficiently, and effectively the first time, then adverse outcomes, due to artificial means of withholding or denying care, would be prevented. Scarce resources would be preserved. Medical need, not means of payment, would determine access to care. A major cause of malpractice would be eliminated.

Systemic barriers to care, set by insurance contracts and often by law, prevent patients' medical need for care from being matched with the resources to deliver necessary services. Seamless access to care, based on medical need, not on one's ability to pay, should be *the* standard for care, because denying medically necessary care constitutes, i.e., defines, malpractice.

Each public medical program and private insurance policy is but one in the United States' tens of thousands of health care delivery systems. Medical decision-making determines a patient's access to, and availability of, diagnoses or treatments. Each and every delivery system's *design* independently decides *if* medical care will be permitted or prohibited—a crude, often cruel, means of *access. Availability* of diagnoses and treatments is set by the allocation and consumption of our planet's scarce resources, thus setting the quantity, and even quality, of deliverable care. *Access* merged with *availability* constitutes the actual practice of medicine.

Deviations from accepted medical practice, i.e., the *medical* standard for care, constitute *malpractice*. Determinations of malpractice are set by courts of law throughout the United States. The resulting *legal* standards for delivered care are as varied as are the numerous jurisdictions making new law, daily. Large malpractice premiums have forced physicians to join new business ventures and to surrender their independence of medical judgment, just to keep practicing medicine. "Malpractice avoidance," a major manipulator of the acceptable practice of medicine, has the circular result of redefining acceptable medical practice, and thereby sets new medical and legal standards of care to which all providers will be held. However, a true, universal and immutable standard can neither redefine nor measure itself.

Delivery systems' designs determine who will receive care, under what conditions, and when. That level of care practiced by, and acceptable to, reasonably competent members of the profession, generally defines the *medical* standard of care. In the United States, two types of medical standards exist: national and local. However, the *legal* standards set by courts of law are neither national nor local. Each state's codes and case law essentially reshape medical standards into judicially enforced *legal* "standards," which vary not only from state to state but from court to court. Even the "federal" standard of care is set by states' courts.[1] Accordingly, the *applied* standard of care is made case by case. The national or local *medical* standard is altered by judicial interpretation, filtered through federal and state case law, under complex rules of courts—all to set a *legal* standard by which to measure medical practice or, rather, its malpractice.

In the United States, each of our tens of thousands of delivery systems, ranging from Medicare and Medicaid to every public and private health insurance policy in force, constitutes its own independent delivery "system." Patients covered by each separate insurance policy can seek or receive medical care from permitted providers, in accordance with limitations set by the underlying, legally binding, *contract*.

Each, within that myriad of independent systems, vies for the same set of scarce resources, providers, and patients. Our scarce, *nonrecyclable* resources are necessarily allocated to, and shared by, all systems. Providers (personnel and institutions) can participate in multiple systems. Patients, however, are "captives" within one system, given that only one insurance policy will pay for a patient's care at a given time for a particular illness.

Our collective sharing of our planet's severely limited resources proves how fragile is every nation's resource allocation. No two patients can occupy the same bed at the same time. Every time one person seeks and/or receives medical care, another person is denied use of those same scarce resources. Additionally, the artificial partitioning of the population by insurance contracts explains why one patient with a particular illness in one locality could, were another insurance policy in force, receive dramatically different delivered care, or none at all.

The structure of each independent delivery system— e.g., health maintenance organization (HMO), managed care organization (MCO), preferred provider organization (PPO), point of service (POS) contract, independent provider association (IPA), etc.—is set by the provisions of the governing insurance contract (or relevant law). Each of those system types functions somewhat differently, due to variations in structure and contractual provisions. For the purposes of this chapter, HMOs and MCOs will be used as proxies for all similar types of systems, given that HMOs and MCOs embody the generic principles upon which the others are built. Actually delivered care is *predictable*. Patients' medical outcomes can be foreseen, based upon the contractual rules of medical decision-making within each delivery system. Both the quantity and quality of to-be-delivered care are fixed *before* the fact.

Delivery systems' designs superseded "doctors' orders." "Accepted medical practice" defines the standard of care. Participating providers within each delivery system constitute a group of licensed physicians, who "accept their practice of medicine" by obeying the terms of their payor-provider contracts. Accordingly, willing providers both *set* and *met* the applicable standard of care. Each independent delivery system *contractually designs* its own standard of care. Providers' contractual compliance automatically prevents malpractice. Courts cannot redefine the standard or find fault with providers' compliance.

Were patients' medical needs properly met through these artificially contrived means of decision-making, then systemic medical malpractice would not exist. "Malpractice avoidance" would thereby require that the valid standard of delivered medical care be set, and measured, by patients' medical needs, rather than by acceptable medical practice, as measured by actually delivered care.

ACCESS

Eligibility for care based on payment ability, not by medical need

Patients, providers, and payors ("the 3 P's") are the necessary elements of all delivery systems. Medical care delivery is most viable when the providers, payors, and patients are independent and equally powerful, each as to the other. As analogy, our forefathers dreamed that their triangular design of the federal government would have the independent legislative, executive, and judicial branches as mutual watchdogs, making each other toe the mark.

However, when independent deals exist between providers and payors—as in the case of HMOs, MCOs, and the like— patients cannot enforce their rights or ensure they receive the care they need. Overridden by a separate provider-payor agreement that excludes them, patients lose the power to force providers and payors to act within the confines of the legally binding insurance contract that jointly governs all three.

Triangles are the most rigid of geometric figures (thus explaining the solidity and durability of the Pyramids). If one angle is changed, or one line altered, its sides are no longer able to meet and the triangle is destroyed. Analogously, when patients, providers, and payors have a mutual relationship, within which all are mutually independent and none is more powerful than any other, their "triangle" remains fixed and known. Potentially deliverable medical care is *foreseeable*, and patients' outcomes are predictable. However, when separate payor-provider contracts exclude patients, both the quantity and quality of delivered care are necessarily compromised. Patients are left powerless, with untreated disease and no recourse.

Systemic architecture

Governing contracts (including Medicare and Medicaid) determine:

1. which patients are eligible to receive care;
2. which providers will deliver care, and when;
3. what particular supplies and services are permitted for use; and
4. the terms of payment for supplies and services.

The particular contract provisions constitute each delivery system's design. Traditional fee-for-service (FFS) systems, where solely "doctor's orders" initiate diagnoses and treatments, yield different levels of both quantity and quality of delivered care than can MCOs or HMOs, which restrict available supply (e.g., by preset formulary) and services (e.g., network of permissible providers). Even patients with *access* to medical care—by virtue of their ability to pay, e.g., through insurance coverage—have no guarantee of receiving necessary diagnosis or treatment on the basis of their medical need.

In theory, both HMOs and MCOs serve beneficial ends; but in practice, those delivery systems corrupt the very purposes for which each was conceived. HMOs are intended to provide preventative care, in order to reduce and/or eliminate the need for medical treatment. In reality, HMO contracts are such that providers are generally required to give all medically necessary care for a fixed fee. "All medically necessary" care is usually remedial and curative, not preventative. The limited fees allotted to provide "all" that care are insufficient to pay for the demand, i.e., patients' medical needs, for care. Rather than prevent disease, HMOs are forced to leave existing disease untreated. MCOs were conceived as a means to contain the costs of delivering necessary medical care. Generally, "managed care" is neither "managed" nor "care." MCOs allot *benefits* based upon preset formularies and selected provider networks. Patients' medical needs are not primary factors when MCOs determine permissible care. For MCOs, if a benefit is permitted under the contract, then a covered patient is eligible to receive that benefit. Benefits exist, whether or not eligible patients have corresponding medical needs; patients' medical needs exist, whether or not MCOs permit necessary treatments. Often the twain do not meet, leaving patients with untreated disease. That is malpractice.

Public plan determinations are made by law. For example, Medicaid plans, by law, determine patients' eligibility for medical care based on their financial, not medical, need. Medical care for each state's Medicaid population differs, due to its being set by governing law, not by the practice of medicine. States' laws determining eligibility for Medicaid differ.[2] Persons could live and receive Medicaid in one state, but might not be eligible for Medicaid care were they living in another state. States can apply for federal government Medicaid waivers,[3] as did Oregon and others.

The legislated language of Oregon's unique Medicaid plan[4] ("the Oregon Plan," or simply "the Plan") is particularly instructive in terms of delivery system design and the consequences of systemic medical decision-making.

The Plan is funded biennially by property taxes, and care is restricted in accordance to the *timing* of disease onset. Treatments available for eligible recipients are ranked in a numeric hierarchy, the List.[5] Known statistical incidences of illnesses and the respective costs of permitted treatments determine the List's cutoff of permissible care, available during the particular biennial period associated with each property tax levy.[6] The total of collected property taxes in one biennial period may permit more treatments on the List than a lesser aggregate might allow during another biennial period. So, an ill Medicaid recipient needing "Treatment No. 542" on Oregon's List might receive care in year 2 but not in year 5.

The Oregon Plan also provides financial incentives to providers for better compliance with restricted medical care delivery.[7] Medical care providers participating in the Plan "shall" advise patients of services, treatments, or tests that are medically necessary but not covered under the contract, if an ordinarily careful practitioner in the same or similar community would do so under the same or similar circumstances.[8] Furthermore, physicians who comply with the Oregon Plan "shall not be subject to criminal prosecution, civil liability or professional disciplinary action for failing to provide a service which the Legislative Assembly has not funded or has eliminated from its funding."[9]

The collected language of the Plan indicates that its authors anticipated the state's likely inability to deliver a sufficient quantity and quality of medical services, which would avoid adverse outcomes to patients, i.e., what would qualify as malpractice in another delivery system. The treatment hierarchy in the Oregon Plan was based on cost containment[10] and the general public's preferences regarding medical care.[11] Neither of these is necessarily related to Medicaid patients' real medical needs. Moreover, Medicaid patients are subject to the Plan by force, i.e., by law, not by choice.

In some countries, of which Canada is one, queue lengths for particular types of nonemergency or elective care can be painful sources of delayed medical care delivery. However, Canadian citizenry across the board are guaranteed treatment for serious matters. Canadians have a legal *right* to care.[12] Canada's population of approximately 30 million is geographically spread across a thin, 3000-mile-long strip. All citizens (and eligible others) receive ample quantities of medical care, regardless of age, working status, preexisting conditions, or province of residence. Care is based on patients' medical need. Compare that to the approximately 45 million in the United States who, due to various socioeconomic circumstances, are inherently not eligible for care, due to lack of insurance coverage, private *or* public. Those persons' medical needs are irrelevant. The system prevents their receipt of treatment because they cannot pay.

While Canada maintains thirteen distinct care delivery systems, representing the nation's provinces and territories, the 1984 Canada Health Act mandates some specific requirements for *all* provinces. If that required compliance were absent, federal funding to the delinquent province would be denied. No province's system can endure without federal funding.

Canada's provincial plans contain "captives": all eligible persons are fully covered; all participating providers must obey the laws, which determine not only which treatments will be permitted but also the specific fees that providers are paid. Patients are not permitted to pay physicians for services that are covered. A physician has a disincentive to provide care if the physician must personally subsidize (pay) a portion of its cost (e.g., Ontario's "clawbacks" which penalize physicians for earnings in excess of provincially permitted limits). Provincial fee rates leave physicians little "wiggle room." Some cost-containment measures, regularly used in Canada, would shock Americans' sensibilities (e.g., severely restricting hospital use during holiday periods). On the other hand, given that medical education and technology are essentially the same in both countries, the overall quality of medical care delivery is similar. Therefore, remarkable differences in patient care between the United States and Canada are due to variations in law and differences in systemic decision-making methodologies.

Additionally, in the United States, decision-making by system design establishes acceptable medical practice, as defined by governing insurance contracts and the law. Delivery systems generate medical malpractice, as measured by patients' diseases improperly, or not, treated. Patients neither created nor consented to these new medical practice patterns, which profoundly, and forever, changed medical care delivery. Are we not *all* "patients"?

The unlicensed corporate practice of medicine

Contractual arrangements in public and private systems show the structure and function of medical care delivery systems. Structure and function not only determine patient outcomes, but also cast in concrete the pillars of our collective public welfare. Our population's health, or lack thereof, is *contractually* derived. The "point of no return" is long gone.

How the United States Government pays for public medical care (aged, poor, veterans, Native Americans, et al.) forced new, private delivery systems. Implementation of the DRG (Diagnostic Related Groups) payment system spread two types of *risk*: financial (cost) and medical. Unreimbursed costs of public patients' care had to be borne by insured patients and/or those paying out-of-pocket—*financial* (cost) risk-shifting. Resulting denials of care to patients left diseases untreated—*medical* risk-shifting. Burden-shifting "busted" out all over.

Dramatic increases in delivery costs spread across the board. Reeling from "fiscal fallout," providers scrambled to find guaranteed pools of patients in order to ensure fiscal health. Insurance contracts reined in costs by denying patients' claims. Willing providers (institutions and physicians) struck mutually beneficial deals with health plans, e.g., HMOs and MCOs.

Simple arithmetic necessitated draconian change. Providers' remaining open for business depends on maximization of available cash, i.e., increase revenues, decrease costs. New kinds of provider-payor contracts ensure fiscal health by guaranteeing incoming patients (revenue) while eliminating costs of treatment (expenses). HMOs and MCOs make favorable contracts with corporations, the major source of patient pools. A person can only be included in one patient pool at a time. Corporations exist to make profits (not products). By drastically reducing the premiums available to fund medical care, corporations divided our population into two groups: the working-well versus the unemployed-ill. Those most in need lack medical care. Providers and payors signed mutually beneficial contracts to ensure their survival. Patients bear the "bottom line": untreated disease, premature death. Left, patients have no rights.

Decision-making by HMOs and MCOs is based on cost containment, although HMOs emphasize preventative medicine while MCOs treat disease.

Health plans fix the treatments permitted. The onset of disease in a population is statistically known. Outcomes for the covered population are predictable. Should not health plans be held liable for all foreseeable adverse outcomes, necessitated by the designers of those payor-provider contracts, by which medical decision-making is "fixed"? The ultimate decision-maker is a *contract*. Willing providers, despite their oaths to "do no harm," obey the contract terms by limiting treatments and omitting cures, thereby causing harm.

Providers and payors want ironclad legal grounds, defining negligence and malpractice—i.e., an *inviolate standard* of care—governing all one-size-fits-all health plans. Such is not possible, theoretically or practically. The practice of medicine is more art than science. Individuals and their diseases are not carbon copies of each other. Were it otherwise, medical decision-making by fiat would be accurate, and physicians would no longer have jobs. Computers and textbooks would have all the answers. Accordingly, everybody would be treated identically. By analogy, regardless of the make or model of car, all vehicle repairs would be identical, by recipe. Cure rates would soar to 100%. The cost of medical care would be indistinguishable from the breadbasket necessities of life. The health care *industry* would vanish. In the logical extension of this absurdity, life would be guaranteed and death, an elective.

Medical decision-making depends on two contracts: provider-patient versus provider-payor. The provider is "bound" on both sides of that inequitable equation. Squeezed between treatment choices, the provider is forced into mandatory compliance with both conflicting contracts at the same time. Sometimes the resulting medical "decision" is dictated by the provider's employment contract. When patients—as is usually the case—have no leverage against the payor, providers likely obey provider-payor agreements. Sanctions against providers are more drastic and immediate. Potential malpractice lawsuits remain remote.

Within HMOs, patients have little "immediate" leverage. However, HMO provider-patient contracts obligate physicians to deliver *all necessary* medical care. Patients can force delivery of medically necessary services. MCO provider-payor contracts are more severe. Patients have no recourse against providers for contractually denied care. MCOs also enforce strict provider networks and rigid formularies. Even pharmacists can override "doctor's orders." MCO patients have no recourse. The *payor-patient* contract absolutely prohibits specified care.

Insurance exists, but not because alive patients need medical care. One's ability to purchase care depends on non-medical life circumstances, e.g., working, being poor or disabled, being over 65, having a working spouse or parent, or being independently wealthy. Most insurance premiums are paid through the workplace. Corporations' powerful influence on access to, and availability of, medical care creates "the great divide": sick people, in great need, cannot get medical care; healthy people, despite lesser or absent need, can get all the medical care they want. Only by excluding workplace influences can fragile resource allocation effectively and efficiently serve the sick. Today, medical care is "ordered," not by doctors, but by the unlicensed corporate practice of medicine. Access to medical care is by privilege, not by right.

AVAILABILITY

Supply can never satisfy demand

In a normal free-market industry, supply usually satisfies demand. Health care is not normal. Scarce, nonrecyclable resources can never meet our unlimited demand for medical care. Medical care delivery systems must make access equitable and equal—seamless across the entire population served. Effective resource allocation matched with efficient consumption best benefits a whole society *and* all individuals within it. (Resource allocation and consumption are wholly different from "resource utilization.") Delivery system designs must maximize the benefits of resource consumption across the *whole* population, not just those directly served.

The United States' constitutionally defined political foundation prioritizes individuals' rights: "welfare of the whole" is conceptually absent. In Canada, the primary political premise is "welfare of the whole": enhanced well-being of all individuals within is a necessary by-product. While the quality of medical care (medical diagnosis and treatment) is essentially the same in both countries, resource allocation and consumption differ greatly. By law, Canadians receive medical care simply because they are Canadians. However, queues in Canada for certain kinds of medical care are long. Large numbers of U.S. citizens have no access to care, even though availability of medical care is ample throughout the United States.

Allocation and consumption of resources are set by system design. However, some uncontrollable, independent constraints result from the scarcity of nonrecyclable, nonrenewable resources. That tenuous tug-of-war demands scrutiny in system design, to prevent undue resource waste. Money is not a major constraint. Limitations of nonmonetary resources, such as time, organic matter, some chemicals, and knowledge, are significantly more insidious than insufficient funds will ever be.

Multiple resources (inputs) are necessary to deliver medical care (outputs). If the supply of just one mandatory resource dries up, medical care stops. People die. All delivery systems are obligated to enforce judicious resource allocation and consumption. Scarce, nonrecyclable, and nonrenewable resources, once used, are forever gone.

STANDARDS

Medical, legal, neither, nor

The *design* of medical care delivery systems matches *access* to medical care with *availability* of services. By law, delivered medical services must meet "standards." *Medical* standards of care are, theoretically, set by physicians, and are generally defined as the reasonable care that would be given by a competent physician under similar conditions. Whether a provider has committed malpractice is determined in a court of law by "measuring" the care given against the *applicable* medical standard, thus setting the *legal* standard for care. Providers will adjust their practice of medicine so as to avoid committing malpractice. Therefore, the *legal* standard of care, set by courts, alters the *medical* standard of care, set by doctors. "Legal" standards necessarily differ from court to court and jurisdiction to jurisdiction.

Circular empty standards are created and enforced by system design

What, therefore, are the standards of care that apply to providers? Should *legal* standards, set by courts of law, override *medical* standards, set by licensed medical professionals? Are standards national, local, or both at the same time? Does the standard for a federally employed physician, giving care under a federal program (e.g., veterans, or Indian affairs) differ, were that same physician in private practice treating the same individual and disease? Will a physician employed by an HMO or MCO be held to a different standard, were that same physician treating the same patient within the terms of traditional fee-for-service insurance coverage? Will a physician, employed by and/or treating a patient in an institution, be required to make different treatment decisions than if that same patient's treatment were rendered by the same physician in an independent private office? Will computer-generated practice "guidelines" gain the force of *acceptable recipes* for care, subsequently sustained in a court of law as "*the* standard"? Is there a different standard of care for a specialist who treats a patient over a long distance, by means of a computer hookup, than would be the standard of care were the same patient and same specialist in the same room? If case law is law, then what effect does a judicial determination of malpractice in one state have over federally employed physicians practicing in another state? Are not underlying *medical* standards national in application? Is not a *legal* definition of malpractice state-specific and not national in scope or effect? How will any patient ever be able to secure the requisite quantity and quality of necessary medical care, if there are no "teeth" in enforceable standards and/or malpractice cannot be determined by any court, because sitting judges do not know if any standard applies to the case at their bar today?

Malpractice avoidance: "the" standard?

Malpractice, by definition, is a deviation from the "standard of care." The *standard* has various definitions:[13] e.g., physicians using "that degree of skill and learning normally possessed by doctors in good standing in similar practice and under like circumstances";[14] giving "a course of treatment supported by other physicians in good standing";[15] being "under duty to exercise that degree of care, skill and diligence which physicians in the same general line of practice ordinarily exercise in similar cases";[16] or, as one state's statute requires, the standard is reasonable competent care acceptable to other members of the profession.[17]

Providers are risk-averse. They prefer to act within legally accepted bounds rather than risk a malpractice judgment. "Malpractice avoidance" moves medical decision-making.

Two kinds of malpractice exist: one is due to system design; the other occurs at bedside.

Any willing provider?

Systemic malpractice can be self-catalytic. Provider-payor contracts limit permissible care. Withholding or denying necessary medical care generally violates the standard of care. So, would not physicians who obey provider-payor contracts, by withholding necessary care, have committed malpractice? Did those physicians *not* deviate from the accepted practice of medicine by licensed physicians in similar circumstances? Malpractice avoidance would suggest that "risk-averse" providers comply with the standard, grant the necessary care, and disobey their employment contracts. More to the point, why would a licensed provider sign

a contract that necessitates the commission of malpractice? Or does it?

HMOs, MCOs, and the like are staffed by licensed physicians, who issue orders to deliver treatment. Licensed physicians are assumed reasonably competent. Physicians, delivering care through provider networks, are required to deliver medical services with the same duty and degree of skill as is provided by nonnetwork physicians. Provider-network physicians agree to comply—i.e., to practice medicine—in accordance with their governing provider-payor agreement. The care specifically permitted or prohibited under such contracts may not meet patients' needs, nor even match the long-established national or local standards of care to which licensed, nonnetwork physicians in the same general line of practice are held. Seemingly, network providers know, when signing the contract, that they will be forced to commit malpractice if they wish to remain employed.

Is there an "out"? Third-party employment agreements are signed by all participating physicians. They are licensed physicians in good standing, in similar practice, and under like circumstances. All physicians signed. All collectively agreed. That employment contract, therefore, is its own standard of care. Compliant physicians met the standard. Theoretically, at least, health plans' contracts would render malpractice and malpractice avoidance as one and the same. However, if a health plan physician committed malpractice, were his conduct measured against those long-standing national or local standards, would the doctor's compliance with the plan's contract exonerate him? What would a court decide?

Moreover, we hasten to add that while we have no doubt that all concerned expected the medical services arranged for by the HMOs to be of acceptable quality, . . . It may well be that an employer and an HMO could agree that a quality of health care standard articulated in their contract would replace the standards that would otherwise be supplied by the applicable state law of tort. We express no view on whether an ERISA plan sponsor may thus by contract opt out of state tort law. . . . [18]

On the other hand, the same *Dukes* court also opines, "[P]atients enjoy the right to be free from medical malpractice regardless of whether or not their medical care is provided through an ERISA plan."[19]

Third-party contracts can set the standard for both the quantity and quality of actually delivered medical care. Powerful, network-provider health plans are then *the* "standard" bearers. The *business* of medical practice prescribes the practice of medicine.

King Solomon's dilemma: judicial notice taken

What's a judicial body to do? A health plan can deliver whatever quantity and quality of services are fixed by contract. Life and death are but a business duel. Necessity is "the mother" of microsurgery. Federal judges—board-certified, licensed specialists in semantic hair-splitting—sharpened their double-edged scalpels.

Enter ERISA, the enigma of modern-day medicine. Corporations provide insurance benefits for their workers. Regulation of medical care is governed by states. ERISA generally protects the administration of health plans from malpractice lawsuits. So, is there a judicially bright line between the "denial of medical benefits" (quantity of care), which is protected by ERISA, and the "denial of medical treatment" (quality of care), which is not protected by ERISA? *Dukes v. U.S. Healthcare, Inc.*, is the currently reigning ERISA ruling.[20]

In *Dukes*, the court essentially declared that quantity of care, a sacrificial pawn, is immune from malpractice lawsuits, but quality is queen. The *Dukes* court ruled: claims as to withheld or denied *quantity* of care relate to benefit administration and are preempted by ERISA; claims as to the *quality* of delivered care impinge on the state's role of regulating the practice of medicine, and are not protected in federal courts under ERISA. (The *Dukes* court provides a stellar analysis of the legal issues, as to plaintiffs' claims for recovering benefits due, enforcing rights under, or clarifying rights to future benefits.[21]) The *Dukes* court's ruling is sharply double-edged and ambiguous. If the provider-payor contract is silent about quality of care, then physicians who comply with the contract may be sued for malpractice, using the old, national and local, standards. However, if the health plan's contract language "opts out" of states' laws of tort, then either malpractice cannot exist, by law, or it is protected by ERISA.

Underlying the *Dukes* opinion is an implicit, but tacit, assumption that quantity and quality of delivered medical care are mutually exclusive and wholly unrelated. If the benefit provided by the HMO is medical care itself, then a plaintiff's claims against the HMO for withheld or denied *quantity* of care would not qualify in state courts as a medical malpractice claim, which can only arise from the poor *quality* of care actually provided. The *Dukes* court writes:

Instead of claiming that the welfare plans in any way withheld some quantum of plan benefits due, the plaintiffs in both cases complain about the low quality of the medical treatment that they actually received and argue that the [health plan] should be held liable under agency and negligence principles. . . . We find nothing in the legislative history suggesting that § 502 was intended as a part of a federal scheme to control the quality of benefits received by plan participants. Quality control of benefits, such as the health care benefits provided here, is a field traditionally occupied by state regulation and we interpret the silence of Congress as reflecting an intent that it remain such. . . . [T]here is no indication in ERISA that Congress chose to displace general health care regulation by the states.[22]

What did Congress intend? Congress wanted to protect plan beneficiaries from loss, if corporate funds became insufficient to provide promised benefits.[23]

Were limited monetary resources not the very reason why health plans erupted in the first place? The Government's DRG reimbursement policies passed off financial risk onto the private sector and burdened patients with untreated disease. Unable to fund both the costs of public and private care, corporations restricted the moneys available to fund employees' medical benefits. Increases in costs of care served only to decrease further the amounts of available funds to meet the demand for medical care, which can *never* be satisfied. Congress intended ERISA to protect people from losing benefits, if corporate funding is lacking. Absent corporate funding is the reason people cannot get medical benefits, today. (Exit!, ERISA)

So what did the judicial body do? By assuming that quality and quantity of care are inherently separable, the *Dukes* court overlooked the reality that, when quantity of care is restricted, then quality of care is necessarily compromised. Patients suffer and die. By splitting semantic hairs in order to maintain malpractice avoidance as a positive influence, courts encouraged the "unlicensed corporate practice of medicine" to use contract law to circumvent states' law of torts and ignore legislated congressional intent. Stumbling judicial negotiation of this veritable legal minefield could blast, forever, people's abilities to receive adequate, safe, medically necessary treatment, while simultaneously suppressing patients' rights to protect their very survival.

What is a "standard," anyway?

Malpractice lawsuits are clearly a deterrent against mutually beneficial provider-payor contracts, which prevent delivery of both adequate quantity and quality of necessary medical care. Maintaining a means to measure malpractice requires setting a standard that neither legal contracts nor physicians' conduct can alter.

Standards should be immutable. Standards should be universal, uniform, and fixed. Standards should not be alterable, defined, or set by the very human conduct that those standards are supposed to govern. Is there a unique, universal, uniform standard, applicable to all, in all cases, all the time? In the realm of legal medicine, can one size *ever* fit all?

If the application of standards by courts of law is reduced to arguments over language, differences in judicial procedures, definitions of "expert," rules of evidence, federal laws versus state's rights, or legal technicalities, then the letter of the law will crush its spirit.

CONCLUSION

We have decried our rights to life and liberty, our freedoms, and our cherished autonomy, by participating—actively, or passively in silence—while impersonal, unlicensed corporations do not even bother to blink, when prescribing our lives and deaths. We each have the right, and the concomitant obligation (on the basis of informed consent), to accept, or to refuse, medical care. We each must also have the unbridled independence to select, not from a list of permission slips (formularies and approved networks) offered by impersonal third-party corporations that never attended medical school, but from all reasonably available treatment options. Survival is not guaranteed. Death is not negotiable.

The quantity and quality of delivered medical care defines the well-being of the population served. Use of medical goods and services clearly differs, depending not only on the bases of resource allocation, but also on system design *and* public policy, often set by law. Delivered medical care is determined by both *access*, i.e., system design, and *availability*, i.e., allocation of resources. The traditional economic model of supply and demand cannot adequately explain either the means or the modes of medical care delivery. Taken together, *access* and *availability* are a reasonable proxy for deliverable care, i.e., supply. Patients' medical needs approximate demand. However, in medical care, supply can never satisfy demand.

Medical and legal standards of care are, essentially, nonexistent. Medical standards of care have been molded and filtered by state and federal laws, case by case, judicially applied differently in a multitude of jurisdictions. Payor-provider contracts have rendered malpractice, and malpractice avoidance, barely distinguishable.

When a supposed "standard" sets and measures itself, it is not a standard. A standard, by definition, should be fixed and immutable, universal and uniform.

In medicine, disease reigns. No health plan contract can preempt illness. Laws cannot annihilate it. Only death ends it. Medical need for care is universal and immutable. Not meeting that need constitutes malpractice.

When *access* to the system is universal and *availability* of goods and services causes efficient and effective distribution of limited resources on the basis of medical need, then delivery of care will comply with an immutable *standard*, inherently *preventing* malpractice. Medical care, not just for the privileged, must become a right. *E pluribus unum.*

ENDNOTES

1. *Bellomy v. U.S.*, 888 F. Supp. 760 (S.D. W.Va. 1995); *Donais v U.S.*, 232 F. 3d 595 (C.A.7 (Ill.) 2000); *Dickey v. Baptist Memorial Hospital-North Mississippi*, 146 F. 3d 262 (C.A.5 (Miss.) 1998); *Byrd v. U.S.*, 945 F. Supp. 968 (S.D. Miss. 1996); et al.
2. Poverty laws differ by state, according to law. Medicaid, a federal program, is wholly administered by states, thus creating inherent inequalities for eligible recipients, state to state.
3. 42 U.S.C.S. §1396n(b) and Or. Rev. Stat. §414.829.
4. Or. Rev. Stat. §414.018, *et seq.*
5. Or. Rev. Stat. §414.835.
6. Or. Rev. Stat. §414.710(8).
7. Or. Rev. Stat. §§414.610, 414.630(4), et al.
8. Or. Rev. Stat. §414.725(5).
9. Or. Rev. Stat. §414.745.
10. Or. Rev. Stat. §414.610.
11. Or. Rev. Stat. §414.018.
12. Canada Health Act, 1984.
13. *Peck v. Tegtmeyer*, 834 F. Supp. 903 (W.D. Va. 1992); *Ralph by Ralph v. Nagy*, 749 F. Supp. 169 (M.D. Tenn. 1990); *Torres Nieves v Hospital Metropolitano*, 988 F. Supp. 127 (D. Puerto Rico 1998); *Law v. Camp*, 116 F. Supp. 2d 295 (D. Conn. 2000); *Cortez-Irizarry v. Corporacion Insular de Seguros* (C.A.1 (Puerto Rico) 1997); et al.
14. *Beckman v. Mayo Foundation*, 804 F. 2d 435.
15. Tennessee Code Annotated, §29-25-115; *Ward v. U.S.*, 838 F. 2d 182.
16. *Polozie v U.S.*, 835 F. Supp. 68.
17. *Kroll v U.S.*, 708 F. Supp. 117, *aff'd* 900 F. 2d 253.
18. *Dukes v U.S. Healthcare, Inc.*, 57 F. 3d 350, 359 (3rd Cir. 1995).
19. *Id.* at 358.
20. *See also Moreno v. Health Partners Health Plan*, 4 F. Supp. 2d 888 (D. Ariz. 1998); *Moscovitch v. Danbury Hospital*, 25 F. Supp. 2d 74 (D. Conn. 1998); *Garrison v. Northeast Georgia Medical Center, Inc.* (N.D. Ga. 1999); *Lazorko v. Pennsylvania Hospital*, 237 F. 3d (C.A.3 (Pa.) 2000); et al.
21. *Dukes v. U.S. Healthcare, Inc.*, at 356-61.
22. *Id.* at 357.
23. *Id.*

Research and Experimentation

CYRIL H. WECHT, M.D., J.D., F.C.L.M.

HISTORICAL BACKGROUND
BENEFIT VERSUS RISK RULE
CRIMINAL AND CIVIL LIABILITY
INNOVATIVE THERAPY
RADIATION EXPERIMENTS
QUESTIONABLE HUMAN RESEARCH AND EXPERIMENTATION PRACTICES
CONCLUSION

HISTORICAL BACKGROUND

Few subjects in the medicolegal field have raised as much widespread controversy since World War II as the question of human experimentation and clinical investigation. Exposés of activities by the Central Intelligence Agency (CIA), the Department of Defense, and other federal agencies involving the deaths of innocent victims, who were unknowing, involuntary guinea pigs, have raised many moral and ethical questions for the entire country. Ever since the Nuremberg trials after World War II, medical researchers and other professional scientific personnel involved in clinical investigation have been made aware of the medicolegal hazards and pitfalls of improper, illegal human experimentation. The Declaration of Helsinki and Codes and Guidelines adopted by the American Medical Association and other national professional organizations, as well as by the Department of Health and Human Services (DHHS), have emphasized the importance and necessity of having well-defined principles for all medical experimenters and researchers using human subjects in their studies.

The World Medical Association (WMA) addressed this controversial subject in 1949 at its meeting in London, at which time a rather strict International Code of Medical Ethics was adopted. It said in part: "Under no circumstances is a doctor permitted to do anything that would weaken the physical or mental resistance of a human being except from strictly therapeutic or prophylactic indications imposed in the interest of the patient." However, by 1954, the WMA had become uncomfortable with its commitment exclusively to the individual patient. That year, the organization adopted its "Principles for Those in Research and Experimentation," which, while warning that there must be "strict adherence to the general rules of respect of the individual," also explicitly recognized that experiments may be conducted on healthy subjects.

By 1964 the WMA had clearly abandoned the individual patient-centered commitment of 1949 in a new set of recommendations, "because it is essential that the results of laboratory experiments be applied to human beings to further scientific knowledge and to help suffering humanity."

Today, not only the regulations of the WMA, but also those of the Nuremberg Code and the U.S. government justify a human experiment if the risks compare favorably with the foreseeable benefits to the subject or to others. Hence the Hippocratic tradition regarding human experimentation has been amended to include a concern for suffering humanity and, of course, for scientific progress.

Yet this same commitment to benefit society may also have opened the door for the type of experimentation that includes the injection of hepatitis virus into mentally retarded children, as occurred at Willowbrook State Hospital (see below). Thus a "Willowbrook" becomes possible once experimenters can convince themselves that the risks are outweighed by the possible benefits, including the potential benefits to people who were not included in the experiment.

Some scientific researchers have been irritated by the institution of codes and guidelines and continue to insist that they should be permitted to use their own best moral and ethical judgment as professional people. Although the majority of these persons would, of course, apply a high level of moral and ethical judgment, experience has demonstrated all too frequently that even highly experienced researchers can be carried away with a particular project and engage in activities that not only are in violation of the existing civil common law and criminal codes, but are in opposition to traditional medical morals and ethics. For all these reasons, it is essential that physicians and other scientists who directly or indirectly engage in any kind of experimentation or clinical investigation involving human beings be

After the public disclosures of the Olson and Blauer cases, the news media turned up numerous other instances of unethical experimentation with hallucinogenic drugs on unsuspecting human subjects involving several government agencies. At least 7000 persons had been so treated by the U.S. Army alone. The Rockefeller Commission report had also alluded to experiments on "unsuspecting persons in normal social situations," on both the West and East Coasts during the 1950s and 1960s.[4]

Later, it was learned that the U.S. Atomic Energy Commission, predecessor to the Energy Research and Development Administration, sponsored and monitored various experiments from the 1940s through the 1960s on human subjects, including children, in which the subjects were exposed either to radiation or to the highly toxic metal plutonium. In the radiation tests, 79 inmates of the state penitentiary in Oregon, men and women, were exposed to doses of radiation to determine the effects on the reproductive organs. No follow-up studies had been performed in recent years, but as a result of the disclosure, prison officials agreed to conduct medical evaluations to detect adverse aftereffects.

In the plutonium exposure tests, 18 men, women, and children, all thought to be terminally ill, were injected with plutonium in amounts ranging from 2 to 145 times the maximum permissible dose under current standards. The subjects were not told what the substance was. The injections were performed between 1945 and 1947 at various hospitals in four different states. Astonishingly, although all the subjects were thought to be terminally ill at the time, three were still alive 40 years later.[5] Obviously, aside from the ethics of the experiment itself, such long survival of "terminally ill" patients raises serious questions about the ability of researchers to determine such conditions in their choice of subjects.

LSD

The Justice Department recently settled a lawsuit by nine Canadians who asserted that the CIA, unknowingly to them and their relatives, made them the subjects of mind-control experiments in the 1950s. The plaintiffs were patients of a psychiatrist who received money from the CIA to do research into drugs that could be used to control human behavior. According to government records, the nine plaintiffs were not told they were the subjects of experiments. They were subjected to heavy doses of the hallucinogen LSD, powerful electric shock treatment two or three times a day, and doses of barbiturates for prolonged periods of drug-induced sleep.

Documents that became public showed that the CIA had used private medical research foundations as a conduit for a 25-year, multimillion-dollar research program to learn how to control the human mind. Through a front organization called the *Society for the Investigation of Human Ecology*, the agency funneled tens of thousands of dollars to pay for an array of experiments that involved LSD, electroshock therapy, and a procedure known as *psychic driving*, in which patients listened to a recorded message repeatedly for up to 16 hours.

The Nuremberg Code

Of course, there is nothing new about medical experiments on humans. Galen founded the experimental science of medicine before A.D. 200, and there are references to medical experiments on human subjects in the oldest literature. Nonetheless, public awareness of ethical and legal problems posed by medical research involving human subjects did not coalesce until the post–World War II trials at Nuremberg, where more than 25 "dedicated and honored medical men" were accused of having committed war crimes of a medical nature against involuntary human subjects. According to Telford Taylor, chief prosecutor at the Nuremberg Military Tribunals, the defendants' "advances" in medicine were confined to the field of "thanatology," the science of death. Of the 25 defendants, only 7 were acquitted; 9 were sentenced to prison, and the remaining 9 were sentenced to death.

After it became known, through these trials, what the Nazis had done under the guise of medical and scientific research, there developed what has been referred to as the Nuremberg Code (see Appendix 22-1). The Nuremberg Code was the forerunner of the subsequent codes and guidelines that were adopted by different agencies and organizations in the ensuing decades. It addressed the question of what constitutes valid, legal, moral, and ethical experimentation. However, it did not explicitly deal with the subject of children. Probably nobody at that time thought it would be necessary. But it did deal with the subjects of consent, the voluntariness of consent, the right of a patient to withdraw if he or she wished, and the basic question of doing things in conformance with proper medical standards and safeguards. The Nuremberg Code prompted more interest and concern in these problems.

Declaration of Helsinki

In 1964, the World Medical Association promulgated a code that came to be known as the Declaration of Helsinki (Appendix 22-2). The Declaration of Helsinki was, in essence, adopted and given the imprimatur of the American Medical Association in November 1966. The AMA referred to it as *Ethical Guidelines for Clinical Investigation*. Earlier in 1966, the Public Health Service of the United States had issued some guidelines that were subsequently revised later in the year. Recently, the DHHS has also been attempting to draft some guidelines.

Children as subjects

Apart from international codes, there have also been a number of court decisions in this country bearing on the questions of ethical experimentation and informed fully aware of all the legal ramifications and potential problems associated with this area of professional activity.

The late eminent Harvard Medical School anesthesiologist and medical ethicist, Dr. H. K. Beecher, claimed that human experimentation beyond the boundaries of medical ethics was being carried out to an alarming and dangerous degree by clinical investigators in the United States. He claimed that these investigators were more concerned with furthering the interests of science than with the good of the patient. He found 12 of 100 consecutively reported studies involving experimentation with human subjects, appearing in a highly respected medical journal in 1964, to be seemingly "unethical." Beecher concluded: "If only one fourth of them is truly unethical, this still indicates the existence of a serious situation." In the prestigious *New England Journal of Medicine*, he found 50 examples of unethical experimentation described or referred to in various articles.[1]

Government-sponsored experimentation

Medical experimentation on humans has a long history, but public concern over it is a comparatively recent development. One of the more spectacular recent examples of unethical human experimentation was partially revealed in June 1975 by the Commission on CIA Activities within the United States, the so-called Rockefeller Commission. In its chapter on domestic activities of the CIA's Directorate of Science and Technology, the Commission's report described some of the CIA projects involving drug experimentation on humans, noting that most of the records of such experiments had been destroyed. The report minimized the consequences of the experiments to the subjects involved, many of whom had not even been informed that they were subjects of an experiment. One of the CIA experiments was described more specifically, although still in casual, almost indifferent terms:

The Commission did learn, however, that on one occasion during the early phases of this program [in 1953], LSD was administered to an employee of the Department of the Army without his knowledge while he was attending a meeting with CIA personnel working on the drug project.

Before receiving the LSD, the subject had participated in discussions where the testing of such substances on unsuspecting subjects was agreed to in principle. However, this individual was not made aware that he had been given LSD until about 20 minutes after it had been administered. He developed serious side effects and was sent to New York with a CIA escort for psychiatric treatment. Several days later, he jumped from a tenth floor window of his room and died as a result.

The General Counsel ruled that the death resulted from circumstances arising out of an experiment undertaken in the course of his official duties for the U.S. Government, thus ensuring his survivors of receiving certain death benefits. The Director of Central Intelligence issued reprimands to two CIA employees responsible for the incident.[2]

As if to suggest that the experiment perhaps had to do with the death, the report added a gratuitous fo "There are indications in the few remaining Agency that this individual may have had a history of em instability." The individual was not identified in the mission's report.

The report went on to conclude that "it was clearly gal to test potentially dangerous drugs on unsuspe United States citizens," and recommended that "the should not again engage in the testing of drugs on un pecting persons." Not a word about medical ethics, inter tional codes, or anything else to indicate any genuine mo concern—not even a suggestion that the unknowing su jects of the experiments ought to be located and informe This was how a prestigious governmental commission pe ceived its obligations and performed its duties.

Fortunately, the news media were not satisfied with this incomplete disclosure. The identity of the victim in the specific incident described by the Commission was soon determined to be Dr. Frank Olson, a civilian Army employee. His "history of emotional instability" consisted of visits to a New York psychiatrist, retained by the CIA, after he had been subjected to the CIA's drug experiment. When the detailed circumstances of the experiment and Dr. Olson's death became widely publicized, the President of the United States expressed public apologies to his widow and children. Ultimately, after a suit had been filed, the case was settled privately and quietly by a $2 million payment from the government.

Other examples of governmental drug experimentation on humans also came to public attention. One involved a 42-year-old hospital patient, Harold Blauer, who died in January 1953, approximately 2½ hours after receiving an injection of a mescaline derivative. (Mescaline is a hallucinogenic drug derived from a type of cactus plant and is similar to LSD in its effects on the mind.)

Blauer, along with an undetermined number of other patients, had been given injections of mescaline derivatives during the course of a 29-day project conducted by the New York State Psychiatric Institute under an Army contract. At no time was there knowledge on the part of any of the patients or their families as to the nature of the experiment, nor was any informed consent obtained.

Some comments by the acting Mental Hygiene Commissioner of New York State, Dr. Hugh F. Butts, after disclosure of the circumstances of Blauer's death, are especially relevant:

It was not uncommon practice at that time for medical and psychiatric researchers to use drug treatment without the detailed knowledge and special consent of patients. This was thought necessary to avoid false reactions. Such practices could not occur today because patients are protected by laws and regulations that have been specifically enacted to prevent such occurrences.[3]

consent, particularly in reference to children. Under existing case law, although it is often forgotten, a parent cannot say to a neighbor or friend or a research team of scientists: "Take one of my children and if you wish to do something that is not going to be beneficial or advantageous to him, go ahead and do it anyway because I, the parent, give you permission." A parent cannot legally do that. We are a nation governed by laws, and the law is clear in this regard. Neither parents, legal guardians, administrators of homes and hospitals for retarded children, government officials, nor university research teams, individually or collectively, are empowered to ignore or circumvent a basic and important concept of Anglo-American law, namely, that you cannot commit an assault and battery on another human being.

In 1944 the U.S. Supreme Court, in *Prince v. Massachusetts*, stated: "Parents may be free to become martyrs themselves, but it does not follow they are free in identical circumstances to make martyrs of their children before they reach the age of full and legal discretion when they can make that choice for themselves."[6] *Prince v. Massachusetts* has never been overruled by a subsequent U.S. Supreme Court decision.

Some people refer to an earlier case in Mississippi, *Bonner v. Moran*,[7] in which a 15-year-old boy was apparently conned by an aunt into going to a hospital to give skin transplants for his cousin, the aunt's son, who had been burned. The boy did, but there was some question as to whether the mother of the donor really knew the facts of the treatment and the risks to her own son. She subsequently brought legal action against the hospital, but the court was far less than unequivocal in giving its opinion as to whether or not the mother could recover in damages. That case is sometimes quoted in defense of experimentation without consent, but the circumstances and facts were very peculiar and special for that case. There was good evidence to indicate that although the consent was not originally obtained from the mother, the procedure and risks were subsequently made known to her because the son went back repeatedly for more skin transplants and for treatment.

In any event, until such time as the Supreme Court definitively rules otherwise, or until the U.S. Congress enacts contrary legislation, the law prohibits experimentation on humans without informed consent. Furthermore, it is illegal to conduct experiments that are tantamount to assault and battery.

Rather than considering this subject as an academic or legalistic question, one should consider some specific examples. During and after World War II, physicians developed awareness that excessive oxygen could produce a condition known as retrolental fibroplasia (RLF) in children, which leads to blindness. In most instances, this condition was observed in premature infants who had been placed in an excessive quantity of oxygen. So it was decided to conduct an experiment, with no real informed consent from the parents and obviously not from the babies, in which one group of babies was placed in an excessive quantity of oxygen and another in an atmosphere with a much reduced amount of oxygen. Six of the babies became totally and permanently blind.[8]

Consider another experiment. Red blood cells are broken down in the liver of the human body. In some infants the liver fails to excrete bilirubin, the major degradation product in the breakdown of erythrocytes. Furthermore, in infants, unlike adults, bilirubin has the capacity to pass the blood-brain barrier and to precipitate in the brain a dangerous condition that can lead to permanent brain damage and, in some instances, death. Research had previously established that a chemical found in human breast milk seemed to alter, revise, or impede the biochemical processes within the liver by which bilirubin was normally excreted. The researchers wanted to see if that was also true in vivo. Therefore they prepared an experiment in which this chemical compound was given in significant dosages to babies. The experiment confirmed that there was a rather fast, quite substantial buildup of the bilirubin level in these children, with the possibility of subtle brain damage as a result. There was permanent brain damage in some of those children.[9]

In another situation, at Children's Hospital in Boston, there was great interest in the natural defense mechanisms of the human host in reaction to an organ transplant. Boston is a leader in the medical field, and Children's Hospital is one of its finest health care facilities. Yet here is what they did in designing and conducting an experiment. Without obtaining any kind of an informed consent (in most of the cases, it was questionable whether they even obtained a basic consent, that is, the traditional kind that sufficed before the concept of informed consent developed in the medical malpractice field in the early 1960s), they performed a thymectomy on babies and youngsters who were undergoing surgery for various cardiovascular problems. They took out the thymus gland, which is known to play a role in the body's immunological defense mechanisms. They then attached a piece of skin on these children from unrelated individuals to determine what the bodily reaction of the thymectomized child would be to the skin that had been placed on his or her body. This was very interesting and important research. But was there any possible danger to the thymectomized youngster? And did not the parents, at the very least, have the right to have an intelligent, informed discussion from the physicians about what the possibilities of subsequent damage might be?

At Willowbrook State Hospital, Staten Island, New York, some researchers wanted more information about hepatitis in an epidemiological environment. They reasoned that in such an institution, the patients might get hepatitis anyway at some time in the future. So they took retarded youngsters, with no informed consent and most probably without any kind of consent, and gave them orally a fecal extract containing hepatitis virus to see what the medical results would be. They also did a supplemental clinical investigation in which they directly injected hepatitis virus into still other retarded children.[10]

Here is yet another example. Linoleic acid is known to be an essential nutrient, the deprivation of which has been shown to produce serious problems in animals. The effects of its deficiency have also been noted clinically in children. Nevertheless, at the University of Texas at Galveston, from 1956 to 1962, 445 babies, without informed consent, were deprived of linoleic acid. Seven of those children are known to have died of conditions directly related to the deprivation of this essential nutrient. Many others became seriously ill with a variety of dermatological conditions, pneumonia, and other problems.[11]

In Pennsylvania in 1973 there was an exposé of another deplorable situation at the Hamburg State Home and Hospital in Berks County. It was shown that retarded children, with no consent of any kind obtained from their parents, not even informed consent, were injected with a meningitis vaccine. The vaccine had not been approved by the FDA and was not on the clinical market, but it was given to these children nevertheless. Said the researchers at a later date, "We thought that the administrator of the hospital was the legal guardian for these children for all purposes, and he told us it was all right to go ahead and do it." After hearings before the Department of Health, Education, and Welfare and the Department of Justice in Harrisburg, the Commonwealth of Pennsylvania put an end to that experiment and to other similar experiments that had not received approval or that had not been reviewed by appropriate agencies and authorities.

Ethics and fetal research

For years, scientists who wanted to do research involving human embryos and fetuses have found themselves in a catch-22. They could do their work with impunity and receive federal funds for it, so long as an ethics advisory board approved their proposals. The catch is that the board does not exist, and has not existed for nearly a decade.

The research on fetuses has thrived, although it has remained in the ethical shadows. The testing of new methods for prenatal diagnosis or in vitro fertilization, among other things, has been financed with profits from infertility treatments and standard prenatal diagnosis. The research at issue involves either embryos, including those created by in vitro fertilization, or intact fetuses obtained from miscarriage or hysterotomy, an early form of cesarean birth.

The ethics board was originally created in 1974, partly in response to fetal research in the 1960s and 1970s, which took place without federal restrictions. Although many experiments were unremarkable, some were profoundly objectionable. In the early 1960s scientists at one university immersed 15 fetuses obtained from abortions in a salt solution to see whether they could absorb oxygen through the skin. One lived 22 hours. An experiment at another university examined the fetal brain's metabolism of glucose; the researchers used heads severed from live human fetuses.

At the same time, more researchers were working on in vitro fertilization, in which eggs removed from a woman's body are mixed with sperm and one or more resulting embryos are implanted in her uterus. To develop the method, research with human embryos was required. After the U.S. Supreme Court struck down most restrictions on abortion in 1973, Congress appointed a commission for the protection of human subjects and asked it to rule on fetal research.

The commission ruled that fetal research was permissible. But it also ruled that no one could subject a fetus to be aborted to any more risk than one that was to be carried to term. It was an extremely restrictive policy, the commission recognized, but there was an out: an advisory board would decide, on a case-by-case basis, when this "minimal risk standard" could be waived. However, the ethics board was dissolved before it had a chance to rule on any case, and the DHHS has declined to appoint a new one.

Adult experimentation

Of course, there have been similar problems in experiments with adults. Some of these have been widely publicized.

Between February 1945 and July 1956 at the Brooklyn Jewish Chronic Disease Hospital, injections of cancer cells were given to elderly hospital patients, with no actual or meaningful permission having been obtained from them or their families. Malignant tumor cells were injected directly into the veins of elderly people suffering from advanced parkinsonism, multiple sclerosis, and other kinds of severe neurological disorders. The principal researcher in that case was Dr. Chester M. Southam from Sloan-Kettering Institute, who subsequently had his license suspended temporarily by the state of New York. When asked why he had not injected himself in the experiments since he had said that it was quite safe, he replied: "Well, you know there is always a possibility of some harm and let's face it, there simply are not too many cancer researchers around."[12]

The infamous Tuskegee syphilis study, initiated and monitored by the U.S. Public Health Service, was not terminated until 1972. In Macon County, Alabama, some 400 black men with syphilis, of a total of 600 subjects in the study, were deliberately deprived of treatment from 1932 on, purportedly to study the effects of allowing the disease to take its natural course. At least 28 of these men, and possibly as many as 107, are known to have died as a result of the disease. It has been argued that in 1932, the cure for syphilis was ineffective and sometimes worse than the disease, but certainly this was not true in the 1950s, 1960s, and 1970s, during which time the "experiment was continued and regularly reported."

This incredible experiment was thoroughly evaluated and criticized extensively by a specially appointed committee. In the Final Report of the Tuskegee Syphilis Study Ad Hoc Advisory Panel, Department of Health, Education, and Welfare (Washington, D.C., 1973), one of the panelists, Jay Katz, M.D., stated:

In conclusion, I note sadly that the medical profession, through its national association, its many individual societies, and its journals, has on the whole not reacted to this (Tuskegee Syphilis) study except by ignoring it. One lengthy editorial appeared in the October 1972 issue of the *Southern Medical Journal* which exonerated the study and chastised the "irresponsible press" for bringing it to public attention. When will we take seriously our responsibilities, particularly to the disadvantaged in our midst who so consistently throughout history have been the first to be selected for human research?[13]

In April 1997, President Clinton offered a formal apology to the families and the eight remaining survivors of the Tuskegee syphilis experiments, identifying the experiments as a "blight on the American record." In addition, the U.S. government has paid a total of $10 million in an effort to compensate the victims and family members for the incident.

Geriatric research

In Philadelphia in 1964 and 1965, 13 elderly nursing home patients died as a direct result of drug experiments conducted on behalf of one of the large pharmaceutical manufacturers. The experiment had two stages. One drug was used to induce nervous system disorders and then another was introduced to control them. Although the Food and Drug Administration (FDA) was aware of the experiment and prepared a report on it in 1967, the report was withheld for many years and not released until the *Philadelphia Bulletin* obtained it under the Freedom of Information Act.[14] There was much doubt as to whether informed consent had been obtained in this experiment.

Reporting on his observations from 50 field inspections by the FDA in 1972, Dr. Alan B. Listook, Medical Officer in the FDA's Bureau of New Drugs, stated the following:

We have seen consent forms of senile patients signed "X-(her mark)" and have found others executed posthumously. On one occasion, where the obtainment of consent was the major reason for the FDA to conduct an investigation, we visited the subjects of the study, and discussed their understanding of the document they signed. It turned out that the women were not fully aware that they were participating in an experiment of any kind. They were not aware that they had been given a medication which had not been proven to be safe and effective.[15]

More than 3 years later, exactly the same kind of problem was reported again in a study conducted at a "distinguished university hospital and research center," not otherwise identified.[16] According to this later study, of 51 pregnant women who had signed a consent form in an experiment on the effects of a new labor-inducing drug, 20 did not know they were the subjects of research, even after the drug had been administered, and did not learn of it until they were interviewed by the follow-up investigator. Most of the 51 women had not been aware that any hazards were involved and had been informed only that a "new" drug was being tested, and not that it was an experimental drug. Yet, their own private physicians referred many of these women to the hospital for study. Whether the private physicians were aware of the true nature of the experiment is not stated, but in any case, it is clear that having one's own physician is no safeguard in these matters.

The whole area of new drug investigations is a jungle from the standpoint of research ethics, quite apart from the specific question of informed consent. Again, a quote from the remarks of Dr. Listook is appropriate:

We have had examples of physicians submitting case reports recording the administration to subjects of much more new drug substance than was available to them. We have had police departments report the finding of case lots of investigational drugs by the roadside in trashcans.

On occasion we find records of months of treatment on an index card. We have looked at records of patients reported as having been treated for intractable angina and found no mention of heart disease, no electrocardiograms, and no noted treatment. We frequently find that laboratory results reported to the FDA cannot be substantiated by records in the physician's office or by contact with the clinical laboratory where the work was said to have been done.

In institutions such as mental hospitals or geriatric facilities, we often see therapy prescribed that makes a study impossible to interpret and thus invalid. Major tranquilizers are given during the study of psychoactive compounds; vasodilators are given during the study of drugs being evaluated for the same purpose. Investigational drugs are discontinued without the investigator's knowledge, and adverse reactions go unreported because of lack of communication or lack of awareness on the part of the ward staff.

I could quote horror stories about paroled inmates and discharged mental patients reported as being treated in situ for weeks after their release, of therapy duration and dosage and hospital clinical courses that did not approximate those reported. . . .

We have come across individuals who were able to care for patients in their offices while they were on extended European vacations. Others, while not quite so versatile, have been able to come up with large patient populations for the treatment of widely divergent types of disease. We have the internist who does a study on an antiobesity drug and a few months later is found to be using the same patients in the study of an antihypertensive agent. In our review of the case reports we find no hypertension reported in the first study.[17]

In view of such findings, it would seem that these researchers were not being meticulous about getting informed consent. Yet it is from this very area—the development of new drugs—that we most often hear the arguments being advanced that research must not be fettered and that those of us who insist on adhering to the law are obstructing scientific progress.

BENEFIT VERSUS RISK RULE

In situations in which there is no potential therapeutic benefit to the subjects, it is customary to distinguish four levels of human experimentation.[18]

1. Benefit is reasonably believed to exceed the risk to the patient, and the study involves a patient who consents to this low-risk diagnostic or therapeutic procedure by coming to the physician. The patient is given information and shows that it is understood. He or she is not a subject, but rather a patient, and the needs of the patient come before any effort to gain knowledge. There is no legal problem in such a situation, except, of course, the one that physicians must contend with in all therapeutic situations, namely, obtaining an informed consent.

2. Benefit is reasonably considered to at least equal the risk, if not possibly exceed it. The patient is a volunteer. He or she may be a subject also, but if so, the relationship between the volunteer and the physician is made quite clear. At this level, we have a controlled experiment, but everyone knows what is happening, and there is definitely a strong possibility, in fact a probability, that the project may be of some therapeutic benefit to the patient.

3. The risk exceeds the benefit to the patient, but the risk is balanced by possible benefit to society. Here, the highest possible degree of informed consent is essential. Experiments in this field are still permissible, including those on children, provided the highest degree of informed consent is obtained from the patient or subject.

4. Risk exceeds benefit. The individual is either both the subject and the patient or purely just a subject. Consent from the individual either has not been obtained or has been obtained through deceit, the force of authority, or other improper means.

Usually, the last category is the issue. Because medical research trials commonly require that a convenient, stable subject population be monitored over weeks or months rather than days or hours, the medical scientist naturally turns to "captive" groups whose availability can be controlled. These groups include the following:

- Hospitalized or institutionalized patients
- Children
- Mentally abnormal persons
- Prisoners
- Persons under discipline (armed forces and police force)
- Laboratory assistants and medical students

In all these groups, factors are present that tend to make the individuals involved susceptible to pressures or influences that induce them to give their consent to experimentation. For example, prisoners hope for probation, soldiers for promotion, and students for higher grades. Use of such groups for medical experimentation is not invariably improper, but experiments conducted on such persons raise the question as to whether the consent obtained, if any, may have been the result of coercion or other influences that would place the project in Category 4.

In recent years, medical research in prisons has been prohibited in many states. The National Commission on Protection of Subjects has recently released its recommendations on allowable research on prison inmates. They are very stringent recommendations that would virtually eliminate such research from U.S. prisons.

This problem was particularly relevant in the case of children as experimental subjects. In the Hamburg State Home and Hospital case mentioned earlier, studies were initially undertaken without an informed consent. Indeed, there was no consent obtained at all. The physician in charge of the study "thought" that the administrator of the hospital was the legal guardian of these mentally retarded children!

Some time later, the physicians did send some kind of generalized consent form to the parents, and some of these were signed and returned. However, there is no question at all from a legal standpoint that this kind of consent is not a valid informed consent and would not hold up in the courts of Pennsylvania, even if the parents had been the subjects.

What if the pharmaceutical company involved with that meningitis vaccine believed it was essential to learn what the effects of that vaccine on children would be? Could that company, with its thousands of employees in this country and abroad, including all their research teams and top administrators, have gone to their employees and asked for volunteers?

Inasmuch as the meningitis vaccine that was being tested was of no direct therapeutic benefit to the children who were to receive it, even the parents within the pharmaceutical company could not have given a legal consent for their own children. Such experimentation would be considered assault and battery. And no one—even a parent—can give legal consent to have assault and battery committed on another human being.

Every one of these experiments on children involved subjects who did not have the necessary intellectual capacity to give a truly informed consent. They may have been legally adjudicated *non compos mentis*, or perhaps they merely had been socially and economically deprived to an extreme degree, but invariably they were incapable of giving an informed consent.

It is imperative that everyone in positions of authority within government, medical institutions, health care facilities, and custodial homes appreciate that no matter what the altruistic and projected humanitarian aspects of medical research may be, human beings cannot be subjected to medical experimentation without a proper informed consent having been obtained from them. In the case of minors (especially retarded children), elderly or senile persons who are suffering from serious diseases and do not have a full grasp of their mental faculties, or people who are imprisoned or otherwise subject to coercion, very serious moral and ethical principles must be carefully considered by the research team before undertaking any experiments that place the subjects at risk.

No legitimate reason or justification exists for further delay or governmental procrastination on this subject. There is absolutely no question from a legal standpoint that experiments of this nature are in violation of the law and are against basic concepts of medical morality and ethics. Physicians and scientists, as well as governmental officials in charge of hospitals, homes, and institutions of various kinds, should realize that the civil and criminal laws pertain to them, also.

CRIMINAL AND CIVIL LIABILITY

Although the *Hyman v. Brooklyn Jewish Chronic Disease Hosp.*[19] case makes mention of the "experimentation" question, it is of little value in ascertaining the legal guidelines for experimentation. The court confined itself to the narrow issue of whether a director of a membership corporation has a right to inspect the corporate records. In this case, the court held that possible corporate liability gives the director the right to inspection. As to the liability for the experimentation, the court ventures no unnecessary opinion. Assuming that experimentation is carried on under approved scientific techniques, it may be instructive to consider possible liabilities, viewing a researcher-subject relationship under criminal, tort, and contract law, recognizing that the categories are not always mutually exclusive.

Criminal liability, in the absence of statute, will attach when there is an intended harm constituting homicide or mayhem, or an unintended harm resulting from negligence by commission or omission of such character that it extends beyond ordinary negligence and is considered culpable negligence. If a volunteer dies during or as a result of "experimentation," the criminal liability, if any, would be for homicide—murder or manslaughter.

The Pennsylvania statute (typical of most states) defines the crime of murder as follows:

All murder which shall be perpetrated by means of poison, or by lying in wait, or any other kind of willful, deliberate and premeditated killing or which shall be committed in the perpetration of, or attempting to perpetrate any arson, rape, robbery, burglary, or kidnapping shall be murder in the first degree. All other kinds of murder shall be murder in the second degree. The jury before whom any person indicted for murder shall be tried, shall, if they find such person guilty thereof, ascertain in their verdict whether the person is guilty of murder of the first or second degree.

Murder is the unlawful killing of another with malice aforethought, express or implied.[20]

It is highly unlikely that a properly conceived and reliably approved research project undertaken by a competent specialist would qualify as an act of murder. If the research provides a strong possibility of death or severe injury, known in advance to the scientist in charge, malice may perhaps be implied. The statute provides a further definition: "Manslaughter, however, may be found without malice. Where the practice is such as to constitute a gross ignorance or culpable negligence or such a complete disregard of life or health, the courts have found voluntary or involuntary manslaughter."

Although no case involving experimentation that resulted in a conviction for voluntary or involuntary manslaughter can be found, it has been established that where such charges are brought, consent does not usually constitute a defense to criminal liability.

Professor Kidd of the University of California School of Law raises the question with specific reference to experimentation:

How far can one consent to serious injury to himself? The analogies are not close. Abortion, except for therapeutic reasons, is a crime, and the consent of the woman is no defense for the doctor. A person can not legally consent to his own death; it is murder by the person who kills him. . . . A person may not consent to serious injury amounting to a maim.[21]

In general, criminal negligence in a physician (experimenter) exists when the physician exhibits gross lack of competency, inattention, or wanton indifference to the patient's safety, either through gross ignorance or lack of skill. It is assumed that the same standards would be applicable to scientists engaging in human experiments: "In case of permanent injury or disease rather than death, the possible criminal charge would be mayhem. This crime at common law and by statute generally is also founded on malice and as such would be governed by the same considerations alluded to above."[22]

Basic to the law of torts, a second area of consideration as to the legal consequences of experimentation is the right of the individual to "freedom from bodily harm," so that any unauthorized invasion, or even threat, to the person constitutes grounds for liability. Consent is usually achieved through the use of a release, either written or oral, allowing the patient's person to be physically handled. In the normal physician-patient relationship, there usually is ample basis for finding informed agreement on the part of the patient for ordinary procedures by virtue of the recognized relationship between the parties. It is assumed that the physician is acting in good faith for the personal benefit of the patient who, by seeking professional assistance, may be assumed to consent to the treatment and diagnoses given. In an experimental situation, the inference of consent is not so easily drawn, and there seems to be more of a need for formal consent:

There is scant legal authority on this problem [but] . . . abundant expert testimony is usually available to show that subjecting a patient to experimentation without disclosure and consent is contrary to the customs of surgeons and thus negligent, even though there may be no technical slip in actual performance of the experiment.[23]

Specific to the problem of experimentation, tort liability may arise in cases of nontherapeutic, unnecessary, and legally questionable procedures involving criminal liability and public policy. For instance, in situations such as abortion and euthanasia, cases may be found in which, despite consent, the physician was held to tort liability. In none of these areas has there occurred experimentation by a scientist on humans for nontherapeutic reasons. In some states, a contract action is permitted on the theory breach of an implied agreement to treat with proper care and skill; the essence of the research contract lies in the complete understanding of the parties:

The medical research procedure by definition and by nature is a deviation from normal practice, even though all the specific elements involved may be well established, simply because medical practice ordinarily does not encompass employment of human beings primarily for the advancement of knowledge. There is no implicit understanding that conventional methods will be used and that the patient will be released as soon as his condition warrants. Consequently, the researcher has a more specific responsibility for full disclosure of his purpose, method, and probable consequences. Achieving a meeting of the minds is a far more critical element in the research contract.[24]

Assuming there is a complete understanding, a research contract will probably provide a defense against liability in a reasonable execution of the contract obligation or performance of the experiment. However, such a contract is unlikely to serve as a complete bar to an allegation of negligence. The patient's own performance under the contract will not be the subject of a decree for specific performance by a court of equity as they are for "personal services."

In conclusion, it would seem that medical practice, generally conceived to be diagnosis, treatment, and care, is governed by state statute and supporting administrative licensing and regulatory bodies. Medical research experimentation on human subjects would appear to be outside the scope of these rules:

Case law, insofar as it appears to recognize medically related activity, generally characterizes such research as experimentation and holds it to be outside legitimate medical practice. Reported cases have not yet considered modern controlled medical research as such, and have not yet established limits within which human research may be pursued. Cases which have involved conduct labeled experimentation have been decided basically on issues of disclosure or consent, negligence, lack of qualification, improper activity (quack procedures, medicines or devices) or unlicensed practice of medicine usually arising in cases of departure from accepted diagnosis, therapy or other practice.[25]

Despite the Nuremberg Code, the Declaration of Helsinki, the AMA Ethical Guidelines, and numerous other declarations of similar import, apparently many physicians, scientists, and governmental officials still think that because humane benefits may be derived from these experiments in later years, anything is justified today, particularly if the groups being used as guinea pigs consist of retarded children, senile persons, prisoners, or other unfortunate groups with various physical, psychological, or economic handicaps.

A special national commission has been proposed to review all the various facets of this sensitive, important, and complex matter. This group is to have a dual purpose: first, to establish basic principles and guidelines that would be uniformly applicable in all proposed projects involving human experimentation; and second, to consider, evaluate, and approve each new research proposal involving any kind of experimentation on humans. Legislation would have to be enacted to require that all such proposals be submitted and approved before being implemented. Membership in such a commission should necessarily be broad, extending beyond the medical and scientific professions, and all its decisions and records should be subject to public disclosure.

In 1982 the President's Commission for the Study of Ethical Problems in Medicine and Biomedical and Behavioral Research completed a 2-year examination of federal rules and procedures for conducting research with human subjects. The commission concluded that most government supervisory agencies have insufficient data on compliance, and a review of a few well-documented (and widely reported) cases of misconduct on the part of research scientists showed that government oversight can be improved. However, the public must keep a balanced perspective.

Because successful therapies for humans can be established only by tests on human subjects, medical progress depends on the participation of volunteers in research to test new therapies. The prerequisites for such experimentation include at least the following: a reasonable theoretical base for the belief that therapy may be useful; preliminary tests on nonhuman subjects; a careful weighing of the possible benefits and expected risks of the experimental therapy, as well as an assessment of the available standard therapies; and the genuine voluntary consent of the human subject.

The presidential commission's study demonstrates that federally funded institutions need well-defined procedures for responding to reports of misconduct, ranging from falsified data on patients/subjects' charts to conducting studies with drugs not cleared for tests on humans. Some procedures should protect from reprisal those who report their concern (the so-called whistle-blowers). Such procedures also should protect scientists accused of misconduct from publicity and loss of federal funds, at least until a preliminary finding is made that the accusations have some basis in fact. For the sake of all concerned, the institutional response should be prompt, thorough, and fair. The 23 governmental agencies and institutions involved in research on human subjects (e.g., the DHHS, the National Science Foundation) need clearly defined standards for investigations and sanctions.

INNOVATIVE THERAPY

To understand the concept of innovative therapy, it is useful to consider first the activities referred to as standard medical practice. The National Commission defined standard practice for the Protection of Human Subjects of Biomedical and Behavioral Research as "interventions that are designed solely to enhance the well-being of an individual patient or client and that have a reasonable expectation of success. The purpose of medical or behavioral practice is to provide diagnosis, preventive treatments, or therapy to particular individuals."[26]

The commission was established by Congress.[27] Its purpose was to conduct a comprehensive investigation and study to identify the basic ethical principles that should underlie the conduct of biomedical and behavioral research, evaluate existing guidelines for the protection of human subjects, and make appropriate recommendations to the Secretary of Health, Education, and Welfare concerning further steps, if any, to be taken.

The commission identified innovative therapies as a class of procedures that were "designed solely to enhance the well-being of an individual patient or client," but had not been tested sufficiently to meet the standard of having "a reasonable expectation of success." Innovative therapies have been defined as activities "ordinarily conducted . . . with either pure practice intent or with varying degrees of mixed research and practice intent that have been sufficiently tested to meet standards for acceptance or approval."

Dale H. Cowan[28] has stated that the difference between innovative and standard practices may be simply the difference between a beginning and an advanced level of the practice of medicine. However, as noted by R. J. Levine, in referring to the Belmont Report,[29] the attribute that defines innovative therapies is the "lack of suitable validation of [their] safety and efficacy," rather than their "novelty." A practice might not be validated because there is (1) a lack of sufficient testing to certify its safety and efficacy for an intended class of patients or (2) evidence that previously held assumptions about its safety and efficacy should be questioned.

In general, practices or therapies that are standard or accepted have risks and benefits that are known. Additionally, some basis exists for thinking that the benefits outweigh the risks. By contrast, the potential benefits and risks of innovative therapies are less well known and predictable. Consequently, their use exposes patients to a greater likelihood that the balance of benefits and risks may be unfavorable due either to the therapies being ineffective or entailing greater, possibly unknown, risks. Thus standard medical practice can be distinguished from innovative therapies on the basis of the extent of knowledge that exists regarding their likely risks and benefits.

The commission described experimentation or research as

an activity designed to test a hypothesis, permit conclusions to be drawn and thereby to develop or contribute to generalizable knowledge (expressed, for example, in theories, principles, and statements of relationships). Research is usually described in a formal protocol that sets forth an objective and a set of procedures designed to reach that objective.[30]

Levine defined research involving humans as

any manipulation, observation, or other study of a human being— or of anything related to that human being that might subsequently result in manipulation of that human being—done with the intent of developing new knowledge and which differs in any way from customary medical (or other professional) practice.[31]

The distinction between innovative therapy and experimentation can be drawn by focusing on the four levels of research listed previously. Like research, innovative therapy generally represents a departure from standard medical practice.

Federal regulations require that all research involving human subjects conducted by the DHHS, or funded in whole or in part by a grant, contract, cooperative agreement, or fellowship from DHHS, be reviewed by an institutional review board (IRB) established at each institution in which the research is to be conducted. The regulations define research as "a systematic investigation designed to develop or contribute to generalizable knowledge." The regulations further specify minimum requirements for the composition of IRBs and require that each institution engaged in research covered by the regulations must file a written assurance to the secretary of DHHS that "it will comply with the requirements set forth in [the] regulations."

To approve research by the regulations, IRBs must determine that a number of requirements are satisfied.

1. Risks to the subjects are minimized.
2. Risks to the subjects are reasonable in relation to anticipated benefits, if any, to subjects, and the importance of the knowledge that may reasonably be expected to result.
3. Selection of the subjects is equitable.
4. Informed consent will be sought from each prospective subject or the subject's legally authorized representative.
5. When appropriate, the research plan makes adequate provision for monitoring the data collected to ensure the safety of the subjects.

RADIATION EXPERIMENTS

In December 1993, the U.S. Department of Energy publicly disclosed that for the preceding 6 years it had ignored clear evidence of extensive illegal experiments conducted by distinguished medical scientists in the nation's nuclear weapons industry that took place over three decades after World War II, in which various groups of civilians were exposed to radiation in concentrations far above levels that are considered safe at this time. These experiments, conducted at government laboratories and prominent medical research institutions, involved injecting patients with dangerous radioactive substances, such as plutonium, or exposing them to powerful radiation beams. Allegedly, this work was undertaken to determine what the effect of radiation would be on soldiers and civilians if a global atomic war occurred. The experiments dealing with testing radiation on humans are listed in Table 22-1.

Other experiments of a similar nature took place at a state school in Fernald, Massachusetts, from 1946 to 1956, in which as many as 125 mentally retarded teenage boys were given radioactive iron and calcium in their breakfast cereal. Consent forms sent to the parents indicated that this study was intended to help researchers better understand human metabolism and nutritional needs. No mention was made that radioactive elements would be used.

Records from the Massachusetts Institute of Technology indicate that 23 pregnant women at the Boston Lying-In Hospital (now part of Brigham and Women's Hospital) were injected with radioactive iron in the early 1950s to allow researchers to study maternal-fetal circulation. In yet another experiment conducted around the same time at Massachusetts General Hospital, patients were given radioactive iodine to study thyroid function and body metabolism, even though the researchers acknowledged they did not know what the long-term effects would be.

TABLE 22-1 Radiation experiments on humans

Location(s)	Date	Those affected	Experiments
Vanderbilt University, Nashville	Late 1940s	About 800 pregnant women	Subjects were studied to determine the effect of radioactive iron on fetal development. A follow-up study of children born to the women found a higher-than-normal cancer rate.
Oak Ridge National Laboratory, Oak Ridge, Tennessee	Mid-1970s	Nearly 200 patients with leukemia and other cancers	Subjects were exposed to high levels of radiation. The experiments ended after a 1974 government investigation.
University of Rochester, Oak Ridge Laboratory, University of Chicago, and the University of California Hospital in San Francisco	1945-1947	18 people	Subjects were injected with high concentrations of plutonium, apparently without their informed consent. Many patients were chosen because medical specialists believed they suffered life-threatening illnesses.
Oregon State Prison	1963-1971	67 inmates	Prisoners' testicles were exposed to x-rays to help researchers understand the effects of radiation on production and function of sperm. The inmates signed consent statements indicating that they were aware of some of the risks, but the statements did not mention that radiation could cause cancer.
Washington State Prison	1963-1970	64 inmates	A similar study subjected prisoners to high levels of radiation. The purpose was to determine the minimum dose that would cause healthy men to become temporarily sterile.
Columbia University and Montefiore Hospital in the Bronx	Late 1950s	12 terminally ill cancer patients	Subjects were injected with concentrations of radioactive calcium and strontium-85, another radioactive substance, to measure the rate at which radioactive substances were absorbed into various human tissues.

From The Department of Energy, the Atomic Energy Commission, and Congress.

Altogether, as of early 1994, U.S. government officials acknowledged that more than 30 experiments involving the use of radioactive materials or radiation, in which the subjects or their parents and guardians were not apprised of the true nature of the studies and therefore could not have given legally acceptable informed consent, took place during a three-decade period beginning in 1946. There may well have been more that are yet to be uncovered.

The government had previously resisted paying compensation to any of these individuals. However, from October 1991 to May 1993, the government spent $47.1 million to reimburse the legal expenses of the private corporations that operated its nuclear weapons plants. The then Energy Secretary, Hazel O'Leary, proclaimed her definite intention to obtain compensation for all victims of these unethical experiments.

It is important to note that the General Accounting Office first disclosed some of these tests in 1986 in a report to Congress. However, when Representative Edward J. Markey of Massachusetts, chair of the congressional committee that reviewed this report, asked the government for more information and urged full disclosure of all such experiments, he was firmly and repeatedly rebuffed by both the Reagan and Bush administrations.

A senior official of the Atomic Energy Commission, in a 1950 memorandum to one of the prominent physician-scientists involved with some radiation experiments in the Boston area, observed that these medical experiments might have "a little of the Buchenwald touch." Thus it would appear that both the government officials and medical researchers who planned and conducted these radiation experiments were aware that these studies violated the 1947 Nuremberg Code, which was adopted after the Nazi war crimes trials and is regarded as the universal standard for experiments involving human beings.

Currently the U.S. government is aggressively pursuing settlement with the subjects of the Defense Department's radiation experiments in which the victims were unknowingly injected with uranium or plutonium. The federal government indicates that 16 of the 18 victims of the experiments have received a total of $6.5 million in compensation.

In addition, the Clinton administration sought to expand the current 1990 Radiation Exposure Compensation Act to include the family members of 600 now deceased miners who worked in government-operated uranium mines. The proposed expansion resulted from a presidential advisory committee finding that the high level of exposure to radon experienced by the miners between 1947 and 1991 was due to the government's failure to adequately ventilate the mines.

QUESTIONABLE HUMAN RESEARCH AND EXPERIMENTATION PRACTICES

In addition to the large number of alleged illegal experiments involving radiation and radioactive compounds, several other highly controversial situations have been brought to light in the past few years involving research projects and experimentation, in which informed consent, official and academic guidelines, and other applicable legal and ethical considerations were ignored by the physicians, scientists, and officials in charge of those studies.

The Medical University of South Carolina was accused of testing pregnant women for illicit drug use without their consent and then transmitting that information to local law enforcement officials. This drug testing program was apparently adopted as a means of forcing drug-addicted women who were pregnant to stop using drugs by threatening them with jail if they refused to cooperate with the hospital's regimen of prenatal visits and also attend an established drug treatment program. Almost all the women in the program were African Americans, and several of them were actually arrested and prosecuted for illicit drug use as a result of the disclosure of this information by the university hospital to the police. Dr. Charles R. McCarthy, formerly chief of the Office of Protection of Research Risks at the National Institutes of Health, concluded that this project "fits the definition of an experiment." He indicated that federal rules regarding human experimentation require that subjects give informed consent before being made part of an experiment, and that the patient has the right to refuse to participate and still be given appropriate and necessary medical treatment.

The *Boston Globe* recently reported that the infamous Timothy Leary, the 1960s drug guru, gave inmates at the Concord State Prison in Massachusetts doses of psilocybin, a powerful hallucinogenic drug, without their knowledge or consent. This compound can produce hallucinations, perception distortion, and psychosis and is considered to be psychologically addictive. These tests took place in the 1960s when Leary was a faculty member at Harvard University. He was eventually fired from his position at the prison by state officials, although not until these illegal tests had been under way for many years.

In late 1993 a rash of international articles reported that postmenopausal women were being impregnated with donated eggs fertilized with their husbands' sperm. In England, a 59-year-old woman gave birth to twins, and a 61-year-old Italian woman also gave birth after such a procedure. Numerous cases of a similar nature were also reported in France. Harvested eggs from aborted female fetuses were permitted to mature and then, via artificial insemination, were used to impregnate these elderly women. This experimental process, which had first been utilized in mice by Dr. Roger Gosden, a research scientist in Edinburgh, Scotland, has raised many ethical questions and has precipitated specific legislation in France and elsewhere that would ban the use of such a technique in postmenopausal women.

In the summer of 1993, two French physicians were charged with manslaughter in connection with the death of a child, who died after contracting Creutzfeldt-Jakob disease, a rare viral illness that attacks the brain after a long incubation period. Several other children were thought to have been afflicted also, but had not yet died. This disease, which is incurable and leads to rapid dementia and death, developed after the administration of pituitary gland extracts given to children who suffered from dwarfism. The pituitary glands had been acquired from 1983 to 1988 from corpses in Bulgaria and Hungary. Many of the deceased donors had been patients in psychiatric hospitals and infectious wards.

A current controversy with fascinating legal and ethical overtones is that of human cloning. Federally sponsored research dealing with in vitro fertilization (IVF) has been held in abeyance since 1980, but in 1993 the Clinton administration attempted to gain federal support for research on IVF and the resultant human embryos. The NIH Revitalization Act of 1993 nullified the requirement for ethics board scrutiny of IVF research proposals.

A scientific debate has yet to resolve the question of exactly what a clone is. Dr. Robert Stillman of George Washington University Medical Center reported his findings at a meeting in October 1993 of the American Fertilization Society. He claimed to have cloned human embryos, splitting single embryos into identical twins or triplets. Because human sperm can be frozen and used at a later date, it could be possible for parents to have a child, and years later use a cloned, frozen embryo to give birth to an identical twin, possibly as an organ donor for the older child. A technique has already been developed for making identical twins in animals (e.g., cattle) by dividing the embryo one or more times and letting the new clusters of cells develop into two genetically identical organisms.

In 1993 an internationally known medical researcher, Dr. Peter Wiernik, publicly admitted his role in having provided illegal injections of an experimental drug for 16 brain tumor patients in 1987, using them as human guinea pigs. Wiernik acknowledged a 5-year cover-up in an agreement worked out with federal prosecutors earlier in 1993, whereby he was demoted and reprimanded, but not subjected to criminal prosecution. The patients, all of whom were terminally ill and have since died, were told about the experimental nature of the drug, but were not informed that it lacked approval from the FDA. Wiernik had received FDA approval to use this drug, interleukin-2 (IL-2), in kidney cancer experiments. However, he gave leftover IL-2 to two neurosurgeons for treatment of patients with brain tumors. The FDA had never approved such treatments.

The FDA proposed a major change in the rules for reporting side effects from drug trials in 1993. This proposal came on the heels of publicly released information indicating that several people had died after having been given a new drug for hepatitis B in a series of experimental drug trials. A total of 5 of 15 patients who took the drug for 4 weeks or more died. It was determined in retrospect that five other patients in earlier experiments most probably died as a result of taking that same drug or its experimental predecessor. The drug involved was fialuridine; in the earlier experiments, it was a closely related drug, filacytosine. The scientists or the drug companies reported none of the deaths to the FDA, supposedly because the individuals conducting the experiments assumed that the drug had not caused the deaths.

In late 1993 articles appeared in newspapers throughout the world dealing with the use of cadavers in car crash tests at Heidelberg University in Germany. These experimental studies had been partly financed by the U.S. National Highway Traffic Safety Administration. Similar tests reportedly had been conducted at the University of Virginia and at the Medical College of Wisconsin, and also at Wayne State University in Detroit, the latter at the behest of the Centers for Disease Control and Prevention (CDC). Many questions were raised about whether an informed consent had been obtained by the legal next-of-kin before these corpses were used. The tests in Germany included the dead bodies of 200 adults and 8 children. German law permits the use of cadavers for research as long as the relatives' consent is obtained.

In 1976 John Moore, a 33-year-old man, was diagnosed with hairy-cell leukemia at the Medical Center of the University of California at Los Angeles (UCLA). His treating physician was Dr. David W. Golde, a hematologist and researcher at the UCLA Medical Center. A splenectomy was performed as part of the treatment. Golde recognized the commercial and scientific value of Moore's spleen and other bodily tissues and materials at the time he recommended the splenectomy. The spleen was taken to a hospital research unit to develop a cell line for commercial use. Golde and another researcher, Quan, then developed and patented a cell line from Moore's cells that produced lymphokines, a genetic product of considerable commercial value. The two researchers, a pharmaceutical company, and UCLA entered into a contract with the Genetics Institute worth more than $330,000 for the products that would be developed from this patented cell line over a 3-year period.

After the splenectomy, Moore returned to the hospital on several occasions over 7 years at the request of Golde and had samples taken of his blood, skin, bone marrow aspirate, and sperm. These were done specifically for commercial and not therapeutic purposes. Moore was never informed at any time by Golde of these research activities, or of the commercial value of his cells. When Moore ultimately discovered that his cells had been used to develop this cell line, he sued the researchers, various companies, and UCLA. The trial court dismissed all the claims, but an intermediate appellate court reversed and held that Moore had stated a cause of action for conversion. On appeal, the California Supreme Court, two justices dissenting, reversed and held that Moore had no property interest in his cells and therefore no cause of action for conversion.

However, the court unanimously held that Moore had set forth facts sufficient to state a cause of action for breach of fiduciary relationship and lack of informed consent against Golde for failing to disclose his research and commercial interest before the splenectomy and before the removal of Moore's other body tissues and blood in subsequent visits to UCLA. A petition for writ of certiorari to the U.S. Supreme Court was denied.

In 1994, after the publication of a series of articles on the plutonium injections, President Clinton appointed an advisory committee on human radiation experiments to investigate the matter and gave it access to thousands of secret documents. Jonathan D. Moreno, a biomedical ethicist at the University of Virginia, worked for the committee, and then went on to examine the broad history of experiments that the U.S. Government had secretly conducted on human subjects in the interest of national security from World War II through the Cold War.

During World War II, both military and civilian agencies sponsored numerous experiments with human subjects in connection with investigations of the new antibiotic penicillin, agents against malaria, and protections against poison gases. The subjects were conscientious objectors, prison inmates, hospital patients, students, and Army recruits. Most were volunteers who had been informed of the risks. But others participated without their consent, including tens of thousands of soldiers who were exposed to poison gases to test protective clothing and gas masks.

Despite the Nuremberg Code, the Atomic Energy Commission had no general policy governing experiments with human subjects. The Defense Department had a policy after 1953, at least for experiments in atomic, chemical, or biological warfare, but it was not widely disseminated.[32]

CONCLUSION

A discussion of the liability of a physician for experimental procedures including human research requires an initial examination of the two competing interests that must be balanced in any experimental situation. There is the obvious interest of the patient to be free from the abuses to which uncontrolled experimentation can lead—from the most grotesque examples of the atrocities of Nazi Germany to the violation of the rights of individuals to be free from becoming unwilling participants in any form of experimentation. The interest of the physician and the interest of society as a whole must be balanced against the interest of the individual. If physicians are limited strictly to previously established procedures, all innovation and progress in the field of medicine would cease. The courts have recognized both of these interests in attempting to deal with the problem of when the physician should bear the burden of the effects of experimental procedures.[33] They have laid down the principle that one who experiments with an innovative treatment is responsible for all the harm that follows. Later

cases articulated the need for the advancement of medicine, and in these cases the court stated that it is a recognized fact that, if the general practice of medicine is to progress, a certain amount of experimentation must be carried on.

Complicating the problem of balancing these interests is the difficulty of defining experimentation.[34,35] Courts have confused judgmental decisions and experimentation. In the opinion of one court, a physician is presumed to have the knowledge and skill to use some innovation; yet courts have in the past mislabeled that area of permissible judgment as "experimentation." However, any time a physician's procedures do not follow accepted medical practice, he or she is moving in the direction of experimentation and the distinction between innovation and experimentation becomes blurred. On the other hand, the courts have determined that the mere fact of departure from the drug manufacturer's recommended dose does not make the departure an "experiment." A procedure does not rise to the level of an experiment if the physician has previously used the method successfully, the procedure has been described in the literature, and the choice has been reasonably and prudently calculated by the physician to accomplish the intended purpose. However, surely it is not enough that the intentions of the physician be reasonable to find that a previously unapproved procedure is not an experiment.

When drawing the line between experiment and judgment becomes difficult, the courts are likely to be influenced by the fact that no approved therapy is available. The physician then is faced with the choice of no treatment or innovation. And in examining the type of innovation chosen by the physician, the court will look at the rationale of the physician in making that choice and the extent to which that choice was a significant departure from previous standards of care.

Another factor that has been proposed as being important in deciding what is considered experimentation is the distinction between the curable and the terminally ill patient. It has been argued that the terminally ill patient with no hope of recovery from accepted medical procedures should be free to choose from any form of treatment and should not be restricted in his or her choice by laws that were designed to protect the patient from the risks of experimentation. A distinction between curable and terminally ill patients is not valid, however, when the protection of the rights of an individual from the use of experimental drugs is concerned. It has been held that a physician treating terminally ill patients with an unapproved drug may be subject to criminal penalties.[36] The U.S. Supreme Court has ruled that the Federal Food, Drug and Cosmetic Act, which restricts the use of experimental drugs, contains no exemptions for the terminally ill patient.[37]

Although a number of courts have recognized a legal right to recover for damages resulting from experimentation by the physician, no cases to date have actually turned on the issue of experimentation alone. The courts have seemed reluctant to base liability squarely on the issue of experimentation, perhaps because the issue of experimentation is composed of a number of elements. Instead, they have relied on a number of other legal theories for finding liability.

The first and most important is that of informed consent. One court has stated that without informed consent for an investigational procedure, a physician commits a battery.[38] Liability for experimental procedures has been predicated on the lack of informed consent of the patient in a number of cases.[39] In one case involving psychosurgery on a mental patient and a procedure that was totally novel and unrelated to any previously accepted procedure, lack of knowledge on the subject made a knowledgeable consent impossible.[40] However, most courts have accepted the idea that an informed consent is possible even when the knowledge surrounding the procedure is limited. Some believe absolute liability should be imposed on the physician for experimental procedures because they amount to abnormally dangerous activity under 402(a), Restatement (Second) of Torts. However, informed consent before the administration of an investigational drug amounts to voluntarily encountering a dangerous activity that bars recovery under 402(2).

If a physician adopts a method not recognized as sound by the medical community, the physician may be liable if it injures the patient in any way. Any variance from established standards can lead to liability. This "any variance" approach has been modified by most courts. It is generally recognized that where competent medical authorities are divided, a physician will not be held liable if he or she follows a form of treatment advocated by a considerable number in the profession. This represents the "respectable minority approach."[41]

It is important to consider whether the physician undertook a form of treatment that a reasonable and prudent member of the medical profession would undertake under the same or similar circumstances. This standard is an appropriate one, but in the area of experimentation there is a need for more specific guidelines to be articulated by the courts.[42] For example, the test might include factors such as (1) the qualifications of the physician in question to do the particular procedure involved, (2) the rationality of the procedure based on the extent of departure from accepted procedures and the indication of need for the procedure under the circumstances, and (3) the risk of the procedure versus the benefit to be derived from it.

A third legal theory used in experimentation cases is based on the patient's right of privacy. The right to control one's body is part of the right of privacy inherent in our Constitution. Experimentation has been considered a violation of this right.

The physician may be able to guard against liability for experimental procedures with a covenant not to sue. The patient agrees before treatment not to sue if injured as a result of the experimental treatment. When the procedure, although experimental, may have some value and represents a last chance for help, the physician may secure an agreement not to sue if the procedure is not helpful, provided the patient is fully advised.

In addition to the case law that has developed regarding experimentation, there is some federal and state statutory law in this area. Most important within the federal province is the Federal Food, Drug and Cosmetic Act and the regulations promulgated thereunder. These are designed to regulate the influx of new drugs in the market. Section 505(i) of the Act[43] exempts from premarketing approval drugs intended solely for investigational use if they satisfy certain criteria. Experimental drugs are available only to authorized investigators. At authorized institutions their use (as well as any experimental procedure) is subject to the IRB under the regulations of the DHHS. The board examines (1) the knowledge to be gained from the study, (2) prior experimental and clinical findings to determine the necessity and timeliness of using human subjects, (3) potential benefits to the subjects, (4) potential risks and procedures to minimize them, (5) confidentiality procedures, (6) the consent process, and (7) the proposed subject population.

The approval of a study does not mean that the investigator is then insulated from personal liability for harm suffered by the subjects in the study, but it substantially decreases the risk, especially with regard to liability based on failure to secure a subject's informed consent. These procedures are not universally mandated by law, but they apply when research is supported by DHHS funds or submitted to the FDA.

State statutes designed to protect subjects from the risks of experimentation tend to focus on specific matters rather than setting general guidelines for review of research.[44] These statutes regulate investigational drugs, fetal research, psychosurgery, confidentiality of information, and privacy. Only the state of New York statutorily requires institutional review committees for human research. Their function is basically the same as that of the IRB.[45] The state of Louisiana is the only state that defines the crime of human experimentation.[46] State statutes regulating human experimentation are a reasonable exercise of the state's police power.

ENDNOTES

1. H.K. Beecher, *Ethics and Clinical Research*, N. Engl. J. Med. 37ff. (June 8, 1973). *See also* H.K. Beecher, *Experimentation in Man*, published as a report to the Council on Drugs of the American Medical Association, 169 J.A.M.A. 461-478 (1959) (republished by Charles C. Thomas 1959).
2. Commission on CIA Activities within the United States, *Report to the President* (June 1975).
3. Associated Press dispatch, Washington, D.C. (Aug. 13, 1975).
4. UPI dispatch, Salem, Oregon (Mar. 4, 1976).
5. UPI dispatch, Washington, D.C. (Feb. 22, 1976) (E. Delong).
6. *Prince v. Massachusetts*, 321 U.S. 158 at 170 (1944).
7. *Bonner v. Moran*, 126 F. 2d 121 (D.C. Cir. 1941).
8. Pappworth, *Human Guinea Pigs: Experimentation on Man* (1967).
9. The New Republic, Dec. 3, 1966 at 10.

10. 288 N. Engl. J. Med., 755, 791, 1247 (1973).
11. Med. World News, 4 (Apr. 13, 1973).
12. Med. World News, 6 (June 5, 1964); 151 Science 663 (1966).
13. Med. World News, 15 (Aug. 18, 1972); Curran, *Legal Liability in Clinical Investigations*, 289 N. Engl. J. Med. 730 (1973).
14. The Philadelphia Bulletin 1 (Nov. 16, 1975).
15. Hosp. Trib., 1 (May 14, 1973).
16. Barber, *The Ethics of Experimentation with Human Subjects*, 234 Sci. Am. 25 (Feb. 1976).
17. Hosp. Trib., 1 (May 14, 1973).
18. *Human Experimentation*, Med. World News, 37ff. (June 8, 1973).
19. *Hyman v. Jewish Chronic Disease Hosp.*, 206 N.E. 2d 3381 N.Y. (1965).
20. 18 Purdon's Statutes §2501 *et seq.*; 18 Pa. C.S.A. §2501 *et seq.*
21. Kidd, *The Problem of Experimentation on Human Beings: Limits of the Right of a Person to Consent to Experimentation on Himself*, 117 Science 211, 212 (1953).
22. *Id.*
23. *Id.*
24. *Id.*
25. *Id.*
26. The commission was established by Congress in Title II, Part A, §201(a) of the National Research Service Award Act of 1974, Pub. L. No. 93-348, 88 Stat. 142. The purpose of the commission was to conduct a comprehensive investigation and study to identify the basic ethical principles that should underlie the conduct of biomedical and behavioral research, evaluate existing guidelines for the protection of human subjects, and make appropriate recommendations to the Secretary of HEW concerning further steps, if any, to be taken. *Id.* at §202(a)(1)(A) (hereinafter referred to as *the commission*).
27. *Id.*
28. Dale H. Cowan, *Innovative Therapy versus Experimentation*, Tort and Insurance L.J. (Summer 1986).
29. National Commission, *The Belmont Report: Ethical Principles and Guidelines for the Protection of Human Subjects of Research*, DHEW Pub. No. (OS) 78-0012 (1978) (hereinafter referred to as the *Belmont Report*).
30. *Supra* note 26.
31. R.J. Levine, The Boundaries between Biomedical or Behavioral Research and the Accepted and Routine Practice of Medicine, Belmont Report, Appendix I, Paper No. 1, DHEW Pub. N. (OS) 78-0013 (1978).

32. J.D. Moreno, *Undue Risk: Secret State Experiments on Humans* (W.H. Freeman & Company 1999).
33. *Carpenter v. Blake*, 60 Barb. (N.Y.) 488, *rev'd on other grounds*, 50 N.Y. 696 (1872).
34. *Fortner v. Koch*, 272 Mich. 273, 261 N.W. 762 (1935).
35. *Brooks v. St. Johns Hickey Memorial Hosp.*, 269 Ind. 270, 380 N.E. 2d 72 (1978).
36. *People v. Privitera*, 23 Cal. 3d 697 (1979).
37. *U.S. v. Rutherford*, 582 F. 2d 1234, *cert. granted* 99 S.Ct. 1042, 439 U.S. 1127, *cert. denied* 99 S.Ct. 1045, 439 U.S. 1127, *revised*, 99 S.Ct. 2470, 442 U.S. 544, *on remand*, 611 F. 2d (1979).
38. *Gatson v. Hunter*, 121 Ariz. 33, 588 P. 2d 326 (1978).
39. *Ahern v. Veteran's Administration*, 537 F. 2d 1098 (1976).
40. *Kaimowitz v. Michigan Dept. of Mental Health* (Civil No. 73-19434-AW), Cir. Ct. Wayne Co., Mich. (1973).
41. *Colton v. New York Hosp.*, 414 N.Y.S. 2d 866 (1979).
42. *Fiorentino v. Wegner*, 272 N.Y.S. 2d 557 (1966).
43. Federal Food, Drug and Cosmetic Act, §501(i), 21 U.S.C. 335(i).
44. California Health and Safety Code §§24176-24179.5 and 26668.4.
45. New York Public Health Law 2440-2446 (Supp. 1976).
46. La. Stat. Ann. Title 14, 872 (1974).

GENERAL REFERENCES

A *Doctor's Drug Studies Turn into Fraud*, The New York Times, A1/Col 1 (May 17, 1999).

Rebecca Dresser, *Time for New Rules on Human Subjects Research?* Hastings Center Report (Nov./Dec. 1998).

Drug Trials Hide Conflicts for Doctors, The New York Times, A1/Col 1 (May 16, 1999).

Gregg Easterbrook, *Medical Evolution*, The New Republic 20–25 (Mar. 1, 1999).

David M. Morens, *Should the Declaration of Helsinki Be Revised*, Letter to the Editor, 341 N. Engl. J. Med. (1999).

Proposed Revisions to the Declaration of Helsinki: Will They Weaken the Ethical Principles Underlying Human Research?, 341 N. Engl. J. Med. (1999).

Eileen Welsome, *Human Guinea Pigs*, The New York Times, Sunday Book Review, 28/Col 2 (Dec. 12, 1999); provides a review of The Plutonium Files.

World Medical Association, *Declaration of Helsinki: Recommendations Guiding Physicians in Biomedical Research Involving Human Subjects*, 277 J.A.M.A. (1977).

APPENDIX 22-1   **The Nuremberg Code**

The Nuremberg Code provides as follows:

1. The voluntary consent of the human subject is absolutely essential. This means that the person involved should have legal capacity to give consent; should be so situated so as to exercise free power of choice, without the intervention of any element of force, fraud, deceit, duress, overreaching, or other ulterior form of constraint or coercion; and should have sufficient knowledge as to enable him to make an understanding and enlightened decision. This latter element requires that before the acceptance of an affirmative decision by the experimental subject, there should be made known to him the nature, duration, and purpose of the experiment; the method and means by which it is to be conducted; all inconveniences and hazards reasonably to be expected; and the effects upon his health or person which may possibly come from his participation in the experiment.

The duty and responsibility for ascertaining the quality of the consent rest upon each individual who initiates, directs or engages in the experiment. It is a personal duty and responsibility which may not be delegated to another with impunity.

2. The experiment should be such as to yield fruitful results for the good of society, unprocurable by other methods or means of study, and not random and unnecessary in nature.

3. The experiment should be so designed and based on the results of animal experimentation and a knowledge

From 1 and 2 *Trials of War Criminals before the Nuremberg Military Tribunals: The Medical Case* (U.S. Government Printing Office, Washington, D.C. 1948).

of the natural history of the disease or other problem under study that the anticipated results will justify the performance of the experiment.

4. The experiment should be conducted as to avoid all unnecessary physical and mental suffering and injury.

5. No experiment should be conducted where there is a priori reason to believe that death or disabling injury will occur; except, perhaps, in those experiments where the experimental physicians also serve as subjects.

6. The degree of risk to be taken should never exceed that determined by the humanitarian importance of the problem to be solved by the experiment.

7. Proper preparation should be made and adequate facilities provided to protect the experimental subject against even remote possibilities of injury, disability or death.

8. The experiment should be conducted only by scientifi-

cally qualified persons. The highest degree of skill and care should be required through all stages of the experiment of those who conduct or engage in the experiment.

9. During the course of the experiment the human subject should be at liberty to bring the experiment to an end if he has reached the physical or mental state where continuation of the experiment seems to him to be impossible.

10. During the course of the experiment the scientist in charge must be prepared to terminate the experiment at any stage if he has probable cause to believe, in the exercise of good faith, superior skill and careful judgment required of him that a continuation of the experiment is likely to result in injury, disability, or death to the experimental subject.

APPENDIX 22-2   The Declaration of Helsinki

The Declaration of Helsinki provides as follows:

It is the mission of the physician to safeguard the health of the people. His knowledge and conscience are dedicated to the fulfillment of his mission.

The Declaration of Geneva of The World Medical Association binds the physician with the words: "The health of my patient will be my first consideration" and the International Code of Medical Ethics, which declares that "Any act or advice which could weaken physical or mental resistance of a human being may be used only in his interest."

Because it is essential that the results of laboratory experiments be applied to human beings to further scientific knowledge and to help suffering humanity, The World Medical Association has prepared the following recommendations as a guide to each physician in clinical research. It must be stressed that the standards as drafted are only a guide to physicians all over the world. Physicians are not relieved from criminal, civil, and ethical responsibilities under the laws of their own countries.

In the files of clinical research a fundamental distinction must be recognized between clinical research in which the aim is essentially therapeutic for a patient, and the clinical research, the essential object of which is purely scientific and without therapeutic value to the person subjected to the research.

BASIC PRINCIPLES

1. Clinical research must conform to the moral and scientific principles that justify medical research and should be based on laboratory and animal experiments or other scientifically established facts.

2. Clinical research should be conducted only by scientifically qualified persons and under the supervision of a qualified medical person.

3. Clinical research cannot legitimately be carried out unless the importance of the objective is in proportion to the inherent risk to the subject.

4. Every clinical research project should be preceded by careful assessment of inherent risks in comparison to foreseeable benefits to the subject or to others.

5. Special caution should be exercised by the physician in performing clinical research in which the personality of the subject is liable to be altered by drugs or experimental procedure.

CLINICAL RESEARCH COMBINED WITH PROFESSIONAL CARE

1. In the treatment of the sick person, the physician must be free to use a new therapeutic measure, if in his or her judgment it offers hope of saving life, reestablishing health, or alleviating suffering.

   If at all possible, consistent with patient psychology, the physician should obtain the patient's freely given consent after the patient has been given a full explanation. In case of legal incapacity, counsel should also be procured from the legal guardian; in case of physical incapacity the permission of the legal guardian replaces that of the patient.

2. The physician can combine clinical research with professional care, the objective being the acquisition of new medical knowledge, only to the extent that clinical research is justified by its therapeutic value for the patient.

From 67 Ann. Intern. Med. suppl. 7 at 74-75 (1967).

NONTHERAPEUTIC CLINICAL RESEARCH

1. In the purely scientific application of clinical research carried out on a human being, it is the duty of the physician to remain the protector of the life and health of that person on whom clinical research is being carried out.

2. The nature, the purpose, and the risk of clinical research must be explained to the subject by the physician.

3a. Clinical research on a human being cannot be undertaken without his free consent after he has been informed; if he is legally incompetent, the consent of the legal guardian should be procured.

3b. Consent should, as a rule, be obtained in writing. However, the responsibility for clinical research always remains with the research worker; it never falls on the subject even after consent is obtained.

4a. The investigator must respect the right of each individual to safeguard his personal integrity, especially if the subject is in a dependent relationship to the investigator.

4b. At any time during the course of clinical research the subject or his guardian should be free to withdraw permission for research to be continued. The investigator or the investigating team should discontinue the research if in his or their judgment, it may, if continued, be harmful to the individual.

The Human Genome Project

STEPHANIE L. ANDERSON, M.D., J.D.

HISTORY OF GENETICS
HISTORY OF THE HUMAN GENOME PROJECT
THE NEW GENETICS AND THE SHADOW OF EUGENICS
GENETIC REDUCTIONISM/DETERMINISM
GENETIC ENHANCEMENT
ACCESS TO GENETIC SERVICES
GENETICS AND PRIVACY: INSURANCE AND EMPLOYMENT
CONCLUSION

A more important set of instruction books will never be found by human beings. When finally interpreted, the genetic messages encoded within our DNA molecules will provide the ultimate answers to the chemical underpinnings of human existence. They will not only help us understand how we function as healthy human beings but will also explain, at the chemical level, the role of genetic factors in a multitude of diseases—such as cancer, Alzheimer's disease and schizophrenia—that diminish the individual lives of so many millions of people.

JAMES WATSON[1]

Medicine in the twenty-first century will be dominated by genetics. The Human Genome Project, the multi-billion-dollar international attempt to map the human genome, which was born of a powerful alliance between governments, private enterprise, and science, has been described as a Holy Grail or Rosetta Stone for deciphering the secrets of humanity and all biology that, until now, nature has adeptly guarded and kept just beyond science's grasp. The working draft human DNA sequence has so far revealed that within the genome's 3 billion bits of information, the expected 100,000 human genes is closer to 35,000—only a little more than twice that of a fruit fly, a mosquito, or a tiny worm. Still, the larger volume of data associated with the larger human genome makes for a considerable increase in complexity. The human genome (the first vertebrate genome) is around 30 times larger than the recently sequenced fly, worm, and mosquito genomes, and 250 times larger than the yeast (the first eukaryotic genome).[2] Most recently, scientists from 27 institutions in six countries have reported the decoding of the complete set of genes of a mouse.[3] The mouse code consists of 2.5 billion base pairs (only slightly smaller than that of a human), 5% of which are identical to humans—perhaps lending some credence to scientists' theory that mice and humans shared a mammalian ancestor.

"What a piece of work," as Hamlet marveled, "is a man."[4] While some view the early successes of the Human Genome Project as a magnificent and powerful basis of discovery that will profoundly alter the way we view ourselves, some fear the Human Genome Project is an attempt to reduce man, that marvelous "piece of work," to biology, which could lead us back to the road of the eugenics of old. Still others warn of a growing unease in the public sphere of a massive control of the processes of life, its potential social dangers, and a "fear of Frankenstein."[5] For every enthusiastic claim of its value, there has been an apocalyptic counterclaim. Notwithstanding what will certainly be an ongoing controversy and debate in scientific, political, theological, and lay circles over the merits of genomics and the role of genes in human life, our understanding of how genes function continues to expand at an almost unfathomable pace. As genetic technology relevant to human biology is developed, society will be challenged by a host of complex ethical, legal, and social issues. Although many of the technologies discussed here and elsewhere related to the Human Genome Project are not yet available, it is not too soon to begin a dialogue and a careful analysis of the potential costs and benefits of future genetic programs and to formulate a tentative plan for how society and medicine might respond.

HISTORY OF GENETICS

Gregor Johann Mendel, an inquisitive Augustinian monk and priest who had studied at university in Olmütz and Vienna, had a passion for tending his pea plants in the gardens of the monastery in Brünn, Austria (now Brno, Czech Republic).[6] In 1856, his fascination with the distinct varieties of plants and the resulting peas led him to begin an 8-year series of experiments that would involve the planting of over 30,000 different plants, the crossing of his pea varieties, and recording the types of plants produced. He discovered the elements of heredity, which he called genes, and some basic rules governing their transmission from generation to generation. In 1865 he would present the results of his work to the Brünn Society for the Study of Natural History and those results were published in 1866 in *Experiments with Plant Hybrids*.[7] Though his work revolutionized biology and experimental science, its importance would not be realized in his lifetime. It was not until 1900 that his work would be rediscovered and later still that he would be hailed as the father of modern genetics.

In 1859, the first edition of Charles Darwin's *On the Origin of Species* was published and sold out in one day. In it he described the modern theory of evolution: adaptation is the result of natural selection. Natural selection is a consequence of hereditary differences among organisms in their ability to survive and reproduce in the prevailing environment.[8] Those best suited to their environment will have better survival and reproductive success than others of their kind and will then pass those advantageous traits to their offspring. Although Darwin could provide a detailed account of how the mechanism of natural selection worked, he was unable to explain how variations could arise in populations or how those characteristics could be transmitted from one generation to the next.[9] Although Darwin and Mendel were contemporaries, neither was apparently aware of the other's work. By 1900, long after the death of both Mendel and Darwin, three botanists working in three different places on different species duplicated Mendel's work before his original paper was rediscovered. In 1918, in Britain, the mathematical genius of Ronald Fisher reconciled Darwinism and Mendelism, proving that Mendel had brilliantly "supplied the missing parts of the structure erected by Darwin."[10]

In 1951, chance threw a precocious, confident 19-year-old American, James Dewey Watson, with a bachelor's degree from Indiana University, into the Cavendish Laboratory at Cambridge University with 35-year-old Francis Harry Compton Crick, a British biophysicist (who had yet to attain a Ph.D.). Both were convinced that genes were made of DNA, not protein—as was commonly believed at the time. Together they began an inquiry into the structure of DNA. Utilizing x-rays and molecular models, by 1953 they proposed the first essentially correct three-dimensional representation of the double helix structure of DNA and could explain how the DNA molecule replicates, controls heredity, and undergoes mutation. Their discovery paved the way for all the major genetic discoveries of the last 50 years. In 1962, Watson and Crick were awarded the Nobel Prize for Medicine, for their "discoveries concerning the molecular structure of nucleic acids and its significance for information transfer in living material," a prize they shared with Maurice Hugh Frederick Wilkins, who simultaneously worked on the structure of DNA along with Rosalind Franklin (deceased and therefore unable to be honored with the Nobel Prize) at King's College in London. Watson and Crick have since been variously characterized as having made the greatest scientific discovery of the twentieth century and one of the greatest discoveries *ever* made.

HISTORY OF THE HUMAN GENOME PROJECT

The Human Genome Project (HGP) was a 15-year effort formally begun in October 1990. At that time, its stated goal was to analyze the structure of human DNA, determine the location of all human genes, and make them available for further biological study, with parallel studies being carried out on selected model organisms to provide the comparative information required for understanding the functioning of the human genome. Another long-range project goal is to determine the complete sequence of the 3 billion DNA base pairs in the human genome, a feat that even with today's technology remains awesome to consider.

The groundwork for the project began in 1985 when Charles DeLisi, Director of the Office of Health and Environmental Research (OHER) at the Department of Energy (DOE), the division responsible for funding most of the life sciences and environmental research for the department, proposed a Human Genome Initiative. His interest in the project grew out of an effort to study DNA changes in the cells of atomic bomb survivors of Hiroshima and Nagasaki, and to augment the ongoing work of the Atomic Bomb Casualty Commission in its study of the biological effects of radiation exposure.[11] The DOE also had an interest in being able to utilize high technology national laboratories and their multidisciplinary teams of scientists.[12]

Soon after the initial proposal, the OHER convened a conference in Santa Fe, New Mexico, to assess the feasibility of a Human Genome Initiative. Following the Santa Fe conference, DOE's OHER announced the Human Genome Initiative. A year later, in 1987, the Congressionally chartered DOE advisory committee, the Health and Environmental Research Advisory Committee (HERAC), endorsed the plan for a 15-year, multidisciplinary scientific and technological undertaking to map and sequence the human genome. In 1990, the DOE and the National Institutes of Health presented a joint HGP plan to Congress and the 15-year program formally began. Also in 1990, recognizing the wider social implications of the HGP, the Ethical, Legal and Social Implications (ELSI) Program was established as part of the HGP to identify problem areas and develop solutions before newly gained scientific information would be integrated into health care practice.[13]

The progression from 1985 to 1990 was not an easy one for the DOE. It would have to explain why the agency should play a major role in the project and explain its connection and expertise relative to the project.[14] Further, as the proposal for the HGP was thrust onto the public policy agenda, the project's goals had to undergo several "redefinitions" to ensure that each hurdle, whether it be in the

Senate or the House or one of many hearings, would be cleared. At least part of the redefinition was aimed at seizing the lay imagination with the excitement of the possibilities of more robust health and cures for disease.

In 1992, amid differing scientific aims and conflicts about his patent rights, NIH scientist Craig Venter resigned his post to head up a new Institute for Genomic Research with hopes of speeding up the project using state-of-the-art automation and avoiding the bureaucracy of operating in the public arena. By 1994, the project had announced that its 5-year goal of genetic mapping was one year ahead of schedule. That same year, the Genetic Privacy Act was written—the first United States HGP legislative product, proposed to regulate collection, analysis, storage, and use of DNA samples and genetic information obtained from them.[15] Still farther ahead of schedule, on June 25, 2000, the HGP leaders, both public and private, and President Clinton announced the completion, 5 years early, of a "working draft" DNA sequence of the human genome.[16] That initial working draft sequence was published on February 12, 2001.[17] Finally, on April 14, 2003, the International Genome Consortium, led in the United States by the National Human Genome Research Institute (NHGRI) and the DOE, announced the successful completion of the HGP more than 2 years ahead of schedule.

THE NEW GENETICS AND THE SHADOW OF EUGENICS

George Santayana, a U.S. philosopher, is credited with penning the dictum, "[w]hen experience is not retained . . . infancy is perpetual. Those who cannot remember the past are condemned to repeat it." Eugenics was the early twentieth-century movement for hereditary improvement that was wrought with virulent racism and atrocious wrongs visited upon vulnerable individuals and populations. Some, remembering the past, fear that mapping the human genome opens up the possibility of widespread nonmedical uses of genetic knowledge. Eugenics and its attendant social and moral failures, promoted by a particular conception of human perfection, led genetics into the bleakest period of its short history.

Although Francis Galton (1822–1911), a cousin of Darwin and a respected and influential British scientist, is given the dubious honor of being the creator of eugenics,[18] the eugenic ideal has been a part of Western discourse at least since Plato, who proposed, in Book Five of the *Republic* (459d), the selective breeding of the guardians to ensure superior offspring (positive eugenics), coupled with the destruction of those deemed inferior (negative eugenics).[19] Plato, however, never garnered the momentum that the eugenic movement achieved on both sides of the Atlantic before World War II. With eminent geneticists poised at the forefront, popular eugenics was rapidly introduced into the public discourse.[20] Further, eugenicists drawing on Darwinian notions of evolution viewed medical care as a frustration to evolution by allowing the unfit to survive and reproduce.[21]

Eugenics came to be viewed as a completely respectable part of American and British biology, taught at universities and incorporated into laws.[22] In the United States, by 1911, six states already had laws allowing forced sterilization of the mentally unfit. By 1917, nine more states had joined them. The Immigration Restriction Act of 1924 was a direct result of eugenic campaigning.[23] That law remained unamended for 40 years. In 1927, Justice Oliver Wendell Holmes of the United States Supreme Court, in his majority opinion in *Buck v. Bell*, ruled that the Commonwealth of Virginia could sterilize Carrie Buck, a 17-year-old girl, deemed feebleminded in light of eugenic theory.[24] Similar sterilizations continued in Virginia until 1972—four were performed that year. The laws allowing those sterilizations are still on the books in Virginia, and similar laws remain in effect in many other states.[25] The Supreme Court has never reversed its decision in *Buck v. Bell*. The United States, where individual liberty is so highly valued, crudely interfered with the rights of individuals to determine their reproductive futures by sterilizing more than 60,000 people for "feeblemindedness" between 1910 and 1935.[26]

Eugenics brings to mind a time when "science" served to justify social prejudice by its obsession with biological improvement of the human race. The evils transpired when the values of a few were mistaken for the values and goals of human beings in general. Though no one may expect a repeat of the grizzly racial policies of Nazism, history does account for a level of mistrust of genetic science. There is a sense that an ethically ambiguous and potentially destructive body of research is taking place, conducted by scientific elites, that promises to alter our lives in some dramatic or undesirable way.[27] Some critics fear that a subtle form of eugenics may slip in through the cultural backdoor.[28] The growing technological abilities to control human genetic makeup could foster the emergence of the image of the "perfect child," and the impact of the social value of perfection will begin to stigmatize and oppress all those who fall short. Knowledge of the past is an indispensable guide to the future. It is not difficult to understand the fear that a benign policy of forestalling disease may become a program for enforcing social prejudice and a new eugenics. Even taking care to remember the past, some question whether society is well enough aware of the problem to avoid it.

GENETIC REDUCTIONISM/DETERMINISM

We cannot allow any barrier to stand in the path of our complete control and thereby understanding of the life phenomena. I believe that anyone will reach the same view who considers the control of natural phenomena is the essential problem of scientific research.

JACQUES LOEB[29]

This sentiment, noted among scientists to some degree since Descartes,[30] has grown into what some refer to as a

Reductionist Revolution in biology, genetics, and the life sciences. As the HGP moves forward toward its goal of identifying each base pair among the 3 billion that comprise the human genome, there is concern that scientists will become more persuaded that genes alone are the control centers, not only of whether we are tall or short, have green eyes or brown, or have a predisposition to develop heart disease, but also whether we behave in certain ways or entertain certain thoughts.[31] Critics argue that humans will be reduced to the sum of their genes—at the formation of the zygote, the future potential of the person it will become will be known or knowable—genes will be equated with destiny, and all will be consigned to the "Trap of Determinism"—condemned to a fate written in their genes before they were born.[32]

Reductionism hearkens back to the Hobbesian notion that human beings are "merely complex machines."[33] It presupposes that all of the phenomena of biology, even that of human nature, obey the laws of chemistry and physics. The previously unimaginable successes of molecular biology realized in the HGP and in our understanding of the machinery of the cell have given the impression that no problem is beyond the analytical power of science—that even the genome is concrete and manageable so that complete knowledge of the entire organism is just around the corner.[34]

Another criticism of the growing trend toward reductionism is the concern that a focus on the "power" of the genes will lead to a lessening of efforts to improve public health by correcting environmental contributors to disease.[35] "The most serious objection to predisposition studies . . . is that they can detract attention from the epidemiological fact that cancer is a disease whose incidence varies according to occupation, diet, socioeconomic status, and personal habits such as smoking." Ignoring such epidemiological relationships would be dangerous in terms of setting public policy. Antipollution laws or laws governing workplace safety might become low priority if it is individuals' genetic composition that really provides the risk.

GENETIC ENHANCEMENT

Health is a state of complete physical, mental and social well-being and not merely the absence of disease or infirmity.[36]

As knowledge and capabilities in genomics mature, there is little controversy that efforts, for the most part, should be directed toward interventions to prevent or cure disease.[37] If health is more than the absence of disease, however, genomics could offer a future that redefines physical, mental, and social well-being. Those new definitions may "ratchet up" the standard for "normal" human functioning, and disability and insurability may likewise be redefined. A difficult question that society will have to consider is whether "genetic enhancement"—that is, use of genomic technology to select height, eye color, temperament, or intelligence of future

offspring—is morally permissible.[38] Genetic enhancement involves no abnormal gene; its goal is to amplify "normal" genes to make them "better." Genetic science has a long way to go before enhancements are developed, are proven safe and effective, and become widely available commercially. Notwithstanding, as the technology required for such genetic enhancements move closer to being realized, should we celebrate the fruits of biotechnology's labors that make it all possible, or should there be limits and controls on their activities and society's choices? The profit motive and the inexorable law of supply and demand are among the strong social forces that will make it extremely unlikely that genetic technology will be limited to preventing and curing disease.[39]

When considering the possibility of making genetic enhancements available, a critical first step will be to ascertain *which* enhancements are best for future children and *who* will decide what kinds of children would be best.[40] The history of the eugenics movement and the frequency of racist attitudes about what characteristics would be desirable should provide reasons for pause.[41] In answering the "who" question, the right to privacy would necessarily extend to enhancement decisions—recognizing the importance, for parents and children, of parents having substantial discretion and freedom to decide how to raise their children.[42] Parents may be just as susceptible as the early proponents of eugenics to such stereotypes and prejudices.[43] At the time when an enhancement decision is being made, it may be difficult to separate out individual "parental" choice from the larger societal influences at play. What may be wrong with eugenics is that the social currents coerce in ways that we scarcely notice—our individual "choices" becoming mere instantiations of prevailing cultural imperatives about what bodies, gender, and capacities of intellect are desirable.[44] Although history provides strong grounds for caution about attempts to perfect our children, if genetic interventions that assure future generations will be beneficiaries of genes that will enable their lives to be better can be pursued justly, they should not be abandoned.[45] Moreover, new molecular knowledge must be evaluated by considering the social surround at the time an enhancement is considered, not with the level of knowledge and understanding we have today. In spite of the past, or perhaps because of it, the moral permissibility of eugenic goals must be addressed on its own terms.

ACCESS TO GENETIC SERVICES

. . . We hold these truths to be self-evident: that all men are *created* equal; that they are endowed by their *creator* with certain inalienable rights; that among these rights are life, liberty and the pursuit of happiness.

Declaration of Independence

Our domestic political history has been dominated by the demand for equality and the resistance to that demand.[46] In a world that tolerates so much inequity in the circumstances into which its children come into being, it is hard to make the argument that there lies a moral distinction between their rights to biological advantages as opposed to social and economic advantages.[47] Because of the urgent social problems present long before the HGP was proposed, the beautiful world that its enthusiasts envisage, of a kind of "genetic utopia," may be a long way from reality.[48] Already we struggle with the fair allocation of vital health care resources in a society marked by great discrepancies in wealth and social status.[49] The likelihood that genetic technologies will be available to some people but not to others, and that a major determinant of access will be wealth, raises profound social issues.[50] Lack of insurance coverage combines with other factors of the delivery system to have a systematic effect on the utilization of health care services.[51]

Wealth-based access to health care has always been a distinct feature of our health care system. Those patients able to afford the service can simply "buy" it, even if it is not covered by a private or public insurance plan. The failure of most insurers to pay for in vitro fertilization will narrow the pool of patients able to access some genetic services to the most wealthy.[52] Likewise, if insurers define genetic enhancements as "not medically necessary," as they do cosmetic surgery, then only those able to purchase them with personal funds will be able to access them; the more expensive the enhancement, the more limited this group may be.[53]

Aside from economic barriers, the benefits of genetic information are likely to be available only to some people: those who know about genetic testing, who know how and where to get it, and who can assimilate the results.[54] Those who are able to access the new technologies will do so as a definitive preventive measure, as a therapy for many disorders, or they will embrace genetic enhancements as a means of gaining socioeconomic advantages. In the worse case scenario, this unequal access could conceivably lead to a "genetic aristocracy" or "genobility"—those with genetically engineered advantages that enable them to monopolize the most lucrative jobs and investment opportunities, thus widening the gulf between them and the "genetic underclass."[55] If, as some argue, the HGP has been oversold, it may be because things have been made to appear simpler than they are.

Norman Daniels, a noted American philosopher, posits that there is something special about health care—something distinguishing it from other social goods such as food or clothing. He suggests that if there is a right to health care, it is because of the kinds of needs it meets.[56] A right then presupposes an obligation on the part of the state to make health care services available on the basis of medical need, without regard to ability to pay or other nonmedical factors.[57] The "specialness" of health care requires that it be treated differently from other social goods, even in a society that tolerates (even glorifies) significant and pervasive inequalities in the distribution of most social goods.[58]

Many agree that it is a requirement of justice for health care to be distributed more equally.[59]

If there is indeed a "right" to health care, is it identical to a right to receive genetic therapy? Assuming some scarcity of resources and the requirement that health needs be met under reasonable resource constraints, would genetic "disease" be a social need that the state would be obliged to insure against, or would it be responsible to provide access only to a basic minimum? Is some level of health care and "genetic care" rationing inevitable? Daniel's theory of *Just Health Care* puts forth a hierarchy of *needs*, suggesting that there may not be an obligation, even in a theoretical world, on the part of the state to provide access to all available services.[60] He maintains that individuals must have a fairly equal opportunity to obtain those health care services that will provide them a "normal range of opportunity." That range of "normality" may change at the same pace as new developments in genetics.[61]

GENETICS AND PRIVACY: INSURANCE AND EMPLOYMENT

Given the rapid progress of biotechnology and bioinformatics in recent years, coupled with the successes of the HGP, the volume of available genetic information is on the verge of an explosion.[62] Because proliferation of such information could result in social stigma and the loss of educational and social opportunities and highly valued freedoms, societies with strong commitments to autonomy and individual rights will be challenged to develop the best strategies for protecting privacy.[63] Scientific, technological, and cultural developments alter the context in which the need for privacy exists. These advances push societies onto uncharted ethical and legal terrains. There is no property so private, no information more confidential, than a person's genetic profile. Therefore, the premium to be placed on an individual's rights is greater when the issue is something as personal and as intimate as their genetic constitution. In the ever-changing, ever-advancing milieu of genetic science, society must adapt and extend privacy protection to conform to the environment.

Inherent features of genetic information make it qualitatively different from other forms of health data. It relates to a range of people, not just one individual. Information revealed about the individual who consented (the proband) to the genetic testing may also reveal personal information about the proband's parents, siblings, and children, and may have implications for the spouses or potential spouses (and future offspring). This gives rise to special concerns for how the information is gathered, stored, accessed, and used. Another feature that distinguishes genetic data from other forms of health information is that it is not merely about one's medical past, but can also furnish information about one's medical future (and that of blood relatives). Because of these unique characteristics of genetic information, many believe that the concern for privacy should be enhanced. Others believe, however, that there should not be a strong unflinching commitment to privacy protection at the expense of other social goods and that individual liberty must yield to the greater needs of the community.[64]

What kinds of harms are threatened by the loss of genetic privacy? At worst, there is a risk that knowledge generated by the HGP, if freely disseminated, could lead to the creation of a subcaste of "genetic lepers" who are refused jobs, insurance coverage, and even possibly the right to marry and have children.[65] Today, a primary concern is that insurers will use information regarding an individual's propensity to develop an illness as a preexisting illness to justify denying, limiting, or canceling insurance policies, or, alternatively, to charge prohibitively high premiums. Another concern is that employers will use genetic information against current workers or to screen potential employees and then use that information to refuse to hire (or as a reason to fire) individuals with genetic predisposition to disease to avoid having to pay for or to supplement the costs of future care.

An individual's autonomy and privacy rights as concerns genetic information mean the right to control what they or others may know about them. The highest level of control may be exerted through controlling the initial production of information. Although the HGP has inspired enthusiastic and hyperbolic descriptions from supporters, when risks of social stigma and loss of insurability are high, and when no medical intervention exists for positive results, one may reasonably decide that the risk/benefit ratio is too high and refuse testing.[66] Protective measures may need to be implemented, however, to assure that those who refuse testing do not suffer repercussions that reverse that risk/benefit ratio. For example, if an employer can refuse to hire based on a prospective employee's refusal to submit to genetic tests, any right to privacy would protect only if being unemployed is a tenable option.

Control of disclosure of genetic information by determining the identity of recipient(s), the purposes for which the information is used, and the period of time within which future disclosures may be made, is often lost after the initial consent to disclose is given. For example, stored Newborn Screening Guthrie cards could become the basis for establishing DNA databases for new and previously unimagined purposes if their use is not regulated.[67] Protections will have to be tailored to account for the unusual predictive power of genetic tests that makes their results useful to third parties whose interests may not always be innocuous.

To date, there has been no federal legislation directed to the novel challenges to privacy that the HGP and associated new technologies will present. However, on February 8, 2000, President Clinton signed an executive order that prevents every federal department and agency from considering genetic information in any hiring or promotion actions, thereby providing some protections for federal employees.

Nearly every state has enacted some form of genetic nondiscrimination laws, none of which is comprehensive.[68] The most likely source of protection against genetic discrimination in the workplace is Title I of the Americans with Disabilities Act of 1990 (ADA), enforced by the Equal Employment Opportunity Commission (EEOC).[69]

The Health Insurance Portability and Accountability Act (HIPAA) provides some protections against genetic discrimination in the realm of insurance, but it applies only to employer-based and commercially issued group health insurance. There is no similar law that protects private individuals seeking health insurance. HIPAA does, however, provide protection for information in a patient's medical record, regardless of their insurance status. The new federal standards limit the nonconsensual use and release of private health information (not specific to genetics) and generally restrict any release to the minimum needed for the intended purpose.

Existing legislation is a move in the right direction, but comprehensive privacy protections will become more urgent as the economic incentive to discriminate based on genetic information increases and the costs associated with genetic testing decrease. Insurance companies are always seeking ways of identifying high risk groups. The insurance industry could rightly claim that stringent privacy legislation would place them at an unfair disadvantage. Those less than optimistic about the efficacy of privacy laws to prevent unauthorized dissemination of genetic information believe that the focus should be on implementing antidiscrimination laws that would proscribe the *use* of genetic information should privacy safeguards fail.

CONCLUSION

Now is not the end. It is not even the beginning of the end. But it is, perhaps, the end of the beginning.

WINSTON CHURCHILL, 1942, after 3 years of war

As the Human Genome Project (HGP) continues toward its goal to identify each of the 3 billion base pairs that make up the human genome, some believe the solution to the mysteries of humanity, the most magnificent and complex biological Rosetta Stone, may be near. The seemingly disparate paths of the sciences of molecular biology, chemistry, and physics have converged to this end. The work of the HGP and the knowledge it spawns will someday reveal a new human anatomy. As James Watson has recognized, "[i]f society is to cope with the consequences of this knowledge, people must learn and become better informed about genetics."

Proponents of the HGP view it as a trustworthy and badly needed step toward improving the health of mankind, but ethical debates must acknowledge the horrors perpetrated in the name of eugenics in the past century. The important dialogue already begun, must continue with a focus on forestalling the threat of creating new forms of discrimination and methods of oppression. Much of the suspicion of the HGP is a presumed hidden agenda to control the future of humanity through manipulating human genes and the reductionist philosophy that humans are "determined" by their genes.

Almost everyone would agree that, for the foreseeable future, new genetic knowledge should be directed toward its use to prevent or cure disease. On the other hand, is there anything wrong with pursuing perfection as a goal of reproduction? Will it be part of medicine's professional responsibility to allow parents to select among traits for their future offspring? Will such choices only be available to those who are able to pay? Without serious considerations of these difficult questions today, society of the future risks being divided into those who are genetically sound and those who are genetically afflicted. There are serious inequalities in the United States in access to medical services which are correlated to both class and race. A world in which genetic testing is widely available might be incompatible with a system of private health insurance. Societies committed to equality and fairness will have to consider measures to ensure that the means to implementing eugenic choices are available to *all* who desire them. Envisaging the future world of genomics reinforces arguments for ensuring all members of society will have access to affordable medical care, so that the new technologies do not compromise the rights and aspirations of vulnerable people.

ENDNOTES

1. R. Lipkin, *The Quest to Break the Human Genetic Code*, Insight 46-48 (Dec./Jan. 1991).
2. Ewan Birney, A. Bateman, M. Clam, & T. Hubbard, *Mining the Draft Human Genome*, 409 Nature 827-28 (2001).
3. National Human Genome Research Institute, NIH News Advisory, *The Mouse Genome and the Measure of Man*, December 4, 2002, available at http://genome.gov/pagecfm?pageID =10005831.
4. William Shakespeare, *Hamlet*, Act II, Scene ii.
5. Jon Turney, *Frankenstein's Footsteps: Science, Genetics and Popular Culture* (New Haven: Yale University Press, 1998).
6. *See* Martin Brookes, *Get a Grip on Genetics*, 36 (1998).
7. *Id.*
8. Daniel Hartl & Elizabeth Jones, *Genetics, Principles and Analysis*, 4th ed. (1998).
9. Tom Wilkie, *Perilous Knowledge: The Human Genome Project and Its Implications*, 198 (1993).
10. Lori Andrews et al., *Genetics: Ethics, Law and Policy*, 6 (2002).
11. A joint Japanese-American investigation of the long-term radiation-bombing effects that was established at the direction of President Truman in 1947 to proceed with a long-term investigation of the effects of atomic radiation. *See* John Beatty, *Genetics in the Atomic Age: The Atomic Bomb Casualty Commission, 1947-1956*, in: K.R. Benson, J. Maienschein & R. Rainger (eds.), *The Expansion of American Biology*, 284-324 (1991).
12. *See* Robert Cook-Deegan, *The Gene Wars: Science, Politics, and the Human Genome*, 92 (1994).
13. ELSI's research areas are: (1) Privacy and fairness in the use and interpretation of genetic information, including prevention of misinterpretation or misuse. (2) Clinical integration of new genetic technologies, including advising on clinical policies related to genetic testing and counseling. (3) Informed consent and other research-ethics review issues related to the design, conduct, participation in, and reporting of genetics research. (4) Education on genetics and related ELSI issues for health professionals, policy-makers, and the general public. More information on ELSI is available at www.nhgri.nih.gov/ELSI.
14. DOE representatives stressed two main reasons why the agency should play a pivotal role in the project: (1) continuity with previous large-scale and largely successful efforts in human genetics funded by the agency and its predecessors, and (2) the agency's success in developing novel technologies, together with its commitment to facilitating commercialization of new technologies through closer relations between its labs and U.S. firms. *See* David Galas, Testimony to Hearing Before Subcommittee on Energy Research and Development (1990), U.S. Senate, 11 July 1990, 18-19, 28-29.
15. The Genetic Privacy Act and Commentary are available at http://www.ornl.gov/hgmis/resource/privacy/privacy1.html.
16. Office of the Press Secretary, The White House, *Remarks by the President et al. on the Completion of the First Survey of the Entire Human Genome Project*, June 26, 2000, available at http://clinton3.nara.gov/WH/EOP/OSTP/html/00626_2.html.
17. The International Human Genome Mapping Consortium, *A Physical Map of the Human Genome*, 409 Nature 934-41 (February 15, 2001); The Celera Genomics Sequencing Team, *The Sequence of the Human Genome*, Science, 1304-51 (February 16, 2001).
18. Francis Galton coined the term "eugenics" in 1885, defining it as the "science of improving stock—not only by judicious mating, but whatever tends to give the more suitable race or strains of blood a better chance of prevailing over the less suitable than they otherwise would have had." *See* Allen Buchanan et al., *From Chance to Choice: Genetics and Justice*, 152 (2000). Galton founded the Laboratory for National Eugenics (now the Galton Laboratory) at University College, London, the first human genetics department in the world. His career also included the scientific study of fingerprints, statistical tests on the efficacy of prayer, and publication of a human-beauty map of the British Isles. Brookes, *supra* note 5, at 59.
19. Phillip Sloan, *Controlling Our Destinies: Historical, Philosophical, Ethical, and Theological Perspectives on the Human Genome Project*, 185 (2000).
20. Daniel Kelves, *Out of Eugenics: The Historical Politics of the Human Genome*, in: Daniel Kelves and Leroy Hood, *Code of Codes*, 3-36 (1992). The National Socialist Program in Nazi Germany, called *Lebensborn*, gave money, medals, housing, and other rewards to persuade "ideal" mothers and fathers to have large numbers of children in order to create a super-race of Aryan children and thus increase the representation of certain genes in the gene pool of future generations (i.e., positive population genetics). *See also* Daniel Kelves, *In the Name of Eugenics* (1995), first published 1985.
21. Buchanan, *supra* note 18, at 32.
22. Barbara Rothman, *The Book of Life: A Personal and Ethical Guide to Race, Normality, and the Implications of the Human Genome Project*, 58 (2001).
23. Concerned that uncontrolled immigration of "racially inferior types" would threaten the genetic health of America, many states imposed quotas on immigrants, favoring those of "better stock," Northern and Western Europeans, while restricting "inferior" people, including Eastern Europeans, many of whom were trying to escape the more extreme racist programs of the Nazis.
24. 274 U.S. 200 (1927); *see also* Paul Lombardo, *Three Generations, No Imbeciles: New Light on Buck v. Bell*, 60 N.Y.U.L. Rev. 30, 50-62 (1985).
25. In May 2002, Virginia Governor Mark Warner apologized to the victims of sterilization for Virginia's role in the eugenics movement.
26. Matt Ridley, *Genome: The Autobiography of a Species in 23 Chapters*, 290 (1999).
27. Sloan, *supra* note 19, at 1.

28. T. Duster, *Backdoor to Eugenics* (New York and London: Routledge, 1990).

29. Jacques Loeb, *Die Umschau* 7 (1903), pp. 21, 25, quoted by Pauly.

30. According to Descartes, the goal of human knowledge and technology is that humans might become the "masters and possessors of nature."

31. Behavior is nearly always influenced by complex sets of genes and the environment, so that the link between the immediate output of these genes and human behavior is extremely tenuous. Similarly, genetic heritage itself cannot determine in advance the content of thinking and reasoning—even if it is the prerequisite of developing these capacities. None of the large and well-funded linkage studies to date have conclusively identified a single specific gene that contributes to individual differences in behavior and what it does in the brain. *See* Dean Hamer, *Rethinking Behavior Genetics*, 298 Science 71-72 (October 4, 2002).

32. Sloan, *supra* note 19, at 92.

33. Thomas Hobbes, *Leviathan* (1651), introduction, ed. E. Curley.

34. Richard Lewontin, *It Ain't Necessarily So: The Dream of the Human Genome and Other Illusions*, 104 (2000).

35. John Harris, *Wonderwoman and Superman*, 188 (1992). "Inevitably as individuals [genetically] protected against environmental pollutants multiply, the perception of the urgency of need to eradicate such pollutants might well recede. The existence of the new breed might thus carry dangers to the environment as a whole as well as to the rest of mankind."

36. Preamble to the Constitution of the World Health Organization as adopted by the International Health Conference, New York, June 19-22, 1946; signed on July 22, 1946, by the representatives of 61 states (*Official Records of the World Health Organization*, no. 2, p. 100) and entered into force on April 7, 1948.

37. Stephanie Anderson, *From Chance to Choice: Genetics and Justice*, 22 J.L.M. 151 (2000) (book review).

38. *Id.*

39. *Id.*

40. Buchanan, *supra* note 18, at 161.

41. Anderson, *supra* note 37.

42. Buchanan, *supra* note 18, at 164.

43. *Id.*

44. Sloan, *supra* note 19, at 224.

45. Buchanan, *supra* note 18, at 60, 163.

46. Lewontin, *supra* note 34, at 189.

47. Sloan, *supra* note 19, at 221.

48. *Id.*

49. The Institute of Medicine, *Unequal Treatment: Confronting Racial and Ethnic Disparities in Healthcare* (2002). Racial and ethnic disparities in health care exist even when insurance status, income, age, and severity of conditions are comparable. These differences in health care occur in the context of broader historic and contemporary social and economic inequality, and persistent racial and ethnic discrimination in many sectors of American life.

50. Maxwell Mehlman et al., *Access to the Genome: The Challenge to Equality*, 87 (1998).

51. Norman Daniels, *Just Health Care*, 3 (1985).

52. Abortion is one method for preventing the birth of a child with a genetic illness or defect. Anticipating the expense of what might come to be known as more conventional gene therapies, abortion is likely to be the "primary preventive" measure that will be available to the poor and uninsured. *See* Mehlman, *supra* note 50.

53. *Id.* at 85.

54. *Id.* at 48.

55. *Id.* at 98.

56. Daniels, *supra* note 51.

57. *Id.* at 12.

58. *Id.* at 11.

59. *See, e.g.*, John Rawls, *A Theory of Justice* (1982), a theory of "justice as fairness" on which Norman Daniel's *Just Health Care* is based. *See also* Robert Nozick, *Anarchy, State and Utopia*, 233-35 (1974), a libertarian view of entitlement to social goods.

60. During his administration, President Clinton proposed the Health Security Act legislation that would have guaranteed health insurance for virtually every American. Under pressure from health insurers and others, his effort failed and there are no plans to revive it. Clinton's plan would not have provided blanket coverage for all health services—insureds would have been guaranteed only a package of basic health benefits.

61. *See generally* Daniels, *supra* note 51. If physical health conditions and mental abilities achievable with genetic technologies come to be regarded as necessary to enable individuals to carry out a life plan with a normal range of opportunity, then it would be unjust to deny individuals that chance.

62. Anderson, *supra* note 37, at 151.

63. Madison Powers, *Privacy and the Control of Genetic Information*, in: Mark S. Frankel & Albert Teich (eds.), *The Genetic Frontier: Ethics, Law and Policy*, 77 (1994).

64. *See generally* Daniel Callahan, *Setting Limits: Medical Goals in an Aging Society* (1995); Willard Gaylin et al., *The Perversion of Autonomy: The Proper Uses of Coercion and Constraint in a Liberal Society* (1996).

65. Wilkie, *supra* note 9, at 11.

66. *See* Graeme Laurie, *Challenging Medical-Legal Norms: The Role of Autonomy, Confidentiality, and Privacy in Protecting Individual and Familial Group Rights in Genetic Information*, 22 J. L. Med. 1-54 (2000).

67. *Id.*

68. *Supra* note 15. The Genetic Privacy Act is a draft bill written in 1995 by George Annas of Boston University School of Public Health, to assist legislators in proposing new legislation in their states.

69. In March 1995 the EEOC provided some guidance by interpreting the ADA as it may relate to genetic information: "Entities that discriminate on the basis of genetic predisposition are regarding the individuals as having impairment, and such individuals are covered by the ADA."

Fetal Interests

JEFFREY L. LENOW, M.D., J.D., F.C.L.M., F.A.A.F.P.

A noted pediatric surgeon, Karlis Adamsons, M.D., proclaimed in a *New England Journal of Medicine* article in 1966, "It appears unlikely that even in the distant future, fetal surgery will become a field of major concern to the clinician. . . ."[1] However, it would only be 14 years before *Williams Obstetrics*, the leading textbook in the discipline, would state in the preface: "Happily, we have entered an era in which the fetus can be rightfully considered and treated as our second patient . . . we are of a view that it is the most exciting of times to be an obstetrician. Who would have dreamed—even a few years ago—that we could serve the fetus as physician?"[2] The era of fetal treatment had arrived.

Bolognese notes, "Perinatologists are the advocates of the fetus. . . ."[3] The notion of the maternal-fetal unit as a single treatment focus would come into question as the developing subspecialty disciplines of maternal/fetal medicine (high risk obstetrics) and neonatology (high risk pediatrics in the newborn period) began to flourish in the early 1980s. In fact the field of fetal therapy and treatment has grown dramatically since Clewell's first report of proposed fetal surgery on a hydrocephalic fetus in the Denver Fetal Treatment program, and Harrison and his team's landmark ex utero surgical approach to a fetus with a posterior urethral valve obstruction, both in 1982.[4] The current ruling principles regarding fetal rights, "personhood," and proper recommendations in the face of very real "maternal-fetal" and "fetal-fetal" conflicts (in multiple gestations) have not changed significantly since the subject had been initially formally reviewed in the literature.[5] There have been nonetheless interesting legal "twists" along the way that warrant review in this chapter. Whether it presages an upheaval in the maternal-fetal rights "balance" is difficult to predict.

The maturation of the field of fetal therapy has been truly remarkable.[6] While it is beyond the scope of this chapter to review with explicit clinical detail the remarkable scientific accomplishments of the fetal treatment teams worldwide,[7] the fact that many such procedures may pass from "experimental/investigational" to accepted standards of reimbursable care suggests that ongoing dialogue about the challenging ethical and legal challenges presented by this discipline is even more critical than ever.[8]

In the following, we explore some key questions/issues arising from the legal review of the fetal patient. This overview first looks at the historical development of the fetus in the eyes of the law historically, with a critical focus on the unavoidably controlling doctrine as defined in the landmark and highly controversial U.S. Supreme Court ruling in *Roe v. Wade*.[9] The chapter then surveys recent trends in the last decade that have offered interesting new perspectives on the issue of fetal personhood and may be predictive of the directions in which the legislatures at the state and federal levels may be moving in attempts to redefine the status of the fetus and, derivatively, the fetal patient.

KEY QUESTIONS/ISSUES

While we can marvel at the truly remarkable progress in the science of fetal treatment, it heightens both critical[10] ethical and legal issues raised by the evolution of this discipline:[11]

- Are the maternal patient and fetal patient separable entities, medically and legally?
- Are the rights of the maternal patient the same as or superseding those of the fetal patient?
- Does the prebirth fetal patient enjoy the same legal protection as the postbirth?
- How to resolve potential of maternal-fetal conflicts (i.e., if the maternal patient should refuse a recommended therapy for the fetus).
- How to resolve fetus-fetus conflict (i.e., can a procedure for a compromised fetus in a multiple gestation scenario be a risk for an unaffected fetus?).

The history of the fetal person in the law

In the context of tort law, a number of states would seem to have recognized fetal rights through their wrongful death determinations.[12] Although most states have come to recognize the concept of wrongful death on behalf of an unborn fetus, the circumstances vary from state to state, and generally recognize such "rights" only after the fetus has been born alive.[13] The seeming contradiction between the right of wrongful death of a fetus as contrasted to the Supreme Court's clearly stated position that the unborn fetus has no constitutional rights is resolved by a clear understanding of Justice Blackmun's explanation. The *Roe* court noted that its decision was not inconsistent with the policy of some states to allow the parents of a stillborn child to file an action for wrongful death as a result of prenatal injuries.[14] Justice Blackmun noted that wrongful death suits were brought to vindicate the parent's right to recover for the loss of "potentiality of life," not of a person "in the whole sense." Since parents bring prenatal wrongful death actions on their own behalf, parental consent to an abortion constitutes a waiver of any parental wrongful death action.[15] It is probably therefore not very useful in a discussion of the recognition of fetal rights to utilize wrongful death cases as an appropriate resource.[16] An interesting event occurred in June 2001, however, when the Arkansas Supreme Court, in allowing a wrongful death claim for an unborn fetus which died during a labor induction, overturned a lower court ruling and did agree that an unborn child meets the legal definition of "a person."[17]

In criminal law some states have begun to recognize feticide statutes in order to prevent abuses such as was evidenced in *Keeler v. Superior Court*,[18] where an individual was not convicted for the death of a viable stillborn fetus as a result of an assault. The *Keeler* dissent noted that the violent act of "stomping the child to death" was no different from killing a newborn because the fetus with its "unbounded potential for life" was entitled to protection.[19] Following this dramatic outcome, the California legislature amended its homicide statute making it unlawful to kill a human being or a fetus regardless of age.[20]

ROE v. WADE: BENCHMARK FOR ANALYSIS OF FETAL RIGHTS

The unique concept of separability of fetus and mother in a legal context is best viewed with an appropriate understanding of the dicta in *Roe v. Wade*.[21] With all that has been written, analyzed, and debated since the ruling in 1973 (including first commentaries on the fetal patient perspective 20 years ago[22]), the primary determinant for any legal discussion on the rights of the fetus and derivatively the fetal patient revolve around the still intact *Roe* case. In determining whether a Texas statute properly applied the word "person" to an unborn fetus, the *Roe* court suggested that the use of the Fourteenth Amendment or any other part of the U.S. Constitution and its amendments was not applicable in the *prebirth* state and for that reason did not confer any constitutional recognition to the unborn fetus. The court, however, recognized

a portion of pregnancy beyond the point of "viability," adopting essentially a medical definition of this term where the state could recognize a "compelling interest" in the well-being of the fetus.[23] Thus the court set the stage for a still hotly debated subject—what did they mean by the use of the clinical term "viability" and could the justices have ever imagined the technological advances soon to arrive that would pit the dicta of the 1970s against the reproductive advances that would soon follow and would challenge the application of fetal rights interpretation in a new scenario.[24]

Viability: why it is a key concept

Viability is a concept "widely used to identify a reasonable potential for subsequent survival if the fetus were to be removed from the uterus."[25] In essence, then, it is a nonlegal definition that is defined in terms of practicality (i.e., how early a fetus can be delivered with hopes of reasonable survival), and since no single factor determines fetal survival, the prediction of viability is at best a moving target and imprecise.[26] The progeny of abortion cases to follow *Roe* would manifest consistency in the court's subsequent avoidance of the viability issues despite the fact that viability would be a major future determinant in any discussion of the fetal patient. In *Planned Parenthood of Central Missouri v. Danforth*, the Supreme Court said, "It is not the proper function of the legislature or the courts to place viability, which essentially is a medical concept, at a specific point in the gestation period . . . and the determination of whether a particular fetus is viable is, and must be, a matter for the judgment of the responsible attending physician."[27] In *Colautti v. Franklin* the court ruled that the attending physician would make a viability assessment on the particular facts of the case before him, "based in part on whether there was a reasonable likelihood of the fetus' sustained survival outside the womb, with or without artificial support."[28] According to a brief filed with the Supreme Court in *Webster v. Reproductive Health Services* by the American Medical Association, the American Academy of Pediatrics, and the American College of Obstetricians and Gynecologists, viability "is dependent upon a large number of factors. . . . The importance of each of these factors and the medically appropriate method of measuring them will vary with the circumstances of the individual pregnancy."[29] In *Planned Parenthood of Southeastern Pennsylvania v. Casey*, the court focused on the precise point of viability as "an imprecision within tolerable limits given that the medical community and all those who must apply its discoveries will continue to explore the matter."[30]

Ultimately the question arises as to the real impact of the viability standard. Does a group of patients exist for whom the "compelling state interest in a viable fetus" clause applies? Data would demonstrate that the number of fetuses aborted beyond the viable state is extremely limited.[31] Clearly the import of the quasi-Constitutional rights conferred by this clause has had little practical import from the perspective of the *Roe* court protecting interests of viable fetuses as a class in the abortion context.[32] However, the justices could never have imagined the "double-edged" impact this clause might have in the near future, with the advent of new fetal treatment modalities and the potential for viable fetal patients to come into conflict with both the maternal patient and also with other fetuses in a multiple gestation setting.[33]

Conflict scenarios (maternal vs. fetal and fetal vs. fetal)

As noted earlier, the advances in fetal therapy, both medical and surgical, are dynamic. Since most of these fetal patients with potentially "correctable" defects manifest well beyond the viable state, issues of conflict when treatment determinations are offered begin to surface. So concerned were the early pioneers in the field of fetal therapy with such conflict potential and the unclear legal issues surrounding them, they convened the first conference to define ethical guidelines and standards for the future.[34] The predictable scenario of pitting the rights and interests of the maternal patient with those of the unborn fetus beyond the point of "viability" when the state might exercise its "compelling state interest" formally manifested itself dramatically in *Jessie Mae Jefferson v. Griffin Spaulding County Hospital*.[35] In *Jefferson* the mother of a 39-week-old fetus suffered from a complete placenta previa,[36] a condition in which the placenta blocks the birth canal. There was a 99% chance that the fetus would die if natural delivery were attempted and a 50% chance that the mother would also not survive. The physicians predicted that both the mother and the child had excellent chances of surviving delivery by cesarean section. The maternal patient objected to surgery on religious grounds. The attending physicians petitioned the court for authorization to perform a cesarean section, sonogram, and blood transfusions on Mrs. Jefferson. In affirming the order of the lower court granting the physician's petition, the Georgia Supreme Court stated that, according to *Roe v. Wade*,[37] the state had a compelling interest in the life of a fetus after the point of viability. It was this interest, the court reasoned, which permitted intrusion on the mother's rights in order to protect the fetus. Justice Hill, in a concurrence to the court's per curiam opinion, noted: "We weighted the right of the mother to practice her religion and to refuse surgery on herself, against her unborn child's right to live. We found in favor of her child's right to live."[38]

Chervenak argues for exceptional situations where forced fetal treatment near term is allowable.[39] The American College of Obstetricians and Gynecologists takes a balanced perspective in this regard.[40] The ACOG Committee on Ethics has come to the following conclusions:

- The role of the obstetrician is that of educator and counselor, who must weigh the risks and benefits to both patients, while realizing that tests, judgments, and decisions are fallible.
- Consultation with others, including an institutional ethics committee, ought to be sought when appropriate.
- Obstetricians should refrain from performing procedures that are unwanted by a pregnant woman.
- The use of the courts to resolve conflicts violates the pregnant woman's autonomy, and is almost never warranted.

This recommendation would become a critical feature in the leading case to date regarding forced fetal therapy, the matter of Angela Carder, or "*In re AC*."[41] In June 1987, a judge in Washington, D.C., ordered a cesarean section to be performed on Angela Carder, who was 26 weeks pregnant and near death from cancer. She had discussed with her physicians the hope that her life could be prolonged to the 28th week of pregnancy, when the potential outcome for the fetus would be much better. When it appeared her death was imminent, however, the hospital, unable to get consent for a cesarean section from the patient or her family, obtained a court order for immediate delivery of the fetus. The cesarean surgery was performed; the infant died within a few hours; Carder died two days later. Three years later, the District of Columbia Court of Appeals noted that it would have deferred to the patient's level of competency to make her own choice. If she had not been competent, the court should have used substituted judgment. The appeals court noted, "We hold that in virtually all cases the question of what is to be done is to be decided by the patient—the pregnant woman—on behalf of herself and the fetus."

The decision holds precedent only for its own jurisdiction, but there have been no higher level determinations of this specificity to date and other courts that may some day face this type of decision are prone to deferring to such judgments. It is a legal determination that aligns with policy statements of both the American College of Obstetricians and Gynecologists (ACOG), the American Academy of Pediatrics Committee on Bioethics,[42] and the American Medical Association (AMA).[43]

In an era of significant achievement in the area of assisted reproductive technologies, scenarios with multiple gestations are not unusual. Postulated is the potential fetus vs. fetus conflict when a procedure to aid a compromised fetus might be considered unnecessarily risky to the unaffected "fetal siblings." What rights in action would the unaffected fetus have in this case and who would represent these interests in a legal challenge? These are indeed rare scenarios, but conjure dilemmas in the analysis. There simply is no precedent in the law, no "on point" case law that answers these situations. If the viable compromised fetal patient has quasi-protected rights under the "compelling state interest" clause of *Roe*, are these "rights" no different for the unaffected sibling(s)? Several examples exist as well where selective fetal reduction via cardiac puncture under ultrasound guidance places two or more fetuses directly in this situation.[44] The closest analogous case law derives from cases of "substituted judgment" as demonstrated in the *Strunk v. Strunk* case, where the court had to determine if a surrogate can make a determination of care for an incompetent individual.[45] In *Strunk*, the Kentucky Court of Appeals, in permitting a kidney transplant from a mentally retarded person to his brother, was willing to imply the consent of an incompetent individual to an intrusive and burdensome procedure on the grounds that the resulting benefits were in the incompetent's best interests. Given that the transplant was necessary for the recipient brother's survival, the court utilized the substituted judgment doctrine and authorized the transplant on the grounds that the brother's death would have an "extremely traumatic effect upon [incompetent]."[46] In *Hart v. Brown*,[47] the Connecticut Supreme Court relied on the *Strunk* precedent and permitted a kidney transplant from one twin to another.[48] The difficulty in applying these cases to the fetus versus fetus conflict scenario is that there must be a demonstrated benefit to the unaffected fetus to "allow" the procedures to occur on the affected fetus. Such demonstration is implausible at best, unless there is evidence of the future benefits of sibling company, love, and attention, or simply evidence of improved existence generally.[49]

Consequences of forced fetal therapy

The specter of *Roe* becoming an unintended vehicle for forced fetal interventions (be they dramatic, such as forcing cesarean sections, or even seemingly limited to the taking of a digoxin pill by the maternal patient to limit the risk of fetal cardiac arrhythmias[50]) is offset by the sobering observation that there may indeed be common law consequences for unsuccessful outcomes ranging from the tort of battery to the damages that ensue from "creation of a peril" and a catastrophic outcome.[51] The suggestion here is that, while perhaps well intended, emotional moves to intervene, above and beyond the wishes of the maternal patient and her family, can result in secondary outcomes that were perhaps unforeseeable but for which reasonable arguments could be fashioned to hold the interveners liable.

NEW CHALLENGES AND THE FUTURE LEGAL STATUS OF THE FETAL PATIENT

There have been numerous attempts at both state and federal levels to institute fetal rights legislation. This is bothersome to abortion rights proponents as they argue that it constitutes what is essentially an "end run" to ultimately prohibit women access to abortion, thus effectively dismantling the current standing of *Roe v. Wade*.[52]

Attempts to limit types of abortion

There have been several rulings at the state court level dealing with the issue of late-term abortions. State Supreme Courts in these jurisdictions (New Jersey, Alaska,

Montana, Arizona, Illinois, Michigan, Arkansas, Nebraska, and Florida) have consistently overturned attempts by state legislatures to ban late-term abortions as unconstitutional and impairing the rights of bodily self-determination outlined in *Roe v. Wade*.[53] In the most recent Supreme Court determination on this subject,[54] the court ruled that this constituted a violation of a woman's right under *Roe* to make the free choice of bodily self-determination. Thus, all attempts to chisel away at the core premise of *Roe v. Wade* have been thus far ineffective.

New criminalization strategies in the prenatal state

There has been considerable attention paid to the issue of fetal rights in the context of crimes against pregnant women. Some 24 states have "unborn victim laws," with another 15 states looking at similar legislation.[55] In April 2001, Congress considered passage of H.R. 503/S. 480, the "Unborn Victims of Violence Act," which would amend the federal criminal code to create a separate offense if a defendant causes the death of, or bodily injury to, an "unborn child" during the commission of a federal crime.[56] The punishment for the separate offense would be the same as if the defendant had caused the death of, or injury to, the woman herself. Opponents of the law argue that such a law creating criminal protection for a pregnancy would establish new and bad precedent, encouraging the extension of "fetal rights" to other areas of the law.[57] There has been a strong editorial condemnation of this law and related state laws.[58]

Pursuit of fetal rights through the vehicle of child abuse, search and seizure issues

There have been several cases in the last few years where various jurisdictions have attempted to protect the unborn fetus from different types of prenatal abuse, such as a history of prior child abuse, drug abuse, and related issues. In *Ferguson v. City of Charleston*,[59] affirming the right to confidential medical care for all Americans, the U.S. Supreme Court struck down a drug-testing scheme targeting pregnant women developed by local police and prosecutors in collaboration with doctors in a South Carolina hospital. In its 6-3 decision in *Ferguson*, the court found that the Medical University of South Carolina drug-testing scheme was in direct violation of the Fourth Amendment, which provides all Americans with protection from unreasonable searches.

The case involved ten petitioners accused of cocaine abuse during pregnancy. One woman was arrested at the hospital shortly after giving birth and another, who had sought prenatal care, was arrested and jailed for 3 weeks until she delivered her child. In arguments before the court, Justice Steven G. Breyer strongly suggested that the hospital's policy would harm fetuses more than it would help by discouraging women from seeking prenatal care.[60]

In May 2001, Regina McKnight was convicted and sentenced to 12 years in prison for killing her unborn child by using crack cocaine during her pregnancy.[61] She was 8½ months pregnant when she delivered the stillborn baby in May 1999. Four doctors who testified at her trial gave differing opinions as to whether her addiction to crack caused the baby's death. In 1997, the South Carolina Supreme Court upheld the conviction of a woman who had been charged with child abuse for using cocaine during her pregnancy, ruling that a viable fetus was considered a person under the state's criminal code. The ruling was the only one of its kind in the country.

A few weeks after the McKnight conviction, in yet another South Carolina prosecution, Brenda Peppers was prosecuted for child abuse, having had a stillborn child after crack cocaine abuse. She challenged her own guilty plea and 2 years probation. She is one of 200 women in 30 states prosecuted for "fetal abuse."[62]

In another case Bristol County, Massachusetts, prosecutors held Rebecca Corneau in a prison hospital in order to protect her unborn fetus.[63] At 9 months gestation, this member of a fundamentalist Christian group that shuns modern medicine had refused to see a physician. Prosecutors were concerned that two other children from this cult, including one of Corneau's, had died from neglect and starvation. Fearing that the fetus she was carrying might meet the same fate as her other child, Attleboro Juvenile Court Judge Kenneth P. Nassif imprisoned Corneau to await the birth and to submit to prenatal medical examinations against the beliefs of what he called her "bizarre and dangerous cult." Her newborn daughter was placed in foster care with her three other children. Nassif's assertion of jurisdiction over the body of a pregnant woman never charged with a crime was never subject to appellate review because Corneau refused legal representation.[64] The Massachusetts Supreme Judicial Court dismissed a challenge to a court-ordered examination. Boston attorney Wendy Murphy, a teacher at the New England School of Law, had unsuccessfully appealed the state juvenile court's ruling. Supported by the National Organization for Women and the ACLU, she argued that jailing a pregnant woman because she has refused medical treatment violated her right to privacy guaranteed in *Roe v. Wade*.[65]

Bush administration's foray into fetal rights

On September 27, 2002, the Bush administration through the Department of Health and Human Services issued final rules for allowing states to define a fetus as a child eligible for government-subsidized health care under the State Children's Health Insurance Program (SCHIP).[66] The Bush administration said it saw no contradiction between the ruling in *Roe v. Wade* that did not recognize the fetus as a "person" under the Fourteenth Amendment of the Constitution and this new SCHIP interpretation.[67] It noted that the rule would not set up "an adversarial relationship between the mother and her unborn child." The DHHS press release promoted the importance of opening health care options to low income mothers regardless of immigration status.[68] The administration calculated the new rule would increase federal spending by $330 million over 5 years and that 13 states would choose to cover "unborn children," with 30,000 fetuses gaining coverage as a result.

CONCLUSION

It has been 20 years since the first reported fetal surgical interventions.[69] With this new class of "viable" fetal patient, the potential for conflicts between mother and fetus continues to manifest. The issue of what constitutes fetal rights is still unsettled despite recent Supreme Court determinations that continue to uphold the original *Roe* protection of a woman's right to bodily self-determination and free right to choose abortion (despite the cloudy meaning of "state compelling interest" in the viable fetus). But as more challenges present to the intent of *Roe*, the likelihood of the viability standard surviving is not great. The court's determination occurred in 1973, before today's technological miracles existed and well before any of the justices or their researchers could have comprehended this new class of patient, the "viable" fetus, let alone the potential for conflict that could manifest. One can only surmise the premise for Blackmun's interpretations, the use of the trimester analysis and the viability discussion. But rapid changes in health care technology are essentially rendering the value of this interpretation more and more ineffectual. Predictions are difficult. With the Bush administration in place, the opportunities to stack the court with conservative viewpoints relative to abortion rights is significant. Additionally, other Supreme Court rulings subsequently have shown language, specifically from Justice Sandra Day O'Connor, which points to the Roe determination's weakest link, the vagueness of the trimester approach.[70] Curiously, Laura Bush, the President's wife, was quoted in January 2001 as suggesting that she did not believe the *Roe* ruling should be undone, implying that the administration should look for other ways to limit the need for abortion.[71]

ENDNOTES

1. K. Adamsons, *Fetal Surgery*, 275 N. Engl. J. Med. 204, 205 (1966).
2. J. Pritchard & P. McDonald, *Williams Obstetrics*, 16th ed. (1980).
3. R. Bolognese, *Medico-Legal Aspects of a Human Life Amendment*, 5 Pa. Law Journal-Reporter 13 (1982) (commenting on attempts by several state legislatures to define life at the moment of conception).
4. W.H. Clewell, M.L. Johnson, P.R. Meier, et al., *Placement of Ventriculo-Amniotic Shunt for Hydrocephalus in a Fetus* [letter], 305 New Engl. J. Med 1955 (Oct. 15, 1981). *See also* Harrison, Golbus, Filly, et al., *Fetal Surgery for Congenital Hydronephrosis*, 306 N. Engl. J. Med. 591 (1982). Surgery was performed in April 1981 and was the first ex utero surgery performed on a fetus.
5. J.L. Lenow, *The Fetus as a Patient: Emerging Rights as a Person?*, 9 Am. J. Law Med. (1983).

6. H.L. Hedrick & T.M. Cromblehome, *Current Status of Fetal Surgery*, Contem. Obstet. Gynecol. (Dec. 2001). *See also* D.S. Walsh & N.S. Adzick, *Fetal Intervention: Where We're Going*, Contemp. Pediatr. (June 2000).

7. N.S. Adzick, M.I. Evans & W. Holzgreve (eds.), *The Unborn Patient: The Art and Science of Fetal Therapy*, 3d ed. (W.B. Saunders, Philadelphia, 2000). Additional information on two leading centers for fetal treatment includes the Fetal Treatment Center of the University of California, San Francisco (http://www.fetus.ucsf.edu/index.htm) and the Center for Fetal Diagnosis and Treatment, The Children's Hospital of Philadelphia (http://fetalsurgery.chop.edu/contact.cfm).

8. J.L. Simpson, *Fetal Surgery for Myelomeningocele: Promise, Profess, and Problems*, 282 (19) J.A.M.A. 1873-74 (1999).

9. 410 U.S. 113 (1973).

10. Barclay, McCormick, Sidbury, et al., *The Ethics of In Utero Surgery*, 246 J.A.M.A. 1550 (1981). *See also* Ruddick & Wilcox, *Operating on the Fetus*, 12 Hastings Center Rep. 10 (Oct. 1982).

11. Lenow, *supra* note 5.

12. A detailed analysis of the historical perspective of property, tort, and criminal law on the question of fetal personhood is evident in Lenow, *supra* note 5, at 3-11.

13. Lenow, *supra* note 5.

14. 410 U.S. 113, at 162.

15. Lenow, *supra* note 5, at 8.

16. Janet Gallagher, *Prenatal Invasions and Interventions: What's Wrong with Fetal Rights*, 10 Harvard Women's Law J. 9, 37, 57 (1987).

17. T. Albert, American Medical News (AMA News) (June 2001).

18. 2 Cal. 3d 619, 470 P. 2d 617 (1981).

19. *Id.* at 663.

20. Cal. Penal Code Section 187 (West 1970 and Supp. 1983).

21. 410 U.S. 113 (1973).

22. Lenow, *supra* note 5. *See also* G. Annas, *Forced Cesareans: The Most Unkindest Cut of All*, 12 Hastings Center Rep. 16 (June 1982).

23. 410 U.S. 113 at 159.

24. Lenow, *supra* note 5, at 10-15.

25. *Williams Obstetrics, supra* note 2, at 587.

26. The choice of 24-28 weeks gestational age or 600-750 grams in fetal weight as the point of viability accruing is arbitrary. The best estimates come from experts in high risk obstetrics and neonatology having observed thousands of premature births and correlating the best evidence to match up to these numbers. Vital to survival is adequate development of the major organ systems. *See* R. Bolognese & N. Roberts, *Amniotic Fluid*, in: *Perinatal Medicine: Management of the High Risk Fetus and Neonate*, 198–203 (2d ed. 1982). *See also* Hershel, Kennedy, et al., *Survival of Infants Born 24–28 Weeks Gestation*, 60 Obstet. Gynecol. 154, 154 (1982), wherein the authors note a 45% survival rate at 26 weeks gestation and a 92% rate at 28 weeks. *See also* Williams, Creasy, Cunningham, et al., *Fetal Growth and Perinatal Viability in California*, 59 Obstet. Gynecol. 624 (May 1982), who conclude that mortality rates are more sensitive to birth weight than to gestational age.

27. 410 U.S. 113 at 159. "When those trained in the discipline of medicine . . . are unable to arrive at any consensus, the judiciary . . . is not in a position to speculate as to when viability occurs."

28. 439 U.S. 379 (1979).

29. *Webster v. Reproductive Health Services*, No. 88-605, October Term, 1988, p. 7. 492 U.S. 490 (1989).

30. *Planned Parenthood of Southeastern Pennsylvania v. Casey*, 112 S. Ct. 2791 (1992).

31. National Center for Disease Control, *Abortion Surveillance Report 1978* (Nov. 1980). Only 0.9% of abortions done (1.2 million in 1978) were performed beyond 21 weeks gestation. *See also* S.K. Henshaw, L.M. Koonin, & J.C. Smith, *Characteristics of U.S. Women Having Abortions, 1987*, 23 Family Planning Perspectives 75 (1991), who noted that half of the 1.5 million abortions in the United States each year today take place within the first 8 weeks of pregnancy; 9 in 10 occur within the first 12 weeks. Less than 1% are performed after 20 weeks. *See also* the Alan Guttmacher Institute, *The Limitations of U.S. Statistics on Abortion* (Washington, D.C., 1997), where it is noted that 300-600 abortions—or up to four one-hundredths of 1%—are performed after 26 weeks.

32. Lenow, *supra* note 5 (term defined by Lenow).

33. Lenow, *supra* note 5.

34. Harrison, Filly & Golbus, *Fetal Treatment 1982*, 307 N. Engl. J. Med. 1651 (1982). Leaders from around the world met in the Santa Ynez Valley, California.

35. 247 Ga. 86, 274 S.E. 2d 457 (1981).

36. A condition where the placenta (afterbirth) lies too low in the uterine wall and over the internal cervical os (opening to the birth canal). This is one of the major obstetrical complications of the latter half of pregnancy and can be the cause of fetal or maternal demise if not quickly and properly treated. Death results when the placenta separates partially from the wall of the uterus and causes hemorrhage. Treatment usually involves strict bed rest, blood replacement if needed, serial ultrasound examinations, and often cesarean section. See *Williams Obstetrics, supra* note 2, at 508.

37. 410 U.S. 113 (1973).

38. 274 S.E. 2d at 460 (Hill J, concurring). Ultimately, a subsequent ultrasound examination revealed an extremely rare shift of the placenta, which enabled the mother to vaginally deliver a healthy girl. It was reported in the *Southern Medical Journal* under the headline, "Mother Nature Reverses on Appeal."

39. F.A. Chervenak, L.B. McCullough, & D.W. Skupski, *An Ethical Justification for Emergency, Coerced Cesarean Delivery*, 82 Obstet. Gynecol. 1029-35 (1993).

40. Committee on Ethics, American College of Obstetricians and Gynecologists, *Patient Choice: Maternal-Fetal Conflict*, Opinion, Aug. 11, 1987 (relying in part on J.L. Lenow, *The Fetus as a Patient: Emerging Rights as a Person?*, *supra* note 5).

41. *In re A.C.*, 573 Atl. Rpt. 2d 1235, 1237 (D.C. Court of Appeals, April 26, 1990).

42. Committee on Ethics, American College of Obstetricians and Gynecologists, *Patient Choice: Maternal-Fetal Conflict*, Opinion, August 11, 1987. (Note that the Academy of Pediatrics has adopted balanced guidelines as well on the subject. *See* American Academy of Pediatrics, Committee on Bioethics, *Fetal Therapy—Ethical Considerations* (RE9817), 103 Pediatrics 1061-63 (May 1999).

43. Law and Medicine/Board of Trustees Report, *Legal Interventions During Pregnancy*, J.A.M.A. 2663-70 (Nov. 28, 1990).

44. Kerenyi & Chitkara, *Selective Birth in Twin Pregnancy with Discordancy for Down's Syndrome*, 304 N. Engl. J. Med. 1525 (1981). *See also* Aberg, Mitelman, Cantz & Gehler, *Cardiac Puncture of Fetus with Hurler's Disease Avoiding Abortion of Unaffected Co-Twin*, 2 Lancet 990 (1978).

45. 445 S.W. 2d 145 (Ky. 1969).

46. *Id.* at 146.

47. 29 Conn. Supp. 368, 289 A. 2d 386 (Conn. Super. Ct. 1972).

48. The use of the benefits rationale to authorize transplants for incompetents has not been unanimously adopted. *See Lausier v. Pescinski*, 67 Wis. 2d 4, 226 N.W. 2d 180 (1975).

49. I. Moilanen, *Are Twins' Behavioural/Emotional Problems Different from Singletons'?*, 8 Eur. Child. Adolesc. Psychiatry, Suppl. 4, 62-67, (Jan. 1999) (suggestion that there may be evidence of fewer behavioral problems in twins).

50. Harrigan, Kangos, et al. *Successful Treatment of Fetal Congestive Heart Failure Secondary to Tachycardia*, 304 N. Engl. J. Med. 1527 (1981).

51. J.L. Lenow, *Prenatal Intervention—Duty vs. Liability*, 3(6) Legal Aspects of Medical Practice (June 1985). Accepted for presentation (25th Annual International Meeting of American College of Legal

United States each year, but organs are actually harvested from only about 15% of these.[7] The increasing need for organs and the inadequacy of initial voluntary efforts have been the driving forces behind much of the legislation concerning transplantation. In 1968 the Uniform Anatomical Gift Act (UAGA) was promulgated to facilitate cadaver donations. Later statutes were amended to allow for donation by a signature on the back of drivers' licenses. Brain death statutes were passed to allow removal of vital organs from artificially maintained bodies. Medicare funding and the Joint Commission on Accreditation of Healthcare Organizations (JCAHO) standards now mandate that hospitals have protocols for routinely approaching families for organ donations. States have passed required request and routine injury laws. Implied consent for corneas from medical examiner cases has been adopted in many states. As the pressure for organs mounts, policymakers will increasingly move away from voluntary to compulsory systems of procurement.

The major legal problems pertinent to transplantation are consent or authorization to donate, the determination of death in the case of procurement from a cadaver, and the rationing of organs and medical resources.

STATE ANATOMICAL GIFT ACTS

The foundation for the law on organ procurement in the United States is the UAGA, which provides the legal authorization for the system of voluntary donations and specifically defines the legal mechanisms for organ and tissue donations. In an effort to promote organ and tissue procurement, the National Conference of Commissioners on Uniform State Laws (NCCUSL) and the American Bar Association, after 3 years of deliberation, drafted the model act in 1968.[8] By 1972 all 50 states, the District of Columbia, and Puerto Rico had adopted the UAGA, spurred on by the excitement over heart transplantation. Many of the states modified the UAGA during enactment or by later amendments. A substantially altered 1987 version of the UAGA, embodying new legal developments and other legislation, has been promulgated by the NCCUSL (Appendix 25-2).[9] As of August 1996 it had been adopted by 19 states (Arizona, Arkansas, California, Connecticut, Hawaii, Idaho, Iowa, Minnesota, Montana, Nevada, New Mexico, North Dakota, Oregon, Rhode Island, Utah, Vermont, Virginia, Washington, and Wisconsin), and the remaining states have all retained some version of the 1968 UAGA. However, many states that have not formally adopted the 1987 UAGA and that effectively repealed the 1968 UAGA have amended their UAGA several times over the years, blurring the distinctions. Therefore every state has adopted some version of the 1987 UAGA.[10]

The UAGA authorizes persons or their families to make an "anatomical gift" of all or part of his or her body to take effect upon death. The legally binding right to direct the disposition of one's own remains after death is a new right created by the UAGA. Previously, as a carry-over from the original common law of England, one had no property rights in his or her body after death. Individuals could not clearly bequeath their bodies, and heirs could nullify or overrule bequests. Even families did not have full property rights in bodies but rather a limited right to possess the body for burial purposes. Bodies were considered "quasi-property."[11,12]

According to the 1968 UAGA, any person 18 years of age or older and "of sound mind" can execute an anatomical gift. Many states have substituted different age requirements. The requirement for a sound mind has been deleted from the 1987 UAGA. An anatomical part includes organs, tissues, eyes, bones, arteries, blood, other fluids, and other portions of the human body. Any condition can be imposed on the gift, but if the condition is inappropriate or unacceptable, it should be declined.

Gifts by a decedent

The decedent's wishes, if known, are to be carried out despite the wishes of the next of kin. Knowledge of religious beliefs may constitute knowledge of the decedent's intentions. In *In re Moyer's Estate* the Utah Supreme Court found that this posthumous control over one's body was "in the public interest" as long as it was not "absurd" or "preposterous."[13] In *Holland v. Metalious*, the deceased willed her eyes to an eye bank and her body to one of two medical schools.[14] The New Hampshire Supreme Court stated that the wishes of the decedent should usually be carried out, but because the medical schools had declined to accept the donation (because of objections of the spouse and children), the court ruled that the surviving spouse could determine the disposition of the body. No survivor has the legal right to veto a valid gift by the decedent; however, as a practical matter, if the family objects to the donation over the expressed desire of the decedent, it may be prudent to decline the decedent's donation.

Gifts by next of kin

When the deceased has not indicated his or her intentions, the UAGA spells out specifically who among those available at the time of death may make an anatomical gift of the body or body parts. The UAGA first designates the spouse, and if the spouse is not available at the time of death, then an adult son or daughter, followed by either parent, then an adult sibling. If none of the aforementioned is available, a guardian of the decedent at the time of the death or any other person authorized or under an obligation to dispose of the body (e.g., the medical examiner or anatomical board) may donate the body or body parts.

Consent by one next of kin (e.g., one brother) is legally negated by the objection of another of the same class of next of kin (e.g., another brother), although inquiry of all in a class is not required to exclude the possibility that someone might object, as confirmed in *Leno v. St. Joseph Hospital.*[15] New York allows any family member to veto a gift by any other family member; in Florida a spouse cannot make a donation over the objection of an adult son or daughter.

The statute does not address the status of divorced or separated spouses, stepparents, stepchildren, other dependents, designated caregivers, those appointed power of attorney, and others. The list of next of kin to be approached for organ donation in the UAGA is not necessarily the same as that for inheritance, autopsy consent, or even required request statutes. Consent by next of kin must be timely; the specified individuals must make the gift "after or immediately upon death." This provides little guidance as to the time and diligence necessary in attempting to contact these persons before considering them "unavailable." Time limits for the harvest of particular organs and tissues are clearly relevant.

Execution of the gift

The gift may be executed by a will or other document. Such provisions in typical estate wills are discouraged because they are usually not immediately available at the time of death. The use of "living wills" is preferred because they are immediately available as part of the medical record. Two witnesses are necessary to validate a gift during the donor's lifetime, but none is required in the case of a gift by next of kin. Some states have relaxed or eliminated (as in the 1987 UAGA) this witness requirement, whereas other states have statutorily specified witness requirements. The next of kin can make gifts by a signed document or by telegraphic or recorded message. The 1987 UAGA would also allow other forms of communication reduced to writing and signed by the recipient. Neither delivery nor public filing is necessary to make the gift effective. The gift can be revoked or amended by a signed statement, an oral statement in the presence of two witnesses, or a statement to an attending physician.

Any card, form, or even sticker may be carried by the donor to evidence the intention of the gift. During the mid-1970s, 44 states incorporated legislation to enable organ and tissue donation by the mere signing of the back of a driver's license. Most organ procurement agencies and transplant surgeons do not accept such a signature by itself (so-called pocket wills) but rather require the contemporaneous consent of the next of kin. They speculate that the decedent may have changed his or her mind since the signing and that they could not afford the negative publicity that might occur in the face of objections by the family. Use of donor cards is mandated in the 1987 UAGA, which requires law enforcement officers and emergency rescue personnel to make a reasonable search for a document of gift and then requires the hospital to cooperate in the implementation of the anatomical gift. Routine inquiry further emphasizes acceptance of documents of a decedent's wishes and provides a mechanism to check the currency of the card.

Persons accepting a gift

Any specified person, physician, hospital, accredited medical school or university, tissue bank, or procurement agency can accept an anatomical gift for education, research, therapy, or transplantation. Several states additionally allow donation to anatomical boards, which generally receive unclaimed bodies for educational purposes. In Connecticut the state commissioner of health must approve recipients. The attending physician is the presumed donee, if a donee is not specified. The attending physician who makes a determination of death is excluded from participating in any part of the transplant procedures, although it does not prevent him or her from communicating with the transplant team. The term *hospital* is substituted for the term *attending physician* in the 1987 version of the act.

The intentions of the donor must be respected, including any condition imposed on the gift. A donee can accept or reject a gift. The donee of the entire body can authorize embalming and funeral services. One provision authorizes any postmortem examination necessary to ensure medical acceptability of the donated organ, including an autopsy. The donee of a part must remove the part without unnecessary mutilation and then relinquish custody to the next of kin or other person under obligation to dispose of the body. The drafters chose not to deal with the issue of compensation for processing the gift.

The UAGA does not qualify in any way the legal right of a physician, organ procurement organization, or transplant team who receives a donated organ to do with it what they perceive as properly carrying out the intentions of the family. It has been argued that the donee holder of an organ is the owner of the organ and thus has the absolute right, limited only by any express covenant of purpose, to choose the ultimate organ recipient. It also has been argued that the intermediary party is an agent of the donor or the donor's family and is liable for failure to comply with their wishes. It has even been espoused that the donee is a public trustee who is liable for negligence (or perhaps conversion) to a prospective recipient for an inappropriate selection.

Medical examiners

Most vital organs are retrieved from patients who are declared brain dead because most natural deaths render organs unsuitable for transplants. Approximately 50% of brain deaths result from motor vehicle accidents or other violence and therefore fall under the jurisdiction of the coroner or medical examiner. The UAGA states that it is subject to other state laws governing autopsies; thus medical examiner and coroner laws take precedence. Comments to the original 1968 NCCUSL act state that it

is necessary to preclude the frustration of the important medical examiner's duties in cases of death by suspected crime or violence. . . . It may prove desirable in many if not most states to reexamine and amend the medical examiner statutes to authorize and direct medical examiners to expedite their autopsy procedures in cases in which the public interest will not suffer.

The 1986 National Task Force on Transplantation also recommended enactment of laws that would encourage coroners and medical examiners to give permission for organ and tissue procurement from cadavers under their jurisdiction.

Many states have "implied consent" statutes that allow harvest of corneas from medical examiner cases when no known objection to the harvest exists. The 1987 version of the UAGA provides that the medical examiner may authorize removal of an organ or tissue for transplant purposes if it will not interfere with the postmortem investigation and if the medical examiner does not know of an objection to the donation after making a reasonable effort, and taking into account the useful life of the part, to find documentation of the decedent's intention and to contact the next of kin.

Immunity

The physician who removes an organ in good faith is protected from civil and criminal liability by the UAGA. Mississippi and Montana grant civil immunity only; South Carolina makes an exception for malpractice. In *Nicoletta v. Rochester Eye and Human Parts Bank,* parties recovering organs were protected when they relied on the good faith belief that a person consenting to donation was a surviving spouse when in fact she was not.[16] This provision of immunity withstood constitutional attack in *Williams v. Hofmann.*[17]

The provision applies only to valid gifts. The UAGA takes effect only after death has been declared; it does not afford protection to the pronouncement of death itself. Failure to comply with the provisions of the act (e.g., no unnecessary mutilation of the body) may demonstrate bad faith. However, the act's provisions are to be construed liberally to achieve its stated goal of promoting organ and tissue donations. In *Ravenis v. Detroit General Hospital* the Michigan Court of Appeals ruled that the protection did not preclude liability for the negligent failure of a hospital to screen a donor adequately for disease that was subsequently transmitted to a recipient.[18] Thus courts may interpret this provision of immunity to be inapplicable to malpractice.

Most states also have protective clauses in their blood banking statutes that specifically maintain that blood transfusions, organ procurement procedures, and transplants are to be regarded as services rather than sales of products; accordingly, members of the transplant team are exempt from strict product liability.

The 1987 UAGA revision

The 1987 NCCUSL model act, among other things, added provisions for routine inquiry, required requests, presumed consent for medical examiner cases, and prohibition of the sale of organs (Appendix 25-2).[19] These substantial new provisions codify in the UAGA legislation what has to some extent been adopted elsewhere. These issues are discussed in the following sections.

ROUTINE INQUIRY OR REQUIRED REQUEST

Possible policy solutions to increase voluntary organ and tissue donations include routine inquiry, required request, and presumed or implied consent legislation. Only 1 of 25 hospital deaths provides material suitable for organ donation, although 24 of 25 deaths provide material suitable for tissue donations.[20] An estimated 17,000 to 26,000 potential organ donors die each year in the United States.[21] Only 15% to 20% of potential donors become actual donors (about 2600 in 1984).[22,23] However, approximately 70% to 75% of families were approached for permission to grant donation.[24] The limiting factor appears to be the inadequate request and referral by the health care team.[25-28]

Recognizing the problem, Arthur Caplan called for "required request" legislation, which would force providers to approach families for donation in appropriate cases.[29] This legislation focuses on the consent of surviving family members. "Routine inquiry," on the other hand, refers to asking a patient on hospital admission if he or she is an organ donor. This method focuses on the advance decision of the individual and his or her right to self-determinism, which is the proper priority according to the UAGA. Furthermore, it saves valuable time by preempting the need to contact the family before procurement. However, some have argued that queries during admission to the hospital are poorly timed because potential patients may feel apprehensive either that the care they receive might be substandard if they fail to comply with a request for donations or that medical providers might be less vigorous in resuscitative attempts if they do comply.[30]

Required request is now found in the laws of most states, in federal Medicare and Medicaid conditions of participation, and in JCAHO standards of accreditation.[31,32] Both the JCAHO and Medicare merely require that a hospital have written protocol. Most current state legislation has been enacted in the form of amendments to state anatomical gift acts and rather closely tracks the federal law. State laws are typically more detailed and sweeping and apply to unaccredited, nonparticipating hospitals. However, state laws are generally weak and vary greatly; few states even require documentation of the request, which would allow for enforcement, and several create institutional exemptions and wide discretionary exceptions for requests. Approximately half the states have weak versions of required request in which the sole requirement is a mere written hospital policy of routine requests of family members. In some states the request must be made by the physician, whereas in others the request must be made by a designated member of the hospital staff or of the regional organ procurement agency. Appropriate training of the requester is sometimes required. Half the states require documentation of the inquiry and its disposition; in many states this documentation is in a log book, a central registry, or a place other than the medical record.

There are numerous exceptions to the requirement of request based on considerations such as medical criteria, known objection, or religion. In Alabama the attending physician can decide that inquiry should not be made. In Massachusetts, exception is allowed when discussion would cause the family undue emotional distress. Lobbying efforts have exempted hospitals in several states.[33]

Early measures requiring request have doubled and tripled overall tissue procurement, but vital organ procurement, which was the target of the legislation, has increased only modestly. Legal sanctions may be imposed if these provisions are not followed or are insufficient. The Health Care Financing Administration (HCFA) is seeking ways to assess compliance with Medicare and Medicaid required request regulations.[34]

The 1987 UAGA has provisions for both routine inquiry and required request (Section 5). Documentation is to be placed in the medical record. The hospital administrator is responsible for implementation, and the Commissioner of Health is responsible for oversight. Furthermore, the legislation mandates that donor cards be sought and respected. Law enforcement agents, emergency personnel, and hospital personnel are to make a reasonable search for a donor card or other documentation of gift at the time of death or "near" the time of death. When evidence of a desire to donate is found, the hospital is to cooperate in the implementation of the gift. Administrative (but not criminal or civil) sanctions are to be imposed.

In an effort to increase public awareness of and improve hospital participation in the donor program, Pennsylvania Act 102 amended the state's UAGA in 1994. The new law changed the way hospitals handle the identification and referral of potential donors and the request for anatomical donations, requiring hospitals to work with the organ procurement organization after every hospital death. In addition to formalizing the process of required request, the new law allows Pennsylvania drivers to indicate donor consent on the front of their driver's license; state Department of Transportation computer records are accessible 24 hours a day. The new law also created an Organ Donation Awareness Trust Fund for educational purposes and set up a contribution system tied to driver's license renewal and state income tax filings. To ensure compliance, Act 102 stipulates that a hospital can be fined up to $500 for every death not reported. The legislation also mandates that the state Department of Health conduct medical reviews to compare organ procurement organizations' referral records to hospitals' death records, which can be used to measure compliance rates.[35]

Pennsylvania's routine referral law has increased referrals and donations dramatically throughout the state. Since the law was enacted, the state has experienced a 26% increase in the number of donors and a 36% increase in the number of transplants.[36] The legislation's success has marked an important milestone in addressing the organ shortage in Pennsylvania and has sent a message to other states that enacting similar legislation may be a key to increasing their donation rates. As of June 1997 at least eight states had enacted routine referral laws, and several more are expected to follow suit.[37]

PRESUMED OR IMPLIED CONSENT

Presumed consent laws, in which consent is presumed in the absence of actual knowledge of objection, are common in Europe. It is a policy of "opting out" instead of "opting in." It has not been a popular notion in the United States, but as demand continues to outstrip the supply for organs and tissues, presumed consent will be increasingly favored by policymakers. Even in countries with implied consent laws, families are regularly asked permission for donations.[38]

A number of states have enacted legislation authorizing medical examiners to have corneas removed based on presumed consent. These laws allow removal of the corneas when the death falls under the jurisdiction of the medical examiner, when removal of the corneas will not interfere with the investigation or disturb the appearance of the body, and when there is no known objection from the next of kin. Maryland passed the first such law in 1975. These presumed consent laws have been highly effective in increasing the supply of corneas.

Statutes vary remarkably in the degree of diligence required in attempting to locate family members. Some states require no effort, others require reasonable effort, some require a good faith effort, some specify attempts for a 4-hour period, and some specify attempts for a 24-hour period unless the organ or tissue would become unfit earlier. Numerous instances of families becoming outraged after corneas have been retrieved from loved ones have resulted in litigation and in Texas in a change in the law.[39]

In *Powell v. Florida* the implied consent statute for removal of corneas by medical examiners was upheld by the Florida Supreme Court.[40] Two sets of parents sued when the corneas of their sons were removed by medical examiners without their consent or without any attempt to give them notice. The court found that the legislation was reasonable, did not violate due process or equal protection requirements, and served a public purpose. It noted that the state of Florida was spending $138 million per year to support its blind citizenry, that corneal transplantation is in great demand, and that it is frequently successful in restoring sight. The court determined that recovery from medical examiner autopsy cases was the most important source of quality tissue and that removal of the corneal tissue, which did not affect the decedent's appearance, was an insignificant bodily intrusion compared with the autopsy itself. The court cited California statistics that approximately 80% of the families of decedents could not be located in time for medical examiners to remove usable corneal tissue. The court further held that the next of kin has no property right in the remains of the decedent but merely a limited right to possess the body for burial purposes. Similarly, medical examiner implied consent statutes have withstood constitutional challenge in Georgia and Michigan.[41,42]

In *Kirker v. Orange County* a mother was awarded damages for the intentional infliction of emotional distress caused by the "mutilation of her daughter's body" when the medical examiner granted permission to remove the child's eyeballs despite an expressed refusal for corneal donation in the medical record.[43] The medical examiner should have known of the objection. An attempted coverup was also shown.

As previously mentioned, the 1987 model act includes a provision authorizing any organ or tissue donation by a medical examiner for transplantation based on a presumed consent provided that a reasonable effort is made to discover any appropriate objection. Maryland and California have expanded presumed consent beyond medical examiner situations to include patients dying in hospitals.

CADAVER ORGANS: DETERMINATION OF DEATH

Most kidneys (80%), most livers (except those from living parental donors), and all hearts for transplantation are harvested from patients who have been declared brain dead and maintained on life support. In such cases a determination of death is necessary. Patients experiencing traumatic deaths often are not brain dead but die of cardiac arrest. An estimated five to six times more donors have no heartbeat than are brain dead.[44] Protocols for such donors have been established in several centers; rapid, timely management of the cadaver may allow organ recovery after the heart has stopped and the patient has been declared dead. The premature removal of organs may subject the physicians to civil and criminal liability.

The law has always held that a person is dead when a licensed physician pronounces him or her dead, if the determination is based on accepted medical standards. Brain death has become an accepted standard, and every court that has examined the question has held it a legally proper determination, regardless of the presence or absence of a state brain death statute. However, medical standards for determination of brain death have become rigorous in many jurisdictions, and failure to adhere to methods for determination specified by such standards may result in liability.

The physician who removes an organ in good faith may be protected from civil and criminal liability by the UAGA. This act appears to take effect only after death has been declared. However, it is to be construed liberally so that its

stated goal of promoting organ and tissue donations may be achieved and conflicts of interest avoided (Section 7). The act specifically states that the physician who makes the determination of death "shall not participate in the procedures for removing or transplanting a part."

In *Tucker v. Lower* the brother of an organ donor alleged that the organs had been removed before the donor was legally dead.[45] At the time, Virginia had not yet adopted a brain death standard. The jury found for the surgeon based on the instruction that death could be determined if there was complete and irreversible loss of brain function.

However, in *Strachan v. John F. Kennedy Memorial Hospital* the court ruled that the hospital was liable for delaying the release of a body while attempting to change the parent's decision not to donate. An emergency department physician had diagnosed brain death 3 days before the official pronouncement of death and disconnection of the respirator.[46]

ORGANS AND TISSUES FROM FETUSES AND ANENCEPHALIC INFANTS

The national organ shortage is much more critical for pediatric organs (especially livers) than for adult organs. Less than 6% of organ donations are from donors 5 years of age and under.[47] It has been estimated that the potential demand each year for infant organs is approximately 1000 livers and 500 hearts and kidneys.[48] This is a conservative estimate because approximately 7500 infants with life-threatening congenital heart defects are born each year.[49] As of June 1997 the United Network for Organ Sharing listed 89 patients under 5 years of age who were waiting for a kidney, 355 patients waiting for a liver, 90 patients waiting for a heart, and 14 patients waiting for a heart-lung block.[50] Half the transplant candidates die before an organ becomes available. In comparison with adults, a very small number of infants and children die with transplant-suitable organs.

Anencephalic infants represent an important potential source of fetal organs. Organs from such infants could meet the bulk of the current demand for infant organs. Organs from stillborns and infants dying from other diseases generally are not suitable for procurement and transplantation.

Anencephaly is an abnormality of primary neurulation commencing within the first month of gestation and resulting in the congenital absence of a major portion of the brain, skull, and scalp. Cranial neural tissue is exposed and often protrudes from the skull defect. Both cerebral hemispheres are absent or unrecognizable. Although some rudimentary cerebral development can occur, there is no functioning cerebral cortex. Anencephalic children cannot reason and presumably cannot suffer. The term *monster* has been applied to this anomaly, which represents the most severe form of neural tube defect (spina bifida). Anencephaly is a universally fatal condition. Two thirds of anencephalic infants die in utero. Very few survive beyond

1 week after birth. Infants provided maximal support may survive somewhat longer, but when strict diagnostic criteria are applied, survival still does not exceed 2 months. Longer survival periods have been reported; however, the diagnostic criteria were not well documented. Cases of amniotic band syndrome, ruptured encephalocele, and iniencephaly are sometimes confused with the diagnosis of anencephaly and probably account for the rare cases of prolonged survival reported in the literature.

Between 13% and 33% of infants born with anencephaly have defects of the nonneural organs. These defects may complicate care and render their organs unsuitable for donation.

Estimates of the incidence of anencephaly have varied from 0.3 to 7 per 1000 births.[51] Differences result from, among other things, different diagnostic criteria, true geographical differences, and prenatal screening programs. Prenatal detection of anencephaly usually results in early termination of pregnancy; thus screening programs can dramatically reduce the incidence of anencephaly at birth. The Centers for Disease Control and Prevention (CDC) cites an incidence of 0.3 per 1000 births (live births and stillbirths).[52] Extrapolation of this figure would indicate that more than 1000 infants are born with anencephaly annually in the United States, but this figure would drop to less than 100 if screening and induced abortion were uniformly applied.

The first transplant of the heart of an anencephalic infant occurred in October 1987 at the Loma Linda University Medical Center in California without legal incident. Subsequently, other parents requested that their anencephalic children be used as donors to help other children. This meant that the pregnancies were carried to term rather than terminated. With parental permission, the live-born anencephalic children were then placed on respiratory support and their organs donated if brain death criteria were fulfilled within 1 week. Only 1 of 12 anencephalic newborns met brain death criteria, and no recipient could be found for his organs; consequently the program was suspended. One of the infants survived for 2 months after the respirator was removed.[53]

The Medical Task Force on Anencephaly reported in March 1990 that it was able to identify 80 anencephalic infants who were involved in transplantation protocols.[54] Only 41 of the infants were used as sources of organs, providing 37 kidneys, two livers, and three hearts.

A major problem with organ donation from anencephalic infants is that legal criteria for brain death are not easily applied. Brain death criteria are derived from the Uniform Determination of Death Act, in which a declaration of brain death is based on irreversible cessation of all brain functions, including those of the brainstem (so-called whole brain death). Although anencephalic infants have no higher cortical function, they may have good brainstem function. Therefore they have intact circulatory and respiratory function; have good reflexes; may cry, swallow, and regurgitate; and may respond to pain, vestibular stimuli, and sometimes sound. Frequent malformations of special sense organs and facial muscles may complicate neurological evaluations or render them impossible.[55]

Although technically incorrect, some have argued that anencephalic infants are "brain absent" and that the brain death concept is not applicable. Others have argued that anencephalic infants have no capacity to reason and thus are not "persons" within the meaning of governing statutes. They may be considered nonviable fetuses. Several states have introduced bills to allow a determination of death in anencephalic infants. One approach is for states to amend their brain death acts to declare anencephalic babies brain dead. Another approach is to change the UAGA so that the term *donor* includes those diagnosed as either brain dead or anencephalic. If an anencephalic child is a person born alive, the Baby Doe handicapped-infant regulations, requiring appropriate nutrition, hydration, and medication, may apply and arguably may prevent organ procurement until natural death.

Many commentators have alluded to a "slippery slope"; that is, creating a special category of brain death for anencephalic infants may open Pandora's box. If anencephalic babies are considered to have a marginal existence that can be sacrificed for the good of society, who else can be sacrificed? Why not extend brain death equivalence to other handicapped infants, particularly to those who are suffering from their handicap? Why limit such rationalization to neonates? What of other "brain-dead" patients, such as those in chronic persistent vegetative states? These commentators believe that the law should be consistent and that less fortunate persons should not be treated with lesser justice. If an anencephalic infant is a person and is alive, he or she is ethically worthy of respect and has legal rights.

The Medical Task Force on Anencephaly noted that anencephaly differs from a persistent vegetative state (PVS) in that (1) anencephaly is an embryological malformation, whereas PVS is an acquired condition with various etiologies; (2) in anencephaly the extent of neurological malformation is readily demonstrable by clinical examination, whereas in PVS the extent of permanent neurological damage is not always observable; (3) anencephaly can be diagnosed with certainty, whereas the diagnosis of PVS may be problematic; and (4) the prognosis for anencephaly is measured in days to weeks, whereas patients with PVS may live for months to years.[56]

The Medical Task Force on Anencephaly recognized four general approaches to organ procurement from infants with anencephaly, as follows:

1. The infant is immediately placed on maximal life-support systems at birth, and the organs are removed as soon as possible without regard to presence or absence of brainstem function.

2. The infant is immediately placed on maximal life-support systems at birth, and the organs are removed after brainstem functions are observed to stop.

3. The infant is given standard (minimal) care until he or she develops hypotension, hypoxia, bradycardia, or cardiac arrest; the infant is then placed on maximal life-support systems, and the organs are removed after brainstem functions are observed to stop.

4. The infant is given standard (minimal) care until he or she dies, and then the organs are harvested.

Of 34 anencephalic infants who were on transplantation protocols and could be thus categorized, the success rate for transplantation was 100% for the first approach but 0% to 11% for the other three approaches.[57] There is a conflict of interest between the clinician's duty to maintain the health of the donor and the duty to preserve organs for a potential recipient.

Fetal tissue has uses other than pediatric organ transplants. Fetal tissue is plastic, immunoprivileged, and available. It has been used to treat diabetes and bone marrow disorders and is a possible consideration for the treatment of Parkinson's disease, Alzheimer's disease, and almost any genetic metabolic disease.

The 1973 *Roe v. Wade* decision did not deprive the fetus of all legal protections, and subsequent regulations and judicial case law have furthered fetal rights. In particular, federal regulations regarding the protection of human subjects may apply. The 1975 Department of Health and Human Services (DHHS) Section 46.201 states that DHHS regulations apply to "research, development, and related activities involving . . . the fetus." The 1985 Health Research Extension Act prohibits federally supported research on nonviable, living fetuses ex utero unless (1) that research is for the benefit or health of the fetus; (2) the research will pose no added risk of suffering, injury, or death to the fetus; and (3) the research cannot be accomplished by other means. Some states limit experimentation on aborted fetal remains, although transplantation research is arguably not research on the remains themselves, within the meaning of the statutes. The Fifth Circuit Court of Appeals has declared Louisiana's statute prohibiting experimentation on an unborn child or a child born as a result of abortion unconstitutional.[58]

Potential sources of human fetal tissue include tissue from stillbirths, ectopic pregnancies, spontaneous abortions, and elective abortions. The tissue must be viable; sufficiently differentiated for use; of sufficient quantity for extraction and implantation; free from major genetic abnormalities or diseases; and free from bacterial, fungal, and viral contamination. These requirements generally render all fetal tissue useless, except that derived from elective abortions. In other words, as a practical matter, only tissue from elective abortions is of sufficient availability and quality to serve as a significant source of fetal tissue for transplantation.

On March 22, 1988, then DHHS Secretary Robert Windom, sparked by a National Institutes of Health (NIH) proposal to implant fetal tissue into patients with Parkinson's disease, imposed a moratorium on further NIH funding of experiments using fetal tissue pending a report from a special NIH advisory panel to examine the medical, ethical, and legal implications of using aborted fetuses for research. After several meetings, 18 of 21 panel members concluded that the use of fetal tissue from induced abortions for transplantation research would be acceptable. The panel recommended that appropriate guidelines be established and that the decision to terminate a pregnancy be kept independent from the decision to use the tissue for research. Nonetheless, on November 2, 1989, DHHS Secretary Louis Sullivan disregarded the panel's recommendations and extended the moratorium indefinitely. He indicated that such research might provide justification for women to decide to have an abortion and would likely result in an increased incidence of abortions across the country.[59-61]

The moratorium did not affect use of fetal tissue not involving transplantation into human subjects with NIH funds. The NIH could fund research using fetal tissue from spontaneous abortions or fund transplants of human fetal tissue (even from induced abortions) into animals. Moreover, the policy letter had no legal bearing on transplantation of any fetal tissue that was not federally funded.

Concern has also been raised over a market in fetal tissue for transplantation, which might result in conceptions and abortions for profit or in manipulation of abortion decisions at the risk of pregnant women. Hana Biologicals of Alameda, California, applied to the Food and Drug Administration (FDA) for permission to market fetal pancreatic tissue. Jeremy Rifkin petitioned the DHHS to declare such a sale prohibited by the NOTA.[62]

The National Institutes of Health Revitalization Act of 1993, enacted to amend the Public Health Service Act and revise and extend programs of the NIH, addresses the issue of research on transplantation of fetal tissue. According to the act, the secretary may conduct or support research on the transplantation of human fetal tissue for therapeutic purposes, regardless of whether the tissue is obtained pursuant to a spontaneous or induced abortion or pursuant to a stillbirth.[63] Under the statute, federally funded projects require a statement in writing from the woman providing the tissue, stating that she is donating the tissue for use in research, that the donation is made without any restriction regarding the identity of any recipients, and that the woman has not been informed of the identity of any recipient. In addition, the attending physician is required to make a statement in writing that the abortion was not planned to coincide with the need for the tissue. The statute also prohibits the purchase of human fetal tissue or the use of donated tissue from a specified donor (e.g., a relative).

In a report issued by the General Accounting Office, extramural projects using fetal tissue that are funded by the NIH follow federal guidelines, including informed consent requirements, and there have been no reports of violations in the methods used to obtain fetal tissue at sites conducting transplantation research.[64]

The NIH awarded more than $6 million to five extramural research projects involving therapeutic uses of human fetal tissue between fiscal 1993 and 1996; of this, $5.9 million supported human fetal tissue transplantation activities. Researchers have found that human fetal tissue can be used to treat a number of illnesses, including juvenile diabetes, leukemia, and Parkinson's disease.[65]

The British Medical Association has promulgated guidelines on the use of fetal tissue, including the condition that tissue may be obtained only from dead fetuses resulting from therapeutic or spontaneous abortion. Death of a fetus was defined as an irreversible loss of function of the organism as a whole.[66]

LIVING DONORS: DONOR CONSENT

Legal requirements for transplantation by a living donor primarily revolve around issues of consent of the donor for organ procurement. The rights of privacy and self-determination demand that adults of legal age and sound mind must give informed consent for donation of their organs or tissues. Competent adults should give consent voluntarily, knowingly, and intelligently after being fully informed of potential risks.

In the typical case the HLA-matched sibling is asked to donate a kidney. The sibling may have considerable trepidation concerning the risk, pain, and disfigurement of the surgery, as well as the potential future compromise of his or her remaining kidney. Although consent is usually granted, the potential donor may decide to refuse. There is no legal duty to be a Good Samaritan. Family and community pressure may significantly cloud the voluntariness of this consent. The issue of living, unrelated kidney donors, which was once viewed with suspicion, has now become common practice. Spousal donation is the most common, but it has been extended to friends. Again the donor shortage has prompted attempts to increase the donor pool. Living-donor protocols include extensive education and psychological evaluation to ensure informed consent.

In the case of *McFall v. Shrimp*, Robert McFall, a victim of aplastic anemia in need of a bone marrow transplant, sued to compel his cousin, David Shrimp, the only person found on initial testing to be a compatible donor, to complete his compatibility testing and if compatible to donate a portion of his marrow.[67] The marrow harvest was described to Shrimp as consisting of inserting a curved needle into his hip at least 200 times. McFall's counsel argued that there is a duty to aid another in peril of his life; the court disagreed. McFall never received a transplant and died shortly thereafter.

In the case of a vital organ transplant, a psychiatric or psychological assessment of the donor and donee may be advisable to negate possible future allegations of duress and also because of the high rates of psychiatric morbidity and suicide in recipients.

Organ donors have failed in their suits against transplant surgeons because of the absence of a physician-patient relationship. In *Sirianni v. Anna* a mother, who donated a kidney to her son after his kidneys were negligently removed by a surgeon, was not allowed to recover against the surgeon for her impairment of health, which she sustained as a result of the loss of her kidney.[68] She undertook the operation with full knowledge of the consequences.

MINORS AND INCOMPETENT DONORS

In the case of minors and incompetent (e.g., mentally impaired) persons a court order is usually necessary for the organ transplantation. Although parents and guardians generally may consent to medical treatment of their children and wards, it is not clear that they have the same authority when surgery is not medically indicated. As a practical matter, most surgeons refuse to perform such surgery without a court order. The consent of guardians or parents is often additionally sought, but the court may overcome their refusal.

In most cases involving intrafamilial transplants, judicial approval has been granted. Judges conducting these hearings in chambers have almost always allowed the harvest procedure and foregone the need for a written explanation of the court's findings. Even where a record is present, courts have not always articulated well the basis for their decision. This may be categorized best as simple judicial approval of parental consent.

In a 1972 Connecticut case, *Hart v. Brown*, the court approved a transplant between two identical 7-year-old twins, considered the medical ramifications, and stated that the parents' motivation and reasoning had met with approval of the guardians ad litem, physicians, clergy, and the court.[69]

Courts also invoke the equitable doctrine of parens patriae to give consent on behalf of minors and incompetent persons. The court often appoints a guardian ad litem in such cases to argue on behalf of the incompetent person.

If the court focuses on the interests of the potential donor with a protective eye, it may find that no objective reason exists for the donor to submit to the risk and bodily intrusion of an organ harvest. It has been argued that the court has no power to authorize the surgery in the absence of specific enabling legislation.

In the 1973 Louisiana case *In re Richardson* a husband brought suit against his wife to compel her consent to the removal of a kidney from their mentally retarded son for donation to his older sister.[70] The Fourth Circuit Court held that neither the parents nor the courts could authorize surgical intrusion on a mentally retarded minor for the purpose of donating organs, that such an authorization would invade the minor's right to freedom from bodily intrusion, and that it was not shown to be in the minor's best interest.

In 1975 the Supreme Court of Wisconsin in *In re Guardianship of Pescinski* held that the court had no power to compel a 39-year-old catatonic schizophrenic patient to donate a kidney to a 38-year-old sister in the absence of any showing of benefit to the incompetent: "[The] incompetent particularly should have his own interests protected. Certainly no advantage should be taken of him."[71] Medical testimony indicated that the risk to the donor at that time was one death in 4000 kidney transplants. The dissent stated that requirement of consent was inappropriate as applied to an incompetent person without lucid intervals.

Other courts have authorized donation by applying a "best interest" test and finding psychological benefit (or absence of detriment) and asserting consent.

In a 1979 Texas case, *Little v. Little*, a mother sought judicial consent for the removal of a kidney from her 14-year-old daughter with Down syndrome for her son.[72] The guardian was opposed. The mother argued that the daughter was the only suitable donor for her brother, that there was no threat to her life, and that the daughter would have wanted this for her ill brother. Medical testimony alleged that the daughter was a perfect match (despite brother and sister not being identical twins) and that the chance of finding a suitable cadaver kidney was extremely remote. The judge authorized the transplant on the basis of "substantial psychological benefit" to the donor.

Courts have increasingly used the doctrine of "substituted judgment" to decide medical cases involving difficult ethical issues with incompetent persons. Specifically, the court must substitute itself, as nearly as possible, for the incompetent person to act with the same motives and considerations as would have moved the individual.

In the 1969 case *Strunk v. Strunk*, the mother of a 27-year-old mentally retarded man with an IQ of 35 petitioned the court for a kidney removal to be used for his 28-year-old brother.[73] The court, based on psychiatric testimony that the death of the donor's brother would have an extremely traumatic effect on the donor, allowed the transplantation to avoid the detriment. The court reached this result despite testimony from the director of the renal division at the local institution; the director stated that, if something happened to the retarded donor's remaining kidney, he would not meet the selection criteria necessary for hemodialysis or transplantation. The dissent stated that "it is common knowledge that the loss of a close relative or a friend to a 6-year-old is not of major importance." Opinions concerning psychological trauma at best are nebulous.

CONFIDENTIALITY OF POTENTIAL DONORS

Potential donors are often HLA matched to find an immunocompatible host and thereby achieve a greater chance of graft survival. Modern immunosuppressive therapies generally obviate this need except in the case of bone marrow transplantation. The need for matched organs has given rise to expensive HLA registries. There is great pressure to give names of those individuals with matching phenotypes to potential recipients.

In the case of *Head v. Colloton* the plaintiff, William Head, had leukemia and sued to demand disclosure of the identity of the only potential donor in the institution's bone marrow transplant registry who had a matching HLA type.[74] The potential donor had been HLA typed as a possible platelet donor for an ill family member. She was telephoned by the registry and asked in general terms if she would be interested in being a bone marrow donor; she responded that she would be interested only if it was for a family member. The court maintained the anonymity of the potential donor and refused further inquiry but did so on narrow legal grounds relating to the interpretation of the Iowa Freedom of Information Act. The plaintiff died during the court proceedings without having had a marrow transplant.

Names of potential donors should be placed on registries only after they have given informed consent, and donors should be able to withdraw their names at any time. Disclosures should be restricted to necessarily involved medical personnel only.

ARTIFICIAL AND ANIMAL TRANSPLANTS

In the immediate future, organs from animals (xenografts), except porcine heart valves, will continue to play only a minor role in transplantation and will remain largely experimental. Important strides have been made in the understanding of xenograft rejection, but a major barrier to this technique remains. Genetically engineered animals, probably pigs, will incorporate human immunological factors. Baboon hearts and livers have always been rejected and thus have fallen from favor. Simians will not meet the need because of low numbers. An additional concern is the transmission of animal diseases (zoonoses).

Artificial hearts also have a poor overall record but are increasingly used for temporary replacement until a human transplant can be performed. Left ventricular assist devices, on the other hand, have become popular.

Failure to obtain adequate informed consent has been a major criticism of most pioneering efforts. Today, this issue is better recognized, and more appropriate consent procedures are being followed. All human experimentation must be reviewed by a medical institution's internal review board. The first artificial heart transplant precipitated a lawsuit, *Karp v. Cooley*, which remains the leading authority on the issue of informed consent for an experimental therapy.[75]

Special considerations exist regarding artificial organs. The Medical Device Amendment enacted in 1976 ensures the safety of medical devices and imposes strict regulations on manufacturers of artificial organs regarding interstate commerce.[76] The DHHS and FDA have responsibility to promulgate regulations under this act. These regulations were not enforced in cases of early artificial heart transplants but have since been and will continue to be enforced. Also, strict product liability may be applied to these implants.

DONOR SCREENING

Donors must be screened to determine suitability of donation. Transmission of disease from an organ or tissue donation is an important concern. Transplantation personnel must maintain constant vigilance against bacterial and fungal infections resulting from organs and tissue derived from septic patients and from contamination during handling. The implant may act as a nidus for infection. Cytomegalovirus (CMV) is the most common problem and can be clinically significant. Other serious diseases that can be transmitted via transplantation include cancer and infections with the human immunodeficiency virus (HIV), hepatitis B, tuberculosis, toxoplasmosis, and Jakob-Creutzfeldt disease. Cancer, except low-grade brain malignancies, obviates a patient as a donor. The organ may be impaired by nontransmissible disease, such as atherosclerosis; however, the donor shortage has led to expanded donor criteria, including older donors (over age 60); treated, controlled hypertensive patients; and even diabetic persons without evidence of renal disease.

Screening for transmissible disease involves chart review, specific laboratory tests, and examination of the donor. The United Network for Organ Sharing, discussed later in this chapter, requires documentation of certain tests and evaluations as minimal acceptable standards for an independent organ procurement agency.

Inadequate screening can give rise to litigation. Ordinary negligence liability results if the disease or defect is discoverable by standard medical practices. Failure to test for HIV antibody would be a breach of standard medical practice in cases of heart transplantation, but it would result in liability only if the donee subsequently developed an HIV infection. If no results were available by the time a transplantation would need to proceed, liability might not attach because a court might find that a surgeon acted reasonably. However, a court may find that the brain-dead cadaver should have been maintained until a result could have been obtained or that, if a risk factor were present in the donor's record, the donation ought to have been declined. Liability should not attach if, as can happen, HIV is transmitted despite a negative HIV antibody test; donor screening is imperfect. Faulty testing or specimen mix-ups may result in incompatible organs being transplanted, in which case liability is likely. The immunity statutes previously mentioned may protect an organ procurement agency or a transplantation team.

In *Ravenis v. Detroit General Hospital* the hospital was found negligent in two cases in which patients lost the sight remaining in an eye after transplantation of an infected cornea.[77] No hospital official was responsible for selection; slit-lamp examinations were not performed despite availability of equipment; and the appropriate information for the surgeon to determine the unsuitability of the tissue for transplantation was missing from the patient's chart.

In *Good v. Presbyterian Hospital* a medical malpractice action was brought under the informed consent theory against a transplant surgeon who performed a heart and lung transplant on a 5-year-old patient.[78] The plaintiff, the patient's mother, alleged that the surgeon failed to advise her that the organs to be transplanted had tested positive for CMV and that the virus caused the 5-year-old child's death. The court found that the transplant surgeon did not violate the New York informed consent standards, since the universal practice of reasonable medical practitioners in 1990 under similar circumstances was not to discuss specifically the CMV status of organs with the patient or the patient's representatives.[79]

FEDERAL LEGISLATION

Health matters are generally the province of state law. Because of ongoing developments in the field, the need for centralized national allocation of organs, and funding issues, however, the federal government has become increasingly involved in transplantation and has attempted to enhance and coordinate private and local government initiatives. For example, the federal government sponsored the establishment in 1983 of the American Council on Transplantation, a group of private sector organizations and individuals to promote organ donation (dissolved in the early 1990s).

The National Organ Transplant Act (NOTA) was enacted in 1984.[80] It called for the creation of a national Organ Procurement and Transplantation Network (OPTN) to match prospective donors to prospective recipients, the creation of a special advisory task force, and the prohibition of the sale of organs. The OPTN was to create a fair and equitable system of organ allocation that could optimize matches between organs and patients throughout the United States by facilitating regional independent organ procurement agencies (IOPAs). Grants for the establishment of new agencies and the improvement of existing IOPAs were authorized to form an adequate base of a truly national network. This network was then to "assist organ procurement organizations in the distribution of organs which cannot be placed locally, to develop organ procurement standards, and to help coordinate transport."

The United Network for Organ Sharing (UNOS), a private, nonprofit entity solely devoted to organ procurement and transplantation, was awarded the federal contract to run the OPTN in September 1986. Federal oversight of UNOS is provided by the Division of Organ Transplantation under the Health Resources and Services Administration, within the Public Health Service and the DHHS.

The Task Force on Organ Transplantation was created by DHHS Secretary Heckler in January 1985. It rendered its final report in April 1986 and was dissolved. The 78 recommendations largely define federal policy.

The Omnibus Budget and Reconciliation Act (OBRA) of 1986 built on the 1984 legislation and the task force's recommendations by amending the Social Security Act.[81] First, it mandated as Medicare and Medicaid conditions of participation that hospitals institutionalize a required request policy (as previously explained) to increase the voluntary supply of organs. Second, also as Medicare and Medicaid funding requirements, it stated that hospitals performing transplantations must be members and must abide by the rules and policies of the OPTN (i.e., UNOS).

The statutory requirement that transplantation centers must be members and abide by the OPTN gives UNOS great regulatory power. Many consider UNOS as a unique experiment in self-regulation within the health care field. UNOS requirements are more stringent than DHHS regulations. The policies of UNOS, equivalent to conditions of participation, are subject to review and approval by the DHHS and are subjected to public "notice and comment" in the *Federal Register*. Despite lip service to the contrary, the system appears to operate in a very centralized manner, rather than the flexible, pluralistic decentralized system originally envisioned in the 1984 NOTA.[82]

Membership in UNOS as a qualified IOPA was a great organizational challenge. The task force recommended that competition between organ procurement organizations be discouraged. IOPAs were required to have defined and exclusive service areas. The response was for all IOPAs in given areas to merge into single entities. A regional system of IOPAs is now in place. Anticipated litigation never materialized.

Membership in UNOS as a transplantation center qualified by procedure will continue to be problematic. To become members, new programs must already have performed a particular procedure many times, which is almost impossible without federal funding. Thus the UNOS membership guidelines tend to entrench existing members who helped establish the guidelines. The governmental umbrella over UNOS might shield its members from antitrust considerations.

Sale of organs

The NOTA of 1984 prohibited the transfer of "any human organ for valuable consideration if the transfer affects interstate commerce."[83] The term *human organ* is defined as the human kidney, liver, heart, lung, pancreas, bone marrow, cornea, eye, bone, skin, and any other organ included by the secretary of the DHHS for regulation. It is not intended to include replenishable tissues, such as blood or semen. The term *valuable consideration* does not include the "reasonable payment associated with removal, transportation,

implantation, processing, preservation, quality control, and storage, or the expenses of travel, housing, or lost wages in connection with donation of the organ."

The commerce clause reflects an attempt to fit the regulation into the federal constitutional commerce powers. In other situations this language has been interpreted so broadly as to include almost any interstate or intrastate transaction. Nonetheless, several states have also passed such prohibitions.

A 38-year-old leukemia patient needed a bone marrow transplant but could not find a suitable donor. His older brother was homeless and earned money by serving as a subject in medical experiments. He initially refused to be tested for compatibility. An anonymous donor offered him $1000 to undergo testing and $2000 to donate. He was tested and was found not to be an HLA match. If he had matched, the prohibition against "the transfer of any human organ for valuable consideration" arguably would have been applicable and would have barred his marrow donation to his brother.[84]

Food and Drug Administration

The FDA has jurisdiction over tissue banking and has maintained a task force on transplantation since 1983. The regulation of the safety and efficacy of human tissue is analogous to regulation of manufactured materials for use in therapy. The agency is developing proposals for regulating cryopreserved semen, dura mater, and heart valves. The FDA is not concerned with solid organs except possibly for disease transmission by improper screening of donors. The FDA is also concerned with organ perfusion solutions.[85]

In October 1993 the U.S. House of Representatives passed H.R. 2659, the Organ and Bone Marrow Transplantation Amendments of 1993, to revise and extend programs relating to the transplantation of organs and bone marrow. The proposals amended 42 U.S.C., Sections 273 and 274. The amendments extended for 3 fiscal years the authorization of appropriations for the NOTA. In November 1995 the Senate favorably reported the proposed Solid Organ and Bone Marrow Transplant Reauthorization Act of 1995 to revise and reauthorize funding for transplantation programs.[86] This legislation, which is administered by the Health Resources and Services Administration of the DHHS, would provide for continued operation of the transplant network and scientific registries and provide rules for transplant network governance and administration. In addition, appropriations would establish a patient advocacy and case management office for the bone marrow transplantation program.

The secretary of the DHHS is required to issue regulations establishing enforceable procedures for the procurement, allocation, and transplantation of solid organs and bone marrow. Such regulations also would establish the criteria that must be satisfied for membership in OPTN. In issuing such regulations, the secretary is directed to consider existing policies and guidelines issued by UNOS and the National Bone Marrow Registry.

The secretary is required to review and approve any changes in the amount of patient registration fees imposed by the private contractor administering the system of solid organ procurement.

Organ allocation policies of the OPTN and the member organ procurement organizations (OPOs) require maintenance of a single list of patients referred for transplants for each solid organ and give preference to patients who are U.S. citizens or permanent resident aliens.

Expansion of the system of patient advocacy for bone marrow transplant patients is provided with an inclusion for case management services. The General Accounting Office is required to perform studies of the National Marrow Donor Program.

Last, the secretary of the DHHS is required to study the feasibility, fairness, and enforceability of allocating solid organs to patients based solely on the clinical need of the patient involved and the viability of organs involved.

Legislation and administrative rule-making in the areas of organ donation and transplantation are undergoing continual revisions. The reader should consult the appropriate federal and state reference source materials, in addition to current medicolegal periodicals, to keep apprised of these revisions and updates.

SELECTION OF ORGAN RECIPIENTS

The scarce supply of organs and tissues relative to demand and the economic considerations of transplantation force the medical community to confront ethical issues on rationing. The public must perceive the allocation of organs as fair and equitable, or the national organ and tissue supply (which depends on voluntary contributions) will be jeopardized.

Regulation of recipient selection for organs is now imposed nationally through funding requirements. The NOTA of 1984 created the OPTN for the equitable distribution of all available organs in the United States.[87] The OBRA of 1986 requires all hospitals to abide by the policies of the OPTN as conditions of Medicare and Medicaid payment.[88] The federal OPTN contract was awarded to UNOS.

The basis of the UNOS system is a computerized point system for allocation. The point system is an objective method of patient selection determined primarily by probability of success, time on the waiting list, logistic factors, and medical need, modified from the proposal by Starzl.[89] Variances can be granted for fair patient selection criteria to accommodate local concerns.

Kidneys require more stringent testing than other solid organs because potential donees can be maintained on dialysis while awaiting an optimal kidney. Difficult choices must be made for nonpaired vital organs. Kidneys will be offered first to the recipient located anywhere in the country who has a perfect antigenic match. Only 15% to 25% of kidneys will have such a match. Otherwise, cadaveric kidneys will be allocated on a point system based on time of waiting, quality of antigen match, and panel-reactive antibody screen (a measure of sensitization). Medical urgency is not considered for kidney allocation.

Extrarenal organs will be allocated based on organ size, ABO typing, time of waiting, degree of medical urgency, and logistic factors. Pancreata will be offered solely on the basis of distance to a potential recipient and time on a waiting list.

Pediatric organs and patients are given special consideration. Dual transplants (e.g., simultaneous kidney-pancreas) are also handled outside the usual schema.

Patients on local waiting lists are offered organs in descending sequence, with the highest number of points receiving the highest priority. Only if an organ is not accepted locally will it be offered regionally, and then nationally. Organ sharing arrangements between interregional and intraregional OPOs may be entered into on approval of UNOS. The OPTN (UNOS) patient waiting list is open only to direct UNOS-member OPOs, and such members cannot offer organs to non–UNOS-member transplantation centers. A potential recipient may be placed on multiple listings, even though this confers some advantage.

The final decision to accept an offered organ remains the prerogative of the transplantation surgeon, physician responsible for the care of the patient, or both. A transplantation center has 1 hour to accept an offered organ, or the offering procurement agency will be free to offer the organ to another recipient.

The issue of whether the patient with the greatest chance of survival or the one with the greatest urgency should receive an organ has been a source of continuing debate. A potential heart recipient deteriorates and becomes suddenly much more ill, so he or she is at once more critically in need of a new heart and less likely to survive the transplantation. This question is largely moot with respect to kidneys because patients can be placed on dialysis (except in the rare case of exhaustion of vascular access sites). However, the issue of deterioration is paramount with respect to hearts and livers. Medical urgency determines the status for liver and heart recipients in the UNOS system. The potential for manipulating the system as a result of its subjectivity has led to extensive efforts to develop listing criteria for liver transplantation. Criteria for all organs are being considered by UNOS and its membership.

Highly sensitized patients, or "responders," have antibodies against most histocompatibility antigens. A negative crossmatch may give a responder his or her only chance to receive a surviving transplantation. However, the chance of organ acceptance is lower than that for similarly matched nonresponders. The transplantation community generally feels an obligation to offer to this patient his or her last small chance at a tolerable organ.

Matching is a significant criterion based on sound immunological principles. HLA compatibility is unavoidably discriminatory against African-Americans and Hispanics (who have a several times higher rate of ESRD) because most available kidneys have been donated by whites. On the basis of histocompatibility alone, most kidneys from large urban centers would go to white suburban areas. HLA compatibility is of debatable significance to other organs.

Other criteria, such as age and lifestyle, although not a part of the UNOS point system, may be locally operative. Valid medical justifications for these gray areas exist; for instance, is a young patient a better surgical risk than an older alcoholic patient who continues to drink and is likely to damage the new liver and unlikely to take medications regularly? However, discrimination based on age or social position raises issues of fairness. Such subjective criteria are also prone to capriciousness. These do not seem to be primary selection criteria.

After a patient receives a transplant, he or she is usually given greater consideration for a subsequent organ, but the chances for long-term success fall as a patient receives more transplants.

Persons from other countries may not come to the United States and pay for a transplant and deplete national organ resources. Payment for organs is now prohibited. Currently, aliens are held to about 5% of current waiting lists, but those on the lists are to be treated as American citizens and not to be discriminated against based on political influence, national origin, race, gender, religion, or financial status. UNOS members are not to enter into contractual arrangements with foreign agencies or governments or perform transplants on nonresident aliens for financial advantage. Exportation and importation of organs are to be strictly arranged and coordinated through UNOS. Although thousands are maintained on the United States waiting lists, several hundred kidneys are shipped abroad because they are unacceptably old by rigorous U.S. standards.

Lawsuits can be filed against hospitals, transplant surgeons, and committees on behalf of patients who fail to obtain vital organs because others have received the organs first. This is increasingly likely because criteria might be attacked as arbitrary, capricious, or otherwise unreasonable. The implication that one recipient is chosen over another for financial reasons might be argued as an illegal sale of an organ and thus a basis of liability. Another problem area involves cases in which a sudden decline in health precipitates a recipient's "jumping the queue" (being ranked higher priority) and receiving an organ that would have gone to another. Although the sudden deterioration may suggest a poorer prognosis, others in the queue are at increasing risk for sudden death. The potential liability for choosing between who lives and dies is enormous, and the absence of suits to date is surprising.

COST AND PAYMENT CONSIDERATIONS

Vital organ transplantation is extremely expensive. The approximate range for a typical kidney transplant is $25,000 to $30,000; for a heart transplant procedure, $57,000 to $110,000; for a heart-lung transplant, $130,000 to $200,000; for a liver transplant, $135,000 to $238,000; and for a pancreas transplant, $30,000 to $100,000.[90]

Transplantation failures and ancillary costs (e.g., transportation and lodging for the patient and family when the patient does not live near the transplantation center) greatly elevate these figures. Almost all vital organ transplant patients require lifelong maintenance on immunosuppressant therapy, although this may be changing. The cost of conventional immunosuppression maintenance (steroids and azathioprine) averages $1000 to $2000 per year and $5000 to $7000 per year for cyclosporine. However, because cyclosporine decreases overall complications, it does not raise overall costs. The OBRA of 1986 enabled Medicare and Medicaid to cover out-patient immunosuppressive therapy, particularly cyclosporine, for 3 years after transplant.[91]

The cost of transplantation is generally prohibitive, and individuals must rely on third-party reimbursement. Furthermore, many if not most of those in need of a solid organ transplant are incapable of employment. Thus transplants can be viewed as treatment for a catastrophic life-threatening illness.

Established in 1972, the Medicare End-Stage Renal Disease Program (ESRDP) provides treatment to patients with kidney failure regardless of their ability to pay.[92] ESRD was the first disease targeted for funding through a special program by the federal government. This program established the standard acquisition charge for transplantable kidneys, allowing each transplant center to predict its organ charges regardless of the location of origin of the organ or complicating expenses attributable to an individual donor. Over the years the method of payment for transplantable kidneys has been extrapolated to all solid organ transplants.

The cost of the ESRDP, primarily for long-term dialysis, continues to escalate as the number of beneficiaries, now 275,000, increases.[93] Transplantation costs in the United States in 1994 were approximately $4 billion, or 0.04% of total health care expenditures.[94] This amount is much greater than anticipated, and the ESRDP is often cited as an expensive program run amok.[95,96]

Kidney transplants are cost effective (with the initial large investment generally being paid back in 3 years) compared with the alternative, hemodialysis. The long-term costs of maintaining patients with functioning grafts are only one third of those for dialysis patients.[97,98] Furthermore, the quality of life is improved, allowing more people to become productive citizens again. No alternative exists for heart or liver transplants.

In this era of cost containment, many find it difficult to justify the expense of transplantation for the few while sacrificing more widespread financing of health care. The juggernaut is not easily stopped because U.S. society typically responds to individual pleas for a specific and lifesaving treatment. Increasingly the federal government is asked to subsidize transplants, but federal fiscal restraints make this difficult.

At present the costs of transplantation are high but not higher than the costs of taking care of the typical AIDS patient or cancer patient, and the results are much better. As a result of the organ shortage, the total costs to the government are now relatively low and predictable. However, the government's ability to pay for organ transplants may not continue, particularly because of a growth in the supply of organs, increase in demand, and technological innovations, such as usable artificial organs. Over time, pressures will grow to relax the standards for patient reimbursement. The history of the ESRDP demonstrates this process of ever more lenient selection standards tending toward universal access.

Medicare coverage of services furnished to individuals with ESRD who require dialysis or kidney transplantation is authorized under Section 1881 of the Social Security Act. Medicare also covers other organ transplants that the HCFA has determined are "reasonable and necessary" (Section 1862) and pays for those transplant and related organ procurement services.[99] Based on a report by the Office of Health Technology Assessment that liver transplants are no longer experimental, the HCFA reported that it will cover the cost of some adult liver transplants, including those needed because of alcoholic cirrhosis.[100] As of February 2, 1995, lung transplants and heart-lung transplants were added to the list of medically reasonable and necessary services covered under Medicare, when specific established criteria were met.[101] Medicare considers pancreas transplantation experimental but will fund the kidney portion of a combined kidney-pancreas transplantation, whereas private insurers cover the entire procedure.

States pay for transplantation procedures for low-income persons through Medicaid (subsidized by the federal government). The states vary greatly in their coverage and payment policies. In 1990, of the 50 states and the District of Columbia, only 12 states reimbursed pancreas transplants, 15 provided for lung transplants, and 23 paid for heart-lung transplants but 40 provided reimbursement for heart transplants, 48 for liver transplants, and 50 for kidney transplants. Only Wyoming offered no transplantation reimbursement.[102]

For Medicare and Medicaid (and most private health insurance plans) the funding eligibility trigger is "medical necessity" for the treatment. Thus the government will pay for a transplantation if, like other medical therapy, it can be shown that the procedure is reasonable and necessary for the illness and that such treatment is not experimental.

Patients have successfully sued for reimbursement from state agencies when policies or administrative regulations have unfairly denied coverage. In *Brillo v. Arizona*, Mrs. Brillo successfully sued the state to provide coverage for her liver transplantation.[103] The service director's policy determination was that the state would not pay for adult liver transplants because they were experimental, although they would pay for pediatric liver transplants. The court found the policy to be arbitrary, capricious, and a denial of equal protection of the law.

In *Allen v. Mansour* the Michigan court ordered Medicaid funding for an alcoholic with cirrhosis, holding that the recipient selection criterion of a 2-year abstinence from alcohol in cases of cirrhosis caused by alcoholism was arbitrary and unreasonable as formulated and applied.[104] The court noted that this criterion was developed on meager experience and that "medical necessity" of the procedure is the touchstone for evaluating the reasonableness of standards in state Medicaid plans.

In *Lee v. Page* the Florida Medicaid program refused to fund a liver transplant to be performed at the University of Nebraska for a medically qualified 26-year-old woman with a fatal liver disease. The state's position was that the high cost of the liver transplant procedure, which would divert substantial funds from other needy persons, and the minimal benefit to the population of all eligible recipients made the refusal to pay reasonable. The court indicated that states have considerable leeway to implement federally backed Medicaid programs. States must adopt "reasonable standards," but they cannot exclude coverage for "medically necessary treatments." A state can legitimately argue in support of its refusal to fund a treatment as unnecessary either because the treatment is experimental or because it is inappropriate. The court held that liver transplantation is no longer experimental. The court also held that an unfavorable cost-benefit determination is not a medical appropriateness criterion and thus is not a reasonable standard from which to refuse funding.

This is not a question of the limits on the amount Medicaid will pay for a procedure, but rather a case where Medicaid refuses to pay the entire amount based on the cost of the procedure. . . .

[Medicaid] cannot eliminate one health-related service while leaving others intact. . . . It does not appear that federal law permits Florida to refuse to fund all liver transplants. . . . Florida voluntarily entered the federal Medicaid cooperative program and must comply with the standards.[105]

In *Todd v. Sorrell*, a Virginia child was determined to be a suitable candidate for a liver transplantation by the Children's Hospital of Pittsburgh.[106] Because of cancer, 85% of the child's liver had been removed, and secondary biliary cirrhosis had developed. The hospital required an advance payment ($162,000). The Virginia Medicaid program refused to pay because its policy was to pay for pediatric liver transplants only in cases caused by biliary atresia. The U.S. Court of Appeals for the Fourth Circuit overturned a district court's holding and granted an injunction ordering the state to pay for the transplantation pending a final three-judge panel review. Nonetheless, citing the high costs of liver transplants ($250,000), other priorities, and the poor outcomes of liver transplants, Virginia decided to stop Medicaid funding of all liver transplants (May 1988).

Oregon decided not to spend Medicaid monies on transplantations except for kidneys and corneas. It reversed its controversial stand after public protest.[107,108]

MALPRACTICE SUITS

For a number of reasons, malpractice suits involving transplantation of vital organs have been almost nonexistent. First, in the past, transplantations were considered largely experimental, and thus customary standards were not well established. Second, failure was a well-recognized risk. Third, the careful attention by physicians in these cases resulted in generally good relationships and good communication with patients and their families. Fourth, the surgeons and institutions involved were of high stature and esteem. Fifth, transplant physicians were few and closely knit, making opposition testimony difficult to find. Sixth, damages were difficult to prove, given the ill health of the patients. However, a marked increase in suits may be anticipated in the future because these conditions will no longer hold true as vital organ transplants become commonplace.

In *McDermott v. Manhattan Eye, Ear & Throat Hospital* the appellate court reversed a lower court's finding of negligent corneal transplant, holding that evidence was insufficient to support a malpractice claim that the surgeon lacked the skill or experience to perform the operation, that the operation was of extreme delicacy with a high incidence of failure, and that the situation was one of desperation.[109]

The degree to which courts are reluctant to find liability in favor of transplant efforts can be found in *State of Missouri ex rel. Wichita Falls General Hospital v. Adolph.*[110,111] A Missouri transplant team flew to Wichita Falls, Texas, to harvest a heart from a donor and then returned to Missouri to transplant the heart into a recipient. During the transplant they discovered that the Texas hospital had incorrectly typed the donor as type A rather than type B. The patient died shortly thereafter, despite a second transplant. A Missouri appeals court refused to allow a Missouri trial court assert jurisdiction over a Texas hospital because of the potential adverse effect on future transplants.

Several problem areas are likely to be litigated in the future, especially the issues of informed consent and suitability of the organ for transplant.

Theoretically, *strict liability* (in which the court may award damages without a finding of fault by the defendant) might apply to injuries sustained from implants of diseased or defective organs as an unreasonably dangerous defective product or from an implied warranty. Plaintiffs in early cases of hepatitis and adverse reactions to transfusions of blood and blood products successfully argued theories of strict liability. Later decisions rejected the notion, holding that provision of blood is a service and not the sale of a product.

Most states now have statutes that specifically protect hospitals and blood banks from strict liability. Such laws hold that transfusions of blood and blood products are not sales, so no warranties attach, and that liability may be imposed only for negligence or willful misconduct. Many statutes further include transplantations of other tissues and organs in these provisions. The states that specifically mention blood but fail to mention other tissues and organs might risk the interpretation that their legislatures intended to exclude organ transplantations from such protection. Otherwise, strict liability is unlikely to be applied to organ transplantation because transplantation will be construed to be a hospital and physician service instead of the sale of a product, in light of the blood banking court decisions and the federal and state proscriptions against sales of organs. Statutory immunity conferred by the UAGA also might apply to negligent procedures, as discussed earlier.

RECENT DEVELOPMENTS

On December 7, 1993, the House of Delegates of the American Medical Association (AMA) adopted a report from the Council on Ethical and Judicial Affairs that was subsequently revised in response to comments received from peer reviewers.[112] This report recommended that mandated choice, in which individuals would be required to state their preferences regarding organ donation when they renew their driver's licenses, file their income tax return, or perform some other task mandated by the state, should be pursued by the AMA in working with state medical societies to draft model legislation for adoption by state legislatures. The report raised ethical objections to the alternative of presumed consent, in which it is assumed that an individual would consent to be an organ donor at death unless an objection from the individual before death or from his or her next of kin after death is known to the health care provider. A federal circuit court has adopted this approach.[113] In this case the circuit court of appeals, in reversing the district court's ruling, determined that a widow could maintain a civil rights action filed against the coroner based on his removal of the decedent husband's corneas for use in transplantation without the widow's consent. The court held that consent was presumed when the coroner claimed a lack of knowledge as to any objection to such removal of organs for transplantation before performing the procedure.

Medical examiners and transplant coordinators are cooperating to maximize the lawful retrieval of organs and tissues for transplantation.[114,115] Representatives from the Association of Organ Procurement Organizations, the North American Transplant Coordinators Organization, the American Society of Transplant Surgeons, and the National Association of Medical Examiners have met to agree on guidelines for their respective members. This need for cooperative efforts is underscored by the estimate that currently approximately one suitable transplant candidate in the United States is dying every 4 hours because of lack of a suitable organ for recommended transplantation. These guidelines are needed to protect concerns that forensic evidence will not be lost or affected by the subsequent transplantation surgery. The results of a retrospective study (from 1990 to 1992) of information received from responding organ procurement organizations indicated that as many as 2979 individuals may have been denied transplants because of medical examiner denials.[116] Such denials were generally the result of a perceived need by the medical examiner to preserve forensic evidence that could be necessary later in documenting the cause of an individual's death.

Multiple efforts to increase organ donation are underway. Virginia has become the latest in a growing number of states to offer an organ donation license plate. In the spring of 1997, Ohio residents were encouraged to discuss their decision to donate over breakfast. As part of a National Organ and Tissue Donor Awareness Week milk cartons carried the donation message. Organ donor networks across the country sponsor a variety of activities from relay races to formalized studies designed to identify and standardize effective strategies that improve donation.[117] The 104th Congress passed the Organ Donation Insert Card Act as part of the health insurance portability law enacted in 1996. The new law required the Treasury Department to include information on organ and tissue donation with each refund check. In addition, the campaign included print ads and radio public service announcements recorded by members of Congress. The new law was enacted with the goal of increasing the number of potential organ donors and encouraging potential donors to discuss their decisions with family members.[118]

In the current managed care environment, with intensified scrutiny of health care costs, questions surround the possible surplus of transplantation centers, as discussed at the first joint annual meeting of UNOS and the DHHS Division of Organ Transplantation.[119] Statistics indicated that 40% of kidney transplant centers were performing fewer than 25 transplants a year and that 40% of liver transplant centers were performing fewer than 15 transplants per year, accounting for only 8% of livers transplanted in the United States. In contrast, the 20 largest liver transplant centers were performing 76% of the liver transplants. Since centers with a higher volume of cases seemed to have better outcomes, performance criteria were suggested as a basis for determining whether a new transplant program should be approved and whether an existing program should be allowed to continue with government support. Evidence also indicated that the cost of a transplant generally decreases as the volume of cases increases at a center. For many U.S. citizens, availability of transplant centers will be determined by these considerations.

The HCFA published a final rule in May 1996 setting performance standards for organizations that procure organs for transplantation under the Medicare and Medicaid programs. The final rule modified some of the requirements contained in the interim final rule, allowing greater flexibility regarding performance criteria. Flexibility is important to transplantation, a field of medicine that continues to develop and adapt.

ENDNOTES

1. United Network of Organ Sharing (UNOS) Update (Richmond, Va., Summer 1997).
2. Tissue Banking Data (Washington Regional Transplant Consortium, Washington, D.C. Summer 1997).
3. *UNOS 1996 Annual Report on The Scientific Registry of Transplant Recipients and The Organ Procurement and Transplantation Network* (Richmond, Va. 1996).
4. UNOS Membership Data, http://www.ew3.att.net/UNOS.
5. 2 The UNOS Bulletin (July 1997).
6. National Task Force on Organ Transplantation, *Organ Transplantation: Issues and Recommendations* (DHHS, Washington, D.C., GPO # 1986-O-160-709, 1986).
7. *Id.*
8. Uniform Anatomical Gift Act (1968), National Conference of Commissioners.
9. Uniform Anatomical Gift Act (1987), National Conference of Commissioners on Uniform State Laws (Chicago 1987); §8A U.L.A. 16 (Supp. 1989).
10. §8A U.L.A. 2 (Supp. 1996); §8A U.L.A. 9 (Supp. 1996).
11. *New Developments in Biotechnology: Ownership of Human Tissues and Cells—Special Report* (Office of Technology Assessment, U.S. Government Printing Office, Washington, D.C. 1987).
12. P. Matthews, *Whose Property?: People as Property*, Current Legal Problems 193-239 (1983).
13. *In re Moyer's Estate*, 577 P. 2d 108 (1978).
14. *Holland v. Metalious*, 198 A. 2d 654 (1964).
15. *Leno v. St. Joseph Hospital*, 302 N.E. 2d 58 (1973).
16. *Nicoletta v. Rochester Eye and Human Parts Bank*, 519 N.Y.S. 2d 928 (1987).
17. *Williams v. Hofmann*, 223 N.W. 2d 844 (1974).
18. *Ravenis v. Detroit General Hospital*, 234 N.W. 2d 411 (1976).
19. *Supra* note 9.
20. Maximus, Inc., *Assessment of the Potential Organ Donor Pool: Report to Health Resources and Services Agency* (DHHS, Washington, D.C. 1985).
21. *Organ Transplantation Q & A* (DHHS, Division of Organ Transplantation, Washington, D.C., DHHS Pub. No. [HRS-M-SP] 89-1, 1988).
22. K.J. Bart et al., *Increasing the Supply of Cadaveric Kidneys for Transplantation*, 31 Transplantation 383-387 (1981).
23. S.W. Tolle et al., *Responsibilities of Primary Physicians in Organ Donation*, 106 Ann. Int. Med. 740-744 (1987).
24. J. Prottas, *The Structure and Effectiveness of the U.S. Organ Procurement System*, 22 Inquiry 365-376 (1985).
25. J.M. Prottas, *The Organization of Organ Procurement*, 14 J. Health Politics, Pol. & L. 41-55 (1989).

to receive organs, in order to facilitate matching the compatibility of such individuals with organ donors,

(F) coordinate, as appropriate, the transportation of organs from organ procurement organizations to transplant centers,

(G) provide information to physicians and other health professionals regarding organ donation, and

(H) collect, analyze, and publish data concerning organ donation and transplants.

Scientific registry

Sec. 274a. The Secretary shall, by grant or contract, develop and maintain a scientific registry of the recipients of organ transplants. The registry shall include such information respecting patients and transplant procedures as the Secretary deems necessary to an ongoing evaluation of the scientific and clinical status of organ transplantation. The Secretary shall prepare for inclusion in the report under section 274b an analysis of information derived from the registry.

General provisions respecting grants and contracts

Sec. 274b. (a) No grant may be made under section 273 or 274a or contract entered into under section 274 or 274a unless an application therefore has been submitted to, and approved by, the Secretary. Such an application shall be in such form and shall be submitted in such manner as the Secretary shall by regulation prescribe.

(b) (1) In considering applications for grants under section 273—

(A) the Secretary shall give priority to any applicant which has a formal agreement of cooperation with all transplant centers in its proposed service area,

(B) the Secretary shall give special consideration to organizations which met the requirements of section 273(b) before the date of the enactment of this section, and

(C) the Secretary shall not discriminate against an applicant solely because it provides health care services other than those related to organ procurement.

(D) The Secretary may not make a grant for more than one organ procurement organization which serves the same service area.

(2) A grant for planning under section 273 may be made for one year with respect to any organ procurement organization and may not exceed $100,000.

(3) Grants under section 371 for the establishment, initial operation, or expansion of organ procurement organizations may be made for two years. No such grant may exceed $500,000 for any year and no organ procurement organization may receive more than $800,000 for initial operation or expansion.

(c) (1) The Secretary shall determine the amount of a grant made under section 273 or 274a. Payments under such grants may be made in advance on the basis of estimates or by the way of reimbursement, with necessary adjustments on account of underpayments or overpayments, and in such installments and on such terms and conditions as the Secretary finds necessary to carry out the purposes of such grants.

(2) (A) Each recipient of a grant under section 273 or 274a shall keep such records as the Secretary shall prescribe, including records which fully disclose the amount and disposition by such recipient of the proceeds of such grant, the total cost of the undertaking in connection with which such grant was made, and the amount of that portion of the cost of the undertaking supplied by other sources, and such other records as will facilitate an effective audit.

(B) The Secretary and the Comptroller General of the United States, or any of their duly authorized representatives, shall have access for the purpose of audit and examination to any books, documents, papers, and records of the recipient of a grant under section 273 or 274a that are pertinent to such grant.

(d) For purposes of this part:

(1) The term "transplant center" means a health care facility in which transplants of organs are performed.

(2) The term "organ" means the human kidney, liver, heart, lung, pancreas, and any other human organ (other than corneas and eyes) specified by the Secretary by regulation and for purposes of section 274a; such term includes bone marrow.

Administration

Sec. 274c. The Secretary shall, during fiscal years 1985, 1986, 1987, and 1988, designate and maintain an identifiable administrative unit in the Public Health Service to—

(1) administer this part and coordinate with the organ procurement activities under Title XVIII of the Social Security Act,

(2) conduct a program of public information to inform the public of the need for organ donations,

(3) provide technical assistance to organ procurement organizations receiving funds under section 273, the Organ Procurement and Transplantation Network established under section 274, and other entities in the health care system involved in organ donations, procurement, and transplants, and

(4) one year after the date on which the Task Force on Organ Transplantation transmits its final report under section 104(c) of the National Organ Transplant Act, and annually thereafter through fiscal year 1988, submit to Congress an annual report on the status of organ donation and coordination services and include in the report an analysis of the efficiency and effectiveness of the procurement and allocation of organs and a description of problems encountered in the procurement and allocation of organs.

Report

Sec. 274d. The Secretary shall annually publish a report on the scientific and clinical status of organ transplantation. The Secretary shall consult with the Director of the National Institutes of Health and the Commissioner of the Food and Drug Administration in the preparation of the report.

TITLE III—PROHIBITION OF ORGAN PURCHASES

Sec. 274e. (a) It shall be unlawful for any person to knowingly acquire, receive, or otherwise transfer any human organ for valuable consideration for use in human transplantation if the transfer affects interstate commerce.

(b) Any person who violates subsection (a) shall be fined not more than $50,000 or imprisoned not more than five years, or both.

(c) For purposes of subsection (a):

(1) The term "human organ" means the human kidney, liver, heart, lung, pancreas, bone marrow, cornea, eye, bone, and skin, and any other human organ specified by the Secretary of Health and Human Services by regulation.

(2) The term "valuable consideration" does not include the reasonable payments associated with the removal, transportation, implantation, processing, preservation, quality control, and storage of a human organ or the expense of travel, housing, and lost wages incurred by the donor of a human organ in connection with the donation of the organ.

(3) The term "interstate commerce" has the meaning prescribed for it by section 201(b) of the Federal Food, Drug and Cosmetic Act.

TITLE IV—MISCELLANEOUS

Bone marrow registry demonstration and study

Secs. 274f and 274g. (a) Not later than nine months after the date of enactment of this Act, the Secretary of Health and Human Services shall hold a conference on the feasibility of establishing and the effectiveness of a national registry of voluntary bone marrow donors.

(b) If the conference held under subsection (a) finds that it is feasible to establish a national registry of voluntary donors of bone marrow and that such a registry is likely to be effective in matching donors with recipients, the Secretary of Health and Human Services, acting through the Assistant Secretary for Health, shall, for purposes of the study under subsection (c), establish a registry of voluntary donors of bone marrow. The Secretary shall assure that—

(1) donors of bone marrow listed in the registry have given an informed consent to the donation of bone marrow; and

(2) the names of the donors in the registry are kept confidential and access to the names and any other information in the registry is restricted to personnel who need the information to maintain and implement the registry, except that access to such other information shall be provided for purposes of the study under subsection (c).

If the conference held under subsection (a) makes the finding described in this subsection, the Secretary shall establish the registry not later than six months after the completion of the conference.

(c) The Secretary of Health and Human Services, acting through the Assistant Secretary for Health, shall study the establishment and implementation of the registry under subsection (b) to identify the issues presented by the establishment of such a registry, to evaluate participation of bone marrow donors, to assess the implementation of the informed consent and confidentiality requirements, and to determine if the establishment of a permanent bone marrow registry is needed and appropriate. The Secretary shall report the results of the study to the Committee on Energy and Commerce of the House of Representatives and the Committee on Labor and Human Resources of the Senate not later than two years after the date the registry is established under subsection (b).

Approved October 19, 1984.

Life Care Planning: Ethical and Legal Issues

ELLEN BARKER, M.S.N., R.N., A.P.N., C.N.R.N., C.L.C.P., A.B.D.A.
MICHAEL F. SAULINO, M.D., Ph. D.

Life care planning is an important and dynamic process that has significant value as a legal tool, a clinical tool, in discharge planning, rehabilitation and post-discharge for patients with long-term or lifetime disabilities.[1] It is a new trend in care planning that has recently emerged as a specialty associated with catastrophic case management.[2] This chapter will introduce and define the specialty of life care planning, describe the life care plan (LCP) process, and review the history of life care planning. Previously published ethics and scope of practice will be included.[3] The reader will learn how life care planning was first introduced in the legal system in the 1980s and how professional life care planners have successfully expanded the practice to include broader applications. Knowledge of the ethical and legal issues of life care planning is important for representatives of the legal profession to understand as they encounter life care plans as accepted instruments in the courts and other legal settings. Unlike other existing medical documents, life care planning outlines the present and future lifetime needs of individuals with catastrophic injury or long-term chronic health needs, including associated costs. The LCP assists the client, their families, and health care providers with a well-defined plan of care to maintain a consistent high level of individualized care with provisions for funding and resources over the expected lifetime of the disabled individual.

LIFE CARE PLANNING PROCESS

Simply put, a life care plan is a document that attempts to estimate what health services and special needs are likely to be required by a particular individual for the duration of their life. It is a dynamic document based upon published standards of practice, comprehensive assessment, data analysis, and research. It provides an organized, concise plan for current and future needs, with associated costs for individuals who have experienced catastrophic injury or have chronic health care needs. Common diagnoses that currently utilize life care planning include conditions such as children with special health care needs, e.g., anoxic encephalopathy or cerebral palsy (CP); traumatic injuries, e.g., traumatic brain injury (TBI) and spinal cord injury (SCI); adults with chronic neurological disorders, e.g., multiple sclerosis; and older adults with conditions, e.g., dementias.

Specific steps are followed after the life care planner has been retained to prepare an LCP. A letter, contract, or verbal agreement initiates the first step in the process. Once both parties have agreed on the terms and conditions, the life care planner obtains written permission to review all records, contact all members of the client's treating team, attend client visits with physicians and other health care providers, and contact teachers, or employers at work sites.

A complete set of medical records is needed from the date of injury/illness to discharge from all facilities, significant past medical records, work records and evaluations, and school records (if the client is a student). All employment and salary records, performance evaluations, attendance records, and sick visits should be made available. Tax records for the past 5 years should be reviewed to establish earnings and assets. Attorneys who request an LCP should submit copies of all legal documents.

One of the most important aspects of the process is the initial interview scheduled when the client, family, and attending caregivers are available. It is important for the life care planner to make an independent evaluation and complete data collection in the home or setting where the client resides.

The four steps that are typically utilized in the formation of an LCP are: (1) determination of the extent of the individual's impairments with their resultant disability and handicap; (2) estimation of short- and long-term prognosis; (3) estimation of the need for and benefit of further medical, nursing, or facility care and rehabilitative interventions; and (4) identify providers of the services, equipment, and other needs with calculation of the costs in the region where the individual lives. This information is obtained in consultation with physicians. The data is organized into tables for easy reference, future reevaluations, and for the economist.

Impairment, disability, and handicap have been defined by the World Health Organization. Impairments are a loss or abnormality of psychological, physiological, or anatomical structure or function. It is the dysfunction caused by the disease process at the molecular, cellular, tissue, organ, or organ system level. Examples would include pain, weakness, confusion, etc. Disabilities are any restriction or lack of ability to perform an activity in the manner or within the range considered normal for a human being that results from impairment. It is dysfunction recognized at the level of an individual. Examples include impaired locomotion, hygiene, dressing, etc. Handicaps are disadvantages for a given individual resulting from an impairment or disability that limits or prevents the fulfillment of a role that is normal for that individual. It is dysfunction that is present at the societal level. Examples might include impaired social interactions or employment possibilities.

The prognostic aspect of an LCP is paramount. Disease processes can have a variety of courses including static, progressive, and relapsing. The LCP must include a statement of disease prognosis both in terms of the primary disease and with regard to comorbidities and sequelae. An astute LCP will also address the interaction of the primary disease process with the normal sequelae of aging. For example, a young patient with chronic paraplegia due to spinal cord injury may easily utilize a manual wheelchair for mobility. As this individual experiences normal neuromusculoskeletal aging, a power wheelchair may be required. Lastly, no prognostic assessment is complete without some estimation of life expectancy. With increasing improvement in medical care, chronically disabled individuals are attaining longer postinjury life expectancy. Estimated life expectancy can be discussed with the physicians and documented in the LCP using published government tables.

The life care planner must develop a comprehensive assessment of a patient's health and functional needs. Items that should be considered may include the following: medications (both prescription and over the counter), medical supplies, durable medical equipment (ambulatory and ADL devices, orthotics, prosthetics, etc.), physician visits, nursing, attendant care at home or facility care, rehabilitative therapies, educational/vocational services, architectural/structural modifications, psychiatric and/or psychological counseling, adapted recreation (hippotherapy, aquatic, or other recreational activities), wheelchairs, case management, transportation, medical care, and identification of potential complications (see Table 26-1).

Once the required components of the LCP are identified, the incurred cost must be quantified. This assessment would include purchase, repair, and maintenance of equipment as well as duration, frequency, and intensity of medication supplies, and provider interactions. The economist should extrapolate these costs across the anticipated life expectancy with an appropriate adjustment for inflation.

HISTORY OF LIFE CARE PLANNING

Deutsch and Raffa introduced the term "life care plan" into the legal literature in 1981 in the publication *Damages in Tort Actions*. This publication identified guidelines for specifying damages in civil litigation cases.[4] In 1985, Deutsch and Sawyer introduced the concept to the rehabilitation profession when they published the classic *Guide to Rehabilitation*. They identified an LCP as a part of the rehabilitation evaluation to project the impact of catastrophic injury on an individual's future.[4] Rehabilitation professionals recognized the value of an LCP. Following numerous requests, Deutsch offered the first educational program to a group of 100 professionals in the fall of 1986 in Hilton Head, South Carolina.

Following the pioneering efforts of Deutsch and others, there were demands for a formalized curriculum and program. Requests came from health care professionals representing various disciplines throughout the United States who requested to enroll in a program that would prepare them as a "life care planner." In 1992, a group of rehabilitation professionals developed the first educational curriculum designed for the life care planning process. An eight-tract, 180-hour training program included tenets, process, methods, medical basics in catastrophic cases, forensic issues, and business and ethical practice.[4] After a successful trial period of course offerings, the founding group of rehabilitation professionals gave this program to the University of Florida. Horace Sawyer, from the faculty, developed the program into a joint public-private relationship between the Rehabilitation

process as early as the acute hospitalization (see Fig. 26-1). They can be refined during the recovery and acute rehabilitative phase. Each phase of rehabilitation requires assessment (which include definition of functional problems), setting of functional goals, ongoing progress reports addressing current status, and an estimation of trajectory for goal attainment (see Fig. 26-1).

The physiatrist's roles in the life care planning process may include medical interventions toward the disease process or "symptom management," integration and leadership of a multidisciplinary team, patient/family education, and communication with external providers (payers, referring physicians, etc.). This LCP may be reevaluated and modified several times during the patient's disease course and in multiple settings (acute hospital, rehabilitation center, outpatient, or home). The LCP can be potentially finalized with a reasonably comprehensive LCP in place by the patient's time of discharge from an acute rehabilitation center.

Life care plans should undergo regular revisions through routine evaluative assessments. Physiatrist or other physician input into a life care plan can ascertain the medical necessity of the entities defined within the LCP that provide the legal system with the required degree of medical expertise.[9]

At subsequent physician visits that will continue for the remainder of the individual's lifetime, the LCP provides physicians with a written organized, comprehensive plan and summary of care that promotes continuity of care. In addition to the physiatrist and neurorehabilitation physicians, the client with severe deficits may have treating physicians from multiple specialties, as indicated in Table 26-2.

REFERRAL SOURCES

An LCP can originate in the rehabilitation setting as described above, or requested by a family member with a disabled child, spouse, or parent; an insurance company with the need to establish a reserve fund for insurance compensation or workers' compensation claims; or an attorney for civil litigation or mediation purposes who represents clients who have sustained severe injuries or illnesses.[1] Other areas where an LCP may be appropriate include:

- Health insurance companies
- Long-term disability cases
- Special needs trust for children or impaired adults
- Workers' compensation
- Elder or older adult care facilities
- Acute or subacute rehabilitation facilities
- Long-term facilities with special populations, e.g., dementia units or supervised living programs.

A child, for example, born with severe congenital deficits may remain in the home setting until adulthood with parents and caregivers providing 24-hour services. As the parents become older adults with the realization that their child's life expectancy is greater than their own lifespans, they often seek legal counsel to prepare for the child's future care after their death. In this scenario, a life care planner can work closely with the attorney and family to prepare an LCP. The LCP can be reviewed and approved by the parents with the reassurance that all the necessary provisions and funds are in place for the child's life expectancy.

Attorneys who specialize in medical malpractice, workers' compensation insurance carriers, and insurance companies are the most common sources of referrals.[5] For example, when an attorney has a client who has suffered an acute SCI, he can rely on a life care planner for the following: (1) assess their client, (2) work with them to ensure that the individual will have a good quality of life after their injury, and (3) develop a cost-effective plan of care to help prevent complications and unnecessary rehospitalizations.

COMPLETION OF THE LIFE CARE PLAN

The LCP continues to emerge as an effective method for the prediction of future care costs. In civil litigation, plaintiff and defense attorneys have increasingly turned to the use of an LCP in medical malpractice for trial preparation. The role and responsibilities of life care planners in litigation, rehabilitation, and other situations described above will continue to evolve and grow. The researched and completed LCP is unparalleled in compiling the most comprehensive assessment and plan of care for disabled individuals. Implementation by the health care providers and continuing case management maximizes continuity of care and quality of life.

THE LIFE CARE PLAN AS A LEGAL DOCUMENT

When attorneys for personal injury litigation request an LCP, the life care planner prepares the document using a format that will be acceptable in the jurisdiction where the

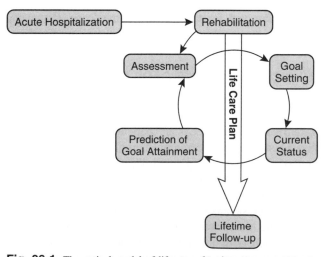

Fig. 26-1. Theoretical model of life care planning process within the medical model.

TABLE 26-2 Life care plan future evaluations: example of future physician and other health care provider's evaluation for client with severe traumatic brain injury (TBI)

Therapy	Age/year to start	Age/year to stop	Frequency of evaluations/year	Annual cost/year	Economic growth trend	Recommended by
Physiatrist	Age 21	Life expectancy	1-2 × year	$120-$200 per evaluation	To be determined by economist	Physiatrist
Neurologist	Age 21	Life expectancy	1 × year	$260 per evaluation	To be determined by economist	Neurologist
Family physician or internist	Age 21	Life expectancy	1-2 × year (beyond the usual yearly exam) abnormalities and complications	$85-$155 per evaluation depending on office procedures/tests	To be determined by economist	Family physician or internist
Orthopedist	Age 21	Life expectancy	Yearly	$260 per evaluation for specialty care	To be determined by economist	Orthopedic surgeon
Pulmonologist	Age 21	Life expectancy	Yearly	$260 per evaluation	To be determined by economist	Pulmonologist
Urologist	Age 45	Life expectancy	Yearly	$260 per evaluation	To be determined by economist	Urologist
Speech/language	Age 21	Life expectancy	Yearly	$85-$100 per evaluation	To be determined by economist	Physiatrist
Physical therapy	Age 21	Life expectancy	Yearly	$85 per evaluation	To be determined by economist	Physiatrist
Occupational therapy	Age 21	Life expectancy	Yearly	$85 per evaluation	To be determined by economist	Physiatrist
Recreational therapy (hippotherapy)	Age 21	Age 35	Yearly	$25-$50 per evaluation	To be determined by economist	Physiatrist
Aquatic therapy	Age 21	Life expectancy	Yearly	$85 per evaluation	To be determined by economist	Physiatrist
Podiatrist	Age 21	Life expectancy	Monthly	$59 per month or $708 per year	To be determined by economist	Physiatrist and case manager
Psychiatrist	Age 21	Life expectancy	Yearly	$150-$200 per evaluation	To be determined by economist	Psychiatrist
Dentist	Age 21	Life expectancy	Every 6 months beyond routine	$85-100 per evaluation	To be determined by economist	Dentist
Neuro-ophthalmologist	Age 21	Life expectancy	Yearly	$250 per evaluation	To be determined by economist	Neuro-ophthalmologist
Nutritionist	Age 21	Life expectancy	Yearly	$120 per evaluation	To be determined by economist	Nutritionist
Independent case manager	Age 21	Life expectancy	20 hours year 1; 12-15 hours per year for the next 10 years; then 52 hours/year thereafter	$50-$100 per hour	To be determined by economist	Independent case manager

LCP is to be presented at trial. Life care planners are listed as either the plaintiff or defense expert and must be fully aware of the legal rules of the court. Before trial, the attorney can assist the life care planner in defining legal terms that may have a different meaning in a courtroom than in the health care system.

Both the plaintiff and defense attorneys may retain the services of a life care planner. Each life care planner may be requested by the attorney to review and critique the LCP of the opposing side. From the perspective of evaluating the needs of the client, the two life care plans may appear very similar if the published standards of life care planning have been applied. Opinions of the life care planner should not be biased on whether the testimony is for a plaintiff or defense case.

Once the life care planner has presented testimony regarding their education, credentials, and background information, the court may be asked to accept the witness as a qualified expert. During testimony the life care planner will educate the court about the client's unique and individualized needs.

Regardless of whether it is a plaintiff or defense life care plan, the life care planner will certainly be able to testify in a persuasive manner. During testimony the life care planner can explain to the jury in a compelling manner the rationale for items included in the LCP and be prepared to defend the LCP against tough questioning during cross-examination. Various methods for exhibits from the LCP can be used during courtroom testimony. Charts can be prepared from the LCP to allow the jury and members of the court to follow the items described during testimony. PowerPoint presentations are possible in some of the newer courtrooms equipped with sophisticated electronic technology. The life care planner should explore the most effective options with the attorney and follow the rules of evidence.

Important legal considerations include the individual's life expectancy, guardianship to control the funds, implementation of the LCP, delineation of health care providers, and how the needs and services will be funded.

LEGAL AND ETHICAL PRINCIPLES

Legal or ethical conflicts of life care planning can be avoided by considering the following:

- Maintain honesty and trustworthiness in all matters. Patient and client confidentiality has become an increased area of liability.
- Strict client confidentiality of all records and client information.
- Obtain informed consent or permission in writing from the client before initiating the LCP.
- Store the LCP for a minimum of 5 years.
- Never inflate costs in order to increase the overall cost of the LCP when researching the cost of services and equipment.
- Physicians or other individuals should not be contacted for opinions or information unless the client has signed written permission forms that can be presented in person or by mail.
- Immediately identify and report any conflicts of interest during the preparation of the LCP.
- Complete the LCP within the agreed-upon time frame to avoid delaying any court or legal proceedings. A "tickler file" should be maintained for all deadlines and completion of the LCP.
- Consider developing written policies or procedures for defining and describing the preparation of an LCP that can be provided to an attorney or individuals requesting services.
- Establish a fee schedule that is mutually accepted by the life care planner and the client retaining the services.

In litigation, life care plans prepared by certified life care planners are used to determine the duration and cost of future medical care. Case examples include *Balance v. Wal-Mart Stores*.[10] Courts frequently rely on life care plans to determine future damages (see, e.g., *Osborne v. United States*).[11] Texas courts have recognized the validity and usefulness of life care plans in *Exxon Corp. v. Starr*.[12] These and other legal citations can be reviewed in an amicus curiae brief prepared by Richard N. Countiss, an attorney in Houston, Texas.[13]

ROLE OF THE ECONOMIST

Development and pricing of an LCP are parts of personal injury litigation. After the final LCP document has been completed by the life care planner, the attorney or life care planner may retain the services of a qualified economist. The economist's role is to use the LCP to prepare the economic report with the final or total price. The economist may also serve as an expert at trial. A forensic economist is retained who can use special techniques to project future costs of services and equipment included in the LCP. Economists who routinely work with life care plans have developed a methodology for projecting the cost of each category at various growth rates.[14] The economist's job is much easier when the life care planner has carefully prepared tables for each category listing associated costs as shown in Table 26-2.

A rehabilitation or vocational counselor will evaluate the individual's ability to work, loss of earning capacity, or loss of the ability to be employed. The economist will use the results of experts as to whether or not to include calculation of lost wages. Economic or special damages, in addition to the cost of all past and projected future medical care, should include lost wages. The medical experts will assess the individual to determine whether or not they are incapable of working or capable of working part- or full-time to earn a living at any time in the future. It is important for the life care planner or attorney representing the client to provide copies of past wages for an adult with a work history, highest educational level achieved, current occupation history, and proof of enrollment in any educational/training programs. Pediatric cases are more difficult for the economist to quantify. Past educational preparation of the parents and their occupations are often entered into the economist's equation in projecting a child's potential occupation or lost wages.

The LCP is always costed in today's dollars, without regard to cost-of-living inflation or other economic factors. It is up to the economist to ensure that the final cost projection conforms to local jurisdiction rulings. Costs should reflect the usual and customary rates in the geographic area proximate to the injured person's home.[15] The combined testimonies and exhibits of the life care planner and economist at trial using a life care plan for clients with extensive and complicated care provides the jury with a simple exhibit to guide their decision on damages.

CONCLUSION

Life care planning is a new specialty in health care and rehabilitation. A valid LCP has many benefits for an individual who is ill or disabled with permanent and lifelong disabilities that require expensive and complicated care. An LCP gives caregivers and families a clear, well-defined individualized plan of care. Major considerations in the cost of funds for an LCP focus on the individual's life expectancy, the level of care needed, where the care will be provided (home versus facility care), whether the individual will ever work, and the need for a barrier-free environment for safety and functional livability. Unlike a typical discharge plan, an LCP includes the management that continues across the life expectancy of the individual with a disability. Additional benefits of an LCP may also include prevention of complications, prevention of future medical emergencies, enhanced quality of life and self-esteem, security in financial planning, availability of funds and resources, and cost-effectiveness for future physical and psychosocial care.

RESOURCES

Commission on Health Care Certification (CHCC)
http://www.cdec1.com

International Academy of Life Care Planners
www.internationalacademyoflifecareplnners.com

Life Care Planning, University of Florida
www.intelicu.com

Neuroscience Nursing Consultants
www.neuronurse.com

The Tailiant Life Care Planning Group
www.tailiant.com/109

ENDNOTES

1. E. Barker, *Legal Issues and Life Care Planning*, in E. Barker (ed.), *Neuroscience Nursing: A Spectrum of Care* (St. Louis: Mosby, 2002).
2. E. Barker, *Evolution/Revolution: The Life Care Plan*, 62(3) R.N. 58-61(1999).
3. S.L. Reavis, *Standards of Practice*, 1(1) Journal of Life Care Planning 49-58 (2002).
4. P. McCollom & R. Weed, *Life Care Planning: Yesterday and Today*, 1(1) Journal of Life Care Planning 3(2002).
5. A.T. Neulicht, S. Riddick-Graham, et al., *Life Care Planning Survey 2001: Process, Methods, and Protocols*, 1(2) Journal of Life Care Planning 97-148 (2002).
6. D.M. Lowell, C. Madison & B. Sibley, *Pediatric and Adult Life Care Planning: The Benefits of a Physician-Driven Clinical Model*, Medical Case Management Convention (MCMC XIV), Denver, CO (Sept. 26, 2002).
7. R. Katz & G. Delancey, *Life Care Planning*, 13 Physical Medicine and Rehabilitation Clinics of North America 287-308 (2002).
8. R.L. Kirby, *Impairment, Disability, and Handicap,* in J. Delisa (ed.), *Rehabilitation Medicine: Principles and Practices*, 2d ed., 40-50. Philadelphia: Lippincott Co. (2002).
9. R.P. Bonfiglio, *The Role of Physiatrist in Life Care Planning*, in R. Weed (ed.), *Life Care Planning and Case Management Handbook*, 15-22 (Boca Raton: CRC Press, 1999).
10. 178 F. 3d 1282 (4th Cir. 1999).
11. 166 F. Supp. 479, 494 (S.D W. Va. 2001).
12. 790 S.W. 2d 883 (Tex. App.-Tyler 1990, no writ).
13. R.N. Countiss, 1(1) Journal of Life Care Planning 9-33 (2002).
14. M.J. Piette, *The Economist's Role in Establishing Damages in Litigation*, 13(3) Journal of Legal Nurse Consulting 16-21 (2002).
15. M. Yudkoff, *The Life Care Planning Expert*, in J.B. Bogart (ed.), *Legal Nursing Consulting: Principles and Practice* (Boca Raton: CRC Press, 1998).

The Process of Dying

BEN A. RICH, J.D., Ph.D.

DETERMINATION OF DEATH
THE DYING PATIENT
CONCLUSION

The subject of this chapter intersects with a wide range of important topics in legal medicine and biomedical ethics. Our survey of the critical concepts and issues related to the process of dying will proceed in the following manner. The first section of the chapter is devoted to the general theme of the determination of death. We begin with a brief analysis of current thinking about the nature of human death and its relationship to medical practice, with special attention devoted to brain death. Next, we consider matters such as certification of death, ascertainment of the cause of death, and issues of consent for autopsy and custody and control of the body.

The second, more extensive section of the chapter is devoted to issues arising out of the care of dying patients. Particularly in the last 10-12 years, issues concerning what constitutes appropriate care at the end of life have received an unprecedented level of attention and critical analysis. We will compare and contrast the traditional and modern views of the goals of medicine and the models of disease, with particular focus on their relevance to the care of dying patients. We then consider the implications for the identification of and care for dying patients inherent in the massive Study to Understand Prognoses, Preferences for Outcomes, and Risks of Treatment (SUPPORT) and the voluminous analysis of the data generated by it. Next, we discuss the concept of medical futility and the role that it plays in decisions to withhold or withdraw life-sustaining interventions such as mechanical ventilation and artificial nutrition and hydration, as well as in the utilization of "do not resuscitate" (DNR) orders. In the final sections of the chapter, we discuss the developing field of palliative medicine and its response to the widespread phenomenon of undertreated pain, in the process of which we briefly consider the newly resurgent doctrine of double effect (DDE) and the distinction between appropriately aggressive palliative interventions and physician-assisted suicide (PAS) or voluntary active euthanasia. We take careful note of an emerging stan-

dard of care for dying patients, as well as the legal implications (administrative, civil, and criminal) of such standards for the physician.

DETERMINATION OF DEATH

There is a strong consensus among experts in medicine and related fields such as biomedical ethics that human death is a process, not an event.[1] Consequently, in adopting and implementing a particular formulation of death and declaring persons dead according to it, we are not discovering but rather deciding that the person is dead. While there is a certain inescapable arbitrariness to such declarations, there need not be any capriciousness so long as the formulations are consistent with the most current scientific knowledge. Such declarations at an appropriate and specific point in time are essential for a host of legal and social reasons. Nevertheless, the relatively rapid move during the 1970s and early 1980s toward the inclusion of brain death as a basis for determining death has not been without residual confusion and controversy.[2] When the traditional cardiopulmonary formulation of death was the exclusive basis upon which to determine death, there was no question that when a physician concluded that there had been complete cessation of cardiopulmonary function, there arose a duty to pronounce the person dead. However, with the advent of the brain death formulation, it could plausibly be suggested that when a physician ascertained that the criteria for brain death had been met, there was simply an opportunity, but not necessarily an obligation, to forthwith declare the person dead.[3] The point at which a patient was declared brain dead not infrequently was the point at which negotiations concerning the withdrawal of "life support" began with reluctant family members. The problem was, in no small measure, a product of the fact that such "patients" looked the same to their families after brain death was declared as they had earlier, when they had been receiving very aggressive treatment.

Brain death

The introduction of the concept of brain death is ascribed to the 1968 report issued by an Ad Hoc Committee of the Harvard Medical School.[4] The objective of the report was "to *define* irreversible coma as a new *criterion* for death."[5] What subsequently came to be known as the "Harvard Criteria" were the following:

1. Unreceptivity and unresponsivity: a total unawareness of externally applied stimuli and inner need and complete unresponsiveness, despite application of intensely painful stimuli.
2. No spontaneous movements or breathing: absence of all spontaneous muscular movements or breathing, as well as absence of response to stimuli such as pain, touch, sound, or light.
3. No reflexes: fixed, dilated pupils; lack of eye movement despite turning the head or ice-water stimulus; lack of response to noxious stimuli; and generally, lack of elicitable deep tendon reflexes.

In addition, the committee advised confirmation of the above criteria by two electroencephalograms (EEGs) administered 24 hours apart, documenting the absence of cortical electrical activity above baseline. It was also considered essential to exclude the presence of any metabolic state, hypothermia, or drug intoxication that might cause or contribute to a reversible loss of brain activity.[6]

Beginning with Kansas in 1970, brain death statutes were, with remarkable rapidity and absence of controversy, adopted by many states. The statutes acknowledged alternative formulations of death—cardiopulmonary (irreversible cessation of circulatory and respiratory functions) and whole brain (irreversible cessation of all functions of the entire brain, including the brainstem)—either of which would support a physician's determination of death based on ordinary standards of medical practice. The Uniform Determination of Death Act (UDDA) has now been adopted by most states, and brain death has become a recognized basis for determining death throughout the United States.[7]

The President's Commission on "Defining Death"

In 1981, the President's Commission for the Study of Ethical Problems in Medicine and Biomedical and Behavioral Research published a report entitled *Defining Death*. In this report, the Commission readily acknowledged that "the basic concept of death is fundamentally a philosophical matter" in that "philosophical issues persist in the choice to define death in terms of organ systems, physiological functions, or recognizable human activities, capacities, and conditions."[8] Nevertheless, in arriving at the conclusion that the prevailing formulation of brain death, consistent with the UDDA, ought to be based on physiological functions, the Commission in essence maintained that the characteristic essentially significant to a human being is the capacity for bodily integration. Essential to this capacity is the brainstem. Hence, the brain death formulation must include permanent cessation of all brain function, including that of the brainstem.

Higher brain death. No discussion of brain death would be complete without at least brief consideration of the whole brain versus higher brain debate. The advocates of the higher brain death formulation, also referred to as neocortical or cognitive death, take issue with the Commission's conclusion as to the characteristic essentially significant to a human being. They maintain that the essential characteristic is the capacity for conscious experience. Cessation of higher brain function as a result of the destruction of the neocortical structures that sponsor consciousness permanently deprives the individual of the capacity for conscious experience and hence the ability to live the life of a person. That, the higher brain death advocates maintain, should be the basis upon which we determine human death, regardless of whether a functioning brainstem continues to support certain physiological functions of the body. Interestingly, Henry K. Beecher, the Chair of the Ad Hoc Committee that offered the original whole brain formulation of brain death, said in a later presentation to the American Association for the Advancement of Science that what is most essential to the nature of human beings is "the individual's personality, his conscious life, his uniqueness, his capacity for remembering, judging, reasoning, acting, enjoying, worrying, and so on."[9]

Another indication that the currently prevailing formulation of brain death does not enjoy universal acceptance is a New Jersey statutory exception to the application of brain death criteria when a physician has reason to believe that to do so would violate the personal religious beliefs of the patient. In such cases, death may not be declared until the cardiopulmonary criteria have been met.[10] At the present time, however, advocates of higher brain death do not have the option of being declared dead according to cognitive criteria or the permanent loss of neocortical function.

Death certificate

After the patient has been pronounced dead, the attending physician should prepare the working copy of the death certificate, which includes such information as name and address of the decedent, age, place and date of birth, names of parents (including mother's maiden name), birthplace of parents, race, and decedent's occupation. These data are included primarily for statistical and epidemiological purposes. A particularly significant feature of the death certificate is specification of the immediate and contributing causes.

When a patient has been receiving appropriately aggressive palliative measures in the terminal phase of an illness or incident to the withdrawal of life-sustaining interventions pursuant to patient or surrogate consent, it is very important to distinguish between the underlying terminal diagnosis and medical measures that are incident to it. This is also a concern with regard to the autopsy, since on occasion medical examiners have concluded that the cause of death in such instances was the result of the withdrawal of life support or the provision of analgesics rather than the patient's terminal diagnosis.[11] The immediate cause of death is not always necessarily the mechanism of death, such as cardiac arrest or ventricular fibrillation, but rather the condition that eventually resulted in death, such as myocardial infarction with arrhythmia.

From this working document, the final death certificate is usually prepared by the mortician, who then presents it to the physician for signature. In most states, disposition of the remains is not permitted until the attending physician has signed the death certificate in complete and final form.

Cause of death

As noted previously, the cause of death on the death certificate should be the immediate cause, i.e., the condition that resulted in death, rather than the mechanism of death. When the cause of death is obscure or the physician has not seen the patient within the time period specified by statute, state law usually requires that the medical examiner or coroner be contacted. Most states specify that such contact is essential when: the patient is a dead-on-arrival (DOA) case; the cause of death cannot be determined, e.g., because of an inadequate hospital stay or when death occurs within 24 hours of admission; sudden, violent, suspicious, unexpected, unexplained, or medically unattended death; all intraoperative or perioperative deaths (including preoperative and immediate postoperative deaths); deaths related to industrial employment; deaths resulting from therapeutic misadventure; death resulting from alleged, suspected, or known criminal activity; and death resulting from vehicular accidents, including train or airplane accidents.

Physician awareness of the circumstances warranting contact of the medical examiner or coroner is essential, as is the willingness to speak with such officials about the case. Requests for the results of the autopsy or a copy of the autopsy protocol for the physician's records are customarily honored.

Custody of the body and authorization for autopsy

Despite what will be said later in this chapter, as well as other chapters of this text, about patient autonomy and the legal and moral authority of advance directives, the pre-death request of a patient that an autopsy be performed is advisory only. Upon death, the next of kin are recognized by law to have a property interest in the decedent's body. Although the order of priority may vary from state to state,

generally it proceeds as follows: surviving spouse, eldest living adult child of the decedent, parent(s) of the decedent, legally appointed guardian, eldest living adult sibling, aunt(s) or uncle(s) of the decedent, or other relatives in order of consanguinity.

The consent for autopsy must follow the formal pronouncement of death, and the request for autopsy form should be executed by the appropriate person prior to the procedure. Consent may be limited to certain portions of the body. However, the physician should advise the consenting party that the quality and definitiveness of the autopsy results may be materially compromised by such limitations. Despite increasing evidence that the percentage of autopsies performed in the United States has steadily declined over the last few decades, the procedure is considered essential to an accurate assessment of the quality of care provided.[12] An autopsy may be necessary in some cases to determine what the patient died from, but it is absolutely essential to determine what the patient died with but had not been diagnosed during the life of the patient. The attending physician must strike a delicate balance in raising the issue of an elective autopsy with the next of kin between coercing consent from the unwilling and discouraging the procedure out of individual or institutional concerns about iatrogenic (physician-induced) conditions that may have resulted in death.

THE DYING PATIENT

Comparing the traditional view with the modern perspective

Historically, physicians were much more comfortable with death, which was viewed as the inevitable consequence of our mortality rather than medical failure. When there was far less that the physician could do to forestall death from a life-threatening illness, the relief of pain and suffering that attended the dying process was openly embraced as a core value and primary responsibility of the physician. With the advent of modern medicine, particularly the technologies that become the focus of the care of patients with life-threatening illness, death became the ultimate enemy of the physician, and the relief of suffering was the stepchild of the procedure-oriented subspecialist, resorted to only when high-tech medicine had "nothing more to offer." Indeed, as a major study of the last decade revealed, given our current preoccupation with critical care medicine, it has become increasingly difficult to determine when or even if a patient is dying.

The SUPPORT Study. The Study to Understand Prognosis, Preferences for Outcomes, and Risks of Treatment (SUPPORT) proposed to "improve end-of-life decision making and reduce the frequency of a mechanically supported, painful, and prolonged dying process."[13] In the Phase I data-gathering, major deficiencies in the care of dying patients in the intensive care units (ICUs) of five major academic medical centers were identified, including a disproportionality between the level of care provided and the patient's prognosis, as well as the pervasiveness of pain in the last days of life and a discontinuity between code status and the patient's or proxy's expressed wishes.[14] In reflection upon and further study of the abject failure of the interventional Phase II of SUPPORT to bring about any demonstrable improvement, the investigators noted that even when state-of-the-art prognostic models were combined with the judgment of highly skilled and experienced physicians, the median predicted chance of survival for 2 months was 17% on the day before death and 51% a full week before death.[15] Thus patients, families, and physicians in ICU settings tended to see the patient as a seriously ill person in need of treatment and not as "terminally ill" and certainly not as "dying." This phenomenon poses serious challenges to the timely provision of palliative interventions that have customarily been reserved for patients who are actively dying.[16] The antidote, it is increasingly suggested, is the concept of "simultaneous care," according to which pain and other troublesome symptoms are aggressively managed even as disease-directed interventions continue.[17]

Forgoing life-sustaining treatment. Issues concerning when, how, and by whose authority life-sustaining measures should be withdrawn continue to be the subject of dispute. In the decades of the 1970s and 1980s, many of the so-called "right to die" cases involved efforts by patients or their families to compel physicians to cease and desist from life-sustaining interventions that the patient/proxy deemed inappropriate or ineffective. Some of these cases were aptly described as examples of "therapeutic belligerence."[18] In 1990, the Supreme Court acknowledged: "The principle that a competent person has a constitutionally protected liberty interest in refusing unwanted medical treatment may be inferred from our prior decisions."[19] The young woman whose care was at issue in that case, Nancy Cruzan, was in a persistent vegetative state (PVS), and it was her parents who, as her surrogate decision-makers, sought the discontinuation of artificial nutrition and hydration.

While the courts have generally acknowledged that a competent patient's right to refuse treatment, including that without which they will die, survives even the permanent loss of decisional capacity, the states have been given wide latitude to impose stringent evidentiary standards on surrogate decision-makers. In imposing such standards, the states exercise their *parens patriae* power over vulnerable individuals. In some instances, the state actually becomes a party to the litigation and asserts one or more of four "countervailing interests" that the court must then balance against the interest of the patient in being free from unwanted medical intrusions. These state interests are consistently identified as: preserving life, preventing suicide, protecting the interests of innocent third parties (minor children), and upholding the ethical integrity of the medical profession.[20]

An important consequence of the right to die jurisprudence of the last 30 years has been a societal and legal consensus on the following propositions. First, the state has no legitimate interest in compelling a seriously ill or dying patient to continue to live when they would prefer to be allowed to die. Second, refusing life-sustaining measures does not constitute suicide. Third, individuals do not forfeit their right to refuse treatment by becoming parents. Fourth, it is not respect for but rather disregard of a patient's right to forgo necessary medical treatment that compromises the ethical integrity of the medical profession.

Medical futility

The pendulum has now begun to swing in the opposite direction, i.e., to cases in which patients or families seek to compel physicians to initiate or continue to provide interventions that are deemed medically inappropriate. The unfortunate term "medical futility" has been applied to such cases. The reason why "unfortunate" is an apt characterization is that efforts to develop a definition of futility that can claim even a modest consensus among physicians have themselves proven futile. One often-cited but also much criticized effort to define futility in the medical context advocates that "the adjective 'futile' be used to describe any effort to achieve a result that is possible but that reasoning or experience suggests is highly improbable and that cannot be systematically produced."[21] The Council on Ethical and Judicial Affairs of the AMA has eschewed any attempts to define futility or to delineate a set of futility criteria. However, it has noted that legitimate issues of futility arise in the context of providing life-sustaining interventions to patients who are permanently unconscious or actively dying.[22]

Despite well-intentioned efforts to distinguish between the quantitative and qualitative aspects of medical futility, the seemingly inescapable fact of the matter is that there is an inherently normative dimension to any conclusion that a particular intervention would be futile that necessarily takes it beyond the realm of purely objective clinical judgment.[23] A recent trend has been to shift the focus from efforts to define medical futility or to arrive at a broad consensus on paradigm cases of it, to multi-institutional policies and procedures for handling such disputes between physicians and patients or families. These process-oriented approaches have several positive features: they recognize and address the fact that such controversies are often the result of a breakdown in communication; they provide a mechanism for the mediation of disputes; and they specify an end-point at which the institution will, under appropriate circumstances, support a physician's decision not to provide measures that he or she deems medically inappropriate.[24]

One reason for the shift from definitions and paradigm cases to the dispute resolution approach may be the ambiguous treatment of futility cases by the courts. Perhaps the most notorious of these was *In re Baby K*,[25] a case in which a hospital and its clinical staff were deemed to be required by the federal Emergency Medical Treatment and Active Labor Act (EMTALA) to provide an anencephalic infant with the medical treatment necessary to stabilize her respiratory deficiencies when brought to the emergency room. The court found no futility exception to EMTALA.

In *Gilgun v. Massachusetts General Hospital*, an unreported case, a jury declined to find negligence on the part of Massachusetts General Hospital or a physician who entered a DNR order and subsequently withdrew life support from a 72-year-old woman over the objection of her daughter. The jury concluded that although there was credible evidence the patient would have wished to have life support continued, given her comorbidities (including significant brain damage) and poor prognosis, such measures were no longer medically appropriate.[26]

DNR orders and futility. A DNR order is unique in medicine in that it is the only instance in which an order must be written that some intervention not be provided. The justification for this anomalous situation is that the custom and practice in medicine is to resuscitate all patients who experience cardiopulmonary arrest. Thus an order is required to ensure that the standard procedure is not followed. While the autonomy of patients has been noted to be asymmetrical, in that a patient may decline medically necessary treatment but may not demand medically inappropriate treatment, institutional policies do not generally reflect this asymmetry. Opting for a risk management, litigation-adverse approach, many hospital policies do not clearly support a physician who, in the *Gilgun*-type situation, writes a DNR order over the objection of a patient with decisional capacity or a surrogate. Because of the vagaries of the concept of medical futility previously noted, a physician is always well advised to inform a patient and/or the patient's family that cardiopulmonary resuscitation is not appropriate under the circumstances and that an order to that effect will be entered in the medical record. Reasonable efforts should be undertaken to address questions or concerns and to clarify misunderstanding. The organized medical staff of each health care facility should advocate for a clearly written policy addressing DNR orders in the absence of patient/family consent.

Withholding and withdrawing treatment from patients without decisional capacity

It is important at this point to note an important distinction between competence and decisional capacity. Competence (or its reciprocal, incompetence) is a legal determination made by a court in a guardianship or conservatorship proceeding. Decisional capacity is a clinical determination that the patient's physician is medically qualified and legally authorized to make. Moreover, while many physicians seek a psychiatric consult (when readily available) prior to making such a determination, one is not required by law. The clinical literature also suggests, however, that the assessment of decisional capacity is not a skill that many physicians possess.[27] One common misunderstanding, for example, is that a diagnosis of depression negates decisional capacity.[28] When making such determinations, physicians should also be mindful that it is a fundamental principle of American jurisprudence that every adult is presumed to possess decisional capacity, and the burden of persuasion falls upon anyone who asserts the contrary.

The role of advance directives. Advance directives can be given orally or in writing. Many patients erroneously assume that oral directives will suffice, and hence do not execute written directives. The extent to which a patient's oral directive will ultimately influence decisions about his or her care varies greatly from case to case and from jurisdiction to jurisdiction. While most states will consider a patient's prior oral statements as indicative not only of their values and priorities, but also of what would be in their best interests, there are some jurisdictions that demand clear and convincing evidence that the patient expressed, during a prior period of decisional capacity, a desire not to receive a particular type of intervention, e.g., mechanical ventilation or artificial nutrition/hydration, when diagnosed with a condition identical or quite similar to the one in which they now find themselves, e.g., PVS, end-stage congestive heart failure.[29] Statutorily recognized advance directives are, at least in part, a legislative response to public demand for a mechanism by which an individual can prospectively exercise the right to make health care decisions during a subsequent period of decisional incapacity.

The first type of advance directive recognized by statute was the living will. In many instances, however, living will statutes promised much more than they delivered. Virtually all required that the patient be certified to be in a terminal condition before the document took effect, thereby excluding their use in some of the very circumstances—permanent coma, persistent vegetative state—that patients sought to avoid through their use. Also, many statutes specifically excluded artificial nutrition and hydration from the medical interventions that could be discontinued pursuant to a living will. Artificial nutrition and hydration is often the only intervention sustaining the life of permanently unconscious patients.

The next generation of advance directives, the durable power of attorney for health care, was not usually subjected to such severe restrictions. Once a patient has lost decisional capacity, in most jurisdictions the designated proxy is fully empowered to make all decisions regarding the patient's medical treatment, including directing that life-sustaining interventions be withheld or withdrawn, subject only to such restrictions as the patient may have incorporated into the document.

In 1990, Congress enacted the Patient Self-Determination Act,[30] requiring all health care institutions participating in the Medicare or Medicaid programs to advise each patient upon admission, or as soon thereafter as practicable, of his or her rights under state law to make decisions about their medical treatment and to execute an advance directive, as well as any policies of the institution or provider respecting the implementation of those rights. If the patient has or subsequently executes an advance directive, that must be documented in the medical record. While the Secretary of Health and Human Services has the authority to exclude noncompliant institutions from the Medicare and Medicaid programs, to date that has never happened.

The latest trend in advance directive legislation has been the adoption by a number of states of the Uniform Health-Care Decisions Act (UHCDA), which is designed to provide individuals with a single document in which they can give instructions for their medical care in the event of decisional incapacity, designate a surrogate, and indicate whether they wish to be an organ donor. There is also a residual decision-making section of the act that applies when there is no written directive. The UHCDA was adopted by the National Conference of Commissioners on Uniform State Laws in 1993 and has subsequently been adopted, in whole or significant part, by seven states.[31]

Despite significant legislative activity during the last 30 years, it remains the case that only about 15% of adults have executed any form of directive. Many reasons have been offered to explain this phenomenon, including physician disinclination to initiate these discussions with patients and patient reluctance to anticipate grave or life-threatening injury or illness.[32]

Care of the dying patient

The decade of the 1990s was one in which many deficiencies in the quality of care provided to dying patients were identified and reforms proposed. In addition to the SUPPORT data previously discussed, the Institute of Medicine published a major report calling for fundamental changes in the care of the dying.[33] One of the major concerns about the quality of care generally provided to dying patients is the widespread phenomenon of undertreated pain.[34] While nationally recognized clinical practice guidelines have been in existence for some time, there is compelling evidence that the custom and practice of most physicians is significantly below these parameters.[35]

Medical malpractice in end-of-life care. To date, two cases have produced jury verdicts for substandard care of a dying patient. The first case, *Estate of Henry James v. Hill-*

haven Corporation,[36] involved a 75-year-old patient who entered a skilled nursing facility with a diagnosis of terminal metastatic prostate cancer. A nursing supervisor declined to administer a pain management regimen developed at the local hospital because she believed the patient was addicted to opioid analgesics. A jury awarded the deceased patient's family $7.5 million in compensatory damages and $7.5 million in punitive damages because of the unnecessary pain and suffering this substandard care inflicted on the patient and his family.

The second case, *Bergman v. Chin,*[37] concerned an 85-year-old man who was hospitalized for 5 days because of severe pain and clinical indications of advanced lung cancer. Nursing records indicated moderate-to-severe pain levels on each day. The patient died 3 days post discharge. The family filed suit under the state elder abuse statute when the state medical board declined to discipline the treating physician despite a finding of substandard pain management. The AHCPR Clinical Practice Guidelines *Managing Cancer Pain* were admitted into evidence.[38] The jury found such an egregious example of undertreated pain in an elderly patient with an advanced terminal condition constituted elder abuse and awarded damages of $1.5 million.[39]

Two additional examples of the changing perspective on end-of-life care should be noted. First, when the U.S. Supreme Court ruled that there was no constitutional right to physician-assisted suicide, five of the nine justices wrote or joined in concurring opinions emphasizing the importance of appropriately aggressive palliative measures to ensure that dying patients do not suffer.[40] Citing the doctrine of double effect, they carefully distinguished between physician-assisted suicide and the increased risk of a hastened death posed by large doses of opioid analgesics.[41] Second, in 1999 the Oregon Board of Medical Examiners became the first such board to pursue disciplinary action against a physician for failure to properly alleviate the pain and distress of seriously ill or dying patients. In combination with *James* and *Bergman*, what has emerged is arguably a new standard of care for dying patients that includes pain relief and symptom management.

Care of the dying patient and the criminal law. A very small number of criminal prosecutions of physicians for withdrawing life-sustaining treatment or providing aggressive palliative interventions have had a disproportionate impact on the level of fear that permeates the medical profession with regard to aggressive management of dying patients. However, in both of two high-profile prosecutions the defendant physicians were ultimately vindicated. In the first, the court ruled that physicians who withdrew life support from a dying patient with the consent of his relatives could not be guilty of murder because the act did not constitute the "unlawful killing of a human being."[42] In the second case, an appellate court reversed the conviction for attempted first-degree murder of a physician who administered high doses of opioid analgesics to a dying patient.[43] The court held that because the defendant physician had presented competent expert testimony in support of his care of the patient, no reasonable jury could have found beyond a reasonable doubt that he had acted with homicidal intent.

CONCLUSION

A number of the topics covered in this chapter, especially those in "The Dying Patient" section, have been the focus of a great deal of recent and continuing litigation, legislative, and regulatory activity at the federal and state level. Health care professionals are well advised to stay up to date on developments in their own jurisdiction so as to ensure that their practice is consistent with current standards and requirements. Some of the topics featured in this chapter are given more extensive discussion and analysis in other chapters of this volume. Among those to which the reader is referred in particular are the chapters on Competency and Capacity (Chapter 4), Physician-Assisted Suicide (Chapter 28), and Pain Management (Chapter 58).

ENDNOTES

1. F. Plum, *Clinical Standards and Technological Confirmatory Tests in Diagnosing Brain Death*, in S.J. Youngner, R.M. Arnold, & R. Shapiro, eds., *The Determination of Death*, 54 (Johns Hopkins University Press, 1999).
2. R.D. Truog, *Is It Time to Abandon Brain Death?*, 27 Hastings Center Report 29 (1997).
3. R.M. Veatch, *The Conscience Clause: How Much Individual Choice in Defining Death Can Our Society Tolerate?* in S.J. Youngner et al., *supra* note 1, at 139.
4. *A Definition of Irreversible Coma: Report of the Ad Hoc Committee of the Harvard Medical School to Examine the Definition of Brain Death*, 205 J.A.M.A. 337 (1968).
5. For a discussion of the importance of carefully distinguishing among terms such as concept, definition, criterion, and test in the context of brain death, *see* Karen Gervais, *Redefining Death* (Yale University Press, 1986).
6. *Id.*
7. Uniform Determination of Death Act, §1, 12 U.L.A. 593 (1996).
8. Report of the President's Commission for the Study of Ethical Problems, *Defining Death: Medical, Legal and Ethical Issues in the Determination of Death*, 55-56 (1981).
9. H.K. Beecher, "The New Definition of Death: Some Opposing Views," unpublished paper presented at the December 1979 meeting of the American Association for the Advancement of Science, quoted in Robert M.Veatch, *Death, Dying, and the Biological Revolution*, 39 (Yale University Press, 1989).
10. N.J. Stat. Ann. 26:6A-5.
11. P.S. Haugen, *Pain Relief for the Dying: The Unwelcome Intervention of the Criminal Law*, 23 William Mitchell L. Rev. 325, 341-343 (1997).
12. G.D. Lundberg, *Severed Trust: Why American Medicine Hasn't Been Fixed*, 249-255 (Basic Books, 2000).
13. The SUPPORT Principal Investigators, *A Controlled Trial to Improve Care for Seriously Ill Hospitalized Patients*, 274 J.A.M.A. 1591 (1995).
14. J. Lynn et al., *Perceptions of Family Members of the Dying Experience of Older Seriously Ill Patients*, 126 Annals of Internal Medicine 97 (1997).
15. J. Lynn et al., *Prognoses of Seriously Ill Hospitalized Patients on the Days Before Death: Implications for Patient Care and Public Policy*, 5 New Horizons 56 (1997).
16. J. Lynn et al., *Defining the Terminally Ill: Insights from SUPPORT*, 35 Duquesne Law Review 311 (1996).
17. *Id.*
18. B.A. Rich, *The Assault on Privacy in Healthcare Decisionmaking*, 68 Denver University Law Review 1 (1991).
19. *Cruzan v. Director, Missouri Department of Health*, 497 U.S. 261 (1990).
20. *Superintendent of Belchertown State School v. Saikewicz*, 370 N.E. 2d 417 (1977).
21. L.J. Schneiderman et al., *Medical Futility: Its Meaning and Ethical Implications*, 112 Annals of Internal Medicine 949, 951 (1990).
22. Council on Ethical and Judicial Affairs, American Medical Association, *Medical Futility in End-of-Life Care*, 281 J.A.M.A. 937 (1999).
23. R. M. Veatch, *Why Physicians Cannot Determine if Care Is Futile*, 42 Journal of the American Geriatrics Society 871 (1994).
24. A. Halevy and B. Brody, *A Multi-Institution Collaborative Policy on Medical Futility*, 276 J.A.M.A. 571 (1996).
25. 16 F. 3d 590 (4th Cir. 1994).
26. No. 92-4820 (Mass. Super. Ct., Suffolk County, Apr. 21, 1995).
27. D.C. Marson et al., *Consistency of Physician Judgments of Capacity to Consent in Mild Alzheimer's Disease*, 45 Journal of the American Geriatrics Society 453 (1997).
28. E.W.D. Young et al., *Does Depression Invalidate Competence? Consultant's Ethical, Psychiatric, and Legal Considerations*, 2 Cambridge Quarterly of Healthcare Ethics 505 (1993).
29. *See, e.g., Cruzan v. Harmon*, 760 S.W. 2d 408 (Mo. Banc 1988); *In re O'Connor*, 534 N.Y.S. 2d 886 (Ct. App. 1988); *In re Martin*, 538 N.W. 2d 399 (Mich. 1995); *Matter of Edna M.F.*, 563 N.W. 2d 485 (Wis. 1997); *Conservatorship of Wendland*, 28 P. 3d 151 (Ca. 2001).
30. Patient Self-Determination Act, 42 U.S.C.A. §1395cc(f)(1) (West Supp. 1994).
31. The states are Alabama, California, Delaware, Hawaii, Maine, Mississippi, and New Mexico.
32. *See* B.A. Rich, *Advance Directives: The Next Generation*, 19 Journal of Legal Medicine 63 (1998).
33. Institute of Medicine, *Approaching Death: Improving Care at the End of Life* (National Academy Press, Washington, D.C., 1997).
34. J.H. Von Roenn et al., *Physician Attitudes and Practice in Cancer Pain Management*, 119 Annals of Internal Medicine 121 (1993).
35. *See, e.g.*, Agency for Health Care Policy and Research Clinical Practice Guidelines, *Managing Cancer Pain* (Department of Health and Human Services, Washington, D.C., 1994)
36. No. 89 CVS 64 (N.C. Super. Ct., Jan. 15, 1991).
37. No. H205732-1 (Super. Ct., Alameda Co., Feb. 16, 1999).
38. Agency for Health Care Policy and Research Clinical Practice Guidelines, *Managing Cancer Pain* (Department of Health and Human Services, Washington, D.C., 1994).
39. Jury verdict reduced by the trial court to $250,000 based upon statutory limits on damage awards for pain and suffering.
40. *Washington v. Glucksberg*, 521 U.S. 702 (1997); *Vacco v. Quill*, 521 U.S. 793 (1997).
41. P.A. Woodward, ed., *The Doctrine of Double Effect: Philosophers Debate a Controversial Moral Principle* (University of Notre Dame Press, 2001).
42. *Barber v. Superior Court*, 195 Cal. Rptr. 484 (Cal. App. 1983).
43. *State v. Narramore*, 965 P. 2d 211 (Kan. Ct. App. 1998).

28 Physician-Assisted Suicide

S. SANDY SANBAR, M.D., Ph.D., J.D., F.C.L.M.
STUART G. SELKIN, M.D., J.D., F.A.C.S., F.C.L.M.

BASIC PRECEPTS AND DEFINITIONS
SUICIDE, ASSISTED SUICIDE, AND EUTHANASIA: ITS GOVERNING LAW IN AMERICA
REGULATING MEDICAL PRACTICE IN THE CONTEXT OF END-OF-LIFE CARE
OREGON'S DEATH WITH DIGNITY ACT AND THE LEGAL SPEEDBUMPS THAT WOULD UNDO IT
OREGON'S DEATH WITH DIGNITY ACT IN ACTION
SOME FINAL THOUGHTS

For centuries, physicians have discreetly helped the terminally ill hasten their deaths.[1] And despite widespread opposition, Americans have tacitly approved.[2] By 1996, popular support for the practice reached 75%.[3] But other than in Oregon, America's laws have condemned it. Here, we present the laws that govern the practice of hastening death of the terminally ill. We present America's law of assisted suicide.

BASIC PRECEPTS AND DEFINITIONS

Federalism defines the division of power between states and the federal government, and the law of assisted suicide invokes its precepts.[4] First, medical practice has long been regulated by the individual states.[5] And second, federal law will preempt state law only where federal and state law conflict.[6] Before making policies that may affect the states, the federal government must first inform the states, then analyzing potential conflicts "with the greatest caution," must defer to state law.[7]

Citizens derive their rights from constitutions, statutes, and the common law. A constitution defines a government's fundamental laws, character, and sovereign power.[8] The United States and each state have a separate constitution and a court that acts as its final arbiter. In the federal system, that court is the United States Supreme Court.

Statutes are laws passed by a legislative body.[9] In our representative republican democracies, we elect state and federal legislators respectively in state legislatures and in Congress. Those legislators enact statutes that govern their constituents' conduct.

American common law devolves from the English law that appears in commentaries dating to the thirteenth century. Instead of constitutions or statutes, the common law appears in judicial decisions.[10] A respected commentator has described common law as "the power of judges to create new law under the guise of interpreting it."[11]

An admixture of constitutional, statutory, and common law has created America's law of suicide, assisted suicide, and euthanasia. Suicide is the taking of one's own life.[12] Assisted suicide is the intentional giving of medical means or knowledge that allows others to take their own lives.[13] In assisting suicide, a physician provides drugs that can end life and instruction in their use. The patient—not the physician—administers the lethal dose. Euthanasia is the causing of death in one suffering from an incurable, usually painful condition—for reasons of mercy.[14] In euthanasia, the physician—not the patient—administers the lethal dose. America's laws treat suicide, assisted suicide, and euthanasia differently.

SUICIDE, ASSISTED SUICIDE, AND EUTHANASIA: ITS GOVERNING LAW IN AMERICA

Under medieval English law, suicide was considered a felony.[15] Thus under the common law, early Colonial American courts punished suicide with forfeiture of the decedent's estate.[16] But later Colonial American courts and legislatures, discerning the injustice in punishing a decedent's family for the decedent's wrongdoing, viewed suicide as a grave public wrong, and not a crime.[17] Currently, no state views suicide or attempted suicide as a crime. But assisting suicide is another matter.

Under the common law and statutes respectively, Colonial American courts and legislatures forbade assisting suicide. Neither the patient's consent, nor extremity of suffering, nor the imminence of death from illness, injury, or condemnation by a jury, provided a defense against criminal charges.[18]

Currently, 44 states and the District of Columbia view assisting suicide as a crime. Conflicting legal doctrine, however, leaves uncertain whether North Carolina, Ohio, Utah, Virginia, and Wyoming view assisting suicide as a crime. Under its Death with Dignity Act, Oregon is the only state that allows assisted suicide—but only by a physician under expressly prescribed and closely monitored circumstances.[19]

Euthanasia involves inducing a gentle and easy death.[20] But no matter how well intentioned, it remains the intentional taking of another human's life. In each of the 50 United States and the District of Columbia, therefore, euthanasia is punishable as murder or as manslaughter.

Thus in 1999, a jury convicted Dr. Jack Kevorkian of second-degree murder. He will spend 10-25 years in prison because, unlike his conduct in his other cases, Dr. Kevorkian, and not the patient, administered the lethal drug.[21]

The law distinguishes refusing medical treatment from suicide.[22] The common law right to preserve one's bodily integrity permits competent adults, defined as those with decision-making capability, to refuse medical treatment.[23]

Before 1976, the relatively few treatment-refusal cases that courts decided involved treatment that the patient's religious beliefs forbade, such as blood transfusion. But with the advent of respirators and artificial nutrition, courtroom battles forced Americans to confront the legitimacy of their right to die.

The seminal case, *In re Quinlan*, was the first state court decision to allow physicians to withdraw a respirator from a patient who was in a persistent vegetative state.[24] Since *Quinlan*, courts have invariably held that no distinction exists between withholding or withdrawing life-sustaining medical treatment.[25] Those who withhold or withdraw life-sustaining medical treatment under relevant state law thus risk no criminal liability.

In a ruling that jolted the medical and legal communities, the *Quinlan* court held that in end-of-life decisions, patients' judgments must prevail over physicians' judgments.[26] Since *Quinlan* was decided in 1976, courts and legislatures have struggled to fix medical management's legal boundaries in the context of end-of-life care.

REGULATING MEDICAL PRACTICE IN THE CONTEXT OF END-OF-LIFE CARE

In *Cruzan v. Department of Health*, in 1990, the Supreme Court made its first foray into end-of-life issues.[27] The court held that should a competent adult become incompetent, states can require clear and convincing evidence of that patient's wishes before allowing the family to discontinue life support.[28] The Supreme Court thus recognized that regulating medical practice in the context of end-of-life care is a right reserved by the states.

In 1997, the Supreme Court reaffirmed that principle. And it did so in reversing decisions in which two federal appeals courts held that state bans on physician-assisted suicide violate the federal constitution.[29] In *Vacco v. Quill* and *Washington v. Glucksberg*, the Supreme Court held that New York's and Washington's bans on physician-assisted suicide do *not* violate the federal constitution.[30]

In *Quill* and in *Glucksberg* respectively, the Supreme Court held that neither the equal protection clause nor the due process clause confer a constitutional right to assisted suicide.[31] But these decisions do not prevent state legislatures from conferring a right to assisted suicide.[32] To the contrary, the court encouraged continued debate over the "morality, legality, and practicality of physician-assisted suicide" by the states.[33] With the Supreme Court's urging states to protect "terminally ill, mentally competent individuals who would seek to end their suffering,"[34] Oregon's legislature did just that.

OREGON'S DEATH WITH DIGNITY ACT AND THE LEGAL SPEEDBUMPS THAT WOULD UNDO IT

When its voters approved the Death with Dignity Act in 1994, Oregon became the first—and only—state to make physician-assisted suicide legal.[35] But responding to a lawsuit, a federal district court quickly prevented Oregon from implementing the act.[36] The injunction continued for 3 years, until a federal appeals court vacated it.[37] On November 4, 1997, Oregon's voters rejected a legislative proposal to repeal the act. By a 60% to 40% margin, voters ensured that obtaining a physician's aid in hastening the death of the terminally ill would remain legal in Oregon.[38]

The terminally ill have incurable, irreversible disease that is expected to cause death within 6 months. Under the Death with Dignity Act, competent, terminally-ill Oregonians may make a written request for self-administered medication to end their lives in a "humane and dignified manner."[39] The patient must sign and date the request, which two unrelated, disinterested individuals must witness. A physician must inform the patient of the alternatives to hastening death, and two physicians must confirm the patient's medical diagnosis and mental competence to make health-related decisions.[40] Physicians who are unwilling to aid suicide have no duty to do so; and physicians and pharmacists who participate in the act risk no civil, criminal, or professional disciplinary actions.[41] Outside the act, aiding suicide is second-degree manslaughter.[42] Health care providers must file reports with Oregon's Department of Human Services documenting their actions taken under the act.[43] Because barbiturates have been the drugs of choice in effecting physician-assisted suicide, Oregon's Death with Dignity Act incorporates the federally enacted Controlled Substances Act.

The Controlled Substances Act

In 1970, Congress enacted the Controlled Substances Act.[44] Enacted to deal with drug abuse in the United States, the act ensures that legally available drugs remain legally distributed and legally used.[45] Physicians who violate the act risk losing their prescribing privileges, and they risk severe criminal penalties.[46]

A 1971 regulation adopted under the Attorney General's limited power to implement the act states that prescriptions for controlled substances must be written for "a legitimate medical purpose."[47] But nothing in the Controlled Substances Act or its implementing regulations defines "a legitimate medical purpose."[48]

A 1984 amendment to the act targeted physicians who divert legitimate prescription drugs to illegitimate uses.[49] The 1984 amendment thus empowers the Attorney General to deny registration under the act for conduct "inconsistent with the public interest."[50] In determining the public interest, the Attorney General must consider compliance with state law and threats to public health.[51] But nothing in the Controlled Substances Act defines conduct "inconsistent with the public interest" or "threats to public health."[52]

The act empowers the Attorney General to place drugs on or to remove drugs from any of the act's five schedules.[53] But first, the Secretary of Health and Human Services must provide a "scientific and medical" evaluation. The Attorney General must accept and follow the Secretary's advice about "such scientific and medical matters."[54]

In the Controlled Substances Act, Congress did not intend to regulate physicians as the states do.[55] Nor did Congress intend to regulate medical practices allowed by state law—and that are unrelated to drug abuse or trafficking.[56] And in determining accepted medical practice, the Attorney General can make no credible claim to expertise.[57]

Assisted suicide's opponents: congressional conservatives

Only a day after voters approved Oregon's Death with Dignity Act—for the second time—congressional conservatives induced the Drug Enforcement Administration (DEA) to act against it. With neither Justice Department nor congressional approval, the DEA proclaimed that physicians who prescribe controlled substances to assist suicide could find their prescribing privileges subject to revocation.[58] And fearing DEA reprisals, Oregon's physicians refused to assist suicide under its duly enacted Death with Dignity Act.

But after a seven-month-long, thorough investigation by the Justice Department, then Attorney General Janet Reno rejected the DEA's position.[59] She ruled that in the Controlled Substances Act, Congress intended to block drug trafficking but not physician-assisted suicide.[60] She upheld that the "morality, legality, and practicality" of physician-assisted suicide was to be resolved in state legislatures.[61] She ruled that "adverse action against a physician who has assisted in a suicide in full compliance with the Oregon Act would *not* be authorized by the Controlled Substances Act."[62]

Only hours after receiving Ms. Reno's ruling, conservatives in both Houses of Congress sprung into action to amend the Controlled Substances Act. Under two separate proposed statutes, an amended Controlled Substances Act would proclaim using controlled substances to relieve pain—even if death follows—legitimate medical practice.[63] But using controlled substances to assist suicide would not be legitimate medical practice.[64] Using controlled substances to assist suicide would therefore subject physicians' federal controlled-substances registration to revocation. And it would subject physicians to criminal prosecution—and a 20-year mandatory prison term.[65] Even complying with the Death with Dignity Act's every provision would not furnish a defense.[66] Ostensibly aimed at pain relief and not the Death with Dignity Act, either proposed federal statute would, if enacted into law, effectively annul it.[67]

The attempts to amend the Controlled Substances Act, first under the Lethal Drug Abuse Prevention Act and later under the Pain Relief Promotion Act, stalled indefinitely in the Senate. Yet the Pain Relief Promotion Act passed in the House of Representatives by a 271-156 majority.[68] Many ascribe that to the position opposing physician-assisted suicide championed by the American Medical Association (AMA).

Assisted suicide's opponents: the American Medical Association

The AMA Code of Ethics condemns assisting suicide for being "fundamentally incompatible with the physician's role as healer."[69] Under the AMA Code of Ethics, even physicians who comply with every provision of Oregon's Death with Dignity Act behave unethically. But when the AMA purports to speak for an entire profession, incongruity surfaces.

First, the AMA position ignores that substantial numbers of America's physicians support assisted suicide.[70] Second, the AMA membership roster claims only a third of America's physicians.[71] Third, the AMA's Council on Ethical and Judicial Affairs, which authors its Code of Ethics, is not elected; instead, it is appointed.[72] And fourth, that unelected Council issues ethical guidelines without polling America's physicians.[73] Still, Congress and the Supreme Court accord AMA positions pivotal deference.[74]

But the recent AMA reasoning, on which Congress relied in debating the Pain Relief Promotion Act, raises constitutional concerns.[75] The AMA supports "providing effective palliative treatment even though it may foreseeably hasten death."[76] The AMA therefore exalted the Pain Relief Promotion Act for "reducing physicians' exposure to criminal investigation and prosecution for legitimate medical practices." [77]

But the Pain Relief Promotion Act would impose a national solution on issues that historically have been handled by the states. DEA agents would intrude into the physician-patient relationship.[78] When physicians prescribe controlled substances, DEA agents would interpret physicians' intent.[79] In settings where even physicians disagree, DEA agents—not physicians—would determine appropriate prescribing practices.[80] Finally, the Attorney General would act as though Oregon's Death with Dignity Act, a duly enacted state law, does not exist.[81] Still this has not lessened the AMA's resolve.[82]

When the Pain Relief Promotion Act died in the Senate, the AMA—and its opposition to assisted suicide—found a staunch ally in Attorney General John Ashcroft.

Assisted suicide's opponents: Attorney General John Ashcroft

Undaunted by their failure to thwart physician-assisted suicide in Oregon, its opponents tried a new tactic—which would avoid the open, thorough legislative debate required by Congress. Seeking refuge with Attorney General John Ashcroft, they tried to "get through the administrative door that which they could not get through the congressional door."[83] They found the Attorney General ready to reverse the Justice Department's earlier interpretation of the Controlled Substances Act with an administrative directive that attempted to rewrite federal law.

Attorney General Ashcroft's closed-door process took only a few months.[84] He acted without public hearings or debate, without warning to the medical community, and without the data or input from Oregon that he had earlier agreed to consider.[85]

In what has become known as the "Ashcroft directive," the Attorney General, who can make no credible claim to medical expertise, defined "legitimate medical purpose." Under the "Ashcroft directive" issued on November 6, 2001, using controlled substances to aggressively manage pain is a "legitimate medical purpose." But under the "Ashcroft directive," using controlled substances to assist suicide is "inconsistent with the public interest" and is *not* a "legitimate medical purpose."[86] Under the "Ashcroft directive," even under Oregon law, prescribing, dispensing, or administering controlled substances to assist suicide violates the Controlled Substances Act.[87]

Under the "Ashcroft directive," the assisted-suicide records required by Oregon law would self-incriminate physicians who obey that law.[88] Under the "Ashcroft directive," physicians who assist suicide, even under Oregon law, risk investigation, prosecution, and punishment. Under the "Ashcroft directive," those physicians risk having their prescribing privileges suspended or revoked—and a 20-year prison sentence.

The "Ashcroft directive," which disclaimed Janet Reno's 1998 ruling that reached the opposite conclusion, effectively annulled the Death with Dignity Act and Oregon's four-year experience in applying it.[89]

In response to the "Ashcroft directive's" unwarranted intrusion into Oregon's sovereign interests, physicians, terminally-ill patients, and Oregon's Government sued to prevent giving the "Ashcroft directive" any legal effect.[90]

The "Ashcroft directive" in a federal district court

In his April 17, 2002, decision, the Honorable Robert E. Jones, a federal judge appointed by the first President Bush, restrained the "Ashcroft directive" permanently.[91] Judge Jones' words deserve echoing. In a decision that sharply criticized Attorney General Ashcroft, Judge Jones wrote: "The determination of what constitutes a legitimate medical practice or purpose traditionally has been left to the individual states. State statutes, state medical boards, and state regulations control the practice of medicine."[92]

Thus in deciding that prescribing controlled substances to assist suicide had no "legitimate medical purpose," Mr. Ashcroft had overstepped his authority. Indeed Judge Jones wrote: " . . . the Ashcroft directive is not entitled to deference under any standard and is invalid."[93]

Judge Jones admonished: "To allow an attorney general—an appointed executive whose tenure depends entirely on whatever administration occupies the White House—to determine the legitimacy of a particular medical practice without a specific congressional grant of such authority would be unprecedented and extraordinary."[94]

Judge Jones emphasized that "Many of our citizens, including the highest respected leaders of this country, oppose assisted suicide." But, he warned, while "opposition to assisted suicide may be fully justified . . . [that] . . . does not permit a federal statute to be manipulated from its true meaning to satisfy even a worthy goal."[95]

On May 24, 2002, the federal government announced its intent to appeal to the Ninth Circuit Court of Appeals. As of this writing, that appeal has not been decided.

OREGON'S DEATH WITH DIGNITY ACT IN ACTION

As the act requires, Oregon's experience with its Death with Dignity Act has been documented, studied, and evaluated in detail.[96] Reports from Oregon and from United States agencies published in the *New England Journal of Medicine* confirm that the Act has worked very well.[97]

Patients who chose to hasten death under the act were educated, overwhelmingly white, and motivated by issues relating to quality of life.[98] Most suffered from end-stage cancers and dreaded their progressive, inexorable loss of body functions, autonomy, and their ability to interact meaningfully with loved ones.[99] Fears that the act would be disproportionately chosen by, or forced on, patients who were poor, uneducated, uninsured, or afraid of the financial consequences of their illness proved unfounded.[100] And the act has reduced the underground practice of physician-assisted dying that was widespread in Oregon—and remains underground throughout the rest of the nation.[101]

The Fourth Annual Report on Oregon's Death with Dignity Act provides statistics amassed over the four years during which assisted suicide has been legal in Oregon.[102]

The Report advises that while prescribing under the act has increased, the number of physician-assisted deaths has not. In 2001, physicians wrote 44 prescriptions for controlled substances in lethal doses. This compares to the 39 prescriptions written in 2000, 33 in 1999, and 24 in 1998.

In 1998, the first year during which terminally-ill patients could hasten their deaths under the Death with Dignity Act, 19 Oregonians died under the act. In 1999, 27 died, in 2000, 27 died, and in 2001, 21 died under the act. Two of the 2001 deaths resulted from lethal ingestion in December 2000. Thus of the 39 prescriptions for lethal doses written in 2001, only 19 patients ingested them. The number of terminally-ill patients ingesting lethal medication under the act has remained small. Fewer than 0.1% of Oregonians die by physician-assisted suicide.

SOME FINAL THOUGHTS

More than two centuries ago, Sir William Blackstone observed that "Law is the embodiment of the moral sentiment of the people."[103] The law of assisted suicide blends ethics, philosophy, and morality with medicine and the law. It touches our fundamental beliefs about life, death, illness, religion, autonomy, and dignity. Thus people of good conscience can disagree about assisted suicide's wisdom.[104]

The legal issues that surround assisted suicide affect the balance of power between the state and federal governments. Those issues especially concern Oregonians facing critical end-of-life decisions—and health care's lawful role in those decisions.[105] Deep disagreements about the limits of legitimate medical practice and of physicians' conduct pervade medical and medical-ethics communities.[106] For physicians, patients, religious groups, ethicists, philosophers, and legislators, whether Oregon's Death with Dignity Act should allow the terminally ill to hasten their deaths therefore understandably ignites controversy.

Many, including the AMA, believe that the Attorney General may interpret the Controlled Substances Act in a way that effectively subverts the Death with Dignity Act. But many, including the American College of Legal Medicine, believe that Attorney General Ashcroft subverts federalism's basic precepts, the Supreme Court's guidance, and Oregon's sovereign interests.[107] In agreeing with that stance, this chapter's authors, however, assert no position on assisted suicide's morality, correctness, or wisdom.

Our thoughts, our beliefs, and our disagreements will affect and then determine how the law of assisted suicide evolves. The only absolute in this ever-changing venue is that the law of assisted suicide in America will affect each of us.

ENDNOTES

1. *Compassion in Dying v. Washington*, 79 F. 3d 790 (9th Cir. 1996) *rev'd sub nom. Washington v. Glucksberg*, 521 U.S. 702 (1997).
2. Wayne Guglielmo, *Assisted Suicide? Pain Control? Where's the Line?*, Med. Economics (Oct. 11, 2002); Diane E. Meier et al., *A National Survey of Physician-Assisted Suicide and Euthanasia in the United States*, 338 New Engl. J. Med. 1193 (1998); Alan Meisel, *Physician-Assisted Suicide: A Common Law Roadmap for State Courts*, 24 Fordham Urb. L. J. 817 (1997) (citing Ezekiel J. Emanuel, *Euthanasia—Historical, Ethical, and Empiric Perspectives*, 154 Arch. Intern. Med. 1890 (1994))
3. Meisel, 24 Fordham Urb. L. J. at 818 (citing polls from the National Opinion Research Center); *Right to Die*, USA Today (Apr. 12, 1996) (citing USA Today/CNN/Gallup Poll).
4. *Black's Law Dictionary* 627 (7th ed. 1999).
5. *Dent v. West Virginia*, 129 U.S. 114 (1889); *Linder v. United States*, 268 U.S. 5 (1925).
6. H.R. 3, 84th Cong. (1955); H.R. 3, 85th Cong. (1957); H.R. 3, 86th Cong. (1959); *Kelly v. Washington*, 302 U.S. 1 (1937).
7. President's Executive Order on Federalism 13132.
8. *Black's Law Dictionary* 306 (7th ed. 1999).
9. *Id.* at 1420.
10. *Id.* at 270.
11. Glanville Williams, *Learning the Law* 29-30 (11th ed. 1982).
12. *Black's Law Dictionary* 1447 (7th ed. 1999).
13. *Id.*
14. *Id.* at 575.
15. John A. Alesandro, *Physician-Assisted Suicide and New York Law*, 57 Alb. L. Rev. 819 (1994).
16. *Glucksberg*, 521 U.S. at 711 (citing Marzen, O'Dowd, Crone & Balch, *Suicide: A Constitutional Right?*, 24 Duquesne L. Rev. 1, 17–56 (1985)).
17. *Glucksberg*, 521 U.S. at 713 (citing 2 Z. Swift, *A System of the Laws of the State of Connecticut* 304 (1796)).
18. Williams, *Learning the Law* 29-30; *see also Blackburn v. State*, 23 Ohio St. 146 (1872); *Commonwealth v. Bowen*, 13 Mass. 356 (1816).
19. Codified at Or. Rev. Stat. §§127.800-127.897 (2001).
20. *Oxford English Dictionary* (2d ed., CD-ROM version 2.0, 2000); Lecky, *European Morals*, I. xi. 233 (1869) ("an abridgment of the pangs of disease").
21. *People v. Kevorkian*, 639 N.W. 2d 291 (Mich. App. 2001).
22. *Vacco v. Quill*, 521 U.S. 793 (1997).
23. *Cruzan v. Director, Mo. Dept. of Health*, 497 U.S. 261 (1990); *Black's Law Dictionary* 278 (7th ed. 1999).
24. *In re Quinlan*, 70 N.J. 10, 355 A. 2d 647, *cert. denied*, 429 U.S. 922 (1976).
25. *Cruzan*, 497 U.S. 261.
26. *Oregon v. Ashcroft*, No. 02–35587, *Brief of Amici Curiae Margaret P. Battin, et al. in support of Plaintiffs-Appellees for Affirmance*, filed Nov. 12, 2002 (citing *Quinlan*, 70 N.J. at 41).
27. *Cruzan*, 497 U.S. 261.
28. *Id.*
29. *Quill*, 521 U.S. 793; *Glucksberg*, 521 U.S. 702.
30. *Id.*
31. *Quill*, 521 U.S. 793 (equal protection); *Glucksberg*, 521 U.S. 702 (due process).
32. *Glucksberg*, 521 U.S. 702.
33. *Glucksberg*, 521 U.S. at 734 (Renquist, C.J.); 521 U.S. at 737 (O'Connor, J., concurring); 521 U.S. at 787 (Souter, J., concurring).
34. *Glucksberg*, 521 U.S. at 737 (O'Connor, J., concurring).
35. Or. Rev. Stat. §§127.800-127.897 (2001).
36. *Lee v. Oregon*, 891 F. Supp. 1491 (D. Or. 1994); *Lee v. Oregon*, 891 F. Supp. 1421 (D. Or. 1994), *rev'd, Lee v. Oregon*, 107 F. 3d 1382 (9th Cir. 1997), *cert. denied*, 522 U.S. 927 (1997).
37. *Lee v. Oregon*, 107 F. 3d 1382 (9th Cir. 1997), *cert. denied*, 522 U.S. 927 (1997).
38. Joy Fallek, *The Pain Relief Promotion Act: Will it Spell Death to "Death with Dignity" or Is it Unconstitutional?*, 27 Fordham Urb. L. J. 1739 (2000); *see* State Wide Special Election at www.sos.state.or.us/elections/nov97other.info/m5abst.htm.
39. Or. Rev. Stat. §§127.800-127.897 (2001).
40. *Id.*

41. *Id.*; Or. Admin. Rule 847-010-0081 (citing Or. Rev. Stat. §§677.190[1], 677.188[4]).

42. Or. Rev. Stat. §163.125[1][b].

43. Or. Rev. Stat. §127.865[1][b].

44. Comprehensive Drug Abuse Prevention and Control Act of 1970, Pub. L. No. 91-513, 84 Stat. 1236 (1970); H.R. Rep. No. 91-1444, 91st Cong., 2d Sess. (1970).

45. *U.S. v. Moore*, 423 U.S. 1222 (1975); 1970 U.S.C.C.A.A.N. at 4590; 1984 U.S.C.C.A.A.N. at 3442.

46. 21 U.S.C. §823-824, 84-846.

47. 21 C.F.R. §1306.04.

48. 21 U.S.C. §802; 21 C.F.R. §§1306.01, 1306.02, 1306.04 (2002).

49. 21 U.S.C. §824 (in *Trawick v. Drug Enforcement Admin.*, 861 F. 2d 42 (4th Cir. 1988).

50. 21 U.S.C. §824[l][4].

51. 21 U.S.C. §§823[b] and [e], 824[a][4].

52. *Id.*

53. 21 U.S.C. §811[b].

54. *Id.*

55. 21 U.S.C. §823[g][2][H][i].

56. 1970 U.S.C.C.A.A.N. at 4590; *Conant v. McCaffrey*, 172 F.R.D. 681 (N.D. Cal. 1997).

57. *Id.*; *see also* 21 U.S.C. §811[b].

58. Letter from Thomas A. Constantine, Administrator of the Drug Enforcement Agency, to Henry J. Hyde, Committee on the Judiciary, U.S. House of Representatives (Nov. 5, 1997).

59. Letter from Janet Reno to Henry J. Hyde (June 5, 1998), available at www.house.gov/judiciary/attygen.htm [Reno letter].

60. *Id.*

61. *Id.*

62. *Id.*

63. H.R. 4006, 105th Cong. (1998); S. 2151, 105th Cong. (1998); H.R. 4006, 105th Cong. §2(c)(2). H.R. 2260, 106th Cong. §101(i)(1) and S-1272 (1999) (amending §303 of the CSA).

64. *Id.*

65. H.R. Rep. No. 106-378, pt. 2, at 10 (1999); 145 Cong. Rec. H10872 (daily ed. Oct. 27, 1999); *see also* 21 U.S.C. §841(b)(i)(C) (1994).

66. H.R. 2260, 106th Cong. §101(i)(1) and S-1272 (1999) (amending §303 of the CSA).

67. H.R. Rep. No. 106-378, pt. 1, at 11 (1999); S-1272; 145 Cong. Rec. H10869 (daily ed. Oct. 27, 1999).

68. Robert Pear, *House Backs Ban on Using Medicine to Aid in Suicide*, N.Y. Times (Oct. 28, 1999) at A1.

69. AMA Code of Medical Ethics §2.211 (issued 1994).

70. Melinda A. Lee et al., *Legalizing Assisted Suicide—Views of Physicians in Oregon*, 334 New Engl. J. Med. 310, 311 (1996) and Jerald G. Bachman et al., *Attitudes of Michigan Physicians and the Public Toward Legalizing Physician-Assisted Suicide and Voluntary Euthanasia*, 334 New Engl. J. Med. 303, 305 (1996); David Orentlicher, *The Legalization of Physician Assisted Suicide*, 335 New Engl. J. Med. 663 (1996).

71. Historical membership chart, American Medical Association.

72. David Orentlicher, *The Influence of a Professional Organization on Physician Behavior*, 57 Alb. L. Rev. 583, 588 (1994).

73. AMA Code of Medical Ethics—Current Opinions with Annotations, at iii (2000–2001) (first stated in 1992 Code, at 87; *see also* Historical membership chart [AMA].

74. *See, e.g., Glucksberg*, 521 U.S. at 730.

75. H.R. Rep. No. 106-378, pt. 1, at 31–39.

76. AMA Code of Medical Ethics §2.20, at 56 (2000-2001).

77. AMA position on the Pain Relief Promotion Act, available at www.ama_assn.org/ama/basic/article/0,1059,199_483_1,00.html.

78. 145 Cong. Rec. H10870; *Oregon v. Ashcroft*, 192 F. Supp. 2d 1077 (D. Or. Apr. 17, 2002); *Oregon's Supplemental Memorandum in Support of Motion for a Preliminary Injunction*, filed Nov. 16, 2001.

79. Meisel, 24 Fordham Urb. L. J. 817 (citing William E. May, *Double Effect*, in 1 *Encyclopedia of Bioethics* 316-19 (Warren T. Reich ed., rev. ed. 1995)).

80. 64 Fed. Reg. 25,073, 25,079 (1999).

81. *Id.*

82. AMA position on the Pain Relief Promotion Act.

83. *Oregon v. Ashcroft*, 192 F. Supp. 2d at 1093.

84. *Oregon v. Ashcroft*, No. 02-35587, *Brief of the Patient Plaintiffs-Appellees*, Nov. 11, 2002; *see also* Memorandum, Justice Department Office of Legal Council, June 27, 2001.

85. *Id.*; *see also* letter to Oregon Attorney General Hardy Meyers, dated Apr. 17, 2001.

86. 66 Fed. Reg. 56,607, 56,608 (Nov. 9, 2001); 21 CFR §1306.04 (2001).

87. *Id.*

88. *Id.*

89. *Id.*; *see also* Reno letter, *supra* note 59.

90. *Oregon v. Ashcroft*, 192 F. Supp. 2d 1077, *Plaintiff's Memorandum in Support of Motions for a Temporary Restraining Order and a Preliminary Injunction*, filed Nov. 7, 2001.

91. *Oregon v. Ashcroft*, 192 F. Supp. 2d at 1077

92. *Id.* at 1092

93. *Id.*

94. *Id.*

95. *Id.* at 1093.

96. Or. Rev. Stat. §127.865.

97. Arthur E. Chin et al., *Legalized Physician-Assisted Suicide in Oregon—The First Year's Experience*, 340 New Engl. J. Med. 577 (1999); Amy Sullivan et al., *Legalized Physician-Assisted Suicide in Oregon—The Second Year*, 342 New Engl. J. Med. 598 (2000); Katrina Hedberg, Oregon Health Division, *Oregon's Death with Dignity Act: Three Years of Legalized Physician-Assisted Suicide in Oregon* (Feb. 22, 2001); Oregon Department of Human Services, *Fourth Annual Report on Oregon's Death with Dignity Act* (Feb. 6, 2002), both www.ohd.hr.state.or.us/chs/pas/htm.

98. *Id.*

99. *Id.*

100. *Id.*

101. *Compassion in Dying*, 79 F. 3d at 811; Guglielmo, *supra* note 2; Meier et al., *supra* note 2.

102. Oregon Department of Human Services, *Fourth Annual Report on Oregon's Death with Dignity Act* (Feb. 6, 2002).

103. Sir William Blackstone, 1723-1780, author of *Commentaries on the Laws of England* (1765-1769). Inscription on the courthouse, Supreme Court, Kings County, New York.

104. Fallek, 27 Fordham Urb. L. J. at 1792.

105. *Oregon v. Ashcroft*, 192 F. Supp. 2d 1077, *Oregon's Supplemental Memorandum in Support of Motion for a Preliminary Injunction*, filed Nov. 16, 2001.

106. *Oregon v. Ashcroft*, No. 02–35587, *Brief of Amici Curiae Margaret P. Battin et al. in support of Plaintiffs-Appellees for Affirmance*, filed Nov. 12, 2002 (citing D. Callahan, *The Goals of Medicine: Setting New Priorities*, Hastings Center Report (Supp.) at 26 (Nov.-Dec. 1996); L.R. Kass, *Regarding the End of Medicine and the Pursuit of Health*, The Public Interest at 40 (1975); F.G. Miller, H. Brody, & K.C. Chung, *Cosmetic Surgery and the Internal Morality of Medicine*, 9 Cambridge Quarterly of Healthcare Ethics 353-64 (2000); E.D. Pellegrino, *The Goals and Ends of Medicine: How Are They to Be Defined?*, in M.J. Hanson & D. Callahan, eds., *The Goals of Medicine* 55-68 (1999); R.M. Veatch & F.G. Miller, *The Internal Morality of Medicine: An Introduction*, 26 J. of Medicine and Philosophy 555-57 (2001).

107. *Oregon v. Ashcroft*, No. 02–35587, *Amicus Curiae Brief of the American College of Legal Medicine in Support of Plaintiffs-Appellees*, filed Oct. 23, 2002; President's Executive Order on Federalism 13132; *Glucksberg*, 521 U.S. at 734, 737, 787.

Professional Medical Liability

Medical Malpractice Overview

The term *malpractice* refers to any professional misconduct that encompasses an unreasonable lack of skill or unfaithfulness in carrying out professional or fiduciary duties. Although the term *medical negligence* may be preferable to medical malpractice, the latter is used in this chapter because of the common and traditional usage of this term.

PLAINTIFFS' THEORIES AGAINST PHYSICIANS

Currently there are a number of legal theories or causes of action by which a patient as plaintiff may bring a lawsuit against a physician. Although negligence is the most common basis for a medical malpractice action imposing liability on a physician, physicians also may be involved in legal actions based on other legal theories. The physician must be aware that a suit often can be brought under several theories. If the plaintiff patient wins under any of these theories, recovery of a monetary award from the defendant physician may result. Alternative plaintiffs' theories against physicians are considered here after a discussion of the basic principles of medical negligence.

Medical negligence

Medical negligence is a breach of the physician's duty to behave reasonably and prudently under the circumstances that causes foreseeable harm to another. For a successful suit under a theory of negligence or in legal terms to present a cause of action for negligence, an injured patient (plaintiff) must prove each of the following four elements by the preponderance of evidence.

Duty. The first element of the negligence theory of liability is duty as created by the physician-patient relationship. This duty requires that a physician possess and bring

The Editorial Committee updated this chapter. The committee gratefully acknowledges the past contribution of Martin B. Flamm, M.D., J.D., F.C.L.M.

to bear on the patient's behalf that degree of knowledge, skill, and care that would be exercised by a reasonable and prudent physician under similar circumstances. In other words, a physician owes the patient a duty to act in accordance with the specific norms or standards established by the profession, commonly referred to as *standards of care*, to protect the patient against unreasonable risk.

A plaintiff may show that the defendant physician failed to exercise the required skill, care, or diligence by commission or omission (i.e., by doing something that should not have been done or by failing to do something that should have been done). It may not matter that the physician has performed at his or her full potential and in complete good faith. Instead the physician must have conformed to the standard of a "prudent physician" under similar circumstances.

There is no clear definition of the duty of a particular physician in a particular case. Because most medical malpractice cases are highly technical, witnesses with special medical qualifications must provide the judge or jury with the knowledge necessary to render a fair and just verdict. As a result, in nearly all cases the standard of medical care of a "prudent physician" must be determined based on expert testimony. In the case of a specialist the standard of care by which the defendant is judged is the care and skill commonly possessed and exercised by similar specialists under similar circumstances. The specialty standard of care may be higher than that required of general practitioners.

Although courts recognize that medical facts usually are not common knowledge and therefore require expert testimony, professional societies do not necessarily set the standard of care. The standard of care is an objective standard against which the conduct of a physician sued for malpractice may be measured, and it therefore does not depend on any individual physician's knowledge. In attempting to fix a standard by which the trier of fact may determine whether a physician has properly performed the requisite duty toward the patient, expert medical testimony from witnesses for both the prosecution and the defense is required. The trier of fact ultimately determines the standard of care, after listening to the testimony of all medical experts.

Breach of duty. The second element of medical negligence that must be proved by the plaintiff is that by failing to act in accordance with the applicable standard of care the defendant physician did not comply with the requisite duty, called *breach of duty*. The applicable standard of care must be proved before the plaintiff can prove that the physician breached that duty.

In most cases expert witnesses for the prosecution and the defense address the question of breach of duty while testifying as to the standard of care owed. Of course there are exceptions to every rule. Expert testimony may not be required if a plaintiff presents evidence showing that the defendant physician's substandard care is so obvious as to be within the comprehension of a layperson. *Res ipsa loquitur*, which literally means "the thing speaks for itself," is a legal doctrine that relieves the plaintiff from the requirement of proving duty and breach of duty through a physician expert witness. In other words, negligent care may be presumed. *Res ipsa loquitur* requires the plaintiff to show only that the outcome was caused by an instrumentality in the exclusive control of the defendant, that the plaintiff did not voluntarily contribute to the result, and that the injury was the type that normally does not occur in the absence of negligent care. After the plaintiff shows these elements, the burden of proof may shift to the defendant physician to prove otherwise. For example, the patient who discovers that a sponge or an instrument was left within his or her abdomen during surgery may have a *res ipsa loquitur* case. Causation and damages still may need to be proved by expert testimony, however.

Causation. The third element that must be proved by the plaintiff is causation. The plaintiff must show that a reasonably close and "causal connection" exists between the negligent act or omission and the resulting injury. In legal terms this relationship is commonly referred to as *legal cause* or *proximate cause*. The concept of causation differs markedly from that of medical etiology in that it refers to a single causative factor and not necessarily the major cause or even the most immediate cause of the injury, as is the case with medical causation or etiology. Although causation may seem to be an easy element for plaintiffs to prove, it is frequently the most difficult and elusive concept for the jury to understand because of the many complex issues.

Legal causation consists of two factual issues—causation in fact and foreseeability. Causation in fact may be stated as follows: An event A is the cause of another event B. If event B would not have occurred but for event A (known as the *but for test*), causation exists. This test is easily passed in some cases but not in others. Consider the following contrasting examples. The patient with an intestinal perforation resulting from a surgeon's failure to remove an instrument from the abdominal cavity may suffer subsequent abdominal abscess, surgery, or death. But for the retained instrument, such a complication would not have occurred. In contrast, a physician's delay in the diagnosis of a highly aggressive malignant neoplasm might not necessarily affect the patient's chance of survival.

Foreseeability is the second causation issue. A patient's injuries and other damages must be the foreseeable result of a defendant physician's substandard practice. Generally the patient must prove only that his or her injuries were of a type that would have been foreseen by a reasonable physician as a likely result of the breach of the medical standard of care.

The law of causation varies widely from jurisdiction to jurisdiction, and its proof is currently in flux. In *Daubert v. Merrell Dow Pharmaceuticals* the U.S. Supreme Court addressed the admissibility of scientific evidence in a case involving expert testimony concerning causation.[1] This decision, which is followed in most jurisdictions, allows judges great discretion in deciding what scientific evidence is or is not admissible, especially as applied to the causation element.

Damages. The fourth element of the medical negligence suit is proof of damages. In general the concept of damages encompasses the actual loss or damage to the interests of the patient caused by the physician's breach of the standard of care. If the patient is not harmed, there can be no recovery. (The exception to this rule is "nominal damages," where a token sum, economically worthless, is awarded a plaintiff who has had his or her honesty, integrity, or virtue challenged and is vindicated by the satisfaction of having his or her claim honored. Although rare, the significance of an award of nominal damages is that it may serve as a prerequisite to the award of punitive damages.)

The purpose of awarding damages in a tort action is to ensure that the person who is harmed is made "whole" again or returned to the position or condition that existed before the tort. Because it is generally impossible to alleviate the effects of an injury resulting from medical malpractice, public policy demands redress through the award of monetary compensation to the plaintiff. The legal fiction is that money makes the damaged patient whole.

Damages may encompass compensation for a wide range of financial, physical, or emotional injury to the plaintiff patient. The law has recognized certain categories of damages, but categorization is often imprecise and inconsistent because some of these categories overlap and are not strictly adhered to by courts of all jurisdictions.

Compensatory damages are awarded to compensate the patient for losses. There are two types of compensatory damages—special and general. General damages are awarded for noneconomic losses, including pain and suffering, mental anguish, grief, and other related emotional complaints without any reference to the patient's specific physical injuries. Special damages are those that are the actual but not necessarily the inevitable result of the injury caused by the defendant and that follow the injury as foreseeable and natural consequences. Typical items of special damages that are compensated by a monetary judgment include past and future medical, surgical, hospital, and other health care–related costs; past and future loss of income; funeral expenses in a case involving death; and unusual physical or medical consequences of the alleged injury, such as aggravation of a preexisting condition.

If a wrong was aggravated by special circumstances, punitive or exemplary damages, in addition to the injured patient's actual losses, may be awarded. Punitive damages, which are rarely awarded in medical negligence cases, are intended to make an example of the defendant physician or to punish his or her egregious behavior. Such damages generally are awarded when the defendant's conduct has been intentional, grossly negligent, malicious, violent, fraudulent, or with reckless disregard for the consequences of his or her conduct.

Other theories

Battery. In medical injury cases battery really is not a negligence action but an intentional tort. The law in general recognizes that an individual should be free from unwarranted and unwanted intrusion. In legal terms touching another person without that person's express or implied consent is a battery. The attempt to touch another person without consent is an assault. Assault can be considered an attempt at battery.

The law in all jurisdictions places considerable importance on this principle of personal autonomy, which traditionally has been reinforced by legislation dealing with patients' rights. In the medical setting, battery most often involves undesired medical treatment or nonconsensual sexual contact. To successfully prove a claim of medical assault or battery, the plaintiff must show that he or she was subjected to an examination or a treatment for which there was no express or implied consent. The treatment provided must be substantially different from that to which the patient agreed. There also must be proof that the departure was intentional on the part of the physician.

Unlike claims made under the negligence theory of consent, which is discussed later, there is no need to prove actual harm in battery cases, although harm may have occurred. The amount of damages of course relates directly to the amount of harm in most cases. For example, an operation that is not consented to but saves the patient's life likely will not result in damages, except in rare cases. However, if the patient suffers painful, crippling, or lingering effects, significant damages may be awarded.

Specific examples of medical battery include the performance of sexual "therapy" by a psychiatrist or other mental health care professional in the name of treatment, the unauthorized extension of a surgery to nonconsented bodily organs unjustified by the original procedure, and the nonconsensual treatment of Jehovah's Witnesses or others whose religious convictions limit therapeutic alternatives. Expert testimony regarding standard of care and breach of standard of care is not necessary in battery cases.

Although in some jurisdictions recovery still may be based on assault and battery theories, through legislation (sometimes as part of reform measures) most jurisdictions have removed the right to bring such an action because it is subsumed under other medical malpractice causes of action. This change is a result of the now nearly universal acceptance of the doctrine of informed consent. A physician may be negligent if he or she diagnoses or treats a patient without obtaining informed consent or an adequate informed consent for such a diagnostic or treatment procedure.

Informed consent. Patients must be capable of giving consent, must possess adequate information with which to reach a decision regarding a diagnostic procedure or treatment, and must be given ample opportunity to discuss alternatives with the physician. A failure to meet the requirements for an appropriate and adequate informed consent may be a departure from the recognized standard of care and may result in an action for failure to obtain "informed consent" against a health care provider.

Consent is a process, not a form. Physicians may fail in their duty to patients when they rely on a form or document for achieving "informed consent." Such a form can never replace the exchange of information between a patient and a health care provider, which is necessary to fulfill the requirements of an adequate informed consent. This topic is covered more thoroughly in Chapter 31.

Abandonment. Generally a physician has no duty to provide care to a person who desires treatment. However, a physician who agrees to treat a patient accepts the duty to provide continuity of care. Legal recognition of this duty follows from the reality that a sick or injured person is at risk until cured or stabilized. No physician can be available at all times and in all circumstances. Yet, physicians must provide an adequate surrogate when unavailable. Many physicians meet this obligation by making arrangements with a partner or nearby colleague in the same or similar field of practice. Backup may be provided by directing ambulatory patients to a nearby, physician-staffed hospital emergency department. Brief lapses of coverage are generally reasonable. For example, it is unlikely that a physician would be successfully sued for failure to attend simultaneous cardiac arrests for which no other physician was available. Physicians are sued when the unavailability of coverage for several hours harms a patient.

This duty to provide care is extinguished when the physician dies, when the patient no longer requires treatment for the illness under consideration, or when the physician gives reasonable notice to the patient of his or her intention to withdraw from the case. In the last case, however, the physician must give the patient time to arrange for care from another qualified physician or must arrange for a substitute physician who is acceptable to the patient. The original physician also must provide emergency care for the patient's condition and related medical problems until the patient has established a relationship with the new physician.

With the accelerated growth of managed health care plans, many physicians have become members of various health care networks. In some cases a physician may opt to leave a network to join another. Such an action per se does not necessarily end a physician-patient relationship, particularly if the patient opts to continue the relationship outside of the network payment scheme. Any physician who wishes to discontinue caring for patients previously seen in such a system may notify those patients of a change in managed care participation and arrange for appropriate transfer of care to a successor physician.

Breach of confidentiality. Physicians have a duty to respect the privacy interests of their patients. Generally, everything said by a patient or his or her family members to a physician in the context of medical diagnosis and treatment is confidential and may be revealed only under certain circumstances. In many states the physician-patient relationship is recognized by a statute that sets forth exceptions to the general rule of confidentiality. Some states rely on common law in this area. Each practitioner should know the rules that apply in his or her state and establish procedures for his or her employees to act accordingly.

In general, health care providers can safely release medical information to other treating physicians or consultants. In life-threatening emergencies, certain information pertinent to the patient's treatment also may be revealed to other medical personnel, even if the patient is unaware. The topic of patient confidentiality is dealt with in more detail in Chapter 32.

Breach of contract or warranty to cure. When a physician promises to effect a cure or to achieve a particular result and the patient submits himself or herself for treatment, the physician is generally liable if the treatment fails to achieve the promised result. The unhappy patient in such a situation can sue the physician in contract rather than in tort. This form of medical malpractice suit has become less common in recent decades. The major advantage for the plaintiff in a contract suit is that a medical standard of care need not be shown. The plaintiff must prove only that a promise was made and relied on, the promise was not kept, and damages resulted because of the broken promise.

The plaintiff in such a suit must prove how he or she was damaged by the physician's breach of promise. A successful plaintiff generally recovers an amount of money that would place him or her in a position comparable to the position he or she would be in had he or she not agreed to treatment. In many cases this amounts to a return of the surgeon's fees, plus a small sum for related expenses. Damages may be exceedingly high in some instances, however, such as when a professional performer is scarred or killed.

Most physicians at one time or another prognosticate for their patients. Courts understand this aspect of medical practice. Breach of contract or warranty actions usually arise when a physician sells a patient on a particular operation. To prevent a plethora of unwarranted suits, many states provide that no legal action may be taken for breach of a contract to cure unless the physician's promise is in writing.

Strict liability for drugs and medical devices. Strict liability (i.e., not negligence-based liability) is imposed on manufacturers, sellers, and distributors of unreasonably dangerous and defective products for injuries resulting from their use. Such liability is independent of negligence law, and a defendant's degree of care is irrelevant in lawsuits based on the concept of strict liability. However, the law recognizes that every drug and device used in medical practice is potentially hazardous. Therefore manufacturers, sellers, and distributors of such products are not liable for damages if they give adequate warnings about how to avoid the risks and make their products as safe as possible. These warnings must be given clearly, prominently, and in a timely manner, and they must be given to the proper person. Overpromotion of a product can negate the effect of otherwise adequate warnings.

Strict liability is dealt with in more detail in Chapter 35. Strict liability is mentioned here because many medical malpractice suits also include claims for harm caused by the physician's alleged failure to inform and adequately warn the patient of a dangerous or defective product in his or her role as "learned intermediary."

Strict liability reduces the plaintiff's burden of proof. It is much easier to prove that a product warning was not given or was inadequate than it is to show that a physician violated the standard of care. The plaintiff must show only that the product was defective or that the warning of its nondefective hazards was faulty and the deficiency of product or warning was a cause of the injury. Foreseeability is not required to make a case of strict liability against a defendant.

A strict liability case also can be brought when a defendant physician is uninsured or underinsured, and a solvent pharmaceutical house or device manufacturer may be found liable to pay a share of any judgment. Sometimes a defendant physician brings the drug manufacturer or device company into the suit as a "third-party defendant," requiring it to pay part or all of the plaintiff's damages, or the defendant treating physician also may be the seller of the drug or device.

Physician liability for the actions of other health care providers

Vicarious liability. Physicians usually employ or supervise other less qualified health care professionals. Physicians therefore owe their patients the duty to supervise nurses, technicians, and other subordinates properly. That duty may create vicarious liability, whereby one person may be liable for the wrongful acts or omissions of another. Several legal doctrines must be discussed in this context.

The simplest such doctrine is known as *respondeat superior* and states that an employer is liable for the negligence of his or her employees. For example, if a physician's office nurse injects a drug into a patient's sciatic nerve, causing injury, that patient may sue the physician for the nurse's negligence.

Physicians also may be held vicariously liable for the negligence of hospital employees they supervise under other legal doctrines. For example, surgeons have been sued for errors and omissions by operating room personnel under the "captain of the ship" doctrine. This doctrine holds a surgeon liable based on the legal action that he or she has absolute control, much like the captain of a ship at sea who is responsible for all the wrongs perpetrated by the crew. This doctrine was intended to offer a remedy to persons injured by negligent employees of charitable hospitals, which were otherwise legally immune from suit under the doctrine of charitable immunity.

The captain of the ship doctrine has been largely replaced by the "borrowed servant" doctrine in such situations. This latter doctrine holds surgeons responsible for hospital employees' negligent acts that are committed under their direct supervision and control.

Negligent referrals. Physicians today frequently request consultations from other physicians, especially regarding hospitalized patients. A referring physician usually is not liable for the negligence of the specialist. However, the referring physician may be liable for the specialist's misdeeds if each physician assumes the other will provide certain care that is omitted by both or if they neglect a common duty (e.g., postoperative care).

Physicians cannot attend or be available to all patients at all times. They have the duty to provide another physician to care for their patients when they cannot. Just as physicians generally are not liable for consultants' malpractice, they need not answer for care provided by other physicians who cover their practice. Exceptions include the use of covering physicians who are also partners and the negligent selection of covering physicians.

False imprisonment

False imprisonment is a tort that protects an individual from restraint of movement. False imprisonment may occur if an individual is restrained against his or her will in any confined space or area. The plaintiff is entitled to compensation for loss of time, for any inconvenience suffered, for physical or emotional harm, and for related expenses.

A physician holding a patient against his or her will, in absence of a court order, could be held liable for false imprisonment. Such situations arise in cases involving involuntary commitment of a patient with a mental disorder, where a patient is held without compliance with laws governing civil commitments.

Defamation

A statement is defamatory if it impeaches a person's integrity, virtue, human decency, respect for others, or reputation and lowers that person in the esteem of the community or deters third parties from dealing with that person. A defamatory statement can be made either in writing, which is called *libel*, or in verbal communication, which is called *slander*.

In general, truth is an absolute defense to defamation. Some jurisdictions have a rule that a statement that is substantially true, when published with good motives and justifiable ends, shall be a sufficient defense, even though it may not be literally true. For example, if a physician states publicly that a nursing home has 50 complaints against it and there were only 30, the statement likely would not be held defamatory.

Failure to warn and control

The failure of a physician to warn the patient or a third party of a foreseeable risk is a separate and distinct negligent act. A physician's duty of care includes the duty to identify reasonably foreseeable harm resulting from treatment and, if possible, to prevent it. It is increasingly recognized that a physician has the responsibility to warn patients of dangers involved in their care. Failure to advise the patient of known, reasonably foreseeable dangers leaves the physician open to liability for harm the patient suffers and injuries that patient may cause to third parties.

The courts have imposed the duty to warn on a physician when medications with potentially dangerous side effects are administered. If an administered drug might affect a patient's functional abilities (such as ambulation), the physician is obliged to explain the hazard to the patient or to someone who can control the patient's movements (e.g., family members or others who can reasonably be expected to have contact with the patient). The same duty is owed to patients engaged in any activity that may be hazardous, such as driving a car or operating machinery.

Similarly, when a physician learns that a patient has or may have a medical condition with dangerous propensities that may impair the patient's control of his or her activities, the physician has a duty to warn the proper persons, such as the patient's family members or others in contact with the patient. This duty to warn may apply whether the condition is completely diagnosed or is still under study.

In a number of cases physicians have been held liable to injured third parties for failure to warn them of the potentially dangerous mental condition of a patient. Similarly, patients' next of kin have successfully sued after the patients committed suicide, which could have been foreseen and potentially prevented by a physician.

"rewarding" persons for their own folly and to reduce the likelihood of collusion in suits between parties.

To avoid the potential for harsh results, however, contributory negligence as a concept has been largely replaced by the doctrine of comparative negligence. This innovation requires the trier of fact to determine the relative negligence of each party to a lawsuit and requires the judge or jury to assess monetary awards accordingly. Some states permit a plaintiff to recover only if the negligence of the plaintiff is less than that of the defendant.

A physician's duty to prevent harming the patient often is considered greater than any duty of the patient's. Only in limited circumstances can a physician escape liability as a result of a patient's negligence. For example, a diabetic patient who continues participation in a hazardous sport, despite a physician's clear warnings to cease participation, and suffers a secondary complication of the diabetes that results in injuries may pose such a case. However, defendant physicians have great difficulty proving negligence of the plaintiff. Rarely do the courts consider such socially destructive acts as smoking and drinking alcohol during pregnancy negligence on the part of the patient.

Comparative fault is a more recent legal doctrine designed by courts to allow apportionment of damages among negligent defendants. Some jurisdictions have experimented with various tests, including allocating damages based on a comparison of causation among all parties. In this case previous rules regarding contribution and indemnification among defendants have been rewritten. This area of the law currently is evolving.

Sovereign (government) immunity

In medieval times the concept that "the King can do no wrong" allowed the state to escape liability. As a consequence, if the state could do no wrong, its employed physicians and government hospitals could not be sued for malpractice. This was the law until relatively recently, when both federal and state governments passed tort claims acts that now allow suits against the sovereign and its representatives with some restrictions and limitations of damages. These statutes permit individuals who have been negligently injured by government workers, including government-employed physicians, to sue and recover from the government sometimes only after special notice or claim is first denied.

Statute of limitation

The idea that misdeeds must be litigated within a reasonable time is the basis for statutes of limitations. Plaintiffs are held to a duty to bring suit before the passage of time makes defense an unreasonable burden. The deadline for filing and serving certain legal claims varies from state to state, and different theories of recovery (i.e., felonies, breach of contract, torts, disputes over land ownership) may have different statutes of limitations.

The statute of limitation for medical negligence is generally the same as for other unintentional torts. If an injured patient sues a physician after the time set forth in the applicable statute of limitation has passed, the defendant may be entitled to dismissal.

The time allowed for filing suit is said to run from the date the negligence is discovered, which may present a special problem when the negligence was an omission or when injuries are apparent only after a long period. Most states stop or "toll" the running of time set forth in the statute during periods when the plaintiff would not be legally competent to commence the lawsuit without great difficulty. Examples include situations in which the plaintiff is a minor or is mentally incompetent. Other causes for such "tolling" include cases in which the physician fraudulently concealed the misdeed or continued to care for the patient beyond the limitation period.

Exculpatory agreements and indemnification contracts

Exculpatory agreements between physicians and patients appear to relieve the physician of liability for negligence. Although such contracts occasionally are upheld in other theories of liability, they are consistently struck down in the medical malpractice context. The rationale for not acknowledging such agreements is simply that they are contracts of adhesion. The fact that an ill patient is not in a position to negotiate terms or to reach a fair meeting of the minds, which is essential for a binding contract equity, dictates such an approach.

Contracts of indemnification usually arise between physicians and other individuals or institutions. For example, a hospital may agree to pay (indemnify) any damages incurred by the president of its medical staff for any liability resulting from carrying out the duties of that office. Conversely the chief of anesthesiology may agree to indemnify the hospital for any malpractice damages arising from the operation of the department, if no hospital employee is found to be negligent. Both types of contracts are generally upheld and effectively transfer enormous financial burdens from one party to another. Although such agreements often are represented as standard terms in an employment contract, they must be considered carefully.

SETTLEMENT OF MALPRACTICE CLAIMS

Practical aspects of defending any particular malpractice claim dictate the need for consultation with counsel and the malpractice insurer. In most cases a malpractice insurer provides counsel under the policy to defend the claim. Although a physician may believe that the best time to settle a malpractice claim (from his or her point of view) is at the time such claim occurs, procedural matters and substantive matters must be considered, and the physician's personal legal counsel may be able to give the best advice on this point.

The physician should contact his or her professional liability carrier as soon as there is even a suggestion of a potential claim and ask for a representative to handle the matter. The physician should always insist that an attorney rather than a claims adjuster handle the matter, even if the physician is willing to admit fault. Private counsel also should be retained to handle potential liability not covered by the policy or to advise the physician regarding negotiating a settlement in the course of the litigation. This advice is particularly important because the Health Care Quality Improvement Act of 1986 requires that the settlement of any medical malpractice claim for any amount in excess of $1 be reported.[2]

In practice, negotiation and settlement of a medical malpractice claim rarely occur before the phase of formal discovery procedures, which occur during the months between the filing of the suit and the scheduled trial. Discovery measures include interrogatories; requests for admissions; requests for production of documents or other items, such as x-ray films or fetal monitoring strips; and depositions of parties and witnesses. These measures are useful for ferreting out information; the prosecution and defense counsel use the same methods to determine the nature of the opposing party's case.

ENDNOTES

1. *Daubert v. Merrell Dow Pharmaceuticals*, 61 U.S. 6W 4805 (1993).
2. Health Care Quality Improvement Act, 42 U.S.C. §§11101 *et seq.* (1986).

30

Physician-Patient Relationship

MATTHEW L. HOWARD, M.D., J.D., F.C.L.M

NATURE AND CREATION
LIMITING THE DUTIES IMPOSED
BREACH OF CONTRACT
SPECIAL SITUATIONS
LIABILITY FOR INJURY TO THIRD PARTIES
RELATIONSHIPS FORMED BY CONTRACT WITH OTHERS
TERMINATION
EXPECTATIONS OF THE FUTURE: TRENDS
CONCLUSION

Physician-patient relationships (PPRs) presumably have been a source of concern since some forgotten ancestor first claimed special talent as a healer. The Hippocratic oath can be thought of as a codification of rules governing the PPR, the existence of which suggests that some physicians at least needed to be bound by oath to enforce adherence to the social norm.[1] The sanctions[2] of the Code of Hammurabi may be the earliest expression of the idea that physicians should be liable for harm to patients.[3]

Modern professional negligence law has arisen by application of elements of English common law of contracts and torts to the same concerns expressed by Hippocrates and Hammurabi.[4] Changes in the structure of the medical profession, which began in 1964 with the passage of Medicare legislation and are proceeding at an increasingly accelerated pace through legislative mandates, corporate initiatives, and technological change, continue to modify the traditional approaches. This chapter is intended to provide an overview of the issues, generally stating the majority view. Case law varies between jurisdictions; both case law and statutes should be examined for variance before taking any action with potential legal consequences.

The PPR traditionally has been considered contractual. Written contracts are the exception; the contract is implied by the actions of the parties in seeking and providing advice and care.[5] The physician is deemed to have promised that professionally acceptable care will be provided, with no guarantee. Unless a specific warranty has been made, courts will not infer that a physician has guaranteed treatment success. The fact that a patient does not pay for services does not affect the existence of the contract or lessen the physician's duties, obligations, responsibilities, or liabilities.[6]

For a person to be professionally liable to another, four conditions must be met. A person claiming compensation for malpractice must show that the professional owed a duty of care to that person (duty owed), the duty was not met (an accepted professional standard of care was breached), and the breach of duty resulted (causation) in otherwise avoidable damages (injury) to the person making the claim. Each one of these elements (duty, breach of the duty, causation, and injury) must be proven for the plaintiff to prevail, which is true whatever the profession. The law applied to physicians or other health care professionals is fundamentally the same as that applied to architects, engineers, and attorneys.

Before a professional duty can be established, the traditional and general rule has been that a professional relationship must exist. Demonstrating the existence of a relationship between the physician and the person claiming to have been harmed is the keystone of every medical malpractice action.[7]

Under certain statutes, duties may arise from hospital-patient relationships, which, once established in accordance with the terms of the law, impose duties on the physician. When a physician becomes involved in a legal problem that stems from a hospital-patient relationship, it is usually because of a special relationship between the hospital and physician. Managed care and telemedicine are further altering the traditional analysis.

NATURE AND CREATION

This chapter discusses the question of the physician-patient relationship entirely in the context of traditional American jurisprudence, which arises out of an Anglo-European tradition. From a legal point of view, that is entirely appropriate as the parameters of the PPR, especially when problems lead to court action, will be defined in that context. The PPR has a cultural aspect also, however. Although space limitations prevent a review of the differences that exist throughout the world, a brief commentary on the issues that arise from immigration to the United States, in a textbook of legal medicine directed at an American audience, is worthwhile. American medical literature has referred with increasing frequency to the Japanese tradition that a patient should not be told of a terminal prognosis. The current American view of the PPR, which is based on a contract entered into by two autonomous and competent adults, requires that the patient be affirmatively told of their prognosis. Many persons do not put their affairs in order until they know the end is approaching. At least one suit has been based on a physician's failure to apprise his patient of the patient's preterminal condition.[8] But many cultures, including Japanese, Italians, Greeks, Korean-Americans, Mexican-Americans, Sephardic Jews, Spanish, Eastern Europeans, and Moroccans, have been reported to believe that such information should be withheld.[9] In all cases, of course, no assumption should ever be made about a person's beliefs based on their ethnicity. For each patient, at the onset of the PPR, the physician should ascertain the level of autonomy and information desired by the individual at hand. The physician should not be surprised to find many Japanese-Americans wanting full disclosure and persons of other ethnic backgrounds preferring to be kept in ignorance. The important point is to be aware of the possibilities and act to obtain necessary information so that the PPR can be satisfactory for both parties. In some instances, requests may be made for services appropriate to the culture but illegal in the United States, as for example when female genital excision (female circumcision) or "female cutting" is requested.[10]

In the absence of a PPR or some other special relationship, physicians are not legally compelled to treat strangers, even during an emergency, in almost all states.[11] When a person seeks the services of a physician for the purposes of medical or surgical treatment, that person becomes a patient and the traditional PPR is established.[12] A contract is implied by the mutuality of the relationship.[13] The physician is not an employee of the patient.[14] This traditional relationship is consensual, meaning the patient has consciously sought out a physician who has affirmatively agreed to provide care. The mutuality of the relationship is independent of who solicits the relationship or who pays for the services provided.[15] As we shall see, many problems arise in situations in which the physician is held to a duty to a person for whom he or she has not consciously agreed to provide care.

Creation of the PPR usually requires some form of physical contact with the patient. It may be created by a single telephone conversation.[16] Pathologists[17] and radiologists,[18] however, have a duty to the patient to exercise reasonable and ordinary skill and care while rendering their services even though they generally have no personal contact with the patient.

Whether a PPR legally exists is a factual determination. For public policy reasons, courts give persons alleging injury from medical malpractice considerable latitude as to the evidence required to establish the existence of the relationship.[19] Courts will determine whether the patient entrusted care to the physician and whether the physician indicated acceptance of the duty to render care. If the circumstances of the contact caused the patient to have a reasonable expectation of treatment or if the physician undertook to render treatment, then the courts will infer the existence of a relationship.[20]

One legal definition of treatment is "the broad term covering all steps taken to effect a cure of an injury or disease. The word includes examination and diagnosis as well as application of remedies."[21] This broad interpretation and the willingness of most courts to interpret almost any action as an undertaking-to-treat may result in a PPR that the physician did not intend to create.

LIMITING THE DUTIES IMPOSED

Once established, unless limited or conditioned by agreement, the relationship continues until the services are no longer needed or are properly terminated. Once the relationship has been terminated, the physician is generally not obligated to follow the patient's progress.[22]

Courts are quick to find a PPR yet generally recognize the physician's ability to qualify or limit the relationship.[23] Agreements to treat may be limited to one particular treatment or procedure.[24] Physician availability may be restricted, if clearly understood and accepted by the patient, to certain times and places.[25]

Physicians generally are free to choose their patients[26] and are not obligated to treat anyone with whom they have no special relationship.[27] Absent statutorily imposed requirements, physicians are not compelled to practice, to practice under terms other than those the physician may choose to accept, or to provide care to any or all prospective patients. This principle is recognized by the Principles of Medical Ethics of the American Medical Association and supported by case law.[28]

An established relationship renders the physician liable for damages legally caused by any breach of the resulting duty. The fundamental duty is to exercise the same degree of knowledge, skill, diligence, and care that an ordinary competent physician would exercise under the same or similar circumstances. There is a concomitant duty to suggest a referral if the physician knows or should know that he or she does not possess the requisite knowledge or skill to properly treat the patient.[29] Failure to make a referral is negligence.[30]

The patient is obligated to cooperate by following reasonable instructions for further evaluation and treatment.[31]

hospitalization.[77] The appellate court reversed a summary judgment for the hospital and remanded for trial on the issue of whether the actions of the insurer led to the death.

Telemedicine

Has a relationship been established by an exchange of information on an Internet site? A court may conclude that an Internet site that appears to have been established for the purposes of bringing in new patients may establish a relationship.

It is a fundamental rule of due process that a court may not exert jurisdiction over a person unless that person has some "minimal contacts" with the state seeking jurisdiction.[73] A person living and working in Illinois who is involved in an automobile accident in Illinois with a California resident cannot be called to a California court to respond to a personal injury suit brought by the Californian. Neither can he or she be called to any court in the United States other than an Illinois court. Where a physician has provided personal services to an out-of-state patient, as happens frequently in our mobile society as patients seek out major medical centers or well-known physicians, the courts treat the resulting malpractice claim as they would the automobile accident.

Jurisdiction resides in the state where the incident took place. However, where the physician has attracted out-of-state patients through marketing schemes, personal jurisdiction in the patient's home state has been established.[74] Where the PPR was based on the mail-order nature of the business, the court found jurisdiction.[75] The applicability of this decision to advice provided over a "chat" site or Internet site should be clear. Several states have enacted statutes that forbid prescribing for patients where the only contact has been by telecommunications, so-called "reaching into another state."[76] Penalties ranging from reprimand to loss of license to practice may apply.[77]

Relationships imposed by statute

An increased duty to treat is being imposed by some states as a condition of licensure. For example, physicians have been forbidden to refuse care to patients who have tested positive for human immunodeficiency virus.[78]

LIABILITY FOR INJURY TO THIRD PARTIES
Nonpatient relationships with physicians

Not every patient contact results in the creation of a PPR. When a physician performs an examination at the request of a third party for sole use by the third party (e.g., to determine eligibility for employment or for the issuance of life insurance), courts differ in their interpretation of the physician's duty to the patient. If a physician is employed to perform preemployment examinations, then the physician's duty is owed to his or her employer; no PPR is implied. Absence of therapeutic intent is often the key issue.[79] Courts have said that the employed physician owes no duty to the examinee other than to avoid causing an injury[80] and is under a duty to use reasonable care to avoid same.[81] Failure to do so may lead to a claim based on ordinary negligence rather than medical malpractice. Another court assumes no duty unless advice is offered.[82] No liability exists for a negligently performed examination, but the employer may be liable to the examinee for the negligent acts of a physician-employee under the doctrine of respondeat superior.[83] The physician may in turn be liable to the company under a contract theory for any resulting damages.

As a general rule, a third-party employed physician is not bound to disclose abnormal findings to an examinee. Possible exceptions to this rule occur if the physician conducts an examination on a person with whom he or she has a prior existing PPR or if the physician completes an attending physician's statement for an insurance company and is paid a fee for doing so (contrast with physician as salaried employee).[84] Under such circumstances, the physician might have a duty to disclose significant findings to the examinee. This traditional rule was explicitly abandoned and physician liability expanded in a case in which a preemployment physical included a chest x-ray examination. The physician, failing to detect what later proved to be a lung carcinoma, reported to the employer that the person was employable. This court ignored traditional intent to treat and patient expectation rules in finding the physician liable.[85]

If a physician gratuitously elects to discuss findings with the examinee, he or she must not misrepresent the examinee's medical condition. If the physician recommends treatment, liability may result if substandard advice causes injury to the examinee.[86] Third parties other than employers may employ physicians to examine or treat a patient. The courts distinguish between liability to the third party (for the examination itself) and liability to the patient (for the treatment once it has begun).[87]

Indirect relationships with physicians

Recognizing the fundamental principle that all must use ordinary care not to injure others, violations of that duty occur when an injury results that is reasonably avoidable and is a foreseeable consequence of a person's actions. All physicians have a duty to warn patients about aspects of their medical condition or treatment that could injure others.[88] The physician treating a seizure patient, for example, may be liable for injury to a nonpatient if the injury is indirectly caused by negligent treatment, failure to diagnose the condition, or failure to advise the patient of the risks of engaging in dangerous activities.[89]

Although the courts reject creating a PPR with the third-party victim, they freely apply ordinary negligence principles and hold that the injury to the nonpatient was a foreseeable consequence of the patient's condition, which imposed on the physician a duty to avoid injury to foreseeable victims.[90] Lack of foreseeability was at issue where a physician treated a police officer for a pituitary gland tumor. A citizen later shot by the officer was not permitted to maintain an action either under malpractice or negligence theories against the treating physician.[91]

Liability has resulted in some cases when physicians have failed to advise patients of the danger of performing certain acts while taking medications, such as driving while using sedatives or decongestants,[92] but there has been no liability in similar circumstances in other courts.[93] Liability has resulted when the physician failed to properly caution patients with communicable diseases to avoid transmitting the disease to third parties.[94] The Court of Appeals considered a suit against a physician brought by the family of a motorist killed in an automobile accident with the physician's patient. The patient had received a sedating medication by injection and was given no warning against driving. The Michigan court permitted the suit to proceed not in negligence as described previously but as a medical malpractice action, ruling that dismissing the suit because of the absence of a PPR between the physician and the deceased would "exalt form over substance."[95] West Virginia has come to a similar conclusion.[96]

Where a patient's relative who was permitted to remain in an emergency department treatment area fainted at the sight of blood and sustained significant permanent sequelae from the resulting head injury, the physician was held to have no liability to the injured relative.[97]

Courts have imposed liability on physicians who bear a special relationship to a dangerous person and a subsequent victim.[98] Such a relationship may support affirmative physician duties for the benefit of a nonpatient third party.[99] The duty to the nonpatient stems from the physician's special relationship with the patient, and the potential for harm to the third party is a result of the patient's behavior. The leading case is *Tarasoff*,[100] which imposed liability on a psychotherapist whose patient had repeatedly expressed hostile intent toward a specific person who was subsequently murdered. Most subsequent cases have limited that liability to the facts of the *Tarasoff* case, although the victim need not be a patient. Where hostile intent has not been limited to a specific, readily identifiable person, no liability has been found when harm subsequently resulted.[101] The duty to protect endangered third persons has been extended to the protection of endangered property.[102]

RELATIONSHIPS FORMED BY CONTRACT WITH OTHERS

If a physician contracts with a third party to treat a patient, then the PPR is not established with the patient until there is some overt undertaking. If the physician does not treat the proposed patient, then no duty to the expectant patient is created. However, physician liability to the third party who relies on the physician's assurance to treat may exist.[103] When a third party contracts with a physician to treat a particular patient and the treatment is undertaken, the PPR is established and the physician's duty is now to the patient rather than the third party.[104] If the physician's agreement to provide care to a patient leads the third party to believe that the patient is being competently cared for, and because they are reasonably restrained by this belief the third party does not seek care elsewhere, then the physician could be liable to both patient and third party. Liability to the patient would be based on medical malpractice, and liability to the third party would be based on breach of contract. Such a situation could arise in the case of a minor student at college being treated at the request of a parent living elsewhere.

A physician employed by a third party for the sole purpose of obtaining evidence to support the third party's challenge to a claim of injury is under no duty to the examinee.[105] The physician is generally under no duty to inform the examinee of the results of the examination and is not liable to the examinee if a negligent examination or negligently prepared report of the examination later causes injury to the examinee, provided the report was not, as postulated, prepared for the use or benefit of the examinee.[106]

TERMINATION

The duties imposed on the physician by the creation of a PPR continue until the relationship is terminated. This termination may occur through completion of the treatment by virtue of patient recovery,[107] dismissal of the physician by the patient, mutual consent, or formal physician withdrawal.[108] Like any other contract, the parties may terminate the agreement by mutual consent. The patient may unilaterally terminate the relationship for any reason and at any time. This termination may be express or implied by the patient's actions.[109] Even though dismissed, the physician is under a duty to warn the patient of any risk of discontinuing treatment. A prudent physician will carefully document the basis and circumstances of dismissal as protection against a later claim by the patient of abandonment. The relationship may be considered terminated once a patient's care has been properly and completely transferred to another physician so that the services of the transferring physician are no longer needed and the duty of continuing care ends.[110] Once services are terminated, the traditional rule has been that the physician is under no duty either to provide future care or to reestablish the relationship.[111] However, some courts have mandated such liability on the grounds that the physician is in a better position than the patient to keep abreast of changing knowledge.[112]

If during the course of treatment a physician concludes that he or she lacks the requisite skill or knowledge to treat the patient competently or for other acceptable reasons determines that the patient would be more properly treated by another physician or at another facility, then the patient should be so informed. As a practical matter, patients readily accede to their physician's judgment in these circumstances and termination of the relationship by a mutually agreed-on transfer usually results. If transfer is declined, then the treating physician is required to inform the patient of the consequences of the refusal, to carefully document the refusal and appropriate counseling, and to continue care until a proper unilateral termination of the relationship has been accomplished.

Unilateral termination by the physician is permitted. The patient must be provided sufficient time to arrange for care to be provided by another physician. Written notice[113] should be provided, preferably by certified mail.[114] The notice should provide an explanation of the patient's condition and the further services needed, as well as a description of the likely consequences of failure to obtain continuing care. The physician should continue to provide care for such time as it will reasonably take for the patient to secure further care, and this length of time should be specified in the notice letter.[115] Improper withdrawal[116] by physicians has resulted in suits for breach of contract,[117] professional negligence, and abandonment.[118]

Abandonment

Abandonment is the unilateral severance of the PPR by the physician without reasonable notice to the patient at a time when continued medical care is still necessary.[119] If physician illness or disability is the cause of the withdrawal, then abandonment has not occurred. Liability for abandonment may be found where the physician intends to terminate the relationship without the patient's consent, as well as where the court finds physician failure to attend the patient as frequently as due care in treatment would demand. Such failure denies the patient the benefit of the PPR and is referred to as *constructive abandonment.*

Abandonment may give rise to an action for either negligence or breach of contract.[120] If a patient is injured because the physician failed to see the patient often enough or if the physician improperly concluded that the patient's condition required no further treatment, the patient has a cause of action in negligence alone.[121] In an action for negligence the patient must present expert testimony; such testimony is not required in an action for breach of contract. The remedies vary, however, and negligence is the action generally preferred. Because abandonment can occur only if there is a valid PPR, it does not result if a physician permissively refuses to enter into such a relationship with a particular person.[122]

EXPECTATIONS OF THE FUTURE: TRENDS

Society's perception of the PPR is generally reflected in the law. During the past several years, both legislation and case law have tended to perceive the physician as being so able to bear the costs of compensation to injured patients that

expansion of physician liability to provide for compensation to more patients has been a justifiable public policy. Recent court decisions support a conclusion that such expansion of physician liability is continuing and equally support a conclusion that the pendulum is beginning to swing in the opposite direction.

Supporting the idea that liability expansion is continuing is the series of cases discussed earlier with regard to EMTALA and its extension beyond the situations that presumably led to its adoption, as well as recent cases in which physicians have been prosecuted under criminal statutes in circumstances that once would have been treated solely as civil professional negligence issues.[123] A case that initially appears to reduce a physician's right to exercise judgment in accepting patients for care, by permitting criminal prosecution for negligently exercising the option to refuse to accept a patient for care, led to conviction of a resident physician. The trial court refused to dismiss the indictment.[124] New York State created a new area of physician liability when its court of appeals found that a physician may be liable in malpractice for providing false testimony during a patient's suit against his or her health insurer.[125] A summary judgment for a physician has been reversed where suit was brought by the children of the patient on grounds that their parent was never informed that his hereditary disease could affect his children.[126] Also supporting the idea that liability is being expanded are two cases where physicians were held liable for inducing patients to accept surgery by exaggerating their experience and training.[127]

Supporting the opposite point of view is a case in which a deceased patient's family brought suit against treating physicians on the theory that the physicians' failure to inform the patient of his prognosis led him to engage optimistically in financial dealings that because of his subsequent early death harmed his heirs.[128] The court declined to hold the physicians liable. Further supporting a view that courts wish to restrain liability was the decision of the Pennsylvania Supreme Court to reverse the decision in *Duttry* [127] on the grounds that misrepresentation is a contract issue, and not a malpractice issue.[129] However, the prudent physician will wish to refrain from "puffery" when responding to patient questions about training and experience.

Telemedicine is likely to be a continuing source of controversy. When will contacts through the Internet or other electronic means suffice to establish a PPR? The offering of specific treatment is likely to be the key factor. More important, where will the case be tried? The trial locale will depend on whether the patient can claim sufficient contact between the physician and the patient's home state.

CONCLUSION

Physician liability depends on the existence of a PPR. Such a relationship may be explicit, implicit, or statutorily imposed. Numerous situations arise in our complex society in which physician, patient, government, and third-party payor interact in ill-defined ways, such that PPRs can arise by implication and without conscious physician intent. Physicians should be cautious in their statements and in their behavior to avoid creating a relationship that contrary to their intentions imposes legal obligations.

The legal obligation imposed is the requirement to exercise ordinary professional care in the discharge of professional duties. The plaintiff patient alleging malpractice must establish the existence of the PPR, a breach of the duty created by that relationship, and the existence of an injury caused by the breach. Reasonable differences of opinion as to these elements may subject the physician to all the financial and emotional stress of a lawsuit and its aftermath. Proof of the elements stated, which requires a mere preponderance of the evidence, will subject the physician to liability, will trigger National Practitioner Data Bank reports, and may precipitate disciplinary action.

ENDNOTES

1. Attributed to Hippocrates, Greek physician, fourth century B.C.E.
2. A physician whose patient loses an eye under treatment has his own eye put out.
3. Hammurabi, Babylonian king, lived in the twenty-seventh century B.C.E., roughly 4700 years before the publication of this work.
4. *Thomas v. Corso*, 265 Md. 84, 288 A. 2d 379 (1972) (abandonment is a contract issue, no expert required).
5. *Pike v. Honsinger*, 155 N.Y. 201, 49 N.E. 760 (1898); *Greenstein v. Fornell*, 275 N.Y.S. 673 (1932).
6. *Vitta v. Dolan*, 155 N.W. 1077 (Minn. 1916) (patient need not pay; physician duty remains).
7. *Kennedy v. Parrot*, 243 N.C. 355, 90 S.E. 2d 754 (1956) (preference for tort law over contract law in "due care" situations).
8. *Arato v. Avedon*, 5 Cal. 4th 1172, 858 P. 2d 598, 23 Cal. Rptr. 2d 131 (1993) (physician's duty does not extend to liability for inaccurate prognosis as to life expectancy).
9. B. Freedman, *Offering Truth*, 153 Arch. Intern. Med. 572-76 (1993) and L.J. Blackhall, S.T. Murphy, G. Frank, et al., *Ethnicity and Attitudes Toward Patient Autonomy*, 274 J.A.M.A. 820-25 (1995).
10. N.D. Cent. Code 12.1-36-01; 1999 Tex. Gen. Laws 3213 (female genital mutilation prohibited).
11. *Childs v. Weis*, 440 S.W. 2d 104 (Tex. 1969) (physician may arbitrarily refuse to render care to a nonpatient).
12. *Traveler's Ins. Co. v. Bergeron*, 25 F. 2d 680, 49 S.Ct. 33 (1928) (relationship established when professional services are accepted by another person for purposes of medical or surgical treatment).
13. *Findly v. Board of Supervisors*, 230 P. 2d 526 (Ariz. 1951) (consensual relationship); *Brumbalow v. Fritz*, 183 Ga. App. 231, 358 S.E. 2d 872 (1987) (patient refused advised admission, then was injured while leaving emergency department; suit against physician dismissed).
14. *In re Estate of Bridges*, 41 Wash. 2d 916, 253 P. 2d 394 (1953) (physician not employee).
15. *Hoover v. Williamson*, 236 Md. 258, 203 A. 2d 861 (1964) (services paid for by employer but duty to employee).
16. *Vitta, supra* note 6 (not necessary for patient to know physician, engage his or her services, or pay for them in ordinary way).
17. *Walters v. Rinker*, 520 N.E. 2d 468 (Ind. Ct. App. 1988) (examination of tumor removed from patient establishes PPR).
18. *Rule v. Cheeseman*, 181 Kan. 957, 317 P. 2d 472 (1957) (radiologist's duty of care).
19. *Vitta, supra* note 16.
20. *Betesh v. United States*, 400 F. Supp. 238 (D.C. 1974) (in the context of a preinduction physical, physician's recall of rejected examinee to check on progression of disease was sufficient act to indicate treatment).
21. *Kirschner v. Equitable Life Assurance Soc.*, 284 N.Y.S. 506 (1935) (defines "treatment").
22. *Fleischman v. Richardson-Merrell, Inc.*, 266 A. 2d 639, 558 N.Y.S. 2d 688 (1990) (no duty to follow patient's progress once relationship is terminated).
23. *Osborne v. Frazor*, 425 S.W. 2d 768 (Tenn. 1968) (relationship by its terms may be limited); *Mozingo v. Pitt County Memorial Hosp., Inc.*, 415 S.E. 2d 134 (N.C. 1992).
24. *Markley v. Albany Medical Center*, 163 A. 2d 539, 558 N.Y.S. 2d 688 (1990) (duty may be limited to those medical functions undertaken by physician and relied on by patient).
25. *Sendjar v. Gonzales*, 520 S.W. 2d 478 (Texas 1975) (physician had right to refuse hospital calls).
26. *Hoover, supra* note 15 (no duty to nonpatient unless physician affirmatively acts).
27. *Hiser v. Randolph*, 617 P. 2d 774 (Ariz. 1980), *overruled on other grounds*, 688 P. 2d 605 (1988) (may refuse to treat patient). The author must distinguish between duty for professional liability purposes, discussed here, and duties imposed as a condition of licensure. In various states, duties as a condition of continued licensure have been imposed that restrict a physician's right to freely choose those for whom he or she will provide care. Included are abstention from balance billing of Medicare patients, acceptance of Medicaid patients, and acceptance of HIV-positive patients. Additional restrictions are created by federal civil rights laws and the Americans with Disabilities Act.
28. *Childs, supra* note 11 (right of physician to refuse intoxicated patient); *Childers v. Frye*, 158 S.E. 744 (N.C. 1931) (may refuse to treat nonpatient); *Coss v. Spaulding*, 126 P. 468 (Utah 1912) (physician employed by third party to examine also gratuitously advised, thereby establishing a relationship).
29. Malpractice: Physician's Failure to Advise Patient to Consult Specialist or One Qualified in a Method of Treatment which Physician Is Not Qualified to Give, 35 A.L.R. 3d 349 (failure to get consultation).
30. *Shoemaker v. Crawford*, 78 Ohio App. 3d 53, 603 N.E. 2d 1114 (1991), *appeal denied*, 64 Ohio 3d 1434, 595 N.E. 2d 943 (1992) (physician's admitted lack of experience in managing postoperative patient establishes negligence where that lack of experience was proximate cause of patient's injury).
31. Malpractice: What Constitutes Physician-Patient Relationship for Malpractice Purposes, 17 A.L.R. 4th 132 (PPR for malpractice purposes).
32. Medical Malpractice: Patient's Failure to Return, as Directed, for Examination or Treatment as Contributory Negligence, 100 A.L.R. 3d 723 (patient contributorily negligent for failure to return).
33. *Truman v. Thomas*, 27 Cal. 3d 285, 611 P. 2d 902, 165 Cal. Rptr. 208 (1980) (physician liable for failure to warn of consequences of refusing Pap smear).
34. *Rule, supra* note 18.
35. *Osborne, supra* note 23 (contractual relationship between patient and physician).
36. *Alexandridis v. Jewett*, 388 F. 2d 829 (1968) (obstetrician breached contract when he did not deliver infant).
37. *Thor v. Superior Court*, 5 Cal. 4th 725, 855 P. 2d 375, 21 Cal. Rptr. 357 (1993) (physician has no duty toward quadriplegic who refuses medically necessary feeding tube).
38. *Laurie v. Senecal*, 666 A. 2d 806, 808 (1995) (physician's duty persists despite refusal).
39. *Guilmet v. Campbell*, 385 Mich. 57, 188 N.W. 2d 601 (1971) (physician's representations interpreted as guarantees); *Stewart v. Rudner*, 349 Mich. 459, 84 N.W. 2d 815 (1957) (family practitioner breached

contract by promising cesarean section that was not performed). N.B. Michigan law was later amended to require such contracts to be in writing.

40. *Greenwald v. Grayson*, 189 S. 2d 204 (Fla. 1976) (ability to recover in contract even though no negligence shown).

41. *Oliver v. Brock*, 342 S. 2d 1 (Ala. 1976) (no obligation to practice or to accept professional employment).

42. *Osborne, supra* note 23.

43. *Ingber v. Kandler*, 128 A.D. 2d 591, 513 N.Y.S. 2d 11 (1987) (informal opinion offered without review of records or even knowledge of patient's name does not establish relationship); *Grassis v. Retik*, 25 Mass. App. Ct. 595, 521 N.E. 2d 411 (1988) (admitting resident not responsible for later negligence of treating physicians where resident had no further contact with patient).

44. *Irvin v. Smith*, 31 P. 2d 934, 939 (Kan. 2001) (physician agreement to provide care in the future does not create a PPR)

45. *NDB Bank v. Barry*, 223 Mich. App. 370, 372-73, 566 N.W. 2d 47 (1997) (multiple telephone conversations between attending physician and consultant do not create a PPR where consultant never examined patient and never accepted decision-making responsibility).

46. *Hickey v. Travelers Ins. Co.*, 158 A.D. 2d 112, 558 N.Y.S. 2d 554 (1990) (cause remanded for trial to determine whether physician was guilty of "negligent omission" for which apparently no liability would be imposed, or "negligent commission" for which liability would be imposed).

47. *Reed v. Gershweir*, 160 Ariz. 203, 772 P. 2d 26 (Ct. App. 1989) (physician not liable for malpractice of covering physician where reasonable care in selecting coverage was exercised).

48. *Blackshear v. Calis*, L-01240-93 (N.J. Super. Ct. Middlesex Cnty., July 16, 1996) (obstetricians left inexperienced resident to do difficult forceps delivery).

49. *Alexandridis, supra* note 36 (obstetrician breached contract when resident delivered infant).

50. *Perna v. Pirozzi*, 457 A. 2d 431 (N.J. 1983) (patient should be informed of substitution in advance).

51. *Baird v. National Health Foundation*, 144 S.W. 2d 850 (Mo. 1940) (substitute physician cannot use other physician's negligence as excuse for own actions).

52. *Bass v. Barksdale*, 671 S.W. 2d 476 (Tenn. Ct. App. 1984) (covering physician signed prescription at request of primary physician).

53. *Steinberg v. Dunseth*, 631 N.E. 2d 809 (Ill. App., 4th Dist. 1994).

54. *McKenna v. Cedars of Lebanon Hosp.*, 93 Cal. App. 282, 155 Cal. Rptr. 631 (1979) (malpractice action against resident physician for emergency care rendered to in-patient with whom resident had no prior contract allowed protection of Good Samaritan statute); *Leathers v. Serrell*, 376 F. Supp. 983 (1979) (intern loses hospital's immunity because he did not function within strict interpretation of statute when he treated nonpatient).

55. *Smart v. Kansas City*, 105 S.W. 709 (1907), *overruled on other grounds; State ex. rel. McNutt v. Keet*, 432 S.W. 2d 597 (Mo. 1968) (where clinical professor examined patient on ward with patient's knowledge, consent, and belief the purpose was for treatment, a relationship was implied).

56. *Rogers v. Horvath*, 65 Mich. App. 644, 237 N.W. 2d 595 (1975) (no relationship because examination not conducted for patient's benefit and no advice offered). But *see also Lownsbury v. VanBuren*, 762 N.E. 2d 354 (Ohio 2002) (physician who agreed to supervise resident physicians at a teaching hospital has PPR with patient with whom he had minimal contact).

57. *Perna, supra* note 50.

58. *Rainer v. Grossmen*, 31 Cal. App. 3d 539 (1973) (lecturing physician gave advice in response to question; no attempt to treat; no relationship).

59. *Pearson v. Norman*, 106 P. 2d 361 (Colo. 1940) (license to practice does not require physician to accept all comers).

60. *Clough v. Lively*, 186 Ga. App. 415, 367 S.E. 2d 295 (1988) (emergency department nurse checked patient's vital signs and drew blood at police request; patient dies after transfer to jail; PPR established by consent to draw blood).

61. *Hiser, supra* note 27; *Thompson v. Sun City Comm. Hosp.*, 141 Ariz. 597, 688 P. 2d 605 (1984) (assenting to hospital bylaws, which required participation in emergency room call, altered physicians' right to refuse to treat a patient).

62. *Wilmington General Hosp. v. Manlove*, 54 Del. 15, 174 A. 2d 135 (1961) (more than public reliance on hospitals to provide care is required to establish PPR); *Weaver v. University of Michigan Board of Regents*, 506 N.W. 2d 264 (Mich. App. 1993) (telephone call to make appointment does not create PPR).

63. *Fabran v. Matzko*, 236 Pa. Super. 267, 344 A. 2d 569 (1975) (telephone contact insufficient to establish relationship); *St. John v. Pope*, 901 S.W. 2d 420 (Tex. Sup. Ct. 1995) (telephone discussion about postoperative fever, followed by physician advice to seek care from surgeon who performed surgery, insufficient to establish relationship).

64. *Hamil v. Bashline*, 224 Pa. Super. 407, 305 A. 2d 57 (1973) (telephone contact constituted advice and treatment); *Lyons v. Grether*, 218 Va. 630, 239 S.E. 2d 103 (1977) (appointment arranged by telephone to treat created duty where patient was not permitted to enter with guide dog).

65. *Swift v. Coleman*, No. 68488 (N.Y. App. Div., 3d Dept., Mar 10, 1994) (anticipation of future treatment created by single telephone call sufficient to establish a "continuous relationship of trust and confidence"); *Cogswell v. Chapmen*, 672 N.Y.S. 2d 460 (App. Div. 1998) (giving medical advice in response to query from patient is sufficient to establish PPR).

66. Council on Ethical and Judicial Affairs, American Medical Association, *Sexual Misconduct in the Practice of Medicine*, 266 J.A.M.A. 2741 (1991).

67. *See, e.g.*, Colo. Rev. Stat. Ann. 12-36-117(1)(r); Fla. Stat. Ann. 458.331(1)(j); Ariz. Rev. Stat. Ann. 32-1401(21)(z); Doering's Calif. Bus. and Prof. Code §756.

68. *Gromus v. Medical Board of California*, 8 Cal. App. 4th 589, 10 Cal. Rptr. 452 (1992) (sexual interaction must breach professional duty in a way "substantially related to the qualifications, functions, or duties of the occupation for which a license was issued."); *Larsen v. Comm. on Medical Competency*, 585 N.W. 2d 801 (N.D. 1998) (consensual relationship for 3 months grounds for revocation of license).

69. *New Mexico Physicians Mutual Liability Co. v. LaMure*, 116 N.M. 92, 860 P. 2d 734 (1993) (insurance company not required to indemnify physician found liable in medical malpractice by jury for sexual misconduct with patient); *Patricia C. v. Mark D.*, 12 Cal. App. 4th 1211, 16 Cal. Rptr. 2d 71 (1993) (psychotherapist not liable in malpractice for sexual misconduct with patient).

70. *Benavidez v. United States*, 177 F. 3d 927 (10th Cir. 1997) (homosexual relations between therapist and patient under the influence of drugs and alcohol is malpractice); *St. Paul Fire and Marine Insurance v. Engelmann*, 2000 WL 33674542 (S.D.) (where physician was acquitted of rape charges, despite admitting to sexual contact, the insurer was required to defend the resulting civil action and may have to pay whatever portion of the judgment is attributable to noncriminal conduct; case remanded for trial for jury to apportion damages between covered negligence and noncovered criminal behavior).

71. *Wickline v. State*, 192 Cal. App. 3d 1630, 239 Cal. Rptr. 810 (1986) (physician has duty to advocate for his or her patient and to challenge inappropriate payor decisions).

72. *Wilson v. Blue Cross*, 222 Cal. App. 3d 660, 271 Cal. Rptr. 876 (1990) (insurer may be liable if refusal to pay for continued hospitalization was clearly contrary to informed medical opinion).

73. *International Shoe v. State of Washington*, 325 U.S. 310, 66 S.Ct. 154 (1945).

74. *Bullion v. Gillespie*, 895 F. 2d 213 (5th Cir. 1990) (mailing drugs to patient in another state attracted to the physician's practice through nationally distributed literature establishes jurisdiction in patient's state).

75. *Kennedy v. Freeman*, 919 F. 2d 126 (10th Cir. 1990) (processing and reading biopsy specimens from out-of-state physicians).

76. *See, e.g.,* Calif. Business and Professions Code §2234(g) (". . . unprofessional conduct includes, but is not limited to, the following: . . . (g) The practice of medicine from this state into another state or country without meeting the legal requirements of that state or country for the practice of medicine.")

77. *In re B.T. Taylor, M.D.*, Action Report, Medical Board of California (Oct. 1999) (reprimand from Medical Board of California after Colorado disciplined physician for prescribing over Internet and by telephone for patients never personally examined by him).

78. *Cahil v. Rosa*, 89 N.Y. 214, 674 N.E. 2d 274 (1997) and *Lasser v. Rosa*, 237 A.D. 361 (N.Y. 1997) (New York State human rights law forbids a dentist from turning away patients because of positive HIV tests).

79. *Lotspeich v. Chance Vought Aircraft*, 369 S.W. 2d 705 (Tex. App. 1963) (employer has liability under respondeat superior to employee for physician's negligence; no PPR); *Mracheck v. Sunshine Biscuit*, 308 N.Y. 116, 123 N.E. 2d 801 (1954) (employer liability for acts of negligent physician; no PPR).

80. *Lotspeich, supra* note 79 (no duty to employee except not to injure); *Mero v. Sadoff*, 31 Cal. App. 4th 1466, 37 Cal. Rptr. 2d 769 (1995) (physician who injuries patient during worker's compensation examination is liable in malpractice even in absence of PPR).

81. *Beadling v. Sirotta*, 41 N.J. 555, 197 A. 2d 857 (1964) (preemployment examination, duty of reasonable care; not entitled to results of examination, but entitled to not be injured during examination).

82. *Fleishman, supra* note 22.

83. *Wilmington General Hosp., supra* note 62.

84. *Dowling v. Mutual Life Ins. Co. of N.Y.*, 168 So. 2d 107 (La. 1964) (prior relationship may impose duty).

85. *Green v. Walker*, 910 F. 2d 291 (1990) (physician has responsibility "to the extent of the tests conducted").

86. *Keene v. Wiggins*, 69 Cal. App. 3d 308, 138 Cal. Rptr. 3 (1977) (no duty where examination is for report to employer but voluntary care or attempt to treat or benefit worker creates a duty).

87. *Maltempo v. Cuthbert*, 504 F. 2d 325 (5th Cir. 1974) (promise to parents to treat imprisoned son).

88. *Myers v. Quisenberry*, 144 Cal. App. 3d 888, 193 Cal. Rptr. 733 (1983) (failure to warn diabetic patient of driving risk).

89. *Lemmon v. Freese*, 210 N.W. 2d 576 (Ia. 1973) (liable for foreseeable injury to third party resulting from failure to warn patient of dangers of seizures).

90. *New Mexico Physicians, supra* note 69.

91. *Joseph v. Shafey*, 580 So. 2d 160 (Fla. 1991) (no duty or privity of contract between citizen shot by officer and officer's physician).

92. *Wilschinsky v. Medina*, 108 N.M. 511, 775 P. 2d 713 (1989) (physician's duty extends to members of the public who may be injured by sedated driver; the duty is met by warning the patient not to drive); *Zavalas v. State of Oregon*, 861 P. 2d 1026, 124 Or. App. 166 (1993) (physician liable in negligence to people injured by patient driving under the influence of drug prescribed by physician); *Kaiser v. Suburban Transportation System*, 398 P. 2d 14 (Wash. 1965) (failure to warn bus driver of sedating effect of decongestant).

93. *Johnson v. Fine*, 45 P. 3d 441 (Okla. Ct. App. 2002) (physician did not owe a duty to the mother of two children who were injured in an automobile accident caused by a patient to whom the physician had prescribed Xanax)

94. *DiMarco v. Lynch Homes Chester County, Inc.*, 559 A. 2d 530 (Pa. 1989) (injured third party relied on incorrect advice provided by physician to patient regarding communicability of hepatitis); *Nold v. Binyon*,

31 P. 3d 274, 278 (Kan. 2001) (physician has PPR with unborn fetus that contracted hepatitis B after failure of attending physician to appropriately treat mother with gamma-globulin to protect fetus).

95. *Welke v. Kuzilla*, 144 Mich. App. 245, 375 N.W. 2d 403 (1985) (malpractice action allowed despite absence of PPR).

96. *Osborne v. United States of America*, No. 30115 (S.Ct. W.Va. July 3, 2002) ("the legislature intended to allow individuals generally to recover damages attributable to medical professional liability regardless of whether they are actually patients") (on a question of state law certified from U.S. District Court).

97. *McElwain v. Van Beek*, 447 N.W. 2d 442 (Minn. Ct. App. 1989) (duty to warn third parties applies only to dangers arising from the patient).

98. *Duvall v. Goldin*, 363 N.W. 2d 275 (Mich. 1984) (special relationship imposes duty on physician that benefits third party).

99. *Id.* (special relationship with dangerous person imposes a duty to warn public).

100. *Tarasoff v. Regents of the University of Calif.*, 17 Cal. 3d 425, 551 P. 2d 344, 131 Cal. Rptr. 14 (1976) (failure to warn third party of known threat presented by patient).

101. *Thompson v. County of Alameda*, 27 Cal. 3d 741, 614 P. 2d 728, 167 Cal. Rptr. 70 (1980) (endangered third party not readily identifiable; no duty to warn); *Sellers v. United States*, 870 F. 2d 1098 (6th Cir. 1989) (no duty to injured third party where in-patient psychiatric service had no knowledge of patient's harmful intent to a particular person).

102. *Peck v. Counseling Service of Addison County, Inc.*, 499 A. 2d 422 (Vt. 1985) (duty to warn nonpatient third party of possible property damage).

103. *Maltempo, supra* note 87

104. *Hoover, supra* note 15, at 250 (relationship between physician and patient no matter who pays).

105. *Davis v. Tirrell*, 443 N.Y.S. 2d 136 (1981) (psychiatrist employed by school district to examine student and advise district about handicap; no PPR).

106. Council on Ethical and Judicial Affairs, *supra* note 66.

107. *Thiele v. Ortiz*, 165 Ill. App. 3d 983, 520 N.E. 2d 881 (1988) (duty to evaluate possible complication of surgery 2 weeks postoperatively exists despite presence of other treating physicians).

108. *Peterson v. Phelps*, 123 Minn. 319, 143 N.W. 793 (1913) (termination of duties).

109. *Millbaugh v. Gilmore*, 30 Ohio St. 2d 319, 285 N.E. 2d 19 (1972) (patient's conduct terminated relationship).

110. *Brandt v. Grubin*, 131 N.J. Super. 182, 329 A. 2d 82 (1972) (referral of psychiatric patient terminates care).

111. *Hoemke v. New York Blood Center*, 720 F. Supp. 45 (S.D.N.Y. 1989) (physician had no duty to contact past recipients of blood tranfusions to warn them that they could be HIV infected and that they could spread the virus to others); *Boyer v. Smith*, 345 Pa. Super. 66, 497 A. 2d 646 (1985) (no duty to contact past recipient of medications when new risks discovered).

112. *Tresemar v. Burke*, 86 Cal. App. 3d 656, 150 Cal. Rptr. 384 (1978) (physician required to notify patients of risks of Dalkon shield once such risks became known).

113. *Burnett v. Laymon*, 181 S.W. 157 (Tenn. 1915) (definition of reasonable notice dictated by circumstances of case).

114. *Groce v. Myers*, 224 N.C. 165, 29 S.E. 2d 553 (1944) (reasonableness of notice).

115. *Miller v. Dore*, 154 Me. 363, 148 A. 2d 692 (1959) (must notify with sufficient time for patient to find substitute).

116. *Collins v. Meeker*, 198 Kan. 390, 424 P. 2d 488 (1967) (improper withdrawal from case).

117. *See* Measure and Elements of Damages in Action Against Physician to Achieve Particular Result or Cure, 99 A.L.R. 3d 303 (breach of contract).

118. *See* Liability of Physician Who Abandons Case, 57 A.L.R. 2d 432.

119. *Stohlman v. Davis*, 220 N.W. 247 (Neb. 1928); *Mucci v. Houghton*, 57 N.W. 305 (Iowa 1894); *Groce v. Myers*, 224 N.C. 165, 29 S.E. 2d 553 (1944) (abandonment defined).

120. *Chase v. Clinton County*, 217 N.W. 565 (Mich. 1928); *Alexandridis, supra* note 36 (causes of action in abandonment).

121. *Thomas v. Corso*, 265 Md. 84, 288 A. 2d 379 (1972) (negligent care distinguished from abandonment).

122. *Easter v. Lexington Memorial Hosp.*, 303 N.C. 303, 278 S.E. 2d 253 (1984) (PPR required).

123. *State v. Warden*, 813 P. 2d 1146 (Utah 1991) (conviction for negligent homicide of infant upheld); *People v. Holvey*, 205 Cal. App. 3d 51, 252 Cal. Rptr. 335 (1988) (statute providing for criminal prosecution for "contributing to death of elderly dependent" is constitutional and applies to physicians; case remanded for trial; subsequently modified with respect to nonphysicians by *People v. Heitzman*, 9 Cal. 4th 189, 886 P. 2d 1229 (1994)).

124. *People v. Anyakora*, 162 Misc. 2d 47, 616 N.Y.S. 2d 149 (1993), *summary affirmation*, 238 A.D. 2d 216, 656 N.Y.S. 2d 253 (1997) (chief obstetrical resident convicted for failure to admit and for falsifying records used to justify refusal; action brought by Committee of Interns and Residents to obtain malpractice defense dismissed), 86 N.Y. 2d 478, 657 N.E. 2d 1315, 634 N.Y.S. 2d 32 (1995).

125. *Aufrichtig v. Lowell*, 85 N.Y. 2d 540, 650 N.E. 2d 401, 626 N.Y.S. 2d 743 (1995) (PPR creates a fiduciary duty that implies requirement to offer truthful testimony); *see also Hammond v. Aetna Casualty & Surety Co.*, 243 F. Supp. 793 N.D. Supp. 793 (1965).

126. *Safer v. Estate of Pack*, 291 N.J. Super. 619, 677 A. 2d 1188 (1996), *appeal denied*, 146 N.J. 568, 683 A. 2d 1163 (1996) (physician has duty to warn those at known risk of avoidable harm from genetically transmissible condition, and duty extends to patient, as well as to members of immediate family of patient who may be adversely affected by breach of duty).

127. *Duttry v. Patterson*, 741 A. 2d 199 (Penn. 1999); *Johnson v. Kokemoor*, 545 N.W. 2d 495 (Wis. 1996)

128. *Arato, supra* note 8.

129. *Duttry v. Patterson*, 565 Pa. 130, 771 A. 2d 1255 (2001)

31 Informed Consent to Medical and Surgical Treatment

THEODORE R. LeBLANG, J.D., F.C.L.M.
ARNOLD J. ROSOFF, J.D., F.C.L.M.
CHRISTOPHER WHITE, M.D., J.D., F.C.L.M.

The requirement that physicians must obtain consent from their patients before proceeding with treatment has been a part of Anglo-American jurisprudence since eighteenth-century England.[1] However, the notion that the patient's consent must be informed in order to be legally effective dates back less than 50 years. It appears the term "informed consent" was first used in 1957 by a California appeals court, which explained: "A physician violates his duty to his patient and subjects himself to liability if he withholds any facts which are necessary to form the basis of an intelligent consent by the patient to the proposed treatment."[2] Since that pronouncement, informed consent has been a fertile ground for litigation.

Although most jurisdictions have sorted out their positions on the major issues arising under the informed consent rubric, some significant questions still remain. Thus, informed consent continues to be an evolving doctrine—with changes in health care practice, health system organization, and information technology, among other factors, bringing forth new issues. This is not yet, and perhaps will never be, a static subfield of legal medicine. Moreover, even though the current generation of physicians have lived their entire lives under a regime requiring informed consent, many are uncertain as to the applicable requirements and how to satisfy them in their daily practice routines. This chapter highlights these requirements and their legal and ethical underpinnings and offers suggestions for satisfying them in ways that are not unduly burdensome or intrusive.

Although informed consent claims are fairly common in malpractice litigation, they rarely stand alone. They are generally appended to an underlying count (or counts) of negligent care, as a "tack-on" or "make-weight" claim. Nonetheless, they can be most troublesome, particularly if the informed consent process has not been adequately documented. While claims of negligent care generally can be addressed, and hopefully disproved, by information routinely kept as part of the patient's medical record, a claim that the patient was not adequately informed prior to treatment can be difficult to address unless the provider is well schooled on the applicable informed consent requirements and has developed a policy and procedure that supports doing the right thing and also documenting it. This is one of those places where education in legal medicine goes significantly beyond standard medical training in preparing practitioners to deal with problems they may encounter in their practice.

ORIGINS OF THE INFORMED CONSENT DOCTRINE

Historically, physical treatment of a patient without his or her consent has been treated as a "battery," an unpermitted touching. This principle is reflected in a famous quote by Judge (later Justice) Cardozo in an oft-cited 1914 New York case: "Every human being of adult years and sound mind has a right to determine what shall be done with his own body; and a surgeon who performs an operation without his patient's consent commits an assault for which he is liable in damages."[3] Among other situations, a battery action can be brought when the patient is incapable of giving valid consent, when the physician goes beyond the limits of the consent without adequate justification, or the one who renders the care is other than the one authorized to do so.

Because battery is an intentional tort, an invasion of a person's bodily inviolability, a claim can be made out even if the medical treatment is well intentioned, nonnegligent, and doesn't cause physical harm. Moreover, punitive damages can be awarded to the victim of a technical battery to vindicate his or her rights and make an example of the wrongdoer. As a practical matter, however, suits are rarely brought to challenge a technical battery if no harm was intended and no significant physical consequence was caused. Nowadays, while lack of "informed" consent could be treated as a battery, and has been on occasion,[4] it generally is treated as a negligent tort and somewhat different principles are applied.

Since around 1960, litigation involving consent issues has often dealt with the nature and extent of the information provided to a patient in the course of obtaining authorization for treatment. An inadequate disclosure, unless deemed to be deliberate misrepresentation, is generally treated as negligence rather than battery. Thus, damages are awarded only when there is significant harm caused to the victim; and punitive damages, seldom awarded, are limited to cases where there is *gross* negligence. In some jurisdictions, the statute of limitations period is longer for a negligent tort than for battery.[5]

The doctrine of informed consent has evolved largely through case law; but, in recent years, about half of the states have defined the doctrine by statute and many have provided statutorily for the standard to be applied in measuring the adequacy of the information provided to the patient. A physician seeking to satisfy informed consent requirements needs, therefore, to check both the statutory and case law in his or her state. Staying current can be challenging because the health care system is still evolving, changing the context in which consent must be obtained. Physicians increasingly practice in group settings, including managed care organizations (MCOs). In a team practice setting, responsibilities for patient care are shared and are subject to the policies and procedures of the sponsoring organization. Thus, questions can arise as to whose responsibility it is to inform the patient, obtain his or her consent to treatment, document that consent, etc. Also, in a changing system, there may be more things that a patient would want or need to know in order to make decisions about his or her care.

The foundation of the doctrine

In the 1957 case of *Salgo v. Leland Stanford, Jr., University Board of Trustees*,[6] the California Appeals Court recognized that a patient's consent to a procedure might not be effective if it were not intelligent or "informed." In *Salgo*, the patient consented to an aortogram without being advised, allegedly, of the risk posed by use of the contrast medium.[7] While *Salgo* set a precedent requiring adequate disclosure to the patient, it gave little guidance as to just what must be disclosed or how, as a general matter, a court would go about judging the adequacy of disclosure in a given instance. Supplying this additional "detail" has proved to be a major undertaking, one that has taken decades and still is not completed.

What must be disclosed?

A long line of cases over the years has distilled a generally accepted list of elements that must be disclosed to the patient—or, more accurately, must be known by the patient—for his or her consent to be adequately informed. Those elements are: the diagnosis; the nature and purpose of the proposed treatment; the risks and consequences of the proposed treatment; reasonably feasible alternatives; and the prognosis if the recommended treatment is not provided. Although there is general agreement that these elements must be disclosed, there is far less agreement on the amount and nature of the detail that must be addressed within each of these areas. Moreover, the list of disclosure elements is not limited to these categories. As discussed below, the basic approach a jurisdiction adopts on informed consent will greatly affect whether additional elements may have to be disclosed.

Two standards for disclosure

In the first decade of development of the informed consent doctrine, courts adopted the same approach as the Kansas Supreme Court in *Natanson v. Kline*,[8] and fixed the required content of a physician's disclosure by reference to that which physicians commonly made when handling a similar case. Under this "professional community" standard, if a physician lived up to the standard of disclosure generally followed by the relevant physician group, he or she was deemed to have satisfied the "duty to disclose." A key consequence of using this approach is that a patient-plaintiff could not make out an informed consent claim without introducing expert testimony as to what other physicians normally tell their patients in similar cases. This posed two obvious problems for prospective plaintiffs. The first was the difficulty of finding physicians willing to testify as expert witnesses against their colleagues on a matter of questionable substance. Second, the *Natanson* approach left the entire question of what should be disclosed up to the discretion of the physician community, which might exercise that discretion with little regard for what patients want to know.

The physician-based approach was rejected in a string of cases starting with the landmark *Canterbury v. Spence*[9] ruling by the U.S. Court of Appeals for the D.C. Circuit in 1972 and followed soon afterward by an equally celebrated California case, *Cobbs v. Grant*.[10] In both cases, the courts ruled that what was needed for an adequate disclosure should be measured by what a reasonable patient would want to know about the proposed treatment, its risks and consequences, and any treatment alternatives before deciding what course to follow. To put it another way, the courts ruled that the physician must disclose all that he or she should reasonably expect to be "material" to the patient's decision-making process.[11]

This patient-based approach to informed consent avoided the two problems inherent in the *Natanson* approach. First, the required content of the physician's disclosure was measured by the patient's informational needs rather than by what physicians might, or might not, choose to tell their patients. By focusing on the patient, the *Canterbury* approach was more faithful to the ideals of patient autonomy and self-determination that were increasingly emphasized and honored in society's values and in related areas of medical jurisprudence, such as the Supreme Court's upholding of a woman's right to have an abortion in its landmark *Roe v. Wade*[12] decision in 1973. Second, using a patient-based standard meant that patient-plaintiffs no longer had to establish by expert testimony what the "standard disclosure" was for a particular condition or treatment. They could simply assert that the undisclosed information was something that an "average, reasonable patient" would want to know. That assertion could go to the jury without expert testimony on disclosure practices.

Not having to produce an expert witness on the "standard disclosure" point greatly changed the dynamics of lawsuits claiming a lack of informed consent. Because plaintiffs could get their cases before a jury without having to leap a sometimes steep evidentiary hurdle, it was much easier for them to prosecute their claims, thus affecting settlement negotiations and, in turn, affecting the propensity of plaintiffs to include informed consent claims in their malpractice suits. The incidence of informed consent claims increased rapidly in the 1970s and 1980s, much more so in states following *Canterbury* than in those holding fast to the older *Natanson* approach.

Throughout the 1970s and 1980s, state after state addressed the question of whether informed consent claims should be adjudicated using one or the other of the above standards. Much of the play was in the courts; but many states also passed statutes that set the standards for measuring physician disclosures. By the end of the 1980s, most states had fallen into one camp or the other. Looking past the small handful of states whose approaches are hybrids or defy classification using the above two schemes, a bare majority of the remaining states follow a physician-based standard, while the others follow some variant of the patient-based, or "materiality," standard. (Appendix 31-1 summarizes the various states' positions on this issue.)

EXCEPTIONS TO THE REQUIREMENT OF INFORMED CONSENT

Full, formal consent from the patient is not always feasible to obtain and is not always required. The law recognizes situations in which something less is acceptable.

Emergency consent

In a medical emergency, a patient may be unconscious, disoriented, sedated, or otherwise incapable of giving an effective consent. When that is so, and no one is available who would be authorized to act on the patient's behalf, the law generally allows the physician to presume that the patient would want to be treated as necessary to preserve his or her life and/or function.

When a patient cannot give consent and care is urgently needed, the physician should attempt to identify and contact the patient's next of kin or other person authorized who might act on the patient's behalf. Other people present should assist so that the physician can stay focused on providing needed care. If possible, another physician or health care provider with appropriate expertise should participate in the assessment, to help establish that there was an emergency, that care was needed immediately, that attempts were made to contact next of kin, and that the care rendered did not go beyond that necessary to preserve the patient until full consent might be obtained. An emergency does not give the physician license to do whatever he or she deems advisable for the patient; it supports only limited measures to preserve the status quo.

The "extension doctrine"

The so-called "extension doctrine" allows the physician to go beyond the care the patient authorized if an unexpected complication arises that makes it medically advisable to do so. An excellent example of the application of the extension doctrine is the 1956 case of *Kennedy v. Parrott*,[13] in which a physician who was performing an appendectomy on a patient determined that she had an ovarian cyst that should be excised. Because the patient was under general anesthetic and no person authorized to speak on her behalf was available, the physician decided it was medically appropriate to treat the cyst as part of the same operation. Had he not done so, a second surgery—with its attendant inconvenience, risks, and cost—would have been necessary at a later time. The North Carolina Supreme Court upheld the physician's decision to proceed, reasoning that he had not only the right to do so but also the duty to do what sound medicine dictated.[14]

The extension doctrine does not apply to elective, or nonessential, procedures,[15] nor does it apply when the possible need for extension of the authorized procedure should have been anticipated by the physician prior to beginning it. In such a case, the physician must inform the patient before the fact of the possible need for extension and obtain the patient's express consent.

Waiver

Just as patients are entitled to have information about their health care, they are also entitled *not* to have such information when they think they would be unduly distressed by it or would simply prefer to let the physician make the necessary treatment decisions. Patients can waive their right to information; but a waiver of information must be knowing and voluntary to be effective. Therefore, the physician must provide enough information that the patient knows the general nature of the information he or she is forgoing. For example, the physician could tell the patient that there are risks inherent in the procedure being recommended. Then, if the patient chooses not to have more complete information on the risks, that would be a legitimate election and the requirement of informed consent would be deemed satisfied.

Obviously, any such waiver should be documented. One way to implement this is to have a two-part consent form. In the first part, the recommended treatment is named and general information is given about it, noting, as may be appropriate, that there are risks, consequences, or alternatives. The form then recites that the patient is entitled to full information and the physician stands ready to provide it. The patient initials either a box that indicates the information is desired or one saying that the patient chooses not to have a more complete explanation.[16] A process and associated form like this allows the patient to choose how much information he or she desires and documents the patient's choice. As with other aspects of "managing" informed consent, doing the right thing is only part of the game; the other, crucial part is being able to prove, if challenged, that the right thing was done.

Therapeutic privilege

Many jurisdictions recognize a physician's right to withhold information from a patient if disclosure would be harmful to the patient. Perhaps the best-known statement of this principle, commonly known as "therapeutic privilege," is in the landmark *Canterbury* case:

[An] exception obtains when risk-disclosure poses such a threat of detriment to the patient as to become unfeasible or contraindicated from a medical point of view. It is recognized that patients occasionally become so ill or emotionally distraught on disclosure as to foreclose a rational decision, or complicate or hinder the treatment, or perhaps even pose psychological damage to the patient. Where that is so, the cases have generally held that the physician is armed with a privilege to keep the information from the patient, and we think it clear that portents of that type may justify the physician in action he deems medically warranted. The critical inquiry is whether the physician responded to a sound medical judgment that communication of the risk information would present a threat to the patient's well-being.[17]

This quote nicely summarizes the commonly articulated rationale for therapeutic privilege. In actuality, however, therapeutic privilege has seldom been applied in the case law; thus it is largely "dictum."[18] One should be wary of relying too heavily on this exception and should do so only in exceptional circumstances. In the *Canterbury* case, the defendant neurosurgeon testified that he generally did not tell patients of the paralysis risk inherent in a laminectomy because he thought they might decline surgery he thought

they truly needed. Rejecting the therapeutic privilege defense upon these facts, the court explained:

The physician's privilege to withhold information for therapeutic reasons must be carefully circumscribed, however, for otherwise it might devour the disclosure rule itself. The privilege does not accept the paternalistic notion that the physician may remain silent simply because divulgence might prompt the patient to forego therapy the physician feels the patient really needs. That attitude presumes instability or perversity for even the normal patient, and runs counter to the foundation principle that the patient should and ordinarily can make the choice for himself. Nor does the privilege contemplate operation save where the patient's reaction to risk information, as reasonably foreseen by the physician, is menacing.[19]

A physician seeking to justify nondisclosure on this ground has the significant burden to particularize its application to the individual patient and not contend that patients in general are unable to handle this kind of information.

Causation issues

While not exactly an "exception" to the requirement of informed consent, a failure to disclose information to the patient is excused if a court believes that no consequence flowed from this failure. Lack of a causal connection between nondisclosure and the harm suffered by the patient defeats informed consent liability. A patient-plaintiff who brings an informed consent claim is essentially contending that if he or she had known the undisclosed information, he or she would not have opted for the treatment in question. Thus, to recover upon an informed consent claim, the patient-plaintiff must prove that the physician knew, or should have known, the information in question, and did not disclose it; that the treatment caused harm to the patient (medical causation); and that she or he would not have chosen the treatment if the information had been revealed ("informed consent" causation). On the last point, "informed consent" causation, the patient is arguing that he or she would have acted differently if properly informed.

Courts have been understandably reluctant to accept such after-the-fact causative assertions in situations where they believe a *reasonable and prudent patient* would have followed the physician's recommendation and accepted the treatment in question, even if fully informed of the risks.[20] Most courts facing the issue thus have opted to use an *objective* standard, asking what an "average, reasonable patient" would have done rather than what *the particular patient* would have done, a *subjective* standard.[21] Using a subjective standard is problematic because there is often no way to know what a given patient would have chosen if things had been different. Once again, the *Canterbury* opinion is instructive:

It has been assumed that the issue [of "informed consent" causation] is to be resolved according to whether the factfinder believes the patient's testimony that he would not have agreed to the treatment if he had known of the danger which later ripened into injury. We think a technique which ties the factual conclusion on causation simply to the assessment of the patient's credibility is unsatisfactory. To be sure, the objective of risk-disclosure is preservation of the patient's interest in intelligent self-choice on proposed treatment, a matter the patient is free to decide for any reason that appeals to him. When, prior to commencement of therapy, the patient is sufficiently informed on risks and he exercises his choice, it may truly be said that he did exactly what he wanted to do. But when causality is explored at a postinjury trial with a professedly uninformed patient, the question whether he actually would have turned the treatment down if he had known the risks is purely hypothetical: "Viewed from the point at which he had to decide, would the patient have decided differently had he known something he did not know?" And the answer which the patient supplies hardly represents more than a guess, perhaps tinged by the circumstance that the uncommunicated hazard has in fact materialized.[22]

Notwithstanding these practical considerations, some courts have reasoned that because the core objective of informed consent doctrine is to support patient autonomy, their decision should turn on what they believe the particular patient would have chosen, not what some hypothetical patient would have done. Thus, a few states apply a *subjective* standard of causation.[23]

WHO CAN GIVE CONSENT?

Although the discussion thus far has largely assumed that it would be the patient himself or herself who either gives or withholds consent, there are occasions in which others may be involved. One has been discussed above, the emergency situation where a patient who would otherwise have the capacity to consent is under some disability blocking that capacity. It is often said that in such situations the patient's next of kin has authority to grant consent. In truth, however, the fact that someone is the next of kin to a patient who temporarily lacks capacity is not enough to bestow decision-making capacity on the relative. Ideally, there should be some order of court designating who can decide on the patient's behalf or a document—such as a durable power of attorney—signed by the patient while he or she was competent, doing the same thing.

Without such a designation by a court or the patient, the next of kin can give valid consent only when time is too short to obtain court designation of a surrogate. When the need for care is too urgent to allow court designation, the provider may assume, absent contrary evidence, that the next of kin has the patient's interest at heart and can make the best projection of what the patient would choose. Moreover, any care beyond what is immediately necessary to stabilize and preserve the patient is not properly authorized. Jurisdictions differ on how much latitude the treating physician has to decide what is immediately necessary; but restraint is advised. As much as the physician may feel motivated to push forward and render all the care he or she thinks the patient ultimately needs, going beyond the point of necessity without court endorsement is risky.

Minors

All jurisdictions have statutes defining the age of majority, generally age 18, outlining what kinds of medical and related care a minor can consent to, and, in some cases, identifying areas of exception to the general rules. Most states have provisions for "emancipated" minors—those living on their own and not dependent on their families for support—to make their own health care decisions. Also, in many states, a "mature" minor—that is, one of sufficient age and discretion to be able to understand his or her situation, the proposed treatment(s), and the consequences likely to flow from the treatment or its alternative(s)—is authorized to make treatment decisions in a situation when care is urgently needed and the minor's parents cannot be involved in the decision process. Generally, such exceptions are recognized in the case law rather than statutory law. It is common, however, for statutes to provide that a minor is treated as an adult for the purpose of health care decision-making if the minor is married or pregnant. Many states also allow minors to consent to birth control counseling and assistance and to diagnosis and treatment for sexually transmitted disease and substance abuse without parental consent or notification.

A physician should find out what the law in his or her state provides with regard to treatment of and consent by minors. Obviously, whenever possible, the minor's parents should be involved in the decision-making and give their consent. Minors are generally held contractually liable for "necessaries," including health care; but, because most minors have limited resources, there is little assurance that care will be paid for if the parents do not authorize it. In many situations, however, payment will be a secondary consideration. The minor's need for care and his or her ability to give legally valid consent will be more compelling. In such cases, the physician should offer all information to the minor that would otherwise have been given to the minor's parents or guardian(s), adapted as necessary to the minor's age and ability to comprehend it. In addition to documenting that appropriate information was given, the physician should document why it was necessary or advisable to proceed without the parents' (or parent's) participation. If there is any basis for doubt that the minor was sufficiently mature to be able to give meaningful consent, then the physician should seek authorization from a court, unless the situation is an emergency requiring immediate action.

REFUSAL OF TREATMENT

The requirement that patients must consent if treatment is to proceed lawfully rests upon the unstated principle that they may withhold their consent and not be treated, even when this runs counter to the physician's convictions as to what is best for the patient. Issues involving the patient's right to refuse treatment and what is necessary for that right to be effectively exercised arise in many different contexts. The following discussion addresses two such issues that arise in more routine treatment situations. Issues of end-of-life care, refusal of life support, assisted suicide, etc., are beyond the scope of this chapter.

"Informed refusal"

Just as a patient needs adequate information to be able to accept proposed treatment, he or she needs information to be able to decline or refuse it. However, because informed consent doctrine grew out of the tort of battery, an unpermitted touching, it has not always been clear that a physician has an obligation to provide information in a situation where the patient is *forgoing* treatment. With informational obligations apparently tied to the provision of care, it is not so obvious that they also apply to the nonprovision of care.

Truman v. Thomas,[24] decided by the California Supreme Court in 1980, is often cited for the principle of "informed refusal." *Truman* held that a physician who recommends a procedure—in that case, a diagnostic Pap smear test—is obliged to ensure that a patient who rejects this recommendation understands the consequences of not having the test. Although the decision has not been widely followed, its core rationale—that a physician should provide the information needed to support the patient's decision-making, even when the decision is to refuse the treatment—is sound. It is consistent with the longstanding convention that when someone leaves a hospital emergency room before receiving all the treatment the personnel there believe is needed, efforts are made to get the patient to sign a form indicating that he or she left "against medical advice." To give good protection against an informed refusal claim, this form should contain a clear statement of the risks and consequences of not getting the recommended care.

Refusal by others on the patient's behalf

The above discussion of who can consent on the patient's behalf dealt mostly with situations where the next of kin purporting to speak for the patient's interest was willing to authorize the treatment in question. Where that is not the case, the provider obviously faces significant risk. If the provider disregards that person's objections and renders the care, and there is a bad outcome, then a lawsuit is to be expected. When time permits, a court order authorizing the treatment should be sought. When there is no time, and the provider feels he or she must proceed anyway, great care should be taken to ensure that the objecting party understands why treatment is urgently needed and to document this. Where possible, confirmation by independent medical personnel is strongly advised. Finally, where the provider

heeds the patient's next of kin and does not provide care, it is still important to document that full information was given to the one rejecting the care on the patient's behalf.

OBTAINING AND DOCUMENTING CONSENT

Successful compliance with informed consent requirements as part of regular practice routines raises numerous issues. The issues in the following sections are the ones most frequently encountered.

Who is responsible to obtain informed consent?

Generally speaking, the physician rendering the care in question is the one who should obtain the patient's informed consent to that care. However, that task may be delegated to another health care provider, e.g., resident, nurse practitioner, etc. If adequate and accurate information is provided and it can be proven that the correct consent was obtained from the patient, it doesn't matter who performed the tasks necessary to achieve this. If the consent falls short in some way, however, then the physician rendering the care bears the primary responsibility and the potential liability that results from this failure. Thus, each person "laying on hands" or otherwise treating the patient must take care that the consent obligations are fully satisfied with regard to his or her aspect of the treatment. One can delegate the function of obtaining adequately informed consent; but if the function is not fulfilled, the delegator cannot avoid the underlying legal responsibility.

Complexity can enter the picture when a major, or primary, treatment being rendered to the patient is comprehensive enough in scope to subsume other ancillary procedures. For example, if a surgeon has assistants helping install a prosthetic device in a patient's leg, separate consents would not be needed for the assistants' actions, even if those actions were medically and factually discrete. The surgeon in charge might use an intern or resident to close and suture the patient after the main part of the operation is complete. In such a case, the surgical consent should be drawn broadly enough to encompass the others who were integrally involved in the overall surgical procedure, particularly—and this is the key—where the surgeon was in charge of the overall procedure and the other participants looked to the surgeon for supervision. The reasonable scope of control of the surgeon should be the determining factor.

To draw a distinction, though, if the patient were also to be put under general anesthesia for the surgery, and if the anesthesia were to be administered by an independent anesthesiologist, then it would be appropriate to have a separate consent for anesthesia. In that case, the anesthesiologist would be responsible to ensure that the consent was adequate for this subset of the overall procedure. If the surgeon provided sufficient information and obtained a broad enough consent to cover administration of the anesthesia, then that would be okay; but if the consent to anesthesia were found to be insufficient, it would be the anesthesiologist, not the surgeon, who would have the principal liability exposure.

Duty of hospitals or other health care institutions

When care is delivered in a hospital or other institutional setting, or under the auspices of a managed care organization, one might try to hold the institution liable for any failure to obtain an adequate informed consent. Courts have been reluctant, however, to find such institutions liable for inadequate disclosure, recognizing the institution's inability to police the details of information transmission and also respecting the close, personal nature of the physician-patient relationship.[25] They have gone so far as to hold the institution obligated to have policies and procedures in place to facilitate and help ensure that adequate consent is obtained, particularly when the institution holds itself out to the public as meeting standards—such as JCAHO accreditation standards—that include assurance of patients' rights.[26] Courts have not gone the additional distance of holding the institution responsible for the *content* of the physician's disclosure to the patient; but they might do so if it could be shown that the institution knew, or had reason to know, either in a particular instance or in general, that the physician was treating a patient (or patients) without adequate consent. Of course, if the physician is employed by the institution, vicarious liability likely would be imposed under *respondeat superior*.[27]

Documenting consent

From a practical standpoint, documentation of adequate patient consent can be as important as the actual satisfaction of the underlying obligation. Often in litigation the question is not whether the right thing was done but, rather, whether that can be proven. That said, a problem with the implementation of informed consent doctrine is that excessive emphasis is often put on the completion of a consent form, sometimes eclipsing concern for the human interaction and two-way information exchange that is supposed to take place. The challenge, then, is to balance the substantive aspects of the consent process with effective documentation while, at the same time, avoiding cumbersome and costly intrusion into day-to-day medical practice and the physician-patient relationship.

Except in a dozen or so states whose statutes put special emphasis on written consent,[28] an oral (spoken) consent is as good as a consent in writing, except that written documentation generally makes it easier to prove that a satisfactory consent actually was obtained. The classic format for written consent is a form signed by the patient, identifying and authorizing the treatment to be administered, naming the provider(s) authorized to render the treatment, and

acknowledging, in a reasonable degree of detail, that information was provided on the required disclosure elements, such as risks and consequences of, and alternatives to, the proposed treatment. The form commonly will recite that the patient was given an opportunity to ask questions and to receive answers and explanations from the physician(s) involved. The form can be specially prepared for a particular patient and treatment situation, or it can be a standardized form, crafted for repeated use with the same treatment, but perhaps tailored to accommodate any special facts or circumstances of the current case. Both types of forms have their adherents and reasonable arguments pro and con for their use.

With either type of form, though, one has to choose between greater or lesser specificity regarding the information the form purports to document. A less specific form that simply says the patient acknowledges having received "full information as to expected benefits, risks and consequences of the proposed treatment, as well as alternatives thereto," leaves it open for the patient to later claim that certain information was, in fact, not disclosed. The form evidences that some risks were disclosed, but it stops short of proving that a particular risk was mentioned. On the other hand, if the form is very specific and attempts to list all the risks that were disclosed, on occasion an undisclosed risk might be omitted from the list. In such a case, the form could serve as persuasive, albeit misleading, proof that the information in question was not provided. Thus, if a specific form is to be used, it must be exactly right every time.

Other approaches to documenting informed consent are also possible. The physician can simply make a note in the patient's record that he or she discussed the nature of the procedure, material risks thereof, reasonable benefits to be expected, and available alternatives. Such a contemporaneous recording in the medical record may be very persuasive to a jury, particularly when a physician is able to testify that such a notation refreshes his or her recollection about the nature and scope of the discussion ordinarily undertaken with patients in similar situations. In sum, then, greater documentation is desirable to guard against informed consent challenges; but the degree of effort put toward documentation must be weighed against the projected risks of a challenge.

CONCLUSION

Informed consent is more than a legal doctrine and a trap for unwary practitioners, it is a concept central to American beliefs about individual rights and the proper relationship between patients and providers. All physicians should look beyond the specifics of the consent requirements discussed here and always be mindful of the larger goal—respect for the dignity and autonomy of individual patients and a commitment to help them participate fully and meaningfully in the decisions that affect their bodies and their lives.

ENDNOTES

1. *Slater v. Baker & Stapleton*, 95 Eng. Rep. 860 (K.B. 1767).
2. *Salgo v. Leland Stanford, Jr., Univ. Bd. of Trustees*, 317 P. 2d 170, 181 (Cal. App. Ct. 1957).
3. *Schloendorff v. Society of New York Hosp.*, 105 N.E. 92, 93 (N.Y. 1914).
4. *See, e.g., Perna v. Pirozzi*, 457 A. 2d 431 (N.J. 1983).
5. *See, e.g., Canterbury v. Spence*, 464 F. 2d 772, 793 (D.C. Cir. 1972).
6. *Salgo*, 317 P. 2d 170.
7. *Id.* at 180-81.
8. 350 P. 2d 1093 (Kan. 1960).
9. *Canterbury*, 464 F. 2d 772.
10. 502 P. 2d 1 (Cal. 1972).
11. *Canterbury*, 464 F. 2d at 786.
12. 410 U.S. 113 (1973).
13. 90 S.E. 2d 754 (N.C. 1956).
14. *Id.* at 759.
15. *See, e.g., Lloyd v. Kull*, 329 F. 2d 168 (7th Cir. 1964) (physician liable for cosmetic excision of a mole on an unconscious patient's thigh while correcting a vesicovaginal fistula).
16. This approach has been suggested by Dr. Ralph Alfidi of the Cleveland Clinic in *Informed Consent: A Study of Patient Reaction*, 216 J.A.M.A. 1325 (1971). It is also the approach required under Oregon's medical consent statute. Ore. Stats. §677.097 (2001).
17. *Canterbury*, 464 F. 2d at 783.
18. *See, e.g.,* Margaret A. Somerville, *Therapeutic Privilege: Variation on the Theme of Informed Consent*, 12 L. Med. & Health Care 4, 11 (1984).
19. *Canterbury*, 464 F. 2d at 789.
20. *See, e.g., Fischer v. Wilmington Gen. Hosp.*, 149 A. 2d 749 (Del. Super. Ct. 1959).
21. *See, e.g., Fain v. Smith*, 479 So. 2d 1150, 1152–54 (Ala. 1985) (citing other jurisdictions that have adopted the objective standard). *See also Ashe v. Radiation Oncology Assocs.*, 9 S.W. 3d 119, 121 (Tenn. 1999) and extensive sources cited therein.
22. *Canterbury*, 464 F. 2d at 790.
23. *See, e.g., Arena v. Gingrich*, 748 P. 2d 547 (Or. 1988); *Spencer v. Seikel*, 742 P. 2d 1126 (Okla. 1987).
24. 611 P. 2d 902 (Cal. 1980).
25. *See, e.g., Smith v. Gaynor*, 591 A. 2d 834 (Conn. Super. Ct. 1991).
26. *See, e.g., Robinson v. Bleicher*, 559 N.W. 2d 473, 476 (Neb. 1997) (duty of hospital to have informed consent procedures in place).
27. *See, e.g., Doctors Mem'l Hosp. v. Evans*, 543 So. 2d 809 (Fla. Dist. Ct. App. 1989); *Campbell v. Pitt County Mem'l Hosp.*, 362 S.E. 2d 273 (N.C. 1987).
28. *See, e.g.,* Fla. Stat. Ann. §766.103 (West 2002); Ga. Code Ann. §31-9-6.1(b)(2) (2002); Idaho Code §39-4305 (2002); Iowa Code Ann. §147-137 (West 2001); La. Rev. Stat. Ann. §40:1299.40 (West 2002). Maine, Nevada, North Carolina, Ohio, Texas, Utah, and Washington, among others, also have statutory provisions regarding written consent.

APPENDIX 31-1   Overview of States' Positions on Disclosure Standard

Note: This Appendix classifies states between the physician-based or patient-based disclosure standard for informed consent and identifies those few states that do not follow either of these standards or cannot be confidently classified. The classification was based upon statutory and case law research updated in February 2003 and is believed to be accurate and up to date as of publication. Readers are cautioned, however, to confirm any classifications herein before relying upon them in any way.

States following a physician-based standard

Alabama	*Fain v. Smith*, 479 So. 2d 1150 (Ala. 1985), applying Ala. Code §6-5-484 (2002 Supp. 1990).
Arizona	*Gurr v. Willcutt*, 707 P. 2d 979 (Ariz. Ct. App. 1985), applying Ariz. Rev. Stat. §§12-561, 12-563 (2002).
Arkansas	*Aronson v. Harriman*, 901 S.W. 2d 832 (Ark. 1995); Ark. Code Ann. §16-114-206 (2002).
Delaware	*Robinson v. Mroz*, 433 A. 2d 1051 (Del. Super. Ct. 1981), applying Del. Code Ann. tit. 18, §6852 (2002).
Florida	*Ritz v. Florida Patient's Compensation Fund*, 436 So. 2d 987 (Fla. Dist. Ct. App. 1983); Fla. Stat. Ann. §766.103 (West 2002).
Idaho	*Shabinaw v. Brown*, 963 P. 2d 1184 (Idaho 1998), applying Idaho Code §39-4304 (2002).
Illinois	*Ramos v. Pyati*, 534 N.E. 2d 472 (Ill. App. Ct. 1989).
Indiana	*McGee v. Bonaventura*, 605 N.E. 2d 792 (Ind. Ct. App. 1993); Ind. Code Ann. §34-18-12-1 (West 2002).
Kansas	*Stovall v. Harms*, 522 P. 2d 353 (Kan. 1974). *But see* Kan. Stat. Ann. §65-6709 (2001) (applying reasonable patient/materiality standard as to abortion).
Maine	*Ouellette v. Mehalic*, 534 A. 2d 1331 (Me. 1988), applying Me. Rev. Stat. Ann. tit. 24, §2905 (West 2002).
Michigan	*Marchlewicz v. Stanton*, 213 N.W. 2d 317 (Mich. Ct. App. 1973).
Missouri	*Baltzell v. Baptist Med. Ctr.*, 718 S.W. 2d 140 (Mo. Ct. App. 1986).
Montana	*Llera v. Wisner*, 557 P. 2d 805 (Mont. 1976).
Nebraska	Neb. Rev. Stat. §44-2816 (2002); physician-based standard criticized but followed in *Eccleston v. Chait*, 492 N.W. 2d 860, 868 (Neb. 1992).
Nevada	*Smith v. Cotter*, 810 P. 2d 1204 (Nev. 1991), applying Nev. Rev. Stat. §§41A.110, 449.710 (2002).
New Hampshire	*Smith v. Cote*, 513 A. 2d 341 (N.H. 1986), applying N.H. Rev. Stat. Ann. §507-E:2 (West 2002).
New York	*Karlin v. IVF America, Inc.*, 712 N.E. 2d 662 (N.Y. 1999), applying N.Y. Pub. Health Law §2805-d (McKinney 2002).
South Carolina	*Baxley v. Rosenblum*, 400 S.E. 2d 502 (S.C. Ct. App. 1991).
Tennessee	*Ashe v. Radiation Oncology Assocs.*, 9 S.W. 3d 119 (Tenn. 1999), applying Tenn. Code Ann. §29-26-118 (2002).
Vermont	*Perkins v. Windsor Hosp. Corp.*, 455 A. 2d 810 (Vt. 1982), applying Vt. Stat. Ann. tit. 12, §1909 (2002).
Virginia	*Tashman v. Gibbs*, 556 S.E. 2d 772 (Va. 2002); Va. Code Ann. §8.01-581.20 (2002).
Wyoming	*Weber v. McCoy*, 950 P. 2d 548 (Wyo. 1997).

States following a patient-based standard

Alaska	*Korman v. Mallin*, 858 P. 2d 1145 (Alaska 1993), applying Alaska Stat. §09.55.556 (2002).
California	*Arato v. Avedon*, 858 P. 2d 598 (Cal. 1993).
Connecticut	*Gemme v. Goldberg*, 626 A. 2d 318 (Conn. App. Ct. 1993).
District of Columbia	*Gordon v. Neviaser*, 478 A. 2d 292 (D.C. 1984).
Georgia	*Ketchup v. Howard*, 543 S.E. 2d 371 (Ga. Ct. App. 2000), applying Ga. Code Ann. §31-9-6.1 (2002). (Note: An appendix to this opinion offers a state-by-state analysis of informed consent approaches.)
Maryland	*Faya v. Almaraz*, 620 A. 2d 327, 334 (Md. 1993).
Massachusetts	*Feeley v. Baer*, 669 N.E. 2d 456 (Mass. App. Ct. 1996).
Mississippi	*Hudson v. Parvin*, 582 So. 2d 403 (Miss. 1991).
New Jersey	*Acuna v. Turkish*, 808 A. 2d 149 (N.J. Super Ct. Law Div. 2002).
New Mexico	*Henning v. Parsons*, 623 P. 2d 574 (N.M. Ct. App. 1980).
North Dakota	*Jaskoviak v. Gruver*, 638 N.W. 2d 1 (N.D. 2002).
Ohio	*Bedel v. University of Cincinnati Hosp.*, 669 N.E. 2d 9 (Ohio Ct. App. 1995); Ohio Rev. Code Ann. §2317.54 (Banks-Baldwin 2001).
Oklahoma	*Spencer v. Seikel*, 742 P. 2d 1126, 1129 (Okla. 1987) (language suggests that a "*subjective* patient standard" might be applied).
Pennsylvania	*Southard v. Temple Univ. Hosp.*, 781 A. 2d 101 (Pa. 2001); 40 Pa. Cons. Stat. §1303.504 (2002).
Rhode Island	*Lauro v. Knowles*, 785 A. 2d 1140 (R.I. 2001); R.I. Gen. Laws §9-19-32 (2002).
South Dakota	*Wheeldon v. Madison*, 374 N.W. 2d 367 (S.D. 1985).
Utah	*Nixdorf v. Hicken*, 612 P. 2d 348 (Utah 1980); Utah Code Ann. §78-14-5 (2002).
Washington	*Backlund v. University of Washington*, 975 P. 2d 950 (Wash. 1999); Wash. Rev. Code Ann. §7.70.050 (West 2002).
West Virginia	*Adams v. El-Bash*, 338 S.E. 2d 381 (W. Va. 1985).
Wisconsin	*Johnson v. Kokemoor*, 545 N.W. 2d 495 (Wis. Ct. App. 1996); Wis. Stat. Ann. §448.30 (West 2001).

States with other approaches or not classified

Colorado	*Gorab v. Zook*, 943 P. 2d 423 (Colo. 1997); Colo. Rev. Stat. Ann. §13-64-401 (West 2002) (physician-based standard, but defendant has burden of proving standard was met).
Hawaii	*Carr v. Strode*, 904 P. 2d 489 (Haw. 1995); Haw. Rev. Stat. §671-3 (2002) (patient-based standard, but with state medical board responsible to develop specific standards for disclosure).
Iowa	Iowa Code Ann. §147.137 (West 2002) makes a written consent containing general information presumptively valid; *Bray v. Hill*, 517 N.W. 2d 223 (Iowa Ct. App. 1994), and other cases recognize a patient-based standard.
Kentucky	*Keel v. St. Elizabeth Medical Ctr.*, 842 S.W. 2d 860 (Ky. 1992), applying Ky. Rev. Stat. Ann. §304.40-320 (Banks-Baldwin 2002) (physician-based standard with a "reasonable individual [patient]" overlay).
Louisiana	La. Rev. Stat. Ann. §40:1299.40 (West 2002) makes a written consent containing general information presumptively valid; *Boudoin v. Crawford & Marshall, Ltd.*, 709 So. 2d 798 (La. Ct. App. 1998), and other cases recognize a patient-based standard.
North Carolina	*Osburn v. Danek Medical, Inc.*, 520 S.E. 2d 88 (N.C. Ct. App. 1999), applying N.C. Gen. Stat. §90-21.13 (2002) (physician-based standard with a "reasonable person [patient]" overlay).
Oregon	*Zacher v. Petty*, 826 P. 2d 619 (Or. 1992), applying Or. Rev. Stat. §677.097 (2001) (physician-based standard applied with regard to use of "therapeutic privilege").
Texas	*Rodgers v. Coleman*, No. 01-93-00372-CV., 1994 Tex. App. LEXIS 370 (not reported in Tex. App. Hous., 1st Dist., 1994), applying Tex. Rev. Civ. Stat. art. 4590i §6.02 (West 2001).

32

Medical Records

FILLMORE BUCKNER, M.D., J.D., F.C.L.M.

STANDARDS OF RECORD-KEEPING
OWNERSHIP AND PATIENT ACCESS
CONFIDENTIALITY AND PRIVACY
PRIVILEGE AND ADMISSIBILITY

The medical record serves several legal functions. It is "the witness that never dies" in professional liability suits against health care providers. Any defense lawyer will assure you that a well-documented, complete, and unambiguous medical record means a case that is infinitely easier to defend. The medical record also functions to document the injuries of crime victims, victims of domestic violence, victims of both elder and child abuse, workplace accident victims, and personal injury litigants. In addition the medical record may play a vital role in courtroom competency issues in a variety of estate, criminal, and civil commitment cases.

STANDARDS OF RECORD-KEEPING

The standards for medical record-keeping are determined by three overlapping bodies or regulations. Individual state statutes or administrative regulations furnish the first layer of requirements. Medical records may be covered under specific health regulations and/or regulations for business records, and detail what should be entered and contained, the mechanics of entry, and the authentication of the records.[1] Local regulations may place some differing burdens on hospital records in contrast to physician or clinic records, but the trend is for all three of the regulating bodies to treat medical record seamlessly from the out-patient setting to the extended care facility. The next layer of control is exerted by JCAHO. JCAHO also has extremely extensive and detailed standards for medical records located in two sections of their accreditation manual, *Assessment of Patients and Information Management Planning*.[2] However, the detail in the JCAHO's standards is more concerned with the content and handling of the medical records entry than with the mechanics of entry. The JCAHO standards also attempt to incorporate the third layer of control, the federal regulations, including those of Medicare.[3] Hospital staffs, managed care organizations, and clinics may assert institutional requirements applicable to their records that exceed or are in addition to the three layers of control described above.

Mechanics of medical record entry

The mechanics of entering data into a medical record are simple and well known, but frequently overlooked by the busy practitioner. First, medical record entries are to be made contemporaneously with the event. The entries are not to be postponed to a more convenient time or to the end of the day. They are to be written or dictated contemporaneously with the care and/or treatment, producing a record in chronological order. There is no justifiable reason for the record not to be in chronological order. Medical record entries should aim at conveying all relevant, objective, accurate information concerning the patient into the record. Subjective conjecture or opinion information should not be entered. Abbreviations and acronyms should be routinely avoided to eliminate the possibility of confusion. Entries must be legible if entered by hand and, in most jurisdictions, may be entered by typewriter or computer to ensure legibility. Most jurisdictions require that the record be written in ink and be in English. The entries should be direct, concise, clear, complete and unambiguous. *No entry should be altered or backdated!* All entries should be signed or otherwise authenticated in a legal manner and timed and dated.*

What should the record contain

Combining the requirements of JCAHO and Medicare/Medicaid leads to the minimal requirements for the contents of medical records containing the following items:
- Identification and demographic information
- Evidence of informed consent
- Evidence of known advance directives
- Admitting complaint or diagnosis
- History of the present illness
- Past history (including social history)

---

* Some states will allow notes to be authenticated with a rubber stamp or some combination of keyboard strokes on the computer.

- Family history
- Orders
- Laboratory reports
- Imaging reports
- Consultations
- Reports of procedures or tests
- Progress notes that include:
    Clinical observations
    Results of treatment
    Complications
- Final diagnosis
- Discharge summary

The contents listed above have not included items that may be required by local statutes or regulations, or a hospital, institution, or specialty organization's specific requirements. In addition, a thoughtful risk manager might add the following requirements:

- Notations concerning lack of patient cooperation, failure to follow advice, or failure to keep appointments, as well as records of follow-up telephone calls and letters.
- For any laboratory, radiographic, diagnostic test or consult ordered, the dates ordered, received, and reviewed.
- Copies of records, instructions, diets, or directions given to the patient or the patient's representative.

Additions, corrections, patient access, and statements of disagreement

A great deal of misinformation has been conveyed to physicians as to how medical record corrections and additions should be made. Remember the admonition made above *that no medical record should ever be altered or backdated.* Corrections and/or additions should be made as outlined in the Uniform Health Care Information Act (UHCIA).[4] The procedure described in the act is quite simple. The health care provider should never expunge or obliterate any material. Instead, the provider should add the correction or addition to the medical record as a new chronological entry. The provider should also mark the corrected or amended record, in its margin, as corrected or amended and indicate where the correction or amendment may be found.[5]

Both the UHCIA and the DHHS regulations, generated in response to the Health Insurance Portability and Accountability Act (HIPAA),* provide for patient access in all but a few circumstances.[6] In addition, over 30 states have statutes allowing patients some access to medical records.[7] Both HIPAA and UHCIA allow patients to copy those records and to seek correction of errors within the record.[8] If the provider agrees with the proposed correction or amendment, the provider corrects or amends the record as described above. If the provider disagrees with the

proposed correction or amendment, the provider must notify the patient of his or her refusal to correct or amend the record and offer the patient the opportunity to add a concise Statement of Disagreement. On receipt of the Statement of Disagreement, the provider enters it in the medical record, marks the disputed entry as disputed, and identifies where the Statement of Disagreement is located. The UHCIA provides for both civil and criminal penalties if the provider denies patients this right.[9] At least one state court has levied sanctions against a provider who failed to allow a patient legitimate access to his or her medical records.[10]

Alteration, destrution, or loss of medical records

In the law of evidence, the loss, destruction, or significant alteration of evidence is termed "spoliation of evidence." Thus, when medical records that have been altered, or had portions removed, or cases in which the record cannot be found come before the court, the evidentiary concept of spoliation of evidence is invoked. The common law evidentiary inference concept or remedy for spoliation is explained by Wigmore as an indication that the spoiler's case is weak, and "operates, indefinitely though strongly, against *the whole mass of alleged facts constituting his cause*" (2 Wigmore (3d ed. 1940) §278 p. 120 (emphasis added).[11]

Therefore, alterations to records can prove to be disastrous. Records with alterations are absolutely deadly in court. Document examination is now a sophisticated science. With skill and uncanny accuracy, experts may be able to determine the time that entries were made in medical records and who made them.[12]

Courts reason that destroying or altering records in anticipation of or in response to a discovery request falls under the umbrella of misuse of discovery. Discovery rules provide a broad range of sanctions for the misuse of discovery. Sanctions can include monetary fines, contempt charges, establishing or precluding the facts at issue, striking pleadings, dismissing all or parts of the action, and even granting a default judgment against the offending party. In addition to these evidence and discovery sanctions, many penal codes include criminal penalties for perjury and spoliation.[13] In several jurisdictions, spoliation of evidence itself is a cause of action in tort.[14]

Therefore, tampering with medical records may make malpractice cases impossible to defend. Further, providers who falsify a patient's record may be found civilly and criminally liable. Proof of such charges will result in loss of hospital privileges and even loss of license to practice.[15]

Retention of medical records

The increased complexity of health care delivery has heightened the importance of medical record retention. It is imperative, apart from any statutory mandates, that a physician

---

* HIPAA is discussed in detail elsewhere in this volume (see Chapter 19).

maintain comprehensive patient records as long as the threat of a medical malpractice suit exists. That means that, if at all possible, medical records should be maintained indefinitely. A general guideline is to maintain medical records for at least 10 years after the *last* time the patient consulted the health care provider. In the case of minors, the medical records should be kept for a minimum of 10 years or until the patient reaches the age of majority plus the applicable statute of limitations, whichever offers the longer period of time. The presence of a latent injury may extend the statute of limitations until the injury is discovered. Discovery rules in some states will extend malpractice liability beyond the statute of limitations. These rules will usually allow a period of time, most often 1 year, after discovery of the malpractice to bring a suit. In states with such discovery rules, minors' records should be retained for sufficient time for the minor to reach majority and for the statute of repose, if there is one, to expire.[16] If there is no statute of repose, minors' records, and adult records as well, must be kept indefinitely because there is no time limit to bringing a suit under the discovery rule.

If it is impossible for a health care provider to retain the medical records indefinitely, records may be stored at a commercial facility or microfilmed.[17] However, both of these alternatives are expensive, especially for the physician leaving practice. Many times local clinical or hospitals will agree to maintain the records of a physician retiring or leaving the community in order to establish at least a marginal contact with the physician's former patients. Either as partial consideration in a sale of medical records or as total consideration for the unremunerated transfer of records, a binding written agreement should be made. The agreement should specify the following at a minimum:

- that the transferee will act as trustee of the records for the transferor;
- that the records must be retained for a specific term of years or indefinitely;
- that the trustee will honor the confidentiality of the patient;
- that the patient's requests for copies of all information will be honored;
- that the original provider, his or her attorney-in-fact, and his or her personal representative will have access to and may copy any record;
- that the records may be microfilmed, scanned, or otherwise reduced or compacted at no expense to the original provider;
- that the agreement is binding on the transferee's successors and assigns.[18]

State regulations. State law may dictate specific medical record retention requirements. For example, employee health records should be retained according to specific state retention requirements.

Federal regulations. Federal regulations governing the Medicare program require participating hospitals to keep patient records and records of building materials; cost report materials; and reviews, reports, and other records[19] for at least 5 years after a Medicare cost report is filed with the fiscal intermediary or that period of time determined by the appropriate state regulation governing the retention of records, whichever is longer.[20] All records pertaining to any reimbursement issue that is on appeal with the Medicare program should be retained until the conclusion of the appeal.[21]

Methadone treatment programs must maintain records traceable to specific patients, showing dates, quantities, and batch or code marks of the drug dispensed for a period of 3 years after the date of dispensing.[22] Likewise, when narcotic drugs are administered for treatment of narcotic-dependent, hospitalized patients, the hospital must maintain accurate records, showing dates, quantities, and batch or code marks for the drug administered for at least 3 years.[23]

The federal Occupational Safety and Health Administration (OSHA) requires that a provider maintain, for 5 years after the end of the year to which it relates, documentation, consisting of a log and descriptive summary; a supplementary record detailing the injuries and illnesses; and an annual summary, which is to be posted, of an employee's occupational injuries and illnesses.[24]

Other regulations, recommendations, and requirements. JCAHO provides that the length of time for which medical records are to be retained is dependent on the need for their use in continuing patient care, legal research, or educational purposes and on law and regulation.[25] A provider may wish to consider the recommendations of professional associations regarding record retention times. For example, three such associations—the American Hospital Association, the American Medical Association, and the American Medical Record Association—have recommended that the complete patient medical record (in original or reproduced form) be retained for a period of 10 years. This period would commence with the last encounter with a patient. These associations further suggest that after 10 years such records may be destroyed, unless destruction is specifically prohibited by statute, ordinance, regulation, or law, and provided that the institution retains certain information for specified purposes.[26]

Destruction of medical records

Some states have specific regulations governing the destruction of medical records.[27] Usually these regulations call for incineration or shredding as a means of protecting patient confidentiality. If a health care entity destroys its own records, it should establish written policies covering the destruction and require a written declaration from the person responsible for record destruction that the prescribed policies were followed. Usually destruction of records will require the use of a commercial document disposal company. It is important that the record destruction by such a commercial entity be covered by a written agreement. That agreement should include provisions that cover the following points:

- the method of destruction;
- warranties that the confidentiality of the records will be honored;
- indemnification for any unauthorized record disclosures;
- a Certificate of Destruction from the commercial entity certifying the date, method, and the complete destruction of the record. The Certificate of Destruction should be retained as a permanent record.

Record security and protection

Although reason would dictate that a certain degree of record security and protection is necessary to prevent unauthorized access to medical records and ensure the integrity of the information contained therein, there are a few specific guidelines regulating record security and protection.[28] The federal regulations protecting confidentiality of alcohol and drug abuse require that the records be maintained in a secure room, locked file cabinet, safe, or other similar container when not in use.[29] Both the HIPAA Standards for the Privacy of Individually Identifiable Health Information and UHCIA call for providers to effect "reasonable" safeguards for the security of medical records, but do not specify what those reasonable safeguards should be.[30] However, the comments to the UHCIA chapter indicate that the safeguards should be reasonable for the sensitivity of the information contained, the type of provider maintaining the information, and other factors particular to the information's environment. The following are minimal requirements that should be part of any record program:

- a written health care management policy with security and protection provisions;*
- a designated individual in charge of record security;*
- background checks and bonding of all record personnel;
- training of all medical record personnel in security and privacy issues;*
- locked door, authorized entry access to records;
- locked, fire proofrecord storage;
- locks changed on a regular basis or with a change of personnel;
- passwords, access codes, or advanced recognition technology and firewalls for automated systems;†
- confidential material should not be kept on a publicly accessible system and a publicly accessible system should not be run on the institution's internal system;*
- passwords and access codes changed on a regular basis;

- written or electronic access and print logs;*
- archival and/or backup records stored off-site;
- a zero tolerance for security violations regardless of the form of the records. No record security violation should go unrecorded or unpunished.‡

Record retrieval

No record system is complete without an organized method for the retrieval of records. Strange as it may seem, there seem to be few if any regulations governing the retrieval system used, but there are cases reflecting damages for retrieval failures.[31]

OWNERSHIP AND PATIENT ACCESS

There is little controversy about who owns the tangible medical record, that is, the paper, film, or recording that contains the medical information: the health care provider who is responsible for creating, compiling, and maintaining the medical record owns it.[32] In facilities where records are compiled by several individual health care providers, the facility is the owner, not the assorted individual health care providers.[33] The ownership is established by statute in several states and by contract in others.[34] However, the ownership interest in the medical record is different from the ownership interest in most other personal property and is governed by a large body of ethical, administrative, statutory, and common law controls. The concept of ownership is further complicated by two federal court cases that hold that the patient has a limited "property right" in the record.[35] However, most court cases reflect the patient's right to access the medical record and the medical information therein rather than their ownership rights to the physical record.

CONFIDENTIALITY AND PRIVACY

The medical record is apt to contain more personal information than any other single document. It contains not only sensitive health care information, but also demographic, sexual, behavioral, dietary, and recreational information. Because of the vast amount of highly sensitive information in the medical record, patients have the expectation that the information therein will be held in privacy. That loss of personal privacy is the greatest concern of over a quarter of our population.[36]

The privacy versus confidentiality conflict

Patient privacy advocates look for a model based on access only by informed patient consent and question the need to circulate the health care information beyond the health care

---

† See Chapter 33 below for a more complete discussion of security for electronic records.

‡ Those requirements marked with * are HIPAA requirements as well. Many of the recommendations are also required by the Centers for Medicare and Medicaid Services (CMS). *See* CMS Security Manual, http://cms.hhs.gov/manuals/.

provider. Professor Alan Westin[37] defines this concept as "privacy."

On the other hand, Westin defines as "confidentiality" the question of how medical data shall be held and used by the provider that collected it, what other further uses will be made of it, and if or when the patient's consent will be required. The confidentiality advocates, hospitals, insurers, managed care organizations, educators, researchers, public health agencies, government agencies, utilization review organizations, and risk managers, hold to the premise that access to and sharing of health care data are critical to a well-functioning, cost-efficient health care system, and essential to the discovery and monitoring of disease trends.

The conflict between the concepts of "privacy" and "confidentiality" then, reduced to its basics, is whether we support privacy, recognizing that the greater social good will be negatively effected, or do we feel that the greater social good is important enough to negatively impact the privacy of the medical records and the information therein. There appears to be little doubt that current legal theory supports the concept of confidentiality, and in this day of third party-payers, fourth-party auditors, and the multiple legitimate needs for health care information, classical patient privacy is a myth.

Constitutional privacy protections

Privacy advocates relying on constitutional privacy protection get little support. First, the right to privacy under the Constitution offers protection only from intrusions by the government.[38] Therefore, constitutional remedies do not reach breaches by private health care information holders. Further, a whole series of federal court cases have demonstrated that even when there is government intrusion into individually identifiable health care information, individuals cannot rely on constitutional protections to preserve their privacy. The strong public interest represented by the need for the information outweighs the individual's need for privacy. The seminal case in this series is *Whalen v. Roe*.[39] In an attempt to stem the illegal distribution of prescription drugs, the New York legislature passed a law requiring all prescriptions for Schedule II drugs to be logged and information concerning the prescription, including the identity of the patient, to be transmitted to the State Department of Health. Public disclosure of the information was forbidden and access to the information was confined to department and investigative personnel. Patients receiving Schedule II drugs and their doctors brought suit questioning the constitutionality of the law. They argued that the doctor-patient relationship was one of the zones of privacy accorded constitutional protection. A unanimous United States Supreme Court held that the patient identification process was reasonable exercise of the state's broad police powers.[40] In *United States v. Westinghouse Electric Corp.*[41] the United States Court

of Appeals for the Third Circuit elucidated the following seven factors to be considered in determining "whether an intrusion into an individual's privacy is justified . . .":

- the type of record requested;
- the type of information it does or might contain;
- the potential for harm in any subsequent nonconsensual disclosure;
- the injury from disclosure to the relationship in which the record was generated;
- the adequacy of safeguards to prevent unauthorized disclosure;
- the degree of need for access;
- whether there is an express statutory mandate, articulated public policy, or other recognizable public interest militating toward access.[42]

The test appears to have survived the test of time[43] and offers pragmatic evidence that even under constitutional protections privacy is dead and confidentiality reigns.

Confidentiality

Section 5.05 of the AMA Code of Ethics adopts a standard for confidentiality.[44] It directs the physician not to reveal information about the patient without the patient's consent or as required by law. It then goes on to say some "overriding social considerations" will make revelations "ethically and legally justified." While the text and the 65 annotations may give a member physician some idea of the scope of the problem, the broadness, vagueness, and double speak of Section 5.05 reflect the current confused state of medical record confidentiality in the United States.

State regulation. State statutes have developed piecemeal across the country. All states require health care providers to report some types of patients to state agencies.[45] However, universality ends with that statement. State confidentiality rules are dramatically inconsistent in their regulations and even their presence.[46] Ohio appears to be the only state with an independent tort for unauthorized disclosure of medical information.[47] In general, states have been largely unsuccessful in finding ways to compensate patients for injury sustained by authorized disclosures.[48] In pre–World War II America this was not a problem. The population was not tremendously mobile and health care information was essentially local. However, since World War II the American population has become increasingly mobile, and coincident with both that mobility and the development of regional and national payers, health care information has crossed state lines as never before. In addition, the expanded use of electronic health care information has no regard for state boundaries. The patchwork effect of strikingly different state confidentiality regulations, or complete lack thereof, became a major problem. Both UHCIA and HIPAA developed in response to this problem.

PRIVILEGE AND ADMISSIBILITY

Provider-patient privilege

An issue closely related to privacy and confidentiality is how confidential health care information is treated by the courts. As might be surmised from the discussions above, it would seem apparent that nowhere is the release of confidential health care information more in the public interest than in the court of law. In addition, there is no doctor-patient testimonial privilege in the common law. It therefore seems incongruous that since 1828 all but three states have passed some sort of provider-patient testimonial privilege statute.[49] The statutes vary widely from state to state but all offer some degree of protection to the patient by not allowing the provider to testify in court about the patient's medical information. Many states do not recognize the privilege in criminal cases, others limit the privilege to psychotherapists, and others include a variety of health care providers in addition to physicians. Under Section 501 of the Federal Rules of Evidence, if a claim in a federal court arises under federal law, no privilege will be recognized.[50] There has been a definite trend in both federal and state courts to look at the health care testimonial privilege skeptically. Even in that bastion of privilege, the psychiatric record, courts have questioned the merits of confidentiality. Critics see the privilege as nothing more than a litigation tactic and doubt that testimony deters people from seeking psychiatric or, for that matter, any health care. The current uses of group therapy and the fact that people in states without privilege seek care at the same rate as in privilege states are frequently asserted arguments.

Nonetheless, a general body of law has developed in regard to the provider-patient privilege. The privilege extends to the entire medical record, including x-rays, laboratory reports, billing records, and all other documents compiled and maintained by the provider.[51] The communication must be made in confidence for the privilege to apply. The communication must also be made within the context of the provider-patient relationship and be made in regard to diagnosis or treatment. Therefore, situations in which the communicator is a nontraditional patient, such as one undergoing an independent medical examination, or relating facts unrelated to diagnosis or treatment, are not covered by the privilege.[52]

The privilege and the benefit thereof belong to the patient, although anyone with an interest may assert it. Only the patient may waive the privilege. The waiver may be express or implied. An express waiver is made when the patient signs an authorization directing the provider to disclose the information. Implied waivers may be made in several different ways. The patient may voluntarily introduce the medical evidence to the court; the patient may voluntarily place his or her medical condition at issue in litigation; or the patient may fail to assert his or her privilege when the medical information is placed into evidence. A good rule of thumb for health care providers is always to assert the privilege when faced with a subpoena that is not accompanied by a patient's authorization to disclose the information. As we have mentioned above, this is required by the federal alcohol and drug regulations and even in cases not involving alcohol or drugs, failure to assert the privilege has resulted in liability in at least one state court.[53]

Admissibility

As is the case with all evidence, medical records must be relevant and material to the issues before the court to be admitted into evidence. However, depending on the document, a variety of objections may be raised to the admission of even relevant and material health care information. In addition to the privilege objection discussed above, some medical information, such as incident reports, may be protected because they were made in anticipation of litigation or fall within the attorney-client privilege or are part of the attorney's work product. However, the most often used objection to admission is that the medical record is hearsay. It is an out of court statement being introduced to prove the truth of the matter asserted in the statement. However, medical records tend to fall into one of a number of exceptions to the hearsay rule. First, medical records are business records[54] or records of regularly conducted activity and fall under that exception in the hearsay rule.[55] Second, statements made for the purposes of medical diagnosis or treatment[56] are exceptions to the hearsay rule. Finally, dying declarations[57] and declarations against interest[58] are also exceptions that may apply to medical records. For practical purposes, records made in accordance with the record-keeping mechanics outlined above will be admitted as evidence over the hearsay objection.

ENDNOTES

1. *See* Washington Administrative Code, Title 246: Department of Health §246-318-440: Records and Reports—Medical Record System.
2. Joint Commission on Accreditation of Healthcare Organizations, *Accreditation Manual for Hospitals*, Standards 5-10, 54-63 (1995).
3. 42 C.F.R. Ch. IV §482.24.
4. National Conference of Commissioners on Uniform State Laws, *Uniform Health Care Information Act*, 9 U. La. Ann. 478 (1988).
5. *Id.* §4-102.
6. *Id.* §4-101; DHHS Standards for Privacy of Individually Identifiable Health Information, 45 C.F.R. §§160-164 10-1-01, Final rule, Federal Register, Aug. 14, 2002, 67(157):53182-53273, to be codified at 45 C.F.R. Parts 160-164; §3-102 UHCIA, *supra*; 45 C.F.R. §164.524 10-1-01 edition, *supra* (note this section was not changed in the final rule of August 2002.); §3-102 UHCIA, *supra*; 45 C.F.R. §164.524 10-1-01 edition, *supra* (note this section was not changed in the final rule of August 2002).
7. For examples, *see* Wn. Rev Code 70.02.080 (1993); Fla. Stat. Ann. §455.241 (1985); Or. Rev. Stat. Ch. 192 §525 (1993); Nev. Rev. Stat. Ch. 629 §061 (1983); N.Y.M.H.L §33.16 (1988).
8. §4-101 UHCIA, *supra*; 45 CFR §164.526 10-1-01 edition, *supra* (note this section was not changed in the final rule of August 2002).

9. §§8-101, 8-102, 8-103, UHCIA, *supra*.

10. *Pierce v. Penman*, 515 A. 2d 948 (1986).

11. *Thor v. Boska*, 113 Cal. Rptr. 296, 302 (1974).

12. *See*, Anderson: *Counterfeit, Forged and Altered Documents*, 32(6) Law Society J. 48 (1994); Fortunato & Steward, *Sentence Insertion Detected Through Ink, ESDA, and Line Width*, 17 J. Forensic Sciences 1702 (1992); Schwid, *Examining Forensic Documents*, 64 The Wisconsin Lawyer 23 (1991).

13. *See* Model Penal Code §241.7

14. F. Buckner, *Cedars-Sinai Medical Center v. Superior Court and the Tort of spoliation of evidence*, 6(1) Legal Medicine Perspectives 1-3 (1999).

15. *Ritter v. Board of Commissioners of Adams County Public Hospital*, 637 P. 2d 940 (1981). *See also* F. Buckner, *Medical Records and Physician Disciplinary Actions*, 11 J. of Medical Practice Management 284-290 (1996); H. Hirsh, *Tampering with Medical Records*, 24 Med. Trial Tech. Q. 450-455 (Spring 1978); Preiser, *The High Cost of Tampering with Medical Records*, Medical Economics 84-87 (Oct. 4, 1986); Gage, *Alteration, Falsification, and Fabrication of Records in Medical Malpractice Actions*, Med. Trial Tech. Q. 476-488 (Spring 1981); Mich. Stat. Ann. §14.624(21) (Callaghan 1976); Tenn. Code Ann. §63-752(f) 14 (Supp. 1976); Tenn. Code Ann. §39-1971 (1975) (making it a crime to falsify a hospital medical record for purposes of cheating or defrauding).

16. In at least one state, such statutes of repose have been struck down making the discovery rule applicable indefinitely. *DeYoung v. Providence Medical Center*, 136 Wn. 2d 136; 960 P. 2d 919 (1998).

17. Several states specifically authorize the microfilming of records. *See*, Cal. Evid. Code §1550 (West 1986).

18. F. Buckner, *Closing Your Medical Office*, 4 J. Medical Practice Management 274-280 (1989).

19. Medicare and Medicaid Guide (CCH) ¶6420.85 (1990).

20. 42 C.F.R. §482.24(b)(1) (1990).

21. *Id.*

22. 21 C.F.R. §291.505(d)(13)(ii).

23. 21 C.F.R. §291.505(f)(2)(v).

24. 29 C.F.R. Chap. XII, §§1904 et seq.

25. Joint Commission on Accreditation of Healthcare Organizations, *Accreditation Manual for Hospitals* (JCAHO, 1990), Standard MR 4.2.

26. American Hospital Association and American Medical Record Association, *Statement on Preservation of Medical Records in Health Care Institutions* (1975).

27. *See* Tenn. Code Ann. §68-11-305 (c) (1987).

28. 42 C.F.R. §2.16.

29. *Id.*

30. §164.530(c) (1 and 2), Standards for the Privacy of Individually Identifiable Health Information, *supra* note 6; §7-101, UHCIA, *supra* note 4.

See also, discussion on HIPAA and electronic medical records (Chapters 19 and 33, this volume).

31. *See Fox v. Cohen*, 406 N.E. 2d 178 (1980); *Bondu v. Gurvich*, 473 So. 2d 1307 (1985).

32. Dewitt et al., *Patient Information and Confidentiality: Treatise on Health Care Law* (Mathew Bender, 1991).

33. *Parsley v. Associates in Internal Medicine*, 484 N.Y.S. 2d 485 (1985).

34. *See* Tenn. Code Ann. §68-11-304 (1990).

35. *See Bishop Clarkson Memorial Hospital v. Reserve Life Insurance, Co.*, 350 F. 2d 1006 (8th Cir. 1965); *Pyramid Life Ins. Co. v. Masonic Hosp. Assn.*, 191 F. Supp. 51 (W.D. Okla. 1961).

36. Wall Street Journal/ABC poll of September 16, 1999, quoted in *Standards for Privacy of Individually Identifiable Health Information: Proposed Rule*, 64 Federal Register 59917 (Nov. 3, 1999) at 59919.

37. Alan Westin, *Computers, Health Records and Patient's Rights* (1976).

38. Barefoot, *Enacting a Health Information Confidentiality Law: Can Congress Beat the Deadline?*, 77 N. C. Law Rev. 283 (1998).

39. 429 U.S. 589 (1977); *see also U.S. v. Miller*, 425 U.S. 435 (1976).

40. *Id.* at 598-604.

41. *United States v. Westinghouse Electric Corp.*, 638 F. 2d 570 (1980).

42. *Id.* at 578.

43. *See Doe v. Southern PA Transportation Authority*, 72 F. 3d 1133 (1995).

44. AMA Council on Ethical and Judicial Affairs, *Code of Medical Ethics: Current Opinions and Annotations*, §5.05 (1997).

45. F. Buckner, *The Uniform Health-Care Information Act: A Physician's Guide to Record and Health Care Information Management*, 5 J. Medical Practice Management 207 (1990).

46. *See* §1-101 UHCIA, *supra* note 4; *see also* Barefoot, *supra* note 38.

47. *Biddle v. Warren General Hospital*, 715 N.E. 2d 518 (1999).

48. *See generally* Frankel, *Do Doctors Have a Constitutional Right to Violate Their Patient's Privacy?*, 46 Villanova Law Rev. 141 (2001).

49. South Carolina, Texas, and Vermont.

50. Rule 501, General Rule, Federal Rules of Evidence for United States Courts and Magistrates Effective July 1, 1975 as Amended to September 1, 1991 (West).

51. *See Tucson Medical Center v. Rowles*, 520 P. 2d 518 (1974).

52. *See Polsky v. Union Mutual Stock Life Ins. Co.*, 436 N.Y.S. 2d 744 (1981); *see also Chiasera v. Mutual Ins. Co.*, 422 N.Y.S. 2d 341 (1979); *Griffths v. Metropolitan St. Ry. Co.*, 63 N.E. 808 (1902).

53. *Smith v. Driscoll*, 162 P. 572 (1917).

54. *See* Fla. Stat. Ann. §90.803(6).

55. Rule 803(6), Federal Rules of Evidence, *supra* note 50.

56. *Id.*, Rule 803(4).

57. *Id.*, Rule 804(b)(2).

58. *Id.*, Rule 804(b)(3).

33

Electronic Records

FILLMORE BUCKNER, M.D., J.D., F.C.L.M.

ELECTRONIC MEDICAL RECORDS AS A LEGAL AID
ELECTRONIC RECORD CRITERIA
SECURITY ISSUES

The electronic medical record is an electronically stored database containing a patient's health care information from one or multiple sources. The health care industry has become the last industry in the United States to be computerized.* In every other industry the electronic record has become the norm. Whether this rejection of the computer is a result of some inbred reactionary trait on the part of the medical profession or truly an objective look at a new technology is open to debate—for surely, electronic records have some well-known problems. Critics cite high initial cost, large training investment, hardware crashes and breakdowns, power failures, software glitches, sabotage of the system by both disgruntled employees and hackers, unauthorized access, viruses, Trojan horses, reluctance of physicians to use the tightly controlled format for notes, and a host of other real and imagined problems.[1]

On the other hand, the health care industry is hard pressed to deny that electronic medical records facilitate and many times are essential to effective quality assurance, analysis of practice patterns, and research activities; speed the retrieval of data and expedite billing;[2] reduce the number of lost records; allow for a complete set of backup records at little or no cost; expedite the transfer of data between facilities, regardless of geographic separation; are a proven long-term cost reducer; and, in most cases, are practice enhancers and a public relations tool. The original claims of significant staff reductions have had to be reduced to claims for modest staff reductions. In some hospitals and clinics the only reduction has been in the number of transcriptionists. The high initial startup cost has been modified by greatly reduced hardware costs, and the introduction of wireless and hand-held devices has greatly increased the

versatility of electronic record entry and retrieval. Advances in natural language processing software have made screening free text records faster and more accurate than previously thought possible, and the field continues to develop.[3]

ELECTRONIC MEDICAL RECORDS AS A LEGAL AID

However, from a legal standpoint, some other factors weigh more heavily in favor of the electronic medical record. First and foremost, an electronic record system will produce a legible record.[4] In the minds of many, this is reason enough to justify the electronic record. Many of the problems of wrong medication, wrong dose, wrong directions, wrong procedure caused by illegible and misinterpreted records will be eliminated. Second, a properly planned medical record system can incorporate practice guidelines that are automatically triggered by a diagnosis or symptom syndrome.[5] Adherence to practice guidelines has been an effective defense in many malpractice actions. Guidelines have also been championed as the most effective method of eliminating unnecessary and costly defensive medicine practices.[6] In a like manner, the effective electronic medical record system will have connections to the pharmacy and pharmacy data banks. Computerized prescriptions and orders will not permit prescriptions or orders for drugs for which the patient has a known allergy, and the system will alert both provider and pharmacist of potentially harmful drug-drug interactions or incompatibilities with the patient's physical or laboratory findings.[7] Adverse drug events are now the number one adverse hospital event[8] and second only to birth injuries in the amount of damages paid in malpractice claims. Reducing these adverse events would be an important risk management accomplishment. Fourth, electronic medical record systems can track ordered laboratory, diagnostic, or imaging tests, alert the provider of abnormal tests, and even notify the patient of the need, or the lack thereof, of future tests, diagnosis, or treatment.[9]

---

* In Great Britain almost all general practices are now computerized. Lusignan, *Does Feedback Improve the Quality of Computerized Medical Records in Primary Care?*, 9(4) Journal of the American Informatics Society 395 (2002).

Fifth, electronic medical records automatically confirm the date and times of all entries and keep a dated and timed log of all individuals who have accessed the record. Many individuals think these features make electronic medical records more secure than paper records. In any case, such entries offer great protection against accusations of Medicare or Medicaid fraud and abuse. Finally, most electronic record systems automatically generate patient educational materials tailored to the patient's diagnosis and treatment. These defensive features are hard to beat in a paper system.

ELECTRONIC RECORD CRITERIA

As was mentioned in the previous chapter, properly compiled and maintained medical records are business records. Electronic medical records too are business records.[10] As such they must meet certain criteria to ensure their admissibility as evidence in court. The most critical element in the admissibility of electronic records is reliability. When a paper record is prepared, it is fixed in form and content. In most cases changes may be detected. The electronic media may be changed and the changed product may be indistinguishable from the original. Therefore, the first criterion to be met is that the electronic medical record must place each entry as made in a "read only" mode. That is, once the entry is made, it cannot be altered. Any changes must be made by a new note entered in order, dated, and timed.

Although no formal criteria have yet been published, the following criteria must be adhered to for electronic data to be considered "records" in the evidentiary sense:

- *Compliant.* Information-keeping must adhere to local jurisdictional requirements for admissibility as "business records."
- *Responsible.* Written policies and procedures for record storage and maintenance must be established and maintained.
- *Implemented.* The written policies and procedures must be employed at all times.
- *Consistent.* Record-maintenance systems must ensure that records stored and maintained are managed in a uniform fashion to ensure credibility.
- *Comprehensive.* All business records must be stored and maintained.
- *Identifiable.* All business records for a discrete transaction must be readily identifiable and accessible.
- *Complete.* Stored records must preserve the content and structure of the business transaction creating them to ensure accuracy and understanding.
- *Authorized.* All maintained records must have been stored under the auspices of an authorized creator.
- *Preserved.* Records must be inviolate to preserve their original content. No records may be audited without a concise audit trail that preserves relevant information of the original content.

- *Removable.* Records may be removed from storage only with the consent of an authorized entity. All removals must be evidenced by an audit trail that preserves the content of the record being removed.
- *Usable.* The information in the stored records must be accessible for general business purposes, for exportation to reporting functions, and for redaction when necessary. Any and all accesses (even simple reading) must create an audit trail.[11]

A careful analysis of these requirements will stress that, in addition to reliability, generally requiring some sort of emergency power source, both a functioning archival system and a secondary, preferably off the premises, backup system are essential to a well-functioning medical records system. Unfortunately, the backup system, one of the electronic medical record's greatest advantages over the paper system, is the most commonly overlooked element of electronic medical records.

The Federal Rules of Evidence have long recognized the admissibility of electronic business records.[12] In addition, the Federal Rules of Evidence recognize a computer printout as an "original" for the purposes of admission.[13] Most state courts have followed the federal leads on both issues.[14]

SECURITY ISSUES

The privacy issue is the most common concern voiced about electronic medical records. As discussed in the previous chapter, privacy can no longer be a consideration in medical records of any type. What the health care industry must consider are reasonable rules of confidentiality. Electronic records have all the confidentiality concerns of their paper counterparts and the added concerns of preserving the integrity of the record and preventing unauthorized remote access to the information. Although medical record security in general has been discussed above, some issues specific to the security of electronic records are discussed below.

Access. With paper records one of the principal security measures employed is limiting access to records to a limited number of individuals and, in some situations, limiting access to only the attending physician. However, one of the great advantages of the electronic medical record is that it can offer seamless recording from any number of sources. It can also offer access to a nonfragmented medical record to the same number of sites. Therefore, traditional criteria of limiting access to a single physician or group of physicians or limiting access by job criteria will limit the benefits of the electronic record. All providers involved in the care of the patient should have access to and be able to record in the record. It is as important for the dentist caring for the patient to know about the patient's rheumatic fever as it is for the pharmacist or clinical pharmacologist to know about the patient's renal function. When the patient comes to the Emergency Department in the middle of the night, the triage person needs immediate access to the complete record. This means access must be spread across a wider range of provider and job categories and cannot be limited by current "attending" criteria.

Authorizations. The access issues described above mandate that a system of blanket category authorizations to enter the system must be made. For instance, "all licensed providers" (which would include LPNs in many states); or "all licensed providers except . . ."; or "all licensed providers and . . . ."

Authentication. In the field of electronic medical records, authentication is defined as the system for determining the identity of an individual seeking access to the system to enter or retrieve data. The simplest authentication system is the combination of user identification name and password. If the individual enters that combination of symbols making up the user name followed by the proper password, entry is allowed. User identification names are usually permanent and are frequently numerical. Passwords are generally changed periodically, monthly, or quarterly. Another relatively simple system combines the user identification name with a smart card not unlike a credit card or mechanized gate card. As computers have become more sophisticated, so have authentication systems. Commercial authentication systems are now available based on "digital signature," fingerprints, retinal patterns, facial biometrics, and voice recognition. Authentication systems need constant upkeep to remove people who leave the system and add people new to the system.

Firewalls. Another advantage of electronic records is that they allow remote access to medical records. Therefore, providers may access and enter data from remote sites such as physician offices and outlying clinics. The access ports for these remote sites are vulnerable to unauthorized individuals entering the system. They must be guarded by firewalls. A firewall is a point of entry for remote users that can be configured and controlled. A firewall normally restricts access by denying entry to incoming messages arising from an unapproved source, and limiting access to approved sources such as a list of approved phone numbers or identified computers. A firewall may also limit the functions it allows an incoming source to perform.

Transmission control protocol wrappers. Wrappers serve somewhat the same function as firewalls. Wrappers may be thought of as functioning within the server rather than at the port of entry, as does the firewall. It too will intercept incoming data and check it against a programmed security protocol. Wrappers can not only deny entry to the system or prevent a proposed function, but can audit the source, date, and time of the entry.

Audit trails. As has been discussed above, an audit trail (a.k.a. audit log) logs all access to electronically stored medical information. An effective audit trail will record not only the identification of the individual accessing the record and the time and date of record access, but also the record or records accessed, the portion of the record accessed, and the action made. The audit trail must be secured against modification and provide for periodic analysis for unauthorized access. Audit trails that meet or exceed these criteria appear to be an effective tool in preventing unauthorized access to records.

Under HIPAA final rules,[15] the patient has the right to request a log of disclosures made for the 6 years prior to the date of the request. That log must contain: the date of disclosure; the name of the entity or individual who received the protected health care information and, if known, their address; a brief description of the health care information disclosed; a brief statement of the purpose of the disclosure or, in lieu of the statement, a copy of the written request for the information.[16] Routine disclosures for the purposes of treatment and care are excepted from this disclosure mandate, as are certain disclosures protected by other HIPAA sections.[17]

Encryption. If health care information is to be sent over public networks such as the World Wide Web, it should be encrypted to ensure confidentiality.

Virus control. Viruses must be controlled by strict rules against downloading unauthorized software programs from the web or bringing in software from home. In addition, antivirus software must be installed and updated on a regular basis. Regular checks of the software configurations and unauthorized service ports will help control the problem as well.

PCASSO

A brief review of the University of California at San Diego Healthcare's Patient-Centered Access to Secure Systems Online (PCASSO)[18] will give the reader a sense of how all the factors mentioned above come together to develop a reasonably secure system with patient and multiple provider access. PCASSO was conceived to empower patients to become active participants and partners in their health care, while satisfying the state and federal regulations (including HIPAA) and the University's IRB. The plan utilizes the Internet to allow both patients and providers to access records from almost anywhere, if they elect to become part of the PCASSO program. Patients are asked to sign the following consent before being enrolled in the program:

The information you will be able to access via the PCASSO system is technical and contained in systems that were originally designed for trained health professionals to use only. As a result, there is a possibility that you will be exposed to information that you do not understand or find startling. PCASSO is not intending to place upon you the burden of interpreting your medical record, nor to cause you to act on the information received without first discussing it with your physician. One of the risks associated with this study is that "a little knowledge is a dangerous thing." By agreeing to participate, you agree to contact your physician to help to resolve any questions or problems that might arise as a result of viewing your medical data online. If you have difficulty contacting your physician, you may contact PCASSO project staff, who will assist you in contacting your physician.[19]

In addition, a hotline and triage system was established to take care of any questions for distraught patients. Such calls were classified as information toxicity and reported to the IRB.

Patients' clinical data is entered into the program's server as divided messages classified as to sensitivity level, as low, standard, public deniable, guardian deniable, or patient deniable. "Low" data is not patient identifiable.[20] "Standard" is health information that is patient identifiable and does not fall into any of the deniable categories. "Public deniable" is information protected by special state or federal statute such as mental health, AIDS and HIV infections, abortion, adoption, substance abuse, and sexually transmitted diseases (STD). "Guardian deniable" is information that can legally be withheld from a guardian about a minor patient, such as abortion, STD, or substance abuse in some states. "Patient deniable" is information that the primary physician believes is capable of causing harm to the patient if it were disclosed to that patient, most often psychotherapy notes.

A firewall separates PCASSO from the remainder of the university system. The user logs in from any of the common web browsers and uses a graphical image keyboard and a combination of authentication procedures, a password, a token, and a public-private key pair. The private key is a diskette that interacts with the server and mutually authenticates the communicators.* An individually held plastic card with a serial number is the final step in the authentication process. If the name, password, number, and key correspond, entry is permitted. A technical support number is available if entry or other problems are encountered. All PCASSO operations are monitored and logged, including any attempted penetrations. Its designers believe it meets all the criteria required by HIPAA.[21] It allows for emergency access, role-based access, encryption, access (including unauthorized attempts) audits and logs, unique identifiers plus password and token, automatic log off, and technical and informational support.

---

* In some systems such disks include the encryption program. In others the encryption program is downloaded as part of the setup procedure.

With authentication completed, a screen customized for patient or provider appears. PCASSO's secure communication system allows authorized patients and providers to access specific information and for the providers to carry out privileged additions to the record. PCASSO does not allow the information to be saved to disk, printed out, or transferred to another application. In many ways the system seems more secure than allowing patients to view paper records. Information labeled "pending" or "interim" is filtered out.

PCASSO was fully operational by the spring of 1999. The system has been judged safe and effective as a medical device by the FDA.[22] The system has repulsed all efforts of hackers, first by security consultants and then by hackers at large. Extensive review by risk managers and the California University System's attorneys concluded that the benefits of the system far outweighed the risks. In practice, a greater percentage of patients used the system than did physicians. Patients thought the access precautions very reasonable while many of the physicians considered them unreasonable or intolerable. However, a majority of both the physicians and patients thought the value of having the records available on the Internet was very high.

In conclusion, PCASSO and, by inference, electronic record systems like it, will provide secure electronic records available to both patients and providers. However, high security, while acceptable to patients, has come at a perceived increased price in time and effort to the provider.

ENDNOTES

1. *See* Loomis et al., *If Electronic Medical Records Are So Great, Why Aren't Family Physicians Using Them?*, 51(7) J. Family Practice 36 (2002).
2. HIPAA regulations on electronic billing practices are covered under 45 C.F.R. Parts 160 and 162. Strangely, the Centers for Medicare and Medicaid Services' *Business Partner's Security Manual* still restricts any Internet health care claims, §5 Internet Security Rev. 02-13-02.
3. *See* Heinze et al., *Mining Free-Text Medical Records*, 254 AMIA Annual (2001).
4. *See* Haskins, *Legible Chart*, 48(4) Canadian Family Physician 768 (2002).
5. *See* van Wingerde et al., *Linking Multiple Heterogenous Data Sources to Practice Guidelines*, 391 AMIA Annual (1998).
6. *See* Kapp, *Our Hands Are Tied: Legal Tensions and Medical Ethics* (Auburn House, Westport, Conn. 1998).
7. *See* Evans et al., *Preventing Adverse Drug Events in Hospitalized Patients*, 28 Ann. Pharmacotherapy 523 (1994).
8. *Id.* at 523.
9. *See* F. Buckner, *The Duty to Inform, Liability to Third Parties and the Duty to Warn*, 100 J. Medical Practice Management (Sept./Oct. 1998).
10. Rule 803(6), Federal Rules of Evidence for United States Courts and Magistrates Effective July 1, 1975 as Amended to September 1, 1991 (West).

    (6) **Records of Regularly Conducted Activity.** A memorandum, report, record, or data compilation, *in any form* of acts, events,

conditions, opinions or diagnoses, made at or near the time by, or from information transmitted by, a person with knowledge, if kept in the course of a regularly conducted business activity . . .

11. From Apgood, *Electronic Evidence*, 53(8) Washington State Bar News 46, 47 (1999).

12. *See* Rule 34, Federal Rules of Civil Procedure; *see also* Rule 803(6), Federal Rules of Evidence, *supra* note 10.

13. Rule 1001(3), Federal Rules of Evidence, *supra* note 10.

14. *See Bray v. Bi-State Development*, 949 S.W. 2d 93 (1997).

15. 45 C.F.R. §164.528 10-1-2001 (Modified Federal Register 67(157) at 53271).

16. *Id*. at 53272.

17. *See* 45 C.F.R. §§164.502, 164.510, 164.512.

18. Masys et al., *Giving Patients Access to Their Medical Records Via the Internet*, 9(2) J. American Medical Informatics Association, 181 (2002). *See also* Masys et al., *A Secure Architecture for Access to Clinical Data Via the Internet*, MedInfo 1130 (1998-99); Baker & Masys, *PCASSO: A Design for Secure Communication of Personal Health Information Via the Internet*, 54(2) Int. J. Medical Informatics 97 (1999).

19. *Id*. at 186.

20. *See* 45 C.F.R. §164.502(d).

21. Masys, *supra* note 18, at 183.

22. *Id*. at 184.

34

Medical Testimony and the Expert Witness

JOSEPH D. PIORKOWSKI, Jr., D.O., J.D., M.P.H., F.C.P.M., F.C.L.M.

GENERAL RULES OF ADMISSIBILITY
SPECIAL CONSIDERATIONS
CONCLUSION

The use of medical experts in litigation has increased dramatically in recent years. In medical malpractice and product liability cases, expert testimony usually is necessary to establish one or more of the essential elements of a civil claim or defense. Similarly, in the criminal context, expert testimony generally is required to support claims of incompetency or insanity, and such testimony may be necessary to resolve issues about a defendant's potential for future dangerous behavior. Even when expert testimony is not required to prove an essential element of a claim or defense, medical experts increasingly are used to explain complex scientific concepts and aid the fact finders' understanding of the evidence.

Much of the popularity of using medical experts undoubtedly stems from the special status the law accords expert witnesses. "Unlike an ordinary witness, . . . an expert is permitted wide latitude to offer opinions, including those that are not based on first-hand knowledge or observation."[1] Because experts today can both offer opinions on ultimate questions of fact and explain fully the bases of their opinions, an expert witness provides a useful vehicle for a skilled trial lawyer to review the evidence on a particular issue and present it in a cogent and concise form for the jury.

At common law the presentation of expert testimony was rather cumbersome. Preliminarily the expert's background, training, and education were reviewed, and the court determined whether the witness was competent to render the proffered opinions. If the witness was found to be competent, the presentation of his or her direct testimony proceeded as a strictly regulated hypothetical question. A Florida court described the common law procedure for presenting an expert witness's direct testimony as follows:

When an expert is called upon to give an opinion as to past events which he did not witness, all facts related to the event which are essential to the formation of his opinion should be submitted to the expert in the form of a hypothetical question.

No other facts related to the event should be taken into consideration by the expert as a foundation for his opinion. The facts submitted to the expert in the hypothetical question propounded on direct examination must be supported by competent substantial evidence in the record at the time the question is asked or by reasonable inferences from such evidence.[2]

The rationale for this procedure was that "[a]dherence to this form for the direct examination of an expert prevents the expert from expressing an opinion based on unstated and perhaps unwarranted factual assumptions concerning the event; facilitates cross-examination and rebuttal; and fosters an understanding of the opinion by the trier of fact."[3] In practice the use of hypothetical questions was tedious and came under harsh criticism. Wigmore's treatise on evidence contains the following sharp critique:

It is a strange irony that the hypothetical question, which is one of the few truly scientific features of the rules of evidence, should have become that feature which does most to disgust men of science with the law of evidence. The hypothetical question, misused by the clumsy and abused by the clever, has in practice led to intolerable obstruction of truth. In the first place, it has artificially clamped the mouth of the expert witness, so that his answer to a complex question may not express his actual opinion on the actual case. This is because the question may be so built up and contrived by counsel as to represent only a partisan conclusion. In the second place, it has tended to mislead the jury as to the purport of actual expert opinion. This is due to the same reason. In the third place, it has tended to confuse the jury, so that its employment becomes a mere waste of time and a futile obstruction.[4]

Rules 702 through 705 of the Federal Rules of Evidence (known as *the Rules*), enacted in 1975, simplify greatly the requirements for the admissibility of expert testimony. The Rules eliminate the requirement that evidence of the facts relied on by the expert be admitted into evidence; indeed the Rules expressly permit an expert to rely on facts that are inadmissible. The Rules also obviate the necessity for using hypothetical questions, although hypothetical questions are still permissible. Most states eventually have followed the lead of the Rules as applied by the federal courts in eliminating at least some of the common law requirements. Although a great deal of variability still exists between states, the general trend since 1975 has been toward fewer procedural restrictions on the admissibility of expert testimony.

The first section of this chapter reviews the courts' approach to resolving frequently raised questions concerning the admissibility of medical or scientific expert testimony. Although this chapter focuses primarily on medical experts, cases interpreting the law dealing generally with expert testimony are discussed where useful. The major issues include (1) whether the subject matter of the expert's opinion is appropriate to the case, (2) whether the expert is sufficiently qualified to render the proffered opinion, (3) what types of information provide a proper basis for an expert witness's opinion, (4) the role of general consensus in the scientific community in evaluating the admissibility of expert testimony, and (5) other limitations that exist regarding the types of opinions experts can express. The second section of this chapter reviews some special considerations, including expert testimony in the form of medical literature, the "reasonable degree of medical certainty" standard, discovery of expert witnesses' opinions, and ethical considerations relating to the use of experts.[5]

GENERAL RULES OF ADMISSIBILITY

The law governing the admissibility of expert testimony should be understood in light of two important background considerations. First, a constant tension exists in the law of evidence between two competing principles. One principle holds that deficient or problematic evidence should be inadmissible. Another principle holds that any problem or deficiency in evidence should affect only the weight given to that evidence rather than its admissibility. In no other area of the law of evidence is this tension so pronounced as in the area of expert testimony. Many of the rules reflect compromises between these two jurisprudential approaches.

Second, the trial judge is accorded broad discretion to determine whether expert testimony should be admitted or excluded in a given case. A trial court's decision of inadmissibility will be affirmed on review unless it is "manifestly erroneous."[6]

The subject matter of the expert's opinion

Under the common law, courts took a restrictive view of when expert testimony was appropriately admitted as evidence. The standard articulated in *Hagler v. Gilliland* represents the traditional test: "The admissibility of expert opinion evidence is governed by the rule that such evidence

should not be admitted unless it is clear that the jurors themselves are not capable, from want of experience or knowledge of the subject, to draw correct conclusions from the facts proved. It is not admissible on matters of common knowledge."[7,8] Stated somewhat differently, courts held that "the subject matter must be so distinctively related to some science, profession, business or occupation as to be beyond the ken of the average layperson."[9] If the subject matter was not beyond the ken of the average layperson, the opinion was deemed unnecessary and therefore inadmissible.

The standard articulated in the Rules, which has been adopted in form or in substance by most state courts, is much less hostile to expert testimony than the common law standard. Rule 702 provides, "If scientific, technical, or other specialized knowledge will assist the trier of fact to understand the evidence or to determine a fact in issue, a witness qualified as an expert by knowledge, skill, experience, training, or education, may testify thereto in the form of an opinion or otherwise, if (1) the testimony is based upon sufficient facts or data, (2) the testimony is the product of reliable principles and methods, and (3) the witness has applied the principles and methods reliably to the facts of the case."[10]

Rule 702, as interpreted by the courts, includes three distinct requirements related to the subject matter of expert testimony in addition to the three enumerated requirements concerning the foundation of an expert's opinion (which are discussed in greater detail below). First, the testimony must be composed of scientific, technical, or other specialized knowledge.[11] Second, the testimony must assist the fact finder in understanding the evidence or resolving a factual dispute in the case.[12] Third, the witness must be qualified to render the opinion.

Requirement one: scientific knowledge. In *Daubert v. Merrell Dow Pharmaceuticals* the U.S. Supreme Court addressed the first of Rule 702's three prongs and noted that "[t]he subject of an expert's testimony must be scientific . . . knowledge."[13] The court explained that

The adjective "scientific" implies a grounding in the methods and procedures of science. Similarly, the word "knowledge" connotes more than subjective belief or unsupported speculation. The term "applies to any body of known facts or to any body of ideas inferred from such facts or accepted as truths on good grounds." Of course, it would be unreasonable to conclude that the subject of scientific testimony must be "known" to a certainty; arguably, there are no certainties in science. But, in order to qualify as "scientific knowledge," an inference or assertion must be derived by the scientific method. Proposed testimony must be supported by appropriate validation (i.e., "good grounds") based on what is known. In short, the requirement that an expert's testimony pertain to "scientific knowledge" establishes a standard of evidentiary reliability.[14]

The *Daubert* court emphasized that the approach to scientific knowledge is flexible.[15] "Its overarching subject is

rather than on a medical diagnosis of plaintiff's condition, their evidence is admissible."[56] Other courts have reached similar conclusions.[57]

In *Gideon v. Johns-Manville Sales Corp.*, the U.S. Court of Appeals for the Fifth Circuit considered whether the trial court properly admitted the testimony of the plaintiff's expert, "a biostatistician and epidemiologist specializing in the study of the causes of disease and its effects upon individuals and the public" in an asbestos case.[58] The defendants had objected that the nonphysician witness had given "medical testimony."[59] The court noted that the witness had not testified about the plaintiff's physical condition or prognosis. In affirming the trial judge's ruling admitting the testimony, the court concluded that the witness was qualified to render opinions about risk of cancer, decreased life expectancy associated with asbestosis, and the date when the toxic effects of inhaling asbestos were first known.[60]

Although courts generally have required that witnesses testifying about medical diagnoses must have medical training, they occasionally have permitted nonphysicians to offer opinions about a diagnosis when the witness's education, training, and experience demonstrate that the witness's opinion will assist the trier of fact. For example, in *Jackson v. Waller*, a case involving the contest of a will, the court permitted an optometrist to testify about the progressive nature of cataracts he observed while examining the testatrix's eyes for the purpose of fitting her for glasses.[61]

Jenkins v. United States involved an appeal of a criminal conviction in a case in which the defendant had relied solely on the defense of insanity.[62] The defendant had introduced the testimony of three psychologists, two of whom testified that the defendant's mental illness was related to his crime. The trial court instructed the jury that "[a] psychologist is not competent to give a medical opinion as to a mental disease or defect." The U.S. Court of Appeals for the District of Columbia Circuit reversed the defendant's conviction, stating: "The determination of a psychologist's competence to render an expert opinion based on his findings as to the presence or absence of mental disease or defect must depend upon the nature and extent of his knowledge. It does not depend upon his claim to the title 'psychologist.'"[63]

The court acknowledged that "[m]any psychologists may not qualify to testify concerning mental disease or defect. Their training and experience may not provide an adequate basis for their testimony."[64] Nonetheless, the court noted that "the lack of a medical degree, and the lesser degree of responsibility for patient care which mental hospitals usually assign to psychologists, are not automatic disqualifications."[65]

One common theme runs through all of these cases: "[T]he trial judge should not rely on labels, but must investigate the competence a particular proffered witness would bring to bear on the issues, and whether it would aid the trier of fact in reaching its decision."[66] When an expert is asked to render multiple opinions, the determination of whether the expert is qualified normally should not be made on an all-or-nothing basis. Rather, "expert opinion must be approached on an . . . opinion-by-opinion basis, and the court must . . . carefully examine each opinion offered by the expert to assess its helpfulness to the jury."[67] An expert may be qualified therefore to render some opinions but unqualified to render others.

In *Flanagan v. Lake*, for example, an appellate court considered whether a registered nurse was qualified to offer expert testimony on the issue of causation.[68] Although the court ultimately agreed with the trial court that the nurse was not qualified to offer such testimony, the court at the same time noted that the nurse would have been qualified to offer expert testimony concerning breaches of the standard of care allegedly committed by the nursing staff.[69]

Similarly, in *Perkins v. Volkswagen of America, Inc.*, a product liability case, the issue was the admissibility of testimony given by a specialist in mechanical engineering who had no experience in designing entire automobiles.[70] The U.S. Court of Appeals for the Fifth Circuit affirmed the trial court's decision to allow the expert to render opinions on general mechanical engineering principles but not to allow him to testify as an expert in automotive design.[71]

The foundation of the expert's opinion

At common law, ensuring that an expert's opinion had an adequate factual foundation presented little problem. Unless the expert was testifying on the basis of first-hand observation (as in the case of a treating physician testifying about his or her patient's diagnosis), the facts on which an expert's opinion was based generally had to be admitted into evidence before the expert could state an opinion. Thus the jury always had before it the expert's opinion, as well as all the testimony, records, and other evidence on which the expert's opinion was based.

The Rules relax the requirement that the underlying facts and data be admissible in evidence. Rule 703 provides that "the facts or data in the particular case upon which an expert bases an opinion or inference may be those perceived by or made known to the expert at or before the hearing. If of a type reasonably relied upon by experts in the particular field in forming opinions or inferences upon the subject, the facts or data need not be admissible in evidence in order for the opinion or inference to be admitted." Facts or data that are otherwise inadmissible shall not be disclosed to the jury by the proponent of the opinion or inference unless the court determines that their probative value in assisting the jury to evaluate the expert's opinion substantially outweighs their prejudicial effect.[72]

Rule 703 thus continues to permit experts to base their opinions on the traditional foundations (i.e., personal knowledge or facts made known to them at trial). However, Rule 703 expands the common law rule by permitting experts to base opinions on facts that have not been admitted into evidence and that are themselves inadmissible. The Advisory Committee explained the rationale behind this modification as follows:

[T]he rule is designed to broaden the basis for expert opinions beyond that current in many jurisdictions and to bring the judicial practice into line with the practice of the experts themselves when not in court. Thus a physician in his own practice bases his diagnosis on information from numerous sources and of considerable variety, including statements by patients and relatives, reports and opinions from nurses, technicians, and other doctors, hospital records, and X-rays. Most of them are admissible in evidence, but only with the expenditure of substantial time in producing and examining various authenticating witnesses. The physician makes life-and-death decisions in reliance upon them. His validation, expertly performed and subject to cross-examination, ought to suffice for judicial purposes.[73]

Rule 703 thus creates the anomalous situation of an expert being permitted to rely on inadmissible facts or data as the foundation for an admissible opinion. To ensure that the basis of the expert's opinion is reliable, the facts or data must be "of a type reasonably relied upon by experts in the particular field in forming opinions or inferences upon the subject."[74] Whether the facts or data are "of a type reasonably relied upon" is to be determined by the trial court. "Though courts have afforded experts a wide latitude in picking and choosing the sources on which to base opinions, Rule 703 nonetheless requires courts to examine the reliability of those sources."[75]

Before *Daubert*, federal courts were divided on the proper level of judicial scrutiny for evaluating whether an expert's opinion was based on facts or data of a type reasonably relied on by experts in the field. Judge Weinstein's decision in *In re "Agent Orange" Product Liability Litigation* summarizes the competing schools of thought:

Courts have adopted two judicial approaches to Rule 703: one restrictive, one liberal. The more restrictive view requires the trial court to determine not only whether the data are of a type reasonably relied upon by experts in the field, but also whether the underlying data are untrustworthy for hearsay or other reasons. The more liberal view . . . allows the expert to base an opinion on data of the type reasonably relied upon by experts in the field without separately determining the trustworthiness of the particular data involved.[76,77]

At issue in *Agent Orange* was whether expert witnesses proffered by the plaintiffs who were relying on symptomatology checklists completed by the plaintiffs and "prepared in gross for a complex litigation" were basing their opinions on facts or data of a type reasonably relied on by physicians.[78] The court found that such checklists "are not material that experts in this field would reasonably rely upon and so must be excluded under Rule 703."[79]

This court's reasoning reflected the restrictive approach.[80] In particular, the court did not defer to the expert on the question of whether the facts or data he relied on were of a type reasonably relied on by experts in the field. Rather, the discussion focused on the pivotal role of the trial judge in assessing the foundation of the expert's opinion. "[T]he court may not abdicate its independent responsibilities to decide if the bases meet minimum standards of reliability as a condition of admissibility. If the underlying data is so lacking in probative force and reliability that no reasonable expert could base an opinion on it, an opinion which rests entirely upon it must be excluded."[81]

Factual foundation. Regardless of the type of information on which an expert's opinion is based, courts generally require that an expert's opinion have an adequate factual foundation. "The trial court's examination of reasonable reliance by experts in the field requires at least that the expert base his or her opinion on sufficient factual data, not rely on hearsay deemed unreliable by other experts in the field, and assert conclusions with sufficient certainty to be useful given applicable burdens of proof."[82]

At common law the trial judge could easily enforce this foundation requirement. If factual assumptions were included in a hypothetical question but no evidence was contained in the record to support the existence of the assumed facts, an objection to the hypothetical question would be sustained and the expert's opinion would not be admitted.

Under the Rules, expert testimony lacking an adequate foundation historically has been excluded by Rule 703 (for reasons discussed previously), Rule 401, Rule 403, or some combination thereof.[83] Rule 403, which is discussed later in the section on Additional Limitations, permits the trial judge to balance the evidence's probative value against other concerns to determine the admissibility of the evidence. Obviously an expert's opinion that has no factual basis has little if any probative value and thus can properly be excluded. "[E]ven if a witness is eminently qualified, even if there is merit to his views, and even if [Rules] 702, 703, 704, and 705 are most liberally interpreted, there must be and ought to be some reliable factual basis on which the opinions are premised."[84] Although expert testimony that lacks a foundation should properly be excluded by the trial court, it is also generally accepted that "the relative weakness or strength of the factual underpinning of the expert's opinion goes to weight and credibility, rather than admissibility."[85]

The decision of the U.S. Court of Appeals for the District of Columbia Circuit in *Richardson v. Richardson-Merrell, Inc.* illustrates how courts assess whether an expert's opinion has an adequate factual foundation.[86] In *Richardson* the plaintiffs alleged that the administration of the antinausea drug doxylamine/pyridoxine (Bendectin) during pregnancy caused their child's birth defects. After a trial resulting in a jury verdict in favor of the plaintiffs, the trial judge granted judgment notwithstanding the verdict in favor of the defendant. The trial court concluded that the plaintiffs' expert's opinion lacked "a genuine basis, 'in or out of the record,'" and "that his 'theoretical speculations' could not sustain the [plaintiffs'] burden of proving causation."[87]

The Court of Appeals in *Richardson* agreed that the plaintiffs' expert's opinions did not have an adequate foundation. The court stated, "Whether an expert's opinion has an adequate basis, and whether without it an evidentiary burden has been met, are matters of law for the court to decide."[88] The court proceeded to analyze the adequacy of the foundation of the plaintiffs' expert's opinion. The court noted that the expert had "predicated his opinion upon four different factors: (1) chemical structure activity analysis, (2) in vitro (test tube) studies, (3) in vivo (animal) teratology studies, and (4) epidemiological studies."[89] The court determined that the first three types of studies "cannot furnish a sufficient foundation for a conclusion that Bendectin caused the birth defects at issue in this case."[90] The court then noted that "the drug has been extensively studied and a wealth of published epidemiological data has been amassed, none of which has concluded that the drug is teratogenic."[91] The plaintiffs' expert was able to establish a statistically significant association between Bendectin and the injury at issue only by "recalculating" epidemiological data previously published in peer-reviewed scientific journals.[92] Several other courts have reached conclusions similar to *Richardson*.[93]

The requirement that an expert's opinion be based upon an adequate factual foundation and be derived using reliable methods and principles were expressly integrated into Rule 702 as part of the 2000 Amendments.[94]

Medical causation. Since *Daubert*, in cases involving medical causation issues courts seem to have changed the heading under which they perform their analyses; rather than considering whether an expert opinion has an adequate factual foundation under Rule 703, courts now appear to be considering whether the opinion is (1) "based upon sufficient facts or data", (2) "the product of reliable principles and methods," and (3) based on the application of "the principles and methods reliably to the facts of the case" under Rule 702.[95] Substantively, however, the analyses appear essentially identical with the critical focus being reliability of the expert's testimony.

In *Porter v. Whitehall Laboratories, Inc.*, for example, the Seventh Circuit considered a trial court's order granting summary judgment based on the need for the plaintiff to prove causation through expert testimony and the inadmissibility of the expert testimony proffered.[96] The case revolved around whether ibuprofen use could cause rapidly progressive glomerulonephritis (RPGN). One expert offered only a "curbside opinion" as opposed to "an analytical, scientific opinion." A second expert could not offer his opinion to a reasonable degree of medical certainty. The third expert "admitted that if his personal hypothesis turned out to be correct, it would be the first case in history in which ibuprofen caused RPGN." A fourth expert admitted that his proffered opinion was outside his area of expertise.[97] The trial court, in holding that the testimony of the proffered experts was inadmissible, had "posited that the expert must be able to compare the data at hand with a known scientific conclusion or relationship."[98] In affirming the ruling the Seventh Circuit stated: "If experts cannot tie their assessment of data to known scientific conclusions, based on research or studies, then there is no comparison for the jury to evaluate and the experts' testimony is not helpful to the jury."[99]

Similarly, in *Chikovsky v. Ortho Pharmaceutical Corp.* the Court considered the admissibility of an expert's opinion that the drug tretinoin (Retin-A) is a teratogen.[100] The court noted that the expert was not aware of any published study or treatise that found that tretinoin caused birth defects.[101] Although the expert testified that the dose is relevant in determining whether a substance can act as a teratogen, he knew of no studies that provided a basis for concluding that the plaintiff could have received a sufficient dose of tretinoin to cause such effects.[102] Finally, although the expert contended that vitamin A (a chemically related compound) could cause fetal harm when administered to pregnant women in some doses, he did not know at what level vitamin A became unsafe and he had "performed no comparisons between the dose of vitamin A in the study and that found in Retin-A."[103] The court concluded "as a matter of law that [the expert's] opinions are not based on scientifically valid principles and, therefore, do not meet the reliability requirements of Rule 702 as interpreted by the Supreme Court in *Daubert*."[104]

The analysis of the adequacy of a scientific expert's factual foundation appears to reach the same conclusion regardless of whether the analysis is conducted under the rubric of Rule 702 or Rule 703.[105] Whether an expert witness's opinion has an adequate factual foundation is an issue that arises most often in the context of medical causation opinions. The issue also can arise, however, in other contexts, such as standard of care opinions.

In *Davis v. Virginian Railway Co.*, for example, the U.S. Supreme Court reversed a judgment in favor of the plaintiff arising from a medical malpractice claim.[106] The court held that "[n]o foundation was laid as to the recognized medical standard for the treatment [at issue]." The court held that the opinion of the plaintiff's expert that "he did not 'think that [the treatment] is proper'" did not provide an adequate foundation for a jury to determine the applicable standard of care.[107]

In *Stokes v. Children's Hospital, Inc.* the court granted judgment as a matter of law in favor of the defendant because the plaintiff's expert "was required to lay the foundation as to 'the recognized medical standard'" but failed to do so.[108,109] The court noted that "[i]n a case in which expert testimony is required, it is insufficient for the expert to state his opinion as to what he or she would have done under similar circumstances. . . . Rather, the jury must be informed of 'recognized standards requiring the proper . . . procedures under the circumstances.'"[110]

The role of "general acceptance" of scientific evidence. For the past several decades, many federal and state courts have held that before medical or scientific expert testimony can be admitted into evidence, the principles from which the expert's opinions were derived must have attained general acceptance within the relevant scientific community. This standard was first articulated in *Frye v. United States*, an appellate decision from the District of Columbia Circuit, and has been referred to as the *Frye test*.[111] The Frye test has been applied to testimonial evidence and all forms of scientific evidence.

In *Frye* the court considered and rejected the admissibility of results of a systolic blood pressure deception test (a precursor of the polygraph). The court stated:

Just when a scientific principle or discovery crosses the line between the experimental and demonstrable stages is difficult to define. Somewhere in this twilight zone the evidential force of the principle must be recognized, and while courts will go a long way in admitting expert testimony deduced from a well-recognized scientific principle or discovery, the thing from which the deduction is made must be sufficiently established to have gained general acceptance in the particular field in which it belongs.[112]

The *Frye* court recognized that jurors can be unduly influenced by evidence that purports to be "scientific." Such evidence by its very nature carries with it an aura of accuracy and reliability. The Frye test was intended to protect jurors from placing excessive stock in scientific evidence until the principles from which the evidence was derived have gained general acceptance in the appropriate scientific community. "The requirement of general acceptance in the scientific community assures that those most qualified to assess the general validity of a scientific method will have the determinative voice."[113]

The Frye test, however, has encountered many difficulties in application.[114] Whether the evidence sought to be admitted has gained general acceptance in the appropriate field can depend on whether the "field" is defined broadly or narrowly. Also, courts have never adequately defined what constitutes "general acceptance." Although courts have recognized that *Frye* "does not require unanimity of view," no clear standard has emerged for measuring "general acceptance" among the relevant scientific community.[115]

The Rules, which were enacted more than half a century after the *Frye* decision, do not mention the Frye test or any need for scientific evidence to be generally accepted as a precondition to admissibility. Federal Courts of Appeal were sharply divided for years on the issue of whether the Frye test survived the enactment of the Rules. Some courts reasoned that no common law of evidence survived the enactment of the Rules and that the drafters of the Rules intended to abolish *Frye*. Other courts reasoned that the Rules were not intended to be an exhaustive codification of the law of evidence. These courts reasoned that the drafters would not have overruled such a well-accepted, long-standing standard without so much as a comment in the Advisory Committee Notes or a statement in the legislative history.

The U.S. Supreme Court finally resolved the question in *Daubert*.[116] The court held that the Frye test was superseded by the adoption of the Rules. The court made it clear, however, that the Frye "general acceptance" test was one of many factors bearing on the reliability of an expert's methodology. The court stated that "'general acceptance' can yet have a bearing" on the question of whether evidence is sufficiently reliable to justify its admission.[117] The court stated:

A "reliability assessment does not require, although it does permit, explicit identification of a relevant scientific community and an express determination of a particular degree of acceptance within that community." Widespread acceptance can be an important factor in ruling particular evidence admissible, and "a known technique which has been able to attract only minimal support within the community," may properly be viewed with skepticism.[118]

The Frye test continues to be important for another reason. State courts, which are not governed by the Rules, may still employ the Frye test. The Supreme Court of Florida, for example, in a post-*Daubert* decision asserted the continuing vitality of *Frye* as the standard for the admissibility of scientific evidence in Florida.[119]

Additional limitations

Three other limitations on the admissibility of expert testimony warrant brief mention. First, expert witnesses are not permitted to offer legal conclusions. Second, expert witnesses cannot express opinions about the credibility of other witnesses. Third, expert testimony, like all evidence, can be excluded if its probative value is substantially outweighed by other specific considerations.

At common law, expert witnesses were prohibited from giving opinions that embraced an ultimate issue; the rationale was that permitting experts to opine on an ultimate issue would invade the province of the jury. Rule 704 modified the common law rule, stating: "[t]estimony in the form of an opinion or inference otherwise admissible is not objectionable because it embraces an ultimate issue to be decided by the trier of fact." Thus under Rule 704 an expert is permitted to offer an opinion on an ultimate issue of fact.[120]

Rule 704 did not, however, open the door to experts opining on legal conclusions. As the U.S. Court of Appeals for the Fifth Circuit explained in *Owen v. Kerr-McGee Corp*:

Rule 704, however, does not open the door to all opinions. The Advisory Committee notes make it clear that questions which would merely allow the witness to tell the jury what result to reach are not permitted. Nor is the rule intended to allow a witness to give legal conclusions. [A]llowing an expert to give his opinion on the legal conclusions to be drawn from the evidence both invades the court's province and is irrelevant.[121]

Despite the seemingly simplistic distinction between permissible expert testimony on ultimate issues of fact and prohibited expert testimony on conclusions of law, courts have had great difficulty distinguishing between the two in practice. Moreover, courts have not been consistent in applying any set of standards to differentiate opinions of ultimate fact from legal conclusions.

The second limitation is that experts cannot express opinions about the credibility of other witnesses.[122] Evaluating the credibility of witnesses is exclusively the function of the jury. Several courts have excluded expert opinions that effectively tell the jury which witnesses to believe; such opinions are deemed both unhelpful and irrelevant.

In *State v. McCoy*, for example, the Supreme Court of Appeals of West Virginia reversed a defendant's rape conviction based in part on the testimony of a psychiatrist who stated that the alleged rape victim was "still traumatized by this experience."[123,124] The court stated that the psychiatrist's "testimony amounted to a statement that she believed the alleged victim and by virtue of her expert status she was in a position to help the jury determine the credibility of the most important witness in a rape prosecution."[125] The court determined that the psychiatrist's testimony encroached "too far upon the exclusive province of the jury to weigh the credibility of the witnesses and determine the truthfulness of their testimony."[126] The court concluded that "admission of her testimony was reversible error."[127]

Courts have held, however, that expert testimony is not inadmissible simply because it may have the indirect effect of bolstering another witness's credibility.[128] "Much expert testimony tends to show that another witness either is or is not telling the truth. That fact by itself does not render the testimony inadmissible."[129]

The third limitation is that, in addition to satisfying the standards on the admissibility of expert testimony imposed by Rules 702 through 705 of the Rules, expert testimony must not violate any of the other rules governing the admissibility of evidence at trial. A frequent obstacle to the admissibility of expert testimony is Rule 403, which provides: "Although relevant, evidence may be excluded if its probative value is substantially outweighed by the danger of unfair prejudice, confusion of the issues, or misleading the jury, or by considerations of undue delay, waste of time, or needless presentation of cumulative evidence."[130]

As the U.S. Supreme Court has noted: "Expert evidence can be both powerful and quite misleading because of the difficulty in evaluating it. Because of this risk, the judge in weighing possible prejudice against probative force under Rule 403 of the present rules exercises more control over experts than over lay witnesses."[131]

Thus even if an expert witness is qualified, the testimony would be helpful, and the basis is proper, the trial court has the discretion to exclude the witness's testimony if it would cause unfair prejudice, confuse the issues, mislead the jury, or waste time.

Preliminary questions of admissibility

An important practical issue with respect to the testimony of medical experts is how a litigant procedurally challenges the admissibility of expert testimony. Courts' practices vary greatly. Some courts require in limine motions concerning such matters to be filed well in advance of trial. Other courts permit challenges to an expert witness's qualifications to be raised for the first time when the witness takes the stand.

Some courts have held that before excluding expert testimony based on Rule 702, 703, or 403 the trial court must hold an in limine hearing to establish a sufficient factual record to support its decision. For example, in *In re Paoli R.R. Yard PCB Litigation* the U.S. Court of Appeals for the Third Circuit reversed a district court's original order granting summary judgment in favor of the defendants because the trial court's rulings excluding evidence pursuant to Rules 702 and 703 were not supported by a sufficiently detailed factual record.[132,133] The Third Circuit also "reversed the district court's Rule 403 determinations, holding that Rule 403 exclusions should not be granted pretrial absent a record which is 'a virtual surrogate for a trial record.'"[134]

On remand in *Paoli*, after a period of discovery, defendants again moved in limine to exclude the opinions of plaintiffs' experts and for summary judgment. The district court, pursuant to Rule 104(a) of the Rules, held 5 days of in limine hearings.[135] At the hearing, three of the plaintiffs' experts testified and 10 physicians and scientists testified for the defense as to the reliability of plaintiffs' experts' opinions.[136] The district court "filed extensive opinions (totalling 330 pages) setting forth not only findings of fact but also its reasons for again excluding the vast bulk of plaintiffs' expert evidence."[137] In affirming in part and reversing in part the district court's rulings, the Third Circuit implicitly approved the manner in which the district court conducted the Rule 104 hearing.[138]

Similarly in *Hall v. Baxter Healthcare Corp*. the court held a hearing pursuant to Rule 104(a) that "spanned 4 intense days" at which "experts on both sides were questioned by counsel, the court, and the [court's] technical advisors."[139,140] (The court appointed as "technical advisors" experts in the fields of "epidemiology, rheumatology, immunology/toxicology, and polymer chemistry.") The issue in *Hall* involved the admissibility of the plaintiffs' experts' opinions that atypical connective tissue disease had been caused by the plaintiff's silicone gel breast implants. In addition to holding an evidentiary hearing, the parties provided the court with videotaped summations and proposed questions to guide the court's technical advisors in evaluating the experts' testimony.[141] The court's technical advisors then submitted reports, and both sides were provided with an opportunity to question them.

In *Kumho Tire*, the U.S. Supreme Court stated that the "abuse of discretion" standard of review applied both to the "trial court's decisions about how to determine reliability" and to "its ultimate conclusion."[142] The Supreme Court noted that "[o]therwise, the trial judge would lack the discretionary authority needed both to avoid unnecessary 'reliability' proceedings in ordinary cases where the reliability of an expert's methods is properly taken for granted and to require appropriate proceedings in the less usual or more complex cases where cause for questioning the expert's reliability arises."[143]

These decisions provide some guidance to trial courts grappling with the appropriate scope of a hearing to decide pretrial motions in limine in a complex case.

SPECIAL CONSIDERATIONS

Use of medical and scientific literature as evidence

All state and federal courts in the United States allow medical literature to be used for some purposes at trial. The traditional rule was that learned treatises and articles could be used during cross-examination to impeach or contradict the testimony of a testifying expert; such materials could not, however, be admitted as substantive evidence because of the prohibition against hearsay.

"Virtually all courts have, to some extent, permitted the use of learned materials in the cross-examination of an expert witness."[144] Courts vary greatly, however, on what threshold requirement must be met before such materials can be used for impeachment. Courts generally permit a treatise or article to be used for impeachment if the witness relied specifically on that treatise or article in forming his or her opinions.[145] Other courts permit a treatise or article to be used for impeachment in the absence of the witness's reliance if the witness acknowledges that the source is a recognized authority in the field. Still other courts permit such material to be used for impeachment even if the witness being impeached does not acknowledge the source as a recognized authority, if the authoritativeness of the source can be established through the testimony of other witnesses or by judicial notice.[146]

The admissibility of medical and scientific literature as substantive evidence has been the focus of heated debate. Opponents of admissibility argue that (1) the field of medicine changes so rapidly that treatises quickly become dated, (2) the trier of fact may be unable to understand complex technical passages that may be presented out of context, (3) the author is not available for cross-examination, and (4) medical literature is unnecessary as substantive evidence when live expert witnesses are available.[147]

On the other hand, proponents of the substantive admissibility of medical literature argue that (1) treatises generally are more up to date than live experts; (2) attorneys will be able to protect against confusion, the selective presentation of material, or passages being presented out of context; (3) cross-examination is not necessary when a live expert is available to explain the treatise or article; (4) the scrutiny of the peer review process lends a high degree of reliability to opinions or conclusions published in peer-reviewed scientific literature; and (5) the author of a treatise or medical article has no interest in the outcome of the particular case at issue.[148]

The proponents of admissibility succeeded in recent years in having the absolute prohibition against the substantive admissibility of medical literature replaced with a more liberal standard in the Rules in about half of the states. Rule 803(18) of the Rules is representative of the prevailing standard.

Although Rule 803(18) creates an exception to the hearsay rule for medical literature, it addresses the concerns of the opponents of admissibility and contains provisions to alleviate some of these concerns. For example, Rule 803(18) requires that the statements in the medical literature sought to be admitted either be "relied upon by the expert witness in direct examination" or "called to the attention of an expert witness upon cross-examination." This requirement ensures that an expert witness is available to explain the passage introduced into evidence, thereby diminishing the concern about the author's unavailability for cross-examination. Rule 803(18) also requires that the proponent of the evidence demonstrate that the source is "established as a reliable authority" through either the testimony of the witness on the stand, another expert witness, or judicial notice. Finally, Rule 803(18) provides that "the statements may be read into evidence but may not be received as exhibits."[149] This provision helps to ensure that the jury does not give undue weight to medical literature vis-à-vis the testimony of live expert witnesses. This requirement also ensures that the jury will not rely on any portion of the treatise or article other than the passages admitted by the court.

The "reasonable degree of medical certainty" standard

Some courts require that an expert hold opinions on causation and prognosis with "a degree of confidence in his conclusions sufficient to satisfy accepted standards of reliability."[150] "A doctor's testimony can only be considered evidence when he states that the conclusion he gives is based on reasonable medical certainty that a fact is true or untrue."[151]

Courts are in general agreement that expert testimony stating that a conclusion is "possible" does not meet the standard for admissibility with respect to the party who bears the burden of proof.[152] "A doctor's testimony that a certain thing is possible is no evidence at all. His opinion as to what is possible is no more valid than the jury's own speculation as to what is or is not possible."[153]

Courts differ, however, as to how much certainty is enough to constitute "a reasonable degree of medical certainty." Some courts have held that the standard requires only that the conclusion is more probably true than not; this formulation renders the phrase synonymous with "more probable than not." Such courts often permit experts to testify in terms of a "reasonable probability."[154] Other courts reject that standard. In *McMahon v. Young*, the court stated:

> Here, the only evidence offered was that [plaintiff's condition] was "probably" caused [by defendant's conduct], and that is not enough. Physicians must understand that it is the intent of our law that if the plaintiff's medical expert cannot form an opinion with sufficient certainty so as to make a medical judgment, there is nothing on the record with which a jury can make a decision with sufficient certainty so as to make a legal judgment.[155,156]

Regardless of which standard they apply, courts generally look to the substance of an expert's testimony rather than the form in determining whether the witness has testified with the requisite degree of certainty. In *Matoff v. Ward* the Court of Appeals of New York stated:

> Granted that "a reasonable degree of medical certainty" is one expression of . . . a standard [of a witness's degree of confidence in his or her conclusions] and is therefore commonly employed by sophisticates for that purpose, it is not, however, the only way in which a level of certainty that meets the rule may be stated. [T]he requirement is not to be satisfied by a single verbal straightjacket alone, but, rather, by any formulation from which it can be said that the witness' "whole opinion" reflects an acceptable degree of certainty. To be sure, this does not mean that the door is open to guess or surmise.[157,158]

Discovery of the expert witness's opinions

The Rules' elimination of many of the common law restrictions regarding the admissibility of expert testimony was premised on the belief that the adversarial system is capable of exposing the deficiencies in an expert's opinions. The drafters of the Rules recognized, however, that advance knowledge of the expert's opinions and the bases of the opinions is "essential for effective cross-examination."[159]

In civil cases, Rule 26 of the Rules "provides for substantial discovery in this area, obviating in large measure the obstacles which have been raised in some instances to discovery of findings, underlying data, and even the identity of the experts."[160] The majority of states also provide for ample discovery of the opinions of testifying experts. However, a few states, such as New York and Oregon, severely restrict pretrial discovery of the identities and opinions of testifying experts.

Under the Federal Rules of Civil Procedure, discovery of expert testimony is governed by Rule 26(a)(2) and Rule 26(b)(4). Rule 26(a)(2)(A) requires a party to disclose to other parties "the identity of any person who may be used at trial to present evidence under Rules 702, 703, or 705 of the Federal Rules of Evidence."[161] Rule 26(a)(2)(B) then requires a more extensive disclosure than that required under the old Rules:

> [T]his disclosure shall, with respect to a witness who is retained or specially employed to provide expert testimony in the case or whose duties as an employee of the party regularly involve giving expert testimony, be accompanied by a written report prepared and signed by the witness. The report shall contain a complete statement of all opinions to be expressed and the basis and reasons therefor; the data or other information considered by the witness in forming the opinions; any exhibits to be used as a summary of or support for the opinions; the qualifications of the witness, including a list of all publications authored by the witness within the preceding 10 years; the compensation to be paid for the study and testimony; and a listing of any other cases in which the witness has testified as an expert at trial or by deposition within the preceding 4 years.[162]

Thus the Rules place an affirmative disclosure obligation on the party who intends to call the expert as a witness at trial; it is no longer incumbent on other parties to obtain such information through interrogatories.

In *Sylla-Sawdon v. Uniroyal Goodrich Tire Co.*, for example, the Eighth Circuit affirmed the district court's decision to limit an expert's testimony where, instead of submitting a report that complied with the court's scheduling order (which was quite similar to the Federal Rules of Civil Procedures), the expert submitted an affidavit that lacked the specificity mandated by the court's scheduling order and a curriculum vitae (CV).[163] The district court had limited the expert's testimony to matters set forth in his affidavit and his CV.[164] The court held that "[t]he failure to comply with the Scheduling Order is not excused because [the opposing party] elected to depose [the expert]."[165]

Rule 26(b)(4)(A) expressly authorizes a party to depose "any person who has been identified as an expert whose opinions may be presented at trial," thereby harmonizing the rule with what has been the customary practice.[166] The Rules also provide that "the court shall require that the party seeking discovery pay the expert a reasonable fee for time spent in responding to discovery."[167]

The Rules also contain a provision governing discovery of nontestifying retained experts. Rule 26(b)(4)(B) provides that "opinions held by an expert who has been retained or specially employed by another party in anticipation of litigation or preparation for trial and who is not expected to be called as a witness at trial" can be discovered only "upon a showing of exceptional circumstances under which it is impracticable for the party seeking discovery to obtain facts or opinions on the same subject by other means."[168]

In criminal cases, Rule 16 of the Federal Rules of Criminal Procedure contains the major provisions governing the discovery of an expert witness's opinions. Rule 16(a)(1)(E) provides:

At the defendant's request, the government shall disclose to the defendant a written summary of testimony the government intends to use under Rules 702, 703, or 705 of the Federal Rules of Evidence during its case-in-chief at trial. . . . The summary provided under this subdivision shall describe the witnesses' opinions, the bases and the reasons for those opinions, and the witnesses' qualifications.[169]

Rule 16(b)(1)(C) requires the defendant to make a similar disclosure at the government's request "[i]f the defendant requests disclosure under subdivision (a)(1)(E) of this rule and the government complies."[170] These subdivisions of Rule 16 were added as part of the 1993 amendments; they represent a major expansion of federal criminal discovery. The Advisory Committee explained that "[t]he amendment is intended to minimize surprise that often results from unexpected expert testimony, reduce the need for continuances, and to provide the opponent with a fair opportunity to test the merit of the expert's testimony through focused cross-examination."[171]

Rule 16 also contains provisions governing discovery of reports of examinations and tests. Rule 16(a)(1)(D) provides:

Upon request of a defendant the government shall permit the defendant to inspect and copy or photograph any results or reports of physical or mental examinations, and of scientific tests or experiments, or copies thereof, which are within the possession, custody, or control of the government, the existence of which is known, or by the exercise of due diligence may become known, to the attorney for the government, and which are material to the preparation of the defense or are intended for use by the government as evidence in chief at the trial.[172]

Rule 16(b)(1)(B) imposes a similar, although somewhat different, disclosure requirement on the defendant "[i]f the defendant requests disclosure under subdivision (a)(1)(C) or (D) of this rule, upon compliance with such request by the government." The defendant's disclosure requirement includes only "results or reports of physical or mental examinations and of scientific tests or experiments made in connection with the particular case."[173] The defendant is required to produce only materials "which the defendant intends to introduce as evidence in chief at the trial or

which were prepared by a witness whom the defendant intends to call at the trial when the results or reports relate to that witness' testimony."[174]

Rule 12.2 imposes a notification requirement on a criminal defendant if the defendant "intends to rely upon the defense of insanity at the time of the alleged offense," or "[i]f a defendant intends to introduce expert testimony relating to a mental disease or defect or any other mental condition of the defendant bearing upon the issue of guilt."[175,176]

Ethical considerations

Two ethical considerations relating to the use of expert witnesses warrant mention. First, paying a contingent fee to an expert witness is not permitted in most jurisdictions. The American Bar Association (ABA) Model Code of Professional Responsibility includes a disciplinary rule that states: "[A] lawyer shall not pay, offer to pay, or acquiesce in the payment of compensation to a witness contingent upon the content of his testimony or the outcome of the case."[177] The ABA Model Rules of Professional Conduct do not expressly prohibit the payment of a contingent fee to an expert witness, but Model Rule 3.4 prohibits offering "an inducement to a witness that is prohibited by law."[178] The Comment to Rule 3.4 also notes that "the common law rule in most jurisdictions is that . . . it is improper to pay an expert witness a contingent fee."[179]

The second ethical consideration relates to ex parte contacts with expert witnesses in civil proceedings. ABA Formal Opinion 93-378, which was issued in November 1993, concluded:

[A]lthough the Model Rules do not specifically prohibit a lawyer in a civil matter from making ex parte contact with the opposing party's expert witness, such contacts would probably constitute a violation of Rule 3.4(c) if the matter is pending in federal court or in a jurisdiction that has adopted an expert-discovery rule patterned after Federal Rule 26(b)(4)(A). Conversely, if the matter is not pending in such a jurisdiction, there would be no violation.[180]

The Committee noted that neither the Model Rules nor the Model Code contains "an automatic bar to lawyers initiating contact with the opposing parties' experts."[181] The Committee characterized Rule 26(b)(4)(A) of the Federal Rules of Civil Procedure and similar state provisions as the "exclusive procedures for obtaining the opinions, and the bases therefore, of the experts who may testify for the opposing party."[182] Because Rule 26(b)(4) and similar state rules make no provision for informal discovery of expert witnesses' opinions, the Committee concluded that "in those jurisdictions a lawyer who engages in such ex parte contacts would violate Rule 3.4(c)'s prohibition against knowingly disobey[ing] an obligation under the rules of a tribunal."[183]

CONCLUSION

The next decade promises to be a dynamic period with respect to the law governing medical testimony and expert witnesses. The U.S. Supreme Court's decisions in *Daubert* and *Kumho Tire* provide general guidance regarding the proper role of the trial court in ensuring the reliability of expert testimony. The full impact of those landmark decisions and their practical effect on the practice of litigation involving medical experts, however, remain to be determined.

ENDNOTES

1. *Daubert v. Merrell Dow Pharms.*, 509 U.S. 579, 592 (1993).
2. *Nat Harrison Assoc's., Inc. v. Byrd*, 256 So. 2d 50, 53 (Fla. Dist. Ct. App. 1971).
3. *Id.*
4. 2 J. Wigmore, *Evidence* §686, at 962 (Chadbourn rev. 1979) (footnote omitted).
5. The American Bar Association Section of Litigation published an excellent treatise entitled *Expert Witnesses*, which was written in part and edited by Professor Faust F. Rossi. The treatise includes three parts—a careful review of the relevant law of evidence, a section that provides general guidance for the litigator on the practical aspects of working with experts, and a section that provides practical guidance on specific types of experts.
6. *Salem v. United States*, 370 U.S. 31, 35 (1962). In *General Electric Co. v. Joiner*, 522 U.S. 136, 118 S.Ct. 512, 515 (1997) the United States Supreme Court clarified that "abuse of discretion" is the appropriate standard that an appellate court should apply in reviewing a trial court's decision to admit or exclude expert testimony under *Daubert*.
7. *Hagler v. Gilliland*, 292 So. 2d 647, 648 (Ala. 1974).
8. *Id.*
9. *Dyas v. United States*, 376 A. 2d 827, 832 (D.C.) (quotation omitted), *cert. denied*, 434 U.S. 973 (1977).
10. Fed. R. Evid. 702.
11. *Supra* note 1, at 579, 600.
12. *Breidor v. Sears, Roebuck & Co.*, 722 F. 2d 1134, 1139 (3d Cir. 1983).
13. *Supra* note 1, at 589-590.
14. *Id.* (quotation and citations omitted).
15. *See id.* at 594-595.
16. *Id.* at 594-595.
17. *Id.*
18. *Id.*
19. *Id.*
20. *Id.*
21. *Kumho Tire Co. v. Carmichael*, 526 U.S. 137, 119 S.Ct. 1167, 1175-1176 (1999).
22. *Id.* at 1175.
23. *Id.* at 1176.
24. *Supra* note 12.
25. *Ellis v. Miller Oil Purchasing Co.*, 738 F. 2d 269, 270 (8th Cir. 1984).
26. *Id.* at 270.
27. *Id.*
28. *Linkstrom v. Golden T. Farms*, 883 F. 2d 269, 270 (3d Cir. 1989) (quoting *In re Japanese Elec. Prods.*, 723 F. 2d 238, 279 (3d Cir. 1983), *rev'd on other grounds*, 475 U.S. 574 (1986).
29. *Carroll v. Otis Elevator Co.*, 896 F. 2d 210, 212 (7th Cir. 1990).
30. *Id.* at 212.
31. *Supra* note 1 (quoting 3 J. Weinstein & M. Berger, *Weinstein's Evidence* ¶702[02], at 702-18[1988]).
32. *See American Tech. Resources v. United States*, 893 F. 2d 651, 656 (3d Cir.), *cert. denied*, 495 U.S. 933 (1990).
33. *Federal Crop Ins. Corp. v. Hester*, 765 F. 2d 723, 728 (8th Cir. 1985).
34. *Supra*, note 29.
35. *Shea v. Phillips*, 98 S.E. 2d 552 (Ga. 1957).
36. *Rodriguez v. Jackson*, 574 P. 2d 481, 485 (Ariz. Ct. App. 1977) (emphasis in original and citation omitted); *but see Harris v. Robert C. Groth, M.D., Inc.*, 663 P. 2d 113 (Wash. 1983).
37. *See McNeill v. United States*, 519 F.Supp. 283, 287 (D.S.C. 1981).
38. In *Falcon v. Cheung*, 848 P. 2d 1050, 1054 (Mont. 1993), for example. The court disqualified an expert who had never practiced medicine in Montana, had never practiced at a rural hospital in another state, and therefore was unfamiliar with the standard of practice in rural Montana.
39. *Frost v. Mayo Clinic*, 304 F.Supp. 285, 288 (D. Minn. 1969).
40. *Baerman v. Reisinger*, 363 F. 2d 309, 310 (D.C. Cir. 1966).
41. *Swanson v. Chatterton*, 160 N.W. 2d 662 (Minn. 1968); *Hartke v. McKelway*, 526 F. Supp. 97, 101 (D.D.C. 1981), *aff'd*, 707 F. 2d 1544 (D.C. Cir.), *cert. denied*, 464 U.S. 983 (1983).
42. *Fitzmaurice v. Flynn*, 356 A. 2d 887, 892 (Conn. 1975).
43. *Supra* note 41 *Hartke*.
44. *Id.* at 101.
45. *Id.*
46. *Northern Trust Co. v. Upjohn Co.*, 572 N.E. 2d 1030, 1041 (Ill. App. Ct.), *appeal denied*, 580 N.E. 2d 119 (1991), *cert. denied*, 502 U.S. 1095 (1992).
47. *Id.* (citation omitted).
48. *Id.*
49. *Smith v. Pearre*, 625 A. 2d 349, 359 (Md. Ct. App.), *cert. denied*, 632 A. 2d 151 (Md. 1993).
50. *Id.*
51. *Id.*
52. *Hedgecorth v. United States*, 618 F.Supp. 627, 631 (E.D. Mo. 1985).
53. *Id.*
54. *Owens v. Concrete Pipe and Prods. Co.*, 125 F.R.D. 113, 115 (E.D. Pa. 1989).
55. *Id.*
56. *Id.*
57. *See Backes v. Valspar Corp.*, 783 F. 2d 77, 79 (7th Cir. 1986); *Roberts v. United States*, 316 F. 2d 489, 492-493 (3d Cir. 1963).
58. *Gideon v. Johns-Manville Sales Corp.*, 761 F. 2d 1129, 1136 (5th Cir. 1985).
59. *Id.*
60. *Id.*
61. *Jackson v. Waller*, 10 A. 2d 763, 769 (Conn. 1940).
62. *Jenkins v. United States*, 307 F. 2d 637, 643-644 (D.C. Cir. 1962).
63. *Id.* at 643, 645.
64. *Id.* at 644.
65. *Id.* at 646.
66. *Mannino v. International Mfg. Co.*, 650 F. 2d 846, 850 (6th Cir. 1981).
67. *Zenith Radio Corp. v. Matsushita Elec. Indus. Co.*, 505 F.Supp. 1313, 1333 (E.D. Pa. 1980), *aff'd in part and rev'd in part*, 723 F. 2d 238 (3d Cir. 1983), *rev'd on other grounds*, 475 U.S. 574 (1986).
68. *Flanagan v. Lake*, 666 A. 2d 333 (Pa. Super. Ct. 1995).
69. *Id.* at 335.
70. *Perkins v. Volkswagen of Am., Inc.*, 596 F. 2d 681, 682 (5th Cir. 1979).
71. *Rimer v. Rockwell Int'l. Corp.*, 641 F. 2d 450, 456 (6th Cir. 1981) (permitting a pilot to testify about experiences as a pilot, experiences of other pilots, and a forced landing that he made as a result of a fuel siphoning problem in a plane similar to that at issue in the case, but excluding pilot's opinion that the plane's fuel system had been defectively designed).
72. Fed. R. Evid. 703.
73. Notes of Advisory Committee on 1972 Proposed Rules, Fed. R. Evid. 703.
74. *Supra*, note 72.
75. *Soden v. Freightliner Corp.*, 714 F. 2d 498, 505 (5th Cir. 1983).

76. *In re "Agent Orange" Prod. Liab. Litig.*, 611 F.Supp. 1223, 1244 (E.D.N.Y. 1985), *aff'd*, 818 F. 2d 187 (2d Cir. 1987), *cert. denied*, 487 U.S. 1234 (1988).

77. *Id.* at 1243-1244 (citations omitted).

78. *Id.* at 1247.

79. *Id.* at 1246.

80. The U.S. Court of Appeals for the Third Circuit, for example, adopted the liberal approach to Rule 703 in *DeLuca v. Merrell Dow Pharmaceuticals, Inc.*, 911 F. 2d 941, 952 (3d Cir. 1990). In that case the court determined that an expert who had relied on his own reanalysis of published epidemiological data was basing his opinions on the same epidemiological data that the defendant's expert used in formulating her opinions. *Id.* at 953. The court held that Rule 703 did not require the plaintiff's expert to accept the conclusions of the authors of the studies upon whose data he relied. The court concluded that there was no basis for excluding the plaintiff's expert's opinion under Rule 703. In *In re Paoli R.R. Yard PCB Litigation*, 35 F. 3d 717, 747-749 (3d Cir. 1994), *cert. denied*, 115 S.Ct. 1253 (1995), however, the Third Circuit overruled *DeLuca* and its liberal approach to Rule 703. The court stated, "Judge Weinstein's view is extremely persuasive, and we are free to express our agreement with it because we think that our former view is no longer tenable in light of *Daubert.*" *Id.* at 748. Although the Supreme Court's holding in *Daubert* was based on Rule 702 and not Rule 703, the Third Circuit nonetheless held that "[i]t makes sense that the standards are the same, because there will often be times when both Rule 702 and Rule 703 apply." *Id.* Thus after *Paoli*, U.S. Courts of Appeals are in agreement that "it is the judge who makes the determination of reasonable reliance." *Id.*

81. *Supra* note 76.

82. *Id.*

83. *Lynch v. Merrell-National Lab.*, 830 F. 2d 1190, 1196-97 (1st Cir. 1987).

84. *Johnston v. United States*, 597 F.Supp. 374, 401 (D. Kan. 1984) (quoted in *In re Agent Orange*, 611 F.Supp. at 1250).

85. *Taenzler v. Burlington N.*, 608 F. 2d 796, 798 n.3 (8th Cir. 1979).

86. *Richardson v. Richardson-Merrell, Inc.*, 857 F. 2d 823 (D.C. Cir. 1988), *cert. denied*, 493 U.S. 882 (1989).

87. *Id.* at 829.

88. *Id.*

89. *Id.*

90. *Id.* at 830.

91. *Id.* at 832.

92. *Id.* at 831.

93. *See Brock v. Merrell Dow Pharms., Inc.*, 874 F. 2d 307, 313 (5th Cir. 1989), *modified on reh'g*, 884 F. 2d 166 (5th Cir. 1989), *cert. denied*, 494 U.S. 1046 (1990); *supra* note 83.

94. Fed. R. Evid. 702.

95. *Id.*

96. *Porter v. Whitehall Labs., Inc.*, 9 F. 3d 607 (7th Cir. 1993).

97. *Id.* at 614-615.

98. *Id.* at 614.

99. *Id.*

100. *Chikovsky v. Ortho Pharm. Corp.*, 832 F.Supp. 341 (S.D. Fla. 1993).

101. *Id.* at 345.

102. *Id.*

103. *Id.* at 346.

104. *Id.*

105. *See Glaser v. Thompson Med. Co.*, 32 F. 3d 969, 975 (6th Cir. 1994) (reversing lower court's decision to exclude expert testimony based on studies that had undergone peer review, were published in reputable medical journals, and had "clearly explained, solid scientific methodologies"); *Sorensen v. Shaklee Corp.*, 31 F. 3d 638, 649 (8th Cir. 1994) (affirming lower court decision excluding expert opinion where "the experts . . . reasoned from an end result in order to

106. hypothesize what needed to be known but what was not"; no reliable evidence that alfalfa tablets contained ethylene oxide or that ethylene oxide causes mental retardation); *see also Wheat v. Pfizer, Inc.*, 31 F. 3d 340, 343 (5th Cir. 1994) (in affirming summary judgment, court stated that proffered testimony was a hypothesis that lacked an empirical foundation and had not been subjected to peer review and publication and was therefore inadmissible).

106. *Davis v. Virginian Ry., Co.*, 361 U.S. 354, 357-358 (1960).

107. *Id.*

108. *Stokes v. Children's Hosp., Inc.*, 805 F.Supp. 79, 82-83 (D.D.C. 1992), *aff'd without op.*, 36 F. 3d 127 (D.C. Cir. 1994).

109. *Id.* at 82 (quoting *supra* note 106).

110. *Id.* (omissions in original) (quoting *Levy v. Schnabel Found. Co.*, 584 A. 2d 1251, 1255 [D.C. 1991] [citation omitted]).

111. *Frye v. United States*, 293 F. 1013 (D.C. Cir. 1923).

112. *Id.* at 1014.

113. *United States v. Addison*, 498 F. 2d 741, 743-744 (D.C. Cir. 1974).

114. *See* Gianelli, *The Admissibility of Novel Scientific Evidence: Frye v. United States, a Half Century Later*, 80 Colum. L. Rev. 1197, 1208 (1980).

115. *Massachusetts v. Lykus*, 327 N.E. 2d 671, 678 (Mass. 1975).

116. *Supra* note 1.

117. *Id.* at 594.

118. *Id.* (citations omitted).

119. *Flanagan v. Florida*, 625 So. 2d 827 (Fla. 1993). *See Fielder v. Magnolia Beverage Co.*, 757 So. 2d 925, 937 (Miss. 1999) (continued vitality of *Frye* test in Mississippi); *California v. Leahy*, 882 P. 2d 321 (Cal. 1994) (reaffirming use of general acceptance test of admissibility of scientific evidence in California); *Nebraska v. Carter*, 524 N.W. 2d 763 (Neb. 1994) (affirming continuing vitality of "general acceptance test" of admissibility in Nebraska); *Arizona v. Bible*, 858 P. 2d 1152, 1183 (Ariz. 1993) (continuing to apply general acceptance test in Arizona "notwithstanding legitimate criticism of *Frye*"), *cert. denied*, 114 S.Ct. 1578 (1994); *Washington v. Cissne*, 865 P. 2d 564, 569 (Wash. Ct. App. 1994) (acknowledging that Washington courts continue to employ *Frye* when determining admissibility of evidence based on novel scientific procedures), *review denied*, 877 P. 2d 1288 (Wash. 1994).

120. Rule 704(b) includes a specific limitation that is applicable only to cases in which an expert witness is testifying with respect to "the mental state or condition of a defendant in a criminal case." This rule precludes an expert witness from stating "an opinion or inference as to whether the defendant did or did not have the mental state or condition constituting an element of the crime charged or of a defense thereto." Fed. R. Evid. 704(b).

121. *Owen v. Kerr-McGee Corp.*, 698 F. 2d 236, 240 (5th Cir. 1983).

122. *Henson v. Indiana*, 535 N.E. 2d 1189, 1192 (Ind. 1989).

123. *West Virginia v. McCoy*, 366 S.E. 2d 731 (W. Va. 1988).

124. *Id.* at 737.

125. *Id.*

126. *Id.* (quoting *Kansas v. McQuillen*, 689 P. 2d 822 [Kan. 1984] [C.J. Schroeder, dissenting]).

127. *Id.*

128. *Minnesota v. Meyers*, 359 N.W. 2d 604 (Minn. 1984).

129. *Id.* at 609.

130. Fed. R. Evid. 403.

131. *Supra* note 1, at 579, 595 (quoting Weinstein, *Rule 702 of the Federal Rules of Evidence is Sound: It Should Not be Amended*, 138 F.R.D. 631, 632 [1991]).

132. *In re Paoli R.R. Yard PCB Litig.* ("Paoli I"), 916 F. 2d 829 (3d Cir.), *cert. denied*, 499 U.S. 961 (1991).

133. *Id.* at 855-859.

134. *In re Paoli R.R. Yard PCB Litig.*, 35 F. 3d 717, 735 (3d Cir. 1994) (quoting Paoli I, 916 F. 2d at 859-860).

135. *Id.* at 736.

136. *Id.*

137. *Id.* at 732.

138. *Id.* at 738-741.

139. *Hall v. Baxter Healthcare Corp.*, 947 F.Supp. 1387 (D. Or. 1996).

140. *Id.*

141. *Id.*

142. *Supra* note 21 at 1167, 1176.

143. *Id.*

144. McCormick, *Evidence* §321, at 900 (3d ed. 1984).

145. *Id.*

146. *Id.*

147. *See* 6 J. Wigmore, *Evidence* §1690 (1979); J. King, *The Law of Medical Malpractice in a Nutshell* 100-103 (1977); F. Rossi, *Expert Witnesses* 135-136 (1991).

148. *Id.*

149. Fed. R. Evid. 803(18).

150. *Matott v. Ward*, 399 N.E. 2d 532, 534 (N.Y. 1979).

151. *Palace Bar, Inc. v. Fearnot*, 381 N.E. 2d 858, 864 (Ind. 1978).

152. *See Cohen v. Albert Einstein Med. Ctr.*, 592 A. 2d 720 724 (Pa. Super. Ct. 1991), *appeal denied*, 602 A. 2d 855 (Pa. 1992).

153. *Supra* note 151.

154. *See Parker v. Employees Mut. Liab. Ins. Co.*, 440 S.W. 2d 43, 46 (Tex. 1969).

155. *McMahon v. Young*, 276 A. 2d 534, 535 (Pa. 1971).

156. *Id.* (citation omitted).

157. *Supra* note 150.

158. *Id.* (citation omitted).

159. Notes of Advisory Committee on 1972 Proposed Rules, Fed. R. Evid. 705.

160. *Id.*

161. Fed. R. Civ. P. 26(a)(2)(A).

162. Fed. R. Civ. P. 26(a)(2)(B).

163. *Sylla-Sawdon v. Uniroyal Goodrich Tire Co.*, 47 F. 3d 277 (8th Cir. 1995), *cert. denied*, 116 S.Ct. 84 (1995).

164. *Id.* at 284.

165. *Id.*

166. Fed. R. Civ. P. 26(b) (4) (A).

167. Fed. R. Civ. P. 26(b)(4)(C).

168. Fed. R. Civ. P. 26(b)(4)(B).

169. Fed. R. Crim. P. 16(b)(1)(C).

170. Fed. R. Crim. P. 16(b)(1)(E).

171. Notes of Advisory Committee on 1993 Amendment, Fed. R. Crim. P. 16.

172. Fed. R. Crim. P. 16(a)(1)(D).

173. Fed. R. Crim. P. 16(b)(1)(B).

174. *Id.*

175. Fed. R. Crim. P. 12.2(a).

176. Fed. R. Crim. P. 12.2(b).

177. ABA Model Code DR 7-109(C).

178. ABA Model Rule 3.4(b).

179. Comment 3 to ABA Model Rule 3.4.

180. ABA Formal Opinion 93-378 (Nov. 8, 1993).

181. *Id.*

182. *Id.*

183. *Id.* (brackets in original).

35

Liability of Health Care Entities for Negligent Care

SAL FISCINA, M.D., J.D., F.C.L.M.

Corporate liability for negligent care and treatment on the part of health care providers was historically limited so that the corporation was responsible only for its employees, acting within the scope of their duties; for the hazardous conditions of its physical plant; and for the equipment it provided. The hospital was considered a facility where physicians, usually contracted privately by patients before their arrival, could practice medicine restricted only by the state regulatory boards. It was the physician rather than the hospital who was licensed to practice medicine. Under these circumstances the physician was considered an independent contractor from whom the patient could seek compensation in case of injury caused by professional negligence.

When the health care provider was a direct employee of the hospital, however, the hospital also could be held liable for injuries to the patient under the doctrine of respondeat superior. In this regard the hospital was treated similarly to other corporate entities whose employees offered services to the public. Where the employee acted within the scope of his or her duties, the employer was held responsible for the outcome. In earlier times some hospitals were run as charitable institutions (eleemosynary), and as such either they were held immune from liability or their damages as a result of liability were greatly reduced on the theory that the charitable contributions were not intended to be used by the donors as compensation for fault. Later, as health care institutions became insured and began accepting other sources of income, the rationale for these exemptions or restrictions dissolved. Other institutions, such as government-run hospitals, escaped liability under the sovereign immunity doctrine. No lawsuit could be brought against the state unless the state gave its permission. With growing recognition of the unfairness of the exemption, local, state, and federal legislation allowed claims to be brought for the negligent acts of its employees, albeit with numerous and varied restrictions, conditions, and caps on selected damages.

In the modern era the law is no longer simply concerned with the corporate responsibility of hospitals. It also must deal with the rapidly emerging variants, mutations, and affiliations of corporate health care, including managed care organizations (MCOs), permutations of all of these types based on their internal organizations, and the increasingly popular professional associations (PAs) or professional corporations (PCs), under which one or more physicians can own and be employed by a self-owned third party.

Hospitals traditionally enjoyed exemption from liability because they have evolved from charitable institutions into sophisticated corporations operating primarily on a fee-for-service basis, while assuming the role of a comprehensive health center with responsibility for arranging and coordinating the total health care of its patients. This has established duties to its patients, including the duty to use reasonable care in:

- The maintenance of safe and adequate facilities and equipment.
- The selection and retention of competent physicians.

- The oversight of clinical performance of health practitioners within its walls.
- The formulation, adoption, and enforcement of adequate rules and policies to ensure quality care for the patients.

Statements and citations mentioning "the hospital" as the corporate entity usually apply to the newer forms of health care organizations and even if they are not perfectly applicable, should at least be considered as a potential bellwether of developments.

Hence the responsibility of the health care institution for proper selection, retention, and supervision of professionals on its staff has assumed more corporate hazards. No longer can the hospital simply delegate to a volunteer staff committee the responsibility to examine a staff applicant's credentials and prior performance before granting clinical privileges. Nor can the physician on staff be allowed to practice without reasonable and prudent continuous supervision or review of performance. Under the modern doctrine of corporate negligence a health care organization may share responsibility with the negligent physician for the consequences of his or her acts or omissions.

LEGAL BASIS FOR THE HOSPITAL'S DUTY TO PATIENTS

The scope of a hospital's independent duty of care to its patients has expanded, and now imposes on the hospital the responsibility for monitoring and supervising the quality of, medical care of its independent medical staff. The negligence of its health care personnel may be imputed to the hospital under doctrines such as respondeat superior and ostensible agency, making the hospital jointly liable with the negligent staffer.

The corporate liability doctrine requires a hospital to properly credential and monitor its staff physicians for clinical privileges as part of the implied contract between the patient and the hospital.[1] The hospital may even have a duty to intervene to prevent a negligent staff physician from endangering hospitalized patients.

Traditionally a hospital's liability for negligent acts of members of its medical staff depended on the legal relationship between the hospital and the physician. At one end of the legal continuum was the salaried physician who was a hospital employee. Under the doctrine of respondeat superior the hospital would be jointly liable for the physician's negligence.[2,3] At the other end of the continuum was the independent staff physician who admitted patients under his or her care to the hospital. In the past the hospital was seldom liable for an independent staff physician's negligence, even if the negligent actions occurred within the hospital.[4,5]

Whether a physician is considered an "employee" may depend less on the written contract between the institution and the physician than on actions and appearances. Thus, if the hospital provides supplies, equipment, uniforms, meals,

parking spaces, billing services, and ancillary personnel, a physician who claims to be an independent contractor may be held to be a de facto employee, particularly if the physician does not maintain an office elsewhere. The conditions set by the Internal Revenue Service may have significance here and should be considered.[6] If a patient seeks treatment directly from the hospital rather than from the physician who negligently caused the injury, or if the hospital does not allow the patient to choose a physician to provide a therapeutic service, that physician may be viewed as an employee and the doctrine of respondeat superior may apply, even if the treating physician is considered an independent contractor for other purposes. If a hospital represents to the patient that a physician is a hospital employee but the doctor actually is an independent contractor, a court may still hold the hospital vicariously liable for the physician's acts under a theory of liability referred to as *ostensible* or *apparent* agency. A plaintiff relying on an ostensible agency theory need show only that he or she looked to the hospital for treatment and that the assigned attending physician negligently injured the patient in the provision of the treatment sought.

To hold a hospital liable on a corporate liability theory, a plaintiff must show that the hospital knew or should have known that the physician whose negligence caused the plaintiff's injury was providing substandard care.

Previously a hospital's liability for the negligence of a hospital-based physician, such as an anesthesiologist or pathologist, was referred to the contractual arrangements between the physician and the hospital in determining whether the physician was more like an "employee" or an "independent contractor," ordinarily a question of fact for the jury to decide.[7-9] Under the ostensible agency doctrine the contract issue is moot. The theory of apparent agency is applicable where a hospital holds out a physician as its agent or employee, and a patient accepts treatment from that physician in the reasonable belief that it is being rendered on behalf of the hospital.[10-12]

Case law

Pederson v. Dumouchel recognized the need for a hospital to adhere to its own rules and regulations designed to control and regulate a staff physician's conduct.[13] In this case an injured child was examined by a physician who diagnosed a fractured mandible. A dentist was called in to perform oral surgery, and the physician left the hospital. The operation was performed without a physician in the operating room. The child sustained intraoperative cerebral anoxia and permanent brain damage. The hospital was liable because it had not enforced its own rules, which required that no surgery be performed without a physician present.

The case most often cited as extending and expanding hospital responsibility to include a direct duty to patients, however, is *Darling v. Charleston Memorial Hospital.*[14]

In this case a general practitioner who had not treated a leg fracture in several years cast a patient's fractured tibia. As a result of negligence, the leg had to be amputated. The hospital was liable for failing to require the physician to obtain a consultation. *Darling* came to engender the seminal concept that a patient is entitled to expect that the hospital will reasonably monitor and oversee the treatment provided by physicians practicing within its structure.

Fiorentino v. Wenger held that a hospital may be liable if it allows a physician to provide services to its patients when those in charge of granting clinical privileges know, or should know through reasonable inquiry, that the physician is likely to commit malpractice.[15] This knowledge may consist of notice that the physician's staff privileges were rescinded at another hospital because the physician had conducted improper and radical surgery.

Mduba v. Benedictine Hospital held that a nonsalaried physician, despite his contract to the hospital to operate the emergency room, was an employee of the hospital.[16] The rationale was that the physician's fees were based on rates guaranteed by the hospital and that the physician was subject to the rules and regulations of the hospital's governing board.

Corleto v. Shore Memorial Hospital noted that the hospital was ultimately responsible for the care of its patients, and therefore it had a duty to act when it had reason to know that malpractice would probably occur. Therefore, a hospital could be liable for permitting a known incompetent physician to perform an operation and failing to prevent him from treating a patient after his incompetence became obvious to the hospital.[17]

Corporate liability

Under the corporate negligence theory a hospital may be liable for negligently failing to establish adequate procedures to ensure the safety of patients, where the hospital knew or should have known that the physician who caused injury to the patient was not qualified to practice in the hospital but nevertheless granted or renewed the physician's hospital privileges. Earlier, some courts limited the hospital's duty to supervise staff physicians to situations involving only employee physicians or to situations of gross negligence by the hospital. Apparently these courts were concerned that the imposition of a broad duty of hospitals to supervise care would impair independent physicians' discretion in purely medical decisions. Other jurisdictions have imposed a duty on hospitals to use reasonable care in the selection of staff physicians if detectable information exists about a physician's incompetence or lack of qualifications. Such notice can be inferred from records related to denying or restricting privileges at other hospitals or the existence of prior malpractice claims against the physician. If there is no notice of a physician's incompetence and no

apparent reason to rescind or deny privileges, a hospital may escape liability. A physician's membership on the medical staff does not by itself create corporate liability for the hospital or health care organization.

NONDELEGABLE DUTY

Under the theory of corporate negligence the hospital may be held responsible for the acts and omissions of its apparent (ostensible) agents under certain circumstances, even when they were thought to be nonemployees or independent contractors. This theory recognizes that the hospital has a nondelegable duty to provide reasonable and safe health care to its patients and that direct liability can arise for negligent care. In addition, liability for employees may arise out of the doctrine of vicarious liability, in which a person may be held responsible for the actions of others whom he or she has the right to control.

Jackson v. Power is a landmark decision that enunciated that a hospital had a nondelegable duty for the acts of a nonemployee, independent contractor emergency department physician.[18] In this case, a man who fell from a cliff was airlifted to a hospital where he was examined by an independent contractor physician. Severe internal injuries allegedly went untreated as a result of the physician's negligence. The court discussed whether a patient transported to the hospital without their specific request for a designated physician established that such a physician was an ostensible agent of the hospital, or whether such a patient should have known the treating physician was not an employee of the hospital. Although the court said that this determination was a question for the jury, the court held that a general acute care hospital has a *nondelegable* duty to provide nonnegligent physician care in its emergency department. As an acute care facility the state mandated the hospital to provide a physician in the emergency department at all times. The hospital had received Joint Commission on Accreditation of Hospitals (JCAH) accreditation, which imposed standards for operation of the emergency department. The hospital bylaws had rules and regulations governing emergency department performance. In these statutes, standards, and rules, the court found that the hospital had to provide physician care in its emergency department. Seeking guidance in determining the questions of whether that duty could be delegated, the court turned to a case involving the principles governing safety of passengers on common carriers in which it was held that the principal carrier would not be allowed to avoid liability by engaging in separate subcontracts to provide food, perform maintenance, or even supply crews.[19] Seeing similarities in the responsibility of hospitals in supplying various services to patients, the court held that the duty to provide physicians and nonnegligent care for patients in its emergency department was nondelegable. Such a duty does not extend, however, to situations in which a patient is negligently treated in the emergency department by a physician of the patient's own choice.

Insinga v. LaBella held that a hospital has a duty to select and retain competent physicians who, even though they are independent practitioners, would be providing hospital care in the exercise of their clinical staff privileges. The hospital's responsibility for the physician's acts, however, does not extend to acts outside the hospital.[20] This concept probably is not applicable where hospitals enter into direct associations with the physician or purchase the staff physician's private practice and continue to refer patients to him or her. Under those limited circumstances there may be an inducement of the patient to visit the physician's "private" office because of the referral or the endorsement of the care by the hospital.

STANDARDS TO MEASURE HOSPITAL CONDUCT

Many courts have distinguished the facts involved in determining a hospital's standard of care from those of *Darling*, thereby blunting the impact of that case on the hospital's requisite standard of care. Some courts have refused to extend *Darling*'s holding that a hospital is liable for malpractice by an independently retained physician, unless it had reason to anticipate that the act of malpractice would take place. *Lundahl v. Rockford Memorial Hospital* distinguished the facts of *Darling* on the grounds that the physician in *Lundahl* had been an employee of the hospital and assigned to the emergency department.[21] In this case, a boy was examined by a physician employed by the hospital, and then referred to a staff orthopedist who was not a hospital employee. After the orthopedist replaced a moleskin traction strip with a floating splint, a blood clot formed, eventually requiring an amputation. The plaintiff claimed that the hospital had a duty to review the *medical* care being given to him by the orthopedist. The court ruled that the decision to treat a patient in a particular manner was a medical question to be made solely by the treating physician, not by the hospital.

Other courts have held that the only way a hospital could be liable for negligent clinical performance by a member of its staff would be if the plaintiff proved that the hospital had been negligent in its original selection of an unskilled physician.[22] *Pogue v. Hospital Authority of DeKalb County*, however, involved a partnership under contract to staff an emergency department.[23] Although the contract required that the services performed would be "subject to surveillance by the medical staff of the hospital," and be in keeping with "good medical practice," the contract also specifically provided that the partners were "independent contractors." The hospital was not liable for negligence of a member of the partnership because it had no right to direct specific medical techniques employed by emergency physicians. It was not liable when the physician's negligence related to a matter of professional judgment as long as the hospital did not have the right to control the physician's diagnosis and treatment of the patient.

Even though *Vanaman v. Milford Memorial Hospital* had facts similar to *Darling*, a court came to an opposite conclusion.[24] A mother brought her child to the emergency department with a fractured leg. Her own physician could not be located, therefore she asked to see the on-call physician, who set the leg, applied the cast, and provided follow-up treatment in his office. The on-call physician, not the hospital, billed for his services. When permanent disability of the leg resulted, the parents sued both the physician and the hospital. In finding that the hospital was not liable, the court said that the medical staff was an organized body with qualifications and privileges approved by the governing board of the hospital for patient care. The court held that the hospital had functioned only as a referral service and had not practiced medicine itself. This viewpoint has become outdated.

Most courts, however, have recognized and reaffirmed the concept of liability enunciated in *Darling*. In *Ohligschlager v. Proctor Community Hospital* a patient experienced severe pain and swelling in her arm near an intravenous infusion insertion site.[25] The patient informed a nurse's aide of the pain, but the aide did nothing. Skin necrosis, requiring skin grafting, resulted from infiltration of the intravenous medication, which the physician had ordered in an incorrect concentration. The patient charged that the hospital's negligence was the proximate cause of her injuries. The court said that there was sufficient evidence to require submission to the jury of the issues of whether the hospital had failed to heed the patient's complaints and whether it failed to properly supervise the injection ordered by the physician. Citing *Darling*, the court said that the hospital was under the duty to "conform to the legal standard of reasonable conduct in the light of the apparent risk."

Ensuring medical staff competence

Tucson Medical Center v. Misevch restated the duty of the hospital, acting through appropriate committees, to ensure the competence of members of its medical staff.[26] The hospital was responsible to a patient if failure to properly supervise an incompetent physician results in the patient being injured. In this case the plaintiff contended that a physician staff member was negligent in administering anesthesia during surgery, and as a result the patient had cardiac arrest and died. The key contention against the hospital was that the anesthesiologist was under the influence of alcohol during the operation and that the hospital was negligent in retaining him on its medical staff. The court pointed out that a hospital owes a duty to its patients to ensure the competence of its medical staff by supervision of the physicians on its staff. The court stated that a hospital and its governing body may be held liable for injuries resulting from negligent supervision of members of its medical staff. The court reasoned that a hospital assumed certain responsibilities for the care of its patients and thus was required to meet the standards of responsibility commensurate with that trust.

A hospital would be negligent if its medical staff were negligently supervised by its members or failed to recommend action by the hospital's governing body before a patient's injury. When a hospital's negligence is predicated on an omission to act, the hospital will not be held responsible unless it had reason to know that it should have acted to fulfill its duty to the patient. Therefore, knowledge (actual or constructive) is an essential factor in determining whether the hospital exercised reasonable care under the circumstances. The court quoted JCAH, which stated that "the medical staff is responsible to the governing body of the hospital for the quality of hospital patient care. It therefore evaluates the qualifications of applicants and members to hold staff privileges and recommends curtailment and exclusion when necessary."

A hospital may be liable for not becoming aware of medical staff members' incompetence if the hospital, through due diligence, could have acquired such knowledge and acted so as to prevent the plaintiff's injury but failed to do so. *Gonzales v. Nork* held that a hospital had a duty to its patients to protect them from the malpractice of an independently retained member of its staff if the hospital knew, had reason to know, or should have known that the surgeon's negligent acts were likely to occur.[27] In this case a private physician member of the medical staff admitted to performing unnecessary and negligent spinal surgery on a 27-year-old hospital patient who had suffered from back pain after being injured in an automobile accident. Three years after this operation the hospital administrator heard a rumor that the surgeon's malpractice insurance had been canceled. Because the hospital required staff physicians to have such insurance, it investigated and found that the rumor was true. The hospital promptly placed the surgeon in a monitoring program under which he was forbidden to operate without another qualified surgeon present. During the trial, the surgeon admitted to performing at least 26 other unnecessary operations over 9 years. The court indicated that the hospital's liability was based on its duty to protect its patients from malpractice by members of its medical staff. Although the hospital had no knowledge of the surgeon's propensity to commit malpractice, it was negligent because it had failed to investigate an earlier malpractice case in which the surgeon had been sued. The court concluded that mere compliance with the prevailing JCAH standards did not discharge the hospital from its duty to its patients because those standards furnished no effective means of detecting a fraudulent physician. The court also concluded that the hospital's peer review of the quality of patient care was random, casual, subjective, and uncritical and therefore at the time of the patient's surgery the hospital had no actual knowledge of the surgeon's fraud and incompetence. The court held that the hospital governing board was corporately responsible for the conduct of its medical staff because it had a duty to protect its patients from malpractice by members of its medical staff.

Hospital standard of care

The standard of care that the hospital must meet to discharge this duty was detailed and illustrated in *Johnson v. Misericordia Community Hospital*, a case involving the credentialing of a physician member of the medical staff.[28] In this case a patient contended that the hospital was negligent in appointing the surgeon to the medical staff and in granting him surgical privileges. Testimony established the surgeon's negligence and that the surgeon misrepresented the truth on his application and authorized the hospital to verify all information given. The hospital's administrative records were devoid of any procedures used in the appointment of the surgeon to the medical staff organization. The court concluded that these procedures would have uncovered that at two hospitals the surgeon's privileges were revoked; at another hospital he was denied privileges; he was neither board certified nor board eligible; and that 10 malpractice suits had been filed against him. The court held that the hospital had a duty to exercise reasonable care to grant clinical privileges only to competent physicians and surgeons. It concluded that had the hospital exercised ordinary care in the staff selection process, it would not have appointed the surgeon to its medical staff, and thus the patient would not have been negligently injured. In enunciating that a hospital owes a duty of care of its patients to refrain from any act that will cause foreseeable harm or an unreasonable risk of danger, the court interwove the concept of institutional responsibility with foreseeability.

Granting privileges

Although a hospital is not the ensurer of competence of its medical staff, it will be charged with evaluating the knowledge that would have been acquired had it exercised ordinary care in investigating its medical staff applicants.

In addition to judicial recognition of the direct duty of a hospital to exercise reasonable care in selecting and retaining staff physicians, some courts have enunciated a duty to *supervise* the health care provided by physician staff members. The hospital's duty to promulgate regulations to oversee the clinical performance of physicians was enunciated in *Bost v. Riley*, which adopted the concept of corporate negligence for failure to supervise medical treatment.[29] The plaintiff contended that inadequate physician progress notes were evidence of negligent care that resulted in the patient's death. The court held that hospitals have a duty to make a reasonable effort to monitor and oversee the treatment prescribed and administered by physicians practicing in the hospital. Therefore, the hospital may have breached its duty to the patient by failing to enforce its own internal rule requiring the keeping of accurate progress notes.

Supervision of performance

Other legal decisions have refused to extend or expand a hospital's duty to supervise medical treatment. In *Cox v. Haworth* the patient was hospitalized so that his privately retained physician could perform a myelogram.[30] During the course of treatment, the patient sustained permanent injury to the spinal cord. The patient alleged that the hospital was negligent in not obtaining informed consent before the medical procedure was performed. No negligence by the hospital personnel during performance of the myelogram was alleged. The court refused to interpret the doctrine of corporate liability as imposing a duty on a hospital to inform and advise the patient of the nature of medical procedures that are to be privately performed.

The limitations placed on the expansion of the doctrine of corporate liability probably represent judicial recognition that hospitals are not well equipped to supervise patient care actively and concurrently. The personal nature of the physician-patient relationship requires that the physician exercise necessary discretion in the diagnosis and treatment of the patient's condition. Moreover, it would be impractical for the hospital to *personally* supervise the quality of medical care rendered by each medical staff member.

Oversight of quality

Overseeing the quality of physician performance is a different matter. A hospital's *review* of medical staff clinical performance is not a concurrent duty but one involving a retrospective process performed through delegated medical staff committees (such as quality assurance, risk management, and credentials). To project future performance, the committees use a historical data base describing the physician's training, experience, and prior performance. Some courts have conditioned a hospital's duty to ensure the competence of its staff on the hospital's knowledge (actual or constructive) and awareness of a physician's incompetent acts. This approach adopts the agency law principle that a corporation is bound by the knowledge acquired by, or by the notice given to, its agents or officers, who are within the scope of its authority in reference to matters to which its authority extends.

Fridena v. Evans held that a negligent physician was an officer of the hospital who held a medical administrative position as chief of the medical staff.[31] This relationship became the linchpin for imputing knowledge of the physician's incompetence to the hospital. Holding that the hospital had "actual" notice of the physician's incompetence, the court concluded that the hospital had been negligent in failing to supervise the physician's performance.

Elam v. College Park Hospital provides insight into the law's reluctance to create the unusually difficult task of supervising physicians as a responsibility of hospital staffs.[32] The court indicated that the hospital had a duty of "continuing evaluation" of the staff physicians' clinical performance, apparently a less onerous and more achievable modification of the requirement that a hospital supervise the *actual* medical care. Such a requirement did not necessarily require concurrent supervision and on-line intervention.

Pickle v. Curns expresses additional modifications of the hospital's duty to supervise physicians.[33] The court rejected the contention that a hospital has a duty to ensure that physicians practicing on its premises never commit negligent acts. Instead, the court formulated the hospital's duty as one to prevent injuries resulting from negligence of its staff physicians when it knew, or should have known, that the physician would perform a negligent act.

The trend evinced by these cases is to impose a duty on the hospital to supervise clinical performance only when the hospital has been put on notice by past negligent acts. Thus, it does not impose on hospitals a duty to concurrently supervise the administration of medical care but rather to monitor a physician's provision of medical services through patient care assessment committees.

Policy and procedures

In addition to responsibilities to patients regarding medical staff conduct, hospitals must have developed adequate policies to protect the welfare of patients receiving care in their institutions and must establish an organizational structure to carry out those policies.

Polischeck v. United States illustrated a violation of this duty. A hospital was held liable for failing to have a patient with a severe headache examined or her chart reviewed by a physician prior to discharge from an emergency department.[34] The hospital permitted emergency department patients to be admitted and discharged by physician assistants, who under state law were not considered qualified to make such determinations.

Ravenis v. Detroit General Hospital imposed direct liability on the hospital for failing to have appropriate standards of care related to handling tissues to be transplanted from donor cadavers.[35] Several patients were injured as a result of contaminated cornea transplants because the hospital had no policy that required the performance of necessary tests on the donor or the donor tissue.

In Andrews v. Burke, the plaintiff contended that an incomplete physician's note of a failed resuscitation effort made the hospital corporately negligent per se because it violated hospital regulations adopted by governing boards regarding hospital record-keeping rules.[36] The state regulatory code required the adoption of minimum standards and regulations to govern the operation of hospitals, and the state administration code directed hospitals to establish governing bodies to govern such regulations. The court rejected the contention that a physician staff member's violation of hospital regulations amounted to negligence per se. The plaintiff argued that the physician failed to comply with the hospital record-keeping rules. The court noted that privately adopted standards are generally admissible to establish the standard of care when relevant and reliable, but they do not have the force of law. The court rejected the contention that the hospital had been corporately negligent because the plaintiff did not assert that the defendant physician was incompetent, or identify any negligent act that the hospital should have prevented in properly exercising its corporate responsibility. Therefore, the physician's failure to comply with hospital record-keeping rules did not establish that the hospital's failure to enforce this rule contributed to the patient's death.

MEDICAL STAFF SELECTION, MONITORING, AND SUPERVISION

Courts have recognized the hospital's duty to select, monitor, and supervise independent contractor members of the medical staff. Although a hospital's overall monitoring system is closely examined when a hospital is named in a suit, the hospital is not considered to be guarantor of the adequacy of medical care rendered in its facility. Isolated negligent acts of an otherwise competent independent contractor physician generally are not evidence of negligence on the part of the hospital.

Selection

The hospital is responsible for obtaining reasonably available information on prospective staff members regarding their credentials and any prior negligent conduct. In *Joiner v. Mitchell County Hospital Authority* a patient complaining of chest pain was examined at the hospital by an independent contractor member of the medical staff.[37] The physician advised the patient that the condition was not serious and sent the patient home. Shortly after he returned home, the patient's condition worsened and he died. The patient's estate sued the hospital directly for its negligence in permitting an allegedly known incompetent physician to continue to serve on its medical staff. The court rejected the hospital's contention that it was relieved of liability by delegating its authority to screen medical staff applicants to the members of the existing staff, reasoning that the medical staff simply acted as an agent for the hospital in screening applicants. The court held that because the hospital knew or because, based on information in the hospital's possession, it was apparent that the physician was incompetent, the hospital did not act with reasonable care in permitting the physician to remain a member of the staff.

A hospital also may incur liability if it has implemented a data system for evaluating the qualifications of its staff members but has failed to use this system to restrict the clinical privileges of a physician who has demonstrated incompetence. *Purcell v. Zimbelman* ruled that the hospital had "notice" of the surgeon's incompetence, based on evidence that prior similar operations performed by the surgeon had resulted in lawsuits against him and other hospitals.[38] Significantly the court concluded that the failure of the hospital surgical department, which had reviewed the surgeon's various mishaps in the operating room, to take any corrective action against the surgeon did not relieve the hospital of its duty to protect the patient.

Monitoring

If a hospital has not implemented review procedures to properly credential and appraise staff physicians' clinical performance, plaintiffs must demonstrate that review procedures would have placed the hospital on notice. *Reynolds v. Mennonite Hospital* involved a negligence lawsuit against a hospital for damages caused by allegedly unnecessary surgery.[39] The plaintiff claimed that the hospital failed to comply with certification and review procedures. The court said, however, that such failure, even if the surgery was unnecessary, was insufficient to prove that the hospital was directly negligent. The hospital had no notice of any flaw in the qualifications or background of the surgeon or of any circumstances existing before the plaintiff's surgery that would have caused the hospital to limit or revoke the surgeon's privilege to operate. The court pointed out that a hospital is not an ensurer of a patient's safety; therefore because nothing in the record indicated that an evaluation of the surgeon's capabilities would have disclosed substandard practices, the hospital was not negligent.

Supervision

In *Braden v. St. Francis Hospital* the plaintiff alleged that an unnecessary amputation was performed by a staff surgeon, that the hospital had a duty to exercise proper supervision to prevent unnecessary and wrongful surgery, and that it breached this duty.[40] The court pointed out that statistics themselves do not indicate a proclivity on the part of the staff surgeon to perform unnecessary amputations because multiple surgeries do not necessarily support a reasonable inference that any one procedure, including the procedure in this case, was unnecessary or negligently performed. The plaintiff offered statistics showing that the staff surgeon had performed significantly more amputations than the average number of amputations performed by other surgeons on the hospital staff. The plaintiff also referred to the hospital's bylaws, which documented an elaborate administrative structure of supervision and monitoring to ensure quality care. The court held that a hospital does not generally expose itself to liability for negligence unless it knows or should know of a physician's propensity to commit negligent acts.

EXPANDING HOSPITAL LEGAL DUTIES

Kirk v. Michael Reese Hospital expanded a hospital's liability beyond its patients to individuals affected by the actions of patients.[41] In this case the hospital discharged a patient on medication that should not be combined with alcohol, especially if the patient intended to drive. The patient consumed alcohol and injured a pedestrian, who sued both the patient and the hospital. The court ruled that the hospital had an obligation to that pedestrian, an individual who had not been admitted or treated in the hospital.

Physician offices

In general, hospitals do not have a duty to ensure that its staff physicians render medical care competently outside the hospital setting. *Pedroza v. Bryant* held that a hospital is not liable for injuries resulting from malpractice committed in the private office of a nonemployee physician before the patient was admitted to the hospital.[42] The plaintiff charged that the hospital was negligent in not ensuring that its staff physician, the patient's private physician, was competent. Noting that the physician's negligent acts had occurred entirely outside the hospital, the court stated that for the plaintiff to prevail, the court would have to extend the hospital's corporate duty of care to patients treated by staff members in their private offices, where the hospital is not involved. The court declined to do so, pointing out that negligence committed by staff physicians outside the hospital is relevant *only* if the hospital has actual or constructive notice of it and negligently fails to take action. A hospital is not an inspector or ensurer of the private office practices of its staff members. Within the hospital, the hospital's delineation of staff privileges may reasonably affect staff members.

Notification requirement

The doctrine of corporate liability may encompass a duty for the hospital to inform a patient when it is aware of a deviation from the standard of care that has caused an injury. When a hospital knows that a deviation from the standard of care has caused an injury, the failure to inform the patient or the patient's survivors may constitute fraudulent concealment. *Kruegar v. St. Joseph's Hospital* held that whether fraudulent concealment was present was a question of fact for the jury to determine.[43] In this case the plaintiff was advised by her husband's physicians that he had died of heart failure during an operation. Three years later, it was anonymously disclosed to his spouse that intraoperative malfunction of respiratory equipment had contributed to the cause of death. The patient's estate sued, alleging that the hospital had a duty to inform her of this fact and was therefore precluded from asserting the statute of limitations as a defense. The court noted that fraud can exist even when no false statement is made. The suppression of a material fact, which a party is bound in good faith to disclose, is equivalent to a false representation.

Failure to warn of disease

A hospital must be sensitive to emerging areas of liability for failure to warn, particularly in areas involving the adverse side effects of radiation therapy and possibility of contact with communicable diseases. Case law principles governing a hospital's duty to warn in these instances are still developing. *Knier v. Albany Medical Center Hospital* dealt with the hospital's duty to warn the general public that one of its employees had come in contact with a patient who had scabies, a communicable disease.[44] A nurse's family sued the hospital for failing to warn them that the nurse had been exposed to a contagious disease. The court ruled that the hospital did not have an obligation to warn her family, friends, or the public at large that she had been exposed to scabies.

Far more dangerous than scabies is the threat of AIDS. The hospital's duty to warn patients that a surgeon was HIV-positive was explored when the hospital restricted the surgeon's privileges until he provided proof of informed consent from his patients. The duty of confidentiality to the surgeon as patient was pitted against the duty of the hospital to protect other patients from "risk of harm." Although the restriction and temporary suspension of surgical privileges may not violate state law against discrimination,[45] further developments are needed before a health care corporation may take such action without exposure to liability. AIDS, considered to be a handicap in many states, is protected by special laws of confidentiality in others, and is a reportable disease (although not with disclosure of the patient's name) everywhere. How these competing issues will play out remains to be seen.[46]

Thompson v. Nason Hospital imposed an additional responsibility on hospitals to control independent medical staff members.[47] This case involved emergency department treatment of a trauma patient by a private staff physician who was not a member of the department, nor "on call" to the department. When negligent treatment of intracerebral hemorrhage caused the patient permanent dysfunction, the patient sued both the physician and the hospital, claiming that the physician was an ostensible agent of the hospital, and therefore the hospital had a responsibility to ensure that care given in the emergency department was not negligent.

The court pointed out that a hospital has a corporate responsibility to a patient to supervise hospital care, even medical services rendered by physicians whose only relationship with the hospital is as a member of the medical staff. The court also pointed out that hospitals have changed as the structure of the health care system has changed. The practice of medicine is now being carried out by hospitals that have many full-time physician employees. Present-day hospitals now undertake to treat the patient through their physicians and nurses, rather than simply to procure them to act upon their own responsibility. Their manner of operation demonstrates that hospitals do far more than furnish facilities for treatment. People who avail themselves of hospital facilities expect that the *hospital* will attempt to cure them, not that employees will act on their own responsibility.

This case raises the question of whether hospitals can refuse to grant clinical privileges to physicians without due process on the grounds that hospitals must protect themselves from corporate liability. This development is likely to create tension with antitrust issues that would further expose a hospital to liability.

An important predicate, in determining whether a hospital was negligent, is the demonstration that the hospital knew of an ongoing aberration in the clinical care of its patients. A hospital fulfills this duty by recognizing the established responsibility of hospital employees (such as nurses and technicians) to notify the hospital of unusual orders, treatments, or decisions observed in the course of a patient's care. Failure to give such notice would be a liability burden just as the negligence itself is such a burden.

MANAGED CARE ORGANIZATIONS

An MCO is designed to facilitate the financial management of health care while delivering services to its enrolled members. The most common type is the HMO, which in turn may consist of groups of physicians under contract to an employer or an insurer, independent practice networks, staff model organizations with direct employment of physicians, and open-ended networks that allow enrollees to seek services from within and from outside the organization. Regardless of the variant, MCOs share a common goal to provide health care services at reduced costs through consumer competition.

Cost-containment measures may include direct incentive payments to physicians to decrease patient-initiated use of services, deselection of physician involvement where overuse can be demonstrated, fixed fees for identified procedures, and capitation payment. These cost-containment services may require the physician to restrict or deny some health care measures requested by the patient. Conflicts may arise when the patient feels harm has resulted from the restriction or denial of care, especially when the restrictions are contrary to the treating physician's own medical judgment.

The MCO may face liability for the improper selection and retention of the physicians or other professionals with whom it contracts to provide services to enrollees. This area of liability is similar to that of corporate liability for a hospital's negligence in providing hospital staff privileges. Because the MCO may function as the provider, the payor, and the quality reviewer, it may be exposed to liability for breaches in each of these areas.

Harrell v. Total Health Care, Inc. found that an HMO had failed in its duty to properly select the physician whose care allegedly injured an enrollee because the physician had a history of malpractice and incompetence.[48] The Missouri Supreme Court found the HMO free of liability on statutory grounds but did not reject the theory of corporate liability.

McClellan v. Health Maintenance Organization of Pennsylvania refused to apply the doctrine of nondelegable duty to an HMO that did not provide on-site health care services.[49] Nevertheless, the court apparently recognized the theory of corporate liability for negligent staff selection and retention of HMO physicians.

Because MCOs may be employers, the theory of respondeat superior is applicable to hold the HMO liable for the negligence of its employees and agents acting within the scope of their duties. Therefore, a staff model HMO was held liable for acts of its physicians in *Robbins v. HIP of New Jersey*.[50] The hallmark of such action is the HMO's right to control the physician's activities. Thus, in *Sloan v. Metropolitan Health Council, Inc.*, the HMO was liable because it exercised control over an allegedly negligent physician.[51] In *Schleier v. Kaiser Foundation Health Plan of Mid-Atlantic States*, the HMO was held liable for the acts of a physician who was a consultant rather than an employee because the HMO had "controlled" the physician through its medical director.[52]

Mitts v. HIP of Greater New York, however, found physicians to be independent contractors because the HMO did not directly treat patients; therefore negligence was not imputed.[53] A similar conclusion was reached in *Chase v. Independent Practice Association* in which an HMO contracted with an IPA and had no direct control over medical decisions. In this case the court refused to apply respondeat superior.[54]

Ostensible agency

Under the theory of apparent or ostensible agency, HMOs have been held liable for negligent acts of affiliated physicians who were not directly employed by the HMO. Judicial considerations include: whether the HMO "held out" the physician as an agent; whether the patient looked to the HMO rather than the designated physician for care; whether the physician was chosen from lists supplied by the HMO; and whether the HMO restricted the patient's choice of physician.[55] However, HMOs were not held liable where the HMO exercised no professional control over the physician, or where the state law prohibits the HMO from practicing medicine.[56,57] If an HMO physician specifically promised a given result and the patient relied on that promise, the HMO could be held liable for breach of contract when the result was not forthcoming from the treatment.[58]

Cost-containment measures

In *Wickline v. State of California* a patient was prematurely discharged from a hospital because of a utilization review decision to deny additional hospitalization, resulting in the amputation of her leg.[59] She sued the state Medicaid program for its interference with her physician's judgment to keep her hospitalized. Although holding that only the physician could be held responsible for the patient's premature discharge, the court allowed that the program could be held liable if a defect in the MCO's cost-containment measures caused harm. In *Wilson v. Blue Cross of So. California* the utilization review organization of a private insurer refused extension of a patient's hospitalization for depression.[60] The patient committed suicide after discharge. The court said the utilization review organization, the insurer, and the utilization review physician could be held liable. Unlike in *Wickline*, in *Wilson* there was no clear public policy expressed in the statute that required a cost-containment utilization review process. The private insurance provisions requiring cost-containment review and restriction of services were not the products of public policy.

ERISA

Claims of malpractice against an MCO by an enrollee may be preempted under the Employee Retirement Income Security Act of 1974 (ERISA),[61] where a qualified health plan is offered to an employee as part of a benefit package. The preempted malpractice claims usually are those resulting from defective design or implementation of cost-containment or claims-handling systems, or those resulting from vicarious or direct liability for negligence by a health care provider. At present there does not seem to be a sense of urgency by courts to preempt medical malpractice claims against MCO providers (*DeGenova v. Ansel*).[62] However, the issue may become more prominent with further federal involvement in health care and attempts to correct so-called malpractice crises.[63]

DIRECT LIABILITY OF MANAGED CARE ORGANIZATIONS

MCOs may be subject to direct liability for corporate negligence, such as in cases for negligent selection and retention of incompetent physicians who are held out to subscribers on its list of specialists.[64] The theory applied is similar to that of corporate liability of the hospital.[65]

As courts continue to view MCOs as "health care providers," particularly in delivery models where care is dispensed instead of merely financed, direct liability for negligent supervision and control of MCO physicians will probably increase. A coherent and consistent standard of care for MCOs may be difficult and as yet remains unclear.[66] The federal government's efforts to reform health care nationwide may attempt to set practice parameters that some courts may interpret as "standards."

Vicarious liability

Courts have found health plans vicariously liable for the actions of physicians they hold out as their own. *Lancaster v. Kaiser Foundation Health Plan* took the next step and found that institutional negligence should be applied to HMOs that do *not* hold out physicians as their own.[67] The Illinois Supreme Court has been influential in establishing direct corporate liability for hospital staff, and vicarious liability for independent contractor physicians and has extended liability for corporate negligence to MCOs.

In *Jones v. Chicago HMO Ltd. of Illinois*, an enrollee of an IPA model HMO was assigned a physician because public assistance enrollees were not allowed to choose their own physicians.[68] The physician negligently failed to diagnose bacterial meningitis in the enrollee's daughter. As a result, the daughter became permanently disabled. An ensuing lawsuit charged the HMO with institutional negligence for assigning a primary care physician who was serving an overloaded patient population, and for negligently adopting procedures that required enrollees to call first for an appointment before visiting the physician's office or obtaining emergency care.

Because the HMO was an IPA model that both assigned physicians to enrollees and supervised the care provided to them, the ERISA preemption was not mentioned by the court. The court stressed that institutional negligence was just an extension of traditional tort law where institutions take on responsibilities that include the possibility of injuring people through tortious conduct. This conclusion was driven by recognition that MCOs are heavily involved in patient care decisions that go beyond the provision of insurance services.

Proof of institutional negligence

The plaintiff did not need expert testimony on allegations of negligently assigning more enrollees to the PCP than he was capable of serving, and adopting procedures requiring the enrollee to call first for an appointment before visiting the PCP's office, because other evidence established the appropriate standard care and the defendant indicated that there should be a primary care physician for every 3500 patients, and in its contract with the state to provide services promised to have a PCP for every 2000 patients. Since the defendant's medical director testified that patient load could influence the standard of care, and since the defendant's own records and other testimony indicated that the PCP might be assigned to more than 4500 patients, the court found that this raised an issue for the jury and summary judgment was inappropriate.

CONTRACT AND WARRANTY THEORIES

Dissatisfied enrollees may seek relief in the courts via legal theories other than negligence, including breach of contract or warranty or misrepresentation by the MCO. *Williams v. Health America* and *Boyd v. Albert Einstein Medical Center* provide examples, albeit unsuccessful at the time, of these theories.[69,70] The more the MCO becomes a "provider" of health care for its enrollees, the more it can be expected that a court will find contractual or fiduciary relationships between it and the enrollee.

PROFESSIONAL SERVICE CORPORATIONS

Professional service corporations, variously known as a PC or PA, are products of state legislatures. Specific regulations, restrictions, limitations, and liabilities for these corporations and their shareholders, agents, and employees should therefore be researched in the applicable state statutes.

In most states, professionals, such as physicians and lawyers, may incorporate for the sole purpose of rendering specific professional services, provided that the shareholders are duly licensed to render the same service.[71] Motivation for incorporation by professionals includes tax benefits, pension plans, group ownership of property or contracts, and reduction of liability exposure. Although the corporation cannot legally provide professional medical services, it can be owned by the licensed professionals and contract with others as a provider of health care services, own and convey property, employ persons (who need not be licensed) for managerial purposes, employ licensed professionals who need not be shareholders, sue, and be sued.

Under these professional service corporation arrangements the individual professionals are not necessarily shielded from liability for their own acts, but the corporation may assume liability for the professional acts of its employees, including the individual licensed professional, up to a specific amount of its property.[72]

The PA may purchase professional liability insurance to cover all of its professional employees and others acting within the scope of their duties, and each licensed professional may purchase individual liability coverage. Strict attention should be paid to these variables by all seeking to purchase coverage for the corporation, its shareholders, or both and for the employees, as well as by all those to whom professional employment is offered. The terms may vary significantly from state to state.

Conversely the liability of individual shareholders for the "nonmalpractice" liability of the professional corporation has been held in some jurisdictions to be limited to an extent similar to that of shareholders of nonprofessional corporations. For example, the assets of the individual shareholders should be exempt for ordinary business debts or nonprofessional contracts entered into solely in the name of the corporation. Compare *We're Associates Co. v. Cohen et al.*, where individual shareholders of a professional corporation of attorneys were not held responsible for the corporation's default on its lease, with *South High Dev. Ltd. v. Weiner et al.*, where the bar rules made the individual lawyers guarantors for the acts of their professional corporation when professional duties were concerned.[73,74]

In the sale or lease of a piece of expensive medical equipment, the prudent vendor may require that the individual professionals as shareholders cosign with the corporation itself. Notification of the professional corporation at the time of notice to a shareholder in a malpractice action is customary or required in many states, but failure to do so is not necessarily fatal because the intent of the state legislature allowing professional corporations was not to provide an escape mechanism for the errant individual.

CONCLUSION

The role of the health care corporations who provide patient care has significantly changed. No longer is the hospital simply a physician's workplace that merely furnishes room, board, operating rooms, sophisticated equipment, nurses, attendants, and other personnel. Today, health care corporations play a role in the treatment of the patient as a health care center that is ultimately responsible for the health care provided within its walls. The public expectation is that the hospital will act to ensure the overall quality of care rendered. The doctrine of corporate liability is an attempt to pragmatically focus the law on the modern relationships between legal doctrine and socioeconomic reality. The courts are moving away from an overly strict application of traditional but archaic doctrinal rules in recognition of these changing relationships among the hospital, health care corporation, patients, subscribers or enrollees, and physicians.

A common thread running through those legal cases that have applied the corporate negligence theory is the court's role in identifying and analyzing the organizational structure of the hospital. This approach recognizes that hospitals have assumed the dual role of delivering services and monitoring the physicians they appoint to their staff. The duty, however, does not automatically render the hospital liable for all malpractice committed by physicians if the hospital has been reasonable in its procedures and has carefully selected and monitored its medical staff. The movement to assign responsibility for all types of professional malpractice, including acts of independently practicing physicians, to the hospital corporation itself has developed slowly, considering that it has been the most common form of legal responsibility in most aspects of "enterprise liability" in American law during the past century.

ENDNOTES

1. *Insinga v. LaBella*, 543 So. 2d 209 (1989) (Fla.).
2. *Bing v. Thunig*, 143 N.E. 2d 3 (1957) (N.Y.).
3. *Sepaugh v. Methodist Hospital*, 202 S.W. 2d 985 (1946) (Tenn.).
4. *Byrd v. Marion General Hospital*, 162 S.E. 738 (1932) (N.C.).
5. *Moon v. Mercy Hospital*, 373 P. 2d 944 (1962) (Colo.).
6. 1992–22 I.R.B. 59.
7. *Carroll v. Richardson*, 110 S.E. 2d 193 (1959) (Va.).
8. *Seneris v. Haas*, 291 P. 2d 915 (1957) (Cal.).
9. *Brown v. Moore*, 247 F. 2d 711 (1957) (Pa.).
10. *Cuker v. Hillsborough County Hospital Authority*, 605 So. 2d 998 (1992) (Fla.).
11. *Orlando Regional Medical Center v. Chmielewski*, 573 So. 2d 876 (1990) (Fla.).
12. *Arthur v. St. Peter's Hospital*, 405 A. 2d 443 (1979) (N.J.).
13. *Pederson v. Dumouchel*, 431 P. 2d 973 (1967) (Wash.).
14. *Darling v. Charleston Memorial Hospital*, 211 N.E. 2d 253 (1965) (Ill.).
15. *Fiorentino v. Wenger*, 227 N.E. 2d 296 (1967) (N.Y.).
16. *Mduba v. Benedictine Hospital*, 384 N.Y.S. 2d 527 (1976) (N.Y.).
17. *Corleto v. Shore Memorial Hospital*, 350 A. 2d 534 (1975) (N.J.).
18. *Jackson v. Power*, 743 P. 2d 1376 (1987) (Ala.).

19. *Alaska Airlines v. Sweat*, 568 P. 2d 916 (1977) (Ala.).
20. *Supra* note 1.
21. *Lundahl v. Rockford Memorial Hospital*, 235 N.E. 2d 671 (1968) (Ill.).
22. *Clary v. The Hospital Authority of the City of Marietta*, 126 S.E. 2d 470 (1962) (Ga.).
23. *Pogue v. Hospital Authority of DeKalb County*, 170 S.E. 2d 53 (1969) (Ga.).
24. *Vanaman v. Milford Memorial Hospital*, 262 A. 2d 263 (1970) (Del.).
25. *Ohligschlager v. Proctor Community Hospital*, 303 N.E. 2d 392 (1973) (Ill.).
26. *Tucson Medical Center v. Misevch*, 545 P. 2d 958 (1976) (Ariz.).
27. *Gonzales v. Nork*, No. 228566 (Cal. Sup. Ct., Sacramento Co.) (1974) (Cal.).
28. *Johnson v. Misericordia Community Hospital*, 301 N.W. 2d 156 (1980) (Wis.).
29. *Bost v. Riley*, 262 S.E. 2d 391 (1980) (N.C.).
30. *Cox v. Haworth*, 283 S.E. 392 (1981) (N.C.).
31. *Fridena v. Evans*, 622 P. 2d 463 (1981) (Ariz.).
32. *Elam v. College Park Hospital*, 183 Cal. Rptr. 156 (1982) (Cal.).
33. *Pickle v. Curns*, 435 N.E. 2d 877 (1982) (Ill.).
34. *Polischeck v. United States*, 535 F.Supp. 1261 (1982) (Pa.).
35. *Ravenis v. Detroit General Hospital*, 234 N.W. 2d 411 (1976) (Mich.).
36. *Andrews v. Burke*, 779 P. 2d 740 (1989) (Wash.)
37. *Joiner v. Mitchell County Hospital Authority*, 189 S.E. 2d 412 (1972) (Ga.).
38. *Purcell v. Zimbelman*, 500 P. 2d 335 (1972) (Ariz.).
39. *Reynolds v. Mennonite Hospital*, 522 N.E. 2d 827 (1988) (Ill.).
40. *Braden v. St. Francis Hospital*, 714 P. 2d 505 (1985) (Colo.).
41. *Kirk v. Michael Reese Hospital*, 513 N.E. 2d 387 (1987) (Ill.).
42. *Pedroza v. Bryant*, 677 P. 2d 166 (1984) (Wash.).
43. *Kruegar v. St. Joseph's Hospital*, 305 N.W. 2d 18 (1981) (N.D.).
44. *Knier v. Albany Medical Center Hospital*, 500 N.Y.S. 2d 490 (1986) (N.Y.).
45. *Estate of William Behringer, M.D. v. The Medical Center at Princeton, et al.*, 592 A. 2d 1251 (1991) (N.J.).
46. G.A. Reed & S.W. Malone, *Acquired Immunodeficiency Syndrome*, Ch. 13 in *Healthcare Facilities Law* (A.M. Dellinger ed., Little Brown and Company, Boston, 1991).
47. *Thompson v. Nason Hospital*, 591 A. 2d 703 (1991) (Pa.).
48. *Harrell v. Total Health Care, Inc.*, 781 S.W. 2d 58 (1989) (Mo.).
49. *McClellan v. Health Maintenance Organization of Pennsylvania*, 604 A. 2d 1053 (1992) (Pa).
50. *Robbins v. HIP of New Jersey*, 625 A. 2d 45 (1993) (N.J.).
51. *Sloan v. Metropolitan Health Council, Inc.*, 516 N.E. 2d 1104 (1987) (Ind.).
52. *Schleier v. Kaiser Foundation Health Plan of Mid-Atlantic States*, 876 F. 2d 174 (1989) D.C.
53. *Mitts v. HIP of Greater New York*, 478 N.Y.S. 2d 910 (1984) (N.Y.).
54. *Chase v. Independent Practice Association*, 583 N.E. 2d 251 (1991) (Mass.).
55. *See Boyd v. Albert Einstein Medical Center*, 547 A. 2d 1229 (1988) (Pa.); *Dunn v. Praiss*, 606 A. 2d 862 (1992) (N.J.); *Decker v. Saini*, 88-361768 NH (1991) (Mich.).
56. *Raglin v. HMO Illinois, Inc.*, 595 N.E. 2d 153 (1992) (Ill.).
57. *Williams v. Good Health Plus, Inc.*, 743 S.W. 373 (1987) (Tex.).
58. *Depenbrok v. Kaiser Foundation Health Plan, Inc.*, 144 Cal. Rptr. 724 (1978) (Cal.).
59. *Wickline v. State of California*, 239 Cal. Rptr. 810 (1986) (Cal.).
60. *Wilson v. Blue Cross of So. California*, 271 Cal. Rptr. 876 (1990) (Cal.).
61. 29 U.S.C.A. §1001-1461.
62. *DeGenova v. Ansel*, 555 A. 2d 147 (1988) (Pa.).
63. W.A. Chittenden III, *Malpractice Liability and Managed Health Care: History and Prognosis*, Tort & Ins. L. J. 451-496 (Spring 1991).
64. *See Darling v. Charleston Community Hospital*, 211 N.E. 2d 253 (1965) (Ill.); *Purcell v. Zembelman*, 500 P. 2d 335 (1992) (Ariz.); *Corleto v. Shore Memorial Hospital*, 350 A. 2d 534 (1975) (N.J.); *Elam v. College Park Hospital*, 183 Cal. Rptr. 156 (1982) (Cal.); *Blanton v. Moses Cone Memorial Hospital*, 354 S.E. 2d 455 (1987) (N.C.).
65. *Harrell v. Total Health Care Inc.*, *supra* note 48.
66. See D. Kinney & M. Wilder, *Medical Standard Setting in the Current Malpractice Environment: Problems and Possibilities*, 22 U.C. Davis L. Rev. 421 (1989).
67. *Lancaster v. Kaiser Foundation Health Plan*, 958 F.Supp. 1137 (1997) (Va.).
68. *Jones v. Chicago HMO Ltd. of Illinois*, 730 N.E. 2d 1119 (2000) (Ill.).
69. *Williams v. Health America*, 535 N.E. 2d 717 (1987) (Ohio).
70. *Boyd v. Albert Einstein Medical Center*, *supra* note 55.
71. Ch. 621 Florida Stat. (1991).
72. Ch. 621.07 Florida Stat. (1991).
73. *We're Associates Co. v. Cohen et al.*, 480 N.E. 2d 357 (1985) (N.Y.).
74. *South High Dev. Ltd. v. Weiner et al.*, 445 N.E. 2d 1106 (1983) (Ohio).

Liability of Managed Care Organizations

MILES J. ZAREMSKI, J.D., F.C.L.M.

LEGISLATIVE EFFORTS
CASE LAW
CONCLUSION

In the previous (fifth) edition of this text, this author wrote (in Chapter 46) about the liability exposures facing managed care organizations. Though that chapter and its discussion of legal theories and their application are as relevant today as they were when the text was published three years ago (and for that reason the text of this chapter is included within the electronic materials accompanying the publication of this sixth edition), that which follows can properly be viewed as a supplement to that chapter. But the current materials highlight the present direction for establishing such liability, legislatively and through ad hoc case law determinations, and what may likely be the end result in this arena for managed care entities.

So, just what has occurred with respect to liability exposure of managed care liability over the last two or three years? The answer depends upon when the question is asked, and in what venue, i.e., in legislative bodies or in appellate courts.

LEGISLATIVE EFFORTS

Considerable efforts occurred on Capitol Hill in the 107th Congress (2000-2002) concerning patients' bill of rights ("PBOR") legislation, which included accountability for managed care entities. This was found in the remedies section of the two bills that were the focus of the Senate and the House, S.1052 and H.R. 2653, respectively. Both bills passed their respective chambers. Table 36-1[1] lists the comparisons between both versions of the remedies section within these bills. However, even though each bill passed its respective chamber, neither became law, mainly

because of partisan views regarding the contents of the remedies sections.

As this chapter is being written during the early months of the 108th Congress, it is difficult to say just what will be introduced[2] and what will proceed through the halls of Congress—yet, alone, what may even pass into federal law. Regardless, this author has put forth a "blueprint" for congressional consideration in the area of accountability for managed care organizations.[3]

Last congressional term, the White House wanted to establish some sort of uniform federal standard to be applied to health plans alone within a PBOR remedies section. It had also indicated a willingness to have cases based upon decision-making to determine medical necessity, now called medically reviewable events, or quality-of-care decisions per court decisions, adjudicated in state court.[4] Remember, concomitantly, that while all this is being advocated, physicians and hospitals (more often than not "joined" with health plans as potentially accountable parties) are still subject to culpability in malpractice suits in state courts according to state laws. How can there really be one case involving a plaintiff and certain defendants in state court under state law, but as against a health plan there too but using federal law as to the plan?

A federal standard can be established: just ensure that the federal standard follows state procedural law. Why? Because it is not realistic to continue to believe that a mixed eligibility and treatment case can be litigated and tried to verdict according to some as yet undefined federal law in the same (state) courtroom as the same case against a physician or hospital subjected to state law for the same or similar treatment decisions. What law should be applied to pleadings, discovery, statutes of limitations, evidence and burdens of proof? State rules and procedures? A new federal standard as yet created (remember, ERISA [the Employee Retirement Income Security Act of 1974] is not a federal medical malpractice law)? A hybrid of state and yet to be

The author wishes to recognize with great appreciation the research efforts of Priscilla M. Dragoi, J.D., a graduate of the Chicago-Kent College of Law, Chicago, Illinois, and who is with Kamensky & Rubinstein. In addition, he acknowledges the editorial assistance of Ms. Shirley Walker-Moore and Mr. Gary Johnson, also of Kamensky & Rubinstein, in the preparation and assembly of this chapter.

TABLE 36-1 Comparison of House and Senate liability provisions

Provision	Senate	House
ERISA preemption/access to state law remedies	Amends ERISA to allow state law causes of action and to expand federal law causes of action for denials of benefits.	Amends ERISA to expand federal causes of action; allows state courts to have concurrent jurisdiction over health care–related claims.
Federal law claims	New federal cause of action against ERISA fiduciary who fails to exercise ordinary care in making an administrative coverage determination.	New federal cause of action against health plan's designated decision-maker who fails to exercise ordinary care in denying the initial claim for benefits or denying the claim during the internal review process, or fails to comply with the external reviewer's decision to reverse the claim denial, if that failure is the proximate cause of personal injury or death.
State law claims	Amends ERISA to allow medically reviewable decisions to be adjudicated in state court.	Allows state courts to hear cases involving new federal cause of action against designated decision-maker, but does not allow state law claims based on benefit of denials.
Damages—federal claims	Defendant is liable for economic and noneconomic damages but not exemplary or punitive damages, if it failed to exercise ordinary care causing personal injury or death.	Allows additional assessment, not to exceed $5,000,000, if claimant can establish by C&C evidence doctor's conduct demonstrated bad faith and was a proximate cause of the personal injury or death that is the subject of the claim. Designated decision-maker is liable for economic and noneconomic damages. Noneconomic damages may not exceed $1,500,000; punitive damages may not exceed $1,500,000.
Damages—state law claims	State economic, noneconomic, and punitive damages are allowed.	If new federal cause of action is tried in state courts, a state may further limit damages than the amounts listed above.
Severability	None	If one provision is unconstitutional, all remedy provisions are unconstitutional.
Standard of proof	Preponderance of the evidence.	Clear and convincing evidence in court if administrative decision upholds decision of plan.

developed federal law? Stop trying to put a square peg in a round hole: use state procedural law to be applied to all here, in state court.[5]

Further, decisions made to determine medical necessity—to determine whether a proposed treatment is investigational or experimental or even necessary—must be made by physicians. The standards to be applied should be medical standards. Let courts determine, as a matter of law in states that have not already done so, whether such decision-making constitutes medical practice. From discussion of case law, *infra*, in this chapter, we certainly now know that the practice of medicine is state governed, and medical necessity decisions are inclusive of the practice of medicine.

With respect to punitive damages, Democrats should consider this a "throw away," to be conceded to the White House. Ask anyone from the American Trial Lawyers Association how many times punitive damages are awarded in a medical malpractice case—few occasions to none.

Regarding caps on noneconomic damages,[6] how can caps on damages be placed on HMO-type entities for the same acts or omissions as offending physicians or hospitals may have committed or who are subjected to state law with

different ceilings than those proposed in H.R. 2563? Answer: there cannot be any, absent a claim of denial of equal protection. However, both sides can set the bar on damages high enough or be consistent with state law so that it will not matter to any constitutional scholar asked to opine on such a provision.

As to severability, in H.R. 2563 there is a clause that states if one provision of the remedies section is declared unconstitutional, the entire remedies section is unconstitutional. In most legislation, typically if one provision or section is declared unconstitutional, all others survive. That needs to be done here or with any subsequent legislative efforts on point.

Issues of burden of proof and relationship between administrative decisions made by internal/external decisions of a health plan/outside reviewer and legal action should be dealt with as procedural rules of the state in the state court where the case is being litigated.

An external review process relating to internal review decisions made by a plan[7] should be created for use so that those who comprise external review panels are independent of the plan and its administration. Consistent with this thinking is that independence is the *sine qua non* for a reviewer not basing his or her opinion *solely* on how a plan defines what is medically necessary. In cases where a reviewer sides with the health plan, the plan enrollee should not have to show in a court of law that that decision was erroneous by "clear and convincing" evidence as required by H.R. 2563. American jurisprudence uses the "preponderance of the evidence" rule in proving wrongdoing in medical professional liability cases; that same standard should be applied to health plans where the claims are solely treatment related or treatment mixed with an eligibility decision. Such rules of evidence should be based upon state law.

Cases against a health plan based, in whole or in part, on medical decision-making of the variety described in this chapter, should not be preempted by ERISA, and removal to federal court for adjudication should be precluded. Claims based solely on a coverage decision, absent a state independent reviewer statute where the independent reviewer reverses the decision of a plan on medical necessity or benefit determination, will remain venued, as they are now, under ERISA and remain, again as they are now, in federal court. The damages for such actions are limited presently to the loss of the benefit denied, although PBOR bills in the 107th Congress increased those ceilings of recovery.

Federal court is not the venue in which to try medical malpractice cases against managed care entities. Besides some of the nation's best and brightest health care law scholars, attorneys, physicians, and jurists all saying so, envision, if you will, a plaintiff suing a health plan in federal court for, to put it simply, medical malpractice based on faulty medical decision-making and then having to file a second suit against a physician/hospital/nurse in state court who is/are involved in the same circumstances giving rise to a claim against a health plan.[8] This will not maximize judicial economy and reduce taxpayer expense.

Finally, employers are a business force whose needs require recognition. In general, and for the most part, they are not sued for medical malpractice. At least this author could not find any such reported cases. Yes, a small percentage of employers (typically, the very large ones) do administer plans and make decisions like a health plan, like a physician. Here is a solution. Before any such entity can be joined as a party defendant in any case, require a hearing with proofs (according to state law). Based upon a determination of the court, an employer will, or will not, be so joined.

Also intertwined with the issue of accountability for HMO-like organizations is the so-called "next round" of the medical malpractice "crisis" (it seems once a decade or so such a crisis occurs due to the cost and availability of medical malpractice insurance), and what to do about it. As of this writing, there is much discussion in Congress and from the White House about limiting malpractice awards, caps on noneconomic damages, e.g., pain and suffering, and the like.[9] At first blush, holding HMOs accountable might be the antithesis to the present thinking of the majority in both chambers of Congress; a critical inspection, however, reveals holding managed care companies accountable for medical necessity decision-making is not related to federal efforts to limit accountability for all those who care and treat all patients, i.e., caps on noneconomic damages.

CASE LAW

Case law is instructive in determining which way the pendulum of liability is swinging for managed care organizations. This "sword of Damocles" is surely coming closer to those entities than ever before. Let's see how.

Two cases from the Illinois Supreme Court are illustrative of this thinking. The first is *Petrovich v. Share Health Plan*.[10] The issue in this case was fairly straightforward. Can an HMO be held vicariously liable for the negligence of its independent-contractor physicians under the doctrine of apparent authority? In answering in the affirmative, the court recognized that whether or not an HMO can be held liable for medical malpractice was an issue of first impression in that state. The defense asserted that to allow for such exposure would increase health care costs and make health care inaccessible to a large number of the state's population. The court found this position unpersuasive, since it is fundamental jurisprudence that organizations are accountable for their tortious actions and those of their agents.[11] The court also opined that HMO accountability is essential to counterbalance the HMO goal of cost containment.[12] The court also held, "To the extent that HMOs are profit-making entities, accountability is also needed to counterbalance the inherent drive to achieve a large and ever-increasing profit margin. Market forces alone 'are insufficient to cure the deleterious (e)ffects of managed care on the health care industry'" (citations omitted).[13] . . . "Indeed the national trend of courts is to hold HMOs accountable for medical malpractice under a variety of legal theories. . . . "[14]

The second case is *Jones v. Chicago HMO*.[15] This is quite notable since it established for the first time in the country the liability of an HMO under the theory of corporate or institutional negligence.[16] The court held that it was a question of fact whether an HMO negligently assigned more patients to a physician under contract with it than that physician was capable of seeing and handling.[17]

In holding as it did, the Illinois Supreme Court found in this case that the doctrine of institutional negligence had equal applicability to HMOs as it (institutional negligence) did 35 years earlier to hospitals.[18] An HMO, so found this state high court, arranges for, and provides, health care services to its members by an amalgam of various individuals who play various roles within an HMO structure.[19] An HMO, in other words, has a duty to its members, and to fulfill this duty, it must act "reasonably careful . . . under the circumstances."[20]

Next, managed care organizations have used the ERISA law as a shield against imposition of liability. But, just as the Illinois Supreme Court characterized managed care entities, above, so have federal courts. Two cases out of the United States Supreme Court are pertinent here, though neither squarely faced the issue of liability for decision-making, notably what is, or is not, medical necessity. The first case is *Pegram v. Herdrich*.[21] *Pegram* pertained to whether it was a breach of a fiduciary duty by a health plan under ERISA to not disclose any financial incentive arrangements between a plan and a provider who is under contract to that plan. In declining the invitation to make such a finding, the court, per Justice Souter, stated that "ERISA was not created to federalize malpractice litigation,"[22] that ERISA will not preempt the area of health care (an area of state regulation) absent clear congressional intent clearly expressed to the contrary, and that ERISA does not preempt medical malpractice litigation.[23]

Notably, the court broke down decisions made by managed care entities into those solely administrative in nature, those solely medical, and, for the majority of decisions they make, those involving a mixture of eligibility and treatment (quality of care). This is what this author coins *Pegram*'s "trichotomy." But within the court's discussion is the point that the area of health care is one traditionally left for the states to administer, and medical decision-making is clearly within the practice of medicine which, in turn, is clearly inclusive of health care.

Yet, the question remains, if a decision is made to provide or not provide certain medical care or treatment per a health plan's benefit structure, i.e., is the treatment medically necessary or not, is it an administrative decision (in which case the remedies to the patient are confined to what ERISA provides (the loss of the benefit denied), is it solely a medical, "quality of care" decision (common tort law remedies apply), or is it both (which would make questionable the remedies to be provided)? The case of *Rush Prudential HMO, Inc. v. Moran, et al.*,[24] handed down by the United States Supreme Court two terms after *Pegram*, is instructive—particularly as to the latter type of decision.

The *Rush Prudential* court affirms the lower court's holding, finding that ERISA did not preempt an Illinois statute providing for independent review of disputes between primary care physicians and health maintenance organizations over the medical necessity of a covered service. The language of Section 4-10 of the Illinois HMO Statute (the "Act")[25] reads as follows:

Each Health Maintenance Organization shall provide a mechanism for the timely review by a physician holding the same class of license as the primary care physician, who is unaffiliated with the Health Maintenance Organization, jointly selected by the patient . . . , primary care physician and the Health Maintenance Organization in the event of a dispute between the primary care physician and the Health Maintenance Organization[26] regarding the medical necessity of a covered service proposed by a primary care physician. In the event that the reviewing physician determines the covered service to be medically necessary, the Health Maintenance Organization shall provide the covered service.

To arrive at the conclusion that a statute like the Illinois HMO Act is not preempted by ERISA, one must, as the majority did, travel a maze of interrelating insurance law, an analysis of what constitutes the business of insurance, a determination of whether HMOs are in the business of insurance, and ERISA's preemptive reach in this regard.

ERISA preempts state laws that relate to any employee benefit plan.[27] But state laws that regulate insurance, banking, or securities are "saved" from being preempted.[28] Section 4-10 was clearly found to "relate to" employee benefit plans within Section 1144(a) of ERISA. But it could only be saved from preemption if the Illinois Act was found to regulate insurance. Now comes one of the interesting points in the case. Is an HMO in the business of insurance and, therefore, does it regulate it for the area(s) in which it operates?

An approach, labeled by the court as "common sense," states "a law must not just have an impact on the insurance industry, but must be specifically directed toward that industry. . . ." The court takes this approach and interweaves it with the three-prong test (under the McCarran-Ferguson Act) used to ascertain whether insurance laws are saved from preemption to determine if the Illinois HMO Act is saved from preemption.[29] The answer is "yes." Why? Because Illinois law tells us so. An HMO "provide(s) or arrange(s) for . . . health care plans under a system which causes part of the risk of health care delivery to be borne by the organization or its providers."[30] While Rush states it is not an insurer, as it is a health care provider, the court disagrees. Rush is in the business of both: "[Rush] provides health care, and it does so as an insurer."[31] A managed care entity provides health care and is, therefore, a provider in today's era of health care delivery. As the court continues, the (federal) HMO Act of 1973, for example, encouraged "the development of HMOs as a *new form* of health care delivery system."[32]

Further, the operation of the savings clause within ERISA is not defined by multiple functions of an HMO "as long as providing insurance fairly accounts for the application of state law."[33] An HMO receives dollars for each patient enrolled pursuant to the terms of a contract to provide health care. The HMO assumes the financial risk of providing benefits, and if the enrollee never uses those benefits, then the HMO does not sustain a loss; if the enrollee becomes sick, then the HMO must pay for what is provided under the contract. HMOs also manage risk and are defined, in part, by reference to risk. These notions define the typical insurer, underwriting and spreading of risk. The court went on to say: "Rush cannot checkmate common sense by trying to submerge HMOs' insurance features beneath an exclusive characterization of HMOs as providers of health care."[34]

Rush's additional arguments for why it should not have been considered in the business of regulating insurance were not persuasive. These included that it may not have any risk at all, as the risk may be borne by providers with which it contracts to provide patient care, or that a plan may provide only "administrative" or other services for self-funded plans. The court still perceives the HMO as *providing* medical care, regardless of the ability of physicians or third-party insurers to honor their contracts with the HMO.

The Illinois HMO Act also qualifies as regulating insurance under the McCarran-Ferguson test. In its analysis, the court looked to the role of the independent reviewer. That role is seen as including the application of a standard of medical care (medical necessity) and "characteristically, as in this case,"[35] construction of policy terms because the independent reviewer affects the "policy relationship" between the HMO and covered persons.[36] Moreover, the Court states that Section 4-10 of the Act is within the policy relationship between an HMO and insured because this section provides a legal right to the insured to determine the HMO's medical obligations.

Thus, whether an HMO claims to do only administrative work, or considers itself a mere "matchmaker" (matching up plans with enrollees), an HMO does business as an insurer particularly because it (the HMO) has taken over "much business formerly performed by traditional indemnity insurers."[37] But, again, it must be emphasized that an HMO represents a new form of health care delivery that combines medical care with other functions, unlike the role of insurers of decades past. As the court states: *"Thus, virtually all commentators on the American health care system describe HMOs as a combination of insurer and provider, and observe that in recent years, traditional 'indemnity' insurance has fallen out of favor . . ."*[38] (emphasis added). The linchpin to the court's analysis, and the focus of the dissent, rested with whether the Illinois Act supplanted the enforcement mechanisms found within ERISA.

In the view of the court, the independent review mechanism mandated by the Illinois Act is a state regulatory scheme that provides no new cause of action under state law and authorizes no new form of ultimate relief under ERISA. The Act does not enlarge that which is already provided for by ERISA—the cost of the benefit denied. The dissent finds problems with this interpretation because it leaves HMOs and similarly situated entities subject to the laws of each jurisdiction (about 40 states have such external review laws) that chooses to provide independent reviews.

Justice Souter countered, "Such disuniformities . . . are the inevitable result of the congressional decision to 'save' local insurance regulation. . . ."[39]

In addition, the dissent likens the independent review to an arbitral procedure. As such, it would bypass the remedial scheme provided by ERISA. The majority focuses on the independent reviewer doing one thing—determining whether the medical procedure at issue is medically necessary. There is no admission of evidence or contract interpretation by an independent reviewer in the classic sense of what a judicial review of a health care plan's decision to deny care should be predicated. The majority also equates an independent review to more of a second opinion practice to ensure sound medical judgments than anything else. Because the external, independent review process arises from the Illinois Act, which, additionally, mandates that the HMO provide the necessary treatment, and the Act then becomes part of the contract as it regulates the HMO as an insuring entity, the mandate placed upon the HMO by the Act would be no different than a mandated-benefit regulation.[40] Moreover, the decision of the independent reviewer would precede judicial scrutiny in any event. While such thinking may be questioned, particularly the court's characterization of an independent reviewer, the logic is a means to an end—to confirm that an HMO cannot escape from its role in being a provider of medical care.

The facial importance of this decision is that state statutes providing for external, independent reviews, not arbitral in nature, where the decisions of independent reviewers are akin to second opinions, taking into account the definition of "medical necessity" in plan documents, are not now preempted by ERISA. There is, however, additional value in the court's view of the role an HMO-type entity plays in health care delivery and whether its responsibilities to enrollees of a plan are analogous to those of hands-on, treating practitioners. Such "telescoping" of thought can be found in the following observation: "In the field of health care, a subject of traditional state regulation, there is no ERISA preemption without clear manifestation of congressional purpose."[41] Justice Souter again writes, "regulating insurance tied to what is medically necessary is probably inseparable from enforcing the quintessentially state-law standards of reasonable medical care."[42] He then adds: "[R]ecall the ways States regulate insurance in looking out for the welfare of their citizens. Illinois has chosen to regulate insurance as one way to regulate the practice of medicine, which we have previously held to be permissible under ERISA."[43] Of additional importance is the court's description of an HMO in *Pegram*. The court explained "that when an HMO guarantees medically necessary care, determinations of coverage cannot be untangled from physicians' judgments about reasonable medical treatment."[44] The Illinois Act operates in this fashion because "the independent examiner must be a physician with credentials similar to those of the primary care physician . . . and is expected to exercise independent medical judgment in deciding what medical necessity requires."[45]

Notwithstanding that HMOs are likened to insurers (in a new era of health care delivery), for purposes of being saved from preemption under ERISA, the court's statements in the preceding paragraphs provide a crystal ball look into the future of legal precedent considered essential by health plans faced with being accountable for medical necessity determinations. Even though this medical necessity decision-making occurs within a benefits determination or within administrative duties in a plan's business office, this decision-making still constitutes a form of providing medical care—decisions relating to medical practice according to state law standards of reasonable medical care. *Rush Prudential* certainly instructs us on such decision-making in the insurance context.

Of particular interest, moreover, is the *Pegram* court's emphasis that mixed eligibility decisions by an HMO come about through its physicians, that these "physicians . . . draw on resources held for others and make decisions to distribute them in accordance with entitlements expressed in a written instrument (embodying the terms of an ERISA plan)," that "treatment judgments are what physicians, reaching mixed decisions do make, by definition," and "physicians through whom HMOs act make just the sorts of decisions made by licensed medical practitioners millions of times every day, in every possible medical setting."[46] It would appear that the court is describing an HMO medical director.

Two final comments here. First, some observers would say the Supreme Court, in *Rush Prudential*, has announced that damages, in whatever context they are raised, are limited to the cost of the benefit denied when a beneficiary disputes a decision of a plan based upon denial of care, in turn based upon whether that care is medically necessary. After all, we now know, these observers would further say that this type of damage, once only enforceable in an action brought under ERISA's civil enforcement scheme,[47] still can be pursued only in federal court under ERISA with the same damage cap. This is making pronouncements with blinders affixed.

The *Rush Prudential* decision is a benefits case; it is that simple. When a beneficiary of a plan wants his or her treatment covered, without claiming any further damages, then the relief now could arguably be found under state law in a state court providing for independent reviews of health plan decisions premised on medical necessity. That is, what the court arguably does, in a practical sense, is perhaps suggest a shifting of forums for resolution of a benefits claim involving an independent reviewer's determination from federal court under ERISA to state court for violation of an independent reviewer statute (again, should the reviewer decide against the HMO and the HMO does not wish to follow the decision of the independent reviewer). Others, perhaps would differ here, opining that, where federal courts have, at a minimum, concurrent jurisdiction with state courts, the ultimate arbiter for benefits, even based upon a state statute that has been violated, remains federal court under ERISA. Nonetheless, a beneficiary knows that, regardless of the forum used, an independent review provided by state statute cannot be preempted by ERISA, and that deference will not be given to how plan documents define "medical necessity." In possibly allowing for this, the court affirms the precept that the area of health law is traditionally venued within state jurisdictions.

The court neither opines nor implies, nor even suggests, that a person will be denied all damages in fact scenarios that go beyond strictly a claim for benefits, for example, from fact patterns involving delays or denials of care based on medical necessity that lead to injury or death. To reiterate, the court's language (about what an HMO does, how it goes about doing it, and the process of making its decisions, including those, now, of the independent medical reviewer) offers still another road map, or a beacon of light, for characterizations leading to the conclusions put forth in this chapter about what an HMO really provides, or does in conjunction with other activities. This is true regardless that such characterizations are put forth in a context where the beneficiary merely seeks to obtain the cost of the benefit denied.

Again, nonetheless, while indications from it seems clear, the U.S. Supreme Court does not answer the precise question of whether or not ERISA is intended to preempt state laws holding accountable those who or which make decisions determining whether a patient should receive a particular medical treatment. Additional lower court rulings carry this banner, and in so doing, cement a determination for liability exposure of managed care health plans.

In *Cicio v. Vytra Healthcare*,[48] the plaintiff was employed by a local bank, the North Fork Bank, and received health care coverage for herself and her husband through Vytra Healthcare ("Vytra") purchased by the bank. Vytra administered the plan.

In March 1997, Carmine Cicio was diagnosed with multiple myeloma, a potentially fatal form of cancer. On January 28, 1998, the plaintiff's treating doctor, an Edward Samuel, determined that it was medically necessary for his patient to receive high-dosage chemotherapy combined with peripheral blood stem-cell transplantation in a tandem double transplant. This procedure would potentially save Mr. Cicio's life. Dr. Samuel contacted Vytra requesting approval for this medical treatment. Dr. Samuel wrote that the "likelihood of maintaining (Mr. Cicio's) disease under control (through other means) . . . is low for any sustained period of time" and that the proposed treatment "demonstrated superiority in over-all survival and disease-free survival."

Vytra received the request the following day, January 29; it did not respond until February 23, 1998, through its Medical Director, Dr. Brent Spears. Dr. Spears denied the requested treatment as "experimental/investigational." With his patient's consent, Dr. Samuel appealed this decision in writing on March 4, 1998, requesting reconsideration of the denial and still wanting his patient to have the double transplant. In that correspondence, Dr. Samuel stressed that the procedure was not experimental/investigational. Numerous articles from major medical journals were cited in support. Vytra did not reply until March 25, 1998, three weeks later. Significantly, Vytra then reversed itself, in part. It approved an alternative: a single stem-cell transplant. The double transplant was denied. No mention was made of whether the single transplant was experimental/investigational or whether the single transplant was a benefit within the coverage provided. However, at this time, Mr. Cicio dropped out of being a suitable candidate for any transplant due to his worsening condition. He died on May 11, 1998.

The health plan that North Fork Bank purchased and had administered for itself provided that medically necessary services were to be covered, but excluded "[a]ny procedure or service which in the judgment of Vytra's Medical Director, is experimental or is not generally recognized to be effective for a particular condition, diagnosis or body area."

A lawsuit was commenced on May 3, 2000, alleging 18 causes of action arising under New York state law. Theories included medical malpractice involving the plan.

The federal magistrate's report concluded that the Vytra plan was one falling within the ambit of ERISA, even taking the language of *Pegram* into account. It then reviewed whether the state law claims "related to" an ERISA plan and, therefore, were appropriate for removal and federal preemption. After an analysis of regulation of insurance as being saved from preemption, the lower court concluded that the plaintiff was attempting to enforce a health plan " . . . in a manner outside the exclusive scope of ERISA's civil enforcement mechanisms by alleging that Vytra failed to perform its obligations under the policy and intentionally misconstrued the terms of the policy."[49] By circumventing Section 502(a), the plaintiff triggered ERISA preemption under Section 514(a). Federal jurisdiction thus became proper, and certain of the counts providing for alternative relief to ERISA were dismissed. In light of *Rush Prudential*, such thinking must be seriously questioned.

The court's treatment of the state law claims, including medical malpractice, is more problematic. This centers around Vytra's refusal to find medically necessary what Dr. Samuel requested,[50] and in a timely fashion.

The underpinning of the plaintiff's position was that Vytra is a medical service provider and its actions were based on medical decision-making, not on administrative decisions. In other words, Vytra made decisions akin to the decisions in the role served by Dr. Samuel.

The district court opined that *Pegram* was not controlling. In *Pegram*, the defendant HMO and the physician were one and the same. Vytra, on the other hand, acted solely in the role of a plan administrator and was not the medical services provider. It did not, in other words, provide medical treatment.

Vytra's role was limited to determining whether the proposed treatment qualified as an experimental procedure under the terms of the plan. Although Vytra's benefits determination may have involved some medical judgment, this may be said of countless medical administrative-made decisions every day. There is no evidence that Congress intended that these quasi-medical/administrative decisions made by a plan administrator survive ERISA preemption. Vytra's coverage determination cannot be separated or construed apart from the ERISA plan. Vytra functioned solely as a plan administrator and bore no responsibility as a provider of medical services in this action. For this reason, the challenge here does not target the quality of care but rather attacks the benefits decision that was made. This determination is preempted by ERISA.

The district court looked to the Fifth Circuit U.S. Court of Appeals in *Corporate Health Ins. v. Texas Dept. of Insurance*,[51] for guidance. Specifically, the court held that Texas law providing for independent review of medical necessity determinations made by an HMO was preempted by ERISA. However, with the decision in *Rush Prudential*, the precedential effect of this (Fifth Circuit) decision has been undermined.

Finally, the district court in *Cicio* was not persuaded by the plaintiff's effort to point to many (actually, by this author's research, more than 140) cases where medical malpractice cases survive ERISA's preemptive reach. The court distinguished those cases because they involved as a defendant the treating physician and/or his employer or agent. These cases must be distinguished, so said the district court, from cases, as here, where the plan administrator and medical director did not provide direct medical services.

The conclusion of the district court in Cicio is misplaced and, therefore, its conclusion is incorrect. It is hornbook law, and *Rush Prudential* and *Pegram* confirm this again, that health care is an area traditionally left to states to control, absent congressional intent clearly expressed to the contrary. ERISA does not preempt the practice of medicine, one form of which is, to reiterate, medical decision-making for what is medically necessary or not; nor does ERISA, by its history, language, or wording, preempt decisions that involve, in whole or in part, medical decision-making of the variety that HMOs make in determining whether a particular treatment is medically necessary. But this notwithstanding, can a health plan escape accountability if its medical director is not the treating physician?

In many states, New York included, medical directors must be licensed as physicians. This is regardless of the

AT&T/Lucent employed-physician; if the two had a qualified doctor-patient relationship, the court explained, then the plaintiff would have standing to sue Lucent for the medical malpractice of its agent under a vicarious liability theory. The court also noted that the evidence presented did not clearly illustrate whether Lucent was acting as a service provider or administrator when it delayed responding to Duong's requests for further advice and evacuation. As a result, the court found "unconvincing" evidence that Lucent was acting as an administrator; moreover, it was unable to weigh evidence on summary judgment.[108] "What matters is what [Lucent] was wearing during the time it committed the acts of which [the plaintiff] complains." Here, the plaintiff had shown a general issue of material fact as to whether Lucent was wearing its service provider hat or its administrator hat when its physician initially communicated with Duong and thereafter when he delayed in responding to Duong's further requests.[109] Accordingly, the appellate court reversed the lower court's decision to grant summary judgment to the defendants as to these issues. The Ninth Circuit Court of Appeals held that "*ERISA does not preempt claims of medical malpractice against medical service providers for decisions made in the course of treatment or . . . evaluation. That is true even if those medical service providers also serve, at other times, as administrators*"[110] (emphasis added).

Thornton v. Shah

Another case from an Illinois appellate tribunal provides an interesting twist to the "shield" traditionally asserted by managed care organizations faced with liability exposure. This case is *Thornton v. Shah*.[111] There, the parents of a child who died in utero sued an HMO and a physician for medical malpractice predicated on breach of contract and negligent spoliation of evidence. The HMO moved to dismiss in the trial court based upon the exhaustion of the 2-year limitations period applicable to a *breach of contract for damages of injury or death arising out of patient care* (emphasis added). The trial court granted the motion and the appellate court affirmed.

Because the HMO asserted that the plaintiffs' cause of action was time barred, it is logical to assume that if the lawsuit was filed within the proper time period, a proper cause of action would have been stated, i.e., that an HMO (at least in Illinois) does provide patient care and treatment. This would be consistent, in other words, with characterizations of HMOs found by the United States Supreme Court decisions in *Pegram* and *Rush Prudential*, previously discussed in this chapter, and in other cases described in the preceding pages. Concomitantly, this Illinois court here equates an HMO with a physician, dentist, registered nurse, or hospital licensed under Illinois law for purposes of the statute of limitations at issue that applies to the latter categories of patient caregivers (relying, as well, upon the Illinois Supreme Court pronounce-ments in *Petrovich* and *Jones*, also previously discussed in this chapter).

Marks v. Watters

In another federal decision, the court in *Marks v. Watters*[112] held that where utilization review was limited to determining whether to provide plan coverage, and not to determine what type of treatment should be rendered, preemption by ERISA will apply. In so holding, the Fourth Circuit concurs, nonetheless, with the dictates in the *Pegram* case, viz., " . . . when an HMO diagnoses and treats a patient's condition with an appropriate medical response, even if it is at the same time also making an eligibility determination, it does not act as a fiduciary under ERISA because the mixed eligibility and treatment decisions as a practical matter reduce to the stuff of state malpractice claims and not to traditional breach of fiduciary duty claims."[113]

The facts in *Marks* reveal that the defendant 'Mainstay' managed the behavioral health care component of the PPO plan insured by an entity that subcontracted certain duties to Mainstay to those insured by the plan. One of those insured was the deceased on behalf of whom the lawsuit was brought. Mainstay, in other words, was contracted as a utilization agent that did not treat patients but which managed care provided by others to accommodate the benefits of the plan, perform network development, credential health care providers, and perform quality assurance functions. Under Mainstay's utilization review program, it supplied case managers, one of whom was a Shelley Watters, also a named defendant. Watters was never engaged to actually provide treatment or to make treatment decisions for the insured-deceased; all she did was confirm with health care providers that the health care being delivered or proposed was approved for payment under the patient's health care plan. If Watters, as a case manager, was unable to confirm this coverage upon reviewing the specifics of the patient's health care plan and the applicable medical necessity criteria, she was required to refer the matter to Mainstay's medical director. Because of these duties, shown by the facts, what Watters did was not "practically inextricable" from treatment decisions made by those in a different setting.

(How would this case "square" with the Second Circuit's ruling in *Cicio*? The principal distinction is that the medical director in *Cicio* made a decision to deny a specific treatment, and then provide a different treatment. Even if done in an office setting, the medical director still made a medical treatment decision, and one intertwined with eligibility criteria. In *Marks*, no such treatment decisions were made, just administrative ones by a nonmedical doctor.)

KAHP v. Miller

Finally, the most recent case out of the Supreme Court that may provide additional guidance to whether or not liability matters involving health plans should remain in state courts according to state laws is *Kentucky Association of Health Plans, Inc., et al. v. Miller*.[114] This decision, rendered in April 2003, held that ERISA does not preempt "any willing provider" state statutes (laws that preclude providers who are willing to accept the terms and conditions of a health plan from being barred from becoming members of a plan's panel). While its analysis focused on insurance laws and whether health plans are in the business of insurance, which, by being so, can be regulated by an AWP statute, the impact of the court's decision goes beyond its written words and holding. First, it is the first decision in the ERISA preemption/managed health care arena authored by other than Justice Souter. The court's decision was written by Justice Scalia, a member of the conservative wing of the present court. Second, the decision was unanimous, indicating, at least in this author's view, that the conservative and liberal factions of the court are coming together in recognizing that the so-called shield that health plans have raised in recent years, *à la* the Illinois external review statute in *Rush Prudential*,[115] is becoming more and more of a paper tiger. This should provide a further beacon for plans that continue to posture that they should also be shielded by ERISA's preemptive reach in cases involving professional liability issues, certainly ones involving decisions of medical necessity. Moreover, the court in *KAHP* gives further credence through its analysis and outcome that the area of health care remains venued within states to regulate, absent clear congressional intent to the contrary.

CONCLUSION

The "circle" is nearly "complete" for analyzing liability exposure for managed health care plan organizations. It has taken only 30-plus years to do so. That is to say, HMO-like entities and ERISA health plans came about in the 1970s as an alternative to traditional indemnity insurers whose expenditures in paying for health care charges were becoming unmanageable and sky-high. Managed health care, so was the prevailing thought at the time of their creation, would reduce reimbursement costs and make health care delivery more manageable and less costly. While this lofty goal appears not to have been met, what arose, at least with some emphasis in the early 1990s, was a shield behind which plans stood: a protection against exposure to liability—notably, professional liability claims and lawsuits premised upon medical necessity decision-making. Plans asserted that the decisions they make, whether from determining what is, or is not, medically necessary treatment or by physicians viewed as their agents, were administrative ones pursuant to the ERISA law (and not based on quality of care subject to state laws in state courts). Consequently, the only exposure plans faced per ERISA was the loss of the benefit denied. As the distinction between quantity of care provided under plan documents and quality of that care being rendered became blurred and has been refined and narrowed considerably by courts nationwide, what has become clear is that plans can be held accountable for medical care and treatment decisions undertaken by its agents, i.e., treating physicians who are part of their panels, but held out by plans to enrollees of their (plans') doctors. Plans, at least viewed through the prism provided by the Illinois Supreme Court, can even be held responsible for corporate decisions, like how many enrollees can be seen by one of its panel physicians.

The murkiest area for liability exposure, and the last vestige for health plans to assert the shield claimed to be afforded them by the ERISA law, is decision-making by plan personnel as to what treatment is medically necessary for the enrollee and when that treatment should be rendered. To preclude exposure to this kind of accountability, plans have been forced to assert that such decisions are made in an administrative context. As such, these determinations, so plans assert, are cloaked with ERISA law protection with the maximum liability exposure being the loss of the benefit denied. A fortiori, all plans do is make decisions in order to reimburse charges and benefits provided for within plan documents. But such thinking harkens back to what traditional indemnity insurers did *before* HMO entities came to the forefront of the health care delivery system: pay for treatment covered by the insurance policy. Thus, as stated atop this concluding section, that circle would seem to now be complete: even though plans were created to supplant indemnity insurers, plans now claim, at least for liability concerns, that they are *just like* indemnity carriers. As a result, clarity in the ERISA statute must be made (if not, we will only be able to rely on court decisions, made solely on an ad hoc basis). Can an amendment to the ERISA law be drafted to clarify whether or not managed care plans should be accountable for decisions of medical necessity they make? Certainly. Will those members in Congress in the 108th Congress (2002–2004) enact such a law? Who knows.[116] One thing is certain, however: absent a legislative amendment to ERISA that is signed into law, we will have to rely on court decisions, whose beacon of light (drawn from the likes of decisions in this chapter) grows ever stronger.

ENDNOTES

1. Compiled by Julie A. Barnes, King, Pagano & Harrison, Washington, D.C.
2. Legislation was introduced in 2003 to place caps on damages in medical malpractice lawsuits. The bill, which passed the House in 2003, is one on tort reform affecting professional liability and contains a cap of $250,000 on noneconomic damages. Up to submitting page proofs for this chapter (the Fall session, 2003), the analogous version in the Senate, S.11, has been unable to muster enough votes to overcome a filibuster. Neither bill focuses upon accountability for managed care entities. In fact, patients rights legislation, with provisions for such accountability, is not presently viewed as important among federal legislators.
3. 23 Journal of Legal Medicine 547-62 (American College of Legal Medicine, Dec. 2002, Taylor & Francis publication). It is reproduced, in

part, with permission in the text that accompanies and follows this footnote.

4. With a Republican majority in Congress and a Republican administration in the White House, it is problematic just what the White House will now pursue. *See* note 111, *infra*.

5. *See Pegram v. Herdrich*, 530 U.S. 211, 236-37, 120 S.Ct. 2143, 2158 (2000).

6. In an address President Bush gave in January 2003 at the University of Scranton (Pa.), he emphasized the need for caps on damages and related this need (incorrectly so to this author) to the availability and affordability of medical malpractice insurance for physicians. Legislation has already been introduced in the House to place caps on noneconomic damages in medical malpractice cases. *See also* note111, *infra*.

7. See note 24, *infra*, and accompanying text.

8. This approach of "duplicity of lawsuits" repeats what Congress did with the EMTALA law that it enacted in the late 1980s. EMTALA provides a statutory cause of action in federal court against hospitals that transfer/discharge a patient in an unstable condition. Proof of this really is the same for a state-based medical malpractice case. Though EMTALA is not a federal medical malpractice statute, recoverable damages are based on damages allowed for by state law. And an EMTALA suit does not preclude a state malpractice suit against the very same hospital (named in the EMTALA case).

9. *See* note 116, *infra*.

10. 188 Ill. 2d 17, 719 N.E. 2d 756 (1999).

11. *Id.* at 29, 635, 764.

12. *Id.*

13. *Id.*

14. *Id.* at 30, 635, 764.

15. 191 Ill. 2d 278, 730 N.E. 2d 1119 (2000).

16. This decision is similar in its progressive thinking to what that same state high court did when it eliminated charitable immunity for hospitals in *Darling v. Charleston Community Hospital*, 33 Ill. 2d 326, 211 N.E. 2d 253 (1965).

17. *See KAHP v. Miller, infra* at note 114 and accompanying text.

18. *See also Shannon v. McNulty*, 718 A. 2d 828 (Pa. Super. Ct. 1998).

19. 191 Ill. 2d at 293, 1128, 663.

20. *Id.* at 1129, 664.

21. 530 U.S. 211, 120 S.Ct. 2143 (2000).

22. 530 U.S. at 236, 2158.

23. *Id.* at 236-37.

24. 122 S.Ct. 2151 (2002).

25. 215 Ill. Comp. Stat. Ch. 125, §4-10 *et seq.*

26. In the health care industry, the term "Health Maintenance Organization" has been defined as "[a] prepaid organized delivery system where the organization *and* the primary care physicians assume some financial risk for the care provided to its enrolled members. . . ." "Rush's Certificate of Group Coverage," issued to employees who participate in employer-sponsored plans, promises that Rush will provide them with "medically necessary" services. The certificate specifies that a service is covered as "medically necessary" if Rush finds:

"(a) [The service] is furnished or authorized by a Participating Doctor for the diagnosis or the treatment of a Sickness or Injury or for the maintenance of a person's good health.

(b) The prevailing opinion within the appropriate specialty of the United States medical profession is that [the service] is safe and effective for its intended use, and that its omission would adversely affect the person's medical condition.

(c) It is furnished by a provider with appropriate training, experience, staff, and facilities to furnish that particular service or supply."

122 S.Ct. at 2158.

27. 29 U.S.C. §1144(a).

28. *Id.*, §1144(b)2(A).

29. Under the McCarran-Ferguson Act, one or more factors to consider to see whether or not a law regulates insurance include: (1) does it target the effect of transferring or spreading a policyholder's risk; (2) is it an integral part of the policy relationship between insured and insurer; and (3) is it limited to entities within the insurance industry.

30. 215 Ill. Comp. Stat., ch. 125, §1-2(9) (2000).

31. *Rush Prudential*, 122 S.Ct. at 2160.

32. *Id.* (emphasis added).

33. *Id.*

34. *Id.* at 2162. It is recognized by some that the court's characterization of an HMO as a provider cannot be equated to that of a treating, primary care physician as a provider. The error for those who may wish to think this way is that when an HMO makes a decision on medical necessity, it typically uses a medical director who undertakes the same thought processes as a physician in a medical office. Both rely upon reasonable standards of medical care to make a decision. Thus, the description "provider of medical care" aptly would apply to both.

35. *Id.* at 2163.

36. *Id.*

37. *Id.*

38. *Id.* at 2161 (citations omitted).

39. *Id.* at 2167 (citation omitted).

40. *Id.* at 2170.

41. *Id.* at 2171.

42. *Id.* (citing *Pegram*, 530 U.S. at 236).

43. *Id.* at 2170 (citation omitted).

44. *Pegram*, 530 U.S. at 229.

45. *Rush Prudential*, 122 S.Ct. at 2168. In another case before the U.S. Supreme Court and argued in January 2003, the court was asked to decide whether ERISA also preempts "AWP" (any willing provider) statutes on the grounds that these state statutes are not saved from preemption by ERISA because they do not regulate the business of insurance. *See KAHP v. Miller, supra* note 17. While, from oral arguments, the court seemed predisposed to affirm the lower court which found that these statutes were saved from preemption, this author does not see, from an analytic viewpoint, much difference in a state's external review statute decided in *Rush Prudential* and an AWP statute: both are within the penumbra of areas of what is considered to be the practice of medicine . . . which is part of health care traditionally regulated by the states.

46. *Id.* at 231-32. *See also Oregon v. Ashcroft*, 192 F.Supp. 2d 1077, 1092 (D. Ore. 2002) (no violation of federal Controlled Substances Act by physicians who assist suicide of terminally ill patients pursuant to Oregon's Death with Dignity Act: "The determination of what constitutes a legitimate medical practice or purpose traditionally has been left to the individual states. State statutes, state medical boards, and state regulations control the practice of medicine . . . the practice of medicine is based on state standards.") An appeal of this decision is pending, but was orally argued in the 9th Cir. in Portland, Or., on May 7, 2003.

47. *See* 29 U.S.C. §1132(a); *Moran v. Rush Prudential*, 230 F. 3d 959, 971 (7th Cir. 2000).

48. 208 F.Supp. 2d 288 (E.D. N.Y. 2001).

49. *Id.* at 297.

50. In its brief filed in the Second Circuit, Vytra claimed its March 25 letter confirmed Dr. Samuel's request of March 4 (quoted in the text herein) that he only wanted a single transplant. It would not appear this is correct from a reading of the quoted language.

51. 20 F. 3d 641 (5th Cir. 2000).

52. 321 F. 3d 83 (2d Cir. 2003), pet. cert. filed July 11, 2003, and pending as of Sept. 23, 2003, U.S. Supreme Court.

53. 2002 W.L. 1461710 (S.D. Ind. 2002).

54. *Id.* at 1-2.
55. *Id.*
56. *Id.*
57. *Id.* at 2.
58. *Id.* at 5.
59. *Id.* at 6.
60. *Id.* at 8.
61. 307 F. 3d 298 (5th Cir. 2002). Although four plaintiffs participated in this lawsuit, special attention will be paid to the claims of Calad and Davila, since it is upon their claims that the court focuses its discussion. With respect to Thorn and Roark's claims, the court rejected the first two arguments made by the defendant in response to those claims simply because it was not proper for that court to consider those issues upon an ultimate finding that this case was not completely preempted. Further, the defendant relied on cases decided prior to *Pegram*, and the court noted this chronology.
62. It is important to note that the Court of Appeals addressed two other issues in the case. The first was determining whether the ERISA civil enforcement provision completely preempted the appellants' breach of contract claims. The second required the court to examine the ERISA conflict-preemption provision to determine whether the appellants' medical malpractice claim was preempted under that provision. For purposes of this chapter, more attention is given to the medical malpractice issues related to mixed decisions of eligibility and treatment.
63. *Id.* at 301.
64. *Id.* at 4.
65. *Id.*
66. *Id.*
67. *Id.*
68. *Id.* at 5.
69. *Id.*
70. *Id.*
71. *Id.*
72. *Id.*
73. *Id.* at 7.
74. *Id.*
75. *Id.* at 8.
76. *Id.*
77. *Id.* at 10.
78. *Id.* at 13.
79. *Id.* at 10.
80. 310 F. 3d 1143 (9th Cir. 2002).
81. *Id.*
82. Apparently, AT&T/Lucent employees were required to surrender their passports upon entering Saudi Arabia. The passports were then returned to them in preparation for returning to their respective home countries. *Id.* at 1146 n.2.
83. *Id.* at 1147.
84. *See Dukes v. U.S. Healthcare, Inc.*, 57 F. 3d 350, 356-58 (3d Cir. 1995); *Corporate Health Ins., Inc. v. Tex. Dept. of Ins.*, 215 F. 3d 526, 534-35 (5th Cir. 2000), *vacated on other grounds sub nom. Montemayor v. Corporate Health Ins.*, 122 S.Ct. 2617 (2002); *Pacificare of Okla. Inc. v. Burrage*, 59 F. 3d 151, 153-55 (10th Cir. 1995).
85. *Bui*, 310 F. 3d at 1147.
86. *Id.* at 1148.
87. *Id.*
88. *Id.* at 1148-49.
89. *Id.* at 1149.
90. *Id.*
91. *Id.* at 1150. *See also Roach v. Mail Handlers Benefit Plan*, 298 F. 3d 847 (9th Cir. 2002).
92. *Bui*, 310 F. 3d at 1150.
93. *Id.*
94. *Id.*
95. *Id.* at 1150-51.
96. *Id.* at 1150.
97. *Id.*
98. *Id.*
99. *Id.*
100. *Id.* at 1150 n.27.
101. *Id.* at 1151.
102. *Id.*
103. *Id.*
104. *Id.*
105. *Id.* at 1152.
106. *Id.*
107. *Id.*
108. *Id.* at 1152-53.
109. *Id.* at 1153. *See, e.g., Corporate Health*, 215 F. 3d at 534 (stating that, when wearing "their hats as medical care providers," managed care providers are subject to state law claims for malpractice).
110. *Bui*, 310 F. 3d at 1153.
111. 333 Ill. App. 3d 1011, 777 N.E. 2d 396 (2002).
112. 322 F. 3d 316 (4th Cir. Mar. 14, 2003).
113. *Id.* at 324.
114. 123 S.Ct. 1471 (Apr. 2, 2003).
115. *Supra*, note 24.
116. *See, e.g.*, that portion of President Bush's State of the Union Address delivered on January 28, 2003, concerning improvements to the health care system. He stated, in pertinent part, "Instead, we must work toward a system in which all Americans have a good insurance policy, choose their own doctors, and seniors and low-income Americans receive the help they need. Instead of bureaucrats and trial lawyers and HMOs, we must put doctors and nurses and patients back in charge of American medicine" and . . . "To improve our health care system, we must address one of the prime causes of higher cost, the constant threat that physicians and hospitals will be unfairly sued. Because of excessive litigation, everybody pays more for health care, and many parts of America are losing fine doctors. No one has ever been healed by a frivolous lawsuit. I urge the Congress to pass medical liability reform." See http://www.whitehouse.gov/news/releases/2003/01/print/20030128 –21.html. *See also* H.R.5, the House version of a medical malpractice reform bill that passed the House in 2003 and which contained provisions pertaining to managed care organization liability. The counterpart in the Senate to H.R.5 was S.11.

The Honorable Charlie Norwood (R-Ga.) introduced legislation early in the 108th Congress to preclude preemption by ERISA of state causes of action based on the existence or extent of coverage of any coverage of any item or service under a health plan to the extent that the administration is of whether or not the item or service is medically necessary or appropriate as a treatment recommendation. This bill is known as the ERISA Clarification Act of 2003. Its status remained unclear as of submission of this chapter for publication.

Medical Product Liability

MICHAEL S. LEHV, M.D., J.D., F.C.L.M.

INDUSTRY BACKGROUND
LIABILITIES AND DEFENSES
SPECIAL ISSUES

Liability for medical products (medical devices and pharmaceuticals) is governed by the concepts of strict liability that eliminate the need to prove negligence for an injury caused by a defective product.[1] However, policy interests have shaped the unique nature of medical products case law to provide multiple exceptions to the standard rules of strict liability. Some of the exceptions favor plaintiffs.[2] In such cases manufacturer liability is easier to prove and is often decided with minimal evidence.[3] Other exceptions favor the defendants in such litigation. The most notable exception is comment k to Section 402A of the Restatement (Second) of Torts.[4,5] Comment k distinguishes some pharmaceuticals from most other manufactured products by stating that the manufacturer is not held liable for injury resulting from consumption of drugs that are seen as unavoidably unsafe. Use of these drugs is justified in spite of the apparent medical risks. Certain products are unavoidably dangerous and are incapable of being made safe when manufactured properly. Currently, a majority of courts agree with the Restatement's view and find some drugs dangerous by nature, but it is unclear which drugs are unavoidably unsafe.[6]

While comment k's text and lone example seem to focus on drugs, Section 402A concerns "any product" and the comment actually pertains to "unavoidably unsafe products." Thus, the legal treatment of medical devices is generally similar to that of drugs, although there are regulatory differences. This chapter will use the term "medical products" to encompass both medical devices such as pacemakers and surgical instruments, and pharmaceuticals, including drugs and vaccines.

The courts treat medical products differently than other manufactured products. One reason for this different treatment is the interaction between the patient's body and the drug or device. When a drug is ingested or a device is implanted, the response of an individual patient is difficult to predict. Every effect and each adverse reaction is unique. Frequently the response depends more on the individual's

physiology than on the product design. Therefore a safely designed medical product for every situation or every individual may be illusory. Some commentators[7] and the Restatement (Third) of Torts: Products Liability[8] (Restatement (Third)) consider the medical products industry sufficiently unique to be categorized separately from all other forms of product liability. Others believe the manufacturers should be held to the same form of strict liability as other industries.[9] Still others contend that the companies should be strictly liable for their products but define the role of liability differently, usually holding manufacturers to a lesser standard.[10]

INDUSTRY BACKGROUND

Pharmaceuticals

The drug industry in America has changed dramatically since the 1930s and 1940s. Early pharmaceutical companies generally produced a complete line of medication to serve pharmacists' needs.[11] These companies spent little money on research, development, and advertising. Customarily the basic drug ingredients constituted 75% of corporate expenditures.[12]

The impetus for change was the increasing efficacy of drugs.[13] In the early part of the century, even with hundreds of compounds on the market, few "cures" could be credited to pharmaceuticals.[14] Most drugs sold were used for supportive care and did little to affect the course of illness directly. However, by the late 1940s and early 1950s drugs took the offensive against disease.[15] Penicillin and other broad-spectrum antibiotics heralded a new age in which medicine could directly attack foreign cells without harming the host. Because most drugs are effective against only one or two conditions, hundreds of drugs are sold. In the United States, thousands of physiologically active compounds are available.[16] These compounds in turn are mixed with other compounds that produce hundreds of thousands of products.[17]

Adverse reactions are unwanted interactions between a drug and a recipient's physiology. Multiple forms of adverse reactions are possible with any drug. Hypersensitivity or allergic reactions, drug interactions, excessive amounts of the desired effect, unavoidable side effects, and activation of physical illness are a few of the adverse reactions possible. Wherever possible, a manufacturer should seek to discover and eliminate these unwanted side effects. Adverse reactions to drugs remain one of the major causes of hospitalization, illness, and death in the nation. Some authors believe that more than 140,000 deaths per year are caused by adverse drug reactions in the United States.[18] As might be expected, that is highly beneficial to millions of patients may be deadly to a few. Most commentators agree that a prescription drug should not be considered defective simply because an unusually sensitive user develops an adverse reaction.[19]

Medical devices

Prior to the mid-twentieth century, medical devices consisted mostly of relatively simple mechanical surgical instruments. There were but a few implants such as metal or plastic plates used for cranial reconstruction and these were usually fabricated intraoperatively by the surgeon from raw materials. Manufacturers' liability generally resulted from the inopportune breakage of a surgical instrument.

In the last 50 years, the routine surgical implantation of synthetic materials has been made feasible by the development of antibiotics and advanced techniques of surgical asepsis. Parallel with these advances, manufacturers have become capable of fashioning and packaging a wide array of implantable devices from an ever-increasing variety of metals and plastics. With the appearance of pacemakers, joint implants, heart valves, and breast implants, medical device liability has become a major issue for manufacturers. Not only do these devices need to function as contemplated, but they must do so over the entire life of the patient. The latter requirement has led to a number of unexpected long-term device failures such as broken pacemaker leads, failing cardiac valves, disintegrating joint implants, and leaking breast implants. No longer are manufacturers just liable for simple manufacturing defects, but they are now additionally responsible for latent defects both in the device materials and in device design. Liability also accrues for manufacturers' failure to warn of known, unknown, and intentionally undisclosed device defects.

As in the case of pharmaceuticals, many of these devices perform life-saving functions and/or greatly enhance the quality of life of their recipients. As such, removal from the market is undesirable. Thus, medical devices are usually designated along with drugs as "unavoidably unsafe" in qualifying for Section 402A, comment k's exception to strict liability.

LIABILITIES AND DEFENSES
Overview

Most courts categorize rules of liability that apply to medical products differently than rules for other products. Some courts have held that the rules of strict liability should not apply,[20] other courts apply a limited form of strict liability with less stringent rules, while still others do not differentiate between medical and other manufactured products.[21]

The Restatement (Second) of Torts, Section 402A, comment k, describes some drugs as "incapable of being made safe." For example, "the vaccine for the Pasteur treatment of rabies" often "leads to very serious and damaging consequences when it is injected." Such a drug is "properly prepared, and accompanied by proper directions and warning, is not defective, nor is it unreasonably dangerous."[22] Comment k does not seek to prevent all suits against drug manufacturers. Although it protects drug manufacturers against liability for design defects, it does not immunize them against suits for manufacturing defects or inadequate warnings.

Multiple policy considerations are behind the adoption of strict liability in torts. Some of these considerations include compensation or spreading of the loss between all consumers of a product, deterrence, encouraging useful conduct by both parties to an action, protecting consumer expectations, and improving the allocation of resources.[23] Multiple approaches have been used by the courts in the development of the concept of defectiveness. One approach is the consumer expectation test, which weighs whether a product is unreasonably dangerous beyond the danger contemplated by the ordinary consumer.[24] This test has fallen from favor in a majority of courts because it relies on the term *unreasonable* as a requirement of defectiveness. Reasonableness is a negligence concept.[25] If a danger generally is known to the ordinary consumer, the product is not per se defective.[26]

Another approach is the risk/utility test,[27] which balances the risk of danger associated with a product and the utility of the product to the consumer. This test is the approach used most often to determine defectiveness.[28] The emphasis is on the safety of the product rather than the reasonable or unreasonable action of the manufacturer. Some of the factors considered in a risk/utility analysis include the severity of the risk, the likelihood of harm, the benefits of the product, and the feasibility of an alternative design.[29] Once a product is determined to be dangerous, the court must then balance the product's utility against its dangers. Many courts refuse to classify a drug as unreasonably dangerous if the drug or device's utility to mankind is considered greater than the potential for injury to an individual.[30] Lastly, some jurisdictions offer an alternative test that uses a bifurcated standard—either consumer expectation or risk/utility.[31] Use of the disjunctive expands recovery potential for plaintiffs.

In 1988, the California Supreme Court in considering a DES[32] case, *Brown v. Superior Court*,[33] analyzed many of these approaches and arrived at what it considered to be the consensus view for prescription drug liability. That view is that drug manufacturers are not strictly liable for injuries caused by their products so long as the drug was "properly prepared" and accompanied by appropriate warnings that were "either known or reasonably scientifically knowable."[34]

Types of defects

Overview. A variety of possible defects might affect a medical product. First, a manufacturing defect might cause one "batch" of the product to deviate from the norm. This might include a faulty casting of a surgical instrument or a contaminated lot of vaccine. Second, a design defect, such as an intrinsic flaw in the chemical or mechanical design, could exist. For example, serrations on a surgical instrument designed for handling nerves might damage nerves, or a vaccine could cause a high incidence of liver damage. Lastly, where the manufacturer knows of dangers associated with the normal use of the product, a warning is required. "A product sold without such warning is in a defective condition."[35] Thus, the instrument manufacturer may be required to warn of its use on small nerves, or the vaccine manufacturer be required to warn of its use in those with previous liver disease.

Manufacturing defects. Manufacturing defects are those that deviate from the manufacturer's design or specifications and thus are different than the usual product that "comes off the assembly line."[36] Manufacturing defects typically are easy to identify because the products are flawed. Even though the cause of the manufacturing defect usually is negligence, difficulty in proof mandates a strict liability standard, without regard to the manufacturer's reasonableness in protecting its process from error. The consumer expectation test is used because the consumer expects a product to be free of defects.

Design defects. Whereas a manufacturing defect involves an isolated deviation from the norm, a design defect involves the entire line of products. Such a product is manufactured according to specifications but remains unreasonably dangerous for its intended use.[37] Difficulty in determining a design defect situation arises when the courts attempt to define "reasonable danger."[38]

If a design is defective, all of the products manufactured using that design are defective. The evaluation of design defect by the jury is based on a four-prong test involving (1) feasibility of an alternative design (2) which at the time of manufacture was (3) commercially available and (4) would not destroy the product's productivity.[39] Some courts hold that the "FDA's decision of product marketability disposes of the defect issue."[40] These courts conclude that, if the FDA approves a product, "the product must be considered unavoidably unsafe as a matter of law and thus outside the parameters of strict liability for defective design."

Failure to warn of known adverse reactions. Pharmaceutical manufacturers are required to warn adequately of known dangers in the administration of their product.[41]

Unknown adverse reactions. Perhaps more serious than known side effects are those that remain undiscovered until an adverse reaction occurs in the ultimate consumer. Although no national consensus exists, some courts consider an undiscovered side effect a defect and impose the same strict liability as with other defects.[42] Others look to comment k of Section 402A and insulate medical products from standard product liability.[43]

Causation

As in negligence actions, causation must be proved in strict tort liability. Professor Prosser states that "[s]trict liability eliminates both privity and negligence; but it still does not prove the plaintiff's case."[44] The standard elements of proof, as enumerated in Section 402A of the Restatement (Second) of Torts, are (1) proof that the product was defective, (2) proof that the defect existed at the time it left the control of the defendant, (3) proof that the defect created a product that was unreasonably dangerous for the intended or foreseeable use, and (4) proof that the defect caused the injury.[45] Within the pharmaceutical industry, causation is most commonly proved through epidemiological and statistical studies, expert testimony, direct or circumstantial evidence, or a combination of these methods.[46]

In situations in which the plaintiff is unable to identify the defective product's specific manufacturer, an industry-wide liability has been devised.[47] Liability may be imposed on every manufacturer of a generic product. It is then the responsibility of the various defendants to prove that they did not supply the defective product.[48]

On the other hand, a design defect is easier to prove because all of the same types of drugs are equally defective and available for testing. In a failure-to-warn case the plaintiff must prove that lack of proper warning was the proximate cause of the injury. The failure to warn must be the direct link between the product and the injury. The plaintiff must further show that the manufacturer either knew or should have known about the danger of harm from the drug.[49] Defendant liability may be severed by the introduction of an intervening cause. In strict liability litigation, courts are willing to view intervening causes as unforeseeable.[50]

Most courts view the terms *user* and *consumer* liberally. Historically, privity was required before permitting recovery. Today, the end user may be far removed from the initial privity of contract.[51] If it is foreseeable that an individual will be a user, that individual is a potential plaintiff.[52] If, for example, the patient were to ingest multiple drugs, each drug might be viewed as a cause-in-fact of the subsequent harm. At least one court has held a manufacturer of one defective drug liable for the entire injury sustained by the ingestion of multiple drugs.[53]

The foreseeability of the harm caused by a product is an issue in many courts.[54] Some courts now reject the foreseeability of harm approach and instead examine the foreseeability of use.[55]

Damages

Similar to negligence litigation, strict liability provides for property and personal damage recovery.[56] With both negligence and strict liability, damage is part of a prima facie case.[57] Commentators differ in their views regarding punitive damage awards in strict liability litigation. Some assert that punitive damage awards should be granted as punishment for wanton, willful, reckless, malicious, or outrageous conduct.[58] Other jurisdictions grant punitive damage awards to deter others who might commit the same outrageous conduct.[59] Most jurisdictions use punitive damages for any combination of the preceding reasons.[60]

Punitive damage awards are common in strict liability litigation involving pharmaceutical products.[61] The plaintiff has the burden of proving the defendant's outrageous conduct by presenting clear and convincing evidence.[62] Punitive damage awards punish inappropriate manufacturing practices and deter product suppliers from making economic decisions but do not remedy the product's defects.[63] The most common type of drug cases in which punitive damages are granted are those in which the manufacturer had knowledge of adverse reactions but failed to properly warn of the danger.[64]

Defenses

Assumption of risk. The Restatement (Second) of Torts describes assumption of the risk as "the form of contributory negligence which consists of voluntary and unreasonable encounter of a known danger."[65] If the consumer knew of the product's defect but disregarded the danger and used the product, he or she is barred from seeking to recover against the defendant. The defendant must prove that the plaintiff knew and understood the danger and "voluntarily and unreasonably" consented to being exposed to it.[66]

Assumption of the risk is an essential concept in pharmaceutical litigation defense. If adequate warning is given to the physician and the physician disregards these dangers, then the physician and patient have assumed some of the risk for potential adverse reactions.

Comparative fault. Comparative fault measures the plaintiff's fault in comparison to the manufacturer's fault and places a percentage value on each. Most states with comparative negligence systems have applied a comparative fault scheme to strict tort liability litigation.[67] In a pure comparative fault system a plaintiff may recover the percentage of damage caused by the defendant, regardless of the fault attributable to the plaintiff.[68]

A goal of strict tort liability is to avoid making the manufacturer an insurer for product-induced injuries. Comparative fault provides more equity in allocating risks and preventing manufacturers and innocent consumers from sharing in the costs attributable to those who fail to use products carefully. Most courts that have permitted a comparative fault defense also have permitted defenses of assumption of the risk and misuse.[69] The jury usually is instructed to combine the percentage from each of these defenses and award the percentage of fault as the sum of the three.[70]

Product misuse. The product misuse defense is permissible when the plaintiff has used a product for a purpose not reasonably foreseeable to the manufacturer.[71] The Restatement (Second) of Torts recognizes the defense of product misuse. Comment h of Section 402A provides that "if the injury results from abnormal handling, . . . the seller is not liable."[72] Product misuse arises when the plaintiff's misuse of the product was a contributing cause of the injury.[73] To assert this defense, the plaintiff's misuse of the product must be unforeseeable. The definition of the term *unforeseeable* is the important issue. Taking four times the standard dose of a medication may be foreseeable but taking five times may be unforeseeable. There is no standard, fixed, arbitrary cutoff. The fact-finder must determine foreseeability on a case-by-case basis.

Blood and device shield statutes. Section 402A makes clear that any seller of a defective product, even a mere "retailer," is strictly liable. This holds true even if the seller in not "engaged solely" in selling. Statutes have been passed in most states to protect hospitals and other health care providers from liability for unknowingly "selling" defective blood products to patients.[74] These so-called "blood shield" laws posit that in providing blood to patients for a charge, hospitals and blood banks are not "selling" but rather providing a service.[75] These laws do not apply to manufacturers of defective blood products that have been prepared from whole blood collected from multiple donors.[76]

The concept of protecting health care providers from sellers' liability has been expanded to include protection for those providers supplying breast implants[77] and, more commonly, orthopedic implants.[78]

Learned intermediary. As discussed below under Warnings, a prescription drug or device manufacturer's duty to warn is usually satisfied by providing information to the physician rather than the patient. Provision of warnings to this "learned intermediary" is an adequate defense to failure-to-warn claims regardless of whether the physician has actually heeded them in his or her prescription or otherwise passed them on to the patient. Exceptions may exist where the product is usually prescribed on a commodity basis, such as with birth control pills[79] or contraceptive devices,[80] and vaccines.[81] The defense may also not be available in cases where prescription drugs are marketed directly to consumers, such as nicotine patches,[82] or in cases in which the drug's usage has been promoted for an off-label indication.[83]

Federal preemption of state law tort claims. Both the pharmaceutical and medical device industries are subject to intense federal regulation by the FDA. Chapter 15 of this volume provides a general discussion of these regulations, but we are here concerned with their utility in the defense of medical product tort claims. First, by maintaining full regulatory compliance, manufacturers may claim to have produced a product that is, as a matter of law, free of design defects and provides adequate warnings.[84] Second, manufacturers frequently defend state law liability actions by claiming federal preemption under the Food, Drug, and Cosmetic Act of 1938[85] (FDCA) and Medical Device Amendments[86] (MDA) to the FDCA. In practice, these two defenses are often merged under the general label of preemption.

MEDICAL DEVICES. The currently controlling decision on federal preemption of medical device claims is *Medtronic Inc. v. Lohr*, handed down by a sharply divided U.S. Supreme Court in June 1996.[87] Lohr filed suit in Florida state court against Medtronic based on the failure of a pacemaker lead. The case was removed to federal court, where the district court granted Medtronic's summary judgment on the grounds that Lohr's claims were preempted by the MDA.

Under *Lohr*, a determination must first be made as to whether the device underwent full FDA review either with a pre-MDA "new drug application" (NDA) or a modern day "pre-market approval" (PMA) versus simple approval under MDA Section 510(k). The latter is granted to devices that are "substantially equivalent" to other devices already on the market and does not subject the device to a detailed review of safety and effectiveness. When the device has been subjected to a PMA-equivalent process, state law tort claims that would require a design or warnings inconsistent with those approved by the FDA are preempted under MDA Section 360(k). Those devices marketed under a 510(k) process, as was the pacemaker in *Lohr*, may be subject to state warning requirements. For the most part, both federal and state courts have followed this interpretation of *Lohr* for both design[88] and warning[89] defects, although there have been exceptions.[90]

PHARMACEUTICALS. Although the FDA regulation of the content of pharmaceutical warnings is exercised at the same word-for-word level of scrutiny as for PMA devices, there is no equivalent 360(k) federal preemption for drugs.[91] Thus, virtually all courts consider the FDA-mandated pharmaceutical warnings to be minimal standards, permitting state law failure-to-warn actions to proceed.[92] This situation persists despite the fact that it would be difficult for manufacturers to maintain different labels for different jurisdictions or to predict what warnings would immunize it from every conceivable state jurisdiction failure-to-warn claim.[93] Defects in the design or formulation of drugs similarly lack any federal preemptive protection.[94]

SPECIAL ISSUES
Warnings

Duty to warn. Products that are both properly designed and correctly manufactured may still be dangerous and will be considered defective if not accompanied by proper warnings.[95] The supplier of any product, including the manufacturer of pharmaceuticals, is under a duty to use reasonable care to adequately warn of the risks associated with the use of its product.[96] This duty extends to the risks about which the manufacturer knows and to those about which, through reasonable care, it should have known.[97]

The duty of a pharmaceutical manufacturer to warn arises when the product is known to cause a particular side effect. The manufacturer is not responsible for unforeseeable or unknown dangers it is unable to discover with reasonable care.[98] Nor is the company a guarantor of the safety of a product that causes an unusual hypersensitivity reaction if that reaction was not a known side effect of the product.[99]

The "unavoidably dangerous" protection afforded prescription medical products under the Restatement (Second) of Torts, Section 402A, comment k, applies unless the manufacturer has provided an adequate warning of potential adverse reactions.[100] The protection does not extend to those manufacturers who have failed to follow FDA guidelines for testing and marketing of their product.[101]

Drugs and medical devices are an exception to the rule requiring a warning of danger to the ultimate consumer.[102] The drug manufacturer's duty to warn includes a warning to physicians of the special risks that accompany normal use.[103] In the majority of cases there is no duty to warn the patient directly.[104] In the case of pharmaceutical warnings the physician is considered the "learned intermediary," and as such, in most instances the duty to warn ends when an adequate effort is made by the company to instruct physicians of the drug's potential side effects.[105,106] The pharmaceutical manufacturer has no obligation to warn the ultimate user of danger propensities "where there is an intermediary who is not a mere conduit of the product, but rather administers it on an individual basis."[107] After the manufacturer has given the physician the necessary information, it is then the physician's duty to warn the patient.[108]

The manufacturer's duty to warn does not end with the purchase of the drug by the patient. Postsale warnings also are required. The manufacturer is considered an expert with regard to its product.[109] As an expert, the manufacturer has the duty to stay abreast of new scientific information in the field and the further duty to warn physicians of newly discovered hazards caused by the product.[110]

If an unknown hazard is discovered after the drug has reached the end user, the manufacturer is required to make reasonable efforts to inform the consumer.[111] This requirement usually is satisfied with warnings to physicians in the form of "Dear Doctor" letters or via detail persons. One court has stated that "[a]lthough a product may be reasonably safe when manufactured . . . risks thereafter revealed by user operation and brought to the attention of the manufacturer or vendor may impose upon one or both a duty to warn."[112,113]

The manufacturer is responsible for performing studies of its product when adverse reactions are reported. The results of these studies, if adverse to the product, must be reported to the public (i.e., physicians).[114] This duty to report new adverse findings extends to more than the research of the manufacturer and includes all industry knowledge (i.e., the state of the art). Constructive knowledge of potential side effects is presumed with the publication of articles in scientific journals that relate to the product.[115]

Although the duty of drug manufacturers to provide warnings usually extends only to the physician, in cases in which the manufacturer knows that the product will reach the public without individualized medical intervention the drug manufacturer also must warn the public at large.[116,117] An example is immunizations; everyone is administered a standardized dose of the vaccine without individualized dosing by the physician.[118] Likewise, birth control pills are often prescribed without much individual attention. Therefore no protection exists for the drug manufacturer under the learned intermediary rule in situations in which the producer had actual or constructive knowledge of the potential for the public to acquire the product without significant physician intervention.[119]

Adequacy of warning. The adequacy of the warning is a major issue in determining reasonableness. If the warning is adequate, the defendant drug producer will usually prevail, even if the product is unavoidably unsafe.[120] The warning is adequate when it is obviously displayed, when it gives a fair appraisal of the extent of the danger, and when it properly instructs the user in how to use the product.[121] Likewise, a warning is adequate when it "warns with the degree of intensity demanded by the nature of the risk."[122] A warning, however, may be inadequate if it is "unduly delayed, reluctant in tone or lacking in a sense of urgency."[123]

Even if an adequate warning of the risk is given, it will not insulate the manufacturer from liability when the defect could have been cured with little effort. Moreover, statements that lead the user to minimize the importance of the warning may diminish the value of an adequate warning. For example, one manufacturer's warning concerning birth control pills contained studies showing an increased incidence of thrombosis in British women taking the pill. The court held that having a study dealing with British women did little to amplify concern of thrombosis in American women and therefore did not adequately warn this group.[124]

In addition, most courts require warnings to be given if an allergic reaction may affect a substantial number of people.[125] Some courts have imposed a duty to warn of rare adverse reactions if the end result would be exceedingly serious.[126] The Restatement (Second) of Torts states that "[w]here . . . the product contains an ingredient to which a substantial number of the population are allergic . . . the seller is required to give warning . . . and a product bearing such a warning, which is safe for use if it is followed, is not in defective condition, nor is it unreasonably dangerous."[127]

In 1993 the California Supreme Court held in *Anderson v. Owens-Corning Fiberglass* that a manufacturer was strictly liable for injuries caused by its failure to warn of dangers known to the scientific community at the time the product was manufactured and distributed.[128] In 1996 the same court held in *Carlin v. Sutter County Superior Ct.* that prescription drug manufacturers may be strictly liable under state law for failure to warn, so long as the risk of injury is either actually known or scientifically ascertainable at the time of the drug's distribution.[129] In 1996 in *Wagner v. Roche Laboratories* the Ohio Supreme Court held that expert testimony that a drug manufacturer knew or should have known of the synergistic side effects of its drug and certain antibiotics was specific enough and of sufficient probative value to create under state product liability law a question of fact as to the adequacy of warnings contained in an FDA-approved package insert.[130]

Methods of warning. Warnings may be satisfied in a number of ways. Labeling, package inserts, advertising, and interaction with drug company detail persons all may act as adequate warnings to decrease liability.

LABELING. The FDA has numerous requirements for the labeling of pharmaceuticals.[131] These are minimum requirements only and do not relieve the manufacturer of its duty to fully warn of dangers of which it has actual or constructive knowledge.[132] The basic labeling rule as promulgated by the FDA is that all material facts relating to the drug are to be presented on the package.[133]

PACKAGE INSERTS. The package insert is the method developed by the FDA for instructing physicians and patients about the makeup, side effects, indications, and dosing of a product.[134] The most important feature of the package insert is the requirement that the information contained therein be completely based on substantial evidence. No "hype" or promotion is permitted to be included. Because physicians have almost unlimited access to drug information through a variety of sources, the package insert is not intended to be the most current repository of information concerning the benefits of a drug. Instead, its purpose is to inform the physician of any substantial evidence relating to the drug's benefits or side effects.

The package insert contains information based on data submitted to the FDA by the manufacturer dealing with the safety and efficacy of the drug.[135] A physician is not required to follow the instructions on the package insert. However, if the physician chooses not to follow the instructions, he or she should be concerned about increased liability.[136] This fear leads many physicians to practice "cookbook medicine" (i.e., following the product insert instructions implicitly without regard to the patient's individual reactions). In general, however, most physicians do not dispense drugs; thus they do not see the product inserts, which can be problematic. Likewise, although pharmacists have access to inserts, they usually rely on computer-provided details for the majority of their product information.

Some courts construe a manufacturer's failure to comply with rules requiring package inserts as constituting negligence per se.[137] Other courts have held that failure to follow statutory regulation concerning inserts is not a controlling issue.[138]

ADVERTISING. The emphasis on product promotion is one of the more controversial activities of the pharmaceutical industry. Manufacturers spend more than one fourth of their gross income from drug sales on marketing.[139] The majority of this money is spent on advertising and the use of detail persons. The Pharmaceutical Manufacturers Association, realizing the importance of this issue, has promulgated the Code of Fair Practices in the Promotion of Drug Products. But, as with many such professional ethical codes, the written word is often overlooked for an improved bottom line.

For most prescribing physicians, drug manufacturers are the dominant, if not the only source of information regarding drug risks and benefits. Other independent sources of information, such as medical journals, may be reluctant to publish research that is critical of drug manufacturers' products because drug advertising accounts for the largest share of medical journals' revenue.[140]

Courts have held drug manufacturers liable for advertisements that dilute proper warnings or reduce the physician's reliance on the package insert.[141] Furthermore, a company incurs liability if it causes a prescribing physician to disregard the warnings mandated by the FDA.[142] Some courts have also held the manufacturer liable, even when the physician acted in a negligent manner, if the physician's actions were induced through overpromotion.[143]

Drug manufacturers may be held to a warranty standard based on their advertising. They rarely expose themselves to liability by expressly warranting their products.[144] Instead, exposure to breach of warranty liability most often arises through implied warranty and misrepresentation.

DETAIL PERSONS. Detail persons are the sales representatives for ethical drugs and occupy a position different from those of other salespersons. Their potential misrepresentation of the product, rather than being harmless fluff, may lead to death or illness of the ultimate consumer. Detail persons, acting as the liaison between physicians and the manufacturer, are the most common transmitters of new information concerning pharmaceuticals. The pharmaceutical industry employs almost 40,000 detail persons.[145]

Detail persons are frequently torn between a desire to increase the profits of the drug manufacturer and a duty to inform the physician of the product's side effects and possible contraindications.[146] There is great potential for detail persons to mislead physicians in an attempt to increase sales. Manufacturers are vicariously liable for the actions of their detail persons who are acting within the scope of their employment.[147] Some courts have held that the liability extends even beyond the scope of employment.[148] An otherwise adequate warning provided by the company can be nullified by an overzealous detail person. High-pressure sales by intense, occasionally knowledgeable detail persons often determine physician use patterns. Even though the oral communications of detail persons are difficult to monitor as to completeness or accuracy, drug companies cannot escape liability for the improper overpromotion of a product by detail persons.

If a detail person convinces the physician to disregard warnings provided by the manufacturer, the company may be held liable should an injury ensue.[149] At least one court has held that detail persons have a duty to warn of potential adverse reactions.[150] Liability is possible because the physician might otherwise have been aware of the risks that were involved had the detail person given adequate warnings.[151]

Government intervention

Occasionally the government accepts responsibility for drug defects. In 1976 the U.S. government statutorily accepted liability for any adverse reactions to the swine flu immunization.[152] The government took the position of the manufacturer for the purpose of liability.[153] This legislation was repealed in 1978.[154] A similar program of "no-fault compensation" was created by the National Childhood Vaccine Injury Act.[155] This legislation has a dual purpose. First, it allows easier access to compensation for those children who have suffered hypersensitivity reactions to vaccines.[156] Second, it provides liability protection for manufacturers of a vaccine, allowing them to continue their production.[157]

Physician and pharmacist liability

Many physicians and pharmacists are not fully informed of the potential side effects associated with the drugs they prescribe. One study revealed that less than 13% of drug use was evaluated as rational, 21.5% was considered questionable, and amazingly, more than 65% was judged irrational.[158] Because of the prevalence of drug use in the treatment of disease, many malpractice cases have pharmaceutical components.

The application of traditional liability rules to pharmaceutical manufacturers is problematic. For example, the defined consumer of prescription drugs is the physician, not the patient. The patient has little input into the drug selected by the physician. The physician holds a position as the "learned intermediary" and as such, takes on some of the manufacturer's liability even in the case of a product defect.[159]

Physicians and pharmacists who find themselves targeted in a suit resulting from a defective product have some recourse.[160] There is a potential tort action against the manufacturers of the defective product both for the injury to the patient and for damage to reputation and earnings.[161] In many circumstances this action leads to plaintiffs playing one potential defendant against another.[162]

Mass tort litigation

Overview. Mass tort litigation is a term denoting the legal circumstance in which a product is alleged to have actually caused, or to have the potential to cause, future injury to a large number of individuals. Typically, multiple legal actions are filed in both state and federal courts which may eventually result in formal class certification at either the state or federal level.[163] Because of the often serious nature of these injuries and the widespread use of prescription drugs and medical devices, pharmaceutical and medical device manufacturers are frequent targets of mass tort litigation. Even a casual awareness of legal events will bring to mind litigation surrounding Bendectin, breast implants, the Dalkon Shield contraceptive device, DES, HIV-contaminated blood products, penile implants, defective pacemaker leads, defective heart valves, and the FenPhen diet drugs. Numerous other medical products have been the subjects of such litigation with less publicity. The majority of these cases have arisen in the past 15 years.[164]

It is beyond the scope of this chapter to discuss the complexities of class actions as they relate to medical product liability. Perhaps the best-known example of these cases, the breast implant litigation, is summarized below. Mass tort litigation has drawn the frequent attention of legal commentators and scholars. Several recent citations are provided for the interested reader.[165]

Silicone breast implants. In 1997 Dr. Jack Snyder published an exhaustive law review article on the subject of silicone breast implants in which he noted that breast implant litigation had reshaped the concept of compensable "soft tissue injury" in the 1990s.[166] Snyder noted that between 1977 and 1992 breast implant product liability cases were primarily resolved on evidentiary or procedural grounds. Plaintiffs alleged negligence, strict liability, fraudulent misrepresentation, and breach of express and implied warranty. His analysis of past, present, and future breast implant lawsuits included the potential defendants, causes of action and defenses, causation hurdle, case management (including the traditional case-by-case method), consolidation, bifurcation, multidistrict litigation, class actions, dormant dockets, future injuries, and federal-state coordination.

In 1988 the FDA reclassified breast implants in the category of the most strictly regulated medical products.[167] In 1991 the FDA learned that Dow Corning Corporation had not disclosed evidence suggesting it had safety concerns about breast implants. In 1993 the commissioner of the FDA, D. David Kessler, announced that the availability of silicone breast implants would be severely limited. What followed was a flood of litigation resulting in billions of dollars in judgments and settlements. The breast implant cases are cited, reviewed, and superbly discussed by Snyder.

Restatement (Third) of Torts: Products Liability

It is rare to find a medical products liability case that does not at some point reference section 402A of the venerable 1965 Restatement (Second) of Torts.[168] Nonetheless, in 1998, the Restatement (Third) of Torts: Products Liability[169] was published by the American Law Institute. This Restatement differs considerably from its predecessor in its treatment of medical products liability. To date, no published medical products liability case has been decided on the basis of the Restatement (Third)[170] and only two references to it have appeared.[171] One can reasonably expect, however, that with time, various states will either codify, or accept through case law, the new rule. On the other hand, given this Restatement's significant divergence from its predecessor, some jurisdictions are likely to decline its adoption.

Section 2b of Restatement (Third) initially provides that all products are defective in design "when the foreseeable risks of harm posed by the product could have been reduced or avoided by the adoption of a reasonable alternative design. . . ."[172] This language replaces the strict liability approach of the Restatement (Second) with a negligence concept. In addition, Section 6,[173] is specifically devoted to "Defective Prescription Drugs and Medical Devices" and departs from Section 2's alternative design approach to design defects. Section 6c states:

A prescription drug or medical device is not reasonably safe due to defective design if the foreseeable risks of harm posed by the drug or medical device are sufficiently great in relation to its foreseeable therapeutic benefits that reasonable health-care providers, knowing of such foreseeable risks and therapeutic benefits, would not prescribe the drug or medical device for any class of patients.[174]

This definition does away entirely with patient expectations[175] as to the safety or efficacy of a drug or medical device, placing those determinations entirely in the presumably more objective views of the "reasonable health-care provider." At first blush, this definition would seem to greatly ease the burden for a manufacturer defending a defective design claim. How the various states will treat the new Restatement's retreat from strict liability and its physician-judged design defect standard remains to be seen.

The public should be free to purchase goods without fear of defect. Strict tort liability has been a valid means to ensure that products function without causing injury. On the other hand, it is unreasonable to expect all products to be totally safe and risk-free for consumers. A knife with a dull blade might be safer than one with a sharp blade, but part of the sharp knife's efficacy is due to the cause of its dangerous propensity, namely, its sharpened edge. Ice cream would be safer without the heavy cholesterol content, but the joy of eating it comes from its richness, which clogs our arteries. Medication and medical devices are unique because they are used with the knowledge that despite their enormous benefits, in a certain number of individuals there will be serious side effects. Restatement (Third): Products Liability appears to be an acknowledgment of that fact.

ENDNOTES

1. *Greenman v. Yuba Power Prod.*, 59 Cal. 2d 57, 377 P. 2d 897, 27 Cal. Rptr. 697 (1963); Restatement (Second) of Torts §402A(1) (1965).
2. *See* Comment, *DES and a Proposed Theory of Enterprise Liability*, 46 Fordham L. Rev. 963 (1978).
3. *See Wells v. Ortho Pharmaceutical Corp.*, 788 F. 2d 741 (11th Cir. 1986), *cert. denied*, 479 U.S. 950 (1986).
4. Restatement (Second) of Torts §402A, comment k (1965).
5. At the time this chapter was written (December, 2002), no published state or federal medical product liability case had been decided on the basis of the Restatement (Third) of Torts: Products Liability (1998). Therefore, Restatement (Second) of Torts (1965) continues to be cited and discussed as the sole controlling authority. *See* discussion of Restatement (Third) of Torts under Special Issues.
6. *See, e.g., McElhaney v. Eli Lilly & Co.*, 575 F.Supp. 228 (D.S.D. 1983).
7. *See, e.g.,* Scott, *Medical Product and Drug Causation: How to Prove It and Defend Against It*, 56 Def. Couns. J. 270 (1989); Leighton, *Introduction to the Symposium on Chemical and Food Product Liability*, 41 Food Drug Cosm. L. J. 385 (1986); Schwartz, *Unavoidably Unsafe Products*, 42 Wash. & Lee L. Rev. 1139 (1985).
8. Restatement (Third) of Torts: Products Liability §6(c) (1998).
9. McClellan, *Drug Induced Injury*, 25 Wayne L. Rev. 1 (1978); Maldonado, *Strict Liability and Informed Consent: "Don't Say I Didn't Tell You So,"* 9 Akron L. Rev. 609 (1976); Merrill, *Compensation for Prescription Drug Injuries*, 59 Va. L. Rev. 1 (1973); Keeton, *Product Liability: Drugs and Cosmetics*, 25 Vand. L. Rev. 131 (1972).
10. Britain, *Product Honesty Is the Best Policy: A Comparison of Doctor's and Manufacturer's Duty to Disclose Drug Risks and the Importance of Consumer Expectations in Determining Product Defect*, 79 N.W.U. L. Rev. 342 (1984); Fink, *Education in Pharmacy and Law*, 26 J. Legal Educ. 528, 538 (1974).
11. *See* Staudt, *Determining and Evaluating the Promotional Mix*, Modern Medicine Topics 8 (July 1957).
12. *See* E. Ackerknecht, *Therapeutics from the Primitives to the 20th Century* (Hafner Press, New York 1973).
13. *Id.* at 144-145.
14. *Id.* at 145.
15. *Id.* at 30.
16. U.N. Industrial Development Organization, *The Growth of the Pharmaceutical Industry in Developing Countries: Problems and Prospects*, at 23, U.N. Doc. ID/204, U.N. Sales No. E.78.II.B.4 (1978).
17. Halberstrom, *Too Many Drugs?*, F. on Med. 3 (Mar. 1979).
18. Tally & Laventurier, *Drug-Induced Illness*, 229 J.A.M.A. 1043 (1974).
19. *See, e.g.,* Restatement (Second) of Torts §402A, comment c (1965).
20. *See, e.g., Johnson v. American Cyanamid Co.*, 239 Kan. 279, 285, 718 P. 2d 1318, 1323 (1986) (quoting Restatement (Second) of Torts §402A, comment k [1965]).
21. *See, e.g., Brochu v. Ortho Pharmaceutical Corp.*, 642 F. 2d 652 (1st Cir. 1981).
22. Restatement (Second) of Torts §402A, comment k (1965).
23. D. Fisher & W. Powers Jr., *Products Liability: Cases and Materials* 50-51 (1988).
24. Restatement (Second) of Torts §402A, comment g (1965).
25. *Id.* at §395 (1965).
26. *Id.* at §402A, comment i (1965).
27. *See, e.g., Boutland of Houston, Inc. v. Bailey*, 609 S.W. 2d 743, 746 (Tex. 1980).
28. *See, e.g., Phillips v. Kimwood Mach. Co.*, 269 Or. 485, 525 P. 2d 1033 (1974); *Dosier v. Wilcox-Crittendon, Co.*, 45 Cal. App. 3d 74, 119 Cal. Rptr. 135 (1975).
29. Wade, *On the Nature of Strict Tort Liability for Products*, 44 Miss. L. J. 825, 829 (1973).
30. *See contra, supra* note 21.
31. *Barker v. Lull Engineering Co.*, 20 Cal. 3d 413, 573, P. 2d 443, 143 Cal. Rptr. 225 (1978) (permitting the use of either the consumer expectation test or the risk/utility test).
32. DES is a drug that was administered to pregnant women to prevent miscarriage. It was subsequently found to cause vaginal cancer in their daughters, an entire generation after its use.
33. *Brown v. Superior Ct.*, 751 P. 2d 470 (1988).
34. *Id.* at 482.
35. Restatement (Second) of Torts §402A, comment h (1965)
36. *Barker, supra* note 31, at 225, 241.
37. Comment, *Can a Prescription Drug Be Defectively Designed?: Brochu v. Ortho Pharmaceutical Corp.*, 31 De Paul L. Rev. 247 (1981).
38. Birnbaum, *Unmasking the Test for Design Defect: From Negligence to Strict Liability to Negligence*, 33 Vand L. Rev. 593 (1980).
39. Isaacs, *Drug Regulation, Product Liability, and the Contraceptive Crunch: Choices Are Dwindling*, 8 J. Leg. Med. 533 (1987) (strict liability and duty to warn).
40. *See, e.g., Collins v. Ortho Pharmaceutical Corp.*, 195 Cal. App. 3d 1539, 231 Cal. Rptr. 396 (1986).
41. Restatement (Second) of Torts §402A, comment j (1965)
42. *See, e.g., Brochu, supra* note 21.
43. *See, e.g., Johnson, supra* note 20.
44. Prosser, *The Fall of the Citadel (Strict Liability to the Consumer)*, 50 Minn L. Rev. 791, 840 (1966).
45. Restatement (Second) of Torts §402A (1965).
46. Middlekauff, *The Current Law Regarding Toxic Torts: Implications for the Food Industry*, 41 Food Drug Cosm. L. J. 387, 404-05 (1986).
47. Comment, *Industry Wide Liability*, 13 Suffolk U. L. Rev. 980 (1979); *Mulcahy v. Eli Lilly & Co.*, 386 N.W. 2d 67 (Iowa 1986) (DES market share liability).
48. Comment, *The Market Share Theory: Sindell's Contribution to Industry Wide Liability*, 19 Hou. L. Rev. 107 (1982).
49. Restatement (Second) of Torts §402A.
50. *See generally* D. Fischer & W. Powers Jr., *supra* note 23, at 409-411.
51. Restatement (Second) of Torts §402A, comment l (1965).
52. *Winnett v. Winnett*, 57 Ill. 2d 7, 310 N.E. 2d 1 (1974).
53. *Basko v. Sterling Drug*, 416 F. 2d 417, 426 (2d Cir. 1969).
54. *Helene Curtis Indus. v. Pruitt*, 385 F. 2d 841, 859-864 (5th Cir. 1967); *Bigbee v. Pacific Tel. & Tel. Co.*, 34 Cal. 3d 49, 665 P. 2d 947, 192 Cal. Rptr. 857 (1983).
55. *See, e.g., Baker v. International Harvester Co.*, 660 S.W. 2d 21 (Mo. Ct. App. 1983).
56. See Restatement (Second) of Torts §402A (1965).
57. *See generally* W. Prosser, *Law of Torts* §96 (4th ed. 1971).
58. *See* Restatement (Second) of Torts §908(2) (1965).
59. *See, e.g., Malcolm v. Little*, 295 A. 2d 711 (Del. 1972).
60. *See, e.g., Miller v. Watkins*, 200 Mont. 455, 653 P. 2d 126 (1982); *Newton v. Standard Fire Ins. Co.*, 291 N.C. 105, 229 S.E. 2d 297

(1976); *see also* W. Keeton et al., *Prosser and Keeton on Torts*, §2, at 9 (5th ed. 1984).

61. *See Hoffman v. Sterling Drug*, 485 F. 2d 132, 144-147 (3d Cir. 1973).

62. *Acosta v. Honda Motor Co.*, 717 F. 2d 828, 833 (3d Cir. 1983).

63. *Neal v. Carey Canadian Mines*, 548 F.Supp. 357 (E.D. Pa. 1982), *aff'd*, *Van Buskirk v. Carey Canadian Mines*, 791 F. 2d 30 (3d Cir. 1986).

64. *See G.D. Searle & Co. v. Superior Court*, 49 Cal. App. 3d 22, 122 Cal. Rptr. 218 (1975); *Roginsky v. Richardson-Merrell, Inc.*, 378 F. 2d 832 (2d Cir. 1967); *Toole v. Richardson-Merrell, Inc.*, 251 Cal. App. 2d 689, 60 Cal. Rptr. 398 (1967).

65. Restatement (Second) of Torts §402A, comment n (1965).

66. *Smith v. Clayton & Lambert Mfg. Co.*, 488 F. 2d 1345, 1349 (10th Cir. 1973).

67. *Daly v. General Motors Corp.*, 20 Cal. 3d 725, 575 P. 2d 1162, 144 Cal. Rptr. 380 (1978).

68. *Mulherin v. Ingersoll-Rand Co.*, 628 P. 2d 1301, 1303-1304 (Utah 1981).

69. *See generally* Fischer, *Products Liability: Applicability of Comparative Negligence to Misuse and Assumption of the Risk*, 43 Mo. L. Rev. 643 (1978).

70. *See, e.g., Duncan v. Cessna Aircraft Co.*, 665 S.W. 2d 414 (Tex. 1984).

71. *Perfection Paint & Color Co. v. Konduris*, 147 Ind. App. 106, 107, 258 N.E. 2d 681, 682 (1970).

72. Restatement (Second) of Torts §402A, comment h (1965).

73. *Basko, supra* note 53.

74. *See Roberts v. Suburban Hosp. Assn.*, 532 A. 2d 1081, 1086 (Md. 1987).

75. *See, e.g., Chauvin v. Sisters of Mercy Health*, 818 So. 2d 833 (La. 2002); *id.*

76. *See, e.g., JKB v. Armour Pharmaceutical Co.*, 660 N.E. 2d 602 (In. 1996); *In Re Factor VIII or IX Concentrate Blood Products Litigation*, 159 F. 3d 1016 (7th Cir. 1998).

77. *See, e.g., In re Breast Implant Product Liability Litigation*, 503 S.E. 2d 445 (S.C. 1998).

78. *See, e.g., Cafazzo v. Central Medical Services*, 668 A. 2d 521 (Pa. 1995); *Budding v. SSM Healthcare System*, 19 S.W. 3d 678 (Mo. 2000); *Royer v. Catholic Medical Center*, 741 A. 2d 74 (N.H. 1999).

79. *See, e.g., MacDonald v. Ortho Pharmaceutical Corp.*, 394 Mass. 131, 475 N.E. 2d 65 (1985), *cert. denied* 474 U.S. 920 (1985).

80. *See, e.g., Hill v. Searle Laboratories*, 884 F. 2d 1064 (8th Cir. 1989), *but see In re Norplant Contraceptive Products Liability Litigation*, 165 F. 3d 374 (5th Cir. 1999).

81. *See, e.g., Davis v. Wyeth Laboratories, Inc.*, 399 F. 2d 121 (9th Cir. 1968).

82. *Edwards v. Basel Pharmaceuticals*, 933 P. 2d 298 (Okla. 1997).

83. *Proctor v. Davis*, 682 N.E. 2d 1203 (Ill. 1997).

84. Products Liability Symposium, *Statutory Compliance and Tort Liability: Examining the Strongest Case*, 30 U. Mich. J. L. Ref. 461 (Spring 1997).

85. Federal Food, Drug, and Cosmetic Act (21 U.S.C. §355 et seq. (West Group 2002).

86. Medical Device Amendments to the Federal Food, Drug, and Cosmetic Act of 1938 (21 U.S.C. §360c et seq. (West Supp. 1996).

87. *Medtronic Inc. v. Lohr*, 116 S.Ct. 2240 (1996).

88. *See, e.g., Mitchell v. Collagen Corp.*, 126 F. 3d 902 (7th Cir. 1997); *Richman v. Gore*, 988 F.Supp. 753 (S.D. N.Y. 1997); *Martin v. Telectronics*, 105 F. 3d 1090 (6th Cir. 1997); *Worthy v. Collagen Corp.*, 967 S.W. 2d 360 (Tex. 1998); *Martin v. Medtronic*, 254 F. 3d 573 (5th Cir. 2001).

89. *Brooks v. Howmedica*, 273 F. 3d 785 (8th Cir. 2001).

90. *See, e.g., Niehoff v. Surgidev Corp.*, 950 S.W. 2d 816 (Ky. 1997); *Goodlin v. Medtronic*, 167 F. 3d 1367 (11th Cir. 1999).

91. *Eve v. Sandoz*, 2002 W.L. 181972, 2 (S.D. Ind. 2002).

92. *Motus v. Pfizer*, 127 F.Supp. 2d 1085, 1096 (C.D. Cal. 2000).

93. *Id.* at 1095.

94. *See, e.g., Abbot v. American Cyanamid Co.*, 844 F. 2d 1108 (4th Cir. 1988).

95. *See, e.g., Basko, supra* note 53; *see also Jacobson v. Colorado Fuel & Iron Corp.*, 409 F. 2d 1263, 1271 (9th Cir. 1969).

96. Restatement (Second) of Torts §12 (1965).

97. *See, e.g., Lindsay v. Ortho Pharmaceutical Corp.*, 637 F. 2d 87 (2d Cir. 1980); *Sterling Drug, Inc., v. Cornish*, 370 F. 2d 82 (8th Cir. 1966); *Incollingo v. Ewing*, 444 Pa. 263, 282 A. 2d 206 (1971), *rev'd on other grounds*, 491 Pa. 561, 421 A. 2d 79 (1977).

98. *Griggs v. Combe, Inc.*, 456 So. 2d 790 (Ala. 1984); *Freeman v. United States*, 704 F. 2d 154 (5th Cir. 1983).

99. *Gravis v. Parke, Davis & Co.*, 502 S.W. 2d 863 (Tex. Civ. App. 1973).

100. *Davila v. Bodelson*, 103 N.M. 243, 704 P. 2d 1119 (App. 1985).

101. *Id.*

102. *See, e.g., Buckner v. Allergan Pharmaceuticals*, 400 So. 2d 820 (Fla. Dist. Ct. App. 1981); *Lindsay, supra* note 97; *id.* at 91.

103. *See, e.g., Fellows v. USV Pharmaceutical Corp.*, 502 F.Supp. 297 (D. Md. 1980) (the manufacturer has a duty to provide warnings to physician, but the duty does not extend to the patient); *Ezagui v. Dow Chemical Corp.*, 598 F. 2d 727 (2d Cir. 1979).

104. *Id.*

105. *Reyes v. Wyeth Laboratories*, 498 F. 2d 1264 (5th Cir.), *cert. denied*, 419 U.S. 1096 (1974).

106. *See Leesley v. West*, 165 Ill. App. 3d 135, 518 N.E. 2d 758 (App. Ct.), *appeal denied*, 119 Ill. 2d 558, 522 N.E. 2d 1246 (1988); *Stone v. Smith, Kline & French Laboratories*, 447 So. 2d 1301 (Ala. 1984); *Mauldin v. Upjohn Co.*, 697 F. 2d 644 (5th Cir. 1983).

107. *Bacardi v. Holzman*, 182 N.J. Super. 422, 424, 442 A. 2d 617, 618 (1981).

108. *See Crain v. Allison*, 443 A. 2d 558, 562 (D.C. App. 1982); *Salis v. United States*, 522 F.Supp. 989, 1000 (M.D. Pa. 1981).

109. *Barson v. E.R. Squibb & Sons*, 682 P. 2d 832 (Utah 1984).

110. *Id.* at 834 (citing *McEwan v. Ortho Pharmaceutical Corp.*, 270 Or. 375, 528 P. 2d 522 (1974)).

111. *Schenebeck v. Sterling Drug*, 423 F. 2d 919 (8th Cir. 1970).

112. *Id.*

113. *Cover v. Cohen*, 61 N.Y. 2d 261, 268, 461 N.E. 2d 864, 871, 473 N.Y.S. 2d 378, 385 (1984) (citations omitted).

114. *See Schenebeck, supra* note 111; *O'Hare v. Merck & Co.*, 381 F. 2d 286 (8th Cir. 1967).

115. *Feldman v. Lederle Laboratories*, 97 N.J. 429, 479 A. 2d 374 (1984); *see also* Gilhooley, *Learned Intermediaries, Prescription Drugs, and Patient Information*, 30 St. Louis L. J. 633 (1986).

116. *See Brochu, supra* note 21; *Dyer v. Best Pharmacal*, 118 Ariz. 465, 577 P. 2d 1084 (Ct. App. 1978).

117. *See Reyes, supra* note 105; *Davis, supra* note 81.

118. *Brazzell v. United States*, 788 F. 2d 1352 (8th Cir. 1986).

119. *Williams v. Lederle Laboratories*, 591 F.Supp. 381 (S.D. Ohio 1984).

120. *Formella v. Ciba-Geigy Corp.*, 100 Mich. App. 649, 300 N.W. 2d 356 (1980).

121. Madden, *The Duty to Warn in Products Liability: Contours and Criticism*, 89 W. Va. L. Rev. 221, 310-20 (1987); *Richards v. Upjohn Co.*, 95 N.M. 675, 679, 625 P. 2d 1192, 1196 (Ct. App. 1980).

122. *Seley v. G.D. Searle & Co.*, 67 Ohio St. 2d 192, 198, 423 N.E. 2d 831, 837 (1981).

123. *Id.* at 837.

124. *McEwan v. Ortho Pharmaceutical Corp.*, 570 Or. 375, 528 P. 2d 522 (1974).

125. *Kaempfe v. Lehn & Fink Prods. Corp.*, 21 A.D. 2d 197, 249 N.Y.S. 2d 840 (App. Div. 1964), *aff'd*, 20 N.Y. 2d 818, 231 N.E. 2d 294, 284 N.Y.S. 2d 818 (1967).

126. *Tomer v. American Home Prod. Corp.*, 170 Conn. 681, 368 A. 2d 35 (1976); *Crocker v. Winthrop Laboratories*, 514 S.W. 2d 429 (Tex. 1974).

127. Restatement (Second) of Torts §402A (1965).

128. *Anderson v. Owens-Corning Fiberglass*, 810 P. 2d 549.

129. *Carlin v. Sutter Court Superior Ct.* (No. S045912, 8/30/96).

130. *Wagner v. Roche Laboratories* (No. 95-1209, 11/13/96).

131. 21 C.F.R. §201 (1990).

132. *Feldman, supra* note 115.

133. 21 C.F.R. §201.5.10 (1990).

134. *Pharmaceutical Mfr. Ass'n. v. Food & Drug Admin.*, 484 F.Supp. 1179 (D. Del. 1980).

135. 21 C.F.R. §201.5 (1990).

136. *Ohligschlager v. Proctor Community Hosp.*, 55 Ill. 2d 411, 303 N.E. 2d 392 (1973).

137. *Lukaszewicz v. Ortho Pharmaceutical Corp.*, 510 F.Supp. 961, *amended*, 532 F.Supp. 211 (E.D. Wis. 1981).

138. *See MacDonald, supra* note 79.

139. Harrell, *Pharmaceutical Marketing*, in *The Pharmaceutical Industry* 80 (C. Lindsay ed. 1978).

140. *See* S. Greenberg, *The Quality of Mercy* 267-283 (Atheneum, New York 1971).

141. *Love v. Wolf*, 226 Cal. App. 2d 378, 38 Cal. Rptr. 183 (1964); *Wolf*, 226 Cal. App. at 399-400, 38 Cal. Rptr. at 196 (citation omitted).

142. *See Toole, supra* note 64.

143. *See, e.g., Stevens v. Parke, Davis & Co.*, 9 Cal. 3d 51, 507 P. 2d 653, 107 Cal. Rptr. 45 (1973).

144. *But see Spiegel v. Saks 34th Street*, 43 Misc. 2d 1065, 252 N.Y.S. 2d 852 (Sup.Ct. 1964), *aff'd*, 26 A.D. 2d 660, 272 N.Y.S. 972 (1966).

145. Pharmaceutical Manufacturers Association, *Prescription Drug Industry Fact Book* 56 (Washington, D.C. 1986).

146. *See generally* J. Lidstone, *Marketing Planning for the Pharmaceutical Industry* (1987); R. Norris, *Pills, Pesticides and Profits* (1982).

147. Restatement (Second) of Agency §229 (1958).

148. *See, e.g., Schering Corp. v. Cotlow*, 94 Ariz. 365, 385 P. 2d 234 (1963).

149. *Stevens, supra* note 143.

150. *Incollingo, supra* note 97.

151. *See, e.g., Schenebeck, supra* note 111; *Krug v. Sterling Drug, Inc.*, 416 S.W. 2d 143 (Mo. 1967).

152. National Swine Flu Immunization Program of 1976, Pub. L. No. 94-380, 90 Stat. 1113; *see also Ducharme v. Merrill-Nat'l Labs.*, 574 F. 2d 1307 (5th Cir.), *cert. denied*, 439 U.S. 1002 (1978).

153. 90 Stat. 1116.

154. Health and Services Amendments of 1978, Pub. L. 95-626, 92 Stat. 3551.

155. Pub. L. 99-660, 100 Stat. 3755 (codified at 42 U.S.C. §§300aa-1 to 33 [1986]).

156. 100 Stat. 3758 (codified at 42 U.S.C. §300aa-10 (1988)).

157. 100 Stat. 3758-59 (codified at 42 U.S.C. §300aa-11 (1988)).

158. M. Silverman & P. Lee, *supra* note 48, at 289-290.

159. Comment, *Strict Tort Liability/Negligence/Prescription Drugs: A Pharmaceutical Company Owes No Duty to a Non-Patient Third Party to Warn Doctors or Hospitals of the Side Effects of a Drug and a Hospital or Doctor Owes No Duty to a Non-Patient Third Party to Warn a Patient of the Effects of a Prescription Drug*, 77 Ill. B. J. 227 (1988); Comment, *Torts: Duty to Warn—Incorrect Prescription of Unavoidably Unsafe Drugs*, 22 Kan. L. Rev. 281 (1984).

160. See Merrill, *Compensation for Prescription Drug Injuries*, 59 Va. L. Rev. 1, 50-68 (1973).

161. *See, e.g., Oksenholt v. Lederle Laboratories*, 294 Or. 213, 656 P. 2d 293 (1982); Mobilia, *Allergic Reactions to Prescription Drugs: A Proposal for Compensation*, 48 Alb. L. Rev. 343, 364-365 (1984).

162. *See* Willig, *Physicians, Pharmacists, Pharmaceutical Manufacturers: Partners in Patient Care, Partners in Litigation?*, 37 Mercer L. Rev. 755 (1986).

163. Norman, *Class Actions: A Practitioner's Tool*, 31-WTR Brief 48 (2002).

164. Cabraser, *Class Action Update 2002: Mass Tort Trends, Choice of Law Rule 23(F), Appeals, and Proposed Amendments to Rule 23*, SH009 ALI-ABA 1189 (2002).

165. *See, e.g.*, Nahrstadt, *Getting It Together: A Guide to Understanding Mass Tort Litigation*, 11-OCT BUSLT 19 (2001); Lysaught, *Forces Shaping Mass Tort Litigation: Strategies for Defense Counsel*, 67 DEFCJ 165 (2000); Cabraser, *New Issues and Key Rulings in the Certification, Trial, Settlement, and Appeal of Class Actions*, N01CACB ABA-LGLED B-1 (2001).

166. J.W. Snyder, *Silicone Breast Implants: Can Emerging Medical, Legal, and Scientific Concepts Be Reconciled?*, 18 J. Legal Med. 133-220 (1997).

167. C.F.R. §878.3540 (1990).

168. Restatement (Second) of Torts (1965).

169. Restatement (Third) of Torts: Products Liability (1998).

170. Westlaw search, Dec. 31, 2002.

171. *Gerhart v. Don Lengle Inc.*, 1999 W.L. 1273729 (Pa. 1999); *Ehlis v. Shire Richwood*, 2002 W.L. 31769691 (D.N.D. 2002).

172. Restatement (Third) of Torts: Products Liability, §2b (1998).

173. *Id*. at §6.

174. *Id*. at §6c.

175. Conk, *Is There a Design Defect in the Restatement (Third) of Torts: Products Liability?*, 109 Yale L. J. 1087 (2000).

Electronic Mail Communication with Patients

FILLMORE BUCKNER, M.D., J.D., F.C.L.M.

ADVANTAGES OF E-MAIL
E-MAIL AS A TOOL IN PHYSICIAN-PATIENT COMMUNICATION
DISADVANTAGES OF E-MAIL
GUIDELINES FOR USE OF E-MAIL FOR PHYSICIAN-PATIENT COMMUNICATIONS
ADMISSIBILITY OF E-MAIL
CONCLUSION

Electronic mail (e-mail) occupies a singular position in health care law. Because of its unique properties it is part of telemedicine law, part of medical records law, has many of the legal attributes of the telephone in health care law, and mimics the evidence problems of traditional mail. The discussion below will concern external e-mail—that e-mail common to the vast majority of providers and patients based on the modem, wireless, or cable access to the Internet through an Internet service provider (ISP) and transmitted from one user to another via the Internet. It is by far the fastest growing means of communication worldwide. The speed, ease, and low cost of sending information over the Internet has made it the communication media of choice of industry and commerce and it is rapidly becoming the patient's method of accessing health care information.

Regardless of the ISP, at the time of registration, users must agree to a terms of service agreement, a set of operating rules. These operating rules govern the user's communications and the contents therein. What is implied by such regulations, and which may or may not be explicitly expressed, is that the ISP reserves the right to inspect traffic in and out of its site. The ISP has the legal right to do so. The Electronic Communications Privacy Act of 1986[1] specifically covers e-mail and provides criminal and civil penalties for the interception of electronic data. However, it carefully spells out an exception for providers of electronic communications service such as an ISP.[2]* That means any external e-mail communication has a built-in gap to guaranteed confidentiality.

---

* This would hold equally true for employers who act as their own Internet service providers.

ADVANTAGES OF E-MAIL

E-mail is an underappreciated technology. E-mail has the advantage of extremely low cost. The e-mail user pays either a very low monthly fee to an ISP or elects to use an organizational, institutional, or commercial ISP that offers Internet access at no fee at all. That means it is cheaper than overnight letter services or sending long-distance faxes. Messages then can be sent to any location on the globe with no surcharge per message.

Like the telephone, e-mail is fast. Messages travel thousands of miles in milliseconds rather than in days via the Postal Service. E-mail is more convenient than the telephone. It is easily typed from the computer keyboard at any time; there is never a busy signal. It is asynchronous, it requires neither the recipient's presence nor their availability; therefore it completely eliminates the time-consuming telephone tag with which busy providers are plagued. E-mail messages are also tagged on the recipient's screen to indicate what action has been taken in regard to that message. Therefore, an e-mail message is less likely than a telephone message to get lost, ignored, or forgotten. In addition, unlike the telephone, it is a written, not a spoken, message. That means it is an edited, more formal, and hopefully more carefully crafted communication than a phone conversation or voice-mail.

E-mail is particularly well suited to transmit to the patient anything the patient would have to write out if it were transmitted orally. E-mail also provides a ready-made permanent record that has the capability of being printed out to become part of a patient's paper medical record or being exported electronically to the patient's electronic medical record without manual recopying. As mentioned above, the message may be forwarded to other interested parties without retyping. Because it is essentially a typed message, illegible messages are eliminated. Finally, e-mail

417

allows embedded links to recommended or appropriate educational sites on the web.

E-MAIL AS A TOOL IN PHYSICIAN-PATIENT COMMUNICATION

E-mail has taken on a distinctive role in physician-patient communications. With the expanding use of computers by the public, the majority of patients now have access to e-mail.[3] Of the patients who own computers or are planning to purchase them within 6 months, a substantial majority would like to use e-mail to interact with their physician.[4] E-mail has been exploited by only a small minority of physicians to improve communications with patients. Among the various physician-patient interactions via e-mail that have been advocated or adopted are the following: postoperative checks on patients;[5] giving directions and educational materials to patients;[6] answering prescription refill requests;[7] appointment requests, reminders, and changes;[8] receiving and answering referral requests;[9] receiving and answering medication questions;[10] reporting adverse drug reactions;[11] transmitting laboratory and diagnostic test results to the patient;[12] exchanging insurance information;[13] reporting home-generated results (glucose levels, urine volumes, blood pressures, etc.);[14] and even get well cards or birthday greetings.[15]

In addition, e-mail allows the physician to send out a series of standardized letters to both patients and colleagues such as thank you letters for referrals, notices of office hour changes, holiday greetings and closures, changes in coverage, new phone numbers, and a myriad of similar notifications.

DISADVANTAGES OF E-MAIL

E-mail is a marvelous communication tool, but one marked by security defects with no currently known solution. E-mail resembles a postcard rather than a letter. It is open to its carrier or carriers. The message is sent through many connections and networks during transmission. The message is usually fragmented and, while it is theoretically possible for it to be seized and read anywhere in the milliseconds along the way, its practical vulnerability lies in the ISP or ISPs of the sender and the recipient and upon the desktop of the sender and recipient. There it is intact and stored and may be easily and legally accessed by ISP personnel, office personnel, family members, or third parties able to access an unattended computer terminal. At these points it is most vulnerable to hackers. Personal information may be read, copied, altered, or forwarded without the sender or recipient ever knowing of the intrusion. E-mail is infinitely easier to forge than is regular mail. There is no handwriting or scripted signature to compare, and rare type fonts and graphic identifiers may be readily scanned and duplicated on a computer.

Encryption[16] or the use of a secure messaging service such as Medem™ would help security, but neither method provides absolute security and each diminishes the practicality of e-mail in the communication between physician and patient.[17]* Both physician and patient must use the same encryption program. At present, such software must be purchased by the physician, but may be downloaded by the patient.[18] This immediately presents a problem for the patient who is unable to download or cannot adjust to a program that alters his or her routine use of e-mail. Secure messaging services are protected ISPs that become the service for both physicians and patients. Many provide encryption/de-encryption for all messages sent. These are commercial ventures and therefore add a cost to what has previously been a free, or practically free, means of communication. Both encryption and secure messaging services have been touted as necessary to satisfy the Department of Health and Human Services Standards for Privacy of Individually Identifiable Health Information,[19]† the final regulations for which were published in 2002.[20] Based on these relaxed final rules and the Department of Health and Human Services discussion of the rules,[21] it would appear that with proper consent unencrypted messages may be sent through regular ISPs.

In addition, it is inherently easier to send material to the wrong address in e-mail than with regular mail. To send an e-mail, the sender usually clicks on a name on a list and the letter is automatically addressed. All computer users have experienced the frustration of discovering that the cursor was one line up or one line down from the intended item on a menu. Therefore, e-mail is more frequently misaddressed than is regular mail. The "Reply to All" or "List Send" can also create a problem by revealing the name of every patient to every other patient. Eli Lilly recently settled a case based on this very happening.[22]‡ The recipient, with little more than the push of a button, may forward the message to any individual or individuals anywhere in the world without recopying or securing the sender's permission. Another potential problem results from the fact that ISPs routinely make backup copies of all messages. These backup copies may remain in the system long after the message has been erased from both the sender's and recipient's memories and computers.[23] Finally, there is a measure of social inequality in the distribution of e-mail capability. E-mail service is directly correlated to income and distributed unevenly across racial and ethnic groups.[24]

---

* In addition to their lack of practicality, neither technique may be necessary to preserve the physician-patient privilege or a fiduciary duty of confidentiality. Recent court cases indicate that e-mail, like a telephone conversation, will preserve the attorney-client privilege and be considered ethical practice. *See also* ABA Standing Committee on Ethics and Professional Responsibility Formal Opinion 99-413, http://www.abanet.org/cpr/ethicopinions.html.

† *See* Chapter 19 (this volume).

‡ Because Eli Lilly was not considered a health care provider, the case was brought by the FTC and not under the Health Insurance Portability and Accountability Act (HIPAA).

GUIDELINES FOR USE OF E-MAIL FOR PHYSICIAN-PATIENT COMMUNICATIONS

Do these disadvantages mean that e-mail should not be used for physician-patient communications? The answer is a resounding no. Every mode of communication carries some risk of unauthorized interception and disclosure. It simply does not make sense to refuse to make use of this superb means of communication because of the remote possibility of loss of confidentiality, especially when the unauthorized use or dissemination of that information is illegal. You have a reasonable expectation of privacy in communicating via e-mail even though you cannot guarantee security.[25] What is needed is adequate informed consent from the patient and adherence to carefully crafted guidelines.

American Medical Informatics Association (AMIA) Guidelines

In 1997, the AMIA adopted the guidelines proposed by their task force on clinical use of electronic mail with patients. This was published as their White Paper, *Guidelines for the Clinical Use of Electronic Mail with Patients*.[26] The guidelines were presented in a dual approach, guidelines for effective communication with patients and risk management or medical-legal guidelines. These guidelines are summarized in Tables 38-1 and 38-2 taken directly from the AMIA White Paper.[27] Unfortunately, these guidelines do not satisfy many legal commentators, and several alternative sets of guidelines have been published or generally outlined in law review articles.[28]

Defining a turnaround time is essential for successful e-mail communication. One of the essentials is to be conservative in stating a turnaround time. If there is a chance that on busy days the e-mail will only be checked once per day, it is important that the provider not warrant that it will be checked more often than that. The AMIA guidelines envisioned a 2- to 3-day turnaround time for e-mail. Present practice would indicate that e-mail has attained a next-day turnaround in most offices, and in many offices messages received during one business day are processed that day. AMIA guidelines ask for provider assurances of privacy and security in multiple guidelines. The current thought is described above; there is a reasonable expectation of privacy on e-mail but the provider has no control of the security and/or the integrity of the e-mail communication and should make no assurances as to confidentiality or integrity or distinguish degrees of sensitivity of messages. The remainder of the communication guidelines are as valid today as they were in 1997.

Unfortunately the medical-legal guidelines have not fared as well in the ensuing years. Certainly an informed consent and e-mail practice policies are as important today as then, but the recommended content of those documents has changed with time. Today the consent form must conform to the consent requirements of HHS's Standards for Privacy of Identifiable Health Information.[29] The essence of the informed consent agreement still should be that the provider is making no assurances of e-mail confidentiality or security and that the patient desires that the communications of the types enumerated be communicated by e-mail. The consent should also carefully, and conspicuously, detail whether or not the e-mail messages will be encrypted. Certainly the fact that the provider will make the e-mail transmission part of the written or electronic medical record is still an essential part of the consent but, in these days of multiple providers and shifting personnel, the hours of e-mail service are more important to detail than trying to detail who will service the communication. Also as discussed above and in Chapter 32, the security of internal networks should never be compromised by allowing patients' e-mail accounts on the internal network, a possibility suggested in the AMIA White Paper.

Other risk management suggestions

No single set of guidelines incorporates all of the issues one must contemplate in order to develop a comprehensive set of

---

TABLE 38-1 Summary of communication guidelines

- Establish turnaround time for messages. Do not use e-mail for urgent matters.
- Inform patients about privacy issues. Patients should know:
  - Who besides addressee processes messages during addressee's usual business hours, and during addressee's vacation or illness.
  - That message is to be included as part of the medical record.
- Establish types of transactions (prescription refill, appointment scheduling, etc.) and sensitivity of subject matter (HIV, mental health, etc.) permitted over e-mail.
- Instruct patients to put category of transaction in subject line of message for filtering: "prescription," "appointment," "medical advice," "billing question."
- Request that patients put their name and patient identification number in the body of the message.
- Configure automatic reply to acknowledge receipt of messages.
- Print all messages, with replies and confirmation of receipt, and place in patient's paper chart.
- Send a new message to inform patient of completion of request.
- Request that patients use autoreply feature to acknowledge reading provider's message.
- Maintain a mailing list of patients, but do not send group mailings where recipients are visible to each other. Use blind copy feature in software.
- Avoid anger, sarcasm, harsh criticism, and libelous references to third parties in messages.

TABLE 38-2 Medicolegal and administrative guidelines

- Consider obtaining patient's informed consent for use of e-mail. Written forms should:
    Itemize terms in communication guidelines.
    Provide instructions for when and how to escalate to phone calls and office visits.
    Describe security mechanisms in place.
    Indemnify the health care institution for information loss due to technical failures.
    Waive encryption requirement, if any, at patient's insistence.
- Use password-protected screen savers for all desktop workstations in the office, hospital, and at home.
- Never forward patient-identifiable information to a third party without the patient's express permission.
- Never use patient's e-mail address in a marketing scheme.
- Do not share professional e-mail accounts with family members.
- Use encryption for all messages when encryption technology becomes widely available, user-friendly, and practical.
- Do not use unencrypted wireless communications with patient-identifiable information.
- Double-check all "To:" fields prior to sending messages.
- Perform at least weekly backups of mail onto long-term storage. Define "long-term" as the term applicable to paper records.
- Commit policy decisions to writing and electronic form.

risk management guidelines, and some include some extremely questionable advice. For example, Speilberg[30] suggests that e-mail from patients is so sensitive it should not be included in the patient's regular medical record—a recommendation that is hard to take seriously when the meassage has been transmitted over an acknowledged insecure network and the patient has consented to its inclusion in the medical record. An edited compendium of the current recommendations is given below.

Informed consent. The informed consent should emphasize that the provider can make no guarantees of confidentiality because the transmission has the possibility of being monitored in transit, but that e-mail may be a convenience for the type of communication the provider wants to use e-mail for. The patient should be warned that even deleting the message may still make it available to anyone else using the same computer. The types of communications should be enumerated and there should be a blanket prohibition of any other type of communication. Unless the provider specifically wants to receive emergency communications via e-mail, emergencies should be specifically prohibited and the proper procedures for notifying the provider of emergencies given. The fact that all e-mail communications will become part of the medical record should be included. The informed consent should include a specific request from the patient that the patient desires e-mail for the enumerated communications. The consent should also contain a signed acknowledgment of the accuracy of the patient's e-mail address. Some commentators suggest adding an agreement that e-mail communications will only be made from terminals within the state—an attempt to avoid the licensure issues of medical practice across state lines.*

Written e-mail policies and procedures. Detailed e-mail policies and procedures should be written and distributed to all staff. Those portions of the policies and procedures applicable to patients should become part of the provider's new patient brochure or distributed to patients at the time they request e-mail communication. The patient's receipt of that brochure or written policy statement should be documented in the patient's medical record. Placing the patient policies on an easily accessed website is an additional method of ensuring that the patient has realistic expectations of the e-mail service. The patient-related policies and procedures should include the following:

1. *Realistic hours.* Although e-mail may be sent on a 24-hour basis, in most cases it will be processed during business hours. Therefore, reasonable hours during which e-mail will be accessed for processing and a cutoff hour after which no messages will be accepted for processing must be set for each business day.

2. *Reasonable turnaround time.* Although same-day turnaround is rapidly becoming the norm, set a turnaround time that is routinely possible in the specific provider's practice. If a 1-, 2-, or 3-day turnaround is the best you can guarantee, do not promise more.

3. *Specific provider and patient ID.* Set a specific signature character set or logo to be included in each message from the provider. Request that patients use a simple designation in addition to their names in each communication.†

4. *Specific "subject" line categories.* Specific wording in the subject listing on patients' messages allows for easier triage and helps direct the message to the proper individual in the provider office. The same use on the provider's messages reinforces the categories. Simple categories, such as "prescription," "laboratory," "information," "appointment," or "billing," are recommended.

---

* In Northern practices with numbers of "snowbirds," e-mail is considered an ideal way for patients spending the winter in the Sunbelt to keep in touch with their regular providers, and these practices tend to accept or ignore the possible risk.

† Several medical societies, including the AMA, are experimenting with digital IDs that can satisfy this requirement.

5. *Clear notice that only consent e-mail is accepted.* There should be a clear notice that e-mail will not be accepted from patients who have not signed an e-mail informed consent. The provider's e-mail software can be programmed to accept messages only from the e-mail addresses acknowledged on the informed consent.

6. *Replies requested.* Request that patients acknowledge receipt of provider communications. (On most e-mail programs, this can be accomplished by a single keystroke or two and a copy of the message received will be included with the acknowledgment.) This provides complete documentation of the request, the action on the request, and the patient's notification of the action.

Policies and procedures for staff should include the following:

1. Receipt of all incoming messages from patients should be acknowledged. This lets the patient know the inquiry is being processed, prevents needless follow-up calls, and instills confidence in the system.

2. All patients should be informed when their requests are completed.

3. All patient messages, the replies thereto, and patient acknowledgments should be printed out and placed in the patient's paper medical record or should be transferred into the patient's electronic medical record.

4. All e-mail programs have the ability to maintain an e-mail address list and make mass e-mail messages. These lists are extremely convenient and real time-savers. However, they are extremely prone to two types of errors. First, unless the computer operator is vigilant, it is easy to click on the name above or below the intended addressee. Therefore, the address on the message must be double-checked on every transmission. Second, sending a message to the entire address book without adequate precautions will reveal the names of every patient on the list to every other patient on the list. This can be solved using the blind carbon copy feature on the e-mail program (View bcc on Microsoft Outlook™, for instance). A message about an office closure could be sent to every patient on the provider's list by addressing the message to the provider, one of the provider's personnel, or the hospital and transferring the entire patient list to bcc. Each patient would get the message but none would be aware of any name but that of the addressee.

5. Closely related to the address book problems is the proximity of the "reply" button to the "reply to all" button on most e-mail programs. Therefore, all personnel must be carefully coached to watch that messages are sent only to the patient sender.

6. Patient e-mail must be protected from other patients visiting the provider's office. If there are computer terminals in patient areas, they must be equipped with password or smart-card protected standby or screen savers.

7. Consider the use of headers and footers on all outgoing messages marking the message as a privileged and confidential communication intended only for the designated recipient. However, remember such messages attract the attention of those attempting to intercept messages during transmittal. Certain types of transmissions attract hackers more than others, and marking a message as secret or confidential can have the effect of turning a boring health care provider message into something worth a hacker's time to retrieve.

8. Establish iron-clad forwarding criteria. Secure the patient's consent for all forwarding or for all forwarding except forwarding to other treating providers or third-party payers. Make sure personnel know the hazard of electronic data transfer without patient's permission unless it is in the context of treating or collecting for treatment.

9. The policy and procedures statement should spell out exactly who is responsible for handling each type of triage category messages and who is responsible for entering the messages, replies, and acknowledgments into the patient's medical record.

10. Develop your triage system with the entire staff. Keep it within the bounds of your e-mail system. A simple and effective system can be worked out using only the patient ID and the one-word subject line headings.

11. Remember each and every e-mail message you send may become a written record and will remain a retrievable electronic message for the foreseeable future. Be discrete in what you write. Do not SCREAM (all capital messages). Avoid anger, sarcasm, demeaning or defamatory language, "emoticons,"* and attempts at humor.

12. Develop templates for frequently asked questions or for frequently sent messages.

13. Confine your graphics to necessary diagrams and aids to instructions. Graphics take tremendous memory and your patient's computer may not be able to handle elaborate illustrations.

14. The same caution should be applied to attachments. Many e-mail programs handle attachments with difficulty. Make sure your patient and the patient's e-mail program can handle attachments before sending needed information via attachment.

15. If in doubt about sending a communication via e-mail, don't do it. The whole idea of adopting technology is to make life easier for you. Worrying about the

---

* Emoticons are various character groups used by e-mail users to convey emotion—the happy face, etc.

appropriateness of using it just complicates your life. Adopt the technology for the tasks that you are certain about. Add additional tasks as you become comfortable with the technology and the legal issues surrounding the medical use of the technology become clarified.

16. Finally, read every message and the address line before hitting the "send" button.

ADMISSIBILITY OF E-MAIL

In general, e-mail as a part of the medical record is treated no differently than any other part of the paper or electronic medical record. It is treated as part of the business record as discussed in Chapter 32 and admitted into evidence as such. However, e-mail communications not part of the medical record or accounting records,[31] face a problem of authentication.[32] The Internet made no provision for authentication of e-mail when the program began and has added none since. Although each e-mail message contains the header described above, it is evidently easy for those with expertise to create anonymous messages, without header information, or to forge false header information. There is also the problem of messages coming from compromised accounts where the account name and password have been accessed by a hacker. Such cases have come to court[33] but have not resulted in authentication challenges. From the cases thus far, it would appear that the header information, despite its ease of forgery, and barring evidence to the contrary, will serve as authentication for e-mail's admission under Federal Rule of Evidence 902.7. Jablon[34] compares the use of the header for authentication to the court's use of an oriental "chop" mark for authentication.[35] The recent cases of *United States v. Siddiqui*[36] and *Bloom v. Commonwealth of Virginia*[37] have clarified the evidence necessary to establish that an e-mail was sent and identify the sender. Such evidence should include one or more of the following:

- A witness or entity received the e-mail.
- The e-mail bore the e-mail address of a particular individual.
- The e-mail contained the name or nickname of this individual in the body of the e-mail.
- The e-mail recited matters that would normally be known only to the individual who is alleged to have sent it (or to a discrete number of persons including this individual).
- Following receipt of the e-mail the recipient witness had a discussion with the individual who purportedly sent it and the conversation reflected this individual's knowledge of the contents of the e-mail.[38]

CONCLUSION

E-mail is an extremely valuable communication tool that is replete with security flaws. Its use is a fact of life. Its efficiency demands that the health care provider learn to deal with his or her resistance to change and adopt its use. It can increase the bonding between provider and patient by providing a superior tool to carry out routine, but essential, communication tasks. The key to its successful use is to have well-crafted informed consents and e-mail guidelines in place.

In this chapter, we have dealt with communications between the provider and patients where the provider-patient relationship was established and after an informed consent had been signed by the patient. The inadvertent establishment of a provider-patient relationship and resultant or potential malpractice situations have not been discussed. The interested reader is referred to the discussion of telephone liability in Chapter 39 below for thorough coverage of that issue. Electronic medical records are discussed in Chapter 33 and practice across state lines also is discussed in Chapter 39.

ENDNOTES

1. Pub. Law 99-508 codified in various sections of 18 U.S.C.
2. *Id.* §101(c)(6).
3. Bauchner et al., *"You've Got Mail": Issues in Communicating with Patients and Their Families by E-Mail*, 109(5) Pediatrics 954 (2002). *See also* Kleiner et al., *Parent and Physician Attitudes Regarding the Use of Electronic Mail in Pediatric Practices*, 109(5) Pediatrics 740 (2002).
4. Mold et al., *Patient-Physician E-Mail Communication*, 91(6) Journal of Oklahoma Medical Association 331-4 (1998).
5. Ellis et al., *Use of Electronic Mail for Postoperative Follow Up After Ambulatory Surgery*, 11(2) Journal of Clinical Anesthesia 136-9 (1999).
6. *See* Eysenbach & Diepgen, *Responses to Unsolicited Patient E-Mail Requests for Medical Advice*, 280(15) J.A.M.A. 1333-5 (1998).
7. Roemer, *Letter to Editor*, 282(8) J.A.M.A. 729 (1999).
8. *Id.*; *see also* Sherman, *Patients and E-Mail*, 98(3) W.M.J. 66 (1999).
9. *Id.*
10. Sherman, *supra* note 8.
11. Henkel, *E-Mail, Snail Mail, Phone or Fax*, 32(6) FDA Consumer 7 (1998).
12. Heusner, *The E-Mail Connection*, 82 Minnesota Medicine 22 (1999).
13. Kane et al., *Guidelines for the Clinical Use of Electronic Mail with Patients*, 5(1) Journal of the Medical Informatics Association 104 (1998).
14. *Id.*
15. Nordhaus-Bike, *Patient Relations: Get Well E-Mail*, 1(1) Hospital Health Network 14 (1999).
16. *See* Kiuchi et al., *Using a WWW-Based Mail User Agent for Secure Mail Service for Health Care Users*, 37(3) Methods of Information in Medicine 247 (1998).
17. *See* Loscalso & Simmons, 35(2) Trial 20 (1999); Brienza, 35(7) Trial, 112 (1999).
18. *See* Terry, *E-Mail Patients? Don't Be Nervous. Do Be Careful*, Medical Economics 86-91 (Sept. 3, 2001) for some specific suggestions as to software and secure messaging services.
19. 45 C.F.R. Part 164.
20. *See* 67 Federal Register (Aug. 14, 2002) Final Rule, Standards for Privacy of Individually Identifiable Health Information. *See also* Proposed Rules, 67 Federal Register 14776 (2002) (to be codified at 45 C.F.R. Parts 160 and 164).
21. Department of Health and Human Services, Office of Civil Rights, Office of the Secretary, 45 C.F.R. Parts 160 and 164, Rin: 0991-AB14,

Standards for Privacy of Individually Identifiable Health Information. Action: Final Rule.

22. Young, *FTC-Lilly Settlement Sheds Light on E-Mail Privacy with Patients*, 59 American Journal of Health System Pharmacy 509 (2002); Current Developments, *Eli Lilly Settles FTC Charges Concerning Disclosure of E-Mail Addresses of Prozac Users*, 19 The Computer & Internet Lawyer 27 (2002).

23. *See* Kolker, *This File Will Not Destruct*, 24 American Lawyer 11 (2002).

24. Mandl et al., *Social Equity and Access to the World Wide Web and E-Mail: Implications for the Design and Implementation of Medical Applications*, Proceedings of AMIA Symposium 215 (1998).

25. Brienza, *supra* note 17.

26. Kane & Sands, *Guidelines for the Clinical Use of Electronic Mail with Patients*, 5(1) Journal of the American Informatics Association 104 (1998).

27. *Id.* at 106.

28. *See* Heusner, *supra* note 13; Jurevic, *When Technology and Health Care Collide: Issues with Electronic Medical Records and Electronic Mail*, 66 U.M.K.C. Law Review 809 (1998); *see also*, Bernstein, *Why and How to Use Technology*, 33(1) Trial 93 (1997); Speilberg, *Online Without a Net*, 25 American Journal of Law and Medicine 267 (1999); Subscriber's Manual, www.medem.com (2002).

29. *See* 45 C.F.R. §164.506.

30. Speilberg, *supra* note 28, at 275.

31. *See* Cavenaugh, *Fax and E-Mail Qualify as "Documentary Evidence" for Sec. 274*, 29(4) The Tax Advisor 210 (1998).

32. *See* Joseph, *Internet and E-Mail Evidence*, The Practical Litigator 45 (2002); Jablon, *"God Mail": Authentication and Admissibility of Electronic Mail in Federal Courts*, 34(4) American Criminal Law Review 1387 (1997).

33. Jablon, *supra* note 32, at 1390-91.

34. *Id.*

35. *See Zenith Radio Corp. v. Matsushita Electric Industrial Co.*, 505 F.Supp. 1190 (1980).

36. *United States v. Siddiqui*, 215 F. 3d 1318 (11th Cir. 2000).

37. *Bloom v. Commonwealth of Virginia*, 542 S.E. 2d 18 (2001).

38. Joseph, *supra*, note 32, at 52-53

Telemedicine

FILLMORE BUCKNER, M.D., J.D., F.C.L.M.
RAYMUND C. KING, M.D., J.D., F.C.L.M.

TELEMEDICINE
LEGAL ISSUES
CONCLUSION

TELEMEDICINE

Telemedicine is specifically defined as the application of telecommunications to the care of the individual.[1] However, in general medical parlance, the terms "telemedicine" and "telehealth" have come to mean the convergence of the burgeoning technology of the telecommunications industry and the health care professions. Reduced to its simplest terms, telemedicine is nothing more than the electronic transfer of health care information from one site to another.[2] Telemedicine can probably trace its historic roots back to the Civil War when Union Army physicians telegraphed for medical supplies. However, the term "telemedicine" was introduced almost 40 years ago when the Bureau of Indian Affairs used telephone and video programs to train paramedics on the reservations. Today, the status of telemedicine far exceeds the expectations one arouses with a statement about its origins or the simple transfer of data.

Probably nothing has contributed to the advances in telemedicine more than digital imaging. Digital photographs work with light sensitivity just like standard film photography does. However, in digital imaging the image is captured on a chip instead of on film and the digital image can capture approximately 16 million colors and 250 shades of gray. When digital imaging is coupled with image enhancement, the electronic image produced can be clearer and sharper than what the on-site observer can visualize with the unaided eye. In addition to digital imaging, the development of fiber optic transmission and data compression techniques has aided the speed of transmission and helped prevent contamination of the signals. Virtual reality techniques have added the possibility of a three-dimensional image evaluation, and satellite transmissions have added an international and intercontinental and even an interplanetary scope to telemedicine.[3] Now, streaming video has improved video teleconferencing and further enhanced telemedical practice.

The term "telemedicine" is currently used to cover a wide variety of health applications, and more are developing rapidly. It is estimated that by the turn of the next century the majority of American physicians will be involved with telemedicine in some way.

EKG and EEG transmission

The use of telephone lines and facsimile machines to transfer EKG and EEG tracings was probably the earliest application of what we now call telemedicine. Although only providing a static picture and usually accompanied by the scantiest of medical information about the patient, the technique became well established and gave a preview of what was possible in the future.

CME and administrative conferences

Another early and continued widespread use of telemedicine is its use to allow large health provider organizations communicate over an intraorganizational network. Using videoconferencing, a large clinic or hospital can hold administrative or business meetings with their outlying or rural clinics or branches. These video conferences can be as effective as face-to-face meetings and have the advantage of saving the time and expense of transporting personnel between facilities. Continuing medical education (CME) programs originating at the central facility can be viewed by staff throughout the system. Not only can these sessions present lectures, but complicated procedures can be demonstrated and taught. The availability of state-of-the-art CME in rural areas has the potential of making those areas more attractive to young physicians who might hesitate to practice in "educational backwaters" otherwise. The addition of "chat lines" and online journal clubs can also help remote physicians feel connected with mainstream medicine.

Teleradiology

Radiology was the first of the clinical specialties to realize the potential of telemedicine. Remote interpretation of medical imaging is now an established medical procedure. The American College of Radiology has established medical standards as to the qualifications, credentialing, equipment, and quality assurance necessary for telemedicine. Not only can the images be transmitted by digital graphic techniques, but those same techniques are making it possible to save the huge areas of space formerly devoted to the storage of x-ray films. No longer must a rural or outlying physician suffer for the lack of a radiologist to read an emergency film. The image can be transferred to an on-call radiologist digitally and electronically in minutes. In addition, valuable radiology oncology information may be exchanged rapidly between the radiation physicist, the radiology oncologist, and the diagnostic radiologist in the rural or feeder hospital. On the downside, these teleradiology techniques are working so well that many local radiologists are now complaining of competition from the larger, better-known radiology centers. Rural, small community, and suburban clinics are finding it easier to send images electronically to the remote center than to carry films to the local hospital for interpretation.[4]

Patient medical records and medical data banks

Telemedicine networks allow the transfer of patient medical information from clinic to clinic and inpatient facility to inpatient facility. With open access to all health providers involved in a patient's care, such systems cut down on duplicative and contradicting therapies and help eliminate adverse drug reactions. Medical data banks[5] available at the provider's fingertips encourage the use of such data banks and their recommended treatment plans or guidelines. The existence of such programs with the patient's complete medical history makes research into outcomes and total care experiences possible across a wide variety of system facilities.

Videoconsultation, diagnosis, and treatment

This is the area of telemedicine that has taken the lion's share of the attention directed to the subject. Magenau[6] indicates that despite the progress in this field in the United States, Europe, which is free of many of our barriers, is far ahead. With the videoconsultation and modern telemedicine techniques it is possible to have a consultation between a treating physician, the patient, and the telemedicine consultant in which the telemedicine physician meets the patient, views the patient, reviews the medical records, pathology, laboratory, medical imaging, listens to the patient's heart and lungs, and can even palpate the patient via virtual reality gloves.[7] Dermatology consults in particular have thrived in the videoconsultation environment.

Videoconsultation techniques are a godsend in remote or rural medical situations. They can be adopted to help with emergency service care and ambulance transfer to the hospital. Prisons and jails can use the techniques to avoid transferring prisoners to extramural medical facilities. The military can use the techniques in treating frontline casualties. In fact, the military is one of the largest current users of videoconsultations and has satellite connections to over 70 remote sites. The military is now experimenting with remote-controlled battle front surgery using three-dimensional virtual reality screens and robot or surrogate surgeons. There have also been proposals to adapt these techniques to allow patients to be followed in home health care programs.

Telepathology, telecolposcopy, and physician reluctance

The same digital imaging and image enhancement techniques used above can be used for microscopic views, the basis of both histology and colposcopic exams. For several reasons, the techniques, although useful, have not become as popular as teleradiology. Pathologists cite the lack of the gross specimen, the ability to make their own representative "cuts," and loss of depth perception as their principal objections. Colposcopists bring up their disappointment with cervography, a previous imaging technique. It appears, however, that both techniques are effective and will bring an additional method of consultation to underserved areas, but telemedicine's failure to win widespread use in these two procedures illustrates a major problem: physician reluctance to use telemedicine. The usual argument is that the only way to practice medicine is face to face and in person. This defeats one of the principal aims of telemedicine, which is to provide care where that face-to-face in person meeting is not possible. It is also very apparent that a large number of physicians are reluctant to use what they see as new technology. It is easy to write this off to cultural lag, but critics of the profession promote this as further evidence of a profession striving to hold onto the status quo and adopting technologies long after the technology is obsolete. This reluctance to accept telemedicine is likened to the professions' previous failures in the field of heath informatics.

Along with the reluctance of physicians to use telemedicine, other barriers prevent its rapid implementation in the United States. The first is the lack of the communications infrastructure in the American hinterlands to permit rapid, inexpensive, undistorted transmission of medical data. The second is the presence of state licensing requirements, and the third is a series of other legal concerns. In the United States, telemedical practice has flourished in locales such as Hawaii or Alaska where geography presents unique challenges to conventional health care delivery.

Rural telecommunications infrastructure and site equipment

A fully developed and sophisticated communications infrastructure is necessary to transport telemedicine information between rural patients and central specialists. This infrastructure is absent in many of the areas most in need of telemedicine. At the present time, there is no clear-cut method of funding the development of the needed infrastructure. Furthermore, the general economic recession of 2002 has had a tremendous impact upon telecom companies in the United States. If the local carrier does the infrastructure buildout, local access and transport areas rate schedules make the cost of telemedicine prohibitive or, at best, too expensive to be practical. The Telecommunications Act of 1996[8] attempts to secure universal service[9] in regard to health, education, and safety for everyone in the United States regardless of location. The act aims to place telemedicine services at the disposal of rural residents at the same rates as those paid by urban residents. The act instructed the FCC to set up a Joint Working Group on Telemedicine, and Section 709 calls on the Joint Working Group to cooperate with the Department of Health and Human Services in a report to Congress. The FCC went one step further and set up a Telecommunications and Health Care Advisory Committee. It behooves anyone truly interested in telemedicine to read the act carefully and to secure the reports of the working group and the committee created by the FCC.

Although sophisticated equipment is needed at each remote site and providers have worried about potential liability for equipment failure, these problems do not appear to be the barrier some expected them to be. First, the cost of site equipment has dropped more rapidly than anyone could have predicted even 3 to 4 years ago and the one-time outlay today is often comparable to one month's transmission costs in a busy clinic. Second, the general rule for health care providers is that the provider is liable for injuries resulting from negligence in the care, maintenance, or use of the equipment but the manufacturer and seller are liable for injuries resulting from latent defects in the equipment. There seems little reason to believe this general rule will not apply to telemedicine equipment as well.

LEGAL ISSUES

FDA regulation as a medical device

The FDA was given the authority to regulate medical devices in 1976 under the Medical Device Amendments of 1976.[10] The Safe Medical Device Act of 1990[11] built upon the 1976 foundation and created an extensive FDA regulatory scheme to ensure the safety of medical devices. The scheme is a cumbersome one requiring registration, premarketing notification, inspection of the manufacturing facility, warnings to purchasers, and reporting of adverse events for all devices and premarket approval of all new devices. Premarket approval is a lengthy process requiring proof of the safety and efficacy of the device. Section 321(h) of the Food, Drug, and Cosmetics Act defines a medical device very broadly.[12] It would appear that both the telemedicine systems and their components fall under the definition of a medical device as established by Section 321(h). It also appears that the FDA will assume a regulatory role in telemedicine.

The FDA has shown great interest in teleradiology and is already regulating the hardware of teleradiology systems and the software connected with medical imaging systems.[13] To date, FDA regulation appears to be dependent upon whether the device is promoted as a medical device or not. Equipment marketed for general communication purposes has escaped FDA attention. In fact, the FDA's approach has been thoughtful and helpful. However, if the FDA acts as most administrative regulatory agencies are so inclined, it will gradually extend its authority over all aspects of telemedicine. If the FDA attempts to regulate telemedicine systems as a whole, it could be a disastrous turn of events for the development and use of telemedicine. The Byzantine nature of the FDA approval system could wreak havoc on upgrading systems, as well as discouraging manufacturers of communications hardware and software from entering the telemedicine field. One can envision the rapidly evolving telemedicine technology suddenly brought to the glacial pace that only an administrative agency may invoke. We should watch this area of regulation closely.

Licensing and credentialing

State licensing laws are highly individual and set up a barrier to the practice of telemedicine across state lines. Each state has the right to license physicians to practice medicine as part of the state's police power to protect the health of its citizens. This police power is granted the states by the Constitution[14] and two Supreme Court decisions.[15] Therefore, there is a presumption that the state will find anyone examining, diagnosing, or treating a state resident practicing medicine within that state. The Federation of State Medical Boards (FSMB) has maintained the necessity of individual state licensure in its Model Act to Regulate the Practice of Medicine by Other Means Across State Lines.[16]

At the time of this writing in 2002, there are 21 states in the United States that statutorily require full medical licensure in the state where a physician is practicing telemedicine.[17] By default, states that have not specifically addressed telemedical practice by statute will require a physician to have a valid state license in the state where they are practicing medicine via telemedicine. At present, there are numerous telemedicine-related bills being considered in several state legislatures. Only time will tell when all states have finally codified some form of telemedicine law. In addition, there are 6 states that require a special purpose license.[18] For example, Texas law provides that a person shall be considered to be "practicing medicine" if the person is physically located in another jurisdiction and through any medium performs an act that is part of patient care service initiated in Texas that would "affect the diagnosis or treatment of a patient."[19] The "special purpose license" is required for a physician who is actively licensed in another state and certified in a medical specialty.[19] The law also requires that an applicant for a special purpose license pass the Texas Medical Jurisprudence examination, and practice is limited to the medical specialty upon which the license is granted.[19] A special purpose license is not required for a limited number of "episodic consultations" to a Texas physician who practices in the same medical specialty, consultation services provided to a Texas medical school, or for medical assistance if no charge is made.[19]

The FSMB Model Act would permit a duly licensed practitioner in one state to obtain a limited license in another state solely for the purpose of practicing medicine across the state line. The FSMB Model Act has been criticized in telemedicine circles because it permits the adoption of somewhat different standards by each of the states. California has eliminated licensure requirements for the consultant who "shall not open an office, appoint a place to meet patients, receive calls from patients within the limits of this state, give orders, or have ultimate authority over the care or primary diagnosis of a patient who is located in this state"[20]—a limited relief at best. Several other states have introduced licensing requirements applicable to telemedicine or had preexisting statutes that might be applied to telemedicine.[21] However, none of the states appear to have adopted the FSMB Model Act in its entirety. At this time it would appear that four rather shaky conclusions can be drawn concerning interstate licensure (see Box 39-1)

Credentialing

Little attention has been directed to the credentialing of telemedicine specialist physicians either by their specialty organizations[22] or by the organizations (hospitals and/or MCOs) of the treating physician and, to date, it appears that existing consultation criteria control. The Joint Commission for the Accreditation of Health Care Organizations has delineated no credentialing criteria specifically for telemedicine consultants. Several bills have been introduced within state legislatures pertaining to telemedicine consultants and practice within state-regulated hospitals, but the content and progress of those bills is currently not available to the authors.

Confidentiality

Fears that the confidentiality of patient medical information would be violated has also acted to slow the spread of telemedicine. While true confidentiality of medical information is probably a myth in this age of multiple providers, third-party payors, and fourth-party auditors, it has been one of the legal issues most commonly raised in discussions of telemedicine. Moreover, the protection of the integrity of the medical information is commonly lumped with confidentiality as a single issue. Indeed the fear of "hackers," who are capable of not only observing teleconsultations and medical records but of altering the records as well, seems to be the primary concern of many commentators.[23] The fact that a readily accessible paper record is subject to the same sort of scrutiny, alteration, or destruction by a much less sophisticated trespasser seems to have been forgotten in the wake of widespread reports of hacker prowess. As the National Research Council notes, attention must center on methods of protecting the confidentiality and integrity of sensitive electronic health care data rather than opposing its use in health care.[24]

To think that electronically transferred information cannot be protected or to forbid information transfer done for the benefit of the patient because it may violate some state confidentiality regulation makes no sense. Electronic patient data is transferred across state lines daily just as information in all fields of modern endeavor is. Today, information knows no state boundaries. The benefit to the patient and to society as a whole of permitting the electronic transfer of health data makes state confidentiality regulations obsolete. The 1986 Electronic Privacy Act[25] prohibits the interception of any electronic communication but offers no practical protection criteria.

Telemedicine needs practical guidelines as to what steps it must take to protect personal medical information from unauthorized persons or institutions. Congress has addressed that issue in the Health Insurance Portability and Accountability Act (HIPAA) of 1996.[26] The final HIPAA directive on the subject, entitled *Standards for Privacy of Individually Identifiable Health Information*, was published in late 2002.[27]

Malpractice insurance

The telemedicine consultant must carefully determine whether he or she is covered by malpractice insurance.[28] Some malpractice insurance carriers specifically exclude

---

BOX 39-1

State law still controls licensure and no federal preemption is likely to occur in the near future.

Irregular, infrequent physician to physician consults will not require a license in most states.

Regular, frequent consults, direct patient contacts, and patient interventions will require either a limited or full license.

The state licensure statutes vary to such a degree that the relevant statutes should be carefully reviewed before accepting any of the generalities listed above.

coverage for telemedicine. These exclusion clauses are usually based largely on the licensure issue, although there is no doubt that the physician-patient relationship and conflict of laws issues discussed below enter into the carrier's decisions.

Malpractice issues

Fortunately, there have been few malpractice cases involving telemedicine. Unfortunately, those malpractice cases that have arisen have reached settlement and we are unaware of any that have reached the appeals level. Dalton reports the same lack of precedents in the European Union.[29] Therefore, there are no binding precedents in telemedicine law. Despite this lack of precedents, physicians continue to worry and lawyers continue to speculate about the potential of malpractice actions for telemedicine activities. The foremost of the issues is whether a telemedicine physician assumes a duty of care for the remote patient. In other words: does a physician-patient relationship exist?

Physician-patient relationship

Classically, the physician who discusses a patient with the treating physician does not establish a physician-patient relationship with the patient.[30] There is nothing inherent in the electronic aspect of such discussions that should change that concept. However, when telemedicine is used for remote diagnosis, interactive videoconsultations and remote physicians take a more active role in the treatment of the patient, perhaps even including surgery, the physician-patient relationship may well be established. Someday, the definition of a patient-physician relationship may also reflect the changed health care delivery systems possible with telemedicine.[31]

There are a long line of telephone cases, certainly an early form of telemedicine, that establish that a physician-patient relationship exists when a physician attempts to diagnose, advise, or treat a patient via the phone.[32] There are also a long line of cases that establish a physician-patient relationship for physicians such as pathologists, radiologists, and electrocardiologists who are active in the care of the patient but that never have a face-to-face meeting with the patient.[33] The reasoning in these case lines would appear to be directly applicable to comparable telemedicine cases and indicate that a physician-patient relationship will exist in many telemedicine situations. The physician-patient relationship appears particularly clear in situations where the telemedicine physician meets with both the treating physician and the patient via the videoteleconference and takes part in developing the history and physical examination of the patient through the use of various media and then participates in developing a treatment plan.

Jurisdiction

It is a principle of conflicts of law that in a personal injury case the situs of the injury determines the jurisdiction unless some other state has a more significant relationship. These dual factors make it likely that the patient would have no difficulty instituting suit in his or her state of residence and may be able to bring suit in the telemedicine physician's state if the forum was more appealing. Diversity of residence and the value of the case may also add the possibility of the federal court system as an applicable forum. The possibility of the plaintiff being able to bring suit in any state the telemedicine physician has electronic ties to, and thus have an almost unlimited opportunity to forum shop, although widely speculated on in the medical literature, does not appear to be a serious concern at this time.

More complicated conflict of laws situations may exist in malpractice cases where the patient is a resident of a country other than the United States and has no local provision for malpractice litigation, or in patients treated in space. A wide variety of cases will have to reach the appellate level before all these jurisdictional issues become clear-cut.

Abandonment

While most legal commentators think it is highly unlikely that a telemedicine physician would be held to have abandoned a patient still under the care of the treating or referring physician, the telemedicine physician must be sure to document the items listed in Box 39-2.

Reimbursement

Most physicians have a difficult time securing reimbursement for telemedicine services. At this time, there is no consistent national policy on reimbursement for telemedicine services. Most telemedicine is currently supported by demonstration grants from federal, state, or private sources. In general, insurers have refused to pay for telemedicine services. Medicare will pay for teleradiology providing the films are transmitted and read according to the standards established by the American College of Radiology. On July 1, 2001, the Health Care Financing Administration (HCFA) was renamed the Centers for Medicare and Medicaid Services (CMS). CMS will allow Medicare to pay for telemedicine in designated health care shortage areas, and will allow Medicaid areas to establish their own telemedicine policies. CMS has been directed to establish national standards for telemedicine reimbursement and has set up several test areas to test plans. Once Medicare

---

BOX 39-2

The patient and treating physician know of the need for any continuing treatment.
All parties know and agree on who will provide that care.
The patient knows who to call in an emergency.
The treating physician knows how and when to contact the telemedicine physician.

and Medicaid have such a standard, it is likely that private insurers will adopt a similar payment scheme.[34]

CONCLUSION

Telemedicine has demonstrated its potential to offer widespread access to sophisticated medical care, curtailed health care delivery costs, and homogeneous health and health-related education opportunities. However, progress in telemedicine has revealed a variety of potential barriers to its widespread application once the technical infrastructure is well established. These barriers include technical limitations, reimbursement issues, equipment and networking costs, and appropriate scientific studies to document efficacy and cost-effectiveness. These issues may prove to be only transient disincentives that can be surmounted.

In addition, a number of medical and legal issues exist that may not be as readily resolved by traditional methods of analysis. Some examples include: (1) the potential need to redefine the nature of the physician-patient relationship; (2) the protection of patient privacy and confidentiality; (3) the balance between federalism and states' rights in determining the medical licensure status of physicians who practice telemedicine; and, (4) the political and regulatory obstacles that are sure to require solutions based on national consensus. The practice of telemedicine will change the interactions and relationships between physician/patient, physician/physician, and physician/third-party payor.

One thing is certain: telemedicine enhances man's ability to deliver medical care. Perhaps the real question is: What price is mankind willing to pay to provide health care without boundaries? At this point, all we know is that the answer lies somewhere between here and cyberspace.

ENDNOTES

1. *See* U.S. Federal Food and Drug Administration, Center for Devices and Radiological Health, *White Paper on Telemedicine Related Activities* (1996); *see also* Joint Working Group on Telemedicine, *Executive Summary: Telemedicine Report to Congress* (Jan. 1997), http://www.ntia.doc.gov/reports/telcmcd.

2. *See* California Telemedicine Development Act of 1996, 1996 Cal. Stat. 864 §1(d).

3. Dalton mentions intercontinental programs in pathology, obstetrics, radiology, cardiology, oncology, dermatology, surgery, laparoscopy, and endoscopy. K. J. Dalton, *Legal Aspects of Telemedicine Across State Borders*, L.L.M. Dissertation, Cambridge University (Aug. 28, 1998); M.R. Campbell, *Surgical Care in Space*, 70 Aviation, Space and Environmental Medicine 181 (1999).

4. *See* D.F. Meek, *Telemedicine: How an Apple (or Another Computer) May Bring Your Doctor Closer*, 29 Cumberland L. Rev. 173, 175 (1998).

5. Examples of such data banks include the highly successful Helix data bank for clinical geneticists and several regional data banks dealing with diabetes and diabetic complications. *See* P. Tarcyz-Hornoch et al., *Creation and Maintenance of Helix, a Web Based Database of Medical Genetics Laboratories*, 1998 Proceedings of AMIA, 341; T.H. Williamson & D. Keating, *Telemedicine and Computers in Diabetic Retinopathy Screening*, 82 British Journal of Ophthalmology 5 (1997); P.C. Jones et al., *Nationwide Telecare for Diabetics*, 1998 Proceedings AMIA, 346.

6. Jeff L. Magenau, *Digital Diagnosis: Liability Concerns and State Licensing Issues Are Inhibiting the Progress of Telemedicine*, Communications and the Law 25 (Dec. 1997).

7. Several examples of virtual gloves are currently undergoing clinical evaluation.

8. Pub. L. No. 104-104 (codified in scattered sections of 47 U.S.C.).

9. *Id.* §§253 and 254.

10. 21 U.S.C. §§360c-360k.

11. Pub. L. No. 101-629, 104 Stat. 4511 (1990)

12. 21 U.S.C. §321(h) defines a medical device as: an instrument, apparatus, implement, machine, contrivance, implant, in vitro reagent, or other similar or related article including any component part or accessory, which is
    (1) recognized in the official National Formulary, or in the United States Pharmacopeia, or any supplement to them,
    (2) intended for use in the diagnosis of disease or other conditions, or in the cure, mitigation, treatment or prevention of disease in man or other animals, or
    (3) intended to affect the structure or any function of the body of man or other animals, and which does not achieve its primary intended purpose through chemical action within or on the body of man or other animals and
    (4) which is not dependent upon being metabolized for the achievement of its primary intended purpose.
    Only one of the three elements must be met to classify the object as a medical device.

13. *See* FDA, Center for Devices and Radiological Health, *Guidance for the Content and Review of 501(K) Notifications for Picture Archiving and Communications Systems and Related Devices* (1997).

14. U.S. Const. Amend. X.

15. *Dent v. West Virginia*, 129 U.S. 114 (1889); *Hawker v. New York*, 170 U.S. 189 (1898).

16. See Appendix 39-1 below.

17. These 21 states are: Arizona, Arkansas, California, Colorado, Connecticut, Florida, Georgia, Hawaii, Illinois, Indiana, Missouri, Mississippi, Nebraska, New Hampshire, North Carolina, North Dakota, Oklahoma, South Dakota, Utah, Virginia, and West Virginia.

18. These 6 states are: Alabama, Montana, New Mexico, Oregon, Tennessee, and Texas.

19. *See* 22 TX ADC §174.2 and TX OCC §151.056.

20. Senate Bill 1665 §3, 1996-97 Reg. Ses. (Cal. 1996) (Enacted), codified in various sections of the Business and Professions Code, Health and Safety Code, Insurance Code, and Welfare and Institutions Code.

21. Maryland's statute, while not specific to telemedicine, provides much the same protections as does California's statute (Md. Ann. Code §14-302); Colorado (Col. Rev. Stat. §12-36-106(b), Delaware (Del. Code Ann. §1726), Indiana (Ind. Code Ann. §25-22.5-1-2 (4)) Missouri (Mo. Ann. Stat. §334.010), Vermont (Vt. Stat. Ann §26-23-1313), and Nevada (Nev. Rev. Stat. §630.047) allow consultations across state lines; Alabama, while specifically stating that telemedicine is the practice of medicine (Ala. Code §34-24-501(2)), also allows practice across state lines if it occurs less than 10 times per calendar year (Ala. Code §34-24-505(b)); Oklahoma's Telemedicine Act (Okla. Stat. Ann. §6801), while covering reimbursement and informed consent, does not deal with licensing directly; Mississippi's statute on telemedicine (Miss. Code Ann. §73-25-34) specifically requires a state license for the practice of telemedicine across state lines (although the Mississippi Attorney General has rendered an opinion that radiologists interpreting films sent outside the state are not practicing medicine in Mississippi); Texas (Tex. Rev. Stat. Ann. Art. 4495(b) §3.06(I)), South Dakota (S.D. Codified Laws §36-4-41), and Florida (Fla. Stat. Ann. §458.3255) have provisions that closely resemble Mississippi's; Minnesota (Minn. Stat. Ann. §147.081) and Oregon (Or. Rev. Stat. §677.085) define the practice of medicine in a way that indicates a license is required for telemedicine; Kansas and Ohio have licensing provisos that may permit a telemedicine practitioner to receive a limited license to practice.

charging of Vo with murder or manslaughter of the fetus. The court concluded that: "Legislature did not intend to include a fetus in the definition of 'person' or 'human being' contained in murder statute; thus, killing of a fetus does not constitute first-degree murder."[17]

The court further clarified their opinion by stating that it was the responsibility of the legislature if they intended to include a fetus in the definition of a person[18] for purposes of the homicide statutes. Of note, the Arizona legislature did subsequently respond by passing legislation[19] that expanded the definition of manslaughter to include a fetus. The classification of manslaughter included one who ". . . knowingly or recklessly causing the death of an unborn child at any stage of its development by any physical injury to the mother of such child which would be murder if the death of the mother had occurred." This broader concept of unlawful homicide expanded the legal rights of a fetus.

If the fetus is subsequently born alive

Civil law. In the context of civil law, the situation in which a fetus is harmed and then subsequently born alive is often quite similar to the situation in which any other person is harmed. Just because the injury is inflicted prenatally does not generally limit the civil options available to the newborn or the estate. If there is a prenatal injury resulting in a postnatal lawsuit, these suits are often directed against obstetricians and hospitals. Failure to diagnose, failure to treat, and delayed treatment are common malpractice complaints. These lawsuits are quite similar to the situation when the fetus does not survive until parturition. However, there are more causes of action and remedies available when the fetus survives to become a live-born baby. Causes of action, such as negligent infliction of emotional distress, can generally be maintained. A surviving newborn has essentially the same civil rights as any other "person."

WRONGFUL DEATH. If there is a prenatal injury, and the child is born alive and subsequently dies as a result of those injuries, a wrongful death action can be maintained. Unlike the situation when the fetus dies in utero, there is not the same interstate variability in these cases. If the child is born alive, wrongful death suits are generally allowed.

Criminal law. When a newborn dies as a result of criminal activity,[20] courts have largely refused to make a distinction based on timing of the injury. Following *Vo*,[21] various states adopted legislation to address the situation where a fetus is harmed in utero.[22]

In a 2000 case, the Superior Court of Maricopa County addressed the specific problem of an in-utero injury resulting in a neonatal death. The court was faced with a defendant who shot and killed a woman who was 8½ months pregnant. The child was born and lived for 1 day. The prosecution argued that reckless manslaughter statutes should apply, and that the defendant would be guilty of an unlawful killing, even though the injury took place prior to parturition. The court held,[23] and the appellate court affirmed,[24] that the homicide statutes apply to the killing of a child that is born alive, even if the fatal injuries were inflicted prenatally. The court further held that the statutes were not rendered impermissibly vague, and due process was not violated by applying the homicide statutes to this defendant.

EXTREMELY PREMATURE INFANTS

If an infant is born with a heart rate, respiratory effort, or voluntary muscle movement, the baby is considered to be a live birth.[25] However, this does not mean that the medical or legal issues are completely resolved. Ironically, some of the most renowned medical malpractice cases concerning newborns are brought specifically because the baby survived, and the parents had expressed their wishes that the baby not be resuscitated after birth. With respect to the tiniest newborns, "born alive" may be a state of being that lasts only seconds or minutes. Babies born during the middle part of the second trimester can be born with a spontaneous pulse and some brief respiratory effort. Technically, these babies are born alive, and therefore they are persons. Medically, the technology does not exist that can offer them reasonable assistance. Legally, these tiny entities often exist in a "gray zone."

Complications of extreme prematurity include death, intracranial hemorrhage, retinopathy of prematurity, blindness, cerebral palsy, deafness, developmental delay, mental retardation, failure to thrive, chronic lung disease, recurrent pulmonary (and other) infections, reactive airway disease, and other severe chronic diseases.[26] With improved technology has come increased survival rate for the tiniest babies. However, many authors, health care providers, and parents wonder if this increased survival comes at the unacceptable price of the substantially increased incidence of moderate to severe handicaps.

A normal pregnancy generally lasts 40 weeks. An infant is considered to be premature when the gestation is less than 37 weeks.[27] Birth weight less than 2500 grams is considered to be low birth weight.[28] If a newborn weighs less than 1500 grams, this is considered to be very low birth weight.[29] There are a variety of causes of prematurity and low birth weight including maternal hypertension, multiple gestation, and inadequate prenatal care. In many cases, the etiology is unknown. However, maternal smoking, low socioeconomic status, and African-American race have been causally linked to low birth weight.[30]

With the advent of newer therapies and technologies, including antenatal corticosteroids,[31] surfactant replacement therapy,[32] high-frequency[33,34] and other modes of mechanical ventilation,[35] and advances in all aspects of NICU care, it is not unusual for babies weighing 1 lb. to survive.

Unfortunately, the complications of prematurity can be profound. The complications of prematurity tend to occur in the smallest and most premature babies. Although survival for extremely low–birth weight babies has improved over the last 20 years, the incidence of complications is substantial. Recent data published by D'Angio et al.[36] shows that surviving infants of less than 29 weeks gestation now have greater than 50% of having at least one severe disability.[37] For many years it has been known that otherwise "normal" premature babies will often have subtle neurological abnormalities, such as cognitive deficits, which can be difficult to diagnose prior to the child reaching school age.

Recent data in the *Journal of Perinatology*[38] demonstrate improvements in survival and outcome for babies with a birth weight of 500 to 800 grams. These data were compiled by the prestigious Committee on the Fetus and Newborn, a section of the American Academy of Pediatrics. In this series, the majority of newborns survived, even when the smallest babies (500-599 gram cohort) were evaluated. The majority of the babies in this study survived until discharge. As is often seen in outcome studies of extremely premature newborns, some of the complications seen in the tiniest survivors included intracranial hemorrhage, periventricular leukomalacia, abnormal tone, poor suck and swallow, seizures, abnormal EEGs, and retinopathy. Given the long-term outcome data reported by Hack et al.[39] and other groups, strong concern remains among neonatal practitioners that significant challenges face the tiniest of survivors.

In this sense, new technology can be seen as a "double-edged sword." Tiny, fragile newborns that would have likely died 15 years ago now have an improved chance of survival. But significant and often profound complications can arise. Because long-term morbidity may not be readily apparent, there is often a staggering burden on the family and the health care team when there is the high potential for a 1 lb. baby to be born. Given the high likelihood of death or severe deficits, should the baby receive resuscitative efforts?

Given this background of uncertainty,[40] health care practitioners, parents, and the courts face considerable challenges in attempting to draft meaningful guidelines for the care of the smallest babies. *Roe v. Wade*[41] established the right to terminate a pregnancy under certain circumstances. However, the justices addressed the complexities inherent in efforts to determine "when life begins":

We need not resolve the difficult question of when life begins. When those trained in the respective disciplines of medicine, philosophy, and theology are unable to arrive at any consensus, the judiciary, at this point in the development of man's knowledge, is not in a position to speculate as to the answer.[42,43]

This observation may or may not be a satisfactory answer in determining the gestational age at which abortion is "allowed." Perhaps more importantly, it does not shed light on the question of when an extremely premature infant is considered "previable" and when the infant is considered to be deserving of full resuscitative efforts.[44]

The progeny[45,46] of *Roe* further defined the limits of the right to terminate an undesired pregnancy. In 1992, in *Planned Parenthood of Southeastern Pennsylvania v. Casey*, the court explicitly reaffirmed that the "line should be drawn at viability."[47] So, "previable" fetuses are not accorded the same rights as fetuses that have passed 23-24 weeks gestation. Previable is generally viewed as gestation at which the fetus is not capable of independent existence outside of the uterus. Premature fetuses that can be kept alive only with the use of technology are *not* considered to be "previable." Only fetuses at a gestation that could not survive with modern NICU care are considered previable.

What if the child is born alive at 22-24 weeks gestation? In general, the fetus could have been aborted at this gestation.[48] However, if the child is born alive, the law may be considerably more complex.

The survival rate at 23 weeks gestation has recently been reported to be in the 10-30% range, with an approximately 50% incidence of moderate or severe handicap for the survivors.[49] Two widely respected groups, the Committee on the Fetus and Newborn and the Neonatal Research Network, have recently published data in the journal *Pediatrics*.[50]

Data, such as these recent publications, are often presented to families when they are facing the extremely difficult decision of whether or not to forgo resuscitation. Health care providers have striven to provide families with the most accurate and up-to-date information to facilitate informed decision-making.

CARING FOR PREMATURE INFANTS AGAINST PARENTS' WISHES

HCA v. Miller

On August 17, 1990, Karla Miller was admitted to an HCA Texas hospital in premature labor. Gestation was estimated at 23 weeks.[51] Because Mrs. Miller had an "infection," the obstetrician determined that aborting the pregnancy would be unsafe for the mother. An obstetrician and neonatologist met with the Millers to discuss the outlook for babies delivered at this gestation. After these discussions, the Millers orally requested that no heroic measures be provided. Initially, the health care providers supported the parents' decision. However, subsequent meetings took place with the obstetrician and hospital representatives. It was decided that if the baby was born alive and weighed more than 500 grams, then the baby would receive resuscitative efforts.[52]

The obstetrician explained this to Mr. Miller, who again reiterated the parents' wishes that the baby not be resuscitated. The baby was born "alive," and was resuscitated. Sidney Miller survived. She now suffers from "severe physical and mental impairments, and it is predicted that she will never be able to care for herself."[53]

The Millers sued HCA (the treating hospital was a subsidiary of HCA), under a theory of vicarious liability. The parents sued because their daughter was treated without their consent, and they also asserted that the HCA hospital had vicarious liability because the hospital had a policy mandating treatment of all newborns weighing greater than 500 grams, even without parental consent. Finally, the parents asserted that HCA had direct liability because the hospital did not have policies in place to prevent this unwanted treatment of their daughter. The hospital asserted that parents had no right to refuse life-sustaining measures.

At the trial court level, the Millers were awarded a total verdict exceeding $60 million.[54] In overturning this verdict, the appellate court ruled that the parents did not have the right to refuse consent for resuscitation. In making their decision, the court referred to the Advanced Directives Act. If life-supporting care is withheld or withdrawn, the Advanced Directives Act protects physicians, health care professionals and institutions from civil and criminal liability. However, a patient must be certified as "terminal" before the health care providers are protected under the act.[55] The court ruled that the condition of Sidney Miller could not be certified as "terminal" under the Advanced Directives Act.[56] Therefore, there was no parental right to deny " . . . urgently needed life-sustaining medical treatment, and no court order was needed to overcome their refusal to consent to it."[57]

In reaching their decision, the Texas Appellate Court discussed three legal issues and potentially competing interests:

1. Parents have the right to consent for their children's medical care.
2. Parents have a legal duty to provide needed medical care for their children.
3. The state has an interest in guarding the well-being of minors.

Each of these issues is discussed below.

Parents' right to consent. In general, parents are responsible for the care, custody, and control of their children. This liberty interest is a fundamental right and it is protected by the due process clause of the Fourteenth Amendment.[58] If care must be provided on an urgent basis, then the "emergency exception" may apply. In these situations, a health care provider generally will be shielded from liability based on lack of consent, because the provided care was too urgent to obtain proper consent. The limits of the emergency exception were examined in a 1920 case, *Moss v. Rishworth*. A doctor obtained consent for a tonsillectomy from a sibling. Although the surgery was indicated and no negligence was found with the care, the parents prevailed based on their claim of lack of informed consent.[59]

The *Miller* court pointed out that the right for parents to consent is a fundamental right, but *not* an absolute one.[60] An extensive list of examples was presented in which the state was allowed to interfere with parental decision-making. Instances when the state can interfere with absolute parental

rights include mandatory newborn screening, mandatory syphilis testing, mandatory immunizations, mandatory hearing and visual exams, mandatory attendance at school, prohibition on parents putting their children in the workforce, and court-ordered transfusions for children.

The justices also noted that inherent in the right to consent is the corollary right to *not* consent.[61] The *Cruzan* decision largely empowered families and health care providers to decide to forgo life-sustaining care in cases of terminal illness or futility. Consistent with *Cruzan*, parents generally have the right to make these surrogate decisions for their own children.[62] Given this background of parents' right to determine the care and custody of their children, the court then examined the two other competing legal issues.

Parents' legal duty to provide needed care to their children. Part and parcel of a parent's right to make health care decisions for their children is the balancing duty of parents to ensure that their children are receiving necessary care. The *Miller* court cited the Texas Family Code,[63] and noted that failure to meet this duty may constitute a criminal act on the part of the parent.[64]

States' interest in guarding the well-being of minors. Acting as parens patriae, the state has this interest. It is clear that this interest can directly conflict with parents' rights and authority. As noted above, the court recited a partial list of instances when the state may interfere with parental decision-making. Parents' fundamental rights and authority may be restricted by the state, and, in the case of children, the state has considerable authority to oversee the care of children. After a detailed discussion of parents' rights, the right to refuse medical treatment, and the state's interest, the court articulated the issue as: Does a parent have a right to deny urgently needed life-sustaining medical treatment to their child, i.e., to decide, in effect, to let their child die?

While the Texas legislature has granted parents the right to withhold medical treatment if their child is terminal, this right does not exist because the child is otherwise disabled or impaired. In overturning the $60 million verdict, the appellate court held that " . . . as a matter of first impression, a health care provider is not liable in tort for administering urgently needed life-sustaining medical treatment to newborn infant contrary to pre-birth instructions of parents not to do so."[65]

The appellate court does conclude that perhaps an exception should be made for extremely premature babies that are likely to be born in such critical condition that sustaining their life is not justified. Having stated this, the majority points out that such an exception, if desirable, would be a result of new legislation or a higher court.[66,67] Of note, the Texas Supreme Court has granted certiorari.

Wrongful birth and wrongful life in the Miller case. The court discusses the concepts of wrongful birth and wrongful life. Contrasts are drawn with other cases, and then these issues are dismissed.[68,69] The court relies upon an earlier case and quotes: "The principal reason for this holding was the impossibility of rationally determining whether the child had actually been damaged by the birth because to do so would require weighing the relative benefits to her of an impaired life versus no life at all."[70]

Dissent. The dissent in *HCA v. Miller* noted that no emergency existed. The physicians did not attempt to transfer care to another doctor who would have honored the parents' wishes. Also, the dissent notes that the hospital and physicians had 11 hours to either obtain a court order or discuss their thinking with the parents. The dissent points out that this was not an "emergency," and it was the appellant's indecision and delay that led to the "emergency" nature of the care being provided. The dissent also noted that the most important issue is "the best interest of the child,"[71] and having a court hearing regarding the resuscitation would have allowed an impartial panel to make a decision.

The Messenger case

On February 8, 1994, Gregory and Traci Messenger had a similar experience to the Millers. When Traci Messenger threatened to deliver at 25 weeks gestation, the parents considered the very high rate of severe complications for their son. The parents requested that their child not be intubated and ventilated. The physician assistant at the Lansing, Michigan, hospital disregarded the parents' request and intubated the baby boy. At approximately 1 hour of age, Gregory Messenger, a dermatologist, removed his son from the ventilator and placed the baby in his mother's arms. Without mechanical ventilation, the baby died. The attending physician wrote "homicide" on the death certificate. Dr. Messenger was subsequently charged with manslaughter.[72] Almost exactly 1 year later, Dr. Messenger was acquitted of manslaughter in the death of his newborn son.[73,74]

The court cited authority for parents to withdraw care for their terminally ill children.[75] *In re Guardianship of Barry* addressed the issue of parents withdrawing care and letting their terminally ill children die. In this case, the child was a 10 month old who was terminally ill and "wholly lacking in cognitive brain functioning." The parents, as guardian, petitioned the court to allow the withdrawal of life support. The trial court granted this request. The district appellate court noted that the trial court, in making their decision to allow the withdrawal of care, correctly applied the doctrine of "substituted judgment."[76]

HANDICAPPED NEWBORNS

Baby Doe

There has been considerable interface between the legal system and those who care for "handicapped" newborns. The very definition of handicap, the allowable limitations on care provided for handicapped newborns, and the remedies available to babies, families, hospitals, and the state have been extensively debated and, in some cases, litigated.

During the early 1980s a series of court cases brought the issue of handicapped newborns to the mainstream.

Baby Doe only lived for 6 days. His brief life precipitated tremendous controversy[77] and plunged the neonatal community into a prolonged debate. Within 3 years of his death, the American Medical Association, the American Academy of Pediatrics, the Reagan Administration, and the United States Supreme Court would be involved in the debate. In 1983, when the U.S. Supreme Court denied certiorari,[78] the matter was far from resolved. More than 20 years after his death, the legacy of Baby Doe still affects the care provided to handicapped newborns all over the country.[79]

Infant Doe was born with Down's syndrome on April 9, 1982, in Bloomington, Indiana. Despite the fact that children with Down's exhibit a wide range of developmental delay, Down's syndrome is not considered to be a fatal syndrome. As is often the case with babies with Down's syndrome, Infant Doe had an anomaly of the gastrointestinal tract. Although not the most common atresia associated with Down's syndrome, Infant Doe had esophageal atresia.[80] This anomaly prevents the enteral intake of fluid and nutrition. Without surgical correction, the baby would die. After the health care team spoke with the parents, the decision was made to withhold food and water until the baby died. Absent the diagnosis of Down's syndrome, deferring surgical correction would not even have been considered as an option.

Baby Doe had a correctable surgical problem and an underlying syndrome that would lead to mental retardation. The baby was allowed to die because he had Down's syndrome. Many observers felt that the decisions to defer surgery and to withhold nutrition were unreasonable. Many questioned the parents' rights to make such a decision for a child with a nonfatal syndrome such as Downs. A national controversy erupted following the baby's death. Amidst the controversy, advocates for the handicapped relied upon Section 504 of the Rehabilitation Act of 1973,[81] which prohibits discrimination based on handicap.

Subsequently, the Department of Health and Human Services issued guidelines that were designed to prevent handicapped newborns from being deprived of life-saving therapies solely because they were handicapped. At the request of President Reagan, a strong federal role was suggested in ensuring care be provided for handicapped newborns. Hospitals that received federal funds were required to post "in a conspicuous place"[82] a notice that a "hotline" was available for anyone to report a violation of the law to the Department of Health and Human Services. The American Academy of Pediatrics and other groups contested these guidelines. Ultimately, the guidelines were declared invalid.

Baby Jane Doe

On October 11, 1983, Baby Jane Doe was born with meningomylocoele, hydrocephalus, and other anomalies.[83] The baby's parents refused to give the hospital consent to repair the spinal defect and to drain the hydrocephalus. The parents opted for nutritional support and antibiotics with the hope that the skin would grow over the defect and protect it. An attorney, who was unrelated to the family, filed for the appointment of a guardian *ad litem* for the baby. The federal government subsequently brought suit, under Section 504 of the 1973 Rehabilitation Act,[84] to discover whether or not the baby was the victim of discriminatory withholding of medical care based on her handicap.

The district court held that the federal government could compel access to the medical records in this case. This holding was overturned during the appellate process. The Second Circuit of the United States Court of Appeals affirmed[85] that the Department of Health and Human Services lacked the statutory authority to conduct the investigation and to access the medical records of Baby Jane Doe. This court also affirmed that the hospital was honoring the reasonable medical decision-making of the parents.

This case reached the U.S. Supreme Court in 1986. As noted above, in the original Baby Doe case, the United States Supreme Court denied certiorari. However, the High Court did ultimately consider the issue of the care of handicapped newborns.[86] In this case, the court not only reviewed the facts of the present case, Baby Jane Doe, but they also recapped the judicial history of Baby Doe.

The United States Supreme Court found (1) the parents had made a reasonable medical decision that could have been consistent with the best interests of the child, (2) withholding the surgical treatment was not discriminatory, and (3) the trial court had abused their discretion by allowing the proceedings to go forward.[87]

The Supreme Court ruled that in order to violate Section 504, an "otherwise qualified" would have to be denied care "solely by reason of his handicap." The Supreme Court concluded that, absent parental consent, the withholding of treatment from a handicapped infant cannot violate Section 504.[88]

ANENCEPHALY

Baby K

Anencephaly is a neural tube defect[89] that leads to profound abnormality of brain development. The skull is incompletely formed and part of the brain is exposed to the amniotic fluid. In general, there is complete absence of the cerebral cortex and other vital neural structures. If the pregnancy is not terminated through spontaneous or surgical abortion, the newborns generally live for a few days or weeks. Absent heroic intervention, these babies generally die very soon after birth.[90]

On October 13, 1992,[91] Baby K was born with anencephaly. The baby had respiratory distress. She was placed on mechanical ventilation so that her diagnosis could be confirmed, and so that the situation could be completely explained to her parents. Because of the extremely grim prognosis, the doctors recommended that the baby only receive warmth, fluids, and nutrition. The mother, based on her firm religious beliefs, insisted that the baby receive mechanical ventilation if needed to sustain the baby's life. The hospital's efforts to transfer the baby to another facility were unsuccessful. After she no longer required intensive care, Baby K was transferred to a nursing home.

Baby K was readmitted to the original hospital on three occasions for respiratory distress. Each time, the mother insisted on intubation and mechanical ventilation. The hospital felt that providing this care was morally and unethically inappropriate, and they sought judicial intervention to allow them to stop providing what they perceived to be futile treatment. The hospital wanted clarification if they were obligated to provide emergency medical care for Baby K. Baby K's guardian and her father joined in the action, as they also felt that the baby should not be offered mechanical ventilation.[92] The mother prevailed. The case reached the 4th Circuit of the United States Court of Appeals in 1994.[93] This 4th Circuit affirmed the findings of the lower court, namely, that the hospital was obligated to provide the requested care under the Emergency Medical Treatment and Active Labor Act[94] (EMTALA). This act requires that participating hospitals provide emergency stabilizing treatment to any person with any emergency medical condition if that treatment is requested on their behalf. This act was known as "antidumping" legislation to prevent hospitals that received federal funds from withholding treatment or transferring unstable patients based on the patient's ability to pay.

The courts found that an anencephalic baby was handicapped and disabled,[95] and that the hospital could not circumvent the mother's request for life-saving intervention. The sole reason to withhold therapy would be the anencephaly, and this withholding would violate EMTALA as well as the American with Disabilities Act (ADA).[96]

ETHICS

In neonatology, as in most medical specialties, there is considerable crossover between law and ethics. Those who take care of sick newborns regularly deal with concepts such as informed consent, autonomy, the right to die, surrogate decision-making, beneficience, nonmalfeasance, truth-telling, etc. On a daily basis, health care providers and families must face extremely sensitive issues while caring for the most fragile of patients. The overall trend has been toward parental autonomy as long as reasonable decisions are being made.

While a detailed review of perinatal and neonatal ethics is beyond the scope of this chapter, complex ethical issues are inherent in all of the court cases contained herein. The very essence of "personhood" or being "born alive" is a fundamental issue in many of the most challenging NICU cases. What are the limits on a parent's right to make health care decisions for their newborns? When is it acceptable to forgo resuscitation on an extremely premature baby?[97] What are the limits of viability? At what gestation, if any, should a physician (or judge) be able to "overrule" a parent's request?

While some difficult questions have been addressed by the legislative and judicial branches, many more complex issues await resolution. In some cases, such as *Baby K*,[98] physicians have been given the clear message that they cannot be solely guided by their own ethical principles. Yet in other cases, such as *Miller*, the parents' rights and ethical convictions were overruled. Given the available information, it appears that the Millers made a loving, informed, and heart-breaking decision regarding the care of their child. Because of legal uncertainties, the Millers' ethical convictions were discarded by the health care system and the judicial system.

One notable, guiding ethical principle that has emerged from the last 20 years of neonatal cases is the "best interest" standard. In a case brought before the District of Columbia Court of Appeals, a neglected child's guardian determined that a "do not resuscitate" (DNR) order was in the best interest of that child. The court supported the guardian's decision and ruled that the "best interests" of the child standard, rather than the "substituted judgment" standard, applied with respect to DNR determination.[99]

For many years, the "substituted judgment" standard was used. In a situation where the patient is unable to communicate their own wishes, the "substituted judgment" principle compelled the guardian or decision-maker to determine, as best they could, the appropriate course of action based on what the incapacitated individual would have decided. Because a sick newborn has never been able to communicate their intentions, a guardian makes essentially all the health care decisions. This case clarified that the "best interest" standard was most appropriate. This test simply asks if the decisions being made are consistent with the child's best interest.

SUMMARY AND CONCLUSIONS

At the border of fetal existence and "personhood" is a largely undefined legal transition. The critically ill newborn often exists at this legal crossroads. As a fetus, *Roe v. Wade* and progeny govern. After being born alive, the sick newborn can still be distinguished from other persons. There is a small, but growing, body of law that governs the "never-aware" and the "never-competent."

On the one hand, various courts have said that the parents do not necessarily have the right to refuse resuscitation. The courts based their holding on the fact that extreme prematurity is not necessarily "terminal," and therefore withholding or withdrawing care is not an available option to the parents or guardians. On the other hand, Dr. Messenger removed his own son from the ventilator and was found innocent of manslaughter. How does one reconcile the *Miller* case and

the *Messenger* case? If an extremely premature baby is resuscitated against the parents' wishes and the baby is tremendously damaged as the result of that prematurity, then the parents cannot sustain a cause of action. However, if an extremely premature baby is resuscitated against the parents' wishes, and the father removes the baby from the ventilator, no homicide has been committed. So what is the legal standing of a critically ill newborn? In one case, these babies can be cared for against parents' wishes with no liability for the caregivers. In the other case, the infant can be removed from support by the parents against the caregivers' wishes, and there is no liability for the parent.

The *Baby K* case serves to further complicate the legal picture. Given the extremely grim prognosis for anencephalic babies, this case was largely seen as a strong vindication of parents' right to determine the care of their children. The case also sent a clear message to doctors and other health care providers that their personal ethics will be subjugated to parental wishes, even if the parental request is perceived as extremely unreasonable. Providing ventilatory support to a child without a cerebral cortex was mandated by the court.

For thousands of years, medical care has been provided based on benefit to the patient.[100] In the case of *Baby K*, the court mandated that doctors provide what is largely viewed as futile and inappropriate care. In the *Miller* case, the court found that the parents could not recover when their daughter received care that the parents felt was futile and inappropriate. In the *Messenger* case, the court found that the father was not criminally liable for an unauthorized termination of care that he felt was futile and inappropriate.

The *Miller* majority gave a clear articulation of the need for legal clarification:

> Having recognized, as a general rule, that parents have no right to refuse urgently-needed life-sustaining medical treatment to their non-terminally ill children, a compelling argument can be made to carve out an exception for infants born so prematurely and in such poor condition that sustaining their life, even if medically possible, cannot be justified.[101]

Perhaps, when the Texas Supreme Court consider *HCA v. Miller*, the justices will provide needed direction for neonatologists, obstetricians, staff, hospitals, and parents of sick newborns. Perhaps the legislature will intervene. Until a higher court or legislature deals definitively with this issue, the care, withholding of care, and withdrawal of care for critically ill newborns will continue to be surrounded by legal uncertainty.

ENDNOTES

1. Albert R Jonsen, *Issues in Procreational Autonomy: Transition from Fetus to Infant: A Problem for Law and Ethics*, 37 Hastings Law Journal 697 (1986).
2. AL Code 1975 §26-21-2 and 26-22-2 (2001).
3. MO ST §193.015.

4. AK ST §18.50.950 (2001).

5. AZ ST §36-301 (2001).

6. ME ST T.22§1596.

7. 65 A.L.R. 3d 413 (1975) (proof of live birth in prosecution for killing newborn).

8. *Greco v. United States*, 111 Nev. 405, 893 P. 2d 345 (1995). The court discussed the complexity of trying to decide if the child would be better off had he never been born. The court notes that they would have to weigh the harms of being handicapped against the "utter void of non-existence." *See also* Marc Franklin & Robert Rabin, *Tort Law and Alternatives* 258 (1996).

9. *Turpin v. Sortini*, 32 Cal. 3d 220, 643 P. 2d 954 (1982).

10. The majority of states now allow a wrongful death cause of action for a fetal death. For cases and statutes on point in Nevada, Minnesota, Indiana, and Georgia, *see White v. Yup*, 458 P. 2d 617, Nev. 527 (1969), 229 Minn. at 370-71, 38 N.W. 2d at 841, *Bolin v. Wingert*, 764 N.E. 2d 201, Ind. (2002), and *Shirley v. Bacon*, 267 S.E. 2d 809.

11. *Farley v Sartin*, 466 S.E. 2d 522 W.Va. (1995).

12. Ca: Const. Art. 1, §7; *see also Justus v. Atchison*, 19 Cal. 3d 564, 565 P. 2d 122 (1977).

13. *Dillon v Legg*, 68 Cal. 2d 728, 441 P. 2d 912, 69 Cal. Rptr. 72 (1968). The California Supreme Court discussed the foreseeability of emotional injury.

14. C.C.P. §377.34.

15. *Vo v. Superior Court in and for County of Maricopa*, 836 P. 2d 408 (1992).

16. At oral arguments in *Vo*, counsel informed the court that the fetus was 23 weeks gestation at the time of the death.

17. *Vo, supra*, at 206.

18. *Id.*

19. AZ ST §13-1103, subsection A.5. Manslaughter classification to include "knowingly or recklessly causing the death of an unborn child at any stage of its development by any physical injury to the mother of such child which would be murder if the death of the mother had occurred."

20. A.L.R. 1975, *supra* note 7.

21. Vo, *supra* note 15.

22. AZ ST §13-1101, *supra* note 19.

23. *Maricopa County*, Cause No. CR 97-09388, Thomas Dunevant, III, J.

24. *State v Cotton*, 5 P. 3d 918, Ariz. App. Div. 1 (2000).

25. Definitions of live birth, *supra* notes 3-7.

26. Avroy A. Fanaroff & Richard J. Martin, *Neonatal-Perinatal Medicine: Diseases of the Fetus and Infant*, 7th ed., 936, 939 (Mosby, 2002).

27. Robert K. Creasy & Robert Resnik, *Maternal-Fetal Medicine*, 4th ed., 498 (W.B. Saunders, 1999).

28. *Id.*

29. Fanaroff, *supra* note 26, at 21.

30. *Id.* at 22.

31. *Id.* at 309.

32. Thomas E. Wiswell & Steven Donn (eds.), *Update on Mechanical Ventilation and Exogenous Surfactant*, 28(3) Clinics in Perinatology (W.B. Saunders, 2001). The reader is referred to *Biology of Surfactant* by Alan Jobe & Machiko Ikegami on p. 655 of this journal, and *see also Current Surfactant Use in Premature Infants* by Gautham K. Suresh & Roger F. Soll on p. 671.

33. Mark C. Mammel & Stephen J. Boros, *High Frequency Ventilation*, in Jay P. Goldsmith & Edward H. Karotkin (eds.), *Assisted Ventilation of the Neonate*, 3d ed., 199, 202, 203 (W.B. Saunders, 1996).

34. David R. Gerstmann, Steven D. Minton, et al., *The Provo Multicenter Early High-Frequency Oscillatory Ventilation Trial: Improved Pulmonary and Clinical Outcome in Respiratory Distress Syndrome*, 98(6) Pediatrics 1044 (1996).

35. Steven M. Donn & Joanne Nicks, *Special Ventilatory Techniques and Modalities I: Patient-Triggered Ventilation*, in *Assisted Ventilation of the Neonate, id.* at 215, 216, 222.

36. Carl T. D'Angio, Robert A. Sinkin, et al., *Longitudinal, 15-year Follow-up of Children Born at Less than 29 Weeks' Gestation After Introduction of Surfactant Therapy into a Region: Neurologic, Cognitive, and Educational Outcomes*, 110(6) Pediatrics 1094 (2002). This study presented data at age 7 years and 14 years. While there has continued to be refinement of NICU care since these children were born in the mid-1980s, this study included babies born at 27 and 28 weeks gestation. It is worth noting that some larger infants also suffered a significant intracranial hemorrhage and/or now have significant neurological deficits.

37. *Id.* at 1097.

38. Rita G. Harper, Khalil U. Rehman, et al., *Neonatal Outcome of Infants Born at 500 to 800 Grams from 1990 Through 1998 in a Tertiary Care Center*, 22(7) Journal of Perinatology 555, 559 (2002).

39. Maureen Hack & Avroy Fanaroff, *Outcomes of Extremely Immature Infants: A Perinatal Dilemma*, 329(22) New England Journal of Medicine 1649 (1993).

40. Joyce L. Peabody & Gilbert I. Martin, *From How Small Is Too Small to How Much Is Too Much: Ethical Issues at the Limits of Neonatal Viability*, 23(3) Clinics in Perinatology (Gary E. Freed & Joseph R Hageman, eds.), 473–489 (1996). This article provides a detailed analysis of a multitude of ethical issues in newborn care. Readers are also referred to the endnotes of this article. Many of the landmark papers concerning neonatal outcomes are cited.

41. *Roe v. Wade*, 410 U.S. 113, 93 S.Ct. 705 (1973).

42. *Id.* at 159.

43. Jonsen, *supra* note 1. This treatise discusses the sanctity and quality of life issues, and addresses some of the "border" issues concerning fetuses and newborns.

44. Roe, *supra* note 41. In this 1973 case, Justice Blackmun does note that viability was generally considered around 28 weeks and possibly as early as 24 weeks.

45. *Akron v Akron Center for Reproductive Health*, 462 U.S. 416 (1983).

46. *Planned Parenthood of Southeastern Pennsylvania v. Casey*, 505 U.S. 833, 112 S.Ct. 2791 (1992).

47. *Id.*

48. *Id.*

49. Hugh McDonald and the Committee on the Fetus and Newborn, *Perinatal Care at the Threshold of Viability*, 110(5) Pediatrics (Nov. 5, 2002). This article reviews important outcome statistics and suggests some guidelines for counseling of families facing the birth of an extremely premature child. *Also see* J.A. Lemons, C.R. Bauer, W. Oh, et al., *Very Low Birth Weight Outcomes of the National Institute of Child Health and Human Development Neonatal Research Network, January 1995 Through December 1996*, 107(1) Pediatrics (2000).

50. *Id.*

51. *HCA, Inc. v. Miller ex rel. Miller*, 36 S.W. 3d 18, 190 (2000).

52. *Id.* at 190.

53. *Id.*

54. This value represented the sum of $29,400,000 for past and future medical expenses, $13,500,000 in punitive damages, and $17,503,066 in prejudgment interest.

55. *Health Care Law*, 55 S.M.U.L. Rev. 1113, 1153 (2002).

56. Advanced Directives Act. V.T.C.A., Health & Safety Code §§166.002(13), 166.031, 166.035.

57. *HCA v. Miller, supra* note 51, at 195.

58. *Troxel v. Granville*, 530 U.S. 57, 120 S.Ct. 2054, 2060, 147 L. Ed. 2d 49 (2000). This case cites the Fourteenth Amendment to the U.S. Constitution as the basis for this parental interest. The U.S. Supreme Court has described this liberty interest as a fundamental right. Justice O'Connor with the Chief Justice and two Justices concurring states that "custody, care, and nurture of child reside first with parents, whose primary function and freedom include preparing for obligations the state can neither supply or hinder."

59. *Moss v. Rishworth*, 222 S.W. 225 Tex. Com. App. 1920 (June 2, 1920).

60. *Prince v. Massachusetts*, 64 S.Ct. 438 U.S. 1944.

61. *Cruzan v. Director, Mo. Dep't of Health*, 497 U.S. 261, 270, 110 S.Ct. 2841, 111 L. Ed. 2d 224 (1990).

62. V.T.C.A., Health & Safety Code §166.035.

63. Texas Family Code Ann. §151.003(a)(3).

64. Texas Penal §22.04.

65. *HCA v Miller*, *supra* note 51, at 187.

66. *Id.* at 195.

67. John J. Paris & Frank Reardon, *Bad Cases Make Bad Law: HCA v. Miller is not a Guide for Resuscitation of Extremely Premature Newborns*, 21(8) Journal of Perinatology 542 (2001). This journal article comprehensively discusses the case, and urges that decisions regarding resuscitation and care of extremely premature babies lie with the parents. Father John Paris has written extensively on the issues of neonatal ethics as well as many other topics in biomedical ethics.

68. *Nelson v. Krusen*, 678 S.W. 2d 918 (1984).

69. *Jacobs v. Theimer*, 519 S.W. 2d 846, 847 (1975).

70. *Nelson, supra* note 68, at 925. In *Nelson*, parents and minor son sued doctor and medical center alleging that doctor was negligent in assuring them that mother was not a carrier of neuromuscular disease.

71. *HCA v. Miller, supra* note 51, at 197.

72. *People v. Messenger*, No. 94-67694-FH, 30th Judicial Circuit Court for County of Ingham (Michigan), decided Feb. 2, 1995 (Judge Harrison's Court).

73. Independent (London) 39,40,42 (Nov. 11, 2000) WL 26289589. Copyright 2000 Independent Newspapers (UK) Limited.

74. *Man Acquitted in Son's Death*, N.Y. Times Abstracts 10 (Feb. 4, 1995).

75. *In re Guardianship of Barry*, 445 So. 2d 365 Fla. App. 2 Dist. (1984). This case involved a terminally ill 10-month-old child who had essentially no cognitive function or chance of improvement. The parents, as guardians, petitioned to have life support removed. The request was granted.

76. *Id.* For a more detailed discussion of "substituted judgment" versus "best interest," the reader is referred to the Ethics section of this chapter.

77. *Infant Doe v. Bloomington Hospital*, 104 S.Ct. 394.

78. *Infant Doe v. Bloomington Hospital*, 464 U.S. 961 (1983).

79. 45 C.F.R. §84.55, Code of Federal Regulations Part 84, Nondiscrimination on the Basis of Handicap; Sec. 84.55 Procedure relating to health care for handicapped infants (2002). These regulations encourage facilities that receive federal funds to establish Infant Review Committees.

80. Marshall H. Klaus & Avroy A. Fanaroff, *Care of the High-Risk Neonate*, 5th ed., 180-181 (W.B. Saunders, 2001). Duodenal or jejunal atresia are more commonly seen in association with Down's syndrome. All of these atresias are generally surgically correctable. Surgical correction of esophageal atresia can be more problematic, but this surgery is routinely done at children's hospitals nationwide.

81. 29 U.S.C.A. §794.

82. 48 Fed. Reg. 9630. Notices were to be prominently posted in delivery wards, maternity wards, pediatric ward, and each nursery.

83. *United States v. University Hospital of the State University of New York at Stony Brook*, 575 F.Supp. 607, 610 (1983). Judicial history includes *Weber v. Stony Brook Hospital*, 95 A.D. 2d 587. *See also Weber v. Stony Brook Hospital*, 60 N.Y. 2d 208.

84. *Supra*, note 81.

85. *U.S. v. University Hosp., State University of New York*, 729 F. 2d 144 (1984). As noted, the 2d District also noted the abuse of discretion by the trial court.

86. *Bowen v. American Hospital Assn.*, 476 U.S. 610 (1986).

87. The Appellate Division of the Supreme Court of the State of New York noted the abuse of discretion by the trial court.

88. *Id* • • •

89. Fanaroff, *supra* note 26, at 816. The neural tube is a primitive embryological structure from which the central nervous system develops. Abnormalities in the neural tube lead to a variety of conditions including anencephaly.

90. *Id.* at 833.

91. *In the Matter of Baby K*, United States District Court, Civ. A. 93-68-A, 4 Nat. Disability Law Rep. 219.

92. *Id.* at 1026.

93. *In the Matter of Baby K*, United States Court of Appeals, 4th Circuit, 62 U.S.L.W. 2504 at 592.

94. 42 U.S.C. §1395dd.

95. 29 U.S.C.A. §794. The baby lacked cognitive function, and was "disabled" and "handicapped" within the meaning of the Rehabilitation Act of 1973, §504.

96. 42 U.S.C.A. §12102(2).

97. Ehrnle W. Young & David K. Stevenson, *Limiting Treatment for Extremely Premature, Low Birth-Weight Infants (500-750 Grams)*, 145(11) American Journal of Diseases in Children 1223 (1990).

98. *Baby K, supra* note 91.

99. *In re K.I.*, 735 A. 2d 448 (1999).

100. Janna C. Merrick, *Critically Ill Newborns and the Law*, 16 Journal of Legal Medicine 189 (1995).

101. *HCA v. Miller, supra*, at 194 and 195.

41

Liability of Ophthalmologists

PHILIP A. SHELTON, P.A., M.D., J.D., F.C.L.M.

RECOGNIZED COMPLICATIONS OF REFRACTIVE SURGERY
THEORIES OF RECOVERY FOR INJURY-CAUSING COMPLICATIONS FROM REFRACTIVE
  SURGERY
CONCLUSION

"Refractive eye surgery" (or just "refractive surgery") is the general name for a variety of techniques, none more than about 30 years old, for correcting the corneal abnormalities at the root of refraction-related vision problems—myopia, hyperopia, and astigmatism. All of these surgical techniques involve reshaping the cornea so that (in the ideal case) eyeglasses or contact lenses are no longer necessary for bringing images into focus at the retina.

The first type of refractive surgery, radial keratotomy (RK), was developed in Japan and Russia in the 1970s. In RK, the surgeon uses a diamond-tipped blade to make spoke-like incisions in the peripheral cornea, causing the central cornea to flatten. RK's commonest use today is to correct myopia left undercorrected after photorefractive keratectomy (PRK).[1]

In PRK, the next major advance after RK, the surgeon scrapes off the cornea's epithelial layer to expose the stroma, and then reshapes the cornea by employing a laser to vaporize, or ablate, small amounts of stromal tissue.

In laser-assisted in situ keratomileusis (LASIK), currently the dominant form of refractive eye surgery in the United States, the surgeon employs a microkeratome (knife) to cut a flap on the surface of the cornea. With the flap pulled back on its hinge, the stroma is exposed. As in PRK, the surgeon then employs a laser to reshape the cornea by vaporizing, or ablating, small amounts of stromal tissue. Once that is finished, the flap is laid back in place.

Because glasses or contacts remain a fully adequate corrective for most people with refraction errors, any type of refractive surgery is almost always elective, with the election driven more by cosmetic and lifestyle considerations than the health benefits to be gained from surgery. (For example, in *Stasack v. Capital Dist. Physicians Health Plan, Inc.*,[2] the court held that an insurance plan properly denied coverage for refractive surgery on grounds that it was not medically necessary.) Nonetheless, with millions of Americans exhibiting refraction errors, and with a surge in cosmetic procedures overall, there has been no shortage of patients willing to pay out of their own pockets. LASIK is now among the most frequently performed elective surgeries in the United States.[3]

There has also been no shortage of patients alleging *some* degree of adverseness in the result of refractive surgery.[4] The American Academy of Ophthalmology, in a January 2002 assessment of the safety and efficacy of LASIK, concluded that "serious adverse complications leading to significant visual loss . . . *probably* occur *rarely* in LASIK procedures,"[5] but also that "annoying side effects such as dry eyes, night time starbursts, and/or reduced contrast sensitivity occur relatively frequently."[6] The assessment recognized that these "annoying side effects" can be severe, though some patients may be prone to overstating the annoyance "because their corrected visual acuity was most likely excellent before the procedure and because they elected to have surgery."[7]

Anecdotal evidence from the courthouse confirms that there are some serious injuries from refractive eye surgery and belief by at least some lawyers that the injuries are widespread. With respect to the first point, the press has reported recent jury verdicts of $4 million (to a commercial airline pilot who had to give up his career after LASIK degraded his night vision,[8] though a retrial was pending as of this writing[9]) and $1.7 million (to a patient who went legally blind in one eye[10]). With respect to the second point, such verdicts have led to predictions of more and more similar lawsuits. *Lawyers Weekly USA*, reporting on the $1.7 million verdict, headlined its story, "$1.7M for Botched Laser-Eye Surgery Suggests New Mass Tort," and quoted a lawyer saying that "awards of this kind will certainly bring LASIK cases to the attention of medical malpractice attorneys and [make them] realize that a lot of these cases are meritorious and should be taken."[11]

RECOGNIZED COMPLICATIONS OF REFRACTIVE SURGERY

The following are some of the possible complications from refractive surgery as recognized in reputable literature:

- Dry eyes. This is the most common complication of refractive surgery.[12]
- Visual perturbations such as glare, halos, and starbursts. The authors of one study concluded that "[t]here are a number of potential causes" of these and similar side effects: "irregular corneal topography"; "residual and surgically induced astigmatism"; "decentration of the treatment zone"; "large pupils"; "corneal surface microirregularities," including surgery-associated folds in the flap; and "corneal haze," including haze resulting from conditions at the interface between the flap and the stromal bed.[13]
- Reduced contrast sensitivity.[14]
- Errors in cutting the flap. When the surgeon has cut an incomplete flap, "[t]he recommended management . . . is not to attempt treatment or manual extension, but to replace the flap, wait approximately 3 months, and recut a new flap."[15] Even so, "this complication does have some negative impact on quality of vision, and surgeons are wise to take all reasonable measures to avoid a poor keratectomy."[16] One authority suggests that surgical experience is the best indicator of a proper keratectomy, but concludes that unspecified anatomical features of some eyes make them more prone to keratectomy problems, and that the Hansatome microkeratome is more prone to causing a certain kind of improper cut.[17] In cases where bilateral surgery was planned, an error in cutting the first flap should result in postponement of surgery on the second eye.[18]
- Errors in replacing the flap. A correctly cut flap may be replaced incorrectly, causing folds in the flap that may affect visual acuity or contrast sensitivity.[19] When the flap has been cut completely free of the cornea (a variety of poor keratectomy), the surgeon may continue with ablation and replace the flap.[20]
- Infection between the flap and the stromal bed.[21]
- Epithelial growth into the interface between the flap and the stromal bed.[22]
- Disruption of fusion, leading to strabismus and diplopia.[23] One authority suggests a connection between diplopia and irregular astigmatism and/or forme fruste keratoconus.[24] "Until there is further information, we would suggest using caution in treating such patients and consider factors such as topographic power, thin corneas, topographical superior/inferior disparity, and decreased BCVA before treating."[25]
- Distortion of the cornea due to thinning or keratectasia. According to one authority, "[t]here is increasing concern regarding the occurrence of keratectasia after LASIK, . . . but the cause and mechanism remain unknown."[26] Multiple retreatments are another possible risk factor for corneal scarring.[27]
- Overcorrection and undercorrection, such that the patient will continue to require glasses or contacts (or additional surgery, which itself is a risk factor for complications), and may not achieve even the level of preoperative visual acuity.

With improvements in knowledge and equipment, particular complications may become more avoidable and, for those already affected, perhaps even remediable. For example, the U.S. Food and Drug Administration in late 2002 approved the use of custom-contoured ablation pattern, a method for correcting the consequences of off-center ablation in a previous laser (LASIK or PRK) refractive surgery.[28] Off-center ablation occurs when the cornea and the laser are not properly aligned during surgery and its typical consequences are glare, halos, and diplopia. Wavefront technology, or custom cornea, offers additional hope for elimination of visual perturbations.[29]

THEORIES OF RECOVERY FOR INJURY-CAUSING COMPLICATIONS FROM REFRACTIVE SURGERY

Preoperative negligence in screening patients for refractive surgery

Proper screening of surgical candidates has emerged as a key issue in refractive surgery lawsuits. In a number of recent cases resolved by verdicts or sizeable settlements, there was evidence that the ophthalmologist was negligent in conducting a preoperative examination to determine whether the patient was a suitable candidate or a candidate who might face increased risk of an adverse result. Where the evidence shows that proper screening would have resulted in a better assessment of the relevant risk and, based on that assessment, a decision to avoid refractive surgery, then the patient may have a claim for presurgical negligence due to lack of informed consent.

The largest-to-date verdict in a LASIK case ($4 million, though a new trial was pending as of this writing) grew out of poor pre-operative screening. In *Post v. University Physicians, Inc.*,[30] the patient was a 32-year-old commercial airline pilot with myopia whose LASIK resulted in significantly reduced night vision and disqualification from his well-paying career. For the type of damage he suffered, there is currently no approved corrective surgery in the United States. Post alleged that he was not a good candidate for LASIK because his pupils tended to remain relatively large in dim light and that increased incidence of loss of night vision is a recognized complication for people with that tendency.

Indeed, the medical literature has clearly recognized pupil size as an important consideration:

Pupil size measurement in low light conditions should be performed, because increasing pupil size may be correlated with increased postoperative vision disturbances such as halos and glare. Many surgeons consider that a pupil size greater than 7 mm in dim illumination increases the risk of corneal refractive surgery, especially in highly myopic or astigmatic eyes, although the allowable size may vary with the diameter of the treatment and blend zones of the laser ablation. The goal is to have an effective treatment zone at least as large as the scotopic pupil.[31]

Likewise, information on LASIK recently available on the website of the federal Food and Drug Administration lists large pupils as a risk factor and advises the following:

Large pupils. Make sure this evaluation is done in a dark room [in order to maximize the dilation]. Younger patients and patients on certain medications may be prone to having large pupils under dim lighting conditions. This can cause symptoms such as glare, halos, starbursts, and ghost images (double vision) after surgery. In some patients these symptoms may be debilitating. For example, a patient may no longer be able to drive a car at night or in certain weather conditions, such as fog.[32]

Thus, the plaintiff in *Post* alleged that negligent presurgical screening failed to measure properly his pupil size in dim light and, as a result, that no one realized his higher risk for a complication that might have dissuaded him from surgery if it had been disclosed (especially in his case, given his profession). The defense argued unsuccessfully that Post's loss of night vision was not connected with his pupil size but, rather, to spherical aberrations in the shape of the eye that sometimes degrade night vision after LASIK, and that these risks were fully disclosed. But the defense will have a second opportunity because the judge ordered the case retried after the plaintiff's medical expert revealed that his testimony was based on an erroneous assumption about the equipment used to measure Post's pupil size.[33]

Other factors to be considered in a thorough preoperative assessment are:

- The patient's refractive error. "A cycloplegic refraction should be performed even if treatment may be based on the dry manifest refractive error."[34] Also, surgeons should use "extreme caution . . . in treating eyes with high or extreme corrections. . . ."[35]
- Refractive stability. The patient should exhibit less than 0.5 diopters of change over at least 1 year "to help ensure that the correction will be appropriate in the future."[36]
- Previous refractive surgery: "[E]yes . . . undergoing multiple retreatments, particularly hyperopic retreatment after initial myopic or astigmatic PRK or LASIK," face increased risk for "[s]erious complications such as scarring with ectasia. . . ."[37]
- Contact lens-induced corneal warpage. "Rigid contact lenses should be removed for several weeks and soft lenses for several days to weeks before [preoperative] examination."[38]

- Ophthalmic pathologies, including Fuchs corneal endothelial dystrophy (which has been associated with decompensation of the cornea as well as poor flap adhesion), corneal epithelial basement membrane dystrophic changes (which have been associated with epithelial sloughing, epithelial growth into the interface between the flap and the stromal bed, and diffuse lamellar keratitis), significant blepharitis (which has been associated with postoperative infection and interface inflammation), and retinal tears.[39]
- Systemic autoimmune disease. It "has been associated with corneal melting after PRK and may therefore increase LASIK risks, although the peer reviewed literature on this topic is sparse."[40]
- Preexisting dry eyes. Refractive surgery may aggravate the condition.[41]
- Active participation in contact sports "in which blows to the face and eyes are a normal occurrence."[42] The patient's profession or leisure activities might not otherwise be a risk factor, but they may well be a factor. For example, the fact that the plaintiff in *Post* was a commercial airline pilot did not put him at greater risk for a complication than anyone else with large pupils. But the fact that he was an airline pilot did put him at greater risk for dire consequences resulting from the complication. A careful surgeon should consider the patient's profession and lifestyle during the process of obtaining informed consent.
- Corneal topography. "[A]ssess[ing] corneal shape is a critical feature of the pre-LASIK evaluation."[43] A careful topography can detect irregular astigmatism, keratoconus or asymmetrical steepening, inferior corneal steepening (forme fruste keratoconus), and flat corneas, all of which are associated at least to some extent with complications.[44] The authors of another study advised special caution in treating "[p]atients showing inferior steepening on topography, particularly if associated with steep keratometry," and note that such patients "may require more customized ablation, such as performing a spherical treatment of the steeper area of the cornea *and careful patient counseling*."[45]

Failure to detect keratoconus underlay another high-damages case, *Cofsky v. Goosey*,[46] which settled for $1.75 million. Cofsky had been a patient of Maltz, an optometrist, since 1988. In 1998, Cofsky consulted Maltz on LASIK. Maltz told Cofsky that he was a good candidate and referred him to Goosey, an ophthalmologist with whom Maltz shared fees. The surgical result was adverse, particularly to Cofsky's left eye, where his vision deteriorated to 20/400. Two bilateral corneal transplants eventually restored his vision to useful levels. Cofsky alleged that Maltz erred in designating him a good candidate because he suffered from keratoconus and that Maltz should have known this from the corneal topographies he had performed in each of the 5 years preceding the referral to Goosey. He also alleged that Maltz failed to provide the topographies to Goosey for review, and that Goosey was negligent in failing to detect the keratoconus in the topographies that Goosey himself ordered and reviewed prior to surgery. The defendants alleged that Cofsky's keratoconus was, at all times prior to the original surgery, subclinical and beyond detection except by topography.

- Corneal thickness. Even absent the corneal thinning that may be associated with keratoconus, the cornea should be thick enough after ablation "to leave a central bed beneath the microkeratome flap that will allow corneal stability and prevent bulging or ectasia. . . . While the minimum safe bed thickness is not known with certainty, it is thought to be least 250 μm, and many surgeons recommend leaving 275 or 300 μm."[47] The authors of another study recommend that surgeons "always calculate the preoperative pachymetry even in low myopias, and based on present knowledge, attempt to leave 250 μm of stromal bed."[48]

  Consequently, the surgeon must know how thick a flap the microkeratome will cut. This may not always be possible because "average flap thickness does not predictably follow the manufacturer's label due to instrument variability and other operative factors," and has varied an average of 16 to 30 μm, depending on the study.[49] Therefore, the surgeon must consider the variability of flap thickness in determining whether the patient will retain the recommended minimum of stromal bed.

The previous list of risk factors is not definitive, as researchers disclaim to have isolated all the risks that can be detected preoperatively for unsuccessful refractive surgery. According to one study published in 2000, "[w]e are unable to draw definite conclusions as to the avoidable factors for serious complications of LASIK and PRK based on this study."[50] According to the U.S. Food and Drug Administration, insufficient study has been done to determine the safety and efficacy of refractive surgery on patients with the following: (1) herpes simplex or herpes zoster (shingles) near or involving the eyes; (2) glaucoma, glaucoma suspect, or ocular hypertension; (3) eye diseases such as uveitis or iritis; and (4) history of previous eye injury.[51]

This situation complicates surgeons' quest for a protocol of adequate, nonnegligent preoperative screening. It also complicates the task of plaintiff and defense counsel seeking, in any particular case, similar understandings of the appropriate standard of care and, thus, of the liability risk.

Informed consent

Before a physician begins any invasive procedure, the process of informed consent must be complete. Informed consent is the patient's permission granted after the patient has had an opportunity to understand the risks of the procedure, the risks of not electing the procedure, and any alternative procedures and therapies. In the absence of informed consent, a patient having suffered an adverse surgical result can sue the physician for damages regardless of whether the physician was negligent; all the plaintiff has to prove is that a reasonable person would not have elected surgery if the risks of surgery had been adequately disclosed in the informed consent process. This may in fact be difficult to prove in the case of surgery for life-threatening or serious conditions. The defense can often win by arguing persuasively that even if the risks of surgery had been adequately disclosed, the risks of not electing surgery were too great for a reasonable person not to elect surgery. Not so in the case of refractive eye surgery, where patients generally do not run any risks in not electing the procedure. Because all of the risks are on the side of having surgery, it is relatively easy for a damaged patient to claim that he or she would not have elected surgery if the risks had been adequately disclosed.[52]

Another reason has contributed to making informed consent the most significant issue in litigation over the results of refractive surgery. Ophthalmologists often provide all of their surgery patients with the same informed consent documents instead of customized risk assessments based on the degree to which a specific patient presents any of the recognized risk factors. It is arguably inadequate to tell a patient that he or she faces a certain numerical risk of poor night vision, where the number reflects the average incidence of that result, without also telling the patient that he or she faces an above-average risk of that result because of a certain risk factor as determined in a preoperative assessment. Indeed, the average risk and the risk to a specific patient with a specific risk factor can vary immensely. Consequently, the process of obtaining informed consent must include discussion of the patient-specific risks, ideally in terms of percentages (based on current research) expressing the complications that may result from the identified risk factors. Otherwise, the patient's consent is hardly meaningful.

Assuming proper disclosure of risks, the defendant should prevail. For example, in *Lehrer v. McClure*,[53] the plaintiff's preoperative best uncorrected vision was 20/400; after surgery, his best uncorrected vision was 20/40 and he alleged that he could not read as well as before, had problems with nighttime driving, and also experienced halos and blurry vision. The jury found that the three-page informed consent document adequately disclosed these risks and issued a verdict for the defense. Similarly, in *Bawa v. Garabet*,[54] the microkeratome cut the flap completely free of the cornea. Following the standard of care, the surgeon proceeded to ablation, then reseated the corneal flap and bandaged it with a contact lens, with instructions to the patient not to remove the lens or rub the eye and to return for a follow-up examination. When the plaintiff returned, the contact lens bandage and the corneal flap were both gone, so the physician performed a lamellar keratoplasty. The plaintiff claimed that his particular complication was the cause of uncorrected vision of 20/60 in the affected eye and was an undisclosed material risk. The defendant argued that the informed consent material provided to the plaintiff disclosed the risk of free flaps and, in any event, was irrelevant because the plaintiff testified that he did not read the material or view a companion videotape. The jury rendered a verdict for the defense.

Counsel involved in an informed consent case must review the informed consent documents to determine whether the complication at issue was disclosed.

Surgical negligence

"Complications occur in LASIK as in any other surgical procedure."[55] Such complications may generally be related to the surgical equipment or the surgical technique. The federal Food and Drug Administration approves lasers for specific types of refractive treatment (LASIK, PRK, etc.) of patients with refraction errors falling within certain parameters. For example, a certain laser may be approved for LASIK correction of myopia of less than −9.0 diopters (but not any degree of hyperopia), with or without astigmatism of −0.5 to −3.0 diopters. The same laser might be approved for PRK correction of myopia up to −10.0 diopters (but not any degree of hyperopia), with or without astigmatism of up to −4.0 diopters. Another laser may be approved only for PRK correction of certain degrees of hyperopia.

The investigation of any adverse outcome should consider whether the surgeon used the equipment to treat a condition beyond its licensed specifications. The FDA's list of approved lasers, and the indications for which each has been approved, is available on its website.[56] (The FDA has not approved any laser for LASIK on a minor.[57]) In January 2001, the FDA reached a settlement with a company and four of its executives for $1.5 million (the executives were held personally liable for a third of the amount) on claims that the company sold software that allowed ophthalmologists to program lasers for treatments exceeding the terms of their FDA licenses.[58]

While it may seem that the obvious claim to make in the case of misused equipment is that of negligence, the issue may be presented as one of informed consent. In *Anonymous v. Anonymous*,[59] the plaintiff obtained a $1.03 million settlement after LASIK for mild hyperopia (20/70 and 20/50) left him with severely degraded vision (20/200 and 20/400). The evidence would have shown, allegedly, that the defendant had not informed the patient that, at the time of surgery in 1996, the FDA had not approved any laser for LASIK correction of hyperopia.[60]

The technician and surgeon should check the surgical equipment (the laser, suction ring, microkeratome, and blade) before a procedure.[61] The second-largest known LASIK verdict, $1.7 million, involved negligent setup of the equipment.[62] Tonya Oliver underwent a generally successful LASIK for myopia in her left eye, and about 6 months later a second procedure to fix an astigmatism in the same eye. The second surgery, however, increased Oliver's astigmatism. The plaintiff's theory of the case was that the ophthalmologist transposed her refraction, with the result that he programmed the laser to make corrections to the wrong axis of her eye. Preoperative notes supported the transposition theory, as did medical testimony that the observed damage to Oliver's vision was exactly what would be expected from corrections made along the wrong axis. Oliver also had testimony from one of the ophthalmologist's former employees, who allegedly heard Oliver say after the surgery that "the prescription didn't add up." The surgeon scheduled Oliver for enhancement surgery only 1 week later. (This in itself was problematic: enhancement surgery "can be performed once the refraction is stable for at least 1 month after surgery, but generally is not performed before 3 months."[63]) After that and a fourth surgery, and then a corneal transplant, Oliver remained legally blind in her left eye.

Other equipment-related problems that have turned into lawsuits include:

- Placing the microkeratome upside down, which caused shredding of the corneal flap.[64]
- During retreatment to correct halos and double vision in one eye, failure to lock the depth plate, as a result of which the laser perforated the cornea and iris, ruptured the globe, and penetrated into the anterior chamber, leaving plaintiff with vision of 20/400.[65]
- Keeping the laser on for too long and gouging a hole beneath the corneal flap, causing the patient to require a lamellar keratoplasty, which restored his uncorrected vision to presurgical levels.[66]
- Failing to seat the spacing plate into the keratome machine, as a result of which the keratome removed approximately 70% of the iris in the patient's right eye.[67]

With respect to surgical technique, refractive surgery (the laser-assisted varieties) generally involves topical anesthetic of the operative eye, placement of a speculum to hold the lids open, marking the cornea to assist in aligning the flap after ablation, placement of a suction ring on the eye to induce intraocular pressure of greater than 65 to 70 mmHg, creation and reflection of the flap, ablation, repositioning of the flap and verification of alignment, removal of the speculum, and then reexamination of the flap about 30 minutes later to verify alignment.[68] A mistake can occur at any stage, particularly in creating the flap and in repositioning and aligning the flap after ablation (*see* text at notes 15-20). The literature clearly advises not to proceed with surgery "[i]f the flap created during the . . . procedure is irregular, incomplete, or buttonholed."[69]

CONCLUSION

Wavefront technology, also called custom cornea, offers hope that some adverse results previously experienced by surgical patients can be avoided, and *perhaps* that some adverse results still suffered by patients can be ameliorated (if their corneas are not too scarred or ectatic for retreatment). In the meantime, surgeons should continue to exercise caution, especially in the areas where litigation has proven them most vulnerable: in conducting preoperative screenings in a non-negligent manner; and in communicating with their patients, in the process of obtaining informed consent, a realistic assessment of patient-specific risks with reference to the results of preoperative screenings.

ENDNOTES

1. RK for purposes other than retreatment of previous refractive surgery may be per se below the standard of care. In *Doe v. Roe Ophthalmologist*, 2001 WL 1849090 (Cal. Super. Ct. June 4, 2001), the parties settled for $150,000 the patient's claim that RK was outdated at the time of his surgery in 1998.

2. 736 N.Y.S. 2d 764 (N.Y. App. Div. 2002).

3. "More than three million Americans have undergone laser vision correction . . . since the procedure first became available in the U.S. in 1995." Antonio Regalado, *Zapping the Flaws in Laser Eye Surgery*, Wall Street Journal (Dec. 12, 2002) at D1.

4. *See, e.g.*, http://www.surgicaleyes.org (last visited Dec. 16, 2002) and http://www.lasikdisaster.com (last visited Dec. 16, 2002).

5. Alan Sugar et al., *Laser In Situ Keratomileusis for Myopia and Astigmatism: Safety and Efficacy*, 109 Ophthalmology 175, 181 (2002) (footnotes omitted; emphases added).

6. *Id.* (footnotes omitted). The study also noted the difficulty in distinguishing between "a complication compared to a minor nuisance or annoying side effect," *id.*

7. *Id.*

8. Diana Digges, *$4M Award Over Laser-Eye Surgery Breaks New Ground*, Lawyers Weekly USA (May 27, 2002) at A1.

9. *Record $4M Verdict in LASIK Case Overturned by Judge*, Lawyers Weekly USA (Dec. 9, 2002) at A3.

10. Elizabeth Amon, *The View Is Clear: More Laser Lawsuits*, Nat'l Law J. (Dec. 10, 2001) at A4.

11. Genevieve Haas, *$1.7M for Botched Laser-Eye Surgery Suggests New Mass Tort*, Lawyers Weekly USA (Dec. 10, 2001) at A1.

12. Sugar, *supra* note 5, at 181.

13. Peter S. Hersh, *Photorefractive Keratectomy Versus Laser In Situ Keratomileusis: Comparison of Optical Side Effects*, 107 Ophthalmology 925, 931-32 (2000).

14. Sugar, *supra* note 5, at 181.

15. Simon P. Holland et al., *Avoiding Serious Corneal Complications of Laser Assisted In Situ Keratomileusis and Photorefractive Keratectomy*, 107 Ophthalmology 640, 651 (2000) (footnote omitted). *See also* Vivien M.-B. Tham, *Microkeratome Complications of Laser In Situ Keratomileusis*, 107 Ophthalmology 920, 922 (2000) ("making another microkeratome pass after 3 months and attempting to complete the LASIK procedure is generally safe").

16. Tham, *supra* note 15, at 922.

17. *Id.* at 923.

18. Holland, *supra* note 15, at 651.

19. Sugar, *supra* note 5, at 181. *E.g.*, in *Wilger v. Faulkner*, No. A9800710, 2001 WL 718554 (Ohio Ct. C.P. Apr. 19, 2001), the surgeon performing automated lamellar keratoplasty replaced the patient's flap inverted and upside down; the jury awarded $325,000.

20. Sugar, *supra* note 5, at 181.

21. *Id.*

22. *Id.*

23. *Id.* at 182.

24. Holland, *supra* note 15, at 650.

25. *Id.*

26. *Id.* at 646 (footnotes omitted).

27. *Id.* at 651 ("[c]aution is also advisable before performing a third or fourth retreatment for under- or overcorrection").

28. 67 Fed. Reg. 67629, 67630 (Nov. 6, 2002).

29. Regalado, *supra* note 3.

30. 22 No. 6 Verdicts, Settlements & Tactics 248 (Ariz. Dist. Ct. May 9, 2002).

31. Sugar, *supra* note 5, at 176. *See also* Hersh, *supra* note 13, at 932 ("[i]n low illumination, a disparity between the dilated pupil size and treatment zone may allow unfocused noise light into the eye").

32. http://www.fda.gov/cdrh/LASIK/when.htm (last visited Sept. 19, 2002).

33. *$4M Verdict, supra* note 9.

34. Sugar, *supra* note 5, at 176.

35. Holland, *supra* note 15, at 646.

36. Sugar, *supra* note 5, at 176.

37. Holland, *supra* note 15, at 651.

38. Sugar, *supra* note 5, at 176.

39. *Id.*

40. *Id.*

41. *Id.*

42. http://www.fda.gov/cdrh/LASIK/when.htm (last visited Sept. 19, 2002).

43. Sugar, *supra* note 5, at 176.

44. *Id.*

45. Holland, *supra* note 15, at 651 (emphasis added).

46. 22 No. 7 Verdicts, Settlements & Tactics 297 (Texas Dist. Ct. Apr. 30, 2002).

47. Sugar, *supra* note 5, at 176 (footnotes omitted).

48. Holland, *supra* note 15, at 646.

49. Sugar, *supra* note 5, at 177.

50. Holland, *supra* note 15, at 651.

51. http://www.fda.gov/cdrh/LASIK/when.htm (last visited Sept. 19, 2002).

52. "[A]ny potentially vision-threatening complication is of great importance in such an elective procedure, with readily available alternatives for correcting the refractive error." Holland, *supra* note 15, at 640.

53. No. 01-CC-02195, 2002 WL 1918295 (Cal. Super. Ct. May 17, 2002).

54. No. BC-238080, 2001 WL 1849087 (Cal. Super. Ct. Sept. 26, 2001).

55. Sugar, *supra* note 5, at 181.

56. http://www.fda.gov/cdrh/LASIK/lasers.htm (last visited Sept. 19, 2002).

57. http://www.fda.gov/cdrh/LASIK/when.htm (last visited Sept. 19, 2002).

58. Diana Digges, *Laser Eye Surgery Settlement Sends Warning That Feds Are Watching*, Lawyers Weekly USA (Feb. 19, 2001) at B1.

59. 21 No. 7 Verdicts, Settlements & Tactics 302 (N.C. Dist. Ct. Apr. 23, 2001).

60. *See also Cody v. Garabet*, No. BC-196910, 1999 WL 1069219 (Cal. Super. Ct. Sept. 27, 1999) (jury awarded $48,000; plaintiff alleged that surgeon never told patient that equipment was not FDA-approved).

61. Sugar, *supra* note 5, at 177.

62. *Oliver v. Abell*, No. 99-CI-1816 (Ky. Cir. Ct. Nov. 1, 2001). The facts presented here are drawn from Amon, *supra* note 10.

63. Sugar, *supra* note 5, at 177.

64. *Anonymous 38 Year Old Female v. Anonymous Eye Surgeon*, 2001 WL 1854266 (Va. Cir. Ct. 2001) (settled for $235,000).

65. *McLeod v. York*, No. SC-059561, 2000 WL 33800665 (Cal. Super. Ct. Dec. 1, 2000) (settled for $275,000).

66. *Doe v. Dr. Roe*, 2000 WL 33143769 (Cal. Super. Ct. Nov. 14, 2000) (structured settlement with present-day cash value of $350,000).

67. *Scott v. Wong*, No. 99-07375, 2000 WL 33719626 (Texas Dist. Ct. Nov. 6, 2000) (settled for $200,000).

68. Sugar, *supra* note 5, at 177.

69. *Id.; see also* text, *supra*, at note 15.

42

Liability of Otolaryngologists

RAYMUND C. KING, M.D., J.D., F.C.L.M.

OTOLOGY
RHINOLOGY
LARYNGOLOGY
CONCLUSION

Every medical specialty has its own unique set of medical malpractice issues that, more often than not, correspond with the complications associated with procedures or treatments commonly performed by that particular specialist. The field of otorhinolaryngology/head and neck surgery (or ear, nose, and throat medicine and surgery) is no different. As in other medical specialties, it is not uncommon to see otorhinolaryngology-related lawsuits that result from a mere difference of expectations, the patient's expectations of surgical outcome typically being more optimistic or at least "different" than the physician's expectations. Often, the differences in expectations between the two parties can be resolved by obtaining true informed consent.

Three factors unique to otorhinolaryngology must be taken into consideration when litigating a medical malpractice suit (Box 42-1).

The purpose of this chapter is to educate the reader about some of the medical malpractice issues in otorhinolaryngology. Please note that the terms "otorhinolaryngology," "otolaryngology," and "ENT" will be used interchangeably throughout this chapter. The chapter has been divided into malpractice issues dealing with otology, rhinology, and laryngology, respectively. There are so many different types of surgical and medical treatments in this specialty that this chapter is by no means comprehensive. However, actual court cases have been selected to help illustrate some of the more common malpractice issues seen in otolaryngology.

OTOLOGY

Although not all otologic liability or complications are due to surgery, a majority of the medical malpractice suits seen by this author result from surgical complications. Generally, a postoperative complication is defined as a postoperative state that does not meet the expected goal of the surgical procedure, particularly with regard to healing, anatomy, or function. From a purely objective academic standpoint, the difficulty with evaluating trends in postoperative otologic

---

BOX 42-1. MEDICAL-LEGAL PEARL

Otorhinolaryngologic treatment has the potential to affect one's ability to experience and interact with the environment through one's ability to hear, smell, speak, or swallow. Therefore, any event that adversely affects these abilities may have a dramatic impact upon one's quality of life.

Otorhinolaryngology typically involves the face, the part of the body that most people associate with one's identity. Therefore, any disfigurement or impairment inflicted upon the face may have potentially devastating psychological consequences

Otorhinolaryngology is a specialty that is constantly evolving with new instruments, techniques, and modifications to instruments and/or techniques. Therefore, the definition of "standard of care" is also constantly evolving.

---

surgical complications is the fact that analyses from one physician to another or one institution to another are not always consistent. For example, some ear surgeries are staged and require multiple procedures. Each procedure is technically a separate surgical case, although complications resulting from these procedures may all be lumped into one general complication.

In contrast, the difficulty with evaluating trends in lawsuits stemming from otologic complications is the fact that the chances of a lawsuit being filed or settled—despite the severity of the otologic complication—are often influenced by numerous subjective medical and legal factors: (1) from the medical perspective, some important subjective factors include hearing sensitivity, vertigo, patient attitudes, and physician rapport with the patient; and (2) from the legal perspective, some critical factors include credibility of the parties and witnesses, adequacy of medical documentation, and extent of the damages (both actual and perceived).

For this reason, it is crucial for the otolaryngologist to document not only the objective time lapses between surgery and the development of complications, but also the subjective complaints, findings, and apparent patient "attitudes" that accompany the stages of the procedure or procedures all the way to full recovery. In addition, the attorney representing the otolaryngologist should be mindful of the factors that affect the strength of each case.

Unfortunately, many postoperative complications are unavoidable or the result of surgical intervention. For example, some of the more common causes of otologic complications associated with middle ear surgery are illustrated in Table 42-1.

For an attorney defending an otolaryngologist being sued for medical negligence after an otologic procedure, the lawyer must be cognizant of the numerous possible reasons for the complication that are not necessarily the result of negligence or malpractice. For the otologic surgeon, preoperative patient counseling (i.e., truly informed consent), preoperative patient evaluation (e.g., audiogram, auditory brainstem response testing), and preoperative planning are just as critical to the successful outcome of the procedure as the surgeon's technical skill, experience, and awareness of possible subtle variations in patient anatomy.

The otologist must be aware of some of the more common technical errors and complications that lead to medical malpractice suits. These are listed in Table 42-2.

Another common complication in otologic surgery is associated with recurrent pathology of the ear. Not surprisingly, medical malpractice cases related in some way to recurrent pathology are typically associated with a "negligent informed consent" issue. The following case example, which resulted in a defense verdict, illustrates this point.[1]

The plaintiff brought a medical malpractice action against the defendant otolaryngologist, alleging that the defendant negligently damaged his ear while performing surgery to correct an inner ear problem allegedly caused by the plaintiff's repeated exposure to ocean water. The plaintiff additionally asserted that the defendant physician failed to obtain his informed consent prior to surgery.

The plaintiff, an avid surfer, was diagnosed with exostosis of the inner ear, associated with the formation of bony growths along the ear canal. The diagnosis was made in September 1998, and the condition was causing the plaintiff discomfort, hearing impairment, recurring ear infections, and other problems. The defendant otolaryngologist recommended surgical removal of the growths.

The plaintiff's expert otolaryngologist opined that the defendant deviated from the standard of care by opting to enter the ear canal through an approach that failed to provide the defendant with optimal visibility of the affected structures of the external auditory canal. The plaintiff's expert contended that the defendant's technique traumatized and injured the ear canal. The plaintiff maintained that

TABLE 42-1 Common causes of otologic complications with middle ear surgery

Residual bone disease	Some complications of new bone formation include: (1) osteoma and eburnated mastoid, (2) ossicular ankylosis (usually of the stapes and the head of the malleus), and (3) obliteration of the oval window secondary to residual otosclerosis, tympanosclerosis, or osteitis. Chronic or persistent osteitis may cause further lysis or necrosis of the ossicles or even of the preserved posterior wall or a portion of it. Residual osteitis can appear anywhere in the middle ear, and sometimes may be responsible for progressive damage of the osseous labyrinth. Another possibility is the risk of long-term suppuration when bone dust is left in an infected area.
Residual cholesteatoma	Often related to the care and skill given to the removal of the matrix or any "unsafe" tissue, which includes ossicular remnants. For this reason, many otologists advocate the taking of a second look in a staged procedure.
Residual tubal dysfunction	Often dependent upon the preoperative care and treatment of the rhinopharynx. An endoscopic preoperative examination of the eustachian tube is performed by some otolaryngologists, and idiopathic tubal dysfunction is also a known disorder. Incomplete removal of disease in this area (such as polyps, cholesteatoma, or scarred occlusive folds) occurs relatively frequently when the anterior remnant of the tympanic membrane has been left in place.
Residual mucosal disease	Involves the mucosal lining of the middle ear cleft. Frequently dependent upon the immune status of the patient. The proportion of normal to diseased tissue remaining in the middle ear often directly affects the risk of residual disease evolution. One commonly sees persistent or nonspecific infections wherein the immune system probably has an underlying critical role. Examples: fibrous inflammatory hypertrophy of the basal mucosal lining, absence of self-cleaning activity secondary to the disappearance of ciliary cell activity, increase of secretory and mucous glandular cell population, mucosal degeneration, granulomatous metaplasia, residual cholesterol granulomas, and fibrosis of aeriform spaces of the middle ear cleft when a large area of mucosa is removed. Syndromes or disorders such as Wegener's granulomatosis, and nonspecific inflammatory granulomas (such as histiocytosis X, eosinophilic granuloma, or xanthogranuloma) should be considered.

TABLE 42-2 Common technical errors and otologic complications that lead to medical malpractice suits

Acoustic trauma	Labyrinthine injury may be caused by extremely high sound energy. This occurrence can happen with any kind of bur; perhaps more prevalent with cutting burs that may make contact with ossicles that are still connected with the inner ear. Heavy suction applied to the stapes or to the oval window may also be hazardous.
Exposed bony areas	A poorly replaced skin flap or meatal skin graft may cause exposed bony areas on the external auditory canal; may result in complications such as obliteration of the lateral space of the hypotympanum leading to a concave, scarred, and nonfunctioning tympanic membrane.
Graft defect	Careful selection and evaluation of the implanted material is critical; perforations or small dehiscences in an implanted tympanic membrane may lead to early postoperative perforation.
Lateral displacement of an implanted tympanic membrane	May occur when a fascia graft is applied using an underlay technique when the fibrous annulus has not been correctly replaced or in an overlay technique when the fibrous annulus has been removed and the graft fails to make good contact. Choice of anesthesia may have an effect on the outcome: a partial gas pressure of nitrous oxide or even pure oxygen may have consequences for the tympanic membranes.
Postoperative care complications	Ear packing is probably associated with the most common postoperative care complications. Lateral displacement of the inferior part of the external meatal skin secondary to bleeding under the replaced meatal skin leading to overgrowth of epithelium and fibrous obliteration of the inferior sulcus. A stenotic ring may result from removing the packing too early or poor replacement of external skin on top of the graft. Patient education is key. For example, patient should be advised not to insert any blunt instruments (such as a Q-tip) in the ear and should avoid the intrusion of water or other liquid into the ear canal.
Audiologic complications	Decreased hearing sensitivity or deafness following surgery. The ultimate postoperative vestibular and auditory function is of critical importance in successful ear surgery and of more critical importance in avoiding malpractice liability. Documentation of the postoperative audiometric and vestibular outcomes is crucial. Outcomes are typically assessed by measuring hearing level by air and bone conduction and measurement of air-bone gap, as well as speech discrimination tests and tympanometry.

as a result of the defendant's alleged negligence, he suffers from permanent diminished hearing in the left ear, tinnitus (ringing in the ears), and chronic ear infections.

The defendant denied negligence and maintained that surgery was properly performed. In addition, the defendant contended that the plaintiff was fully advised of the risks and alternatives to surgery. The defendant contended that the patient was noncompliant with regard to postoperative care and specifically failed to follow the physician's instructions regarding water-related activities. The jury also found for the defendant.

This case deals with exostosis in the external auditory canal. Nodular bony outgrowths from the osseus meatus, usually sessile, multiple, and bilateral, are common incidental findings on otoscopic examination. The term "exostoses" typically refers to discreet nodules, whereas the term "hyperostoses" is typically applied to more diffuse bony elevations of the wall of the osseus meatus. Van Gilse first described exostoses of the meatus, related to swimming in cold water.[2] So close is the relationship between cold-water exposure and exostoses of the inner end of the osseus meatus that the otologist is seldom mistaken in concluding that the patient has been an ardent swimmer in relatively cold water. Multiple exostoses are almost always bilateral and appear as hard, smooth, rounded, whitish nodules that lie close to the sulcus tympanicus, resulting in a greater or lessor narrowing of the osseus meatus. This rarely causes

the occlusion of the ear canal. When exostoses cause sufficient narrowing of the bony ear canal (osseus meatus) to produce retention of epidermal debris and conductive hearing impairment, surgery should be performed. Patient compliance after surgical treatment is key to avoiding recurrence.

In this case, the otolaryngologist was sued based upon allegations that ear damage occurred following surgery and because the physician allegedly failed to obtain informed consent prior to surgery. Despite the plaintiff's expert's contentions, the key to defending this case rested upon proper documentation of informed consent as well as documentation of the patient's noncompliance in the postoperative period.

RHINOLOGY

Rhinology involves the treatment of diseases involving the nose. In the field of otolaryngology, this includes treatment of the sinuses. In this author's experience, it is rare to find rhinologic malpractice cases asserting solely damages of anosmia (inability to smell) or ageusia (lack or impairment of taste). Although epistaxis (nosebleed) is one of the most common rhinologic problems seen emergently by the otolaryngologist, the majority of lawsuits associated with rhinology are related to cerebrospinal fluid (CSF) rhinorrhea (CSF leaking from the nose) following nasal or endoscopic sinus surgery (ESS). In addition, lawsuits secondary to complications from ESS, such as infection leading to meningitis, are common. In fact, if one reviews the otolaryngology-related verdicts and settlements reported in 2002 in the *National Jury Verdict Review & Analysis* publication, the most frequently reported type of rhinology-related malpractice suit is associated with a CSF-leak complication of ESS.

CSF rhinorrhea may result from trauma, congenital abnormalities, septal surgery, or sinus surgery. Leakage may become apparent immediately following surgery after dural injury, or the leak may reveal itself many days later after tissue swelling has subsided. During nasal septal surgery, the anterior skull base is at risk if care is not taken to protect the cribriform plate from direct trauma. During ESS with septal surgery, the perpendicular plate of the ethmoid and the attachment of the middle turbinate are often manipulated, which also places the skull base at risk. Certainly, the risk of intraoperative skull base damage and/or dural damage is diminished by using only sharp instruments to divide the perpendicular plate of the ethmoid or the middle turbinate before removing these structures. This precaution decreases the chance of applying unnecessary torque to the cribriform plate when these structures are being manipulated.

CSF rhinorrhea may first become evident after the patient experiences an episode of acute meningitis, chronic headache, or some other acute intracranial pathologic process. Some related clinical findings may include hoarseness, chronic cough, positional cephalgia, or altered taste sensations (such as a salty or sweet taste in the mouth). CSF rhinorrhea typically tends to be intermittent and position-dependent. Often, it is difficult to localize the source of leakage.

The laboratory examination for CSF leak should be more involved than just a dipstick test for glucose because this method gives many false positive results secondary to the normal glucose content of nasal secretions. A CSF sample should be sent to the lab for quantification of glucose. A glucose level equal to or greater than 50 mg per 100 ml is typically diagnostic.[3] Perhaps beta- or tau-transferrin testing is most specific for CSF rhinorrhea. Localization of the CSF leak may be clinically difficult to determine, and radiologic studies may be indicated. Studies using metrizamide, a radiographic contrast medium, as well as high-resolution CT scanning may assist with localization.

Statistically, about 70% of postoperative CSF leaks resolve spontaneously.[4] Conservative treatment includes elevation of the head and avoidance of straining or sneezing. This may be combined with lumbar punctures or subarachnoid lumbar drain placement. If spontaneous closure does not occur, surgical intervention is indicated. If the site of an anterior cranial skull base leak is localized, then extracranial modes of closure are usually preferred. On the other hand, if the leak is persistent and cannot be well localized, then an intracranial approach is indicated. The following case illustrates a common ESS complication scenario.[5]

The male plaintiff, who suffered from chronic sinusitis, came under the care of the defendant otolaryngologist, who recommended an endoscopic ethmoidectomy. The plaintiff contended that the defendant doctor inadvertently perforated the thin membrane separating the sinus cavity and the brain. Furthermore, the plaintiff asserted that the tear was negligently repaired, allowing subsequent infection to develop.

The plaintiff was subsequently diagnosed with meningitis and resulting brain damage. Although the plaintiff survived the meningitis, he was left with permanent cognitive deficits such as short-term memory problems, personality changes, and difficulty processing abstract thought. The plaintiff also claimed that he was permanently disabled from returning to work in his previous occupation as a self-employed plumber. The plaintiff claimed a lost earning capacity of $45,000 annually for the remainder of his life expectancy.

The plaintiff's experts were prepared to testify that the sinus cavity is situated adjacent to the cranial cavity, separated by only a thin sheath of tissue, and that tearing or perforation of the sheath or tissue is a recognized risk of surgery that can occur in the absence of negligence on the part of the treating surgeon. In addition, the experts were prepared to testify that the defendant deviated from the standard of care, not in tearing the tissue, but in failing to properly repair the injury. The plaintiff's experts would testify that the subsequent infection was caused by the alleged negligent repair undertaken by the surgeon.

The defendant otolaryngologist denied liability and maintained that his care and treatment of the plaintiff comported with the standard in all aspects of the procedure. Nevertheless, this case from Cuyahoga County, Ohio, resulted in a $2,600,000 settlement prior to trial.

Although this case probably had extenuating circumstances that led to the large settlement, one thing is sure: the propensity for lawsuits associated with ESS is such that any otolaryngologist should be extremely vigilant in every aspect of patient care when this surgery is contemplated. Very critical to the defense of these types of cases is the medical documentation in the preoperative, intraoperative, and postoperative periods. The following case also depicts CSF rhinorrhea.[6]

A female plaintiff brought this action against the defendant otolaryngologist to whom she presented with complaints of recurring ear infections. The plaintiff claimed that the defendant negligently failed to attempt less invasive alternative treatments to surgery and negligently failed to perform all the necessary diagnostic studies prior to proceeding with surgery on the plaintiff's sinuses. The surgery left the plaintiff with a continual "runny nose." Ultimately, it was determined to be CSF rhinorrhea resulting as a complication of the surgery. The plaintiff underwent surgical repair of the leakage, but was left with permanent neurologic damage as noted above.

The plaintiff contended that the defendant otolaryngologist ordered a CT scan at the time of her initial presentation, during which time she also complained of recurrent earaches (otalgia). She claimed that after receiving the CT scan results, the defendant advised her that she would require surgery to her sinuses as a first step to alleviating her recurrent otalgia. According to the plaintiff, the defendant offered no alternative course of treatment at the time. The plaintiff further alleged that the surgery was scheduled for November of 1996, but that she decided to postpone the surgery.

The plaintiff testified that she contacted the defendant again approximately 9 months later complaining of worsening ear complaints. The sinus surgery was rescheduled for July 1997. The surgery proceeded as scheduled, but sometime shortly thereafter, the plaintiff began experiencing drainage of clear fluid emanating from her left nostril. Leakage continued from her nose even after she returned home. The plaintiff contended that the otolaryngologist failed to address her new symptoms of fluid drainage from the nose.

Upon presenting to her family physician, the clear drainage from the plaintiff's nose was tested, and was determined to be cerebrospinal fluid, suggesting that the defendant otolaryngologist had perforated the ethmoid sinus intraoperatively. The plaintiff's condition necessitated surgical repair, but she was left with permanent neurologic damage resulting from trauma to the olfactory nerve thought to have occurred during the course of the repair surgery. In addition, the surgery resulted in loss of taste and smell as well as partial facial paralysis.

The plaintiff's medical expert testified that the defendant deviated from the standard of care by proceeding with the surgery based upon one clinical exam, one CT scan study, and without first attempting less invasive means of treatment of the plaintiff's ear complaints, including a trial by antibiotic therapy alone or in conjunction with other medications. The plaintiff's expert emphasized the serious risks associated with the surgical procedure, as evidenced by the plaintiff's unfortunate outcome. The plaintiff's expert supported the contention that less invasive treatment measures should have been attempted prior to subjecting the patient to such surgery.

Meanwhile, the defendant otolaryngologist contended that the surgery was indicated based upon the extensive history provided by the plaintiff's medical record, combined with the results of the CT scan study and clinical examination. The jury found for the plaintiff and returned a verdict of $1,900,000.

In this medical malpractice case, the sinus surgery may or may not have been indicated. It is also unclear from the report as to the actual cause of the facial hemiparesis. Regardless of whether or not surgery in this case was indicated—even if a CSF leak had occurred—the jury outcome may have been different if there was evidence that the physician had carefully followed the procedures listed in Box 42-2.

It is highly unlikely that all of the above occurred in this case, and it is very likely that the jury was aware of this

---

BOX 42-2. MEDICAL-LEGAL PEARL

. . . explained to the patient the differential diagnosis for conditions that cause her clinical symptoms;

. . . explained to the patient the possible medical and surgical treatments that follow based upon the otolaryngologist's shared consideration of the differential diagnosis;

. . . presented the patient with a list of potential viable treatment options and alternatives (both medical and surgical) that would logically treat the conditions contemplated in the differential diagnosis;

. . . explained to the patient the potential risks, benefits, and complications associated with each viable treatment option;

. . . documented all of the above, and demonstrated that the treatment chosen resulted from truly informed consent from the patient.

---

fact. As alluded to previously, many medical malpractice lawsuits could be avoided just by educating the patient about the specific pathologic processes occurring in their body. Indeed, patient education should be a fundamental component to obtaining informed consent for any surgical procedure or medical treatment.

LARYNGOLOGY

The larynx is the musculocartilaginous structure situated at the top of the trachea and below the base of the tongue and the hyoid bone. It is the essential air passageway that guards the entrance into the trachea, and functions secondarily as the organ of voice. Not surprisingly, most medical malpractice lawsuits associated with the larynx include cases involving acute airway emergencies or cases involving some type of voice impairment. Anytime an otolaryngologist is emergently consulted, it is usually because of an acute airway situation or some type of acute bleeding. The following case illustrates an airway issue.[7]

Mr. M, complaining of difficulty in breathing, went to the emergency room at approximately 3:00 A.M. He was placed under the care of Dr. VH, the emergency room physician on duty. Dr. VH's physical examination of M revealed swollen lymph nodes, inflammation of the pharynx, enlarged, swollen tonsils covered with pus-like exudate, and a muffled, hoarse voice. M also had stridor. After examining M, Dr. VH asked the nurse to telephone the on-call otolaryngologist.

Pursuant to the emergency room's procedure, its answering service telephoned the defendant, a board-certified otolaryngologist, and left a message. When the defendant returned the telephone call at 3:15 A.M., he spoke to Dr. VH. The defendant had never treated M. The defendant described his telephone conversation with Dr. VH, in part, as follows:

[Dr. VH] told me he had seen a patient, 31-year-old obese male, come in with sore throat. . . . He had stridor, he had tonsillitis, and he had a positive strep test. . . .

He then asked me how our group treated our patients with tonsillitis. And I replied, "Did you say he had stridor? Did you—is this guy's airway obstructed? Is the patient in acute airway distress?"

He said, "No, the patient's airway is not obstructed, he's not in acute airway distress. In fact, he's walking around and he's talking, and has normal O2 sats. on pulse oximetry."

I said, "Well, is he having noisy breathing?" He said ["Y]es.["] I then asked him what did he see on his exam. He said he had large, inflamed tonsils that were almost touching. I asked him if one tonsil was larger than the other. . . . He said ["N]o, they were both symmetrically enlarged and almost touching.["]

And then I said, "Well, you had told me that you had given him a shot of penicillin and that you had ordered a breathing treatment." And he said, "That's correct. I've already given him the penicillin shot."

I said, "Well, what we normally do with our patients is to give them a gram of Rocephin . . . and give them Dalalone. . . ."

. . . .

I said it probably wouldn't hurt to give him the—you know, an additional shot of the other antibiotic, and that I said, "You needed [sic] to observe the patient, especially after giving him the shot and the breathing treatment."

And he asked me how long we observed patients, and I told him that we usually, at least with the shot, have them wait 20 minutes; and with the breathing treatment, it could be 30 minutes to an hour.

. . . .

I then told him that . . . if anything changed, to call me, let me know. I reminded him that it took me about 25 minutes to get in to the hospital.

. . . .

And then I said, "Why don't you just give me a call after he finishes the breathing treatment and let me know how he's doing." And that was the end of the call. And the next call I received came later that morning sometime before 6:00 [A.M.].

. . . .

Dr. VH said that he was going to refer the patient to me. I said that was fine, to have the patient call me, set up an appointment that morning.

. . . .

He said that—"Would it be all right if I referred the patient to you?" I said that's—that's—that would be fine, to ask the patient to call me in the morning to set up an appointment, to tell him—try to set that appointment up for that—for that morning.

During his deposition, Dr. VH explained some of his reasons for contacting the defendant:

Q: What time did you call Defendant?
A: About 3:15 [A.M.].
Q: And that would be after your examination?
A: After the examination.
Q: And when you finished your examination, you just weren't comfortable about what problem Mr. M might have?
A: Yes, I had an understanding of his problem.
Q: But you weren't entirely sure; is that correct?
A: You are never sure about anything.
Q: All right. So you consulted with someone who was a specialist in the area of your concern?
A: That's correct.
Q: And your number one concern was that the fact that you heard stridor?
A: That's correct.

. . . .

Q: And you knew stridor was bad, could be?
A: Could be.
Q: And so you wanted to call an ENT specialist; is that correct?
A: That's correct.

Later that morning, Mr. M stopped breathing and arrested in the emergency room. Dr. VH attempted to intubate him, was unsuccessful, and then performed an emergency tracheotomy. In the interim, the defendant was called and was asked to come to the hospital to assist Dr. VH. When the defendant arrived, he examined Mr. M for the first time and transferred him to the intensive care unit. A subsequent EEG showed that Mr. M had no brain activity. Three days later, Mr. M died.

Mrs. M sued the otolaryngologist for medical malpractice. The case above ultimately resulted in a defense verdict for the otolaryngologist when the Texas Court of Appeals held that the otolaryngologist did not take an affirmative action to treat Mr. M sufficient to create a physician-patient relationship, and therefore owed no duty to Mr. M. This case should remind the otolaryngologist to be particularly diligent with medical documentation whenever there is a consultation regarding a potential acute airway patient.

Although production of voice is the secondary function of the larynx, it is of critical importance in one's ability to communicate. More importantly, voice-related liability issues are also commonly seen in the courtroom. Here is another case example.[8]

The plaintiff was a 54-year-old college professor. On April 21, 1978, she was referred to otolaryngologist Dr. MT for treatment of a lump in her throat. Dr. MT's diagnosis was a thyroglossal duct cyst, and he continued the plaintiff on antibiotics as prescribed by the referring physician. When the antibiotics failed to effect improvement, Dr. MT recommended removal of the cyst by surgery. The plaintiff signed the appropriate consent form and surgery was performed on May 9, 1978.

After incision the cystic mass was visualized as extending from the cricothyroid membrane to the infrahyoid area. A second mass was identified as either a projection of the thyroid gland or a pyramidal lobe. After removing the second mass, Dr. MT utilized blunt and sharp dissection to retract the thyroglossal duct cyst on its upper end. The lower end of the tract turned 180° superiorly behind the thyroid cartilage.

The inferior half of the thyroid cartilage was incised, and the tract visualized as penetrating the underlying membrane for 2-3 mm. The entire tract, including the cyst, was excised in one piece. The edges of the thyroid cartilage were reapproximated with a No. 30 wire. Before concluding the operation Dr. MT performed a laryngoscopic examination that revealed the presence of a possible mucosal laceration, 3-4 mm in length, near the anterior commissure.

Postsurgical progress was uneventful; the sutures were removed and the vocal cords moved well. However, when examined on July 12, 1978, the plaintiff complained of hoarseness. Dr. MT found no objective basis for the complaint as the vocal cords appeared normal and moved satisfactorily. Dr. HM, an associate of Dr. MT, noted a slight edema (swelling) of the vocal cords but otherwise movement was good. The plaintiff was given a prescription for Valium and told to consult a speech therapist for problems with articulation and phonics. It was the plaintiff's last visit with Dr. MT.

The plaintiff sought treatment from Dr. LT, an otolaryngologist, on September 27, 1979, for congestion in her ears associated with postnasal drainage and chronic sore throat. She informed Dr. LT of hoarseness and vocal cord dysfunction since the operation of May 9, 1978. Examination revealed a slightly atrophic right vocal cord. Dr. LT intervened surgically on October 16, 1979, using a laser to divide scar tissue, which was believed to be pulling down slightly on the right vocal cord. No improvement was noted. A second diagnostic laryngoscopy revealed a small web of scar tissue involving the right vocal cord and the anterior commissure, and the left vocal cord was atrophic and scarred. A sterile glycerine solution injected into the left vocal cord to increase its bulk effected no demonstrative improvement. A final laryngoscopic exam on April 23, 1980, revealed the posterior commissure rotated to the left. Dr. LT referred the plaintiff to a speech therapist.

From April through June of 1980, the plaintiff was treated by Dr. OV, a psychiatrist, for depression with anxiety secondary to the loss of her normal vocal capabilities. She filed suit on September 25, 1980, claiming the hoarseness and vocal cord dysfunction impacted on her ability to teach and to support herself and her family. The central issues at trial were whether the thyroglossal duct cyst operation was negligently performed and whether, as a proximate result of negligence, the plaintiff suffered injuries that would not otherwise have been incurred.

The proceedings in this case resulted in a classic courtroom "battle of the experts," wherein testimony from multiple plaintiff's experts and defendant's experts was pitted against each other before the judge in order to determine which experts were more credible. The defendant's surgical treatment and management were meticulously scrutinized in this lawsuit, but the defendant prevailed. However, there are two important factors to note in this case: (1) the importance of establishing the standard of care through credible expert witness testimony, and (2) the potentially devastating impact that voice impairment can have upon a patient (or plaintiff).

Otolaryngologists who specialize in voice procedures emphasize the importance of proper preoperative as well as postoperative management of voice patients. Dr. Robert Ossoff, a prominent laryngologist from Vanderbilt University School of Medicine, recommends a preoperative assessment by a speech and language pathologist, a vocal pedagogue, and a gastroenterologist in order to maximize the success of any voice procedure.[9] In addition, Dr. Ossoff recommends a preoperative voice recording as well as a videostroboscopic examination and photograph as the minimum necessary preoperative assessments for patients undergoing vocal surgery or any surgery that may affect one's ability to phonate, particularly if the patient's livelihood is dependent upon their ability to speak or sing.[9] Although this author realizes that these documentation measures and resources may not be readily available to a typical small ENT practice, it is this author's belief that a "high risk" patient or a patient who appears litigious should be referred to a facility that is equipped to perform a complete and adequate preoperative assessment.

Finally, informed consent for voice procedures should include patient education about potential complications such as chipped or broken teeth, bleeding, infection, voice hoarseness, and voice whisper. The patient should be aware that poor vocal outcomes may occur even if surgery is performed perfectly, and they should be educated that healing after vocal surgery is a *process*, not an *event*. This process may typically take anywhere from 3 to 18 months, depending upon the surgery.[9]

CONCLUSION

In any medical malpractice lawsuit, negligence is defined by treatment that falls below the so-called "standard of care." Perhaps the most difficult aspect of litigating an otolaryngology-related case is the fact that this specialty is always in a state of evolution with new techniques, new instrumentation, and new "standards" as clinical data are accumulated about the new techniques and new instruments. For example, there are numerous ways to perform a tonsillectomy. Tonsils can be removed by wire snares, electrocautery, laser, and even sharp or blunt dissection. All techniques work, and all are acceptable techniques that are often dependent upon the skill and experience of the operator, as well as the basic health, education, and comprehension ability of the patient.

In the courtroom, however, if the plaintiff's expert testifies that electrocautery is the *only way* that tonsils should be removed and that any other technique falls below the standard of care, then electrocautery becomes the "standard of care" for that courtroom until contrary evidence is produced from the opposing expert witness. Otolaryngologists should be aware that new instruments and new techniques are often fraught with potential "new complications," and that medical documentation is often the physician's best defense in a medical malpractice suit.

For the attorney representing an otolaryngologist in a medical malpractice suit, the lawyer should be aware of otolaryngology's constant evolution, and that proper education of the judge or jury about the current standard of care is critical to each case. One common denominator in many malpractice suits is that of informed consent. The reader should note that standard of care and informed consent issues are addressed in other chapters of this text, and should refer to those chapters for a more in-depth discussion.

ENDNOTES

1. *Conn v. Purcelli, M.D.* (Case No. SC059122, Mar. 15, 2001), 16(7) National Jury Verdict Review & Analysis 17 (2001).
2. P.H.G. Van Gilse, *Des Observations Ultérieures sur la Genèse des Exostoses du Conduit Externe par l'Irritations d'Eau Froide.* 26 Acta Oto-Laryngol. 343 (1938).
3. JR. Chandler, *Traumatic Cerebrospinal Fluid Leakage.* 16 Otol. Clin. North Am. 623-632 (1983).
4. D.L. Myers & R.T. Sataloff, *Spinal Fluid Leakage After Skull Base Surgery*, 17 Otol. Clin. North Am. 601-612 (1984).
5. Citation withheld by reporter, 17(1) National Jury Verdict Review & Analysis 18 (2002).
6. *McKibben v. Baldone* (Case No. 98CCV A06-4535 Sept. 2001), 17(8) National Jury Verdict Review & Analysis 16 (2002).
7. *El Majzoub v. Appling*, 2002 WL 31521130, Tex. App.-Hous. (1 Dist.).
8. *Pernia v. Trail*, 519 So. 2d 231.
9. Telephone interview with Robert Ossoff, D.M.D., M.D., Aug. 7, 2002.

Liability of Radiologists

MICHAEL M. RASKIN, M.D., M.S., J.D., M.P.H., M.A., F.C.L.M.

THE PROBLEM
MANAGING RISK
TYPES OF ERRORS
THE SOLUTION
CONCLUSION

THE PROBLEM

The probability of a physician being sued for medical malpractice in the United States is about one out of four. The incidence of lawsuits has increased for all fields of medicine. What is most alarming is the increase in the number of million dollar or higher jury awards. Approximately 45% of jury awards from 1998 to 1999 were a million dollars or more compared to 39% from 1997 to 1998. This overall increase in jury awards has raised the *median* malpractice award from $750,000 in 1998 to $800,000 in 1999, and to $1 million in 2000. The average jury award for medical malpractice more than tripled between 1994 and 2000, from $1.1 million to $3.5 million.

Going to trial in a medical malpractice case is an expensive ordeal for both sides. When going to trial for the specific liability of childbirth injuries, missed diagnosis of cancer, or delayed treatment, the median award was over $1 million in the year 2000. Settling out of court for these three specific liabilities was less costly, with the median settlement of $750,0000 for childbirth injuries and $665,000 for delayed treatment. The overall median settlement for all categories was $500,000 in the year 2000.[1]

Indeed, we face a medical malpractice liability insurance crisis in the United States. This is especially true in states that have no cap on noneconomic damage awards. The frequency of million dollar awards in Florida is well above the national average and 63% higher than in California, which passed medical liability reform legislation in 1975.[2] Many medical liability insurers have left high-risk states and several have stopped underwriting medical malpractice liability insurance entirely. Others set narrow guidelines defining the physicians they are willing to insure. Larger jury awards are just one of the factors in this crisis. Lower interest rates, which translate into a lower return on investments insurers make to cover claims, rate cuts by the Federal Reserve, and a highly competitive insurance market have also contributed to the medical malpractice mess we are in today.[3]

The public has become desensitized to think of a million dollars as a large sum of money. Sports figures routinely make several million each year, with an increasing number making tens of millions. This is also fueled by the lottery as well as popular television quiz shows. Jurors seem to have no problem making someone a millionaire even if they cannot become a millionaire themselves. The jury awards keep going up, with the median award in the year 2000 over $1 million. Settlement medians are significantly lower, making it somewhat more attractive for insurers to settle rather than risk greater exposure at a jury trial, not to mention the extra costs of defending a case to jury verdict.

Radiology has its own special problem with liability insurance. While the average indemnification has doubled in the last 15 years for all physicians, it has tripled for radiology. Furthermore, one-third of all medical malpractice claims are lost by the radiologist. If a "missed diagnosis" is alleged, 41% are lost. The most commonly missed diagnoses are breast cancer, lung cancer, and fracture of the spine.[4]

MANAGING RISK

A very practical reason for studying risk management is to attempt to understand why we get sued. The risk of being sued is high in all of medicine, not just radiology. However, there are some positive risk management steps that you can take to reduce the possibility of being sued and losing. The more you understand the risk management process, the better you will be able to minimize or manage your risk. Risk management involves the identification, analysis, and evaluation of the risk and selecting the most advantageous method of addressing it. From a practical standpoint, this means identifying situations where you are at greatest risk of being sued and doing something to minimize that risk.

The first step of the risk management process involves identification of the risk. This may vary depending upon the practice. For example, if the practice involves interpreting studies from a busy trauma center or a mammography center, the practice involves higher risk than a free-standing MRI center. Once the risk is identified, it needs to be analyzed. Do the lawsuits occur with certain radiologists, during the evening, or during teleradiology reads? Once the risk is analyzed, implementation of risk management techniques needs to be instituted. Should radiology staffing be changed to address these risks? Finally, there needs to be a method to monitor the results. If not, you won't know if any change you made was effective or not.

Certain areas of radiology practice are associated with a significantly higher incidence of lawsuits, and risk management techniques can be effective in reducing the risk of being sued and losing. In general, there are four main reasons why radiologists get sued: errors in perceptions, errors in interpretation, failing to suggest the next appropriate procedure, and failure to communicate.[5]

TYPES OF ERRORS

Perception errors

Unfortunately, perception errors occur quite often and are the most common reason why radiologists get sued.[6] With perception errors, the abnormality is seen in retrospect but it is missed by the radiologist when interpreting the initial study. Some perception errors occur because the radiologist does not possess sufficient knowledge. Whether the abnormality is subtle or not may depend upon whether the observer error falls below the standard of care. This is despite the fact that the error rate in radiology is approximately 30%.[7] Ultimately, it will depend upon the final outcome of the missed findings. Lawsuits involving perception errors are usually settled by the radiologist since the radiologist loses approximately 80% of these cases if it goes to a jury verdict.

Of course, the abnormality is always perceived in retrospect, but the real question is: was it below the standard of care for the radiologist not to have seen the abnormality?[8] Although there have been a few cases in which the jury was convinced that missing a radiographic abnormality was not malpractice, they have been few and far between. In 1997, a Wisconsin Court of Appeals determined that errors in perception by radiologists viewing x-rays can occur in the absence of negligence. To require the average radiologist to see all abnormalities, even subtle ones, would elevate the standard to which the radiologist is held to perfection.[9] However, this concept has not been accepted in other jurisdictions. It may be difficult to defend the radiologist before a jury when the radiologist has failed to perceive an abnormality that even the jurors can see. Indeed, it is unfortunate, but the public seems to believe that every radiology perception error represents a negligent act.[10]

An additional source for error results from the influence a radiology report has over another radiologist. This type of perceptual error, sometimes called an alliterative error, occurs because the radiologist reads the old report first before looking at the imaging study and is more apt to adopt the same opinion as that rendered previously.[11] If the first radiologist missed it, the next radiologist will often miss it as well.

Interpretation errors

With interpretation errors, the abnormality is perceived but it is incorrectly described. This is not a perception error because, in this situation, the abnormality is identified, but it is called the wrong thing. Interpretation errors most often occur due to lack of knowledge or faulty judgment. This is also called a "misdiagnosis" and most often occurs when a malignant lesion is incorrectly attributed to a benign finding. A misdiagnosis can also occur when a normal structure, or variant of normal, is called abnormal. This situation occurs more commonly in ultrasound and computed tomography studies. When lawsuits involving interpretation errors go to trial, approximately 75% are found in favor of the radiologist.

Having an appropriate differential diagnosis can be of great help here, especially if the correct diagnosis is included in your differential diagnosis. This is especially true if the actual abnormality is extremely rare but your differential was at least "in the ballpark." However, a "blanket diagnosis," such as "probably benign, but malignancy cannot be ruled out," is usually not successful if the results are grave.

Error of failing to suggest the next appropriate procedure

While some radiologists might suggest additional studies to increase referrals, the prudent radiologist will suggest the next appropriate study or procedure based upon the findings and the clinical information. One of the criticisms raised when a radiologist recommends or suggests an additional study or procedure is that the referring physician does not want to "feel forced" to order a study or procedure merely to minimize his or her potential liability. If the radiologist fails to recommend or suggest the next appropriate study or procedure for fear of upsetting the referring physician, the radiologist may become a defendant in a lawsuit for not suggesting the very procedure or study the referring physician did not want recommended. This should not be construed as self-referral or "auto-referral" but merely good medical practice.[12] Some of the newer modalities, such as functional MRI scans for cognitive dysfunction, diffusion MRI scans for recent infarction, and PET scans for recurrent metastases, are ones of whose efficacy and appropriateness the ordering physician may be unaware. Radiologists must ensure that the recommendations or suggestions for any additional diagnostic studies or procedures are appropriate and will add meaningful information to clarify, confirm, or rule out the initial impression. Sometimes the next appropriate procedure may merely be a follow-up study.

In 1993, the American College of Radiology (ACR) realized that there would be a premium placed on the efficient use of resources in health care, especially involving the appropriate use of radiologic services. The ACR recognized the need for nationally accepted, scientifically based appropriateness criteria to assist radiologists in referring physicians in making appropriate imaging decisions. The ACR Appropriateness Criteria were thus created for this purpose. The ACR established these guidelines based upon validity assessment to determine if they would lead to better outcomes. It should be emphasized that the ACR Appropriateness Criteria are used as clinical practice guidelines to apply to the majority of patients. Be aware that ACR Appropriateness Criteria may suggest a nonradiologic procedure such as transthoracic or transesophageal echocardiography. Also, the complexity and severity of a patient's clinical condition may dictate the selection of appropriate imaging procedures and treatments. Furthermore, the availability of equipment or trained personnel may influence the timely selection of appropriate imaging procedures. The ultimate decision on the appropriate use of any imaging procedure should be made by the referring physician in consultation with the radiologist in consideration of the clinical circumstances.[13]

A radiologist is usually not expected to follow up on a recommendation or suggestion to obtain additional procedures or studies. However, a recent Missouri Supreme Court decision held that a radiology group has a duty of continuing care, including follow-up, to ensure that the treating physician acts on unexpected or adverse findings. This duty arose because the radiology group did not formally withdraw from a physician-patient relationship but rather kept interpreting the images on three separate occasions. Therefore, the court held that the "continuing care" exception to the medical malpractice statute of limitations applied. However, the court noted that if a physician specifically advises a patient that his or her relationship with the patient has ended, the statute of limitations will run from that date forward.[14] This is only one state and, as such, does not suggest a trend. However, it does show the court's willingness to consider all physicians to share responsibility for the care of the patient, which would place the radiologist in the same position as a primary health care provider.

Error of failure to communicate

The final written report has always been considered to be the definitive means of communicating the results of an imaging study or procedure to the referring physician. However, there are times when direct or personal communication of results must be made immediately and can vary with the nature of the urgency of the clinical problems. At times, this may require the radiologist to immediately communicate the results directly to the referring physician. Failing to communicate in a timely and clinically appropriate manner has been evolving as an increasing reason why radiologists are sued. In addition to rendering an official interpretation, the radiologist is responsible to communicate these findings directly to the referring physician, other health care provider, or appropriate representative in situations in which the radiologist feels immediate patient treatment is indicated. In nearly a third of cases, failure to communicate was the major factor in the error in diagnosis.

The American College of Radiology (ACR) Standard for Communication indicates that direct communication can be accomplished in person or by telephone to the referring physician or an appropriate representative.[5] This is an oral report that should be documented, as a final written report does not substitute for direct communication of the need for emergent care. Prior to 2002, the ACR Standard for Communication required direct communication for both significant unexpected findings as well as for urgent findings. Since then, the radiologist can communicate significant unexpected findings to the referring physician, other health care provider, or an appropriate individual in a manner that reasonably ensures receipt of the findings. After January 1, 2002, the radiologist no longer has to directly communicate significant unexpected findings. However, the radiologist who insists that the written report provides all the information the referring physician needed will be perceived as uncaring and callous if a simple telephone call could have averted a bad outcome. Furthermore, written reports are inaccurate in 18% of cases, affecting outcome in almost half of these cases. In 10% of cases, the written report was not issued in a clinically appropriate or timely manner, affecting outcome in 75% of these cases.[1]

In some practices, a preliminary report or a "wet read" is issued by the radiologist or the emergency room physician prior to the preparation of the final report. Any significant change between the preliminary report or wet read and the final report should be reported directly to the referring physician and documented in the final report.

If the author of an interpretive report is not available to sign the report, a colleague will often sign the report, substituting their signature for the author's signature. There is a danger to signing a colleague's interpretive report because, if he or she is sued for malpractice, you will almost certainly be sued as well. If you are signing a colleague's report, you should review the images and make corrections to the report, if necessary, with the full understanding that you will most likely be held responsible for the contents of the report.[16]

Correctly diagnosing an abnormality may not be enough if the findings are not directly communicated. A radiologist who correctly diagnosed a radial head fracture of a child, which was missed by the emergency room physician, argued that his liability should end when he correctly dictated the report. The Court of Appeals of Ohio disagreed and noted that radiologists have direct obligations to patients even though they may never see them personally. The court stressed that the communication of a diagnosis, if it is to be beneficial, is sometimes as important as the diagnosis itself.[17] This case is probably the origin of the ACR Standard for Communication. Similarly, a New Jersey Appellate Court has held that communication of an unusual finding so that it may be beneficially utilized is as important as the finding itself.[18] The Arkansas Supreme Court held that a radiologist cannot escape the duty to immediately communicate with the referring physician when they discover a misplaced endotracheal tube on a chest radiograph. It does the patient little good if the radiologist discovers this condition but does not inform those responsible for his care.[19] Attempts to show that the ACR Standards are merely "guidelines" and only one of the factors to be considered in determining the standard of care have been largely unsuccessful. The ACR acknowledges that the ACR Standards are not rules, but are guidelines that attempt to define principles of practice that should generally produce high-quality radiologic care. Whether you like it or not, the ACR Standards will be interpreted to mean "reasonable care"—anything less will be *below* the standard of care.[20]

The ACR Standards may be a double-edged sword for some. Certainly, the ACR Standards can be used against you if you deviated from them and did not document why you did so. You may be justified in not following the ACR Standards based upon the clinical situation. The ACR Standards are minimal, but you must document why you chose not to follow them. On the other hand, the ACR Standards may result in a case being dismissed against you if you can demonstrate that you followed the ACR Standards. Also, the term "standard" carries more weight and respect than the term "guidelines" and creates a positive effect on the perception of the ACR in the community.[21]

THE SOLUTION

Improve perception

Studies have shown that perception errors will occur even with the best-trained radiologist. However, some perception errors can be minimized by paying proper attention to clinical information when it is given, or obtaining clinical information when it is not. Knowledge of pertinent clinical history has been shown to increase the accuracy of the interpretation. Also, look at the films before reading prior reports. A "negative" prior report makes it easier for you to arrive at the same conclusion too.

Provide a meaningful interpretation

Errors in interpretation can be reduced through continuing education. Attending conferences and meetings and reading journals will help broaden your horizon and improve your

differential diagnosis. The ACR Standard for Communication indicates that a precise diagnosis should be given whenever possible and that a differential diagnosis should be given when appropriate. Having an appropriate and meaningful differential diagnosis will reduce your exposure. Your chances of losing are less if the actual diagnosis is included in your differential diagnosis.

Do not attempt to interpret studies in an area in which you do not feel comfortable or have not had sufficient training. Be aware that the ACR Standards have criteria for qualification as well as maintenance of competence and continuing medical education requirements for various imaging studies and procedures. Unfortunately, studies have shown that more things are missed because they are not thought of, rather than what is known.

Suggest the next appropriate procedure

When it is appropriate, a radiologist should not be reluctant to indicate that an additional study or procedure may be of diagnostic or confirmatory value when the initial diagnosis is not clear or in doubt. In fact, it is recommended to do so in the ACR Standard for Communication. With many of the newer diagnostic and therapeutic modalities now available in diagnostic imaging, not all referring physicians will be familiar with what procedures to do next. Most ordering physicians actually do know the next appropriate procedure to order when an abnormality is found on the study they originally ordered. However, if they are named in a lawsuit for failing to order that procedure, they will certainly blame it on you if you did not recommend it.

The keyword here is "appropriate." The radiologist should read the ACR Appropriateness Criteria and be familiar with the next appropriate procedure. It is usually, but not always, a radiologic study or procedure that can help define or amplify the initial findings. The radiologist should be aware of all imaging modalities, even if that modality is not offered in their department, institution, or office. If a deviation from the ACR Appropriateness Criteria is made due to the clinical circumstances or availability of equipment, it is recommended that the justification for the deviation be documented in the report.

Communicate the results

Lack of appropriate and timely communication appears to be one of the greatest problems confronting radiologists today. This is made even more burdensome by the difficulty in being able to quickly speak to a busy referring physician and the increasing workload that radiologists now have to bear. However, this is the one area in which the radiologist can dramatically improve the odds against being sued, and that is by communicating and documenting the communication.

The radiologist needs to be especially careful in communicating a "significant unexpected finding" on a "routine" or "pre-op" chest radiograph. Referring physicians may be less likely to expect abnormalities and might not even receive the written report prior to discharge of the patient.[22] Especially under these circumstances, the radiologist should make sure the communication is in a manner that reasonably ensures receipt of the findings. A federal court in Indiana found a radiologist negligent for correctly interpreting a skull fracture on Christmas Day in a child but not calling the referring physician when the radiologist knew that the report would not be transcribed for 2 days. The radiologist should have foreseen that the 2-day delay would have prevented the referring physician from instituting treatment in a timely manner.[23]

The ACR Standard on Communication recommends that direct communication be documented. Even though it is only a recommendation, the lack of documentation has been used in court to imply that the urgent or significant unexpected finding was not directly communicated. If the official report has already been dictated, then an addendum documenting the direct communication should be performed. This should be done contemporaneously with the direct communication. Finally, the ACR Standard for Communication should be thoroughly read and completely understood and implemented by every radiologist.

CONCLUSION

Obviously, there is no "solution" but merely recommendations: pay attention to clinical information or obtain it when not given; be qualified to interpret or perform a procedure and maintain your competence; suggest the next appropriate study or procedure; use the ACR Appropriateness Criteria; when appropriate, suggest a follow-up study; directly communicate findings when immediate patient treatment is indicated and document the communication; read, understand, and implement the ACR Standard for Communication into your practice. Adhering to these measures certainly will not prevent you from being sued. It will, however, reduce the risk of being sued and losing.

ENDNOTES

1. *Physician Insurers Association of America and the American College of Radiology Practice Standard Claim Survey* (Physician Insurers Association of America, Rockville, MD, 2000).
2. R.P. Hartwig, *Don't Blame Rate Hikes on the Stock Market* (Letter to the editor), Miami Herald (Jan. 6, 2003) at 10B.
3. T. Albert, *Liability Insurance Crisis: Bigger Awards Just One Factor*, 45 Am. Medical News 1-2 (2002).
4. M.M. Raskin, *Suing Radiologists* (editorial), 30 Applied Radiol. 5 (2001).
5. M.M. Raskin, *Why Radiologists Get Sued*, 30 Applied Radiol. 9-13 (2001).
6. L. Berlin, *Perceptual Errors*, 167 Am. J. Roentgenol. 587-90 (1996).
7. L. Berlin & R.W. Hendrix, *Perceptual Errors and Negligence*, 170 Am. J. Roentgenol. 863–67 (1998).
8. L. Berlin, *Does the "Missed" Radiographic Diagnosis Constitute Malpractice?*, 123 Radiology 523-27 (1977).
9. L. Berlin, *Missed Radiographic Diagnoses Do Not Constitute Negligence, Wisconsin Court of Appeals Rules*, 554(3) ACR Bulletin 20-23, 30 (1998).
10. L. Berlin, *Malpractice Issues in Radiology: Defending the "Missed" Radiographic Diagnosis*, 176 Am. J. Roentgenol. 317–32 (2001).
11. L. Berlin, *Malpractice Issues in Radiology: Alliterative Errors*, 174 Am. J. Roentgenol. 925–31 (2000).
12. M.M. Raskin, *"Auto-referral" and self-referral*, 24 Applied Radiol. 19-20 (1995).
13. American College of Radiology, *ACR Appropriateness Criteria*, i-ii (American College of Radiology, Reston, VA, 2001).
14. *Montgomery v. South County Radiologists, Inc.*, 49 S.W. 2d 191 (2001).
15. American College of Radiology, *ACR Standard for Communication: Diagnostic Radiology*, in *Standards*, 1-3 (American College of Radiology, Reston, VA, 2001).
16. M.M. Raskin, *Substituted Signature*, 30 Applied Radiol. 19-21 (2001).
17. *Phillips v. Good Samaritan Hospital*, 416 N.E. 2d 646 (1997).
18. *Jenoff v. Gleason*, 521 A. 2d 1323 (N.J. Super. Ct. App. Div., 1987).
19. *Courteau v. Dodd*, 773 S.W. 2d 436 (1989).
20. P. Cascade & L. Berlin, *American College of Radiology Standard for Communication*, 173 Am. J. Roentgenol. 1439-42 (1999).
21. R. Chesbrough, *Strategic Approach Fends Off Charges of Malpractice*, 24 Diagnostic Imaging 46-51, 87 (2002).
22. L. Berlin, *Radiology and Malpractice*, in J. Taveras & J. Ferrucci, (eds.), *Radiology*, Vol. II, chap. 100, 1-25 (Lippincott Williams & Wilkins, Philadelphia, PA, 2002).
23. *Keene v. Methodist Hospital*, 324 F.Supp. 233 (1971).

Legal Issues of Prehospital Emergency Medical Systems

SPENCER A. HALL, M.D., J.D., F.C.L.M.

DISPATCHERS
EMERGENCY MEDICAL TECHNICIANS (EMTs)
MEDICAL DIRECTORS
CONCLUSION

Providing emergency treatment and transportation to a hospital is an important component of our health care delivery system. Reality TV in prime time impresses us with "the speed with which the ambulances reach the sick and injured, bringing help that literally wrests the sufferer from the jaws of death, as the last flickering spark of life is leaving the body."[1] This is a relatively new area of medicine that has been developing over the last 30 years or so, and, as may be expected, the legal issues are still in a state of flux.

The important thing to remember about EMS is that it is local. EMS laws and regulations vary from state to state, and often from county to county.[2]

Although there is some overlap, prehospital care providers may be divided into three general classes: dispatchers, emergency medical technicians, and medical control physicians. These groups, and the legal issues specific to each, will be considered in turn.

DISPATCHERS

The first contact most patients have with the emergency medical services (EMS) system is the dispatcher who answers their call to 911. Dispatchers are almost always governmental employees and usually are responsible for the dispatch of law enforcement and fire personnel in addition to EMS.

Initially, the 911 operator was responsible only for getting the address of the caller and dispatching the appropriate resources to that location. Now, the standard of care is emergency medical dispatch (EMD) where the dispatcher, after sending resources, begins patient care by delivering instructions to the caller over the telephone. It is not unusual to hear of lives being saved by these instructions.

Legal issues surrounding dispatchers (individuals and/or the agency they represent) are almost solely those of tort liability. A public entity owes a duty not only to properly design and implement a 911 system, but to correctly use it as well.[3] Most lawsuits against dispatchers fall into two general theories of negligence, the failure of or delay in sending a response, or sending it to the wrong place.

Generally, most of these lawsuits are unsuccessful. Dispatchers benefit from several significant protections. These are sovereign immunity, statutory immunity, and the special duty doctrine.

Sovereign immunity

Sovereign immunity protects a governmental agency from the torts of its officers or agents in the absence of a constitutional or statutory provision creating a liability. State tort claims acts delineate the areas where immunity is waived.[4] Tort claims acts typically do not excuse willful or wanton conduct.

For example, the Texas Tort Claims Act states liability "applies to a claim against a public agency that arises from an action of an employee of the public agency or a volunteer under direction of the public agency and that involves providing 9-1-1 service or responding to a 9-1-1 emergency call only if the action violates a statute or ordinance applicable to the action."[5] A Texas dispatcher who sent an ambulance to an incorrect address after repeatedly being informed of the correct address was found to have violated a local ordinance that outlined the standard of care for emergency action and thus did not qualify for immunity.[6]

Immunity was also not available to a Maryland dispatcher who ignored and mishandled a series of 911 calls about a heart attack victim while she was engaged in a personal phone call. The jury awarded $1.7 million.[7]

Statutory immunity

Some states have specific immunity statutes that include dispatchers, often along with other EMS providers. In Indiana, a statute specifically provides immunity for losses arising

The author would like to thank the Lexis-Nexis Group for research support.

out of the "development, adoption, implementation, operation, maintenance, or use of an enhanced emergency communication system."[8] This law completely shielded dispatchers who never sent an ambulance to a heart attack victim, despite saying they had during four 911 calls.[9]

Special duty doctrine

Even if there is no other immunity, the legal principle of special duty still operates in many jurisdictions. Generally, although governments are responsible for providing protective services such as police, fire, and EMS, they owe this duty to the population as a whole, rather than specific individuals. Individuals may claim a duty from the government only when a "special duty" is established.

Establishing this special duty requires finding that a special relationship has formed between a caller and the governmental entity. This includes the open assumption by the entity to act on behalf of an injured party, knowledge on the part of the entity's agents that inaction could lead to harm, direct contact between the agents and the injured party, and the injured party's justifiable reliance on the entity's help.[10] For example, a single call to a dispatcher, from someone with a headache who was advised to try aspirin and was later found to have a stroke, was not sufficient to establish a special duty,[11] while a series of two phone calls to another dispatcher was.[12] Similarly, an ambulance dispatched to an incorrect address never established a special duty toward an unconscious victim because the victim never relied on the dispatcher's promise to send an ambulance.[13]

Special duty is not widespread, and is quite likely to vary between jurisdictions. New York and the District of Columbia, for example, have series of cases discussing special duty, while New Mexico has eliminated the public duty/special duty distinction by statute.[14]

EMERGENCY MEDICAL TECHNICIANS (EMTs)

EMTs are a cosmopolitan group, ranging from volunteers with the minimal training (usually about 120 hours) required to qualify as basic emergency medical technicians (EMT-Bs) who render care that is largely first aid, to professional paramedics (EMT-Ps) with more than 1000 hours of training who may perform invasive procedures and administer drugs—often actions that used to be restricted to physicians. Although most legal issues relating to responders concern medical negligence, there are other concerns as well.

EMTs are employees, and as such may become plaintiffs in many areas of general employment law. Americans with Disabilities Act (ADA)[15] lawsuits have been filed by EMTs alleging employment discrimination on the basis of obesity[16] or congenital deformity,[17] and have been routinely dealt with by the courts. Family Medical Leave Act (FMLA)[18] lawsuits have occurred,[19] as well as actions under the Uniformed Service Employment and Reemployment Rights Act (USERRA).[20]

There is one area unique to EMT employment. Many EMTs are also trained as firefighters. The Fair Labor Standards Act (FLSA)[21] provides that a public employer need not pay overtime for "individuals engaged in fire protection" until they have worked more than 212 hours in 28 consecutive days (53 hours per week).[22] This was commonly used as a cost savings measure by public employers until courts clarified that in order to qualify for these savings, ambulance and rescue personnel had to be "regularly dispatched" to fires,[23] a factor that will now be determined on a case-by-case basis.[24]

EMTs have been the target of civil rights (42 U.S.C. §1983) lawsuits as well. These are usually unsuccessful. There is no constitutional right to be taken to a hospital of the patient's choice.[25] Moreover, a recent federal case reviewed an alleged right to competent rescue and found that "states have no constitutional obligation to provide competent rescue services" and "there is no federal constitutional right to rescue services, competent or otherwise."[26] An *en banc* rehearing of this case is pending.[27]

Response

Generally, decisions about situating or staffing response units is discretionary, although local regulations may set minimum requirements. There still may be liability when the system fails to function properly. An example of this is *Brooks v. Herndon Ambulance Service, Inc.* A student in gym class began seizing and then arrested.[28] The responding basic life support ambulance had difficulty finding the address, equipment malfunctioned on scene, and finally the ambulance broke down en route to the hospital with the patient. Ten minutes from the school was a fire department with a paramedic unit that was never notified.

Often, complaints against services have to do with response times. Regardless of facts, patients often perceive that it took too long for an ambulance to respond to their call.[29] Sometimes this is justified: a Honolulu jury awarded $1,987,705 against the city for a 2-hour delay in ambulance arrival.[30] Even a delay of transport due to prolonged scene time (20 minutes for someone with chest pain) may be a cause of loss of a decedent's chance of survival and result in a jury award.[31]

Transport issues

The area with the greatest number of lawsuits concerns patient transport. Failure to transport a patient, patient refusal of transport, and transporting a patient against their will each present complex dilemmas balancing autonomy and paternalism that often lead to legal actions when there is a poor outcome.

Patients denied transport or convinced by field personnel to forgo ambulance transport have been a source of numerous claims within EMS.[32] Research indicates that a significant number of individuals who refuse transport are eventually seen by physicians,[33] and a high number of patients who are refused transport by EMS personnel are eventually admitted to hospital.[34]

Refusal of transport. There is no question that any competent individual has a right to refuse any medical intervention, including transport, even if the refusal of treatment may result in death.[35] This must be an "informed" refusal. The patient must be informed of their diagnosis, the recommended treatment and alternatives, and what is likely to happen if treatment is refused. This is problematic in the prehospital setting. First, although EMS providers are trained that they cannot "diagnose" illness, here they must determine whether a patient is mentally "competent," a determination that is both a diagnosis and a legal conclusion.[36] Second, prehospital providers have only basic training in assessing mental capacity that may be insufficient for evaluating mental status and providing information to patients for purposes of informed refusals. Third, there is no clear demonstration of the validity of any mental status evaluation made outside a clinic or hospital environment.[37]

Generally courts have upheld the right of patients to refuse transport in the prehospital setting. Failure to properly fill out a run report during a patient's initial refusal of transport after her son called the ambulance did not constitute a negligent breach of the standard of care and led to overturning a wrongful death action against the medics for her subsequent death.[38] Similarly, EMTs escaped liability in allowing a patient with abnormal physical findings from a leaking brain aneurysm, after consultation with a medical control physician, to refuse transport to a hospital.[39] Negligence in performing a complete physical exam on an uncooperative patient who refused transport and wanted to go home did not constitute the gross negligence necessary to overcome a Michigan immunity statute.[40]

Failure to transport. The trend is less favorable when EMTs make the decision not to transport. In *Green v. City of Dallas*, paramedics failed to transport a 35-year-old male patient complaining of chest pain.[41] Because of the patient's age, the fact that he was on no medications, and their impression that he was exhausted from playing basketball, the paramedics reasoned that the pain was not cardiac in nature. Five minutes after the crew departed, the man arrested; the ambulance was sent back to the scene, but the man could not be resuscitated. The city avoided liability only through sovereign immunity.

Wright v. City of Los Angeles outlined paramedic duties in another incident of failure to transport.[42] Police summoned EMS personnel for a man found lying on the sidewalk who appeared to have been involved in an altercation. The paramedic did only a cursory assessment and decided ambulance transport was not necessary. The paramedic thought that the patient was simply intoxicated while, in fact, he was in sickle-cell crisis. The court held that if the paramedic had conducted an examination consistent with the standard of

care, he should have been able to determine that the patient was in need of immediate treatment. The paramedic made no contact with medical control for approval of the decision not to transport; the paramedic testified that he "saw no symptoms indicating such a call was necessary."[43] Minutes after the paramedic left the scene, the patient arrested and died. The court found that the failure of the paramedic to provide "even a scant amount of care" was an "extreme departure from the standard of care for a paramedic in such a situation." Governmental immunity did not shield the defendant from liability in this state court ruling because the conduct was deemed grossly negligent.

In *St. George v. City of Deerfield Beach*, an ambulance was summoned by a visitor of a man found bleeding extensively from a tooth extraction.[44] The paramedics failed to transport the man, who was "obviously drunk and bleeding, but [who] absolutely and continually refused examination or treatment." The visitor called 911 a second time about 20 minutes later, but the dispatcher refused to send another ambulance. The appellate court rejected the defendant's motion to dismiss, ruling that sovereign immunity did not apply. Additionally, the court determined that the service owed a "special duty" toward the patient based on the repeated phone calls.

On the other hand, there was no reason to find that a failure to transport contributed to the death of a patient who had suffered a lethal gunshot wound to the head and was not transported by paramedics.[45]

Transporting a patient against their will. A few states have statutes that provide legal authority for peace officers to direct EMS personnel to take a person to a hospital if it reasonably appears that medical treatment is needed. Such statutes usually require a peace officer or transporting personnel to act in "good faith" to gain the protections of immunity.[46] In other states, statutes may allow EMS personnel this authority. New Mexico allows transport upon a "good faith judgment" by the EMS provider that it is needed.[47] These types of statutes provide both authority and legal protection in the unwilling transport situation. Immunity was not available for paramedics who forcibly took an allegedly suicidal patient to a Wyoming hospital against her will, although they were acting under the state's valid emergency detention statute.[48] The "reasonableness" of their actions in carrying the patient, naked, uncovered, and handcuffed, to an ambulance, was left for a jury to decide. In a similar circumstance, the city of Louisville was forced to go to trial to determine if their actions of transporting a patient to the hospital and inserting an IV against her will constituted false imprisonment and battery.[49] Similarly, a New York statute immunizes EMTs from all but gross negligence in involuntarily transporting psychiatric patients.[50]

A special class of patients transported against their will is prisoners. There has been a large increase in recent years of cases involving "in custody death," or "positional asphyxia" cases.[51] Although most of these cases are against law enforcement, EMS personnel are occasionally named. Lack of evidence showing that they acted with "deliberate indifference to any serious medical needs" protected EMTs under a state immunity statute when an obese, intoxicated individual they were transporting face down under a canvas restraint device known as the "blue monster" died.[52] On the other hand, Cincinnati did not escape trial in a civil rights action for unreasonable seizure and right to reasonable medical care in another prone restraint death.[53]

Negligence

Most actions against EMTs are simple malpractice. EMTs share with dispatchers the protections of sovereign immunity, statutory immunity, and special duty. There are some differences. Often tort claims acts waive immunity for incidences involving equipment and/or vehicles. For example, the Texas legislature has waived such immunity in certain limited circumstance, including:

(1) property damage, personal injury, and death proximately caused by the wrongful act or omission or the negligence of an employee acting within his scope of employment if:
  (A) the property damage, personal injury, or death arises from the operation or use of the motor-driven vehicle or motor-driven equipment; and
  (B) the employee would be personally liable to the claimant according to Texas law; and
(2) personal injury and death so caused by a condition or use of tangible personal or real property if the governmental unit would, were it a private person, be liable to the claimant according to Texas law.[54]

This removed immunity from El Paso EMS personnel who left a patient strapped to a backboard, considered "tangible property," in the middle of an intersection where he was struck by a passing car.[55] In Tennessee, EMTs are considered "health-care providers" and are also removed from immunity under the state tort claims act.[56] In a recent New Jersey case, documenting patient care was not considered part of "rendering intermediate life support services" and was not included under a state immunity statute.[57]

Good Samaritan immunity. In most states, EMTs fall under Good Samaritan statutes. While traditional Good Samaritan statutes cover care rendered without remuneration, nominal payment does not exempt some volunteer organizations. EMS providers have been specifically included in others. Sometimes the results are confusing. In Connecticut, the Good Samaritan statute specifically includes paid firefighters who have completed a first-aid course, while EMTs have no immunity unless they are performing services for free.[58] Firefighters who are also EMTs thus do not have immunity.[59] A federal circuit court has ruled that U.S. Border Patrol agents performing rescue and

first-aid actions fall under Good Samaritan immunity because even though they are paid, they are paid for law enforcement, not EMS, activities.[60]

There is a limited federal Good Samaritan law. The Aviation Medical Assistance Act of 1998 immunizes qualified individuals from liability in state or federal court unless they are guilty of "gross negligence or willful misconduct" in their response to an in-flight medical emergency.[61]

Loss of chance. The loss of chance theory has expanded into EMS cases. Despite lack of negligence on the part of the EMTs, an ambulance provider was found liable for the loss of chance of a patient when a defibrillator failed to function, despite any evidence as to the cause of the patient's collapse and subsequent death.[62] Low probability of survival did not sustain a motion for summary judgment for dismissal in a negligence case against EMTs who cared for a pulseless and apneic individual after prolonged bystander CPR.[63]

MEDICAL DIRECTORS

Medical directors are licensed physicians who provide a range of services for EMS. These may range from delivering direct medical control to simply providing quality assurance or training. Most commonly, however, medical directors provide protocols that outline the treatment patients receive based on their complaints. These protocols, or medical guidelines, provide a framework for treatment of a given condition. At least one jurisdiction has recognized that following protocols is "following the directions of a physician."[64] Because the medical director is rarely present in the field when protocols are implemented, he or she must depend on the training and experience of the EMT to apply the proper treatment based on the field assessment. Additionally, the medical director, as well as emergency department personnel, often provide "on-line" medical control wherein they advise treatments for a patient based on descriptions of that patient's condition as relayed by EMTs over a radio or telephone.

Medical directors are required by statute in only 35 states,[65] and may differ widely in training and experience. They may be board-certified emergency medicine physicians who have received training in medical control or local generalists who are the only physicians in town. There are different regulatory structures and varying degrees of specificity in different jurisdictions.[66] For example, some state laws provide little more than a short definition of the medical director as a licensed physician responsible for the supervision and training of EMS personnel. Some regulations only state the responsibilities of the medical director in general terms, while in other states, regulations identify the responsibilities of the medical director in detail. Florida requires, for example, that the medical director "establish a quality assurance committee to provide for quality assurance review of all emergency medical technicians (EMTs) and paramedics under his supervision."[67] Medical directors are encouraged to ride with the ambulance services in

Oregon.[68] In Washington, rules expressly provide that the "medical program director" is certified by the EMS regulatory authority and can be terminated for failure to perform the duties of the position.[69] Clearly, trends are emerging in the regulatory arena to abolish the "paper doc" and mandate quality supervision and involvement.

Increasingly, states are attaching qualifications to the role of medical director beyond mere state licensure to practice medicine. In Oregon, the Board of Medical Examiners must review and approve an application for the position of prehospital medical director.[70] Board certification in emergency medicine, family practice, internal medicine, or surgery, or certification in both advanced cardiac life support and advanced trauma life support, are required in Missouri.[71] Now that medical director training is available at the national level,[72] certain states now require their medical directors to undergo certification. New Mexico requires that new medical directors receive, within 2 years, either a nationally recognized EMS medical director course, a state-approved course, or local orientation provided by a regional or state medical director.[73]

Vicarious liability

The legal relationship between the EMT and their medical control physician depends on the jurisdiction. Currently, most EMTs are licensed. Licensure recognizes their training and gives them the authority to function within a given area, usually known as a scope of practice. Even licensed EMTs usually require medical control for invasive treatments, however.

The status of the EMT is important to bear in mind during any consideration of liability. The more closely an EMT is linked to a physician under state law, the easier it would be to find the physician vicariously liable for that EMT's actions. There have not been many vicarious negligence claims against medical control physicians in the prehospital setting, but expanding notions of physician responsibility may change this.

Until recently, "no court in the country has heretofore held a private physician liable for injuries suffered by an individual whom he has never treated, never met, and never agreed to treat."[74] This has changed. North Carolina found a nontraditional physician-patient duty formed between a physician and a patient seen only by residents the physician had contracted to supervise.[75] Although the reasoning in this case has been criticized,[76] the trend has continued. A Missouri surgeon agreed to be on call for the emergency room at the same time he was attending a medical conference out of town. A patient was injured in an accident and suffered complications from a delay in obtaining surgical treatment due to the absence of the surgeon. An appeals court determined that even in the absence of a traditional physician-patient relationship, public policy and the foreseeability of harm to patients supported finding a duty on the part of the on-call surgeon.[77] An Arizona Court of Appeals has recently determined that a physician had a duty to a patient he had never seen or treated just by providing an informal, or "curbside," consultation about an EKG.[78] The court determined that the consultant physician was in the best position to prevent future harm to the patient by giving correct advice, no matter how informal the request. These lines of reasoning could extend to physicians providing medical oversight to EMTs.

Civil rights claims

Civil rights claims are increasing against medical directors. Many of these claims are due to the somewhat unique role of the EMS medical director in EMT employment. Although the physician is rarely the EMT's employer, their decision on whether or not to provide medical control for a given individual may determine whether or not that EMT will have a job. Defending these cases may be quite expensive for physicians. Traditional malpractice insurance typically does not cover these claims, and special policies covering medical directors for these "administrative" liabilities are becoming harder to obtain.

In *Baxter v. Fulton-DeKalb Hospital Authority*, a federal court ruled on the due process claims of a paramedic whose medical director refused to reinstate him after he had been cleared of misconduct following a hospital investigation of a protocol violation.[79] The court ruled that the paramedic's claim against the hospital and medical director should not be dismissed because the paramedic was deprived of substantive due process by the arbitrary and groundless decision of the medical director.

The authority of medical directors to determine who may practice under their license was also the focus of a ruling from the state of Minnesota.[80] A county paramedic who was a member of a union had been terminated because of patient care concerns and an arbitrator subsequently determined that the paramedic should be reinstated. On appeal the medical director stated that he could neither trust the paramedic nor be certain that the paramedic would perform safely and appropriately even on probation. The appellate court ruled that the medical director could not be forced to authorize the paramedic to work under his medical license. The unique relationship requiring the medical director to extend his license to the paramedic could "impose potential tort and disciplinary liability on the medical director for actions of unfit paramedics." Therefore the medical director could exercise "medical judgment" to decide who should or should not work as a paramedic.

A New Mexico physician found himself charged with federal civil rights violations after he withdrew medical control from a couple of EMS providers who were already suing him for medical malpractice.[81] The providers claimed that they had a "right" to medical control. The case settled.

A Kentucky physician was named as a defendant in a state lawsuit alleging violation of rights under the Family Medical

Leave Act as well as for civil rights violations because he withheld medical control for a paramedic in a delegated practice state.[82] The physician refused to extend medical control to the paramedic after the paramedic tried to return to work after treatment for alcoholism and depression; the medical director had a long list of prior complaints against this individual, unrelated to his illness, and was in the process of bringing them to the attention of the state licensing authority.

Fraud and abuse

There are other statutory risks for a medical director; merely signing the medical necessity form stating a patient needed transport by ambulance could subject a physician to fines, damages, and civil monetary penalties under false claims[83] and Medicare fraud and abuse acts[84] that have been targeted by government investigators, including FBI task forces, in recent years. These penalties are most commonly levied against the owners or operators of the ambulance service, however.

CONCLUSION

EMS law remains local. EMS activities are controlled by state and local laws. These laws and regulations outline the responsibilities of each actor in prehospital medicine as well as determining which of the many immunities and protections may be available to EMS personnel.

Dispatchers and EMTs often have significant immunities. The medical control physician, on the other hand, may not enjoy all these protections. Additionally, medical directors face additional legal threats from their administrative roles via civil rights and false claims acts.

EMS law may be one of the most rapidly evolving areas of health law. Each new technology or treatment may open new areas of legal relationships, responsibilities, and concerns. Political decisions affect it as well; as the United States becomes more concerned with homeland defense, the impact on prehospital personnel will likely become significant.

ENDNOTES

1. *The Ambulance in American Cities* (editorial), 28 J.A.M.A. 36-37 (1897).
2. *See, for example,* G.C. Wydro et al., *Legislative and Regulatory Description of EMS Medical Direction: A Survey of States*, 1(4) Prehosp. Emerg. Care 233-37 (1997).
3. *See, for example, Ma v. San Francisco*, 2002 Cal. App. LEXIS 790 (2002).
4. All state tort claims acts are referenced in Restat. 2d of Torts, §895B (1979).
5. Tex. Civ. Prac. & Rem. Code Ann. 101.062(b).
6. *City of Temple v. Stephan Peterson*, 1998 Tex. App. LEXIS 3435 (1998) (unpublished opinion).
7. R. Castaneda, *Pr. George's Must Pay $1.7 Million*, Washington Post (Sept. 25, 2002) at B02.
8. Ind. Code §34-4-16.5-3 (17) (later (18)).
9. *Thomas Barnes, City Council of Gary, Indiana, City of Gary Fire Department and City of Gary Police Department v. Rose Ann Antich*, 700 N.E. 2d 262 (1998).
10. *Johnson v. District of Columbia*, 580 A. 2d 141 (1990).
11. *Wanzer v. District of Columbia*, 580 A. 2d 127 (1990).
12. *St. George v. City of Deerfield Beach*, 568 So. 2d 931 (1990).
13. *Sarah Fried et al. v. Kim Archer et al.*, 775 A. 2d 430 (2001).
14. *Schear v. Board of County Commissioners*, 687 P. 2d 728 (1984).
15. Pub. L. 101-336, codified at 42 U.S.C. 12101 (1990).
16. *Keel v. Hopkinsville*, 1997 U.S. App. LEXIS 35777 (1997).
17. *Kelly A. Gillen v. Fallon Ambulance Service, Inc.*, 283 F. 3d 11 (2002).
18. Pub. L. 103-3, codified at 29 U.S.C. 2601 (1993).
19. *Hagen v Anderson*, Anderson Circuit Court, Commonwealth of Kentucky, No. 98-CI-00259, complaint filed Oct. 23, 1998.
20. Pub. L. 103-353, codified at 38 U.S.C. 4301 (1994). *See, for example, Rogers v. San Antonio*, 211 F.Supp. 2d 829, 2002 U.S. Dist. LEXIS 13003 (2002).
21. 29 U.S.C. 201 *et seq.*
22. 29 C.R.F. 553.201.
23. 29 C.R.F. 553.215.
24. See also 116 A.L.R. Fed. 143 for an extensive review of this topic.
25. *Wideman v. Shallowford Community Hospital, Inc.*, 826 F. 2d 1030 (1987).
26. *Brown v. Commonwealth of Pennsylvania Department of Health Emergency Medical Services Training Institute*, U.S. Court of Appeals for the Third Circuit, No. 01-3234, filed Aug. 8, 2002.
27. *Id.*, petition for *en banc* rehearing, filed Sept. 9, 2002.
28. 475 A. 2d 1319 (1985).
29. A.L. Harvey et al., *Actual vs. Perceived EMS Response Time*, 3(1) Prehosp. Emerg. Care 11-14 (1999).
30. *Cooper v. City of Honolulu*, 1st Cir. Ct. (Haw. 1992).
31. *Ambrose v. New Orleans Police Department Ambulance Service*, 627 So. 2d 233 (1993).
32. From H. Handler, Vice President, the American Agency (1988) and S. Forry, Director of EMS Programs, VFIS/AIS (1997).
33. A. Sucov et al., *The Outcome of Patients Refusing Prehospital Transportation*, 7(4) Prehosp. Disaster Med. 365-71 (1992).
34. B.S. Zachariah et al., *Follow-up and Outcome of Patients Who Decline or Are Denied Transport by EMS*, 7(4) Prehosp. Disaster Med. 359-64 (1992).
35. *Schloendorf v. Society of New York Hospital*, 105 N.E. 92 (1914).
36. K. Kaplan et al., *The Clinician's Role on Competency Evaluations*, 11 Gen. Hosp. Psychiatry 397-403 (1989).
37. L. Zun, *A Survey of the Form of the Mental Status Examination Administered by Emergency Physicians*, 15 Ann. Emerg. Med. 916-22 (1986).
38. *Holt v. City of Memphis*, 2001 Tenn. App. LEXIS 524 (2001).
39. *Kyser v. Metro Ambulance, Inc.*, 764 So. 2d 215; 2000 La. App. LEXIS 1678 (2000).
40. *Ingesoulian v. City of Lincoln Park*, 2002 Mich. App. LEXIS 130 (2002) (unpublished opinion).
41. 665 S.W. 2d 567 (1984).
42. 268 A. 2d 309 (1990).
43. *Id.*
44. 568 So. 2d 931 (1990).
45. *Larry Clark v. City of Shreveport et al.*, 726 So. 2d 1042; 1999 La. App. LEXIS 34 (1999).
46. *See, for example,* Fl. Stat. §396.072 (1) (1979).
47. §24-10B-9.1 NMSA (1978).
48. *Moore v. Wyoming Medical Center*, 825 F.Supp 1531 (1993).
49. *Mistelle Cathey v. City of Louisville, Joseph Schiess, and Lee Schmid*, 1999 Ky. App. LEXIS 108 (1999).
50. *Woody v. Astoria General Hospital, Inc.*, 264 A.D. 2d 318; 1999 N.Y. App. Div. LEXIS 8610 (1999).
51. K.N. Lewis, *Fit To Be Tied? Fourth Amendment Analysis of the Hog-Tie Restraint Procedure*, 33 Ga. L. Rev. 281 (1998).
52. *Melendez v. Howard County*, 1997 U.S. App. LEXIS 21859 (1997).
53. *Johnson v. City of Cincinnati*, 39 F.Supp. 2d 1013; 1999 U.S. Dist. LEXIS 3661 (1999).
54. Tex. Civ. Prac. & Rem. Code Ann. §101.021 (Vernon 1997).

55. *Borrego v. City of El Paso*, 964 S.W. 2d 954; 1998 Tex. App. LEXIS 1587 (1998) (*cert. denied*).

56. *Mooney v. Snead*, 30 S.W. 3d 304; 2000 Tenn. LEXIS 572 (2000).

57. *De Tarquino v. City of Jersey City*, 800 A. 2d 255 (2002).

58. Conn. Gen. Stat. §52-557b.

59. *Bolivar v. Town of Manchester*, 2002 Conn. Super. LEXIS 1420 (2002).

60. *Ortiz v. U.S. Border Patrol*, 2000 U.S. App. LEXIS 6664 (2000).

61. Public Law 105-170 §5(b). This includes "any person who is licensed, certified, or otherwise qualified to provide medical care in a State, including a physician, nurse, physician assistant, paramedic, and emergency medical technician."

62. *Haynes v. Calcasieu Medical Transportation, Inc.*, 702 So. 2d 1024; 1997 La. App. LEXIS 2645 (1997).

63. *Meck v. Paramedic Services of Illinois*, 695 N.E. 2d 1321; 1998 Ill. App. LEXIS 332 (1998).

64. *Falkowski v. Maurus*, 637 So. 2d 522 (La. App. 1st Cir. 1993).

65. Jacob L. Hafter, *The Relationship Between the Comprehensiveness of EMS State Legislation and Geographic Distribution of EMS Providers*, Dissertation, Cleveland State University (2001).

66. *See, for example*, Wydro, *supra* note 2.

67. Florida Public Health Law 401.265.

68. Board of Medical Examiners: Oregon Administrative Rule 847-35-025.

69. Wash. Stat. RCW 18.71, WAC 246-976920, revised 1990.

70. Board of Medical Examiners: Oregon Administrative Rule, Ambulances and Emergency Medical Personnel, 847-35-020 (2).

71. Missouri Rule, 19 C.S.R. 30-40.160, updated Feb. 25, 1995. A requirement for pediatric advanced life support is pending.

72. The National Association of EMS Physicians (NAEMSP) provides a 7-hour course at least twice yearly.

73. §9.3.2, 7 NMAC 27.3, Medical Direction for Emergency Medical Services (1996).

74. *Mozingo v. Pitt County Memorial Hospital*, 415 S.E. 2d 341, 347 (N.C. Sup. Ct. 1992).

75. *Id.* For a good review of this case, *see* Sharon M. Glenn, *Liability in the Absence of a Traditional Physician-Patient Relationship: What Every "On Call" Doctor Should Know: Mozingo v. Pitt County Memorial Hospital*, 28 Wake Forest L. Rev. 747 (1993).

76. *Rivera v. Prince George's County Health Department*, 649 A. 2d 1212 (Md. App. 1994) and Glenn, *supra* note 75.

77. *Millard v. Corrado*, Missouri Court of Appeals Eastern District, 14 S.W. 3d 42; 1999 Mo. App. LEXIS 2405 (1999). Reviewed in *Could Somebody Call a Doctor? On-Call Physicians and the Duty to Treat*, 65 Mo. L. Rev. 1055 (2000).

78. *Diggs v. Arizona Cardiologists, Ltd.*, Arizona Court of Appeals Division 1, 1 CA-CV 99-0508, filed Aug. 8, 2000.

79. 764 F.Supp 1510 (1991).

80. *County of Hennepin v. Hennepin County Association of Paramedics and Emergency Medical Technicians*, 464 N.W. 2d 578 (1990).

81. *Atwater v. Caruana*, U.S. District Court of the District of New Mexico, No. CIV 96-1218JP.

82. *Hagan v. Anderson et al.*, Anderson Circuit Court, Commonwealth of Kentucky, No. 98-CI-00259, complaint filed Oct. 23, 1998.

83. False Claims Act, 31 U.S.C. 3729.

84. Medicare and Medicaid Fraud and Abuse Act, 42 U.S.C. 1320a-7d.

Professional Liability in Emergency Medicine

HOWARD A. PETH, Jr., M.D., J.D., F.C.L.M.

PROFESSIONAL LIABILITY CLAIMS
THE "DUTY" ELEMENT OF PROFESSIONAL LIABILITY CLAIMS
CONCLUSION

The largest study into adverse patient events ever performed identified the emergency department (ED) as the hospital entity with the highest incidence of adverse patient events due to negligence.[1] When one considers the complex factors at play in the emergency medicine milieu, it should come as no surprise that emergency medicine is near the pinnacle of the ultra-high-risk specialties. Let us look at some of those factors.

First, emergency medicine operates 24 hours a day, 7 days a week, including weekends, nights, and holidays at times when many resources are unavailable. In addition, access to a patient's critically important medical records, prior EKGs, x-rays, diagnostic studies, and laboratory tests, as well as other vital information, may not be possible. It is also difficult or impossible to contact a patient's personal physician to discuss the patient's past medical history, medication history, or allergy history after "regular business hours" and on holidays.

Second, unlike virtually every other medical specialty, there is no limit to the number of unscheduled patients who may present for emergency care at any given time; the emergency physician and nurse may be responsible for the simultaneous care of a potentially unlimited number of critically ill or injured patients. In terms of sheer volume, our nation's emergency departments are faced with the crushing burden of serving as America's safety net. Emergency department visits have increased 15% since 1990 and today more than 100 million Americans annually depend on our EDs to come through for them in their hour of need. 42.6 million Americans had no health insurance in 1999[2] and the ED is their only source of medical care. In addition, another several million homeless Americans with no other source of health care depend on our nation's EDs for their medical care.[3]

Third, in addition to caring for the enormous volume of patients presenting to our nation's EDs, emergency physicians care for patients who are suffering from illnesses or injuries of much greater acuity than most other specialties. For example, 40% of all hospital admissions nationwide originate in the ED.[4]

Fourth, emergency physicians must operate within a very narrow window of time (minutes to hours) in which to determine whether a patient is suffering from a potentially catastrophic condition. Furthermore, emergency patients, who may be suffering from a host of comorbid conditions, are virtually unknown to their emergency physicians and emergent treatment must be initiated with only limited and often no information available about a patient's past medical or surgical history.

Finally, and perhaps most importantly, the difficulties routinely faced by emergency physicians and nurses are further compounded by the fact that many of the highest risk emergency diagnoses, such as acute appendicitis,[5-11] myocardial infarction,[12-18] pulmonary embolism,[19] abdominal aortic aneurysm,[20,21] or subarachnoid hemorrhage,[22,23] may have atypical or ambiguous presentations (Table 45-1).

PROFESSIONAL LIABILITY CLAIMS

Failure to diagnose

The majority of professional liability actions against emergency physicians arise under a "failure to diagnose" claim, i.e., where an ED patient's diagnosis is either missed entirely or the diagnosis is made but in a delayed fashion (Table 45-2). Specifically, the high-risk presentations of chest pain, abdominal pain (in a patient of any age or gender), febrile infants, headache, fractures, and wound management constitute 70% of professional liability claims against emergency physicians.[24,25] Two important factors that contribute to the missed emergency diagnosis are (a) a failure to initiate an appropriate diagnostic evaluation, and (b) an atypical or ambiguous manifestation of the high-risk presentation may obscure the nature of the illness.

TABLE 45-1 Factors contributing to risk
in emergency medicine

1. Emergency patients are usually unknown to their emergency physicians; emergency medicine operates at times when vital patient records are inaccessible.
2. There are no limits to the numbers of patients that must be seen in emergency medicine.
3. Emergency patients suffer from illnesses and injuries of greater acuity than most other medical specialties.
4. Emergency physicians have a very narrow time frame within which to identify a life-threatening condition.
5. Many of the highest risk emergency diagnoses present in an ambiguous or atypical manner.

TABLE 45-2 Factors that contribute to a delay or
a failure to diagnose the high-risk patient

1. Failure to initiate an appropriate diagnostic workup.
2. Atypical presentations of a high-risk diagnosis.
3. Failure to properly interpret diagnostic tests.
4. Failure to obtain a consult.
5. Failure to receive results of diagnostic tests.
6. Refusals of treatment.

Failure to initiate appropriate workup. Since each one of the above high-risk presentations suggests the possibility of a catastrophic illness, the emergency physician's evaluation of such presentations will ordinarily consist of an extensive workup appropriately tailored to the patient's complaint. Failure to initiate an appropriate workup of the high-risk patient may result in a delayed or a missed diagnosis and result in a professional liability claim against the physician.[26-28] A typical jury instruction in a "failure to diagnose" case highlights the issue:

If you find from the evidence that the defendant doctor did not exercise the appropriate degree of skill and care, as to which you have been instructed, in making his/her diagnosis of the ailment which is the subject of this action, and that such erroneous diagnosis resulted in injury to the patient, you may find that defendant's inaccurate diagnosis or failure to diagnose the ailment constitutes malpractice.[29]

Therefore, it is incumbent upon the emergency physician to demonstrate that he or she took the high-risk presentation seriously, and a mere cursory examination on the part of the physician in such patients is a recipe for disaster. However, an extensive diagnostic evaluation in the ED does not guarantee that a catastrophic diagnosis will be excluded, and a definite percentage of catastrophic diagnoses go undetected in the absence of any negligence, and despite an appropriate ED evaluation. For example, despite increased utilization of such technological advances as abdominal and pelvic computerized tomography (CT), ultrasonography, and laparoscopy, the timely and accurate diagnosis of appendicitis has not improved.[30] This technology has improved the diagnostic accuracy of appendicitis in children.[31] It should be noted, however, that even with the availability of advanced technology the diagnosis of appendicitis in children remains difficult.[32,33] The appropriate emergency evaluation and treatment of high-risk presentations is obviously beyond the scope of this chapter and the reader may wish to refer to a variety of references focusing on the high-risk patient.[34]

Atypical manifestations of the high-risk presentation. A catastrophic illness may present with atypical or ambiguous symptoms that can lead to a delay or failure to diagnose. Many high-risk patients, particularly those at both extremes of age, will present to the ED with an atypical presentation of their illness. In addition, most of the potentially catastrophic illnesses share symptoms or signs with benign conditions that can lead to ambiguity in the high-risk patient's presentation. This will often result in the ED physician forgoing a particular diagnostic test that would have been routine had the presentation been "classic" for the high-risk illness. For example, it is estimated that at least 25% of myocardial infarctions occurring in patients over the age of 65 years have no chest pain.[35-37] For another example, consider that the "classic" presentation of acute appendicitis with initial onset of poorly localized visceral pain in the periumbilical region and subsequent migration to the right lower quadrant of the abdomen occurs in only 60% of cases.[38,39]

Other factors contributing to delay or failure to diagnose. Other factors that have been cited as contributing to a delay or failure to make the high-risk diagnosis include misinterpretation of laboratory data or diagnostic studies, failure to receive the results of a diagnostic study, and failure to obtain a consult with a specialist.

Treatment refusals: a guaranteed missed diagnosis

Patients who are brought to the ED and who refuse evaluation are extremely high-risk in that it is a virtual certainty that the patient's illness will not be diagnosed. Great care must be made in these cases to ensure that the patient's refusal of care is voluntary and fully informed and is not based on an underlying organic process that may impair the patient's sensorium. The estate of a patient who dies shortly after he has been discharged from the ED against medical advice may have a valid claim against the emergency physician if it can be proved that the patient died of a condition that would have made it likely that he did not possess adequate decision-making capacity or was not in full command of his mental faculties at the time of his refusal of treatment. An understanding of the law concerning the management of patients who refuse emergency treatment is vital if we are to reduce the incidence of missed diagnoses in patients who refuse care (Table 45-3).

TABLE 45-3 Management of treatment refusals

1. A mental status examination must be performed on every ED patient who refuses treatment to assess the patient's decision-making capacity.
2. Patients who possess adequate decision-making capacity based upon the emergency physician's mental status examination may refuse treatment even if their refusal may result in their death.
3. Patients who do not possess adequate decision-making capacity may not refuse emergency medical treatment and treatment will proceed on the basis of the emergency exception to the general consent theory.
4. Suicidal patients may not refuse emergency medical treatment, even if they pass their mental status examination.
5. Documentation in the medical record must reflect the basis upon which the emergency physician either accepted or rejected a patient's treatment refusal.
6. Emergency treatment of a minor should never be delayed because there is difficulty in obtaining consent.

(For excellent in-depth reviews of general consent theory and the evaluation of patient competence, the reader is referred to Chapters 4 and 31 of this volume.)

Most ED patients present for care of their own volition and are cooperative and eager to receive treatment. However, many patients are brought to the ED by paramedics or police not of their own choice but by virtue of an injury or illness that initiated an emergency medical services (EMS) response. Such patients may be uncooperative and refuse treatment and are often referred to as "difficult patients" in the medical literature.[40-47] Many difficult patients brought to the ED are suffering from subtle or profound mental impairment due to a traumatic head injury, the influence of alcohol or drugs, or an acute psychosis,[48] and their impaired sensorium renders them lacking in the decision-making capacity requisite to an informed treatment refusal.[49,50]

A major tenet of Anglo-American law is the respect accorded individual autonomy and the protections afforded the integrity of one's person. This respect for individual autonomy is translated into our modern consent theory, very clearly expressed in the immortal words of the great Justice Benjamin Cardozo nearly one hundred years ago: "Every human being of adult years and sound mind has the right to determine what shall be done with his body."[51]

Emergency physicians may proceed with treatment and evaluation of their patients only after obtaining the patient's permission.[52-57] In the case of a minor patient, authority to consent is transferred to the patient's legal guardian or closest available relative.[58] Emergency treatment of a minor, however, should never be delayed because of difficulty in obtaining consent. In essence, no treatment may be initiated on behalf of a patient until the physician has explained the material facts concerning the treatment, including its risks and its alternatives (including nontreatment). The objective is then to obtain the patient's competent, voluntary, and understanding permission to proceed.[59-65] The corollary to the informed consent theory is the doctrine of "informed refusal" whereby a patient's refusal of a recommended diagnostic or therapeutic course of action must be based on a full understanding of the risks associated with that refusal.[66]

In order for a patient to give a valid consent for treatment, he or she must be legally competent to do so. Competence is a *legal* and not a medical concept. All adults are presumed by law to be competent, and only a judge may declare an individual incompetent, usually in the setting of a formal judicial proceeding. If a patient presenting for treatment has been declared *incompetent* by a judge, consent must be obtained from the patient's designated conservator or guardian *ad litem* prior to initiating treatment. Otherwise, every adult patient is presumed to be legally competent to accept or refuse treatment. With notable exceptions, minors are legally incapable of giving consent[67-69] (see Chapters 4 and 52 of this volume).

Capacity, on the other hand, is a *medical* concept and is the basis by which physicians can determine whether a patient is capable of granting an understanding and informed consent (or refusal) to treatment.[70] Capacity implies that the patient is in sufficient command of his or her mental faculties to understand the ramifications of the proposed diagnostic workup or treatment regimen and is capable of giving his or her informed consent. There are many medical conditions, acute and chronic, that may impair an individual's capacity to adequately understand the nature of his or her illness and the recommended course of treatment. These conditions are never at greater play than in the emergency department.

The emergency privilege. Many patients presenting to the ED for care are unable to provide a valid refusal or consent to treatment because they are suffering from an organic process that renders them lacking in capacity. For example, patients with cardiac arrest, ventricular fibrillation, diabetic ketoacidosis, shock, or status epilepticus are unable to consent to treatment. Obviously such patients will suffer catastrophic consequences if emergent treatment is delayed or withheld on the basis of a lack of consent. To avoid such an unfortunate result, the law has created a legal fiction known as the "emergency privilege" or "emergency exception to the consent doctrine" that allows for the treatment of emergency patients to proceed in such cases without the patient's informed consent.[71-75] Three requirements must be met in order for the emergency privilege to apply:

(a) the patient must be unconscious or without capacity to make a decision, while no one legally authorized to act as agent for the patient is available; (b) time must be of the essence, in the sense that it must reasonably appear that delay until such time as an effective consent could be obtained would subject the patient to a risk of a serious bodily injury or death which prompt action would avoid; and (c) under the circumstances, a reasonable person would consent, and the probabilities are that the patient would consent.[76]

A mental status examination must be performed on every patient who refuses treatment in the ED to determine whether he or she possesses adequate decision-making capacity.[77-79] Any patient who on the basis of an emergency mental status examination is found to lack decisional capacity may not give a valid refusal of emergency treatment and the emergency physician should reject the patient's refusal and proceed to treat on the basis of the emergency exception to the consent doctrine.[80-82] On the other hand, if the patient has a normal mental status examination and can articulate understanding of the risks and benefits of the proposed evaluation or treatment, the patient may refuse treatment even if the patient's refusal may result in his or her death.[83] It is vital that the emergency physician carefully document the results of the mental status examination and the basis on which the physician either accepted or rejected the patient's treatment refusal. The following short paragraph is one method of documenting the basis upon which a physician has accepted a patient's treatment refusal:

The patient has refused any further evaluation or treatment in the emergency department. I have carefully explained the risks (including death) as well as the benefits of my proposed treatment and evaluation and I have answered each one of the patient's questions pertaining to my proposed care. The patient has articulated understanding of the risks and benefits, which I have explained to his/her satisfaction. Based upon the patient's completely normal mental status examination [which must be documented in the medical record] I have determined that the patient possesses adequate decision-making capacity and I have accepted the patient's refusal of emergency evaluation and treatment. The patient is discharged from the emergency department against medical advice (AMA) according to his/her wishes.

The following language may express the basis for an emergency physician's rejection of a patient's treatment refusal and should be included in the patient's medical record:

The patient has refused any further evaluation or treatment in the emergency department but is unable to articulate understanding of the risks of his/her treatment refusal. Based upon the patient's mental status examination, which he/she failed, [the mental status examination must be documented in the record] I have determined that the patient lacks adequate decision-making capacity and may not refuse treatment in view of the potentially serious nature of his/her illness/injuries. I have initiated emergency treatment and evaluation for the patient on the basis of the emergency exception to the general consent doctrine.

THE "DUTY" ELEMENT OF PROFESSIONAL LIABILITY CLAIMS

The four elements of a professional liability claim* have been reviewed in considerable detail in Chapter 29, but it is highly worthwhile for physicians practicing emergency medicine to acquaint themselves with two potential landmines that can extend physician liability under the "duty" element of professional liability actions: (a) admission orders written by ED physicians, and (b) coverage of in-house emergencies by ED physicians.

When physician's duty to patient is terminated

The "duty" element of professional liability actions against physicians is not a major point of contention in most medical malpractice claims, and in most cases it is fairly clear whether a doctor-patient relationship has been created or terminated. The general rule is that a physician's duty to a patient ends when the patient's care is entrusted to another physician.[84-87] However, when ED physicians write admitting orders[88] or respond to in-house (i.e., non-ED) emergencies,[89] ambiguities may arise that cloud the issue of which physician is responsible for a patient's care and make it difficult to ascertain when the doctor-patient relationship was terminated.

Admission orders. Emergency physicians do not admit inpatients to hospitals nor do they care for inpatients following admission to the hospital. Rather, responsibility for inpatient care lies with the patient's admitting and consulting physicians. However, as a service to its admitting physicians, many hospitals have policies whereby ED physicians write admission orders as a courtesy to admitting physicians on behalf of patients admitted from the ED. Such orders have the potential of creating an ambiguity as to who is responsible for the patient's ongoing care and may extend the liability of the emergency physician based upon a continuation of the doctor-patient relationship. The American College of Emergency Physicians has delineated a wise policy concerning the writing of admission orders by emergency physicians and opposes such orders if they "extend, or appear to extend, [emergency physician] control and responsibility for the patient beyond treatment in the emergency department to the inpatient setting."[90] It is prudent for emergency physicians to clearly indicate on the admission orders who is responsible for the patient's inpatient care and to limit admission orders from the ED to items that address only urgent

---

* The four elements that a plaintiff must prove in a professional liability action against a physician are: (1) the physician owed the patient a duty of reasonable care to conform to a certain standard of conduct; (2) the physician must have breached that duty; (3) a causal connection between the physician's conduct and the resulting injury, i.e., legal or "proximate" cause; and (4) actual loss or damage to the patient. (W.P. Keeton, D.B. Dobbs, R.E. Keeton, et al., *Prosser and Keeton on the Law of Torts*, 5th ed., 164-65. St. Paul, MN: West Publishing Co., 1984).

46

Liability of Neurologists

JAMES C. JOHNSTON, M.D., J.D., F.C.L.M.

MALPRACTICE LIABILITY
NONMALPRACTICE LIABILITY
LIABILITY OF THE FORENSIC NEUROLOGIST
CONCLUSION

This chapter provides an overview of the liability issues affecting neurologists. It focuses on current trends in malpractice law. Illustrative management strategies are provided for several common recurring claims involving stroke, epilepsy, and headache. Nonmalpractice liability issues are discussed with particular attention to the unique risks engendered by the expert witness.

MALPRACTICE LIABILITY

Current trends

Medical malpractice claims in the United States are generally increasing in frequency and severity, with a disproportionately adverse impact on neurology.[1] The following data from one insurance consortium review of 2607 neurology claims between 1985 and 2000 paints a disturbing picture.[2] The percentage of neurology claims to total claims increased 63% between 1990 and 2000. The payment ratio (percentage of paid claims to total claims closed) for claims closed in 2000 was 28%, a 10% increase over the past decade. Neurology had the highest average indemnity payment of all specialties including neurosurgery during the 1985-2000 period. A trend analysis of claims by close year demonstrates a dramatic increase in neurology indemnity payments over the last few years. The 1995 average neurological indemnity paid was 42% higher than the average for all physician specialties ($255,431 versus $179,996). In 2000, it was 52% higher ($439,556 versus $288,637). The average neurology indemnity increased 72% (53% adjusted for inflation) during that 5-year period. Moreover, the expenses paid to defend neurology claims in 2000 exceeded that of all specialty groups.

There are several unique factors inherent to the specialty of neurology that may explain these alarming statistics. First, the unprecedented growth of sophisticated neurodiagnostic tests (functional neuroimaging, neurogenetic testing),

the proliferation of powerful neuropharmacological agents (antiepileptic drugs, triptans), and the advent of more invasive procedures (botulinum toxin injection, deep brain stimulation) raise the standard of care, increasing the level of accountability and hence likelihood of suit. Second, neurologists confront a diverse array of legal issues beyond the scope of traditional practice involving, *inter alia*, brain death, genetic testing, competency issues, neurotoxic insults, and evaluation of the neurologically impaired child. These varied conditions—governed by expanding legal doctrines, evolving regulatory control and political whims—expose the neurologist to a variety of often novel claims. Third, neurology engenders liability beyond the physician-patient relationship to include a host of third parties. Neurologists may face tort liability for negligence to a patient that also injures a fetus, child, or spouse. In addition to the duty to warn of imminently dangerous patients, there is now a duty to warn third parties of communicable diseases. Neurologists have a duty to warn patients of medical conditions that may impair driving (epilepsy, sleep disorders, stroke); they may also be required to warn others directly, either by statute or an imposed tort duty to warn of foreseeable harm. The result is an ever-expanding pool of potential claimants. Fourth, the very nature of neurological disease or injury spells a grave outcome for many patients and this is reflected in the indemnity payments. The confluence of these factors may herald a fundamental shift transforming neurology from a low-risk specialty to one plagued by malpractice claims.

Neurological misadventures and claims against neurologists

The most prevalent neurological misadventure is diagnostic error, occurring in almost one-third of claims.[3] The most frequent incorrectly diagnosed condition is malignant neoplasm of the brain, followed by intracranial and intraspinal abscess, subarachnoid hemorrhage (SAH), headache, and

The author deeply appreciates the support and assistance of Uli.

vertebral fracture.[4] Other prevalent misadventures include (in decreasing order of frequency): no medical misadventure (no allegation of inappropriate medical conduct against the named neurologist); improperly performed procedure; failure to supervise or monitor case; medication error; procedure performed when not indicated or contraindicated; delay in performance; not performed; failure to recognize a complication of treatment; and failure or delay in referral or consultation.[5]

In general. Providing care that meets or exceeds the prevailing standard may not shield the neurologist from a lawsuit. A solid physician-patient relationship, valid consent, and proper medical record documentation are essential for successful risk management and malpractice defense. Although the root of a malpractice claim is injury or perceived injury, most suits are actually triggered by a breakdown in the physician-patient relationship due to poor communication. A thorough understanding of this relationship, as outlined in Chapter 30 of this volume, is essential; meeting patient expectations through effective communication significantly reduces the risk of suit.[6] Informed consent issues are a frequent source of malpractice suits, wholly unrelated to negligence claims. The legal theories of informed consent detailed in this volume are applicable to all specialties, and are therefore not repeated in this chapter. Poor documentation is the leading factor in the forced settlement of most malpractice suits. The literature is replete with recommendations for ensuring that records are clear, accurate, legible, complete, and timely without alterations or other evidence of spoilation.[7] It is unnecessary to reiterate good record-keeping principles in this chapter, but one legal maxim cannot be overemphasized: "If it is not in the record, it never happened."

Specific claims. The scope of neurological malpractice liability precludes a compendium of potential claims. Moreover, any such listing would be outdated before publication, as emerging diagnostic and therapeutic options open the door for new claims. It is, however, instructive to consider the most prevalent patient conditions generating suits against neurologists (in decreasing order of frequency): displacement of intervertebral disc; back disorders; convulsions; cerebrovascular accident; headache; malignant neoplasm of the brain; epilepsy; SAH; intracranial and intraspinal abscess; and encephalopathy.[8] Intervertebral disc displacement and related spine disorders are not discussed because these claims are predominantly straightforward diagnostic errors, only a small percentage result in an indemnity payment, and the total indemnity is a small fraction (2.9%) of the total paid for all neurology claims.[9] Encephalopathy is not reviewed because it is usually a secondary diagnosis, poorly defined and least prevalent among the top ten claims. This section outlines several management strategies for the more common claims involving the remaining conditions, arbitrarily grouped together as stroke, epilepsy, and headache, the latter

subsuming brain tumor and SAH. It is impossible in an introductory chapter to provide a discussion of the widely disparate malpractice suits involving these conditions. Therefore, several particular topics were selected because they are frequently seen by neurologists and nonneurologists alike, affect a large segment of the population, generate recurring claims, and have the potential for devastating outcomes with exceptionally high indemnity payments or judgments.

Stroke. Cerebrovascular disease is the third leading cause of death in the United States with approximately 200,000 fatalities annually; there are more than 700,000 individuals newly diagnosed with stroke every year.[10] Stroke therapy has changed dramatically over the last decade with the development of specific treatment options (thrombolysis) and prevention strategies (anticoagulation, carotid endarterectomy). These recent advances create a heightened expectation of proper stroke management and, combined with the catastrophic impact of stroke, portend increasing litigation in this area.

THROMBOLYSIS. The administration of tissue plasminogen activator (tPA) within 3 hours of ischemic stroke onset significantly improves functional outcome in selected patients.[11] The therapeutic window is narrow and strict adherence to the approved protocol inclusion and exclusion criteria is imperative.[12] tPA thrombolysis represents the neurological standard of care for acute ischemic stroke, despite the fact that a low percentage of eligible patients receive the drug at this time. The hospital, emergency department, and neurology consultant should establish a dedicated stroke team capable of responding to every acute ischemic stroke patient in a timely fashion and, if indicated, administering tPA. Alternatively, tPA-eligible patients must be promptly transferred to another institution for definitive treatment. Failure of the hospital to provide appropriate facilities and personnel (streamlined emergency room pathways, CT technicians available 24 hours) may create liability for all parties including the neurologist.

The failure to recommend or administer tPA to an eligible patient may constitute negligence, unless it can be proven that tPA would not have made a material difference in the patient's outcome. The neurologist deciding not to use tPA in an acute ischemic stroke should clearly document the reasons for that decision in the medical records. It is equally important for the neurologist to resist pressure from the emergency physician or family to use tPA unless the patient meets all inclusion and exclusion criteria. The evidence demonstrates that modification of the criteria, especially the 3-hour time constraint, decreases the benefits of tPA and increases the risk of intracerebral hemorrhage.[13] Thus it is crucial to determine the time of stroke onset. A common error is to consider the onset time as the time when symptoms were first observed rather than the last time the patient was known to be well. For example, if the patient awakens with deficits, then the onset time must be considered to be the last time the patient was known to be well (usually the night before), not when the symptoms were first noticed upon wakening. The same is true if the patient is unable to communicate the onset time. Additionally, neurologists must be attentive to patients with stroke-related neglect syndromes who cannot reliably observe the time of onset. Another frequent error is the administration of anticoagulants or antiplatelet agents during the first 24 hours after tPA administration, which greatly increases the risk of intracerebral hemorrhage. Again, it is imperative to follow the protocol guidelines. There are cases, however, where the neurologist may consider all of the risks and benefits, and decide it is in the patient's best interest to deviate from the protocol. This decision should be discussed with the patient or legal representative and family, and thoroughly documented in the records.

The failure to obtain valid consent may precipitate a malpractice action separate from negligence.[14] Informed consent mandates a frank discussion regarding the benefits and risks of tPA, including the potential for hemorrhage, coma, and death.[15] The acute stroke patient may not be able to fully participate in the process due to communication deficits or cognitive impairment. Options should then be discussed with a close family member and documented, but only a legal representative (guardian or person with written power of attorney) can give consent. If the patient is unable to give consent and no legal representative is available, the neurologist may proceed with tPA when it is the most reasonable option. Courts will recognize an implied consent; there is an assumption that a competent individual would have agreed to the procedure.[16]

ANTICOAGULATION. The use of heparin to prevent an impending stroke remains controversial, although considerable evidence supports immediate anticoagulation for fluctuating basilar artery thrombosis and impending carotid artery occlusion, as well as in certain cases of cardioembolic cerebral infarction. Warfarin is probably beneficial in the first few months after an ischemic event, but there is no definitive evidence that the benefits of long-term anticoagulation for thrombosis or embolism outweigh the potential risks except in patients with atrial fibrillation (AF). AF is present in more than 2 million Americans and the incidence increases with age; it is the leading cause of ischemic stroke in patients older than 75 years.[17] The 5% annual rate of ischemic stroke in untreated AF patients increases with high risk factors such as hypertension, left ventricular dysfunction, transient ischemic attack (TIA), or prior stroke.[18] Anticoagulation with warfarin significantly reduces this risk of stroke, and represents the standard of care for stroke prevention in these patients. In fact, 11 separate guidelines advocate anticoagulation for AF patients with additional risk factors conferring high risk of stroke.[19] These guidelines differ in the classification of risk criteria; however, every guideline statement labels prior stroke or TIA high risk, and recommends anticoagulation. If warfarin is contraindicated, or the patient is at low risk of stroke, then antiplatelet therapy is the appropriate treatment.

Neurologists may be reluctant to use warfarin because of the amount of monitoring and follow-up required or they may inappropriately minimize the medication dosage out of undue concern about bleeding. This is a frequent subject of litigation, with the claim that a major stroke would have been prevented if the patient was properly anticoagulated. It is imperative, therefore, to identify patients at risk for stroke in accordance with established clinical guidelines. Accurate diagnosis is essential and neuroimaging to rule out intracranial hemorrhage must be performed before initiating therapy. The reasons for or against anticoagulating a patient at risk should be documented in the medical records. For example, if the increased risk of bleeding due to gait instability outweighs the potential benefits of anticoagulation, then careful documentation may protect against litigation if the patient suffers a massive embolus. Patient and family education concerning the management of anticoagulation is crucial, and should be clearly documented. Certain medication increasing the risk of bleeding should be avoided or used with extreme caution (i.e., aspirin, barbiturates, cephalosporins, sulfa drugs, and high-dose penicillin). Establish and follow written procedures for monitoring patients on warfarin, or enlist one of the anticoagulant management services.

CAROTID ENDARTERECTOMY. Almost one-quarter of recently symptomatic patients with a high-grade carotid stenosis (greater than 70% diameter reduction) will suffer an ipsilateral stroke within 2 years, despite appropriate management of risk factors and antiplatelet therapy. Carotid endarterectomy (CEA) significantly reduces the incidence of cerebral infarction in these patients, and represents the standard of care.[20] There must be careful patient selection (i.e., exclusion of patients with a high-grade tandem lesion in the ipsilateral intracranial arteries or severe contralateral carotid artery stenosis or occlusion), and skill of the surgical team is paramount. The most common malpractice claim is the failure to diagnose TIA or minor stroke, or failure to perform a workup for carotid stenosis, allowing the patient to suffer a recurrent or massive stroke. Every patient with a TIA or stroke should have a carotid doppler or magnetic resonance angiography (MRA) unless surgery is plainly contraindicated. Patients with symptomatic carotid artery stenosis greater than 70% should be offered CEA. Delay in referring a TIA patient with high-grade stenosis for definitive treatment may also constitute negligence, since a high percentage of strokes occur within 48 hours of the TIA. Surgery should be offered as soon as possible after a TIA. Premature surgical intervention following stroke creates a liability risk; once a stroke occurs, CEA must be delayed 4-6 weeks to avoid extension or hemorrhagic conversion of the infarction. Informed consent issues are critical, and all decisions should be thoroughly documented in the records.[21]

Epilepsy

DRIVING. Every state restricts issuance of a driver's license to individuals who have suffered a loss of consciousness. The laws differ among the states, but generally require that an individual be seizure-free for a period of time before obtaining a driver's license. The seizure-free interval is variable within individual state jurisdictions, ranging from no fixed duration to one year. The trend is toward a shorter time frame, with consideration of individual factors (seizure due to physician-directed medication changes or a temporary condition, an established pattern of nocturnal seizures). A physician's evaluation must be submitted to the state before a license will be issued.

Neurologists are rightfully concerned about their potential liability when certifying to the state that a patient with epilepsy is capable of driving. Some states grant immunity to the physician, although the level of immunity varies among the jurisdictions, ranging from "good faith" immunity to immunity from suit. In other states, physicians are not granted statutory immunity from liability for the information they provide to the state or for damages arising out of a seizure-related accident. In states without physician immunity laws, courts may still refuse to impose liability on the neurologist who exercised reasonable care in reporting to the state.[22]

Six states—California, Delaware, Nevada, New Jersey, Oregon, and Pennsylvania—have express mandatory reporting statutes requiring physicians to report patients with epilepsy (or other disorders associated with a loss of consciousness or impaired ability to drive) to the state.[23] All other states have voluntary reporting statutes. The neurological standard of care for the epileptic patient varies according to the laws and regulations of each state. It is incumbent upon neurologists to know the relevant statutes of their jurisdiction, and have an understanding of the common law trends for any ambiguous issues. The neurologist has a duty to advise patients of the legislation in their particular state, and emphasize the importance of complying with the law. If the state has an explicit self-reporting requirement, patients should be advised in writing to comply, with a copy of the letter kept in the medical records. The discussion of driving restrictions as well as restriction on other activities, the effect of discontinuing or reducing dosage of a drug, and possible side effects of medications in relation to driving should be clearly documented in the records. These issues should be reiterated and documented upon any change in medication, due to the increased risk of breakthrough seizures.

If an epileptic continues driving because the neurologist either failed to report where reporting is mandatory or failed to instruct the patient in a voluntary reporting state, then a seizure-related accident may trigger a malpractice suit by the patient or patient's estate. Therefore it is imperative that the neurologist clearly document patient instructions in the medical records, and keep a copy of any notification sent to the state. It is also advisable to record any factors that may mitigate liability for not filing a report. The patient who drives against medical advice is a special concern for every neurologist, especially in voluntary reporting states. *Tarasoff* reasoning may be applied to the neurologist who advises a patient not to drive, learns the patient continues driving, and fails to take any further action.[24] In this situation the neurologist should inform the patient in writing about the potential consequences of driving, and consider filing a voluntary report with the appropriate state agency. There may be statutory protection for a voluntary report that is made in good faith and consistent with the prevailing standard of care. However, the level of protection varies among jurisdictions, and it is advisable to consult legal counsel.

Neurologists may be liable to third parties for failing to report a patient or certifying a patient to drive. This is an emerging area of liability, and most decisions turn on whether the neurologist owes a duty to the third party. Courts have ruled in both directions and the issue is far from settled.[25] Neurologists should adapt practice patterns to comport with the relevant legal trends in their jurisdiction, but even third-party liability is minimized by effective patient discussions, proper reporting, and thorough documentation as outlined above.

TERATOGENESIS. There are over 1 million women with epilepsy of childbearing age in the United States; 3-5 births per thousand are to epileptic mothers.[26] Epilepsy is the most common neurological disorder in pregnant women and it raises a number of legal and medical issues. However, the most serious concern is the potential for congenital malformations in the offspring of mothers taking antiepileptic drugs (AEDs). These mothers have a 7% risk of bearing a child with congenital malformations, threefold higher than nonepileptic mothers.[27] Although this higher risk is probably multifactorial with genetic and social components, AEDs are clearly implicated as human teratogens.[28] All conventional AEDs—phenytoin, phenobarbital, carbamazepine, and sodium valproate—share an increased risk of congenital malformations, which commonly include orofacial clefts (cleft lip or cleft palate or both), congenital heart disease, neural tube defects, skeletal abnormalities, and urogenital malformations.[29] Carbamazepine and valproic acid are associated with a significantly higher incidence of neural tube defects.[30] Trimethadione is absolutely contraindicated during pregnancy due to an exceptionally high incidence of fetal malformation.[31] Termination of pregnancy should be considered if the mother ingested this drug in the first trimester. The teratogenic potential of the newer AEDs remains unknown, and these drugs should be avoided in pregnancy.

Malpractice suits for AED-induced fetal malformations have the potential for extraordinarily large settlements or judgments, and tolling of the statute of limitations is commonplace. The neurologist must address a variety of complex issues in epileptic women who take AEDs during their reproductive years in order to minimize liability for these claims.[32] Detailed counseling early in the reproductive years should include a discussion of the increased risk of seizures during pregnancy, importance of medication compliance, necessity of regular follow-up with AED levels, risk of malformations, folic acid and vitamin K supplementation, and the importance of avoiding coteratogens. Prior to pregnancy, it is important to determine whether AEDs are necessary; for example, if the patient is receiving an anticonvulsant for migraine, depression, or some other disorder, it may be possible to discontinue the drug. Additionally, if the patient with a single type of seizure has been in remission for 2-5 years, and has a normal neurological examination with no EEG abnormalities, then it may be reasonable to gradually withdraw the drug. The withdrawal must be performed slowly over months, and completed 6 months before conception, since recurrence of seizures is most likely during this time. If treatment is indicated, every effort should be made to place the patient on monotherapy with the most suitable AED (providing optimal seizure control with the least side effects) at the lowest effective dose. Frequent daily dosing will avoid high peak levels which may increase the potential for teratogenesis. The administration of folic acid in the earliest stages of pregnancy reduces the incidence of neural tube defects and should be given to all women of childbearing potential. Optimal dosage for epileptics is controversial, and data must be extrapolated from studies of nonepileptic women; the author recommends 4.0 mg/day combined with vitamin B_{12}.

It is not uncommon for women with epilepsy to present to the neurologist after becoming pregnant. In general, the risk of uncontrolled epilepsy is greater than the risk of AED-induced teratogenesis, and drug treatment must be continued throughout pregnancy. For several reasons, it is a serious albeit common error to change medications for the sole purpose of reducing teratogenic risk. First, there is a risk of precipitating seizures that may reduce placental blood flow and impair fetal oxygenation. Second, the critical period of organogenesis has usually passed, and discontinuing an AED does not lower the risk of congenital malformations. Third, exposing the fetus to a second agent during the crossover period increases the teratogenic risk. Thus, if an epileptic woman presents after conception on effective monotherapy, the AED should not be changed. In a related matter, hemorrhagic disease of the newborn may occur in neonates exposed to hepatic enzyme-inducing AEDs and requires special attention, including maternal

administration of oral vitamin K_1 20 mg/day during the last month of pregnancy.

The free (non–protein-bound) AED levels should be monitored at least preconception, at the beginning of each trimester, the last month of pregnancy, and 2 months postpartum. Pregnancy screening should include serum alphafetoprotein at 16-18 weeks and a level II ultrasound at 18-20 weeks. If indicated, amniocentesis may be offered at 18-20 weeks. The patient should be properly counseled if there is a serious malformation, and provided with the option to terminate the pregnancy.

Headache. Headache is arguably the most common patient complaint in the outpatient neurology setting. It may be of little clinical significance or, paradoxically, herald a catastrophic illness, such as brain tumor, SAH, or meningitis. A complete and accurate diagnosis of the headache patient requires a detailed history coupled with a full neurological and general medical examination. The single most important step in the evaluation is to classify the type of headache and, *pari passu*, ascertain whether it is acute, long-standing, or with recent change. This practical approach will allow the neurologist to determine the need for any diagnostic testing and initiate a proper treatment plan, all with the appropriate degree of urgency. Too often, the inexperienced, poorly trained, or hurried neurologist distorts a patient's history or fails to perform an adequate examination, resulting in the wrong diagnosis. Accordingly, headache remains one of the most prevalent conditions in recurring malpractice claims against neurologists. These claims seem to run the gamut: failure to diagnose brain tumor; failure to identify and treat rebound phenomenon; failure to diagnose and treat temporal arteritis; failure to diagnose and treat sphenoid sinusitis; avascular necrosis secondary to steroids; and inappropriate use of triptans or ergotamines.[33] There are two areas of particular concern that warrant further discussion: neuroimaging in the patient with headache and the failure to diagnose SAH.

The role of neuroimaging in the patient with headache and a normal neurological examination remains a controversial area. The American Academy of Neurology (AAN) Practice Guidelines state that "neuroimaging is not usually warranted in patients with migraine and a normal neurological examination," but should be considered in patients with an abnormal neurological examination or "patients with atypical headache features or headaches that do not fulfill the strict definition of migraine or other primary headache disorder."[34] These parameters presuppose an accurate diagnosis of the patient's headache, which is frequently not the case. For example, it is not uncommon for the neurologist to diagnose a patient with migraine or chronic headache in the absence of neuroimaging, only to find that subsequent evaluation reveals a brain tumor.[35] Arguments that earlier diagnosis would not have materially affected the outcome are generally unsuccessful. There may be absolutely no relationship between the headache and brain tumor, but the trier of fact will likely find otherwise if the neurologist failed to order a timely imaging study. Thus, the decision to forgo neuroimaging in a patient with headaches requires a great deal of experience and clinical acumen. For many neurologists, it would simply be prudent to perform an imaging study on every headache patient early in the evaluation. Of course, there is no point in repeating a test if it was already performed, assuming there is no change in the patient's condition. There are no evidence-based recommendations for the relative sensitivity of MRI as compared with CT in the evaluation of migraine or other nonacute headaches. However, MRI is probably a superior choice in most circumstances given its sensitivity and ability to visualize the posterior fossa. Unfortunately, concerns over deselection and negative capitation may deter the neurologist from ordering these studies, and the failure to diagnose brain tumors will probably remain one of the most common malpractice claims.

The failure to diagnose SAH consistently results in the highest average and highest total indemnity for all claims involving diagnostic error.[36] The neurologist must maintain a high index of suspicion for patients presenting with a severe headache of sudden onset (thunderclap headache), neck stiffness or low back pain suggestive of meningeal irritation, focal neurological deficits, cognitive impairment, or a history of premonitory symptoms suggestive of a sentinel bleed or expansion of an aneurysm. A good history of the current headache is essential, because even known migraineurs may suffer a SAH. The patient with a history or exam suggestive of a SAH should have an immediate CT scan of the brain, followed by a lumbar puncture (LP) even if the CT is negative for blood.[37] The LP should include measurement of the opening pressure as well as evaluation for xanthochromia. Based on the clinical history, sequence of events, and time of presentation, as well as CT and LP results, it may be reasonable to proceed with MRA or arteriography.

NONMALPRACTICE LIABILITY

Neurologists must be cognizant of the morass of laws and regulations affecting their practice, which raise the specter of adverse licensing actions, civil penalties, and criminal prosecution. This nonmalpractice liability penumbra generically includes credentialing disputes (professional licensure, hospital privileges, professional organization membership), reimbursement issues (fee disputes, program exclusion, denial of managed care contracts), and a myriad of *ad personam* (assault, manslaughter, homicide), economic (anti-kickback, self-referral, and antitrust violations; false claims) and regulatory (violation of Americans with Disabilities Act, Health Insurance Portability and Accountability Act, Emergency Medical Treatment and Labor Act) crimes.[38] The relevant legal principles governing these diverse areas are substantially the same for all specialties and are detailed elsewhere in this volume. Several examples underscore this broad liability:

- Increasingly, medical malpractice is subject to criminal prosecution. The facts of most emerging cases are *sui generis*, but the underlying theme is criminalization of gross negligence.[39]
- A "whistleblower" complaint under the False Claims Act *qui tam* provision leads to criminal and civil prosecution of a neurologist performing excessive electrodiagnostic testing procedures.[40]
- Economic credentialing may take many forms: a hospital surreptitiously discredits the staff neurologist who refused to participate in a fraudulent billing scheme involving neuroimaging studies.[41]

LIABILITY OF THE FORENSIC NEUROLOGIST

Many neurologists have responded to managed care constraints by expanding their practice to include medical record reviews, independent medical examinations, and expert witness services. These lucrative activities generally do not invoke a physician-patient relationship (thus precluding a medical malpractice claim), but pose unique risks for administrative penalties, civil lawsuits, and criminal prosecution. Of note, malpractice insurance policies may not cover these services without a special rider.

Expert witness

Anecdotal reports of neurologists advancing specious complaints are legion. One study of malpractice suits against neurologists over a 10-year period documented improper testimony in 37% of cases.[42] It is "alarmingly common for accomplished neurologists to hire themselves out for [one-sided testimony]."[43] These partisan experts have flourished behind the common law expert witness immunity shield and lack of professional oversight. Today, the pendulum is swinging back toward accountability with increased expert witness liability.[44] Friendly expert lawsuits (suits against experts by the party that retained them) are increasing.[45] The traditional immunity is not absolute,[46] and the majority of states ruling on this issue have carved out exceptions to hold the expert liable for professional negligence. One state Supreme Court explained that an "absence of immunity will . . . protect the litigant from the negligence of an incompetent professional."[47] Several legal authorities suggest this may represent the most effective means of stemming the proliferation of negligent experts.[48] Courts have also upheld suits against opposing and independent experts. Some jurisdictions continue to favor immunity for testimony,[49] but that does not necessarily extend to nontestimonial expert activity (discovery of facts, literature search). Nor does it protect the expert from criminal prosecution for improper testimony or misrepresentation of a degree or license. The expert neurologist may also be liable for defamatory communications and negligent or intentional spoliation of evidence.

Expert testimony and related activities are subject to increased scrutiny by state licensing boards and professional organizations. The American Medical Association considers testimony to be the practice of medicine and subject to peer review, and supports state licensing boards in disciplining physicians who provide fraudulent testimony or false credentials.[50] Some boards have expanded the definition of medical practice to include expert testimony, allowing disciplinary action if warranted.[51] The AAN adopted *Qualifications and Guidelines for the Physician Expert Witness*,[52] promulgated a code of professional conduct for legal expert testimony,[53] and established a formal disciplinary procedure for errant neurologists with potential sanctions ranging from censure to expulsion.[54] AAN disciplinary actions may trigger the American Board of Psychiatry and Neurology to revoke certification. A recent Seventh Circuit Court of Appeals' decision validated this type of disciplinary policy and stated in dicta that the American Academy of Neurological Surgeons had a duty to discipline a neurosurgeon for irresponsible testimony.[55]

This complex, evolving area of law will create a more perilous liability climate for the future expert. The standard of care for expert services varies with the particular facts of each case, but salient guidelines applicable to all circumstances are listed in Box 46-1. It is important to remember that all deposition and trial testimony constitutes a permanent public record, which may be accessed any time from national repositories.[56]

CONCLUSION

The malpractice climate is increasingly adverse; nonmalpractice liability issues continue intruding into clinical practice. Integrating this chapter with an understanding of the entire volume will provide the neurologist with a guide to meet today's legal challenges, thereby improving patient care and minimizing malpractice and nonmalpractice liability.

BOX 46-1. GUIDELINES FOR EXPERT TESTIMONY

1. Fulfill the AAN qualifications before accepting a case.
2. Review all relevant medical information in the case.
3. Review the standard of care for the time of occurrence.
4. Perform adequate discovery of the facts.
5. Review and understand the relevant literature.
6. Properly assemble and present the case.
7. Avoid losing or destroying any evidence.
8. Provide accurate, impartial, and truthful testimony.
9. Avoid conflicts of interest.
10. Do not discuss the case outside the course of litigation.
11. Compensation must be reasonable, not contingent on outcome.

ENDNOTES

1. Approximately 95% of medical malpractice claims are settled before or during trial; of those going to a jury, plaintiffs are winning more often (38% of the time) and the median jury award continues to increase ($1 million in 2000). Med. Econ. (May 10, 2002) at 18 (citing Jury Verdict Research report).

2. Physician Insurers Association of America, *A Risk Management Review of Malpractice Claims (Neurology)*, 2000 edition.

3. *Id.* at v (Exhibit 5).

4. *Id.*

5. *Id.*

6. S.F. Olson, *Risk Management for Neurologists*, AAN Education Program Syllabus 5BS.003 (2002).

7. *See, e.g.,* M.I. Weintraub *Documentation and Informed Consent*, 17(2) Neuro Clin. 371-81 (1999).

8. *Supra* note 2, at vi (Exhibit 6).

9. *Id.*

10. *See generally* Centers for Disease Control (www.cdc.gov) and American Heart Association (www.americanheart.org).

11. The National Institute of Neurological Disorders and Stroke rt-PA Study Group, *Tissue Plasminogen Activator for Acute Ischemic Stroke*, 333 N. Engl. J. Med. 1581-87 (1995).

12. *See* American Academy of Neurology, *Report of the Quality Standards Subcommittee: Practice Advisory: Thrombolytic Therapy for Acute Ischemic Stroke (Summary Statement)* (1996).

13. *See* S.L. Hickenbottom & W.G. Barsan, *Acute Ischemic Stroke Therapy*, 19(2) Neuro Clin. 379-97 (2000) (reviewing the National Institute of Neurological Diseases and Stroke tPA Stroke Study, European Cooperative Acute Stroke Study I and II, and the Altepase Thrombolysis for Acute Non-Interventional Therapy in Acute Stroke Study).

14. *See, e.g., Backlund v. University of Washington*, 975 P. 2d 950 (1999) (negligence and informed consent are alternative theories of liability).

15. A Position Paper of the American Academy of Neurology Ethics and Humanities Subcommittee, *Consent Issues in the Management of Cerebrovascular Diseases* (1999).

16. *See Canterbury v. Spence*, 464 F. 2d 772 (D.C. Cir. 1972), *cert. denied*, 408 U.S. 1064 (1974) and its progeny.

17. S. Palacio & R.G. Hart, *Neurologic Manifestations of Cardiogenic Embolism*, 20(1) Neuro Clin. 179-93 (2002).

18. R. Llinas & L.R. Caplan, *Evidence-Based Treatment of Patients with Ischemic Cerebrovascular Disease*, 19(1) Neuro Clin. 79-105 (2001).

19. R.G. Hart & R.D. Bailey, *An Assessment of Guidelines for Prevention of Ischemic Stroke*, 59 Neurology 979-82 (2002). *See* American Academy of Neurology, *Report of the Quality Standard Subcommittee: Practice Parameters: Stroke Prevention in Patients with Nonvalvular Atrial Fibrillation* (1998).

20. For the North American Symptomatic Carotid Endarterectomy Trial Collaborators, *Beneficial Effect of Carotid Endarterectomy in Symptomatic Moderate or Severe Stenosis*, 325 N. Engl. J. Med. 445-53 (1991); European Carotid Surgery Trial, *Interim Results for Patients with Severe (70-99%) or with Mild (0-29%) Carotid Stenosis*, 337 Lancet 1235-43 (1991).

21. *Supra* note 15.

22. *Krejci v. Akron Pediatric Neurology, Inc.*, 511 N.E. 2d 129 (Ohio App. 1987).

23. *See, e.g.,* Or. Rev. Stat. §807.710. The Epilepsy Foundation of America (www.efa.org) provides a review of the laws in each state.

24. *Tarasoff v. Regents of the Univ. of Cal.*, 551 P. 2d 334 (Cal. 1976). *See Osborne v. United States of America*, No. 30115 (W. Va. July 3, 2002).

25. *See Harden v. Dalrymple*, 883 F.Supp. 963 (D. Del. 1995). *Cf. Praesel v. Johnson*, 41 Tex. Super Ct. J. 630 (1998).

26. American Academy of Neurology, *Neurologic Disorders and Pregnancy*, 6(1) Continuum 8-63 (Feb. 2000).

27. R.H. Finnell, H. Nau & M.S. Yerby *General Principles: Teratogenicity of Anti-Epileptic Drugs*, in *Anti-Epileptic Drugs*, 4th ed., 209-30 (New York: Raven Press, 1995).

28. *Supra* note 26 at 19.

29. N. Foldvary, *Treatment Issues for Women with Epilepsy*, 19(2) Neuro Clin. 409-25 (2001).

30. A. Delgado-Escueta, D. Janz & G. Beck-Mannagetta, *Pregnancy and Teratogenesis in Epilepsy*, 42 (Suppl. 5): Neurology 1-160 (1992).

31. *Id.*

32. American Academy of Neurology, *Report of the Quality Standard Subcommittee: Practice Parameter: Management Issues for Women with Epilepsy (Summary Statement)* (1998).

33. *See, e.g.*, J.R. Saper, *Medicolegal Issues: Headache*, 17(2) Neuro Clin. 197-214 (1999).

34. American Academy of Neurology, *Report of the Quality Standards Subcommittee: Practice Parameter: Evidence-Based Guidelines for Migraine Headache (An Evidence-Based Review)* (2000).

35. *See, e.g., Richter v. Northwestern Memorial Hospital*, 532 N.E. 2d 269 (Ill. App. 1988) (neurologist treating a headache patient for 6 years did not order an imaging study and failed to diagnose a cerebellopontine angle tumor; settled malpractice suit for $6 million).

36. *Supra* note 2, at v (Exhibit 5).

37. American Academy of Neurology, *Headache and Facial Pain*, 1(5) Continuum 8-26 (1995) (CT can miss SAH in up to 25% of cases; MRI is unreliable in acute SAH).

38. *See* H.R. Beresford, *Neurology and the Law: Private Litigation and Public Policy* (F.A. Davis Co., Philadelphia, 1998).

39. *See* J.A. Filkins, *"With No Evil Intent": The Criminal Prosecution of Physicians for Medical Negligence*, 22 J. Legal Med. 467-99 (2001).

40. *See* J.C. Johnston, *New Frontiers for Qui Tam Litigation in Health Care* (July 22, 1997), unpublished manuscript submitted in Health Law Seminar, University of Oregon School of Law (neurologists should adopt a well-organized compliance plan in accordance with the Office of the Inspector General's recommendations in order to avoid prosecution for billing mistakes).

41. Personal knowledge regarding Tenet Healthcare Corporation (documentation on file with author).

42. *See* G.N. McAbee, *Improper Expert Medical Testimony: Existing and Proposed Mechanisms of Oversight*, 19 J. Legal Med. 257-72 (1998) (citing A. Safran, B. Skydell & S. Ropper, *Expert Witness Testimony in Neurology: Massachusetts Experience 1980-1990*, 2 Neurology Chron. 1-6, 1992).

43. S. Holtz, *The Neurologist as an Expert Witness*, AAN Education Program Syllabus 7DS.003 (2002).

44. *See, e.g.*, R.K. Hanson, *Witness Immunity Under Attack: Disarming "Hired Guns,"* 31 Wake Forest L. Rev. 497 (1996).

45. *See, e.g., Aufrichtig v. Lowell*, 650 N.E. 2d 401 (N.Y. 1995).

46. *Butz v. Economou*, 438 U.S. 478 (1978). *See also* Restatement (Second) of Torts §588 (limiting immunity to statements that have "some relation to the proceeding").

47. *Marrogi v. Howard*, 805 So. 2d 1118, 1132 (La. 2002).

48. *See, e.g.*, Henderson-Garcia, *Expert Witness Malpractice: A Solution to the Problem of the Negligent Expert Witness*, 12 Miss. Coll. L. Rev. 39 (1991).

49. *Gustafson v. Mazer*, 113 Wn. App. 770; 54 P. 3d 743 (2002).

50. M.I. Weintraub, *Expert Witness Testimony*, 17(2) Neuro Clin. 363-69 (1999).

51. *See, e.g., Joseph v. D.C. Board of Medicine*, 587 A. 2d 1085 (D.C. App. 1991). *Cf. Missouri Board of Reg. for the Healing Arts v. Levine*, 808 S.W. 2d 440 (Mo. App. 1991).

52. American Academy of Neurology, *Qualifications and Guidelines for the Physician Expert Witness* (1998).

53. AAN Code of Professional Conduct §6.4, 59(5) (Suppl. 1) Neurology (2002).

54. Articles and Bylaws of the AAN §§19, 20, 59(5) (Suppl. 1) Neurology (2002).

55. *Malpractice Experts: The Penalty for Bearing False Witness*, Med. Econ. (Aug. 9, 2002) at 36-43.

56. Some professional organizations, e.g., the Defense Research Institute in Chicago, Illinois, and the Association of Trial Lawyers of America in Washington, D.C., maintain copies of expert witness depositions and court testimony.

Nursing and the Law

JUDITH A. GIC, R.N., J.D.

PROFESSIONAL NEGLIGENCE
WORKPLACE TORTS OTHER THAN PROFESSIONAL NEGLIGENCE
PROBLEMS ASSOCIATED WITH OFF-SITE NURSING
NURSING LICENSURE

In a concise format, this chapter overviews significant topics in nursing practice: professional negligence (including the consequences of civil and possibly criminal liability, and being reported to the National Practitioner Data Bank); workplace torts other than professional negligence, such as batteries against patients and breaches of patient privacy and confidentiality; problems associated with off-site nursing; and licensure. Each of these topics could support a lengthier treatment than space constraints have allowed here. Our purpose, therefore, has been to sketch out broad outlines and, where appropriate, to direct the reader to other useful sources.[1]

PROFESSIONAL NEGLIGENCE

The substantive basis for a negligence claim

Most lawsuits based on claims of professional negligence are creatures of state laws, which may vary in detail from state to state, rather than of a federal law that is uniform across the nation. Nonetheless, negligence *generally* means—i.e., above the level of varying details—the same thing in all state and federal courts: failure to act as a reasonable person would act in the same situation.[2] More particularly, in the profession of nursing, the law of negligence examines a nurse's conduct against the standard of "what a reasonable and prudent nurse would have done in the same or similar circumstances. . . ."[3] As one court stated (with respect to a specialist nurse):

A nurse who practices her profession in a particular specialty owes to her patients the duty of *possessing the degree of knowledge or skill* ordinarily possessed by members of her profession actively practicing in such a specialty under similar circumstances. It is the nurse's duty to *exercise the degree of skill* ordinarily employed, under similar circumstances, by members of the nursing profession in good standing who practice their profession in the same specialty and to use reasonable care and diligence, along with his/her best judgment, in the application of his/her skill to the case.[4]

For example, a nurse may be sued for injuries resulting from failure to check a patient's temperature every hour, if hourly checking was professionally appropriate given the facts and the circumstances of that patient. All professional negligence claims are built on some variation of this type of double allegation: that a particular nurse did or failed to do a particular thing, and that such conduct was a deviation from the standard of reasonable and prudent care.

There are other elements to a claim of professional negligence besides whether the nurse's act or omission was a deviation from the standard of care, such as whether the nurse owed a duty to the patient and whether the deviation caused any damages that the patient actually suffered. These elements, however, are usually not as much in the nurse's control as *knowing* the standard of care and *applying* it correctly.

Knowing the standard of care. To say, as we have above, that a nurse's conduct should be reasonable and prudent is not particularly helpful in the context of a *specific* case, once the parties start zeroing in on the facts. At that point, the plaintiff must have evidence (usually in the form of opinion testimony by experts) establishing exactly what was expected of the nurse in the circumstances of the case; and the defending nurse may present expert testimony setting forth a different standard of care.

In telling the jury what a reasonably prudent nurse would have done, the parties' experts should be able to point to authorities that support their versions of the standard of care. These authorities may include current textbooks, treatises, and articles on the particular aspect of nursing at issue in the case; treatment standards issued by the American Nurses Association or any association for the type of nursing at issue in the case; treatment standards issued by the Joint Commission on Accreditation of Healthcare Organizations and by the hospital or health care provider that employed the nurse;[5] doctors' orders pertaining to the patient;[6] and the expert's own experience in dealing with similar situations and in watching others deal with similar situations. Some combination of these authorities may speak generally or directly to the question of what the defendant nurse should have done. An expert's role is to synthesize these sources and, by drawing on qualifications rooted in "knowledge, skill, experience, training, or education,"[7] to give an opinion about what a reasonably prudent nurse would have done when faced with the same circumstances as the defendant nurse.

For example, the patient may allege an injury resulting from substandard conduct involving anesthesia. In deciding whether the nurse was negligent, the court would need to compare the nurse's behavior with that of a reasonably prudent nurse. Its first question might be, was the nurse a nurse anesthetist or a general RN specially tasked to work with anesthesia?[8] A nurse anesthetist would probably be held to a higher standard. Nurse anesthetists are organized into a professional association (the American Association of Nurse Anesthetists) that has issued protocols for patient treatment.[9] A nurse anesthetist would be expected to satisfy those standards, whereas a general RN might not. Many other nurse specialists are organized similarly—the Association of Women's Health, Obstetrical and Gynecological Nurses, the Emergency Nurses Association, the American Association of Operating Room Nurses, and the American Subacute Care Association, to name a few. A court may agree that these specialist associations may help define the appropriate standard of care for nurses regularly practicing within that specialty.[10]

In some cases, the standard of care is clear-cut. For example, if the patient's physician ordered a particular injection and the nurse failed to give it when nothing contraindicated the physician's order, the nurse was probably negligent because a reasonably prudent nurse implements physician's orders. In such a case, the nurse may agree with the patient's evidence on standard of care; instead of presenting evidence of a different standard, the nurse may focus his or her defensive energies on other issues, such as whether there is any evidence of deviation from the standard as set forth by the patient, whether any deviation caused damages, etc.

In other cases, the standard of care is not clear-cut, with both the patient and the nurse presenting conflicting evidence of what would have been the reasonably prudent course of action. For example, in *Ravi v. Williams*[11] the patient sued a surgical nurse (among others) for damages caused by leaving a sponge inside him after an operation. The question on appeal was whether accounting for sponges before closing an incision was the responsibility of the surgeon or the nurse. In other words, was counting sponges before and after something that a reasonably prudent surgical nurse would do? The question was divisive enough that the state's supreme court ended up providing the definitive answer for Alabama. Likewise, the Wisconsin Supreme Court was called upon to

decide in *Mosey v. Mueller*[12] whether, under that state's law, the standard of care for surgical nurses includes retrieving all surgical instruments from the patient's body. It concluded that "[t]he evidence established that the surgical nurses had no responsibility to count or account for surgical instruments during a surgical procedure and that such accountability was the sole responsibility of the surgeon."[13] As a result, the nurse was exonerated. Contentious questions about the standard of care may also arise when a nurse works in an area of new treatment or with new technology: in either situation, the nurse may encounter a scenario for which there is not yet a textbook response.

An issue sometimes litigated is whether the standard of care to which the nurse should have conformed was a national standard or a local standard. If the issue comes up, it does so in connection with the qualification of a particular expert witness to testify for the patient or the nurse. In a case involving a local standard of care, an expert not familiar with standards and practices in the locality where the patient was treated is not in a position to testify about what a reasonably prudent nurse in that locality would have done. On the other hand, in a case involving a national standard of care, location-specific standards and practices are irrelevant, with the result that an out-of-town expert is competent to testify. The effect of there being a local standard at issue in a case, rather than a national standard, is that the experts who can testify for the patient are both fewer in number and drawn from the same locality as the defendant nurse. In small localities, this may translate into a real difficulty in finding an expert to testify against the defendant nurse.[14]

In general, the standard of care will be national if the standard allegedly breached was derived either from a nursing specialty or, at the other extreme, from basic nursing. For example, in *Ross v. Chatham County Hospital Authority*,[15] injury resulted from leaving a surgical instrument inside a patient. The court had to decide whether to apply a local standard that might excuse the defendant's failure to count the instruments before and after surgery. It decided not to because "the ability of an operating room employee to count the surgical instruments present at the beginning and end of an operation obviously would not be affected by the size or location of the hospital."[16]

Whatever local or national standard applies, doctor's orders will supplement the standard of care and, in some cases, override it. If a physician instructs a nurse to perform a certain action and the nurse fails to do it, resulting damages will be charged to the nurse's negligence; on the other hand, following the orders generally shields the nurse from liability even where the result of the ordered treatment is adverse. "[A] hospital [or its employee nurses] generally cannot be held liable for a patient's injury on the theory that nurses or other members of the hospital staff should have known that the treatment generated by a physician was inadequate or improper and therefore should have intervened."[17] In *Moore v. Carrington*,[18] an emergency room doctor and nurse failed to resuscitate a child. Neither the nurse nor her employer, the hospital, could be held liable because the nurse had done as the doctor instructed. The hospital also could not be held liable for any fault of the doctor because he was an independent contractor, not an employee. Consequently, it was legally possible for only the doctor to be held liable (although the jury, after looking at the facts, decided that the doctor had not committed malpractice).

A nurse may, at times, doubt a doctor's judgment. Though without authority to alter the doctor's treatment,

the nurse is not prohibited from calling on or consulting with nurse supervisors or with other physicians on the hospital staff concerning those matters, and when the patient's condition reasonably requires it *the nurse has a duty* to do those tasks when they are within the ordinary care and skill required by the relevant standard of conduct.[19]

Though a nurse may have some concern of being fired because of questioning treatment decisions that do not appear to be in the patient's best interest, he or she may (if indeed fired) have a claim against the employer for termination in violation of public policy.[20]

General areas in which nurses may be found in breach of a standard

How a nurse may breach the appropriate standard of care is a question with innumerable answers, and any catalog of today's possible errors would start becoming outdated tomorrow as new technologies and treatments offer new pitfalls for professional negligence. Instead, we will briefly consider the commonest types.

Patient monitoring and communication. A nurse's key role is to monitor patients and to convey patient information mainly through chart notes and direct communication with physicians and other nurses. "[N]urses must perform a competent nursing assessment of the patient to determine those signs and symptoms presented by the patient that are significant in relation to the attending physician's tasks of diagnosis and treatment."[21] In *Miles v. Box Butte County*,[22] parents on behalf of their minor son successfully sued a nurse for contributing to injuries resulting from hypoxia during labor and delivery. Two of their claims were that the nurse's chart notes reflected an incorrect interpretation of the tracings from the fetal heart monitor (the fetus's condition was much more endangered than the nurse realized) and that the physician had only the chart notes to rely upon because the nurse did not show the tracings to the physician. With respect to showing the tracings, the court agreed that "a hospital [through its staff] has a duty to notify a physician of significant changes in a patient's medical status."[23]

As an example of this duty, the court in *Louie v. Chinese Hospital Association*[24] found a nurse liable for neglecting to tell a physician that a patient had become restless and confused. Some time later, the patient fell while trying to get out of bed. The doctor testified that he might have changed the patient's medicine if he had been told about the patient's mental state. Similarly, the court in *Merritt v. Karcioglu*[25] affirmed a nurse's share of liability for failing to report the confused condition of a patient who later fell while trying to crawl out of bed (when found at the foot of the bed, she said she was trying to get to her kitchen to make dessert for her family).[26]

But the *Miles* court concluded that the duty to give notice had limits:

[W]hen a physician is present at a hospital and is seeing a patient, and when the physician is clearly aware of available information which may be relevant to the diagnosis and treatment of that patient, it is unreasonable to require hospital personnel to make sure that the physician does, in fact, review that information.[27]

Consequently, the nurse in *Miles* was not negligent in not setting the tracings before the physician—the physician knew the tracings existed (the chart notes referenced them) and he could have asked to see them. But, adverse to the nurse, the court also held that the nurse's negligent misinterpretation of the tracings contributed to the physician's decision not to ask for the tracings. The bottom line was that liability resulted from the nurse's faulty monitoring of the patient's condition as reflected in her chart notes on the tracings, not the failure to provide the tracings themselves.[28] Likewise, in *Berdyck v. Shinde*,[29] the nurse's failure to report the maternity patient's persistent high blood pressure and other symptoms indicative of preeclampsia (due in part to a lack of knowledge of preeclampsia that was unacceptable in an obstetrics nurse) contributed to the occurrence of an eclamptic seizure that left the patient partially paralyzed.

Patient-handling errors. As discussed above, nurses may be negligent for patient falls and other injuries resulting from failure to report confused mental states that a physician might have chosen to treat with medication or restraints. Apart from such failure, a nurse may be negligent for falls and other injuries that might have been avoided if the nurse had been reasonably prudent. For example, a reasonably prudent nurse might see, without the need for doctor's orders, that a particular patient's bed rails should be raised to prevent the patient from trying to get up,[30] or they should not be allowed to use the bathroom alone.[31]

Medication errors. A significant number of nursing negligence cases involve the delivery of medication to patients: giving the wrong medicine or the wrong dose, omitting a dose or giving the dose to the wrong patient, or administering it incorrectly (for example, orally instead of by injection), among other mistakes. Various circumstances may delay discovery of the mistake until the onset of serious consequences. Such consequences having occurred, the court may allow the jury to infer negligence through the principle of *res ipsa loquitur*, which expresses the idea that some results cannot have occurred without negligence. (For example, in *Thomas v. New York Univ. Med. Ctr.*,[32] the patient sued for injuries suffered when he fell off the operating table. The court found the hospital liable without any further proof of negligence: "it can hardly be debated that anesthetized patients do not fall from operating tables in the absence of negligence."[33])

Transfusion errors. Similar to medication errors is giving a patient the wrong type of blood. A nurse may mix up two patients' different blood types,[34] type the blood incorrectly,[35] retrieve the wrong type of blood from the blood bank,[36] or think the doctor ordered one type when in fact the doctor ordered another, among other mistakes. It goes without saying that whatever the cause of the mistake, its consequences can be severe, including death.[37]

Liable parties

Any suit against a nurse may be against only that nurse or (which is more likely) against the nurse and variety of other parties, such as other nurses responsible for the patient's care, physicians, other health care providers, and entities such as hospitals, medical practices, etc.

Nurse's own liability. A nurse who has committed malpractice is primarily liable for the damages. The fact that the patient may focus the effort to collect damages from a wealthier codefendant, such as the nurse's employer, does not eliminate the nurse's liability (or the possibility that the nurse's employer will take some adverse job action, such as discipline or termination, or that the state licensing board will suspend or revoke the nurse's license). A nurse must be satisfied that he or she has malpractice insurance, either self- or employer-provided. In selecting the amount of coverage, the nurse should be aware of any caps or limits on damages that exist under state law.

Employer liability. A nurse's employer may incur vicarious liability for the nurse's professional negligence pursuant to the ancient doctrine of *respondeat superior*. *Respondeat superior* makes employers in all lines of work responsible for the negligent (and in some cases, even the intentional) misdeeds of their employees when they act in the course and scope of their employment.[38] "Hospitals, *like all other employers*, may be held liable for the negligent conduct of its [*sic*] employees, including nurses, committed while acting in the course and scope of their employment under the doctrine of respondeat superior."[39] The patient has the option of seeking the full damages for which the nurse has been judged responsible from either the nurse or the employer, or some fraction of those damages from both.[40]

In some instances, a nurse's employer may have been negligent with respect to nursing services regardless of whether any individual nurse employee was negligent. Here, the employer's negligence is not vicarious but its *own* (and the liability is its own). This can happen where, for example, the employer fails to maintain an adequate nursing staff.[41] In *HCA Health Services v. National Bank*,[42] a day-old infant suffered cardiac and respiratory arrest in a hospital nursery. The nurses were partly negligent for not keeping a better eye on the infant, but the hospital was negligent on its own account for not having sufficient nurses on duty: "the hospital administration had been told of an ongoing need for more nurses in the nursery and . . . the number of staff on duty . . . [on the night in question] was below the hospital's own standards. . . ."[43] Likewise, in *Landry v. Clement*,[44] the hospital was partly liable for violating its own policy against assigning nurses to work in its obstetrical department without having first trained the nurses on the use of a fetal heart monitor.[45]

Physician liability. A physician may incur vicarious liability for a nurse's negligence if the physician was either the nurse's actual employer or, during the procedure in question, exercised such supervision and control that a court will *treat* the physician *as if* he or she had been the actual employer. In that case, the nurse is said to be the physician's "borrowed servant."[46]

In *Hunnicut v. Wright*,[47] the plaintiff sued for injuries caused by a screw and washer that fell off a medical instrument and stayed in his body. The evidence showed that a hospital-employed scrub technician failed to tighten the screw after sterilizing it and that if he had done so, the screw and washer would not have fallen off. The surgeon was not the scrub technician's actual employer, so the plaintiff argued that the surgeon should be *treated as* the actual employer. But the court concluded that the surgeon did not have sufficient supervision or control over the scrub technician's sterilization and reassembly of the instrument to be treated as that person's actual employer and to be held liable for his negligence:

The routine acts of treatment which an attending physician may reasonably assume may be performed in his absence by nurses of a modern hospital as part of their usual and customary duties, and execution of which does not require specialized medical knowledge, are merely administrative acts for which negligence in their performance is imputable to the hospital.[48]

On the other hand, the necessary degree of supervision and control were present in *Hudmon v. Martin*[49] for a nurse to be a physician's borrowed servant. In that case, the surgeon and scrub nurse were working together to prepare a patient for surgery and the surgeon directed the scrub nurse to fill a syringe with a certain fluid. The nurse filled it with the wrong fluid, which injured the patient when the surgeon injected it.

Nursing negligence and the National Practitioner Data Bank

A nurse involved in a case of professional negligence may, in certain circumstances, be reported to the National Practitioner Data Bank (NPDB). Congress created the NPDB in 1986 because of concerns that state oversight of health care providers (including nurses) was fragmented and that information about providers who may have been negligent in one state was not being shared with other states, thus allowing negligent practitioners to continue simply by moving.[50] The NPDB legislation requires, in part, that any entity (including an insurance company) paying a settlement or a judgment on a written medical malpractice claim is to report the name of any licensed professional on whose behalf the payment is made, the amount of payment, the name of any hospital with which the person is affiliated, and a description of the acts/omissions and the injuries alleged.[51] The fact that money was paid in settlement (rather than judgment) is not to be construed as presumptive evidence that malpractice occurred.[52] The NPDB legislation allows hospitals to request NPDB reports on applicants for nursing employment.[53] Practitioners may self-query to obtain their own NPDB file.[54]

NPDB entries are permanent, but the subjects of such records are entitled to present their own statement along with the payor's report and/or to dispute the accuracy of information reported on them to the NPDB.[55] In general, the Secretary of the Department of Health and Human Services will mail to the person affected a copy of any NPDB report submitted. The person affected then has 60 days to dispute in writing the accuracy of the report as submitted. The practitioner must try to resolve the dispute with the reporting entity, which is primarily responsible for making a change to a submitted report. If the dispute is not resolved, the practitioner may request review by the Secretary of DHHS, who will determine whether the report as submitted was accurate and whether the report should have been submitted in the first place.

Nursing negligence and criminal liability

In rare but well-publicized instances, negligence in nursing has been so extreme that criminal charges have resulted. In *State v. Winter*,[56] a registered nurse was convicted of simple manslaughter and sentenced to 5 years in prison after she mistakenly transfused a patient with the wrong blood and then intentionally took several steps to conceal the error, "including failing to inform the patient's doctor of her error, secreting and disposing of the remainder of the blood upon realizing her mistake, and changing notations on . . . [the patient's] chart to mask the effects of the transfusion reaction."[57]

Even when it ends with acquittal of the defendant nurse, a prosecution by itself may be expensive and devastating to a career. In *Caretenders, Inc. v. Kentucky*,[58] the state tried two RNs, one LPN, and their employer (a home health agency) for knowing and willful neglect of a patient. The patient, when admitted to a hospital, was dirty and covered with extensive bedsores. Evidence showed that agency employees did not turn the patient as ordered, did not keep her clean, and kept bad records of their patient care activities, and it also showed that the agency failed to train and supervise its employees properly. Even though the nurses were acquitted (while the agency was convicted and fined $8,333.33), their employment prospects must have suffered.

WORKPLACE TORTS OTHER THAN PROFESSIONAL NEGLIGENCE

Torts against patients

Nurses and their employers may be held liable for behavior other than substandard practice that constitutes professional negligence. Some of these torts include:

Patient battery. Intentional mistreatment of patients may be a basis for liability. Operators of nursing homes and other facilities for long-term, subacute patients must be particularly careful in screening, retaining, and training employees. An Oklahoma jury awarded $1.25 million in damages against a nursing home because a drunk aide harshly slapped a patient while trying to bathe him.[59]

Breach of patient privacy and confidentiality. Privacy is a broad right that everyone enjoys with respect to personal information, and invasion of privacy is a widely recognized basis for filing a lawsuit. Confidentiality is a somewhat narrower right, as it is rooted specifically in a patient's medical records. Together, the rights of privacy and confidentiality preserve the nondisclosure of patients' medical records, as well as other private information regardless of whether it has been documented in a medical record. While nurses must be careful to preserve the confidentiality of both records and other nonrecorded private information, they should be particularly on guard concerning the second. Nurses' jobs, especially in institutional or home health settings, often bring them into relatively informal contact with patients' visiting family and friends. These contacts present a dangerous opportunity for a nurse to reveal confidential patient information to a person not entitled to receive it. Such inadvertent disclosures should ordinarily be considered within the course and scope of the nurse's employment, with the result that the nurse's employer should have to share any civil liability under the principles of *respondeat superior*, as discussed above.

But a nurse may have to bear alone the liability for a purposeful breach. In *Jones v. Baisch*,[60] the nurse's employer was dismissed as a defendant in a case based on a nurse's breach of confidentiality. The nurse told friends about a specific patient with herpes. The court ruled that the nurse was not acting in the course and scope of employment when she made the disclosure.

Torts against nurses

Spectacular incidents of crime in the workplace have focused attention on the risks that Americans face as employees. Nurses are certainly not immune from these risks as their jobs bring them in contact with patients who may be unstable or otherwise under significant stress. Employers of nurses may be liable for violence against their nurse employees, just as they may be liable for the workplace injuries of other employees.[61] Depending on the applicable state law and the facts of the case, an injured nurse's recovery against the employer may be through workers' compensation (plus whatever insurance and disability benefits may be available).

PROBLEMS ASSOCIATED WITH OFF-SITE NURSING

Nursing practice today is not limited to the hospitals, medical offices, or other facilities where the nurse is actually employed. Nurses are more and more called upon to travel and to provide care at off-site locations, such as their patients' homes, assisted-living facilities, hospices, etc.

One of the primary challenges of this kind of nursing practice is discharging the basic standard-of-care obligation to keep the patients' physicians informed about their conditions. Obviously, the possibility of miscommunication or of no communication is much greater where the nurse divides time among many patients in different locations and, because of this dispersal, is not in regular face-to-face contact with the patients' physicians. But communication is just one concern. Before assigning nurses to relatively unsupervised duties, employers must be certain of their overall competence and judgment. When an employer fails to do so, it may be held liable not just under *respondeat superior* for the nurse's malpractice, but for its own negligence under a theory such as negligent hiring, retention, or training.

Nontraditional nursing also multiplies the potential liability for torts not directly related to patient treatment. For example, nurses who travel among patients are probably more likely to be involved in traffic accidents within the course and scope of their employment than nurses who generally work at one fixed location. Applicable state law may allow injured persons to hold nurses' employers liable for such course-and-scope accidents.

NURSING LICENSURE

States regulate nurses by legislating the requirements for getting and keeping a license to practice.[62] These regulations vary from state to state, so a nurse must be familiar with the requirements in the state(s) where he or she practices. License requirements cannot violate state and federal constitutional requirements. For example, a state probably could not make getting a nursing license significantly harder for out-of-state nurses solely for the purpose of preserving nursing jobs for current state residents. A state also probably could not enact a license revocation procedure that did not provide any procedural standards or any opportunity for appeal.

In the absence of such constitutional problems, federal law has very little to say about nursing licensure. However, federal law may affect a nurse's employability with an employer that receives federal funds. For example, federal law requires that nursing care in a skilled nursing facility "must meet professional standards of quality."[63] In a similar vein, federal law provides that home health agencies shall employ only those who meet competency standards established by the federal Department of Health and Human Services and who are actually competent to serve patients.[64]

Federal courts provide an unlikely forum for seeking damages where a nurse believes that a state wrongly revoked[65] his or her license. In *O'Neal v. Mississippi Board of Nursing*,[66] two Mississippi nurses unsuccessfully sued state board members under federal law for wrongly revoking their licenses. The board revoked their licenses for false or negligent record-keeping. Mississippi state law allowed the nurses to appeal the board's decision to the state courts. The first-level state court affirmed the board's revocation, but the second-level state court reversed and restored the nurses' licenses.

With their licenses restored, the nurses then sued in federal court, alleging that the board's mistake in revoking their licenses amounted to a violation of constitutional rights. They sued both the board itself and individual board members. The district court dismissed the claims against all defendants and the Fifth Circuit affirmed. It concluded that suing the board itself was equivalent to suing the state in federal court, which the Eleventh Amendment to the Constitution prohibited. It also concluded that board members could not be held liable because of the doctrine of absolute quasijudicial immunity. This doctrine immunizes public officials when they act in the role of judges or prosecutors, which is how the court held the board members acted when they decided that the evidence warranted revocation of the nurses' licenses (even though the decision was ultimately found to be wrong).[67]

ENDNOTES

1. An excellent book-length treatment of legal issues facing nurses is Marcia Andrews, Kathy Goldberg & Howard Kaplan, eds., *Nurse's Legal Handbook*, 4th ed. (Springhouse, 2000).
2. "Unless the actor is a child, the standard of conduct to which he must conform to avoid being negligent is that of a reasonable man under like circumstances." Restatement (Second) of Torts §283 (1965).
3. Steven E. Pegalis & Harvey F. Wachsman, *American Law of Medical Malpractice*, 2d ed., §2:10, at 71-72 (Clark Boardman Callaghan, 1992) (footnote omitted).
4. *King v. Dep't of Health & Hospitals*, 728 So. 2d 1027, 1030 (La. Ct. App.) (emphases added), *writ denied*, 741 So. 2d 656 (La. 1999).

5. "[P]olicy and procedure manuals are hospital-specific and can be viewed as setting the standard of care for that institution." *Mills v. Angel*, 995 S.W. 2d 262, 269 n.25 (Tex. Ct. App. 1999). In *HCA Health Services v. National Bank*, 745 S.W. 2d 120 (Ark. 1988), the Arkansas Supreme Court held that the trial court erred in dismissing negligence claims against two nurses. The evidence showed that the patient, a day-old infant, suffered cardiac and respiratory arrest in a hospital nursery that the nurses had failed to staff according to hospital policy. The policy required at least one nurse in every room of the three-room nursery and could have been complied with if the nurses on duty had moved all the babies into one room. As they did not, the infant was in a room that was not attended.

6. "[T]he hospital and its employees have a duty to follow the orders of an attending physician. . . ." *Berdyck v. Shinde*, 613 N.E. 2d 1014, 1023 (Ohio 1993).

7. Fed. R. Evid. Ann. 702 (West, 2001).

8. Tasking a general RN to function as a nurse anesthetist might itself be negligence, but it would be chargeable to the person responsible for not having a CRNA available, not to the nurse.

9. American Association of Nurse Anesthetists, Scope and Standards for Nurse Anesthesia Practice, at http:www.aana.com/crna/prof/scope.asp (last visited Dec. 5, 2002); American Association of Nurse Anesthetists, Standards for Office-Based Anesthesia Practice, at http:www.aana.com/crna.prof/obstandards.asp (last visited Dec. 5, 2002).

10. *See, e.g.*, Pegalis, *supra* note 3, §6.14, at 290.

11. 536 So. 2d 1374, 1376 (Ala. 1988).

12. 218 N.W. 2d 514 (Wis. 1974).

13. *Mosey*, 218 N.W. 2d at 519.

14. "The fact that a 'conspiracy of silence' in the plaintiff's locality could effectively preclude a possibility of obtaining expert medical testimony has been cited as a basis to abolish the 'locality rule' applicable to medical specialties." Pegalis, *supra* note 3, §2:10, at 71-72 (footnote omitted).

15. 408 S.E. 2d 490 (Ga. Ct. App. 1991).

16. *Ross*, 408 S.E. 2d at 493.

17. *Miles v. Box Butte County*, 489 N.W. 2d 829, 839 (Neb. 1992).

18. 270 S.E. 2d 222 (Ga. 1980).

19. *Berdyck v. Shinde*, 613 N.E. 2d 1014, 1024 (Ohio 1993) (emphasis added).

20. *Cf. Warthen v. Toms River Comm. Mem. Hosp.*, 488 A. 2d 229 (N.J. Super. Ct. App. Div. 1985) (nurse who not only questioned but also refused to provide certain treatment was lawfully fired).

21. *Berdyck*, 613 N.E. 2d at 1022.

22. 489 N.W. 2d 829 (Neb. 1992).

23. *Miles*, 489 N.W. 2d at 839.

24. 57 Cal. Rptr. 906 (Cal. Dist. Ct. App. 1967).

25. 668 So. 2d 469 (La. Ct. App. 1996).

26. *Merritt*, 668 So. 2d at 473, 478.

27. *Miles v. Box Butte County*, 489 N.W. 2d 829, 839 (Neb. 1992).

28. *See also Landry v. Clement*, 711 So. 2d 820 (La. Ct. App. 1998), where the nurses failed to inform the physician of decelerations in the fetal heart rate. The failure to do so effectively misrepresented the patient's condition and possibly contributed to the physician's failure to review the tracings.

29. 613 N.E. 2d 1014, 1024 (Ohio 1993).

30. *Robbins v. Jewish Hosp. of St. Louis*, 663 S.W. 2d 341, 346 (Mo. Ct. App. 1983) (nurse recognized that patient should not get out of bed without assistance, but failed to implement that insight by raising bed rails).

31. *Cf. Simon v. N.Y. Univ. Med. Ctr.*, 700 N.Y.S. 2d 31 (N.Y. Ct. App. Div. 1999) (without any indication that the patient was fatigued or unsteady, the nurse did not violate any standard of care in leaving him unattended once he was seated on the toilet).

32. 725 N.Y.S. 2d 35 (N.Y. Ct. App. Div. 2001).

33. *Thomas*, 725 N.Y.S. 2d at 36.

34. *Parker v. Port Huron Hosp.*, 105 N.W. 2d 1 (Mich. 1960).

35. *Redding v. United States*, 196 F.Supp. 871 (W.D. Ark. 1961); *Berg v. New York Soc. for Relief of the Ruptured and Crippled*, 136 N.E. 2d 523 (N.Y. 1956) (medical technician's error).

36. *Parker v. St. Paul Fire & Marine Ins. Co.*, 335 So. 2d 725 (La. Ct. App.), *writ denied*, 338 So. 2d 700 (La. 1976); *Kyte v. McMillion*, 259 A. 2d 532 (Md. 1969).

37. *National Homeopathic Hosp. v. Phillips*, 181 F. 2d 293 (D.C. Cir. 1950); *Ward v. Orange Mem. Hosp. Ass'n, Inc.*, 193 So. 2d 492 (Fla. Dist. Ct. App. 1966).

38. Restatement (Second) of Agency §§219, 243, 245 (1958).

39. *Ewing v. Aubert*, 532 So. 2d 876, 880 (La. Ct. App. 1988) (emphasis added).

40. "A person whose liability is imputed based on the tortious acts of another is liable for the entire share of comparative responsibility assigned to the other. . . ." Restatement (Third) Apportionment of Liability §13 (2000).

41. *See generally* Thomas M. Fleming, Annotation, *Hospital's Liability for Injury Resulting from Failure to Have Sufficient Number of Nurses on Duty*, 2 A.L.R. 5th 286 (1992 & Supp. 2002).

42. 745 S.W. 2d 120 (Ark. 1988).

43. *HCA Health Services*, 745 S.W. 2d at 125. *See also Merritt v. Karcioglu*, 668 So. 2d 469 (La. Ct. App. 1996) ("the jury could have concluded that Tulane was negligent in understaffing the ward and in requiring [the nurse] . . . to be in two places at the same time").

44. 711 So. 2d 820 (La. Ct. App. 1998).

45. *Landry*, 711 So. 2d at 834.

46. The borrowing physician, meanwhile, is said to be the "captain of the ship." Pegalis, *supra* note 3, §3:14, at 178.

47. 986 F. 2d 119 (5th Cir. 1993).

48. *Hunnicut*, 986 F. 2d at 123.

49. 315 So. 2d 516 (Fla. Dist. Ct. App. 1975).

50. 42 U.S.C.A. §11101 (1995). The statutes setting up the NPDB are codified at 42 U.S.C.A. §§11101-11152 (1995); NPDB regulations are at 45 C.F.R. §§60.1-60.14 (2002).

51. 42 U.S.C.A. §11131 (1995).

52. 42 U.S.C.A. §11137(d) (1995); 45 C.F.R. §60.7(d) (2002).

53. 42 U.S.C.A. §11137(a) (1995).

54. For assistance with a self-query, call the NPDB Help Line during normal business hours at (800) 767-6732.

55. 42 U.S.C.A. §11136(2) (1995); 45 C.F.R. 60.14 (2002).

56. 477 A. 2d 323 (N.J. 1984).

57. *Winter*, 477 A. 2d at 324.

58. 821 S.W. 2d 83 (Ky. 1991).

59. *Rodebush v. Oklahoma Nursing Homes, Ltd.*, 867 P. 2d 1241 (Okla. 1993).

60. 40 F. 2d 252 (8th Cir. 1994).

61. *See generally* Wade R. Habeeb, Annotation, *Liability of Hospital for Injury Caused through Assault by a Patient*, 48 A.L.R. 3d 1288 (1973 & Supp. 2002).

62. *Semler v. Oregon State Bd. of Dental Examiners*, 294 U.S. 608, 611 (1935).

63. 42 U.S.C.A. §1395i-3(b)(4)(A) (West 1992 & Supp. 2002).

64. 42 U.S.C.A. §1395bbb(a)(3)(A) (West 1992 & Supp. 2002).

65. *See generally* Emile F. Short, Annotation, *Revocation of Nurse's License to Practice Profession*, 55 A.L.R. 3d 1141 (1974 & Supp. 2002).

66. 113 F. 3d 62 (5th Cir. 1997).

67. Absolute quasi-judicial immunity also protected medical board members in *Watts v. Burkhart*, 978 F. 2d 269 (6th Cir. 1992); *Bettencourt v. Bd. of Registration in Medicine of the Commonwealth of Massachusetts*, 904 F. 2d 772 (1st Cir. 1990); and *Horwitz v. State Bd. of Medical Examiners of the State of Colorado*, 822 F. 2d 1508 (10th Cir.), *cert. denied*, 484 U.S. 964 (1987).

48 Dental Litigation: Triad of Concerns

BRUCE H. SEIDBERG, D.D.S., M.Sc.D., J.D., D.A.B.E., F.A.C.D., F.P.F.A., F.A.A.H.D., F.C.L.M.

STANDARD OF CARE
COMMON LITIGATION AREAS
TRIAD OF CONCERNS
EMERGENCY CARE
ADDITIONAL AREAS OF CONCERN
CONCLUSION

Local dental societies, dental districts, and dental peer review committees have seen an increase in the number of complaints about dentists.[1] The National Society of Dental Practitioners[2] has identified 12 bases for dental malpractice claims (Box 48-1). To minimize the liability risk, dentists must communicate properly and keep good dental records. Dentists must improve the cooperation amongst members of the dental team, generalists and specialists, and improve the trust and satisfaction of patients and their families (Boxes 48-2 and 48-3).

STANDARD OF CARE

Standard of care is defined as the reasonable care and diligence ordinarily exercised by similar members of the profession in similar cases and like conditions, given due regard for the state of the art. Initially an analysis of local community standards was implied. A dentist was held liable only for the level of competence, concern, and compassion that society would expect of the average dentist in the community in which that dentist practiced. James and co-workers[3] defined the legal concept of standard of care from a community standard to a national standard. Curley[4] also addressed the definitions of standard of care. Today the dentist must meet the national standard because several courts have found that the conduct of a specialist should be measured against national standards of care.[5]

The ethical basis of standard of care is beneficence (i.e., to recommend the best therapy while minimizing potential harm and to avoid placing a patient in a situation in which there is an unreasonable risk of harm).[6] General practitioners are required to exercise the same degree of care and skill as a specialist acting in the same or similar circumstances, locality notwithstanding. In *Taylor v. Robbins*[7] the dentist failed to use accepted treatment techniques, and in *Perry*[8] the locality rule was nullified when sufficient foundation was recognized that the local and national standards did not differ.

COMMON LITIGATION AREAS

The scope of dental litigation touches every phase of dentistry, some more than others (Table 48-1). Common reasons for litigation include, but are not limited to, failure to refer to a specialist; failure to diagnose and treat periodontal disease; dissatisfaction with prosthetics; endodontic failures and mishaps; extraction errors, including the extraction of the wrong tooth; implant failure; adverse consequences, such as paresthesia; temporomandibular dysfunction; poor crown margins; failure to pretreat the patient with antibiotics when medically necessary; failure to obtain the patient's medical history; writing an improper prescription; child abuse; sexual harassment; and inappropriate use of intravenous sedation (Box 48-4).

In a 1994 study by Beckman,[9] 54% of plaintiffs who settled malpractice suits filed between 1985 and 1987 indicated that another health care provider suggested maloccurrence. In addition, 71% identified problematic doctor-patient relationships (DPRs). A poor interpersonal relationship with a patient usually is the result of communication barriers set up by the dentist's staff or by office policy. Markus[10] and Dorn[11] address methods for handling disputes between dentist and patient. Both authors suggest that conflicts must be understood, escalation checked, and resolution skills developed.

TRIAD OF CONCERNS

Doctor-patient relationship

The DPR is a fiduciary relationship in which mutual trust and confidence are essential.[12] Any time a professional gives advice or expresses an opinion to a patient, duties are incurred. When there is no contact and the involvement is limited to a simple observation regarding the patient, with limited suggestions being offered, no direct duty to the patient is assumed.[13] The relationship is based on contract

---

BOX 48-1. **TWELVE WAYS TO GET SUED**

1. Neglect to pay a fee.
2. Refuse to negotiate the return of a fee.
3. Guarantee or promise a result.
4. Exceed your level of competencies.
5. Fail to obtain informed consent.
6. Be inaccessible to a patient with complaints.
7. Be unavailable, or fail to provide coverage for patients of record.
8. Fail to refer.
9. Fail to diagnose or treat a pathological condition.
10. Fail to prescribe or prescribe incorrect medications.
11. Fail to meet a reasonable standard of care.
12. Make treatment errors (e.g., treat the wrong tooth).

From National Society of Dental Practitioners, 12; 4; 97.

BOX 48-2. **HOW TO AVOID LAWSUITS**

Be professional and courteous.

Keep good, accurate records.

Communicate with patients and colleagues, especially those who are confused or unsure.

Obtain adequate informed consent.

Predict an appropriate prognosis.

Do not be egotistical about second opinion diagnoses.

Do not be greedy (i.e., do not overbill).

BOX 48-3. **HOW TO APPROACH A DENTAL MALPRACTICE CASE**

Do not try to settle the matter on your own.

Do not discuss the case with colleagues.

Do not be short-changed by your defense counsel.

Do not be your own private detective.

Do not rely on hold-harmless agreements.

Do not alter records.

Treat patients who have a need; do not treat patients to satisfy greed.

Learn from the experience.

Modified from Edwin Zinman, *What to Do When a Patient Plans to Sue,* Dent. Mgm't. 32-35 (March 1986).

BOX 48-4. **SPECIAL TYPES OF DENTAL NEGLIGENCE**

Abandonment

Failure to refer

Failure to obtain informed consent

Failure to warn

Failure to follow a manufacturer's directions

TABLE 48-1 Claim data from various insurance sources

Procedure	Claims (%)
Endodontics	15-25
Extraction, simple	12-15
Crown/bridge work	15-20
Fixed partial denture	8-15
Routine dental care	8-17
Extraction, surgical	8-12
Removable partial dentures	3-8
Comprehensive orthodontics	3-8
Complete dentures	3-8
Periodontics	5-12
Paresthesia	8-12
Other (e.g., failure to refer, failure to diagnose, implant failures, temporomandibular joint pain, failure to give a patient with subacute bacterial endocarditis antibiotics)	3-15

---

law, with rights and obligations affecting all concerned. The fiduciary principle relates to the fact that the dentist has knowledge and skill based on which the patient entrusts his or her care. It promotes open disclosure of all specifics and encourages the free flow of information between the individuals. The mutuality of contract principle originates when a patient requests services and the dentist agrees to render the services. Consideration, usually in the form of a professional fee, binds the contract. In most cases gratuitous treatment and advice can establish a relationship and invoke all the duties of that relationship. No money has to change hands. Once the relationship begins, the patient is endowed with various rights that include but are not limited to freedom from bodily harm, the right to choose and consent to treatment, the right to refuse treatment, and the right to privacy and confidentiality. To reduce the liability risk, the dentist must strive to improve cooperation between members of the health care team, which includes staff and prior and subsequent caregivers. The dentist also must endeavor to improve the trust and satisfaction of their patients and their families. Once the relationship begins, a series of communication skills must be practiced: a proper history is taken, the case is presented, informed consent is obtained, referrals are made if necessary, and the patient is told what to expect.

The relationship can be terminated without incurring liability for abandonment only if the patient withdraws from treatment voluntarily, the patient no longer requires care, or the provider is unable or unwilling to provide continued care and gives reasonable notice to the patient. Failure to

Date
Patient's Name
Address

Dear_____,
I will no longer be able to provide dental care to (you/your children). If (you/your children) require dental care within the next_____days, I will be available, but in no event will I be available after _____, 2001.

To assist (you/your children) in continuing to receive dental care, I will make records available as soon as you authorize me to send them to another dentist.

Sincerely,

Dentist's Name

Fig. 48-1. Sample letter of withdrawal.

terminate the professional relationship in an appropriate manner can lead to legal action for abandonment. For example, if improper unilateral termination of the DPR by the practitioner occurs at a time when there is a need for continuing care, abandonment may be alleged. Before termination of care for a patient, a dentist must ensure that the patient is not in the middle of a procedure. Whatever treatment has been started must be completed and emergent care must be provided for a reasonable time. See Figs. 48-1 and 48-2 for sample letters.

Date
Patient's Name
Address

Dear_____,
This letter will confirm our conversation of today in which you discharged me as your dentist. In my opinion your condition requires continued dental care. If you have not already done so, I suggest that you employ another dentist without delay.

You can be assured that, at your request, I will furnish the dentist you select with information or copies of your records regarding the diagnosis and treatment that you have received from me.

Very truly yours,

Dentist's Name

Fig. 48-2. Sample letter confirming patient termination of relationship.

BOX 48-5. **PRINCIPAL LEGAL DUTIES OF DENTISTS**

Duty to care
Duty to inform
Duty to maintain confidentiality
Duty to maintain accurate records

Good communication with a patient usually ensures a relationship without conflict. Staff members must be taught how to communicate with a patient without suggesting that any previous treatments were questionable, poor, or improper (Box 48-5).

Informed consent

In the past, patients possessed full confidence in treatments provided by doctors. Smith[14] reviewed current literature from various sources to develop a general sense and understanding of informed consent. He found that the doctrine of informed consent had significantly influenced relationships among health care practitioners and their patients in the last 25 years. He also identified an erosion of the paternalistic approach leading to an increase in patient sovereignty and decision-making. The approach now must be the sharing of information that patients want to know.

The foundation of modern-day informed consent was established by Judge Cordozo in 1914 in the case of *Schloendorff v. Society of New York Hospitals*, when he said, "every human being of adult years and sound mind has the right to determine what shall be done with his own body." The standard for informed consent was established in *Canterbury v. Spence* in 1972. The reasonable person (patient) must have disclosed to them what a practitioner knows, or should know, about the risks for the treatment proposed, allowing a reasonable and intelligent informed decision to be made. There must be explanation to the patient, including enough information for the patient to understand the nature and extent of the treatment, the alternatives, consequences, risks, and effects. The patient must also be informed of the risks if the recommended treatments are not followed. The elements of consent evolving from various court decisions that every health care provider must be knowledgeable of, and of their application, include but are not limited to: a diagnosis in layman's language explaining the nature of the problem and proposed treatment; feasible alternative treatments; and the expected prognosis if treatment is or is not provided.

Consent, therefore, is an ongoing dialogue between the health provider and the patient in which both parties exchange information, ask questions, and come to an agreement on the course of specific dental/medical treatments. When the patient agrees on a specific course of treatment, the dialogue has reached its goal; however, the dialogue does not end there.

BOX 48-6. ELEMENTS OF AN INFORMED CONSENT LAWSUIT THAT COULD CONSTITUTE NEGLIGENCE

1. A patient-physician relationship is proved to have existed.
2. The provider had a duty to disclose information.
3. There was a failure to provide information.
4. If the information had been supplied, the patient would not have consented to treatment.
5. Failure to disclose was the proximal cause of the plaintiff's injury and damages claimed.

Consent and communication about the process of obtaining consent are not limited to obtaining permission for treatment. It continues throughout the course of treatment and alterations of the course of treatment, during follow-up evaluations, and as unexpected results or procedural mishaps occur. It must occur between the person who will perform the procedures and the recipient patient, especially for any invasive procedure. Staffs do not harbor the authority to obtain consent. The provider has a responsibility to assess each clinical situation and patient need to determine the scope of disclosure.

A patient who is not properly informed is likely to launch subsequent litigation over undisclosed complications that develop. An informed consent lawsuit assumes that a doctor-patient relationship exists, there was a failure by the doctor to provide information, and that had the doctor provided the patient with the undisclosed information, the patient would not have consented to the treatment. The doctor's failure to disclose the information must be the proximate cause of the plaintiff's injury and damages claimed (Box 48-6).

The patient's signing documents does not replace the process of the dentist obtaining informed consent; it only serves to memorialize the process. It is appropriate for the

---

BOX 48-7. BASIC ELEMENTS OF CONSENT

1. Date and time of the consent process.
2. Diagnosis in layman's language explaining the problem.
3. Nature and purpose of proposed treatment in language understandable by the patient.
4. Explanation of risks and consequences.
5. Probability of success.
6. Feasible alternative treatments.
7. Expected prognosis if treatments are not accepted.
8. Statement that patient was given the opportunity to ask questions or that the patient's questions have been answered.
9. Signature of patient or legal guardian and a witness.
10. Signature of the health provider.

---

provider to present the facts, follow the elements of the process, and conclude with the patient signing a form acknowledging the process (Box 48-7).

Documentation

"From the facts, the issues arise. Without the facts, there are no issues." This maxim essentially states that, if nothing has been written, there are no facts, and therefore it is considered that nothing has been done. Patient records are considered legal documents, as well as business records. It is the presumption in law that all entries are accurate, are truthful, and were entered in a timely manner.

A dentist's written records can be his or her best friend or worst enemy. If subpoenaed, the records continue to testify long after the dentist has gone. The records end up in the jury room, where the jurors can review them more carefully than the testimony heard on the witness stand. They serve to record prior history, diagnosis, and therapies rendered. They provide continuity between providers (generalists and specialists, partners in group practices, and interested third parties). They also allow transfer of vital information when a patient changes dental providers.

There are many facets of a dental record.[15,16] Aside from containing the patient's demographics and personal identification information, the record should include a current and thorough medical questionnaire. There also must be a current dental history; notations of a complete oral, head, and neck examination; documentation of diagnostic tests and results; a memorialization document of informed consent; and notes regarding any changes in the treatment plan. In addition, copies of letters, laboratory reports, and termination of care documents and notes regarding telephone calls, questions, complaints, pharmacy prescriptions and refills, and canceled or missed appointments are part of the dental record. Diagnostic evidence, such as radiographs, photographs, and study models, are other integral parts of a dental record (Box 48-8).

Reviewing the medical history with the patient is just as important as disclosing information during the informed consent dialogue. At this point in the examination or consultation the dentist can determine whether any of the patient's medical conditions would interfere with or impact dental care. In the event that there is a question about an entry on the medical record or a medication the patient is taking, the dentist is obligated to consult the patient's physician before commencing with treatment.[17] It is important to receive instructions from the patient's physician regarding the use of premedication antibiotics and/or anticoagulant therapy prior to proceeding with dental treatment.

Records should be well written, legible, and accurate. There should be no words inappropriately scratched out, no words covered with correction fluid or tape, and absolutely no improper alteration in any form. Any inappropriate alteration

---

BOX 48-8. UNIVERSALLY ACCEPTED RECORD-KEEPING FORMAT: SOAP

Subjective data

This section of the record contains the patient's chief complaint or complaints. It should state how the patient says he or she feels, what his or her symptoms are, and what specifically has resulted in this visit to the dental office.

Objective findings

What does the dentist observe, see, or find in examination of a patient? This area involves the critical clinical examination and all of the diagnostic tests and results.

Assessment

Taking into consideration all of the comments made by the patient and all that he or she has observed, the dentist makes an assessment of the patient. The subjective and objective data guide the provider's diagnostic and treatment thought process.

Plans

The thought process materializes in this section, and a treatment plan is determined. When presentation of this plan is prepared for the patient, there should be an ideal treatment plan and a secondary treatment plan that would work well for the patient. Often, secondary plans are chosen because of economic issues. Patients also prefer to make choices.

---

is frowned upon and is detrimental to the dentist's credibility. Spoliation[18] is the premature destruction or loss of records which can impair the patient's ability to prove negligence or other tortious conduct in a malpractice lawsuit against the provider. In such a claim, the court may instruct the jury that had the records actually existed and been produced, they would have proved the fact favorable to the plaintiff.

The dentist has custodial rights to the record; the patient has proprietary rights. Records cannot be withheld from patients for any reason when they are requested; however, only copies should be provided. The dentist should receive a proper authorization before releasing copies of records. The dentist must never part with the original dental records or any of the original components. Most states allow a minimum fee per page for copies; however, records cannot be withheld from the patient for payment of a dental bill.

EMERGENCY CARE

Every office must establish a policy for handling emergency calls during and after office hours. When a patient or potential patient telephones the office and speaks with the dentist or a staff member, certain information, such as the medical history, premedical requirements, and nature of the complaint, must be gathered. Emergency services, specifically for patients of record, are the responsibility of the dental practitioner, and thus the office must have a policy. Every dentist must have at least an answering service, answering machine, a mechanism of reachability, and available coverage. Every dental practitioner must be available for, and must respond to, the emergent needs of patients of record in a timely manner. Before prescribing any medication, over the counter or prescription, the dentist must be familiar with the patient and his or her medical history.

ADDITIONAL AREAS OF CONCERN

False claim acts (fraud)

False claim acts involve a claim for compensation by a federal government agency that is fraudulent. The areas of concern are improper coding or upcoding, double billing, billing for services not yet rendered (phantom billing), improper unbundling or bundling of services, waiver of deductibles and/or co-insurance, and the alteration or destruction of records.

Dental areas of consideration

General dentistry. The dentist should provide the patient with treatment options and should not try to "sell" a specific treatment plan; he or she should explain the plan in layman's terms so that the patient comprehends the proposal. Consent should be obtained for every procedure to be done but is specifically important for invasive procedures. During efforts at restoration, the dentist must be observant to avoid overhanging margins, poor reconstruction, an overbite or underbite, and improper post insertions. Other litigation concerns for general dentists are the failure to diagnose periodontal disease, endodontic problems, or cancerous and other medical conditions. Failure to refer to a specialist when necessary is also actionable.

Periodontics. Gingival health, retaining dentition, and cosmetics are goals of periodontal care. There are periodontal procedures that will alter the gingival appearance, hence lengthening teeth and affecting cosmetics and function. If such alterations become a necessity, the patient must be informed before treatment. The patient must participate in discussions about the treatment plan, clearly understand the periodontist's goal, and recognize that he or she must comply with good oral hygiene or the goal cannot be accomplished. At times periodontal care involves the cooperation of other dental specialists, as well as the general dentist. Paresthesia is a concern but not as much as in other phases of dentistry. Periodontists are now included in the team of specialists who place implants and they must specifically describe all aspects of implantology to the patient.

Oral and maxillofacial surgery. Common areas of lawsuits regarding surgery pertain to the extraction of the wrong tooth. Although the oral surgeon receives a prescription for a service to be rendered, the onus is on the oral surgeon to ensure that the diagnosis is correct and that the patient understands which tooth will be extracted before performing the procedure. After an extraction, unforeseen circumstances, such as dry sockets or sinus involvement, could present. Root tips can be left behind, jaws fractured, and foreign bodies aspirated. These possibilities should be discussed as potential risks before the procedure is performed. Paresthesia is a common basis for litigation. Some procedures are more difficult than others and can place stress on the jaw structures, causing trismus, temporomandibular joint dysfunction, or both. Failure to biopsy, diagnose suspicious areas with appropriate follow-up care, and inform patients accordingly have led to litigation. Patients are knowledgeable that dentists (doctors of the oral cavity) are usually first in line to diagnose cancerous lesions of the mouth.

Implantology. Patient selection, implant selection, and implant team member selection are of utmost importance in this area of dentistry. Expectations should be discussed and no guarantees made. Strict informed consent procedures must be adhered to so that all of the known risks are outlined for the patient, and team records must be accurate and consistent. Patients must understand that they have to comply with all instructions given by the implant team. Possible concerns include sinus perforations, mandibular canal perforations, and paresthesia. The patient should be told how much time and commitment are involved with this procedure, the potential longevity of the effect, and the prognosis.

Endodontics. Endodontic procedures can be successful in more than 98% of cases when the condition is properly treated, the restoration of the tooth is appropriate, and the tooth is periodontally sound. Yet, problems and mishaps occur in endodontic therapy. The root canal system anatomy varies from tooth to tooth and patient to patient. Many patients' root canal systems are tortuous, narrow, and constricted or calcified. With newer techniques including microscopes, enhanced vision aids, light sources, and instrumentation, the ease of endodontic therapy has

increased. However, difficulties (usually related to the anatomy and chronological age of the teeth and the more heavily restored and involved teeth) are encountered in many cases. Endodontic fills that extend beyond the anatomical apex of a tooth have been criticized and been the subject of litigation; these fills must be determined as to the extent of three-dimensional sealing capabilities. The material used must be of accepted tolerances. Irrigating solutions that may escape through any of the portals of exit within the anatomical structures have also been implicated in malpractice lawsuits. Perforations of tooth structure in the chamber or root surfaces, the sinus, and the mandibular canal are not uncommon in the challenged anatomy. It is best for an endodontist to prepare a post space within the anatomy of a canal. When the restorative dentist does not follow the path of canal anatomy in preparation for the post placement, failure can follow; however, an altered path is not necessarily negligence. Other concerns in endodontic care are crown and bridge fractures occurring during access preparations, paresthesia, instrument breakage, and the swallowing of instruments if the proper rubber shield is not used.

Fixed prosthetics. Fixed prosthetics are more commonly referred to as *crowns* and *bridges*. Considerations in this area of dentistry include improper margin adaptation, unrealistic cosmetic expectations, occlusal problems, and retention problems. Before preparing and treating teeth by applying fixed prosthetics, the practitioner should perform a complete endodontic and periodontal examination and be comfortable with the status of each. Litigation has resulted from cases in which teeth with evidence of existing periapical pathology have been restored. Once crowns and bridges have been permanently cemented, endodontic therapy and periodontal therapy are possible but much more difficult. After the recent cementation of crowns, periodontal treatment risks the exposure of root structure. In addition, endodontic treatment performed after a final cementation can cause alteration or breakage of the crown, the bridge, or even the abutment.

Removable prosthetics. The most common concern among patients with removable or partially removable prosthetics (dentures) is a poor fit, which usually results from loss of bony ridge structure and poor impression techniques. In patients with removable partial dentures, poor fit can be a result of poorly designed rest areas and clasps. Improper stress on abutments can cause endodontic and periodontal pathology. Additional concerns in this area of dentistry are the mobility of abutments, failure to meet the cosmetic expectations of a patient, temporomandibular joint involvement, and defects of various products.

Orthodontics. Orthodontics used to be for the young, but now increased attention is paid to adult orthodontics aimed at correcting patients' cosmetic defects. Orthodontics deals with improving jaw development and ensuring appropriate occlusal contact. Some of the problems in this area are failure to meet the patient's cosmetic expectations, external apical root resorption, internal resorption, root canal system calcifications, temporomandibular joint problems, injury associated with the appliances, and untoward facial changes.

Pedodontics. Children are sometimes difficult to treat. Some methods of physical restraint can be construed as child abuse. Problems arise due to the patient's age and behavioral problems. Additional difficulties involve improper parental consent to various treatments and the tendency for young patients to neglect oral hygiene.

Paresthesia. Paresthesia is in a category of its own because it can result from any invasive procedure in oral surgery, endodontics, periodontics, or implantation. It can result from a poorly directed mandibular inferior alveolar nerve injection, improper surgical flapping of tissue in the mandible, involvement of the mental nerve, third molar extraction, or recklessness of care. Nerves commonly involved are the inferior alveolar nerve, lingual nerve, chorda tympani nerve, and mental nerve, as well as the peripheral sensory nerve branches. Paresthesia can involve the lower lip, a portion of the tongue, and the chin. It also can cause diminished taste and slurred speech. The dentist should be acutely aware of this possibility because paresthesia can be a temporary and transient situation or a permanent situation. The practitioner should discuss this risk with the patient before discussing the invasiveness of a procedure. Corrective treatment should be recommended when necessary. The patient should be afforded all means of communication, and all conversations and recommendations should be accurately recorded in the dental record.

Additional issues. Failure to recognize medical problems; improper use of nitrous oxide; failure to diagnose[19] and refer; complications with anesthesia; failure to recognize the depressed patient's normal functions during treatment; and improperly monitoring and charting bodily functions, such as blood pressure, cardiac function, and respiration when necessary, also can lead to lawsuits.

CONCLUSION

When all risks are considered in dentistry, most are rare and are not a basis for negligence legal actions. Good communication, obtaining appropriate informed consent for treatment, and keeping accurate and appropriate dental records are the dentist's best preventions and defenses. Included is a list of case citations and references supporting this thesis.

ENDNOTES

1. New York State Education Department, *Disciplinary Cases for Dentistry from 1994-1997* (New York State Education Department, Albany, NY).

2. Burton Pollack, *Risk Management Newsletter* (National Society of Dental Practitioners 1999-2000).

3. A.E. James, S. Perry, R.M. Zaner, J.E. Chapman & T. Calvani, *The Changing Concept of Standard of Care and the Development of Medical Imaging Technology*, 7 Humane Medicine (Oct. 1991).

4. Arthur Curley, *Standard of Care Definition Varies*, 53 J. Am. Coll. Dent. (Fall 1986).

5. R. Shandell & P. Smith, *Standard of Care: The Preparation and Trial of Medical Malpractice Cases*, 1.01 Law J. Press (2000); *Advincula v. United Blood Services*, 176 Ill. 2d 1, 678 N.E. 2d 1009, 1018 (1996).

6. Bruce Weinstein, *Ethics and Its Role in Dentistry*, Gen. Dentistry (Sept./Oct. 1992).

7. *Taylor v. Robbins,* Tex., Harris County 281st Judicial District, No. 85-28095 (May 4, 1988).

8. *Perry v. Magic Valley Regional Medical Center*, Idaho Supreme Court, opinion No. 13 (Feb. 28, 2000).

9. Beckman, *Doctor-Patient Relationship and Malpractice*, 154 Arch. Med. 1365 (1994).

10. L. Markus, AMA News (Mar. 2, 1992).

11. B. Dorn, AMA News (Mar. 2, 1992).

12. F. Buckner, *The Physician-Patient Relationship*, Med. Pract. Mgmt. (Sept./Oct. 1994).

13. ACLM, *Liability Arising from Consultation*, 8 Med. Leg. Lessons (June 2000).

14. T.J. Smith, *Informed Consent Doctrine in Dental Practice: A Current Case Review*, 1 J. Law and Ethics in Dent. (1988)

15. *Morgan v. Olds*, 417 N.W. 2d 232, 235 (Iowa 1987).

16. P.J. Oberbreckling, *The Components of Quality Dental Records*, Dent. Econ. (May 1993).

17. P.G. Stimson & L.A. George, *How to Practice Defensive Dentistry*, 61 J. Greater Houston Dent. Soc. (March 1990).

18. F. Buckner, *Spoliation of Evidence: The Destruction, Alteration, or Loss of Medical Records*, Med. Pract. Mgmt. (Sept./Oct. 1993).

19. R. Shandell & P. Smith, *Failure to Diagnose: The Preparation and Trial of Medical Malpractice Cases*, 1.01 Law J. Press (2000), *St. George v. Pariser*, 253 Va. 329, 484 S.E. 2d 888, 891 (1997).

RELATED CASE CITATIONS

ATLA, *Case Summary Survey 1986-1991*, Professional Negligence Law Reporter.

Avgerakis v. Sweet, Middlesex County, N.J., Docket No. L787293, Jury Verdict Review Dental Liability Alert 6:3 (Nov. 2002).

Brimm v. Malloy, Mich., Oakland County Circuit Court, No. 85 298 750 NO (Aug. 5, 1987) (orthodontics, improper use of dental appliances).

Campbell v. Virginia Park Dental Ctr., Mich., Wayne County Circuit Court, No. 90-004143-NH (Aug. 1, 1991) (wrongful death).

Canterbury v. Spence, 464 F. 2d 722 (D.C. Cir., 1972), *cert. denied*, 409 U.S. 1064 (1974).

Chang v. Frigeri, 76 A.D. 2d 643.

Coert v. Ryan, Wis., Milwaukee County Circuit Court, No. 657-296 (July 1, 1987) (informed consent, failure to consider alternatives).

D'Amour v. Board of Registration in Dentistry, 567 N.E. 2d 1226 (Mass. Sup. Jud. Ct., Mar. 19, 1991). Dentist's license was suspended for gross misconduct (taking nude photographs of a patient in the name of science); the decision was remanded for reconsideration. The dentist contended that there was a relationship between temporomandibular joint pain and scoliosis.

Dillard v. MacGregor Dental Centers, Inc., Tex., Harris County 127th Judicial District Court, No. 85-50994 (July 14, 1987) (paresthesia, general dentistry, wisdom teeth extraction).

German v. Nichopoulos, 577 S.W. 2d 197 (Tenn. Ct. of App.) (requires disclosure to patient regarding the risks incident to a proposed diagnosis for treatment).

Ginsburg v. Golden, Md., Health Cl. Arbitration, No. 93-107 (Feb. 25, 1994) (orthodontics, failure to diagnose root resorption).

Graddy v. New York Medical College, 19 A.D. 2d 426.

Harrison v. Bradley, Md., Health Claims Arbitration No. 84-498 (Mar. 13, 1986) (orthodontics, failure to x-ray).

Isaksen v. Protopappas, Cal., Orange County Superior Court, No. 40-28-06 (June 20, 1986) (medical history, wrongful death).

Johnson v. International Dental, Ariz., Pima County Superior Court, No. 227157 (Apr. 10, 1987) (paresthesia, wisdom tooth removal).

Kavanaugh v. Nussbaum, 71 N.Y. 2d 535.

Koslowski v. Sanchez, La., East Baton Rouge Parish District Court, No. 313, 459, Div. "B" (Nov. 11, 1988) (paresthesia, Sargenti paste).

James Lantier, *Vicarious Responsibility*, personal correspondence.

Limongelli v. State Board of Dentistry, 616 A. 2d 945 (N.J. Superior Ct., Dec. 1, 1992).

McCormack v. Gerren, N.Y., Albany County Supreme Court, No. 1454-86 (Apr. 13, 1988) (improperly fitting dentures).

McGrath v. State Board of Dentistry, No. 25 C.D. 1993, Pennsylvania Commonwealth Court (Oct. 19, 1993). Pennsylvania appeals court upholds license suspension of dentist convicted of Medicaid fraud.

Moore v. Curry, 577 So. 2d 824 (La. Ct. of App., Apr. 3, 1991). Dentist found not negligent in failing to diagnose ameloblastoma.

Morgan v. MacPhail, Pa. Lexis 2739 (Dec. 24, 1997). Informed consent doctrine applies to surgical procedures alone; courts maintain the surgical/nonsurgical distinction for informed consent.

Nathanson v. Kline, 186 Kan. 393, 350 P. 2d 1093 (1960).

Ong v. Department of Professional Regulation, 565 So. 2d 1384 (Fla. Dist. Ct. of App., Aug. 23, 1990). Dentist reprimanded, fined, and given a 90-day license suspension for negligent treatment of a patient's chronic periodontitis.

Pady v Shannahan, Bergen County, N.J., Docket No. L1160291, Jury Verdict Review, Dental Liability Alert 6:3 (Nov. 2002).

Pasquale v. Siegel, N.Y., Queens County Supreme Court, No. 15103/86 (Mar. 19, 1990) (failure to give antibiotics, subacute bacterial endocarditis).

Pastorelli v. Saltzman, N.Y., Queens County Supreme Court, No. 14620/80 (June 27, 1991) (delayed diagnosis of cancer).

Pelnar v. Neumeier, Mich., Menominee County Circuit Court, No. 86 4472 CZ (Nov. 13, 1989) (failure to diagnose, periodontics).

Puglissi v. Klein, U.S. District Court, D. Del, No. 88-481-JJF (Sept. 19, 1989) (failure to diagnose: decay).

Ross v. Fulp, Bucks County, P., Case No. 94-10069-0902, Jury Verdict Review, Dental Liability Alert 6:3 (Nov. 2002).

Schloendorff v. Society of New York Hospital, 105 N.E. 92 (N.Y. 1914).

Bruce H. Seidberg, *Case Summaries* (personal files of dental-legal consultant), Mediation Committee, Onondaga County Dental Society.

Simpson v. Davis, Kansas Supreme Court, 549 P. 2d 950 (endodontics, swallowed instrument, deviation of standard of care).

St. Paul Fire & Marine Ins. Co. v. Shernow, 610 A. 2d 1281 (Conn. 1992) (sexual abuse).

State: Dental Rings Defrauded Medicaid, Robert, LaMendola, Florida Sun Sentinel (Sept. 1, 2002).

VanTreese v. Whitcomb, U.S. District Court, E. D. Mich., No. G88-629-CA7 (Oct. 22, 1990) (failure to refer).

Walter v. Smith, Mo., Jackson County Circuit Court, No. CV-89-23467 (Oct. 26, 1992) (fraud to patient).

Woitalewicz v. Wyatt, Neb., Hall County District Court, No. 86-152 (Sept. 13, 1986) (oral surgery, osteomyelitis).

REFERENCES

A. Bernstein, *Avoiding Medical Malpractice* (Pluribus Press, Chicago 1991).

W. Harold Bigham, *A Lawyer's View of the Legal Implications of Periodontal Disease Recognition*, J. Tenn. Dent. Assoc. (Apr. 1985).

Sherry Case, *Terminating the Doctor-Patient Relationship*, N.Y. State Dent. J. 18-19 (Apr. 1993).

Bruce R. Donoff, *Dentists as Physicians of the Mouth*, 125 J.A.D.A. 20-25 (Jan. 1994).

F. Edwards, *Medical Malpractice* (Henry Holt, New York 1989).

W.W. Feuer, *Medical Malpractice Law* (Lawprep, Irvine, Calif. 1990).

R.M. Fish, M.E. Ehrhardt & B. Fish, *Malpractice Managing Your Defense* (Medical Economics, Oradel, N.J. 1990).

D. Foreman, *Dental Law* (Directed Media 1990).

D. Foreman, *How to Become an Expert Witness* (Directed Media, 1989).

B. Friedland, *Physician-Patient Confidentiality*, 15 J. Legal Med. 249-277.

Paul Gerber, *Can Your Records Withstand the Malpractice Test?* Dent. Mgmt. (Apr. 1985).

Albert Good, *Statute of Limitations in Dental Malpractice Actions*, LIX W. Va. Dent. J. (Jan. 1985) (limitation period does not begin to run until the patient knows or has reason to know of the malpractice).

H.B. Jacobs, *The Spectre of Malpractice* (Medical Quality Foundation 1988).

H.B. Jacobs, *Understanding Medical Malpractice and Maximizing Recovery in All Medical Malpractice and Personal Injury Cases* (Medical Quality Foundation 1988).

J.H. King, *The Law of Medical Malpractice in a Nutshell* (West Publishing, St. Paul, Minn. 1986).

M.D. McCafferty & S.M. Meyer, *Medical Malpractice: Bases of Liability* (Shepard's/McGraw-Hill, Colorado Springs, Colo. 1987).

W.O. Morris, *A Lawyer's View as to How A Dentist Can Keep His House in Order*, 72 N.W. Dent. 45-48 (Sept./Oct. 1993).

Elliott B. Oppenheim, *Presenting an Objective Standard of Care in Med-Mal Litigation*, Med. Malp. Law & Strategy 4-6 (Feb. 1998).

B.R. Pollack, *Handbook of Dental Jurisprudence and Risk Management* (PSG Publishing, Littleton, Mass. 1987).

D. Poynter, *The Expert Witness Handbook* (Para Publishing 1987).

Prosser, *The Law of Torts* §§18, 32 (5th ed. 1984).

F. Rozovsky, *Consent to Treatment* (Little Brown, Boston 1990).

N. Schafler, *Medical Malpractice Handling of Dental Cases* (Shepard's/McGraw-Hill, Colorado Springs, Colo. 1991).

Julian Steiner, *The Dental Malpractice Crisis: What It Means for the Dental Assistant*, 55 Dent. Assist. (Mar./Apr. 1986) (record-keeping accuracy and confidentiality, physician-patient relationship, vicarious decisions and treatment recommendations by the dental assistant).

49 Criminalization of Medical Negligence

JAMES A. FILKINS, M.D., J.D., Ph.D., F.C.L.M.

THE DIFFERENCES BETWEEN CIVIL NEGLIGENCE AND CRIMINAL NEGLIGENCE
THE FLAW IN THE CURRENT APPROACH TO PROSECUTING CRIMINAL MEDICAL
   NEGLIGENCE
PATTERNS OF CONDUCT ASSOCIATED WITH PROSECUTIONS FOR MEDICAL
   NEGLIGENCE
RECOMMENDATIONS
CONCLUSION

Although the criminal prosecution of physicians for medical negligence remains relatively rare, the incidence of such prosecutions has been increasing for nearly a decade. In 1990, the American Medical Association (AMA), commenting upon the dismissal of criminal charges against a Pennsylvania surgeon for medical negligence, noted that the prosecution of physicians for clinical mistakes was "almost unknown."[1] Just 3 years later, the prosecutions of several physicians for medical negligence led the AMA to adopt a resolution at its interim meeting "to insure that medical decision making, exercised in good faith, does not become a violation of criminal law."[2] In 1995 the AMA adopted a more sharply worded resolution opposing the "attempted criminalization of health care decision-making, especially as represented by the current trend toward criminalization of malpractice. . . ."[3] At the time of the 1995 resolution, the AMA estimated that only about 10 physicians nationwide had been prosecuted for medical negligence,[4] but the organization feared the beginning of a trend leading to increasing numbers of physician prosecutions.[5]

The AMA's fears could prove well founded. On November 29, 1999 the Institute of Medicine for the National Academy of Sciences (NAS) issued a report, *To Err Is Human*, estimating that medical errors cause between 44,000 and 98,000 deaths each year.[6] The newspaper *USA Today* put the numbers in perspective by declaring in a front-page headline "Medical Mistakes 8th Top Killer."[7] On

December 7, 1999, President Clinton publicly embraced the report and ordered a task force to report to him within 60 days on plans to improve patient safety.[8] That same day Senator Edward Kennedy of Massachusetts announced that he would introduce a bill in Congress to put the report's recommendations into effect.[9]

Recent prosecutions have, predictably, engendered a certain degree of controversy.[10] Although the AMA cited the NAS report with approval,[11] AMA spokesperson Nancy Dickey, M.D., stated in January 2000 that "[t]he matter of accountability for negligent or incompetent actions is already established in our health care and judicial systems. State and Federal courts, state licensing boards, and accrediting bodies all maintain accountability and standards."[12] Recent criminal prosecutions of physicians for medical negligence, however, suggest that the "matter of accountability" is far from settled. Many commentators agree that an increasing number of physicians are being prosecuted for clinical mistakes, but explain the trend by pointing to the medical profession's failure to police itself by, for example, failing to revoke the licenses of incompetent physicians.[13] Others blame managed care and the loss of more personal physician-patient relationships for the trend.[14] Still others comment that, with the loss of public respect for physicians, there is less reluctance to demand severe penalties when bad outcomes do occur.[15]

Whatever the explanation, the criminal prosecution of physicians for medical negligence is nothing new.[16] Nor are the legal theories on which these prosecutions are based particularly novel. The prosecution of physicians for medical negligence occurs within a well-settled legal framework that resolves, albeit imperfectly at times, guilt for all matters of reckless or negligent criminal acts—without specifying *medically* reckless or negligent conduct. To the

The opinions expressed in this chapter are those of the author alone and do not necessarily reflect the opinions of the Department of Law of the City of Chicago or the Office of the Medical Examiner of Cook County, Illinois. The author also wishes to express his deep appreciation to Judith Ann Gic, R.N., C.R.N.A., J.D., F.C.L.M., for her contributions to this chapter.

extent that certain physicians may appear to have been singled out unfairly, the blame lies with the individual prosecutors and not with the laws they seek to enforce.

This chapter identifies the factors that tend to bring about criminal prosecutions for medical negligence and which, in turn, result in convictions following trial. Although a bad outcome is always at the core of any criminal prosecution for medical negligence, even an unconscionably bad outcome is insufficient to explain by itself the successful prosecution of some medically negligent acts. Certain patterns of conduct appear more commonly associated with criminal prosecutions for medical negligence. By avoiding these patterns of conduct, physicians can reduce the likelihood that they will become defendants in a criminal prosecution.

Additionally, the elements of standard of care and causation become problematic because they should first be established much as they would in any civil lawsuit for medical malpractice. Logically, if there is no departure from the standard of care or if causation cannot be established, then there can be no prima facie criminal case that will satisfy the requirements of due process.[17] Nevertheless, successful criminal prosecutions of medical negligence have taken place in the absence of any clearly defined standard of care or established causation.[18] Accordingly, this chapter recommends that screening panels similar to those employed in civil medical malpractice litigation be used to assure that prosecutors have objective medical advice before bringing an indictment.

THE DIFFERENCES BETWEEN CIVIL NEGLIGENCE AND CRIMINAL NEGLIGENCE

Medical negligence defined

Medical negligence is an act or omission by a physician rendered in the course of treating a patient, which is the cause in fact of harm to the patient and which fails to meet the appropriate standard of care, but which is rendered without any deliberate intent to injure the patient.[19] This definition obviously excludes cases in which a physician uses medical treatment to mask a deliberate injury to the patient.[20] If the physician is to be found liable for a negligent act, causation and a deviation from the standard of care must be proven. Causation, or cause in fact, means the "particular cause which produces an event and without which the event would not have occurred."[21] Standard of care is "the degree of care which a reasonably prudent person should exercise in same or similar circumstances."[22]

Recognizing criminal medical negligence

Gross deviation from the standard of care. Criminal negligence requires a more serious deviation from the standard of care than does ordinary civil negligence. Typically, criminal negligence requires some gross or flagrant deviation from the standard of care.[23] The determination of whether a physician's conduct deviated from the standard of care, and if so, whether that deviation amounted to a gross deviation, is made by reference to an external or objective standard. As the jurist Oliver Wendell Holmes explained, "If a physician is not less liable for reckless conduct than other people, it is clear . . . that the recklessness of the criminal no less than that of the civil law must be tested by what we have called an external standard."[24] A physician's failure to foresee consequences contrary to those the physician intended is "immaterial, if, under the circumstances known to him, the court or jury, as the case might be, thought them obvious."[25] In other words, a jury should look to what it believes a reasonable physician would have done under the same or similar circumstances.[26]

A culpable state of mind. A criminally culpable state of mind, that is, *mens rea*, is an element of most criminal acts, including criminal medical negligence.[27] The physician guilty of criminal medical negligence must not only have committed a gross deviation from the standard of care, but must have done so with a criminally culpable state of mind. Section 2.02 of the Model Penal Code identifies four criminally culpable states of mind: "purposely," "knowingly," "recklessly," and "negligently."[28] The latter two states of mind—recklessly and negligently—are the *mens rea* applicable in the criminal prosecution of medical negligence. Confusion sometimes arises because courts in different jurisdictions use terms such as "criminal negligence," "gross negligence," and "recklessness" more or less interchangeably.[29]

Although this chapter will use criminal negligence to embrace both criminal negligence and criminal recklessness, the distinction between the two lies not in the degree of the defendant's deviation from the standard of care—it is a gross deviation in either case—but in the defendant's state of mind.[30] Criminal negligence is the disregard of a substantial and unjustifiable risk of which the defendant *should have been aware*, but was not.[31] Criminal recklessness is the disregard of a substantial and unjustifiable risk *of which the defendant was aware*.[32] Criminal recklessness requires the defendant to be subjectively at fault. The defendant must have known that he or she was taking a substantial and unjustifiable risk, but consciously ignored the risk and continued the dangerous conduct.[33] In criminal negligence, the defendant's risk-taking is merely inadvertent.[34]

In neither situation does the physician intend deliberately to cause harm. The AMA has indicated a willingness to accept recklessness as a basis for criminal liability, as well as purposeful misconduct and criminal intent, but not negligence.[35] Although this position is consistent with the opinions of those commentators who oppose any criminal liability for negligent conduct,[36] there is no reason for a jurisdiction that has enacted negligence as a basis for criminal liability to create a special exemption for medical professionals.[37]

THE FLAW IN THE CURRENT APPROACH TO PROSECUTING CRIMINAL MEDICAL NEGLIGENCE

The flaw in the current approach to prosecuting criminal medical negligence lies in the difficulty in establishing causation and the standard of care, especially when complex medical issues are involved. The accused physician's intention, his state of mind—rather than causation or the degree of any deviation from the standard of care—often becomes the touchstone against which the jury evaluates any acts or omissions in deciding whether the defendant physician's conduct rises to the level of a criminal offense. It is often easier for the jury in a criminal prosecution for medical negligence to put the cart before the horse and to decide that the negligence in question actually amounted to a criminal act when the jury has first decided that the defendant physician possessed a culpable state of mind. Rather than wrestle with causation and standard of care, the jury may simply adopt the expedient, noted by one British commentator, of asking, in effect: "Did the accused Give a Damn?"[38]

This approach may be appropriate in distinguishing criminal recklessness from criminal negligence once a gross deviation from the standard of care has been established because the distinction between the two offenses lies in the defendant's state of mind. Such an approach as a means of distinguishing *civil* negligence from *criminal* negligence risks doing substantial injustice to the accused because the threshold questions of causation and standard of care are bypassed. If the defendant physician's conduct suggests to the jury that the accused was irresponsible or indifferent, then the physician may be found guilty even if the prosecution fails to establish causation or the standard of care.[39] Additionally, the acts or omissions that lead the jury to infer criminal intent may be distinct in time or place from the acts or omissions that directly caused the injury to the patient. The jury will sometimes take a broad view of any other acts or omissions relevant to the defendant physician's medical practice to establish a pattern of conduct from which a culpable state of mind may be inferred.

PATTERNS OF CONDUCT ASSOCIATED WITH PROSECUTIONS FOR MEDICAL NEGLIGENCE

Table 49-1 identifies 13 cases since 1976 in which a physician was prosecuted for medical negligence.[40] Additionally, there is one case in which a corporation was prosecuted[41] and two that prompted investigations, although criminal charges were never filed.[42] An examination of these cases suggests that certain patterns of conduct may be more likely to lead to criminal prosecutions for medical negligence and to result in convictions. Evidence of any of these patterns of conduct may tempt the jury to skip over the more difficult and more aggressively disputed issues of causation and standard of care and to equate a culpable state of mind with criminal negligence. These patterns are summarized in Table 49-2 and discussed briefly below.

Disregarding past experience

In these cases, the jury found a culpable state of mind existed and convicted the defendant physician because he had ignored *repetitions of the same problem* with the same or different patients. The jury was able to avoid the complexities of causation or standard of care by concluding that the defendant physician had sufficient knowledge based on his previous experience of the problem to have known the problem would cause danger, but the physician ignored the danger.

TABLE 49-1 Recent prosecutions of medical negligence

Defendant	Jurisdiction	Charge	Trial date	Verdict	Appellate decision
Benjamin	New York	2nd degree murder	1995	Guilty	Upheld
Billig	Military	2nd degree murder	1985	Guilty	Reversed
Biskind	Arizona	Manslaughter	2001	Guilty	Upheld
Chavis	California	N/A	N/A	N/A	N/A
Chem-Bio	Wisconsin	Reckless homicide	1995	*Nolo contendere*	N/A
Einaugler	New York	Reckless endangerment	1993	Guilty	Upheld
Klvana	California	2nd degree murder	1989	Guilty	Upheld
Matory	California	N/A	N/A	N/A	N/A
Naramore	Kansas	1st degree murder; attempted murder	1996	Guilty	Reversed
Pignataro	New York	Negligent homicide	1998	Guilty plea	N/A
Schug	California	2nd degree murder	1998	Dismissal by court	N/A
Steir	California	2nd degree murder	2000	Guilty plea	N/A
Verbrugge	Colorado	Reckless manslaughter	1995	Not guilty	N/A
Warden	Utah	Negligent homicide	1988	Guilty	Upheld
Wood	Oklahoma (federal)	1st degree murder	1998	Guilty	Reversed and remanded
Youngkin	Pennsylvania	Involuntary manslaughter	1977	Guilty	Upheld

TABLE 49-2 Culpable acts

Defendant	Culpable act	Disregarding past experience	Failing to limit harm	Improper motive
			Patterns of conduct	
Benjamin	Perforated uterus		×	×
Billig	Coronary artery bypass	×		
Biskind	Perforated uterus		×	
Chavis	Outpatient liposuction		×	×
Chem-Bio	Misread pap smears			×
Einaugler	Misplaced feeding tube		×	
Klvana	Mismanaged deliveries	×	×	×
Matory	Outpatient liposuction		×	×
Naramore	Improper administration of medications			×
Pignataro	Outpatient breast reduction		×	×
Schug	Sent ill patient to another hospital		×	
Steir	Perforated uterus		×	×
Verbrugge	Slept during anesthesia	×		
Warden	Failed to follow up on home delivery		×	×
Wood	Improper administration of medications			×
Youngkin	Barbiturate prescription	×		

Failing to limit harm in a timely manner

In these examples, the jury concluded that the defendant physician possessed a culpable state of mind and convicted because the physician failed to act in a timely fashion to limit the danger to the patient. The failure to act, not the initial negligence, was the decisive issue. This is the most commonly encountered pattern associated with criminal prosecutions for medical negligence.

The appearance of improper motive

Finally, the appearance of any improper motive in the defendant physician's conduct will enable the jury more readily to find a culpable mental state. Practicing medicine in defiance of license restrictions, practicing outside of one's area of expertise, or practicing in a manner that suggests more interest in financial gains than patient well-being are common examples.

RECOMMENDATIONS

Avoiding a criminal prosecution for medical negligence

Practice medicine conscientiously. The physician who wishes to avoid becoming a defendant in a criminal prosecution for medical negligence should observe the old adage, "first do no harm." Physicians should be aware that certain patterns or practices are more likely to lead to criminal prosecutions and convictions for medical negligence. A physician should scrupulously comply with any restrictions that have been imposed on his or her license to practice medicine. Even if a physician has no license restrictions, or complies with any restrictions that have been imposed, the physician must be careful not to exceed his or her expertise. A physician qualified to practice in one area of medicine may not be qualified to perform procedures in other areas of medicine. A physician qualified to practice in a specialty may not be qualified to treat every patient whose presenting complaint falls within that specialty or to perform every procedure that another physician certified in that specialty might be qualified to perform. Any tendency to practice outside of the scope of one's specialty or to treat problems beyond one's expertise should be strictly avoided, particularly if the work appears to be undertaken more for financial gain than patient welfare. The failure to follow up appropriately on one's patients figures prominently in many criminal prosecutions for medical negligence. The physician who fails to follow up conscientiously on his or her patients risks being viewed as a physician who should be punished when something goes wrong, regardless of issues of causation and standard of care.

Avoid inadequate resources. Settings in which the available medical resources are inadequate to meet reasonably foreseeable emergencies impose a further hazard. As more physicians perform surgeries or other invasive procedures away from hospitals—ostensibly as a means of reducing health care costs and providing medical care to underserved areas—criminal prosecutions for medical negligence may increase. The physician whose office or clinic lacks the equipment to handle cardiopulmonary arrest, acute bleeding, or other complications that can precipitously arise during an invasive procedure risks becoming a defendant in a criminal prosecution should something go wrong. The inadequacy of the resources makes the occurrence of a negligent act more likely, while exposing the physician to blame for having failed to anticipate and to prepare for the problem in the first place. Outpatient abortions or the delivery of infants at home or in a clinic may place the patient at a significant risk of harm if something goes wrong, although the risk may not become apparent until the problem arises. Outpatient cosmetic surgery is another example of this problem.[43]

Pre-indictment screening panels

Most states require some form of screening by physicians before a medical malpractice case can be filed in court.[44] States also usually require that a claim of medical malpractice be proven through expert medical testimony.[45] These mechanisms safeguard the defendant in a civil medical malpractice case from lay juries that are unqualified to evaluate complex issues of patient care. Obviously, physicians who are charged with criminal medical negligence should be charged carefully and only when there is evidence to support both a gross deviation from the standard of care and the requisite state of mind. Accordingly, requiring prosecutors to present their cases to a medical review panel before obtaining an indictment would reduce the likelihood of unmeritorious prosecutions for criminal medical negligence.[46] Prosecutors would have to convince the panel of the merits of a particular case and, in turn, would receive the panel's expert medical opinion regarding the potential defendant's deviation from the standard of care and whether the acts in question were the cause in fact of harm to the patient.[47] Pre-indictment screening panels would also help prevent criticism that certain prosecutions are politically motivated.[48]

CONCLUSION

Criminal prosecutions of physicians for medical negligence will likely continue to increase. The legal framework underlying prosecution for criminally negligent or reckless acts is well established. Logically, there is no reason why physicians or other health care professionals should be exempt from liability for medically reckless or negligent acts. Physicians themselves can do much to reduce their chances of becoming defendants in a criminal prosecution by avoiding certain practices. To ensure that only meritorious prosecutions of physicians for medical negligence are brought, causation and a breach of the standard of care must first be established just as they would in any civil proceeding for medical malpractice. If the physician's actions did not cause the harm to the patient or did not breach the standard of care, then the physician cannot have committed medical negligence, let alone criminal medical negligence. Much greater attention should be given by all concerned—prosecutors, defense attorneys, judges, and juries—to the fundamental issues of causation and standard of care. To this end, prosecutors should be required to present cases of criminal medical negligence to medical screening panels, similar to those used in civil medical malpractice cases, before obtaining an indictment. Only if the defendant physician's actions are shown to be the cause of the patient's harm, and only if the physician's actions in causing that harm breached the standard of care, is an indictment for criminal medical negligence appropriate.

ENDNOTES

1. *Pennsylvania Prosecutor Finds No Grounds for Charges Against Surgeon*, Am. Med. News (June 1, 1990) at 5.
2. Morton M. Kurtz, M.D., Criminalization of Medical Judgment, Resolution 223, Proceedings of the American Medical Association, Interim Meeting (Dec. 1993).
3. Criminalization of Health Care Decision-Making, Resolution 202, Proceedings of the American Medical Association (June 1995).
4. *Criminal-Negligence Charges Rarely Filed Against Doctors*, Seattle Times (Jan. 15, 1998) at A14 (citing the AMA).
5. Jodie Snyder, *When Doctors Bury Mistakes, Criminal Charges May Follow*, Ariz. Rep. (Dec. 15, 1998) at A1.
6. Robert Pear, *Group Asking U.S. for New Vigilance in Patient Safety*, N.Y. Times (Nov. 30, 1999) at A1.
7. Bob Davis & Julie Appleby, *Medical Mistakes 8th Top Killer*, USA Today (Nov. 30, 1999) at 1.
8. *Moving Fast on Patient Safety*, N.Y. Times (Dec. 8, 1999) at A30.
9. *Id.*
10. *See, e.g.*, Alexander McCall Smith, *Criminal or Merely Human? The Prosecution of Negligent Doctors*, 12 J. Contemp. Health L. & Pol'y 131 (Fall 1995); Paul R. Van Grunsven, *Medical Malpractice or Criminal Mistake? An Analysis of Past and Current Criminal Prosecutions for Clinical Mistakes and Fatal Errors*, 2 DePaul J. Health Care L. 1 (Fall 1997); Kara M. McCarthy, *Doing Time for Clinical Crime: The Prosecution of Incompetent Physicians as an Additional Mechanism to Assure Quality Health Care*, 28 Seton Hall L. Rev. 569 (1997); James A. Filkins, *"With No Evil Intent": The Criminal Prosecution of Physicians for Medical Negligence*, 22 J. Legal Med. 467 (Dec. 2001).
11. Nancy W. Dickey, M.D., *AMA on Improving Patient Safety*, AMA Statement (Nov. 30, 1999).
12. Nancy W. Dickey, M.D., *Creating a Culture of Patient Safety*, AMA Statement (Jan. 26, 2000).
13. Thomas Maier, *More Doctors Face Prosecution: Crimes Charged in Cases of Deadly Error*, Newsday (Apr. 18, 1995) at A35.
14. *Malpractice or Homicide?*, Wash. Post (Apr. 18, 1995) at A16.
15. *Id.*
16. The earliest example of a criminal prosecution for medical negligence in the United States identified in the course of research for this chapter was *Massachusetts v. Thompson*, 6 Mass. 134, 1809 W.L. 1120 (Mass. 1809).
17. *Utah v. Warden*, 813 P. 2d 1146, 1154 (Utah 1991) (Stewart, J. dissenting). If there is competent conflicting expert testimony that the defendant physician's actions were medically appropriate, then arguably there should be reasonable doubt. *See also Kansas v. Naramore*, 965 P. 2d 211, 223-24 (Kans. Ct. App. 1998).
18. *See, e.g., United States v. Billig*, 26 M.J. 744 (1988).
19. *See, e.g., Black's Law Dictionary* 959 (6th ed. 1990) ("Failure of one rendering professional services to exercise that degree of skill and learning commonly applied under all the circumstances in the community by the average prudent reputable member of the profession with the result of injury, loss or damage to the recipient of those services . . . ").

20. *See, e.g.*, James B. Stewart, *Blind Eye* (1999) (examining the case of Michael Swango, M.D., who allegedly poisoned his patients with arsenic).

21. *Black's Law Dictionary* 221 (6th ed. 1990).

22. *Id.* at 1404-05.

23. Joshua Dressler, *Understanding Criminal Law* 113, 116 (2d ed. 1995).

24. *Massachusetts v. Pierce*, 138 Mass. 165; 1884 W.L. 6544, at *9 (Mass. 1884).

25. *Id.* at *10.

26. Dressler, *supra* note 23, at 115.

27. *See id.* at 101-03.

28. 1 Model Penal Code & Commentaries §2.02 (1985). *See also* Dressler, *supra* note 23, at 105-17 *passim*.

29. Dressler, *supra* note 23, at 113.

30. *Id.* at 116.

31. *Id.* at 113, 116.

32. *Id.* at 116.

33. *Id.*

34. *Id.*

35. *See* Judith Ann Gic, R.N., C.R.N.A., J.D., F.C.L.M., "The Criminalization of Medical Malpractice," Presentation to the American College of Legal Medicine (Mar. 9, 2002).

36. Dressler, *supra* note 23, at 113-14.

37. Gic, *supra* note 35.

38. Paul Monks, *Frankly My Dear, I Don't Give a Damn*, 36 Med., Sci. & Law 185 (July 1996). The criminal prosecution of physicians for medical negligence is not unique to the United States. *See, e.g., Regina v. Adomako*, 3 All E.R. 79 (H.L. 1994) (a notable case from Great Britain).

39. For example, the Court of Military Review in *United States v. Billig* observed that the prosecution "[i]n an attempt to establish the necessary element of culpable negligence in the involuntary manslaughter specifications" introduced "evidence . . . which essentially amounted to a smear campaign to portray Dr. Billig as a bungling, one-eyed surgeon who should have known better than even to enter an operating room because of his past mistakes and poor eyesight." 26 M.J. at 758. The review court noted, however, that the standard of care controlling Dr. Billig's conduct remained "elusive" and "nebulous." *Id.* at 759.

40. *See, e.g., New York v. Benjamin*, 705 N.Y.S. 2d 386 (N.Y. App. Div. 2000); *United States v. Billig*, 26 M.J. 744 (1988); Susie Steckner & Jodie Snyder, *Biskind Charged with Manslaughter*, Arizona Republic (Jan. 13, 1999); *New York v. Einaugler*, 618 N.Y.S. 2d 414 (N.Y. App. Div. 1994); *California v. Klvana*, 15 Cal. Rptr. 512 (Cal. App. 1992); *Kansas v. Naramore*, 965 P. 2d 211 (Kan. App. 1998); Dave Condren, Buff. News (Aug. 7, 1998) at C1 (Pignataro); Linda O. Prager, *Keep-*

ing Clinical Errors out of Criminal Courts, Am. Med. News (Mar. 16, 1998) (Schug); Raymond Smith, *Doctors on Trial*, The Press-Enterprise (Riverside, Cal.) (Feb. 1, 1998) at A1 (Steir); *Colorado v. Verbrugge*, No. 98 C.A. 0262, 1999 W.L. 417965 (Colo. App. June 24, 1999); *Utah v. Warden*, 813 P. 2d 1146 (Utah 1991); *United States v. Wood*, 207 F. 3d 1222 (10th Cir. 2000); *Pennsylvania v. Youngkin*, 427 A. 2d 1356 (Pa. Super. Ct. 1981).

41. David Doege, *Laboratory to Pay $20,000 Fine*, Milw. J. Sentinel (Feb. 23, 1996) at 1A (Chem-Bio).

42. Julie Marquis, *Medical Board Forms Panel to Probe Cosmetic Surgery*, L.A. Times (July 31, 1997), at A12 (Chavis and Matory).

43. Dr. Patrick Chavis, a Los Angeles, California, area obstetrician/gynecologist, had his license suspended as the result of his negligent care of three liposuction patients, one of whom died. Julie Marquis, *Doctor's License is Suspended*, L.A. Times (June 20, 1997), at B1. The Chavis case, along with the death of another liposuction patient who died after 11 hours of liposuction surgery performed by Dr. W. Earle Matory, prompted the California Medical Board to investigate the practice of cosmetic surgery in California. Marquis, *supra* note 42, at A12. Although no criminal prosecution followed the actions of Dr. Chavis or Dr. Matory, Dr. Anthony Pignataro was not so fortunate. In 1998, Dr. Pignataro, a Buffalo, New York, plastic surgeon, pled guilty to criminally negligent homicide in causing the death of his patient, Sarah Smith. Dave Condren, Buff. News (Aug. 7, 1998), at C1. Mrs. Smith, 26, suffered a fatal heart attack while undergoing breast enlargement surgery in Dr. Pignataro's office. *Id.* The court sentenced Dr. Pignataro to 6 months in jail, a $5000 fine, 250 hours of community service, and 5 years probation. *Id.*

44. In Illinois, for example, in a civil action for medical negligence, an affidavit must be filed with the complaint certifying the plaintiff or plaintiff's attorney has conferred with a health professional who has reviewed the relevant medical records and has determined in a written report that there is a "reasonable and meritorious cause" for filing the action. 735 ILCS 5/2-622 (2000).

45. Illinois, for example, has long required standard of care in a medical negligence lawsuit to be established by expert medical testimony. *See Ritchey v. West*, 23 Ill. 329 (1860); and more recently, *Higgins v. House*, 288 Ill. App. 3d 543 (4th Dist. 1997). The same is true of causation. *See Moline v. Christie*, 180 Ill. App. 334 (1913); *St. Gemme v. Tomlin*, 118 Ill. App. 3d 766 (4th Dist. 1983).

46. *See* Gic, *supra* note 35, at 15 (citing Linda O. Prager, *Keeping Clinical Errors Out of Criminal Courts*, Am. Med. News, Mar. 16, 1998).

47. *Naramore*, 965 P. 2d at 225 (Brazil, C.J. dissenting). This would require a legislative act in most jurisdictions. *Id.*

48. Gic, *supra* note 35, at 15.

Crimes by Health Care Providers

STAN TWARDY, J.D., LL.M.

UNDERSTANDING CRIMINAL LAW
FRAUD
CRIMES AGAINST THE PERSON

UNDERSTANDING CRIMINAL LAW

Modern criminal law recognizes two major classes of crimes and a number of miscellaneous offenses and violations. By definition a *felony* is a crime punishable by imprisonment for 1 year or more. Felonies include crimes such as murder (e.g., unauthorized withdrawal of a comatose patient's life support), manslaughter, rape, robbery, larceny, kidnaping, arson, burglary, most narcotics and insurance frauds, and sex with a minor. Misdemeanors are crimes that are punished with imprisonment of no more than 1 year. The term *misdemeanor* is applied to the widest range of criminal activity and includes the broadest gradation of offenses and degrees of unpermitted activity (e.g., failure to report child abuse, refusal to allow patients to examine and copy their medical records, willful disclosure of health care information to unauthorized people). Another category of criminal and quasicriminal offenses—both felonies and misdemeanors—are the so-called strict liability offenses. The major significance of such offenses is that certain defenses, such as mistakes, are generally unavailable. These are usually offenses that are part of regulatory schemes (e.g., practicing medicine or nursing without a license, writing prescriptions without a valid registration from the Drug Enforcement Agency [DEA] or narcotics license from the state).

In the health care field, federal and state agencies, under delegation from Congress or state legislatures, have created a multitude of rules and regulations, the violation of which may be punishable as a crime. These rules and regulations include the DEA's wide-ranging regulations on the licensing and the supervision of prescribing, storing, and dispensing controlled substances; IRS regulations; and various regulations by the health departments, including reporting requirements of certain contagious diseases. Violations of these regulations may be enforced either criminally or administratively by revocation of licenses and heavy fines. In most states there is a third category of offenses and violations, or *prohibited acts*, as they are sometimes called. These acts, although technically crimes, are so minor in nature that the law refuses to classify them as misdemeanors. These include a host of activities such as violating minor traffic laws, allowing dogs to be unleashed, spitting in public, and littering.

The defendant is found guilty when each and every element of the crime prescribed by the legislature and the culpability of the suspect is proved beyond a reasonable doubt to the trier of facts: a jury, judge, or both. At trial the accused may (1) plead guilty, thus obviating the need for an actual trial; (2) plead not guilty and be tried; or (3) plead *nolo contendere* (meaning, "I will not contest the charges"), which although not a guilty plea, is a tacit confession of guilt.

Essential elements of a crime

The essential elements of a crime are (1) intent (*mens rea*) and (2) the act (*actus reus*). To constitute a crime, the act must be volitional, and the intent must be to accomplish the criminal purpose. In the case of misdemeanor offenses and violations the law does not always inquire whether the criminal intent was present. (For example, the traffic court judge does not inquire into the intent of a person who went through a red light, failed to stop at a stop sign, or made a left turn without signaling.) However, "pulling the plug" on a patient without complying with living will and other statutes, presupposes the intent to kill combined with an act to further that purpose. For misdemeanors and petty offenses the element of intent is not normally a consideration. Lack of intent is not a defense for the category of crimes committed while the defendant was intoxicated or under the influence of drugs. The law takes the position that such acts are voluntary and that a misconduct in such a state is predictable; therefore criminal liability should be attached.

Vicarious liability

The physician may be vicariously liable for the acts of his or her employees when allowing them unsupervised access to controlled substances, when allowing them to call in

503

prescriptions without consulting him or her, or when inducing, encouraging, or ordering them to fill out fraudulent insurance claims or commit other criminal acts. Secretaries and bookkeepers often have been prosecuted as accomplices for helping falsify billing records or as accessories after the fact for helping cover up Medicare frauds. The accessory after the fact is treated differently and is not liable for acts performed before his or her involvement. However, when threatened with criminal prosecution, office workers almost invariably make deals with prosecutors. They are either not prosecuted or plead to lesser offenses in exchange for providing testimony against the physician. Such former employees are often the most devastating witnesses against physicians, clinics, and hospitals.

Accessory after the fact

An accessory after the fact is anyone who renders assistance to a felon after an offense has been committed, even though the accessory had no prior knowledge of the commission of the crime. In Medicare and insurance fraud cases, this often involves helping falsify or destroy medical and/or billing records. In modern American jurisprudence, failure to report a felony generally no longer makes one an accessory after the fact.

Conspiracy

Conspiracy is a separate and distinct crime from the substantive criminal acts committed pursuant to the plan. Conspiracy consists merely of an agreement or plan by two or more people who have the specific intent to commit a crime or engage in dishonest, fraudulent, or immoral conduct that is injurious to public health and morals. Previously, in addition to intent, it was required that some overt act in furtherance of the conspiracy must have been committed. This requirement has been virtually abandoned in American jurisprudence. For instance, if a hospital administrator and a physician agree to fill hospital beds with nursing home patients (who do not require hospitalization) to create revenue for the hospital, the administrator may be convicted of conspiracy even though his or her acts in furtherance of the conspiracy consisted only of a telephone call or no act at all. It may be sufficient that the administrator and the physician tacitly agreed to defraud Medicare or an insurance carrier. In most states, proof of the agreement would have been sufficient even if it had not been made in person and there had been no act such as the telephone call. Manufacturers, sellers, and prescribers of unapproved drugs have been convicted of conspiracies.[1]

A factual impossibility to commit a crime (e.g., when conspirators agree to kill somebody who is already dead) is no defense. However, there can be no conspiracy when the objective of the conspiracy is not illegal. The concept of conspiracy involves the accomplishment of an objective prohibited by law. Conspiracies may be punished as criminal and civil acts. Thus a conspiracy to destroy a physician's practice by excluding that physician from hospitals or otherwise defaming or disgracing him or her may be punishable as a crime, even though the mere denial of privileges would not have been a criminal offense. The physician may concurrently seek civil remedies in a lawsuit for damages. In practice, however, unless the circumstances of the case involving civil wrongs are particularly outrageous, the district attorney usually refrains from prosecution, letting the victim seek remedy in civil law.

Causation

Before a criminal defendant can be convicted, it must be shown that his or her act was indeed the cause of the criminal result or was a substantial contributing factor in causing the criminal result. Whereas the mind may get lost in the labyrinth of contributory factors to the crime, modern jurisprudence focuses on the sine qua non, or the so-called but-for test. This test determines whether without such an act the crime would not have happened.

Criminal law recognizes both acts of commission and acts of omission as causes of crime. The gravity of the crime varies if the physician or nurse who had the duty to care for a patient failed negligently or intentionally to provide life-sustaining medications or deliberately provided an overdose, causing that patient's death. For purposes of criminal law, a victim's preexisting conditions do not release the defendant from liability. For instance, victimizing a person who has the unusual and unknown fragility of hemophilia or heart disease is a risk that the wrongdoer takes, even though the same act might not have caused death or serious injury to a healthy individual.

Mistakes of law

The following are a few exceptions to the rule that ignorance of the law is no excuse:

1. When the government has not made information about the law reasonably available to all those who may be affected. This exception usually applies to situations in which the laws punish inaction or omission, such as failure to renew a license or permit or failure to file certain information with appropriate governmental agencies (e.g., if reporting venereal diseases, AIDS, or certain birth defects is mandatory).

2. When there is reasonable reliance on an official government pronouncement and the defendant has made reasonable efforts to find out about such a law and reasonably believes that his or her conduct is not criminal.

3. When the defendant reasonably relies on erroneous official interpretation of the law by a public officer or agency responsible for the interpretation and enforcement of the law, such as an erroneous interpretation of controlled substance laws by ranking officials of the DEA.

Entrapment

The defense of entrapment excuses the commission of a crime if a law enforcement officer, federal or state, actually instigates or induces an otherwise innocent person to commit the crime. The test of entrapment is the subjective disposition of the defendant before police involvement. This is often the case when undercover agents prevail on gullible physicians to prescribe pain medications without proper examination or need. The defense of entrapment is not available in cases involving personal violence.

Attempts

Attempted crimes are criminal offenses if some significant act with the intent to commit a criminal act is established. Mere preparation to commit a crime is not enough. A person can be convicted of attempted murder for pulling the plug, even when the plug was reinserted and the patient did not die.

Intentional and negligent conduct

The health care provider may become a criminal defendant in many ways, sometimes even inadvertently. Most often, prosecutions result from multifaceted problems, such as kickbacks from referrals of phantom patients to specialists, physical therapy, and laboratories for tests; billing frauds, including oft-repeated "mistakes" or visits; use, dispensing, and theft of medications; writing of false or fictitious prescriptions; Medicare and Medicaid frauds; rape; homicide (death resulting from surgery, administration of medications, abandonment, improper care, improper prescription or injection of medications, or drug or alcohol intoxication during surgery); death or injuries resulting from refusal or failure to provide medical or surgical treatment; reckless nursing or pharmaceutical errors; excessive restraints; abuse of children or the elderly; criminal malpractice; income tax fraud; "rebates" from pharmacies; conspiracies; practicing without a license or with a suspended or revoked license; intimacy with minors or psychiatric patients; assault and battery by inappropriate touching during examination or treatment of a female patient; abortion and fertility problems; and most recently the wide-ranging debate about assisted suicide and euthanasia.

The criminal liability of physicians, dentists, nurses, and pharmacists frequently results from a high degree of reckless and negligent conduct. What the law calls *criminal negligence* is largely a matter of degree, incapable of a precise definition. Whether or not criminal negligence exists is a question for the trier of fact. The law requires a showing of "gross lack of competency or gross inattention, or wanton indifference to the patient's safety, which may arise from gross ignorance of the science of medicine and surgery or through gross negligence, either in the application and selection of remedies, lack of proper skills in the use of instruments, and failure to give proper attention to the patient"

(e.g., "practicing fraudulently with gross incompetence and gross negligence" by failing to take and record vital signs of a patient to whom the physician administered anesthesia, using investigational and non-FDA-approved substances).[2] The fact that the patient consented to a specific treatment or operation is no defense to the criminal action against the physician. The courts have been very careful not to hold physicians criminally responsible for patient deaths resulting from a "mere mistake of judgment" in the selection and application of remedies or for inadvertent deaths.[3] However, willful and wanton conduct is clearly criminal.

FRAUD

The federal government and the states have created new units specializing in health care fraud and have embarked on vigorous programs of criminal prosecutions, example setting, and fraud prevention.[4] The most notable of such new units are within the FBI and state attorneys generals' Medical Fraud Control Units (MFCUs). Local and state prosecutors also are increasingly deputized as special assistant U.S. attorneys, enabling them to more fully enlist the aid of federal law enforcement and to prosecute their cases in federal courts. In addition to health care frauds, these prosecutorial activities also focus heavily on many aspects of drug abuse. Boards licensing health care professionals also are allowing many of these special prosecutors to press for suspensions and revocations of physicians', nurses', and pharmacists' licenses in conjunction with criminal proceedings. When criminal convictions are difficult to obtain, prosecutors usually succeed in getting professional license revocations or at least suspensions or revocations of narcotic licenses. Such proceedings, although not criminal in nature, can be professionally devastating and require a much lesser burden of proof than criminal prosecutions. The Inspector General of the Department of Health and Human Services is now actively pursuing health care frauds by focusing mostly on revocations and suspensions of federal reimbursements. Because these revocations and disqualifications from federal reimbursements range in the hundreds of millions of dollars and can last for years, they are a strong deterrent to both institutions and individual practitioners.

One of the more vigorously prosecuted areas is submission by health care providers of false and fraudulent claims under the Medicaid and Medicare programs. It is a felony to knowingly make false and material statements in the processing of Medicare claims.[5–8] Furthermore, physicians who defraud the government or private insurance companies and use the U.S. Postal Service to do so face additional penalties for mail and wire fraud.[9] A physician who is prosecuted in a criminal case may subsequently be left defenseless in a civil action[10] because factual matters litigated in the criminal action will act as a bar to their relitigation in civil action through collateral estoppel.[11,12]

In most instances, criminal prosecutions for health care fraud usually involve the federal government. Physicians also should be aware that criminal responsibility may arise from any material false statements made to the federal or state governments and to private insurance companies. Conviction for such frauds generally also results in suspension or revocation of a medical license. Medical fraud also may involve misrepresentations of certain therapies, other treatments, or untested remedies that allegedly produce miraculous cures. Criminal prosecutions are often carried out against physicians who offer these false cures to patients either verbally or through the mail, and severe penalties are often invoked. In *People v. Privitera*,[13] several groups challenged California's prohibition on using amygdalin or vitamin B_{17} (Laetrile) to treat cancer. The defenses of vagueness regarding that portion of the law prohibiting the "prescribing, selling, or administering of any unapproved drug, medicine, compound, or device to be used in the diagnosis, treatment, or alleviation of cancer" were contradicted by evidence.

Cases regarding billing errors usually center on massive, flagrant, and pervasive general fraudulent billing and mail and wire fraud. These frauds are usually perpetrated on numerous patients, insurers, and the government with the clear intent to rip off the health care system through "creative billing" over an extended time. These billing error cases primarily include charges for services that were never performed; repetitive patterns of unnecessary procedures, hospitalizations, or both; giving and receiving of kickbacks, bribes, or rebates; and false representations for certification of hospitals, nursing homes, intermediate care facilities for the mentally retarded, and home health agencies. Most frequently, individual physicians are charged with fraud for using higher billing codes or for "unbundling" Current Procedural Terminology (CPT) codes. Each CPT code specifically describes the procedure performed. When a physician uses a higher code (called *upcoding*), he or she is misrepresenting what was actually done and is billing and getting paid for services that were not performed. Patient visits under the coding system are categorized as brief, limited, intermediate, comprehensive, and extended. These categories are based on the amount of time spent and the services performed. If a physician charges for 30 minutes for writing a prescription and designates it as an "extensive" consultation instead of a "minimal" consultation, this is usually recognized as fraud. The hospital records or office notes also would indicate what else the physician did. If he or she consistently used the highest codes, the criminal modus operandi will be obvious. Testimony that each case was very complex and required the physician to spend an inordinate amount of time with patients is easily refuted. When a physician is "unbundling" codes, he or she is double-billing for services performed. The physician is paid once for the whole job (called a *global fee*, which includes all the services rendered)

and a second time for the specific things the physician did. The defense of making "mistakes" in using the incorrect codes is not very credible when it can be shown that the same mistakes were made over and over again on numerous patients and always in favor of the physician. Billing for treatment given to dead patients is increasingly picked up by computers that record the date and time of death.

Other fraudulent transactions have included double-billing for fees as attending physician and as a consultant on the same patient at the same time. This is double-billing for the same service by any name. Another fraud involves billing separately for different medications prescribed to the same patient because the physician was already paid for his diagnosis and treatment, which includes prescribing.

In virtually all cases of Medicare and Medicaid fraud the courts have ordered full restitution. In addition, heavy fines were imposed in conjunction with jail terms or probation. Federal sentences are based on mandatory guidelines, which leave little discretion to judges.

The ongoing unprecedented scrutiny, aided by a high level of computerization and widespread use of undercover agents, has brought to light a variety of crimes committed by physicians, nurses, pharmacists, hospitals, clinics, nursing homes, and other health care practitioners and facilities. Even though small in number, these pill pushers, quacks, and welfare cheats can give the medical profession a "black eye." Their creativity in stealing appears to be unlimited in both scope and ingenuity. An overview of some of these schemes in the annual reports by the National Association of Attorneys General (NAAG) lists the following examples of fraud in fee-for-service health care:

1. Overutilization: using treatments, including office visits, laboratory tests, therapy, and prescriptions, that are not required.

2. Pharmacy fraud: billing for prescriptions and supplies not delivered or providing lower-priced or generic products and billing for higher-priced medications or supplies.

3. Billing fraud: billing for services not needed or not performed, billing for nonexistent patients, or billing for products not needed or not supplied. Another form of billing fraud is the "intentional mistake." Hospitals are frequently caught in this web of billing fraud. The use of cumbersome billing procedures providing incredible detail, covering everything from the room charge to aspirin tablets, can conceal charges of intentional mistakes that frequently escape payor scrutiny.

4. Marketing and enrollment frauds: enrolling ineligible or nonexistent individuals or misrepresenting the availability of medical equipment and rehabilitative procedures.

5. Frauds in the procurement of Medicaid contracts: falsifying financial solvency and misrepresenting

staffing or assisted daily living activities such as eating, bathing, toileting, turning, and positioning.

6. Durable equipment or supplies fraud: selling and purchasing (by the payor for the patient) of long-use or durable medical equipment (DME), such as a wheelchair or another device, that is not needed or is of a lesser quality than that for which billed. The sale of DME is a source of regular and heavy abuse.

7. Supplies fraud: billing the patient for nondurable items, such as dressings not delivered or not used by the patient, or billing for supplies not needed but delivered and charged nonetheless. The provider may be the direct victim of supplies fraud (such as when a supplier delivers a lesser quantity or lesser quality than that for which the payor is billed). Whatever costs the hospital may incur in the area of supplies, it will pass on—together with the fraud—to the patient and the ultimate payor.

8. Unbundling: charging separately for procedures that are usually combined or "bundled" into a single charge (diagnosis-related group) in which the single charge is less than the sum of the separate charges.

9. Upcoding: billing for a more expensive procedure than the one used or using a more expensive procedure when a less costly one could have been used. This is a type of billing fraud.

10. Legal scams: engaging in worker's compensation fraud and filing false injury claims, such as faked accidents. The success of such scams requires that the "victim" and his or her lawyers work with physicians, therapists, and other health care providers to secure compensation for false accident or injury claims. Lawyers have also created fictitious companies and instigated or covered up fraudulent billing, sometimes for nonexistent services and facilities.

11. Kickbacks: receiving payments in the form of rebates and referral fees used as business inducements. Most are illegal under the antikickback statutes adopted by the federal government and many state governments.

Fraud in managed care differs primarily in the incentive for underutilization, which is fraudulent when used to deny patients access to contracted services merely to line the pockets of providers. Managed care frauds also include, among others, submission of false cost data to justify higher capitation payments, registration of fictitious enrollees or those who have left the area, payment of kickbacks for referral of healthy patients, avoidance of unhealthy and high-risk groups, and denial of necessary contracted services. In addition, numerous MCOs have been convicted of the following types of fraud: falsifying or misrepresenting professional credentials, providing "quack" treatments, overenrolling patients, charging a single patient to more than one MCO, failing to remove deceased patients from capitation

lists, paying kickbacks for referrals, and giving referrals to laboratories and specialized services in which the provider has a financial interest.

The legal definition of *kickbacks* is extremely broad. The federal antikickback statute makes it a felony for any person (or organization) to offer or pay "remuneration" (bribe or rebate) to any person or induce the person either to purchase a product or to refer a patient for whose care the government would be ultimately responsible. Thus a physician, a pharmacist, or a physical therapist receiving a referral from anyone who may gain from it is subject to prosecution. "Safe harbor" exceptions include employees, certain consultants, investments, and equipment rentals; these are strictly construed, and legal advice should be sought in almost all cases.

CRIMES AGAINST THE PERSON

Homicide is the killing of a human being by another human being. As far as the law is concerned, a homicide may be criminal or innocent. It may be caused by an act of commission (the actual killing) or omission (when one has a duty to take life-saving action but does not do so). The criminal act constitutes an act causing the death of another human that must be committed with criminal intent and without lawful excuse or justification. The law divides criminal homicides into three main categories, as follows: (1) murder, (2) voluntary manslaughter, and (3) involuntary manslaughter. Modern American jurisprudence embraces any unlawful causation of death and extends the period to as long as 3 years. Deaths resulting from negligent medical treatment, failure to provide treatment, or provision of improper or inadequate treatment are seldom treated as murder despite pressure from distraught family members. Absent outrageous or severely aggravating circumstances, even grossly negligent physicians usually are charged with only involuntary homicides. To sustain a conviction of criminal homicide, the prosecution must establish that the victim was alive at the time of the death-causing act by another person. These thorny questions of when life begins and ends, together with euthanasia, are largely a matter of expert medical testimony and state law, and they carry with them a Pandora's box of medical and legal problems that will continue to be hotly debated within both professions for some time.

From the standpoint of medical law, one of the most frequently encountered types of homicide is infanticide. Most states still adhere to the rule that there is no homicide unless the child has been born alive. The traditional determination of a live birth for purposes of a homicide conviction requires that the child must be physically separated from the mother and must give clear signs of independent viability, such as breathing or crying. This definition has been repeatedly challenged by prosecutors with the help of medical testimony that seeks to establish that a living fetus is indeed a human being. Allegations of criminality for failure to treat infants with spina bifida have been dismissed. A physician may encounter infanticide under a great variety of circumstances. Sometimes, he or she may be deemed to have caused the death of the child, and if the death was the result of neglect or willful misconduct, the physician may be found guilty.

In other cases, suffocation of infants may be disguised as "crib death." Infant deaths also may have been caused by parents through acts of abuse, such as drowning, scalding, or starving. Prenatal injuries to the infant resulting from drug abuse by the mother during pregnancy have also led to criminal prosecution in several states. If the physician is aware or suspects such infanticides, he or she is legally obligated to report them. Unfortunately, in the majority of cases, physicians are unwilling to become involved, and most infanticides are allowed to pass as "accidents."

There are two types of euthanasia. The first type, called *active euthanasia* or *mercy killing*, is a crime in every state. In such cases the physician takes an active role in the death of a patient by disconnecting a life-support system or administering a lethal dose of a medication. In the second type, called *passive euthanasia*, a crime may not have been committed, particularly in jurisdictions in which the concept of a "living will" has been approved by the state legislature. Passive euthanasia simply means no further measures (e.g., therapy) are taken against the patient's wishes. Instead, the patient is kept merely as comfortable as possible, and nature is allowed to take its course. In California, two respected practitioners faced murder charges, which were later dismissed on technical grounds, for disconnecting the life-support system of an allegedly terminally ill patient.[14]

A physician is also capable of imparting an element of criminality to an otherwise lawful act. This is particularly true in cases in which a physician attempts to spare a family's feelings but causes further hardship and suffering by issuing an incorrect death certificate or failing to report deaths under suspicious or unusual circumstances to the medical examiner or coroner. Such crimes arise many times in the cases of "overdoses." In most states it is a misdemeanor to fail to report death under unnatural circumstances to the coroner or medical examiner. In many states, there are also misdemeanor charges for failure to report (1) all manner of violent deaths, including those caused by thermal, chemical, electrical, or radiation injuries;

(2) deaths caused by criminal abortion, whether apparently self-induced or not; (3) deaths occurring without a physician in attendance; (4) deaths of people after unexplained comas; (5) medically unexpected deaths during the course of a therapeutic procedure; (6) deaths of prisoners at penal institutions; and (7) deaths of those whose bodies are to be cremated, buried at sea, transported out of state, or otherwise made unavailable for pathological study. Civil and criminal penalties also may be imposed for failure to report diseases that constitute a threat to public health.

Improper or immoral conduct by physicians or dentists toward patients may result in criminal prosecution for rape or child molestation. Such crimes also may lead to disciplinary measures, including loss of licensure to practice.[15] The courts have repeatedly stated that offenses relating to moral turpitude are not relegated only to actions in the lines of professional practice.[16]

The substance of the criminal laws and procedures involving criminal trials and convictions is governed by the strict application of the constitutional standards of due process and equal protection. These concepts are constantly redefined by the courts in a tug-of-war between liberal, socially oriented standards and more conservative approaches that balance the rights of the accused against the more important rights of society and victims of crime.

ENDNOTES

1. *People v. Privitera*, 591 P. 2d 919, *cert. denied*, 444 U.S. 949.
2. *State v. Lester*, 149 N.W. 297.
3. *Cole v. New York State Dept. of Education*, 465 N.Y.S. 2d 637.
4. *Health Care Fraud in a Managed Care Environment*, Report by the National Association of Attorneys General (Apr. 1996).
5. *State of Wisconsin v. Kennedy*, 314 N.W. 2d 884 (Wis. Ct. App. 1981).
6. *United States v. Matank*, 482 F. 2d 1319 (9th Cir. 1973).
7. *People of the State of New York v. Montesano*, 459 N.Y.S. 2d 21, 445 N.E. 2d 197 (1982).
8. *People of the State of New York v. Chaitin*, 462 N.Y.S. 2d 61 (1983).
9. *United States v. Perkal*, 530 F. 2d 604 (4th Cir. 1976).
10. *See, e.g.*, under 31 U.S.C.A., §231, 323[a].
11. *United States v. Zulli*, 418 F.Supp. 252.
12. *Id.*
13. *People v. Privitera*, 55 Cal. App. 3d Supp. 39, 128 Cal. Rptr. 151 (1976).
14. American Medical News (Sept. 16, 1993).
15. *Cadilla v. Board of Medical Examiners*, 103 Cal. Rptr. 455
16. *Barski v. Board of Regents*, 111 N.E. 2d, *aff'd*, 347 U.S. 442.

51 Countersuits by Health Care Providers

BRADFORD H. LEE, M.D., J.D., M.B.A., F.A.C.E.P., F.C.L.M.

POLICY CONSIDERATIONS
MALICIOUS PROSECUTION
ABUSE OF PROCESS
DEFAMATION
NEGLIGENCE
INTENTIONAL TORTS
CONSTITUTIONAL MANDATE
PRIMA FACIE TORT
APPEALS RESULTS
CONCLUSION

Recent years have seen a precipitous increase in the incidence of medical malpractice litigation. This increase has taken the form of a dramatic rise in the number of suits filed and in the size of judgments and settlements. Although many of the suits filed have some legitimate basis, physicians and their insurance carriers have noted a rise in the number of actions filed that lack substantial merit. To counteract these nonmeritorious claims, physicians have sought recourse through countersuits.

Physician countersuits have been conspicuously, although not uniformly, unsuccessful. Countersuits for abuse of process, malicious prosecution, intentional infliction of emotional distress, defamation, barratry, and negligence have been consistently rejected by the courts for numerous reasons.

POLICY CONSIDERATIONS

State and federal courts must weigh a number of opposing public policy issues when deciding whether to permit countersuits. On one hand, courts have recognized a policy favoring protection of individuals from unjustified and oppressive litigation. On the other hand, courts have sought to protect the public interest by providing injured parties with free and open access to the courts. Countersuits exert a chilling effect on injured persons who would seek legal redress.

When an individual with a meritorious claim is faced with the possibility of a countersuit, many legal scholars and members of the judiciary believe that the potential plaintiff's right of access to the courts is threatened. In this situation the nation's legal system for redress of wrongs would be threatened with failing to protect the rights of the individual, and many meritorious claims for damages would not be pursued. The end result could well be to leave the injured party without adequate remedy. On the whole, courts have given far greater weight to preserving the peace by favoring free access to the courts. This policy choice renders it extremely difficult for wrongfully sued physicians and others to seek an effective remedy via countersuits.

Most physician countersuits are brought against the physician's former patient (plaintiff in the original medical malpractice action) and the patient's attorney. As the countersuit litigation progresses, the focus usually shifts from the former patient to the attorney. This shift occurs because the patient frequently raises the defense that he or she relied on legal advice from the attorney regarding the merits of the case. As a practical matter, because most unsuccessful medical malpractice plaintiffs have limited resources, a judgment against a former patient is rarely collectible. The patient's attorney, however, is frequently covered by a legal malpractice liability policy; thus a judgment against a defendant attorney, if covered in the policy, usually is paid. The attorney's insurance carrier may be more willing and able to settle than the insured. The attorney's defense is weaker than that of the former client. The attorney usually can claim only that, before initiating the medical malpractice action, he or she relied on information from the client. The attorney will then claim that such information was inaccurate and led to an unjustified medical malpractice action. Another defense is that the attorney acted reasonably, obtained the advice of medical experts, and relied on their advice before filing suit.

Unlike the tort of malicious prosecution, abuse of process does not require proof of prior favorable determination or lack of probable cause. The principal difficulty faced when prosecuting this cause of action is proof of an ulterior purpose. To establish this element, the physician must demonstrate that the original use of legal process in bringing the medical malpractice action, although justified initially, was later perverted and that the process itself was employed for a purpose not contemplated by the law.

Note that institution of a meritless lawsuit is not sufficient by itself to state a cause of action for abuse of process. Physicians sometimes allege that the original, groundless medical malpractice suit was brought merely to coerce a nuisance settlement. However, a majority of courts have rejected this argument as insufficient to fulfill the requirement of an improper ulterior purpose.

In 1980 the Nevada Supreme Court upheld a countersuit based on an abuse of process.[10] In that case the defendant physician was alleged to have been negligent in the treatment of bed sores that the patient developed while under the physician's care. A thorough review of the facts indicated that there was absolutely no basis for initiating or prosecuting the medical malpractice action. Shortly before trial, the patient's attorney attempted to settle for the nominal sum of $750. The physician refused to settle. The case was tried without the plaintiff's attorney having retained an expert witness, and the plaintiff lost the malpractice case.

The Nevada Supreme Court found that the plaintiff's attorney had used an alleged claim of malpractice solely for the ulterior purpose of coercing a nuisance settlement. His offer to settle for $750, his failure to investigate the facts properly before filing suit, and the absence of essential expert testimony at trial supported a case for abuse of process. Although this court recognized the threat of litigation to coerce a settlement as satisfying the ulterior purpose element, it is unlikely that other jurisdictions will expand on this holding because of the great weight that courts place on the public policy of providing injured parties free and open access to the courts.

DEFAMATION

The tort of defamation can be committed when an oral or written false statement is made to a third party about another person and is damaging to that person's reputation and good name. Countersuits based on the tort of defamation rely on the principle that an unfounded suit attacks the professional reputation of the defendant physician.

Defamation has not proven effective as a cause of action on which to base a countersuit because of an underlying privilege covering oral and written statements made in the course of judicial proceedings. That privilege immunizes patients and their attorneys from liability for any reasonable communication made in the course of a lawsuit. The purpose of this privilege is to permit the free expression of facts and opinions necessary to decide the merits of a lawsuit.

The threat of defamation lawsuits would have a chilling effect on access to the courts and on honest testimony and would be contrary to the public interest in the free and independent operation of the courts.

However, in a 1963 countersuit based on defamation, a California intermediate appellate court ruled in favor of the physician.[11] On the other hand, the fact pattern in this case was unusual *and subsequent decisions have criticized the court's ruling.* In the original medical malpractice action the defendant physician was charged with negligent diagnosis and treatment of a child, resulting in the child's death. A local reporter contacted the office of the plaintiff's attorney for information. That attorney reiterated his formal allegations and added additional, unsubstantiated charges. Those charges were incorporated into a subsequent newspaper article. The defendant physician read that article and contacted the newspaper, demanding that the false allegations be formally retracted in a subsequent article. A newspaper official contacted the attorney who had made the original allegations and asked if the facts set forth in the article were true. The attorney assured the newspaper official that they were true and later supported his claims with formal, written correspondence with the newspaper.

The physician sued for defamation and prevailed at trial. The judgment was upheld on appeal because the attorney's statements to the newspaper were not made in pursuit of the underlying malpractice litigation. The wrongfulness of the attorney's false statements was compounded by his failure to retract them when the newspaper contacted him to substantiate his allegations. Defamation may be a viable form of action in countersuits in which erroneous statements are made outside of usual judicial proceedings. In such circumstances the privilege covering judicial proceedings will not protect an attorney or a patient who makes false statements that are injurious to a physician.

NEGLIGENCE

The law of negligence requires that individuals do not subject other persons to unreasonable risks of harm. A countersuit based on negligence alleges that the patient's attorney was negligent in unreasonably bringing an unfounded lawsuit against the physician. However, under negligence law the plaintiff must prove that the defendant owed him or her a duty. No physician has succeeded with a countersuit based on negligence and prevailed at the appellate level.

Courts have consistently held that an attorney owes no duty to a party, other than his or her client, unless that party was intended to benefit from the attorney's actions. In the usual medical malpractice action an attorney owes a duty to the client (the patient) to zealously represent him or her and to prosecute the claim. Requiring a concurrent duty to a physician not to file an unjustified suit would create a conflict of interest between attorney and client, denying the latter a right to effective counsel and free access to the courts.

INTENTIONAL TORTS

Intentional torts alleged by physicians in their countersuits against plaintiffs and their attorneys from a prior medical malpractice action include invasion of privacy, intentional infliction of emotional distress, and barratry (persistent incitement of lawsuits). Although the courts have, in dictum, lauded the application of these causes of actions as being novel and innovative, they have consistently rejected them.

CONSTITUTIONAL MANDATE

Some jurisdictions do not recognize the common law countersuits. Innovative attorneys in those states have attempted to create new theories of liability to permit physicians to bring successful countersuits. In other states in which there are major stumbling blocks to countersuits, attorneys have sought to establish such novel theories.

For example, Illinois courts require proof of a "special injury" to prove malicious prosecution. This requirement effectively prevents physicians from winning a countersuit of this nature. However, the Illinois Constitution specifically provides that "every person shall find a certain remedy in the laws for all injuries and wrongs which he receives to his person, privacy, property, or reputation. He shall obtain justice by law, freely, completely, and promptly."

An attorney representing a radiologist who was sued unsuccessfully seized on this wording and attempted to fashion a new cause of action based on constitutional mandate. He argued that, because Illinois case law required a showing of special injury, physicians were precluded from successfully bringing a malicious prosecution action. Therefore any wrongs suffered from unjustified malpractice suits had no remedy. This attorney argued that the Illinois Constitution gives a broad remedial right to such plaintiffs who are unable to obtain remedies by more conventional common law causes of action.

An intermediate appellate court in Illinois found that the pertinent section of the Illinois Constitution was merely a philosophical expression and not a mandate for a legal remedy.[12] The court ruled that, as long as some remedy for the alleged wrong exists, this constitutional section does not mandate recognition of any new remedy. It so held in spite of the fact that a physician wrongfully sued is effectively precluded from countersuing. Because the common law remedy of malicious prosecution technically is available to him or her, the courts will not create a new cause of action based on constitutional mandate.

PRIMA FACIE TORT

A form of countersuit recently relied on by creative attorneys attempting to carve out a new countersuit cause of action is the prima facie tort. The elements of this tort are intentional infliction of harm, without excuse or justification, by an otherwise lawful act, causing special damages to the physician.

Innovative attorneys had to resort to this cause of action because of the clear failure of the more conventional causes of action. Charges that the patient's attorney was negligent in failing to ascertain the merits of the case before filing suit have been summarily dismissed because the patient's attorney is not considered to have a duty of care to an adverse party—the physician. As for claims based on the attorney's breach of the attorney's oath not to bring frivolous suits, courts generally consider that private citizens are not proper parties to enforce such oaths and that any disciplinary action must come from the organized bar. Charges of barratry (i.e., the practice by an attorney of habitually pursuing groundless judicial proceedings) have been dismissed on the ground that barratry is a criminal offense with only a public remedy, not a private one.[13] Casting about for some means of avoiding the strictures of these closely defined causes of action, attorneys in three recent malpractice countersuits have laid before the courts a more novel form of action—the prima facie tort. Although in all three instances the physicians ultimately lost, the cases point the way for possible future physician countersuits.

Prima facie tort is a remedy of fairly recent origin; it grew out of an opinion delivered in 1904 by Supreme Court Justice Oliver Wendell Holmes in a case involving a conspiracy among several Wisconsin newspapers to draw away the advertising customers of a rival paper. In appealing their conviction the defendants pointed out that their stratagems had been, strictly speaking, perfectly legal and that they were really being tried for their motives. They argued that motive alone is not a proper line of inquiry for the court. Justice Holmes disagreed, holding that even lawful conduct can become unlawful when done maliciously and that such conduct becomes actionable even when it does not fit into the mold of an existing cause of action.[14]

Out of these general principles there eventually grew the specific cause of action known as *prima facie tort*. Unlike malicious prosecution, abuse of process, or the other torts described earlier, prima facie tort has not been accepted or even introduced in all jurisdictions. Ohio, New York, Georgia, Missouri, and Minnesota have recognized the tort by name, whereas Massachusetts recognizes the principle without the label. Oregon, on the other hand, once enforced the action but has since discarded it.

No appellate court has thus far upheld a countersuit judgment based on a prima facie tort theory. The reason generally stated is that prima facie tort should not be used to circumvent the requirements of a traditional tort remedy, such as malicious prosecution. The courts stress the need for open access to the judicial system and state that the prima facie tort should not become a catch-all alternative for every countersuit that cannot stand on its own. Appellate courts have refused to accept prima facie tort when relief technically is available under traditional theories of liability.

APPEALS RESULTS

Approximately 30 physician countersuits have been decided by appellate courts in recent years. In nearly all of these suits the courts have ruled against countersuing physicians and in favor of medical malpractice plaintiffs and their attorneys. At least four appellate decisions have favored physicians who brought countersuits. Specifically there have been at least two successful appeals of malicious prosecution actions, one successful appeal of an abuse of process action, and one successful appeal of a defamation action.

CONCLUSION

Although the absolute number of medical malpractice claims has increased dramatically in recent years, there has been no concomitant increase in the number of successful physician countersuits. Because the courts recognize the strong public policy interest in ensuring that injured parties have free and open access to the judicial system, they are extremely reluctant to allow countersuits because it is believed that countersuits would have a chilling effect on a party's ability to seek legal redress. Despite the application of many innovative and novel causes of action, physician countersuits have been and will probably continue to be conspicuously, although not uniformly, unsuccessful.

ENDNOTES

1. *Raine v. Drasin*, 621 S.W. 2d 895 (Ky. 1981).
2. *Lackner v. La Croix*, 25 Cal. 3d 747, 159 Cal. Rptr. 693, 602 P. 2d 393 (1979).
3. *Peerman v. Sidicaine*, 605 S.W. 2d 242 (Tenn. App. 1980).
4. *Supra* note 1.
5. *Mahaffey v. McMahon*, 630 S.W. 2d 68 (Ky. 1982).
6. *Nelson v. Miller*, 233 Kan. 122, 660 P. 2d 1361 (1983).
7. *Etheredge v. Emmons*, no. A014929 (Cal. App. 1985).
8. *Williams v. Coombs*, 179 Cal. App. 3d 626 (1986).
9. *Sheldon Appel Co. v. Albert & Oliker*, 47 Cal. 3d 863 (765 P. 2d 498) (1989).
10. *Bull v. McCuskey*, 615 P. 2d 957 (Nev. 1980).
11. *Hanley v. Lund*, 32 Cal. Rptr. 733 (1963).
12. *Berlin v. Nathan*, 381 N.E. 2d 1367 (1978).
13. *Moiel v. Sandlin*, 571 S.W. 2d 567 (Tex. Civ. App. 1978).
14. *Aikins v. Wisconsin*, 195 U.S. 194 (1904).

GENERAL REFERENCES

Logan, *Physician Countersuits*, 32 Med. Trial Tech. Q. 153 (1985-1986).

M.D. McCafferty & S.M. Meyer, *Medical Malpractice Bases of Liability* (Shepard's/McGraw-Hill, Colorado Springs, Colo. 1985).

S.R. Reuter, *Physician Countersuits: A Catch-22*, 14 U. of San Francisco L. Rev. 203 (1980).

W.E. Shipley, *Medical Malpractice Countersuits*, 84 A.L.R. 3d 555.

Linda A. Sharpe, *Medical Malpractice Countersuits*, 61 A.L.R. 3d 555 (supersedes the previous A.L.R. citation).

M.J. Yardley, *Malicious Prosecution: A Physician's Need for Reassessment*, 60 Chi. Kent L. Rev. 317 (1984).

VI

Care of Special Patients

Children as Patients

JOSEPH P. McMENAMIN, M.D., J.D., F.C.L.M.
EUGENE LINWOOD KASTELBERG, Jr., M.D.
KATRICE TAYLOR, B.A.

STATE INTERVENTION
CHILD ABUSE

Although much of the law governing the medical care of children is indistinguishable from that governing the medical care of adults, certain features of the former are unique. These features arise in large part because minors are seen to need special protection from others and from themselves and are generally deemed incompetent (except in specific circumstances) to grant valid consent for their own treatment. The law's solicitude for the special needs of minors sometimes gives rise to poignant conflicts between the desires and values of parents, often inviolable in other settings, and those of the child or those of the state as *parens patriae*. Resolution of these conflicts often falls to the courts. In this chapter, some of the legal issues peculiar to the care of children are explored.

STATE INTERVENTION

The standard of care applicable to parents obliged to provide medical attention for their children is analogous to the standard of care for physicians accused of malpractice. As the New York Court of Appeals wrote when construing a state statute, "The standard is at what time would an ordinarily prudent person, solicitous for the welfare of his child and anxious to promote its recovery, deem it necessary to call in the services of a physician."[1]

In many jurisdictions, statutes permit the state to take custody of a *neglected* or *dependent* child, terms that are variously defined[2] but which have been construed to include a child deprived of medical services by the parents.[3] Examples of such deprivation include the denial of smallpox vaccination viewed by the parents as "harmful and injurious,"[4] refusal to submit to surgery necessary to save the life of a fetus,[5] refusal to permit blood transfusion required for surgery to correct congenital heart disease,[6] and withholding chemotherapy from a child suffering from malignancy.[7] Statutes finding neglect under such circumstances have been upheld against attacks under the freedom of religion clauses of federal and state constitutions and under the due process clause of the

U.S. Constitution.[8] In such circumstances, however, courts may instruct state authorities to respect the religious beliefs of the parents and to accede as much as possible to their wishes without interfering with the court-ordered medical care.[9]

Although the precise limits of the requirement for the provision of medical care by parents are difficult to set, the Illinois statute construed in *Wallace v. Labrenz*[10] may be fairly typical:

[T]he statute defines a dependent or neglected child as one which "has not proper parental care." . . . Neglect, however, is the failure to exercise the care that the circumstances justly demand. It embraces willful as well as unintentional disregard of duty. It is not a term of fixed and measured meaning. It takes its content always from specific circumstances, and its meaning varies as the context of surrounding circumstances changes. . . . [I]t is of no consequence that the parents have not failed in their duty in other respects.[11]

In many jurisdictions, a child treated in good faith solely by spiritual means in accordance with the tenets of a recognized religious body is exempt from the definition of a neglected child.[12] Such statutes do not necessarily prevent a court from concluding in a proper case that spiritual treatment alone is insufficient or from ordering conventional medical therapy where needed, including, if necessary, ongoing monitoring after the acute problem is rectified.[13] These statutes may, however, raise thorny equal protection, First Amendment, and other constitutional issues, because they may give preference to one group of potential offenders over others based on that group's self-proclaimed religious tenets and because they may involve the state in excessive entanglement with such questions as what a recognized religious body is, what its tenets are, and whether the accused acted in accord with such tenets.[14] Some courts, however, have no trouble finding that a parent's decision to "let God decide if the child is to live or die" is not the kind of religious belief protected under such statutes.[15]

Where medical intervention may be deemed elective, parental refusal of such intervention may be permitted if the court does not find neglect or dependency.[16] In some instances, courts have refused to intervene despite medically compelling circumstances. The Illinois Appeals Court, for example, declined to find a child neglected whose sibling had been sexually abused at home, who herself had twice gone into diabetic ketoacidosis probably because of "misuse of insulin" at home, and whose mother—suffering from a psychiatric disorder exacerbated by the stresses of child care—had a history of suicide attempts, sexual promiscuity, and placing the diabetic child in a foster home.[17]

Where, however, a parent's refusal to provide medical care is deemed egregious, criminal liability may be found.[18] Religious beliefs are no defense to neglect of this magnitude.[19] Significant neglect, however, even including neglect sufficient to cause death, may not necessarily be sufficient to sustain a charge of manslaughter.[20] This appears to be particularly true where the neglect is not shown to be willful.[21]

Parens patriae

The power that permits courts to intervene to mandate medical care for children whose parents fail to provide it is known as *parens patriae*.[22] This is distinct from the police power that justifies, for example, fluoridation of water:

The rationale of *parens patriae* is that the State must intervene . . . to protect an individual who is not able to make decisions in his own best interest. The decision to exercise the power of *parens patriae* must reflect the welfare of society as a whole, but mainly it must balance the individual's right to be free from interference against the individual's need to be treated, if treatment would in fact be in his best interest.[23]

The *parens patriae* power allows the state constitutionally to act as the "general guardian of all infants."[24] Its origins are found in antiquity:

In ancient Times the King was regarded as "Parens Patriae" of orphaned or dependent infants. . . . Under our system of government the state succeeds to the position and power of the King. Both King and State exercise this power in the interests of the people. Society has a deep interest in the preservation of the race itself. It is a natural instinct that lives of infants be preserved.[25]

Under the doctrine of *parens patriae*, courts are empowered to consent to treatment when the parents are unavailable to do so. Examples arise where the parents have abandoned the child[26] or where they are just temporarily unavailable.[27] Court intervention in mandating therapy need not be predicated on an immediate threat to life or limb.[28] Although the criteria vary, one frequently invoked standard is the substituted judgment test: "In this case, the court must decide what its ward would choose, if he were in a position to make a sound judgment. Certainly, he would pick the chance for a fuller participation in life rather than a rejection of his potential as a more fully endowed human being."[29] Not only can the court overrule objections of both parent and child, but also under the right circumstances it can overrule the objection of the surgeon who is to perform the procedure.[30]

A serious threat to life, however, is not per se grounds for the intervention of the court under the *parens patriae* doctrine. If, for example, an infant is born with myelomeningocele, microcephaly, and hydrocephalus, and failure to operate would not place the infant in imminent danger of death, surgery may not be ordered over parental objection despite its efficacy in significantly reducing the risk of infection. In *Weber v. Stony Brook Hospital* the court noted:

Successful results could also be achieved with antibiotic therapy. Further, while the mortality rate is higher where conservative medical treatment is used, in this particular case the surgical procedures also involved a great risk of depriving the infant of what little function remains in her legs, and would also result in recurring urinary tract and possibly kidney infections, skin infections, and edemas of the limbs.[31]

The court concluded that the child was not neglected even though the parents had chosen the arguably riskier of two alternatives, both of which were considered valid choices by the available expert medical testimony.

Life-threatening situations. The most commonly accepted situation in which medical therapy may be ordered for children over the wishes of their parents is where the life of the child is at stake.[32] In life-threatening situations, courts will generally find that the parents are violating state statutes concerning child neglect or endangerment if they withhold medical treatment.[33] Courts have concluded that the strong interests of the state, coupled with the best interests of the child, outweigh the parents' religious beliefs and rights.[34]

Such intervention may be ordered even when the likelihood of success is only 50%.[35] State intervention, however, may be predicated on less critical medical need. Parental objection is insufficient in most states to overcome state requirements for prophylaxis against gonococcal ophthalmia neonatorum.[36] Surgery has been ordered, despite opposition by the patient's father, where necessary to stabilize and prevent aggravation of a deformed foot when the surgery was deemed to be in the best interest of the child.[37] Even a tonsillectomy may be ordered over the objections of parents with religious reservations about the procedure, at least where the child is in the hands of a state department of social service.[38] Over parental objection, a court may order medically necessitated dental attention, including plastic surgery for treatment of cleft lip and cleft palate.[39] Surgery may also be ordered if, despite the absence of a present threat to physical health, the court considers it necessary for the psychological well-being of the child.[40] Accordingly, surgery has been ordered even though it was dangerous and offered only partial correction without cure of a facial deformity.[41] In addition, an autopsy may be ordered, notwithstanding religious proscription, where state law requires the authorities to determine the cause of death.[42]

Non-life-threatening situations. Parental refusals of medical intervention are most likely to be upheld where the child's condition is not life-threatening and where the treatment itself would expose the child to great risk.[43] Such refusals are sometimes upheld even when the proposed therapy would offer great benefit to the child.[44] The court may also stay its hand if it is persuaded that the child is antagonistic to the proposed therapy and that his or her cooperation would be necessary to derive any benefit from the treatment.[45]

Most of the time, a court will avoid intervening when the malady sought to be treated is not life-threatening.[46] As we have seen, though, courts sometimes fail to intervene even in the presence of disorders that are clearly life-threatening. In *In re Hofbauer* the parents of a 7-year-old boy with Hodgkin's disease treated him not with radiotherapy and chemotherapy but with nutritional or metabolic therapy including Laetrile.[47] There was expert testimony that Laetrile is effective and the father indicated he would agree to conventional therapy if the physician prescribing the placebos advised it. Persuaded that the parents were concerned and loving and that the child was not neglected, the court held that "great deference must be accorded a parent's choice as to the mode of medical treatment to be undertaken and the physician selected to administer the same."[48] The statute at issue in *Hofbauer* allowed the following interpretation:

Adequate medical care does not require a parent to beckon the assistance of a physician for every trifling affliction that a child may suffer. . . . We believe, however, that the statute does require a parent to entrust care to that of a physician when such course would be undertaken by an ordinarily prudent and loving parent, "solicitous for the welfare of his child and anxious to promote its (*sic*) recovery."[49]

The court refused to find that as a matter of law the boy's parents had undertaken no reasonable efforts to ensure that acceptable medical treatment was being provided him, given the parents' concern about side effects from medical management, the alleged efficacy of the nutritional therapy and its relative lack of toxicity, and the parents' agreement that conventional treatment would be administered to the child if his condition so warranted. So long as they had provided for their child a form of treatment "recommended by their physician and not totally rejected by all responsible medical authority" as, implied the court, treatment with Laetrile had been, the parents' position would be upheld.[50]

A different approach was taken in *Custody of a Minor*.[51] Applying the best interest of the child rule, the court decided that the trial court was justified in concluding that "metabolic therapy was not only medically ineffective [in the management of leukemia] but was poisoning the child . . . and, contrary to the best interests of the child."[52] This conclusion, in the court's opinion, justified the finding that the child was without necessary and proper medical care and that the parents were unwilling to provide the care required of them by the parental neglect statute.

The best interest of the child may justify intervention even when life itself is not threatened, as illustrated by *In re Karwath*.[53] There, the parents had given their child up for adoption because of the mother's emotional illness and the father's unemployment and financial problems. Concern about possible hearing loss and rheumatic fever prompted the child's physician to recommend a tonsillectomy, but the father demanded that surgery be withheld unless necessary beyond the shadow of a doubt.[54] Although the court's opinion does not elaborate on the point, this position was based on the father's religious faith. The father would agree to surgery as a last resort and only after the failure of chiropractic procedures and medicine. The father also requested that the court require second and third opinions to confirm that the procedure was "necessary with reasonable medical certainty to restore and preserve the health of these wards of the State" before surgery could be undertaken.[55] Despite the father's wishes, the court ordered that the surgery be performed.[56] The fact that the parents' objection was religiously based made no difference.

Our paramount concern for the best interest and welfare of the children overrides the father's contention that absolute medical certitude of necessity and success should precede surgery. Nor is it required that a medical crisis be shown constituting an immediate threat to life and limb.[57]

Transfusions

Only flesh with its soul—its blood—YOU must not eat. And, besides that YOUR blood of YOUR souls shall I ask back. From the hand of every living creature shall I ask it back; and from the hand of man, from the hand of each one who is his brother, shall I ask back the soul of man.[58]

If anyone at all belonging to the house of Israel or the proselytes who reside among them eats any blood at all, against the person who eats blood I will set my face, and I will cut him off from his people; the life of every creature is identical with its blood.[59]

These and other scriptural passages[60] provide the theological underpinning for the belief of certain religious groups, notably the Jehovah's Witnesses, that blood transfusions are contrary to the law of God. Since transfusions are a well-accepted component of the therapeutic armamentarium, many cases have examined the right of the state as *parens patriae* to protect the health of children within its jurisdiction as against the right of parents to raise their children according to their religious beliefs. *Parens patriae*, defined in this context as "a sovereign right and duty to care for a child and protect him from neglect, abuse and fraud during his minority," has been the basis in a number of cases for compelling transfusion of a child whose parents objected on religious grounds.[61] As we have seen in other instances, the courts distinguish between religious beliefs and opinions, which are held inviolable, and "religious practices inconsistent with the peace and safety of the state."[62] One court, in justifying such a decision, wrote:

[I]t was not ordered that he eat blood, or that he cease to believe it is equivalent to the eating of blood. It is only ordered that he may not prevent another person, a citizen of our country, from receiving the medical attention necessary to preserve her life.[63]

A party seeking court intervention to authorize transfusion over parental objection is not exposed to civil liability.[64]

As in other areas where religious beliefs and children's welfare may conflict, a court may stay its hand "where the proposed treatment is dangerous to life, or there is a difference of medical opinion as to the efficacy of a proposed treatment, or where medical opinion differs as to which of two or more suggested remedies should be followed."[65] At least one court refused to order transfusions where the patient had no minor children, the patient had notified the physician and hospital of his belief that acceptance of transfusion violated the laws of God, the patient had executed documents releasing the doctor and hospital from civil liability, and there appeared to be no clear and present danger to society.[66] Even where a child is involved, a court may refuse to order transfusions if the child is not faced with a threat to his or her life.

If we were to describe the surgery as "required" like the Court of Appeals, our decisions would conflict with the mother's religious beliefs. Aside from religious considerations, one can also question the use of that adjective on medical grounds since an orthopedic specialist testified that the operation itself was dangerous. Indeed, one can question who, other than the Creator, has the right to term certain surgery as "required." The fatal/nonfatal distinction also steers the courts of this Commonwealth away from a medical and philosophical morass: If spinal surgery can be ordered, what about a hernia or gall bladder operation or a hysterectomy? . . . As between a parent and the state, the state does not have an interest of sufficient magnitude outweighing religious beliefs when the child's life is not immediately imperiled by his physical condition.[67]

A court will be most inclined to order a transfusion when life is threatened. In some situations, this has been done even when the patient was an adult.[68] As a general matter, the willingness of the court to intervene increases in the case of a minor,[69] notwithstanding parents' arguments on due process[70] and free exercise grounds.[71] Although courts are generally more reluctant to order transfusion for adults, when the adult is an expectant mother the court may well ignore the question of the right to transfuse the adult and proceed with the transfusion order based on the right to treat the child.[72]

Where a child's life is in danger, the court may adopt streamlined procedures to preserve life that would not be followed or tolerated under other circumstances. For example, a transfusion can be ordered first and the hearing on the propriety of the order may be held later.[73] A hearing may be held in advance of the need for transfusion, for instance, where a mother near term has a history of Rh incompatibility and has given birth in the past to other children with erythroblastosis fetalis requiring transfusion.[74] Even in a state where a statute provides immunity from criminal prosecution for parents treating their children in accordance with their religious beliefs, the state may nevertheless appoint a guardian to approve transfusions when necessary to save the life of the child.[75] This is the mechanism by which most courts enter transfusion orders.

While courts ordinarily find neglect only where parents abandon their children or otherwise fail to provide for their basic needs, such a finding can be and often is reached where transfusion is required over the religious objections of parents, notwithstanding the sincerity and depth of the parents' beliefs. In *State v. Perricone* a child was afflicted with congenital heart disease that, from the court's description, suggests tetralogy of Fallot.[76] Transfusions were required for proper management of his condition. The parents, who were Jehovah's Witnesses, refused to permit such transfusions, and they were found guilty of neglect of their son even though the court found them to have "sincere parental concern and affection for the child."[77]

A group of Jehovah's Witnesses in the state of Washington brought a class action seeking to have declared unconstitutional a state statute that declared a child dependent, and hence eligible for appointment of a guardian, where transfusion was or could be vital to save the patient and the parents refused to permit it.[78] The court upheld the statute as constitutional, and the Supreme Court of the United States affirmed per curiam.[79] That parents "have not failed in their duty to the child in other respects provides them no more shelter under such a statute than does the sincerity of their religious beliefs."[80] In analyzing the tension between the free exercise clause and statutes of this type, the court in *People v. Pierson*[81] wrote: "We place no limitations upon the power of the mind over the body, the power of faith to dispel disease, or the power of the Supreme Being to heal the sick. We merely declare the law as given us by the legislature."[82]

A threat to the very life of a child is not always deemed necessary for a court to order transfusion over parental objection. Where brain damage was threatened by rising bilirubin in a child with erythroblastosis fetalis, the court found sufficient grounds to order transfusion, even though no mention was made of an actual threat to life.[83] In *In re Sampson* the parents did not oppose plastic surgery required for palliation of massive disfigurement of the right side of the face and neck secondary to von Recklinghausen's disease (neurofibromatosis) in a 15-year-old boy;[84] they did, however, object to the transfusions that such extensive surgery would require. Although there was no threat to life and although the physicians, to diminish the surgical risks, advised delay until the boy was old enough to consent, the trial court ordered surgery and was upheld on appeal. The court rejected as too restrictive the argument that it could intervene only where the life of the child is endangered by a failure to act. The court of appeals distinguished its earlier opinion in *In re Seiferth*, noting that *Seiferth* turned on the question of a court's discretion and not the existence of its power to order surgery in a case where life itself was not at stake.[85] The court had no trouble finding that religious objection to transfusion does not "present a bar at least where the transfusion is necessary to the success of the required surgery."[86]

Where a child is approaching the age of maturity, and where his or her life is not in imminent danger, the minor patient may have the right to express an opinion about the morality of transfusions and his or her willingness to submit to them. In *In re Green* a 16-year-old boy with scoliosis required surgery to prevent his eventually becoming bedridden.[87] His parents, Jehovah's Witnesses, opposed the use of transfusions that the surgery would necessitate. The record did not disclose whether the patient himself was a Jehovah's Witness or planned to become one. The court wrote:

Unlike *Yoder* and *Sampson*, our inquiry does not end at this point, since we believe that the wishes of the sixteen-year-old boy should be ascertained; the ultimate question, in our view, is whether a parent's religious beliefs are paramount to the possibly adverse decision of the child. While the record before us gives us no indication of his thinking, it is the child rather than the parent in this appeal who is directly involved which thereby distinguishes *Yoder*'s decision not to discuss the beliefs of the parents vis-à-vis the children. In *Sampson* the family court judge decided not to "evade the responsibility for a decision now by the simple expedient of foisting upon this boy the responsibility for making a decision at some later date. . . . " While we are cognizant of the realistic problems of this approach . . . we believe that [the child] should be heard.[88]

More recently, however, both the Illinois and the United States Supreme Courts stopped short of imposing their authority when an unborn child's life was endangered because the mother refused, on religious grounds, to undergo a cesarean section. The Illinois Supreme Court declined to review an appellate court decision that upheld a Pentecostal's right to refuse a cesarean section delivery, even though physicians deemed it essential for her unborn child's survival, and the United States Supreme Court, in *Baby Boy Doe v. Mother Doe*, followed suit by declining to order the lower court to convene an emergency hearing in the case.[89]

Police power

Certain public health measures are enacted pursuant to police power and upheld by the courts despite various parental objections. The two best examples of this in the health care arena are the vaccination of schoolchildren and fluoridation of water supplies, performed primarily for the benefit of children. *Police power* is an umbrella term not readily susceptible to precise definition:

While it is perhaps almost impossible to frame a definition of the police power which shall accurately indicate its precise limits, so far as we are aware, all courts that have considered the subject have recognized and sanctioned the doctrine that under the police power there is general legislative authority to pass such laws as it is believed will promote the common good, or will protect or preserve the public health. And the power to determine what laws are necessary to promote or secure these objects, rests primarily with the general assembly, subject to the power of the courts to decide whether a particular enactment is adapted to that end.[90]

Often, regulations are promulgated not by the legislature but rather by a municipality, a board of public health, or some other arm of the state. In general the courts will give deference to determinations made by these bodies:

[D]etermination by the legislative body that a particular regulation is necessary for the protection or preservation of health is conclusive on the courts subject only to the limitation that it must be a reasonable determination, not an abuse of discretion, and must not infringe rights secured by the Constitution.[91]

Under this standard, most regulations such as this one will be upheld, because "abuse of discretion" is seldom found.

Vaccinations

Some health professionals today may be surprised to learn that there is a long history of disputes, continuing to recent times, concerning the validity of state and local regulations that require vaccination of school children as a prerequisite for attendance in public schools.[92] A number of early decisions upheld these regulations only because epidemics of smallpox in some communities warranted vaccination as an emergency measure.[93] In some cases the constitutionality of the vaccination requirement was upheld only because the court construed it to mean not that vaccination was mandated but rather that school attendance without vaccination was not permitted.[94] More recently, it has been held that a child has no absolute right to enter school without immunization, and the school board has full authority to compel it.[95]

Questions of federal constitutionality, at least, were essentially laid to rest in the case of *Jacobson v. Massachusetts*.[96] In *Jacobson*, an adult who apparently feared side effects as a consequence of a bad experience with immunization as a child refused to submit to vaccination under a compulsory vaccination law. The court upheld his conviction:

There is, of course, a sphere in which the individual may assert the supremacy of his own will, and rightfully dispute the authority of any human government . . . to interfere with the exercise of that will. But it is equally true that in every well-ordered society charged with the duty of conserving the safety of its members the rights of the individual in respect of his liberty may at times, under the pressure of great dangers, be subjected to such restraint, to be enforced by reasonable regulations as the safety of the general public may demand.[97]

The court found no violation of equal protection in the statute's exception favoring children who are medically unfit to be vaccinated, despite the absence of such an exception for adults in like condition, both because there was no reason to suspect that an unfit adult would be required to submit to vaccination and because regulations appropriate for adults are not always safely applied to children.[98] Few cases before and apparently no cases after *Jacobson* have found vaccination requirements to be unconstitutional.[99] The courts have rejected constitutional attacks on both equal protection and due process grounds.[100]

Despite the special solicitude of the courts for First Amendment rights, compulsory vaccination has been upheld even when it conflicts with the religious beliefs of citizens.[101] This is true even where, under state law, a board of education was empowered, although not required, to exempt a child whose parents object to immunization on religious grounds.[102] Personal liberty, including freedom of religion, is a relative and not an absolute right, which must be considered in the light of the general public welfare.[103] The right to practice religion freely does not include liberty to expose the community or the child to communicable diseases or the latter to ill health or death.[104] Nevertheless, some courts, generally in earlier cases only, have found it necessary to point out that vaccination requirements do not prevent children from attending schools, and children who are thereby excluded are excluded by their own consciences.[105] In other cases the courts have questioned whether the plaintiff's religious beliefs really did compel the conclusion that vaccination was immoral.[106] Clearly, the courts have enforced the state's strong public policy interest in universal vaccination, an interest that may need even more vigilant protection today as a result of unfounded concerns about alleged ill-effects from vaccination.[107]

Where, however, a statute provides an exemption for members of a recognized church or religious denomination whose tenets conflict with the practice of vaccination, a mother's opposition based on her personal belief in the Bible and its teachings was sufficient to entitle her and her children to the exemption.[108] A similar statute was held not applicable to a man objecting to immunization because one of his children had earlier contracted hepatitis secondary to a diphtheria shot. In so holding, the court found no violation of equal protection or due process.[109] Where exemptions are enacted for persons religiously opposed to vaccination, a local school board may not be given discretion to determine who can qualify.[110]

The vaccination regulations have been repeatedly upheld as a reasonable exercise of the police power.[111] There need no longer be evidence of an epidemic,[112] or even of a single case,[113] to warrant imposition of the regulation. The regulation does not involve the state in the practice of medicine.[114] Evidence impugning the value of vaccination need not even be considered by the courts because such evidence is more appropriately presented to the legislature or its duly constituted agencies, such as the state board of health.[115]

Finally, there is no violation of the right to a free public education, nor is it a violation of state compulsory education laws, to make vaccination a prerequisite to school attendance: "[H]ealth measures prescribed by local authorities as a condition of school attendance do not conflict with statutory provisions conferring on children of proper age the privilege of attending school, nor with compulsory education laws."[116] This is true even though it leads to the exclusion of children whose physical condition precludes vaccination.[117] It has been held that, where a father did nothing to prevent the vaccination of his son, the child was not neglected under a regulation that barred him from school because he was unvaccinated.[118] More often, however, failure to provide for vaccination of a child may warrant a finding of parental neglect and the resultant appointment of a guardian to consent to and arrange vaccination.[119]

CHILD ABUSE

The magnitude of the problem

Sadly, the mistreatment of children is limited neither by time nor space. The problem is found in every nation and in every period.[120] Here, however, we focus upon the problem of abuse in the United States.

In 1998, the most recent year for which national statistics are available, there were reports of more than 2.8 million cases of suspected child abuse and neglect in the United States.[121] Between 2000 and 5000 children are said to die every year as a result of intentionally inflicted injuries.[122] Neglect is probably the commonest form of child abuse and the one most likely to cause fatalities.[123] Reliable statistics, however, are hard to find. There is risk of error in both directions: underreporting and overreporting (see below). McClain et al.[124] reported that 85% of the deaths attributable to child abuse and neglect were not recorded as such, resulting in serious underestimates of fatalities from abuse and neglect. Historically, however, only about 40% of reports have been substantiated.[125]

One reason for uncertainty, undoubtedly, is that there is no universally accepted definition of child abuse. Statutes may impose liability for "excessive corporal punishment," "drug related activity," or require "reasonable suspicion," or "mental injury," yet may fail to define such terms.[126] Some definitions of neglect classify a failure to provide for a child's needs as negligence, whereas others require a harmful outcome or at least the potential for same before neglect can be found. Still others demand that there be a societally available alternative to the deprivation before neglect can be established. Even physical abuse, which may seem a fairly straightforward concept, is not an unambiguous term. Some states define physical abuse as actions resulting in actual injury, whereas others define it to include mere potential for injury.[127] The harms to a developing fetus from maternal substance abuse during the pregnancy are well described,[128] but whether the mother is abusing the baby as she abuses her substances is debated.[129] Psychological abuse is even less amenable to ready definition. In one report, 45% of parents in a nationally representative sample of 1250 parents reported insulting or swearing at their children that year.[130] Whether such behavior is abusive may depend on the severity and frequency of such conduct, but may also depend upon subjective judgments on the proper rearing of children. Sexual abuse may also be a concept more elusive than it appears. Statutory rape, for example, may or may not fit the definition of sexual abuse.[131]

Even assuming one knows what is and is not abuse, child protection workers and health care providers often disagree about the nature of appropriate reports and the relevant legal requirements for making them.[132]

Religious exemptions

Many groups eschew medical interventions on religious or philosophical grounds. Among those best known in the United States are Christian Scientists and Jehovah's Witnesses. Somewhat less well known are the General Assembly and the Church of the First Born, the Faith Tabernacle Church, the Church of God of the Union Assembly Incorporated, and the No Name Fellowship and Faith Assembly Church.[133] Members of these faiths may believe that a proposed medical intervention forces them to choose between obeying the law of man and obeying the law of God.

Some religious groups promote female circumcision.[134] Under fundamental First Amendment principles, religious practices are seldom scrutinized, and rarely constrained, by American law. Nevertheless, the lack of any medical value from the procedure and its potential for significant harm have resulted in its general condemnation.[135]

Certain traditional ethnic remedies may be worse than merely ineffective. They may be dangerous, as with lead used for constipation and other problems.[136] The consequences of reliance upon folk remedies or faith healing can be quite serious. One author claims that since 1975, at least 165 children have died because of their parents' refusal to utilize conventional medical treatment based on their religious beliefs.[137]

The tension between our deeply cherished First Amendment rights and our moral duty and cultural imperative to protect children is not easy to resolve. Except for Hawaii, Maryland, and Massachusetts, all states are said to have some form of religious exemption to child abuse and neglect laws.[138] These provisions often exempt parents who rely upon prayer from requirements to provide medical care for their minor children. For the most part, religious exemption laws originated after enactment of the Child Abuse Prevention and Treatment Act of 1974, 42 U.S.C. Section 5101, *et seq.*[139]

[A] parent or guardian legitimately practicing his religious beliefs who thereby does not provide specific medical treatment for a child, for that reason alone shall not be considered a negligent parent or guardian; however, such an exception shall not preclude a court from ordering that medical services be provided to the child, where his health requires it.[140]

States failing to create such exemptions may be ineligible to receive federal funds appropriated to fulfill the intent of the act: to establish preventive programs to reduce the incidence of child abuse.[141] In regulations promulgated in 1983, HHS said that "[n]othing in this part should be construed as requiring or prohibiting a finding of neglect when a parent practicing his or her religious beliefs does not, for that reason alone, provide medical treatment for a child."[142] On the other hand, the Department of Health and Human Services has required the states to provide that, regardless of religious belief, all cases of medical neglect be reported and investigated.[143]

State courts have taken inconsistent approaches to the cases. In *Walker v. Superior Court*,[144] the California Supreme Court held parents criminally liable for trying to treat meningitis with Christian Science. In Minnesota, however, a different result obtained. Its second-degree manslaughter statute defines manslaughter in the second degree as arising from, among other circumstances, "the person's culpable negligence whereby the person creates an unreasonable risk, and consciously takes chances of causing death or great bodily harm to another. . . ."[145] In *State v. McKown*,[146] Christian Science parents were charged with second-degree manslaughter for the death of their diabetic child, who died without benefit of medical care. The parents relied upon Minnesota's child neglect statute, under which

A parent . . . who willfully deprives a child of necessary food, clothing, shelter, health care, or supervision appropriate to the child's age . . . [which] deprivation harms or is likely to substantially harm the child's physical, mental, or emotional health . . . [shall be] guilty of neglect of a child. If a parent . . . in good faith selects and depends upon spiritual means or prayer for treatment or care of disease or remedial care of the child, this treatment shall constitute "health care."[147]

Because the manslaughter and child neglect statutes had different purposes, however, the court refused to read them together, and held that the religious exemption defense could not be applied to the manslaughter charge. Nevertheless, it also held that the manslaughter indictments violated the parents' due process rights because "the child neglect statute did not provide fair notice" of the potential criminal liability they could face by actually relying on the alternative healing methods that the neglect statute clearly prohibited.[148] Ironically, the minor child's father successfully sought compensatory damages for negligence causing the death of the child.[149]

For health professionals, reliance upon faith healing and other nonscientific approaches may seem irrational and barbaric. Certainly the outcome can be appalling. But religious freedom is rightly seen as one of the great achievements of Western liberal thought.

Diagnosis

The work of Hefler and Kempe remains an excellent guide to diagnosis. In their classic article, they wrote that "the syndrome should be considered in any child exhibiting evidence of fracture of any bone, failure to thrive, soft tissue swellings or skin bruising, and any child who dies suddenly, or where the degree and type of injury is at variance with history given regarding the occurrence of the trauma."[150] They supplied additional details:

The battered-child syndrome may occur at any age but, in general, the affected children are younger than three years. . . . [T]he child's general health is below par and he shows evidence of neglect including poor skin hygiene, multiple soft tissue injuries, and malnutrition. One often obtains a history of previous episodes suggestive of parental neglect or trauma. A marked discrepancy between clinical findings and historical data as supplied by the parents is a major diagnostic feature. . . . The fact that no new lesions . . . occur while the child is in the hospital . . . lends added weight to the diagnosis. . . . Subdural hematoma, with or without fracture of the skull, is . . . an extremely frequent finding. . . . The characteristic distribution of these multiple fractures and the observation that the lesions are in different stages of healing are of additional value in making the diagnosis.[151]

The authors have since concluded that knowledge of the symptoms and signs of child abuse has greatly increased within the health care community.[152]

In children 9 months of age or less, any soft tissue injury suggests possible abuse.[153] In children over age 1 year, accidental bruises tend to be found over bony prominences.

Bruises in less typical locations, such as the abdomen, suggest abuse.[154] Retinal hemorrhages are deemed to be nearly diagnostic of child abuse.[155] Pattern scars or bruises, such as cigarette or immersion burns; lacerations or abrasions of areas not normally so injured, such as the palette or external genitalia; and behavior changes (noncompliance, anger, isolation, destructiveness, developmental delays, excessive attention-seeking, and lack of separation anxiety) are also characteristic.[156]

In contrast to physical abuse, neglect is more apt to present as malnutrition, recurrent pica, chronic fatigue or listlessness, poor hygiene, inadequate clothing for the circumstances, or lack of appropriate medical care, such as immunizations, dental care, and eyeglasses.[157] Behavioral signs, including poor school attendance, age-inappropriate responsibility for tasks such as housework, drug or alcohol abuse, and a history of repeated toxic ingestions, may also be present.[158]

Sexually abused children may have difficulty walking or sitting; thickened or hyperpigmented labial skin; torn, stained, or bloody underclothing; bruised or bleeding private parts; vaginal discharge, pruritus, or both; recurrent urinary tract infections; venereal disease; pregnancy; and lax rectal tone. It is reasonable to believe that these unfortunate children may be at increased risk for acquired immunodeficiency syndrome (AIDS), although the most common cause in children is undoubtedly maternal-fetal infection.[159] A vaginal opening greater than 4 mm in horizontal diameter is said to be characteristic of the sexual abuse of prepubescent girls.[160] Victims of sexual abuse may also have poor self-esteem, attempt suicide, display regressive behavior such as enuresis, masturbate excessively, engage in sexual promiscuity, withdraw from reality, express shame or guilt, and experience distortion of body image.[161]

If the child's caretaker was abused as a youngster, the child in his care is at higher risk. Abusive mothers are often themselves victims of physical abuse by a spouse or partner.[162] Adult sex offenders are also often themselves victims of abuse.[163] An Iowa study indicated that 58% of shaken baby syndrome patients had evidence of prior abuse, and 33% had been shaken before, corresponding to a 33% recidivism rate reported for child abuse generally.[164] A 1999 study by the National Center on Addiction and Substance Abuse found children of substance-abusing parents 3 times more likely to be abused and 4 times more likely to be neglected than children of non-substance-abusing parents.[165]

Abuse most often occurs at the hands of parents. In more than 75% of the reported cases, the parents are the perpetrators, and in another 10%, the perpetrators are other relatives of the victim.[166] People in other care-giving relationships to the victim, such as foster parents, account for only about 2% of all reported cases of child abuse.[167] About 80% of all perpetrators are under age 40, with women more likely to be perpetrators of physical abuse and men more often perpetrators of sexual abuse.[168] Physicians concerned about possible child abuse may wish to inquire about caretakers' tendencies toward alcoholism, drug abuse, sexual promiscuity, unstable marriages, and criminal activity.

The examining physician should strive to strike an appropriate balance, and set the index of suspicion neither too high nor too low. Not all cases present in classic fashion, and typical findings are not always caused by child abuse. "Any one may coincidentally show a variety of types of physical marks (e.g., a black eye, cut lip, bruised ears, scratches and diaper rash burns), even though their parents may be loving, concerned and reasonably careful."[169] Thus, the diagnosis may not be straightforward, particularly since the history is unlikely to be obtained easily from intimidated young patients or from their guilt-ridden parents.

Differential diagnosis. To explain head injuries, parents will often report accidents such as falls from small heights. This explanation is suspect: such injuries are likely to result from abuse.[170] "When children who are said to have had minor falls are found to have life-threatening multiple or severe injuries, the reliability of the history should be seriously questioned."[171]

Some disorders can mimic abuse, but they are rare. Osteogenesis imperfecta ("OI") is "an inherited disorder of connective tissue resulting from abnormal quality and/or quantity of Type 1 collagen."[172] Sometimes referred to as "brittle-bone disease," OI is said to occur in 1 in 15,000 to 1 in 16,000 births and to have four main features: (1) abnormal bone fragility with osteoporosis, (2) blue sclerae, (3) defective dentition (dentinogenesis imperfecta) (a defect in the number, kind, and arrangement of teeth), and (4) presenile hearing impairment.[173]

Glutaric aciduria is a metabolic disorder caused by an enzyme deficiency (glutaryl-coenzyme A dehydrogenase) characterized by an often fatal inability to process amino acids. The condition affects 1 in every 30,000 births. Glutaric acid is an intermediate in the degradation of lysine, hydroxyglycine, and tryptophan. Symptoms are said to mimic those of child abuse.[174] Colorado now requires that all infants be tested for glutaric aciduria at birth.[175] Menkes disease, an X-linked inherited disorder of intestinal copper absorption, can be complicated by progressive macrocephaly following development of subdural hematomas, which can be confused with shaken baby syndrome.[176]

A theory that is sometimes offered with but little justification is that failed CPR could cause retinal hemorrhage.

Reporting laws

At common law, there was no duty to report, even when child abuse was recognized.[177] Today, all states obligate specified individuals to report suspected cases of abuse or neglect to local child protection officials. Among others required to report may be house staff, dentists, podiatrists, nurses, and mental health professionals.[178] For a collection of the statutes obliging physicians to report child abuse, see the National Clearinghouse on Child Abuse and Neglect at http://www.calib.com/nccanch/statutes/index/cfm.[179] Teachers are often required to report as well.[180] Federal law provides for funding to the states for surveillance, prevention, treatment, training, and law enforcement functions related to child maltreatment.[181] Federal funding for state child abuse programs depends upon state enactment of reporting requirements.[182] Evidence of the severity of the problem may well have contributed to the decision to require reporting.[183]

In general, the reporting statutes identify those who must report, describe how such reporting should occur, and limit or abrogate certain privileges. The statutes are far from uniform, however. Consider the statutes mandating reports of sexual abuse. Some states require reports of abuse and neglect only by parents, family members, or caretakers.[184] Others include abuse by nonfamily members.[185] Others include statutory rape, but grant the health care provider some measure of discretion in whether to report.[186]

Most states grant immunity to any professional who reports such information as is required by law.[187] The immunity is typically a powerful bullwark against attack. In *Myers v. Lashley*,[188] for example, a father and grandmother wrongly identified as child abusers brought separate claims against a clinical psychologist for slander, negligent infliction of emotional distress, intentional infliction of emotional distress, and professional negligence. The plaintiffs attempted to describe their claim as one for malpractice. The court rejected this characterization, because such a claim would seek vindication for injury to the children, whereas the plaintiffs sought to recover for injury to themselves. The privilege shielding medical and other professionals from claims arising out of statutorily mandated reporting, however, extended across all cognizable theories of liability. The court held that plaintiffs' failure to prove that the defendant psychologist had reported in bad faith, and that he released the report before submitting it to the state agency, barred recovery. In Pennsylvania, a plaintiff alleging a false report must similarly allege that the defendant acted in bad faith when filing it. In *Heinrich v. Conemaugh Valley Mem. Hosp'l*,[189] the court noted that under Pennsylvania Constitution Statute Section 6318(b), Immunity from Liability, it should and did presume the reporter's good faith. The plaintiff would need to overcome this presumption to recover.[190]

Observing swelling around a child's eye and ear, ER physicians suspected child abuse. Without discussing their suspicions with the patient's mother, his pediatrician, or any staff pediatrician, the emergency physicians notified the state's Department of Children and Youth Services. Eventually, pediatricians established that an accidental fall, rather than an abusive blow to the head, had caused

child, because no doctor-patient relationship existed between the parent and the psychologist or another psychologist because she never evaluated the child.[231] At a custody hearing, Dr. Sternlof had testified that the child may have been sexually abused by the father. The father later sued Sternlof, as well as the child psychologist referring the patient to Sternlof, for professional negligence. The court construed Paulson's professional negligence claims and allegation that Sternlof had no right to conduct an evaluation of the child to mean that the evaluation he conducted was done negligently. Sternlof owed no duty to Paulson, however. Moreover, since Sternlof's evaluation was conducted for purposes of a court proceeding, his communications were made preliminarily to proposed judicial or quasijudicial proceedings and were absolutely privileged, and an action for intentional infliction of emotional distress was barred.[232]

Some courts have held that no private right or action arises under the child abuse reporting statutes. In *Cechman v. Travis*, an administratrix sued a hospital and treating physicians on behalf of a deceased child who was killed by her abusive father after being treated at the defendant institution.[233] Although a criminal statute required that a licensed physician report suspected cases of abuse, the court held that the statute created no private right of action in tort in favor of an abused victim. Moreover, the physician had no common law legal duty to protect the child from the father, and thus no common law medical malpractice claim would lie.[234]

In *Valtakis v. Putnam*,[235] the Minnesota Court of Appeals held that Minnesota's Child Abuse Reporting Act did not create a private right of action.[236]

State liability. Some state agencies have been held liable under the reporting statutes for abuse by foster parents they have selected when the agencies knew or should have known of the abuse.[237]

A mother brought a wrongful death action against a psychologist after discovering that the father had murdered their child. As part of a court proceeding that the mother initiated to modify child custody in response to allegations that the father had abused the child, the psychologist had examined the mother and father. A social worker's alleged failure to properly investigate child abuse allegations against the father did not violate the child's due process right to be free from bodily harm caused by third parties, even though the father later murdered the child. Social workers had authority and discretion in how to conduct their investigation, and they had no special or fiduciary relationship to the child, who was not in state custody. The child was not injured by a state act or a state-created danger. The psychologist had no confidential relationship with the mother that would establish a duty to disclose any facts about the father's relationship with the child. Thus, the psychologist did not violate any duty to disclose for purposes of extending the

statute of limitations pursuant to fraudulent concealment doctrine.[238]

Liability for reporting. Just as a health care professional may be held liable for failing to report, there are circumstances under which liability can be imposed for reporting. In *Russell v. Adams*,[239] for example, an adult patient's mother alleged that the therapist had falsely told the daughter that the mother had abused her and that the therapist had recommended that the daughter sever all ties with her. The court ruled that the statute of limitations had not run on the mother's claim of an infliction of emotional distress. The defense raised the fact that the therapist was not the plaintiff's treater. The court wrote:

We are aware that the treatment of the emotional problems of the patient may, in some instances, have adverse consequences on the patient's relationships with others. . . . It does not follow, however, that the affected third party should have a cause of action for malpractice against the health care provider. Health care providers must "be free to recommend a course of treatment and act on a patient's response to the recommendation free from the possibility that someone other than the patient might complain in the future."

In *Tuman v. Genesis Assoc.*,[240] the plaintiffs sued the therapist treating their 20-year-old daughter, Diane. They alleged that the defendants had implanted false memories to the effect that the plaintiff belonged to a Satanic cult and had ritually murdered Diane's twin brother and that her father had raped and impregnated her. The parents had paid for the therapy, and the court declined to dismiss their claim for breach of contract. Based on specific undertaking to the parents, the court found the negligence claim to be viable together with reasonably foreseeable harm to them. The court rejected the argument that the plaintiffs' theory required the doctor to serve two masters. The court wrote:

The therapist's two duties dovetail to a singular duty to provide reasonably acceptable mental health therapy to the patient. . . . Further, my narrow holding does not subject therapists to negligence liability whenever parents experience emotional injury that may result when a child seeks mental health counseling. There is a vast difference between using acceptable therapy to help a patient understand emotional wounds suffered as a result of her parents' inadequate caregiving, and negligent techniques that create false memories of severely abusive parenting that necessarily injure the parents and the patient.

The court went on to find that even if the defendants owed no duty to the plaintiffs with respect to Diane's mental health counseling, the defendants did have independent duties not to intentionally inflict emotional distress upon plaintiffs.

In *Caryl S. v. Child & Adolescent Treatment Services*,[241] the court upheld a cause of action by grandparents against a therapist who had alleged that the grandmother had sexually abused their grandchild.

Munchausen's syndrome by proxy ("MSP"). MSP is generally characterized by parent-produced symptoms of illness. The child is frequently subjected to many unnecessary and potentially harmful medical procedures.[242] Diagnosis is difficult.[243] Symptoms may seem inconsistent with a previously rendered diagnosis or fail to respond to treatment. Test results may be bizarre or clinically impossible. Puzzling symptoms may spontaneously disappear whenever the child is separated from the parent.[244] The child may be overdependent.[245] The mothers are often depressed.[246] The offending parent, usually the mother, may seem very concerned, articulate, knowledgeable, and supportive. There may be other siblings with perplexing illnesses and perhaps a death under unexplained circumstances of a sibling. The array of symptoms possible may be very broad and include failure to thrive, seizures, apnea, vomiting, diarrhea, irritable bowel syndrome, osteomyelitis, and blood-borne infections. In *People v. Phillips*,[247] a mother deliberately manipulated her adopted infant daughter's electrolyte levels by adding sodium bicarbonate to the baby's formula. The child aspirated and died. Not until a second adopted infant began to develop identical symptoms did the medical staff become suspicious. The two girls, after all, were unrelated.

Typically, courts react to MSP by making the child a ward of the state.[248] Foster care is an alternative, but not free of risk.[249]

ENDNOTES

1. *People v. Pierson*, 68 N.E. 243, 244 (N.Y. 1903); *see also Owens v. State*, 116 P. 345 (Okla. Crim. App. 1911); *see also People v. Edwards*, 249 N.Y.S. 2d 325 (N.Y. Co. Ct. 1964); *see, e.g., In re Carstairs*, 115 N.Y.S. 2d 314 (N.Y. Dom. Rel. Ct. 1952).
2. *See, e.g.*, Ala. Code §12-15-1 (10) (2002); *see also Jehovah's Witnesses v. King County Hosp. Unit No. 1*, 278 F.Supp. 488 (W.D. Wash. 1967), *aff'd*, 390 U.S. 598 (1968).
3. *See, e.g., Heinemann's Appeal*, 96 Pa. 112, 42 Am. Rep. 532 (Ct. App. 1880); *see also Mitchell v. Davis*, 205 S.W. 2d 812 (Tex. Civ. App. 1947).
4. *In re Marsh*, 14 A. 2d 368 (Pa. Super. Ct. 1940).
5. *Jefferson v. Griffin Spalding County Hosp. Auth.*, 274 S.E. 2d 457 (Ga. 1981).
6. *See State v. Perricone*, 181 A. 2d 751 (N.J.), *cert. denied*, 371 U.S. 890 (1962); *In re Santos*, 227 N.Y.S. 2d 450 (N.Y.A.D. 1 Dept.), *appeal dismissed*, 185 N.E. 2d 552 (N.Y. 1962).
7. *See Custody of a Minor*, 393 N.E. 2d 836, 846 (Mass. 1979); *but see Newmark v. Williams*, 588 A. 2d 1108 (Del. 1991).
8. *See State v. Perricone, supra* note 6, at 757; *see also Levitsky v. Levitsky*, 190 A. 2d 621 (Md. 1963); *but see Osier v. Osier*, 410 A. 2d 1027 (Me. 1980).
9. *See In re Hamilton*, 657 S.W. 2d 425 (Tenn. App. 1983).
10. *People ex rel. Wallace v. Labrenz*, 104 N.E. 2d 769 (Ill.), *cert. denied*, 344 U.S. 824 (1952).
11. *Id.* at 773.
12. *See, e.g., In re Eric B.*, 235 Cal. Rptr. 22 (Cal. App. 1987), *review denied*.
13. *See id.* The court need not "hold its protective power in abeyance until harm to a minor child is not only threatened but actual. The purpose of dependency proceedings is to prevent risk, not ignore it." *Id.* at 26. *See*

14. *See State v. Miskimens*, 490 N.E. 2d 931 (Ohio Com. Pl. 1984).
15. *See e.g., In re Application of Cicero*, 421 N.Y.S. 2d 965, 966 (N.Y. Sup. 1979).
16. *See, e.g., Newmark, supra* note 7; *In re Frank*, 248 P. 2d 553 (Wash. 1952).
17. *See In re Gonzales*, 323 N.E. 2d 42, 46-47 (Ill. App. 1974); *see also People in the Interest of D.L.E.*, 614 P. 2d 873 (Colo. 1980).
18. *State v. Chenoweth*, 71 N.E. 197 (Ind. 1904); *see also Stehr v. State*, 139 N.W. 676 (Neb.), *aff'd*, 142 N.W. 670 (1913); *see also Beck v. State*, 233 P. 495 (Okla. Crim. App. 1925); *see also People v. Vogel*, 242 P. 2d 969 (Cal. App. 4th Dist. 1952); *see also State v. Dumlao*, 491 A. 2d 404 (Conn. App. 1985); *see also State v. Clark*, 261 A. 2d 294 (Conn. Cir. A.D. 1969); *see also State v. Staples*, 48 N.W. 283 (Minn. 1914); *see also State v. Beach*, 329 S.W. 2d 712 (Mo. 1959); *see also State v. Watson*, 71 A. 1113 (N.J. Sup. 1909); *see also Pennsylvania v. Barnhart*, 497 A. 2d 616 (Pa. Super. 1985), *appeal denied*, 538 A. 2d 874 (Pa.), *cert. denied*, 488 U.S. 817 (1988); *see also New York v. Edwards*, 249 N.Y.S. 2d 325 (N.Y. Co. Ct. 1964); *State v. Barnes*, 212 S.W. 100 (Tenn. 1919); *Oakley v. Jackson*, 1 K.B. 216 (1914); *Rex. v. Lewis*, 6 Ont. L. 132 1BRC 732-CA (1903). *See Nozza v. State*, 288 So. 2d 560 (Fla. App.), *cert. denied*, 295 So. 2d 301 (Fla. 1974); *Faunteroy v. U.S.*, 413 A. 2d 1294 (D.C. App. 1980); *State v. Zobel*, 134 N.W. 2d 101 (S.D. 1965), *cert. denied*, 382 U.S. 833 (1965), *overruled on other grounds*; *State v. Waff*, 373 N.W. 2d 18 (S.D. 1985).
19. *See* cases cited *supra* note 18.
20. *See Eversley v. State*, 748 So. 2d 963 (Fla. 1999); *see also Singleton v. State*, 35 So. 2d 375 (Ala. 1948); *Craig v. State*, 155 A. 2d 684 (Md. 1959); *New York v. Osborn*, 508 N.Y.S. 2d 746 (1986), *appeal denied*, 505 N.E. 2d 251 (N.Y. 1987); *New York v. Northrup*, 442 N.Y.S. 2d 658 (1981).
21. *See Watson, supra* note 18, at 1114; *see also State v. Osmus*, 276 P. 2d 469 (Wyo. 1954); *Howell v. State*, 350 S.E. 2d 473 (Ga. App. 1986); *Justice v. State*, 42 S.E. 1013 (Ga. 1902); *Michigan v. Mankel*, 129 N.W. 2d 894 (Mich. 1964); *Missouri v. Shouse*, 186 S.W. 1064 (Mo. 1916); *In re Appeal in Chochise County*, Juvenile Action No. 5666-J, 650 P. 2d 459 (Ariz. 1981). *But see State v. Clark, supra* note 18; *Eaglen v. State*, 231 N.E. 2d 47 (Ind. 1967); *State v. Williams*, 484 P. 2d 1167 (Wash. Ct. App. 1971).
22. *Parens patriae* empowers the state to "care for infants within its jurisdiction and to protect them from neglect, abuse, and fraud. . . . That ancient, equitable jurisdiction was codified in our Juvenile Court Act, which expressly authorizes the court, if circumstances warrant, to remove the child from the custody of its (*sic*) parents and award its custody to an appointed guardian." *Wallace, supra* note 10.
23. *In re Weberlist*, 360 N.Y.S. 2d 783, 786 (1974).
24. *Hawaii v. Standard Oil Co.*, 405 U.S. 251, 257 (1972).
25. *Morrison v. State*, 252 S.W. 2d 97, 102 (Mo. Ct. App. 1952).
26. *See Commissioner of Social Servs. re D.*, 339 N.Y.S. 2d 89 (N.Y. Fam. Ct. 1972); *see also Weberlist, supra* note 23; *In re Tanner*, 549 P. 2d 703 (Utah 1976). *See, e.g., People v. Sorensen*, 437 P. 2d 495 (Cal. 1968); *Karin T. v. Michael T.*, 484 N.Y.S. 2d 780 (Fam. Ct. 1985); *Wener v. Wener*, 312 N.Y.S. 2d 815 (1970). *But see Pamela P. v. Frank S.*, 443 N.Y.S. 2d 343 (Fam. Ct. 1981), *aff'd*, 462 N.Y.S. 2d 819 (1983).
27. *See Browning v. Hoffman*, 111 S.E. 492 (W. Va. 1922).
28. *See, e.g., Commissioner of Social Servs.* and *Tanner, supra* note 26; *Weberlist, supra* note 23.
29. *Weberlist, supra* note 23, at 787.
30. *In re Sampson*, 317 N.Y.S. 2d 641, 658 (Fam. Ct. 1970), *aff'd*, 323 N.Y.S. 2d 253 (N.Y. App. Div. 1971), *appeal denied*, 29 N.Y. 2d 486 (1971).
31. 467 N.Y.S. 2d 685, 686-87 (App. Div.), *aff'd*, 456 N.E. 2d 1186 (N.Y.), *cert. denied*, 464 U.S. 1026 (1983).

32. *In re Eric B.*, 189 Cal. App. 3d 996 (Ct. App. 1987); *People ex rel. D.L.E.*, 645 P. 2d 271 (Colo. 1982); *In re Ivy*, 319 So. 2d 53 (Fla. Dist. Ct. App. 1975); *Wallace, supra* note 10; *Custody of a Minor, supra* note 7; *Morrison, supra* note 25; *In re Willmann*, 493 N.E. 2d 1380 (Ohio Ct. App. 1986); *In re Clark*, 185 N.E. 2d 128 (Ohio C.P. 1962).

33. *See, e.g., People ex rel. D.L.E., supra* note 32 (interpreting a Colorado state statute and holding that an epileptic child was neglected when her mother failed or refused to provide medical care because of her religious beliefs).

34. *See In re McCauley*, 565 N.E. 2d 411, 414 (Mass. 1991).

35. *See In re Vasko*, 263 N.Y.S. 552 (1933).

36. *See* Office of Attorney General, No. 81-57, slip op. (Utah Dec. 14, 1981).

37. *See In re Rotkowitz*, 25 N.Y.S. 2d 624 (Dom. Rel. Ct. 1941).

38. *See In re Karwath*, 199 N.W. 2d 147, 150 (Iowa 1972).

39. *See In re Seiferth*, 127 N.E. 2d 820 (N.Y. 1955); *see also In re Gregory S.*, 380 N.Y.S. 2d 620 (1976).

40. *See In re Ray*, 408 N.Y.S. 2d 737 (City Fam. Ct. 1978); *see also In re J.M.P.*, 669 S.W. 2d 298 (Mo. App. 1984).

41. *See Sampson, supra* note 30.

42. *See Snyder v. Holy Cross Hosp.*, 352 A. 2d 334 (Md. App. 1976).

43. *See In re Hudson*, 126 P. 2d 765 (Wash. 1942); *accord Custody of a Minor*, 379 N.E. 2d 1053 (Mass. 1978).

44. *See Custody of a Minor, supra* note 43, at 1062.

45. *See Seiferth, supra* note 39, at 822.

46. *See Hudson, supra* note 43, at 778; *see also* Wash. Rev. Code Ann. §26.44.020 (2002). *See Comment, Relief for the Neglected Child: Court-Ordered Medical Treatment in Non-Emergency Situations*, 22 Santa Clara L. Rev. 471 (1982).

47. 393 N.E. 2d 1009 (N.Y. 1979).

48. *Id.* at 1013.

49. *Id.* (quoting *Pierson, supra* note 1).

50. *Id.* at 1014.

51. *Custody of a Minor, supra* note 7.

52. *Id.* at 845.

53. *Karwath, supra* note 38.

54. *Id.* at 149.

55. *Id.* at 150.

56. *Id.*

57. *Id.*

58. Genesis 9:4-5 (quoted in *Perricone, supra* note 6, at 756).

59. Leviticus 17:10-14 (quoted in *Morrison, supra* note 25, at 99).

60. *See* Leviticus 3:17, 7:26, 27; Deuteronomy 12:23; 1 Chronicles 11:16-19; 2 Samuel 23:15-17; Acts 15:28, 29, 21:25; 1 Samuel 14:32, 33 (cited in *Sampson, supra* note 30, at 646).

61. *See Perricone, supra* note 6, at 758; *see also Hoener v. Bertinato*, 171 A. 2d 140 (N.J. Juv. & Dom. Rel. Ct. 1961).

62. *Hoener, supra* note 61, at 143.

63. *Morrison, supra* note 25, at 100.

64. See *Harley v. Oliver*, 404 F.Supp. 450 (W.D. Ark. 1975), *aff'd*, 539 F. 2d 1143 (8th Cir. 1976); *see also Staelens v. Yake*, 432 F.Supp. 834 (N.D. Ill. 1977).

65. *Morrison, supra* note 25, at 102.

66. *See In re Brooks' Estate*, 205 N.E. 2d 435 (Ill. 1965).

67. *In re Green*, 292 A. 2d 387, 392 (Pa. 1972), *appeal after remand*, 307 A. 2d 279 (Pa. 1973).

68. *See Application of President & Directors of Georgetown College, Inc.*, 331 F. 2d 1000, *reh'g denied*, 331 F. 2d 1010 (D.C. Cir.), *cert. denied*, 377 U.S. 978 (1964). *But see In re Conroy*, 486 A. 2d 1209, 1224 (N.J. 1985).

69. *See Wallace, supra* note 10; *see also Application of Brooklyn Hosp.*, 258 N.Y.S. 2d 621 (Sup. Ct. 1965); *In re Clark*, 185 N.E. 2d 128 (Ohio C.P. 1962); *see also Perricone, supra* note 6.

70. *See In re Clark*, 148 N.E. 2d 138 (Ohio C.P. 1962).

71. *Id.*

72. *See Raleigh Fitkin-Paul Morgan Mem Hosp. v. Anderson*, 42 N.J. 421, *cert. denied*, 377 U.S. 985 (1964).

73. *See Clark, supra* note 32.

74. *See Hoener, supra* note 61.

75. *See Perricone, supra* note 6.

76. *Id.*

77. *Id.* at 759.

78. *See Jehovah's Witnesses, supra* note 2.

79. *Id*

80. *Hoener, supra* note 61, at 143.

81. *Pierson, supra* note 1.

82. *Id.* at 247.

83. *Muhlenberg Hosp. v. Patterson*, 320 A. 2d 518 (N.J. Super. 1974).

84. *Sampson, supra* note 30.

85. *Seiferth, supra* note 39.

86. *In re Sampson*, 278 N.E. 2d 918 (N.Y. 1972); *see also Santos v. Goldstein*, 227 N.Y.S. 2d 450 (N.Y. App. Div. 1962), *appeal dismissed*, 232 N.Y.S. 2d 1026 (N.Y. 1962).

87. *Green, supra* note 67.

88. *Id.* at 392.

89. *Baby Boy Doe v. Mother Doe*, 632 N.E. 2d 326, *cert. denied*, 510 U.S. 1168 (1994).

90. *State ex rel. Milhoof v. Board of Educ.*, 81 N.E. 568, 569 (Ohio 1907).

91. *DeAryan v. Butler*, 260 P. 2d 98, 102 (Cal. App. 1853), *cert. denied*, 347 U.S. 1012 (1954).

92. *See, e.g., McCarney v. Austin*, 293 N.Y.S. 2d 188 (Sup. Ct. 1968), *aff'd*, 298 N.Y.S. 2d 26 (App. Div. 1969); *In re Elwell*, 284 N.Y.S. 2d 924 (Fam. Ct. 1967); *State ex rel. Mack v. Board of Educ.*, 204 N.E. 2d 86 (Ohio Ct. App. 1963); *State ex. rel. Dunham v. Board*, 96 N.E. 2d 413 (Ohio), *cert. denied*, 341 U.S. 915 (1951).

93. *See Hagler v. Larner*, 120 N.E. 575 (Ill. 1918); *Hill v. Bickers*, 188 S.W. 766 (Ky. 1916); *State ex rel. Freeman v. Zimmermann*, 90 N.W. 783 (Minn. 1902); *City of New Braunfels v. Waldschmidt*, 207 S.W. 303 (Tex. 1918); *see also Rhea v. Board of Educ.*, 171 N.W. 103 (N.D. 1919).

94. *See, e.g., McSween v. Board of School Trustees*, 129 S.W. 206 (Tex. Civ. App. 1910).

95. *Mack, supra* note 92.

96. 197 U.S. 11 (1905).

97. *Id.* at 29.

98. *Id.* at 30, 39.

99. *See, e.g., French v. Davidson*, 77 P. 663 (Cal. 1904); *Abeel v. Clark*, 24 P. 383 (Cal. 1890); *Bissell v. Davison*, 32 A. 348 (Conn. 1894); *Hagler, supra* note 93; *Board of Educ. v. Maas*, 152 A. 2d 394 (N.J. Super. 1959), *aff'd*, 158 A. 2d 330 (N.J.), *cert. denied*, 363 U.S. 843 (1960); *Sadlock v. Board of Educ.*, 58 A. 2d 218 (N.J. 1948); *State ex rel. Milhoff v. Board of Educ.*, 81 N.E. 568 (Ohio 1907); *Field v. Robinson*, 48 A. 873 (Pa. 1901); *Commonwealth v. Pear*, 66 N.E. 719 (Mass. 1903), *aff'd sub nom. Jacobson v. Massachusetts* 197 U.S. 11 (1905); *State ex rel. Cox v. Board of Educ.*, 60 P. 1013 (Utah 1900); *see also Ritterbaud v. Axelrod*, 562 N.Y.S. 2d 605 (N.Y. Sup. 1990).

100. *See, e.g. Maas, supra* note 99.

101. *See, e.g., Mosier v. Barren County Bd. of Health*, 215 S.W. 2d 967 (Ky. 1948) (chiropractors); *Mannis v. State ex rel. DeWitt School Dist.*, 398 S.W. 2d 206 (Ark.); *cert. denied*, 384 U.S. 972 (1966) (members of the General Assembly and Church of the First Born); *see also Wright v. DeWitt School Dist.*, 385 S.W. 2d 644 (Ark. 1965); *Dunham, supra* note 92.

102. *See Maas, supra* note 99.

103. *See Sadlock, supra* note 99.

104. *See Pierson, supra* note 1; *accord In re Whittmore*, 47 N.Y.S. 2d 143 (N.Y. 1944); *Wright v. DeWitt School Dist.*, 385 S.W. 2d 644 (Ark. 1965); *Cude v. State*, 377 S.W. 2d 816 (Ark. 1964).

105. *See Staffel v. San Antonio*, 201 S.W. 413, 415 (Tex. Civ. App. 1918).

106. *See Maas, supra* note 99; *see also McCartney v. Austin*, 293 N.Y.S. 2d 188 (Sup. Ct. 1968), *aff'd*, 298 N.Y.S. 2d 26 (App. Div. 1969); *In re Elwell*, 286 N.Y.S. 2d 740 (Fam. Ct. 1967).

107. *See, e.g.*, Bernard et al., *Autism: A Novel Form of Mercury Poisoning*, 56 Med. Hypothesis 462 (2001). Among many articles that have demonstrated the fallacies in the Bernard articles is Nelson and Bauman, *Thimerosal & Autism?*, 111 Pediatrics 674 (2003).

108. *See Dalli v. Board of Educ.*, 267 N.E. 2d 219, 223 (Mass. 1971); *accord Maier v. Besser*, 341 N.Y.S. 2d 411 (N.Y. Sup. 1972); *see also Kolbeck v. Kramer*, 202 A. 2d 889 (N.J. Super. Ct. 1964); *Davis v. State*, 451 A. 2d 107 (Md. 1982); *accord Campain v. Marlboro Cent. School Dist.*, 526 N.Y.S. 2d 658 (App. Div. 1988).

109. *See Itz v. Penick*, 493 S.W. 2d 506 (Itec.); *appeal dismissed*, 412 U.S. 925, *reh'g denied*, 414 U.S. 882 (1973).

110. *See Avard v. Dupius*, 376 F.Supp. 479 (D.N.H. 1974).

111. *See, e.g.*, *Zucht v. King*, 260 U.S. 174 (1922); *Duffield v. Williamsport School Dist.*, 29 A. 742 (Pa. 1894); *Hartman v. May*, 151 So. 737 (Miss. 1934); *State v. Hay*, 35 S.E. 459 (N.C. 1900); *McSween, supra* note 94.

112. *See Maas, supra* note 99; *Mosier, supra* note 101; *Hartman v. May*, 151 So. 737 (Miss. 1934).

113. *See Maas, supra* note 99, at 405; *Pierce v. Board of Educ.*, 219 N.Y.S. 2d 519 (Sup. Ct. 1961).

114. *See State v. Drew*, 192 A. 629 (N.H. 1937).

115. *See Seubold v. Fort Smith Special School Dist.*, 237 S.W. 2d 884 (Ark. 1951); *Wright, supra* note 101

116. *Maas, supra* note 99, at 408; *accord Viemeister v. White*, 72 N.E. 97 (N.Y. 1904); *Blue v. Beach*, 56 N.E. 89 (Ind. 1900); *Hartman, supra* note 111; *McSween, supra* note 94; *Staffle v. San Antonio Sch. Bd.*, 201 S.W. 413; *Zucht, supra* note 111; *City of New Braunfels, supra* note 93; *Freeman, supra* note 93; *Hay, supra* note 111; *Bissell, supra* note 99; *Morris v. Columbus*, 30 S.E. 850 (Ga. 1898); *Duffield, supra* note 111.

117. *See Hutchins v. School Committee*, 49 S.E. 46 (N.C. 1904).

118. *See State v. Dunham*, 93 N.E. 2d 286 (Ohio 1950).

119. *See Elwell, supra* note 92; *Cude, supra* note 104; *In re Marsh's Case*, 14 A. 2d 368, 371 (Pa. Super Ct. 1940); *Mannis, supra* note 101.

120. *See, e.g.*, Radbill, *Children in a World of Violence: A History of Child Abuse*, in R.E. Helfer & R.S. Kempe, eds., *The Battered Child*, 3 (4th ed. 1987).

121. Department of Health and Human Services, Administration on Children, Youth and Families, *Child Maltreatment in 1998: Reports from the States to the National Child Abuse and Neglect Data System*, available at http://www.acf.dhhs.gov/programs/cb/publications/cm98 /cpt3.htm.

122. American Medical Association Council on Scientific Affairs, *AMA Diagnostic and Treatment Guidelines Concerning Child Abuse and Neglect*, 254 J.A.M.A. 796 (1985).

123. Wissow, *Child Abuse and Neglect*, 332 N. Engl. J. Med. 1425 (1995).

124. McClain et al., *Estimates of Fatal Child Abuse and Neglect, United States, 1979-1988*, 91 Pediatrics 338 (1993)

125. National Center on Child Abuse and Neglect (NCCAN), National Child Abuse and Neglect Data System (NCANDS), *Working Paper One, Summary Data Component* (1990).

126. *See, e.g.*, Alaska Stat. 47.17.290(2) (1996); *Wojcik v. Town of North Smithfield*, 874 F.Supp. 508 (D. R.I. 1995), *aff'd*, 76 F. 3d 1 (1st Cir. 1996).

127. *See* Kini & Lazoritz, *Evaluation for Possible Physical or Sexual Abuse*, 45 Ped. Clin. N. Amer. 205, 207 (1998). For an argument that parental smoking can be deemed abuse of a child in the family's home, *see* Anderson, *Parental Smoking: A Form of Child Abuse?*, 77 Marquette L. Rev. 360 (1994) (citing, among other things, cases in which parental smoking was considered by courts deciding custody disputes).

128. *See, e.g.*, Chasnoff, *Prenatal Cocaine Exposure is Associated with Respiratory Pattern Abnormalities*, 143 Am. J. Dis. Child. 583 (1989); Meyer et al., *Perinatal Events Associated with Maternal Smoking*, 103 Am. J. Epidemiol. 464 (1976).

129. *See, e.g.*, Coady, Comment, *Extending Child Abuse Protection to the Viable Fetus: Whitner v. State of South Carolina*, 71 St. John's L. Rev. 667 (1997).

130. Daro & Gelles, *Public Attitudes and Behaviors with Respect to Child Abuse Prevention*, 7 J. Interpersonal Violence 517 (1992).

131. *See* English & Teare, *Statutory Rape Enforcement and Child Abuse Reporting: Effects on Health Care Access for Adolescents*, 50 DePaul L. Rev. 827 (Spring 2001).

132. *See, e.g.*, Deisz et al., *Reasonable Cause: A Qualitative Study of Mandated Reporting*, 20 Child Abuse and Neglect 275 (1996).

133. *See* Hartsell, *Mother May I . . . Live? Parental Refusal of Life-Sustaining Medical Treatment for Children Based on Religious Objections*, 66 Tenn. L. Rev. 499, 502 (1999).

134. American Medical Association Council on Scientific Affairs, *Female Genital Mutilation*, 274 J.A.M.A. 1714 (1995).

135. Council on Scientific Affairs, *supra* note 134. *See also* Baker et al., *Female Circumcision: Obstetric Issues*, 169 Am. J. Ob. & Gyn. 1616 (1993).

136. Anonymous, *Lead Poisoning Associated with Use of Traditional Ethnic Remedies—California, 1991-1992*, 270 J.A.M.A. 808 (1993).

137. Hartsell, *supra* note 133, at 502, citing Roger Munns, *Christian Science Challenged: Ill Children's Rights Debated*, New Orleans Times-Picayune (Apr. 25, 1996) at A-12.

138. Swan, *Children, Medicine, Religion and the Law*, 44 Adv. in Pediatr. 491, 519 (1997).

139. *See* Wadlington, David C. Baum Memorial Lecture, *Medical Decision Making for and by Children: Tensions between Parent, State, and Child*, 1994 U. Ill. L. Rev. 311, 324 (1994), citing 42 U.S.C. §5101 (1988 & Supp. III 1991).

140. 45 C.F.R. §1301.31A(b)(1) (1975).

141. Wadlington, *supra* note 139.

142. *See* 45 C.F.R. §1340.2(d)(2)(ii) (1983).

143. Hardy, Letter to Congressman Berkley Bedell (July 18, 1983), cited in Swan, *supra* note 138, at 513.

144. 763 P. 2d 852 (1988)

145. Minn. Stat. §609.205 (1988).

146. *State v. McKown*, 475 N.W. 2d 63 (Minn. 1991).

147. Minn. Stat. §609.378(a)(i) (1988).

148. *McKown, supra* note 146, at 65.

149. *Lundman v. McKown*, 530 N.W. 2d 807 (Minn. Ct. App. 1995).

150. Hefler & Kempe, *The Battered Child* at 105 (1968).

151. *Id.* at 106. *See also* Kempe et al., *The Battered Child Syndrome*, 181 J.A.M.A. 17 (1962).

152. Hefler et al., eds., *The Battered Child* (5th ed. 1997).

153. Sugar et al., *Bruises in Infants and Toddlers: Those Who Don't Cruise Rarely Bruise*, 153 Arch. Pediatr. & Adolesc. Med. 399 (1999).

154. *See* Carpenter, *The Prevalence and Distribution of Bruising in Babies*, 80 Arch. Dis. Childhood 363 (1999).

155. Reece & Sege, *Childhood Injuries: Accidental or Inflicted?*, 154 Arch. Pediatr. & Adolesc. Med. 11, 14 (2000).

156. Council on Scientific Affairs, *supra* note 122, at 797, 798.

157. *Id.* at 798.

158. *Id.*

159. *Id.*

160. *See* Cantwell, *Vaginal Inspection as it Relates to Child Sexual Abuse in Girls under Thirteen*, 7 Child Abuse and Neglect 171 (1983).

161. Council on Scientific Affairs, *supra* note 122, at 798.

162. U.S. Preventive Service Task Force, *Guide to Clinical Preventive Service* (2d ed. 1996) at Section 1.

163. Katz, *Psychosocial Adjustment in Adolescent Child Molesters*, 14 Child Abuse and Neglect 567 (1990).

Domestic Violence Patients

JACK W. SNYDER, M.D., J.D., M.F.S., M.P.H., Ph.D., F.C.L.M.

CIVIL PROTECTION ORDERS
CRIMINAL DOMESTIC VIOLENCE PROSECUTIONS
IMPACT OF DOMESTIC VIOLENCE IN OTHER AREAS OF LAW
CONCLUSION

Domestic violence occurs when one intimate partner uses physical violence, coercion, threats, intimidation, isolation, and/or emotional, sexual, and economic abuse to maintain power and control over the other intimate partner.[1] Domestic violence is also described as a "pattern of interaction" in which one intimate partner is forced to change his or her behavior in response to the abuse or threats of the other partner.[2] Synonyms for domestic violence include partner violence, relationship violence, dating violence, teen dating violence, intimate partner abuse, spouse abuse, domestic abuse, wife abuse, wife beating, and battering.[3]

Persons most likely to experience domestic violence include (1) women who are single or who have recently separated or divorced, (2) women who have recently sought an order of protection, (3) women who are younger than 28 years of age, (4) women who abuse alcohol or other drugs, (5) women who are pregnant, (6) women whose partners are excessively jealous or possessive, (7) women who have witnessed or experienced physical or sexual abuse as children, and (8) women whose partners have witnessed or experienced physical or sexual abuse as children.[4] Domestic violence affects people from all races, religions, age groups, sexual orientations, and socioeconomic levels.[5]

Despite its widespread occurrence,[6] most domestic violence is largely unrecognized or ignored by professionals, including physicians,[7] family therapists,[8] psychotherapists,[9] and law enforcement officials.[10] Importantly, health care professionals can play a crucial role in the diagnosis, treatment, and referral of victims, helping to break the often intergenerational cycle of domestic violence.[11] Physicians can screen,[12] assess, and intervene efficiently and effectively by eliciting a history of violence,[13] asking specific questions when battering is suspected,[14] documenting the physical findings that often accompany domestic violence,[15] assessing the victim's immediate and future safety,[16] and communicating to the victim all realistic options.[17] A few states have enacted laws that specifically require medical staff to report suspected domestic violence,[18] but many experts suggest that it is "absolutely contraindicated" to report cases of domestic violence to any agency or authority without the victim's direct request and consent.[19] These experts believe that mandatory reporting of domestic violence often increases the survivor's sense of powerlessness and may increase the risk of further harm, including the risk of homicide.[20] The theory that mandatory reporting may deter victims from seeking medical care is not well supported by available empirical observations.[21]

CIVIL PROTECTION ORDERS

In all U.S. jurisdictions the victim of domestic violence can obtain by statute a civil protection order (CPO).[22] Most states authorize emergency or temporary (2- to 4-week) CPOs if the victim (at an ex parte hearing) can prove immediate danger of future violence.[23] Courts also issue longer (1- to 3-year) CPOs after a full hearing, by consent, or by default.[24] Although statutes of limitation typically do not apply to persons requesting CPOs, some courts may not grant an order if the most recent threat or incident of abuse occurred several months before the filing of a petition for a CPO.[25] In most states an abused adult can file on his or her own behalf.[26] An adult also can file on behalf of a child or decision-incapable adult.[27] A few states allow minors to petition for protection on their own behalf.[28]

Basis for granting

State laws define the relationships that must exist between the parties before a CPO will be granted. Recognized targets of a CPO include current or former spouses,[29] family members who are related by blood or marriage,[30] current or former household members,[31] persons who share a child in common,[32] unmarried persons of different genders living as spouses,[33] persons in same sex relationships,[34] persons in dating or intimate relationships,[35] and persons offering refuge to victims of domestic violence.[36]

Courts and legislatures have identified several types of acts as abuse sufficient to support the issuance of a CPO.[37] Acts of abuse against the petitioner include threats,[38] interference with personal liberty,[39] harassment,[40] stalking,[41] emotional abuse,[42] attempts to inflict harm,[43] sexual assault,[44] marital rape,[45] assault and battery,[46] burglary,[47] criminal trespass,[48] kidnapping,[49] and damage to property (including pets).[50] The standards of proof for issuance or extension of a CPO include "preponderance of the evidence," "preponderance of the evidence that the petitioner is facing a clear and present or imminent danger," and "reasonable cause or grounds to believe" that abuse occurred, that there is an emergency, or that the petitioner is in immediate and present danger.[51]

Contents

CPOs typically require that the respondent shall[52] (1) not molest, assault, harass, or in any manner threaten or physically abuse the petitioner and/or his/her child(ren);[53] (2) stay 150 yards away from the petitioner's home, person, workplace, children, place of worship, and day care provider;[54] (3) not contact petitioner and/or his/her children in any manner (personally, in writing, by mail or telephone, or through third parties);[55] (4) vacate the residence at (location) by (date and time) (the police department shall stand by and shall give respondent 15 minutes to collect his or her personal belongings, which include clothes, toiletries, and one set of sheets and pillowcases; no other property may be removed from the premises without petitioner's permission; the police shall take all keys and garage openers from respondent, check to see that they are the right ones, and then turn keys over to the petitioner);[56] (5) relinquish possession and/or use of the following personal property as of (date and time);[57] (6) turn over to the police any and all weapons that the respondent owns or possesses and all licenses the respondent has authorizing the possession of or purchase of weapons;[58] (7) participate in and successfully complete a counseling program;[59] (8) relinquish custody of minor children to petitioner until further order of the court or the expiration date of the order;[60] (9) have rights of visitation with minor child(ren) under specified conditions;[61] (10) pay spousal and child support as designated;[62] and (11) pay for specified repairs, medical or health insurance costs, attorney's fees, and court costs.[63]

Enforcement

In the majority of states, violation of a CPO is a crime for which the police can arrest the offender, even if the violation did not occur in the presence of the officer.[64] The statutory trend is to augment civil or criminal contempt enforcement with misdemeanor charges and to heighten the criminal classification for violation of a CPO.[65] CPOs can and do remain in effect despite the parties' reunification or the petitioner's invitation to the abuser to enter her residence.[66]

In *United States v. Dixon*[67] the Supreme Court ruled that double jeopardy would not bar a battered woman from enforcing her CPO through criminal contempt proceedings while the state proceeds with a criminal prosecution for crimes the respondent committed against the battered woman at the time he violated the CPO, as long as the contempt proceeding and the criminal prosecution each require proof of additional elements.[68]

Consequences of violation

The sentencing of an individual after a criminal contempt conviction or a trial for crimes committed against family members has several important goals, including (1) stopping the violence; (2) protecting the victim, the children, and other family members; (3) protecting the general public; (4) holding the offender accountable for the violent conduct; (5) upholding the legislative intent to treat domestic violence as a serious crime; (6) providing restitution for the victim; and (7) rehabilitating the offender.[69] State courts have upheld a variety of sentences, including jail terms, monetary sanctions, bonds, probation, community service, electronic monitoring, and injunctions.[70]

The Violence Against Women Act

The Violence Against Women Act (VAWA), which amends various sections of the United States Code and Rule 412 of the Federal Rules of Evidence, was signed by President Clinton on September 13, 1994. This comprehensive legislation accomplished the following:

1. Established a federal civil rights cause of action for victims of gender-motivated crimes of violence.[71]
2. Provided that protective orders (including ex parte orders) issued in one state are enforceable in other states as long as due process requirements are met in the issuing state.[72]
3. Required that the U.S. Postal Service protect the confidentiality of addresses of domestic violence shelters and abused persons.[73]
4. Permitted battered immigrant spouses and children of U.S. citizens and legal residents to self-petition the Immigration and Naturalization Service for legal resident status or to file for legal resident status even if their marriage to a U.S. citizen or lawful permanent resident is legally terminated after the petition is filed.[74]
5. Permitted battered immigrant spouses and children of U.S. citizens and legal residents and parents of battered children of U.S. citizens and legal residents residing in the U.S. for at least 3 years to obtain suspension of deportation if deportation would result in extreme hardship to the alien or the alien's parent or child.[75]
6. Created federal criminal penalties for crossing a state line to violate a protection order or to commit domestic violence against a spouse or intimate partner.[76]

7. Mandated restitution enforceable through suspension of federal benefits, and an opportunity for the victim to inform the court regarding the danger posed by pretrial release of the defendant.[77]

8. Funded a continuously operating toll-free hotline that provides the caller with names of local shelters, referrals, and domestic violence programs.[78]

Regarding federal sex crimes, VAWA provides for pretrial detention,[79] payment for testing for sexually transmitted diseases,[80] and increased sentences for repeat sex offenders or where the victim of a federal sex offense is under 16 years of age.[81] VAWA also amends Federal Rule of Evidence 412 to prohibit introduction of evidence regarding the victim's sexual history.[82]

Most courts confronted with constitutional challenges to VAWA have found the act to be a valid exercise of congressional power under the Commerce Clause.[83] However, in *U.S. v. Morrison/Brzonkala v. Morrison*[84] the Fourth Circuit United States Court of Appeals held that rape and other violent crimes against women are not economic or commercial activities and are not individually connected to interstate commerce. Consequently, the court ruled that these crimes could not be regulated under the act. The Supreme Court of the United States heard oral argument in this matter on January 11, 2000.

CRIMINAL DOMESTIC VIOLENCE PROSECUTIONS

When police have probable cause to believe that domestic violence has occurred, many states mandate and others permit warrantless arrests.[85] Exigent circumstances also may give rise to constitutionally permissible warrantless searches.[86] Respondents in domestic violence cases have been criminally prosecuted for a broad range of acts.[87] Until recently, most federal cases involving domestic violence have been prosecuted under the Assimilated Crimes Act (ACA).[88] This act authorizes federal prosecutions for crimes not contained in the United States Code when a criminal offense under state law is committed within a federal enclave or in an area under the exclusive jurisdiction of the United States. Under the ACA, state substantive law is incorporated into the federal prosecution, and the federal prosecutor steps into the shoes of the state prosecutor for purposes of the charged offense.[89] Cases involving criminal racketeering also incorporate state law crimes of violence, including murder or kidnapping.[90] As of 1996, amendments to the Gun Control Act of 1968 prohibit persons convicted of domestic violence offenses from possessing firearms in or affecting commerce.[91]

In most states a defendant is justified in killing an attacker if the defendant did not provoke the attack, reasonably believed the attacker posed an imminent or immediate threat of death or serious bodily harm, and used only force proportionate to the force used or threatened against the defendant.[92] The defendant's belief that the attack was imminent and that the response was necessary for protection must have been reasonable; moreover, the defendant must have been under no duty to retreat or unable to retreat.[93]

For most of the twentieth century, victims of repeated acts of domestic violence who killed their partners could not prove self-defense because courts believed that the attack was not necessary, the use of deadly force was excessive, and the victim was the aggressor in the events immediately preceding the killing.[94] In the 1970s, however, psychologist Lenore Walker studied several hundred women in an effort to explain the psychological and behavioral patterns that commonly appear in women who have been physically and psychologically abused by an intimate partner over an extended period. Analogizing to scientific research on dogs, Walker theorized that the experience of repeated and unpreventable abuse, along with the social conditioning of women to be subservient, created in battered women a state of "psychological paralysis" that rendered them unable to seek escape or help, even when it might be available.[95] Walker coined the term *battered woman syndrome*, which soon provided the basis for expert testimony designed to convince a jury that the defendant reasonably believed she had to kill to save herself, even during an ebb in violence.[96]

Invoking the syndrome, however, may not always advance justice for battered women who kill.[97] Experts therefore have encouraged a redefinition of the "battered woman" because testimony concerning the experiences of battered women refers to more than their psychological reactions to violence and because battered women's diverse psychological realities are not limited to one particular "profile."[98] As the debate over the proper role of domestic violence expert testimony continues in the legal and scientific literature, courts have begun to admit behavioral science evidence in domestic violence cases.[99]

IMPACT OF DOMESTIC VIOLENCE IN OTHER AREAS OF LAW

The role of law in domestic violence cases extends beyond CPOs and criminal prosecutions. Children must be supported, as well as protected; the rights and benefits of employment must be maintained; tort actions may be appropriate; and the validity of prenuptial agreements may be imperiled. Policies having the potential to discriminate against victims of domestic violence may raise constitutional issues of equal protection or due process.[100]

Child custody and support

Batterers often assault their children, and the risk of child abuse and kidnapping increases when a marriage is dissolving.[101] The physical and emotional consequences for children who experience domestic violence include medical problems, substance abuse, suicide attempts, eating disorders, nightmares, fear of being hurt, loneliness, bed wetting, and delinquent behavior such as fighting, prostitution, truancy, crimes against other people, running away, dropping out of school, teenage pregnancy, cognitive disorders, and low self-esteem.[102]

To prevent the offender from using custody and support litigation as a means to extend or maintain control and authority after separation from the victim, courts have been advised to draft orders that (1) specify times of visitation, telephone calls, and participation in school or extracurricular activities; (2) designate the circumstances of exchange or transfer of the children; (3) provide for the safety of the children and the vulnerable parent, including, for example, supervised visitation, injunctions against threatening conduct, and prohibitions against asking the children about the activities of the other parent; (4) account for the current and future needs of the children and the custodial parent; (5) require the offender to participate in educational services designed for batterers; and (6) specify circumstances or conditions under which custody or visitation orders may be altered.[103] All states permit courts to consider domestic violence in relationship to "the best interest of the child."[104] Congress and some states have adopted a presumption against award of joint or sole custody to the abusive parent.[105] Judges may be required to permit testimony about domestic violence and its impact on children and the nonabusive parent.[106]

Prenuptial agreements

Domestic violence may influence prenuptial agreements in three ways. First, battering may provide a defense to the enforcement of an otherwise valid prenuptial agreement.[107] Second, domestic violence may give rise to tort claims that may offset preclusions of equitable economic distribution found in many prenuptial agreements.[108] Third, a prenuptial agreement can include a provision that the occurrence of domestic violence invalidates the terms of the contract.[109]

Employment issues

Many victims of domestic violence are harassed at work by their former or current spouses or partners.[110] Victims also may miss work because of injuries, court dates, or the need to cooperate with criminal investigations.[111] Job performance may be undermined by depression, fear, and other psychological effects of battering.[112]

Employers may incur liability if domestic violence occurs in the workplace or if they fail to respond properly.[113] Theories of liability may include the Occupational Safety and Health Administration's "general duty" clause,[114] *respondeat superior*, duty to warn,[115] wrongful discharge in violation of public policy[116] or an employee's privacy rights, and negligent hiring, retention, security, and/or supervision.[117]

Employees who are victims of domestic violence also are protected by workers' compensation statutes,[118] unemployment insurance or benefit laws,[119] and statutes that preserve benefits for persons cooperating with the judicial process.[120] Perhaps the biggest challenge for employers dealing with domestic violence is to balance employer interests in protecting employees and ensuring workplace safety with employee interests in privacy and freedom from defamation and discrimination.[121]

CONCLUSION

All medical and legal professionals must improve their abilities to identify and confront domestic violence. Appropriate and effective recognition and intervention require vigilance, a knowledge of and a willingness to ask the right questions, and a sense of obligation to help society end this undesirable phenomenon. Knowledge of legal considerations should improve the collaboration of health care workers, legal professionals, and community programs seeking to control domestic violence—a major public health problem.

ENDNOTES

1. Valente, *Domestic Violence and the Law*, in *The Impact of Domestic Violence on Your Legal Practice* 1-1–1-7 (Goelman, Lehrman, & Valente eds., 1996).
2. Dutton, *The Dynamics of Domestic Violence: Understanding the Response from Battered Women*, 68 Fla. Bar J. 24 (1994). Most victims or survivors of domestic violence are women, and most batterers or perpetrators are men. *See* Bureau of Justice Statistics, U.S. Department of Justice, *Violence Between Intimates* 2-3 (1994).
3. Alpert, *Domestic Violence*, in *Current Diagnosis* 105-109 (9th ed., Conn, Borer, & Snyder eds., W.B. Saunders, Philadelphia, 1997).
4. *Id*. at 106.
5. *Id*. at 105.
6. National surveys estimate that at least 2 million women each year are battered by an intimate partner, and crime data from the Federal Bureau of Investigation record about 1500 murders of women by husbands or boyfriends each year. Overall, the Bureau of Justice Statistics reports that women sustained about 3.8 million assaults and 500,000 rapes a year in 1992 and 1993; more than 75% of these violent acts were committed by someone known to the victim, and 29% of them were committed by an intimate—a husband, an ex-husband, a boyfriend, or an ex-boyfriend. These figures are believed to be underestimates. *See* Panel on Research on Violence Against Women, National Research Council, *Understanding Violence Against Women* (Crowell & Burgess eds., National Academy of Sciences, 1996). *See also* Abbott et al., *Domestic Violence Against Women: Incidence and Prevalence in an Emergency Department Population*, 273 J.A.M.A. 1763 (1995).
7. *See, e.g.*, Council on Ethical and Judicial Affairs, American Medical Association, *Physicians and Domestic Violence: Ethical Considerations*, 267 J.A.M.A. 3190 (1992); Sugg & Inui, *Primary Care Physician's Response to Domestic Violence: Opening Pandora's Box*, 267 J.A.M.A. 3157 (1992); McLeer & Anwar, *A Study of Battered Women Presenting in an Emergency Department*, 79 J. Public Health 65 (1989).
8. *See, e.g.*, Avis, *Where Are All the Family Therapists? Abuse and Violence Within Families and Family Therapy's Response*, 18 J. Marital Family Ther. 225 (1992); Harway & Hansen, *Therapist Perceptions of Family Violence*, in *Battering and Family Therapy: A Feminist*

Perspective, 42, 52 (Hansen & Harway eds., Sage Publications, Newbury Park 1993).

9. *See, e.g.*, Hansen & Harway, *supra* note 8, at 45-47; Sesan, *Sex Bias and Sex-Role Stereotyping in Psychotherapy with Women: Survey Results*, 25 Psychotherapy 107 (1988).

10. *See, e.g.*, L.W. Sherman, *Policing Domestic Violence: Experiments and Dilemmas* 25-27 (Free Press, New York 1992).

11. *See, e.g.*, *supra* note 3, at 105; Warshaw, *Identification, Assessment and Intervention with Victims of Domestic Violence*, in *Improving the Health Care Response to Domestic Violence: A Resource Manual for Health Care Providers* 49 (Family Violence Prevention Fund, 1995).

12. A letter to the *Journal of the American Medical Association* reported the following experience with initiating screening protocols:

> I asked eight consecutive patients who had arrived at the clinic with routine gynecologic complaints unrelated to domestic violence whether they had ever been physically abused. The results were horrifying. All eight women had been physically assaulted by their intimate partners within the past year. One patient, who had come to the office for an oral contraceptive pill refill, went directly to the district attorney's office after talking about her dangerous situation at home. Another patient started to cry as she related the details of her physical and emotional injuries. Review of the otherwise thorough charts of these women made it apparent that no physician had asked whether these patients had ever been threatened or harmed. The women were waiting for their physicians to inquire; they showed no hesitancy in talking about their experiences.

Tracy, *Domestic Violence: The Physician's Role*, 275 J.A.M.A. 1708 (1996).

13. *Supra* note 3, at 106. Appropriate questions for eliciting a history of violence include: (1) Have you ever been hit, hurt, or threatened by your husband or boyfriend or partner? (2) What happens when you and your partner have a disagreement at home? (3) Have you ever been threatened, intimidated, or frightened by your partner? (4) Are you afraid for your safety or for that of your children because of anyone you live with or are close to? (5) Would you leave your partner if you could? (6) Do you feel safe in your home? (7) Have you ever needed to see a doctor or go to an emergency room because someone did something to hurt or frighten you?

14. *Id.* at 107. Appropriate additional questions when domestic violence is suspected include: (1) How were you hurt? (2) Has this happened before? (3) Could you tell me about the first episode? (4) How badly have you been hurt in the past? (5) Have you ever gone to an emergency room for treatment? (6) Have you ever been threatened with a weapon, or has a weapon ever been used on you? (7) Have your children ever seen you threatened or hurt? (8) Have your children ever been threatened or hurt by your partner?

15. *Id.* at 107. Objective manifestations of domestic violence may include (1) bilateral or multiple injuries, (2) injuries in different stages of healing, (3) evidence of rape or sexual assault, (4) an explanation by the victim that is inconsistent with the type of injury, (5) delay between the time of injury and the arrival of the victim at the health care facility, and (6) prior repetitive use of emergency services for trauma.

16. *Id.* at 107. Indicators of escalating risk include an increase in the severity or frequency of assaults, increasing or new threats of homicide or suicide by the partner, the presence or availability of a firearm, and the abuser's known criminal record of violent crime.

17. *Id.* at 108. Health care professionals (HCPs) can help the victim understand that she does not deserve to be hurt or threatened by anyone under any circumstances, particularly by someone she loves. The only provocation that justifies the use of physical force against another is an initial act of violence that puts the person attacked in reasonable fear of imminent danger. In other words, only batterers are responsible for their violence.

HCPs also can (1) convey their concern for the victim's safety; (2) advise or refer for specific medical treatment, psychological counseling, safety planning, legal assistance, support groups, or emergency shelter or funds; (3) minimize the prescription of sedating or tranquilizing medications; and (4) evaluate the need to report the violence to a governmental agency.

See American Medical Association, *Domestic Violence: A Directory of Protocols for Healthcare Providers* (1992); American Medical Association, *Diagnostic and Treatment Guidelines on Domestic Violence* (1992); American Medical Association, *Diagnostic and Treatment Guidelines on Family Violence* (1995).

18. *See, e.g.*, Cal. Penal Code §11161 (West 1996).

19. *Supra* note 3, at 107; Hyman, Schillinger & Lo, *Laws Mandating Reporting of Domestic Violence: Do They Promote Patient Well-Being?*, 273 J.A.M.A. 1781 (1995).

20. *Id. See also Policy Statement of the American College of Emergency Physicians on Mandatory Reporting of Domestic Violence to Law Enforcement and Criminal Justice Agencies*, 30 Ann. Emerg. Med. 561 (1997).

21. Houry, Feldhaus, Thorson & Abbott, *Mandatory Reporting Laws Do Not Deter Patients from Seeking Medical Care*, 34 Ann. Emerg. Med. 336 (1999).

22. Klein & Orloff, *Civil Protection Orders*, in *The Impact of Domestic Violence on Your Legal Practice* 4-1–4-5 (Goelman, Lehrman & Valente, eds., 1996). *See also* Keilitz, *Civil Protection Orders: A Viable Justice System Tool for Deterring Domestic Violence*, 9 Violence and Victims 79 (1994).

23. Klein & Orloff, *Providing Legal Protection for Battered Women: An Analysis of State Statutes and Case Law*, 21 Hofstra L. Rev. 801, 1031-43 and accompanying notes 1420-1509 (1993).

24. *Supra* note 22, at 4-1.

25. *Supra* note 23, at 900-905 and accompanying notes 599-632.

26. *Id.* at 842-847 and accompanying notes 204-226. For an extended discussion of efforts to improve accessibility to the courts for battered women appearing *pro se, see id.* at 1048-1065 and accompanying notes 1541-1632.

27. *Id.* at 846.

28. *Id.* at 844.

29. *Id.*, at 814-816 and accompanying notes 38-48.

30. *Id.* at 816-820 and accompanying notes 49-69.

31. *Id.* at 838-842 and accompanying notes 182-203.

32. *Id.* at 824-829 and accompanying notes 94-127.

33. *Id.* at 829-832 and accompanying notes 128-149.

34. *Id.* at 832-835 and accompanying notes 150-168.

35. *Id.* at 835-837 and accompanying notes 169-174.

36. *Id.* at 837-838 and accompanying notes 175-181.

37. *See, e.g., Knuth v. Knuth*, 1992 Minn. App. LEXIS 696 (Minn. Ct. App. June 19, 1992).

38. *Supra* note 23, at 859-863 and accompanying notes 316-353.

39. *Id.* at 858-859 and accompanying notes 308-315.

40. *Id.* at 866-869 and accompanying notes 367-406.

41. *Id.* at 874-876 and accompanying notes 445-465.

42. *Id.* at 869-873 and accompanying notes 407-437.

43. *Id.* at 864-866 and accompanying notes 354-366.

44. *Id.* at 854-858 and accompanying notes 296-307.

45. *Id.*

46. *Id.* at 849-854 and accompanying notes 237-295. Case law indicates that battery is the most common criminal ground for issuance of a CPO. Courts have issued CPOs for shoving an infant's face against a door; physically restraining, striking, kicking, punching, choking, slapping, or throwing cold water on the petitioner; yanking the petitioner by the hair; pulling out the petitioner's pubic or other hair; throwing the petitioner on the floor; bruising a child's back, legs, and buttocks; twisting the petitioner's wrist; pounding the petitioner's head on the floor; attempting to

push the petitioner's face in the toilet; and ordering trained dogs to attack the petitioner.

47. *See, e.g.*, N.J. Stat. Ann. §2C:25-19 (West 1992); Wash. Rev. Code Ann. §10.99.020 (West 1992).

48. *See, e.g.*, Del. Code Ann. tit. 10, §945 (1993); N.J. Stat. Ann. §2C:25-19 (1992).

49. *Id.*

50. *Supra* note 23, at 873-874 and accompanying notes 438-444.

51. *See, e.g., id.* at 1043-1048 and accompanying notes 1510-1540.

52. *Supra* note 22.

53. For extended discussion of "no further abuse" clauses, *see, e.g., supra* note 23, at 914-918 and accompanying notes 712-743.

54. For extended discussion of "stay away" provisions, *see, e.g., id.* at 918–925 and accompanying notes 744-782.

55. For extended discussion of "no contact" provisions, *see, e.g., id.* at 925-931 and accompanying notes 783-822.

56. For extended discussion of "orders to vacate," *see, e.g., id.* at 931-936 and accompanying notes 823-856.

57. For extended discussion of "property rights," *see, e.g., id.* at 937-941 and accompanying notes 857-886.

58. For extended discussion of orders concerning weapons *see, e.g., id.* at 941-944 and accompanying notes 887-909.

59. For extended discussion of treatment and counseling issues, *see, e.g., id.* at 944-949 and accompanying notes 910-950.

60. For extended discussion of custody issues, *see, e.g., id.* at 949-981 and accompanying notes 951-1140.

61. For extended discussion of visitation issues, *see, e.g., id.* at 982-990 and accompanying notes 1141-1208.

62. For extended discussion of spousal and child support issues, *see, e.g., id.* at 997-1000 and accompanying notes 1244-1263.

63. For extended discussion of other forms of monetary relief, *see, e.g., id.* at 990-996 and accompanying notes 1209-1243. *See also id.* at 1000-1006 and accompanying notes 1264-1300.

64. *See id.* at 1095-1099 and accompanying notes 1828-1851.

65. *Id.* at 1097-1098 and accompanying notes 1840-1841. For extended discussion of acts constituting civil and criminal contempt, *see, e.g., id.* at 1102-1112 and accompanying notes 1871-1939.

66. *See, e.g., Cole v. Cole*, 556 N.Y.S. 2d 217 (Fam. Ct. 1990); *City of Reynoldsburg v. Eichenberger*, No. CA-3492, 1990 Ohio App. LEXIS 1613 (Apr. 18, 1990); *People v. Townsend*, 538 N.E. 2d 1297 (Ill. App. Ct. 1989); *State v. Kilponen*, 737 P. 2d 1024 (Wash. Ct. App. 1987); *supra* note 23, at 1112–1117 and accompanying notes 1940-1973.

67. 509 U.S. 688 (1993).

68. For extended discussion of the contemnor's due process rights, *see, e.g., supra* note 23, at 1120-1129 and accompanying notes 1992-2039.

69. See N.D. Lemon, *Domestic Violence: A Benchguide for Criminal Cases* 151 (1989).

70. For extended discussion of sentencing issues in domestic violence cases, *see, e.g., supra* note 23, at 1129-1142 and accompanying notes 2040-2105.

71. 42 U.S.C. §13981 (1994). Victims may sue in federal or state court and seek compensatory and punitive damages, an injunction or a declaratory judgment, and attorney's fees. A prior criminal action is not required to pursue the civil remedy.

72. 18 U.S.C. §2265 (1994).

73. 42 U.S.C. §13951 (1994).

74. 8 U.S.C. §1151 (1994).

75. 8 U.S.C. §1254 (1994).

76. 18 U.S.C. §§2261, 2262 (1994). In *U.S. v. Page*, No. 96–4083 (6th Cir. 1998), the Sixth Circuit held that the Violence Against Women Act does not criminalize domestic violence that occurs before interstate travel. Rather the statute covers only domestic violence occurring "in the course of or as a result of" such travel. Consequently the statute criminalizes the aggravation of injuries inflicted before interstate travel only so long as the worsening of the injuries was caused by intentional violent conduct during interstate travel.

77. 18 U.S.C. §§2263, 2264 (1994).

78. 42 U.S.C. §10416 (1994).

79. 18 U.S.C. §§2241-48 (1994).

80. 42 U.S.C. §14011 (1994).

81. 18 U.S.C. §2245 (2) (1994).

82. 28 U.S.C. §2074 (1994).

83. *See, e.g., U.S. v. Lankford*, No. 98–10645 (5th Cir. 1999); *U.S. v. Page*, 167 F. 3d 325, 334 (6th Cir. 1999); *U.S. v. Gluzman* 154 F. 3d 49, 50 (2d Cir. 1998), *cert. denied*, 119 S.Ct. 1257 (1999).

84. *U.S. v. Morrison/Brzonkala v. Morrison*, 169 F. 3d 820 (1999).

85. *Supra* note 23, at 1148-1158 and accompanying notes 2151-2201. *See also* Wanless, *Notes: Mandatory Arrest: A Step Toward Eradicating Domestic Violence, But Is It Enough?*, U. Ill. L. Rev. 533 (1996). One of the goals of mandatory arrest statutes is to change police officers' attitudes that domestic partners should be left to resolve their disputes privately and that domestic violence is not a serious crime.

86. *Supra* note 23, at 1157.

87. *See, e.g., id.* at 1142-1148 and accompanying notes 2106–2150.

88. 18 U.S.C. §13 (Repl. 1997).

89. *United States v. Kearney*, 750 F. 2d 787 (9th Cir. 1984).

90. 18 U.S.C. §1961 (Repl. 1997).

91. 18 U.S.C. §922 (g)(9). The constitutionality of these amendments has been upheld in *Gillespie v. City of Indianapolis*, No. 98-2691 (7th Cir. 1999).

92. *See, e.g., People v. Evans*, 259 Ill. App. 3d 195, 197 Ill. Dec. 278, 631 N.E. 2d 281 (1994); Stone, *Defense*, in *The Impact of Domestic Violence on Your Legal Practice* 7-5–7-8 (Goelman, Lehrman & Valente, eds., 1996); W.R. LaFave & A.W. Scott, *Criminal Law*, 454-463 (2d ed., West, St Paul, Minn. 1986).

93. *Id.*

94. *See, e.g., State v. Nunn*, 356 N.W. 2d 601 (Iowa App. 1984); *Commonwealth v. Grove*, 363 Pa. Super. 328, 526 A. 2d 369 (1987); *People v. Aris*, 215 Cal. App. 3d 1178, 264 Cal. Rptr. 167 (1989); *State v. Stewart*, 243 Kan. 639, 763 P. 2d 572 (1988).

95. L.E. Walker, *The Battered Woman* 42-55 (1979); L.E. Walker, *The Battered Woman Syndrome* 95-104 (1984). Walker suggested that an abusive relationship can be described as a cycle with three phases: (1) the tension-building phase, characterized by slight instances of physical or emotional abuse; (2) the acute battering phase, characterized by more frequent and escalated instances of violence; and (3) the loving contrition phase, characterized by the offender's apologies and repeated promises to change his behavior. The term *battered spouse* refers to a woman who has been through the cycle at least twice. In phase one the woman's tendency to avoid the batterer may reinforce the pattern of abusiveness. Women in phase two tend to cope with frenzies of violence and wait for an ebb in the flow of abuse. Relief and dread are common to women in phase three; this lull in the abuse may inflict the most severe psychological trauma on the woman. *See* L.E. Walker, *Terrifying Love: Why Battered Women Kill and How Society Responds* 43-62 (1989).

96. *See, e.g., Developments in the Law: Domestic Violence*, 106 Harvard L. Rev. 1574 (1993); Schneider, *Describing and Changing: Women's Self-Defense Work and the Problem of Expert Testimony on Battering*, 9 Women's Rights L. Rep. 195 (1986).

97. The profiles of battered women who kill their partners often do not fulfill the criteria of "learned helplessness" or "psychological paralysis." *See, e.g.*, Meier, *Notes from the Underground: Integrating Psychological and Legal Perspectives on Domestic Violence in Theory and Practice*, 21 Hofstra L. Rev. 1295 (1993); Allard, *Rethinking Battered Woman Syndrome: A Black Feminist Perspective*,

1 U.C.L.A. Women's L.J. 191 (1991); Schopp et al., *Battered Woman Syndrome, Expert Testimony, and the Distinction Between Justification and Excuse*, 1 U. Ill. L. Rev. 45 (1994); Stark, *Re-presenting Woman Battering: From Battered Woman Syndrome to Coercive Control*, 58 Alb. L. Rev. 973 (1995); Maguigin, *Battered Women and Self-Defense: Myths and Misconceptions in Current Reform Proposals*, 140 U. Pa. L. Rev. 379 (1991); Dutton, *Understanding Women's Response to Violence: A Redefinition of Battered Woman Syndrome*, 21 Hofstra L. Rev. 1191 (1993); Callahan, *Will the "Real" Battered Woman Please Stand Up? In Search of a Realistic Definition of Battered Woman Syndrome*, 3 Am. U. J. Gender and L. 117 (1994).

98. *See, e.g.*, Walker, *Battered Woman Syndrome and Self-Defense*, 6 Notre Dame J. L. Ethics and Pub. Policy 321 (1992) (defining battered women's syndrome as a form of posttraumatic stress disorder); Stark, *supra* note 97, at 1201 (suggesting that battered women are subject to entrapment or coercive control by the perpetrator); Dutton, *supra* note 97. Dutton proposes that (1) descriptive references should be made to "expert testimony concerning battered women's experiences," rather than to "battered woman syndrome" per se; (2) the scope of testimony concerning battered women's experiences should be framed within the overall social context that is essential for explaining battered women's responses to violence; and (3) evaluation and testimony concerning battered women's psychological reactions to violence should incorporate the diverse range of traumatic reactions described in the scientific literature, and should not be limited to an examination of learned helplessness, posttraumatic stress disorder, or any other single reaction or "profile."

99. *See, e.g., State v. Kelly*, 97 N.J. 178, 478 A. 2d 364 (1984); *State v. Gallegos*, 104 N.M. 247, 719 P. 2d 1268 (Ct. App. 1986); *Commonwealth v. Stonehouse*, 521 Pa. 41, 64, 555 A. 2d 772, 784 (1989); *State v. Koss*, 49 Ohio St. 3d 213, 551 N.E. 2d 970 (1990); *Arcoren v. United States*, 929 F. 2d 1235 (8th Cir. 1991) (holding that Federal Rule of Evidence 702 encompasses the use of psychiatric and psychological evidence).

100. In *Navarro v. Block*, No. 96-5569 (9th Cir. 1999), the Ninth Circuit addressed the issue of whether domestic violence crimes result in severe injury or death less frequently than nondomestic violence crimes that are considered 911 emergencies. Citing a lack of evidence supporting an assumption that domestic violence crimes are less injurious than nondomestic violence crimes, the court reversed and reremanded a trial court ruling that 911 dispatcher policy equating domestic violence calls with "not-in-progress" calls, and equating nondomestic violence calls with "in-progress" calls, was rational and reasonable.

101. Bowker et al., *On the Relationship Between Wife Beating and Child Abuse*, in *Perspectives on Wife Abuse* 158, 164 (Yllo & Bograd eds., 1988); Pagelow, *Effects of Domestic Violence on Children and Their Consequences for Custody and Visitation Agreements*, 7 Mediation Q. 347 (1990); P.G. Jaffe et al., *Children of Battered Women* 2 (1990); Mahoney, *Legal Images of Battered Women: Redefining the Issue of Separation*, 90 Mich. L. Rev. 1, 5 (1991); G.L. Greif & R.L. Hegar, *When Parents Kidnap* 30 (1993); Edleson, *Mothers and Children: Understanding the Links Between Woman Battering and Child Abuse*, in *A Report of the Violence Against Women Research Strategic Planning Workshop* (Nat'l Inst. of Justice, Washington, D.C. 1995).

102. Judicial Subcommittee, Commission on Domestic Violence, American Bar Association, *Judicial Checklist*, in *The Impact of Domestic Violence on Your Legal Practice* 13-7 (Goelman, Lehrman & Valente eds., 1996).

103. *See, e.g.*, Hart & Hofford, *Child Custody*, in *The Impact of Domestic Violence on Your Legal Practice* 5-1–5-6 (Goelman, Lehrman & Valente eds., 1996). For a discussion of child support issues in the context of domestic violence, see Haynes, *Child Support*, in *The*

Impact of Domestic Violence on Your Legal Practice 5-7–5-10 (Goelman, Lehrman & Valente eds., 1996).

104. *See, e.g.*, Dakis& Karan, *Judicial Intervention*, in *The Impact of Domestic Violence on Your Legal Practice* 13-1–13-9 (Goelman, Lehrman & Valente eds., 1996).

105. *See, e.g.*, H.R. Con. Res. 172, 101st Cong., 2d Sess. (1990); *see also* National Council on Juvenile and Family Court Judges, *Family Violence: A Model State Code* 33 (1994).

106. *Supra* note 104, at 13-1.

107. *See Foran v. Foran*, 834 P. 2d 1081 (Wash. Ct. App. 1992) (holding that, even where evidence of premarital domestic violence was not sufficient to support a finding that the wife was coerced into signing, it could show that it inhibited her willingness to seek independent counsel).

108. *See, e.g., Snedaker v. Snedaker*, 660 So. 2d 1070 (Fla. Dist. Ct. App. 1995) (upholding award of $125,000 for assault and battery claims despite valid prenuptial agreement that severely limited battered woman's recovery in divorce).

109. *See* Berner & Klaw, *Prenuptial Agreements*, in *The Impact of Domestic Violence on Your Legal Practice* 6-1–6-3 (Goelman, Lehrman & Valente eds., 1996).

110. *See, e.g.*, New York Victim Service Agency, *The Cost of Domestic Violence: A Preliminary Investigation of the Financial Cost of Domestic Violence* (1987). In 1992 nearly 20% of the women killed in the workplace were murdered by a current or former husband or male partner. Bureau of Labor Statistics, National Census of Fatal Occupational Injuries (Aug. 3, 1995).

111. See, e.g., Alaska Stat. §12.61.010(5) (1995); 18 Pa. Cons. Stat. §4957(a).

112. *See, e.g.*, Kuperberg & Lieblein, *Corporate Liability*, in *The Impact of Domestic Violence on Your Legal Practice* 10-6–10-10 (Goelman, Lehrman & Valente eds., 1996).

113. *Id.* at 10-6.

114. Occupational Safety and Health Act of 1970, §5(a)(1), 29 U.S.C. §651, §654(a) (1994) (requiring an employer to "furnish each of his employees employment and a place of employment free from recognized hazards that are causing or likely to cause death or serious physical harm to his employees").

115. *See, e.g.*, 82 Am. Jur. 2d *Workers' Compensation* §73 (1992).

116. *See, e.g., Tart v. Colonial Penn. Ins. Co.*, No. 2019 (Pa. C.C.P. Sept. 1985) (holding that a cause of action existed).

117. *Supra* note 112, at 10-7.

118. 82 Am. Jur. 2d *Workers' Compensation* §§358, 359 (1992 & Supp. 1995); Cal. Lab. Code §3208.3 (Deering 1995) (holding that California's workers' compensation statute encompassed compensation for a victim's psychiatric injury caused by work-related violence).

119. *See, e.g.*, Me. Rev. Stat. Ann. tit. 26, §1193 (1)(A)(4) (West 1995). Unemployment benefits may not be denied, for example, if a domestic violence victim is discharged after being absent from work due to injuries from battering, because the absence would not reflect an "intentional disregard of the employer's interests." *See Boynton Cab Co. v. Neubeck*, 296 N.W. 636 (Wis. 1941).

120. *Supra* note 104.

121. *See, e.g.*, Keller, Snell & Wilmer, *Workplace Violence: The Employer's New Catch-22* (1995); Larson, *Employment Screening*, §§2.10, 3.04(1)(a), 3.04(2)(a)(b), 9.11 (1995). Also, as of 1996, at least 13 states had enacted laws designed to restrict insurance discrimination on the basis of domestic violence. These states are Arizona, California, Connecticut, Delaware, Florida, Indiana, Iowa, Maine, Massachusetts, Minnesota, New Hampshire, Pennsylvania, and Tennessee. *See* Fromson, *Insurance Discrimination Against Victims of Abuse*, in *The Impact of Domestic Violence on Your Legal Practice* 10-21 (Goelman, Lehrman & Valente eds., 1996).

Geriatric Patients

MARSHALL B. KAPP, J.D., M.P.H., F.C.L.M.

ELDER MISTREATMENT
GUARDIANSHIP AND ITS ALTERNATIVES
RESEARCH WITH OLDER HUMAN PARTICIPANTS
FINANCING MEDICAL CARE FOR GERIATRIC PATIENTS
ELDER LAW AS A GROWING SPECIALTY

Medical advances enable more Americans to live longer than their predecessors. The segment of our population that is over 65 years old continues to increase astronomically. This growth may be summarized briefly as follows.[1] Persons 65 years or older numbered 34.5 million in 1999, representing 12.7% of the U.S. population or one in every eight Americans. The number of older Americans increased by 3.3 million or 10.6% since 1990, compared to an increase of 9.1% for the under-65 population. About 2 million persons celebrated their 65th birthday in 1999 (5422 per day); in the same year, over 1.8 million persons 65 or older died, resulting in a net increase of 200,000 (558 per day).

The older population itself is getting older. In 1999, the 65-74 age group (18.2 million) was eight times larger than in 1990, but the 75-84 group (12.1 million) was 16 times larger and the 85 and older group (4.2 million) was 34 times larger.

A relatively small number (1.47 million) and percentage (4.3%) of the over-65 population lived in nursing facilities in 1997. However, the percentage increased dramatically with age, ranging from 1.1% for persons 65-74 years to 4.5% for persons 75-84 years and 19% for persons 85 and older.

The likelihood of developing chronic health problems increases sharply with age. Most older persons have at least one chronic condition and multiple conditions are not uncommon. The most common chronic conditions in persons aged 65 and older are arthritis, hypertension and other heart problems, sensory impairments, orthopedic impairments, sinusitis, and diabetes. Other problems include memory loss, dementia, and depression. Mental stress often creates serious physical complications in the aged. The major causes of death for older people are heart disease, stroke, and cancer.

Most of the generic chapters in this volume are fully pertinent to care of the elderly, although general medicolegal concepts frequently take on special nuances as applied specifically to older persons. For instance, the requirement of informed consent to medical interventions applies to persons of all ages, but when older persons are involved, special attention must be paid to issues of decisional capacity and (especially when the patient is institutionalized) the voluntariness of decisions.

The current chapter does not, however, comprehensively discuss the particular application of generic concepts to older persons. Instead, the purpose here is to outline a few selected topics involving the intersection of law and medicine in the care of the elderly population.

ELDER MISTREATMENT

Only in the last few decades have we been willing to publicly admit, let alone begin to address, the phenomenon of serious mistreatment of older persons both within home and community-based settings and institutional environments. The problem is a prevalent one[2] and is by no means limited to the United States[3] or to any particular racial or ethnic group.[4]

The definition of elder abuse and neglect is a matter of state law. Each state has enacted its own statutory schema in this arena, with substantial variation among particular definitions and procedures as a consequence.[5]

The American Medical Association has described elder abuse and neglect as "actions or the omission of actions that result in harm or threatened harm to the health or welfare of the elderly."[6] These actions or inactions may take place in the elder's own home or that of a relative, at the hands of an informal caregiver,[7] or in an institutional setting.[8] A single incident may constitute abuse or neglect in most states, although usually a repeated pattern is discovered and in some jurisdictions is necessary to meet statutory definitions of abuse and neglect. Random criminal assaults of older persons by strangers (e.g., in the context of a robbery) generally are excluded from the category of elder mistreatment as it is being considered in this chapter.

Among the different forms of elder mistreatment are: physical (e.g., assault, forced sexual contact, overmedication, inappropriate physical restraints); psychological or emotional (e.g., threats); denial of basic human needs by the caregiver (e.g., withholding indicated medical care or food); deprivation of civil rights (e.g., freedom of movement and communication);[9] and financial exploitation.

In addition, a significant proportion of reported cases of elder mistreatment fall into the category of self-neglect by older persons living alone, without any informal (i.e., unpaid family or friends) or formal (i.e., paid) caregivers. Examples of self-neglect may include an individual's failure to maintain adequate nutrition, hydration, or hygiene, use physical aids such as eyeglasses, hearing aids, or false teeth, or maintain a safe environment for himself or herself. Self-neglect may be suspected in the presence of dehydration, malnourishment, decubitus ulcers, poor personal hygiene, or lack of compliance with basic medical recommendations.

A few states have enacted distinct statutes dealing with cases of institutional abuse and neglect of older residents. Terms of these statutes may apply to nursing facilities, board and care homes, and assisted living arrangements. Even without such precisely focused legislation in a particular jurisdiction, resident mistreatment by long-term care institutional staff is condemned by federal regulations,[10] including restrictions on the use of involuntary mechanical and chemical restraints,[11] as well as by state institutional licensing statutes and common law tort standards.[12] Also, a number of states explicitly lump together institutional and informal caregiver mistreatment in the same statutes, rather than legislatively handling them distinctly.

Every state has exercised its *parens patriae* power to protect those who cannot fend for themselves by enacting a statute dealing with the reporting of elder mistreatment suspicions by health care professionals to specific public welfare or law enforcement authorities.[13,14] Some state statutes single out the elderly, while others just use age 18 and vulnerability to mistreatment as the criteria for reporting and intervention. At least 43 states plus the District of Columbia mandate reporting of suspected elder abuse and neglect, with criminal penalties and/or civil fines specified for noncompliance in most statutory schemes. A private tort action may also be brought by a mistreatment victim whose injuries were exacerbated by the professional's failure to report in timely fashion.

The remaining jurisdictions make reporting a voluntary matter, with legislation stating that a report "may" rather than "shall" be filed. Whether reporting of mistreatment cases is required or only permitted, all of the statutes immunize the mandated or authorized reporters against any potential liability (e.g., for breach of the duty of patient confidentiality or for defamation) for making the report, as long as the report was made in good faith and without malicious intent.[15,16]

In recognition of the potential for elder abuse and neglect, the states have created a wide variety of programs under the general heading of adult protective services (APS). The basic definition of this concept is a system of preventive and supportive services for older persons living in the community to enable them to remain as independent as possible while avoiding abuse and exploitation by others. Good APS programs are characterized by the coordinated delivery of services to adults at risk and the actual or potential authority to provide surrogate decision-making regarding those services.[17]

GUARDIANSHIP AND ITS ALTERNATIVES

While the law presumes that adults are capable of making voluntary, informed, and understanding decisions that affect their lives, sometimes this presumption is not accurate.[18] A significant minority of older individuals have impaired ability to make and communicate their own choices about personal (including medical) and financial matters in a rational and authentic manner. The prevalence of dementia and other severe mental disabilities among the aged indicates the strong probability that this phenomenon will expand in the future. One important device within the legal system for dealing with the problem of cognitively incapacitated individuals, and the concomitant need for some form of surrogate decision-making on their behalf, is guardianship.

Guardianship is a legal relationship, authorized by a state court, between a ward (the person whom a court has declared to be incompetent to make decisions) and a guardian (whom the court appoints as the surrogate decision-maker for the ward). Terminology regarding this relationship varies somewhat among jurisdictions; in some states, for example, this concept is referred to as conservatorship.

Judicial appointment of a guardian to make decisions on behalf of a person who has been adjudicated incompetent ordinarily occurs in response to a petition filed by the family, a health care facility, or an APS agency. The legal proceeding involves review by the court of the sworn affidavit or live testimony of a physician who has examined the alleged incompetent person. An adjudication of incompetence means that the ward no longer retains the power to exercise those decisional rights that have been delegated to the guardian.

The legal system historically has treated guardianship as an all-or-nothing proposition, global findings of incompetence being accompanied by virtually complete disenfranchisement of the ward. Lately, however, states have amended their statutes to recognize the concept of limited or partial guardianship, which accounts for the decision-specific nature of mental capacity and the ability of some people rationally to make certain kinds of choices but not others.[19] Because creating total or "plenary" guardianship usually entails an extensive deprivation of an individual's basic personal and property rights, the "least restrictive/least intrusive alternative" doctrine makes limited or partial guardianship preferred.

The modern trend in surrogate decision-making has been toward the substituted judgment standard. Under this approach, the guardian is required to make the same decisions that the patient would make, according to the patient's own preferences and values to the extent they can be ascertained, if the patient currently were able to make and express competent decisions. The substituted judgment standard is highly consistent with respect for patient autonomy. When it cannot reasonably be ascertained what the patient would have decided if competent, the guardian is expected to rely on the traditional best interests standard. That test mandates that decisions be made in a manner that, from the guardian's perspective, would confer the most benefit and the least burden on the ward.

A number of alternatives to plenary, private guardianship exist for assisting older individuals with cognitive impairments to navigate through the vicissitudes of daily life. Some of these alternatives involve advance planning, while others are imposed on the individual in the absence of such planning.

A variety of legal and financial strategies have evolved that enable individuals, while still mentally and physically capable of rationally making and expressing their own choices, to plan ahead for the contingency of future incapacity. These advance planning mechanisms promote the principle of autonomy by permitting an individual to prospectively direct or shape subsequent personal decisions even if contemporaneous expression of wishes has become impossible.

Many of these devices pertain to prospective influence over monetary matters; they include joint bank accounts, automatic deposits, living trusts, personal money management services, powers of attorney, and durable powers of attorney. The chief advance planning mechanisms available for future medical decisions are the living will and the durable power of attorney for health care. These written directives are discussed in depth elsewhere in this text.

Although it usually works reasonably as intended, advance financial and health care planning sometimes goes badly awry. The geriatric clinician may become aware, for instance, of an agent named under a now-incapacitated patient's durable power of attorney who is misusing or exploiting the patient's finances, abusing the patient, or grossly neglecting the patient's medical needs. In such circumstances, the clinician confronts ethical quandaries about whether to initiate a guardianship proceeding or otherwise request court involvement. When the clinician sees no other effective, less restrictive means of dealing with such scenarios,[20] referring the situation to the legal system, through official notification of the local adult protective services (APS) agency, is probably the best course to follow.

There also is evidence that physicians not infrequently fail to honor patients' advance medical directives.[21] A number of initiatives have been launched in a concerted effort to educate both medical professionals and the general public about the significance and expectations of advance medical planning.

The majority of people who become decisionally incapacitated have failed to take advantage of the advance planning mechanisms just outlined. For this bulk of the cognitively impaired population, alternatives to standard plenary, private guardianship fall into two categories: alternative forms *of* guardianship (e.g., limited and/or temporary) and alternatives *to* guardianship.

For a growing number of older persons whose cognitive impairments would technically qualify them for guardianship, plenary or limited, the most pressing practical problem is the unavailability of family members or close friends who are willing and able to assume guardianship responsibilities. In the absence of a state public guardianship system, local volunteer guardianship program, or sufficient assets to hire a private, proprietary professional guardian, the cognitively incapacitated individual with no family or friends (the "unbefriended") often literally "falls between the cracks." Important decisions, including those involving medical treatment, may by default go without being made until an emergency has developed and the doctrine of presumed consent applies.

Even in the absence of advance planning for incapacity by the individual, some form of official guardianship for the cognitively incapacitated older person is by far the exception rather than the rule. Unplanned alternatives to guardianship include: representative payees for government benefit payments, adult protective services (APS) (including their emergency intervention powers), family consent statutes, and the informal but universally accepted practice of asking next of kin for authorization to provide or withhold specific interventions.

RESEARCH WITH OLDER HUMAN PARTICIPANTS

The generic legal aspects of conducting biomedical or behavioral research involving human participants is dealt with elsewhere in this volume. However, given the disproportionate prevalence of dementias and other severe mental disabilities among the elderly, the legal and ethical Catch 22 of conducting biomedical and behavioral research using older human participants who are severely demented or otherwise cognitively compromised presents a particular dilemma.[22] On the one hand, progress in developing effective treatments and cures for medical and psychological problems associated with dementia requires that research projects be done in which individuals suffering from the precise problems of interest be the basic units of study. At the same time, paradoxically, those very problems that qualify an individual for eligibility as a subject in such a research project often make it impossible for that person to engage in a rational and autonomous decision-making process about his or her own participation as a research subject.[23] This irony is exacerbated by the fact that research participants generally are more vulnerable to possible exploitation, and hence need more protection, than patients in therapeutic situations because of, among other things, the researchers' potential conflicts of interest.

Federal regulations covering biomedical and behavioral research require that informed consent for participation be obtained from the "subject or the subject's legally authorized representative."[24] However, a subject's legally authorized representative is defined in circular fashion to mean an "individual or judicial or other body authorized under applicable [presumably state] law to consent on behalf of a prospective subject."[25]

A number of alternative possibilities for proxy decision-making in the research context have been identified. These devices include: the durable power of attorney for research participation, reliance on family consent statutes, informal reliance on available family members as surrogate decision-makers, guardianship with specific authorization for research decisions, explicit prior court orders authorizing the incapacitated subject's participation in research protocols on a case-by-case basis, an independent patient advocate supplied by the organization sponsoring the research or by a government agency, and selection of a surrogate by the institutional review board (IRB) or a long-term care facility's resident council.

Some have suggested that special procedural safeguards are necessary to protect vulnerable, cognitively impaired human volunteers from injury due to research participation. These safeguards might encompass: heightened IRB involvement in the protocol approval process, enhanced IRB activity in the postapproval ongoing monitoring and supervision phase of the research, including serving as a forum for appeals and objections, and requiring individual participant assent (i.e., giving participants a veto power) even when informed proxy consent to research participation has been obtained. An important question, especially since the participants of interest are mentally impaired, concerns the definition of assent to be used, namely, whether the failure to actively object to participation in a protocol is enough to be interpreted as a tacit or implied form of assent or whether some more affirmative indication of agreement is necessary.

In 1998, the National Bioethics Advisory Commission (NBAC) issued a report[26] recommending, among other things, that when the potential human participants in a research protocol are mentally impaired:

- For any protocol involving greater than minimal risk, there be an independent assessment of each potential subject's decisional capacity.
- For any protocol involving greater than minimal risk, the IRB require the investigator to explicitly describe to the IRB the process to be used to assess the decisional capacity of potential human participants.
- For protocols involving greater than minimal risk and no prospect of direct benefit to that study's human

participants (a category into which most research seeking to enroll the mentally impaired elderly probably falls), the protocol be reviewed and approved by a newly created national IRB, or under guidelines established by that national IRB, and that the participant's legally authorized representative consents.

At the time this chapter is written, no legislative or regulatory action has been taken on any of NBAC's proposals in this sphere.

FINANCING MEDICAL CARE FOR GERIATRIC PATIENTS

Medical care (acute and chronic) for geriatric patients currently is financed through a crazy-quilt combination of personal out-of-pocket payments, Medicaid (primarily for nursing facility care and for some home and community-based long-term care under various state waiver programs), payments from private Medicare supplementary insurance policies purchased individually by the patient (i.e., "Medigap" policies), and Medicare. Medicare Part A mainly pays for inpatient hospital care and Part B primarily covers physicians' services. Medicare Part C was enacted by Congress as part of the 1997 Balanced Budget Act (BBA).[27] This new program created the Medicare + Choice Program (MCP), which provides an array of private health insurance options for Medicare beneficiaries. These options include: health maintenance organizations (HMOs), competitive medical plans (CMPs), provider-sponsored organizations (PSOs), medical savings accounts (MSAs), and private fee-for-service (PFFS) plans. Under the BBA and implementing regulations,[28] each eligible older and disabled individual now has the right to choose between remaining in federally regulated Parts A and B or enrolling in one of the Part C Medicare + Choice market-oriented options available in the individual's local area.

The chief deficiency of the current Medicare program is its failure to cover the cost of prescription drugs, which amounts to a sizable expense for many older patients. As this chapter is being written, Congress and the state legislatures continue to grapple politically with this gaping hole in the health care safety net for older Americans.

Earlier explicit suggestions that certain aspects of medical care be rationed categorically according to a patient's age[29] have, in general, been soundly rejected in public policy debate. However, there is growing evidence that medical care actually is rationed by age de facto, in the sense that older people in many circumstances are treated less aggressively than younger counterparts from whom they cannot be distinguished in terms of prognosis or other relevant medical criteria.[30]

ELDER LAW AS A GROWING SPECIALTY

Over the past three decades, the field of elder law as a specialty of attorney practice has burgeoned.[31] Educational institutions offer specialized courses and other learning opportunities in this sphere for both attorneys and other professionals, focused textbooks and practice handbooks have proliferated, journals have arisen, and national and state organizations devoted to the field have developed and grown.[32]

The content of elder law is expansive. Matters falling within this area include, at least, advice to and representation of older persons, their families, and physicians and other service providers regarding Social Security retirement and disability benefits; other federal and state benefits; Medicare and Medicaid (including asset sheltering and divestiture for eligibility purposes); housing issues, financial management (e.g., trusts), and estate planning; medical treatment decision-making and advance planning; judicial and nonjudicial forms of substitute decision-making; elder abuse and neglect; employment discrimination; and tax counseling. Elder law practice is necessarily interdisciplinary and interprofessional in nature, entailing cooperation among the attorney, physicians and other health and human services providers, governmental agencies, and nonlegal advocacy and support organizations.

ENDNOTES

1. United States Department of Health and Human Services, Administration on Aging, *A Profile of Older Americans* (DHHS, Washington, D.C. 2001).
2. R.S. Wolf, *The Nature and Scope of Elder Abuse*, XXIV Generations 6-12 (Summer 2000).
3. M. Bradley, *Elder Abuse*, 313 Br. Med. J. 548-550 (1996).
4. T. Tatara, ed., *Understanding Elder Abuse in Minority Populations* (Taylor & Francis, Philadelphia 1999).
5. S. Loue, *Elder Abuse and Neglect in Medicine and Law: The Need for Reform*, 22 J. Legal Med. 159-209 (2001).
6. American Medical Association, Council on Scientific Affairs, *Elder Abuse and Neglect*, 257 J.A.M.A. 966-971 (1987).
7. G.J. Anetzberger, *Caregiving: Primary Cause of Elder Abuse?*, XXIV Generations 46-51 (Summer 2000).
8. L. Mosqueda, J. Heath & K. Burnight, *Recognizing Physical Abuse and Neglect in the Skilled Nursing Facility: The Physician's Responsibilities*, 2 J. A. Med. Directors Assn. 183-186 (2001).
9. M.B. Kapp, *Restraining Impaired Elders in the Home Environment: Legal, Practical, and Policy Implications*, 4 J. Case Mgt. 54-59 (1995).
10. 42 Code of Federal Regulations §§483.10, 483.15, 483.25.
11. M.B. Kapp, *Restraint Reduction and Legal Risk Management*, 47 J. Am. Geriatr. Soc. 375-376 (1999).
12. P.W. Iyer, ed., *Nursing Home Litigation: Investigation and Case Preparation* (Lawyers and Judges Publishing Company, Tucson, Ari. 1999).
13. K.C. Kleinschmidt, *Elder Abuse: A Review*, 30 Ann. Emerg. Med. 463-472 (1997).
14. M.D. Velick, *Mandatory Reporting Statutes: A Necessary Yet Underutilized Response to Elder Abuse*, 3 Elder L. J. 165-190 (1995).
15. E. Capezuti, B.L. Brush & W.T. Lawson III, *Reporting Elder Mistreatment*, 23 J. Geront. Nurs. 24-32 (1997).
16. D.E. Rosenblatt, K.-H. Cho & P.W. Durance, *Reporting Mistreatment of Older Adults: The Role of Physicians*, 44 J. Am. Geriatr. Soc. 65-70 (1996).
17. J.M. Otto, *The Role of Adult Protective Services in Addressing Abuse*, XXIV Generations 33-38 (Summer 2000).
18. T. Grisso & P.S. Appelbaum, *Assessing Competence to Consent to Treatment* (Oxford University Press, New York 1998).
19. L.A. Frolik, *Promoting Judicial Acceptance and Use of Limited Guardianship*, 31 Stetson L. Rev. 735-755 (2002).
20. W.C. Schmidt, Jr., *Guardianship: The Court of Last Resort for the Elderly and Disabled* (Carolina Academic Press, Durham, N.C. 1995).
21. SUPPORT Principal Investigators, *A Controlled Trial to Improve Care for Seriously Ill Hospitalized Patients: The Study to Understand Prognoses and Preferences for Outcomes and Risks of Treatments*, 274 J.A.M.A. 1591-1598 (1995).
22. M.B. Kapp, *Regulating Research for the Decisionally Impaired: Implications for Mental Health Professionals*, 8 J. Clin. Geropsychol. 35-51 (2002).
23. R. Dresser, *Dementia Research: Ethics and Policy for the Twenty-First Century*, 35 Georgia L. Rev. 661-690 (2001).
24. 45 Code of Federal Regulations §46.116 and 21 Code of Federal Regulations §50.20.
25. 45 Code of Federal Regulations §46.102(d) and 21 Code of Federal Regulations §50.3(m).
26. National Bioethics Advisory Commission, *Research Involving Persons with Mental Disorders That May Affect Decision-Making Capacity* (NBAC, Washington, D.C. 1998).
27. Public Law No. 105-33 (1997).
28. 64 Federal Register 7968 (1999).
29. D. Callahan, *Setting Limits: Medical Goals in an Aging Society* (Simon & Schuster, New York 1987).
30. M.B. Kapp, *De Facto Health Care Rationing by Age: The Law Has No Remedy*, 19 J. Legal Med. 323-349 (1998).
31. L.A. Frolik, *The Developing Field of Elder Law Redux: Ten Years After*, 10 Elder L. J. 1-14 (2002).
32. S.J. Hemp & C.R. Nyberg, *Elder Law: A Guide to Key Resources*, 3 Elder L. J. 1-87 (1995).

Oncology Patients

MELVIN A. SHIFFMAN, M.D., J.D., F.C.L.M.

FAILURE TO DIAGNOSE CANCER
PATHOLOGY REPORTS
RADIATION THERAPY
CHEMOTHERAPY
GENETICS
GENETIC COUNSELING
UNORTHODOX CANCER TREATMENTS
CONCLUSION

FAILURE TO DIAGNOSE CANCER

As a result of a failure to obtain an adequate history, a physician may not include the diagnosis of certain cancers in the differential diagnoses or may not give it proper consideration. Family and racial history is important in cancer screening and for obtaining proper tests in certain symptomatic patients.[1]

Occupational exposure and social habits, such as alcoholism or smoking, significant x-ray exposure, or other radiation exposures, chemical exposure, and exposure of parents to certain drugs or carcinogens are important factors. Failure to inquire of these historical factors, warn of dangers, and give guidelines to the patient may be considered negligent.[2]

Overreliance on certain facts obtained in taking the medical history may be just as significant in certain cases as failure to take an adequate history. Failure to detect the clues of certain symptoms as related by the patient because of a history of "cancerophobia" has been a factor in certain failures to diagnose cancer cases.[3]

Physical examination

Failure to perform a physical examination, performing an inadequate examination, overreliance on a negative examination, or failure to perform a follow-up examination may also lead to claims for failure to diagnose cancer. In the 1985 case of *Gorman v. LaSasso*,[4] a Colorado jury awarded $1 million to a woman in her thirties who complained about the presence of a lump in her breast for 6 months, which was not investigated until the fourth time she complained about it.

Referral and testing

A physician has an affirmative duty to obtain or perform appropriate tests in the diagnosis of a suspected cancer. In *Barenbrugge v. Rich*,[5] a gynecologist did not order a mammogram on his 28-year-old patient after she presented with a breast lump later proven cancerous. A 1985 Illinois jury returned a verdict for $3 million in favor of the patient. Failure of a physician to refer to another physician or specialist for a suspected cancer may also be a negligent act of omission. In the case of *O'Dell v. Chesney*,[6] a doctor of chiropractic treated a 63-year-old man for rectal bleeding and diabetes for 2 years. He was held negligent for failing to refer the patient to a medical doctor after the plaintiff died from colorectal cancer.

Failure of a physician to read the test report or consultant's recommendations or to communicate the report or recommendations to the patient may be negligent. In *Mehalik v. Morvant*,[7] a 42-year-old Louisiana woman was referred by her physician for a mammogram to evaluate a breast lump. Her physician told her that the mammogram report was negative, although the radiologist reported a suspicious mass and recommended follow-up monitoring. Relying on this report, she did not return for follow-up evaluation. A large breast cancer was confirmed later at biopsy, and the patient sued her physician for damages, with a resultant settlement.

Failure to repeat a test, perform indicated studies, or refer for biopsy when an initial test is negative may be negligent when clinical suspicion should be high that cancer may be present. A Massachusetts jury in the 1985 case *Brown v. Nash*[8] awarded $3 million to a woman because a surgeon failed to diagnose her breast cancer when he relied on a negative mammogram report, despite a changing physical abnormality noted in her breast. Relying on the false-negative report, he elected not to do a biopsy of an area later shown to be cancerous.

In *Glicklich v. Spievack*,[9] another Massachusetts court awarded $578,000 to a woman who was not referred by her primary care physician to a surgeon for a biopsy, even though he relied on a false-negative mammogram report and a negative needle biopsy of a breast lump later diagnosed as malignant.

Failure to follow recommended protocol

The American Cancer Society and other professional specialty organizations have published guidelines for physicians, suggesting schedules or protocols for early cancer detection. Failure to follow these protocols is not necessarily negligent. However, it is common in litigation involving cancer diagnosis for attorneys to use compliance or noncompliance with published guidelines for health care, whether called "standards" or not, as evidence of the required standard of care. Box 55-1 shows the guidelines for cancer-related checkups recommended by the American Cancer Society.[10]

Delayed diagnosis of breast cancer

Delayed diagnosis of breast cancer is the most frequent cause of litigation related to cancer. Analysis of medicolegal cases shows that breast cancer is involved in 36.7% of cases of delayed diagnosis of cancer.[11] An inordinate delay in the diagnosis of breast cancer may result in a worse prognosis than if there were no delay. Patients tend to perceive any delay in the diagnosis as decreasing their chance of survival.[12]

Haagenson et al.[13] found the following errors by physicians, which resulted in delay in the diagnosis of breast cancer:

1. Failure to examine a breast containing an obvious tumor while treating the patient for an unrelated disease.
2. Failure in palpation of the breast to recognize the tumor of which the patient is complaining.
3. Mistaking a cancer for a breast infection.
4. Wrongfully diagnosing a breast cancer as a benign lesion and failing to advise a biopsy or excision.
5. Disregarding a history of acute and sharp pain in the breast.
6. Disregarding a sign of retraction.
7. Failure to determine the cause of nipple discharge.
8. Relying on a normal aspiration biopsy.

Early treatment of breast cancer is sound practice because the success of treatment, such as surgery, chemotherapy, radiotherapy, and immunotherapy, is predicated on minimal tumor burden.[14]

PATHOLOGY REPORTS

The pathology report on a surgical specimen is one of the most important aspects of the clinical record. The pathological status of the tumor allows a determination of whether there is a malignancy, whether the neoplasm is cured, probably cured, or unlikely to be cured, as well as being an indicator for the type of future therapy and follow-up care.

Since the pathology results are so vital, the report should contain all the information needed by the attending physician(s) to make decisions. All information must be

---

BOX 55-1. GUIDELINES FOR CANCER-RELATED CHECKUPS

1. Health counseling and cancer checkup to include examination for cancers of the thyroid, testicles, prostate, ovaries, lymph nodes, and skin every 3 years after the age of 20 and every year after the age of 40
2. Sigmoidoscopy after the age of 50 to include two normal examinations 1 year apart and then every 3 to 5 years
3. Stool guaiac slide test every year after the age of 50
4. Digital rectal examination every year after the age of 40
5. In women
   a. Papanicolaou test every year after age 18 or before age 18 if sexually active (After three consecutive normal examinations, test may be performed less frequently at physician's discretion.)
   b. Pelvic examination every year after age 18 or before age 18 if sexually active
   c. Endometrial tissue sample at menopause in women at high risk with a history of infertility, obesity, failure to ovulate, abnormal uterine bleeding, or estrogen therapy
   d. Breast self-examination monthly after the age of 20
   e. Breast examination every 3 years between ages 20 and 40 and every year after the age of 40
   f. Mammography every 1 to 2 years between ages 40 and 49 and every year after the age of 50

Data from American Cancer Society, *Survey of Physicians' Attitudes and Practices in Early Cancer Detection*, 35 CA 197-213 (1985); Woo, *Screening Procedures in the Asymptomatic Adult*, 254 J.A.M.A. 1480-1484 (1985); C. Metlin & C.R. Smart, *Breast Cancer Detection Guidelines for Women Ages 40 to 49 Years: Rationale for the American Cancer Society Reaffirmation of Recommendations*, CA-A Cancer J. for Clinicians 248-255 (1994); and A.M. Leitch et al., *American Cancer Society Guidelines for the Early Detection of Breast Cancer: Update 1997*, 47 CA-A Cancer J. for Clinicians 150-153 (1997).

---

clearly stated in the pathology report. An incomplete report or error in the report may result in disastrous consequences to the patient. Although diagnostic decisions may be difficult for the pathologist, the clinician must rely on that pathology report for decision-making.

The Association of Directors of Anatomic and Surgical Pathology (ADASP) has formed several committees for the purpose of developing recommendations concerning the content of surgical pathology reports for various common malignant tumors.

RADIATION THERAPY

More than half of all cancer patients will ultimately need radiation therapy. The physician and the patient must weigh the benefits of therapy against the possible complications. Newer techniques have been developed with the use of the electron and proton beams to allow more accurate placement of the treatment with less damage to surrounding tissues.

Complications

Proper radiation may result in skin burns consisting of erythema (redness) or desquamation (dry or wet).[15] Ulceration with necrosis may be seen with prolonged healing time and scar deformity. Permanent pulmonary fibrosis in the treatment field for cancer of the breast does occur at times. Development of radiation enteritis after treatment of intraabdominal malignancies is not unknown. Excessive radiation has been one source of litigation.

In *Duke v. Morphis*,[16] radon seeds were implanted in the supraclavicular area for treatment of a malignancy. The patient suffered myelopathy and paralysis, blaming the radiation treatment plan and the manner of supervision. The plaintiff was awarded $266,700. In *Rudman v. Beth Israel Medical Center*,[17] paralysis after radiation treatment of a head and neck cancer brought a $2 million settlement. In *Barnes & Powers v. Hahnemann Medical College and Hospital*,[18] a patient with cervical cancer was treated with radiation therapy and radium implants. After a radical hysterectomy she suffered radiation cystitis, vesicovaginal fistula, radiation fibrosis of the ileum, and radiation fibrosis of the vagina. Multiple further surgeries were necessary to correct these problems. The case was settled for an undisclosed amount.

CHEMOTHERAPY

Medical oncology is a changing field, and new chemotherapeutic agents and new combinations of agents are being investigated at a rapid pace. No other medical specialty handles extremely dangerous drugs on an almost daily basis. Many of the antineoplastic drugs are mutagenic, teratogenic, and carcinogenic in animals.[19] Exposure to these agents can result in the appearance of mutagenic substances in the urine.[20] There have been reports of an increased incidence of acute myelogenous leukemia in patients treated with alkylating agents,[21] and bladder cancer[22] has been associated with the use of cyclophosphamide, especially in low doses over prolonged periods.

Chemotherapeutic agents can be fetotoxic and therefore potentially dangerous to health care personnel. Drugs that have been associated with fetal malformations include folate antagonists, 6-mercaptopurine, and alkylating agents,[23] as well as the MOPP (nitrogen mustard, vincristine, procarbazine, prednisone) treatment for Hodgkin's disease.[24] Personnel safety guidelines have been established to protect personnel who are mixing and administering antineoplastic drugs.[25]

Complications

Hypersensitive reactions may occur with edema, rash, bronchospasm, diarrhea, and hypotension.[26] In *Lefler v. Yardumian*[27] there was a leak of intravenous chemotherapy

agents into the subcutaneous area of the arm. Tissue ulceration and damage to the tendons of the left hand occurred. Inadvertent overdose has been a source of litigation. In *Newman v. Geschke*,[28] a patient with throat cancer was given 12-15 mg of vincristine by the office nurse. This amount was 9 to 10 times the normal prescribed dosage. He developed neuropathies, bowel and bladder incontinence, weight loss, and alopecia and required 3 weeks of hospitalization. The case was settled for $450,000.

GENETICS

The recent rapid evolution of genetics in cancer research has provided physicians with the means of identifying individuals and their family members who are at high risk for developing cancer. Ethical, legal, and social implications of genetic abnormalities have become the medical community's new challenge.[29] Some of the genes associated with hereditary cancers are listed in Table 55-1.

GENETIC COUNSELING

Genetic counseling is necessary before genetic testing and includes education on the natural history of genetic disorders, genetics, and surveillance. The individual and high-risk family members who have been counseled may then submit to DNA testing, if this is available; the DNA test results are revealed on a one-to-one basis by the physician or genetic counselor,[30] and management recommendations are discussed.

Familial adenomatous polyposis

Colonic adenomas are likely to occur in patients with a mutant adenomatous polyposis coli (APC) gene (90% penetrance). Adenomas are manifested in 15% of gene carriers by age 10, 70% by age 20, and 90% by age 30.

Screening recommendation for patients who test negative for the APC gene in families with familial adenomatous polyposis (FAP) is flexible sigmoidoscopy at ages 18, 25, and 35 years. The lifetime risk for colon cancer is the same as for the general population (3% to 5%), and offspring will not be at risk for FAP.[31]

If testing is positive for the APC gene, annual flexible sigmoidoscopy should begin at age 10 or 11 years. When adenomatous polyposis is present, the patient is counseled to prepare for eventual colectomy, and upper gastrointestinal screening for polyposis should be performed every 1 to 3 years. Offspring will be at 50% risk for FAP.[32]

Hereditary nonpolyposis colorectal cancer

In hereditary nonpolyposis colorectal cancer (HNPCC), colonoscopy is initiated in high-risk individuals at 25 years of age and repeated biennially through age 35 and annually

TABLE 55-1 Genes associated with hereditary cancers

Cancer	Chromosome	Gene
Breast and ovarian cancer	BRCA1	17q21
Breast cancer	BRCA2	13q12-13
Li-Fraumeni syndrome/SBLA	p53	17p13
Lynch syndrome/HNPCC	MSH2	2p
Melanoma	MLM	9p21
Medullary thyroid	RET	10q11.2
Neurofibromatosis	NF1	17q11.2
Retinoblastoma	RB1	13q14
Turcot's syndrome		
Predominance of glioblastoma	PMS2	7p22
Multiform	MLH1	3p21.3-23
Predominance of cerebellar medulloblastoma	APC	5q21
Familial adenomatous polyposis	APC	Distal to 5'
Hereditary flat adenoma syndrome	APC	Proximal to 5'
von Hippel-Lindau disease	VHLS	3p25
Wilms' tumor	WT1	11p13

HNPCC, Hereditary nonpolyposis colorectal cancer; *SBLA*, sarcoma, breast and brain tumors, leukemia, laryngeal and lung cancer, and adrenal cortical carcinoma.

thereafter. If DNA testing has shown one of the HNPCC abnormalities, annual colonoscopy is started at age 20.[33]

If a patient develops colorectal cancer, subtotal colectomy is recommended because of the high incidence of multiple colorectal cancers. Women with colorectal cancer who have completed their families may submit to prophylactic hysterectomy and bilateral salpingo-oophorectomy at the same time as the colon surgery to prevent cancers that may develop under the Lynch II syndrome. Patients with DNA-proven HNPCC mutation have the option for prophylactic subtotal colectomy.[34]

Familial breast cancer syndromes

Familial breast cancer syndromes are heterogeneous and require a thorough family history (both maternal and paternal). Hereditary breast cancer is more likely in women with family members who have had early-onset breast or ovarian cancer (before age 50), bilateral breast cancer, or two or more affected first-degree relatives with breast or ovarian cancer.[35] Breast cancer gene (BRCA1) predictive testing is available only under research studies, and BRCA2 testing, although cloned, is unavailable as of yet. Women at high risk for breast or ovarian cancer may have close surveillance that includes monthly breast self-examination, annual diagnostic mammograms, and physician breast examinations every 4 to 6 months.[36] The tamoxifen chemoprevention trial is currently available for high-risk women over the age of 35 years. Prophylactic bilateral mastectomy may be an option, depending on the patient's choice after adequate counseling.[37]

Women who are at high risk for breast or ovarian cancer (BRCA1) may have surveillance with transvaginal ultrasound and CA125 measurement every 6 months.[38] They can be offered prophylactic oophorectomy after completing childbearing following counseling.[39]

Multiple endocrine neoplasms

In affected members (chromosome 10q11.2 abnormality) of families with multiple endocrine neoplasms (MEN) 2A (and 2B) or a familial medullary carcinoma, C-cell hyperplasia (the precursor to carcinoma) occurs in 100% of patients by age 30.[40] The average age at which C-cell hyperplasia or medullary thyroid carcinoma is detected by biochemical screening (Pentagastrin and calcium stimulation tests) in at-risk subjects is 10 years.[41]

Prophylactic thyroidectomy is performed when the annual screening test becomes positive or by the age of 3 to 12 years.[42] Treating thyroxine deficiency is relatively easy.

Pheochromocytoma usually becomes evident about 10 years later than C-cell hyperplasia and medullary carcinoma. Early biochemical abnormalities include an increase in urinary epinephrine or norepinephrine. Screening should begin at the time of thyroidectomy.[43] Tumors can also be identified by computed tomography, magnetic resonance imaging, or ^{131}I-labeled metacodobenzylguanidine imaging, even in patients with no biochemical abnormality. However, repeated imaging studies are expensive and radiation exposure may become a hazard. Adrenalectomy is performed when a tumor is identified. Bilateral adrenalectomy is usually necessary because tumor is frequently found in the contralateral adrenal gland.

Periodic measurement of ionized serum calcium is essential to diagnose hyperparathyroidism. The involved gland should then be surgically removed. Genetic counseling is available for any hereditary cancers in which the implicated gene has been identified.

UNORTHODOX CANCER TREATMENTS

Despite persistent efforts to achieve early detection and exhaustive research aimed at developing effective treatment modalities, cancer continues to be a leading cause of death in the United States. Conventional cancer therapy includes surgery, chemotherapy, and radiation therapy in various combinations, depending on the nature and extent of disease involved in each particular case. Elaborate treatment protocols have been developed for virtually every stage of every type of cancer. These medical advances have undoubtedly resulted in increased survival or improved quality of life for some cancer patients. For many others, however, conventional cancer therapy has simply come to mean a sequence of painful, even disabling, experiences that does not in any way alter the inexorable course of the disease and does not make the patient more comfortable, productive, or fulfilled during the time that remains.

For many years, cancer victims have attempted to seek out whatever ray of hope may be offered, even in the form of treatment that the medical establishment finds to be unproven, ineffective, or even fraudulent. These include metabolic therapy, diet therapies, megavitamins, mental imagery applied for antitumor effect, and spiritual or faith healing.[44] Despite recent technological advances in orthodox medical care, unorthodox cancer treatments are increasing in popularity.[45]

Cancer victims, particularly those who are terminally ill, are vulnerable to exploitation because of their predicament. Desperate for any glimmer of hope, they are easy prey for charlatans intent on financial gain. Traditionally, the law has protected those unable to protect themselves on the basis of *parens patriae*. This rationale has most frequently been applied to juveniles and the developmentally disabled.

However, the state's interest in protecting its citizens must be balanced against an individual's right to have control over his or her own body and to make decisions regarding his or her own medical care. Most cancer patients are adults in full control of their mental faculties, which distinguishes them from other citizens the state seeks to protect under the *parens patriae* rationale.

It is this basic conflict between the state's interest in the health and welfare of its citizens and the right of the individual to make decisions affecting his or her health that has confronted legislatures and courts attempting to deal with the problem of unorthodox cancer treatments.

To date, this conflict has not been resolved uniformly. Considerable variation currently exists among the various states with regard to regulation of unorthodox cancer treatment. Interestingly, where there has been legislative action, most legislatures have granted the individual some measure of freedom in selecting cancer treatment that is unproven. In most states that have acted legislatively, however, this freedom is not unlimited. When courts have considered the subject of unorthodox cancer treatment, they have focused more on the state's right to regulate the lives of its citizens under the police power.

Legislative approaches

The overwhelming majority of legislation dealing with unorthodox cancer treatment has concerned Laetrile (amygdalin). Nineteen states have enacted legislation authorizing the manufacture, sale, and distribution of Laetrile.[46] Other unorthodox cancer treatments that have received legislative protection include DMSO (dimethyl sulfoxide),[47] Gerovital H3 (procainamide hydrochloride with preservatives and stabilizers),[48] lily plant extract,[49] and prayer.[50]

Most states that have legislatively authorized the use of Laetrile have placed concurrent restrictions on its accessibility. Twelve states require that the treatment be prescribed by a licensed physician.[51] Three states allow the use of Laetrile only as an adjunct to conventional medical therapy.[52] Many of the states that require a licensed physician's prescription of the unorthodox treatment also require that the patient first sign a consent form indicating that the physician has explained that Laetrile or DMSO has not been proved to be effective in the treatment of cancer or other human diseases, that it has not been approved by the Food and Drug Administration for the treatment of cancer, that alternative therapies exist, and that the patient requests treatment with Laetrile or DMSO.[53]

Several states have attempted to maintain a precarious balance between police power and individual rights by reserving the right to prohibit unconventional cancer treatment when it is found to be harmful as prescribed or administered in a formal hearing before the appropriate state board.[54]

The most sweeping exercise of police power has been enacted in California, where it is a crime to sell, deliver, prescribe, or administer any drug or device to be used in the diagnosis, treatment, alleviation, or cure of cancer that has not been approved by the designated federal agency or by the state board.[55] As discussed later, the statute has been upheld by the California Supreme Court against a constitutional challenge based on the right of privacy.[56]

Judicial determination regarding unorthodox cancer therapy

The lack of uniformity among the states in regulating the use of unorthodox cancer treatments has created an environment in which patients who reside in states that do not authorize the manufacture, sale, or distribution of Laetrile or other unconventional therapies have attempted to obtain those substances from other states, or even from neighboring countries.[57] In several instances, patients have resorted to legal action in attempting to obtain Laetrile.

The most extensively litigated case has been *Rutherford v. United States*, which has generated eight federal court opinions,[58] including one from the U.S. Supreme Court.[59] The Supreme Court did not consider the right of privacy issue. It held that, under applicable statutory law, Laetrile was not a "safe and effective" drug, and therefore FDA approval was required before interstate distribution. The court felt that if an exception were to be made in the case of terminally ill cancer patients, that decision was for the legislature rather than the courts to make.[60]

While *Rutherford* was being litigated, the California Supreme Court had occasion to consider the question of whether the state's police power could be used to restrict an individual's right of access to drugs of unproven effectiveness. *People v. Privitera*[61] involved prosecution of a physician and other individuals for conspiracy to sell and to prescribe an unapproved drug—Laetrile—intended for the alleviation or cure of cancer, in violation of applicable California statutory law.[62] The defendants appealed on the grounds that the statute was unconstitutional, and that the state and federal constitutional rights of privacy encompassed a right to obtain Laetrile.

The court, by a 5 to 2 majority, held that Laetrile was a drug of unproven efficacy and is not included in either the federal or state constitutional rights of privacy. The court further held that the statute prohibiting the prescription or administration of any drug not approved by the FDA or state board was a permissible exercise of the state's police power because it bore a reasonable relationship to the achievement of the legitimate state interest in the health and safety of its citizens.[63]

CONCLUSION

Despite a massive resource outlay directed at early detection and effective treatment of cancer, millions of cancer-related deaths are reported each year. Virtually none of the treatments labeled by orthodox medicine as ineffective has been the subject of well-controlled scientific studies.[64] The scope of research must be broadened to include all modalities in which there appears to be substantial public interest.[65] As a broader range of information becomes available, patients will be able to make more informed decisions regarding treatment. Although some states have enacted legislation allowing patients to obtain certain types of alternative cancer therapies, the majority of state legislatures remain silent on this issue. Diagnosis and treatment of cancer are governed by common law tort principles and the "loss of chance" doctrine.

ENDNOTES

1. Anderson, *Counseling Women on Familial Breast Cancer*, 37 Cancer Bull. 130-131 (1985).
2. Mills, *Prenatal Diethylstilbestrol and Vaginal Cancer in Offspring*, 229 J.A.M.A. 471-472 (1974).
3. *Burke v. United States*, No. M-84-425 (Md. 1984). In 1 Med. Mal. Verdicts, Settlements and Experts 9 (1985).
4. *Gorman v. LaSasso*, No. 83-CV-6311, Denver Dist. Ct. (Colo. 1983). In 1 Med. Mal. Verdicts, Settlements and Experts 17 (1985).
5. *Barenbrugge v. Rich*, No. 81L8949, Cook County Cir. Ct. (Ill. Oct. 25, 1984). In 2 Med. Mal. Verdicts, Settlements and Experts 17 (1986).
6. *O'Dell v. Chesney*, No. 118-496, Riverside County Ct. (Cal. Jan. 15, 1982).
7. *Mehalik v. Morvant*, No. 45173, Lafourche Parish Ct. (La. 1981) (Note: This case was settled on Dec. 9, 1985).
8. *Brown v. Nash*, No. 63471, Suffolk Super. Ct. (Mass. June 19, 1985). In 2 Med. Mal. Verdicts, Settlements and Experts 13 (1986).
9. *Glicklich v. Spievack*, No. 80-2150, Middlesex Ct. App. (Mass. Dec. 8, 1983).
10. C. Metlin & C.R. Smart, *Breast Cancer Detection Guidelines for Women Ages 40 to 49 Years: Rationale for the American Cancer Society Reaffirmation of Recommendations*, CA-A Cancer J. Clinicians 248-255 (1994).
11. K.A. Kern, *Medicolegal Analysis of the Delayed Diagnosis of Cancer in 338 Cases in the United States*, 129 Arch. Surg. 397 (1994).
12. I.C. Henderson & D. Danner, *Legal Pitfalls in the Diagnosis and Management of Breast Cancer*, 3 Hematol. Oncol. Clin. North Am. 823 (1989).
13. C.D. Haagenson et al., *Breast Carcinoma: Risk and Detection* (1981).
14. K.A. Kern, *Historical Trends in Breast Cancer Litigation: A Clinician's Perspective*, 3 (1) Surg. Oncol. Clin. North Am. 1 (1994).
15. G. Fletcher, *Textbook of Radiotherapy* 284 (Lea & Febiger, Philadelphia 1980).
16. *Duke v. Morphis*, Superior Court, Tarrant County (Tex.), No. 352-62434-80. In 4 Med. Mal. Verdicts, Settlements and Experts 43 (1988).
17. *Rudman v. Beth Israel Medical Center*, Supreme Court of the State of New York, County of New York (N.Y.), No. 4764/86. In 4 Med. Mal. Verdicts, Settlements and Experts 46 (1988).
18. *Barnes & Powers v. Hahnemann Medical College and Hosp.*, Common Pleas Court of Philadelphia (Pa.) No. 4031, 1982. In 3 Med. Mal. Verdicts, Settlements and Experts 35 (1987).
19. International Agency for Research on Cancer (WHO), 26 *IARC Monographs on the Evaluation of the Carcinogenic Risk of Chemicals to Humans* 37-384 (International Agency for Research on Cancer, Lyon, France 1981).
20. K. Falck et al., *Mutagenicity in Urine of Nurses Handling Cytostatic Drugs*, 1 Lancet 1250-1251 (1979); T.V. Nguyen et al., *Exposure of Pharmacy Personnel to Mutagenic Antineoplastic Drugs*, 42 Cancer Res. 4792-4796 (1982).
21. D.E. Bergsagel et al., *The Chemotherapy of Plasma-Cell Myeloma and the Incidence of Acute Leukemia*, 301 N. Engl. J. Med. 743-748 (1979); R.R. Reimer et al., *Acute Leukemia after Alkylating Agent Therapy of Ovarian Cancer*, 297 N. Engl. J. Med. 177-181 (1977).
22. P.H. Plotz et al., *Bladder Complications in Patients Receiving Cyclophosphamide for Systemic Lupus Erythematosus or Rheumatoid Arthritis*, 91 Ann. Intern. Med. 221-223 (1979).
23. H.O. Nicholson, *Cytotoxic Drugs in Pregnancy: Review of Reported Cases*, 75 J. Obstet. Gynaecol. Br. Commonw. 307-312 (1968).
24. M.J. Garrett, *Letter: Teratogenic Effects of Combination Chemotherapy*, 80 Ann. Intern. Med. 667 (1974).
25. R.B. Jones et al., *Safe Handling of Chemotherapeutic Agents: A Report from the Mount Sinai Medical Center*, 33 CA-A Cancer J. Clinicians 258-263 (1983).
26. R.B. Weiss & S. Bruno, *Hypersensitivity Reactions to Cancer Chemotherapy Agents*, 94 Ann. Intern. Med. 66, 71 (1981).
27. *Lefler v. Yardumian*, Superior Court, Pinellas County (Ill.) No. 83-14700. In 3 Med. Mal. Verdicts, Settlements and Experts 35 (1987).
28. *Newman v. Geschke*, Superior Court, Multnomah County (Ore.), No. A8609-05800. In 4 Med. Mal. Verdicts, Settlements and Experts 46 (1988).
29. E.W. Clayton, *Removing the Shadow of the Law from the Debate about Genetic Testing of Children*, 57 Am. J. Med. Genetics 630 (1995); J.H. Fanos & J.P. Johnson, *Barriers to Carrier Testing for Adult Cystic Fibrosis Sibs: The Importance of Not Knowing*, 59 Am. J. Med. Genetics 185 (1995); L.D. Gostin, *Genetic Privacy*, 23 J. Law Med. Ethics 320 (1995); D.E. Hoffman & E.A. Wolfsberg, *Testing Children for Genetic Predisposition: Is It in Their Best Interest?*, 23 J. Law Med. Ethics 331 (1995); M. Powers, *Privacy and the Control of Genetic Information*, in *The Genetic Frontier: Ethics, Law, and Policy* 77-100 (M.S. Frankel & A.S. Teichs, eds., American Association for the Advancement of Science Press, Washington, D.C. 1994); S.M. Suter, *Whose Genes Are These Anyway?*, *Familial Conflicts Over Access to Genetic Information*, 91 Michigan Law Rev. 1854 (1993); S.M. Wolf, *Beyond "Genetic Discrimination": Toward the Broader Harm of Geneticism*, 23 J. Law Med. Ethics 345 (1995).
30. H.T. Lynch & J.F. Lynch, *The Lynch Syndrome: Melding Natural History and Molecular Genetics to Genetic Counseling and Cancer Control*, 3 Cancer Control 13 (1996)
31. G.M. Petersen & J.D. Brensinger, *Genetic Testing and Counseling in Familial Adenomatous Polyposis*, 10 Oncology 89 (1996).
32. *Id.*
33. 29 U.S.C. §§791 et seq.
34. *Id.*
35. O.I. Olopade & S. Cummings, *Genetic Counseling for Cancer: Part I*, 10 (1) Principles Practice Oncology Updates 1 (1996).

36. P.R. Billings et al., *Discrimination as a Consequence of Genetic Testing*, 50 Am. J. Human Genetics 476 (1992); N.S. Jecker, *Genetic Testing and the Social Responsibility of Private Health Insurance Companies*, 21 J. Law Med. Ethics 109 (1993); J.E. McEwen & P.R. Reilly, *State Legislative Efforts to Regulate Use and Potential Misuse of Genetic Information*, 51 Am. J. Hum. Genetics 637 (1992).

37. *Supra* note 31.

38. *Id.*

39. M.C. King et al., *Inherited Breast and Ovarian Cancer: What Are the Risks? What Are the Choices?*, 269 J.A.M.A. 1975 (1993).

40. D.F. Eastose et al., *The Clinical and Screening Age-at-Onset Distribution for the MEN 2 Syndrome*, 44 Am. J. Human Genetics 208 (1989).

41. R.F. Gagel, *Multiple Endocrine Neoplasia*, in *Williams Textbook of Endocrinology* 1537-1553 (J.D. Wilson et al., eds., 8th ed., W.B. Saunders, Philadelphia 1992).

42. C.J.M. Lycs et al., *Clinical Screening as Compared with DNA Analysis in Families with Multiple Endocrine Neoplasia Type 2A*, 331 N. Engl. J. Med. 828 (1994); R.D. Utiger, *Nodular Thyroid Carcinoma, Genes, and the Prevention of Cancer*, 13 N. Engl. J. Med. 870 (1994); R.F. Gagel, *Multiple Endocrine Neoplasia*, in *Williams Textbook of Endocrinology* 1537-1553 (J.D. Wilson et al., eds., 8th ed., W.B. Saunders, Philadelphia 1992); R.L. Telalander et al., *Results of Early Thyroidectomy for Medullary Thyroid Carcinoma in Children with Multiple Endocrine Neoplasia Type 2*, 21 J. Pediatr. Surg. 1190 (1986).

43. Utiger, *Medullary Thyroid Carcinoma, Genes, and the Prevention of Cancer*, 331 N. Engl. J. Med. 870 (1994).

44. Cassileth, *Contemporary Unorthodox Treatments in Cancer Medicine*, 101 Ann. Intern. Med. 105-112, 107 (1984).

45. *Id.*

46. Alaska Stat. 08.64.367; Ariz. Rev. Stat. Ann. 26-2452; Del. Code Ann. 16-4901-05; Fla. Stat. Ann. 500.1515 (West); Idaho Code 18-7301A; Ind. Code Ann. 16-8-8-1-7 (Burns); Kan. Stat. Ann. 65-6b; Ky. Rev. Stat. Ann. 311.950 (Baldwin); La. Rev. Stat. Ann. 40:676; Md. Code Ann. 18-301; Mont. Code Ann. 50-41-102; Nev. Rev. Stat. 585.495; N.J. Stat. Ann. 24:6F-1 (West); N.D. Cent. Code 23-23.1; Okla. Stat. Ann. 63-2-313; Or. Rev. Stat. 689.535; Tex. Rev. Civ. Stat. Ann. 71, article 4476-5a; Wash. Rev. Code Ann. 70.54.1310; W. Va. Code 30-5-16a.

47. Fla. Stat. Ann. 499.035 (West); Kan. Stat. Ann. 65-679a; La. Rev. Stat. Ann. 40-1060 (West); Mont. Code Ann. 42-102; Okla. Stat. Ann. 363-2-313.12; Tex. Rev. Civ. Stat. Ann. 71, article 4476.5b.

48. Nev. Rev. Stat. 585.495.

49. Okla. Stat. Ann. 63-2-313.7 (West).

50. Colo. Rev. Stat. 12-30-113 (2).

51. Alaska, Delaware, Florida, Indiana, Maryland, Montana, Nevada, New Jersey, North Dakota, Oklahoma, Texas, and Washington.

52. Idaho, Indiana, and Oklahoma.

53. Arizona, Indiana, Louisiana, New Jersey, Oklahoma, Texas, and Washington.

54. Alaska, Colorado, Delaware, Louisiana, and Maryland.

55. California Health and Safety Code 1701.1 (West 1979).

56. *People v. Privitera*, 23 Cal. 3d 697, 153 Cal. Rptr. 431, 591 P. 2d 919 (1979).

57. Marco & Laetrile, *The Statement and the Struggle*, in *Legal Medicine* 121-136 (C.H. Wecht, ed., 1980).

58. *Rutherford v. United States*, 399 F.Supp. 1208 (W.D. Okla. 1975), 542 F. 2d 1137 (10th Cir. 1976), 424 F.Supp. 105 (W.D. Okla. 1977), 429 F.Supp. 506 (W.D. Okla. 1977), 438 F.Supp. 1287 (W.D. Okla. 1977), 582 F. 2d 1234 (190th Cir. 1978), 616 F. 2d 455 (10th Cir. 1980).

59. *Rutherford*, 442 U.S. 544.

60. *Id.* at 559.

61. *People v. Privitera*, *supra* note 56. For a judicial decision that reached a different conclusion, see *Suenram v. Society of the Valley Hospital*, 155 N.J. Super. 593, 383 A. 2d 143 (1977). The *Suenram* court was not considering a statute, however, and in fact the New Jersey legislature authorized the use of Laetrile shortly after the court's opinion was rendered.

62. California Health and Safety Code 1707.1, which provides as follows: "The sale, offering of sale, holding for sale, delivering, giving away, prescribing or administering of any drug, medicine, compound or device to be used in the diagnosis, treatment, alleviation or cure of cancer is unlawful and prohibited unless (1) an application with respect thereto has been approved under 505 of the Federal Food, Drug and Cosmetic Act, or (2) there has been approved an application filed with the board setting forth: (a) Full reports of investigations have been made to show whether or not such a drug, medicine, compound or device is safe for such use, and whether such drug, medicine, compound or device is effective in such use; (b) A full list of the articles used as components of such drug, medicine, compound or device; (c) A full statement of the composition of such drug, medicine, compound or device; (d) A full description of the methods used in, and the facilities and controls used for, the manufacture, processing and packaging of such drug, medicine, or compound or in the case of a device, a full statement of its composition, properties and construction and the principle or principles of its operation; (e) Such samples of such drug, medicine, compound or device and of the articles used as components of the drug, medicine, compound or device as the board may require; and (f) Specimens of the labeling to be used for such drug, medicine, compound or device and advertising proposed to be used for such drug, medicine, compound or device."

63. *People v. Privitera*, 153 Cal. Rptr. 431, 433.

64. For an example of a well-controlled study of the effect of an "unorthodox" cancer treatment, *see* Johnston, *Clinical Effect of Coley's Toxin: I. A Controlled Study*, 21 Cancer Chemotherapy Reports (Aug. 1962).

65. *Supra* note 44.

Brain-Injured Patients

CLARK WATTS, M.D., J.D., F.C.L.M.

PRIMARY CAUSES OF BRAIN IMPAIRMENT: DIAGNOSIS
TRAUMATIC BRAIN IMPAIRMENT
LEGAL CONSIDERATIONS

When referencing the brain, the general term *injury* should be considered in its broadest context. The brain is considered injured when it sustains pathology from whatever cause. Although this is the context in which the term will be used in this chapter, the primary focus will be on the traumatically brain-injured patient because most of the medicolegal implications of brain injury apply to this group of patients.[1]

It is very important for the legal practitioner to understand how the physician will arrive at a diagnosis in these patients, through the process of creating a differential diagnosis. Equally important for the legal practitioner representing brain-injured patients is an understanding of how the brain recovers, and how the injury and the recovery are quantitated. Of additional importance to the legal practitioner is an awareness of obstacles to coverage of brain injuries.

PRIMARY CAUSES OF BRAIN IMPAIRMENT: DIAGNOSIS

General considerations

Prior to any discussion of the differential diagnosis of primary causes of brain impairment, it is helpful to understand how one arrives at a differential diagnosis. A differential diagnosis is simply a listing, usually by probabilities, but often without mathematical designations, of diseases that it is reasonable to consider in a person suffering from brain impairment. The process of arriving at the differential diagnosis is a relatively simple one, but often poorly understood. It begins, as with all contacts between physicians and patients, with a history and elicitation of signs and symptoms from the patient and a physical examination. This is followed by a correlation of the signs and symptoms with the anatomy and physiology of the portion of the brain that seems to relate to those signs and symptoms. The process of time over which the signs and symptoms have been present is factored in, and the most likely disease cate-

gories, based on general pathology, are then extracted from the process. Confirmation of the conclusions at this point is obtained by laboratory tests and, finally, a differential diagnosis of specific pathology is created.

The process

Signs and symptoms. Symptoms are those complaints the patient presents to the physician. *Signs* are those findings the physician elicits by physical examination. In eliciting the signs and symptoms of a patient with suspected brain disease, it is important to keep in mind that the brain could express itself in response to disease in only a few ways. The brain may respond to disease by an alteration of the *mental status* of the patient. Usually, the alteration of mental status is in the level of consciousness. The patient may appear conscious and be awake and alert, lethargic, or obtunded. Or the patient may present in or deteriorate into an unconscious state. An important subset of the mental status examination is a search for any derangements of intellect, orientation, self-awareness, or memory.

The patient with impaired brain function may present with *motor* symptomatology. Most patients with this group of signs and symptoms will be noted to have certain patterns of paresis, or weakness of muscle function. Some will present, however, without significant weakness, but instead will have abnormal movements created by disorders of the nervous system such as spasticity or seizure disorders. The muscles may be flaccid, unusually rigid, or uncoordinated in action. The abnormal movements may be noted during voluntary or involuntary activity.

Pain, such as headache, is the most common form of *sensory* complaint. The patient may also complain of abnormal sensation, as with parasthesis, or electric-like painful phenomena, or numbness, the presence of dulled sensation. The complaint may be present spontaneously, or only when the physician, in examining the patient, obtains an admission of the symptom. Other sensory complaints may involve visual or hearing difficulties.

Disturbances of *language* are common with brain impairment. Language disorders can be categorized in several ways, but generally they can be placed into three separate groups, called aphasias. In expressive aphasia the person has, as the name implies, trouble expressing himself, that is, trouble making coherent, understandable sentences. The person suffering from receptive aphasia has difficulty receiving communication input and processing it into meaningful language. The verbal expressions of these individuals may appear normal, even quite articulate, but they have no relationship to input received. The person with global aphasia has elements of both and, in the worst cases, may be mute.

Finally, afflictions of the brain may also reveal associated mental *disorder*, including signs and symptoms concerned with emotions, disturbances of reality, and alterations of self-image.

It is rare that the patient will present with a single group of symptoms; more often there will be a constellation of symptoms. For example, a patient presenting with injury involving the left side of the brain may complain of lethargy, headaches, numbness and weakness of the right arm and leg, blindness in certain portions of the field of vision, expressive aphasia, and depression.

Consideration of anatomy/physiology. The brain consists of four parts, which are connected anatomically and physiologically. The largest mass of the brain is the *cerebrum*, composed of the two lateral cerebral hemispheres. Each has a frontal lobe anteriorly, a parietal and a temporal lobe laterally, and an occipital lobe posteriorly. The two frontal lobes in association with structures connecting the two cerebral hemispheres in the midline (portions of the limbic "lobe") are functionally related to personality, emotion, and self-image. The posterior aspects of each frontal lobe provide voluntary motor function for the opposite side of the body, whereas the anterior aspects of both parietal lobes provide conscious sensory function to the opposite side of the body. Brain auditory function is served by temporal lobes, as is memory when the temporal lobes are interacting with the frontal lobes. In most individuals, voluntary and conscious speech function is located in the left frontotemporoparietal area of the left cerebral hemisphere, whereas visual-spatial orientation function is lateralized to the right cerebral hemisphere, particularly the right parietal lobe.

The second element of the brain is the *cerebellum*, located posterior, beneath the cerebrum. This paired structure is responsible, primarily, for involuntary actions of coordination.

Descending down from the middle of the base of the paired cerebral hemispheres, passing anterior to the cerebellum on its way into the spinal canal where it continues as the spinal cord, is the *brainstem*, the third part. It serves as a major pathway for nervous impulses to leave the brain and enter the spinal cord, and to pass from the spinal cord to the brain.

Finally, there are the *cranial nerves*, which pass from the various other elements of the brain to structures peripheral to the skull. They conduct impulses to the brain that provide the senses of vision, smell, taste, and hearing; the voluntary functions of the face, such as mastication and sensation; and certain automatic functions of the body, such as rhythmicity of the heart and autonomic bowel function.

An example of the importance of considerations regarding localization can be seen in the patient who complains of visual disturbances. If that patient were also complaining of weakness in the left hand, one would consider a lesion in the right cerebral hemisphere that is affecting the nerve fibers of vision as they pass from the eyes in front to the occipital lobe in the posterior aspects of the cerebral hemisphere where vision is recognized. On the other hand, if the patient with visual disturbances were also complaining of problems with smell or taste, one might look more anteriorly, to the region of the eyes, where the eyes are more closely associated with nasal and oral mucosa from which taste emanates.

Considerations of time. In arriving at a differential diagnosis, one must not only consider the patient's signs and symptoms and anatomical/physiological correlations, but one must also factor in the time course over which the symptoms and the signs are present. For example, the patient may very well have a headache precipitated by a minor episode of head trauma. The headache would come on suddenly coincident with the trauma and persist appropriately. A headache similar in intensity and location, however, may have gradually developed over several weeks or months in a patient with a brain tumor. Likewise, a brain tumor may cause hand weakness progressively and slowly over several months, whereas a stroke, secondary to cerebral vascular embolization, may cause a sudden onset of hand weakness.

The differential diagnosis

After the physician works through the process of analysis in considering the patient's presenting signs and symptoms, the anatomical and physiological localization of the suspected lesion, the time course for the development and presentation of the suspected lesion, and the general pathological nature of the suspected lesion, the etiology of the brain impairment may preliminarily be placed into one or more categories of diseases from which a more specific differential diagnosis may be extracted. Below, definitions and examples of the major categories of neurological diseases will be presented. Then, the traumatic diseases will be categorized in order to illustrate the process of developing a specific differential diagnosis.

Disease categories. Brain impairment may occur as a result of disease categorized as follows: genetic, congenital/developmental, degenerative/metabolic, infectious, traumatic, neoplastic, vascular, immunological, psychogenic, and idiopathic. As with any arbitrary classification, overlapping of categories may occur, as will be apparent in the following discussion.

Most of the primary diseases of the brain associated with *genetic* disorders are characterized by an underlying error of metabolism. To understand this concept, it is helpful to look at one of the earliest recognized and best understood primary brain disorders produced by a genetic abnormality, phenylketonuria. This disorder, untreated, is seen primarily in children and is highlighted by mental retardation, seizures, and imperfect hair pigmentation, and is transmitted as an autosomal recessive condition. Due to a well-defined genetic disorder, the gene necessary for the activation of an enzyme, phenylalanine hydroxylase, is disturbed and the enzyme is almost completely lacking. As a result, the normal conversion of phenylalanine to tyrosine does not occur. Instead, phenylalanine is converted to phenylpyruvic acid, phenylacetic acid, and phenylacetylglutamine. With the accumulation of these metabolites in the brain, there is interference with normal maturation of the brain, neurofibers within the brain are not properly myelinated (a process of normal insulation), and other widespread and diffuse anomalies develop. Fortunately, in children born with this disorder, urine and blood levels of phenylalanine rise in the first few days and weeks of life and can be detected by a simple screening test.

In general, *congenital/developmental* disorders are those created by a deleterious effect of the environment, either in utero or following birth, upon the developing brain. Some years ago, a number of the genetic disorders were placed in this category. However, as specific abnormalities in the genome have been identified, the corresponding disorders have been removed from this category. The term cerebral palsy refers to a general condition caused by a number of different environmental insults to the developing brain. While its most common presentation is a spastic weakness of all four extremities, some children may experience mental retardation and seizure disorders. The characteristic of this type of congenital disorder is that it is not progressive, although it may appear to be so as the child grows and becomes progressively more disabled in comparison with his or her peers. The etiological insult may occur before birth, in the perinatal period, or in the first few years of life. Cerebral palsy is believed to be caused by any number of insults including abnormal implantation of the ovum, maternal diseases, threatened but aborted miscarriages, external toxins, or metabolic insults such as maternal alcohol ingestion.

The category of diseases termed *degenerative/metabolic* disorders is usually reserved for those conditions that develop in individuals with previously normal brain development. It is appropriate today to exclude conditions with known genetic bases, even though they express themselves later in life, such as Huntington's chorea, or conditions that are congenital or developmental and, as noted previously, appear to progress as the affected individual is compared with developing peers. Alzheimer's disease was at one time believed to be a classic condition in this category. Individuals in the prime of their senior years develop dementia associated with specific neuropathological changes in the brain of unknown etiology. The dementia occurs much earlier than would be expected based simply on senility. Aside from Alzheimer's disease, the most studied degenerative/metabolic disease of the nervous system is Parkinsonism. This condition is characterized by a progressive uncontrollable tremor with an associated dementia. The motor disability created by the tremor often progresses much more rapidly than the dementia, so that patients, well aware of their limitations, suffer substantial depression. For some reason, certain cells within the brain are unable to manufacture an appropriate amount of the agent, dopamine, which is metabolically necessary for cell function. The etiology of the condition in most patients today is not at all clear. A syndrome identical to Parkinsonism has been described in a group of drug abusers who have used *n*-methyl-4-phenyl-1,2,3,6-tetrahydropyridine, both intravenously and by inhalation.

Most known *infectious* agents have been reported to cause infections of the brain. Meningitis is a term used to refer to infections of the coverings of the brain, whereas encephalitis is used to refer to an infection of the substance of the brain. In addition to the generalized widespread infectious processes these terms suggest, localized brain infections, or abscesses, can also occur. This category of disease lends itself to a simplified discussion of how the physician might use the earlier presented scheme of analysis. A patient who has the fairly rapid development of brain impairment associated with a fever might be considered to have a disease within this category. If widespread impairment ensues that is characterized by nonfocal deficits and suppression of the mental status of the patient, one might consider meningitis or encephalitis. If, however, the disease process appears to be focal in nature, resulting in a partial paralysis (e.g., hemiparesis or weakness on one side of the body), one might consider the presence of a more focal infectious process such as a brain abscess.

The traumatic category of diseases encompasses everything associated with acute brain trauma. This includes not only diseases caused by disruption of brain tissue, but also diseases caused by systemic illnesses secondary to the traumatic episode, whether or not this trauma directly involves the head. For example, not uncommonly, following trauma to the head, the patient experiences a period of apnea, or diminished respiratory effort. If this is not corrected quickly, the patient may suffer hypoxia, or a lack of oxygen, which can damage brain cells. A more comprehensive discussion of traumatic brain disease appears later in this chapter to provide more details of the application of principles for defining a specific differential diagnosis of primary brain impairment.

The category of *neoplastic diseases* contains all tumors that are progressive in development, whether benign or malignant. It includes those tumors that arise primarily within the brain and those that metastasize to the brain from extracranial sites. As suggested by the foregoing comments, it is traditional to describe tumors as benign or malignant. A benign tumor is one that grows more slowly, does not extend beyond the confines of the tumor mass itself, and does not metastasize or spread through the vascular system. A malignant tumor is a more aggressive tumor. It has a shorter time course and may spread to other parts of the brain or the body by way of the vascular stream. The malignant tumor characteristically results in death in a shorter period of time than the benign tumor. However, this concept may be deceiving in that a histologically benign tumor, placed in a critical location within the brain, may cause death quicker than a malignant tumor placed within the brain in a location that is not as critical. All tumors cause impairment by one of two mechanisms. They may produce direct pressure on the surrounding brain. Additionally, they develop a volume that cannot be accommodated safely within the fixed cranial vault. Consequently, generalized increased intracranial pressure occurs, which adversely affects the flow of blood to sensitive areas of the brain not directly contiguous with the mass itself.

Most diseases in the *vascular* category affect the blood vessels directly or indirectly. Primarily congenital or developmental conditions, such as aneurysms and arteriovenous malformations, can produce sudden brain impairment by hemorrhage. Arteriosclerosis of the vessels, a degenerative/metabolic condition, may cause sudden impairment by creating an occlusion of the vessels, causing death of tissue from lack of circulating oxygen and nutrients. Occlusions may also occur with embolization of cerebral vessels by arteriosclerotic debris from other sites such as diseased heart valves.

Immunological diseases are caused by disturbances of the immune system. Multiple sclerosis is such a condition. It is characterized by repeated and progressive bouts of demyelinization of nerve cells and their axons, extensions of nerve cells that connect with other cells. These extensions ordinarily contain an insulating material called myelin. As a result of disturbances in the immune system not completely understood, the myelin is recognized by the body as a foreign substance and is placed under lymphocytic attack and destruction. Presentation of the patient will depend on the area of the brain affected, with virtually any combination of signs and symptoms possible.

The category *of psychogenic* diseases refers to those recognized and characterized as diseases of the mind associated with personality disorders, disturbances of emotion, and problems of self-image that may or may not be related to one of the preceding categories. Certainly, patients may be depressed as a result of head trauma or disabling conditions such as Parkinsonism.

Iatrogenic diseases are those produced as a result of treatment by the physician. A patient who develops a blood clot following surgery for a brain tumor due to inadequate hemostasis by the surgeon has developed an iatrogenic hemorrhage.

Idiopathic diseases are those for which there is no known, or reasonably suspected, etiology. As a result of dramatic recent advances in the neurosciences, especially in neuroimaging, these are now few in number.

TRAUMATIC BRAIN IMPAIRMENT

The diagnosis

The diagnosis of traumatic brain disease usually begins with the identification of a traumatic episode resulting in either blunt or penetrating head injury.[2] Penetrating head injuries generally produce less of a problem in the differential diagnosis because the penetrating object (usually a bullet) will produce primary brain disruption and hemorrhage. More challenging is the establishment of a differential diagnosis of traumatic brain disease following blunt trauma.

During blunt trauma, the brain is subjected to forces secondary to acute acceleration and deceleration of the brain within the skull, which is itself undergoing acute acceleration and deceleration. As the result of these forces, a number of pathological processes ensue. The brain may be "stunned" by relatively minor head injury without any anatomical or pathological changes, producing the so-called "concussion." Renewed interest in this condition has occurred because of the exquisite detail of neuroimaging created by MRI. Some believe that through this modality previously unrecognized changes in the limbic lobe, the medial temporal lobe, and the upper brainstem may occur in concussion, accounting for the characteristic findings of transient loss of consciousness, some degree of retrograde amnesia, and difficulty with mental energy (e.g., lack of motivation), which may exist for weeks or months following the injury. Blood vessels, including both arteries and veins, may be torn, resulting in hemorrhage. This hemorrhage may occur exterior to the brain or within the brain substance. Some portions of the brain may move through greater distances than other portions of the brain, creating shearing injuries at the interface of these moving areas—not too dissimilar from the activity at the fault line during an earthquake. Brain tissue may be disrupted. Mentioned earlier is the fact that, following some severe head injuries, apnea, or loss of normal respiration, may ensue, resulting in hypoxia and other metabolic changes that cause direct injury to nerve cells.

With both CT scanning and MRI scanning, intracranial hemorrhages following head trauma are easily identified.

Epidural hemorrhages are arterial in nature and are located beneath the skull but external to the most outer membrane lining the brain, the dura mater. These hemorrhages are usually associated with a skull fracture that lacerates an artery lying between the dura mater and the skull. The hemorrhage may develop rapidly over a period of 2 to 3 hours, creating increased intracranial pressure and focal pressure on the brain. Recovery is excellent in patients who are operated on with evacuation of the hematoma prior to developing coma, whereas the prognosis is extremely poor in someone who develops coma prior to surgery.

The subdural hematoma forms beneath the dura mater but external to the arachnoid membrane, which is the intermediate covering of the brain. The blood usually comes from torn veins, and develops more slowly than an epidural hematoma. It is less well localized and is often associated with other injuries to the brain because the force required to tear veins is actually greater than the force required to cut an artery following a skull fracture, leading to an epidural hematoma. As the result of the more widespread brain injury that is associated with an acute subdural hematoma, the mortality rate for subdural hematomas is higher than that for acute epidural hematomas in that more patients with acute subdural hematomas are comatose at the time of surgery. Often associated with acute subdural hematomas are intracerebral hematomas, blood clots within the substance of the brain. Although rarely an indication for surgery, their presence does adversely affect prognosis.

Subarachnoid hemorrhage (SAH) occurs between the arachnoid membrane and the surface of the brain (the pia mater). It is rarely focal in presentation and may occur with minor head injuries. While SAH, in and of itself, rarely produces primary brain impairment, it may be associated with the development, days or weeks later, of hydrocephalus, which is caused by the excessive accumulation of cerebral spinal fluid that has been normally produced within the brain but is unable to be absorbed normally because of the presence of blood in the subarachnoid space.

Focal injuries produced by shearing forces within the brain are rarely severe. However, if they are widespread throughout the brain, they can produce significant brain impairment, which is treatable only through the provision of primary support to the patient during the recovery and rehabilitation process. Prognosis of the patient with this condition depends on the location and how widespread the lesions are.

Hypoxia and other adverse metabolic stresses suffered by the brain in the posttraumatic period are a major cause of death or residual disability. When brain cells are subject to these stresses, they may continue to function relatively normally (or lack of function cannot be detected clinically); they may die and the patient will suffer permanent deficit; or they may live but not function normally. It will require time for cells to rejuvenate to recover from the insult, and to begin functioning again.

Posttraumatic epilepsy. A discussion of head injuries is not complete without some mention of posttraumatic epilepsy. The condition is due to the creation of hyperexcitable areas in the brain by the underlying disorder, or the removal of the normal inhibition of excitable brain by the disorder. Although epilepsy may be focal in presentation, it is such a generalized nonspecific response to trauma that it has little value in distinguishing the underlying brain pathology.

The treatment

As alluded to previously, treatment[3] of the brain-injured patient begins with the establishment of a differential diagnosis: a general differential diagnosis based upon the history and physical and a more specific differential diagnosis based upon laboratory studies, including brain imaging. The general principles for the treatment of brain-injured patients are relatively uniform regardless of the etiology of the injury.

Treatment of the initial injury may require the surgical debridement of skull fractures and brain lacerations or the evacuation of hematomas. The causes of secondary injury fall into two general categories: loss of vital metabolic substrates, and compression. Failure to adequately oxygenate the patient or to maintain adequate blood pressure will result in poor delivery of oxygen, glucose, and other essential nutrients to the brain, which will result in further cell injury and death. Local compression by bone fragments or hematomas may cause direct injury to nervous system tissue, or may impede the flow of blood to nervous system tissue. Secondary injury may result in cerebral edema, or the excessive accumulation of fluid both in injured cells and in the interstitial space between the cells. Due to the nondistensible nature of the skull, this may lead to increase in intracranial pressure which may further cause direct brain injury or injury secondary to the interference of cerebral blood flow.

It is important in certain patients, particularly those who are unconscious from head injury or who have evidence of hematomas or cerebral edema on imaging studies, to have the intracranial pressure monitored through the use of various surgically implantable intracranial monitoring devices. A medication useful in the treatment of cerebral edema is intravenous mannitol, which will remove interstitial edema in the brain.

Other medications may be useful in the treatment of the brain-injured patient. Antibiotics may be helpful, especially if the brain has been contaminated by an open wound. There is some evidence that the prophylactic use of anticonvulsants during the first week after a disruptive brain injury may reduce the rate of seizure activity following trauma. While at one time, steroids such as Decadron were routinely used in patients with traumatic brain injury, this drug is no longer recommended for this use.

Brain recovery

At one time it was believed that brain cells either functioned or did not function—an all-or-none phenomenon.[4] Increasingly, it is becoming obvious that such cells may function at various levels of activity, depending on influences from surrounding cells.[5] This is an explanation for one phenomenon seen in recovery as the result of rehabilitation. During the time period of rehabilitation, more and more brain cells move from the idling state to the active state. As they do, they exert their influence on surrounding cells, increasing the activity of the cell pool and thus improving the neurological status of the patient. A second phenomenon of rehabilitation is that of relearning. A patient's "weakness" may improve because of the increase in activity of the cell pool as mentioned earlier, or as the result of more efficient utilization of the existing cell pool through repetitive behavior during rehabilitation. It is believed, with regard to the first phenomenon, that 90% of the ultimate recovery of brain function will be seen within the first 6 months following injury and the remaining 10% will be seen in the next 1.5 years. The time frame for the second phenomenon is not understood as well and may proceed for years.

A major factor in the rehabilitation of brain-injured patients is the management of the patient's frustration and accompanying depression. As the brain-injured patient recovers and becomes aware of his limitations, especially that of residual short-term memory deficit, frustration ensues. If this is not adequately managed, it will become institutionalized into the patient's thought and decision-making processes.

Neuropsychological testing may be useful; however, a note of caution. Although some believe that, through careful neuropsychological testing, it is possible to quantitate neuropsychological abnormalities in patients with no deficits on neurological examination and neuroimage evaluation, others believe that adequate research has not been conducted to establish standards for such distinctions.[6] In evaluating these matters, the lack of correlation between neuropsychological testing and neuroimaging confirmation of underlying residual brain impairment, may indicate preinjury evidence of neuropsychological abnormalities. In most cases, preinjury neuropsychological studies are not available on individual patients. Therefore, postinjury results must be related to preinjury performance, such as school grades, community achievement, mentor evaluations, and indirect evidence of neuropsychological performance.

LEGAL CONSIDERATIONS

In general, the legal considerations for the brain-injured patient vary little from those generally present in common and statutory law related to personal injury torts and contracts. Issues of informed consent generally concern the incompetent. Increasingly patients, particularly the elderly, have created advance directives, either a durable power of attorney or a living will. The laws related to these matters are generally state-specific.[7] The exception is the Patient Self-Determination Act of 1990, a federal law mandating that hospitals that receive federal funds must inform patients of their right to create advance directives and to have them followed.[8]

The question often arises as to how to handle a matter of termination of treatment to include termination of life support in patients who do not have advance directives. This is of particular note in situations where the patient is in the persistent vegetative state with no hope of recovery and, potentially, years of survival. The U.S. Supreme Court in *Cruzan v. Director* held that, although a competent adult has a right to terminate treatment, the state may establish the standard of proof in matters involving the incompetent patient such as one in the persistent vegetative state.[9] In *Cruzan* the Supreme Court upheld the state of Missouri's requirement that the proof be "clear and convincing."

Most distressing and costly in terms of dollars and emotional capital is the patient in a persistent comatose state. While a number of these states have been defined, the one with the most recent exhaustive study is the persistent vegetative state.[10] This patient is unconscious; the patient is not aware of his environment nor can he or she react appropriately to that environment.

Of major concern to head-injured patients and their families is denial of coverage under health insurance policies.[11] Often the portion of the policy that relates to chronic care or rehabilitation is ambiguously worded. As can be anticipated from the previous discussion, there are no bright lines between acute care, rehabilitation, and custodial care.[12] These terms and phrases are often self-defined after the fact by adjusters to provide denial. It is important that legal practitioners help medical practitioners understand the legal implications of conclusions such as "no further medical required" or "medically stabilized."

ENDNOTES

1. A number of excellent treatises are available to which the reader may refer to expand the knowledge of the material in this chapter. Especially recommended are (a) R.K. Narayan, J.E. Wilberger, Jr. & J.T. Povlishock, *Neurotrauma* (McGraw-Hill, New York, 1996), (b) G.T. Tindall, P.R. Cooper & D.L. Barrow (eds.), *The Practice of Neurosurgery*, 3 vols. (Williams & Wilkins, Baltimore, 1996), and (c) L.P. Roland (ed.), *Merritt's Textbook of Neurology*, 9th ed. (Williams & Wilkins, Baltimore, 1995).

2. Space does not permit a discussion of the special circumstances surrounding the diagnosis and treatment of brain injury in the neonate and the very young child. A comprehensive review of this subject may be found in A. Towbin, *Brain Damage in the Newborn and its Neurological Sequels: Pathologic and Clinical Correlation* (PRM, Danvers, MA, 1998).

3. In addition to the texts referenced (*supra* note 1), the legal practitioner might wish to review *Guidelines for the Management of Severe Head*

Injury published by the American Association of Neurological Surgeons, Chicago; telephone: 708-692-9500.

4. For a comprehensive review of this subject, especially of the role that rehabilitation plays, see the report of the NIH Consensus Development Panel on Rehabilitation of Persons with Traumatic Brain Injury, *Rehabilitation of Persons with Traumatic Brain Injury*, 282 J.A.M.A. 974 (1999).

5. P. Bach-y-Rita, *Recovery from brain damage*, 6 J. Neuro. Rehab. 191-199 (1992).

6. As evidenced by the conflicting positions contained in the following references, it behooves any lawyer representing clients with brain injuries to become familiar with the subject matter of neuropsychological testing: (a) M.D. Lezak, *Neuropsychological assessment*, 3d ed. (Oxford University Press, New York, 1995), (b) G.P. Prigatano, *Principles of Neuropsychological Rehabilitation* (Oxford University Press, New York, 1999).

7. *See* A.D. Liberson, *Advance Medical Directives* (Clark, Broadman, Callaghan, New York, 1992). See also Chapter 27, this volume.

8. Omnibus Budget Reconciliation Act of 1990, Pub. L. 101-508, §4206, 4751.

9. *Cruzan v. Director, Missouri Dept. of Health*, 110 S.Ct. 2841 (1990).

10. See the publications by the Multi-Speciality Task Force, *Medical Aspects of the Persistent Vegetative State*, 330 N. Engl. J. Med. 1499, 1572 (1994).

11. *See, for example*, S. McMath, *Insurance Denial for Head and Spinal Cord Injuries: Stacked Deck Requires Health Care Reform*, 10 HealthSpan 7-11, 1993 (July/Aug.), and C. Rocchio, *Social Security Continued Disability Review Requires Action*, 2 TBI Challenge 4 (1998), published by the Brain Injury Association.

12. *See Anderson v. Blue Cross/Blue Shield*, 907 F. 2d 1072 (11th Cir. 1990).

Patients with HIV Infection and AIDS

MIKE A. ROYAL, M.D., J.D., F.C.L.M.
MICHAEL A. SHIFLET, J.D.

TREATMENT
VACCINE DEVELOPMENT
DISCRIMINATION
TESTING
STATISTICS AND PRIVACY ISSUES
"SAFE NEEDLE" REGULATIONS
AIDS RESEARCH INVOLVING PRISON INMATES
MEDICAL USE OF MARIJUANA TO TREAT AIDS-RELATED SYMPTOMS
CONCLUSION

What began as a little-noticed report of five homosexual men from Los Angeles with *Pneumocystis carinii* pneumonia in the June 4, 1981, Centers for Disease Control newsletter became an epidemic spanning the globe, killing millions, and affecting the lives of tens of millions.[1] Cases in homosexual men, intravenous drug users, hemophiliacs, and sexual partners of people in high-risk groups soon were reported across the United States. Newly absent T-helper cells seemed to be the common theme connecting these disparate groups. Lack of normal immune function left affected individuals vulnerable to opportunistic infections.

By 1984, human immunodeficiency virus (HIV) was established as the cause of this progressive T-helper cell destruction. Blood tests became widely available and presented the bad news that for every case of acquired immunodeficiency syndrome (AIDS), there were thousands of asymptomatic HIV-positive individuals who were able to transmit the virus to others. By 1988, 90,000 individuals had been diagnosed with AIDS, of whom about 50,000 had died.[2] By 1995, 500,000 had been diagnosed with AIDS, of whom more than 50% had died.[3]

In 1996, newly identified protease inhibitors (PIs) and precisely timed drug cocktails started to reverse symptoms even in seriously ill patients. In 1996 the death rate in the United States fell by 23% compared with that of 1995, and it dropped another 40% in 1997.[4] In this era of highly active antiretroviral therapy (HAART), PIs in combination with nucleoside reverse transcriptase inhibitors (nRTIs) and nonnucleoside transcriptase inhibitors (NNRTIs) have been able to reduce the amount of HIV in plasma to unde-

tectable levels in many patients and increase life expectancy to 36 years in white men with HIV and 11 years in those with AIDS.[5] The combinations also seemed to prevent the progression to AIDS. There were 6% fewer AIDS cases in 1996, 15% fewer in 1997, and 25% fewer in 1998, leading many experts to predict a relatively normal life expectancy for those with HIV or AIDS.[6] What once was a virtual death sentence had become treatable. With new breakthroughs in antiviral therapy and transmission prevention, hopes for a cure with a vaccine are now voiced more frequently.

But to paraphrase Dickens, it has been the best of times and the worst of times in our efforts to treat HIV infection and AIDS. Because of economics (on average HAART costs $17,000 per year), only Western nations have seen the benefits. Unfortunately, AIDS-related illness is now the fourth leading cause of death worldwide.[7] An estimated 50 million individuals have been infected, of whom 33 million are still alive.[8] By November 1999 estimates, 1600 babies are born with HIV or are infected via consumption of breast milk each day.[9]

A total of 19 of 20 new cases of seroconversion and AIDS deaths occur in developing countries, with sub-Saharan Africa (particularly Botswana, Namibia, and Zimbabwe) being responsible for nearly 70% of the world's HIV infections despite representing only 10% of the population.[10] In these regions, seroconversion is almost entirely a result of heterosexual and mother-to-child transmission. In 1998 and 1999, 22 million and 23.3 million, respectively, of those positive for HIV lived in this region, compared with only 500,000 in Western Europe.[11] Life expectancy in the sub-Saharan region, which was 59 years in the 1990s, is now expected to drop to 45 years by 2005 to 2010.[12] By 2005, one of five workers in this part of the world will be HIV positive.[13]

The nations of the former Soviet Union had a greater than 30% increase in the number of HIV conversions in 1999 (estimated at 360,000), with the majority resulting from intravenous drug use.[14] In Moscow there were three times the number of cases in the first 9 months of 1999 as in all prior years combined.[15] Other regions also have been hard hit by this epidemic, with Asia now representing the fastest growing seroconversion rate, heralding a potential explosion in numbers.

The biggest problems continue to be poor access to treatment (mostly because of cost), poor understanding of basic sex education concepts, promiscuity among men who are indifferent to potential heterosexual transmission, and transmission to babies. In sub-Saharan Africa, more women than men are now HIV positive, with African girls ages 15 to 19 years five to six times more likely than boys to be seropositive.[16] This problem will cripple countries whose economies cannot match the resources of the United States or Western Europe. In 1997, for example, the United States spent $1 to $3 billion on HIV/AIDS-related illnesses, whereas sub-Saharan Africa spent only $165 million despite having almost 70% of the world's cases. For these countries the only viable option is a vaccine to prevent further transmission.

The dramatic improvements in life expectancy resulting from new drug combinations in the United States and Western Europe have created other issues of concern. Although less of a problem than in developing countries, the cost of new combination therapies may reduce access to treatment or encourage noncompliance. Adverse events from multiple drug treatments and comorbidities, such as increased susceptibility to opportunistic infections and some cancers, are greater concerns with increased life expectancy. Increasing the pool of seropositive individuals under treatment increases the potential for transmitting the virus to noninfected individuals. Failure to adhere to strict drug regimens substantially increases the chance for mutation, resistance, and tolerance.[17] Resistant strains can be passed on to others, as has been documented in 80 newly infected individuals who showed a 16.3% prevalence of HIV-1 variants with known resistance-conferring genotypes to any retroviral agent.[18] The presumption is that these cases represent transmission of treatment-resistant strains from previously treated patients.

It has been estimated that an adherence rate of 95% is necessary for optimal results.[19] This level of patient compliance is rarely achieved even in the best of situations. Noncompliance rates may approach 30%, allowing for more resistant HIV strains to emerge. Even if the cost was far less than the current $1000 to $2000 per month, other factors encourage incomplete dosing regimens. Multiple drugs must be taken at fixed times, some with food and some without, and side effects, such as malaise, nausea, and vomiting, are common.

TREATMENT

Many hoped that HIV infections could be eradicated if viral replication could be completely suppressed and chronically infected cells could be allowed to die. Using estimates of an infected cell's half-life of 10 to 14 days, it was suggested that eradication might be achievable in 2 to 3 years. These hopes dissipated in the face of newer data indicating that low-level viral replication may occur even with combination therapy at plasma HIV-ribonucleic acid (RNA) levels below detection (<50 copies/ml).[20]

As of December 1999 the consensus regarding specific antiretroviral therapy as reviewed by the International AIDS Society-U.S.A. Panel is to use initial regimens of two nRTIs and one PI, two nRTIs and one NNRTI, or two PIs and two nRTIs.[21] No definitive superiority of one regimen over another has been noted. Early treatment is recommended, but perceived benefits must be balanced against long-term adverse events. Plasma HIV-RNA levels and CD4+ counts are good predictors of outcome.

Current antivirals approved by the U.S. Food and Drug Administration (FDA) include the following:[22]

- nRTIs: Zidovudine (AZT, Retrovir), didanosine (Videx), zalcitabine (Hivid), stavudine (Zerit), lamivudine (Epivir), and abacavir (Ziagen).
- NNRTIs: Nevirapine (Viramune), delavirdine (Rescriptor), and efavirenz (Sustiva).
- PIs: Saquinavir (Fortovase), ritonavir (Norvir), indinavir (Crixivan), nelfinavir (Viracept), and amprenavir (Agenerase).

HAART regimens have reduced HIV to undetectable levels in some patients, raising hopes of eradication, but recent studies have shown a swift resurgence by HIV on discontinuation with or without interleukin-2 (IL-2) added to activate resting memory cells.[23] In one study, 12 patients received HAART for a mean of 20.8 months and 14 patients received HAART for a mean of 20.1 months with IL-2 for a mean of 39 months. CD4+ counts fell even before HIV could be detected, demonstrating a continual low-level "whittling away" of CD4+ even during HAART.

Despite these disappointments, further research has opened doors for new approaches. Transactivator of transcription (Tat) is a small HIV protein essential for both viral replication and the progression of HIV.[24] It increases the transcription rate of viral mRNA by thousands (burst effects), helping to produce full-length transcripts of HIV genes. Tat can be excreted into plasma and enter other cells to trigger immediate transcription of all viral genes. Tat may be immunosuppressive as well by increasing susceptibility of T cells to HIV infection and making them more sensitive to apoptosis (programmed cell death). Individuals with the highest levels of anti-Tat antibodies are among those with the slowest disease progression.

Two other encouraging approaches include HIV-1 fusion inhibitors[25] and integrase inhibitors. HIV-1 fusion inhibitors are designed to block infection by preventing HIV fusion with host cells, thereby preventing insertion of viral deoxyribonucleic acid (DNA). Integrase is an enzyme crucial for insertion of HIV genetic material into the host's own DNA. In January 2000, researchers announced that two compounds, both diketo acids, blocked the enzyme's action in laboratory tests.[26]

VACCINE DEVELOPMENT

Traditional vaccine development typically involves the production of a weakened or attenuated virus that is injected into uninfected hosts to produce an immune response in hopes that, with subsequent exposure, immunological memory will bolster defenses. Unfortunately, traditional approaches have not worked well in HIV prevention. HIV has proved to be a formidable foe to vaccine research. It weakens host antibody responses and makes the cells it inhabits less noticeable to immunological surveillance by constantly changing the structure of peptide antigens (spikes) by which cytotoxic T cells recognize infected cells.[27] These spikes also can be shed into circulation, much like countermeasures released by planes or submarines to attract missiles.

The inherent limitations of current antiretroviral therapy underscore the need to develop effective vaccines, the most feasible and economical way of halting the worldwide epidemic. Several different vaccine strategies have been tested, largely in animals. These strategies include subunit vaccines, inactivated virus vaccines, attenuated live-virus vaccines, and DNA vaccines. Unfortunately, none of the vaccines tested has shown a significant effect on patients' conditions, CD4+ T cell counts, or HIV burden in the blood.[28] Because of the obvious concerns of transmission with some vaccines, the Joint United Nations Programme on HIV/AIDS (UNAIDS) has published recommendations on ethical guidelines for vaccine research.[29]

A group of prostitutes in Kenya that was thought to be immune to HIV despite numerous exposures (from which an antibody was developed) has now become infected.[30] This unfortunate turn of events has raised concerns that immunity may be reliant on continued exposure and any vaccine developed would have to be given repeatedly, certainly not a feasible approach for mass prevention programs. To help coordinate international cooperation on HIV vaccine development, the World Health Organization (WHO) and UNAIDS have created a new initiative (HIV Vaccine Initiative) to provide an independent forum for all researchers on HIV vaccines to collaborate.[31]

DISCRIMINATION

Although all 50 states offer some disability protection, discrimination against persons with HIV continues to be a major issue. Two significant disability discrimination statutes—the Vocational Rehabilitation Act of 1973[32] and the Americans with Disabilities Act of 1990 (ADA)[33]—continue to be enforced at the federal level. The ADA bars discrimination in employment,[34] government-provided services,[35] and public accommodations.[36] It applies to state and local governments, and employment provisions cover private employers with 15 or more employees.[37] Although the ADA does not specifically include HIV seropositivity, the U.S. Supreme Court has determined that it is a disability, even if the patient does not yet exhibit symptoms of AIDS.[38]

Protection from discrimination in insurance remains a great concern for HIV-positive individuals, for whom access to costly treatment regimens may become a life-or-death issue. Most of the legal developments that concern the financing of AIDS care involve efforts by insurers to limit or escape liability, as well as efforts by persons afflicted by AIDS to obtain coverage to which they feel entitled under their insurance plan. Although the ADA prohibits discrimination in employer-based health insurance,[39] it does allow decisions on underwriting to be based on actuarial risk.[40] Of course, the employer must show that it provides a bona fide insurance plan and demonstrate that the plan is not a "subterfuge" for disability discrimination.[41]

TESTING

The first tests for HIV antibody—enzyme immunosorbent assay (EIA) and Western blot (WB)—were developed in 1985.[42] With their development, calls for mandatory testing surfaced. But it was clear that, even ignoring the huge cost, mandatory universal testing was not a viable option. As with all diagnostic testing, the sensitivity and specificity of the test (rate of false-negative and false-positive results) must be considered. Without 100% accuracy, the emotional harm to individuals testing falsely positive and the false sense of security given those testing falsely negative outweigh any potential benefits to society. In addition, the period between infection and detectable antibody development (now about 25 days) increases potential for false-negative results.[43] Voluntary testing programs designed to encourage testing by preventing discrimination through strict confidentiality provisions and to decrease the spread of disease through awareness of HIV status and education regarding appropriate safety measures continue to be the primary testing emphasis.

Because of recent sales of home HIV tests claiming to be approved by the WHO or FDA, the FDA and Federal Trade Commission (FTC) have sent warning letters to numerous companies.[44] The WHO does not license or approve HIV test kits, and the FDA has not approved any home-use test kit. Other than the standard tests, a rapid test (5 to 30 minutes) with sensitivity and specificity as good as EIA is the only one licensed by the FDA.[45] Saliva tests are being developed and may be available soon.

HIV transmission during medical procedures almost exclusively has been from infected patient to health care worker.[46] Prospective studies of health care workers estimate the average risk of transmission after a percutaneous exposure to HIV-infected blood is about 0.3% and after mucous membrane exposure, 0.9%.[47] The risk after skin exposure is probably less than that for mucous membrane exposure, but no data are available to better quantify the number. As of June 1997 the Centers for Disease Control and Prevention (CDC) had received 52 reports of health care workers in the United States with documented seroconversion after occupational exposure, and an additional 114 episodes were considered possible occupation transmissions.[48] Of the 52 documented episodes, 47 were exposed to HIV-infected blood, 1 to bloody body fluids, 1 to an unspecified body fluid, and 3 to concentrated virus in a laboratory setting. A total of 45 exposures were the result of needle punctures (41) or cuts with a broken glass vial (2) or other sharps (3) and 5 were mucocutaneous.

The well-recognized occupational risk has prompted the CDC to issue recommendations for postexposure prophylaxis (PEP) that include a basic 4-week regimen of two drugs (zidovudine and lamivudine) for most exposures and an expanded regimen including a PI (indinavir or nelfinavir) for exposures that pose an increased risk of transmission or where resistance to an nRTI is suspected. PEP's efficacy in reducing seroconversion has support in both animal and human studies, with some studies showing up to an 80% reduction.[49] Postexposure health care workers need not modify patient care responsibilities to prevent transmission to patients based solely on the exposure.[50] If seroconversion occurs despite PEP, the health care worker's work status should be evaluated according to published recommendations. (The 1991 CDC guidelines suggest that an expert committee could restrict a health care worker from performing "exposure prone" procedures.[51])

Despite the widely acknowledged low risk of transmission to patients from seropositive health care workers, courts have frequently upheld the decision to restrict the practice of seropositive health care workers.[52] In cases where HIV-infected health care workers have been prevented from continuing their occupations, the courts have held that the risk of harm to others must be "significant."[53] To evaluate the significance of the risk, four factors must be considered: (1) the nature of the risk, (2) the duration of the risk, (3) the severity of the risk, and (4) the probability that the disease will be transmitted.[54]

STATISTICS AND PRIVACY ISSUES

New federal guidelines published by the CDC for tracking HIV cases have raised concerns about the privacy of the patient health care records.[55] Some fear that individuals may become more afraid of being tested or that current patients may fear losing health insurance or employment.[56] The guidelines instruct states to track the number of cases and to attach the patient's name or some other identifying code to each case.[57]

Confidentiality is important if voluntary testing programs are to succeed. At the federal level, surveillance data are protected by several statutes and by removal of names and encryption of data transmitted to the CDC.[58] In addition, receipt of federal funding for state surveillance activities requires that states show an ability to guarantee security and confidentiality of reports. All states and many localities have legal safeguards for confidentiality of government-held health data that provide greater protection than laws protecting information held by private health care providers.[59] However, because the degree of protection varies from state to state, in some cases being somewhat minimal, the Model State Public Health Privacy Act[60] was developed at Georgetown University and, if enacted by states, would ensure greater confidentiality of surveillance data.

Since 1985, following CDC recommendations,[61] many states have implemented HIV case reporting as part of their comprehensive HIV/AIDS surveillance programs. As of November 1, 1999, 34 states and the Virgin Islands had done so using a confidential system for name-based case reporting for both HIV infection and AIDS.[62] Four states (Illinois, Maine, Maryland, and Massachusetts), the District of Columbia, and Puerto Rico use a coded identifier rather than the patient's name.[63] Washington state reports by patient name to enable public health follow-up and converts the name to codes after services and referrals are offered.[64] In most other states, HIV case reporting is under consideration, or laws, rules, or regulations enabling HIV surveillance should be implemented soon.

In contrast, the Department of Health and Human Services (DHHS) proposed regulations in late 1999 that aim to protect patients' electronic medical records by imposing federal regulations that would apply in any state with less protective measures for patients' electronic medical records.[65] Federal regulation would be a new approach because health care organizations have traditionally dealt primarily, if not exclusively, with the varying regulations of each state.[66] Under the new regulations, electronic (but not paper) medical records could be obtained only via a search warrant, subpoena, or other legal authorization without the patient's consent.[67] Similar protection for nonelectronic medical records would require passage of additional legislation.[68]

"SAFE NEEDLE" REGULATIONS

Intravenous drug use can be linked to nearly one of three AIDS cases and approximately half of all hepatitis C cases in the United States.[69] However, many states restrict the possession and distribution of hypodermic needles to health care workers and those who have a prescription for such devices, often on the grounds that to do otherwise would imply that drug use is acceptable.[70] Individuals and organizations that want to distribute clean needles to intravenous drug users to combat the spread of HIV often experience legal barriers, including criminal prosecution, that prevent them from doing so.[71] To address these concerns, the American Medical Association, the American Pharmaceutical Association, the Association of State and Territorial Health Officials, the National Association of Boards of Pharmacy, and the National Alliance of State and Territorial AIDS Directors have jointly urged states to coordinate efforts across professional disciplines and reduce regulatory barriers to improve access to sterile syringes and needles.[72]

In areas that allow some form of needle distribution to drug users, some groups have found innovative ways to operate. One Chicago organization, the Chicago Recovery Alliance, has instituted a paging system in which a drug user can call a pager number to obtain sterile syringes and blood testing.[73] Chicago Recovery Alliance is one of only two organizations approved under Illinois law to distribute needles to drug users and is not publicly funded, except for purposes of providing drug counseling.[74]

Approximately 600,000 to 800,000 health care workers suffer accidental needle injuries each year.[75] Health care workers often handle a patient's blood products without knowing the patient's HIV status. Even if the health care worker knows that the patient is HIV-positive, under a 1998 Supreme Court ruling, the patient cannot legally be denied health services for that reason alone.[76] To help protect health care workers from the risk of accidental injury and HIV infection by needles used in the treatment of patients, some state legislatures have recently begun implementing or considering legislation requiring the use of retractable needles.[77] California has already passed such laws, and at least 21 other states and the District of Columbia are considering similar legislation.[78] The Occupational Safety and Health Administration (OSHA)[79] and the CDC[80] also advocate the use of retractable needles by medical employers to reduce the number of needle-related injuries.

AIDS RESEARCH INVOLVING PRISON INMATES

Interest is developing in the medical community to expand AIDS research among prison inmates.[81] Despite more than a 50% drop in the number of AIDS cases in U.S. prisons from 1995 to 1997,[82] the rate of HIV infection among prisoners is still more than five times higher than that of the general population.[83] A study at Canadian correctional facilities involving face-to-face interviews in 439 men and 158 women in 1996 and 1997 points to high-risk behaviors as the reason for the prevalence of seropositivity, especially injection drug use and sexual behavior.[84] Nearly one third of the inmates had injected drugs in the year preceding their current sentence. Among those sexually active, more than half had two or more sex partners before being incarcerated and the majority rarely used condoms.

A team at the Brown University HIV/Prison Project has developed preliminary guidelines for clinical tests involving prison inmates.[85] The idea has been met with some strong resistance because of abuses that occurred in inmate research programs during the 1950s and because some states simply outlaw inmate research altogether.[86] Advocates say the research is needed to help find treatments for AIDS and also to allow inmates access to cutting-edge treatments.[87] Administratively, such programs may be aided by a January 2000 U.S. Supreme Court decision. The court declined to review, and thus left standing, an Eleventh Circuit Court decision that allows inmates with HIV to be segregated from the rest of the prison population.[88] However, the primary concern in any research program, whether or not involving prisoners, is that it be conducted in a medically ethical manner.[89]

MEDICAL USE OF MARIJUANA TO TREAT AIDS-RELATED SYMPTOMS

Despite warnings from a recent study that support what many have long suspected, that smoking marijuana increases the risk of cancer almost as much as smoking tobacco,[90] laws have been approved in at least six states to allow the use of marijuana by seriously ill patients, including AIDS patients, to alleviate pain and other symptoms of disease.[91] Some AIDS patients report significant relief of pain and other AIDS-related symptoms from smoking marijuana—relief that they allegedly cannot obtain from taking dronabinol (Marinol) or other treatments.[92] Although some states now recognize that marijuana has some legitimate medical use, the federal government shows no signs of changing its position against the widespread use of marijuana for medical purposes.[93] The Justice Department is currently challenging the medical marijuana laws in five states,[94] and possession and distribution of marijuana remain federal crimes, outside of an approved federal trial program. The U.S. Attorney General also is challenging a federal Ninth Circuit Court of Appeals ruling that would allow a defense of "medical necessity"—a criminal act done to prevent more serious harm—as a defense to violating the federal laws prohibiting the possession of marijuana.[95] The implication of the court's decision is that the medical need to treat patient symptoms in certain cases by prescribing marijuana may be a "lesser evil" than the violation of laws against the possession and distribution of marijuana.

CONCLUSION

Medicine has come a long way in the ability to treat AIDS and HIV-related infections. New antiretroviral treatments have erased what was once a virtual death sentence.

Unfortunately, the epidemic is rapidly accelerating in nonindustrialized nations that do not have the resources to cope with the problem. Vaccine research, although promising, offers only a hope for a future solution.

As more has been learned about HIV/AIDS and the infection has become treatable and is more often the result of intravenous drug use and heterosexual or mother-to-fetus transmission, the fear and hysteria bred by misunderstanding have slowly been replaced by reason and thoughtful concern over how to reduce transmission. Issues of discrimination seem to have shifted more to concerns over privacy of information and maintenance of insurance and medical treatment, but the longer life expectancy resulting from more aggressive treatment regimens provides more opportunities for individuals to suffer discrimination of some type. Moving forward into this new millennium, there is much to do, but desperation has given way to hope—hope for a cure, hope for a vaccine, and hope for greater understanding of and compassion and respect for individuals coping with HIV infection.

ENDNOTES

1. Good places for additional reading are the HIV/AIDS What's New webpage maintained by the CDC at www.cddnpin.org/hiv/whatsnew.htm, the HIV/AIDS Resources webpage maintained by the National AIDS Clearinghouse/CDC at www.cdcnpin.org/, the UNAIDS (Joint United Nations Programme on HIV/AIDS) webpage at www.Unaids.org/, and the HIV and AIDS webpage of links to other sites (including MEDLINE and AIDSline at igm.nlm.nih.gov/) maintained by the FDA at www.fda.fov/oashi/aids/other.html. The CDC's Morbidity and Mortality Weekly Report (MMWR) is available free of charge in electronic format; send an e-mail message to listserv<listserv.cdc.gov. The body content should read, "SUBscribe mmwr-toc."

2. Centers for Disease Control and Prevention, *Update: Trends in AIDS Incidence—United States, 1996*, 46 M.M.W.R. 861-867 (1997).

3. *Id.*, at 165-173.

4. UNAIDS/WHO: *HIV/AIDS Situation December 1996*, reported at www.us.unaids.org/highband/document/epidemio/situat96.html. *See also, The Status and Trends of the Global HIV/AIDS Pandemic* (Vancouver, July 5-6, 1996).

5. R. Sherer, *Summary of the 39th Interscience Conference on Antimicrobial Agents and Chemotherapy*, reported at www.ama-assn.org/special/hiv/newsline/conferen/icaac99/sherer.htm (posted Oct. 25, 1999).

6. Centers for Disease Control and Prevention, *CDC Guidelines for National Human Immunodeficiency Virus Case Surveillance, Including Monitoring for Human Immunodeficiency Virus Infection and Acquired Immunodeficiency Syndrome*, 48(RR-13) M.M.W.R. 2-3 (1999); *see also* P.L. Fleming, J.W. Ward, J.M. Karon, et al., *Declines in AIDS Incidence and Deaths in the USA: A Signal Change in the Epidemic*, 12(Suppl. A) AIDS S55-S61 (1998).

7. UNAIDS/WHO: *Press release*, www.unaids.org/whatsnew/press/eng/pressarc99/london231199.html (posted Nov. 23, 1999).

8. *Id.*

9. UNAIDS/WHO: *AIDS Epidemic Update: 1999*, www.unaids.org/publications/documents/epidemiology/ surveillance/wad1999/embaee.pdf.

10. UNAIDS/WHO: *Press release*, www.unaids.org/whatsnew/press/eng/ny10100.htm (posted Jan. 10, 2000).

11. *Id.*

12. *Supra* note 7.

13. *Id.*

14. *Supra* note 9.

15. *Id.*

16. *Id.*

17. G. Fatkenheuer, A. Theisen, J. Rockstroh, et al., *Virological Treatment Failure of Protease Inhibitor Therapy in an Unselected Cohort of HIV-1 Infected Patients*, 11 AIDS F113-F116 (1997). This study documented up to 30% to 50% resistance rates in treated individuals.

18. D. Boden, A. Harley, L. Zhang, et al., *HIV-1 Drug Resistance in Newly Infected Individuals*, 282 J.A.M.A. 1135-1141 (1999).

19. Panel on Clinical Practices for Treatment of HIV Infection convened by the Department of Health and Human Services, *Guidelines for the Use of Antiretroviral Agents in HIV-Infected Adults and Adolescents*, www.hivatis.org/guidelines/adult/pdf/A&ajani. pdf (posted Jan. 28, 2000).

20. L. Zhang, B. Ramratnam, K. Tenner-Racz, et al., *Quantifying Residual HIV-1 Replication in Patients Receiving Combination Antiretroviral Therapy*, 340 N. Engl. J. Med. 1605-1613 (1999).

21. *Updated Recommendations of the International AIDS Society-USA Panel*, 283 J.A.M.A. 381-390 (2000). *See also supra* notes 5 and 19.

22. The FDA maintains an updated list of antivirals at http://www.fda.gov/oashi/aids/virals.html. A nice overview by M. Schutz and A. Wendrow covers antivirals, side effects, mutations, resistance, and problems with drug-drug combinations, including antituberculous agents and methadone. This report can be found at http://hiv.medscape.com/updates/quickguide. A good coverage of PIs can be found in M.A. Dietrich, J.D. Butts & R.H. Raasch, *HIV-1 Protease Inhibitors: A Review*, 16 Infect. Med. 716-738 (1999).

23. A.S. Fauci, 5 Nat. Med. 561-565 (1999).

24. D. Blakeslee, *Tat: HIV's Achilles' Heel*, www.ama-assn.org/hiv/newsline/briefing/achilles.htm (posted Nov. 16, 1999).

25. J. Stephenson, 282 J.A.M.A. 1994 (1999).

26. D.J. Hazuda, P. Felock, M. Witmer, et al., *Inhibitors of Strand Transfer that Prevent Integration and Inhibit HIV-1 Replication in Cells*, Science 646-650 (2000). *See also* S. James, *Fusion Inhibitors, T-20: Chemokine Variants; Tat and Interferon Antibodies: Gallo Describes Three New Treatment Approaches*, AIDS Treatment News 4-5 (1998).

27. D. Blakeslee, *HIV and Antibodies*, www.ama-assn.org/special/hiv/newsline/briefing/antibody.htm (posted May 11, 1999).

28. P. Fast & W. Snow, *HIV Vaccine Development: An Overview*, http://www.ama-assn.org/special/hiv/treatment/vacessay.htm (posted Mar. 25, 1997).

29. UNAIDS Guidance Document: *Ethical Considerations in HIV Preventive Vaccine Research*, www.unaids.org/publications/documents/vaccines/vaccines/Ethicalresearch.doc.

30. BBC News,news.bbc.co.uk/hi/english/health/newsid_619000/619316.stm (Jan. 26, 2000).

31. www.unaids.org/whatsnew/press/eng/geneva2120200.html (posted Feb. 21, 2000).

32. *See* 29 U.S.C.A. §§701-796 (West 1999).

33. *See* 42 U.S.C.A. §§12101-12213 (West 1999).

34. *See* 42 U.S.C.A. §§12111-17 (West 1999).

35. *See* 42 U.S.C.A. §§12131-12165 (West 1999). This prohibition includes employment discrimination. *See* 35 C.F.R. §35.140 (1992).

36. *See* 42 U.S.C.A. §§12181-12189 (West 1999). Examples of public accommodations include hotels, restaurants, theaters, stadiums, convention centers, parks, museums, private schools, malls, hospitals, and health care providers.

37. *See* 42 U.S.C.A. §12111 (West 1999).

38. *See Bragdon v. Abbott*, 524 U.S. 624 (1998).

39. *See* 42 U.S.C.A. §12112(a)-(b)(2) (West 1999).

40. *See* 42 U.S.C.A. §12201(c)(1)-(3) (West 1999).

41. *See* 42 U.S.C.A. §12201(c)(2) (West 1999).

42. www.cdc.gov/nchstp/hiv_aids/hivinfo/vfax/260310.htm.

43. *See id.*

44. www.fda.gov/oashi/aids/testwarn.html and www.ftc.gov/opa/1999/9911/cyberlink.htm.

45. www.cdc.gov/nchstp/hiv_aids/hivinfo/vfax/260310.htm.

46. K. Henry & S. Campbell, *Needle Stick/Sharps Injuries and HIV Exposure Among Health Care Workers*, 78 Minn. Med. 41-44 (1995).

47. D.M. Bell, *Occupational Risk of Human Immunodeficiency Virus Infection in Health Care Workers: An Overview*, 102 (Suppl. 5B) Am. J. Med. 9-15 (1997).

48. *Public Health Service Guidelines for the Management of Health-Care Worker Exposures to HIV and Recommendations for Postexposure Prophylaxis*, 47(RR-7) M.M.W.R. 1-28 (1998) posted at aepo-xdv-www.epo.cdc.gov/wonder/prevguid/m0052722/m0052722.htm.

49. *Id.*

50. *Id.*

51. Centers for Disease Control and Prevention, *Recommendations for Preventing Transmission of HIV and Hepatitis B to Patients During Exposure Prone Invasive Procedures*, 40 M.M.W.R. 3-4 (1991).

52. *See, e.g., Doe v. University of Maryland Medical System Corporation*, 50 F. 3d 1261 (4th Cir. 1995) (neurosurgery resident); *Bradley v. University of Texas M.D. Anderson Cancer Center*, 3 F. 3d 922 (5th Cir. 1993), *cert. denied*, 114 S.Ct. 1071 (1994) (surgical technician); *Goetz v. Noble*, 652 So. 2d 1203 (Fla. Dist. Ct. of App., Mar. 29, 1995; *rehearing denied*, May 2, 1995) (orthopedic surgeon).

53. *School Bd. of Nassau County, Fla. v. Arline*, 480 U.S. 273, 107 S.Ct. 1123, 94 L.Ed. 2d 307 (1987).

54. *Id.*

55. *See* Russ Bynum, *Guidelines Urge States to Collect HIV Cases with Names*, Associated Press Newswires (Dec. 10, 1999), available in WestLaw AllNewsPlus database.

56. *See id.*

57. *See id.*

58. *Id.* at 11.

59. L.O. Gostin, Z. Lazzarini, V.S. Neslund & M. Osterholm, *The Public Health Information Infrastructure*, 275 J.A.M.A. 1921-1927 (1996).

60. L.O. Gostin & J.G. Hodge, *Model State Public Health Privacy Act* (Georgetown University, Washington, D.C. 1999).

61. Centers for Disease Control and Prevention, *supra* note 6 at 1-31.

62. *Id.* at 2-3.

63. *Id.*

64. *Id.*

65. *See The Coming Revolution: Proposed Patient Privacy Rules May Dramatically Change Daily Operations, Add Compliance Demands*, 10(12) Physician Manager (Nov. 12, 1999), available in 1999 W.L. 13419985.

66. *See Clinton Unveils Limited Privacy Protection for Electronic Medical Records, supra* at 60.

67. *See id.*

68. *See id.*

69. *See* C.W. Henderson, *Groups Seek Better Access to Sterile Syringes*, Health Letter on CDC (Nov. 15, 1999), available in WestLaw, 1999 W.L. 11593596.

70. *See* C. Clark, *Needle Exchange Advocates Strive Anew for County Assent*, San Diego Union & Tribune A1, available in WestLaw, 1999 W.L. 29195430 (quoting San Diego health care supervisor Dianne Jacob, responding to efforts to implement a needle exchange program, "No, no, no. A thousand times, no. It's wrong for governments to say it's OK to use illegal drugs as long as you use a clean needle. Clean needle exchanges send the wrong message to our kids.")

71. *See Medical Emergency Declaration to Be Sought for Needle Swaps*, Los Angeles Times, A33 (Dec. 18, 1999); *see, e.g.*, Cal. Bus. & Prof. Code §4326(b) (West 2000), available in WestLaw, 1999 W.L.

26206731 (making the distribution of needles without a prescription a misdemeanor punishable by fine and/or imprisonment.)

72. *See supra* note 69.

73. *See* M.T. Galo, *Drug Users Have Link to Sterile Needles: Pager System Starts in Northwest*, Chicago Tribune 1 (Dec. 24, 1999), available in WestLaw, 1999 W.L. 31273900.

74. *See id.*

75. *See* Lauran Neergaard, *CDC Urges Use of Safer Needles to Protect Workers*, Washington Post Z07 (Nov. 30, 1999), available in WestLaw, 1999 W.L. 30305865.

76. *See Bragdon v. Abbott*, 524 U.S. 624 (1998).

77. *See Scott-Levin Announces Sharp Ideas: Preventing Occupational Contamination by Needles*, Business Wire (Dec. 10, 1999), available in WestLaw AllNewsPlus database.

78. *See id.* California is also actively enforcing its regulations in this area by issuing fines for noncompliance. *See Fed and State OSHAs Step up Needlestick Safety Enforcement*, Business Wire (Nov. 3, 1999), available in WestLaw AllNewsPlus database.

79. *See* M.F. Conlan, *OSHA Wants Safer Needles Used to Protect Workers*, 143(23) Drug Topics 1 (1999), available in WestLaw, 1999 W.L. 10022313.

80. *Supra* note 75.

81. *See* D. Rising, *Medical Tests on Inmates Reassessed*, AP Online (Oct. 14, 1999), available in WestLaw 1999 W.L. 28128332.

82. *See AIDS Death Rate for Inmates Drops*, Los Angeles Times A31 (Nov. 4, 1999), available in WestLaw, 1999 W.L. 26192733.

83. *See* S. Sternberg, *$7M to Fight AIDS, Drugs In Minorities Behind Bars*, USA Today 07D (Oct. 5, 1999), available in WestLaw, 1999 W.L. 6858143.

84. L. Calzavara & A. Burchell, *HIV/AIDS in Prisons*, 5 HIV/AIDS Policy & Law (1999) posted at www.aidslaw.ca/Newsletter/FallWin99/prisons.htm.

85. *See* D. Rising, *Medical Tests on Inmates Addressed: Team Suggests Guidelines for AIDS and Hepatitis Trials for Prisoners*, Orange County Register A13 (Oct. 16, 1999), available in WestLaw, 1999 W.L. 30109100.

86. *See id.*

87. *See supra* note 81.

88. *See Onishea v. Hopper*, 171 F. 3d 1289 (11th Cir. (Ala.) 1999), *cert. denied, Davis v. Hopper*, No. 98-9663, 2000 W.L. 29361 (U.S., Jan. 18, 2000).

89. *See supra* note 81. Rising references 1950s-era research programs in which "[i]nmates were injected with herpes, hepatitis and syphilis. Some had their testicles radiated; others were inflicted with wounds to see how they healed."

90. *See Marijuana Use Linked to Cancer*, N.Y. Times News Service D6 (Jan. 14, 2000).

91. *See* H.T. George, *Medicinal Marijuana Users Wary Despite Win in Washington State*, Chicago Tribune 38 (Dec. 10, 1999), available in WestLaw, 1999 W.L. 2940383.

92. *See, e.g., supra* note 90; R. George, *Gay Activist Has One Last Cause: The Right to Smoke Marijuana for Medical Reasons*, Sun-Sentinel (Ft. Lauderdale, Fla.) 1E (Oct. 10, 1999), available in WestLaw, 1999 W.L. 20287971.

93. *Supra* note 91.

94. *See id.*

95. See B. Egelko, *Lockyer Backs "Necessity" Defense, Asks Feds to Drop Opposition*, Associated Press Newswires (Oct. 14, 1999), available in WestLaw AllNewsPlus database; *United States v. Oakland Cannabis Buyers' Cooperative*, 190 F. 3d 1109 (9th Cir. 1999).

Pain Management

L. JEAN DUNEGAN, M.D., J.D., F.C.L.M.

BASIC PRECEPTS AND DEFINITIONS
PROCESSES FOR AND RESULTS OF RECENT MANDATES
TREATMENT CHOICES: WHEN AND HOW TO USE THEM
THE CHRONIC PAIN PATIENT
LIABILITY WHEN PAIN IS NOT ASSESSED/TREATED WELL
THE FUTURE OF PAIN MANAGEMENT

Pain is a more terrible Lord of mankind than even death itself.
ALBERT SCHWEITZER

BASIC PRECEPTS AND DEFINITIONS

Pain

This quote by Albert Schweitzer may well support the argument that the death penalty does not deter crime. The Latin word for pain is *poena*, meaning punishment. Indeed the infliction of physical pain in the early Roman Empire was a form of punishment much worse, presumably, than the more civilized guillotine used during the French Revolution 1800 years later. The guillotine offered a quick death with a mercifully brief pain compared to the intense, blinding pain used to break the spirit and cause the recipient to beg for a quick death when relentless physical pain was inflicted. In those times this infliction of pain was used to maintain the status quo and the sufferer was to be personally blamed for his pain. It follows that the infliction of physical pain might well deter crime but, thankfully, the advancement of civilized governments has led not to corporal punishment but more to psychosocial pain infliction (i.e., imprisonment, isolation, loss of social position, etc.); pain not attributable to one's own errors is now attributable to illness or injury. The fear of pain, however, is just as controlling of man's actions now as it was then, and despite our advancements in maintaining man's welfare and contentment, there are still those who suffer such pain or are afraid of such pain that they would rather have their lives end (by suicide or mercy killing) than go on trying to live with the pain they now endure or might later endure.

Pain is an unpleasant sensory and emotional experience associated with actual or potential tissue damage. Its management has preoccupied society since antiquity. Records show the use of opioids beginning in 2250 B.C. Although the sensory component of pain lends itself to the *science* of medicine, the emotional component relegates pain, at least in part, to the *art* of our profession. Pain is the major impetus behind most patient-doctor interactions and thus would logically be the aspect of medicine that each clinician has the most experience in. Alas, it is most physicians' least favorite malady to treat, especially if the therapy involves prescription opioid medications. If the measurement of pain were objective, pain management would be without controversy, and evidence-based treatment protocols would be readily available. The subjective nature of pain has relegated this aspect of illness to the more challenging and controversial realm of our work. When opioids are used for pain management, the objective is to provide analgesia without deleterious side effects. Adequately treating around-the-clock moderate to severe pain requires a reexamination of how pain has been treated for decades in modern medicine, and an admission that perhaps that approach has been neither successful nor warranted. For a thorough review of pain pathophysiology and pharmacology, the reader is referred to *The Handbook of Pain Management*.[1]

Acute/chronic pain

Acute pain comes on abruptly (within 1 second of insult) and is the most frequent reason for patients to take over-the-counter medications or to seek medical attention from the profession.

Chronic pain is also attributable to a physical cause but persists well beyond a normal healing period and has been present a part of each day for a period of 6 months or more during the prior year. Many clinicians (surgeons among them) feel that chronic pain management falls outside their realm, since they "never have patients with pain 6 months or longer." Such clinicians often say that they need not get education about pain assessment and treatment as that realm belongs to the pain management specialists. Therefore, a better definition for chronic pain might be: any pain moderate to severe, not necessarily related to activity, which interferes with a patient's quality of life and may be cyclical or persistent on a daily basis. For instance, the abdominal pain from chronic pancreatitis or sickle-cell crisis or the pain of a cluster migraine headache lasts less than 6 months with each recurrence, but its treatment should be the realm of the general and family physician, and should not necessarily be relegated to only "pain specialists."

PROCESSES FOR AND RESULTS OF RECENT MANDATES

The undertreatment of pain is a major health problem in the United States and throughout the world. More than 20 million people miss at least 20 days of work a year because of the same cyclical nagging pain, at the cost of $50 billion annually.[2] If you add to that the cost of replacement employees for those who miss that much work, it's $85 billion annually. Three-fourths of cancer patients report suffering pain.[3] The quality of patients' lives when they suffer moderate to severe pain is abysmal and patients often contemplate or commit suicide rather than go on living with that pain. On January 1, 2001, we entered the Decade of Pain Control and Research as declared by the Pain Care Coalition (made up of the American Pain Society, the American Academy of Pain Medicine, and the American Headache Society). On that same date, the pain standards of the Joint Commission on Accreditation of Healthcare Organizations (JCAHO) came into effect. By now these standards are "old hat" by most health care institutions and the details can be found at the JCAHO website.[4] These standards were the outgrowth of a 2-year collaboration between JCAHO and the University of Wisconsin.

A summary[5] of the standards/mandates is as follows: (1) Since patients have a right to assessment and treatment of pain, health care organizations have a responsibility to respect and support these rights. (2) Pain should be assessed as warranted based on the reason the patient is presenting for care. (3) Educational materials regarding pain assessment and treatment should be available for patients and staff and all appropriate disciplines should participate in developing policies and procedures for education about pain management. (4) A treatment plan for assessed pain must be developed and such plan should take into account a patient's values/choices and should allow for the patient's active participation. (5) The prescribing and ordering of pain medications must follow established procedures and there must be appropriate procedures for controlling sample medications. (6) Postoperative contact with a patient must include assessment and documentation of pain and treatment response (in the ambulatory setting, a level of

pain assessment for discharge criteria must be achieved with follow-up assessment by phone for an established percentage of patients the following day). (7) Pain management must be a part of a discharged patient's treatment whether he goes to a rehabilitation center, hospice, nursing home, or to his own home (family education concerning pain treatment must be a part of discharge instructions in the latter case).

A November/December 2002 progress report in the American Pain Society's *Bulletin* admits that concern has been voiced about the burdens these standards place on members of the profession.[6] The most common deficiency is failure in the initial assessment standard. The JCAHO standards cannot by themselves improve the quality of pain management, but they have—along with recent liability issues for clinicians who fail to efficaciously treat pain—generated much interest in the field of pain management. Things are changing for the better in this field of the profession.

TREATMENT CHOICES: WHEN AND HOW TO USE THEM

The framework upon which the choices for pain medications rest is, since 1986, the WHO (World Health Organization) pain ladder. Originally developed for cancer pain, there is now worldwide consensus favoring use of the ladder for pain of any etiology. Adjuvants are on all steps of the WHO pain ladder; these refer to medications that are coadministered to manage an adverse effect of the chosen medications or they are medications added to the chosen medications to enhance analgesia (multi-modal approach).[7]

Step 1

Step 1 contains *nonopioids* for the treatment of *mild* to *moderate* pain (pain that is 1-6 on a numeric scale of 0 to 10) and consists of three classes of medication (acetaminophen, salicylates, and NSAIDs). It cannot be overemphasized that nonopioids are to be utilized and titrated *before* opioid pain medications are prescribed. The overuse of short-acting opioid medications prescribed for prn use has conditioned many patients to the associated euphoria with the absence of pain/analgesia; this has led to unintended harm to many of these patients (see under Constant Dosing below).

Over-the-counter (OTC) medications. All medication classes on Step 1 are OTC and the higher dosages of NSAIDs are available by prescription. Safety issues related to the use of two classes of OTC analgesics were recently given FDA attention: (1) potential hepatotoxicity related to the use of acetaminophen and (2) potential gastrointestinal bleeding and renal insufficiency related to the use of aspirin and other OTC NSAIDs.[8]

ACETAMINOPHEN. Acetaminophen is a clinically proven analgesic and antipyretic. In effect this product has no antiinflammatory activity. There occur about 100 deaths and

2000 hospitalizations from acetaminophen-induced hepatotoxicity each year.[9] A recent article in *Hospital Physician*[10] stated that "It is the physician's responsibility to warn of possible liver damage with as little as 2.6 g (some say 4.0 g[11]) of acetaminophen daily over extended periods of time." As will be discussed under Step 2 of the WHO pain ladder, the combination medications for pain often add acetaminophen to an opioid medication, thereby giving a ceiling effect to that product, which severely curtails the possibility of titration for that patient's pain control.

ASPIRIN. Aspirin is an antiinflammatory as well as an antipyretic. Since it interferes with platelet aggregation and clotting, it has a wonderful niche in prevention of cardiovascular disease,[12] but, for those same reasons, it has the same precautions as do OTC NSAIDs as regards bleeding.

OTHER OTC NSAIDs. These medications at lower than prescription doses give little, if any, antiinflammatory effect, making them much less efficacious for pain control than the prescription dosages of NSAIDs.

Prescription NSAIDs. These include both the general class of NSAIDs (inhibiting both cyclo-oxygenase type 1 and type 2) and the newer Cox-2s (inhibiting only type 2 cyclo-oxygenase). The first generation Cox-2 inhibitors were launched in 1999 when Pfizer began marketing celecoxib (Celebrex). In that same year, Merck's Cox-2 inhibitor valdecoxib (Vioxx) was FDA approved. Both products have been widely prescribed and although they can also be associated with peptic ulcer disease (and were given the same warnings as the nonselective Cox inhibitors), the risk is considerably lower.[13] After 3 years of widespread use, the issues of toxicity from hypertension and/or renal effects have been raised. A recent study from the Johns Hopkins University concluded that patients taking antihypertensive therapy and receiving Cox-2s should be monitored for the development of cardiorenal events. It went on to say that patients taking celebrex experienced less edema and less destabilization of blood pressure control compared with those receiving rofecoxib.[14]

From a surgical standpoint the advantage of the Cox2s is their lack of interference with platelet aggregation and concomitant risk of bleeding. A recent study demonstrated the Cox2s' opioid-sparing effects in patients undergoing hip arthroplasties,[15] showing 40% less morphine use in the first 48 hours post-operation when rofecoxib was used pre- and postoperatively.

Valdecoxib, a second-generation Cox-2 specific inhibitor, was launched by Pfizer in 2001 (approved by the FDA in November 2001 for OA, RA, and the pain of dysmenorrhea). A water-soluble prodrug (paracoxib/Dynastat), which is rapidly hydrolyzed to the active drug valdecoxib, and is the only Cox-2 specific parenteral NSAID, was granted a Marketing Authorization in the European Union in March of 2002 for the short-term treatment of postoperative pain and has been launched in the United Kingdom.[16] This product has not been granted FDA approval but it is expected soon and is eagerly awaited, since the other parenteral, general class NSAID (ketorolac/Toradol) has lost favor due to its delete-rious effects. Although valdecoxib (Bextra) has not been FDA approved for pain, there is evidence to believe it should be considered for pain. A recently published study found that valdecoxib at doses of 20 and 40 mg was effective for the pain associated with dental surgery (extraction of two or more third molars requiring bone removal). Pain relief occurred 25 to 35 minutes after dosing and the patients receiving 40 mg of valdecoxib had pain relief comparable to the pain relief for the patients receiving oxycodone 10 mg/1000 mg acetaminophen, with fewer opioid-related side effects (nausea/vomiting and dizziness).

Step 2

The patient whose pain is not relieved with maximum doses (without prohibitive side effects) of the medications on Step 1 can continue those medications and add one or more choices from Step 2, or can discontinue the Step 1 medications (especially if their side effects are troubling or their accumulated costs are an issue) and use only Step 2 medications. On this step, designed to give choices for the treatment of moderate pain, opioids are introduced; many products combine an opioid with another analgesic (e.g., acetaminophen) or an antiinflammatory medication (e.g., an NSAID to give synergism for analgesia), but many clinicians prefer to titrate each ingredient independently using a pure opioid medication (to avoid a ceiling effect when titrating the product to analgesia) and then an antiinflammatory (e.g., ibuprofen or a prescription NSAID) or second analgesic medication (e.g., acetaminophen) of their own choosing.

Opioids. For the last four decades it was accepted that "Drugs are bad!" As a result we were all taught to seriously underdose this class of medications and to be proud of it, hoping our patients would just "tough it out, like we would if we were in their shoes!" As a class, opioids are conjugated in the liver and excreted in the kidney with peak plasma concentration (C_{max}) in 60 minutes after oral, 30 minutes after parenteral (sub q or IM injection), and 6 minutes after IV injection. The half-life of opioids ($t_{1/2}$) depends on the rate of renal clearance and if normal it is 2 to 4 hours. (When dosed repeatedly, a steady state is achieved in plasma after 4 or 5 $t_{1/2}$'s or after 1 day.) Two principles are now fairly well accepted (at least on paper if not in practice) regarding the management of around-the-clock (ATC) moderate to severe pain not necessarily related to activity:

(1) *Constant dosing* rather than prn prescribing. When the clinician essentially makes the patient their own physician, by prescribing "one or two every four to six hours," the patient will get peaks and valleys of opioid concentration at least 4 to 6 times a day. The adverse consequences for the patient will be in both the troughs and the peaks of the plasma levels.

The trough of plasma concentration of the drug, when it falls below the patient's threshold for pain, causes the patient to reexperience the very pain we commit to controlling (if not for the ethical reasons, then surely for the best quality and functionality of the patient's existence). When a patient must discern whether to take one or two pain pills, they are forced to find the pain threshold where two pills are required, and they never "forget" the pain, leading often to anxiety about what the directions mean (the average number of pain pills prescribed is often 30 with one refill and the patient often gets involved in a "I must hold out, as these won't last long enough if I take 2 every 4 hours" situation).

In the peak levels of the plasma concentration are the deleterious side effects of opioid medications (e.g., drowsiness, respiratory depression, nausea and vomiting, inability to concentrate or do basic physical maneuvers, and euphoria); these effects remit over 2 to 3 days when constant dosing is used.[17] One of the most compelling reasons for constant dosing is to deter the euphoric effect of opioid medications; this deleterious effect is directly related to both the rapidity with which one gets the rise of opioid in the plasma and the final level of the peak of opioid after each dose. When patients "pop two," after waiting or holding out for 6 to 8 hours, the sudden peak of opioid medication in the plasma can cause a recurrent euphoric sensation which, over time, can condition the patient to associate that euphoria with the analgesia. Many of the patients who frequent emergency rooms with the chronic, recurrent pain of migraine headaches, pancreatitis, and sickle-cell crisis (exhorting us to give them meperidine/ Demerol because "nothing else works") are an example of this same conditioning. These patients are most often not physically dependent on meperidine (they get it only occasionally), but rather are conditioned to believe that unless the euphoria is present, the pain is not adequately relieved. All patients treated for chronic pain using opioids should be screened for vulnerability to the deleterious side effect of euphoria. The patient who historically "knows euphoria" (from opioids, or alcohol, or illicit drugs such as marijuana) is vulnerable to this conditioning. Peaks and valleys of opioid medication should be avoided as this patient is at considerable risk of having the benefits of opioids outweighed by the long-term deleterious effects.

(2) *Titration*. Most clinicians have "magic" numbers of pain pills prescribed, and often have "magic" daily levels of opioid above which they will not titrate. The efficaciousness of each medication can only be maximized by progressively increasing the total daily dose over time, reaching satisfactory analgesia or prohibitive side effects. In general, a chronic pain patient's routine should be constant enough that breakthrough pain medication should be briefly used (1 or 2 days) and then incorporated into the constant dosing schedule. This results in avoidance (as much as possible) of peaks and troughs of opioid concentration and effects maximal functionality.

The choices on Step 2 include codeine, hydrocodone, oxycodone, dihydrocodeine, propoxyphene, and tramadol hydrochloride (Ultram).

CODEINE. Codeine is a semisynthetic derivative of morphine and is considered a weak opioid about 1/12th as potent as morphine; although it was often used as an antitussive, it carries a high incidence of GI side effects and is seldom prescribed in its pure form. Codeine's demethylation to morphine is responsible for its analgesic property, and patients who lack the cytochrome p450 (genetically determined) get no analgesia from codeine as they are unable to convert it to morphine.

HYDROCODONE. Hydrocodone is only available in short-acting, combination form with acetaminophen (as Vicodin, Lorcet, or Lortab) or aspirin; because it has less GI disturbance than codeine, is a Schedule III controlled substance, and is somehow considered weaker than other opioids except codeine, but it is the most widely used and most widely abused opioid in the nation. The abuse attributed to this medication is primarily related to its universal prn dosing rather than to its deleterious effects (if constant dosed in ATC pain conditions, the deleterious effects would remit). Its potency is similar to that of oxycodone.

OXYCODONE. Oxycodone is on both Steps 2 and 3, is available short- or long-acting, is available pure or in combination products, and is thus a very versatile opioid medication. It has a higher bioavailability than morphine but analgesic potency comparable to it. The extended-release pure form (Oxycontin) has a biphasic absorption pattern with an initial half-life of 0.6 hours and a second of 6.9 hours and, unlike morphine, its absorption is not pH-dependent nor does it carry potential hepatorenal toxicity concerns (as does morphine). Extended-release oxycodone requires less frequent dosing, improving compliance, adherence, and efficacy as well as achieving best analgesia for the dose in 2 to 4 days.

The abuse of this product has received widespread press coverage for the last 2 years (beginning in January 2001), prompting some states to blame it and its manufacturer (Purdue Pharma LP) for harms, including death, to those who obtained it (either by obtaining a legal prescription or by participating in diversion of the product, i.e., the physical delivery of a controlled substance to those who would use it not for its medically intended purposes but rather for its euphoric effects or its addiction fulfillment). The first lawsuit against the makers of Oxycontin was filed in June 2001, in Virginia, and dozens followed. In February 2002, in a jury trial, a Florida physician was convicted of manslaughter in connection with the Oxycontin prescribing decisions he made.

In December 2002 a Virginia doctor became the target of a federal Oxycontin probe when it was learned that one of his patients (who pled guilty to charges and plea bargained with authorities) had bought $72,000 worth of Oxycontin over a period of 10 months and that the prescriptions allowed the patient to obtain 1500 Oxycontin pills every 2 to 4 weeks.[18]

Every decade since the 1950s has seen a particular drug whose abuse eventually leads to a law enforcement crackdown.[19] Liability issues for prescribing opioid medications were feared by many clinicians who tended to shy away from use of the medications receiving the adverse publicity (especially the extended-release oxycodone known as Oxycontin). The reaction of many pain management specialists to the lawsuits was concern that a chill factor, against those with legitimate pain, would settle over treating physicians. Although the product (Oxycontin) is to be swallowed whole and is not to have its physical characteristics changed in any way prior to ingesting it (e.g., by crushing, heating, dissolving and shooting, etc.), the higher doses of medication in the extended-release form can peak and subject a patient to euphoria if it is physically abused. This fact, along with oxycodone's legitimacy (as opposed to illegal drugs like heroin), led many patients seeking euphoria to abuse it. This scenario led to a Clash of the Titans: when mandated pain management met the war on drugs. The perspective depended upon the beholder: law enforcement (with its onus to protect the public) sees the utter destruction of lives when legitimate medications are abused, whereas ardent clinicians (who now work under a mandate to both assess and treat pain efficaciously) saw the marked improvement in functionality and thus quality of life that proper pain management using these products brought.

As law enforcement and the medical professionals have begun working together, and as education concerning proper pain management (the use of constant dosing when indicated, the need to recognize possible conditioning when analgesia and euphoria occur simultaneously, and the requisite of good documentation when following pain-treated patients) has been made available to clinicians and law enforcement officials, we are beginning to see not only more publicity about liability (toward clinicians) when proper pain management is *not* offered (see section on Liability), but also less fear concerning the use of any and all medication choices from the WHO pain ladder. A press release from February 2002, entitled "Another Oxycontin Lawsuit dropped,"[20] mentions individuals' lawsuits against the makers of Oxycontin as being dropped in North Carolina, Maine, and Mississippi. In October 2002 a federal judge dismissed the first lawsuit filed against the company that distributes the pain medication Oxycontin, Purdue Pharma LP; in all, more than a dozen similar lawsuits had been dismissed in 2002.[21]

As an example of cooperation between law and medicine, the Attorney General's office of the state of Rhode Island together with Brown University Medical School sponsored a pain management seminar in the fall of 2002 for third-party payers, clinicians, and lawyers. The objective of the seminar was (1) communication among all concerned and (2) the search for common ground between the need for legitimate pain medications and prevention of abuse and diversion of these same medications. Another such example is the educational work being done by the U.S. Attorney General's office in Knoxville, Tennessee. In a recently published article concerning this work,[22] Jennifer Bolen, Assistant U.S. Attorney, said that a physician indicted in a diversion case is typically operating on a cash basis only with parking lot parties and "with people coming out of the office giving high fives because they got a prescription." She also said that cooperation and communication between law enforcement and physicians saves lives.

DIHYDROCODEINE. Dihydrocodeine has a relatively higher analgesic potency than codeine, with less GI disturbance, and in combination form is indicated for moderate pain. This opioid is most often combined with both aspirin and caffeine; the ceiling effect resulting from the combined products, together with the abuse potential if used for long periods of time, make this opioid unpopular for constant dosing/chronic pain settings.

PROPOXYPHENE (DARVON). This is a synthetic opioid similar to methadone which is often combined with aspirin (Darvon Compound) or acetaminophen (Darvocet N-50, Darvocet N-100, Wygesic); its toxicity, especially in the elderly,[23] and its marked euphoria with poor analgesia (unless dosed every 6 hours until accumulation for analgesia is obtained 24 to 48 hours after initiation), have given it a "dubious distinction."[24]

TRAMADOL HYDROCHLORIDE (ULTRAM). This is the non-opioid on Step 2. It is a non-NSAID, centrally acting inhibitor of the reuptake of serotonin and norepinephrine with a low affinity for μ opioid receptors.

Step 3

The opioids on this step, in addition to oxycodone, include morphine, hydromorphone, fentanyl, and methadone. These choices are indicated for the treatment of severe pain and are to be used when a combination of Steps 1 and 2 products is ineffective or they have been titrated to ceiling effect (prohibitive side effects).

MORPHINE. Morphine has long been considered the gold standard for the treatment of severe pain, but it is increasingly recognized as having serious limitations because of its potential for sensitivity reactions, limited versatility due to poor transmucosal and transdermal absorption characteristics, and its active, potentially toxic, metabolites.[25] Extended-release morphine has proven efficacious for moderate to severe ATC pain if dosed continuously, and prohibitive side effects are absent. Titration is difficult, however, due to the different rates at which plasma concentrations are achieved and maintained in any given patient.[26]

HYDROMORPHONE (DILAUDID). This is 7 to 10 times as potent as morphine, with fewer GI and CNS side effects.

FENTANYL. Fentanyl is 75 to 125 times as potent as morphine, is more lipid soluble than morphine, and, unlike morphine, it does not cause histamine release. It is available in parenteral form or in transdermal form (Duragesic) but cannot be given orally. The parenteral form of fentanyl is a preferred agent for outpatient sedation because of its quick onset (1 to 2 minutes) and its short duration (20 to 30 minutes). Although the transdermal form of this opioid has an excellent niche for chronic ATC pain when the GI tract is not available, the absorption is dependent upon body fat, and ambient temperature and its long high life makes it difficult to titrate.

METHADONE. Methadone has recently been promoted for use in chronic pain syndrome treatment, despite the difficulty in titration (because it has a long half-life of 15 to 20 hours, plasma concentrations tend to rise with repeated dosing).[27] Since this opioid blocks the NMDA receptors, it is a useful alternative to morphine when the latter causes intolerable side effects which do not abate with dose reduction[28] or when the patient has developed consequential opioid tolerance. The potency of methadone is similar to that of morphine in single dose administration, but with repeated dosing (for ATC pain treatment) its potency is erratic and can be deadly; the Florida Department of Law Enforcement recently issued a public alert to raise awareness of the fact that methadone-related deaths rose 31% (from 194 to 254) in the first 6 months of 2002 as compared to the last 6 months of 2001.[29] Of the 254 methadone-related deaths where methadone was present, it was listed as the cause of death in 133.

One impetus for the recent rise in the use of methadone for chronic pain treatment may well be the adverse publicity that abuse of extended-release oxycodone received during the past 2 years. As many clinicians who treat chronic pain patients shied away from oxycodone products, they began prescribing the lesser known opioids with extended half-lives (and thus better suitability for chronic pain treatment); it is interesting to note that the same article quoted above also mentions that "although the number of deceased persons who had oxycodone or hydrocodone in their systems increased, the number of times an overdose of those drugs was seen as the cause of death decreased (20% and 14%)."

When opioid medications are utilized for pain management, the issue of conversion, from one administration route or from one opioid class to another, becomes pertinent. The equi-analgesic table below (Table 58-1) shows one such approximation from the EPEC project supported in part by the American Medical Association. Use of the table when converting from one opioid to another involves solving for x by setting up ratios of the two opioids.

THE CHRONIC PAIN PATIENT

Chronic pain is often defined as pain that lasts more than 3 to 6 months. This definition of chronic pain is not conducive to the real clinical world. Many diseases are associated with pain that may wax and wane periodically (sickle-cell disease, osteo- or rheumatoid arthritis, pancreatitis, etc.) and there are

TABLE 58-1 The equi-analgesic table

Oral/rectal dose (mg)	Analgesic	Parenteral dose (mg)
100	Codeine	60
—	Fentanyl	0.1
15	Hydrocodone	—
4	Hydromorphone	1.5
2	Levorphanol	1
150	Meperidine	50
10	Methadone	5
15	Morphine	5
10	Oxycodone	—

When converting to or from transdermal fentanyl patches, published data suggest that a 25 μg patch is equivalent to 45-135 mg oral morphine/24 hours. However, clinical experience suggests that most patients will use the lower end of the range of morphine doses, i.e., for most patients 25 μg is about equivalent to 45-60 mg oral morphine/24 hours.
©EPEC Project, American Medical Association, 1999. Permission to reproduce for educational purposes granted.

nonspecific diagnoses associated with cyclical pain (cluster migraine headaches, low back pain, etc.). The chronic pain patient is any patient who experiences frequent, cyclical bouts of moderate to severe pain, not necessarily related to activity, which significantly interfere with their quality of life/functionality. Between the bouts of cyclical moderate to severe pain the chronic pain patient may have lesser pain or the absence of pain.

The treatment of the chronic pain patient is challenging and frustrating, but is frequently rewarding. The six *principles of chronic pain management* are as follows:

1. Perform and document a thorough history/physical eliciting any possible clues that euphoria is or was a part of the patient's regular life (e.g., regular ingestion of opioids such that there are peaks of it in his plasma 3 or 4 times a day, regular use of illicit drugs like marijuana, frequent DUIs) and consider such a patient to be at an increased risk for associating analgesia with a sense of euphoria.

2. Diagnose the patient as completely as possible, insisting on appropriate testing and/or psychiatric evaluation (for personality disorder, depression, anxiety, etc.) if indicated.

3. Form a plan of treatment, using the multi-modal approach, and educate the patient about how to take pain medications, the side effects, and the need to avoid peaks and valleys of opioids in the plasma.

4. Use a pain treatment agreement with a time frame (e.g., 3 or 6 months) which can be renewed as needed. (See model agreement, Box 58-1 below.)

5. Incorporate a definition of "success" which answers the question, "Where will I end up if I walk with you on your road of pain?" or "Where are you going?" This will allow the physician to insist on commitment from the patient to improve their functionality and their quality of life. Often it allows the physician not

---

BOX 58-1. MODEL PAIN TREATMENT AGREEMENT

I recognize and understand agreement that I have certain responsibilities that I must meet in order to receive treatment for pain. I also acknowledge that the purpose of this agreement is to create a safe and controlled treatment plan. I accept the fact that the opioid medications I will be given under this contract may not completely resolve my pain but should improve my functioning and significantly decrease my pain. If my ability to function improves and my pain decreases satisfactorily, I will be given the pain medication for as long as my pain continues, provided I do not break the terms of this agreement.

I understand that by changing the medications' intended physical characteristics (by crushing, liquefying, injecting, etc.), or by taking more medication than is prescribed, I may cause myself great harm (i.e., coma, organ failure, psychological dependence, or even death); and furthermore, if I abruptly stop taking my medication (by not planning ahead, etc.) I could go into withdrawal which can be very distressing, uncomfortable, and dangerous. I agree to notify my treating physician if I become pregnant, as the opioid medication would pose risks to an unborn child (including opioid addiction or withdrawal symptoms at birth).

I agree to stop any use of illegal, recreational drugs, and agree to stop alcohol consumption to the point of inebriation during my pain treatment under this contract. The terms of this contract include: (1) Only one pharmacy (name and phone number) will be used for filling my prescriptions. (2) I will plan ahead so that I will have no need to get refills during "off hours" (nights, evenings, weekends, holidays). (3) I agree and will sign a release to allow my treating physician to communicate with other physicians that I may see for unrelated problems. (4) I agree and will sign a release to allow my treating physician to communicate with my spouse, significant other, and/or employer if such communication is needed to gauge my progress in reaching my goals (see "definition for success" below). (5) I agree to allow unannounced urine or blood drug screens to monitor my treatment. (6) I agree to waive my right to privacy regarding any prescription medications that I take. (7) I will contact and rely on my treating physician for all opioid and other pain-related problems, and if I have significant side effects/problems during off hours, I will go to the nearest emergency room. (8) At such time I have failed to demonstrate improved function and quality of life as agreed upon by me and my treating physician, I agree to termination of this agreement.

Definition for success:

Improved function: _____

Improved quality of life: _____

Signatures:

Patient _____   Date ——

Treating Physician _____   Date ——

---

to accept the status quo for that patient but rather something better.

6. Follow the patient in a timely fashion, note definition of "success" and whether it is being pursued, consider reevaluating medications and dosages periodically to meet the patient's needs. Interview family members, caretakers, etc., if needed.

When the clinician judges his efforts to treat the chronic pain patient insufficient for the patient's needs, he may wish to get a consultation with a pain specialist at a multidisciplinary pain center. Especially in the realm of workmen's compensation claims for injury/disability, these centers have improved return to work rates by 30% and have thus decreased the overall cost of care.[30]

LIABILITY WHEN PAIN IS NOT ASSESSED/TREATED WELL

The current health care system is obviously flawed when an HMO forces a patient in severe pain to turn to the professionals in black robes, rather than those wearing white coats, for relief.

RICHARD F. CORLIN, M.D.

Although the initial fear (following the negative press coverage of the use of extended-release opioids) was that the use of opioids for chronic pain carried risks of liability for the prescribers, the issues of liability for *not* adequately treating pain have been a major impetus for marked improvement in pain management throughout the nation.

From the standpoint of liability against a physician's license, a landmark case marked the first time a physician's license was sanctioned for a pattern of care that showed that he failed to adequately assess and manage pain. In 1999 a board-certified Oregon pulmonologist had his license to practice medicine sanctioned for 1 year for failure to adequately assess and treat at least five patients who suffered severe pain. This case occurred 2 years before mandated pain management protocols were a requisite for accreditation of health care institutions (via JCAHO), but it was a signal that pain in all patients could no longer be ignored or passed off as something that must be endured; the technology (behavior modification, procedures, medications, etc.) for safe and efficacious pain management is available and should be used.

In the case of *Bergman et al., v. Eden Medical Center*, Alameda County, California, a jury found a physician guilty of elder abuse for not adequately assessing and treating a patient. They awarded the now deceased patient's family $1.5 million. The case was not filed under medical malpractice (in California, under medical malpractice, pain and suffering dies with the patient) but rather under civil negligence. The facts of the case show that Mr. Bergman was given various opioid medications by the defendant physician (meperidine hydrochloride for back pain while hospitalized, hydrocodone bitartrate/acetaminophen and skin patches for discharge analgesia at home) despite his brief respiratory arrest after morphine when he presented to the emergency room on admission. These facts led many to harshly criticize the verdict, claiming that the physicians are essentially being squeezed between a "rock and a hard place" (they can now be punished for both over- and undertreating pain!).

The vulnerability in the case, however, points to a lack of both communication and documentation (the same major vulnerabilities that exist in most lawsuits wherein the plaintiff/patient prevails against the defendant/physician). The records would suggest that pain was not seriously regarded (no SOAP notes concerning the symptom of pain, for example, so as to track the progression of analgesia) and that there was no plan (consultation with another physician, for example) if the pain was not relieved. Our medical colleagues also questioned the lack of responsibility assigned to the patient ("Why wait until the patient is dead, then retrospectively go after his physician? If the patient was dissatisfied with his pain treatment, why didn't he pick up the phone and make an appointment with another physician?"). Mr. Bergman was 87 years old, and the generational difference between the elder and the younger patients may well have a great deal to do with whether one confronts the physician (one of the results of JCAHO's mandates for pain management has been an empowering of patients to seek their "right" to the relief of pain) regarding failure to relieve pain. The family, on behalf of Mr. Bergman, did seek improved analgesia, but evidence that the patient did so on his own behalf is sparse.

Shortly after the verdict in the *Bergman* case, the state of California passed legislation requiring all physicians wishing to obtain or renew a license to practice medicine to document 12 credit hours of CME in end-of-life and pain management issues. More states are expected to follow California's lead.

A Michigan surgeon now faces felony charges for treatment choices he made for three nursing home patients. He is the first physician to be criminally charged under a 4-year-old law designed to protect senior citizens against elder abuse. Under that law,[31] a person is vulnerable for adult abuse in the second degree if he performs a reckless act or a reckless failure to act that causes a vulnerable adult to suffer serious mental and/or physical harm. Conviction can result in 4 years in prison and/or a $5000 fine on each count. The case

revolves around debridement of chronic wounds and, according to a quote from Michigan's newly elected governor, Jennifer M. Granholm (when she was Michigan's Attorney General and brought the charges), the patients to whom the debridements were done had agonizing pain and "The physician's oath is a sacred promise to care for patients, never to add to their suffering."[32] Again, it is a clinician's lack of regard for a patient's pain and/or a lack of communication about pain management efforts with the patient and family members that is now emerging as a considerable source of liability both from a malpractice and a criminal standpoint.

THE FUTURE OF PAIN MANAGEMENT

"The overuse of opioids for any and all pain by any and all practitioners is finally being challenged, and the pendulum has swung back to a more moderate position."[33] In the use of opioids for moderate to severe ATC pain treatment, three things will continue to advance toward efficacious analgesia with the least deleterious side effects: (1) The use and titration of NSAIDs for their antiinflammatory effects *before* prescribing opioids; (2) the identification of patients who historically know euphoria in their everyday lives and are thus more vulnerable to peaks of opioid with prn treatment; and (3) the use of constant dosing to avoid the harmful effects that prn dosing may cause.

Led by pharmaceutical companies' search for beneficial and profitable new drugs, the neurosciences will continue to advance; as our understanding of the pathways for pain perception improve, we may even see the imminent possibility of genotyping patients' opioid receptors and then designing the individual's pain management "cocktails" based on this information.

Advance testing of patients on opioids so as to track their compliance with prescribed regimens may well reduce abuse and diversion. CQ Monitoring is the trademark tool of a company called U.D. Testing. It is a prescription monitoring, management, and reporting system proven helpful in follow-up for patients at higher than normal risk of addiction, abuse, or diversion.

Education for all health care professionals and prosecuting attorneys who work in drug enforcement is paramount for the continued improvement in quality of life for patients who suffer chronic pain. The schools must incorporate this education into their curriculums and must insist upon certain levels of expertise (in pain management) prior to graduation with a degree in any kind of patient care.

Outcomes-based research is crucial for the advance of protocols for pain management, as the results of these studies will "objectify" pain treatment for many clinicians. Outcomes research in the realm of chronic pain relief is hampered by our ignorance about the pathways by which one develops chronic pain, but we must focus on the environment in which the chronic pain sufferer works and plays; we must also focus on making the chronic pain patient their own manager/partner in their treatment. As clinicians we must continue to fight for multidisciplinary pain treatment reimbursement, convincing the third-party payers that such care is markedly cost-effective in the long, if not the very short, run.

We have come a long way toward efficacious pain treatment throughout our nation; the road ahead will only get brighter for those whose quality of life is decreased because of pain.

ENDNOTES

1. L.J. Dunegan, *The Handbook of Pain Management*, 2d ed. (2002), available at www.A2pain.com.

2. NIH Institute of Neurological Diseases.

3. R. Bernabi et al., *Management of Pain in Elderly Patients with Cancer*, 279 J.A.M.A. 1930 (1998).

4. www.jcaho.org/standard/pm_frm.html.

5. Dunegan, *supra* note 1.

6. J.L. Dahl & D.B. Gordan, *Joint Commission Pain Standards: A Progress Report*, APS Bulletin (Nov./Dec. 2002) at 1, 11.

7. *The Michigan Physician Guide to End-of-Life Care* (2001) at 19.

8. D. Carr, S. Chao, R. Polomano & J. Schaffer, *Restricting Dosage or Availability of OTC Analgesica: A Model for Analysis*, APS Bulletin, (Sept./Oct. 2002).

9. S.J. Landers, *Labels on Common OTC Pain Remedies to Include Heightened Risks*, American Medical News (Oct. 14, 2002) at 25.

10. R.B. Supernaw, *Pain Management: Important Principles in the Drug Management of Pain*, Hospital Physician 45-52 (Aug. 2002).

11. S. Bolesta & S.L. Haber, *Hepatotoxicity Associated with Chronic Acetaminophen Administration in Patients Without Risk Factors*, 36 Annals of Pharmacotherapy 331-33 (2002).

12. C.H. Hennekens, *Update on Aspirin in the Treatment and Prevention of Cardiovascular Disease*, A supplement to Resident and Staff Physician (Dec. 2002).

13. F.E. Silverstein et al., *Gastrointestinal Toxicity with Celecoxib vs. Non-steroidal Anti-inflammatory Drugs for Osteoarthritis and Rheumatoid Arthritis. The Class Study: A Randomized Controlled Trial*, 284 J.A.M.A. 1247-55 (2000).

14. A. Whelton, J.G. Fort, J.A. Puma, et al., *Cyclooxygenase-2-Specific Inhibitors and Cardiorenal Function: A Randomized, Controlled Trial of Celecoxib and Rofecoxib in Older Hypertensive Osteoarthritis Patients*, 8(2) American Journal of Therapeutics, 85-95 (2001).

15. F. Camu, T. Beecher, D.P. Recker & K.M. Verburg, *Valdecoxib, a Cox-2 Specific Inhibitor, is an Efficacious, Opioid-Sparing Analgesic in Patients Undergoing Hip Arthroplasties*, 9(1) American Journal of Therapeutics, 43-51 (2002).

16. *Valdecoxib Receives Positive Opinion in Europe from Committee for Proprietary Medicinal Products*, July 29, 2002 (news release on July 25, 2002, Peapack, N.J., found at: http://www.pharmacia.co.jp/news_e/data/20020729095349.html).

17. R.K. Portenoy, *Opioid Therapy for Chronic Nonmalignant Pain: A Review of the Critical Issues*, 11 J. Pain and Symptom Manage. 203-17 (1996).

18. M. Barakat, *Va. Doctor is the Target of a Federal Oxycontin Probe*, Associated Press (Dec. 2002).

19. T. Albert, *Florida Physician Guilty of Manslaughter*, American Medical News (Mar. 11, 2002).

20. American Medical News (Feb. 25, 2002) at 9.

21. *Oxycontin Lawsuit Dismissed*, American Medical News (Oct. 21, 2002) at 18.

22. A. Robeznieks, *Prosecutor Seeks Physicians' Help in Halting Drug Diversion*, American Medical News (Nov. 18, 2002) at 11, 15.

23. A.L. Wan, B.J.M. (1997).

24. J.L. Dahl, *Focus on Pain: Darvon, A Drug with Dubious Distinction*, Cancer Pain Update (Summer 1998) at 6.

25. P.G. Fine, *Opioid Selection: Plaudits, Pitfalls, and Possibilities*, 2(4) Journal of Pain, 195-96 (2001).

26. N.I. Cherny, *Opioid Analgesics: Comparative Features and Prescribing Guidelines*, 51 Drugs, 713-37 (1996).

27. P. Staats & R. Johnson, *New Perspectives on the Pharmacology of Opioids and Their Use in Chronic Pain* (Dec. 2001).

28. B.A. Chizh, H. Schultz, M. Scheede & W. Englebeerger, *The n-Methyl-d-Aspartate Antagonistic and Opioid Components of d-Methadone Antinociception in the Rat Spinal Cord*, 296 Neuroscience 117-20 (2000).

29. A. Robeznieks (AMNews staff), *Prescription Drug Abuse Deadlier Than Use of Illegal Drugs*, American Medical News (Dec. 2002).

30. B. McCarberg, *Establishing a Pain Service Within Managed Care*, 8(3) APS Bulletin 6-10 (1998).

31. Michigan Penal Code, Ch. 750, Sec. 145N(2).

32. *Doctor Indicted Under Michigan Adult Abuse Law for Recklessness*, American Medical News (Aug. 27, 2002).

33. R.N. Harden, *Chronic Opioid Therapy: Another Reappraisal*, 12(1) APS Bulletin 1, 8 (2002).

Sports Medicine

RICHARD S. GOODMAN, M.D., J.D., F.A.A.O.S., F.C.L.M.

Legal aspects of sports medicine is one of the most dynamic fields in the interphase between law and medicine. *Sports medicine* can be defined as the science or practice of diagnosis, treatment, and prevention of diseases associated with a physical activity that involves exertion, is governed by rules or customs, and is often competitive. Sports medicine is accepted as a medical discipline and a medical subspecialty. Related organizations include the American Society of Sports Medicine and the American Osteopathic Academy of Sports Medicine. Publications include the American, British, and international journals of sports medicine; *Isokinetics and Exercise Science; Journal of Athletic Training; Journal of Biomechanics; Journal of Sports Medicine and Physical Fitness; Journal of Sports Traumatology and Related Research*; and *Medicine and Science in Sports and Exercise*. Other publications, such as the *American Journal of Knee Surgery, Orthopedics, and Orthopedic Review*, routinely cover sports medicine. The *Yearbook of Sports Medicine* abstracts the leading articles in the field.

Laws provide a set of rules to govern those who practice any aspect of medicine that affects participants in a sporting event. Medical law is specific for those who practice medicine that affects sports participants.

This concept—the need for a set of rules to govern medical decisions that affect an athlete—contrasts with the ruling by Judge Cardozo in the famous amusement ride case: "One who takes part in such sport accepts the dangers so far that they are obvious and necessary just as a fencer accepts the risks of a thrust by his antagonist or a spectator at a ball game the chance of contact with the ball."[1]

The courts are now being asked, "What are obvious and necessary risks?" Is the risk of contracting human immunodeficiency virus (HIV) or being exposed to HIV by competing against an opponent who is HIV positive an "obvious and necessary risk," even if it is a small or minimal risk? Is the risk of incurring a catastrophic injury, or the risk of *any* injury, an obvious risk? Is participating in a sport while handicapped or impaired and then being injured an obvious and necessary risk? Can a participant sign away his or her right to sue in response to a catastrophic injury, or to sue for *any* injury, in exchange for the right to participate? Is the risk of a catastrophic injury caused by poor coaching, poor refereeing, or poorly maintained or substandard equipment obvious and necessary?

These questions, as yet unanswered, are the province of legal aspects of sport medicine. Abrasions, bumps, bruises, contusions, and fractures may be considered part of many sports, including contact sports (e.g., football, basketball, soccer) and noncontact sports (e.g., skiing, rollerblading, gymnastics), as well as cheerleading and golf. However, catastrophic injuries, such as death, paraplegia, quadriplegia, permanent brain damage, or HIV infection, are *not* considered part of most sports and are not expected or assumed risks by the average or reasonable participant.[2-8]

One case asked whether schools can be held negligent for substantial injuries during cheerleading practice.[9] The court held that the doctrine of primary assumption of risk, as well as the failure to breach the school's duty to supervise the cheerleader and the signed release by the cheerleader's mother, barred any action.

Medical providers now include any person who acts, appears to be acting, or is assumed to be acting in the role of a health care provider, including but not limited to physicians, chiropractors, trainers, physical therapists, and physician assistants. When a participant in a sport incurs a catastrophic injury or any other injury, a question arises as to the cause of the injury or the level of treatment provided after the injury. On occasion there are reasonable grounds for the injured party to assume that the person providing or appearing to provide health care is knowledgeable in medical care or the need

The author extends his appreciation to Norman Samnick of Strook, Strook, and Levan for his extensive research and for use of his facility in legal aspects of sports medicine.

for medical care. When the care is not provided and results in a catastrophic injury, a growing tendency is to hold the responsible party liable for the lack of care or the improper care.

Among those now being held responsible for these injuries are coaches, supervisors, gym teachers, physical education instructors, trainers, the on-scene or on-call physician, and even the physician who provided the preparticipation athletic physical examination and gave clearance to participate. The providers, as well as the lessors and the maintainers of equipment (including golf carts, which can be proved to be faulty), can also be held responsible as the causal agent for the catastrophic injury.[10,11]

The field of legal aspects of sports medicine is therefore a review of the trend to expand the liability for catastrophic injuries and other injuries sustained by sports participants to those who provide equipment or maintain playing fields as well as those who are practicing sports medicine directly or indirectly. This aspect of sports law—the assignment of responsibility for any of these injuries—focuses on the potential exposure to and limits of liability of the medical and paramedical staffs; the coaching staff and the umpiring, refereeing, or officiating staff; and the suppliers of equipment and playing fields. Their potential liability has now come to the forefront in sports medicine law.

This potential liability of the coaching staff, officials, trainers, and instructors arises from their frequent role as the on-site provider of health care.[12] From a review of the cases cited, the coach is potentially liable if a catastrophic injury can be related to failure of the on-scene supervisor or health provider to do the following:

1. Provide appropriate training instruction.
2. Maintain or purchase safe equipment.
3. Hire or supervise competent and responsible personnel.
4. Give adequate warning to participants concerning dangers inherent in a sport.
5. Provide prompt and proper medical care.
6. Prevent the injured athlete from further competition that could aggravate an injury.

The coach can also be held liable if the injury can be related to the inappropriate matching of athletes with dissimilar physical capabilities and dissimilar skill levels.

Cases in which the failure to properly supervise resulted in severe injuries include the student hit by a golf club because of excessive proximity of another golf student, the wrestler injured by a teammate of much greater skill and weight, and the unpadded football player struck by a teammate's helmet.[13-16] A failure to teach proper technique to avoid injury leaves the instructor at risk. A subsequent injury (e.g., in a football game, to a cheerleader) may be related to the improper technique.[17]

Staff members also have been held responsible for improper use of or failure to insist on proper use of equipment, including golf carts, the design of paths for golf carts,

and installation and maintenance of lightning warning devices. They may also be liable for subsequent injuries.[18]

Another sports medicine issue involves the responsibility for allowing an athlete to participate or the adequacy of the "release" documentation. Releases include parental "permission to participate" for minors, "clearance to participate" by physicians, "permission to allow transportation" for minors, adequacy of preparticipation medical histories and physical examinations, and allowing nonconforming athletes who have a known greater exposure to significant injuries to participate.

These aspects of liability have been tested when they conflict with (1) exculpatory agreements; (2) the concept of the sovereign immunity applied to towns, states, and governmental bodies; and (3) an individual's civil rights. Journals such as the *University of Miami Entertainment and Sports Law Review* and *Entertainment and Sports Law* cover the field of questions regarding the liability of operators or owners (e.g., indoor sports arenas, baseball parks, bowling alleys, skating rinks), proprietors (e.g., racing facilities), and promoters (e.g., boxing contests) for the safety of the patrons.[19-24]

The liability of a physician, coach, trainer, or referee who allows an athlete to participate conflicts with the other aspect of sports law—civil rights. Refusing to allow a participant to enter a sport or continue his or her participation because of the potential for a significant injury can be held as a violation of his or her civil rights or right to continue in the sport.

The legal requirement of sports medicine is to document adequately the participation or lack of participation as well as the prescribed roles of the involved parties. Any person who is a de facto provider of health care to an athlete must have a facility to document the preparticipation process, including the assumption of ordinary risks by the participant or his or her guardian; sufficient preparticipation medical clearance; adequate training in sport safety; proper equipment and playing field; and sufficient umpiring to prevent ordinary, unnecessary trauma.

ENDNOTES

1. *Murphy v. Steeplechase Amusement Co.*, 250 N.Y. 479, 482 (1929).
2. M.J. Mitten, *Amateur Athletes with Handicaps or Physical Abnormalities: Who Makes the Participation Decision?*, 71 N.E.B.L. Rev. 987 (1992).
3. D.M. Weber, *When the "Magic" Rubs Off: The Legal Implications of AIDS in Professional Sports*, 2 Sports Law 1 (1995).
4. C.J. Jones, *College Athletes: Illness or Injury and the Decision to Return to Play*, 40 Buff. L. Rev. 113 (1992).
5. P.M. Anderson, *Cautious Defense: Should I Be Afraid To Guard You? (Mandatory AIDS Testing in Professional Team Sports)*, 5 Marq. Sports L. J. 279 (1995).
6. T.E. George, *Secondary Break: Dealing with AIDS in Professional Sports After the Initial Response to Magic Johnson*, U. Miami Ent. & Sports L. Rev. 215 (1992).
7. J.L. Johnston, *Is Mandatory HIV Testing of Professional Athletes Really the Solution?*, 4 Health Matrix 159 (1994).

8. M.J. Mitten, *Aid-Athletes*, 2 Seaton Hall J. Sports L. 5 (1993).

9. *AARIS v. Las Virgenes Unified School Dist.*, 75 Cal. Rptr. 2d 801.

10. S. Berheim, *Sports: Recreation Injuries. A Seminar for Personal Injury Lawyers, School Attorneys and General Practitioners*, Suffolk Academy of Law (Nov. 1996).

11. M. Flynn, *Cart 54, Where Are You? The Liability of Golf Course Operators for Golf Cart Injuries*, 14 Ent. & Sports L. 127-151.

12. *A Guide to the Legal Liability of Coaches for a Sports Participants Injuries*, 6 Seaton Hall J. Sports L. 1, 7-127 (1996).

13. *Brahatecek v. Millard School District*, 273 N.W. 2d 680 (Neb. 1979).

14. *Stehn v. Bernard MacFadden Food*, C.A. 4398 (M.D. Tenn. (1996) 434 F. 2d 811 (6th Cir. 1970).

15. *Leahy v. School Board of Hernando County*, 450 S.D. 2d 883 (Fla. Dist. Ct. App. 1984).

16. *Massie v. Persson*, 729 S.W. 2d 448 (Ky. Ct. App. 1987).

17. *Woodson v. Irvington Board of Ed.*, Docket ESX-L-56273 (N.J. Super. Ct. Law Div., Jan. 1988).

18. *Supra* note 11; *Baker v. Briarcliff*, 613 N.Y.S. 2d 660 (N.Y. App. Div. 1994).

19. *Uline Ice, Inc. v. Sullivan*, 88 U.S. App. D.C. 104, 187 F. 2d 82.

20. *Neinstein v. Los Angeles Dodgers, Inc.* (2d Dist.), 185 Cal. App. 3d 176.

21. *Ackerman v. Motor Sales and Services Co.*, 217 Minn. 309, 14 N.W. 2d 345.

22. *Thomas v. Studio Amusements, Inc.*, 50 Cal. App. 2d 538, 1223 P. 2d 552.

23. *Hotels El Rancho v. Pray*, 64 Nev. 591, 187 P. 2d 568.

24. *Parmentiere v McGinnis*, 157 Wis. 596, 147 N.W. 1007.

60

Competitive Athletes: Cardiovascular Preparticipation Screening

TIMOTHY E. PATERICK, M.D., J.D., M.B.A., F.C.L.M.
GERALD F. FLETCHER, M.D.
GARY LANE, M.D.
MIKE COOPER, M.D.

Competitive athletes are often viewed as the healthiest members of our society. The unexpected death of an athlete during competition is a tragic event, not only affecting family, friends, and the local community, but also often gaining national media attention. In the past few decades, several high-profile athletes have died during competition, including Olympic volleyball player Flo Hyman in 1986, basketball players Hank Gathers of Loyola Marymount in 1990 and Reggie Lewis of the Boston Celtics in 1993, and Olympic gold medal skater Sergei Grinkov in 1995. One obviously wonders whether these and other sudden deaths in athletes could have been prevented. This discussion will review the definition, epidemiology, and common causes of sudden cardiac death in athletes; the physiological, electrocardiographic, and echocardiographic changes in the normal athlete's heart; and the role of preparticipation screening in preventing cardiac deaths on the athletic field.

DEFINITION

Sudden death is defined as "witnessed or unwitnessed natural death resulting from sudden cardiac arrest occurring unexpectedly within six hours of a previously normal state of health." A competitive athlete is defined as a person who participates in an organized team or individual sport in which regular competition is a component.[1]

EPIDEMIOLOGY

Sudden death in competitive athletes is an exceedingly rare event. This fact, along with the large number of competitive high school and collegiate athletes in the United States, makes estimating the incident of sudden death during competition or training very difficult. There are approximately 8 million competitive high-school-age athletes (grade 9-12), 500,000 collegiate athletes, and 5000 professional athletes in the United States. The prevalence of athletic field deaths is in the range of one in 200,000 to one in 300,000 athletes, with a disproportionate number being males. Sudden death in older athletes is more common, with estimated prevalence being one in 50,000 marathon runners to one in 15,000 joggers.[2] One study evaluated 215,413 marathon runners spanning a cumulative 30-year period, to find four deaths during or immediately after competition. Three of the deaths were due to atherosclerotic coronary artery disease (CAD) and the other to an anomalous left main coronary artery.[3] Another study evaluated a 12-year period of Minnesota high school athletics and calculated that over a 3-year high school career the risk of sudden cardiac death was 1:72,500.[4]

DEMOGRAPHICS

A demographic profile of high-risk athletes has been developed by analyzing several different factors that seem to be found most commonly in athletes who have died during competition. In a systematic review of sudden death on the athletic field from 1985 to 1995, 158 deaths were identified.[5] This study identified 134 athletes who died of cardiac causes who were under 46 years of age. The median age was 17 years and the vast majority of these athletes were male.[6] The most common sports in which an athlete died were football and basketball (68%). Only 24 of these athletes (18%) had prodromal symptoms during the 36 months before their death. The majority of the deaths were due to structural heart diseases, a large proportion of which were congenital. The most common cause of death in this group was hypertrophic cardiomyopathy (HCM), which was more common in Afro-American male athletes than in any other group.

THE ATHLETE'S HEART

There are "normal" changes that occur in the athlete's heart based upon the type of exercise performed. Athletes who are involved in isotonic exercises (running, cycling, or swimming) place an increased volume load on the heart. The increased venous return causes an increased left ventricular end-diastolic diameter, which allows for larger stroke volume and cardiac output. In response to this increased volume demand, the left ventricle thickens in an eccentric fashion so that the mass-to-volume ratio is unchanged. The other type of myocardial adaptation that occurs is seen in weightlifters, shot-putters, and other athletes who participate in resistance and isometric exercise. Left ventricular wall thickness increases because of the pressure demand placed on it by brief increases in systemic blood pressure. The myocardium hypertrophies in a concentric fashion so that the mass-to-volume ratio increases. The symmetric quality of myocardial hypertrophy and reversibility with deconditioning distinguish the athletic heart from HCM.[7]

Several ECG changes can be seen in the athletes, with the majority being secondary to increased vagal tone, reduced sympathetic tone, and physiological hypertrophy.[1] Changes due to increased resting vagal tone include sinus bradycardia, first-degree atrioventricular (AV) block, Mobitz I AV block, and junctional rhythms, all occurring more frequently in well-trained athletes. Changes secondary to physiological hypertrophy include increased P-wave amplitude, increased QRS voltage, and early repolarization (J-point elevation). The finding of increased QRS voltage, manifesting as left ventricular hypertrophy (LVH) or right ventricular hypertrophy (RVH), is present in up to 80% of well-conditioned athletes.[7] This should be considered a normal variant in normotensive, asymptomatic patients with a normal cardiac examination.

The main echocardiographic finding in athletes is an increased left ventricular (LV) mass index. Athletes who participate in aerobic activities also may exhibit an increased LV end-diastolic volume. LVH in an athlete can

be reversed with deconditioning as early as 1 week after cessation of exercise. In contrast, LVH that persists after deconditioning may indicate pathological hypertrophy.[1] Again, the two echocardiographic "red flags" that may indicate abnormal pathology are asymmetric hypertrophy and persistence of hypertrophy after deconditioning.

CAUSES OF SUDDEN DEATH IN ATHLETES

The most frequent cause of sudden death in athletes depends greatly upon the age of the athlete. The vast majority of deaths in athletes older than 35 years of age are due to atherosclerotic coronary artery disease.[8] To the contrary, sudden cardiac death in young athletes (<35 years old) is almost always due to congenital cardiac abnormalities. While these conditions may occur fairly frequently in young athletes dying suddenly, they are extremely uncommon in the general population.[8] These congenital abnormalities include HCM, anomalous coronary arteries, idiopathic LVH, aortic dissection, myocarditis, aortic stenosis, and cardiac conduction diseases.

Younger athletes

Hypertrophic cardiomyopathy. HCM is the most common cause of sudden cardiac death in young persons, including athletes. Its prevalence is estimated at 1:500 persons.[9] In a study of 134 athletes who died of sudden cardiac death during competition from 1985 through 1995, 48 (36%) had probable or definite evidence of HCM.[5] HCM is an autosomal dominant inherited disease, in which the left ventricle is asymmetrically hypertrophied in the absence of other causes of left ventricular hypertrophy. Pathological features include distorted cellular architecture of the myocardium and an increased number of intramural coronary arteries with thick walls and narrowed lumen.[9]

Symptoms that may be seen in HCM are chest pain, dyspnea, light-headedness, and syncope. However, most athletes who die exhibit no prodromal symptoms or functional limitations prior to death.[9] The cause of death in these patients is thought to be malignant ventricular arrhythmias. Physical exam findings in a teen with the obstructive form of HCM include a loud systolic murmur (that increases with maneuvers that decrease preload, such as Valsalva), a fourth heart sound, and a brisk carotid upstroke. The diagnosis of HCM is confirmed by echocardiography where the hallmark is disproportionate thickening of the ventricular septum.

Congenital coronary artery anomalies. Congenital coronary artery anomalies unassociated with atherosclerosis are frequently associated with sudden death in young athletes. Congenital coronary artery abnormalities accounted for the death of 34 (25%) athletes in one review, with an anomalous origin of the left main coronary artery from the right sinus of Valsalva being the most common anomaly.[5] In a group of children who were prospectively studied with two-dimensional echocardiography, a prevalence of 0.17% (4:2388) was determined.[10] Unfortunately, this coronary malformation is usually not identified until autopsy. Of patients with this disease, 75% die before age 20 and the vast majority of these deaths occur during physical exertion.[9] People with anomalous coronaries may experience syncope or angina. Because of the lack of physical findings, the clinician must have a high index of suspicion in athletes with these symptoms. One postulated mechanism of ischemia in these patients is that the anomalous coronary artery contains a slit-like ostium that narrows with aortic dilation during exercise.[7] Echocardiography can be used to demonstrate the origin of the left main coronary artery and sometimes the right coronary artery. If identified, these anomalies are surgically correctable.

Idiopathic left ventricular hypertrophy. Idiopathic LVH accounts for approximately 10% of all sudden death in young athletes.[1] This disease exhibits increased cardiac mass without the myocardial fiber disarray seen in HCM. Other distinguishing factors in idiopathic LVH include a symmetric pattern of hypertrophy and the absence of a family history of SDS.[9] Despite these distinguishing factors, idiopathic LVH and HCM may be part of the same broad disease spectrum.

Aortic dissection and rupture. Aortic dissection and rupture can lead to sudden cardiac death with or without cardiac tamponade. In young athletes, this is most commonly associated with a weakened aortic wall seen in Marfan's syndrome. This weakness is caused by cystic necrosis of the aortic media.[1] The physical stigmata of Marfan's syndrome include arachnodactyly, scoliosis, lens dislocation, myopia, elevated hard palate, wingspan greater than height, anterior chest wall defects, and hyperextensible joints. Thoracic aortic aneurysmal dilation, if large enough, can be seen on plain chest radiography.

Myocarditis. Myocarditis is an inflammatory disease of the myocardium that is most commonly viral in nature. Cocksackie B virus is the causative organism in greater than 50% of cases.[7] Characteristic symptoms include decreased exercise tolerance, dyspnea, cough, and orthopnea, preceded by a prodromal illness. Athletes with myocarditis may die with active or healed disease, and therefore should be withheld from athletic competition for at least 6 months after this diagnosis is made.[11]

Aortic stenosis. Aortic stenosis (AS) in young people results from a congenital bicuspid aortic valve. Symptoms are the same as seen in adults with AS: angina, dyspnea, and syncope. This is a cause of sudden cardiac death that should be easily identified by physical examination. Physical exam findings in a teen include a harsh systolic ejection murmur at the base of the heart with a delayed and slow carotid upstroke. The murmur of AS can be distinguished from HCM because it decreases with maneuvers that decrease preload, whereas the murmur of HCM is accentu-ated by these maneuvers. Aortic stenosis can be confirmed by echocardiography, and cardiac catheterization may be necessary to distinguish moderate from severe disease.[1]

Ion channel diseases. Ion channel diseases including Wolff-Parkinson-White syndrome (WPW) and prolonged QT syndrome can also lead to sudden cardiac death. WPW is present in approximately 1:500 people and increases the risk of sudden death in an athlete.[7] Symptoms include palpitations, light-headedness, and syncope. Electrocardiography shows a short PR interval, the presence of delta waves, and a wide QRS complex. Sudden death occurs from the development of atrial fibrillation, which can deteriorate into ventricular fibrillation in some of these patients.

Long QT syndrome. Long QT syndrome involves prolonged ventricular repolarization and can lead to polymorphic ventricular tachycardia (torsades de pointes). It can be either congenital or acquired (secondary to metabolic causes, i.e., medications or electrolyte abnormalities such as hypocalcemia, hypokalemia, or hypomagnesemia). Athletes with a familial prolonged QT syndrome may have a family history of sudden death. When a prolonged QT interval syndrome is diagnosed, the athlete should be restricted from competitive sports.

Other causes of sudden cardiac death in young people that should be mentioned include mitral valve prolapse, premature CAD, dilated cardiomyopathy, and arrythmogenic right ventricular dysplasia.

Older athletes

While structural and congenital heart diseases constitute the majority of sudden cardiac deaths in young athletes, atherosclerotic CAD accounts for the majority of deaths (80%) during competition in older athletes.[12] In contrast to the previously discussed entities, over half of these athletes have prodromal symptoms or known CAD. While regular exercise is known to decrease risk of cardiac events, vigorous physical activity does transiently increase the risk of myocardial infarction and cardiac arrest.[2] Despite this transiently increased risk, the protection that regular exercise provides is demonstrated by comparing the relative risk of death during exercise in sedentary people (10.7) versus the relative risk of death in people who exercise five times per week (2.4).[12]

SCREENING

The issue of preparticipation screening elucidates several important points regarding the group of cardiac diseases responsible for most of the sudden deaths in young athletes. First, medical history is limited by the fact that most athletes who die during competition have no prodromal symptoms or physical limitations. Physical exam in a teen is limited because many of these diseases are clinically silent; however, congenital AS, the obstructive form of HCM, and Marfan's syndrome should be detectable. An extensive review of 134 athletic field deaths demonstrates the shortcomings of preparticipation history and physical exam in a teen. Of the 115 athletes who were exposed to standard screening exams, fewer than 5% were suspected of having cardiovascular disease and less than 1% were accurately diagnosed.[5]

The routine use of noninvasive tests in young athletes is not recommended based on issues of cost and practicality.[2] For example, the cost of screening echocardiography can be estimated as follows: given a cost of $500 per test, and a prevalence of HCM of 1:500 (the most common cause of sudden cardiac death in young people), it would cost $250,000 to detect one case of previously undiagnosed disease.[2]

Guidelines from the American Heart Association (AHA) and the American College of Cardiology (ACC) recommend that all high school and college athletes undergo a complete history and physical exam in a teen prior to participation. Cardiac history should include a history of chest pain, dyspnea, palpitations, light-headedness, and syncope. Cardiovascular physical exam in a teen should include blood pressure measurement, evaluation of the carotid pulse, radial-femoral pulse evaluation for delay (aortic coarctation), and cardiac auscultation performed with maneuvers to distinguish benign from pathological murmurs.[1]

Despite the inherent limitation of screening in prevention of sudden cardiac death, a full history and physical exam in a teen should be performed on both young and old athletes. Older athletes with significant risk factors for atherosclerotic CAD or suggestive symptoms should undergo further testing for occult CAD before undergoing vigorous exercise programs.[2] Diagnosing one case of HCM or AS in a young athlete or significant CAD in an older athlete could make a huge impact by potentially preventing the death of an athlete.

THE FIDUCIARY RESPONSE

The law of agency attaches certain duties of performance to the agent (physician). First, the agent (physician) is responsible to the principal (patient) as a fiduciary.[13] A fiduciary duty arises out of a relationship of trust and confidence. The law provides for such a relationship between a physician and patient.

There is a general consensus that within a benevolent society a responsibility exists by the medical community to initiate prudent efforts to identify life-threatening conditions in athletes to minimize the risk associated with competitive sport.[13,14] There should also be an implicit obligation of educational institutions and professional sports entities to provide cost-effective strategies to ensure that athletes are not subject to unacceptable and unavoidable medical risk.[15] The extent to which preparticipation screening can be supported is mitigated by the elusive nature of the causes of sudden death, and by cost-efficiency given the prevalence, number of participants, and the cost of extensive evaluation. It is important to acknowledge the

limitations of preparticipation screening. An informed public that understands the elusive etiologies of sudden death, the low prevalence of the etiologies, the large number of participants, and the cost limitations will not harbor misconceptions regarding the efficacy of athletic screening. There must be a public awareness that it is not possible to achieve zero-risk circumstances when screening competitive athletes.

There are no universally accepted standards for screening of competitive athletes. There are no certification procedures for the health care professionals who perform screening examinations.[2] Some forms of medical clearance by a physician or a trained health care professional usually consist of the history and physical exam. This appears most customary for high school and college athletes. There is no uniform agreement among the states as to the precise format of the preparticipation medical evaluation. Some states do not require the process and some do not have a recommended standard medical form.[2] In the absence of binding requirements established by state law of athletic governing bodies, most teams and institutions relay on the team physician to determine the appropriate medical screening process.

Preparticipation screening by history and physical exam in a teen does not have sufficient power to guarantee protection against many critical cardiovascular abnormalities in a large population of young competitive athletes. This fact reinforces the need for awareness by the public that it is not possible to achieve a zero-risk circumstance in competitive sports through preparticipation screening efforts. The support for low expectations of standard screening is provided by an awareness of the elusive nature of the diagnostic etiologies, the low prevalence of these etiologies, and the cost limitations in trying to define etiologies in a large number of athletes where the prevalence is low. The most common etiology of sudden death in young athletes is HCM. Detection of HCM by standard screening history and physical is unreliable because most patients have the nonobstructive form, which characteristically has a soft murmur.

THE HISTORY AND PHYSICAL EXAMINATION

In general, the most important aspect of the complete cardiovascular examination is the history (Table 60-1). In the case of the competitive athlete at risk of sudden death, the history is often unrevealing. The physical exam in a teen, particularly auscultation, is most likely to provide a clue that cardiovascular structural abnormality is present (Table 60-2). The most common cause of sudden death in competitive athletes is HCM. The auscultatory findings often include a rapid rise in the arterial pulse, a soft systolic murmur that is accentuated on standing and becomes fainter with squatting. There may be an S-4 and a presystolic movement with palpation. The findings of pulsus alternans or gallop rhythm

TABLE 60-1 History

1. Family history of sudden death.
2. Family history of congenital heart disease: explore HCM, DCM, Marfan's syndrome, long QT syndrome.
3. Morbidity from CV disease in relatives < 50.
4. Personal history of hypertension, heart murmur, exertional chest pain/pressure, SOB, irregular rhythm or syncope.

TABLE 60-2 Physical exam

1. HCM: rapid rise in arterial pulse, soft systolic murmur accentuated with standing and fainter with squatting.
2. Myocarditis: pulsus arternans and gallop rhythm.
3. DCM: gallop rhythm, displaced PMI, and pulsus alternans.
4. Bicuspid aortic valve: early to mid-systolic murmur with early ejection sound.
5. Marfan's syndrome: diastolic murmur, systolic ejection sounds, systolic murmur, and accentuated A_2.
6. MVP: systolic click and MR murmur.

should raise the issue of myocarditis. The finding of gallop rhythm, pulsus alternans, and displaced point of maximal impulse should suggest cardiomyopathy. An early to mid-systolic murmur of harsh quality with an ejection sound in early systole suggests bicuspid aortic valve and congenital AS. The physical appearance of the tall, thin, and long arm span, long supple fingers and joints, high arched pallet, and "thick glasses" should make Marfan's syndrome a consideration. Associated auscultatory findings include diastolic murmur, systolic ejection sounds, systolic murmur, and accentuated aortic second sound. Marfan's patients can have mitral rather than aortic valve diseases as the prominent lesion. Blue sclera and brittle bones with a tendency to bone fractures are clues to osteogenesis imperfecta. Systolic click and varying degrees of mitral regurgitation should bring to consideration mitral valve prolapse. Sudden death due to ventricular fibrillation can occur in patients with MVP. Congenital coronary anomalies, right ventricular dysplasia, intramural coronary arteries, long QT syndrome, and primary rhythm disturbances will not be diagnosed by auscultation (Table 60-3). The variability of auscultatory findings often leads to a low sensitivity in detecting the most common causes of sudden death in competitive athletes.

TABLE 60-3 Conditions not diagnosed by auscultation

Congenital coronary anomalies	Normal exam
Right ventricular dysplasia	Normal exam
Intramural coronary arteries	Normal exam
Long QT syndrome	Normal exam
Primary rhythm disturbance	Normal exam

Because athletes must entrust their physical well-being to their physicians to predict the risk of untoward events when involved in competitive sports, the physician-athlete relationship is characterized as fiduciary. This suggests the physician has a legal obligation to act for the athlete's health benefit in connection with medical matters. There is currently little precedent in the forms of statutes or case law to establish the legal duties of a physician providing cardiovascular care.[2] Negligence requires proof that a physician deviated from customary or accepted medical practice in performing preparticipation screening of athletes. Malpractice liability for failure to discover a latent, asymptomatic cardiovascular condition requires proof that a physician deviated from customary medical practice in his or her specialty in performing preparticipation screening of the athlete and that the use of established diagnostic criteria and technique would have disclosed the condition. The medical profession is allowed to establish the appropriate nature and scope of preparticipation screening of athletes based on the exercise of its collective medical judgment.[15] The ACC recommendations for cardiovascular preparticipation eligibility of athletes, described in the 26th Bethesda Conference, represent a consensus panel of recommendations.[6] These guidelines could establish a legal standard of care if generally accepted and customarily followed by physicians.

AHA RECOMMENDATIONS

The 1996 AHA consensus panel recommendation states that some form of preparticipation in cardiovascular screening for high school and college student athletes is justified based on ethical, legal, and medical rationale.[2] It is believed that noninvasive testing can improve the diagnostic power of the standard history and physical. The panel does not recommend the routine use of noninvasive testing for the detection of cardiovascular disease in large population of athletes with low prevalence of disease. This recommendation is based upon low yield and cost considerations. The issue of many false-positive results adds further support. Such results could lead to psychological stress and unjustified exclusion from competition. This argument is predicated upon the fact that the low incidence of disease will yield more false positive than true positive results.

The standard is a complete personal and family history and physical exam in a teen designed to identify those cardiovascular lesions known to cause sudden death in a competitive athlete. Such cardiovascular screening is an attainable objective and appears to represent the customary standard of care. The cardiovascular histories include key questions to determine prior exertional chest pressure, dyspnea, or syncope. There should be recognition of prior heart murmur and hypertension. There should be an assessment of premature death in relatives, and morbidity from cardiovascular disease in relatives less than 50 years of age. Current cardiovascular conditions in family members such as

HCM, dilated cardiomyopathy, Marfan's syndrome, long QT syndrome, and life-threatening arrhythmias should be documented. In-depth questioning is mandatory in the search for details of specific conditions. The physical exams in a teen should emphasize auscultation and palpation of the arterial pulse to exclude HCM, assessment of brachial femoral pulses to exclude coarctation, recognition of the physical stigmata of Marfan's syndrome, and assessment of arterial blood pressure.

CONCLUSION

Exercise-related sudden death in competitive athletes is a major American tragedy usually due to a variety of unsuspected cardiovascular disease conditions. The low prevalence of the cardiovascular conditions causing sudden death and the extreme limitations in diagnosing many of the causes of sudden death through the history and physical reflect the limitations of preparticipation screening of competitive athletes. It is clear after careful analysis of the causes of sudden death in competitive athletes that many of these causes cannot be detected by preparticipation screening even if an extensive evaluation is conducted. Accepting these limitations, it is of utmost importance that the "screener" understand the clues from the history and physical that allow suspicion of HCM, dilated cardiomyopathy, myocarditis, aortic stenosis, mitral valve prolapse, coronary disease, and Marfan's syndrome.

The large number of competitive athletes and the low prevalence of the diseases causing sudden death leave any screening strategy with limited power. There must be a public awareness that it is impossible to achieve a zero-risk circumstance when screening competitive athletes. Despite the limitations in screening, the AHA guidelines define what should be the customary practice in screening athletes.[2] Close adherence to these guidelines should allow physicians to maintain fiduciary duty to the competitive athlete. These guidelines suggest that the standard of care should include a complete personal and family history and a physical exam in a teen designed to identify the cardiovascular lesions known to cause sudden death in athletes. The guidelines recognized the extreme limitations of the history and physical in preparticipation screening.

ENDNOTES

1. F.C. Basilico, *Cardiovascular Disease in Athletes*, 27 Am. J. Sports Med. 108-21 (1999).
2. B.J. Maron, P.D. Thompson, J.C. Putten, et al., *Cardiovascular Preparticipation Screening of Competitive Athletes. A Statement for Health Professionals from the Sudden Death Committee (Clinical Cardiology) and Congenital Cardiac Defects Committee (Cardiovascular Disease in the Young), American Heart Association*, 94 Circulation 850-56 (1996).
3. B.J. Maron, L.C. Poliac & W.O. Roberts, *Risk for Sudden Cardiac Death Associated with Marathon Running*, 28 J. Am. Coll. Cardiol. 428-31 (1996).
4. B.J. Maron, T.E. Gohman, & D. Aeppli, *Prevalence of Sudden Cardiac Death During Competitive Sports Activities in Minnesota High School Athletes*, 32 J. Am. Coll. Cardiol. 1881-84 (1998).
5. B.J. Maron, J. Shirani, L.C. Poliac, et al., *Sudden Death in Young Competitive Athletes: Clinical, Demographic, and Pathological Profiles*, 276 J.A.M.A. 199-204 (1996).
6. P.D. Thompson, F.J. Klocke, B.D. Levine, et al., *26th Bethesda Conference: Recommendations for Determining Eligibility for Competition in Athletes with Cardiovascular Abnormalities. Task Force 5: Coronary Artery Disease*, 24 J. Am. Coll. Cardiol. 888-92 (1994).
7. J.A. Drezner, *Sudden Cardiac Death in Young Athletes: Causes, Athlete's Heart, and Screening Guidelines*, 108 Postgrad. Med. 37-50 (2000).
8. B.J. Maron, *Risk Profiles and Cardiovascular Preparticipation Screening of Competitive Athletes*, 15 Cardiol. Clin. 473-83 (1997).
9. B.J. Maron, *Triggers for Sudden Cardiac Death in the Athlete*, 14 Cardiol. Clin. 195-210 (1996).
10. J.A. Davis, F. Cecchin, T.K. Jones, et al., *Major Coronary Artery Anomalies in a Pediatric Population: Incidence and Clinical Importance*, 37 J. Am. Coll. Cardiol. 593-97 (2001).
11. B.J. Maron, J.M. Isner & W.J. McKenna, *26th Bethesda Conference: Recommendations for Determining Eligibility for Competition in Athletes with Cardiovascular Abnormalities. Task Force 3: Hypertrophic Cardiomyopathy, Myocarditis and Other Myopericardial Diseases and Mitral Valve Prolapse*, 24 J. Am. Coll. Cardiol. 880-85 (1994).
12. J.N. Wight, Jr. & D. Salem, *Sudden Cardiac Death and the "Athlete's Heart,"* 155 Arch. Intern. Med. 1473-80 (1995).
13. See Restatement (Second) of the Law, Agency §13.
14. A. Pelliccia & B.J. Maron, *Pre-participation Cardiovascular Evaluation of the Competitive Athlete: Perspective from the 30 Year Italian Experience*, 75 Am. J. Cardiol. 827-31 (1995).
15. B.J. Maron, R.W. Brown, C.A. McGraw, et al., *Ethical, Legal, and Practical Considerations Affecting Medical Decision Making in Competitive Athletes*, in B.J. Maron & J.H. Mitchell, eds., *Recommendations for Determining Eligibility for Competition in Athletes with Cardiovascular Abnormalities: 26th Bethesda Conference*, 24 J. Am. Coll. Cardiol. 854-60 (1994).

61

Impairment, Disability, and Work Issues

E. LYLE GROSS, M.D.

DEFINITION OF IMPAIRMENT AND DISABILITY
COMMUNITY LIMITATION IN ASSESSING IMPAIRMENT AND DISABILITY
SOURCES OF IMPAIRMENT AND DISABILITY REQUESTS
QUANTIFICATION OF CHRONIC PAIN (IS THERE IMPAIRMENT?)
THE MEDICAL LEGAL REPORT
IMPAIRMENT, DISABILITY, AND SCIENTIFIC EVIDENCE
CONCLUSION

Impairment ratings and disability determination are critical elements of any medical legal practice. In a medical legal practice, impairment and disability also carry a slightly different meaning than the definition given by the World Health Organization. Impairment ratings are used to determine the financial damages to be awarded to an individual who has suffered measurable physical or psychological loss following injury. The monetary award given may therefore result in conflict, particularly regarding the degree of loss. This places significant stress on the clinical system of evaluation and establishes the grounds for an adversarial system.

In contrast to impairment, disability is a description of ability or inability of an individual to function, preferably at their expected level of function. When patients fail to reach their expected level of function, clinicians consider numerous factors contributing to the state of disability. There are as many as 20 factors contributing to the disabled state, and these will be discussed in detail.

Impairment is also not as straightforward as describing the objective loss on clinical examination. Physicians of differing specialty and training see physical and psychological loss differently.

The tools of measurement (such as the goniometer or inclinometer in assessing joint motion) may also leave room for a variety of opinions. The simple standardized measurement of joint range of motion can vary as much as 10 to 30 degrees from one examiner to another. Accuracy in the medical legal field is paramount, and significant effort, time, and money is directed to documenting the most consistent opinion possible for both impairment and disability. Once the impairment rating has been calculated and disability determined, the loss is extrapolated to a monetary figure. This monetary conversion is completed using a number of standardized guides that are set by the respective state or jurisdiction, such as in worker's compensation injury and state guides or tort where the American Medical Association *Guides to the Evaluation of Permanent Impairment* provide guides to extrapolate the objective clinical findings into a percentage of the whole person. This number is then used in a preset formula to calculate the monetary award to the patient. Some medical conditions are not easily translated. Soft tissue injuries and arthritis are two examples of clinical conditions that vary depending on the examiner, the timing of the examination (even during the day when one has "warmed up their muscles," for example), and method of measurement, and, as a result, controversy may exist creating an adversarial setting.

Causation is another important term and this can also be the subject of confusion, especially in conditions such as fibromyalgia, chronic fatigue, and even debilitating back pain.

The intellectual debate around the determination of impairment, disability, and causation of loss is normally contained behind the protective medical scenes with only glimpses observed by the lay community. The medical legal field, however, exposes this normal exchange of ideas, leaving the impression that the field of determining loss is confusing and inaccurate. This is particularly stressful to the clinical examiner given the need for an exact science.

The information gathered from the medical legal examination is also used to determine available vocational options. If dispute exists regarding the impairment rating, then this dispute can trickle down to the vocational inventory (or in other words, what actual work a person can or cannot complete based on many factors, including impairment disability, job interest, educational level, and experience). The transparency of a medical legal practice results in a very public process where patients and laypersons may observe the assessment and interpretive stresses facing the clinical community.

In the context of the worker's compensation system, impairment may be extrapolated into dollars as remuneration for measurable loss following the accident, and in a tort system, which follows common law principles, dollars are calculated from the figures given by clinicians and as a result the characteristic adversarial nature of the medical legal discipline sets it apart from the traditional practice of medicine.

In order to minimize the potential conflict and perceived disarray that can arise following dispute of the information gathered by and recorded by clinicians, we have established a common terminology aimed at lessening the confusion with respect to the needs of the third party. A number of other factors have been set forth to try to optimize the communication and minimize conflict potential for the divergent fields of medicine, insurance, law, unions, associations, employers, and others.

While medicine strives to improve on the accuracy and consistency of the diagnosis (the medical test), any claim for damages must also pass the legal test before "loss" is accepted by the parties responsible for disbursement of monetary awards. The legal test defines the policy or regulations concerning the responsibility of the third party to the injured party. The independent medical examination (IME) is discussed in detail elsewhere, and for the purpose of this chapter, this examination is intended to clarify conflicting medical information as it pertains to residual impairment, disability, features of causation, and costs associated with future care. The institution of the IME, however, is fraught with controversy, and a lot has been written on the standards of the ethical medical legal report.

Many steps have been taken to optimize information exchange and to ensure accuracy of information transfer before drawing in the IME. Positive steps have attempted to create a level of fairness and accuracy for the patient and the referring client alike.

Among the vehicles to improve medical legal information exchange are:

1. Clear understanding of medical legal terminology.
2. Clear definition of the third-party policy.
3. Continued educational exchange through workshops and conferences.
4. Establishment of independent bodies for quality assurance of the independent medical examination, qualified rehabilitation consultant, and others providing medical legal reporting.
5. Establishment of recovery guidelines (evidenced-based medicine).
6. Be aware of *Daubert* and other court decisions that guide us in establishing which facts to and from whom should be accepted.
7. Standardize guidelines for the extrapolation of impairment into quantifiable terms (such as the American

Medical Association's *Guides to the Evaluation of Permanent Impairment*).
8. When providing an opinion, stay within one's field of expertise.

The factors that will result in conflict include:

1. The very nature of medicine and law results in divergent principles and practices and may even place the clinician in an unethical position (for example, in law the principle of privileged information contradicts all of medicine's commitment to shared information).
2. The often nebulous or cloudy nature of many medical conditions. Even today, medicine has a diagnostic test for only about 40% of all medical conditions.
3. The fact that dollars may be the core emphasis rather than a functional endpoint.
4. The independent medical examination may not be as independent as it seems.

This chapter focuses on the factors that optimize and those that may compromise our understanding and application of impairment and disability.

DEFINITION OF IMPAIRMENT AND DISABILITY

Impairment is defined as the measurable loss that exists at the end of the period of healing; however, this may or may not represent the maximal functional recovery. Impairment is objective and represents both the psychological and residual physical loss. Impairment is determined by a sole clinician (often a physician) and in the confines of an office. Radiological findings, laboratory tests, and other tools of investigation support the clinical impression in determining impairment. The determination of impairment requires that each physiological and anatomical system be considered individually. The AMA *Guides to the Evaluation of Permanent Impairment* have provided clinicians with a very useful tool to approach loss and document it in measurable terms (Tables 61-1 and 61-2).

Disability is defined by those factors contributing to an individual's inability to return to the expected (as expected by the patient's clinicians) maximal level function. The determination of disability is a comprehensive one and the disability profile lists the causative factors responsible for the failure to reach the expected level of function. It is the expected level of function that presents the complicating features of this state. The disability profile includes the following factors:

1. Time greater than 90 days. Time has been found to have a direct correlation to return to work following injury or illness. Most injured and ill (about 80%) return to work within 90 days. The success in return to work as time progresses is proportionally related, and if the patient fails to return to work by 2 years, then the return to work rate is 0% unless a comprehensive treatment program is made available.
2. Vocational rehabilitation counselor is assigned.

TABLE 61-1 Examples of impairment based on the 5th edition of the American Medical Association *Guides to the Evaluation of Permanent Impairment*

System	Examination
Musculoskeletal system	Joint range of motion, stability, strength, alignment, DJD, amputation, muscle spasm
Nervous system	Dermatome/peripheral distribution, strength, reflex loss, CNS loss (cognitive/perceptual loss)
Cardiovascular system	Rhythm, regularity, peripheral sign symptoms, energy expenditure, peripheral vascular disease, valvular dysfunction, peripheral central pressure
Gastrointestinal system	Weight, colon rectal function, upper GI function, liver and biliary tract dysfunction, hernias
Genitourinary system	Upper urinary tract function, neurogenic, myogenic bladder, sexual dysfunction
Psychiatric system	Mental and behavioral change, impact of pain, impact of cosmetic deformity
Integument system	Skin function and dysfunction
Visual system	Visual acuity, visual field
ENT	Speech, hearing, swallowing, allergies, sinus dysfunction
Respiratory system	Dsypnea, FVC, FEV_1 lung bronchial function
Endocrine system	Hypothalamic-pituitary axis, thyroid, parathyroid, adrenal cortex, pancreas, sexual (hormonal) dysfunction, bone density
Hematopoietic system	Anemia and polycythemias, bleeding disorders

TABLE 61-2 Relationship between causation, impairment, and PPD

Causation	Examination findings	Percent whole person impairment (PPD)
Cervical myalgia following vehicular accident	Muscle spasm and loss of 5 to 10 degrees range of motion in each plane	Depending on exact range of motion 5-10% PPD
Back injury from a fall	Lumbar discectomy without residual sensory/motor loss	7% whole person PPD
Trauma to elbow in farming accident	Elbow injury, sensory/motor loss/skin abnormality	Sensory 10% of upper extremity, motor loss 7% of upper extremity, % are combined rather than added (table found at back of book), 16% PPD of UE and convert to whole according to table, 8% whole person, 8% combined with 2% whole (skin loss), 10% whole person PPD

3. Age.
4. Gender.
5. Educational level.
6. Socioeconomic status.
7. Modified return to work programs.
8. Motivation.
9. Cultural features.
10. English as a second language.
11. Multiple medical problems.
12. Job to return to.
13. Past success or failure in rehabilitation.
14. Multiple job-related injuries.
15. Disproportionate patient symptoms for the physical condition.
16. Litigation.
17. Medication overuse.
18. Lack of medical legal familiarity on the part of attending clinicians.
19. Blind advocacy on the part of the clinician.
20. Third-party policy that does not support investing in return to work.

Disability can and does result from any one of these factors; however, no one factor should be considered in isolation. To date, time has been shown to be the only consistent factor that has a direct bearing on successful return to work. There are some disability profile features that have shown strong association but require further in-depth study. These factors include vocational rehabilitation consultant, socioeconomic status, motivation, and modified return to work programs.

The complexity of disability makes it difficult for any one clinician to answer the question, "Is their patient disabled from returning to their job, and if so what can they do?" In order to address the question of whether a patient is disabled and why, all the above profile factors must be considered with equal weighting. There needs to be more research examining the relations and interrelationship of the disability profile factors. Our "system" to date is not well structured to answer the question of how disabled patients are. The most comprehensive environment to answer this is in a hospital rehabilitation setting where the full assessment team exists. The approach to assessing the work injury or loss from a motor vehicle accident is no different from answering the same question for a spinal cord patient, closed head injured, and other classic rehabilitation patients. The classic rehabilitation setting is, however, found in the hospital setting and few free-standing ambulatory rehabilitation centers exist. Currently we rely on a disjunct community health care to answer the question regarding the extent of complex disability such as in the low back pain patient gone awry, the fibromyalgia patient, and the patient with cervical injury from whiplash who fails to return to their welding job (Fig. 61-1).

COMMUNITY LIMITATION IN ASSESSING IMPAIRMENT AND DISABILITY

Impairment

There are few if any limitations in the community retarding the determination of impairment. The limiting factor with accuracy, however, originates with the familiarity of the clinician carrying out a purely objective physical or psychological examination on their patient. The clinical examination is first learned in medical school or specialty

training. Knowledge of the subsequent tests for the normal routine workup to define the measurable loss is acquired as training advances. As a result, the statement of objectives can be carried out with the most basic knowledge base. For example, on musculoskeletal examination, joint range of motion (ROM) is recorded according to goniometric or inclinometer measurement in degrees of range, and the dermatomal or peripheral sensory loss is stated by the patient and recorded based on our knowledge of the anatomy, physiology, and innervation of nerves.

What become challenging (or potentially) is the explanation of conditions that are less clear-cut. Examples of grayer conditions have already been mentioned, but another that illustrates the potential for explanation based on our history, presentation of complaints, and knowledge of anatomy and physiology is thoracic outlet syndrome.

Patients who have suffered a cervical injury from a "whiplash" event (such as in a vehicular accident) will have a

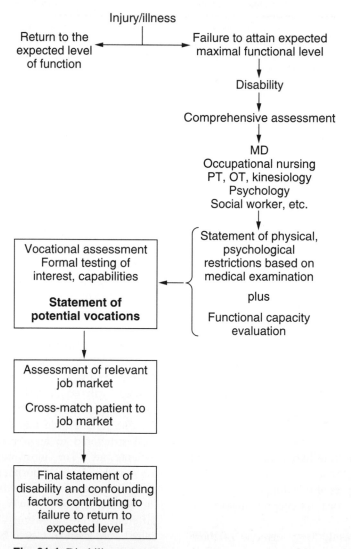

Fig. 61-1. Disability assessment.

history of acceleration and deceleration forces following impact. The initial complaints to the clinician may be neck pain and on examination there may be loss of range of motion and some evidence of muscle spasm. Over time the patient is treated with conservative measures for posttraumatic cervical myalgia and the residual complaints at the end of the period.

In the community at large, the preferred approach to the assessment of disability may not be possible unless an integrated unit exists within the community. Clinicians will, however, be asked by a third party to address impairment and disability in its complete sense. It rests with the clinician to choose the path that can best answer the questions posed. In a clinician's office, most of the factors contributing to disability can be found somewhere in the clinical materials forward. The clinical workup or the demographic material will add detail to the disability profile. The physician's contribution to disability is limited to:

1. A statement of causation regarding injury or illness.
2. A statement of medical risk factors and a statement regarding prognosis of injury or illness.
3. A statement of treatment, investigations, and other clinical matters.
4. The medical opinion should meet the standard of peers.
5. A statement of the medical restrictions based on the injury by any physician (and this is as close as a physician should be to describing a specific job).
6. Finally, a statement of the prognosis can be made.

Limitations on the statement of disability

The complexity of disability requires a comprehensive clinical assessment of the patient and the available services rest outside the physician's office. The cost of a complete assessment is expensive, particularly if completed in the hospital setting, and this can be a significant limitation.

The adversarial nature of the third-party field may retard exchange of information and by definition disability assessment requires complete information. This may therefore compromise the determination of disability. Also, failure by insurers first to recognize the complexity of disability and second to approve treatment may delay the rehabilitative process and the reduction of the ultimate functional level (this may be a case of failure to mitigate).

There may be a poor understanding of what defines disability, and as a result primary clinicians may try to answer all the questions not considering the true nature of disability.

SOURCES OF IMPAIRMENT AND DISABILITY REQUESTS

Worker's compensation

The many jurisdictional variations in the rules and regulations governing worker's compensation extend beyond the focus of this chapter. There is, however, a common thread for all income replacement programs and this lies on the reliance of assessing impairment and disability. Once the objective physical and psychological loss is recorded and the statement of impairment given, worker's compensation will use this information and extrapolate the loss into a percentage impairment as it relates only to work injury.

The AMA guides are the resource most often used to express the loss as a percentage. Some states, however, have developed their own tables and rely on these. The percentage impairment is typically converted into dollars and paid to the injured in keeping with either precedent or legislated formulas. At times the percentage impairment is used to calculate what additional financial support will be given to the injured worker for vocational rehabilitation.

Disability in the worker's compensation may be better understood and funded than any other third-party system because of the emphasis on vocational return. Many work compensation insurers have assessment teams and rehabilitation programs to rehabilitate the worker back to work again. The risk for dispute, however, is greater because most disability is a comprehensive profile that includes work-related loss and non-work-related factors. This is the failing of a system that recognizes "loss of limb" rather than a whole person approach.

Differentiating preexisting or unrelated loss to the stated work-related injury and loss of function is a complex task. It is here that thin skull versus crumbling skull positions are taken. Law also exists to ensure the fair assessment of patients, particularly in light of the difficult issues of health and disease. Separating the human body for purposes of fiduciary obligation with respect to treatment may also be problematic when unrelated work injury medical conditions exist.

Worker's compensation faces many fiscal challenges, and cost-containment strategies are felt at every level of adjudication and approval for treatment. Where impairment is concerned, a cost-containment strategy exists that may be particularly discriminatory. "Up front" cost containment is seen in the approval or denial based on the diagnosis alone. In the AMA *Guides to the Evaluation of Permanent Impairment*, impairment can be determined based on DRE or diagnostic-related evidence. For instance, in some policies fibromyalgia may not be a compensatable condition. The diagnosis of fibromyalgia, however, is in large part medical specialty related. An injured person, for instance, who sustains a neck injury may initially seek out the opinion of a rheumatologist. The diagnosis of fibromyalgia may be made whereas the same clinical condition could be labeled by a physiatrist as posttraumatic cervical myalgia. An orthopedic surgeon may diagnose acceleration-deceleration injury. In this example, the patient who received the fibromyalgia diagnosis will not satisfy the legal test and the claim will not be accepted. Describing only the objective loss to the third-party source and avoiding the connotations of diagnostic labels can avert this potential problem.

Social security disability insurance

The definition of impairment remains the same for social security insurance; however, issues of causation and issues of whether injury is work-related or not lessen the potential for debate. Using the same example, in some government programs, fibromyalgia may not be viewed as a compensatable condition. Social security is the largest disability program in the United States, assisting between 33% and 50% of all persons qualified as disabled. The disabled state, however, must be so severe as to incapacitate that person from engaging in any substantial activity by reason of a medical physical or psychological impairment. The terminology impairment and disability become blended. It may be immediately seen that a problem will arise when considering impairment alone. A cerebral tumor may result in severe impairment, whereas some will be able to return to an active vocational lifestyle and others not. The discriminating feature differentiating these two populations may be features found in the disability profile such as age, English as a second language, and academic level. Therefore, in answering the question of social security disability, a clinician can answer according to the clinical condition alone or, if the information is available, in a comprehensive statement detailing all the factors contributing. This approach is in keeping with the acceptable standards established for assessing classical rehabilitation patients such as the spinal cord injured or brain injured.

Insurance carriers and employers for short- and long-term disability

Insurance carriers are concerned with disability, although in some policies impairment may illustrate the severity of the medical condition and carry weight for claim acceptance. Short- and long-term disability insurance can be purchased and the major features to appreciate about short- and long-term disability are that there are two distinct definitions. Short-term disability is defined as disability from one's own occupation. The length of disability, depending on what is purchased, can extend from 90 to 120 days. Long-term disability, on the other hand, is defined as total disability from all occupations.

Only about 25% of all employers carry long-term disability. Long-term disability requires the complete inventory of all vocational alternatives. By way of a case example: A 29-year-old welder sustains an injury at home while cutting the lawn. He requires an amputation of the nondominant right hand. By definition, the individual is likely disabled from his own occupation (satisfying STD). As the eligibility period runs out and long-term disability must be considered, the physician writes that his patient is totally disabled from all occupations because of neuronal pain and pain secondary to

skin breakdown and scarring. Clearly the individual suffers from medical issues that have complicated the presentation; however, in order to accurately determine the true vocational options, all aspects need be considered including physical medical restrictions, any psychological limitations, past vocational experience, current vocational interests and abilities, and extent of intervention to assist in the return to an appropriate vocation. The economic issues and funding responsibilities are beyond the focus of this chapter.

Tort action

In tort action both impairment and disability become issues of extreme accuracy. Impairment represents the measurable loss directly attributed to the accident in question. The objective loss is then extrapolated into a percentage impairment (termed permanent partial disability or PPD). The AMA guidelines are the most commonly used tool of conversion. Disability examines the current, desired, and potential vocational level comparing preaccident levels with the current postaccident state. This ultimately converts to loss of salary and income, and when a younger individual sustains loss that is lifelong then there may be loss of income for many years. This is where much of the financial loss exists (Figs. 61-2 and 61-3).

PPD (permanent partial disability) is a confusing term. The correct term is probably PPI (permanent partial impairment), and this illustrates the ongoing challenge to keep channels open between the third party and the clinical field.

QUANTIFICATION OF CHRONIC PAIN (IS THERE IMPAIRMENT?)

Chronic pain is by definition nonmeasurable and as a result does not constitute measurable impairment. It is important, however, to discuss pain in any chapter on impairment and disability. Pain is the most frequent condition facing clinicians and is the most common cause for not being able to return to work. When patients recover from injury or illness and they "have" pain, the impact of pain can lead to one of two paths. Pain, in keeping with the degree of organic loss, is defined as chronic pain. Pain that is disproportionate to the degree of impairment directs clinicians to examine the features behind the disabling pain and explain the failure to reach the expected maximal functional level based on the disability profile. Disability is favored as the descriptive term. Clinically the condition is defined as chronic pain syndrome and represents disabling pain that results in disability 3 to 6 months beyond the expected normal period of recovery. The assessment of the "impairment" for pain has been proposed and is reflective of the impact of chronic pain syndrome on the individual, combining the direct objective loss physically and psychologically and the direct impact on our behavior and psychological state (Fig. 61-4).

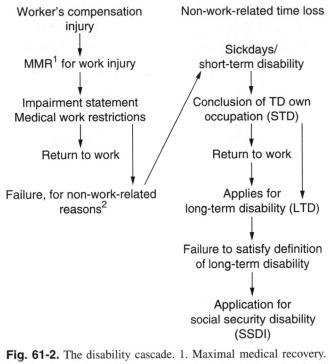

Fig. 61-2. The disability cascade. 1. Maximal medical recovery. 2. When a worker fails to return to work for non-work-related problems, they will access the employer-based system, which may begin with sick days accumulated or the lowest program available.

THE MEDICAL LEGAL REPORT

The medical legal report represents a significant tool of communication between the clinician and third parties. In some cases this may be the only tool, and as a result it is important that accuracy prevail. It is in the nature of clinicians to "please" the patient—in this case the referral source. However, it is critical to avoid the blind advocacy role. Given the challenges surrounding impairment determination (particularly in the gray clinical conditions), the report should remain informative. The complexity surrounding disability determination also deserves similar respect. The following principles have been established as critical to the ethical medical legal report:

1. *Remain a physician first of all.* Even though the independent medical examiner is restricted in role, it is critical that patients not be compartmentalized into a worker's compensation patient, a disability patient, or a third-party patient. While the report is prepared for the referral source and information is tailored to the request, the physician's role cannot be compromised.

2. *Avoid unnecessary alienation of the patient referred for assessment.* The role of any examiner is to optimize information gathered, and if the adversarial setting establishes the clinical examination, then optimal information will be difficult to obtain.

3. *Avoid the use of controversial diagnoses* and endeavor to stick to the objective findings on examination and knowledge of anatomy and physiology (in short, medical school knowledge is often adequate to answer many of the questions regarding impairment determination).

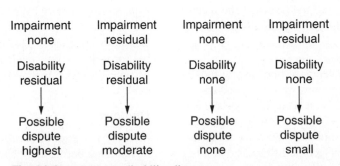

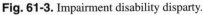

Fig. 61-3. Impairment disability disparty.

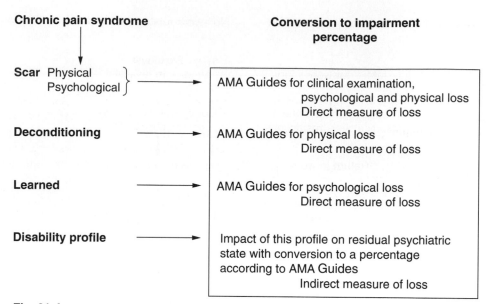

Fig. 61-4. Residual pain following maximal medical recovery and direct and indirect extrapolation to a percentage impairment rating.

4. *Prepare each third party report* as if it were being reviewed by peers.

5. *Use simple terminology* and describe the manner in which conclusions are determined.

6. *Should incidental pathology be noted on examination*, then the obligation is to see that this information is relayed to the attending physician.

IMPAIRMENT, DISABILITY, AND SCIENTIFIC EVIDENCE

Those who by choice or requirement become apart of the medical legal community will at some point in time have to defend their report to an adjudication body. In doing so, it is important to appreciate the applied principles behind "our" evidence being accepted by a court of law. *Daubert* reset the standards.

Daubert "sets out" the rules for the legal system to evaluate the individual and the evidence that is given in a court of law. A physician, as a scientist, represents qualities of paramount importance to the court of law and to the field of medicine, and this is aptly stated by Sir William Osler: "Acquire the art of detachment, the virtue of method, and the quality of thoroughness, but above all the grace of humility."

Frye v. United States

Frye represented the "general acceptance rule" in law and the standard of evidence. Expert testimony must be based upon a scientific principle or discovery and there must be general acceptance in the particular field in which it belongs. *Frye* had many areas of weakness: not only does the *Frye* test prove questionable and vague in specific instances, but it has also been described as "scientific nose counting."

Frye appealed his murder conviction on a novel defense that attempted to apply a relatively new scientific approach (theory), being the application of blood pressure to indicate innocence (possibly one of the first "lie detectors"). The systolic blood pressure would show if he (Frye) were lying. The test was the systolic blood pressure "deception test." The defense claimed that fear and rage would result in a blood pressure rise, while no change in blood pressure would occur in the "truthful man." The underlying basis of this "science" was that truth was spontaneous and a product of calm, unconscious effort. The court struggled (as it has today in fibromyalgia). Where is the line between scientific principle and discovery, between experimental and demonstrable? Frye failed in his bid as the appellate court refused to admit this "systolic blood pressure test," since it had not yet gained "such standing and scientific recognition among physiological and psychological authorities as would justify the courts in admitting expert testimony deduced from the discovery, development, and experiments thus far made."

This test establishes that the *evidence must have gained sufficient popularity* by way of standing and recognition in the "scientific community" so that the court admits the testimony as reliable. This legal test was, however, found to be (or felt to be) inadequate, and eventually *Daubert* became the benchmark case for admissibility of scientific evidence.

Daubert

In 1993, the case of *Daubert v. Merrill Dow Pharmaceuticals* came before the courts and this decision concluded that trial judges should act as gatekeepers. The following needed to be satisfied in order to accept evidence as scientific:

1. Has the *scientific theory or evidence been tested*?
2. Has the *scientific theory or evidence been published* or subject to review?
3. What is the *error rate of the theory* or technique and are there standards?
4. Has the scientific community *generally accepted the theory*?

The Carmichael decision

In *Kumho Tire Co. Ltd. v. Patrick Carmichael*, the *Daubert* decision was revisited. In this case, a "tire expert" was hired by Carmichael. The claim was that a defect existed in a tire, thus resulting in the death of one of the passengers. The methodology used was:

(a) Shoulder treads wear.
(b) Bead groove pattern on the tire.
(c) Sidewall deterioration
(d) Marks on the tire rim flange.

Kumho moved to exclude the expert testimony, stating that the methodology was nonscientific and therefore unreliable. The *Daubert* decision, it was felt, interpreted that the guidelines for admission of "scientific evidence" were applicable to scientists but not to other experts.

In *Daubert*, there was the potential for breakdown in the definition of who was and who was not an expert and to whom *Daubert* applied. The following example was used to further illustrate the point. In a small town in Texas, a farming community, a new chemical was introduced. The newness of it resulted in a lack of data on side effects and complications. Several patients became ill. The judge stated: "No peer reviewed literature is yet available . . . and several cases have come up where credible patients presented with history of exposure and evidence of injury . . . the doctor who treated those patients is credible—but 'Daubert' (*sic*) faces him."

Kumho Tire Co. Ltd. et al. v. Carmichael dealt with the specific issues and provided reasonable and ethical interpretation of *Daubert*. The Supreme Court stated that while the Daubert criteria are intended to serve as a tool to examine the reliable basis of an expert prior to admitting the expert's testimony (applied to all experts), *Daubert* was not exclusive to the "expert" alone. The *Kumho* decision clarifies the *Daubert* decision and clearly states that it is the judge's discretion to decide where and if to use the *Daubert* criteria and when to admit an expert's testimony based on professional experience and methodology used in that specialty.

Impairment can result in confusion when addressing clinical conditions of controversy. When appearing in a court of law, the clinician can make a stronger case when defending the established diagnosis following the principles established by *Daubert*. Disability is an emerging field of study and as a result requires close adherence to evidence-based medicine.

CONCLUSION

The depth of knowledge necessary to assess most impairment can be found at a very basic level of medical school education. A basic science approach within each physiological system generates a methodical approach to address two relatively simplistic terms, impairment and disability. Blind advocacy, extending beyond our boundary of scientific confidence and training, second-guessing the referral source, and failing to adhere to the basics will result in a vulnerable position or exposed opinion. Impairment and disability assessment by clinicians remains critical to our community, and all clinicians should be familiar with the medical legal concepts and the strengths and weakness within.

REFERENCES

R. Katz, *Major U.S. Disability and Compensation Systems Graphically Compared*, in *Disability Evaluation*, Physical Medicine and Rehabilitation Clinics of North America 499 (Aug. 2001).

E.L. Gross, *Injury Evaluation: Medicolegal Principles* (Butterworths, 1991).

N. Hadler, *Occupational Musculoskeletal Disorders*, 2d ed. (Lippincott Williams & Wilkins, 1999)

D. Ogilvie-Harris, *Personal Injury: A Medico-Legal Guide to the Spine and Limbs* (Canada Law Book, Inc., 1986).

B. Ficarra, *Medico-Legal Examination, Evaluation and Report* (CRC Press, Inc., 1987).

M. Shiffman (ed.), *Ethics in Forensic Science and Medicine* (Charles C. Thomas, 2000).

Guides to the Evaluation of Permanent Impairment, 5th ed. (American Medical Association, 2000).

P. Reed, *The Medical Disability Advisor Workplace Guidelines for Disability Duration*, 3d ed. (Reed Group Ltd., Boulder, CO, 1977).

G.M. Aronoff, *Evaluation and Treatment of Chronic Pain*, 2d ed. (Williams & Wilkins, 1992).

L.C.G. Persson, *Pain Coping, Emotional State and Physical Function in Patients with Radicular Neck Pain*, 23(8) Disability and Rehabilitation 325-335 (2001).

P.D. Kiester, *Eight Signs to Nonorganic Back Pain*, 106(7) Postgraduate Medicine (Dec. 1999).

R.N. Jamison, *Empirical Derived Symptoms Checklist 90 Subgroups of Chronic Pain Patients: A Cluster Analysis*, 11(2) J. Behav. Med. 147-158 (1988).

Monika Quessar, Principal Investigator, OECD, Paris, France, personal communication (Dec. 2002).

E. Chaplin, *Chronic Pain: Sociobiological Problem*, 15(1) PM&R State of the Art Reviews (Feb. 1991).

M. Lonstein, *Standardized Approaches to the Evaluation and Treatment of Industrial Low Back Pain*, in *Spine, Occupational Back Pain*, vol. 2(1) (Hanley & Belfus, Inc., Sept. 1987).

R. Mitchell, *Results of a Multi-Center Trial Using an Intensive Exercise Program for the Treatment of Acute Soft Tissue and Back Injuries*, 15(6) Spine (June 1990).

L.F. Miller, *Medical and Legal Evaluation of Disability in Personal Injury Cases* (Yearbook Medical Publ. Inc., 1962).

L. Hashemi, *Length of Disability and Work Compensation Low Back Pain Claims*, 39(10) J.O.E.M. (Oct. 1997).

D. Elisburg, *Workers Compensation*, chapter 6, *Disability Evaluation*.

J. Mather, *Social Security Disability Systems*, chapter 7, *Disability*.

H. Pace, *Ability to Work: The Social Security Viewpoint*, N.Y.S.J. of Med. 1726-1729 (Nov. 1982).

S. Moorhead, *Jumping Through Hoops: Fibromyalgia and Disability Insurance*, 9(2) Arthritis News 12-16 (1991).

P. Baldry, *Myofascial Pain and Fibromyalgia Syndromes* (Churchill Livingstone, 2001).

J. Latham, *The Socio-Economic Impact of Chronic Pain,* 16(1) Disability and Rehabilitation 39-44 (1994).

T. Guidotti, *Occupational Health Services: A Practical Approach* (American Medical Association, 1989).

7th Annual Conference on Medicolegal Issues in Work Injury (Toronto, 1995).

E.L. Gross, *Chronic Pain*, chapter 10 in *Injury Evaluation* (Butterworths, 1991).

J.C. Mohr, *Doctors and the Law* (Oxford University Press, 1993).

D. Sackett, *Evidence Based Medicine: What It Is and What It Isn't,* 312 B.M.J. 13 (Jan. 1996).

P.C. Giannelli, *The Admissibility of Novel Scientific Evidence: Frye v. United States, a Half Century Later*, 80 Columbia Law Review 1197-1250 (1980).

William Daubert, et al., etc., Petitioners v. Merrill Dow Pharmaceutical, Inc., Supreme Court of the United States, No. 92-102.

Frye v. United States, 293 F. 1013, 1014 (United States Court of Appeals).

F.J. Wilfling, *Disability and the Medical/Legal Process*, 42 The Advocate 183 (1984).

W. Fordyce, *A Behavorial Perspective on Chronic Pain*, British Journal of Clinical Psychology 313 (1982).

VII

Legal Aspects of Public Health

Occupational Health Law

CAROLYN S. LANGER, M.D., J.D., M.P.H.

THE OCCUPATIONAL SAFETY AND HEALTH ACT
KEEPING THE WORKER INFORMED
DISCRIMINATION IN THE WORKPLACE
TORT LIABILITY
LEGAL LIABILITY OF THE OCCUPATIONAL HEALTH CARE
    PROVIDER: MEDICAL MALPRACTICE
CONCLUSION

Occupational medicine is a branch of preventive medicine that "focuses on the relationship among" workers' health, "the ability to perform work, the arrangements of work, and the physical, [biological], and chemical environments of the workplace."[1]

From a medicolegal standpoint, occupational medicine is unique among the medical specialties. In no other specialty do regulatory and legislative mechanisms shape and drive the practice of medicine to the extent found in occupational health. Indeed an entire federal agency, the Occupational Safety and Health Administration (OSHA), has been established within the Department of Labor to safeguard the rights of this particular class of patients (the worker) and to specifically prevent or minimize the incidence of work-related disorders.

Providers of occupational health services also face unique challenges arising out of their dual loyalty to patients and employers. Can the occupational physician strive to uphold traditional notions of patient confidentiality, informed consent, and personal autonomy while simultaneously advancing the employer's goals of increased productivity; public goodwill; decreased workers' compensation costs; and promotion of worker, coworker, and customer health and safety? Although dual loyalties to employer and employee create the potential for conflict and impairment of medical judgment, in reality incidents of conflict occur far less frequently than might be anticipated.[2] Occupational health care providers (whether company employees, independent contractors, or private physicians) can most effectively limit their own liability, promote the health and safety of their patients, and preserve the legal and moral rights of workers through familiarization with occupational health laws and regulations and by adherence to good medical and risk management principles.

THE OCCUPATIONAL SAFETY AND HEALTH ACT

In 1970 Congress passed the Occupational Safety and Health Act (OSH Act) "to assure so far as possible every working man and woman in the Nation safe and healthful working conditions and to preserve our human resources."[3] This legislation created OSHA, the primary functions of which are (1) to encourage employers and employees to reduce workplace hazards, (2) to promulgate and enforce standards that lessen or prevent job-related injuries and illnesses, (3) to establish separate but dependent responsibilities and rights for employers and employees with respect to achieving safe and healthful working conditions, (4) to maintain a reporting and record-keeping system of occupational injuries and illnesses, (5) to establish research and training programs in occupational safety and health, and (6) to encourage development of state occupational safety and health programs.

Coverage

The OSH Act covers all employees and all employers (defined as any person engaged in a business affecting commerce who has employees) with the following exceptions:

1. Self-employed individuals.
2. Farms on which only immediate family members of the employer work.
3. Working conditions or workplaces regulated by other federal agencies under other federal statutes (e.g., Mine Safety and Health Act of 1969, Atomic Energy Act of 1954, Department of Transportation regulations).
4. Government employees.

Federal employees receive protection by an executive order that mandates federal compliance with OSHA regulations. State and municipal government employees may be protected if their states have OSHA-approved state plans that explicitly grant them coverage.

Standard setting

OSHA standards encompass four major categories: general industry, construction, maritime, and agriculture. In the absence of a specific OSHA standard for a particular working condition or workplace, employers must adhere to Section 5(a)(1) of the OSH Act, or the general duty clause. The general duty clause directs each employer to furnish "to each of his employees employment and a place of employment which are free from recognized hazards that are causing or are likely to cause death or serious physical harm."[4] Where OSHA has promulgated specific standards, the specific duty clause, Section 5(a)(2) of the OSH Act, mandates that employers "shall comply with occupational safety and health standards . . . promulgated under this chapter."[5]

Section 6(b) of the OSH Act authorizes the Secretary of Labor (hereinafter the Secretary) to promulgate, modify, or revoke any occupational safety and health standard. In adopting standards the Secretary must first publish a "Notice of Proposed Rulemaking" in the Federal Register and allow for a period of public response and written comments (at least 30 days, although usually 60 days or more). At the request of any interested party, OSHA will also schedule a public hearing. After the close of the comment period and public hearing, the Secretary must publish the final standard in the Federal Register.

Enforcement

The OSH Act authorizes OSHA to conduct workplace inspections. As a result of a 1978 U.S. Supreme Court decision, however, OSHA compliance officers may no longer conduct warrantless inspections without the employer's consent.[6] Because OSHA has only about 2100 inspectors to police more than 6.5 million employers with a total of about 100 million workers, the agency has established a priority system for inspections.[7] From highest to lowest, these priorities are (1) imminent danger situations, (2) catastrophes and fatal accidents, (3) employee complaints, (4) programmed high-hazard inspections, and (5) follow-up inspections.

After an inspection, the area OSHA director may issue the employer a citation indicating the standards that have been violated and the length of time proposed for abatement of those violations. The area director also proposes penalties for these violations. The employer must post a copy of the citation in or near the cited work area for three days or until the violation is abated, whichever is longer. Table 62-1 summarizes the types of violations that OSHA may cite and the concomitant penalties that it may propose.

Employers may contest a citation, proposed penalty, or abatement period by filing a "Notice of Contest" within 15 working days of receipt of the citation and proposed penalty. The area OSHA director will forward the case to the Occupational Safety and Health Review Commission (OSHRC), an agency independent of the Department of Labor. An administrative law judge will rule on the case after a hearing. Any party may seek further review by the entire three-member OSHRC. Commission rulings in turn may be appealed to the U.S. Court of Appeals by any party.

KEEPING THE WORKER INFORMED

More than 80,000 chemicals are in commercial use today.[8] Yet the health effects of many of these substances remain unknown. It is estimated that more than 32 million workers may be exposed to toxic agents in the workplace.[9] After passage of the OSH Act, OSHA promulgated a series of regulations to provide workers with more information about the agents present in their workplaces and to enhance the detection, treatment, and prevention of occupational disorders. The following are three of these important provisions:

1. The Hazard Communication Standard.[10]
2. The Recording and Reporting Occupational Injuries and Illnesses Standard.[11]

TABLE 62-1 OSHA violations and penalties

Violation	Penalty*
Other than serious violation (directly related to job safety and health but unlikely to cause death or serious harm)	Discretionary penalty of up to $7000 per violation
Serious violation (substantial probability of death or serious harm, employer knew or should have known of hazard)	Mandatory penalty of up to $7000 per violation
Willful violation (employer intentionally or knowingly committed a violation or was aware of a hazardous condition and failed to take steps to eliminate it)	Minimum penalty of $5000 per violation, up to $70,000 per violation (willful violations resulting in a worker's death may lead to criminal conviction with fines up to $250,000 for an individual and $500,000 for a corporation, imprisonment, or both)
Repeat violation (violation of a previously cited violation)	Fine of up to $70,000 per violation
Failure to correct prior violation (failure to correct a violation before the abatement date)	Penalty of up to $7000 for each day beyond the abatement date

Source: http://www.osha.gov/Firm_osha_data/100008.html.

* OSHA also may issue citations and proposed penalties after conviction for falsification of records, reports, or applications; for violations of posting requirements; or for interference with a compliance officer's performance of duties.

3. The Access to Employee Exposure and Medical Records Standard.[12]

Although employers are ultimately responsible for safeguarding the health and safety of their workers, these regulations have given employees, unions, health care providers, and governmental and nongovernmental agencies a more decisive role in the management of workplace health and safety.

The Hazard Communication Standard

OSHA promulgated the Hazard Communication Standard (HCS) to provide workers with the "right to know" the hazards of chemicals in their workplaces and to enable workers to take appropriate protective measures. Under the HCS, employers must (1) ensure the labeling of each container of hazardous chemicals in the workplace with appropriate identity and hazard warnings, (2) maintain and ensure employee access to Material Safety Data Sheets (MSDSs), and (3) provide employees with information and training on hazardous chemicals in their work areas. MSDSs list the chemical and physical properties of chemical substances, their health hazards, routes of exposure, emergency and first aid procedures, and protective measures for their handling and use. The HCS applies to only chemical agents. Furthermore, MSDSs are not subject to methodical review by regulatory agencies. Thus their quality and adequacy of information vary widely, and they may be of limited use to the clinician in the treatment of exposed workers.

The HCS also contains important provisions for health care provider access to the identities of trade secret chemicals. When a medical emergency exists, the chemical manufacturer, distributor, or employer must immediately divulge the identity of trade secret chemicals to the treating physician or nurse if this information is requested for purposes of emergency or first aid treatment. As soon as circumstances permit, the chemical manufacturer, importer, or employer may subsequently require the physician or nurse to sign a written statement of need and a confidentiality agreement.

In nonemergency situations the chemical manufacturer, distributor, or employer must likewise disclose the identity of trade secret chemicals when requested by a health professional (defined by the regulation as a physician, occupational health nurse, industrial hygienist, toxicologist, or epidemiologist). Before disclosure, however, the health professional shall (1) submit a request in writing, (2) demonstrate an occupational health need for the information, (3) explain why disclosure of the chemical identity is essential (in lieu of other information, such as chemical properties, methods of exposure monitoring, methods of diagnosing and treating harmful exposures to the chemical, etc.), (4) enter into a written confidentiality agreement, and (5) describe procedures to maintain confidentiality of the disclosed information. The HCS is a valuable instrument for providing health professionals with information about patient exposures.

Recording and reporting requirements

Soon after passage of the OSH Act, OSHA promulgated standards to fulfill the Act's mandate for the provision of record-keeping and reporting by employers and for the development of information and a system of analysis of occupational accidents and illnesses. Under 29 C.F.R. 1904, employers with more than 10 workers must maintain a log and summary of all recordable occupational injuries and illnesses. Recordable occupational injuries and illnesses include any fatality, injury, or illness that (1) is work-related, (2) is a new case, and (3) that either meets one or more general recording criteria or certain specific cases. General recording criteria include fatalities (regardless of the span between injury and death, or the duration of illness); restricted work or transfer to another job; medical treatment beyond first aid; loss of consciousness; or a diagnosis by a physician or other licensed health care professional of a significant injury or illness. Specific cases include needlestick injuries or cuts from sharp objects that are contaminated with another person's blood or other potentially infectious material; medical removal of an employee under the medical surveillance requirements of an OSHA standard; occupational hearing loss; tuberculosis infection; or musculoskeletal disorders.

Employers must make entries in a log within 7 calendar days after notification of a recordable injury or illness. The form used to record this information is known as the OSHA 300 form or the Log of Work-Related Injuries and Illnesses (more commonly called the OSHA 300 Log). Employers must also complete an OSHA 301 Incident Report form or an equivalent form, such as an insurance form, to record supplementary information for each recordable injury or illness entered on the OSHA 300 Log. Additionally, at the end of each calendar year, employers must review the OSHA 300 Log and create an annual summary of recordable injuries and illnesses on the OSHA 300-A summary form or equivalent form. These three forms—the OSHA 300 Log, the OSHA 301 Incident Report, and the OSHA 300-A summary form—must be retained for 5 years following the end of the calendar year that these records cover.

In addition to these record-keeping requirements, the standard further imposes a reporting requirement on working establishments. Employers must report all incidents to the nearest area OSHA office within 8 hours when such work-related incidents result in a fatality or the inpatient hospitalization of three or more employees. This requirement applies to all employers, regardless of the size of their workforce.

This standard also grants OSHA, as well as other federal and state agencies, the authority to inspect and copy these logs of recordable injuries and illnesses (although some U.S. circuit courts have upheld the need to obtain a search warrant before such inspections). The regulations also ensure employee access to all such logs in their working establishment. These provisions have proved to be a useful source of epidemiological data to employees, unions, researchers, the Bureau of Labor Statistics, and other agencies.

Access to employee exposure and medical records

Employers have no general duty to collect medical or exposure data on workers. Nonetheless, some specific OSHA standards, such as the lead standard, may require medical surveillance of workers exposed to specific agents. In other cases employers may voluntarily institute biological and environmental monitoring programs even when not mandated by OSHA. Regardless, to the extent that employers do compile medical and exposure records on workers exposed to toxic substances or harmful physical agents, they must ensure employee access to these data.

Employers shall make medical records available for examination and copying within 15 days of a request by an employee or his or her designated representative. The employer is obligated only to provide a worker with access to medical records relevant to that particular employee. Access to medical records of other employees requires the formal written consent of those other employees. Employers also must provide employees or their designated representatives with access to employee exposure records. When an employer lacks exposure records on a particular worker, the employer must provide that worker with exposure data of other employees who have similar job duties and working conditions. Under these circumstances, access to coworkers' exposure records does not require written consent. OSHA has the authority to examine and copy any medical or exposure record without formal written consent.

When medical records do exist on an employee, the employer is required to preserve and maintain these records for the duration of employment plus 30 years. Exposure records must be preserved and maintained for 30 years. Although these record retention requirements are the legal responsibility of the employer, it is recommended that independent contractor physicians who provide occupational health services to companies clarify the custodianship and disposition of medical records, specifying in advance the party to be charged with maintaining the medical records for the required duration.

The three standards discussed in this section—the HCS, the Recording and Reporting Occupational Injuries and Illnesses Standard, and the Access to Employee Exposure and Medical Records Standard—collectively keep employees informed of the nature and risks of hazardous materials in their workplaces and of any resulting exposure or health effects. By communicating these risks to workers, OSHA seeks to (1) encourage employers to select safer materials and engineering controls; (2) enable workers to use better protective measures and handling procedures; (3) familiarize workers and health care providers with valuable emergency and first aid information; and (4) minimize health hazards through earlier detection, treatment, and prevention of occupational disorders.

DISCRIMINATION IN THE WORKPLACE

Americans "with disabilities are a discrete and insular minority who have been faced with restrictions and limitations . . . resulting from stereotypic assumptions not truly indicative of the individual ability . . . to participate in, and contribute to, society."[13] The clinician functions as an important interface between disabled persons and the workplace in a variety of settings (e.g., primary care, preplacement physicals, WC and disability evaluations). It is incumbent on health care providers to make a fair and accurate assessment of workers' functional capabilities in relation to job tasks so as not to reinforce deep-rooted stereotypes about the disabled. Moreover, health care providers can play a key role in safeguarding the rights of workers and in educating employers through familiarization with recent legislative and judicial developments in the areas of employment and discrimination law.

The Americans with Disabilities Act

Congress enacted the Americans with Disabilities Act (ADA) in 1990 to eliminate discrimination against the disabled. Although the ADA addresses five separate areas, this chapter focuses exclusively on Title I, employment discrimination.[14]

Title I of the ADA prohibits discrimination against qualified individuals with disabilities in virtually all employment contexts (i.e., job application, hiring, discharge, promotion, compensation, job training, and other terms, conditions, and privileges of employment). The act defines disability as (1) a physical or mental impairment that substantially limits one or more of the major life activities, (2) a record of such an impairment, or (3) being regarded as having such an impairment. "Physical or mental impairment" is further defined as "any physiological disorder, or condition, cosmetic disfigurement, or anatomical loss affecting one or more . . . body systems."[15] Persons associated with individuals (e.g., family members) with disabilities also receive protection under the ADA.

Under the ADA, qualification standards, tests, or selection criteria that employers administer to job applicants must be uniformly applied, job related, and consistent with business necessity. To be consistent with business necessity, a standard must concern an essential function of the job. An employer who denies an amputee a desk job on the basis of strength testing would be in violation of the ADA if, for example, lifting were not an essential job task. Moreover, even when the qualification standards are job related, the employer must first attempt to make reasonable accommodations before excluding disabled workers on the basis of those tests. Examples of reasonable accommodations may include modified work schedules, job restructuring, equipment modification, design of wheelchair-accessible workstations, and provision of readers or interpreters.

The ADA provides the following three major defenses to employers charged with discrimination:

1. Selection criteria are job related and consistent with business necessity, and a disabled individual cannot perform essential job tasks even with reasonable accommodation.
2. Reasonable accommodation would impose an undue hardship on the employer.
3. A disabled individual poses a direct threat to himself or herself or to the health and safety of others in the workplace.

A regulation of the Equal Employment Opportunity Commission (EEOC) authorizes employers to exclude or refuse to hire an individual when job performance would endanger his or her own health or safety due to a disability. An important U.S. Supreme Court case, *Chevron U.S.A. Inc. v. Echazabal*, 122 S.Ct. 2045 (2002), upheld the EEOC regulation and affirmed an employer's right to exclude workers whose disabilities pose a direct threat to their own health and safety, as well as to the health and safety of other individuals in the workplace.

The ADA has several important implications for health professionals—whether company employees or independent contractors—who are often called on to perform employment physicals of job applicants or return-to-work assessments of injured workers. First, clinicians and employers need to recognize that the ADA bars all preemployment (preoffer) physicals. Employers may continue to administer preoffer nonmedical tests (e.g., language proficiency or strength and agility testing) that are job related, but they may require a medical examination only after extending an offer of employment. This offer may be conditioned on the results of the postoffer, preplacement physical examination provided that all applicants for a particular position are subjected to such an examination regardless of disability.

Second, clinicians should limit their role to advising employers about workers' functional abilities and limitations in performing the essential functions of the job with or without reasonable accommodation and to determining whether these workers meet the employers' health and safety requirements. To make such determinations of functional abilities and limitations, health professionals must insist that employers provide written job descriptions that accurately detail specific and essential job tasks. The employer has the responsibility to make all employment decisions and to determine the feasibility of reasonable accommodation. Nonetheless, health professionals may offer input on ways to achieve reasonable accommodation.

Third, the ADA imposes very strict limitations on the use of information from postoffer medical examinations and inquiries. Such information must be treated as confidential and must be maintained in separate medical files apart from personnel records. The employer must designate a specific person or persons to have access to the medical file. In some instances the release of confidential medical information may be allowable under the ADA, for example, to inform supervisors or first aid personnel about necessary restrictions or emergency treatment; however, a release form from the examinee is always advisable.*

Although the ADA discourages but does not explicitly prohibit clinicians from reporting actual diagnoses to employers, an action for breach of confidentiality may exist under certain state confidentiality laws if a release form is not signed by the examinee. In the absence of a release form, a clinician's best course of action is to inform the employer of functional abilities and necessary work restrictions (e.g., "no working at heights" and "no driving of company vehicles") rather than reporting actual diagnoses (e.g., "epilepsy").

Discrimination denies the disabled the many advantages of employment, including prestige, power, self-esteem, economic well-being, social outlets, and access to health insurance and other job benefits. The ADA will have far-reaching consequences in protecting the rights of the disabled and more fully integrating them into the workplace. Health professionals can play a critical role in fostering patient autonomy and educating employers while simultaneously promoting a safe and healthful workplace.

Gender discrimination, pregnancy, and fetal protection policies

As with the disabled, pregnant workers have often represented a disenfranchised group within the workplace. Although the ADA is broad sweeping, it does not shield these women from employment discrimination because "pregnancy" is not considered a physiological disorder under the Act's definition of disability. Nonetheless, pregnant workers receive ample protection under both legislative and judicial avenues.[16] The Civil Rights Act of 1964 (Title VII) prohibits discrimination on the basis of sex and, as amended through the Pregnancy Discrimination Act of 1978, further prohibits discrimination against "women affected by pregnancy, childbirth, or related medical conditions . . . for all employment related purposes."[17]

Despite the intent of these laws, a number of industries instituted fetal protection policies (FPPs) throughout the 1980s to exclude fertile or pregnant women from the workplace and to avert toxic exposures to the fetus. In some instances, companies went so far as to exclude all women, including postmenopausal women, from jobs or job tracks

---

* Workers sometimes voluntarily disclose their diagnoses to supervisors or first aid responders on their shift to familiarize them with the signs and symptoms of their condition in the event of a medical emergency.

involving potential exposure to toxic substances unless these workers could provide documentation of surgical sterilization. These FPPs were unsound for several reasons.

1. They disregarded reproductive risks to male workers.
2. They assumed that all women in the workplace could or would become pregnant.
3. They essentially required female workers to proclaim their reproductive status to supervisors and coworkers (i.e., women remaining in the workplace were implicitly sterile).
4. They discouraged some women from applying for higher-paying jobs.
5. They encouraged other women to undergo unnecessary surgical sterilization solely to retain their jobs.
6. They overlooked the adverse health effects to the unemployed mother and child from foregone income and health benefits.

In 1991 the U.S. Supreme Court declared these FPPs to be unconstitutional in *International Union, UAW v. Johnson Controls, Inc.*[18] The court held these policies to be discriminatory because they did not apply equally to the reproductive capacity of male employees. Furthermore, the court held that "decisions about the welfare of future children must be left to the parents . . . rather than to the employers who hire those parents."[19]

There are principally only two instances in which employers may discriminate on the basis of gender or pregnancy. Employers may deny employment when gender is a bona fide occupational qualification (BFOQ) reasonably necessary to the normal operation of that particular business or enterprise. Analogous to the ADA, the qualification standards must relate to the essence of the employer's business. For example, a movie producer would be justified in claiming that male gender is a BFOQ when hiring actors for male roles. Under the safety exception, employers may discriminate on the basis of gender in those instances in which gender or pregnancy interferes with the employee's ability to perform the job. For example, airlines are permitted to lay off pregnant flight attendants at various stages of pregnancy to ensure the safety of passengers. In all other instances women should be treated equally with men in the employment setting as long as they possess the necessary job-related skills and aptitudes.

In light of this legislative and judicial history, the following practices that screen out individual women or the entire class of women might be construed as discriminatory:

1. Implementing FPPs or other policies that exclude women from the workplace based on gender or reproductive status.
2. Applying coercion by providing female but not male workers or job applicants with information on reproductive risks or by requiring only female workers to sign waivers absolving the employer of liability in the event of an adverse reproductive outcome.

3. Administering special tests or medical examinations exclusively to women.
4. Using physiological parameters, such as muscle strength, as selection criteria when not a requirement for the job. (For this reason, as with the ADA, job descriptions that accurately reflect job tasks are vital.)
5. Using gender as a proxy for physiological parameters even when specific physiological traits (e.g., anthropometrics and muscle strength) are a requirement for the job and a high correlation exists between gender and ability to perform the job. (Employers must give each individual the opportunity to demonstrate that she meets the job parameters.)

Workers' compensation

Claims. Physicians who evaluate and treat workers with job-related injuries or illnesses must acquire a broad understanding of the workers' compensation (WC) system and an appreciation of their role in the legal disposition of WC claims.

WC systems currently exist in all 50 states and in three federal jurisdictions.[20] WC is a no-fault system that evolved in the earlier part of the twentieth century to promote expeditious resolution of work-related claims. Injured workers relinquished their rights to bring an action in torts in exchange for a rapid, fixed, and automatic payment. The quid pro quo for the employer was a limited and predictable award. WC pays for medical and rehabilitation expenses and typically up to two thirds of wage replacement.

Unlike tort actions, WC claims do not require a showing of employer negligence. Therefore even injuries or illnesses resulting from the employee's own negligence are compensable. Regardless of the cause of the injury, the worker carries the burden of proving by a preponderance of the evidence that a causal relationship exists between an occupational exposure and the resulting injury or illness; that is, the injury or illness must "arise out of or in the course of employment." Employees also are generally entitled to compensation for work-related aggravation of preexisting disorders. To qualify for WC payments, the worker must prove damages, typically by demonstrating a disability or loss in earning capacity. Even when the occupational exposure results in an injury or illness that produces no disability, the employee may still be eligible for an award if the WC laws in that jurisdiction explicitly provide for such coverage, such as payment for scarring, disfigurement, or damage or loss of function of specific organs or body systems.

Physicians who evaluate and treat injured workers must strive to be objective when documenting physical findings and impairments. Although physicians are not discouraged from making assertions about causality, they must be prepared to support their conclusions in a deposition or courtroom should the claim lead to litigation. It is also incumbent on physicians to familiarize themselves with alternative work and transitional duty programs to minimize the length of disability.

Confidentiality. Patients will often present treating physicians with authorization forms requesting release of medical records to the patient's employer, the employer's attorney, or the employer's insurance company in support of a WC claim. By signing these release forms, patients do not waive all rights of confidentiality. It is critical that physicians disclose only information related to the disorder that forms the basis of the WC claim. Several physicians have been sued for releasing confidential information about HIV status that was unrelated to the WC claim, such as ear and sinus problems or head injury with back pain.[21,22] Patients sued these physicians under various theories, such as negligence, breach of confidentiality, breach of contract, and invasion of privacy.

TORT LIABILITY

Many WC statutes contain "exclusive remedy provisions" that hold that WC shall provide the exclusive remedy for injuries and illnesses arising out of or in the course of employment. The goals of these provisions are to foreclose litigation and to limit the employer's liability to WC. During the last few decades, however, workers have been attempting to circumvent the exclusive remedy provisions of WC laws and pursue tort suits. As in WC cases, plaintiffs in tort suits may recover for medical expenses and lost earnings, but because tort actions are more likely to take into account future promotions and job advancements, they may yield a higher award for wage replacement. Moreover, tort suits offer the additional advantage of recovery for certain types of damages unavailable under WC, such as pain and suffering, punitive damages, and loss of consortium.

Despite the greater financial incentive to bring a tort suit, the courts have been reluctant to carve out exceptions to the WC exclusive remedy provisions. The most common doctrines under which employees file tort suits are as follows:[23]

1. Third-party and product liability suits.
2. Intentional harm committed by an employer.
3. Injury by a coemployee (injuries by coemployee health care providers are discussed in the following section on medical malpractice).
4. Dual capacity doctrine (the employer assumes a second role or capacity sufficiently distinct from its role as employer such that workers injured by the employer while acting in this second capacity may recover outside of the WC system).

Theoretically, both WC and tort liability should provide employers with the incentive to promote a safe and healthful workplace. However, given the employer's ability to insure and to pass on some of these costs to consumers, the extent to which these goals are accomplished remains unclear.

LEGAL LIABILITY OF THE OCCUPATIONAL HEALTH CARE PROVIDER: MEDICAL MALPRACTICE

What is the legal liability of a health care provider who commits medical malpractice while under contract to provide occupational health services to a company's employees? Management hires physicians, nurses, and other health care professionals—company salaried and independently contracted—for the benefit of the company (i.e., to ensure workers' fitness for duty).

Historically, health care providers salaried by a company were considered coemployees of other workers. Consequently their negligent acts and the resulting injuries were regarded as arising out of and in the course of employment. The exclusive remedy provisions of WC laws therefore limited injured workers to recovery under the WC system. However, if the workers could establish that the health care providers were not under the control of the company but rather were functioning as independent contractors, they could avail themselves of a remedy in torts.

The distinctions between coemployees and independent contractors have been problematic for the courts. Health care providers often have greater latitude than other employees in their exercise of judgment. At what point do their actions transcend the control of their employers and exceed the scope of employment? Some companies authorize and encourage occupational health care providers to furnish primary care services to employees and even to their families. At what point does the occupational health professional establish a health care provider–patient relationship, no longer acting solely for the benefit of the employer but also for the benefit of the employee?

The courts have developed two tests to determine whether an occupational health care provider is the coemployee of an injured worker (in which case the negligent act is covered by the employer's WC policy) or an independent contractor (and therefore subject to tort liability). Under the control test, health care providers are more likely to be presumed company employees when management exerts greater control over their function, operation, and judgment. For example, clinicians act under the control of the company when they must follow predetermined guidelines and protocols in conducting physical examinations (e.g., which forms to use or which laboratory tests to conduct).

Under the indicia test, the court analyzes various indices of control that normally signify employee status. For example, health care providers are more likely to be categorized as company employees rather than independent contractors if they receive a salary, health insurance, and other company benefits; fall under the company's WC and pension programs; work out of company offices; have regularly scheduled work hours; and report to the company's chain of command.[24]

Despite these two tests, the immunity of occupational health care providers continues to erode. Although the control and indicia tests provide useful guidelines concerning the potential liability of the occupational health care provider, their application results in some uncertainty because many professionals only partially meet these criteria. For example, some clinicians who have a part-time private practice may request workers to follow-up after duty hours in their private offices. Other clinicians may work out of their own offices but see exclusively company employees. Furthermore, courts appreciate that workers often rely on the results of employment physicals to their detriment and that health professionals have a high degree of skill and training and are in a better position to warn patients of harm and to insure against losses. Thus, although courts were traditionally reluctant (even in the independent contractor setting) to hold that a physician-patient relationship existed between a prospective or actual employee and the physician conducting the examination at the employer's request and for the employer's benefit, more courts are willing to recognize that the "examination creates a relationship between the examining physician and the examinee, at least to the extent of the tests conducted."[25]

Therefore the wisest approach for occupational health care providers, whether company employees or independent contractors, is to conduct examinations and treatment with due care and to disclose the results from any tests or examinations performed to the patient. Health care providers must be cautious in following up with patients because attempts to offer advice or to treat may establish a health care provider–patient relationship and place their actions beyond the scope of employment. Health care providers who want to ensure that employees receive adequate follow-up without risking tort liability should consider sending certified letters to patients advising them of the results and of the need for follow-up with their own private family physicians or other specialists as appropriate. See Box 62-1 for more detailed risk management principles. Health care providers would be prudent to delineate these responsibilities in their contracts with employers. Furthermore, occupational health care providers employed by companies should not rely solely on employers' WC policies but also should be covered by malpractice insurance.

CONCLUSION

Occupational health care providers are in a unique position to ensure worker health and safety. Because they interact with injured workers at every phase of employment—preplacement, preinjury, and postinjury—they have a profound impact on the disposition of job applicants and employees in the workplace. Occupational health professionals place a strong emphasis on prevention. Familiarization

---

BOX 62-1. RISK MANAGEMENT PRINCIPLES FOR OCCUPATIONAL HEALTH CARE PROVIDERS

1. Request job descriptions that reflect essential job functions.
2. For company-employed physicians, provide medical services only:
   - To employees (to employees' dependents only if company authorizes in contract and provides malpractice coverage)
   - During normal business or duty hours
   - On company premises (if available)
   - To the extent delineated in employment contract
3. Adhere to company policies.
4. Evaluate necessity and purpose of components of physical examinations and medical surveillance programs.
5. Do not order unnecessary tests.
6. Ensure that all tests are interpreted by qualified individuals.
7. Inform patients of results of all tests.
8. Ensure adequate/reasonable follow-up (appropriate to circumstances).
9. Keep good records—document, document, document.

---

with judicial, legislative, and regulatory mandates will enable them to preserve the health and uphold the rights of workers, to educate employers, and to minimize their own liability.

ENDNOTES

1. From the ACGME Special Requirements for Residency Education in Occupational Medicine, effective Jan. 1, 1993.
2. J.A. Gold, *The Physician and the Corporation*, 3 Bioethics Bull. 1(Fall 1989).
3. 29 U.S.C. §651(b) (1988).
4. 29 U.S.C. §654(a)(1) (1988).
5. 29 U.S.C. §654(a)(2).
6. *Marshall v. Barlow's, Inc.*, 436 U.S. 307 (1978).
7. http://www.osha.gov/oshinfo/mission.html.
8. http://www.cdc.gov/od/ohs/sympsium/symp71.htm.
9. OSHA 3110, Access to Medical and Exposure Records 1 (1989).
10. 29 C.F.R. 1910.1200.
11. 29 C.F.R. 1904.
12. 29 C.F.R. 1910.1020.
13. 42 U.S.C. §12101(a)(7) (Supp. IV 1992).
14. Americans with Disabilities Act of 1990: Title I, Employment; Title II, Public Service/Public Transportation; Title III, Public Accommodation & Services Operated by Private Entities; Title IV, Telecommunications; Title V, Miscellaneous Provisions.
15. Note that current drug abusers receive no protection under the ADA because illegal drug use is not considered a disability under the act. However, alcoholics and fully rehabilitated drug abusers may be protected under the ADA (unless they fail to meet productivity and other performance standards that cannot be corrected by reasonable accommodation).
16. 42 U.S.C. §2000e-2(a) (1988).
17. 42 U.S.C. §2000e(k) (1988).
18. *International Union, UAW v. Johnson Controls, Inc.*, 111 S.Ct. 1196 (1991).

19. *Id.* at 1207.

20. L.I. Boden, *Workers' Compensation*, in *Occupational Health: Recognizing and Preventing Work-Related Disease* 202 (B.S. Levy & D.H. Wegeman eds., Little, Brown & Company, Boston 1995).

21. *Doe v. Roe*, 190 A.D. 2d 463 (1993).

22. *Urbaniak v. Newton*, 277 Cal. Rptr. 354 (Cal. App. 1 Dist. 1991).

23. Modified from S.L. Birnbaum & B. Wrubel, *Workers' Compensation and the Employer's Immunity Shield: Recent Exceptions to Exclusivity*, 50 J. Products Liability 119 (1982).

24. *See, e.g., Garcia v. Iserson*, 33 N.Y. 2d 421, 309 N.E. 2d 420 (1970), holding that worker's exclusive remedy fell under WC law. The plaintiff could not maintain a malpractice action against a company physician because the injuries arose out of and in the course of employment since the company employed the physician at a weekly salary and took the usual payroll deductions, required the physician to work on company premises during certain scheduled hours, and included the physician in the company's medical plan and WC policy. See also *Golini v. Nachtifall*, 38 N.Y. 2d 745, 343 N.E. 2d 762 (1975), holding that WC provided the exclusive remedy to the plaintiff injured by a physician who received company salary and benefits and worked in company facilities.

25. *Green v. Walker*, 910 F. 2d 291 (5th Cir. 1990), holding that physician who was under contract to perform annual employment physicals was liable for malpractice in failing to diagnose and report cancer to examinee.

GENERAL REFERENCES

N.A. Ashford & C.C. Caldart, *Technology, Law, and the Working Environment* (Van Nostrand Reinhold, New York 1991).

B.P. Billauer, *The Legal Liability of the Occupational Health Professional*, 27 J. Occup. Med. 185-188 (1985).

J. Ladou, ed., *Occupational Medicine* (Appleton & Lange, Norwalk, Conn. 1990).

Public Health Law

JAY A. GOLD, M.D., J.D., M.P.H., F.C.L.M.

THE BASIS OF PUBLIC HEALTH AUTHORITY
COMPULSION VERSUS INDIVIDUAL RIGHTS
CONTROL OF THE PERSON
CONTROL OF PROPERTY
COMBATING UNHEALTHFUL CONDITIONS
GATHERING DATA
PUBLIC HEALTH LAW AFTER 9/11

Of all medical specialties, that of public health is the most intertwined with the legal system. The function of public law is to place the authority of the community behind actions that are taken on behalf of the public good. As public health encompasses the health of the entire community, not merely of individuals, every public health activity must be grounded in the legal structure.

This chapter will cover the following key points:
- The legal basis of public health authority in the police power, the Constitution, and in administrative law.
- The need and the legal authority in public health for both compulsion and the protection of individual rights.
- The legal mechanisms in public health law for the control of people's behavior.
- The legal mechanisms in public health law for the control of property.
- The law of nuisance in combating unhealthful conditions
- The law of public reporting of vital statistics and other data.
- Public health law in the aftermath of 9/11.

THE BASIS OF PUBLIC HEALTH AUTHORITY

In the United States, the locus of government authority to protect the public health resides in the states. Such authority is based on the "police power"—the power to provide for the health, safety, and welfare of the people. The police power is considered an inherent power of government; it is not spelled out in the Constitution, although the Supreme Court has acknowledged its reach.[1] The states then delegate the exercise of the police power to counties, to municipalities, and to other lower levels of government. It is the police power that forms the basis for state and local regulations such as health and sanitary codes.

In addition, public health has come to have a greater and greater presence at the federal level. Federal public health

law does not have its basis in the police power, since the Constitution does not grant such power at the federal level. Rather, federal public health powers arise from the power of Congress to "regulate commerce . . . among the several States"[2] and on the taxing and spending power.[3] The interstate commerce clause provides the basis for federal laws that protect the public health, from the Federal Food, Drug, and Cosmetic Act to the Americans with Disabilities Act.

Even more important than constitutional law to the operation of public health is administrative law. Given the scientific and technical nature of the health sciences, and the continual new developments in the field, it usually makes no sense for public health standards to be adopted directly into legislation. Instead, public health agencies are established with general grants of authority that enable them to take appropriate steps to protect the public health. Under these grants, agencies set technical standards through regulation, with notice to the public, opportunity for public comment, and often hearings. An agency may be given the power to pursue administrative remedies such as licensure, inspection, or abatement orders, and may be authorized to bring civil or criminal charges against violators.

Federal public health law is overseen by administrative agencies that have been set up to deal with particular public health issues. Such agencies include the Department of Health and Human Services and its subdivisions, the Department of Agriculture, the Food and Drug Administration (discussed in Chapter 15), the Environmental Protection Agency, and others.

COMPULSION VERSUS INDIVIDUAL RIGHTS

In no field are compulsory measures more essential than in public health. Health authorities must have powers of compulsion in order to prevent disease and to provide medical treatment. Quarantine and isolation require the limitation of the ability to move about at will. Immunizations (particularly of schoolchildren) are required. Surveillance may impinge on people's privacy. For this reason, the protection of individual rights plays an important role in public health law.

In particular, the Constitution offers important protections against the excesses of state action. Two dominant concepts are found in the Fourteenth Amendment: the due process clause and the equal protection clause.

The due process clause (which appears also in the Fifth Amendment) says that no state shall deprive any person of life, liberty, or property without due process of law. This provision requires basic fairness in the procedural application of the law. For example, someone who is charged with an offense has the right to notice, to a hearing, and to defend him or herself.

The equal protection clause says that no state shall deprive any person within its jurisdiction of the equal protection of the laws. This provision requires that any distinction in the legal treatment of different categories of people must have a rational basis, being substantially related to a legitimate governmental objective. Where the classification is "suspect," the interest in promulgating the distinction must be shown to be compelling. For example, a publicly supported hospital may not limit the admission of patients to members of a particular race.

A number of the amendments that constitute the federal Bill of Rights have special relevance to public health. For example, freedom of religion under the First Amendment has not prevented government from forcing compulsory vaccination against those who protest on religious grounds,[4] but *has* been used by members of certain religions to avoid blood transfusions. The Fourth Amendment prohibition on unreasonable searches and seizures limits the conduct of health inspections. The Eighth Amendment ban on cruel and unusual punishment has been held to define an acceptable minimum level of medical care for prisoners.

CONTROL OF THE PERSON

Much of public health law seeks to affect people's behavior through exercise of the police power. There are two traditional examples of this category of public health powers: the control of communicable disease, and the protection of people who suffer from mental illness. A third example has become important in recent years, the prevention of substance abuse and the treatment and rehabilitation of substance abusers.

The classic legal actions for control of communicable disease were *quarantine*, confinement of patients until infectiousness had passed, and *isolation*, confinement for a brief period to allow care and attention until other measures were needed. Such actions are less common these days, though not unheard of. Other legal powers of government continue to be relied upon, particularly compulsory examination of suspected cases and carriers, and compulsory

immunization.[5] In this regard, some of the most discussed issues in recent public health law have been those surrounding the AIDS epidemic: confidentiality versus the need to notify partners, mandatory versus voluntary neonatal testing, discrimination, and others. These are explored at length in Chapter 57.

State laws authorize the involuntary civil commitment of the mentally ill. The chief purpose for such commitment is where continued liberty would pose a danger either to the mentally ill person him or herself or to others. Procedural requirements for commitment under the due process clause, and the existence of a right to treatment of those who are committed, vary by state. The U.S. Supreme Court has taken a moderate position on the standard of proof for involuntary civil commitment.[6]

The issues of law enforcement and control of supply and demand for illicit drugs, therapeutic drugs, and alcohol have become some of the most prominent public health issues. ("Substance abuse," of course, also includes the abuse of nicotine.) Legislatures have struggled with the definition of conditions for compulsory treatment, and with methods of treatment in both residential facilities and communities. In addition, legislation is needed to allow transfer of the substance-dependent person from the criminal justice system into effective treatment programs.

The U.S. Supreme Court has upheld a data surveillance system that was set up to control both overprescribing by physicians and "doctor-shopping" by patients seeking prescription drugs, against a legal challenge based upon the right to privacy.[7] It also has upheld a government testing program requiring a urinalysis test from employees who seek transfer or promotion to certain positions, against a Fourth Amendment challenge.[8] And the courts have treated favorably school requirements for drug testing of students in certain circumstances in the absence of suspicion.[9]

CONTROL OF PROPERTY

Under the police power, public health authorities may, in certain circumstances, invade what otherwise would be a clear right to have one's property remain undisturbed. In the case of real property, public health officials are authorized or required to conduct inspections of a variety of facilities, that is, to visit them in order to determine whether conditions exist that create a risk to health. The U.S. Supreme Court has held that inspections by civil authorities fall under Fourth Amendment protection.[10,11] However, as inspections are not criminal searches, Fourth Amendment requirements are much easier to satisfy than are those established for police searches. Where a facility operates under a public license or permit, the courts will assume that the inspection is being conducted for a legitimate purpose. If not, a general "area warrant" is deemed sufficient.

In the case of goods and products, authorities may employ seizure, embargo, and condemnation. Seizure is the taking of goods or products from the possession of the owner. In an embargo, the goods are left with the owner but cannot be used or disposed of. After judicial proceedings, the owner may be given the opportunity to bring the goods into compliance with the relevant standards. If the owner does not do so, or if it is impossible, the goods may be destroyed.

COMBATING UNHEALTHFUL CONDITIONS

The law offers methods to eliminate conditions that have an adverse impact on public health, particularly the law of public nuisance. In general, where there is a public health emergency, officials have broad power to act quickly. In the absence of an emergency, the proposed actions of health officials may be contested in court before they are implemented, but the courts will uphold even the closing of businesses if they believe the public health is at stake.[12] If actions in abatement of a public nuisance are upheld by the court, the government need not compensate the owner for loss of property.

Courts may order a variety of remedies in nuisance cases:

- *Damages* are awarded primarily to plaintiffs in private nuisance cases.
- *Land use remedies* require a defendant either to shut down in that particular location or, in a private nuisance suit, to buy out the plaintiff.
- *Technological remedies* require a defendant to install the best control technology and to operate it at maximum efficiency.
- *Operational controls* require that the defendant act differently—with greater skill or care, in a different manner, or at a different time.

GATHERING DATA

The requirements for reporting health information are an important part of public health law. Health care workers are required to report certain data to local or state officials, and all states by voluntary agreement send these statistics to the National Center for Health Statistics of the Centers for Disease Control and Prevention. The information whose reporting is required includes vital statistics (births and death certification, the latter with cause of death), communicable diseases, child abuse, gunshot wounds, and other matters that may vary by state. Such matters are not considered a confidential part of the physician-patient relationship, and those who make these reports are immune from such liability as might arise from them.

PUBLIC HEALTH LAW AFTER 9/11

In the aftermath of the events of September 11, 2001, certain aspects of public health law have taken prominence, particularly the law of mass immunization and other defenses against bioterrorism. These aspects of public health law are discussed in detail in Chapter 64. In response to the issues surrounding 9/11, Lawrence O. Gostin and colleagues have offered the Model State Emergency Health Powers Act[13] in order to modernize state public health laws to deal with the present crisis. The Model Act has been the subject of considerable controversy.[14] Unfortunately, we can expect dealing with terrorism to be a prominent topic in public health law for the foreseeable future.

ENDNOTES

1. *See, e.g., Holmes v. Jennison*, 39 U.S (7 How) 283, 340-41 (1840).
2. United States Constitution, Article I, Section 8, Clause 3.
3. United States Constitution, Article I, Section 8, Clause 1.
4. *Prince v. Commonwealth*, 321 U.S. 158 (1943).
5. *Jacobson v. Massachusetts*, 197 U.S. 11 (1904).
6. *Addington v. Texas*, 441 U.S. 418 (1979).
7. *Whalen v. Roe*, 429 U.S. 589 (1977).
8. *National Treasury Employees Union v. Von Raab*, 489 U.S. 656 (1989).
9. *Board of Education v. Earls*, 122 S.Ct. 2559 (2002); *Vernonia School Dist. v. Acton*, 515 U.S. 646 (1995).
10. *Camara v. Municipal Court*, 387 U.S. 523 (1967).
11. *See v. City of Seattle*, 387 U.S. 541 (1967).
12. *Grossman v. Baumgartner*, 271 N.Y.S. 2d 195 (N.Y. 1966).
13. 288 J.A.M.A. 622-28 (2002).
14. *See, e.g.*, E.P. Richards et al., *Review of the Model State Emergency Health Powers Act*, 10 Legal Medicine Perspectives 3-5 (2002).

64

Legal Aspects of Bioterrorism

GEORGE J. ANNAS, J.D., M.P.H.

THE ANTHRAX ATTACKS
THE "MODEL" STATE EMERGENCY HEALTH POWERS ACT
FEDERAL PUBLIC HEALTH

A chapter on bioterrorism is a new addition to this book and was made necessary by 9/11 and its aftermath. Although terrorism has been a worldwide scourge for decades (and in international law can be traced back to the pirates), large-scale terrorism on American soil is more recent, and 9/11 signaled what seems to have been a change in kind rather than degree. This chapter concerns the legal aspects of a specific kind of terrorism, "bioterrorism." It should be read as a preliminary overview of the most immediately relevant legal issues rather than as a final or definitive catalog of them.

Medicolegal experts are not usually called on for their views on terrorism in general, but are needed to explain and explore the variety of legal and ethical issues raised by its biological aspects, especially in the context of using pathogens to spread disease and terror. In this regard we can view legal responses from the perspective of legal jurisdictions. Ultimately, the most important response is to strengthen prevention efforts, most centrally by strengthening the Biological and Toxin Weapons Convention at the international level. This is a long-term strategy that merits wide support. In this chapter, however, I will concentrate on the United States exclusively, and examine legal responses at the federal and state levels. Although public health has historically been primarily a matter of state law, it now seems inevitable that responses to the threat of bioterrorism, because they are primarily concerned with national security and the federal defense powers, will be overseen and controlled by the federal government. Also, because we are concerned with the "bio" in bioterrorism, federal efforts will be directed primarily at the development and deployment of vaccines and drugs that can be used to prevent widespread harm from various pathogens.

Public fear of a possible bioterrorist attack on the United States has been high since 9/11, and this fear has fueled many legal initiatives at both the state and federal levels. In exploring the legal issues raised by the possibility of a bioterrorist attack on the United States, it is useful to examine the response to the post-September 11 anthrax attacks, proposals for new state laws, and initial decisions about vaccinating U.S. citizens against smallpox.[1] A central question to consider is whether in our new reality, modern medical law, complete with informed consent and human rights, will be more effective in responding to threats of bioterrorism than reverting to nineteenth-century public health laws that are based on increased levels of state coercion.[2] Put another way, must we give up some civil liberties to increase our security?

THE ANTHRAX ATTACKS

In the anthrax attacks via the mails after 9/11, 22 people developed anthrax (about half inhalation and half cutaneous) and 5 died.[3] More than 10,000 people were advised to take antibiotics on the presumption that they were at risk for inhalation anthrax.[4] In late December 2001, the Food and Drug Administration (FDA), the Department of Defense (DOD), and the Centers for Disease Control and Prevention (CDC) together released the anthrax vaccine, previously only available to the military, and approved by the FDA only to prevent cutaneous anthrax, for use by those exposed to anthrax in the attacks.[5] Of the 10,000 people eligible to take the vaccine, only 152, or a remarkably low 2%, did.[6]

The anthrax bioterrorist (still unidentified as of early 2003) was extremely effective in meeting his goal: not mass killing (the goal in biowarfare), but terrorizing the civilian population. It is important to understand the belated response of the federal government in making the anthrax vaccine available, and why the public rejected its use, in order to be better prepared for the next bioterrorist attack or similar public health emergency. The basic rules regarding the use of investigational drugs in biowarfare, the closest analogy to bioterrorism, go back to the Gulf War.

Investigational drugs in war and biowarfare

Just prior to the Gulf War, the Pentagon sought an FDA waiver of informed consent requirements for the use of specific investigational drugs and vaccines on U.S. troops in the Gulf.[7] Informed consent is, of course, required for all human experiments, including the use of investigational drugs and vaccines. Specifically, the DOD sought waivers of informed consent under FDA rules so they could use an investigational drug (pyridostigmine bromide, to be used as a pretreatment against an attack by the nerve gas soman) and an investigational vaccine (botulinum toxoid, a protective against *Clostridium botulinum*) without obtaining informed consent from the soldiers.[8]

The basis of the DOD waiver request was that informed consent was not feasible because the military mission could be compromised if individual soldiers could opt out of taking these agents.[9] The FDA adopted a new regulation permitting waiver of consent for military operations, and approved the requested waivers under the provisions of the new regulation.[10] The FDA did, however, require the military to make information sheets on the agents available to the troops, and to collect, review, and report on adverse experiences.[11]

Because it was an approved drug, the military use of pyridostigmine bromide as a "pretreatment" for a gas attack could have alternatively been legally justified as use of an approved drug for an unapproved indication, based on the argument that it was a safe drug, even if not proven effective for this particular use.[12] Moreover, the military command ultimately decided to make botulinum toxoid vaccination voluntary.[13] Nonetheless, the FDA's 1990 waiver-of-consent rule itself cannot be legally justified on the facts. Obtaining consent was feasible in the Gulf, and failure to obtain it in the case of investigational drugs and vaccines is a direct violation of the consent requirements of the Nuremberg Code that the military had adopted as their own in 1953.[14] The FDA policy also turned out to be counterproductive and dangerous. It led to a situation in which the troops were put in much more jeopardy by taking pyridostigmine bromide than they would have been by not taking it. This is because while the drug may protect against soman (the agent that US intelligence thought Iraq had), the nerve gas the Iraqis were actually ready to use was sarin— and pyridostigmine can make sarin more deadly to humans.[15]

The FDA and DOD defended their waiver of consent actions after the Gulf War, but almost no one else did. Ultimately, Congress passed a law that repealed the FDA's military combat exception to informed consent, and put sole authority to grant any future wartime exception to informed consent in the hands of the President.[16] Currently, only the President can authorize the military to use an unapproved or investigational drug or vaccine in wartime without consent, and to do so the President must find, in writing, that obtaining consent is not feasible, is contrary to the best interests of the military, or is not in the interests of national security.[17] The FDA has also adopted regulations to help the President and his advisers make this decision.[18]

A more basic medicolegal question regarding drugs and vaccines designed for emergency use in events like biowarfare and bioterrorism remains, however: Assuming that it is impossible to ethically test the efficacy of a drug or vaccine designed for a bioterrorist or biowarfare agent (because it would be unethical to expose human volunteers to a potentially lethal agent), should there be an alternative way for the FDA to approve such agents for use in a war or other national emergency?

In 1999 the FDA proposed a set of new rules to permit the approval of such agents upon demonstration of safety in human subjects, and efficacy in appropriate multiple animal studies, and these rules were finalized in mid-2002.[19] Using multiple animal models for efficacy testing seems reasonable in this context, since the FDA is right to conclude that it would be unethical to expose human subjects to toxins that could be lethal to them (this would, for example, violate another provision of the Nuremberg Code). But the ethical rule requiring the informed consent of competent adults before they are subjected to drugs or vaccines that have not been demonstrated effective in human populations is equally applicable. No soldier or civilian should be required to take any such drug or vaccine (which would be offered on the basis that it could be effective) where the only scientific support for efficacy is the result of animal studies.

Informed consent to the anthrax vaccine

Anthrax vaccine has been approved for use to prevent cutaneous anthrax and was mandatorily given to the troops in the Gulf War on the basis that it was an approved agent that could be given for an unapproved but closely related use (inhalation anthrax).[20] This vaccine was developed in 1970. After the Gulf War, the DOD signed a sole source contract with a new company, Bioport, to produce anthrax vaccine.[21] In 1998, Secretary of Defense William Cohen ordered that all active-duty troops be given the anthrax vaccine, which was to be delivered in a series of six injections over an 18-month period.[22] Some soldiers refused, and challenged the orders, arguing that the vaccine was experimental and thus could not be given without informed consent. Many of them were court-martialed, and this defense has so far not succeeded.[23]

The bioterrorist anthrax attacks in the United States were on civilians, none of whom had been vaccinated. The recommended course of treatment for exposure to anthrax is 60 days of antibiotics, and antibiotics were made available to the 10,000 people potentially exposed.[24] The anthrax vaccine was not available to civilians in the immediate aftermath of the October 2001 anthrax attacks. In late December 2001, however, the DOD agreed to supply sufficient vaccine to vaccinate the 10,000 exposed civilians. Since the anthrax vaccine was an investigational drug when used for postexposure inhalation anthrax, it could only be used in the context of a clinical trial, and then only with the informed consent of the subjects.[25]

The FDA and CDC designed a consent form, together with a counseling process, for use in obtaining the consent of the exposed civilians to participate in the research project. Unlike the case of the military in the Gulf War, or even the peacetime military with the anthrax vaccine, in which the government required soldiers to be vaccinated, the choice was left entirely to the individual civilians. Government officials did not even make a recommendation as to what they thought any individual should do. No survey of the exposed civilians has been conducted. Nonetheless, it seems likely that the potential subjects mostly decided for themselves that their 60 days (or less) of antibiotics was sufficient protection.

It is also unlikely that anyone who actually read and understood the information in the consent forms provided (for adults, adolescents, and children) would have chosen to take the vaccine. Specifically, the consent forms (which are essentially identical), are five-page, single-spaced documents. Designed for a clinical trial, the forms are nonetheless captioned "Anthrax Vaccine and Drugs Availability Program for Persons Possibly Exposed to Inhaled Spores." Most of the form is in regular typeface, but the following information is in bold:

- Anthrax vaccine has <u>not</u> been shown to prevent infection when given to people after exposure to anthrax spores. . . .
- The vaccine that you will receive in this program has <u>not</u> been approved by the Food and Drug Administration (FDA) for this use and is considered investigational. . . .
- FDA has not approved this lot of vaccine (Lot FAV-063) because the company's license to produce the vaccine is under review. . . .
- You should not consider the vaccine as a treatment for anthrax. . . .
- You may have undesirable side effects from taking the vaccine.

. . . DHHS is <u>not</u> making any recommendation whether you should or should not take this vaccine. . . .[26]

The form also tells potential subjects that the vaccine is to be given in three injections, once every 2 weeks, and is to be supplemented by 40 days of additional antibiotics, although taking antibiotics is not required to obtain the vaccine. A 2-year follow-up is planned.

The fact that it is unethical to expose human subjects to potentially lethal toxic agents does not, of course, mean that studies cannot be undertaken with individuals who have been exposed by a terrorist and who may need an investigational drug or vaccine that has not been approved. The FDA's new regulations make provisions for such research, and appropriately so.[27] The FDA reasonably recognized that this investigational anthrax vaccine should be made available to exposed civilians only with their informed consent.[28] In this respect, the FDA learned from its experience in the Gulf War that there is no justification for waiving informed consent for competent adults, even in the face of a bioterrorist attack and uncertainty about the usefulness of the anthrax vaccine. Informed consent for research on competent adults is always feasible and is always ethically required. Informed consent is also required for medical treatment of competent adult civilians—only military personnel agree to accept reasonable and necessary approved medical procedures without specific consent.[29] That is only one reason why it is dangerous to civilians to argue that after 9/11 "we are all soldiers now."

The anthrax attacks convinced Congress and the public that the United States does not have sufficient safe and effective drugs and vaccines available to respond to a bioterrorist or biowarfare attack on civilians. The primary reason for the drastic increases in NIH funding, for example, are to increase research in areas that might lead to better bioterrorist-related drugs and vaccines.[30] Congress agrees with the FDA that these new agents should be approvable on the basis of animal studies of efficacy.[31]

A related drug and vaccine question is whether there should be a new, narrower category of FDA approval for products that cannot be tested for efficacy, and whose use would be limited to certain populations in specific circumstances. Although there is no precedent for this, teratogenic drugs like accutane and thalidomide have labeling that attempts to limit their prescription to people taking effective birth control measures.[32] This is reasonable. Similarly, when drugs and vaccines are developed for the use of soldiers in war it seems reasonable to restrict their use to competent adults, and to exclude children. It also seems reasonable to limit the use of the agent to military personnel—at least if combat and the military mission are the rationales used to approve the use—and to require that the product be labeled "For Military Use Only."[33] If such a restriction is not made, there is at least the potential for the drug to be used for other reasons (since once the drug or vaccine is approved for one purpose, physicians can lawfully prescribe it for others if it is available to civilians), although the primary reason shortcuts were taken in its testing was military necessity. The labeling of bioterrorist drugs and vaccines is more complicated because the consumers are primarily civilians. A label like "For Use Only in the Event of a National Emergency or Bioterrorist Attack" might not be sufficient, although that will be the primary reason the drug or vaccine has been approved without the usually required human efficacy studies. To permit it to be used by physicians for other purposes is thus not ethically or legally justified.

There is no sufficient reason to require civilians (or soldiers) to trade safety for liberty in an emergency in which unapproved or partially tested drugs or vaccines are made available. The choice to use these agents should continue to be theirs, as it properly was for civilians in the case of the anthrax vaccine. It seems reasonable to insist, nonetheless, that public health or military authorities that make these drugs and vaccines available be prepared to recommend their use. Otherwise the decision to make them available becomes purely a political one, made to cover the behinds of government officials, not a medical or public health one.[34]

THE "MODEL" STATE EMERGENCY HEALTH POWERS ACT

In the immediate aftermath of 9/11 and the subsequent anthrax attacks, hospitals, cities, states, and federal officials began developing or revisiting plans for future biological attacks. The federal response almost immediately emphasized stockpiling drugs and vaccines that could be used to respond to a future attack, especially one involving smallpox.[35] Other initiatives have proposed enhancing the public health infrastructure of the country (especially its ability to monitor emergency department diagnoses and pharmacy sales of relevant drugs), and the training of first responders to recognize and treat the diseases most likely to be caused by a bioterrorist attack (such as anthrax, smallpox, and plague). Major efforts are also underway to improve coordination and communication among local, state, and federal officials responsible for emergencies, and to more clearly delineate lines of authority involving "homeland security." All of these are reasonable and responsible steps our government should take.

On the other hand, planning for mass quarantine and forced vaccination—likely with investigational vaccines—may be unreasonable steps that are more likely to foster public panic and distrust in a real attack. Mass quarantine was a staple of public health from the fourteenth century to the end of the nineteenth century, and its implementation has been historically justified by labeling those groups quarantined as not only dangerous but almost diabolical.[36]

Properly worried that many state public health laws are outdated and perhaps inadequate to permit state officials from effectively containing an epidemic caused by a bioterrorist attack, in the wake of 9/11 the CDC advised all states to review the adequacies of their laws with special attention to quarantining people in the event of a smallpox attack.[37] In addition, the CDC released a proposed model law for the states, entitled the "Model State Emergency Health Powers Act" (model act) on October 23, 2001.[38] The proposal was written under extreme time pressure and in the state of high emotion.

The draft act permits the Governor to declare a public health emergency, after which the state's public health officials are given extraordinary power to essentially take over all of the health care facilities in the state, order physicians to act in certain ways, and order citizens to submit to examinations and treatment on the threat of being quarantined or criminally punished for refusing. Under the act, public health officials, and those working under their authority, are immune from liability for their actions (except for gross negligence and willful misconduct), including those that cause permanent injury or death. Specifically, the act defines a public health emergency (the condition that permits the Governor to declare a state of public health emergency) as "an occurrence or imminent threat of an illness or health condition, caused by bioterrorism, epidemic or pandemic disease, or novel and highly fatal infections agent or biological toxin, that poses a substantial risk of a significant number of human fatalities or incidents of permanent or long-term disability."[39]

An emergency declaration permits the Governor to suspend state regulations, transfer personnel, and mobilize the militia. All public health personnel will be issued special identification badges, which they shall wear "in plain view" and that "shall indicate the authority of the bearer to exercise public health functions and emergency powers. . . ." In regard to health care facilities, public health personnel may "compel a health care facility to provide services or the use of its facility if such services or use are reasonable and necessary for emergency response . . . includ[ing] transferring the management and supervision of the health care facility to the public health authority. . . ."[40]

Public health personnel are given exceptionally broad powers for the examination and testing of citizens, and failure of physicians and citizens to follow their orders is a crime that can be punished by having the order immediately enforceable by a police officer. For example:

Sec. 504(b) **Vaccination and treatment.** Individuals refusing to be vaccinated or treated shall be liable for a misdemeanor. If, by reason of refusal of vaccination or treatment, the person poses a danger to the public health, he or she may be subject to isolation or quarantine. . . . (c) An order of the public health authority . . . shall be immediately enforceable by any peace officer.[41]

Of course, state public health, police, fire, and emergency planners should be clear about their authority, and to the extent the model act encourages states to review their emergency laws, this is constructive. On the other hand, many of the provisions of this draft act, especially those giving authority to public health officials over physicians and hospitals, and authority to quarantine without meaningful standards, seem to be based on the assumption that neither physicians nor the public are likely to cooperate with public health officials in the aftermath of a bioterrorist attack. This assumption itself seems to be based on the results of tabletop exercises involving simulated bioterrorist attacks, including TopOff and Dark Winter. TopOff involved a simulated bioterrorist attack on Denver by using aerosolized *Yersinia pestis*, the bacteria that causes plague.[42] Dark Winter was a tabletop exercise that simulated a smallpox attack on Oklahoma City.[43] Using these simulated cases as a basis for legislation, however, is unreasonable, given the overwhelming voluntary cooperation of the public, physicians, and hospitals to both 9/11 and the anthrax attacks.

Excessive reliance on coercion was perhaps inevitable in the immediate aftermath of 9/11, but this reliance suggests three major objections to the initial draft of the model act. First, it is far too broad, applying as it does not just to a smallpox attack, but to nonemergency conditions as diverse as our annual flu epidemic and the HIV epidemic.[44] Second, although it may make sense to put public health officials in charge of responding to a smallpox attack, it may not make sense to put them in charge of responding to every type of a bioterrorism event. This is because although the state public health department has a major role to play in limiting the public's exposure to a bioterrorist agent, contact identification, information gathering and dissemination, most of the actual treatment of affected individuals, and preventive actions at the level of identifiable patients will be done by physicians, nurses, emergency medical personnel, and hospitals.[45] The primary role of public health authorities will usually be, as it was after the anthrax attacks, to provide guidance to the public and other government officials about how to identify and deal with the disease, and to provide laboratory facilities to assess exposure and definitively establish diagnoses.

The third objection is that there is no evidence from either 9/11 or the anthrax attacks that physicians, nurses, or members of the public are reluctant to cooperate in responding to a bioterrorist attack, or are reluctant to take drugs or vaccines recommended by public health or medical officials. Quite the opposite, physicians and hospitals in the areas affected universally volunteered their time, space, and expertise to respond to 9/11, and the public lined up to be tested for anthrax and stockpiled ciprofloxacin. Instead of resisting treatment or testing, the public actually wanted treatment and testing so much that the CDC had to publicly recommend against both.[46] Another important lesson learned from 9/11 was that Americans are primarily concerned about the safety of their families—and it will not be possible to separate people from their families, even by threats of force, if they do not believe separation is in their family's best interests.

Of course anthrax is not spread from person to person like smallpox. The response could have been different in a Dark Winter-type smallpox attack, or if thousands or tens of thousands of people had become infected with anthrax. Nonetheless, there is no empirical evidence to suggest that a draconian state criminal quarantine law of the type authorized in the act is necessary or desirable. Individuals with smallpox, for example, are most infectious only after they develop fever and a rash; and then they are usually so sick and immobile that they will likely accept whatever care is available.[47] Moreover, the "long incubation period (10-17 days before a rash develops) almost ensures that some persons who are infected in the [smallpox] attack will have traveled great distances from the site of exposure before the disease is recognized or quarantine could be implemented."[48] The key to an effective public health response is making voluntary treatment available. Without a sufficient supply of smallpox vaccine, for example, even police-supported quarantine would not likely be effective. People who do come to centers will come for diagnosis and treatment; they will avoid centers if they do not want diagnosis or treatment, especially if all that is offered is confinement and separation from their families.

It is, nonetheless, reasonable to conclude that a limited quarantine law could be useful to respond to a bioterrorist-induced emergency (e.g., by permitting the few unwilling Americans, if there are any, to be treated, vaccinated, or quarantined). Such a law, however, should be a federal law, not a state law. This is because bioterrorism is a matter of national security, not just state police powers. Existing federal quarantine law based on the commerce clause (and which has special provisions for cholera, plague, smallpox, typhus, and yellow fever) could usefully be examined and updated to deal with bioterrorism.[49] Moreover, to the extent that the federal government funds "dual use" public health infrastructure, federal public health officials will be able to dictate its use.

Civil liberties and public health emergencies

The draft act is based on the almost universal assumption that in public health emergencies there must be a tradeoff between protecting civil rights and effective public health interventions.[50] There is, of course, precedent for this belief, and the preamble to the act cites the 1905 case of *Jacobson v. Massachusetts* for the proposition that "the whole people covenants with each citizen, and each citizen with the whole people, that all shall be governed by certain laws for the 'common good.'"[51] *Jacobson* involved a Massachusetts statute that permitted local boards of health to require vaccinations when they deemed it "necessary for the public health or safety." There were no quarantine provisions in that law, and refusal was punishable by a $5 fine. Vaccination refusals at the beginning of the last century—before the Flexner report—were anticipated because vaccination itself remained controversial, there were no antibiotics, physicians were not universally trusted, science and medicine were in their infancy, and hospitals were seen primarily as "pest houses."[52] Tradeoffs between civil liberties (the right to refuse treatment) and public health (mandatory vaccinations) seemed necessary in such circumstances. There was no FDA, no such thing as an investigational drug or vaccine, and the doctrine of informed consent would not be articulated for more than half a century.

The U.S. Supreme Court cited the military draft as precedent for upholding the Massachusetts law.[53] The point is not that the constitution does not give both state and federal government wide latitude to respond in times of war and public health emergencies—it does; the point is that civil rights tradeoffs are not always required for effective public health response, and draconian responses are likely to be counterproductive today. Just as we have been able to abolish the draft and go to all-volunteer armed forces, so it seems reasonable to think that we can predictably rely on well-informed Americans—who are not the enemy in a bioterrorist attack—to follow the reasonable instructions of government officials for their own protection.

Almost one hundred years after *Jacobson*, neither medicine nor constitutional law is what it was. We now take constitutional rights much more seriously, including the constitutional right of a competent adult to refuse any medical treatment, even life-saving treatment.[54] Of course, we still would permit public health officials to quarantine individuals who have a serious communicable disease who either cannot or will not accept treatment for it or agree to stay in their home, and who threaten to infect others with it, such as active tuberculosis. Even then, however, we require public officials to use the "least restrictive alternative" and resort to quarantine only after other interventions, such as directly observed therapy, have failed.[55] Confinement is also accompanied by other procedural due process protections, including the right to legal representation and to a hearing.[56] At the very least, the individual with a contagious disease should have the option of identifying a qualified examining physician of their own, and if isolation is necessary, isolating him or herself in their own home. Requiring physicians to treat patients against their will and against their medical judgment under penalty of criminal law has no precedent at all, and makes no sense. Governors already have broad emergency powers; there is no compelling reason to expand them.[57]

Public trust is critical to effective response to a bioterrorist attack, and insofar as the act undermines public trust, it will be counterproductive and induce panic. Unlike 1900, for example, we now have 24-hour-a-day news television, the Internet, cell phones, and automobiles. These make effective large-scale quarantine impossible unless the public is convinced that it is absolutely necessary to prevent the spread of fatal disease and is fairly and safely administered. Former Senator Sam Nunn, who played the president in the Dark Winter exercise, accurately observed after it was over: "There is no force on earth strong enough to get 250 million Americans to do something they do not believe is in their own best interests or that of their families."[58] Treating our fellow citizens as the enemy, and using police tactics or martial law to force treatment and isolate them, is much more likely to cost lives than to save them. This is one reason why there has not been a large-scale quarantine in the United States for more than 80

years, and why bioterrorism experts doubt that such a quarantine could be effective.[59]

The revised model act

On December 21, 2001, a revised version was released. The new draft is labeled simply a "draft for discussion," and does "not represent the official policy, endorsement, or views" of anyone, including the authors themselves and the CDC.[60] Although the revised draft, still the one being pushed on state legislatures as of early 2003, is a modest improvement, all the fundamental problems remain. Failure to comply with the orders of public health officials for examination or treatment is no longer a crime but results in isolation or quarantine. Criminal penalties continue to apply for failure to follow isolation or quarantine "rules" that will be written at a future time. Physicians and other health care providers can still be required "to assist" public health officials, but cooperation is now coerced as "a condition of licensure" instead of a legal requirement with criminal penalties for noncompliance. The quarantine provisions have been improved, with a new requirement that quarantine or isolation be imposed by "the least restrictive means necessary" and stronger due process protection, including hearings and legal representation for those actually quarantined. Nonetheless, on the basis of a written directive by a public health official, a person can still be quarantined for 15 days before a hearing must be held, and the hearing itself can be for groups of quarantined persons rather than individuals.[61] Perhaps most critically in the real medicolegal world, nothing in the revised act distinguishes between approved drugs and vaccines and investigational agents, even though the latter are the most likely to be used, and even though state law cannot override federal drug laws that govern their use and informed consent requirements.[62]

Some of the revised quarantine provisions have been improved, but others are even more arbitrary. For example, quarantine can be ordered when the person's refusal to be examined or tested "*results in uncertainty* regarding whether he or she has been exposed to or is infected with a contagious or possibly contagious disease or otherwise poses a danger to public health."[63] This is no standard at all, and simply permits public health authorities to quarantine anyone who refuses to be examined or treated, for whatever reason, since all refusals will result in uncertainty—if you were already certain, you wouldn't order the test. Vague standards are especially troublesome because the act's incredible immunity provision remains unchanged. All state public health officials and all private companies and persons operating under their authority are granted immunity from liability for their actions (except for gross negligence or willful misconduct), even in the case of death or permanent injury. The immunity provision serves only to promote arbitrary state action and thus to undermine the public's trust in public health authorities. Citizens are not soldiers, and should never be treated against their will by their government. But if they ever are, they should be fully compensated for injuries suffered as a result.[64]

Uniform bioterrorism law necessary?

There is no chance that every state, or even many states, will adopt the suggested act as written, so that if uniformity is seen as necessary or desirable, only a federal statute can provide it. Obviously, it is also much more important what states like New York and California (large states that are likely bioterrorist targets) do than what states like Montana, Wyoming, or Arkansas do. As of late 2003, only a few states, including Delaware, Oklahoma, and South Carolina, had adopted the suggested act wholesale. More typically states have ignored it or, like California and New York, had considered it and rejected it outright. Other states, like Minnesota, modified their quarantine laws, but updated them to be consistent with contemporary medical ethics and constitutional rights, rather than making them more arbitrary.

Under the new Minnesota law, for example, even in a public health emergency, "individuals have a fundamental right to refuse medical treatment, testing, physical or mental examination, vaccination, participation in experimental procedures and protocols, collection of specimens and preventive treatment programs."[65] The law further requires a health care provider to "notify the individual of the right to refuse."[66] When isolation or quarantine are necessary, family members are specifically given the right to choose to enter the isolation or quarantine area to visit. Most of the other provisions of the suggested act, including the immunity provisions, were referred to the Minnesota commissioner of health for further study.[67]

Sensible public health and bioterrorism legislation must be drafted in a calm atmosphere, in a transparent, public process. Perhaps most importantly, as Ken Wing has noted, "statute drafting is a technical and instrumental job—one that should follow, not precede the more fundamental task of deciding what the statute ought to say."[68] Public health must ultimately rely not on force but on persuasion, and never on blind trust. Trust itself must be based on transparency, accountability, democracy and human rights.

The challenge remains to draft and debate a twenty-first-century federal public health law that takes constitutional rights seriously, unites the public with its medical caretakers, treats medicine and public health as true partners, and moves us in the direction of global cooperation. The revised act can be useful as a checklist or template for action, but only if it is continuously subject to scrutiny and improvement, and is redrafted to be consistent with federal statutory, regulatory, and constitutional law.

FEDERAL PUBLIC HEALTH

At the outset of the twenty-first century, bioterrorism, although only one threat to public health, can be the catalyst to effectively federalize and integrate much of what is now uncoordinated and piecemeal state and local public health programs. This should include a renewed effort for national health insurance, national licensure for physicians, nurses, and allied health professionals, and national patient safety standards.[69] Federal public health leadership will also encourage us to look outward, and to recognize that prevention of future bioterrorist attacks and even ordinary epidemics will require international cooperation.[70] In this regard the threat of bioterrorism not only demonstrates the need to federalize public health, but to globalize it as well.

The smallpox threat

No one can quantify the risk of a smallpox bioterrorism event; it is very low, but its potential for harm is so great should it happen that it cannot be ignored.[71] Current planning to attempt to mitigate the effects of a smallpox attack illustrates how dramatically the locus of public health planning has shifted from the states to the federal government, and federal law is likely to be central to a new public health law paradigm for the twenty-first century. Specifically, all major discussions and development of plans for such an attack have been done at the federal level, especially at the CDC.[72] Stockpiles of existing smallpox vaccine have been created by the federal government, tests to dilute the vaccine have been sponsored by the federal government, and the development of new smallpox vaccines is being financed by the federal government.[73] All of the existing and proposed supply of smallpox vaccine will be owned and controlled by the federal government.[74] Not only will the individual states have no say as to whether or not smallpox vaccine will be available to them, but decisions about whom the vaccine will be available to (such as military personnel, emergency department nurses, physicians and other employees, first responders, etc.), will be made by federal officials, not by individual governors or other state officials. The most difficult decision, whether and when to make smallpox vaccine available to members of the public prior to an attack, will be made by the President.[75]

Two points about smallpox preparation merit emphasis: first, this is a federal public health activity with the states playing only a supporting role;[76] and second, smallpox vaccination is likely to remain an entirely voluntary decision. A possible exception is military personnel slated to go to a war zone, but even this military exception can be put in place (without presidential order) only after the vaccine itself is properly licensed by the FDA.[77] Reportedly, federal officials have also learned from the anthrax vaccine experience and will not make smallpox vaccine available to the public unless and until they are ready to recommend its use.[78] As mentioned at the beginning of this chapter, the next step is to take a leadership role in strengthening international treaties to prevent the manufacture, storage, and use of biological toxins.[79]

ENDNOTES

1. For a more detailed discussion, *see* G.J. Annas, *Blinded by Bioterrorism: Public Health and Liberty in the 21st Century*, 13 Health Matrix 33 (2003).

2. G.J. Annas, *Bioterrorism, Public Health, and Human Rights*, 21 Health Affairs 94-97 (2002), and G.J. Annas, *Bioterrorism, Public Health, and Civil Liberties*, 346 New Engl. J. Med. 1337-42 (2002).

3. J.L. Gerberding, J.M. Hughes & J.P. Koplan, *Bioterrorism Preparedness and Response*, 287 J.A.M.A. 898 (2002).

4. *Id.*

5. T.V. Inglesby et al., *Anthrax as a Biological Weapon*, 287 J.A.M.A. 2236, 2243-44 (2002).

6. S. Twomey, *Vaccine Offer Draws Few Postal Workers*, Washington Post (Dec. 28, 2001) at A6.

7. For a more detailed discussion of the Gulf War waiver, *see* G.J. Annas, *Protecting Soldiers from Friendly Fire: The Consent Requirement for Using Investigational Drugs and Vaccines in Combat*, 24 Am. J. Law & Med. 245 (1998).

8. *Id.*

9. Informed Consent for Human Drugs and Biologics; Determination that Informed Consent is not Feasible, 55 Fed. Reg. 52,814 (1990) (codified at 21 C.F.R. Part 50).

10. *Id.*

11. Human Drugs and Biologics; Determination that Informed Consent is NOT Feasible or is Contrary to the Best Interests of Recipients; Revocation of 1990 Interim Final Rule; Establishment of New Interim Final Rule, 64 Fed. Reg. 54,180, 54,184 et seq.

12. Annas, *supra* note 7. The use of other drugs during the Gulf War was apparently justified on this basis.

13. *Supra* note 11.

14. Memorandum of Secretary of Defense C.E. Wilson dated February 26, 1953, and reprinted in *The Nazi Doctors and the Nuremberg Code: Human Rights in Human Experimentation*, 343-45 (George J. Annas & Michael A. Grodin, eds., Oxford University Press, 1992).

15. R.W. Haley & T.L. Kurt, *Self-Reported Exposure to Neurotoxic Chemical Combinations in the Gulf War*, 277 J.A.M.A. 231, 232 (1997); I. Koplovitz et al., *Reduction by Pyridostigmine Pretreatment of the Efficacy of Atropine and 2-PAM Treatment of Sarin and VX Poisoning in Rodents*, 18 Fundamental & Applied Toxicology 102, 103-5 (1992).

16. 10 U.S.C. 1107(f) (2000).

17. *Id.*

18. *Supra* note 11.

19. New Drug and Biological Drug Products; Evidence Needed to Demonstrate Efficacy of New Drugs for Use Against Lethal or Permanently Disabling Toxic Substances When Efficacy Studies in Humans Ethically Cannot be Conducted, Proposed Rule, 64 Fed. Reg. 53,960 (1999); and New Drug and Biological Drug Products; Evidence Needed to Demonstrate Effectiveness of New Drugs When Human Efficacy Studies Are Not Ethical or Feasible; Final Rule, 67 Fed. Reg. 37,988 (2002).

20. The vaccine has been shown to protect rhesus monkeys from inhalation anthrax. *See* T.C. Dixon, M. Meselson, J. Guillemin & P. Hanna, *Anthrax*, 341 New Engl. J. Med. 815, 822 (1999)

21. *See* Thomas V. Inglesby et al., *Anthrax as a Biological Weapon: Medical and Public Health Management*, 281 J.A.M.A. 1735, 1740 (1999).

22. S. L. Myers, U.S. *Army Forces to Be Vaccinated Against Anthrax*, New York Times (Dec. 16, 1997) at Al.

23. K. Morris, *U.S. Military Face Punishment for Refusing Anthrax Vaccine*, 353 Lancet 130 (1999), and L. Johannes & M. Maremont, *Worries about Safety of its Anthrax Vaccine Put the Army in a Bind*, Wall St. J. (Oct. 12, 2002) at A1.

24. L. Altman, *Many Workers Ignored Anthrax Pill Regimen*, New York Times (Oct. 30, 2002) at A14.

25. L. Altman, *In Offering Anthrax Vaccines, Officials Admit to Unknowns*, New York Times (Dec. 25, 2001) at B5. Bioport's contract with the Pentagon may also permit it to sell up to 20% of its annual production to others. J. Miller, *Anthrax Vaccine Maker Calls Finances Shaky*, New York Times (Aug. 5, 2002) at A10.

26. Consent forms available on the CDC website at http://www.cdc.gov/od/oc/media/adult.pdf (adult); http://www.cdc.gov/od/oc/media/adolescent.pdf (adolescent); and http://www.cdc.gov/od/oc/media/parental.pdf (pediatric).

27. *Supra* note 19.

28. S. Vedantam & M. Flaherty, *CDC Pushed Paperwork for Anthrax Vaccinations*, Washington Post (Dec. 22, 2001) at A10.

29. And it is probably time to reexamine this policy, at least in peacetime, as well. Moreover, the anthrax vaccine seems to be used currently in the military as a protection against cutaneous anthrax (which it is licensed for, but which is no real risk to soldiers) rather than as a protection against inhalation anthrax (which it is not licensed for, but which is a combat risk).

30. *NIH Breaks Down How it Will Spend Bioterrorism Funds*, Wall Street Journal (Feb. 19, 2002) at A4.

31. Congress required the FDA to adopt the regulation cited in note 19 by legislation; *see* H.R. 3448 (2002), Public Health Security and Bioterrorism Response Act of 2001, and S. 1765 (2001), Bioterrorism Preparedness Act of 2001, both of which contained this language and which became law in 2002.

32. *See* G.J. Annas & S. Elias, *Thalidomide and the Titanic: Reconstructing the Technology Tragedies of the Twentieth Century*, 89 Am. J. Public Health 98 (1999).

33. During the Gulf War, pyridostigmine bromide (as a pretreatment for a poison gas attack) was labeled "For military use and evaluation" instead of the usual IND label, "Caution: New Drug—Limited by Federal Law to Investigational Use." *See supra* note 19.

34. In this regard there are many lessons to be learned from the 1976 attempt to vaccinate all Americans against swine flu. *See, e.g.*, Richard E. Neustadt & Harvey V. Fineberg, *The Swine Flu Affair: Decision-Making on a Slippery Disease* (U.S. Dept. HEW, Washington, D.C., 1978). *See also* Gina Kolata, *Flu: The Story of the Great Influenza Pandemic and the Search for the Virus that Caused It*, 129-95 (Farrer Straus & Giroux, 1999).

35. W. Broad, *U.S. Acts to Make Vaccines and Drugs Against Smallpox*, New York Times (Oct. 9, 2001) at D1.

36. Howard Markel, *Quarantine! East European Jewish Immigrants and the New York City Epidemics of 1892* (Johns Hopkins University Press, 1997)

37. CDC, Smallpox Response Plan and Guidelines, available at www.bt.cdc.gov/agent/smallpox/response-plan/index.asp. *And see* J. Gillis & C. Connolly, *U.S. Details Response to Smallpox: Cities Could Be Quarantined and Public Events Banned*, Washington Post (Nov. 27, 2001) at Al.

38. This model was released on October 23, 2001, to great fanfare, but has since been removed from the sponsor's website. A copy is on file with the author.

39. Model Act, sec. 104(f).

40. *Id.*, sec. 402(b).

41. *Id.*

42. TopOff (Top Officials) was a Congressionally mandated exercise, to simulate three simultaneous attacks: chemical in New Hampshire, nuclear in Washington, D.C., and biological in Denver. The most dramatic was the scenario involving the aerosol release of pneumonic plague at the Denver Performing Arts Center and the 4-day sequel played out in May 2000, which included the closing of Colorado's borders on day 3. Among the questions raised by Denver TopOff were: who is in charge, how to handle drug supply, how to avoid a hospital crisis, whether and how to quarantine those infected,

whether to close city and state borders to contain the disease. *See* www. biohazardnews.net/scen_plague.htm.

43. Dark Winter, played out June 22 and 23, 2001, was a simulated small-pox attack on Oklahoma City. The exercise resulted in five major "learning points," including that biological weapons could threaten vital national security interests, current organizational structures are not well suited to managing a biological attack, there is no surge capacity in our health system, dealing with the media is critical, and finally, "Should a contagious bioweapon pathogen be used, containing the spread of disease will present significant ethical, political, cultural, operational and legal challenges." *See* www.homelandsecurity.org/darkwinter/index.cfm.

44. See W. Parmet & W. Mariner, *A Health Act That Jeopardizes Public Health*, Boston Globe (Dec. 1, 2001) at A15.

45. D.A. Henderson, "Public Health Preparedness," Committee on Science, Engineering and Public Policy, *Science and Technology in a Vulnerable World*, 33-40 (AAAS, 2002); M. Hamberg, *Addressing Bioterrorist Threats: Where Do We Go from Here?*, 5 Emerging Infectious Diseases 564 (1999).

46. J. Bor, *Americans Are Taking Antibiotics into Own Hands in Case of Anthrax*, Baltimore Sun (Oct. 13, 2002) at 5A; *and see* Tara O'Toole, *Terrorism Through the Mails: Testimony Before U.S. Senate Comm. on Government Affairs* (Oct. 31, 2001), Fed. News Service.

47. *See, e.g.*, D. A. Henderson et al., *Smallpox as a Biological Weapon: Medical and Public Health Management*, 281 J.A.M.A. 2127 (1999).

48. J. Barbera, A. Macintyre, L. Gostin, et al., *Large-Scale Quarantine Following Biological Terrorism in the United States: Scientific Examination, Logistic and Legal Limits, and Possible Consequences*, 286 J.A.M.A. 2711 (2001).

49. Public Health Service Act, 42 U.S.C. 264 (1983), and Quarantine, Inspection, Licensing: Interstate Quarantine, 42 C.F.R. 70.1-8 (2000). Of course, bioterrorism is fundamentally a global issue as well. *See* W. Mariner, *Bioterrorism Act—The Wrong Response*, National Law Journal (Dec. 17, 2001) at A21, and D. F. Fidler, *Bioterrorism, Public Health and International Law*, 3 Chi. J. Int'l L. 7 (2002).

50. J. Hodge, *Bioterrorism Law and Policy: Critical Choices for Public Health*, 30 J. Law, Med. & Ethics 254 (2002).

51. *Jacobson v. Massachusetts*, 197 U.S. 11 (1905).

52. Charles Rosenberg, *The Care of Strangers: The Rise of America's Hospital System* (Basic Books, 1987).

53. *Jacobson, supra* note 51.

54. *See* G. J. Annas, *The Bell Tolls for a Constitutional Right to Physician-Assisted Suicide*, 337 New Engl. J. Med. 1098 (1997) (discussing *Washington v. Glucksberg*, 521 U.S. 702 (1997) and *Vacco v. Quill*, 521 U.S. 793 (1997)). *See also Sell v. U.S.*, 2003 U.S LEXIS 4594 (June 16, 2003).

55. *See, e.g., Greene v. Edwards*, 164 W.Va. 326, 263 S.E. 2d 661 (W.Va. 1980); *City of Newark v. J.S.*, 279 N.J. Super. 178 (1993); and G. J. Annas, *Control of Tuberculosis: The Law and the Public's Health*, 328 New Engl. J. Med. 585 (1993). The analogy modern courts have adopted is to the due process protection now constitutionally required to confine a person to an institution because they are mentally ill and dangerous.

56. *Id.*

57. *See supra* note 44.

58. Quoted by Tara O'Toole, oral presentation, Boston University School of Public Health (Oct. 18, 2002).

59. *See supra* note 48. Those quarantines that were undertaken in the past century primarily involved recent immigrants and ethnic minorities.

60. The text of the December 21, 2001 version is available at www.publichealthlaw.net/MSEHPA/MSEHPA2.pdf.

A comparison of the cover pages of the two versions of "The Model State Emergency Health Powers Act" is both instructive and deeply disturbing. The **October 23, 2001, version** contains the following language immediately under the act's title and the date: "Prepared by The Center for Law and the Public's Health at Georgetown and Johns Hopkins Universities For the Centers for Disease Control and Prevention In collaboration with the: National Governors Association, National Conference of State Legislatures, Association of State and Territorial Health Officials, National Association of City and County Health Officers, and National Association of Attorneys General."

The cover page of the **December 21, 2001, version** (apparently the final one) reads as follows after the title of the Act: "Draft as of December 21, 2001. A Draft for Discussion Prepared by: *The Center for Law and the Public's Health at Georgetown and Johns Hopkins Universities* For the Centers for Disease Control and Prevention [CDC] To Assist: National Governors Association [NGA], National Conference of State Legislatures [NCSL], Association of State and Territorial Health Officials [ASTHO], and National Association of County and City Health Officials [NACCHO].

The cover page also contains a footnote to the title of the Act which reads: "Members of the National Association of Attorneys General (NAAG) also provided input and suggestions to the drafters of the Model Act. The language and content of this draft Model State Emergency Health Powers Act do not represent the official policy, endorsement, or view of the *Center for Law and the Public's Health*, the CDC, NGA, NCSL, ASTHO, NACCHO, or NAAG, or other governmental or private agencies, departments, institutions, or organizations which have provided funding or guidance to the Center for Law and the Public's Health. This draft is prepared to facilitate and encourage communication among the various interested parties and stakeholders about the complex issues pertaining to the use of state emergency health powers."

61. *Id.*, sections 605(a) and (b).

62. *Supra* notes 16 to 34 and accompanying text.

63. Section 602(c).

64. *See, e.g.*, G.J. Annas, *The Nuremberg Code in U.S. Courts: Ethics vs. Expediency*, in *The Nazi Doctors and Nuremberg Code, supra* note 14, at 201, 212-19. A good example of how arbitrary power tends to be used in emergencies is the use of potentially lethal gas by Russian commandos to "rescue" hostages held by Chechen nationals in October 2002. *See* S. Myers, S. Travernise & M. Wines, *From Anxiety, Fear and Hope, the Deadly Rescue in Moscow*, New York Times (Nov. 1, 2002) at A1.

65. Minn. Stat. §12.39 (2002).

66. *Id.*

67. *Id.*

68. K.Wing, *The Model Act: Is It the Best Way to Prepare for the Next Public Health Emergency?*, 19 Northwest Public Health 10 (2002). Epidemiological models for responding to a smallpox attack did not begin to appear in the literature until almost a year after the model act was drafted. Controversy continues about which model is most likely to mirror reality, and all are based on assumptions about the number of people each person with smallpox is likely to affect. As one commentator put it, "Without appropriate data, models cannot indicate whether we should target contacts for quarantine or vaccination when those contacts have been made in households, schools, workplaces, at public events, or under other circumstances." J. Koopman, *Controlling Smallpox*, 298 Science 1342, 1343 (2002). *And see* M.E. Halloran et al., *Containing Bioterrorist Smallpox*, 298 Science 1428 (2002) and S.A. Bozzette, R. Boer, V. Bhatnagar, et al., *A Model for a Smallpox-Vaccination Policy*, 348 New Engl. J. Med. 416 (2003). Of course, developing an effective legal strategy is dependent upon reasonable epidemiology, and without it legal plans are likely to be unresponsive or irrelevant to real world epidemics—whether naturally occurring or terrorist-created.

69. *See* Annas, *supra* note 2.

70. Although I have argued in this chapter that modern public health will from now on be considered primarily a federal rather than a state

responsibility, it would be even better if it were treated as a global issue, since epidemic diseases know no geographic boundaries and effective public health measures demand international action. *See generally* Laurie Garrett, *Betrayal of Trust: The Collapse of Global Public Health* (Hyperion, 2000), Institute of Medicine, *Microbial Threats to Health in the United States* (National Academy Press, 1992), and L. Asher, *Confronting Disease in a Global Arena*, 9 Cardozo J. Int'l & Comp. L. 135 (2001).

71. *See, e.g.,* G. Kolata, *With Vaccine Available, Smallpox Debate Shifts*, New York Times (Mar. 30, 2002) at A8.

72. E.g., CDC Smallpox Response and Guidelines, Draft 3.0, Sept. 21, 2002 (available at www.bt.cdc.gov/agent/smallpox/response-plan).

73. R. Pear, *Frozen Smallpox Vaccine Is Still Potent, Officials Say*, New York Times (Mar. 30, 2002) at A8.

74. L. Altman, W. Broad & D. Grady, *White House Debate on Smallpox Slows Plan for Wide Vaccination*, New York Times (Oct. 13, 2002) at 10.

75. *Id. And see*, M. Chase & G. Hitt, *Ugly Side Effects of Smallpox Vaccine Color Terror Plans*, Wall Street Journal (Oct. 21, 2002) at Al. Homeland Security Director Tom Ridge has also been quoted as saying, "The president on down—everyone—recognizes in this life-and-death decision that the president has to make, there will be some families that endure losses and others that endure permanent injury. There has to be some way to compensate them." *Id.* The new Homeland Security Act, passed by Congress on November 19, 2002, provides that all lawsuits involving the smallpox vaccine must be filed against the federal government. H.R. 5710, 107th Cong. (2002).

76. The Homeland Security Act (H.R. 5710), enacted in late 2002, made special provisions for the administration of "any substance used to prevent or treat smallpox" to civilians. Specifically, if the Secretary of Health and Human Services issues a declaration "concluding that an actual or potential bioterrorist incident or other actual or potential public health emergency makes advisable the administration" [of smallpox vaccine or treatment], a "covered person shall be deemed to be an employee of the Public Health Service with respect to liability arising out of administration of a covered countermeasure against smallpox." Covered person is defined to mean not only the "qualified person" who administers the drug or vaccine, but also the manufacturer, the health care entity under whose auspices the smallpox vaccine or treatment is administered, and any "official, agent or employee" of the manufacturer, health care entity, or person administering the treatment or vaccine. A "qualified person" (i.e., the one administering the vaccine or treatment) "means a licensed health professional or other individual who is authorized to administer such countermeasure under the law of the State in which the countermeasure was administered." All lawsuits for injury would have to be filed against the U.S. (Sec. 304).

77. Altman et al., *supra* note 74. *And see* L. Altman & S.G. Stolberg, *Smallpox Vaccine Backed for Public*, New York Times (Oct. 5, 2002) at A1.

78. *See Smallpox: Federal Officials Debate Whether to Recommend, or Simply Offer Vaccine*, Vaccine Weekly (Nov. 13, 2002) at 18. Military vaccination is, however, expected to be ordered. B. Graham & M. Allen, *Military Smallpox Vaccination Planned*, Washington Post (Nov. 15, 2002) at A16.

79. *See, e.g.*, B. Alberts & R.M. May, *Scientist Support for Biological Weapons Control*, 298 Science 1135 (2002).

VIII Forensic Science and Medicine

65

Forensic Pathology

CYRIL H. WECHT, M.D., J.D., F.C.L.M.

AUTOPSIES
FORENSIC PATHOLOGY VERSUS HOSPITAL PATHOLOGY
RAPE
PATERNITY
CHILD ABUSE
DRUG ABUSE
CONCLUSION

Forensic pathology is a unique and fascinating medical specialty. The training to become a forensic pathologist, as with any medical specialty, is highly specific and comprehensive, including 1 year of formal instruction in medicolegal investigation after completion of 4 years of residency training in anatomical and clinical pathology. Although scientifically specialized, the actual practice of forensic pathology cuts across a wide spectrum of everyday life, from the investigation of sudden, violent, unexplained, and medically unattended deaths (the basic jurisdiction of the forensic pathologist) to sex crimes, paternity lawsuits, child abuse, drug abuse, and a variety of public health problems. The range and diversity of such a practice provide constant intellectual stimulation and challenge.

AUTOPSIES

Autopsies should be performed for many reasons, including a variety of benefits to the family of the deceased (e.g., identifying familial disorders, assisting in genetic counseling), information for insurance and other death benefits, and indirect help to assuage grief. Benefits to the public welfare include discovering contagious diseases and environmental hazards, providing a source of organs and tissues for transplantation and scientific research, and furnishing essential data for quality control and risk assessment programs in hospitals and other health care facilities. Autopsies benefit the overall field of medicine through the teaching of medical students and residents, the discovery and elucidation of new diseases (e.g., legionnaires' disease, acquired immunodeficiency syndrome [AIDS]), and the ongoing education of surgeons and other physicians regarding the efficacy of particular operations and medications. Additional benefits to the legal and judicial systems include determining when an unnatural death (accident, suicide, or homicide) has occurred and enabling trial attorneys and judges to make valid decisions pertaining to the disposition of civil and criminal cases.

In light of the significant medical contributions and substantial scientific data that have been derived directly and indirectly from postmortem examinations over the past three centuries, it is unfortunate that in the United States the Joint Commission on Accreditation of Healthcare Organizations (JCAHO), in 1970, dropped its long-standing requirement that hospitals perform autopsies in a certain percentage of patient deaths (teaching hospitals, 25%; other, 20%) to maintain JCAHO certification. Moreover, this is disturbing considering the increasing number of wrongful death cases involving medical malpractice and other personal injury and product liability claims, as well as the thousands of homicides, suicides, and drug-related deaths occurring each year, all of which require definitive and complete autopsy findings.

Areas of concern

A surprisingly high percentage of clinicians, hospital administrators, and even pathologists have expressed a general reticence toward any new, concerted effort to increase the number of hospital autopsies performed. The reasons usually given are economic, educational, and legal. Hospital executives and other nonmedical administrative personnel are constantly seeking ways to cut costs, and postmortem examinations cost money. Pathologists are busy with their other responsibilities and are not paid extra for performing autopsies. Attending physicians and house staff rarely attend autopsies and usually do not even seek information later concerning the autopsy results.

Attending physicians and hospital administrators are concerned that autopsies may reveal evidence of malpractice and may provide additional data for plaintiffs' attorneys in medical malpractice lawsuits. Their reasoning is that in

621

the woman's consent. Ejaculation is not a necessary component, and neither is force. Rape is difficult to prosecute because it pivots on the woman's consent, and usually only the victim and the assailant are present during the commission of the crime; thus the only witness as to consent is the "prejudiced" woman herself. Thorough scientific examinations of the victim and the accused by a forensic pathologist, however, can generate substantive evidence for trial that can assist greatly in accurately determining whether a crime occurred.

Penetration

The condition of the hymen can provide evidence of penetration. Fresh injury to the hymen is usually evidenced by blood clots or hemorrhaging, but the inflammatory process that generally results from injury to other tissues is absent. Although hymenal injury may occur without penetration by way of masturbation or heterosexual sex play, fresh rupture and hemorrhaging of the hymen, especially when combined with testimony of rape, is probative evidence of rape.

The presence of seminal fluid in the woman's vagina is usually considered conclusive evidence that penetration has occurred. This finding neglects, however, the case in which ejaculation occurs while the man is in the mounting position, and the only penetration of the vagina is by the seminal fluid itself. On the other hand, the absence of ejaculatory material at the time of examination is not unusual even when the crime of rape has occurred. Interruption of the act after penetration but before ejaculation can occur, and the rapist is often incapable of achieving ejaculation. The woman's fear of impregnation and disease frequently results in rapid washing with strong antiseptic solutions after the act. These solutions may completely remove all seminal material or introduce factors that interfere with the detection of the constituents of seminal material.

Pathologists factor in all the evidence before reaching a conclusion of penile penetration. The emotionally charged circumstance of an allegation of rape and the resultant pressure to prosecute the rapist demand the utmost restraint and care in investigation by the pathologist to prevent a miscarriage of justice. Physiologically plausible and noncriminal explanations exist for each finding.

Consent

The next component of rape, which is much more difficult to prove, is whether the victim consented to the penetration. When the woman offered little or no resistance, the forensic pathologist is unable to offer much assistance because the investigation focuses on physical findings as opposed to mental intent. Rape, however, is usually accompanied by violence, and the evidence of violence tends to indicate that penile penetration was nonconsensual.

If force was used, there is usually evidence of this on the person or clothing of the victim. Lacerations may occur

from fingernails or other objects, particularly on surface areas of the body where clothing was forcibly removed. Contusions may result from blows by fists or other objects about the face, neck, and forearms in particular. Contusions on the woman's throat caused by throttling attempts are also quite common. Bite marks on the breasts, neck, and face occur frequently, and areas on the woman's thighs may show contusions or lacerations caused by forcible spreading of the legs to achieve penile entry. Signs indicating that the woman actively resisted also may be present. The fingernails may be broken or bent from using them as defensive weapons, and debris, such as clothing fibers, hair, or skin fragments from the assailant, may be present under the nails. Beard hairs and facial epithelium are most common, but any part of the assailant's body surface may be represented.

The absence of wounds may not indicate that consent was given, as when (1) the victim offers no resistance because of fear or resignation to being raped and (2) drugs are involved, e.g., gamma-hydroxybutyrate (GHB), the "date rape drug," a potent tranquilizer that causes central nervous system (CNS) depression, or flunitrazepam (Rohypnol), a benzodiazepine that can cause CNS depression, with the development of euphoria, hallucinations, and memory loss.

Investigative process

The forensic pathologist can aid in the prosecution and investigation of a case of alleged rape in many specific ways, as shown in the following step-by-step review of the investigative process:

1. Examination of the scene. The position of the victim and the state of the victim's clothing at the scene should be carefully noted. Efforts should be made to prevent contamination of the anus or vagina.
2. Photographs of the body at the scene.
3. Examination of the victim and the surrounding area at the scene using UV light or an alternate light source.
4. In fatalities, identification photographs of the body in the autopsy room.
5. Examination of the victim completely undressed using UV light or an alternate light source. Swabs are taken from any suspicious areas.
6. Large and close-up photographs of the injuries, especially of the sexual areas (mouth, vagina, anus).
7. Gentle glove examination of the mouth, vagina, and anus. To prevent contamination, gloves should be changed or washed when moving from one area to another. The physical condition of the hymen should be noted and recorded.
8. Cotton swabbing and aspirates taken from the mouth, vagina, and anus for preparation of microscopic slides, for acid phosphatase testing, and for detection of seminal fluid. A "hanging drop" slide preparation is examined immediately for motile spermatozoa.

9. Speculum examination of the vagina under adequate light to detect the presence of blood, contusions, lacerations, or presence of foreign bodies (e.g., fragments of wood sticks, glass, metal). In fatalities, microscopic sections should be taken from the areas of injury to determine their age, according to the patterns of tissue reactions.

10. Careful examination of the anus to check for presence of injuries. The presence or absence of a patulous or scarred anus indicative of chronic anal intercourse should also be noted.

11. At least 20 hairs plucked in their entirety (and not cut) from the head, axillary areas, and pubic area.

12. Fingernails cut or scraped and marked accordingly, left and right. Examination of the fingernail scrapings may reveal the presence of skin, cloth fibers, or blood that may be matched to that of the assailant.

13. Thorough external examination. Suspected bite marks should be swabbed for saliva typing and imprints lifted if possible.

14. In fatalities, a full internal autopsy, with special attention to the pelvic area, to perforation or other injuries, and to evidence of pregnancy.

15. A full toxicological examination, including analyses for alcohol, barbiturates, sedatives, and narcotics. Specific screening tests for ethanol, GHB, flunitrazepam, and other drugs should also be included.

PATERNITY

An area peripherally related to rape in which the practicing forensic pathologist becomes involved is the identification of the father of a child. Paternity actions were once extremely charged legal actions; the only mode of proof was the testimony of the parties and their witnesses. The high emotion associated with paternity actions has not changed, but the forensic pathologist's ability to contribute to positive identification has increased greatly. The present scientific determination of paternity tends to limit or eliminate the once-common practice of the accused producing a number of men (true or false) who had sexual intercourse at or near the time of conception. Paternity, not promiscuity, is the issue, and scientific testing provides virtually positive proof of fatherhood.

Since the combination of genes peculiar to each person is found in all cells of the body (excluding the egg and sperm), an analysis of blood cells generates the information necessary to establish or exclude paternity. The first approach to scientific proof of paternity is through exclusion techniques, as follows:

- A man can be excluded when both he and the mother lack a gene that the child has, because a child cannot possess a gene lacking in both the parents.
- A man can be excluded when the child does not possess a gene that must have been inherited from the father. (A man with AB blood type cannot have a child with blood type O, because having no other blood genes to contribute, either type A or type B is present in the child of a type AB father.)

Exclusion techniques are reasonably well accepted in U.S. courts because of their finality and long-standing scientific basis. Unfortunately, newer techniques to prove paternity based on both statistical probability and scientific examination are not as well accepted.

Because of the many genetic characteristics that have been identified, sampling only a few of them in the child provides a virtually positive identification index of the father. The subsequent application of mathematical techniques can statistically show whether a given man is the child's father. For example, if one identifies 20 genes in a child that have a frequency of occurrence in the general population of five, and the accused man has those same genes, it is 99.7% likely that the accused is the father.

CHILD ABUSE

The forensic pathologist enters the child abuse drama at the epilogue. The pathologist must identify the pattern of trauma and differentiate abuse from a true accident. This is a great responsibility because the decision of whether to prosecute a suspect often turns entirely on the pathologist's conclusion. A false accusation of child abuse is a traumatic experience, but it is equally distressing to free an abuser. Forensic pathologists therefore must show that the documented injuries are the result of abuse. They also must be able to exclude more natural explanations for their findings.

Recognition and categories of abusers

An association between chronic subdural hematoma and multiple limb fractures of varying ages in young children was first identified in the mid-1940s. Pathologists were unable to correlate the findings with any known disease and were looking for an exotic new disease. The medical profession was psychologically unprepared to accept that parents could seriously maim their children. Not until the mid-1950s was parental violence identified as the responsible modality for these observations. Since then, multiple studies worldwide have clarified the battered child syndrome.

Child abusers can be separated into several categories. *Intermittent child abusers* periodically batter a child but provide appropriate care between episodes. These parents do not intend to hurt their children, but they are driven by panic or compulsion and tend to be sincerely remorseful afterward. Often they are motivated to reform and can be successful in time. The child-victim of these episodes is usually grabbed by an arm or a leg and shaken forcefully, resulting in broken bones and joint dislocations.

One-time child abusers may be distinguished from the previous group, but more likely they are potential repeaters and were only restrained from further abuse by some particular circumstance.

Constant child abusers deliberately beat and mistreat the child. Their intent is to cause harm, usually with the rationalization that they are dispensing appropriate discipline. Such abusers are indifferent to the child's suffering. They often have personality disorders, are detached from the destructive nature of their actions, and are not inclined toward reform.

In this age of alternative lifestyles and broken families, many young mothers have live-in boyfriends. Often these men are affectionate to their girlfriend's children and contribute to their growth and well-being. Frequently, however, the child becomes the innocent victim of an emotional struggle. When resentment builds, either toward the mother or the children, men can become *intermittent habitual child abusers*, with the woman's children becoming the target of hostility.

A child's life generally includes multiple bumps, bruises, lacerations, fractures, and dislocations caused by accidents, making differentiation difficult for the pathologist. Child abuse cases, however, tend to have common findings on examination or autopsy and similar perplexing problems of differentiation.

Common findings

In regard to the hemorrhage produced in the battered child, the pathologist must determine that the trauma resulted from more than one application of force. With head trauma, for example, it may be difficult to surmise that a unilateral subdural hemorrhage is not a result of a fall. If the hemorrhage is multicentric, however, associated with several external lesions (particularly contusions or lacerations) or more than one abrasion, the implication is that the child fell more than once after receiving an initial severe craniocerebral injury, was hit several times, or bounced repeatedly. The pattern and multiplicity of injury help the forensic pathologist reach a conclusion.

Typically, thoracic damage results from a combination of blows and squeezes. Multiple ribs may be fractured, either posteriorly or anteriorly, and may be displaced, resulting in perforated lungs, heart, or liver. These internal injuries can cause excessive hemorrhage into the chest cavity and, if air is sucked into the chest cavity, can produce respiratory difficulty from pneumothorax. With the exception of a pure squeeze, the chest wall contuses more easily than the abdominal wall because the skin is closer to the semirigid ribs. These contusions are common in situations involving an ignorant abuser because the injuries can result from excessive though seemingly innocent squeezing.

The internal organs can receive trauma from any direction, and an unmarked epidermis can hide extensive internal bleeding and disruption of internal organs. The areas most vulnerable are the points of attachment of an internal organ, especially at the sources of blood supply and at points at which blood vessels change direction. One such area is the middle of the superior half of the abdomen, which contains several blood vessels changing direction, particularly the vessels of the celiac trunk and their branches; the hepatic, splenic, and gastric arteries and their branches; and the accompanying veins. The loop of duodenum, the ligament of Treitz, and the pancreas are in the retroperitoneal space, and the stomach and transverse colon are in the triangle located in the peritoneal cavity. *Compression*, whether prolonged, as in a hug or squeeze, or momentary, as from a blow, is the mechanism of trauma. A stretch-stress force of sufficient acceleration and deceleration detaches the jejunum from the ligament of Treitz, lacerates the liver, contuses the intestines or stomach, or ruptures blood vessels crisscrossing the area. Other direct blows include a "kidney punch," which may lacerate the kidney from behind, with bleeding into the space around the kidney and usually surface contusion.

Final determination

The pathologist's ability to explain whether one blow or many caused the damage is more important than being able to explain all the lesions by mechanism. A child dying of multiple internal injuries and manifesting bruises over the entire body, especially if the injuries are of different ages, is more likely to have been beaten than a child with one contusion in an exposed portion of the body, with internal injuries in the same area. A problem arises when the parents allege that the child fell down a flight of steps. In this case, a careful cataloging of all lesions and an on-site study of the premises may resolve the issue.

DRUG ABUSE

The forensic pathologist's task of determining the cause and manner of death is complicated by the problem of drug excess. So many drugs are available and used (illegally or legally) that a demise is often the result of drug combinations rather than the abuse and overdose of a single agent. This problem has become significant in the medical profession and on the street.

Physicians are bombarded on an almost daily basis with new, improved, and modified drugs. The volume of drugs available for use in treatment makes it virtually impossible to remain current with every agent and, more significantly, to be aware of and understand the ramifications of drug combinations. By themselves, most drugs are therapeutic, but when prescribed along with other drugs, potentially lethal combinations and synergisms can result. This is an especially insidious problem when a team of physicians or specialists treats a patient. Although the specialists may be completely familiar with the drugs used within their narrow focus, they may be totally unfamiliar with commonly prescribed drugs for treatment outside their specialty. The result can be an adverse drug reaction or a synergistic action causing untoward effects or death.

Drug death—or not

The frequently subtle differentiation between natural and drug-induced death, or between the death of a person undergoing legitimate medical drug treatment and death from drug abuse, may be impossible to achieve in the absence of some forewarning to the investigating pathologist. Pathological findings that could properly be attributed to natural or non-drug-related etiology may be natural medical complications arising from drug use or abuse. Unawareness of drug-related possibilities could make the forensic pathologist's opinion as to manner of death completely inaccurate. A properly conducted investigation, however, tends to reveal certain factors that alert the pathologist and usually eliminate inaccuracies in the determination.

The pathologist's first hint may come from the deceased. Unexplained coma followed by death or irrational behavior before a bizarre act resulting in death, especially in younger people, raises the possibility of a drug-related death. An investigation of the scene of death often reveals evidence such as needles, tourniquets, spoons for heating or measuring drugs, discarded plastic bags, syringes, burned matches, and other drug-related paraphernalia that may point to a drug-related demise. Even the location of the body when discovered, such as the bathroom (a common place for intravenous injection), may be helpful when combined with other information. Although the autopsy in a suspected drug-related death follows the usual scientific routine, certain findings and observations peculiar to drug users and abusers are often found.

During external examination, special care is taken to find and identify needle marks indicative of drug injection. These marks are often concealed by the abuser to reduce obvious evidence of drug use and may be found interspersed with tattoos, between the toes, in the gums, and in creases and folds of skin anywhere on the body. Abscesses, scarring, and sores are common as a result of scratching of the skin surface with contaminated paraphernalia to inject drugs intradermally (skin popping). Stains on fingertips from capsule dyes may indicate drug abuse, and the color may help identify the abused drug. Froth from the nose and mouth is a common indicator of severe pulmonary edema and congestion, which may result from death caused by depressants.

Internal examination usually generates limited information. The most common finding is pulmonary edema and congestion that, although nonspecific, is almost always present and thus helpful in identifying a drug-related death.

The gastrointestinal contents may reveal traces of pills and capsules, and the dye from capsules may tinge the mucosa with an unnatural color. Examination of the nasal passages and nasopharynx may reveal irritation or even traces of drugs (usually cocaine) inhaled through the nose (snorted).

Microscopic examination tends to be nonspecific in drug deaths, but certain findings are more common in drug deaths than in other kinds of deaths. These findings include pulmonary edema, congestion, focal hemorrhage, bronchitis, and peculiarly, granulomas. Granulomas result from the intravenous injection of foreign substances such as starch, textile fibers, or talcum, either because these substances were used to dilute or cut the drug or because the injection picked up clothing fibers. Other evidence includes thrombosis, thrombophlebitis, and viral hepatitis from the use of needles.

As expected, the most significant finding is made during toxicological analysis. Using GLC, TLC, SPF, and other sophisticated techniques, the forensic toxicologist can identify the presence and concentration of drugs. The samples of choice in these analyses are blood and urine, although nasal secretions, gastric contents, bile, and tissue from the liver, kidneys, or lungs may be necessary to make a definitive determination of drug type and concentration.

CONCLUSION

Virtually any situation involving an interface between law and medicine may call for the expertise of a forensic pathologist. With a background in both law and medicine, forensic pathologists are uniquely qualified to stand at the nexus and serve as the necessary bridge between these two fields.

Court decisions in various jurisdictions have conferred the benefit of governmental immunity on coroners and medical examiners in lawsuits alleging administrative or professional negligence relating to the determination of cause and manner of death. These judicial rulings are based on the premise that both elected coroners and appointed medical examiners are public officers. Therefore, even if their decisions are subsequently proven to have been incorrect, as long as they were made in "good faith" with no evidence of "malice," the pathologist, acting in an official capacity as coroner or medical examiner or their agent, is entitled to governmental immunity. These decisions are consistent with long-standing concepts set forth in administrative law and common law.

66 Forensic Engineering

STEVEN C. BATTERMAN, Ph.D.
SCOTT D. BATTERMAN, Ph.D.

ACCIDENT RECONSTRUCTION
BIOMECHANICS OF INJURIES
PRODUCTS LIABILITY
CONCLUSION

Forensic engineering, defined as the application of engineering principles and methodologies toward the purposes of the law, is a rapidly developing forensics specialty. The field of forensic engineering is extraordinarily broad, since by definition it encompasses all of the engineering disciplines applied in a legal context. Recognizing that it is not possible to cover such a broad field in a short chapter, the purpose of this brief review is to present some relevant forensic engineering applications in some areas of interest to the authors. To name a few, engineering disciplines such as electrical, chemical, civil, metallurgical, and environmental cannot be covered herein. Another purpose of this chapter is to encourage forensic scientists to seek the advice and consultation of forensic engineers in accident cases, or criminal matters, that have resulted in death or serious injury. This focus may come as a surprise to forensic scientists who are unaware that engineering methodology has indeed been successfully applied to understanding the response of human tissues to traumatic loading such as that resulting from impacts, falls, stabbings, bullet wounds, and explosions.

At present, the majority of forensic engineering investigations—but not all—are carried out in a civil litigation context rather than a criminal one. However, consider the example of a plane crash. The cause of the crash can be due to defective design, structural failure, or pilot error, which lie in the realm of civil litigation considerations, but could also be due to terrorist activity, such as a bomb or a hijacking, which are criminal considerations. Initially the cause of a plane crash is often unknown, and only by detailed investigation and engineering analysis can it be determined, if at all. For example, the explosion of Pan Am 103 over Lockerbie, Scotland, on December 21, 1988, was determined by engineers to be due to a small terrorist bomb that was strategically placed in a baggage container adjacent to the fuselage skin just forward of the left wing and was definitely not due to a design defect, malfunction, structural failure, or pilot error. The recovery and analysis of the debris in the

Pan Am 103 disaster, the partial reconstruction of the aircraft, the analysis of the breakup of the aircraft, and the analysis of the biomechanics of the injuries sustained by the passengers stands as a premier model in forensic engineering for analyzing other disasters. In fact, similar techniques were indeed employed 8 years later in order to obtain an understanding of the TWA 800 disaster. When TWA 800 exploded over Long Island on July 17, 1996, the cause was initially thought by some to be due to an onboard bomb or a shoulder-fired missile from a boat on Long Island Sound. Only after a very meticulous reconstruction of a portion of the aircraft, whose fragments were recovered from underwater, along with sophisticated laboratory and engineering analyses, was it determined that the cause was likely due to a center fuel tank defect. Unfortunately, as this chapter was being written, the space shuttle *Columbia* disintegrated in flight over Texas on February 1, 2003, during reentry. Similar techniques will likely be employed on the recovered fragments of the shuttle along with trajectory analyses, laboratory analyses, thermal stress analyses, and the analysis of the data from *Columbia* in order to obtain an understanding of the cause(s) for the disintegration. Although at this writing the cause of the disaster has not been definitely determined, preliminary engineering analyses have ruled out terrorism or criminal activity as likely causes.

Engineering, including forensic engineering, often depends heavily on the use of mathematical analyses. However, this chapter will not focus on the use of mathematics and the presentation will be largely qualitative in nature. A short bibliography is provided for readers who are interested in mathematical detail as well as more in-depth information on forensic engineering.

ACCIDENT RECONSTRUCTION

The field of accident reconstruction is one of the more visible forensic engineering specialties. It is typically thought of as only applying to vehicular accident reconstruction, but it does encompass all types of accidents including vehicular, electrical, industrial, chemical, structural collapses, etc. However, for definiteness and the purposes of this chapter, further attention herein will be focused on vehicular accidents.

Vehicular accident reconstruction may be defined as the scientific process of analyzing an accident using the physical facts and data left at the accident scene in conjunction with the appropriate natural laws of physics, i.e., the laws of classical mechanics stated by Sir Isaac Newton in 1687. The obvious is worth stating: Newton was not thinking about vehicular accident reconstruction since cars and other modern vehicles were not going to be invented for more than 200 years. Although the laws of classical mechanics apply to the motion of all bodies in the universe, Newton was interested in planetary motion, concepts of gravity, and the development of the associated mathematical descriptions. With regard to accident reconstruction, the significance of this is that only qualified engineers and physical scientists should be retained to do accident reconstructions, since they are generally thoroughly educated in understanding and properly applying the laws of physics. Caution is in order, since the advent of user-friendly computer programs and the codification of the laws of physics into "cookbook" type manuals have seen the entry of many less qualified people into the accident reconstruction field, which often does not serve the interests of truth and justice.

General statements of Newton's laws, which are formulated for a particle, are stated below, with more detailed information given in some of the references (Greenwood, Beer & Johnston, Yeh & Abrams):

- *First law*. Every material body continues in its state of rest, or of constant velocity motion in a straight line, unless acted upon by external forces that cause it to change its state of rest or motion.
- *Second law*. The time rate of change of linear momentum (product of mass times velocity) of a particle is proportional to the external force acting on the particle and occurs in the direction of the force. An alternative form of this law, which is the more commonly stated form, is that the resultant force acting on a particle is equal to the mass times the acceleration.
- *Third law*. To every action there is an equal and opposite reaction. Or equivalently, the mutual forces of two bodies acting upon each other are equal in magnitude and opposite in direction.

Although Newton's laws appear to be simple statements, it must be emphasized that there are significant concepts and sophisticated philosophy embedded in the laws, which must be mentioned and which are essential to an understanding and proper application of Newton's laws. First, the laws are vector statements, which means that the magnitude and direction of forces, velocities, and accelerations must be considered and not merely their magnitudes. Second, "motion" and "rest" are relative terms that establish a frame of reference to which the motion of bodies is referred. For vehicular accident reconstruction calculations, the Earth is a suitable fixed reference. However, for space flights, rocket launchings, and general astronomical applications, the Earth would not be a suitable fixed reference and it would be more accurate to use a distant star. Third, Newton's laws mention forces without ever defining them. Force is a very abstract concept and nobody has ever seen a force, which is the action of one body on another. In automobile accidents, apart from forces due to gravity, forces on occupants only arise when an occupant is decelerated (accelerated) such as by contacting another surface or is restrained by a seat belt, air bag, another person, etc. Fourth, Newton's laws are stated only for a particle, which by definition is a mathematical point of constant mass. It requires a rigorous derivation to extend Newton's laws to deformable bodies of finite size such as a crashing automobile. Unfortunately, this is often not appreciated by unqualified accident reconstructionists, who may tend to erroneously oversimplify an analysis. Fifth, the concept of systems of units is defined by Newton's second law. In the SI system, mass is given in kilograms (kg), acceleration in meters per second squared (m/s^2), and force is the defined unit in Newtons (N), where one Newton equals one kg-m/s^2. In the US-British system of units, force is given in pounds (lb), acceleration in feet per second squared (ft/s^2), and mass is the defined unit in slugs, where one slug is equal to one lb-s^2 per ft.

The general philosophy employed in accident reconstruction is to work backward from the final positions of the vehicle(s), to the point(s) of impact or beginning of the occurrence, and if sufficient information exists, prior to the impact(s) or occurrence. Calculations, either by hand or by computer, are performed using the available data in conjunction with Newton's laws. Often Newton's laws are cast in other forms for convenience, such as the work-energy principle or impulse-momentum principle (see references previously cited). In collision problems at the moment of impact, the impulse-momentum principle is particularly useful since the resultant external force acting on the system of colliding bodies is zero. This then leads to the principle of conservation of linear momentum (product of mass times velocity), which states that the linear momentum of a system of colliding bodies is conserved at impact. This principle, combined with the information left at the accident scene and the vehicle data, is often sufficient to solve for the velocities of the vehicles at impact. Examples of the application of the principle of conservation of linear momentum, along with the associated vector concepts and mathematics, are given in Batterman & Batterman (2000), Beer & Johnston, and the SAE Accident Reconstruction Technology Collection. It should also be mentioned that numerous commercially available computer programs exist for accident reconstruction calculations and these programs will not be discussed herein. The programs are based on Newton's laws, as they must be, and many of them contain algorithms specialized for accident reconstruction, e.g., crush damage considerations. As indicated earlier, some of the programs are so user-friendly that it is possible for unqualified people, who do not have an adequate educational background and who do not understand their own limitations as well as those of the programs, to obtain solutions that may not be valid for a particular accident.

Another aspect of accident reconstruction, and undoubtedly the most difficult, is to determine how an occupant moves with respect to the crashing vehicle, i.e., the occupant kinematics. The determination of an occupant's kinematics is often critically related to the injuries that may have been sustained by the occupant. In order to determine the complete occupant kinematics, an enormous amount of physical information is required in addition to the complexities of solving a very difficult problem in dynamics. This physical information includes knowing the properties of the vehicle interior structures that may be contacted by the occupants, the actual contact points in the interior of the vehicle and on the occupant's body, since this will then change the direction of motion of the occupant, the dynamic response of the human body to impact, and the details of how the vehicle is moving as a function of time. It is not surprising that in order to completely solve an occupant kinematics problem throughout the entire crash duration, an enormous amount of information is required as well as assumptions that may influence or bias the outcome.

Sometimes only the initial occupant kinematics may be significant in an injury analysis, and this can often be determined without a complete occupant kinematics analysis. In general, an occupant initially tends to move toward the impact, which is opposite the change in velocity of the vehicle, referred to as delta-v, or opposite the resultant vehicle acceleration (see Batterman & Batterman, 2000). For example, in a frontal crash the occupants will tend to move forward with respect to the vehicle. If the occupants are unrestrained, front-seat occupants can impact the steering wheel, dashboard, or windshield while rear-seat occupants can impact the backs of the front seats. In a rear-end crash, occupants will tend to first move backward into their seats followed by a forward rebound phase. If unrestrained, occupants can then rebound forward into the vehicle structure in front of them while restrained occupants will not exhibit such large excursions. Another important aspect of rear-end collisions is that seat backs can fail, causing occupants to tumble into the rear of a vehicle and thus sustain serious injuries. In a lateral crash, nearside occupants to the crash will move toward the impact and may physically contact the impacting vehicle or a roadside object, such as a pole or a tree. Lap-shoulder belts worn by nearside occupants may not be effective in preventing injuries in this type of crash, but lateral air bags would offer some protection.

However, a restrained farside occupant to a lateral crash may derive benefit from wearing a lap-shoulder belt, which would then limit occupant excursions toward the impact.

BIOMECHANICS OF INJURIES

Biomechanics, which simply means the application of Newtonian mechanics to biology, is a subfield of bioengineering, which can be defined as the application of engineering principles and methodology to biological systems. Bioengineering is a huge and rapidly developing field in the United States and worldwide, with burgeoning numbers of degree programs on the bachelors, masters, and doctorate levels. The field of biomechanics is likewise vast, with applications beyond the vehicular considerations discussed in this chapter. For example, to name a few, biomechanicians are involved in the design of artificial organs, prostheses, bioinstrumentation, medical devices, safety devices such as protective sports equipment, automobile design and restraint system design to minimize injuries in a crash, as well as with understanding the response of tissues, cells, and biological systems to mechanical loading.

Biomechanics of injuries has already been briefly mentioned when initial occupant kinematics was discussed. A complete discussion of injury biomechanics is beyond the scope of this chapter and instead only a few key ideas and concepts will be mentioned. The interested reader is referred to the bibliography, in particular the Stapp Car Crash Conference Proceedings and extensive literature available from the Society of Automotive Engineers.

A concept that frequently appears in automotive injury biomechanics is that of delta-v, which is often correlated with injuries sustained in a crash. Delta-v is defined as the change in velocity (not speed) of a vehicle from its immediate preimpact velocity to its immediate postimpact velocity. Delta-v is a vector quantity, which has both magnitude and direction, and it is generally incorrect to merely subtract speeds in order to determine delta-v (see Batterman & Batterman, 2000). The major reason delta-v is correlated with injury potential is that delta-v is closely related to the vehicle accelerations in a crash and, by Newton's second law, it is accelerations that determine the resultant forces acting on a system. However, it is emphasized that an occupant's body or body segments, in general, will not experience the same delta-v as the vehicle. This is because vehicle and body segment rotations can, and do, greatly influence the velocities and velocity changes an occupant may undergo in a crash.

Correlations of injury with delta-v appear in the biomechanics literature (Mills & Hobbs) and are continuously being collected and updated. It should be noted at the outset that the correlations are statistical in nature, i.e., they give the probability of a certain type of injury occurring as a function of delta-v. Furthermore, to ensure uniformity and standardization of reporting, injuries are typically described utilizing the Abbreviated Injury Scale (AIS) promulgated by the Association for the Advancement of Automotive Medicine (AAAM). The AIS is based on anatomical injury immediately following the accident and does not score impairments or disabilities that may result from the injuries over time. A severity code is used in the AIS which ranges from 0 to 6, as shown in Table 66-1.

In the 1990 AIS, each injury is assigned a seven-digit code with six digits to the left of the decimal and one to the right. The digit to the right is one of the severity codes given above while the six digits to the left specify injury locations to the body region, type of anatomic structure, specific anatomic structure, and level of injury within a specific region and anatomic structure. The interested reader is referred to the detailed instructions for coding injuries given in AIS 90. Furthermore, other injury classification systems exist and are discussed by Pike.

It is again worth emphasizing that injury correlations are statistical and are not absolute. For example, if there is a 60% probability of a certain type and injury severity occurring, this means that in the same crash there is a 40% probability of not sustaining that injury. In addition, a person can be critically injured or killed (AIS 5 or 6) in a moderate delta-v accident, say 15 to 20 m.p.h., but can walk away uninjured or with minor injuries (AIS 0 or 1) in a high delta-v accident, say 35 to 40 m.p.h. Hence, care and discretion must be used when the injury correlation data is to be used in an attempt to predict injuries in a given crash.

It is also worthwhile mentioning a few other key ideas in the field of injury biomechanics. The concept of threshold injury criteria refers to those combinations of kinematic variables, i.e., related to geometry and motion, and kinetic variables, i.e., related to forces that cause the motion, which can cause a traumatic injury to various body tissues. These variables include, but are not necessarily limited to, forces, moments, or torques (rotational effect of forces), accelerations, stresses, strains, and their associated time histories. Time duration of loading (impulses and vibrations) can be very significant; for example, forces and accelerations applied for a short time period may not cause injury while the same forces applied for a longer time period may be injury-producing. In determining threshold injury criteria, an implicit assumption is made that such criteria do indeed uniquely exist and apply across the spectrum of the human population. This should be interpreted with caution, since not only is there expected biological variability between individuals, but factors such as age, disease, preexisting conditions, and other variables can and do influence the response of whole tissues and single cells to mechanical loading.

The concept of threshold injury criteria has entered into the law. The National Traffic and Motor Vehicle Safety Act of 1966 introduced the concept of vehicle crashworthiness, i.e., the ability of a motor vehicle to protect its occupants in a crash. This act led to the creation of the Federal Motor Vehicle Safety Standards (FMVSS), which require a minimum level of crashworthiness for all cars sold in the United States. The FMVSS contain essentially three threshold injury criteria (see Pike), which manufacturers must comply with and which are worth summarizing herein.

The first, known as the Head Injury Criterion (HIC), requires that a certain mathematical expression, i.e., an integral of the resultant acceleration-time history measured at the center of gravity of the head of a restrained ATD (anthropomorphic test device) in a crash test, cannot exceed a value of 1000 or else the vehicle fails the test. There are many deficiencies in the HIC, which include the fact that it does not distinguish between types of head injuries such as skull fractures, subdural hematoma, diffuse axonal injury, and so on (see Newman). In addition, the use of a surrogate such as an ATD may not accurately reflect conditions necessary to cause human injury. However, the HIC may be useful as a screening device, in that a vehicle that results in a lower HIC may be better for head injury occupant protection than a vehicle that results in a higher HIC. The caveat here is that it is indeed possible to walk away from an accident with an HIC greater than 1000, without head injury, while a person can be killed by a head injury in a vehicle where the HIC was significantly less than 1000.

The second criterion refers to a force measurement made in the femur of the restrained ATD. The vehicle fails the test if the force in the femur exceeds 10.0 kN (2250 lb). Again, the deficiency in this criterion is that femoral fracture loads are very variable and compressive fracture loads in human femora can be less than 2250 lb for a significant portion of the population.

The third threshold injury criterion refers to the resultant acceleration measured at the center of gravity of the thorax of the ATD. A vehicle passes this test if the acceleration does not exceed 60 g's (sixty times the acceleration due to gravity) for intervals whose cumulative duration is not more than 3 milliseconds (0.003 seconds). This criterion is an example of where the time duration of loading is significant. Again, a major shortcoming is that it does not account for normal population variability and does not distinguish between types of thoracic trauma such as rib fracture, transected aorta, etc.

This section will be closed by noting that other injury criteria have been proposed and still others are undergoing

TABLE 66-1 AIS severity code

AIS	Severity
0	None
1	Minor
2	Moderate
3	Serious
4	Severe
5	Critical
6	Maximum (currently untreatable, fatal)

intense research investigation. Biomechanics injury research, with its spinoffs to forensic engineering applications, requires the collaboration of engineers, medical researchers, and forensic scientists working toward the goal of understanding whole body and tissue responses to traumatic loading conditions.

PRODUCTS LIABILITY

Products liability is a burgeoning area of forensic engineering investigation. Products liability investigations revolve around the issue of whether a product is defective and if the defect is causally related to any injuries that may have occurred to the user(s) or people in the vicinity of the product. Essentially, the following three types of product defects are recognized in the law, but this may vary according to the jurisdiction of the lawsuit: (1) design defects, i.e., the product lacks those elements that are necessary for its safe and foreseeable uses; (2) manufacturing defects, i.e., the product was not manufactured according to the manufacturer's own specifications or standards; and (3) failure to properly warn or instruct the user in the proper and safe use of the product.

If a forensic engineer is retained on behalf of the person bringing the lawsuit (the plaintiff), the engineer will objectively analyze the product for defects, and if they are found, will determine if the defects are causally related to the plaintiff's injuries. The role of the forensic engineer retained by the defendant, which can often be the engineer(s) who designed the product, will be to objectively defend the product in view of the allegations made by the plaintiff. As part of the defense of the product, the defense forensic engineer(s) may argue that the defect does not exist, and/or the plaintiff grossly misused the product, and/or that the plaintiff's injuries are unrelated to the alleged defect. Products liability investigations can be very long and time-consuming and often require the expenditure of large sums of money for experts on behalf of both plaintiffs and defendants. They can also be very technically challenging, requiring a great deal of calculations, computer modeling, and laboratory testing.

In order to fix ideas, the following examples are presented to illustrate the three types of defects mentioned above. These examples are obviously not intended to be exhaustive and are illustrative only.

Design defects

Consider the phenomenon of vehicle rollover, which may occur during intended and foreseeable use of certain types of vehicles. For example, such vehicles can be all-terrain vehicles (ATVs), designed for off-road use, or sport utility vehicles (SUVs) designed for highway use as well as off-road use. Engineering analyses show that the rollover propensity of these vehicles is in large measure due to the high height of the center of gravity of the vehicle in relation to the track width, which are vehicle parameters under the control of the designer. A plaintiff may be driving an SUV on the highway and suddenly be forced into making a sharp turn or evasive maneuver to avoid an accident, which then leads to the vehicle rolling over, resulting in serious injuries or death to the SUV occupants. The rollover propensity may then form the basis for a design defect lawsuit, and many of these types of cases have indeed been litigated. It is also worth emphasizing that a design defect is an absolute concept, not a statistical one, and it is irrelevant that the same vehicle can be used successfully many, if not millions of, times without rolling over. Note that when TWA 800 exploded, 747s had logged billions of passenger miles prior to the center fuel tank defect manifesting itself. When all physical conditions are satisfied, design defects can spell disaster for SUV occupants when the vehicle suddenly rolls over with little or no warning to the driver.

Manufacturing defects

Simply because a person is injured using a product does not mean that a product defect of any kind exists. Sharp-edged instruments such as knives provide a good example since knives are designed to cut, and the fact that a person may be cut using a knife does not mean that the knife is defective. However, consider the situation where a person is using a knife to carve a turkey and during carving the blade fractures. This causes the person to lose balance, fall forward, and be stabbed by the fractured blade or, perhaps, another person in the vicinity was injured by a piece of the blade. Metallurgical analysis of the blade after the accident revealed that it was weakened by containing inclusions and by improper heat treatment during manufacture. This means that the blade was not manufactured according to the manufacturer's own specifications and was thus defectively manufactured. Manufacturing defect lawsuits are much easier to pursue than design defect lawsuits since the entire product line, which may involve millions of products, is not at issue, but only the single defectively manufactured piece. However, considering the SUV design defect example above, jurors may have a difficult time understanding the physics and mathematics of rollover propensity, or even believing that the design defect exists, especially if they themselves drive SUVs.

Failure to warn

Proper warnings and instructions can be critical to the safe use of a product. For example, properly designed car air bags can be wonderful life-saving devices in a crash. However, a person sitting too close to an air bag can be seriously injured or killed by the air bag front, which can move at speeds up to 320 km/h (200 m.p.h.), i.e., the person may have survived the delta-v of the crash but it was the deploying air bag that caused the serious injury or death. Small adults and children sitting in the front seat of an automobile are particularly vulnerable to impacts by the moving air bag front. If an automobile did not carry prominent warnings about sitting too close to a deploying air bag—and many cars did not when air bags were first introduced—the vehicle would be defective by virtue of a failure to warn. Furthermore, warnings should never be used by a manufacturer to disclaim liability, and in many cases a warning may be interpreted as an admission of a defect that was not designed out of the system. Hence, it is relatively common for allegations of defective design to be coupled with a failure to warn in a lawsuit complaint. For example, in air bag technology, air bags can be designed to be depowered such that the deploying front does not move as fast but still offers occupant protection without as high a risk of injury.

General product design considerations

The goal of design engineering is to design safe products and systems that are free of hazards caused by defects. Engineers must be able to identify hazards in advance, or prospectively, and then design out the hazards, if it is practical and feasible to do so, before the product or system leaves their control. Once an accident due to a design defect occurs, the injured person has essentially identified the design defect and it is too late for a prospective hazard identification analysis. Several hazard identification analysis procedures, and variations of procedures, exist, which should be part of the normal design process and which are routinely employed by engineers in the design stages of a product or system to eliminate defects and improve system reliability. Three of the commonly used identification procedures are:

Failure modes and effects analysis (FMEA). The FMEA is a bottom-to-top basic procedure where the system is examined component by component and a failure or malfunction of any component is traced throughout the entire system. Flow sheets and computer programs are available to assist the engineering design team in this procedure, which screens the entire system. If the component failure results in a hazard that can cause injury, it is identified and necessary design changes should be made to remove the hazard and/or protect the user.

Fault-tree analysis (FTA). The FTA is a top-to-bottom procedure where the undesirable outcome (top event or fault condition) is the starting point. This top event is then traced down through the system and the failures of individual components or events that can lead to the undesirable outcome are identified. Design changes are then made as required to eliminate or minimize the probability of the occurrence of the fault condition. The FTA is a complicated procedure, which is used to analyze complex systems, e.g., a space shuttle; it relies heavily on Boolean algebra techniques and symbols and is most often done on a digital computer.

Product safety audit (PSA). The PSA is basically a checklist containing hundreds, if not thousands, of questions concerning the design of the product. The questions are framed in a manner such that a negative answer triggers

further investigation, which may lead to a design change. The major drawback, as with any checklist procedure, is that if the list of questions is incomplete, a defect can be easily overlooked.

Once the hazards in a product or system are identified by a proper hazard identification analysis, the engineer follows a codified procedure known as the "safety hierarchy" in order to prevent or minimize the probability of personal injury. This hierarchy is not a law of nature or a scientific law but rather a logical procedure that has been adopted by consensus and has the priorities shown in Table 66-2, in the order in which they should be used.

Typically, in products liability investigations applicable to consumer products, only the first three priorities are normally considered part of the safety hierarchy. Furthermore, the line between the first and second priorities can sometimes become blurred, depending on the product and its environment of use. This is because providing a proper guard can be thought of as an integral part of the overall design process, which includes considerations of man-machine interface safety in the concept stage and all design stages of product development. However, if the product is, say, a hand-held circular saw, the rotating blade is essential to the cutting function and obviously cannot be eliminated. Hence, the second priority would call for a blade guard to protect against inadvertent contact with the blade. Whenever a design change is contemplated, it is essential that the engineer examine the alternative design(s) for new hazards which may be introduced by the change(s). The alternative design(s) may not be as safe as the original design and the engineer must decide on which features to include in the final design.

Regarding warnings, it is important to emphasize that properly designed warnings, which can be words and/or pictographs, have to communicate three things to the user, i.e., what the hazard is, the steps the user can take to avoid the hazard, and what the likely consequences can be if the warnings are disregarded. Pictographs may be preferable to words since they can be more dramatic, in addition to eliminating a possible language barrier in locales where more than one language is commonly spoken. It should also be

TABLE 66-2 Safety hierarchy

First priority	Design out the hazard if it is practical and feasible to do so.
Second priority	If the hazard cannot be designed out, guard against the hazard.
Third priority	Provide proper warnings concerning the hazards and instructions for use of the product.
Fourth priority	If applicable, provide training in the safe use of the product or system.
Fifth priority	If applicable, prescribe personal protective equipment.

emphasized that too many warnings on a product may destroy their effectiveness. Furthermore, and very important, warnings should never be used by a manufacturer to disclaim liability and are never ever a substitute for a safe design that is practical and feasible to achieve.

CONCLUSION

The purpose of this short chapter has been to expose the reader to the exciting and rapidly developing field of forensic engineering. In addition, forensic scientists are encouraged to utilize the services of forensic engineers in injury and death investigation cases. The topics discussed in the chapter are necessarily limited in scope and the interested reader is referred to the bibliography for references to further applications and in-depth treatments. The bibliography is provided for representative coverage of the field without endorsement of any publication. An attempt has been made to generally group the bibliography by subject matter, as discussed in the chapter, although there is considerable overlap.

BIBLIOGRAPHY

Forensic engineering

S.C. Batterman & S.D. Batterman, *Forensic Engineering*, in *McGraw-Hill Yearbook of Science and Technology* (2002).

S.C. Batterman & S.D. Batterman, *Forensic Engineering*, in *Medicolegal Death Investigation Manual: Treatises in the Forensic Sciences*, 2d ed., chap. 12 (Forensic Science Foundation Press, 1999).

K.L. Carper (ed.), *Forensic Engineering*, 2d ed. (CRC Press, 2001).

H. Petroski, *To Engineer Is Human: The Role of Failure in Successful Design* (St. Martin's Press, 1985).

N. Putchat, *Forensic Engineering—a Definition*, 29 J. Forensic Sci. 375-78 (1984).

Newton's laws and principles of classical dynamics

F.P. Beer & E.R. Johnston, *Vector Mechanics for Engineers: Statics and Dynamics* (McGraw-Hill, 1977).

D.T. Greenwood, *Classical Dynamics* (McGraw-Hill, 1977).

H. Yeh & J.I. Abrams, *Principles of Mechanics of Solids and Fluids: Particle and Rigid Body Mechanics* (McGraw-Hill, 1960).

Accident reconstruction

Accident Reconstruction Technology Collection, CD-ROM (Society of Automotive Engineers, 2002).

Accident Reconstruction: Human, Vehicle and Environmental Factors, SAE SP-814 (Society of Automotive Engineers, 1990).

S.H. Backaitis (ed.), *Reconstruction of Motor Vehicle Accidents: A Technical Compendium*, PT-34 (Society of Automotive Engineers, 1989).

S.C. Batterman & S.D. Batterman, *Accident Investigation/Motor Vehicle (Accident Reconstruction and Biomechanics of Injuries)*, in J.A. Siegel et al. (eds.), *Encyclopedia of Forensic Sciences* (Academic Press, 2000).

S.D. Batterman & S.C. Batterman, *Delta-v, Spinal Trauma, and the Myth of the Minimal Damage Accident*, 1(1) J. Whiplash & Related Disorders 41-52 (2002).

T.L. Bohan & A.C. Damask (eds.), *Forensic Accident Investigation: Motor Vehicles* (Michie Butterworth, 1995).

R.M. Brach, *Mechanical Impact Dynamics: Rigid Body Collisions* (Wiley, 1991).

R. Limpert, *Motor Vehicle Accident Reconstruction and Cause Analysis*, 2d ed. (Michie, 1984).

Mathematical Simulation of Occupant and Vehicle Kinematics, SAE P-146 (Society of Automotive Engineers, 1984).

Biomechanics of injury

The Abbreviated Injury Scale, 1990 revision (Des Plaines, IL: Association for the Advancement of Automotive Medicine [AAAM],1990).

Automotive Frontal Impacts, SAE SP-782 (Society of Automotive Engineers, 1989).

Biomechanics of Impact Injury and Injury Tolerances of the Head-Neck Complex, SAE PT-43 (Society of Automotive Engineers, 1993).

Biomechanics of Impact Injury and Injury Tolerances of the Thorax-Shoulder Complex, SAE PT-45 (Society of Automotive Engineers, 1994).

A.C. Damask & J.N. Damask, *Injury Causation Analyses: Case Studies and Data Sources* (Michie, 1990).

F.G. Evans, *Mechanical Properties of Bone* (Thomas, 1973).

Human Tolerance to Impact Conditions as Related to Motor Vehicle Design, SAE J885 (Society of Automotive Engineers, 1986).

J.H. McElhaney, V.L. Roberts & J.F. Hilyard, *Handbook of Human Tolerance* (Japan Automotive Research Institute, 1976).

P.J. Mills & C.A. Hobbs, *The Probability of Injury to Car Occupants in Frontal and Side Impacts*, in *Proceedings of Twenty-Eighth Stapp Car Crash Conference*, paper 841652, 223-35 (Society of Automotive Engineers, 1984).

A.M. Nahum & J. Melvin (eds.), *The Biomechanics of Trauma* (Appleton-Century-Crofts, 1985).

J.A. Newman, *Head Injury Criteria in Automotive Crash Testing*, in *Proceedings of Twenty-Fourth Stapp Car Crash Conference*, paper 801317, 703-47 (Society of Automotive Engineers, 1980).

J.A. Pike, *Automotive Safety: Anatomy, Injury, Testing and Regulation* (Society of Automotive Engineers, 1990).

Side Impact: Injury Causation and Occupant Protection, SAE SP-769 (Society of Automotive Engineers, 1989).

Stapp Car Crash Conference Proceedings, CD-ROM (Society of Automotive Engineers, 2002).

Vehicle Crashworthiness and Occupant Protection in Frontal Collisions, SAE SP-807 (Society of Automotive Engineers, 1990).

H. Yamada, *Strength of Biological Materials* (Krieger, 1973).

Products liability

J.J. Phillips, *Products Liability*, 3d ed. (West Publishing Co., 1988).

J.F. Thorpe & W.M. Middendorf, *What Every Engineer Should Know About Product Liability* (Marcel Dekker, 1979).

A.S. Weinstein, A.D. Twerski, H.R. Piehier & W.A. Donaher, *Products Liability and the Reasonably Safe Product: A Guide for Management, Design and Marketing* (Wiley, 1978).

Hazard identification analyses

D.B. Brown, *Systems Analysis and Design for Safety* (Prentice-Hall, 1976).

B.S. Dhillon & C. Singh, *Engineering Reliability, New Techniques and Applications* (Wiley, 1981).

67 Forensic Toxicology

FREDERICK W. FOCHTMAN, Ph.D., D.A.B.T., D.A.B.F.T.

POSTMORTEM FORENSIC TOXICOLOGY
HUMAN PERFORMANCE TOXICOLOGY
ALCOHOL IN THE BODY AND ITS EFFECTS
DRUGS AND DRIVING
FORENSIC DRUG TESTING

When the term toxicology is used, one thinks of poisons or exposure to something that will cause harm to the body. Indeed, toxicology does embrace the study of deleterious effects of substance exposure not only to the human body but also to the environment and all other organisms existing in the environment. Forensic toxicology represents a subset of toxicology where legal issues require toxicology studies to determine the facts. Forensic toxicology has been referred to as toxicology with medicolegal applications. The forensic toxicologist is a scientist with basic training and education most often in chemistry, pathophysiology, and pharmacology and frequently holding an earned graduate degree. Many forensic toxicologists have a Ph.D. degree in pharmacology, toxicology, chemistry, or a related science. Forensic toxicology studies are nearly always analytical in nature because the interpretation of the actions and effects of drugs and toxic substances requires knowing what is present and how much is present. This is true regardless of whether the questions involve postmortem, human performance, or drug-testing interpretations. These are the areas in which forensic toxicologists are routinely involved: postmortem forensic toxicology, human performance toxicology, and forensic drug testing.

POSTMORTEM FORENSIC TOXICOLOGY

Postmortem forensic toxicology involves analyzing body fluids and organs from death cases and interpreting that information. Sudden unexpected and/or unexplained deaths become coroner's cases or fall under the jurisdiction of the medical examiner. Frequently in these cases toxicology studies are useful and necessary for the final decision regarding the cause and manner of death. In nearly every death that remains unexplained after postmortem examination, toxicology studies are sought to rule out poisoning, drug overdose, or therapeutic misadventure.

In some cases there is a history and/or physical evidence to indicate an overdose or poisoning, such as intravenous drug use and drug paraphernalia at the death scene, presence of suicide notes, or empty drug containers. A death from an accidental fire or arson, or exposure to incomplete combustion fumes (motor vehicle exhaust), will indicate that carbon monoxide poisoning should be suspected. In these instances, forensic toxicology studies are necessary to corroborate investigative findings. However, the young or middle-aged therapeutic drug user found dead, the nursing home patient found dead, the science researcher found dead, all without a history or any physical evidence of poisoning or overdose, can present a problem that may be solved by toxicology testing and interpretation.

Forensic toxicologists routinely test postmortem blood and urine specimens when available. Various other fluids, e.g., eye fluid, stomach contents, and bile, also can be analyzed. Samples of organ tissues may have to be tested when bodies are decomposed and fluids are not available. Some forensic laboratories will test both a heart blood sample and a peripheral (femoral) blood sample in order to evaluate postmortem changes in blood concentrations. It is important for toxicology specimens to be properly collected during the autopsy process. Care must be taken that specimens are not contaminated with fluids from other compartments of the body. It is also recommended that a portion of blood specimens be preserved with fluoride to minimize postmortem degradation.

Analytical methodologies used by forensic laboratories vary, but most use a combination of immunoassay and chromatographic methods to identify and quantify drugs and poisons. Alcohol is routinely analyzed in forensic laboratories by gas chromatography. Enzymatic and colorimetric methods occasionally are used as an initial or screening test. Carbon monoxide testing can be performed by spectrophotometric differentiation between oxyhemoglobin, reduced hemoglobin, methemoglobin, and carboxyhemoglobin. Carbon monoxide analysis is also done by a diffusion and colorimetric method, and gas chromatography. Cyanide

635

testing is done by diffusion and colorimetric quantitation. Immunoassay testing can be used for screening both blood and urine specimens for a variety of drugs and drug classes. Opiates, amphetamines, barbiturates, benzodiazepines, and cocaine metabolite are examples of immunoassay testing. Chromatographic methods such as thin layer chromatography (TLC), gas chromatography (GC), high performance liquid chromatography (HPLC), and chromatography interfaced with mass spectrometry (GC/MS, GC/MS/MS, LC/MS, LC/MS/MS) are used for qualitative analysis and quantitative testing of specimens for drugs and poisons. For heavy metal poisoning such as arsenic, mercury, cadmium, and lead, specimens can be analyzed by atomic absorption spectrophotometry.

For the results of toxicology testing to be scientifically valid, the methods and procedures used for analyzing specimens must be validated. The validation process ensures the accuracy, precision, and specificity of the method. The process includes identifying limits of detection and lower and upper limits of quantitation. Included in method validation is testing for possible interfering substances and evaluating carryover from previous tested samples. The method must be able to provide accurate results for reference specimens. The forensic toxicologist must understand the importance of validation and be able to evaluate the effectiveness of the process. Results from scientifically valid methods are necessary to support medicolegal circumstances of criminal or civil cases.

A number of references are available for comparing blood concentrations in order to interpret the results of toxicology testing. Most, if not all, of the reference values for toxic and lethal concentrations of drugs and poisons appearing in the literature are from case reports. For reported reference values a wide diversity exists for methodologies used, condition of the specimens, and the validity of the testing in these reports. This leads to a wide range and frequently overlapping ranges of concentrations reported for toxic and lethal concentrations of drugs and poisons. Accurate and traceable analytical reference values for most scientific comparisons require experimental doses of substances under controlled conditions with validated procedures. Obviously this type of information is not available for toxic and lethal doses in humans. However, for many drugs valid and traceable reference values are available for therapeutic doses. The postmortem forensic toxicologist therefore must make interpretations based on data that in some cases are not scientifically sound. Information and data from case reports, however, is better than having no information available. This emphasizes the importance of experience and training necessary for interpreting postmortem concentrations of drugs and poisons.

Interpretation of combined drug toxicity can be particularly challenging. If the combination includes several or more drugs with similar mechanisms, such as central nervous system depressant action, it may be somewhat easy to interpret. However, when the combination includes drugs with different mechanisms or antagonistic mechanisms, such as selective serotonin reuptake inhibitor, central nervous system stimulant, and central nervous system depressant, the interpretation can be more difficult. This is an area where case reports involving combined drug toxicities can be helpful for interpretation and also the experience and training of the forensic toxicologist.

Blood samples from fatalities of motor vehicle accidents are routinely tested by postmortem forensic toxicologists for alcohol and also frequently for drugs. Alcohol (ethanol) and many different drugs can render a person incapable of safe driving. This is clearly shown by the yearly statistics issued by the National Traffic Safety Bureau on motor vehicle deaths involving alcohol and drugs. A forensic toxicologist's role in interpreting impairment from alcohol and/or drugs is emphasized in human performance toxicology.

HUMAN PERFORMANCE TOXICOLOGY

Human performance toxicology is an area of forensic toxicology that primarily deals with driving under the influence of drugs and alcohol. Human performance toxicology can also be referred to as behavioral toxicology dealing with an inability to perform in the workplace.

The forensic toxicologist is frequently asked to interpret blood alcohol concentration (BAC) and blood drug concentration and the relationship they have with impairment. In addition, since the tested value for alcohol or a drug is not done on a sample taken at the time of the incident (accident or arrest) but at a later time, it is often necessary for the toxicologist to extrapolate what the person's BAC or drug level was at the time of arrest or the accident. This type of interpretation of blood alcohol and drug concentration and the effect on an individual relies on an understanding and knowledge of the physiology and the pharmacology of ethyl alcohol and drugs.

ALCOHOL IN THE BODY AND ITS EFFECTS

Ethyl alcohol, or ethanol, is the active constituent (drug) that is contained in alcoholic beverages. Ethanol concentration in beverages varies from a low of 4% to 5% in beers, 7% to 12% in wines, 20% to 40% in cordials, to a high of 40% to 50% in most distilled beverages (whiskeys, vodkas, rums, etc.). Proof strength stated on the labels of some beverages is a value that is double the percent strength. An example is that a 100 proof beverage would be 50% alcohol. It is necessary for the forensic toxicologist to know the concentration of ethanol in beverages in order to interpret quantities consumed related to blood alcohol concentration.

A person drinking an alcoholic beverage will not absorb alcohol into the blood while the beverage is in the stomach. The stomach's function does not include absorption but merely prepares and liquefies swallowed contents for emptying into the small intestine. When the beverage passes from the stomach to the small intestine (duodenum), absorption into the blood will occur. This process takes approximately 20 to 30 minutes for complete absorption when the stomach is empty. When food is present in the stomach the process takes longer due to food causing the beverage to stay in the stomach longer, thus extending the time of absorption. Depending on the amount of food present in the stomach, the time for complete absorption of alcohol may take an hour or longer.

Once alcohol is absorbed into the blood, it will be distributed to all parts of the body. In the brain, alcohol has its primary pharmacological effect by producing central nervous system (CNS) depression. All of the impairment effects of alcohol are related to the depressant actions on the nervous system. These effects include increased reaction time, decreased visual acuity, decreased peripheral vision, poor judgment, and sensory-motor incoordination. The combined effects are referred to as "impairment" or "under the influence." Scientific studies have shown that impairment from alcohol can be related to the concentration of alcohol in the blood. Various concentrations are used by states and included in their statutes and regulations governing licensed drivers. Most states use a concentration of 0.10% or greater in blood to indicate that a driver is impaired. However, allocation of federal highway funding is being used to influence states to lower the concentration to 0.08%.

Once alcohol enters the blood and is distributed to the liver, it is metabolized first to acetaldehyde and then to acetate, providing calories. Approximately 90% to 98% of alcohol is metabolized, which occurs at a constant rate (zero order). A person's rate of metabolism depends on their experience and frequency of alcohol use. Heavy drinkers will metabolize more rapidly than light or nondrinkers. Metabolism plus the amount of alcohol excreted unchanged represents elimination or dissipation rate. Elimination rates average from 0.015% per hour to 0.02% per hour.

A person's blood alcohol concentration (BAC) can be estimated using the following formulae:

$$150/BW \times A/50 \times B \times 0.025\% = \text{Maximum BAC}$$

$$\text{Dissipation} = \text{Number of hours consuming beverage} \times \text{Elimination rate}$$

$$\text{Maximum BAC} - \text{Dissipation} = \text{BAC}$$

where BW = body weight, A = percent concentration of alcoholic beverage, and B = number of ounces of alcoholic beverage. It is necessary to know the person's body weight, the amount of beverage, and the percent alcohol content in the beverage. Also it is necessary to know when the person started drinking and when they finished to make a meaningful estimation.

Rates of dissipation and absorption of alcohol are also used by the forensic toxicologist to extrapolate back to the time of the arrest or accident. An example is an accident occurring at 8:00 P.M. There is suspicion of driving under the influence of alcohol (DUI). The driver does not pass a field sobriety evaluation and is administered a breath test 2 hours after the accident at 10:00 P.M. The result of the breath test is 0.095% BAC. The driver reports that he has not had anything to eat since lunch and that he stopped drinking 2 hours earlier at 6:00 P.M. Using the information provided and the range of average elimination rates, the driver's BAC at the time of the accident can be estimated. The driver's BAC would have been between 0.125% and 0.135% BAC. These values were obtained by adding to the BAC at 10:00 P.M the dissipation that occurred over 2 hours. Calculations become more complex when drivers have eaten meals recently and continued to drink right up to the accident or arrest. These types of cases present a challenge for the forensic toxicologist.

DRUGS AND DRIVING

For blood drug concentrations and impairment, scientific studies similar to alcohol studies do not exist except for marijuana. Interpreting blood drug concentrations and impairment while driving is more difficult than interpreting impairment with alcohol. Some states utilize trained police officers as drug recognition experts (DREs). The DRE evaluates a suspect by administering a series of tests that are more comprehensive than a field sobriety test, as well as a breath test. In addition, measurements of pulse, blood pressure, and body temperature are taken. After evaluation of all test information the DRE forms an opinion as to what drug or drug class is causing impairment. A blood or urine sample is also taken for toxicology testing to support the DRE's decision. Testing only a urine specimen provides for evidence of prior exposure but cannot provide a direct relationship to impairment. Opinions of forensic toxicology experts regarding impairment from drugs generally rely on blood concentrations and not on urine concentrations.

FORENSIC DRUG TESTING

In 1986, President Ronald Reagan issued Executive Order No. 12564, indicating that the federal government would be a drug-free workplace. Earlier in 1983, a study by the National Transportation Safety Board involving drugs and alcohol use in railway accidents prompted the Federal Railway Administration and the National Institute on Drug Abuse (NIDA) to begin developing drug regulations. Initially the intent was to have guidelines for the Department of Transportation (DOT), but with Reagan's executive order, NIDA continued to investigate the appropriateness of drug testing through studies and conferences. In 1988, NIDA issued mandatory guidelines for federal drug-testing programs. The guidelines were comprehensive, including issues of confidentiality, choice of specimen and collection, chain of custody, procedures for testing, quality control, records, reporting results, and interpretation of results. The regulation guidelines provided for a medical review officer (MRO) to review results before final reporting. Also included were guidelines regarding accrediting laboratories, inspecting laboratories, and proficiency testing for laboratories to maintain accredited status. A National Laboratory Certification Program administered by Research Triangle Institute commenced in 1988 under the auspices of the Department of Health and Human Services through NIDA. Drug testing under the guidelines is applicable only to federal employees and federal agencies, but private-sector drug testing quickly adopted many of the "NIDA guidelines" for their programs.

Although forensic drug testing had been utilized much earlier in the military and Olympics, and also in a small segment of private industry, before 1988, it was Reagan's executive order and subsequent NIDA guidelines that caused a tremendous growth in forensic testing. All types of industry, both large Fortune 500 and smaller companies, began to develop drug-free workplace policies that included drug testing. In addition, many other organizations or specific populations instituted, modified, or increased their use of forensic drug testing to achieve certain objectives. Testing of athletes, both professional and Olympic as well as high school athletes, insurance testing, drug rehabilitation, probation, and parole monitoring are examples of forensic drug testing. Drug testing in hospitals or clinical reference laboratories generally is done for medical purposes, but may become forensic testing when involving legal questions.

Federal regulations specify urine as the specimen for testing. Federal regulations allowed testing urine for five drugs or drug classes: cannabinoids (marijuana metabolites), cocaine (benzoylecgonine), amphetamines (amphetamine and methamphetamine), opiates (morphine and codeine), and phencyclidine (PCP). Nonfederal urine drug testing has been expanded to include barbiturates, benzodiazepines, methadone, LSD, and propoxyphene. Two separate portions (aliquots) of a urine specimen are required to be analyzed for a test to be reported as positive. An initial test on the first aliquot must be an immunoassay method. If the initial test is positive, a confirmatory test that must be a gas chromatograph/mass spectrometry (GC/MS) method is done on a second aliquot. Both the initial immunoassay test and the GC/MS confirmatory test are required to be validated by the laboratory. Validation criteria are discussed above in the postmortem forensic toxicology section.

For each test, the regulations provide cutoff concentrations to indicate a presumptive positive and a confirmed positive result. A specimen aliquot that tests negative on the initial test is reported as a negative and does not require any additional drug testing. The cutoff concentrations were chosen based on experience and recommendations by toxicologists involved with military, postmortem, and clinical testing for drugs. The initial test cutoff values for cannabinoids and opiates were found to be inappropriate and have since been changed. The original urine initial test cutoff for marijuana metabolites was 100 ng/ml. It was shown that this concentration was too high and likely resulted in many false negative reports. Many products promoted to "beat the drug test" that were based on drinking additional water were thought to be effective merely due to dilution of the urine. Subsequently the cutoff for marijuana metabolites was lowered to 50 ng/ml. This value was effective in decreasing the number of false negatives and is high enough to avoid a positive test due to passive inhalation.

The original cutoff for opiates was 300 ng/ml. Foods containing poppy seeds were found to produce positive urine results for morphine. Poppy seeds contain enough morphine to produce urinary concentrations above 300 ng/ml. In addition, cough medicines containing codeine produced urinary concentrations greater than the cutoff for a positive. Prescription analgesics taken by many individuals contain codeine along with a nonopiate analgesic. Chronic use of these prescription analgesics can produce morphine in the urine as a metabolite of codeine. To avoid positives for unintentional exposure and medicinal therapy, the initial test for opiates and confirmatory test cutoff concentrations for morphine and codeine have been changed to 2000 ng/ml for opiates.

Heroin use may be related to a positive result for morphine in the urine. Since heroin is diacetylmorphine and morphine is a heroin metabolite, morphine in the urine can indicate prior use of heroin. Since morphine can be present in the urine from sources other than heroin, the federal regulations allow for a definitive test for heroin use. Urines positive for morphine can be tested for monoacetyl morphine, a metabolite that can only be produced in the urine from heroin use.

Nearly all workplace urine drug testing is done with unobserved collections. This has led to some problems because of numerous attempts to thwart the testing process. The collection process includes monitoring the temperature of freshly collected urine. If there is an attempt to substitute another urine it is difficult to maintain the correct temperature. Various products have been available for sale that can be added to the urine to interfere with testing. They are referred to as adulterants. Some adulterants are very effective and are difficult to detect. In addition, individuals who are intent on "beating the test" will drink large amounts of water or other fluids prior to a test. This will dilute the urine and can cause a false negative when the concentration in the urine is less than the cutoff concentration.

Federal guidelines allow certified forensic laboratories to test for dilution, substitution, and adulteration of urine samples. There are guidelines established for dilution of urine based on creatinine and specific gravity, and for pH regarding adulteration. Most laboratories will test urines for creatinine content and pH. Creatinine concentration in the urine and specific gravity can provide a measure of dilution.

Adulteration of urine is frequently done by addition of an oxidizing substance such as a nitrite salt or pyridinium chromate. These issues present a challenge for the forensic toxicologist.

A medical review officer (MRO) is required to review results of federally mandated drug tests. The MRO can interview and medically evaluate a person with a positive drug test. Based on their findings, the MRO can modify the reported result. An MRO can also request a retest of the specimen.

Specimens other than urine are also being tested for evidence of drug use. Hair is being utilized for testing by some private-sector companies. Oral fluid testing is also being used to detect illicit drug use. These alternative specimens are currently being evaluated as possible substitutes for urine drug testing.

REFERENCES

R.C. Baselt, *Disposition of Toxic Drugs and Chemicals in Man*, 5th ed. (Foster City, CA: Chemical Toxicology Institute, 2000).

Department of Health and Human Services, ADAMHA, *Mandatory Guidelines for Federal Workplace Drug Testing: Final Guidelines*, 53(69) Fed. Reg. 11970-11989 (1988).

M.A. Huestis, J.M. Mitchell & E.J. Cone, *Lowering the Federally Mandated Cannabinoid Immunoassay Cutoff Increases True-Positive Results*, 40(5) Clin. Chem. 729-33 (1994).

C.D. Klaasson, *Casarett and Doull's Toxicology: The Basic Science of Poisons*, 6th ed. (New York: McGraw-Hill, 2001).

Psychiatric Patients and Forensic Psychiatry

MARVIN H. FIRESTONE, J.D., M.D., F.C.L.M.

PSYCHIATRY AND CRIMINAL LAW
PSYCHIATRIC MALPRACTICE
CIVIL RIGHTS

PSYCHIATRY AND CRIMINAL LAW

The purpose and rationale for the system of criminal justice in the United States are based on four fundamental concepts: isolation, retribution, deterrence, and rehabilitation.

As far back as biblical times, the issue of crime and punishment was premised on the notion of intent. The idea of wrongful or criminal guilt inherently required two elements: (1) that the wrongdoer commit an act or misdeed and, more important, (2) that the act was the product of a willing and rational intent. In other words, a crime is made up of two essential components: (1) voluntary conduct (actus rea) and (2) intent or guilty mind (mens rea).

An exception to a finding of criminal guilt historically has been reserved for minors and mentally disabled persons. In Babylonian times, for example, Jewish law held that "it is an ill thing to knock against a deaf mute, an imbecile or a minor: he that wounds them is culpable, but if they wound others they are not culpable."[1] Centuries later, a secular pronouncement was contained in the *Justinian Digest*:

There are those who are not to be held accountable, such is not a madman and a child who is not capable of malicious intention: these persons are able to suffer a wrong but not to produce one. Since a wrong is only able to exist by the intention of those who have committed it, it follows that these persons, whether they have assaulted by blows or insulted by words, are not considered to have committed a wrong.[2]

In 1265 Bracton, Chief Justice of England, wrote the first systematic treatise on English law and in it stated that neither child nor "madman" could be liable because both lacked the felonious intent necessary for an act to be considered criminal. He likened the acts of an insane person, lacking in mind and reason, to be not far removed from that of a brutish animal.[3] Other notable jurists, including Lord Hale, Chief Justice Mansfield, and Chief Justice Holmes in the United States, have all recognized the need to excuse from criminal responsibility any person incapable of forming the requisite criminal intent.[4]

Competency to stand trial

Society's sense of morality dictates that an individual who is unable to comprehend the nature and the object of the proceedings against him or her, to confer with counsel, and to assist in the preparation of his or her own defense may not be subjected to a criminal trial. The oft-quoted legal theorist, Blackstone, in defining this common law rule said:

If a man in his sound memory commits a capital offense, and before arraignment for it, he becomes mad, he ought not be arraigned for it; because he is not able to plead to it with that advice and caution that he ought. And if, after he has pleaded, the prisoner becomes mad, he shall not be tried; for how can he make his defense?[5]

Borrowing from this common-law principle, one of the fundamental tenets of American jurisprudence is the entitlement of every defendant to be afforded a fair and adequate hearing. For this requirement of fairness to be effectuated, the individual litigant must be capable of meaningful participation in the ongoing events of the legal process. The requirement that a litigant be competent to stand trial is of such moral and philosophical importance to the system of justice that it is considered a fundamental element and recognized as a constitutional right. In *Pate v. Robinson* the Supreme Court held "that the failure to observe a defendant's right not to be tried or convicted while incompetent to stand trial deprives him of his due process right to a fair trial."[6]

Despite the constitutional recognition that a defendant must be competent at the time of the trial, the determination and parameters of this fundamental principle have been the source of continued ambiguity. For example, such common mental status criteria as orientation to time and place and

640

the capacity to recollect past events have been found to be insufficient in determining trial competency. Various states have established standards by which to measure a defendant's competency to stand trial. At a bare minimum, it is sufficient to say that the fundamental fairness of law requires at least a finding of competency consistent with the test developed in *Dusky v. United States*: "[T]he test must be whether he has sufficient present ability to consult with his lawyer with a reasonable degree of rational as well as factual understanding of the proceedings against him."[7]

As seen from the general nature of this test, dispute and controversy are not uncommon in a case where a defendant's capacity is at issue. Although numerous federal and state decisions have sought to devise a more objective test, none has been totally successful. As a rule, any substantial impairment that interferes with a defendant's capacity to communicate, testify coherently, or follow the proceedings of the trial with a "reasonable degree of rational understanding" leads to a determination of incompetency.

The determination of competency is essentially a three-fold procedural process. The first step can be characterized as the *trigger stage*. Both the prosecution and the defense, as well as the court, may raise or trigger the issue of incompetency whenever there is a suggestion that the defendant may not be competent to stand trial. In fact, the trial court is under constitutional obligation to recognize and respond to any evidence that the defendant may not be mentally fit for trial. Once the issue has been raised, neither the defendant nor counsel can waive the issue and have the case brought to trial. Fundamental fairness of law requires that a defendant be competent throughout a trial.[8]

After the issue of a defendant's competency is raised, common procedure is for the court to appoint one or more independent experts to conduct a psychiatric examination. Two issues, one procedural and one substantive, are important to note. Although in most jurisdictions a question of competency automatically triggers an impartial psychiatric examination, a defendant has no constitutional right to one. Also, the function of a competency evaluation, as opposed to an insanity defense evaluation, is that the sole issue to be decided is whether the defendant is sufficiently competent "at that time" to proceed in his or her own defense during the trial. Evidence of incompetency, insanity, or other forms of incapacity during the commission of the crime is not germane to the question of competency to stand trial.

After the question of competency is raised, the court then determines whether there is *sufficient evidence* to justify a formal hearing. At this second stage the role of a psychiatrist is vital. Often the results of a psychiatrist's examination are persuasive in the court's determination of competency. For example, in the federal court system and in some states, if a psychiatric examiner concludes that the defendant is likely to be incompetent, a judicial hearing on the issue is required. Although neither the U.S. Supreme Court nor any

state has articulated clearly how much evidence of incompetency is necessary to compel a hearing, as a rule, evidence sufficient to raise a bona fide doubt will suffice the constitutional standards.[9]

At a separate and distinct legal proceeding, the third stage, the *competency hearing*, takes place. The importance of competency to participate in one's own defense is so fundamental to the system of justice that a competency hearing can be held at any time during a trial proceeding. Typically, the psychiatric expert who initially evaluated the defendant is the prime witness at this proceeding. A competency hearing is similar to and different from a normal trial in several respects. It is similar in that it is adversarial in nature. In addition to the findings of the court-ordered psychiatric expert, both the state and the defense may produce their own witnesses (lay and expert) regarding the defendant's competency, along with any other evidence. Also, the defendant has a right to counsel and is permitted to cross-examine the other side's witnesses. However, unlike a normal trial, the defendant has no options regarding adjudication before a judge or jury. A competency hearing is typically before a judge. Also, in most states the defendant must prove incompetency by at least a preponderance of the evidence, although in the federal courts the prosecutor must carry the burden. In another important distinction, because of the special circumstances in which a competency hearing is carried out, the defendant's right to invoke the privilege against self-incrimination is narrowed. The U.S. Supreme Court in *Estelle v. Smith* concluded that a defendant may not claim the privilege against self-incrimination to prevent the examining psychiatrist from testifying about the defendant's competency.[10] However, the court did rule that the privilege against self-incrimination (Fifth Amendment) may bar the disclosure of statements or any resulting psychiatric conclusions from those statements if they were made during the pretrial competency hearing or a subsequent sentencing proceeding.

Although the involvement of the psychiatric expert in this situation might appear to be curtailed, the contribution that expert findings and testimony make in a competency proceeding is invaluable to a system of fundamental justice.

The disposition of persons found incompetent to stand trial is procedurally uniform in the United States. However, differences in state statutes provide for a variety of rights and limitations. Traditionally, defendants found mentally incompetent to be tried were automatically referred to a state institution until they were found to be competent. In effect, a defendant's stay in a mental hospital, often an institution for the criminally insane, could drag on indefinitely and often did. Release could be effectuated only if either the defendant was found to be competent, at which time trial proceedings would then be initiated, or the prosecution dropped the charges. In 1972 the landmark case *Jackson v. Indiana* addressed this traditional practice of indefinite commitment of defendants found incompetent to stand trial.[11] First, the court held that although automatic commitment in and of itself is not prohibited, the length of commitment could not exceed a "reasonable period of time necessary to determine whether there is a substantial probability that he will attain that capacity in the foreseeable future." Also, the court determined that the state would bear the burden of demonstrating progress in the attainment of competency, so that a defendant whose competency does not appear reasonably foreseeable must be either formally committed pursuant to standard civil commitment procedures or released.

Insanity defense

Probably no single issue in the annals of criminal law has stirred more controversy, debate, and comparison among laypersons, as well as jurists, than the insanity defense. The 1982 jury decision finding John Hinckley not guilty by reason of insanity for the shootings of President Reagan and three other persons stunned the nation, and this decision thrust back into the public consciousness questions regarding the viability and fundamental morality surrounding the defense.

By the mid-eighteenth century a significant attempt was made to apply some form of cognizable formula for determining insanity. Judge Tracy in *Rex v. Arnold* suggested that one of the essential requisites for determining criminal responsibility was whether the accused was able to distinguish "good from evil" at the time of the offense.[12]

Later in the century, Hawkins wrote an important treatise on the subject that revised this moralistic standard to the more cognitively based question of "right and wrong."[13] Despite what appeared to be an improvement in providing some form of rule for evaluating insanity, the right-wrong test was short-lived.

In 1800 the interpretation of legal insanity broadened significantly with the inclusion of insane delusions as an acceptable ground for the defense. In *Hadfield's Case* the addition of delusions, or false beliefs that are firmly held despite incontrovertible evidence to the contrary, was first accepted by the common-law court.[14] Hadfield, a soldier who had suffered severe head trauma during the French wars, attempted to shoot King George III to attain martyrdom, which he was convinced was his destiny. Despite the lack of a "frenzy or raving madness," his counsel contended that the delusion was the true character of insanity:

These are the cases which frequently mock the wisdom of the wisest in judicial trials: because such persons often reason with a subtlety which puts in the shade the ordinary conceptions of mankind; their conclusions are just and frequently profound; but the premises from which they reason, when within the range of the malady, are uniformly false—not false from any defect of knowledge or judgment; but, because a delusive image, the inseparable companion of real

insanity, is thrust upon the subjugated understanding, incapable of resistance, because unconscious of the attack.[15]

Following counsel's argument, the court practically preempted the proceeding by ordering an acquittal. Some 40 years later a similar attempt was made on the lives of Queen Victoria and Prince Albert by Edward Oxford. Oxford, like Hadfield, suffered from the delusion of martyrdom and was also acquitted.[16] Despite the notoriety of these two cases, the application of the insanity defense based on delusional beliefs was not widely successful.

In 1843 a significant change in the legal rule used to determine insanity was created. In the trial of Daniel M'Naughton[17] the defendant expressed feelings of great persecution by the pope and Tories, the political party in power at that time. To rid himself of this torment, M'Naughton decided to kill Sir Robert Peel, the prime minister. Not knowing Peel by sight, M'Naughton lay in wait at his residence and mistakenly shot his secretary, Henry Drummond, who was leaving the prime minister's home. In addition to the numerous medical experts who all testified to M'Naughton's insanity, the court also summoned two physicians who were simply observing the trial. Because neither physician was partisan to the proceedings, both were afforded a special degree of credence. On their unanimous conclusion that the defendant was indeed insane, Chief Justice Tindal halted the proceedings, and the jury promptly found M'Naughton "not guilty by reason of insanity." Several days after the verdict, Queen Victoria, herself the target of assassination by the insanity acquittee Edward Oxford, summoned the House of Lords to a special session. The Lords were instructed to clarify and more strictly define the standards by which a defendant could be acquitted by reason of insanity. Out of this session the so-called M'Naughton rule was developed.[18] This rule provides the following:

The jurors ought to be told in all cases that every man is presumed to be sane and to possess a sufficient degree of reason to be responsible for his crimes, until the contrary can be proved to their satisfaction; and that, to establish a defense on the ground of insanity, it must be clearly proved, that, at the time of the committing of the act, the party accused was labouring under such a defect of reason, from disease of the mind, as not to know the nature and quality of the act he was doing or, if he did know it, that he did not know he was doing what was wrong.[19]

In essence, the M'Naughton rule, often referred to as the "right-wrong" test, has three elements that must be proven to establish insanity. The accused, at the time of the crime, must be suffering from some mental illness that caused a defect of reason such that he lacked the ability to understand the nature and quality of his actions or their wrongfulness.

Thus passed the eighteenth-century "good-evil" standard into the right-wrong test of the nineteenth century. Moreover, the M'Naughton decision marked the advent of the psychiatric expert witness as the key figure in defenses based on insanity. Henceforth, psychiatrists would be afforded special latitude in offering retrospective opinions regarding the defendant's state of mind at the time of the offense, whether his or her conduct emanated from some form of mental disease, and whether the defendant was cognizant of the wrongfulness of his or her conduct.

For more than a century the M'Naughton test served as the basic standard by which the insanity defense was judged in the United States and Great Britain. Even today a significant minority of states still apply it in its original form. Despite its extensive utility, it was later criticized. Even with its fairly broad language, the M'Naughton test was often narrowly construed as an evaluation of a defendant's cognitive capacity to distinguish right from wrong. Furthermore, its scope of application was greatly influenced by the perception of many psychiatrists that the concept of disease of the mind encompassed only psychosis, to the exclusion of other pathologies.

As advances in psychiatric theory were made, the M'Naughton rule came under increasing attack as being antiquated. The major argument was that some forms of mental illness affect a person's volition or power to act without impairing cognitive functioning. In other words, although many mentally ill individuals might be able to distinguish between right and wrong, they could not control their wrongful actions. To rectify this perceived deficiency, a number of states broadened the M'Naughton rule to include an additional element known as the "irresistible impulse" test.[20] The irresistible impulse test in essence stated that even though an individual might understand the nature and quality of his or her act and the fact that it is wrong or unlawful, he or she is nonetheless compelled to commit the act because of mental illness. This test basically rests on four assumptions:

[F]irst . . . there are mental diseases which impair volition or self control, even while cognition remains relatively unimpaired; second . . . the use of M'Naughton rule alone results in findings that persons suffering from such diseases are not insane; third . . . the law should make the insanity defense available to persons who are unable to control their action, just as it does to those who fit M'Naughton; fourth, no matter how broadly M'Naughton is construed there will remain areas of serious disorders which it will not reach.[21]

Regardless of whether the irresistible impulse test was developed by state statute or case law, it was never used as a sole standard but as a modification of the M'Naughton test.

Despite the addition of the irresistible impulse concept to the determination of insanity, this too was believed to be too narrow in light of contemporary psychiatry. In 1954

Judge Bazelon, writing for the U.S. Court of Appeals for the District of Columbia in the decision on *Durham v. United States*, rejected the M'Naughton rule as too limited and held the following:

We find as an exclusion criterion the right-wrong test is inadequate in that (a) it does not take sufficient account of psychic realities and scientific knowledge, and (b) it is based upon one symptom and so cannot validly be applied in all circumstances. We find that the "irresistible impulse" test is also inadequate in that it gives no recognition to mental illness characterized by brooding and reflection and so delegated acts caused by such illness to the application of the inadequate right-wrong test. We conclude that a broader test should be adopted.[22]

Accordingly, the court articulated a broader standard that provided that "[a]n accused is not criminally responsible if his unlawful act was the product of a mental disease or defect." Apparently, the purpose of the Durham rule,[23] with the description of mental disease or defect deliberately vague, was to afford greater flexibility to psychiatric testimony to circumvent narrow or psychiatrically inapposite legal inquiries.[24,25] As expected, the Durham rule, or New Hampshire rule as it was sometimes called, created considerable controversy because of its ambiguity and semantically indefinite meaning. It was never widely accepted in the legal system and was adopted in only three jurisdictions: New Hampshire, Maine, and the District of Columbia. Ultimately, the same Court of Appeals for the District of Columbia that created it abolished the Durham rule in 1972.

In the early 1960s the American Law Institute (ALI) drafted a model provision intended to reasonably bridge the narrowness of the M'Naughton rule and the expansiveness of the Durham rule. Incorporated in its Model Penal Code, the ALI standard stated the following:

A person is not responsible for criminal conduct if at the time of such conduct as a result of mental disease or defect he lacks substantial capacity either to appreciate the criminality of his conduct or to conform his conduct to the requirements of the law.[26]

The ALI test differs from the M'Naughton standard in three ways. First, it incorporates a volitional element to insanity, thereby providing an independent criterion, the ability (or inability) to control one's conduct. Second, the ALI substitutes with the phrase, "lacks substantial capacity to appreciate the wrongfulness of conduct," which in effect takes into account a defendant's affective or emotional state instead of simply cognitive comprehension. Finally, the ALI standard does not require a total lack of appreciation of the nature of the defendant's conduct but instead that only "substantial capacity" is lacking. Arguably, the ALI test embraces a broader spectrum of psychiatric disorders sufficient to trigger the insanity defense because it contemplates mental defects as well as diseases.

The ALI test is accepted in a majority of jurisdictions and has been frequently cited as being considerably more applicable than its predecessors. For example, its incorporation of both a cognitive and a volitional element of impairment is viewed as more consistent with the contemporary conceptualization of mental illness in general. Its move away from total (e.g., M'Naughton) to substantial incapacity also appears to be realistic in terms of modern psychiatry. It broadens the role of the psychiatric expert by providing additional questions to be addressed, while leaving the responsibility of the ultimate decision up to the jury.

The ALI standard, despite its improvements in incorporating language indicative of advances in modern psychiatry, leaves the interpretation of "mental disease or defect" wide open. To address this ambiguity, most courts have relied on the definition provided in the case *McDonald v. United States*.[27] In *McDonald* the court defined mental disease or defect as "any abnormal condition of the mind which substantially affects mental or emotional processes and substantially impairs behavior controls."[28] This definition was created to help clarify the Durham standard but turned out to provide guidance for courts using the ALI rule. It is important to keep in mind that the insanity defense under the ALI standard is a two-pronged test. In addition to providing the existence of a mental disease or defect, the defendant then had to show that the disease or defect so impaired judgment that he or she was not able to conform conduct to the requirements of the law (volition element).

In 1984, Congress enacted its first legislation addressing the insanity defense:

(a) Affirmative Defense. It is an affirmative defense to a prosecution under any Federal statute that, at the time of the commission of the acts constituting the offense, the defendant, as a result of a severe mental disease or defect, was unable to appreciate the nature and quality of the wrongfulness of his acts. Mental disease or defect does not otherwise constitute a defense.

(b) Burden of Proof. The defendant has the burden of proving the defense of insanity by clear and convincing evidence.

Other defenses. The development of the two-pronged ALI test, in addition to broadening the range of behavior that would excuse a defendant from criminal responsibility as compared with the M'Naughton test, also has opened the door to other forms of "illnesses" that could be considered to form the basis of an insanity defense.

Posttraumatic stress disorder (PTSD) is a form of mental condition that develops as a result of some traumatic event, such as combat war experience, plane or car crashes, and natural disasters. The most salient symptoms manifested by an individual with PTSD include recurrent elements and phases of the past trauma in dreams, uncontrollable and emotionally intrusive images, dissociative states of consciousness, and unconscious behavioral reenactments of the traumatic situation.

PTSD has been raised most frequently in criminal cases by Vietnam veterans as a form of insanity defense. Typically, the argument is made that the defendant's criminal behavior resulted from combat in Vietnam. Arguably, situations in which the defendant's criminal actions appeared to suggest some causal connection with a reenactment of a former war experience, in the absence of any other plausible explanation, is the most apropos time to raise a PTSD insanity defense. For example, the two murder trials of Vietnam veteran Charles Heads poignantly illustrate this defense. After his return from Vietnam, Heads frequently complained of depression, incessant nightmares, and flashbacks. One day in 1977, Heads, reacting to a fog-laden mist that surrounded a field adjacent to his brother-in-law's home in Louisiana, grabbed a rifle from his car and attacked the house. In the ensuing moments, he fatally shot his brother-in-law. Heads claimed that for an instant he was reliving combat. In his first trial in 1978, however, the jury rejected this temporary insanity claim.[29]

Because of a serious error by the trial judge, the Supreme Court suspended his life sentence and ordered a new trial. In 1981 a second jury heard his characterization of that fateful day and heard testimony from several veterans regarding their experiences of stress emanating from the war. This jury found Heads not guilty by reason of temporary insanity stemming from his past combat experiences.[30] This was the first PTSD defense successfully used in a capital case.

Even when the defendant displays clear signs of PTSD, however, there is no guarantee the defense will be accepted. In addition to demonstrating the existence of the illness, it must also be shown that it so impaired the defendant that it directly caused the criminal act. Although a majority of PTSD criminal cases involve war veterans, the defense is certainly not confined to this group.

Abolition of the insanity defense. Before 1930, Washington, Mississippi, and Louisiana had tried without success to do away with the insanity defense. Even before then, as well as after, numerous commentators had sought to abolish the defense.[31,32]

In 1979, Montana became the first state to constructively limit the use of an insanity plea. It amended its Code of Criminal Procedure to delete the section recognizing the insanity defense, which was substantially consistent with the ALI standard. The legislature substituted a new section that limited the relevancy of mental disease to the determination of mens rea of criminal intent. The Montana section stated: "Evidence that defendant suffered from a mental disease or defect is admissible whenever it is relevant to prove that the defendant did or did not have a state of mind which is an element of the offense."[33]

Three years later Idaho explicitly abolished the use of insanity as a separate defense to charges of criminal acts. As in Montana, however, the Idaho statute recognized that a defendant's mental state may be relevant to the issue of criminal intent:[34] "[N]othing herein is intended to prevent the admission of expert evidence on the issue of mens rea or any state of mind which is an element of the offense, subject to the rules of evidence."[35] Alabama and Utah have followed similar courses in either restricting a plea of insanity to the question of criminal intent or abolishing it altogether.

As alluded to earlier, the change in Montana and Utah to a mens rea approach in effect is a constructive abolition of the use of insanity as a defense because a person must be found so impaired that he or she is incapable of forming the intent to commit the act. For example, if a defendant purposefully shoots and kills a person, the defendant will not avoid criminal responsibility by claiming that his or her conduct was the result of a hallucination, delusion, or some form of thought disorder. A mens rea statute would only relieve persons of responsibility if they were unable to form the requisite intent to commit the crime. To establish the lack of intent, it would be necessary to demonstrate that the defendant was completely unaware of what he or she was doing or did not believe the act being committed (shooting a gun at victim) was actually taking place. A common illustration is that the defendant believed the gun was a banana and that he or she wasn't trying to kill the victim but instead was only squirting the victim with banana seeds.

This degree of impairment indicates the narrowness of the mens rea approach. For any more than a handful of all insanity acquittees each year to be found nonresponsible under this standard is highly doubtful. John Hinckley, Monte Durham, Daniel M'Naughton, Hadfield, and any number of other notable defendants whose insanity trials helped shape the insanity law in this area certainly would not qualify.

Despite this fact, proponents for abolishing the insanity defense argue that there is no constitutional requirement that a defense of mental illness exist at all.[36] Furthermore, allowances for the lack of mens rea comport with the historically held tenet that fundamental morality requires exculpation when a person truly does not know what he or she is doing. It is also argued that the mens rea standard is much easier to administer, thereby reducing the likelihood of confusion and complications frequently arising from contradictory expert testimony. Similarly, abolitionists and proponents of the mens rea test contend that an individual's mental state at the time of the crime still would be considered with regard to treatment, rather than penal alternatives.

The U.S. Justice Department recommended a comprehensive set of changes affecting a variety of areas in criminal justice. Entitled the Comprehensive Crime Control Act of 1984, several provisions pertaining to the insanity defense were included:[37] (1) limiting the (insanity) defense to those who are unable to appreciate the nature or wrongfulness of their acts, (2) placing the burden (of proof) on the defendant to establish the defense by clear and convincing evidence, (3) preventing expert testimony on the ultimate issue of whether the defendant had a particular mental state or condition, and (4) establishing procedures for federal civil commitment of a person found not guilty by reason of insanity if no state will commit defendant.

Guilty but mentally ill. In 1975 Michigan became the first state to adopt the alternative plea "guilty but mentally ill" (GBMI) or "guilty but insane" (GBI). Presumably dissatisfied with the definitional and procedural problems of the insanity defense and the belief that its abolition was not constitutionally sound, Michigan sought a compromise. Also, Michigan sought to decrease the number of successful insanity pleas in its courts, since a 1974 court held that insanity acquittees must be treated the same as civil committees.[38] In effect this 1974 ruling permitted a significant number of insanity acquittees to be released from hospitalization fairly quickly, which raised a concern for public safety. Several other states have enacted similar GBMI legislation, many because of the Hinckley decision.[39]

Because it is at the forefront of this alternative defense plea, Michigan's law has served as a model for other states. Therefore there is sufficient procedural commonality to permit generalization. When an insanity plea is entered, a psychiatric evaluation is required. At the conclusion of the trial, a jury is presented with four possible verdicts: (1) not guilty, (2) guilty, (3) not guilty by reason of insanity, or (4) guilty but mentally ill. The GBMI verdict requires a finding of three factors: the accused was (1) guilty of the crime, (2) mentally ill at the time the offense was committed, and (3) not legally insane at the time of the offense.[40] Most states adopting the GBMI plea require that these factors be proved by a preponderance standard (e.g., 51 out of 100 chances). After a finding of guilty but mentally ill, the court has the discretion to impose any sentence within the statutorily prescribed limits of the crime committed. Typically, sentencing is geared toward psychiatric care within the confines of a prison. If no treatment is available in prison, probation contingent on outpatient treatment is always an option.

Despite the appearance of a novel alternative incorporating both rehabilitative and retributive aspects, the GBMI plea has been heavily criticized, even in its home state.[41] Opponents of the plea state that it is exceedingly difficult to discriminate between a finding of guilty but mentally ill and not guilty by reason of insanity (NGRI) in light of the similarity in definition. A similar concern is that juries will misuse the GBMI plea out of ignorance, thereby finding a defendant guilty when an NGRI finding was more appropriate. Also, the title "guilty but mentally ill" is considered deceptive because it implies some form of mitigation but actually provides no special allowance.

Proponents who tout this alternative on humanitarian grounds because of the treatment element are often confronted by the fact that treatment is not guaranteed, but only part of a criminal sentence.

In effect then, despite a change in name and arguably greater choice of alternatives, a jury's verdict of GBMI is basically no different for a defendant than a verdict of guilty.

PSYCHIATRIC MALPRACTICE

The development and emergence of malpractice lawsuits against psychiatrists have been very gradual and seemingly of recent occurrence. Before 1970, civil actions for psychiatric-related injuries were relatively rare. As a medical specialty, psychiatry was considered almost immune from lawsuits because it was a difficult area to build a case against a practitioner.

Malpractice actions against psychiatrists have steadily increased since the early 1970s, but this fact must be seen in context. The incidence of claims against psychiatrists still remains much lower than against other physicians,[42] and most claims do not result in successful verdicts against the psychiatrist.

Along with the incidence of malpractice actions, the variety of claims against psychiatrists has also increased. Some causes of action reflect acts of negligence or substandard care for which any physician may be found liable. These malpractice areas include negligent diagnosis, abandonment from treatment, various intentional and quasi-intentional torts (assault and battery, fraud, defamation, invasion of privacy), failure to obtain informed consent, and breach of contract. Areas of liability specific to psychiatry include harm caused by organic therapies (electroconvulsive therapy [ECT], psychotropic medication, psychosurgery), breach of confidentiality, sexual exploitation of patients, failure to control or supervise a dangerous patient or negligent release, failure to protect third parties from potentially dangerous patients, false imprisonment, and negligent infliction of mental distress. These claims represent the major causes of action that may be brought against a psychiatrist.

Malpractice actions based on a psychiatrist's use of psychotropic drugs have been fairly infrequent considering the widespread use of this form of treatment during the past 20 years. However, a study of claims filed between 1972 and 1983 against psychiatrists showed that 20% of the actions were related to medication.[43] With managed care, more frequent utilization of the psychiatrist as the prescriber of medication with the psychotherapy, and primary care parceled out to psychologists and other nonmedical therapists, more actions based on medication can be expected.

Relatives of patients who have committed suicide by taking an overdose of medication often file suit, claiming that the psychiatrist was negligent in prescribing the drugs.

In the treatment of suicidal patients a delicate balance exists between providing clinical treatment, which involves certain risks, and applying protective, less therapeutic measures. In recognition of this balance, a psychiatrist will not automatically be found liable if a patient commits suicide with medication provided for treatment. Negligence is likely to be found in high-risk situations in which either the psychiatrist's choice of intervention (e.g., medication) or manner of supervision was unreasonable under the circumstances.

The *Clites v. Iowa* case is one of the first decisions specifically dealing with *tardive dyskinesia* (TD) and aptly illustrates some of the liability considerations inherent in the issue of drug therapy.[44] The plaintiff was a mentally retarded man, who had been institutionalized since age 11 and treated with major tranquilizers from age 18 to 23. TD was diagnosed at age 23, and the plaintiff subsequently sued. He claimed that the defendants had negligently prescribed medication, failed to monitor its effects, and had not obtained his informed consent. A damage award of $760,165 was returned and affirmed on appeal. The court ruled that the defendants were negligent because they deviated from the standards of the "industry." Specifically, the court cited a failure to administer regular physical examinations and tests; failure to intervene at the first sign of TD; the inappropriate use of drugs in combinations, in light of the patient's particular condition and the drugs used; the use of drugs for the convenience of controlling behavior rather than therapy; and the failure to obtain informed consent.

Breach of confidentiality

The duty to safeguard the confidentiality of any communication in the course of psychiatric treatment is the cornerstone of the profession. This obligation of confidentiality is fundamental, but none is more keenly sensitive to its importance than mental health professionals. This point is aptly reflected in the ethical codes of the various mental health organizations. For example, Section 4 of the *Principles of Medical Ethics with Annotations Especially Applicable to Psychiatry* reads in part as follows:

A physician shall respect the rights of patients, of colleagues and of other health professionals, and shall safeguard patient confidences within the constraints of the law . . . confidentiality is essential to psychiatric treatment. This is based in part on the special nature of psychiatric therapy as well as on the traditional ethical relationship between physician and patient. . . . Because of the sensitive and private nature of the information with which the psychiatrist deals, he/she must be circumspect in the information that he/she chooses to disclose to others about the patient. The welfare of the patient must be a continuing consideration.[45]

In essence, confidentiality refers to the right of a person (e.g., patient) not to have communications revealed without authorization to outside parties. The issue of confidentiality in a psychiatric perspective embodies two fundamental rationales. First, a patient has a right to privacy that should not be violated except in certain legally prescribed circumstances. Second, physicians have historically been enjoined (on an ethical basis) to maintain the confidences of their patients. In doing so, patients should feel more comfortable revealing information, which would enhance their treatment.

Psychiatrists have always been susceptible to ethical sanctions if they breach patient confidentiality, but liability for monetary damages is a relatively recent development. Several legal theories allow a patient plaintiff recovery for breach of confidentiality. Besides statutory bases, some courts have upheld a cause of action based on breach of confidentiality on a contract theory.[46] Accordingly, a psychiatrist is considered to have implicitly agreed to keep any information received from a patient confidential, and when he or she has failed to do so, there is a breach of that implied contract term by the psychiatrist. In cases based on this theory, damages typically have been restricted to economic losses flowing directly from the breach, but compensation based on any residual harm (e.g., emotional distress, marital discord, loss of employment) is precluded.[47]

Theories based on invasion of privacy have supported recovery involving breach of confidentiality. The law defines invasion of privacy as an "unwarranted publication of a person's private affairs with which the public has no legitimate concern, such as to cause outrage, mental suffering, shame, or humiliation to a person of ordinary sensibilities."[48] This theory has limited appeal to plaintiffs in jurisdictions requiring a public disclosure of personal facts as opposed to disclosure to a single person or a small group.

A minority of courts has upheld claims for breach of confidentiality based on breach of fiduciary duty of the psychiatrist.[49] Similarly, claims based on violations of medical licensing statutes and physician-patient privilege statutes have provided remedies for unconsented disclosures of confidential information,[50] although with limited success. Such actions, when successful, are presumably based on public policy grounds.

In many states the legal duty to maintain patient confidentiality is governed by mental health confidentiality statutes. These statutes outline the legal requirements covering confidentiality. For example, the Illinois Mental Health and Developmental Disabilities Confidentiality Statute contains 17 sections covering the duty of confidentiality, exceptions to it, rules and procedures for authorizing disclosures, patient and third-party access rules, penalties or violations, and provisions for civil actions by parties injured by unauthorized disclosures.[51]

Failure to warn or protect

Confidentiality was considered sacrosanct by the psychiatric profession until the Supreme Court of California heard the case *Tarasoff v. Regents of the University of California*

in 1976.[52] *Tarasoff* involved a university student from India who became obsessed with a young woman (Tatiana Tarasoff) he met at a dance. She clearly indicated that she had no interest in the young man. Following this rejection, he began individual therapy at the university counseling center. After several sessions the treating psychologist concluded that his patient might try to harm Ms. Tarasoff. The psychologist enlisted the aid of the campus police to detain the patient to ascertain his eligibility for civil commitment. The police interviewed the patient and concluded that he was rational. Based on his assurances that he had no desire to harm Ms. Tarasoff and would refrain from seeing her, they decided not to detain him. The supervising psychiatrist for the case reviewed the facts to that point and concluded there was no basis for commitment. The patient terminated treatment, and 2 months later killed Tatiana Tarasoff.

Tatiana's parents filed a wrongful death action against the university, the treating psychologist, the supervising psychiatrist, and the campus police. The plaintiffs asserted that the defendants owed a "duty to warn" Tatiana of the impending danger that the patient posed to her. The California Supreme Court agreed. In affirming but modifying their earlier holding (1974) the court held the following:

[W]hen a therapist determines, or pursuant to the standards of his profession should determine, that his patient presents a serious danger of violence to another, he incurs an obligation to use reasonable care to protect the intended victim against such danger. . . . Thus [the discharge of this duty] may call for [the therapist] to warn the intended victim or others likely to apprise the victim of the danger, to notify the police, or take whatever other steps are reasonably necessary under the circumstances.

The reaction to both decisions, referred to as *Tarasoff I* and *Tarasoff II*, was immediate, forceful, and frequently vehement. The majority of the early commentary, especially from the psychiatric profession, was critical of the numerous unanswered questions left by the California court. This new theory of liability imposed questions such as the following: Was a duty owed if the threat of danger was not aimed at anyone in particular? What steps did a psychiatrist or therapist have to take to discharge the duty? Was a duty to warn still owed if the potential victim was already aware of the patient's threat or dangerous propensities? How was a therapist's determination of dangerousness to be judged if the profession itself disclaimed the ability to accurately predict future behavior? In some cases these and other questions have been addressed in piecemeal fashion by the numerous "duty to warn/protect" decisions since *Tarasoff*.

The response by the courts following the 1976 California decision has been inconsistent and, at times, confusing. Several courts have followed the holding of *Tarasoff*, concluding that a therapist was liable for not warning an identifiable victim. For example, courts in Kansas and Michigan have ruled that the duty to warn was restricted only to readily identifiable victims.[53] A slightly broader but analogous limitation has been fashioned by decisions in Maryland and Pennsylvania, where the courts have recognized a duty to warn only when the victim is "foreseeable."[54]

The second case to apply the *Tarasoff* ruling, *McIntosh v. Milano*, added a slightly broader twist to the duty-to-warn theory.[55] In *McIntosh* a 17-year-old patient fatally shot a young neighborhood woman. Evidence revealed that the patient had disclosed to the defendant psychiatrist feelings of inadequacy, fantasies of being a hero or important villain, and using a knife (which he brought to therapy one session) to intimidate people. The patient also shared that he had once fired a BB gun at a car in which he thought the victim was riding with her boyfriend. However, the psychiatrist denied that the patient had ever expressed any feelings of violence or made any threats to harm the victim. The parents of the victim claimed that the psychiatrist knew the patient was dangerous and owed a duty to protect the victim. The New Jersey court, in denying a motion for summary judgment, agreed and held that *Tarasoff* applied, based on the therapist-patient relationship. The court found a more general duty to protect society that was analogous to a physician's duty to warn others (in the general public) of persons carrying contagious disease.

Representing the broadest expansion of the *Tarasoff* duty-to-warn theory was a Nebraska decision of *Lipari v. Sears, Roebuck and Co.*[56] A patient, who recently had dropped out of the Veterans Administration (VA) day treatment program, purchased a shotgun from Sears. He resumed treatment, only to drop out against medical advice approximately 3 weeks later. A month after the second termination he walked into a crowded nightclub and randomly discharged the shotgun, injuring the plaintiff and killing her husband. The plaintiff claimed that the VA should have known the patient was dangerous and that the VA was negligent for not committing him. The court held that Nebraska law recognized a duty to protect society, following the holdings of *Tarasoff II* and *McIntosh*. More significantly, they held that foreseeable violence was not limited to identified, specific victims but may involve a class of victims (e.g., the general public at large).

Two other cases, one in Washington State[57] and another in California, have expanded the duty to warn to include victims who were not specified or readily identifiable. In *Hedlund v. Orange County* the victim was a woman in couples therapy with a man with whom she lived.[58] During a session when she was not present, the man told the therapist that he planned to harm her. While in a car with her son next to her, the man shot at her. The woman sought damages for herself and her son, who, she claimed, suffered emotional harm. Rejecting the defendant's argument that they owed no duty of care to the young boy, the California court extended the duty to warn to foreseeable persons in close relationship to the specifically threatened victim.

Fifteen days before the *Hedlund* decision, the U.S. District Court in Colorado decided the case *Brady v. Hopper*.[59] The plaintiffs were all men who had been shot by John Hinckley during his attempted assassination of President Reagan. The plaintiffs alleged that the defendant's psychiatrist, John Hopper, knew or should have known that Hinckley was dangerous. Relying heavily on the *Lipari* decision, the plaintiffs claimed that the defendant should have known that the president was Hinckley's intended victim and that they were a class of people reasonably foreseeable to be at risk because of this danger. The court focused its decision on the issue of foreseeability of the risk to the specific plaintiffs involved. While affirming the duty of therapists to protect third parties, the court's conclusion was prefaced with the admission: "[T]he existence of a special relationship does not necessarily mean that the duties created by that relationship are owed to the world at large." In rejecting the plaintiffs' claims that the defendant was liable to them, the court concluded: "In my opinion, the specific threats to specific victims rule states a workable, reasonable, and fair boundary upon the sphere of a therapist's liability to third persons for the acts of their patients." Therefore, under *Brady*, a determination of dangerousness, in general, will not create a duty to protect without a specific threat to a specific victim. In December 1984 the Court of Appeals for the Tenth Circuit, in a three-page opinion, affirmed the district court's opinion in *Brady*.[60] In essence, it deferred to the discretion of the lower court, stating reversal only could be found if a gross error in the application of the law had occurred.

Cases to date involving some form of the duty-to-warn theory can be viewed as falling somewhere on a continuum based on two common factors: (1) a threat (or potential for harm) and (2) a potential victim. At one end is the *Brady* decision with its "specific threat specific victim" rule, and at the other end is *Lipari*, which held that "foreseeable violence" created a duty to protect "others," regardless of whether the victim was identified or specified. In addition, decisions in Maryland, California, Pennsylvania, and Iowa have refused to apply the theory by either rejecting it outright or finding no liability based on the facts of the case.[61]

At present, most courts have held that in the absence of a foreseeable victim, no duty to warn or protect will be found. Reviewing the cases, a few facts stand out. Most notable is the relative absence of litigation that most commentators thought would occur after the *Tarasoff* decision in 1974.[62]

Whatever the extent of the duty imposed by the *Tarasoff* decision and its progeny, a psychiatrist or therapist cannot be held liable for a patient's violent acts unless it is found that (1) the psychiatrist determined (or by professional standards reasonably should have determined) that the patient posed a danger to a third party (identified or unidentified) and that (2) the psychiatrist failed to take reasonable steps to prevent the violence.

The liability considerations that underlie the treatment and care of the dangerous patient generally differ according to the amount of control a psychiatrist, therapist, or institution has over the patient. As a general rule, psychiatrists who treat dangerous or potentially dangerous patients have a duty of care, which includes controlling that individual from harming other persons inside and outside the facility as well as himself or herself. On the other hand, the outpatient who presents a possible risk of danger to others creates a duty of care, which may include warning or somehow protecting potential third-party victims. Although some facts may require an expansion of the duty of care in one or the other setting (inpatient, outpatient), this general distinction is important to more clearly understand the legal issues and preventive considerations that the dangerous patient presents.

The duty of care owed to dangerous or potentially dangerous patients in an inpatient setting is very similar in principle to those duties governing the treatment of suicidal patients. Causes of action alleged by third parties injured by the dangerous or violent acts of an inpatient generally involve one of two situations. In one situation the inpatient is discharged and shortly thereafter harms a third party. The plaintiff sues whoever made the decision to discharge the patient, claiming that he or she was negligently released. In the second general situation an inpatient escapes from the hospital and then harms someone. The claim in this scenario is typically that the physician or facility in charge of the patient's care was negligent in either supervision or control of the patient.

In both general scenarios the analysis for determining liability is similar. As in cases involving suicide, a treating psychiatrist or other practitioner cannot be held liable for harms committed after a patient's discharge (e.g., negligent release) unless the court determines (1) that the psychiatrist knew or should have known that the patient was likely to commit a dangerous or violent act and (2) that in light of this knowledge, the psychiatrist failed to take adequate steps to evaluate the patient when considering discharge. Similarly, in cases involving third parties injured by a dangerous patient who has escaped, the court evaluates (1) whether the psychiatrist knew or should have known that the patient presented a risk of elopement and (2) in light of that knowledge, whether the psychiatrist took reasonable steps to supervise or control the patient. The actions of a psychiatrist in a negligent discharge or negligent control or supervision claim are scrutinized based on the reasonableness of the actions and the standards of the profession.

Sexual exploitation

From a legal standpoint, the courts have consistently held that a physician or therapist who engages in sexual activity with a patient is subject to civil liability and in some cases

to criminal sanctions. The reason for this overwhelming condemnation rests in the exploitative and often deceptive practice that sex between a health care professional (e.g., psychiatrist, physician, therapist) and patient represents. The fundamental basis of the psychiatrist-patient relationship is the unconditional trust and confidence patients have in the therapist. This trust permits patients to share their most intimate secrets, thoughts, and feelings. As therapy progresses, unconscious feelings of conflict, fears, and desires originating from important relations in the patient's past are said to be "transferred" to the therapist in the present. This *transference phenomenon* is a common occurrence in psychotherapy and often provides a therapist valuable information to analyze and interpret. The transference phenomenon makes a patient vulnerable to the emotions being experienced, such as feelings of love. Therefore the therapist must conduct the treatment with sensitivity and care. A similar phenomenon, *countertransference*, occurs when a therapist experiences unconscious conflicts and feelings toward a patient. As with patient transferences, countertransference feelings should be recognized as important therapeutic information and analyzed to gain insight into how to better understand the patient.

In addition to civil sanctions, a practitioner may face criminal liability if there is evidence that some form of coercion, usually in the form of tranquilizing medication, was used to induce compliance or reduce resistance to the initiation of the sexual activity. A psychiatrist or other practitioner may be charged criminally if the sexual activity involves a child or adolescent patient. In a situation involving a minor, no evidence of force or coercion needs to be demonstrated to support a finding of criminal liability.

In the landmark case *Roy v. Hartogs*, expert testimony concluded that "there are absolutely no circumstances which permit a psychiatrist to engage in sex with his patient."[63]

However, some therapists do attempt to rationalize their actions. Some of the most common defenses, all of which to date have been rejected by the courts, include that the patient consented to having sex, that the sexual relation was not a part of treatment, or that the treatment ended before the sexual relations began.[64]

Abandonment

Once an agreement (explicit or implicit) to provide medical services has been established, the physician is legally and ethically bound to render those services until the relationship has been appropriately terminated. If a physician terminates treatment prematurely and the patient is harmed by the termination, a cause of action based on "abandonment of treatment" may be brought. Generally, in the absence of an emergency or crisis situation, treatment can be concluded safely if a patient is provided reasonable notice of the termination and is assisted in transferring the care to a new physician. Proper transfer of care typically implies that the original psychiatrist or physician prepares and makes available the patient's records as needed by the new physician. It is also prudent for the original care provider to give the patient written and verbal notice to avoid any possible questions regarding the nature, timing, or extent of the announcement of termination. This is particularly important when treating psychiatric patients or persons who are psychologically vulnerable because there may be a tendency to misconstrue or deny a verbal notice.

The issue of abandonment frequently arises when either no notice of termination has been given or the extent of this notice has been insufficient in some way. Although there are no rules or guidelines per se regarding sufficiency of the notice, a therapist who decides to terminate treatment is expected to act reasonably. For example, if few therapists are available in the area to accept transfer of the patient's case, the treating therapist should afford the patient a longer notice period to locate a replacement. If a patient refuses or is unable to locate another therapist, however, the treating psychiatrist or therapist has no obligation to treat the patient indefinitely. The reasonableness of a therapist's notice therefore is judged on the totality of the relevant circumstances.

Patients who are experiencing some sort of crisis or emergency situation require special consideration. For example, a therapist who is treating a patient who is suicidal or presents a possible danger to some third party is not likely to be considered to be acting reasonably if he or she terminates treatment. From a clinical perspective, such a move may exacerbate a patient's already vulnerable feelings and prompt the patient to do something that he or she might not have otherwise done. Legally, the courts are not likely to consider a therapist's decision to terminate treatment reasonable during a time when care is required. Therefore a therapist should be wary of ending therapy during a period of emergency and instead should hold off termination until a more appropriate time.

Patient control and supervision

The treatment of patients who pose a risk of danger to themselves or others presents a unique clinical and legal challenge to the mental health profession.

A lawsuit for patient suicide or attempted suicide is often brought by a patient's family or relatives claiming that the attending psychiatrist, therapist, or facility was negligent in some aspect of the treatment process. Specifically, there are three broad categories of claims that encompass actions stemming from patient suicide. The first is when an outpatient commits suicide or is injured in a suicide attempt. Plaintiffs in this situation claim that the psychiatrist or therapist was negligent in failing to diagnose the patient's suicidal condition and provide adequate treatment, which is typically hospitalization. The second situation is when an inpatient is given inadequate treatment and commits or attempts suicide. Typically, the essence of a negligence claim involving inadequate treatment is that the patient was suicidal and the psychiatrist failed to provide adequate supervision. The last general situation is when a patient is discharged from the hospital and shortly thereafter attempts or commits suicide. Family members, or the injured patient, frequently claim that the decision to release the patient was negligent.

The treatment of suicidal or potentially suicidal patients inherently requires a psychiatrist or other practitioner to make predictions regarding future behavior. The mental health profession has frequently disclaimed ability to predict future behavior with any degree of accuracy. As a result, the law has tempered its expectation of clinicians in identifying future dangerous behavior. Instead of a strict standard requiring 100% accuracy, the law requires professionals to exercise reasonable care in their diagnosis and treatment of patients at risk.[65] Accordingly, a court will not hold a practitioner liable for a patient's death or injury resulting from suicide if the treatment or discharge decision was reasonably based on the information available.

In an attempt to enhance the recovery of patients at risk of suicide, some hospitals use what is known as an *open ward policy*. This policy permits a patient considerable freedom of movement within the hospital and minimizes procedures that are constraining, such as seclusion, physical and chemical restraints, and constant observation. In some cases the courts have recognized the therapeutic value of this procedure and concluded that the professional is in the best position to balance the risks and benefits of increased patient freedom. In doing so, the courts have basically deferred to the judgment of the professional, even though the professional's decision may later prove to be wrong. This deferment to professional judgment is as much an acknowledgment of the difficulties psychiatrists face in attempting to predict future behavior as it is an acceptance of certain practices and procedures of modern psychiatry. A 1981 federal district court decision sums up its conclusion as follows:

[M]odern psychiatry has recognized the importance of making every effort to return a patient to an active and productive life. Thus the patient is encouraged to develop her self-confidence by adjusting to the demands of everyday existence. Particularly because the prediction of danger is difficult, undue reliance on hospitalization might lead to prolonged incarceration of potentially useful members of society.[66]

A few courts have refused to make such a deferment and instead have kept to the more traditional evaluation of the reasonableness of the precautions provided.[67] The issue of reasonableness, whether involving the diagnosis, supervision, or discharge of a patient, is usually measured in terms of the accepted standards of the profession. Expert testimony is needed to establish or disprove that the defendant psychiatrist failed to exercise the reasonable care other psychiatrists would have used in that or similar circumstances. The risk of liability is greatly enhanced when it can be demonstrated that a practitioner or institution failed to follow its own usual practices and procedures for treating a patient at risk for suicide.

CIVIL RIGHTS

Voluntary hospitalization

Mentally ill persons can be admitted to a psychiatric hospital or institution in essentially two ways. The first is to be involuntarily committed. The other and more common means is for the individual to sign in voluntarily, which is similar to a patient entering a general medical facility. In other words, admission is effected through what is legally and clinically presumed to be a free and voluntary action on the part of the patient.

Voluntary or consensual hospitalization of the mentally ill person is a relatively new idea. Massachusetts enacted the first voluntary admission statute in 1881, but other states were slow to follow. By 1949, only 10% of all mental patients were voluntary admissions. For about the next 20 years, states struggled to amend and revise their commitment laws to define and establish realistic procedures for voluntary admission. By 1972 most psychiatric admissions were voluntary.

The purpose of voluntary hospitalization for mentally ill persons is to dispel the coercion, trauma, and stigma normally associated with involuntary hospitalization and to afford the same opportunity for treatment to mentally ill patients that is available to those with physical illness.

One issue of increasing importance in relation to the idea of voluntary hospitalization of the mentally ill person is the question of competency to consent. Presumably, the act of voluntarily entering a psychiatric hospital requires the patient to be legally competent to make such a decision. Many of the first statutes authorizing voluntary commitment made the requirement of competency a specific element. The rationale for such a strict requirement was, at least in part, to prevent clearly incompetent patients from being improperly manipulated by psychiatrists and mental hospitals.

More recent laws, however, designed to encourage voluntary admission and based on a theory that it ensures needed treatment, omit such requirements in most states. The dilemma regarding the issue of a patient's competency to be hospitalized voluntarily remains unresolved. To date, the question of whether a patient by voluntary admission must be competent to exercise an informed consent has not been authoritatively addressed by any court. This lack of judicial scrutiny is largely a consequence of present-day voluntary admission procedures. A person who has been coerced into voluntarily signing in or lacks the capacity to fully comprehend the consequences of the application for admission is unlikely to have any grounds on which to raise either issue since, at any time, a request for discharge can be made. Such an individual would then be either released pursuant to that request or committed pursuant to state involuntary commitment statutes. In either event, at least in theory, the issue of invalid or improper voluntary admission would have been negated, thereby preventing any court from hearing the significant issues surrounding this aspect of the voluntary admission process.

Involuntary hospitalization

Basis and rationale. Involuntary hospitalization or civil commitment refers to state-imposed involuntary detention or restrictions of personal freedom based on a determination that a person is mentally ill and dangerous to self or others or is gravely disabled.

The institution of the civil commitment process is based on two fundamental common-law principles. The first relates to the right of the government, provided by the U.S. Constitution to the individual states, to take whatever actions are necessary to ensure the safety of its citizens. Referred to as the *police power*, this authority is limited by the states' constitutions and by the Fourteenth Amendment of the U.S. Constitution.

The other rationale used to justify the involuntary commitment of mentally ill persons is the *parens patriae* doctrine. This concept, which denotes that the state is acting in place of the parent, prescribes that the "sovereign has both the right and the duty to protect the person and the property of those who are unable to care [for] themselves because of minority or mental illness."[68] From a practical perspective, numerous state statutes and case law, in an attempt to cut back the broadness of certain state commitment provisions, have either abolished the parens patriae rationale or made it contingent on a finding of dangerousness (e.g., thereby invoking the salient purpose of the police power).

Commitment standards. The civil commitment process can be viewed in terms of (1) the criteria or standards governing whether someone is committable and (2) the procedural rules regulating the process.

In most jurisdictions the basic criteria for involuntary civil commitment are the product of a statute. The wording and interpretation of the various commitment laws differ from state to state, but the standards for commitment are similar.

Typically, all states require an individual to demonstrate clear and convincing evidence of at least two separate and distinct elements. The first pertains to the individual's mental condition. Nearly every state requires a threshold finding that a person suffers from some mental illness, disorder, or disease. The second and often more critical requirement is a determination that some "specific adverse consequence" will ensue, as a result of the mental illness, if the person is not confined. Commonly couched in language such as "likely to harm self or others," "poses a real and present threat of substantial harm to self or others," or "dangerous to himself or others," this element is frequently referred to in references as simply the "danger to self or others" requirement. In some states, such as Delaware and Hawaii, this element is extended to harm to property as well as persons.

Closely related to both the mental illness and dangerousness requirements is the standard of "gravely disabled." This standard is somewhat similar to the mental condition requirement in that it typically applies to a person's ability to provide self-care. This is not a uniform standard as are the other two criteria but represents an attempt by a minority of states to provide a broader description of the kind of manifest behavior that may prompt commitment. An example of a state statute applying the gravely disabled standard is the following:

Gravely disabled means that a person, as a result of mental or emotional impairment, is in danger of serious harm as a result of an inability or failure to provide for his or her own basic human needs such as essential food, clothing, shelter or safety and that hospital care is necessary and available and that such person is mentally incapable of determining whether or not to accept treatment because his judgment is impaired by his mental illness.[69]

Least restrictive alternative. Up to the late 1960s, a patient civilly committed to a state institution could expect to remain there for a major portion, if not the duration, of his or her life. Often criticized as mere human warehousing, the majority of mental institutions in America failed at achieving anything remotely therapeutic. Usually, the best that a civilly committed patient could hope for was bare-minimum custodial care. The thought of ever leaving the institution was a fleeting fantasy for many patients, and those who were discharged were rarely any better off than when they were admitted.

Patients legitimately committed due to mental illness and posing risk of danger might remain hospitalized long after the time when one or both of these conditions no longer existed. Because states rarely required the periodic evaluation of those civilly committed, however, a patient could literally waste away in the hospital despite no longer qualifying for detention. This situation represented a serious abridgment of the civil liberties of patients with mental illness and spurred considerable concern by libertarians, scholars, and civil rights activists.

In 1966 the case *Lake v. Cameron* (applying D.C. law) signaled a significant advancement in the recognition of civil rights of mentally disabled persons.[70] *Lake* involved the involuntary commitment of a 60-year-old woman diagnosed as senile but not considered a danger to herself or others. Writing for the majority, Chief Judge Bazelon held that a person could not be involuntarily committed to a

psychiatric hospital if alternative placements could be found that were less restrictive on a patient's constitutional right to liberty. From this opinion the doctrine of the "least restrictive alternative" (LRA) was developed which, at least in theory, recognized and sought to protect the rights to liberty of patients who were so routinely ignored in the past.

After the *Lake* decision, numerous states adopted legislation requiring courts to consider less restrictive alternatives whenever appropriate. In the absence of statutory authority, several lower federal courts upheld the validity of the LRA doctrine based on implied constitutional grounds. This implied reasoning was addressed in the seminal case *Lessard v. Schmidt*:

Even if the standards for an adjudication of mental illness and potential dangerousness are satisfied, a court should order full-time involuntary hospitalization only as a last resort. A basic concept in American justice is the principle that "even though the governmental purpose be legitimate and substantial, that purpose cannot be pursued by means that broadly stifle fundamental personal liberties when the end can be more narrowly achieved. The breadth of legislative abridgment must be viewed in light of less drastic means for achieving the same basic purpose."[71]

The LRA doctrine has been applied to numerous other forms of restraining a patient's liberty within the hospitalization process (e.g., the use of physical restraints and seclusion rooms). In extending the scope of the doctrine to other treatment procedures, respect for a patient's civil rights is acknowledged, the hospitalization experience becomes less stigmatizing, and positive patient-staff relations are fostered.

Despite the social, therapeutic, and psychological value of the LRA doctrine, its application is subject to severe limitations. As Chief Judge Bazelon held in *Lake*, a less restrictive alternative must actually exist in order for the doctrine to apply.

From a practical standpoint this requirement presents a major setback in most cases because such less restrictive alternatives rarely are available. The practical value of the LRA doctrine therefore is limited unless the courts take the initiative to create, or order, alternative placements. In the absence of legislative authority, this development is unlikely.

Rights of the civilly committed patient. The right to treatment and habilitation, to the basic necessities of life, to refusal of treatment, and to treatment in the least restrictive environment have all been litigated and afforded varying degrees of protection.

The concept of a right to treatment was first articulated in 1960 when Dr. Morton Birnbaum proposed that:

The courts, under their traditional powers to protect the constitutional rights of our citizens begin to consider the problem of whether or not a person who has been institutionalized solely because he is sufficiently mentally ill to require institutionalization for care and treatment actually does receive adequate medical treatment so that he may regain his health, and therefore his liberty, as soon as possible; that the courts do this by means of *recognizing and enforcing the right to treatment*; and, that the courts do this, independent of any action by any legislature, as a necessary and overdue development of our present concept of due process of law.[72] [emphasis in original]

A constitutional right to treatment, or to "habilitation," was held to apply to mentally disabled individuals in the landmark case *Wyatt v. Stickney*.[73] The court held that in the absence of the opportunity to receive treatment, mentally disabled individuals in institutions were not patients but were residents with indefinite sentences. Further, the court stated that basic custodial care or punishment was not the purpose of involuntary hospitalization. The purpose, they concluded, was treatment. In its subsequent opinions the court developed an extensive remedial plan that was intended to establish minimum constitutional standards for adequate treatment and habilitation of mentally disabled persons.

A second basic constitutional right, the right to liberty, was addressed in the Supreme Court decision *O'Connor v. Donaldson*.[74] Donaldson had been involuntarily confined in a state mental institution for almost 15 years and was suing the state for depriving him of his constitutional right to liberty. In the first award granted to a mentally ill patient based on a violation of constitutional rights, Donaldson received $20,000 in damages. In addressing the deprivation of liberty that involuntary confinement imposed, the court concluded that three conditions had to be met to justify release: (1) the institution was not offering proper treatment; (2) the patient did not present a danger to self or others; and (3) the person was capable of living in the community with the assistance of family or friends. Although these narrow conditions were illuminated in later litigation, *Donaldson* laid the foundation for future constitutional litigation regarding the rights of the mentally ill.

The U.S. Supreme Court has not yet squarely addressed the issue of the right to refuse treatment. The issue of whether an involuntarily committed patient has a constitutional right to refuse treatment (antipsychotic medication) was before the high court in 1982 in *Mills v. Rogers*,[75] but it was sidestepped and sent back to a lower federal court for reconsideration.

Despite the Supreme Court's refusal to decide *Mills*, several lower federal courts have sought to resolve the issue of right to refuse treatment. In one of the most noted cases, *Rennie v. Klein*, the Court of Appeals for the Third Circuit affirmed the finding that a constitutional right to refuse treatment existed.[76] However, the appeals court differed from the lower court when it adopted a "least intrusive means analysis." Under this analysis, antipsychotic drugs could be forcibly administered in a nonemergency situation to patients who had never been adjudicated incompetent, only if such treatment was the least restrictive mode of treatment available.

A year after *Rennie* the U.S. Supreme Court held in the landmark case of *Youngberg v. Romeo* that mentally retarded residents of state institutions had a constitutional right to the basic necessities of life, reasonably safe living conditions, freedom from undue restraints, and the minimally adequate training needed to enhance or further their abilities to exercise other constitutional rights.[77] Of significant importance to future civil rights cases involving mentally disabled persons was the court's deference to the judgment of qualified professionals to establish minimal adequate training and to safeguard a patient's liberty interests. In seeking to minimize judicial interference in the daily administration of institutions, the court held that "liability may be imposed only when the decision is such a substantial departure from accepted professional judgment, practice or standards as to demonstrate that the person responsible actually did not base the decision on such a judgment."[78]

The full impact of *Youngberg* has yet to be determined, but at least one significant civil rights case, *Rennie v. Klein*, has been redefined because of it. In 1983 the Third Circuit Court of Appeals rejected the "least intrusive means analysis" and adopted the standard of "whether the patient constitutes a danger to himself or others" in determining whether medication can be forcibly administered.[79]

ENDNOTES

1. J. Quen, *Anglo-American Criminal Insanity: an Historical Perspective*, 10 J Hist. Behavioral Sci. 313 (1974).
2. *Justinian Digest* 48, 8.2 (Dec. 533).
3. S. Grey, *The Insanity Defense: Historical Development and Contemporary Relevance*, 10 Am. Crim. Law Rev. 555 (1972).
4. *Id.*
5. 4 W. Blackstone, *Commentaries* 24 (Clarendon Press, Oxford 1769).
6. *Pate v. Robinson*, 383 U.S. 375, 86 S.Ct. 836, 15 L.Ed. 2d 815 (1966).
7. *Dusky v. United States*, 362 U.S. 402, 80 S.Ct. 788, 4 L.Ed. 2d 824 (1960).
8. *Drope v. Missouri*, 420 U.S. 162, 95 S.Ct. 896, 43 L.Ed. 2d 103 (1975).
9. *Id.*
10. *Estelle v. Smith*, 451 U.S. 454, 101 S.Ct. 1866, 68 L.Ed. 2d 359 (1981).
11. *Jackson v. Indiana*, 406 U.S. 715, 32 L.Ed. 2d 434, 92 S.Ct. 1845 (1972).
12. *Rex v. Arnold*, 16 How. Sr. Tr. 695 (C.P. 1742).
13. 1 Hawkins, *Pleas of the Crown* 1 (1824).
14. *Hadfield's Case*, 27 State Trial 1281 (1800).
15. *Id.*
16. R. Reisner, *Law and the Mental Health System* 564 (West 1985).
17. 4 State Tr. N.S. 847, 8 Eng. Rep. 718 (1843).
18. American Psychiatric Association, *Statement on the Insanity Defense* 3 (Dec. 1982).
19. *M'Naughton's Case*, 4 State Tr. N.S. 847, 8 Eng. Rep. 718, 721-22 (H.L. 1843) (per Lord Chief Justice Tindal).
20. A. Goldstein, *The Insanity Defense* 67 (Yale University Press, New Haven 1967).

21. *Id.*

22. *Durham v. United States*, 214 F. 2d 862, 874 (D.C. Cir. 1954).

23. *Id.* at 874-75.

24. D. Weschler, *The Criteria for Criminal Responsibility*, 22 Univ. Chi. Law Rev. 367 (1955).

25. *Supra* note 20.

26. Model Penal Code §4.01 (1962).

27. *McDonald v. United States*, 312 F. 2d 847 (D.C. Cir. 1962).

28. *Id.* at 851.

29. *Heads v. Louisiana*, 370 S. 2d 564 (La. 1979), *remanded for further consideration* 444 U.S. 1008 (1980).

30. *State v. Head*, No. 106, 126 (1st Jud. Dist. Ct., Caddo Parrish, Oct. 1981).

31. M. Guttmacher, *The Role of Psychiatry in Law* (Thomas, Springfield, Ill. 1965).

32. B. Wooten, *Crime and Criminal Law* (Stevens, London 1963).

33. Mont. Code Ann. §46-14-102 (1979).

34. 4 Idaho Code §18-207 Cumm. Supp. (1986).

35. *Id.* at §18-207c.

36. *Supra* note 30.

37. Comprehensive Crime Control Act of 1984 (Government Printing Office, Washington, D.C. 1984).

38. *People v. McQuillan*, 221 N.W. 2d 569 (Mich. 1974).

39. L. Blunt & H. Harley, *Guilty but Mentally Ill: an Alternative Verdict*, 3 Beh. Sci. & Law 49 (1985) [citing Alaska, Delaware, Georgia, Illinois, Indiana, Kentucky, New Mexico, Pennsylvania, South Dakota, Michigan and Utah].

40. Mich. Comp. Laws Ann. 768.36(1), *enacted in* Public Act 1980 of 1975.

41. R. Petrella et al., *Examining the Application of the Guilty but Mentally Ill Verdict in Michigan*, 36 Hosp. and Community Psychiatry 254 (1985).

42. P. Slawson, *Psychiatric Malpractice: A California Statewide Survey*, 6 Bull. Am. Acad. Psychiatry & L. 58 (1978).

43. Clin. Psychiatric News 1 (Oct. 1983).

44. *Clites v. Iowa*, 322 N.W. 2d 917 (Iowa Ct. App. 1981).

45. American Psychiatric Association, *Principles of Medical Ethics with Annotations Especially Applicable to Psychiatry* (APA Press, Washington, D.C. 1985).

46. *Doe v. Roe*, 93 Misc. 2d 201, 400 N.Y. S.Z. 668 (1977); *Clayman v. Bernstein*, 38 Pa. D&C 543 (1940); *Spring v. Geriatric Authority*, 394 Mass. 274, 475 N.E. 2d 727 (1985).

47. Spring, *supra* note 46.

48. Doe, *supra* note 46.

49. *MacDonald v. Clinger*, 84 A.D. 2d 482, 446 N.Y. S. 2d 801 (1982).

50. *Clark v. Geraci*, 29 Misc. 2d 791, 208 N.Y.S. 2d 564 (1960).

51. Illinois Mental Health and Developmental Disabilities Confidentiality Act S.H.A. Ch. 91, §801 (1987); *see also Pettus v. Cole*, 49 Cal. App 4th 402 (1996), interpreting California's Confidentiality of Medical Information Act, Civil Code, §56 *et seq.*

52. *Tarasoff v. Regents of the University of California*, 17 Cal. 3d 425, 529 P. 2d 334, 131 Cal. Rptr. 14, 551 P. 2d 334 (1976).

53. *Durflinger v. Artiles*, 563 F.Supp. 322 (D. Kan. 1981), *ques. cert.* 234 Kan. 484, 673 P. 2d 86 (1983), *aff'd* 727 F. 2d 889 (10th Cir. 1984); *Davis v. Lhim*, 335 N.W. 2d 481 (Mich. App. 1983), *remanded on other grounds* 422 Mich. App. 8, 366 N.W. 2d 73 (1985), *on remand* 147 Mich. App. 8, 382 N.W. 2d 195 (1985), *on appeal* N.W. 2d (Mich. July 1986).

54. *Shaw v. Glickman*, 415 A. 2d 625 (Md. App. 1985); *Leedy v. Hartnett*, 510 F.Supp. 1125 (N.D. Pa. 1981) (interpreting Pa. law).

55. *McIntosh v. Milano*, 168 N.J. Super. 466, 403 A. 2d 500 (1979).

56. *Lipari v. Sears, Roebuck and Co.*, 497 F.Supp. 185 (D. Neb. 1980).

57. *Peterson v. State*, 100 Wash. 2d 421, 671 P. 2d 230 (1983).

58. *Hedlund v. Orange County*, 34 Cal. 3d 695, 194 Cal. Rptr. 805 (1983); (*Bluebook*, p. 179).

59. *Brady v. Hopper*, 570 F.Supp. 1333 (D. Colo. 1983).

60. *Brady v. Hopper*, 751 F. 2d 329 (10th Cir. 1984).

61. *Shaw v. Glickman*, 45 Md. App. 718, 415 A. 2d 625 (1980); *Thompson v. County of Alameda*, 27 Cal. 3d 741, 167 Cal. Rptr. 70 (1980).

62. F. Buckner & M.H. Firestone, *Where the Public Peril Begins: 25 Years after Tarasoff*, J. Legal Med. (Sept. 2000).

63. *Roy v. Hartogs*, 31 Misc. 2d 350, 366 N.Y.S. 2d 297 (Civ. Ct. N.Y. 1975), *aff'd* 85 Misc. 2d 891, 381 N.Y.S. 2d 587 (App. Term 1976).

64. R.I. Simon, *Bad Men Do What Good Men Dream* (American Psychiatric Press, Inc. 1996)

65. *Brown v. Kowlizakis*, 331 S.E. 2d 440 (Va. 1985).

66. *Johnson v. United States*, 409 F.Supp. 1283 (M.D. Fla. 1981).

67. J. Smith, *Medical Malpractice: Psychiatric Care* 504-05 (1986); *Lange v. United States*, 179 F.Supp. 777 (N.D., N.Y. 1960).

68. H. Ross, *Commitment of the Mentally Ill: Problems of Law and Policy*, 57 Mich. L. Rev. 945 (1959).

69. Conn. Gen. Stat. Ann. §17-176 (West 1976).

70. *Lake v. Cameron*, 364 F. 2d 657 (D.C. Cir. 1966).

71. *Lessard v. Schmidt*, 349 F.Supp. 1078 (E.D. Wisc. 1972).

72. Birnbaum, *The Right to Treatment*, 46 A.B.A.J. 499 (1960).

73. *Wyatt v. Stickney*, 325 F.Supp. 781 (M.D. Ala.), *enforced* 334 F.Supp. 1341 (M.D. Ala. 1971), *orders entered* 344 F.Supp. 373, 344 F.Supp. 387 (M.D. Ala. 1972), *aff'd in part, rev'd and remanded in part* sub nom. *Wyatt v. Aderholt*, 503 F. 2d 1305 (5th Cir. 1974).

74. *O'Connor v. Donaldson*, 422 U.S. 563 (1975).

75. *Mills v. Rogers*, 457 U.S. 1119 (1982).

76. *Rennie v. Klein*, 653 F. 2d 836 (3d Cir. 1981).

77. *Youngberg v. Romeo*, 457 U.S. 307 (1982).

78. *Id.*

79. *Rennie v. Klein*, 720 F. 2d 266, 269 (3d Cir. 1983).

Criminalistics

HENRY C. LEE, Ph.D.
ELAINE M. PAGLIARO, M.S., J.D.

STAGES OF EVIDENTIARY ANALYSIS
CLASSIFICATION OF PHYSICAL EVIDENCE
CHALLENGES TO CRIMINALISTICS EVIDENCE

The principles of forensic evidence examination can be applied to recognize, collect, preserve, examine, and interpret various types of physical evidence associated with a crime scene. The crime scene can be a body, a location, or a vehicle. The diverse application of the scientific method, commonly referred to as "criminalistics," provides important, objective information during a case investigation. Analysis of physical evidence may also supply investigative leads through the identification of unknown materials, the comparison to known standards, or by the use of analytical databases to determine a potential source. Criminalists today employ a wide range of tests from microscopic examination to the integration of mass spectrometry with gas or liquid chromatography and computerized image enhancement. Since there are many specialties within criminalistics, the specific analytical approaches, testing procedures, and techniques will vary. The goal of any criminalistics examination, however, is to provide scientific, factual data that, for example, can link a suspect to a case or exonerate the suspect. Cases often go unsolved without objective scientific data to support or to disprove a theory. The results of objective analysis of physical evidence can provide necessary facts that a jury can use to determine the guilt or innocence of a suspect.

Since the divisions of criminalistics are so varied, there are many ways evidence can be classified and analyzed. These classifications commonly include separation by: (1) physical state of the evidence; (2) origin of the evidence, such as evidence from the victim, a witness, or from the suspect; (3) type of evidence examination that is required, such as DNA evidence or latent fingerprint evidence; (4) type of crime, such as homicide evidence or sexual assault evidence; and (5) composition of the evidence, such as biological evidence or chemical evidence.

While criminal investigators and legal practitioners may classify criminalistics evidence differently, the basic approach to the analysis of physical evidence remains the same. Laboratory analyses conducted will ultimately be determined by the nature of the physical evidence and whether evidence items and control samples can be traced to a common origin. For example, evidence removed from the clothing of a homicide victim may be examined to determine the anthropological and body origins of the hair; such information may provide valuable investigative leads for the investigators. More importantly, by microscopic comparison of the questioned hair sample to a known hair sample, one can eliminate or include that person as a potential suspect. On the other hand, it may be most appropriate to compare the DNA profile obtained from that hair with a suspect to provide an individualizing, positive linkage to the contributor of the hair.

STAGES OF EVIDENTIARY ANALYSIS

The central "dogma" of criminalistics examinations involves the recognition, identification, comparison, individualization, and interpretation of evidence. In some cases, after these analytical procedures, reconstruction of the incident events may be required.

Recognition requires that the criminalist have sufficient knowledge and experience to separate inconsequential items from potential physical evidence. This process also includes pattern recognition and documentation of physical characteristics of the objects examined. If the evidentiary nature of an object or pattern is not recognized, information that might have been gained from that evidence will be lost.

Identification uses patterns and class characteristics of the material to determine what the evidence is. These class characteristics may be physical, chemical, or biological in nature. Many types of analysis may be involved to complete these observations. At this stage of the testing process, the criminalist will utilize the most nondestructive and straightforward methods to reach a conclusion. It is also important at this stage to consume or alter a sample as little as possible. Thus, screening tests, instrumental analysis that requires little sample preparation, and microscopic examinations are the common methods employed for identification of physical evidence.

Classification involves the use of further examinations to gain sufficient information to place the evidence in a specific category. This classification may be achieved by comparison to a set of known standards from a database or reference collections, or to a known sample submitted for that purpose. It is at the stage of classification that evidence may be excluded by showing it differs significantly from the known material. Techniques for classification include a variety of instrumental, biochemical, microscopic, and physical methods. When the evidence compares positively with the known standard, analysis may continue to the next stage. However, in many cases the nature of the evidence itself or a legal requirement prevents analysis beyond the level of classification. While this fact causes some confusion and concern among those not conducting criminalistics examinations, it is a reality of the discipline.

When individualization of evidence is possible, it means that evidence can be attributed to a unique source. For example, criminalists make individualizations by comparing fingerprints and other imprint evidence to link that fingerprint or imprint with one and only one source. Forensic DNA analysis may approach individualization in some cases when the profiles obtained and the probability of occurrence is calculated to be sufficiently unique in humans; some laboratories have identified a frequency of occurrence below which an individualization is stated.[1]

Reconstruction does not involve specific analytical techniques, but uses logical analysis of data gained during those procedures to determine the sequence of events or to reconstruct the nature of an incident. Laboratory data is often combined with other information collected during an investigation through a logical, systematic process to arrive at the reconstruction.

Figure 69-1 shows the process of criminalistics analysis and its relationship to other facets of an investigation.

CLASSIFICATION OF PHYSICAL EVIDENCE

It is often useful to classify physical evidence according to its nature by dividing evidence into the following types: transient evidence, conditional evidence, pattern evidence, transfer evidence, and associative evidence.

Transient evidence

Transient evidence, as the name implies, includes those materials and patterns that are temporary in nature. These types of evidence are easily lost or changed by time or circumstances. Examples of transient evidence include heat, odor, surface imprints, rigor mortis, color of bloodstains, and gaseous products, such as smoke. Because transient evidence does readily disperse or change, this type of evidence is often lost unless witnesses or first responders to a scene are acutely aware of its importance and take appropriate steps to document or preserve such evidence.

For example, in one case, the first fire responders to a factory fire noted the large amount of dense, dark smoke and an accelerant-type odor when they arrived at the scene. Once the inception stage of the fire was over, the transient evidence was quickly consumed during the free-burning stage. The acute observations of the firefighters provided factual information useful in the prosecution of an arson-murder case. In another case, the amount of blood present upon arrival by first responders was critical information. The forensic scientist used the witness statements and the initial scene photographs to reconstruct the crime. The victim's husband claimed that he had called 911 as soon as she shot herself and then moved her body from the bed to the floor. The bed and a part of the pillow on the side of the bed where she had been shot were soaked with blood at the time paramedics

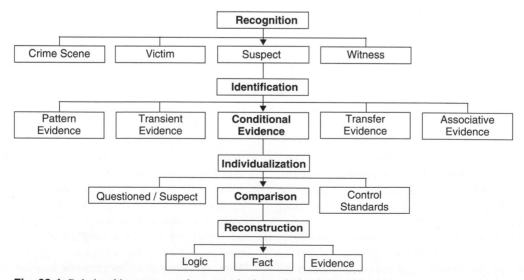

Fig. 69-1. Relationships among various steps in the analysis of physical evidence.

arrived. Based on the amount of blood that had flowed from the body to stain the bed, it was determined that the victim had been shot some time earlier than alleged by her husband.

Conditional evidence

Events or activities of the victim or suspect may result in conditional evidence at the scene or on a body. As with transient evidence, some categories of conditional evidence may be altered by persons, time, or environmental factors. The temperature of a body, the extent of rigor mortis, and the position of the body are all conditions that affect interpretations of the scene. Natural environmental changes can also affect conditional evidence. The impact of environmental factors such as fly larval development and the populations of insects on investigation is well documented.[2] These organisms and the location of the scene are important considerations when interpreting case data and may, themselves, alter significantly the condition and appearance of the physical evidence. Conditional evidence can be key in reconstructing a crime, distinguishing accidental or intentional staging from other causes, or determining the possible sequence of events associated with an incident.

In another case, when a victim's body was found in her bedroom with the air conditioner on high, first responders left the door to the room open. They also turned off the air conditioner because it was too cold to work in the room. By the time the medical examiner and the laboratory scientists arrived at the scene, the ambient temperature of the room had increased notably. This alteration of the scene clearly had a negative impact on the ability of the medical examiner to estimate the time of death based on the body temperature. Thus, the forensic scientist had only witness statements and photographs for scene reconstruction.

Pattern evidence

Pattern evidence includes a large, diverse group of physical patterns. This type of evidence can be produced by static or dynamic contact between two objects, a person and an object, or two persons. Physical patterns from direct contact can be used to determine the type of contact or mechanism that created the pattern. Commonly encountered pattern evidence includes bloodstain patterns, fracture and other damage patterns, burn patterns, patterns of residue deposits, imprints and impressions, patterns of scene activity, and *modus operandi*. Regardless of the type of pattern encountered, there are six steps in the analysis of pattern evidence: (1) recognition of the pattern; (2) documentation of the pattern; (3) enhancement of the pattern; (4) identification of the pattern; (5) comparison of the pattern; and (6) determination of the mechanism of transfer.

Recognition of pattern evidence requires careful observation as part of a logical, systematic approach to the analysis of the crime scene. In addition, experience plays a major role in the ability to perceive and to distinguish similar patterns. Recognition of patterns at a crime scene may play an important role in providing investigative leads. It should be noted that the absence of a pattern may also be significant in case reconstruction. Patterns may also assist investigators to limit false theories based on other information gained from witnesses. Distinguishing between an imprint and an indentation, for example, resulted in controversy during a high-profile criminal case.[3] Thorough observation and careful documentation of the scene at the time of the incident and prior to the admitting of numerous technicians and detectives who walked around the scene might have eliminated this issue during trial. Pattern recognition and preliminary examination can also result in distinguishing between patterns created by types of objects or weapons; this distinction is particularly important when manner and cause of death become an issue. Damage to clothing and human remains caused by animals may often appear to be significant indicators of *modus operandi* to the uninitiated. Marks made by humans that can be detected on bodies would include bite marks, fingerprints, hand prints, and scratch marks caused by nails. The patterns produced by humans demonstrate characteristics different from animal bite or claw marks and insect damage when examined properly. Weapon marks can be distinguished from artificial marks or postmortem damage upon similar careful analysis.

Recognition also involves the determination of whether a pattern is the result of a primary, sometimes called a "direct," transfer or of a secondary action. Activities subsequent to the initial incident, such as transport of a body or evidence, can alter the original pattern, create additional patterns, damage evidence, or transfer chemical residue patterns, such as gunshot residue (GSR). Failure to prevent or to recognize those patterns as secondary in nature could have a serious impact on an incident investigation.

Key to the proper identification and interpretation of pattern evidence is complete and detailed documentation. Documentation in the form of written notes, measurements, photographs, video, and sketches all help to place the pattern evidence in its proper perspective for comparison and reconstruction purposes. In general, thorough photographic documentation must include overall and close-up views of the pattern and its components; these photographs must be taken with and without a scale. This thorough documentation of the patterns prior to alteration of the scene or evidence can help determine if secondary patterns have been produced or if patterns have been altered during collection and transport of the physical evidence. In addition, since many types of pattern evidence may be altered or destroyed by subsequent laboratory analysis, thorough documentation of patterns prior to removing samples provides a complete record for review by other experts or for reconstruction. Since pattern evidence can be a vital part of a case presentation, photographic documentation of the original pattern provides demonstrative evidence for court purposes.

Laboratory techniques applied to the recognition of pattern evidence usually involve macroscopic and low-power microscopic observation of the patterns themselves. In some cases, patterns are enhanced by the use of alternative light sources that will cause some materials to fluoresce at various wavelengths, with or without chemical enhancement. Chemical enhancement techniques have also been successfully used in many situations to develop details of blood and body fluid patterns and for some chemical residues.[4]

Identification is the next step in pattern analysis. Examination of the pattern itself and of photographs using an appropriate scale helps the criminalist identify the possible source of the evidence. Patterns that demonstrate regular, mechanical macroscopic or microscopic characteristics are readily identified as marks made by a tool. Tool mark patterns result from the impact of a manufactured object with a surface. Based on this description, tool mark patterns could include ligature marks associated with a garment or rope, tire marks, finger marks, or typical "tools," such as saws and screwdrivers. Additional examinations, such as higher magnifications using a comparison microscope or scanning electron microscopy (SEM), may be warranted to examine details of impressions or to look at microscopic morphology and minute configurations. While it is often easy to identify a gunshot wound from its macroscopic appearance, for example, in some cases microscopic examination of the excised wound for the presence of gunpowder or metallic residue may be necessary for scientific confirmation. SEM and other microscopic techniques can also help the scientist distinguish whether a specific type of tool caused damage to an object.

The final stage in pattern analysis involves interpretation and comparison of the identified patterns. The experienced criminalist may offer preliminary interpretations based on observations during the earlier steps in the analysis. However, that examiner must have an open mind and be willing to modify any conclusions made prior to extensive examination and testing. Appropriate pattern interpretation requires extremely careful and detailed study. Further chemical, physical, or photographic enhancement of the evidence may be required at this stage for complete interpretation or to effect a comparison. This enhancement can provide additional detail not considered during preliminary examinations. If a known exemplar is submitted for comparison to the questioned pattern, such as with footwear patterns, the same detailed study must be carried out on the exemplar prior to comparison.

Once necessary examinations and comparisons are made, a final reconstruction as to the mechanism and causation of a pattern is offered. These conclusions must always follow the guidelines established by science and logic.

Transfer and trace evidence

The most common type of evidence classification is referred to as transfer evidence. Based on Locard's exchange principle,[5] transfer evidence is among the most diverse and the most useful types of physical evidence in investigations. Trace evidence is material present in small quantity or size. Trace materials are found at scenes, on bodies, or on other pieces of physical evidence. While the terms trace and transfer evidence are often used interchangeably, there are instances in which evidence may be deposited without direct contact transfer. However, these distinctions are generally immaterial for the purposes of recognition, documentation, or laboratory analysis, but may be significant during case reconstruction.

Transfer evidence is often subdivided into several categories. Many categorization schemes are used, often based on the different uses of transfer evidence or the perspective from which the analysis is viewed. A transfer evidence classification system based on the general origin of the evidence would include: (1) biological evidence; (2) physiological evidence; (3) chemical evidence; (4) polymers; (5) mineralogical evidence; and (6) construction materials. Table 69-1 lists some examples of those evidence categories. Trace and transfer evidence has been challenged in court recently as not meeting scientific muster or as having the potential to prejudice a jury that might place more weight on that evidence than is appropriate. A brief description of the analysis of some of the commonly encountered trace materials may provide some insight into the application of analytical techniques to

TABLE 69-1 Examples of trace and transfer evidence

Biological matter	Physiological evidence
Grass	Blood
Leaves	Semen
Wood	Urine
Pollen	Fecal material
Fruits	Tears, milk, bile
Seeds	Tissues, including bone
Hairs	Hair

Chemical evidence	Polymeric evidence
Toxicological—drugs, alcohol, poisons, other chemicals	Fibers
	Paints and finishes
	Plastics
Writing materials—ink, dye, oil, wax, paper	
Household products—cleaners, acids, caustic powders, insecticides	**Construction materials**
	Concrete
Explosives	Cement
Accelerants	Plasters
	Asphalts
	Wood
Mineralogical evidence	Paints and finishes
Soil	Nails, screws, brads, and fasteners
Minerals and ores	
Sands	
Glass	
Metals	
Natural and synthetic crystals	

specific types of evidence and the potential value of transferred materials.

Biological evidence. Biological evidence includes materials that are vegetative or animal in origin and can often be identified and associated with possible sources. The identification of biological substances and comparisons of questioned with known samples can provide useful information for investigative leads or provide cumulative evidence in circumstantial cases. Since the transfer of biological evidence is a common occurrence, many investigators or laboratory analysts may not recognize the value of a particular specimen. Even commonly occurring materials, however, can provide a link between the suspect and the victim or the crime scene or provide valuable information for case reconstruction. In addition, evidence such as pollen is of such a small size that the presence of these materials may be overlooked. In one case, microscopic algae embedded in the fibers of the tee-shirt from a suspect in a homicide case was analyzed by compound and scanning electron microscopy. The presence of these algae led to an association with a pond in the back yard of the victim's house. The murder weapon containing the victim's hair and blood was found in that pond after the association by this transfer evidence.

Recent advances in biotechnology have led to the development of techniques for analysis of plant DNA. Comparisons of DNA profiles obtained from questioned plant materials with known plant samples or databases have resulted in successful individualization, much like the process of human DNA comparisons.[6] Research is currently being carried out at several forensic laboratories to validate DNA testing procedures on marijuana and other plant species.

Physiological evidence. Evidence of physiological origin is among the most significant evidence available for identification, individualization, and association to an individual. Although each type of evidence in this category has its limitations, physiological materials often can provide important investigative leads, support a victim's or suspect's account of an incident, or link a victim, suspect, scene, and/or object.

HAIR. Hairs are often found associated with a victim, suspect, or a crime scene because they are shed as part of the growth cycle of the hair or exchanged during contact and altercation. Hair has the same basic structure whether it comes from a human or some other animal. Chemically, all hair is composed of the protein keratin; thus, current instrumental techniques are not useful to the criminalist in identifying a hair as human in origin. However, microscopic features of hairs can be significantly different. It is the macroscopic and microscopic examination of this basic structure that allows the criminalist to differentiate the animal origin of the hair and, if human, its body origin. All growing hairs have a root, anchored in the hair follicle, a shaft, and a tip. Microscopic examination shows a further division of the hair into three portions: the cuticle, or outer layer; the central medulla; and the cortex, the layer between the medulla and cuticle that contains various structures, such as pigment granules and air spaces. Hair evidence may be damaged or some portions of the hair absent when found on other items or at the scene.

Most hairs that are not of human origin can be identified by examination of the microscopic characteristics of the hair at relatively low magnification. Animal hairs typically demonstrate regular cuticle and medullary patterns, have a relatively wide medulla in comparison to the hair width (often greater than half the width of the hair), and may show banding or other distinct pigment distribution. With sufficient experience and training, forensic microscopists can identify the species of origin of many animal guard hairs. Human hairs, on the other hand, usually demonstrate a relatively thin, irregular cuticle, a narrow or even absent medulla, and, if untreated, an unbanded color appearance. Additional examination of the diameter, cross-sectional shape, and pigment distribution in a human hair may give an indication of the anthropological classification (Caucasoid, Negroid, or Mongoloid). Additional microscopic features of diameter variation, shape, texture, and appearance may lead to identification of the hair as originating from the head, pubic region, or other body origin.

If known hairs are submitted for comparison purposes, such as in a sex crimes evidence kit, microscopic comparison can be conducted. This process involves a painstaking examination of a significant number of known hairs[7] from the root end to the tip end, noting the structure, distribution, and appearance of many microscopic characteristics and structures. It is important to examine a representative sample of known hairs so that the natural variations present within and between hairs are well documented. Unknown hairs are mounted and a similar microscopic examination completed on those hairs. If no gross differences are noted between the known and questioned hairs, microscopic comparison using a double stage comparison microscope follows. If microscopic characteristics noted in the questioned hair fall outside the range of characteristics found in the known sample, the scientist can exclude the known as a source of the questioned hair. If all microscopic characteristics are similar to those demonstrated by the known hair, that known source cannot be excluded. When performed correctly, the process of hair comparison is a long, time-consuming examination. By its nature, microscopic hair comparisons *cannot* link a hair to a particular person or animal.

It cannot be stated strongly enough that microscopic examination of hairs does not serve as a positive means of individualization. Criminalists must be careful not to imply individualization and should make this clear throughout their testimony. Recent highly publicized instances of hair examiners testifying beyond the limitations of the science have made many skeptical of the value of microscopic hair comparison.[8] Fears that a jury will misinterpret the findings when testimony about hair comparisons is offered have led many attorneys to demand the exclusion of this "prejudicial" evidence. However, when hair comparisons are correctly conducted, they can provide valuable leads for investigators. Hair comparisons are also useful as corroborating or excluding evidence.

If a microscopical hair comparison cannot exclude an individual as the source of a hair, more individualizing tests may be possible. If the hair has a root containing sufficient cellular material, nuclear DNA STR profiles may be developed and compared to the possible source. If insufficient cellular material is present or the hair is a fragment, nuclear DNA testing cannot be performed. However, mitochondrial DNA testing can be conducted on hair shafts. Because mitochondria, unlike nuclear DNA, are generally inherited from the mother only, the mtDNA profile will not provide the same level of individualization as nuclear DNA analysis. However, statistics indicate that between 10% and 20% of hairs found to be microscopically similar will demonstrate dissimilar mtDNA sequences.[9]

BLOOD AND BODY FLUIDS. The potential for blood or body fluids to provide individualizing information about the origin of those samples is well known. Advances in DNA technology allow analysis of minute quantities of fluid or tissue. Most physiological materials are suitable for DNA typing. Polymerase chain reaction (PCR) amplification of STR loci provide a valuable tool to the forensic laboratory, since analysis can be conducted in a short period of time. In addition, samples that are degraded may also give reliable DNA profiles using this method. Even small amounts of physiological materials on clothing, jewelry, and other items have provided STR profiles.[10] Because of its sensitivity, STR analysis has been the procedure most commonly utilized in the examination of old, unsolved cases or for postconviction testing.

Before DNA testing can be conducted, however, physiological samples should be identified whenever possible. This is especially important if genetic markers will be used in a case reconstruction. Use of alternative light sources has been shown to be an effective means of locating physiological stains for identification. After macroscopic search for possible body fluid stains, identifying a sample involves a screening test and, when available, a confirmatory test. Absolute identification of blood or a body fluid stain cannot be made based on a screening test alone. The value of a screening test is its ability to distinguish materials that are suitable for further testing.

Once a sample has been identified as blood, semen, saliva, tissue, etc., if sufficient sample exists a species test should also be conducted. Commercially available rapid immunoassay systems for the identification of human hemoglobin, for example, are extremely sensitive and consume very little material. This classification by species in addition to any human DNA quantitation may be information necessary to obtain warrants for known samples from a suspect. Testing a sample for human origin prior to DNA extraction will save time and resources if the results are negative for human blood.

Highly degraded physiological samples and samples such as bone tissue have been successfully typed using mtDNA analysis.

Chemical evidence. Chemical evidence is among the most prevalent in criminalistics laboratories. Forensic chemistry involves the identification of various organic and inorganic materials, including accelerants, explosives, gunpowder residue, drugs, toxic substances, and many other trace materials. The number of recent incidents involving the collection of "white powders" as suspected infectious biochemical weapons illustrates the complex process of analysis of an unknown chemical substance. Once these materials are found not to contain harmful biological agents, such as anthrax, the trace amounts of chemical evidence from those hoax cases are analyzed microscopically and instrumentally. Several different procedures must be utilized before identification of these unknown "white powders" can be effected. Infrared spectroscopy and gas or liquid chromatography coupled with mass spectrometry is usually employed to analyze complex mixtures or identify unknown chemicals. In some instances, quantitation of chemical residues may be important for reconstruction or developing new investigative leads.

GUNPOWDER RESIDUE. Burned and partially burned gunpowder, gases, and soot are released when a weapon is discharged, due to the detonation of the primer and gunpowder in the ammunition. Some of these materials are propelled with the projectile, some are blown back onto the shooter. Deposits of gunshot residue (GSR) may contain components of primer, lubricant, propellant, or ammunition metals. Analytical techniques such as AA, ICP, and SEM/EDX can be used to detect the GSR collected from the hands or clothing of the shooter or victim. In addition, various chemical color tests for those components and infrared photography can be used on target surfaces to estimate the approximate distance between the barrel of the weapon and the target surface.

Historically, GSR was detected on swabbings of hands or surfaces using atomic absorption (AA) methods. Instrumental analysis is now carried out in most laboratories by ion coupled plasma (ICP) techniques. ICP is favored because of its greater sensitivity and more linear calibration. Levels of elements composing primers, typically lead, barium, and antimony, are determined and compared to negative control swabs. High levels of these elements may indicate that gunshot residue is present. However, ICP alone is not conclusive proof that someone discharged a firearm.

SEM analysis of adhesive disks collected from hands or target surfaces can sometimes yield more conclusive results for GSR. SEM/EDX can provide elemental analysis and reveal the morphology of a GSR particle. The combination of a particle possessing characteristic morphology with the presence of lead, barium, and antimony can be interpreted as the presence of GSR. The identification of GSR on a sample from a person's hands only indicates that the person tested might have fired a weapon. GSR can transfer to another surface either through direct contact with the weapon or as airborne particles. Thus, if the individual handled a weapon or was in close proximity when a weapon was discharged, GSR could be deposited in this manner.

Polymer evidence

FIBERS. Fiber transfer evidence is commonly encountered in many types of cases. The likelihood that fibers will transfer depends on the type of fiber, the type of the fabric source, and the nature of the contact surface. Animal fibers, for example, have a tendency to remain adhered to another fabric due to the protruding hair scales of the fiber and electrostatic attraction. Transfer may be through direct (primary) or indirect (secondary) contact.

Fibers are of two general types: natural fibers that occur in the environment or have been used in manufacturing, and synthetic fibers. Fiber examination may involve numerous steps and analyses, depending on the type of fiber and the instrumentation available to the laboratory. Some of the techniques of fiber analysis are destructive; therefore, many laboratories do not conduct those tests in order to preserve the questioned sample for future examination by other experts. Detailed guidelines for the examination of fiber evidence have been compiled by the Scientific Working Group on Material Analysis.[11] A brief overview of the fiber examination process follows.

Initial identification of fibers is carried out using microscopic techniques. Low magnification, compound microscopic examination, and polarized light microscopy will reveal morphology and optical characteristics of the examined fibers. These procedures are nondestructive and are preferred for preliminary examination, identification, and comparison of the fibers. Classification as natural or synthetic fibers is usually easily accomplished through microscopic analysis. Physical characteristics of manufactured fibers, such as the shape, color, diameter variation, inclusions, and surface characteristics, are readily compared by this process. Many fibers that appear similar to each other without magnification may be distinguished by these methods. In fact, the SWG guidelines state that an appropriate microscopic examination provides the most discriminating method of determining if fibers are consistent with coming from the same origin.

For a more conclusive comparison, fiber analysis should include at least two analytical techniques for classification, physical characteristics, and color. To determine those properties, the criminalist commonly employs several instrumental techniques including: visible spectroscopy, to obtain an objective evaluation and comparison of color; pyrolysis gas chromatography, to identify the generic class or subclass of the fiber; and infrared spectroscopy, to identify synthetic fibers.

The value of a fiber comparison is related to the occurrence of that fiber in the environment, the amount of fiber present, and the location of the fiber on the object. Some fibers, such as white cotton, are so common as to make the presence of single white cotton fibers or their comparison meaningless. Others, especially uniquely colored or shaped synthetic fibers or fibers in large quantity, may have greater potential significance.

PAINT. Coatings and paints are often encountered in motor vehicle accidents and burglary investigations, but may be useful information in other case investigations where there can be primary or secondary transfer of paint fragments. Paints are complex mixtures of pigments, binders, plasticizers, carriers, and other components. Some of these components are organic compounds, typically analyzed by FTIR and pyrolysis GC. Other components are inorganic substances suitable for SEM/EDX characterization. Often the paint fragments that are found as trace material contain multiple layers. Microscopic examination can reveal the layer color sequence and texture. Each layer can then be analyzed separately, providing a complex profile of the materials in that fragment. This "profile" can be compared to those of standard paint chips from a known source to determine similarity. The significance of a positive comparison depends on the number of layers present, the nature of the paint in each layer, and the occurrence of that paint in the environment.[12]

Mineralogical evidence.
Soil and other mineral evidence is often overlooked during the collection of physical evidence. Soils can be separated into their organic and inorganic components, as well as the natural and man-made materials present in the sample. Using a petrographic microscope, the criminalist can determine the mineral and elemental composition of soils. Extracts of samples may contain trace amounts of ions and organic chemicals that add to the individual character of a particular sample. Instrumental analysis of these extracts may demonstrate the presence of toxic chemicals in cases of environmental contamination. In addition, if several layers of soil are present, the layer structure of the deposited soil combined with analysis of biological materials present, such as plants, grass, pollens, animal hairs, and insect parts, may also provide useful information concerning the possible origin of the adhering materials. Mineralogical evidence usually has greater value when it involves a comparison to case samples of known origin.

Construction materials.
Transfer evidence related to construction, including wood fragments, plaster, metal shavings, cement, asphalt, etc., can be analyzed and compared to

standard materials. The type of analysis conducted will depend on the chemical nature of the construction material and the size of the sample. Even small wood chips and shavings may provide valuable clues to associate a victim with a crime scene. Differences between treated, preserved, or prepared and natural woods can be easily determined. The species of origin of a wood sample usually can be determined by wood experts, thus tracing the wood samples to their origin. Comparison between known and questioned wood materials collected in a case may provide critical linkage in the investigation.

Associative evidence

Physical evidence is often used to associate the victim or the suspect with the crime scene, an object, or each other. This linkage among various aspects of a crime is often critical and required to provide circumstantial evidence during trial. The actual nature of the evidence in this class will vary, but its primary use is for the purpose of associating various elements or persons. Some types of associative evidence are used to link an object to a specific individual. Paramount among those are vehicles, clothing, shoes, gloves, and tools. Associative evidence used for personal identification includes fingerprints, palm prints, bite marks, tattoos, x-rays, videotapes, and photographs. These associations have been used successfully for many years in investigations and as evidence in courts of law. Of equal importance is the *exclusion* of a person or object by the failure to make an association. Other materials, such as tool marks and firearms evidence, are based on a detailed examination of the individual markings produced when these objects are used. These striae cannot be used to link evidence directly to a specific person, but can provide important corroborating or exculpatory evidence of association or disassociation with two objects.

Valuable associative evidence can be obtained by appropriate use of national and local databases that are now available (Table 69-2). For example, after instrumental analysis is completed on a questioned vehicle paint sample, the national paint database can be searched for identification of the make and model of the automobile. This search can potentially provide key investigative information not available by other means. With the collection of samples from convicted felons, physiological evidence from a no-suspect case can be analyzed and the STR profile searched against the regional or national database. The successful association of individuals with blood and body fluid samples in cases that otherwise could not have been solved is now a common occurrence. DNA databases have been so successful that many states have greatly expanded the class of persons from whom samples are taken. Similar searches of the NIBIN cartridge case database have resulted in the association of previously unrelated crimes involving handguns.

TABLE 69-2 Associative evidence: sources and information

Vehicle	Model, make, shape, logo, sign, damage	VICAP
		MVD request
	Paint, color, license plate	Garage
		Random check
Weapon	Size, shape, color	IBIS/NIBIN
	Bullet	Data check
	Cartridge case	VICAP
	Tool mark	
Clothing	Hat	Photographs
	Shoes	Videotape
	Other clothes	Fiber database
		VICAP
Objects	Mechanism	Manufacturer data
	Tools	UPC labels
	Containers	
Persons	Physical description	Sketch
	ID cards, birthmarks, tattoos, scars	Tattoo records
		Mug shots
	DNA profile	DNA database

CHALLENGES TO CRIMINALISTICS EVIDENCE

Since the Supreme Court decision in *Daubert v. Merrell Dow Pharmaceuticals*,[13] criminalistics has entered a new era. Under the *Frye*[14] standard of general acceptance within the scientific community, criminalists were confident that, if consensus techniques were employed and proficiency tests acceptable, the result obtained was reliable. With long-standing disciplines such as fingerprints, hands-on experience produced a confidence in the absolute individualizations that were made. Initially, only DNA analyses were scrutinized at every stage of the testing process—from validation, to analysis, to quality control. The factors laid out in *Daubert* made it clear to the forensic community that consensus without well-documented validation would not be sufficient for the future. Judges took their role as gatekeepers to bar bad science very seriously.[15]

While some states still retain a version of the *Frye* standard, many have adopted *Daubert*. Some of those courts have held that certain techniques are so well founded in the forensic community that they do not require a *Daubert*-type hearing. However, numerous questions concerning the validation, quality control, peer review, and other factors are still appropriate. Answers to those fundamental questions must be satisfactory or they may still raise serious issues for the jury concerning the reliability of the specific test application in a case.

Clear efforts are being made within the criminalistics community to establish more specific national standards for analysis and quality control guidelines, as evidenced by the creation of numerous scientific working groups and national certification oversight boards. These protocols reflect an awareness of the need for objective, reproducible results obtained within a quality system that can stand up to the rigors of the *Daubert*-type inquiry. Some subjectivity will always be part of the criminalistics process, however. It is the nature of criminalistics itself that scientific comparisons based on the evaluation of objective characteristics are always some part of the analysis. The other aspects of forensic evidence involved in interpretation and reconstruction are based on experience, logic, and objective evaluation.

ENDNOTES

1. For example, the FBI has established a policy that a DNA profile frequency of occurrence of less than 1 in 260 billion would result in a reported individual source for a biological sample.

2. Time of death estimation based on insect species development and persistence has been accepted in numerous courts. For a general reference, *see* K.G.V. Smith, *A Manual of Forensic Entomology* (Trustees of the British Museum, 1986) or J. Byrd & J.L. Castner, eds., *Forensic Entomology: The Utility of Arthropods in Legal Investigation* (1990).

3. *See The State of California v. Orenthal James Simpson*, Case BA097211(1995). *See also* www.courttv.com/casefiles/simpson/new_docs/lee_testimony.html. In that case, questions concerning the identification of additional bloody shoeprints at the scene were raised by the defense. Prosecution experts initially contended that the patterns pointed out by the defense expert were, in fact, indentations in the walkway material and not related to the murder of Nicole Brown. The defense was able to show that the parallel-line type of imprints were, in fact, left by a bloody sole of a size 10 shoe.

4. General protein stains, such as amido black, are used successfully at crime scenes and in the laboratory. Also used is a bloody print enhancement reagent, based on the chemical presumptive test reagent TMB mixed with a plasticizer.

5. Edmond Locard, an early twentieth-century criminalist, postulated that, when objects, persons, or surfaces come in contact with each other, there is a mutual exchange of materials. This transfer may result in identifiable trace materials that can be used to link the objects, persons, or surfaces to each other.

6. *See Bogan v. Arizona* (1993), where a woman's body was dumped in the Arizona desert under a *Palo verde* tree. DNA from seed pods found in the suspect's trunk were matched to the tree under which the victim was found. Also reported in 260 Science (May 14, 1993).

7. While there is no overall agreement on the exact number of hairs necessary, all scientists agree that representative hairs should be removed from all areas of the region of the body being sampled, for example, 25 hairs each taken from the front, back, two sides, and top of the head. Some trace experts suggest examining these hundred hairs and then choosing a representative sample for permanent mounting and comparison to the questioned hairs.

8. Several of these cases have been reported from Oklahoma, where the laboratory examiner gave an opinion that hair evidence showed the accused was physically present at the scene based on her hair comparison results. See *McCarty v. State*, 765 P. 2d 1215 (Okla. Crim. 1988).

9. For a study of mitchondrial DNA typing of hairs previously associated with an individual, *see* Houck et al., *Correlation of Microscopic and Mitochondrial DNA Hair Comparisons*, 47(5) J. Forensic Sci., 964-67 (2002).

10. R.A. Wickenheuser, *Trace DNA: A Review, Discussion of Theory, and Application of the Transfer of Trace Quantities of DNA Through Skin Contact*, 47(3) J. Forensic Sci., 442-500 (2002).

11. *Forensic Fiber Examination Guidelines*, 1(1) Forensic Science Communications (Apr. 1999).

12. For detailed procedures for the analysis of paints, see the SWGMAT Paint Subgroup guidelines in Forensic Science Communications.

13. *Daubert v. Merrell Dow Pharmaceuticals, Inc.*, 509 U.S. 579 (1993).

14. *Frye v. United States*, 293 F. 1013 (1923).

15. *United States v. Plaza et al.*, C.R. 98-362-10,11,12 (Jan. 7, 2002 and Mar. 12, 2002).

Forensic Entomology

NEAL H. HASKELL, Ph.D.

BRIEF HISTORY
SCIENTIFIC PERSPECTIVE AND PRINCIPLES OF APPLICATION
APPLICATIONS
ADDITIONAL APPLICATIONS
IMPORTANCE OF CLIMATOLOGICAL INPUT
IMPORTANCE OF RESEARCH
QUALIFICATIONS OF THE FORENSIC ENTOMOLOGIST
CONCLUSION

Forensic entomology, in the broad sense, is the term applied to the use of entomological (insect) evidence in courts of law. This broad definition includes entomologists who are able to testify about subjects pertaining to proper uses of chemicals or other pesticides, control of fly populations in animal waste, damage to structures from insects, or the contamination of food by insects. These cases are usually adjudicated in civil courts. A more specific meaning of forensic entomology, and that which is focused on in this text, is the use of insects during investigation of crimes or other legal matters where the forensic entomologist will culminate his or her investigation with a report or testimony in court.

In most of these cases, the forensic entomologist becomes involved with the legal system after the initial discovery of a dead body or other crime. This is due to the insects being important in establishing time of death in many cases. It is when the medical examiner/coroner, police, or prosecutor needs additional information regarding insect evidence noticed on the body or at a crime scene, that the forensic entomologist is usually contacted. This is the most desirable scenario from the standpoint of the forensic entomologist, due to the ability of the insect expert to do his or her own recovery of insect evidence at the scene (if called in a timely fashion) or at the very least for a collection to be made during autopsy. The expert is able to gather supporting documentation and request other investigators for help in that quest, to calibrate the microenvironment where the insects were recovered (the scene) with weather stations, and to do additional laboratory studies using live insects freshly recovered from the remains or from the scene.

Secondly, the forensic entomologist may be contacted by the death investigators days, weeks, or even months after a crime has been committed. This is often the case when it was initially determined by the investigators that there was an obvious suspect, or the elements of the crime were known, but then they discovered later that little of the above was actually what had happened. When involved in this way, the forensic entomologist is faced with a greater challenge due to not having the opportunity to collect personally, thus being dependent on others who may have little or no training in recognition or recovery of insect evidence. When significant time has passed, environmental conditions may have changed considerably, so confirmation of climatic conditions at the scene may be impossible. Also, if insects were collected, most often they will be dead, so laboratory rearing for species identification accuracy will be impossible.

The third means by which the forensic entomologist becomes involved is being hired as an expert witness by either the prosecution or defense after charges have been filed. In some cases, the interval of time between being retained and the trial may be as short as $1\frac{1}{2}$ or 2 weeks. This situation presents even greater challenges for the forensic entomologist: first to come up to speed with the case itself, then to educate the trial attorneys on entomology. Insect evidence may be minimal or lacking, supporting documentation may be unobtainable, or time is just not adequate to do the necessary testing and research in order to obtain the most precise results possible. In addition, there may be an opposing forensic entomology expert who has had weeks or months to prepare for the case. Additional preparation of the attorneys regarding the opposing expert (his transcripts, publications, or presentations pertinent to his testimony) is essential if effective cross-examination of the witness is to be accomplished.

Whichever way the forensic entomologist is engaged for the case, the task is to determine what entomological evidence is present and what data are available from the literature or from personal experience for the kind of insects (groups or species) recovered. Once this information is obtained, the forensic entomologist must determine what results and conclusions may be drawn from the combination of the insects and the known information regarding those insect groups. A concise but detailed and well-written report is often the end of involvement in the case. However, continuation of the case as the forensic entomology expert in the courtroom may be an alternative role necessary to answer questions as to the guilt or innocence of a defendant.

It is essential that the forensic entomologist be unbiased regarding the analysis of the entomological evidence. This evidence is derived from a very powerful quantitative scientific methodology gathered by hundreds of researchers over decades of studies, observations, and testing. It must be emphasized that it is not the responsibility of the forensic entomologist to determine the guilt or innocence of the person on trial. The forensic entomologist's only responsibility is to present the conclusions as accurately, honestly, and clearly to the jury as is possible. The criminal justice system is responsible for the judgment.

BRIEF HISTORY

The use of entomology in death investigations dates originally to a thirteenth-century record of a murder where adult blowflies were attracted to the one hand sickle used to kill a Chinese peasant farmer among more than a dozen hand sickles placed upon the ground by other suspects. It became obvious in a matter of minutes which hand sickle retained bits of human tissue, blood, and hair because of the numerous flies orbiting around the murder weapon for a taste of the victim. The owner of the implement soon confessed to the murder.[1]

Reliability in insect growth, development, behavior, and habit proved itself again and again over the following centuries in many experiments regarding questions of spontaneous generation,[2] insect colonization of decomposing human remains in a successional pattern,[3,4] and studies on meat contamination and livestock loss due to parasitic blowflies.[5-9]

Documentation of human death studies records a case from France in the 1850s being solved using the colonization of beetles.[10] A famous case from England in the 1930s gave prominence to the maggots that helped prove that Dr. Ruxton had ample opportunity and time to kill his wife and housekeeper and return to his home within an allotted time frame.[11] It became apparent during the early 1930s that solving murders would benefit by knowing specific information about certain insect groups. J. Edgar Hoover requested work to begin on a monograph focusing on what has become the chief insect indicator group, the blowflies (Diptera: Calliphoridae).[12] It was not until 1948, however, that this work was completed and published by D.G. Hall under the title of *The Blowflies of North America*.[13] This volume satisfied two major needs in entomology, one being the use in death investigation and the other in reducing excessive livestock losses in the southern latitudes of the United States by the primary screw worm (*Cochliomyia hominovorax*).

Due to the pressures of the economic losses caused by this fly, increased research funding was applied to solving this major problem.[6,7,14,15] Vast amounts of data were gathered on this specific species and many of the other closely related blowfly species that cohabitated with *C. hominovorax*. This progression of studies resulted in the most successful biological control and eradication of an insect species in history. After intensive study of the species, it was discovered that there were actually two species of flies (*Cochliomyia hominovorax* and *Cochliomyia macellaria*),[5] in one of which (*C. hominovorax*) the female only mated once. This information indicated that if males could be sterilized, unfertilized eggs would result. This technique was tested in Florida in the mid-1950s and was a great success. A national plan was implemented where tens of millions of male *C. hominovorax* were produced, sterilized, and released.[16] Within the past 40 years of this program's application, the primary screw worm has now been eradicated as far south as Costa Rica. The serendipitous outcome of this intensive research over the past 70 years has been able to provide much knowledge regarding the blowflies, which just happen to be the first insects to colonize dead animal carrion (humans included). Because of this focus on the economic aspects of losses in our livestock industry, forensic entomology is now decades ahead of where it would have been without this early work.

SCIENTIFIC PERSPECTIVE AND PRINCIPLES OF APPLICATION

The basic principles used in most applications where insects are employed to answer questions at a death scene are decades-old, reliable principles of insect behavior, growth, development, and habit. This is due to nearly two and a half centuries of study by hundreds of naturalists, biologists, and entomologists. In a series of studies by Megnin in France in the late nineteenth century,[3] it was observed that as a human body or other animal decomposed, there was a predictable progression to the decomposition. The body changes from a freshly dead condition into a bloated state, then to active decay where body fluids begin to seep from the remains. As more time passes, the body begins to dry out with the fluids becoming more greaselike, and eventually the body dries to the point where any tissues remaining are stiff and leathery. This last bit of mummified tissue eventually disappears until only dry bones remain. It was also noted by Megnin that along with these major physical changes in the human tissues, the tissues were also changing biochemically.

These biochemical changes are the cause of another critical observation that Megnin made. As the biochemicals change, there is a corresponding change in the insect groups and species that appear on the body over the course of the decomposition.

Megnin identified eight specific seral (meaning sere) waves of insects coming to the body, colonizing it for a period of time, and then leaving. With this sequence of insects moving onto the body, feeding for their specific periods of time in the decomposition progression, and then leaving when the tissues had changed biochemically so as not to be attractive to that insect group any longer, it was possible to utilize the food resource entirely. Today, this is known as food (or resource) partitioning. Over the last century, many studies have been conducted on the progression of decomposition of humans and animals from a wide range of different environments and habitats.[17-34]

This sequence or seral wave progression (insect succession) is used today as one of the two major methods of estimation of the time since death or postmortem interval (PMI). What has been learned from the many studies on insect succession is that the timing of the insect groups can be variable given the geographic location (which may be a function of temperature), season of the year (again temperature-related), and habitat. It is important to recognize that in nearly all the studies, even with differing temperatures, varying habitats, diverse geographic locations, and different seasons of the year, the sequence of the insect groups and species (insect taxa) moving onto the carrion (decomposing soft tissues), colonizing the carrion, and then leaving the carrion, were consistent.[17-34] Therefore, if experiments are conducted during different seasons at specific geographic locations within specified habitats, it is possible to obtain very reliable time intervals on how long a dead body has been exposed to the insects. This insect succession method is used when remains have been exposed for long periods of time, such as for weeks or more during summers in the upper latitudes of the United States or for months of exposure during cooler times of the year. This method can be very accurate, but not as precise as the second method used for estimation of the PMI.

The second method used by entomologists for estimation of the time of death is the use of an insect's known growth and development time for a specific species. This is primarily applied to the fly group (Diptera), but not exclusively. As discussed in the historical section above, it is fortunate that much of the early twentieth-century research focused on the blowflies. Since those early years of fly biology research, a resurgence of fly research in the last 40 years has continued to focus on individual species growth and development rates for developing growth tables for several of the most common species of flies to colonize human and animal remains.[35-41] These later studies are becoming more sophisticated regarding temperature variability and the establishment of statistical limits. This

area of research is still one of the most needed areas of data when considering cases from across North America.

The underlying principle in using this means of estimating the PMI is that the blowflies (most species in the group) will colonize immediately upon death if the remains are exposed for access by the flies and the temperatures are above the lower limit flight threshold for the species involved. Also, due to the successional preferences of the different groups, the blowflies will only have one generation developing from any given human or animal remains. This does not mean that there cannot be eggs deposited (oviposition) on a number of successive days or intervals of time where egg-laying by the adult females is inhibited. In the experience of this author, with 20 years of research observations, it has never been seen that a true second generation of blowflies has had the opportunity to colonize a body for the second time. The biochemical condition of the body will pass quickly, as decomposition moves forward, into a form that is not attractive as a food resource.

Specific species developmental time estimates are utilized when there is a shorter PMI in question, usually not longer than 25 to 30 days during warm summer temperatures. This method may be used for periods of weeks or even months if cooler or cold temperatures are prevalent and the specimens have not completed the full life cycle. Great precision can be achieved under this method, being within ± 12 hours in cases of 8 to 15 days duration and ± 48 hours with cases in the 20 to 25 day range.[42]

In general, more advanced flies (evolution based), such as blowflies (Calliphoridae), house flies (Muscidae), flesh flies (Sarcophagidae), and many of the later colonizing flies (e.g. Sepsidae, coffin flies [Phoridae], skipper flies [Piophilidae]), have similar life cycles which include an egg (flesh flies start with a first-stage [instar] maggot), a first-, second-, and third-instar (stage) larva (maggot), a migrating third-instar larva, a puparium (pupa), and finally hatching (eclosing) from the puparium as an adult male or female fly. Many of the beetles associated with carrion have a "complete" life cycle also, with the egg, larva, pupa, and adult, but many beetle species can vary the number of larval stages (instars) if stressed for food or from environmental pressures. Both groups of insects (flies and beetles) have the potential to be used to estimate elapsed time since death by using their individual species life cycles.

As stated earlier, our key insect indicator species group is the blowflies, which is used in the majority of death cases. From data sets (experiments on growth of the flies in the lab or field) on growth and development of the common species of blowflies found in both semitropical and temperate areas of the country, quantification of the temperatures driving that growth and development over time can be derived. The important factors relating to the species are the temperatures at which the specimens were raised to obtain the time it took to complete the different stages of their respective life cycles. In addition, the time is combined with the temperature (temperature × time) to give a product in the units of growing degree days or growing degree hours. A base temperature is also introduced to reflect the lower limit threshold of growth. Below this base temperature there will be no growth or development; therefore in any period of time where the ambient temperatures are below this threshold, no growth occurs and it is denoted as a zero for that value. This method provides a means of dealing with fluctuating temperatures on either an hourly or a daily basis, adjusting for periods of cool temperatures when growth is slowed or for high temperatures when growth is quite rapid, all combined within the same data set of temperatures from any temperature recording station.

Other methods used by practicing forensic entomologists may include data sets that provide a rate of growth at a specified temperature over a given time period. For example, at 80°F it takes 3.5 days for *Phaenicia sericata* (Calliphoridae) to reach the third-instar larva. If you recover third-instar larvae (plural of larva) of *P. sericata* from a body, does that mean that the larva is 3.5 days old? Not necessarily, because the temperatures may be either higher or lower than the rearing data above, and this difference from 80°F has not been taken into account. If the overall average (mean temperature) for the days in question were 80°F even with lower temperatures at some periods and higher temperatures at others, then in this example it could be quite close to the 3.5 days. Therefore, it is critical to know at what temperature the developmental data were derived as well as at what temperature the case specimens are developing.

APPLICATIONS

As we have seen above, the primary application of insects answering questions in death investigation is to estimate when the victim died. This possibility exists due to the insects being the very first organisms to colonize dead animals. Some species within the blowfly group can be found on a dead body within seconds to minutes after the individual died. Eggs or larvae can be deposited within the first hour if temperatures are above the flight and oviposition (egg-laying) minimum temperatures for that particular species. Flight minimum temperatures are around 50°F for temperate climate blowflies and may be slightly higher for the tropical species. There is also a possibility of a delay in colonization after death if conditions are below minima or if there are barriers to the flies accessing the remains. In most cases, death will occur prior to the insect colonization (egg-laying), and the conclusion is that there is an established/calculated minimum of time for the remains to have been dead.

Another application of entomology is using the ranges of a specific insect species' geographic distribution (where it lives) to establish from where a body originated. In a case

from California, the presences of a chigger species on the suspect proved that the suspect had deposited the murdered woman at a location where high populations of this chigger were present. This chigger species is very rare in central California and when found, it only occupies an area of a few hundred yards but is found in very dense aggregations. The chigger was not found in any other location in that part of central California except at the body dump site. This evidence, combined with other testimonial evidence, placed the suspect at the site where the victim was dumped. A conviction resulted in this case.[43] In another case, it was suspected that the murderer had driven from central Belgium to the coast to deposit the body in a tidal estuary, a distance of some 150 miles. Insect evidence (in this case mayflies) was collected from the grill and radiator of the suspect's car. As is customary with the mayflies, they are periodistic (due to their short life as adults) and can be very local in their distribution. Once the mayflies were identified, it was found that they were only found within 20 miles of the coast where the body was deposited and were only out as adults for 4 days. The death of the woman had occurred during this 4-day hatch. The suspect was convicted of the murder.

Carrion insects (primarily blowflies) can be used to identify areas of trauma on badly decomposed remains when major changes have taken place in the appearance of the soft tissues on the body. The larvae of the blowflies have only the nine natural body openings to access the remains, unless there is some means by which the skin of an adult human has been opened or damaged with exposure of underlying muscle or other soft tissue. It has been demonstrated during research that for the first several days of decomposition, the skin is a major barrier to the early-feeding maggots, keeping them from feeding on the underlying soft tissues of the body. Lacking trauma to a body, the preferred site for initial blowfly egg-laying is the face, with the eyes, nose, and mouth as specific locations for finding the first egg masses. This is due to the gases that are being generated within the body purging from the nose and mouth. Compounds carried within these gases are the primary attractants of the blowflies. Head hair that is moist with blood or other natural fluids, and which is close to or in contact with the ground, may have quantities of eggs in as little time as an hour or so of death. The pelvic area will eventually attract female flies for egg laying, but there appears to be a considerable delay from the facial area if trauma to the pelvic area is not present.

Therefore, if a body of only a few days postmortem has colonies of blowfly maggots in locations other than the face or pelvic area, these areas, where there is underlying bone or intact soft tissue, should be examined closely for the presence of some type of wound that opened the skin and exposed the soft tissues to the blowflies. It has also been shown that when there are extensive colonies of maggots in the pelvic area of females, that are as old as or older than the colonies on the face, there is a strong likelihood that some type of trauma has occurred to that region of the body. In cases where there are early stages of maggots in the face and similar-sized maggots on the hands and fingers, and the hands are extended away from the body, an examination of the finger and hand bones (metacarpals and phalange) may reveal cut marks on the bones. Of course, with each case, there are differing circumstances that must be taken into account surrounding the position of the body and the duration of exposure to the blowflies. However, if those variables are considered, a forensic pathologist may discover and arrive at a conclusion in a more timely fashion than if these insect behavior patterns are not known or understood.

The maggots may be used to determine the presence or absence of drugs when human body tissues are too badly decomposed to do toxicology on the human tissues.[44-52] It has been found that maggots feeding on tissues containing many of the controlled drugs will ingest these chemicals and then store them in fat bodies in the insect or in the outer chitein covering of the specimen. Chitein is a protein-like substance that is arranged in a molecular matrix pattern that appears to be ideal for trapping and locking chemical substances within the molecular structure. Actively feeding maggots can hold a number of substances that can be tested for by using normal drug-testing techniques. In one case, empty puparial cases found with skeletal remains were tested and revealed cocaine, which was present in large quantities. The victim had been missing for 4 years, and it was suspected that the decedent had taken an overdose of the drug, but the body had never been found. This new evidence assisted the forensic pathologist in arriving at a cause of death.

Techniques for analyzing molecular DNA structures of insects for species identification[53-61] and the human DNA in insects that feed on humans[62,63] have recently been developed. The major insect groups being studied for these tests include the mosquitoes, lice, fleas, and bed bugs. All of these insect groups may take human blood meals to furnish nourishment to eggs being produced in their bodies or as food for themselves. These human blood meals can be analyzed for individual human DNA testing. As an example, a woman was assaulted and raped by an unknown attacker. The attacker inadvertently transferred pubic lice that he was carrying onto the victim. Fortunately, the lice were collected as evidence and human DNA was extracted and tested. Later, when suspects were being investigated, a match was made between one of the suspects and the DNA sample from the pubic lice recovered from the victim.

In addition to the blood-feeding insects, maggots feeding on decomposing humans have been tested for human DNA and found to retain testable levels.[62] This can be important to an investigation when a body has been removed from a site where decomposition has been extensive enough to leave behind sizable maggots. Even if the remains are never recovered, maggots with a victim's DNA would be proof that the person was dead. Also, this technique could be used to prove if maggots alleged to have come from a crime scene were actually from the remains recovered from that scene and not switched by an opposing expert witness.

ADDITIONAL APPLICATIONS

Insects can also provide considerable information in cases of elderly neglect or child abuse. These types of cases usually involve living as opposed to dead individuals. Children or elderly persons who are under the care of others have been admitted as patients in emergency rooms or doctor's offices with maggots or other insects on them. Questions as to how long since the person has had a bath or how long since a diaper has been changed can often be answered by the presence of fly larvae on the person. The insect fly group is usually the house fly or its relatives. By knowing how long it is required to reach the stage of the fly life cycle collected from the patient, a time interval can be established. In a case from Indiana, house fly maggots of at least 5 days of age were collected from a 3-month-old baby girl. This was proof enough for the county prosecutor to force the parents to enroll in parenting classes. The father was 16 and the mother was 15 at the time of the diaper incident and the child was their second offspring. They truly did not know that a diaper should be changed more than once a week!

The blowflies can answer questions in civil matters such as time of death when payment of an insurance policy is in question. A case from Illinois illustrates this application of forensic entomology. The decedent was last seen around March 24 when he went on a camping trip by himself. He was found dead on approximately April 10. His insurance policy of $100,000 expired on April 1. His 5-year-old child survived him and was the beneficiary of the policy. The county coroner contacted the forensic entomologist and requested assistance in determining when the man died. Blowfly larvae collected from the remains in combination with daily temperature data for the period of March 20 through April 15 proved that the father had died soon after he had last been seen leaving for the camping trip. A report from the forensic entomologist accompanied the coroner's report to the insurance company. The surviving son was awarded the value of the policy within days of the coroner submitting his report.

Yet another situation where blowflies may assist in finding answers to a complicated and horrific occurrence is the identification of human soft tissues in violent air crashes. In recent years, several commercial air disasters have resulted in destruction of the human remains similar to high-velocity military air crashes. With these high-speed crashes, human bodies are literally shredded into small pieces of tissue. Aircraft wreckage and debris are closely intermingled with hundreds of pieces of body parts from the victims. After a few days, the human tissues became very difficult to distinguish from the wreckage (e.g., American Eagle crash, Roselawn, Indiana, October 31, 1994). A way to quickly identify the human soft tissues is to observe where the blowflies are actively feeding and depositing eggs. These insects will only be depositing their next generation on decomposing animal tissue, so recognition of the human remains should be apparent from that of the wreckage with these bright-green and blue flies as signals.

IMPORTANCE OF CLIMATOLOGICAL INPUT

The climatological data, and specifically the temperatures, but including intensity of rainfall, fog conditions, cloud cover, and time of sunrise and sunset, may be important when attempting to determine if insect colonization (especially blowflies) is immediate or if there has been a delay in the insects finding or laying eggs on the corpse. Usually, with bodies in outdoor environments, the data to determine whether there is a delay in colonization or not are available from weather data collected by the National Weather Service (NWS) (there are some private sources available also). The reliability of the NWS is due to the documented standards and protocol directed from oversight committees constantly monitoring the system. There are critical safety issues at stake with NWS data being used by the Federal Aviation Administration, the quality of scientists working for NWS, and the constant monitoring of the data-retrieval equipment all combining together to provide valid, accurate, and trustworthy data. These are the reasons why this author relies heavily on climatological data from this source.

The selection of a weather station or stations for data regarding a specific death scene is of great importance. In most instances, the NWS station will be located at a local or regional airport, in conjunction with the U.S. Forest Service, or at locks, dams, or on lakes as part of the U.S. Army Corps of Engineers, and at major U.S. military bases around the country. Most of the larger airports have data reported on an hourly basis, which can enhance the precision of a PMI estimate in a case. However, the most reliable results from a PMI estimate will come from a station that most closely represents the habitat where the remains were found. If this proximity is an extended distance, then reliance on weather data must accompany a calibration of the death scene and the weather station. This is accomplished by first collecting simultaneous temperatures from both the scene and the weather station and then completing a statistical analysis to calculate the adjustment necessary to make the two locations equal.[64] In many cases, using this method of calibration of the temperature would have nullified many hours of argument in court between the forensic entomologist or meteorologist and the opposing attorney (e.g., the Westerfield trial, San Diego).

The methodology of combining the time with the temperature has been discussed above, but some additional points need discussion regarding degree day and degree hour computations. The degree hour calculations are based upon hourly temperatures, with the degree day calculations based on daily maxima and minima. With the hourly data, a complete data set for a 24-hour period should be available. Therefore, if it is necessary to convert the units from degree hours to degree days, the procedure would be to identify the highest and lowest temperatures from the data set and use those two values as the values for the maxima and minima. This would then give degree day units and would be appropriate. However, *you cannot go the other way*, that is, calculate a daily mean and then multiply by 24. This can be illustrated by using an hourly data set and then taking the daily mean from that data set times 24. They will not be equal! It is incredible that in a case in California the forensic entomologist identified a value of daily temperature mean for what he called the daily temperature median. The median value of a distribution is the very middle number of the number set and has nothing to do with temperature calculations regarding degree days or degree hours. What was additionally interesting in this case was that he had made errors in this computation (of the mean) and the attorney for his side attempted to make up for his errors by stating that he had calculated the median. The end result is that even if he had calculated the "median," it was done incorrectly because he only had the daily maximum and minimum and the median of that data set was the "mean" (the exact middle number of the data).

Another point of degree day and degree hour calculations is the essential element of the base temperature. Again, this author has opposing forensic entomologists who claim that it is not necessary to use a base temperature for these calculations. These individuals have missed the very definition of degree days or degree hours. It is possible to calculate a "value" without a base temperature as long as all the temperatures are above the base. However, once temperatures drop below the base, an overestimation of the growth will result. What is even more interesting is that if the temperatures go below 0°C (32°F), and negative numbers are present, the calculations will suggest that the growing maggot is becoming younger the longer the numbers are in the negative column. This is not biologically possible and would appear as approaching the ridiculous. Could this discovery be the "Fountain of Youth"? (I think not!) However, these same forensic entomologists have insisted while under oath that this method is perfectly valid.

The above calibrations and calculations may require yet another variant. When the maggots are in an aggregation known as the maggot mass, they generate great amounts of exothermic heat.[37,65-67] This is primarily seen during the entire third-instar duration until they move from the remains to initiate migration. Research has shown that when given a range of temperatures to choose from, third-instar blowfly maggots will select a temperature of approximately 90°F.[68] This also is very close to the temperature that provides for the fastest growth. This effect may not be of major significance when ambient temperatures are in the 80s and 90s, but will be of great importance to consider when development is progressing with temperatures in the 30s and 40s. In cases where remains have been recovered and the body placed in the morgue cooler over a weekend prior to autopsy, maggot mass temperatures are still in the 85 to 90°F range after 48 hours of exposure to 40°F temperatures in the cooler.[66,67,69] Therefore, factoring in a temperature of approximately 90°F for 24 hours or so may help compensate for these added energy units. In addition, if 90 to 95°F is at the fastest rate of development, then what has been calculated is the shortest period of time available for growth. Any other temperature would produce a longer period for the development of the maggot.

IMPORTANCE OF RESEARCH

It is fortunate for the forensic entomology community that so much detailed and species-specific research was conducted during the first half of the twentieth century on fly biology, behavior, growth, and development. Without these specific developmental studies, we forensic entomologists would have required another half century to be at the level of knowledge we have today.

Recent forensic entomology studies have been initiated in well-established and many new areas for investigation such as: aquatic insects,[70-72] succession of carrion insects from geographic areas not previously studied,[17,34] comparison of human versus pig carrion,[73] fly DNA cataloging,[58-61,74] human DNA in insects,[61-63] insect preservation,[75] and prehistoric recovery of insect remains on murdered humans,[76] to name just a few.

Still, decades of additional research are required if we are to reach the full potential of the insect evidence recovered from death scenes. Continued studies of growth and development for the forensically important species are needed, with refinements to life stage variability and temperature variations. Studies on variation of the PMI estimates and the influences of temperature data require continuous monitoring. There are many areas where expanding pilot studies must take place, such as the DNA of human blood or tissues in maggots and blood-feeding insects. The investigation into cockroach feeding on humans to determine if there are specific salivary proteins left behind by the cockroaches is yet another area where information is greatly needed. Field studies on the varying habitats and environments across North America must continually be conducted. Detailed population ecology studies on carrion insects are also needed to better understand the effects of insect abundance on colonization and growth rates.

The major drawback to this much-needed research is the limitations of funding for these studies. Very few studies have been funded through national efforts.[73,77] Most studies have had minimal assistance, although whatever assistance is provided is always greatly appreciated, and have been completed only by inventive and nontraditional means (through personal funds and low-budget experimental design). It is hoped that this will change in the near future with the direct link between the use of insects to answer questions in police investigations, the debate over the death penalty, and the direct connection with Homeland Security. It is essential that additional dollars be made available to forensic entomologists attempting to answer questions for science and in courts of law.

Some of the above aspects regarding forensic entomology are discussed in recent popular press publications such as: *Corpse*,[78] *Maggots, Murder, and Men*,[79] *Dead Reckoning*,[80] *A Fly for the Prosecution*,[81] and *Entomology and the Law: Flies as Forensic Indicators*.[82] Other, more technical works on forensic entomology include: *A Manual of Forensic Entomology*,[10] *Entomology and Death: A Procedural Guide*,[83] *Forensic Taphonomy*,[84] and *Forensic Entomology: The Utility of Arthropods in Legal Investigations*.[85] A considerable understanding of the principles of forensic entomology, along with interesting case studies, can be derived from these publications.

QUALIFICATIONS OF THE FORENSIC ENTOMOLOGIST

If a criminal justice agency is in need of a forensic entomologist, the following discussion should help identify the qualifications necessary to select an expert knowledgeable in assessing the time of death of a human based upon insect colonization. First, the most reliable and qualified experts are individuals who possess degrees in entomology and board certification with the American Board of Forensic Entomology (ABFE).[66,67] This board, organized through the American Academy of Forensic Sciences and based upon certification boards of other forensic science disciplines, requires in its certification at least 5 years of study and case involvement in forensic entomology with documentation of published research and case reports. A written test and laboratory practical examination are also necessary to complete with a passing grade before certification is granted. Additionally, board certification within the entomological profession as a board-certified entomologist would show a certain level of competence reached in specified disciplines of entomology. Specific study areas within entomology that would be preferred/required could include: Dipteran (flies) studies, medical and veterinary entomology, insect taxonomy, insect ecology, and, of course, study of forensic entomology. This certification requires several years in the entomological area of study and a 200 point examination with a 70% passing grade or higher to receive certification. An entomology degree at the bachelor's level, but definitely at the master's and Ph.D. levels, in the above study areas would enhance the qualifications of the entomology expert being sought. The Ph.D.-level education in the abovementioned areas of study is the academic degree preferred if the expert is to draw conclusions and then testify to those conclusions in court. Under some conditions, a master's-level entomologist may qualify as a forensic entomology expert in court and do quite well, but this person must show extensive study of the carrion insects with research, publications, and presentation in the forensic entomology arena.

The expert sought must have research areas in one or a combination of the following areas, including: study of carrion insects, fly DNA research, aquatic carrion research, research in carrion insect taxonomy, or specific ecological field studies of carrion and carrion insects. These study areas should generate research papers that would be presented at regional, national, or international entomological or forensic meetings. A track record for such presentations will indicate the individual is willing to share and interact with other participating forensic entomologists. Publication of these papers is also very important because it shows that the research has been reviewed and accepted by his or her scientific peers.

Membership within forensic science and entomological societies or other professional organizations is important. This provides the forum where new ideas can be discussed and old methods reviewed and improved. These are the very places where presentations, interaction with colleagues, and publications of your work as a forensic scientist will take place.

As with any area of expertise, much time, effort, training, education, and experience is foremost in ensuring that the person is truly an expert. This author has seen on a number of occasions where well-meaning college professors, who have studied biology, anthropology, microbiology, or entomology, but are inexperienced in carrion insects, become involved with case work where they have no business becoming involved. Most often these individuals had not put in the required time to study the carrion insects at the level necessary for a well-informed conclusion. They had not established a track record of forensic research, presentations, publications, or involvement with peers in the study of carrion insects. In addition, these academics had not participated in any case studies, either collaborating with an established practicing forensic entomologist or not. These people had only reviewed the entomological literature, but promoted themselves as expert forensic entomologists. In most cases, the results of their analyses were lacking in understanding of basic principles of forensic entomology, with some cases having wrong conclusions. Today, this should not happen due to the information present about qualifications of forensic entomologists with the needs for specialized education and training. This inappropriate selection process must stop for the sake of the courts, the defendants, and the science of forensic entomology.

CONCLUSION

Forensic entomology has a wealth of information to offer the criminal justice system and some of those applications have been presented above. We have been limited in attaining greater knowledge because of the lack of research funding, but that has not deterred us from doing the best we can do with existing resources to answer the most pressing questions facing us at the present time. It is hoped that this chapter has enlightened the reader to the uses of forensic entomology, our strong points, and even some of the areas needing further study.

Those entomologists qualified in the field of forensic entomology have worked for years in field research, spending many summer vacations sweating over the very offensive odors of decomposing humans, pigs, and other animal carrion, and have spent thousands of hours peering through a microscope searching for a hair on a fly or an outcropping on a maggot to identify to which species out of tens of thousands of specimens a fly belongs. We do not deserve the unfair criticism, the attacks, or the insults of "junk science," "voodoo science," or "weirdos" given by self-proclaimed analytical experts on television (e.g., the Westerfield trial, San Diego, 2002). Perhaps the most positive outcome of this undue criticism is that we forensic entomologists worldwide will concentrate renewed conviction, energy, and personal and professional resources in our challenge to seek the truths and understand the science of forensic entomology on a level never before imagined possible.

ENDNOTES

1. McKnight, *The Washing Away of Wrongs: Forensic Medicine in Thirteenth Century China* (1981).
2. Redi, *Esperienze intorno generazione degli insetti*, in *Insegna della Stella* (1668).
3. Megnin, *La faune des cadavres: Application de l'entomologie a la médecine légale*, in *Encyclopédie Scientifique des Aide-Mémoire* (1894).
4. Motter, *A Contribution to the Study of the Fauna of the Grave: A Study of One Hundred and Fifty Disinternments with Some Additional Experimental Observations*, 6 J. N.Y. Entomol. Soc. 201-31(1898).
5. Knipling, *Some Specific Taxonomic Characters of Common Lucilia Larvae—Calliphorinae—Diptera*, 10 Iowa State Coll. J. Sci. 275-93 (1936).
6. Deonier, *Carcass Temperatures and Their Relation to Winter Blowfly Populations and Activity in the Southwest*, 33 J. Econ. Entomol. 166-70 (1940).
7. Deonier, *Seasonal Abundance and Distribution of Certain Blowflies in Southern Arizona and Their Economic Importance*, 35 J. Econ. Entomol. 65-70 (1942).
8. R.A. Wardle, *The Protection of Meat Commodities Against Blowflies*, 8 Ann. App. Biol. 1-9 (1921).

9. J. Wardle, *Significant Variables in the Blowfly Environment*, 17 Ann. Appl. Biol. 554-74 (1930).

10. Smith, *A Manual of Forensic Entomology* (1986).

11. Leclercq, *Entomological Parasitology: The Relations Between Entomology and the Medical Sciences* (1969).

12. Hall & Townsend, *The Blow Flies of Virginia (Diptera: Calliphoridae), The Insects of Virginia*, No. 11, Va. Poly. Inst. and State Univ. Res. Bull., No. 123 (1977).

13. Hall, *The Blowflies of North America* (1948).

14. Cushing & Parrish, *Seasonal Variations in the Abundance of Cochliomyia spp., Phormia spp., and Other Flies in Menard County, Texas*, 31 J. Econ. Entomol. 764-69 (1938).

15. Davidson, *On the Relationship Between Temperature and Rate of Development of Insects at Constant Temperatures*, 13 J. Anim. Ecol. 26-28 (1944).

16. Evans, *Insect Biology: A Textbook of Entomology* (1984).

17. Anderson & VanLaerhoven, *Initial Studies on Insect Succession on Carrion in Southwestern British Columbia*, 41(4) J. Forensic Sci. 617-25 (1996).

18. Baumgartner & Greenberg, *The Genus Chrysomya (Diptera: Calliphoridae) in the New World*, 21 J. Med. Entomol. 105-13 (1984).

19. Baumgartner, *Spring Season Survey of the Urban Blowflies (Diptera: Calliphoridae) of Chicago, Illinois*, 21 Great Lakes Entomol. 130-32 (1988).

20. Braack, *Visitation Patterns of Principal Species of the Insect-Complex at Carcasses in the Kruger National Park*, 24 Koedoe 33-49 (1981).

21. Braack, *Arthropods Associated with Carcasses in the Northern Kruger National Park*, 16 S. Afr. J. Wildl. Res. 91-98 (1986).

22. M Coe, *The Decomposition of Elephant Carcasses in the Tsavo (East) National Park, Kenya*, 1 J. Arid Environ. 71-86 (1978).

23. Goddard & Lago, *An Annotated List of the Calliphoridae (Diptera) of Mississippi*, 18 J. G. Entomol. Soc. 481-84 (1983).

24. Lord & Burger, *Arthropods Associated with Harbor Seal (Phoca vitulina) Carcasses Stranded on Islands Along the New England Coast*, 26 Int. J. Entomol. 282-85 (1984).

25. Reed, *A Study of Dog Carcass Communities in Tennessee, with Special Reference to the Insects*, 59 Am. Mid. Nat. 213-45 (1958).

26. Hall & Doisy, *Length of Time After Death: Effect on Attraction and Oviposition or Larviposition of Midsummer Blow Flies (Diptera: Calliphoridae) and Flesh Flies (Diptera: Sarcophagidae) of Medicolegal Importance in Missouri*, 86 Ann. Entomol. Soc. Am. 589-93 (1993).

27. Haskell, *Calliphoridae of Pig Carrion in Northwest Indiana: A Seasonal Comparative Study*. M.Sc. Thesis, Purdue University (1989).

28. Johnson, *Seasonal and Microseral Variations in the Insect Population on Carrion*, 93 Am. Mid. Nat. 79-90 (1975).

29. Payne, *A Summer Carrion Study of the Baby Pig, Sus scrofa Linnaeus*, 46 Ecology 592-602 (1965).

30. Payne et al., *Arthopod Succession and Decompositon of Buried Pigs*, 219(5159) Nature 1180-81 (1968).

31. Rodriguez & Bass, *Insect Activity and its Relationship to Decay Rates of Human Cadavers in East Tennessee*, 28 J. Forensic Sci. 423-32 (1983).

32. Rodriguez & Bass, *Decomposition of Buried Bodies and Methods That May Aid in Their Location*, 30 J. Forensic Sci. 836-52 (1985).

33. Smith, *The Faunal Succession of Insects and Other Invertebrates on a Dead Fox*, 26 Entomol. Gaz. 277-87 (1975).

34. Grassberger & Reiter, *Atypical Arthropod Succession on Pig Carrion in a Central European Urban Habitat*, in *Proceedings, 1st Euro Forensic Entomol. Sem.*, 149-50, France (2002).

35. Anderson, *Minimum and Maximum Developmental Rates of some Forensically Important Calliphoridae (Diptera)*, 45(4) J. Forensic Sci. 824-32 (2000).

36. Kamal, *Comparative Study of Thirteen Species of Sarcosaprophagous Calliphoridae and Sarcophagidae (Diptera). 1. Bionomics*, 51 Ann. Entomol. Soc. Am. 261-71 (1958).

37. Greenberg, *Flies as Forensic Indicators*, 28 J. Med. Entomol. 565-77 (1991).

38. Nuorteva, *Sarcosaprophagous Insects as Forensic Indicators*, 3 Forensic Med. 1317-33 (1977).

39. Byrd & Butler, *Effects of Temperature on Cochliomyia macellaria (Diptera: Calliphoridae) Development*, 33 J. Med. Entomol. 901-05 (1996).

40. Byrd & Butler, *Effects of Temperature on Sarcophaga haemorrhoidalis (Diptera: Sarcophagidae) Development*, 35 J. Med. Entomol 694-98 (1997).

41. Byrd & Butler, *Effects of Temperature on Chrysomia rufifacies (Diptera: Calliphoridae) Development*, 34 J. Med. Entomol. 353-58 (1997).

42. Haskell, *Criminal Case Studies* 1 (1985-2002).

43. Webb et al., *The Chigger Species Eutrombicula belkini Gould (Acari: Trombiculidae) as a Forensic Toll in a Homicide Investigation in Ventura County, California*, 8(2) Bull. Soc. Vector Ecol. 141-46 (1983).

44. Sohal & Lamb, *Intracellular Deposition of Metals in the Midgut of the Adult Housefly, Musca domestica*, 23 J. Insect Physiol. 1349-54 (1977).

45. Sohal & Lamb, *Storage Excretion of Metallic Cations in the Adult Housefly, Musca domestica*, 25 J. Insect Physiol. 119-24 (1979).

46. Nuorteva & Nuorteva, *The Fate of Mercury in Sarcosaprophagous Flies and in Insects Eating Them*, 11 Ambio 34-37 (1982).

47. Beyer et al., *Drug Identification Through Analysis of Maggots*, 25 J. Forensic Sci. 411-12 (1980).

48. Leclercq & Brahy, *Entomologie et médecine légale: datation de la mort*, 28 J. Méd. Lég. 271-78 (1985).

49. Gunatilake & Goff, *Detection of Organophosphate Poisoning in a Putrefying Body by Analyzing Arthropod Larvae*, 34 J. Forensic Sci. 714-16 (1988).

50. Introna et al., *Opiate Analysis of Cadaveric Blow Fly Larvae as an Indicator of Narcotic Intoxication*, 35 J. Forensic Sci. 18-22 (1990).

51. Kintz et al., *Fly Larvae: A New Toxicological Method of Investigation in Forensic Medicine*, 35 J. Forensic Sci. 204-07 (1990).

52. Goff & Lord, *Entomotoxicology: Insects as Toxicological Indicators and the Impact of Drugs and Toxins on Insect Development*, in Byrd & Castner, eds., *Forensic Entomology: The Utility of Arthropods in Legal Investigations* (2001).

53. Wallman & Adams, *The Forensic Application of Allozyme Electrophoresis to the Identification of Blowfly Larvae (Diptera: Calliphoridae) in Southern Australia*, 46(3) J. Forensic Sci. 681-84 (2001).

54. Sperling et al., *A DNA-Based Approach to the Identification of Insect Species Used for Postmortem Interval Estimation*, 39 J. Forensic Sci. 418-27 (1994).

55. Wallman & Adams, *Molecular Systematics of Australian Carrion-Breeding Blowflies of the Genus Calliphora (Diptera: Calliphoridae)*, 45 Aust. J. Zool. 337-56(1997).

56. Malgorn & Coquoz, *DNA Typing for Identification of Some Species of Calliphoridae: An Interest in Forensic Entomology*, 102(2-3) Forensic Sci. Int. 111-19 (1999).

57. Vincent et al., *Partial Sequencing of the Cytochrome Oxydase b Subunit Gene I: A Tool for the Identification of European Species of Blow Flies for Postmortem Interval Estimation* [published erratum appears in letter from Wells & Sperling, 45(6) J. Forensic Sci. (Nov. 2000)], 45(4) J. Forensic Sci. 820-23 (July 2000).

58. Wells et al., *DNA-Based Identification and Molecular Systematics of Forensically Important Sarcophagidae (Diptera)*, 46 J. Forensic Sci. 1098-1102 (2001).

59. Wells & Sperling, *Molecular Phylogeny of Chrysomya albiceps and C. rufifacies (Diptera: Calliphoridae)*, 36 J. Med. Entomol. 222-26 (1999).

60. Wells & Sperling, *DNA-Based Identification of Forensically Important Chrysomyinae (Diptera: Calliphoridae)*, 120 Forensic Sci. Int. 110-15 (2001).

61. Wells & Benecke, *DNA Techniques for Forensic Entomology*, in Byrd & Castner, eds., *supra* note 52.

62. Wells et al., *Human and Insect Mitochondrial DNA Analysis from Maggots*, 46 J. Forensic Sci. 685-87 (2001).

63. Linville & Wells, *Surface Sterilization of a Maggot Using Bleach Does Not Interfere with Mitochondrial DNA Analysis of Crop Contents*, 47 J. Forensic Sci. 1055-59 (2002).

64. Haskell et al., *The Estimation of Heat Unit Requirement of Developing Larvae Using Statistical Regression of Temperature Measurements from a Death Scene*, in *Proceedings, 1st Euro Forensic Entomol. Sem.*, France (2002).

65. Goff, *Estimation of Postmortem Interval Using Arthropod Development and Successional Patterns*, 5 Forensic Sci. Rev. 81 (1993).

66. Hall & Haskell, *Forensic Entomology: Applications in Medicolegal Investigations*, in C. Wecht, ed., Forensic Sciences (1995).

67. Hall & Haskell, *On the Body: Insects' Life Stage Presence and Their Postmortem Artifacts*, in Haglund & Sorg, eds., *Forensic Taphonomy* (1997).

68. Byrd, *The Effects of Temperature on Flies of Forensic Importance*, M.Sc. Thesis, University of Florida (1995).

69. Higley & Haskell, *Insect Development and Forensic Entomology*, in Byrd & Castner, eds., *supra* note 52.

70. Merritt & Wallace, *The Role of Aquatic Insects in Forensic Investigations, id.*

71. Haskell et al., *Use of Aquatic Insects in Determining Submersion Interval*, 34 J. Forensic Sci. 622-32 (1989).

72. Hawley et al., *Identification of Red "fiber": Chironomid Larvae*, 34 J. Forensic Sci. 617-21 (1989).

73. Schoenly & Haskell, *Testing Reliability of Animal Models in Research and Training Programs in Forensic Entomology*, Nat. Inst. Just. J. 42-43 (NIJ, U.S. Department of Justice, 2000).

74. Wells & Sperling, *Molecular Phylogeny of Chrysomya albiceps and C. rufifacies (Diptera: Calliphoridae)*, 36(2) J. Med. Entomol. 1-4 (2000).

75. Adams & Hall, *Methods Used for the Killing and Preservation of Blowfly Larvae: With Special Reference to Their Effect on Postmortem Length*, in *Proceedings, 1st Euro Forensic Entomol. Sem.*, 119-20, France (2002).

76. Haskell, *Report of Diagnostic Laboratory Examination*, case report requested by Western Cultural Resource Management, Farmington, NM (1999).

77. Wells, *DNA research*, in 'Molecular phylogeny of Chrysomya albiceps and C. rufifacies (Diptera: Calliphoridae)', *supra* note 73, at 42-43.

78. Sachs, *Corpse: Nature, Forensics, and the Struggle to Pinpoint Time of Death* (2001).

79. Erzinclioglu, *Maggots, Murder, and Men* (2000).

80. Baden & Roach, *Dead Reckoning* (2001).

81. Goff, *A Fly for the Prosecution* (2000).

82. Greenberg & Kunich, *Entomology and the Law: Flies as Forensic Indicators* (2002).

83. Catts & Haskell, *Entomology and Death: A Procedural Guide* (1990).

84. Haglund & Sorg, eds., *Forensic Taphonomy* (1997).

85. Byrd & Castner, eds., *Forensic Entomology: The Utility of Arthropods in Legal Investigations* (2001).

71 Forensic Odontology

MICHAEL N. SOBEL, D.M.D., D-A.B.F.O.

In its most literal sense, forensic odontology is the application of the art and science of dental medicine to the resolution of matters pertaining to the law. Some of the diverse facets of this unique discipline can range from the identification of human remains to mass disaster management; from the assessment of bitemark and patterned skin injuries to the use of dental materials in the examination of evidence. This brief introduction only begins to describe the scope that exists within the field of forensic odontology.

Although the practice of forensic odontology is not a recent arrival on the legal scene, it is only within the past 30 years or so that the forensic odontologist has become a distinct specialist, achieving a more visible and productive position within the forensic sciences. At one time, the dental expert was viewed in court primarily as an expository witness in cases involving dental injuries. Today it is not unusual to observe a forensic odontologist working alongside identification teams at an air crash, gathering bitemark evidence at a crime scene, or examining a victim of child abuse.

A practicing dentist can be an important witness in civil cases involving dental injuries. Legal liabilities often arise in these cases as the result of trauma that causes injuries to the teeth, their supporting structures, and other portions of the dentofacial anatomy. Knowledge of oral anatomy and the functional relationships of these parts uniquely qualifies the dentist to give testimony. However, testimony in many criminal cases, involving such matters as critical interpretations in human identification and bitemarks, deserves the attention of a qualified forensic odontologist. This is so because the expertise in these matters is a result of the additional training and experience required to achieve competency as a forensic odontologist.

To be formally perceived as a forensic odontologist, a dentist should have additional training, especially in relevant areas of the forensic sciences, e.g., oral pathology, as well as anthropology, the basic sciences, and the law. Furthermore, he or she should be actively working in the field, preferably connected with a law enforcement agency or a coroner/medical examiner's office. Additional evidence of qualification is indicated in achieving certification by the American Board of Forensic Odontology (www.abfo.org), membership or fellowship in the Odontology section of the American Academy of Forensic Sciences (www.aafs.org), and membership in the American Society of Forensic Odontology (www.asfo.org). The dentist who makes the effort to meet these requirements and become a part of these active organizations is greatly enhanced in qualifying as an expert witness in the courts.

BASIS OF FORENSIC ODONTOLOGY

The most basic concept in forensic odontology is centered on a form of pattern recognition and comparison. This conclusion ultimately arrives at a comparison of the unknown pattern with a known pattern in order to determine the extent of similarity. For example, the dentition described in a set of dental records can exhibit a unique pattern against which to evaluate the dentition of an unknown body. In mass disaster incidents, this problem-solving experience is repeated on a much larger scale.

The same is true in bitemark evaluations. An accurate representation of the bitemark injury, as a pattern, is compared with an accurate representation of the suspect's dentition, both being similarly scaled in measurement.

Of course, the pattern recognition analogy is a simplistic accounting of the core of forensic odontology. Investigator experience, knowledge of testing methodologies, and decision analysis abilities, among other issues, all contribute to successful evidence evaluation and assessment.

DENTAL IDENTIFICATION

The dentition is significant in the human identification process primarily because teeth and the jaw structures can resist even the most severe environmental conditions and trauma. This is so, particularly for the teeth, because of the inherent durability of tooth enamel (the outermost covering of the crowns of teeth) and of cementum (the outer covering of the roots of teeth). As a result, aside from fingerprint analysis, one of the most legally reliable forms of identification of human remains is by comparison of dental structures with dental records.

A consideration should be made of the surprising resistance of teeth and jaws to environmental exposure, such as even the most severe fires. The oral cavity seems to be so well insulated against the high temperature of fires that often even the supporting tissues surrounding the teeth are also well preserved. In addition, the dental restorations are frequently completely intact.

Identification case example 1. A husband suspected his wife of infidelity. He confronted her in a bar with another man and shot them both. The shooter took off with the police in pursuit and returned to his trailer home. The police surrounded the trailer and his car, and the car erupted into flames. When the fire was extinguished, severely burned human remains were discovered. In particular, there was a mandible with only a part of the cranium attached to the maxilla. The question to be answered: was this the shooter they were after or was someone else planted in the vehicle? This author examined the skull and, finding most of the dentition was intact, compared the antemortem dental records with the postmortem remains. There was complete concordance, including a distinctive gold crown and several other dental restorations, thus confirming the identity of the shooter.

The inherent possibilities for uniqueness in the human dentition enable the forensic dentist to determine the degree of concordance between antemortem dental records and the oral structures of specific human remains under examination. The human adult dentition typically consists of 32 teeth, each with 5 surfaces, thus providing 160 possibilities for individual variations of surface anatomy and dental restorations in configuration, size, shape, material, and wear patterns. This does not even take into account, and is not limited to, such factors as decay, missing and extra teeth, alignment of the dental arches, individual tooth positioning, and prosthetic appliances. In fact, in the United States there are many more dental records on file than fingerprint records. The experienced dental clinician can detect many subtleties in observable detail of the teeth and jaws which are most useful in confirming a human identification. Among other distinctive characteristics for

antemortem and postmortem comparisons are maxillary sinus patterns, bone trabeculation patterns, and orbital outlines.

A question often arises as to the number of points of concordance necessary to render a valid decision on a dental identification. However, this is not as significant as the singular quality, or exclusivity, of the points of comparison involved. In addition, when all of the points of concordance in a particular case are considered as a set of aggregate data, the investigator should be able to state, if possible, whether the identification is "positive within reasonable scientific certainty."

The following categories and terminology for body identification are suggested for use in communicating the results of a forensic odontology identification investigation:

> **Positive identification:** The antemortem and postmortem data match in sufficient detail to establish that they are from the same individual. In addition, there are no irreconcilable discrepancies.
> **Possible identification:** The antemortem and postmortem data have consistent features, but, due to the quality of either the postmortem remains or the antemortem evidence, it is not possible to positively establish dental identification.
> **Insufficient evidence:** The available information is insufficient to form the basis for a conclusion.
> **Exclusion:** The antemortem and postmortem data are clearly inconsistent. However, it should be understood that identification by exclusion is a valid technique in certain circumstances.[1]

However, this caveat from the American Board of Forensic Odontology should be noted: "The forensic dentist is not ordinarily in a position to verify that the antemortem records are correct as to name, date, etc.; therefore, the report should state that the conclusions are based on records which are purported to represent a particular individual."[2]

In summary, the forensic odontologist can best be relied upon to render expert opinions concerning identifications based on postmortem evaluation of dental structures, while testing for concordance with antemortem dental records that are as complete as can be obtained.

Identification case example 2. Two white males speeding on a highway ended their trip in a fiery crash. Tracing from the registration of the vehicle, the owner/driver was tentatively identified and witnesses indicated who the male passenger was alleged to be. Dental records were requested from the dentists of the victims for use by this author in the postmortem examinations and comparisons. The driver was readily identified by this process; however, the passenger did *not* match the dental chart furnished, although the family insisted that the passenger victim *had* to be their relative. Further investigation revealed that this victim had loaned his Medical Card to a friend so that the friend could receive unauthorized dental treatment at no charge. Ultimately, another set of dental records was located which did indeed match the passenger victim. Here is an example showing that, while people may lie, the dental evidence does not.

MASS CASUALTY INCIDENTS

Perhaps mass casualty incident identifications are best appreciated as being a greatly extended application of dental identifications as described above. In fact, the most descriptive definition for a mass disaster or mass casualty incident would be: "Any situation, man-made or natural, which overtaxes the normal emergency resources available within a community."[3]

When the typical casualty incident is simultaneously multiplied many times over, and the local consulting forensic odontologist and/or the local dental ID team is incapable of handling the incident because of the number of victims and lack of resources, outside help should be requested. For this reason, the federal government has instituted a program under the NDMS (National Disaster Medical System) and FEMA (Federal Emergency Management Agency) called D-MORT (Disaster Mortuary Operations Recovery Team). Currently, these programs will be coordinated under the Department of Homeland Security.

These teams are set up regionally across the country and are composed of specialists trained in disaster operations, such as pathologists, anthropologists, dentists, and funeral directors. The D-MORT units are prepared for rapid response, complete with supplies, in times of mass casualty incidents to bolster any community's resources when needed. Examples of D-MORT mobilization were seen in the events of September 11, 2001.

BITEMARK EVIDENCE

Another area that utilizes identifying characteristics of the teeth, although on a more functional level, is bitemark analysis. Bites on human tissue may be observed in violent incidents where the attacker may bite the victim or the victim may bite the attacker during defensive responses. In more passive incidents, a person may bite him or herself or an inanimate object left at a scene, e.g., an apple core.

Paramount is the ability to differentiate a patterned injury as a bitemark from a mark made by another source. Here, the forensic odontologist, through training and experience, is the individual most qualified to assess the injury pattern.

Teeth may be considered as tools leaving marks on skin, food, or various other materials. However, there are often more characteristics involved in the analysis of bitemarks than would occur from perceiving of the teeth as merely simple tools. There are class characteristics to be considered, such as which type of tooth inflicted the bite, e.g., incisor, cuspid, etc. The biting surfaces of the individual groups of teeth are related to their function, such as teeth that incise, or tear, or grind. In addition, also seen are individual characteristics, such as rotations, fractures, or missing or extra teeth. The size relationships of the bitemark, as described by the width of the dental arches, could relate to a child or adult bite. Ability to open the mouth maximally may vary from individual to individual. It should be noted that bitemarks can also *exclude* a suspect by revealing a tooth pattern, or opening range, inconsistent with that of a particular person.

The methodologies for preserving and comparing bitemark evidence are crucial to the proper and uniform objective analysis of patterned markings for legal substantiation. Further details may be accessed by reading the ABFO Bitemark Methodology Guidelines.[4]

Bitemark case example 1. An elderly woman was found unconscious beneath a pile of concrete blocks, the victim of a brutal beating and rape. Investigators noticed what appeared to be a bitemark on the victim's right breast. A suspect was apprehended in the area and circumstantially linked to the crime. Permission was granted by the suspect for dental impressions and photographs to be taken. Comparison of a scaled photograph of the bitemark on the victim and plaster models poured from the suspect's dental impressions placed the accused at the scene of violence. Additional comparisons were performed using computer enhancements and overlays. The concordance of the suspect's dentition to the victim's bitemark was able to play a major role in the conviction of the perpetrator.

Bitemark case example 2. A nurse, checking on a middle-aged female patient in a critical care unit, discovered a patterned skin mark on the inner surface of the patient's left thigh. She questioned the patient, who was under sedation, about the marks. The nurse, getting "positive" responses to her questions, suggested that it was a bitemark. A report was filed and the police were notified. The police photographed the patient's injury and made further inquiries, which resulted in charges being filed against her physician on suspicion of molestation. A forensic odontologist was consulted by the police and took impressions on anyone who had contact with the patient during the estimated window of opportunity. All dental models obtained were compared by the prosecution forensic odontologist to the patterned skin mark photos. As a result of the comparisons, the suspect physician was arrested and held for trial on criminal charges. This author was consulted by the defense to evaluate the same materials and found that, although there were characteristics resembling a human bitemark, there were areas on the patterned markings to which the physician's dentition could not be matched positively. In addition, upon reviewing the patient's medical record, the defense odontologist found that an indwelling urinary catheter had been taped to the inner left thigh within the time range of the incident. An overlay of the catheter was then compared to the so-called "bitemark" and a near-perfect outline accounted for all of the patterned marks. When the case came to trial, the judge's verdict (a bench trial) was in favor of the defendant, since the only conclusive evidence was that the urinary catheter was the culprit! ("The only truth that counts in court is that which can be proven.")[5]

MISCELLANEOUS PATTERNED MARKINGS

Often there are patterned markings observed in the course of assaults, rapes, homicides, and child abuse. Marks, such as fingernail scratches, imprints of hands, jewelry, or household objects, can be observed in many cases. This author participated in the first case of fingernail scratch identification admitted to and upheld by the United States courts.[6] In this case, deep fingernail scratches on the neck of a victim of homicide by manual strangulation were recorded by impressions and photography. The suspect was apprehended soon after the murder and his fingernails were able to be matched to unusual curvatures and fractures captured in the marks on the victim's neck. The court admitted the evidence based on the same standards accorded tool marks. The guilty verdict survived appellate review.

Other cases have occurred in which markings on skin were recorded and matched to objects used to strike a victim. Therefore, the expertise of the forensic odontologist in interpreting bitemarks can be transferred to the evaluation of many other patterned injuries to the skin surface and inanimate objects at crime scenes.

HUMAN ABUSE EVIDENCE

Another area in which the forensic odontologist is being consulted more frequently is in cases of alleged human abuse, especially in the case of children. Usually in cases of child abuse with apparent bitemarks, there are only a limited number of persons who could have been able to have intimate enough access to the child to have the opportunity to inflict a bite. This, then, greatly limits the suspect range for comparisons of dentition to the bitemark. Family members, friends of the family, siblings, paramours, and caregivers are most often high on the suspect list in child abuse bitemarks and patterned injuries.

To help determine the physical abuse status, the patterned injuries are usually categorized as recent, healing, and/or healed injuries. This helps to assess whether the abuse status is related to a solitary event or has been continuing over a period of time.

Other types of patterned injuries can be evaluated by the forensic odontologist to assist in determining the instrument of abuse. For example, victims beaten with coiled electric extension cords, belts (with or without buckles), household appliances (electric irons, hair curlers), or ropes can exhibit class characteristics that can be revealing. Cases involving elder and spousal abuse could be examined in like fashion for telling evidence of the instrument of abuse.

Abuse case example. This author was called to a hospital emergency department to examine a 2-year-old child with apparent multiple bitemarks on the body. The mother had gone to work, leaving her daughter in the care of a 14-year-old baby-sitter. After examination, measurement, and photography of the bitemarks, a determination was made that the source of the bitemarks was the young baby-sitter. She was questioned by the police and confessed to the biting activity, evidently a "normal" activity of interplay in the sitter's family. If prosecution instead of counseling had been preferred in this case, the correlation between biter and bitemarks could readily have been demonstrated with admissible legal certainty.

ANALYSIS OF DENTAL EVIDENCE

The profession of dental medicine has become significantly more complex and varied within the past 50 years. Most recently, this is especially true because of the advent of the newer dental materials and technologies that have evolved. The presence of dental prosthetic tooth replacements (including dentures, bridges, partials, etc.) at a crime scene can be analyzed by the forensic odontologist. These materials can potentially yield information such as geography of origin, approximate dating of construction, and even linkage to a particular dentist or dental laboratory. Many unique characteristics and variations exist "labeling" the type, quality, and socioeconomic levels of the dental restorations performed both currently and in the past. These factors and analyses can be helpful in a forensic investigation, both in opening avenues of exploration and for court expert testimony. In a number of cases, the finding of a single tooth or fragment of a tooth has been a pivotal point in assisting in an investigation.

Tooth fragment case example. A portion of an upper right first molar was found adjacent to a badly beaten homicide victim on the north shore of the river. The tooth fragment did *not* belong to this homicide victim. The appearance of the fractured crown was such that this author felt that the tooth fragment had sheared off as the outcome of a traumatic blow to the right side of the mandible, which probably fractured as a result. A bulletin was broadcast to check all treatment facilities for anyone requesting treatment for a mandibular fracture and broken molar. No leads developed until, several days later, another battered homicide victim was found in another area of the city. Upon examination, this victim had a fractured mandible and the tooth fragment matched the broken upper right first molar. Because of the evidence of a single tooth fragment, the two homicides were able to be linked to the same homicide case.

DEVELOPMENTAL APPLICATIONS

The field of forensic odontology continues to advance as a science. The computer is being used more and more in many aspects, from assistance in identification matching (especially mass disaster incidents), to enhancement of x-ray films and bitemark evidence photographs. The scanning electron microscope is being used to amplify details of individual components of bitemark evidence.

Reconstruction of the soft tissue layers of skulls can enable investigators to estimate the actual appearance of a person in life. The caveat here is that certain features, such as eyebrows, eyelids, external nares, and external ears, are subject to extensive conjecture. In many cases, there may be little resemblance to those features in life.

Saliva washings from bitemarks can be serotypic indicators of blood group antigens and can also be a source of DNA for analysis and comparison with a suspect. The downside of saliva washings is that they can be easily contaminated (e.g., by medical treatment at a scene or in the hospital) before being adequately preserved.

Alternative light sources, such as UV range, infrared, etc., can be helpful in the visualization of suspected healed skin injuries. These light sources, in various wavelengths, can penetrate the skin surface, or filter out overlying debris, in order to better document bite or patterned skin mark evidence photographically.

UV light case example. An unknown intruder invaded a woman's apartment and kept her hostage for 8 hours, brutalizing and sexually molesting her. After the incident, she called the police and was taken to the hospital emergency department where she was interviewed, photographed, and treated. One of the photographs showed an apparent bitemark on her left scapular area, which was confirmed by the victim. Five months later a suspect developed, but by now the bitemark had healed. In addition, the original hospital bitemark photograph did not have a reference scale and appeared to have little evidentiary value. Under court order, the suspect submitted to dental impressions and photographs of his dentition. The victim gave permission for new photographs of the healed bitemark site. This author and a colleague felt that reflective UV photography might be able to revisualize the original healed bitemark imprint. This was successfully accomplished with special equipment and a reference scale was included in the photographs. During trial, the court allowed the original hospital photograph to be introduced into evidence as there was demonstrated that there was a 7 mm piping border on the hospital gown the victim was wearing. Comparison of the original hospital photograph, the reflective UV photograph, and the dental models of the suspect indicated significant matching characteristics. A guilty verdict resulted which was upheld on all appeals.[7]

CONCLUSION

Forensic odontology, like most areas of the forensic sciences, is constantly changing and developing in usefulness to the court systems and the world community. The identification and application of a growing subset of forensic matters by qualified forensic odontologists and their team interactions with law enforcement agencies, other forensic scientific specialists, and the legal community can be perceived as a rapidly growing relationship of significant benefit to both the civil and criminal justice systems.

ENDNOTES

1. American Board of Forensic Odontology, *ABFO Body Identification Guidelines*, www.abfo.org.
2. *Id.*
3. A.M. Butman, *Responding to the Mass Casualty Incident: A Guide for EMS Personnel* (Akron, Ohio: Emergency Training, 1982).
4. American Board of Forensic Odontology, *ABFO Bitemark Methodology Guidelines*, www.abfo.org.
5. Paraphrased from the 1997 Dutch film, *Character*.
6. J.A. Perper & M.N. Sobel, *Identification of Fingernail Markings in Manual Strangulation*, 2(1) Am. J. Forensic Med. Pathol. 45-48 (1981).
7. T.J. David & M.N. Sobel, *Recapturing a Five-Month-Old Bite Mark by Means of Reflective Ultraviolet Photography*, 39(6) J. Forensic Sci. 1560-67 (1994).

72

Utilization of Forensic Science in the Civil and Criminal Justice Systems: Forensic Use of Medical Information

CYRIL H. WECHT, M.D., J.D., F.C.L.M.

BRIEF HISTORY OF FORENSIC MEDICINE
THE ADVERSARIAL PROCESS
EXPERT WITNESSES
FORENSIC PSYCHIATRY AND PSYCHOLOGY
ADMISSIBILITY OF EXPERT TESTIMONY

Forensic medicine is the area of medicine concerned with the testimony and information presented in judicial or quasijudicial settings. For example, medical information and testimony presented before hearings and trials, as well as formal legal investigations, would be considered forensic.

Forensic pathology concentrates on autopsies to be reported in legal settings. Other areas of forensic medicine, such as forensic toxicology, forensic surgery, forensic pediatrics, and other health sciences, involve presenting information in a legal forum.

BRIEF HISTORY OF FORENSIC MEDICINE

Medicine as a curiosity, superstition, science, and ultimately a form of self-preservation appears to have originated long before humans organized into communities capable of governing conduct by a legal system consisting of accepted norms. Unfortunately, historical knowledge of the interaction between law and medicine is limited by the slow development of an effective recording system. Thus the origin of forensic medicine can be traced back only 5000 or 6000 years. At that time, Imhotep, the grand vizier, chief justice, chief magician, and chief physician to King Zozer, was regarded as the god of the Egyptians. He was also the first man known to apply both medicine and law to his surroundings.[1]

In ancient Egypt, legal restrictions concerning the practice of medicine were codified and recorded on papyri. Because medicine was shrouded with mysticism, its practice was regarded as a privilege of class.[2] Despite the strong influence of superstition, definite surgical procedures and substantial information regarding the interaction of drugs indicate an awareness that humans, as

opposed to gods or demons, could regulate various bodily responses.

Apparently the Code of Hammurabi (2200 B.C.) was the first formal code of medical law, setting forth the organization, control, duties, and liabilities of the medical profession.[3] Malpractice sanctions included monetary compensation for the victim and forcible removal of the surgeon's hand.[4] Medicolegal principles also can be found in early Jewish laws, which distinguished mortal from nonmortal wounds and investigated questions of virginity.

Later, in the midst of substantial jurisprudential evolution, Hippocrates and his followers studied the average duration of pregnancy, the viability of children born prematurely, malingering, the possibility of superfetation, and the relative fatality of wounds in different parts of the body. Particularly noteworthy is the continuation of an interest in poisons. The Hippocratic Oath includes a promise not to use or advise the use of poisons.[5]

As in Egypt, the practice of medicine in India was restricted to members of select castes. Medical education also was regulated. Physicians formally concluded that the duration of pregnancy should be between 9 and 12 lunar months. Again, the study of poisons and their antidotes was given high priority.[6]

Although little medicolegal development occurred during the Roman era, investigations were conducted regarding the causes of suspicious deaths. This process was sufficiently sophisticated to lead one physician to report that only one of the 23 wounds sustained by Julius Caesar was fatal.[7] In addition, between A.D. 529 and 564 the Justinian code was enacted, regulating the practice of medicine, surgery, and midwifery. Malpractice standards, medical expert responsibilities, and the number of physicians limited to each town were clearly established. Interestingly, although it was recognized that a fair determination of the truth often necessitated the submission of expert medical testimony, such testimony was restricted to the impartial specialized knowledge of the expert.[8] Obviously this evidence was intended to aid the fact-finder, not to replace the fact-finder's independent conclusion.

Throughout the Middle Ages, issues of impotence, sterility, pregnancy, abortion, sexual deviation, poisoning, and divorce provided the backdrop for much medicolegal development. Investigatory procedures advanced as more homicide and personal injury judgments were rendered. In 925 the English established the Office of Coroner. This office much later assumed the responsibility of the investigation of suspicious deaths.

China's contribution to forensic medicine did not surface until the first half of the thirteenth century. Apparently, medicolegal knowledge had quietly passed from one generation to another; the *Hsi Yuan Lu* ("the washing away of wrongs") was so comprehensive that its influence can be noted until fairly recently. It was a treatise detailing procedures for cause-of-death determinations and emphasized the importance of performing each step in the investigation with precision. In addition, the book noted the difficulties posed by decomposition, counterfeit wounds, and antemortem and postmortem wounds and distinguished bodies of drowned persons from those thrown into the water after death. Examination of bodies in all cases was mandatory, regardless of the unpleasant condition of the body.[9]

By the end of the fifteenth century the Justinian code was a lost relic. A new era of European forensic medicine began with the adoption of two codes of German law: the Bamberger code (Coda Bambergensis) in 1507 and the Caroline code (Constitutio Criminalis Carolina) in 1553.[10] The Caroline code, based on the Bamberger code, required that expert medical testimony be obtained for the guidance of judges in cases of murder, poisoning, wounding, hanging, drowning, infanticide, abortion, and other circumstances involving injury to the person.[11]

These works led surrounding countries to question earlier superstitious systems of legal judgment, such as trial by ordeal.[12] Legislative changes followed, particularly in France, and medicolegal volumes began to be published throughout Europe. Most noteworthy among them was Ambroise Pare's book (1575) discussing monstrous births, simulated diseases, and methods to be adopted in preparing medicolegal reports.[13] In 1602 the extent of medical information had grown such that Fortunato Fidele published four extensive volumes. Even more important, between 1621 and 1635, Paul Zacchia, physician to the Pope, contributed his extensive collection, *Questiones Medico Legales*, discussing such issues as death during delivery, feigned diseases, poisoning, resemblance of children to their parents, miracles, virginity, rape, age, impotence, superfetation, and moles.[14] Limited in accuracy by ignorance of physiology and anatomy, the book still served as an influential authority of medicolegal decisions of that time.

In 1650, Michaelis delivered the first lectures on legal medicine at Leipzig, Germany.[15] The teacher who replaced him compiled *De Officio Medici Duplici, Clinici Mimirum ac Forensis*, published in 1704.[16] This text was followed by the extraordinary *Corpus Juris Medico-Legale* by Valenti in 1722.[17] Germany significantly stimulated the spread of forensic medicine, but particularly after the French Revolution, France's system of medical education and appointment of medical experts further defined the parameters of the field.[18]

Despite these remarkable accomplishments, "witchmania," which originated in 1484 by papal edict, was still widely accepted throughout much of the eighteenth century. Thus with the blessing of the medicolegal community, thousands branded as witches were burned at the stake. Despite the repeal of British witch laws in 1736, alleged witches were murdered by mobs as late as 1760, and "witch doctors" practiced as late as 1838. France is known to have held a witch trial in 1818.[19] As Chaillé accurately stated:[20]

[W]ith the impotence of science to aid the law, it adopted miracles as explanations, suspicion as proof, confession as evidence of guilt, and torture as the chief witness, summoning the medical expert to sustain the accused until the rack forced confession.

Nevertheless, in England, medical jurisprudence pushed forward, laying the foundation for the current depth of information. In 1788 the first known book on legal medicine was published in English.[21] The following year, Professor Andrew Duncan of Edinburgh gave the first systematic instruction in medical jurisprudence in any English-speaking university. Recognition by the British Crown was evidenced in 1807, when the first Regius Chair in forensic medicine was established at the University of Edinburgh.[22] Eighty years later, the Coroner's Act defined the duties and jurisdiction of the coroner. As amended in 1926, these obligations included (1) investigation of all sudden, violent, or unnatural deaths and (2) investigation of all prisoners' deaths by inquest.[23] The 1926 amendment also set forth minimum qualifications for the position of coroner and carefully outlined its jurisdiction in criminal matters.[24] It was not until 1953 that the coroner's jurisdiction in civil matters was defined.[25]

Early American colonists brought the coroner's system, intact, to the United States in 1607.[26] Because the position was held by political appointees, most of whom lacked medical training, cause-of-death determinations could be based on little more than personal opinion. Not surprisingly, controversy concerning the validity of death investigations led Massachusetts (in 1877) to replace the coroner with a medical examiner whose jurisdiction was limited to "dead bodies of such persons only as are supposed to have come to their death by violence."[27] Eventually, New York City and other jurisdictions followed suit in an attempt to establish a profession of trained experts qualified to unravel the mysteries behind the violent deaths that increased in number each year as the population expanded. To this end, the medical examiner was given the authority to order autopsies.[28]

During the last half of the twentieth century, considerable advances were made in the area of forensic medicine. Scientific and technological improvements have provided new fabric and groundwork for jurisprudential development. The question at this point, however, is whether such development will proceed. Medicolegal teaching programs are now being offered at many universities, medical schools, and law schools, but they provide only a theoretical foundation. The forum of discussion must now proceed from the world of academia to the practitioner's realm.

THE ADVERSARIAL PROCESS

The legal system in the United States is based on the concept that there is value in the presentation of opposing points of view. The legal process is designed to provide for presentation of opposing points of view and a contest of persuasion. *Forensic medicine* is the study of all the medically related sciences in a way that concentrates on the persuasiveness of information to be presented in the adversarial process that the law applies to the determination of truth. Legal scholars and practitioners believe in the value of the process and support the concept that truth can be found best in a legal setting by allowing the parties to present conflicts regarding the facts and the law.

The concept of reasonable medical certainty is difficult for physicians to understand, but it is a purely legal concept. *Reasonable medical certainty* is a catchphrase meaning "more likely than not in a medical sense." In other words, if the likelihood of an event is more probable than not given the facts, the physician can testify with a reasonable medical certainty. Most physicians believe that "certainty" is misleading, but the legal system has no problem with the word. If a physician understands that the legal system weighs and balances the probity and veracity in terms of "more likely than not," the use of the *certainty* is more easily understood.

Methods and practice in law and medicine are widely divergent. Practitioners in law attempt to apply general principles to specific fact situations, whereas medicine is a highly individualistic and flexible application of general scientific information. Most physicians would not consider themselves empiric scientists operating within a structured environment. Medicine requires great flexibility and artistry.

In the case of law the persuasiveness of an argument always returns to generally accepted principles; therefore there is always an attempt to eliminate the uncertain and mold arguments to fall foursquare on previously accepted legal principles. As a result, when lawyers and physicians attempt to resolve conflicts, they invariably start from different places and sometimes collide before they cooperate.[29]

EXPERT WITNESSES

The layperson, judge, or jury member needs help to establish the truth. As a result, experts are allowed to provide testimony to help the fact-finder. The expert is a person who by reason of training, education, skill, experience, or observation is able to enlighten and assist the fact-finder in resolving factual issues. Experts are allowed to provide specialized information to laypersons only if the court has accepted them as experts in the first place. To be accepted properly as an expert, the court must establish that an individual fits the qualifications as stated. One can be qualified by education or experience, but one must ultimately have enough knowledge to enlighten a layperson. A judge usually makes the determination of whether an individual is an expert, and that determination sometimes is balanced against the potential for prejudice in the presentation of testimony. For example, even if a general practitioner qualifies as an expert on a neurosurgical procedure, his or her expertise must be recognizably less than the expertise of a neurosurgeon. If the judge thinks that the jury will not be able to make that distinction, the court may exclude the testimony and not qualify the expert.[30,31]

The believability and credibility of a forensic scientist are tested in the courtroom and in other legal proceedings. It is no coincidence that the term *examination* is used to describe the process of presenting testimony in a trial or hearing. Direct examination and cross-examination are ultimately a true test of an individual's knowledge of the materials presented. A good cross-examination attempts to test and disprove the assertions that are brought out in the direct examination. The effective and well-prepared attorney is more than qualified to adduce the information that will be relevant and material to the factual issues at hand. The forensic scientist must prepare adequately to present the information clearly in the most persuasive manner possible. Ultimately a forensic scientist in a legal setting is an *advocate*. The individual is tested for professional expertise, thoroughness, accuracy, and honesty.[32,33]

Opinion testimony and hypotheticals

After experts are qualified by the court and accepted to give expert testimony, they can give opinion testimony and answer hypothetical questions. Experts are allowed to give opinion testimony based on facts that are normally used by experts in forming their opinions. Such facts include text and journal information, as well as the evaluation of the facts and the gathering of evidence that is a part of the information used by experts in the field. Frequently, for example, experts can use hearsay evidence in the formation of their opinion.

In court an attorney might present a *hypothetical question* (a question based on stated assumptions) to establish an expert's opinion given certain assumed facts. If an expert is allowed to give an answer to a hypothetical question, it can be used as persuasive testimony by the opposing parties, since factual disputes often cannot be completely resolved. For example, an attorney will ask the expert to assume certain facts that are in dispute and then draw a conclusion. This kind of opinion testimony allows attorneys to advance the version of the facts that their clients offer.

Admission of evidence requires a foundation. Through the use of the witness's testimony, the validity of the physical evidence can be established. For example, a photograph must be a true and accurate representation of the situation of which the witness has knowledge. Retouched photographs and photographs that misrepresent a scene must be tested by laying the foundation so that the information can be accepted into evidence. The typical process involves the labeling of an item as an exhibit, then the foundation being laid by a witness, often the expert witness, or through a process of verification so that the exhibit can be accepted as evidence. Photographs, diagrams, demonstrations, models, slides, films, and tapes can be accepted into evidence, provided that the court finds no attempt to misrepresent or deceive.[34]

Courts generally have a problem with accepting books, texts, journals, and treatises as evidence. The problem is that written material can be so easily abused that the courts generally recognize that in-court testimony by a witness is more easily tested and verified. On the other hand, an effective argument can be made that a journal or book, if considered authoritative, can be used because it is written in a nonadversarial context that makes it more likely to be more believable. Arguments can be made on both sides because, taken out of context, a book can be misleading. In most trial courts, written materials can be used if the expert witness accepts them as authoritative. Textbooks can be used to contradict the testimony of the expert and to support that testimony.[35]

Court-appointed experts

Trial courts have the authority and in some cases have exercised the authority to appoint their own experts. Court-appointed psychiatrists, social workers, and other experts are frequently used in complex cases. This does not rule out the use of experts by opposing parties, but it does allow the court to place more weight on the testimony and evidence presented by the court-appointed expert. The credibility question ultimately still lies in the areas of persuasiveness. For example, an ineffective court-appointed expert can be overcome by an effective, believable expert for the plaintiff or defendant or for the prosecution or the defense. The forensic scientist who is appointed by the court must ultimately stand the test of the courtroom and the direct examination and cross-examination process.[36]

FORENSIC PSYCHIATRY AND PSYCHOLOGY

Psychiatric problems are frequently fraught with legal implications. Forensic psychiatry is critical to determine competence in contract actions, responsibility for torts and crimes, competence to testify, ability to give informed consent to treatment, and particularly competence to stand trial. A related area is *testamentary capacity*, which is the ability of the testator to comprehend that he or she is writing a will, is aware of the property involved and the objects of bounty, and understands to whom the property will descend at death.

The defense to a criminal charge is predicated at times on insanity. Whether the state recognizes the M'Naughton rule, the ALI rule, or the Durham or New Hampshire rule, and whether the defense is diminished responsibility or irresistible impulse, the fundamental questions are whether a mental disease or illness is present and whether it affected the accused person's behavior.

At times the granting of a divorce or annulment and the award of custody, placement, or adoption are based on the presence or absence of a psychiatric problem.

Similarly, in reproduction situations the performance of an abortion or a sterilization procedure is conditioned on the psychiatric state of the patient. Artificial insemination mandates an absence of psychiatric problems in the donor or perhaps in his or her family.

Personal injury and malpractice claims may turn on the presence of traumatic psychoneurosis. In recent years, psychiatric problems related to employment have been the basis for workers' compensation settlements. Strict product liability also has been imposed for psychiatric injury.

Inherent in the etiology and effects of alcoholism and drug habituation and abuse are psychiatric factors; physicians have been held liable for addicting patients to drugs.

Psychiatric problems are often treated along with mental retardation, juvenile delinquency, autism, and hyperactive children. Psychosurgery (i.e., prefrontal lobotomy, brain ablation, electrode implantation) and electroconvulsive therapy may be used only in indicated circumstances with proper consent.

Forensic psychiatry is critical in determining malingering, sociopathy, sexual psychopathy (rape), and other sex-related problems, such as homosexuality, transvestitism, transsexual surgery, pedophilia, and fetishism.

Suicide contemplated because of depression, if recognized, can be prevented. Depression, which can be prevented if anticipated and recognized, often is seen postoperatively, particularly after cardiac surgery, postpartum, in intensive unit care, after transplantation, and incident to dialysis.

Psychiatric malpractice claims frequently involve treatment with medications, usually undertreatment or overtreatment, and toxic reactions (e.g., tardive dyskinesia). Infrequently, misdiagnosis and delayed or erroneous treatment are alleged. Intimate therapy has only recently become a cause célèbre and cause of action.

Psychiatric implications affect patients with psychoneurosis and personality trait or character disorders, but particularly those with schizophrenia, manic-depressive psychosis, the various depressions, and paranoia. Organic brain disease can include epilepsy, cerebral arteriosclerosis, space-occupying lesions, Alzheimer's disease, and a variety of other disorders. These disorders must be distinguished from trauma, infectious metabolic chemical or electrolyte disorders, cortisone intoxication, dehydration and cerebral edema, liver and kidney failure, and other etiologies.

The credibility and qualifications of a psychiatric or psychological expert are subject to the same legal requirements as other expert testimony. Based on adequate and intense investigation and examination of the witness, the opinions of psychiatric experts are admissible for consideration by the fact-finder. There are frequently conflicting opinions about the psychological state of an individual.

The tests of admissibility for psychiatric and psychological evidence in testimony are the same as those applied to all forms of evidence. The credibility of the expert involved is one factor that complicates the admission of forensic psychiatric and psychological information. The opinions of the mental health expert about criminal and civil matters are subject to cross-examination and rebuttal by other experts.[37]

ADMISSIBILITY OF EXPERT TESTIMONY

On the last day of the U.S. Supreme Court's 1992 to 1993 term, the justices' ruling in *Daubert v. Merrell Dow Pharmaceuticals* changed the rules for the admission of testimony by scientific experts in federal courts.[38]

For nearly 70 years, most federal courts judged the admissibility of scientific expert testimony by the 1923 standard of *Frye v. United States* (i.e., are the principles underlying the testimony "sufficiently established to have general acceptance in the field to which it belongs?").[39]

In *Daubert* the Supreme Court unanimously agreed that the *Frye* test was supplanted in 1975 when Congress adopted the Federal Rules of Evidence, which included provisions on expert testimony.

In evaluating evidence of DNA identification, medical causation, voiceprints, lie detector tests, eyewitness identification, and a host of other scientific issues, litigants and courts must now reconsider admissibility questions under *Daubert*.

The Supreme Court did not reject the *Frye* test on grounds that it was a wrong or poor judicial policy. Rather, the court simply concluded that *Frye* "was superseded by the adoption of the Federal Rules of Evidence."

Rule 702 allows opinion testimony by a qualified person concerning "scientific, technical, or other specialized knowledge that will assist the trier of fact to understand the evidence or to determine a fact in issue."

To satisfy that requirement, a court must undertake "a preliminary assessment of whether the reasoning or methodology underlying the testimony is scientifically valid and of whether that reasoning or methodology properly can be applied to the facts in issue," according to Justice Blackmun, who wrote the majority opinion.

Blackmun identified the following four factors that a court should consider in determining whether the scientific methodology underlying an expert's opinion is valid under Rule 702:

1. Whether the expert's theory or technique "can be (and has been) tested."
2. Whether the theory or technique has been "subjected to peer review and publication."
3. What the known or potential "rate of error" is for any test or scientific technique that has been employed.
4. The *Frye* standard of whether the technique is generally accepted in the scientific community.

Blackmun emphasized that the inquiry under Rule 702 "is a flexible one" that focuses on whether an expert's testimony "rests on a reliable foundation."

The full impact of *Daubert* may not be clear for many years, as courts apply its four-factor test to a broad range of expert evidence.

Blackmun criticized *Frye* as being "at odds with the 'liberal thrust' of the Federal Rules and their 'general approach' of relaxing the traditional barriers to 'opinion testimony.'" However, he also wrote that an expert's testimony must be "scientifically valid," which requires an independent judgment of validity by the court.

The potential impact of *Daubert* is vast, and courts will have to reconsider the admissibility of many types of scientific evidence.

The *Daubert* decision will eventually affect court rulings pertaining to such areas as polygraph testing, voiceprint analysis, questioned-documents examination, and so-called expert psychological testimony on such subjects as rape trauma syndrome and posttraumatic stress disorder.

ENDNOTES

1. Polsky, 1 Temple Law Rptr. 15, 15 (1954).
2. Smith, *The Development of Forensic Medicine and Law-Science Relations*, 3 J. Pub. L. 304, 305 (1954).
3. Harper, *The Code of Hammurabi, King of Babylon*, 77-71 (2d ed. 1904).
4. Oppenheimer, *Liability for Malpraxis in Ancient Law*, 7 Trans. Medical-Legal Soc. 98, 103-104 (1910).
5. *Supra* note 1, at 15.
6. *Supra* note 2, at 306.
7. *Id*. at 306-307.
8. *Supra* note 1, at 15.

9. Wecht, *Legal Medicine: An Historical Review and Future Perspective*, 22 N.Y. Law School L. Rev. 4, 876 (1977).

10. *Supra* note 2, at 308.

11. *Supra* note 1, at 16.

12. *Supra* note 2, at 309.

13. *Id*. at 309.

14. *Id*. at 310.

15. *Id*. at 310.

16. Chaill Aae, *Origin and Progress of Medical Jurisprudence*, 46 J. Crim. L. & Criminal 397, 399 (1949).

17. *Supra* note 1, at 16.

18. *Id*. at 17.

19. *Supra* note 16, at 400.

20. *Id*. at 400, note 24.

21. *Id*. at 402.

22. Farr, *Elements of Medical Jurisprudence* (1788). (Translated and abridged from the *Elementra Medicinne Forensis* of Johannes Fridericus Faselius.)

23. Polsky, 3 Medico-Legal Reader 7 (1956).

24. An Act to Amend the Law Relating to Coroners, 16 & 17 Geo. C. 59 (1926).

25. *Id*. at §1.

26. Thurston, *The Coroner's Limitations*, 30 Med-Legal J. 110, 112-113 (1962).

27. Taylor, *The Evolution of Legal Medicine*, 252 Medico-Legal Bull. 5 (1974).

28. Fisher, *History of Forensic Pathology and Related Laboratory Science in Medicolegal Investigation of Death*, in 4 *Guidelines of the Application of Pathology to Crime Investigation* 7 (W. Spitz, ed. 1973).

29. Wecht, *Forensic Sciences* (1984).

30. Lempert, *A Modern Approach to Evidence* (1977).

31. Curran, *Law, Medicine, and Forensic Science* (3d ed. 1982).

32. *Supra* note 29.

33. *Supra* note 31.

34. *Supra* note 29.

35. *Supra* note 30.

36. Hirsch, *Handbook of Legal Medicine* (5th ed. 1979).

37. *Supra* note 29.

38. *Daubert v. Merrell Dow Pharmaceuticals*, 251 F. 2d 1128 (9th Cir. 1991).

39. *Frye v. United States*, 293 F. 1013 (D.C. Cir. 1923).

ADDITIONAL READINGS

R.E.I. Roberts, *Forensic Medical Evidence in Rape and Child Sexual Abuse: Controversies and a Possible Solution*, Clin. Forensic & Legal Med. (Oct. 1997).

R.D. Weber, *Malpractice Expert Witness Statute Held*, Mich. Med. (Oct. 1999).

IX International Contributions

THE LEGAL BACKGROUND

The relevant pieces of legislation that apply to this chapter are as follows:

Statute of Proclamation 1539

Medical Act 1858

European Convention on Human Rights 1950

Medical Act 1983

European Directive 93/16/EEC (Mutual Recognition of Medical Qualifications)

Medical (Professional Performance) Act 1995

European Specialist Medical Qualifications Order 1995

European Primary Medical Qualifications Regulations 1996 (SI 1996/1591)

Human Rights Act 1998

Professional Conduct Committee (Procedure) Rules 1998 (SI 1998/2255)

Health Act 1999

Medical Act 1983 (Amendment) Order 2000 (SI 2000/2052)

European Directive 2001/19/EC (Mutual Recognition of Professional Qualifications)

National Health Service Reform Act 2002

Medical Act 1983 (Amendment) Order 2002 (SI 2002/1803)

In the UK the medical profession was first brought together as a single profession when Parliament enacted the Medical Act of 1858. That Act established what is now called the General Medical Council, and its principal function was to maintain a Medical Register of qualified practitioners so that "persons requiring medical aid should be enabled to distinguish qualified from unqualified practitioners."

To this day, the GMC remains the UK's supreme professional body that regulates the qualifications of practitioners in medicine and surgery, registers them to practice, and governs them in their professional practice.

Since 1858, there have been many amendments to, but few major reenactments of, the Medical Act. The Medical Act 1983 is currently in force, as amended by the Medical (Professional Performance) Act 1995, and also by the Medical Act 1983 (Amendment) Order 2002, which was promulgated as recently as December 17, 2002.

In this chapter I can comment only briefly on the complexity of European medical law that refers to licensing and disciplining of physicians. European medical law derives from three distinct sources.

National law

Each of the 15 EU member states has its own national law, but there may also be subjurisdictions therein, with their own local variant of national law. Only two member states (i.e., the UK and Ireland) follow a common law system, similar to that of the United States. The remainder follow systems of civil law derived from the Napoleonic Code.

It is important to recognize that sometimes the law across the various EU states may be at complete variance with the most fundamental concepts of common law as understood in the United States, in the UK, and in Ireland. For example, in France the doctrine of binding precedent does not usually apply. In Germany the burden of proof may be reversed in medical negligence actions, and so rest on the defendant.

In the UK, medical law may come into force by (1) Act of Parliament, (2) Statutory Instrument, (3) Order in Council, or (4) case law with the force of binding precedent. In England, medical negligence cases are usually heard in the High Court. Appeals are firstly to the Court of Appeal, and finally to the House of Lords. The General Medical Council hears disciplinary cases, and at present appeals are heard by the Privy Council. There may be a further appeal to one of two European courts.

European Union law

EU law applies somewhat uniformly across the 15 member states. Often this derives from Directives of the European Council, which have the force of law. Usually the terms of a Directive are implemented into the law of each member state by specific legislation. But if a state fails actively to adopt the Directive within a specified time after promulgation, the Directive will come into force by default. Under EU law, the final court of appeal is the European Court of Justice (ECJ) in Luxembourg. Appellate decisions made by the ECJ have the force of binding precedent in the UK, whether or not the court of first instance was in the UK.

European human rights law

European human rights law derives from the European Convention on Human Rights, to which more than 30 independent European countries are signatories. (This group of signatories is distinct from, but it includes, the group of 15 EU states.) The Convention was enshrined into English law as the Human Rights Act 1998, and it requires that all UK legislation must be compatible with the European Convention on Human Rights. The final court of appeal is the European Court of Human Rights (ECHR) in Strasbourg. Decisions made by the ECHR have the force of binding precedent in the UK, whether or not the court of first instance was within the UK.

All three systems of law in the UK—national law, EU law, and human rights law—have a considerable impact on its medical jurisprudence, both in theory and in practice. Moreover, the fields of English and European medical law are evolving very rapidly at present, as evidenced by the recent legislation and recent cases cited in this chapter.

REGISTRATION

General registration

British and EU doctors. Article 2 of European Directive 93/16/EEC relates to primary medical qualifications, and it mandates their mutual recognition across the EU, irrespective of whether the doctor speaks the language of the host country in which he is practicing his medicine. This Directive was implemented into English law by the European Primary Medical Qualifications Regulations 1996 (SI 1996/1591).

As a consequence of this, under the Medical Act 1983 (as amended), anyone who holds a primary medical qualification awarded by a recognized body in the UK, or an EU citizen who holds a primary medical qualification from the EU, is entitled to progress to full registration as a medical practitioner in the UK. Depending on the medical school, general medical training will have taken 4 to 6 years. A list of registrable medical qualifications awarded in the EU, and their awarding bodies, is found in the General Medical Council's publication *A Guide to the Registers 2002*.[3]

Non-EU doctors. Until the end of 2002, the GMC had a two-tier system of registration for non-EU qualified doctors. Those qualified at some (but not all) medical schools in Australia, Hong Kong, Malaysia, New Zealand, Singapore, South Africa, and the West Indies had the right to apply for provisional or full registration in the UK. Doctors qualified from other medical schools (e.g., in the United States) could only apply for limited registration, but they could apply for provisional or full registration after working in the UK for a period of time under limited registration. The latter scheme has not changed.

But under the Medical Act 1983 (as amended in 2002), there will now be a single UK system for registering non-EU doctors. In future, the GMC must take into account a doctor's medical qualifications (as before), whether he is of good character, his knowledge or experience, whether this was acquired in Europe or elsewhere, and the acceptance of his medical qualification (if that is the case) by another EU state as qualifying him to practice there. Fast-track provisions to full registration will apply for eligible non-EU specialists and general practitioners. All non-EU medical graduates must show sufficient knowledge of the English language. (But see below for an important exception to this general rule regarding linguistic ability.)

Specialist registration

British doctors. In the UK, the European Specialist Medical Qualifications Order 1995 requires the GMC to keep and publish a register of medical specialists, but not of family general practitioners, who comprise the majority of the profession. For entry onto the specialist register, doctors must first be specialty trained at recognized centres over a specified number of years (minimum 5). In the *early* part of this training (typically after 2 years) they must pass a higher examination, such as that for the Membership of the Royal College of Obstetricians and Gynaecologists. When training has been completed satisfactorily, they will be awarded a Certificate of Completion of Specialist Training (CCST) by the Specialist Training Authority (STA) of the Medical Royal Colleges, and their names will be entered onto the GMC's Specialist Register. Only then may they apply for consultant posts in the National Health Service, and may set up in independent private practice. This stage is approximately equivalent to the American Specialist Boards.

Other EU doctors. By virtue of the European Medical Directive 93/16/EEC, and the European Specialist Medical Qualifications Order 1995, doctors trained in another EU state, and who hold a specialist qualification from that state, would be recognized by the GMC for entry onto the GMC's Specialist Register.

Non-EU doctors. Specialists trained outside the EU may be recognized if the STA deems their qualification to be equivalent to the CCST.

DISCIPLINARY MATTERS UNDER THE "OLD REGIME"

Historical role of the GMC: conduct and health

Historically, the GMC had always restricted its disciplinary concerns to issues of serious professional misconduct, the commission of criminal offenses, and matters relating to the health of medical practitioners. Further, it has always had the legal authority to advise the medical profession on standards of professional conduct or professional performance, and on medical ethics.

Disgruntled patients often make complaints to the GMC, and these have increased 15-fold *(sic)* between 1990 and 2002. Routinely, the courts will report all criminal convictions of doctors to the GMC. In addition, health concerns about doctors may be notified to the GMC by patients, colleagues, employers, legal authorities, or the press. It is only in response to complaints that the GMC can start disciplinary action.

The law relating to the GMC is currently in process of major change, and the new regime will be explained below. Here I shall outline only briefly the present disciplinary regime, so that the future regime (described below) will be understood more easily.

Serious professional misconduct

For issues of professional misconduct, including criminal offenses, hearings take place before the GMC's best-known and most powerful committee, the Professional Conduct Committee. Precise rules of procedure are set out in Professional Conduct Committee (Procedure) Rules 1998 (SI 1998/2255). The key question for this committee is whether the doctor has been guilty of "serious professional misconduct." Its hearings are in public, and the press are allowed to be present. The doctor is legally represented, unless he declines. If serious professional misconduct is found proved, the following sanctions are available: reprimand, conditions on practice, suspension from the Medical Register, or erasure from the Medical Register.

One negligent mistake does not amount to serious professional misconduct. If a doctor has had a single negligent incident in an otherwise unblemished career, this would not necessarily amount to serious professional misconduct. So ruled the Privy Council in the appealed case of *Rao v. GMC*.[4]

Scope of serious professional misconduct. A doctor need not commit an action against a specific person, nor commit a criminal offense, and yet he may still be found guilty of serious professional misconduct. It is likely that this would also apply to the new concept of "impaired fitness to practice" (see below). In the case of *Idenburg v. GMC* (2000),[5] the Privy Council upheld the Professional Conduct Committee's decision that a junior doctor who had left her job without notice or explanation was guilty of serious professional misconduct. She was suspended from the Medical Register for 12 months.

Admissibility of evidence obtained illegally. In *Idenburg*, the Privy Council also held that it made no difference whether the GMC had relied on evidence obtained unlawfully (i.e., confidential medical records disclosed without consent), and it directed that this evidence could be admitted.

Importance of not commenting on nondisciplinary matters. Early in 2003, the GMC's Professional Conduct Committee (PCC) heard the case of Dr. Langdon,[6] a general practitioner. She usually practiced conventional medicine, but occasionally she used homeopathy, and also divining with a swinging crystal in order to confirm her choice of specific homeopathic remedies. Two of her patients (one of them a sick baby brought by her mother) had not expected such unconventional techniques to be used during their consultations, and so they complained to the GMC. The Professional Conduct Committee found Dr. Langdon guilty of failure to obtain the informed consent of her patients before she used homeopathy and divining in their management. She was suspended from the Medical Register for 3 months.

In this case the Professional Conduct Committee said that it had been careful not to give an opinion on whether homeopathy and divining were valid techniques for use in a medical context, as this was not within its remit as a professional disciplinary body. To make an authoritative scientific pronouncement on the validity of homeopathy or divining would have required more extensive evidence and time, and more extensive expertise and legal authority, than was available to them. No doubt, any attempt to have done so would have been overturned by the Privy Council on appeal.

Health issues

For issues relating to doctors' health (e.g., mental illness, alcohol or drug abuse), hearings take place in private before the GMC's Health Committee. The doctor is legally represented, unless he so declines. The key question is whether the doctor's health is such that there is serious impairment of his fitness to practice medicine. If this is found proved, the following sanctions are available: reprimand, conditions on practice, general conditions (see below), or suspension from the Medical Register. Erasure is not available as a sanction for health issues.

Conditions on lifestyle

The conditions imposed on a doctor's registration need not be restricted to his medical practice, but can also relate to his general conduct and lifestyle. In 2001 the GMC's Health Committee determined that Dr. Whitefield's fitness to practice was seriously impaired by depressive illness and alcoholism. It imposed 14 conditions on his registration, including requirements that he abstain from alcohol, submit to random tests of blood and urine, and attend Alcoholics Anonymous. He appealed to the Privy Council, arguing that these conditions would deprive him of enjoyment of social drinking on family occasions or in public, and that they constituted interference with his private life contrary to Article 8 of the European Convention on Human Rights scheduled to the Human Rights Act 1998. The Privy Council dismissed his appeal.[7]

Problems with the "old regime" of disciplinary procedures

There are four principal problems with the "old regime" of disciplinary procedures.

Circular definition. There is no legal definition of the term "serious professional misconduct." In practice, it has come to mean professional misconduct of such a degree that the Professional Conduct Committee considers it to be serious. Although this is clearly a circular definition, the use of the term "serious professional misconduct" has nevertheless stood the test of time unexpectedly well.

Standard of proof. The Professional Conduct Committee will acquit a doctor if the evidence available is not sufficient to reach the criminal standard of proof (i.e., beyond reasonable doubt), even though it might have been sufficient to reach or exceed the civil standard of proof (i.e., on the balance of probability). Then the doctor would legally be free to resume practice, as before, no matter how poor his clinical performance had been. Under such circumstances, his clinical practice could only be challenged through a civil action in negligence, a venture that is lengthy, expensive, and uncertain. This problem has now been resolved, under new performance procedures (see below).

Appeals. Appeal from the decisions and sanctions of the GMC's disciplinary committees—Registration, Health, Conduct, and Performance (discussed below)—are not legally straightforward. The decisions of these committees are neither subject to judicial review nor can they be appealed through the usual court system. Instead, any appeal would leapfrog the High Court, the Court of Appeal, and the House of Lords. Instead, it would be heard by the judicial committee of the Privy Council. But this has the disadvantage of requiring the UK's most senior court to spend time hearing appeals that could often be handled perfectly well by a less senior judge sitting alone. On rare occasions, Privy Council decisions may be appealed to the European Court of Justice in Luxembourg, or to the European Court of Human Rights in Strasbourg.

Categorization. Concerns about a doctor cannot always be categorized simply as issues of *either* conduct *or* health. Often there is an overlap, in that health issues may contribute to problems of conduct. But the Health Committee has had no power to erase a doctor's name from the Medical Register. When there is such an overlap, the Privy Council has held[8] that concerns on conduct may "trump" concerns on health, and so a hybrid case may be heard as a conduct case, with erasure available as a sanction.

Professional performance

During the 1970s there arose increasing concerns about the professional performance of a small minority of doctors. This led Parliament to enact the Medical (Professional Performance) Act 1995. It gave the GMC new powers to investigate and adjudicate on a doctor's professional performance (in addition to his conduct and health), and to impose sanctions if sanctions were considered to be appropriate.

Assessors of clinical performance carry out an on-site assessment of the doctor, interview various people, review his management of patients (from their medical notes, and also using real patients or actors), conduct an assessment of his practical skills, and conduct a verbal and written examination of his knowledge. They would then write a report as to whether they consider that his performance has been so seriously deficient that action should be taken against his registration. If so, they would make appropriate recommendations. For example, they might advise him to stop operative surgery but allow him to continue in office practice, or they might recommend a more serious sanction. The doctor would be invited to accept the recommendations in the assessors' report. If he refused to accept them, the GMC's Committee on Professional Performance would then conduct a formal hearing of his case. If they found his performance to be seriously deficient, they may impose sanctions as follows: reprimand, conditions on practice, suspension from the Medical Register, or erasure from the Medical Register.

The new powers to assess clinical performance came into force on July 1, 1997. For poor clinical performance before that date, the GMC was (and remains) without legal authority to take action against, or impose any sanction on, the doctor.

In the 2000 case of *Krippendorf,*[9] the Privy Council considered the GMC's new legal authority conferred by the Medical (Professional Performance) Act 1995. It held that, even though the GMC now had legal authority to take disciplinary action regarding the *performance* of a doctor, it had no such authority to take action regarding his *competence.* Thus, the GMC's Committee on Professional Performance had erred in law when it judged Dr. Krippendorf incompetent in the practice of medicine, and it had acted *ultra vires* when it erased her name from the Medical Register. Her name was therefore restored. Further, the Privy Council directed that the GMC's performance assessment procedures should focus its attention on the doctor's track record and assess her past performance in the medical work that she had actually been doing. It should not treat the assessment procedure as a theoretical test of the doctor's competence at work that she had never been called upon to perform.

The Privy Council's narrow interpretation of the term "performance" in *Krippendorf* led to the uncomfortable result that a doctor who had been found to be incompetent by the GMC's assessors of clinical performance was nevertheless allowed to carry on practicing medicine. Note that the effect of this Privy Council decision has now been reversed by provisions of the Medical Act 1983 (Amendment) Order 2002 (see below).

RECENT CHANGES IN THE LAW ON THE UK's GENERAL MEDICAL COUNCIL

At the time of writing this chapter, a number of important and far-reaching reforms to the structure and functions of the GMC are in progress. These major changes were approved by Order in Council on December 17, 2002, and they have not yet come into force. But by the time this book is published, they will be in force.

Order in Council

Compared with previous governance (i.e., governance under the Medical Act 1983 as originally enacted by Parliament), a curious legal anomaly now exists in regard to governance of the UK's medical profession. Parliament has enacted this anomaly deliberately, in that the Health Act 1999 (viz., Sections 60 and 62) now gives to the Secretary of State for Health the legal authority directly to amend primary legislation, i.e., the Medical Act 1983, at his discretion, by means of an Order in Council.

Previously, powers to amend the Medical Act, as to amend most other Acts of Parliament, had always been reserved to Parliament. Not surprisingly, the medical profession at first opposed this new extension to the already wide powers of the Secretary of State, but to no avail. Section 60 of the Health Act 1999 was nicknamed "the Henry VIII clause," because such a device was first used in the Statute of Proclamation 1539, to give King Henry VIII the power to legislate by proclamation.

Nevertheless, as we shall see below, there are advantages in having available a mechanism to change the relevant legislation speedily, if the need arises.

THE GENERAL MEDICAL COUNCIL OF THE FUTURE

The Medical Act 1983 (Amendment) Order 2002 (SI No. 1803) reforms the GMC's registration and disciplinary committees. It also states that in future the GMC's main aim will be: "to protect, promote and maintain the health and safety of the public."

The Council of the "new" GMC will have only 35 members. Of these, 16 will be laypersons, appointed by the Privy Council after rigorous interviews. Of the 19 medical members, 17 will be elected on a constituency basis by doctors nationwide. The remaining two medical members will be appointed: one by the Medical Royal Colleges and Faculties, and one by the Council of Heads of Medical Schools.

Most of the GMC's statutory committees that were previously important, and so were mentioned frequently in case law, are now to be abolished. These include: the Registration Committee, the Interim Orders Committee, the Preliminary Proceedings Committee, the Assessment Referral Committee, the Committee on Professional Performance, the Health Committee, and the Professional Conduct Committee. Instead, new committees and panels will be established: an Education Committee, an Investigation Committee, and one or more Registration Decisions Panels, Registration Appeal Panels, Interim Orders Panels, and Fitness to Practice Panels.

Previously only members of the General Medical Council sat on the disciplinary committees, but they will no longer do so. In future, such panels will be populated by coopted medical and lay members. This will mark a clear separation between those committees taking general policy decisions (e.g., the Registration Committee) and those taking disciplinary decisions on individual cases (e.g., a Registration Decision Panel).

License to practice, and revalidation

The Medical Act 1983 (as amended in 2002) will introduce a new license to practice for all doctors who wish to practice medicine. It will also introduce a requirement for a regular revalidation of practice.

Doctors with a license to practice will undergo periodic revalidation to retain it, and so revalidation will demonstrate that a doctor remains up to date and fit to practice. Doctors who do not wish to revalidate will not hold a license to practice medicine, and they will not be allowed to prescribe drugs or exercise the other rights and privileges currently provided by registration. Revalidation will probably come into force in 2005.

The new fitness to practice procedures

Until now, the GMC's various disciplinary committees had considered charges that were variously framed as "serious professional misconduct," "criminal conviction," "seriously deficient performance," or "serious impairment of fitness to practice by reason of a physical or mental condition." But the definition of these terms has been vague, and far from satisfactory, and this has led to many difficulties.

Under the Medical Act 1983 (as amended in 2002) there will now be the single concept of "impaired fitness to practice" by reason of misconduct, deficient professional performance, a criminal conviction, adverse physical or mental health, or a determination of another regulatory body.

The fitness to practice procedures have been reformed. Progress of a case through the new disciplinary process will now be divided into two main stages.

First, an Investigation Committee will investigate allegations suggesting that a doctor's fitness to practice may be impaired. In its investigations, it may legally override the Data Protection Act by requiring confidential documents to be disclosed.

For minor matters, if the Investigation Committee determines that the matter need not be considered further, it has the legal authority to conclude the case by giving a warning regarding the doctor's future conduct or performance. For serious matters, if the Investigation Committee finds that there is a *prima facie* case to answer, then a Fitness to Practice Panel will be appointed to adjudicate.

Whilst a serious case is awaiting formal hearing, the Investigation Panel may refer it to an Interim Orders Panel. This may make an order, to take immediate effect, that a doctor's registration be made conditional or even suspended, pending formal hearing. Such an order is likely to be made if it is necessary for the protection of members of the public, or otherwise in the public interest, or in the interests of the doctor.

In certain circumstances, the GMC may disclose information about a doctor to his actual or potential employers, or to organizations to whom he is providing services. It may also disclose information if it determines that this is in the public interest.

Next, a Fitness to Practice Panel will decide on whether the doctor's fitness to practice is impaired. Its hearings will be adversarial in nature, as with the Professional Conduct Committee now. The panel will usually consist of five members (three is a quorum), at least one of whom must be on the Medical Register, and at least one of whom is a layperson. The panel will have a Legal Assessor, who is usually a senior Queen's Counsel or a retired judge. He advises on matters of law, and any advice that he gives *in camera* must be repeated in public. In the case of *Walker v. GMC* (2002),[10] the Privy Council held, on appeal, that the Legal Assessor should not express an opinion regarding an appropriate sanction, as this might be taken to constitute legal advice.

Procedure and rules of evidence are similar to a criminal trial. Charges are read. Witnesses (both factual and expert) give evidence under oath, and they are cross-examined. If evidence is not in dispute, a statement may be admitted without oral evidence being heard. (Note: depositions are not used in the English legal system.) A criminal standard of proof is required, in that any charge must be proved beyond reasonable doubt. If the panel finds one or more charges proved, any previous disciplinary findings by the GMC will be disclosed, and evidence in mitigation heard. Typically this will be documentary evidence in the form of supporting testimonials, and verbal evidence from witnesses, as to the character of the defendant doctor.

In private session, the Fitness to Practice Panel will then determine whether the doctor has been guilty of "impaired fitness to practice." If it finds against him, it may issue a warning regarding his future conduct or performance, or it may make a direction regarding conditional registration or suspension, or even erase his name from the Medical Register. Erasure or suspension will automatically revoke his license to practice. Even if it finds that a doctor's fitness to practice is not impaired, it has authority to give a warning regarding his future conduct or performance.

Sanctions usually come into force 28 days after the hearing, to allow time to appeal. But a Fitness to Practice Panel has authority to put a sanction into immediate effect, and it is likely to do so when it is satisfied that this is necessary for the protection of the public, or is otherwise in the public interest, or in the best interests of the doctor.

Before 2000, disciplinary sanctions could not be put into immediate effect. But this changed when the Interim Orders Committee was established, with legal authority to impose immediate sanctions (see below). Before this, all stages of the disciplinary mechanism had to be followed through, including allowing 28 days for appeal, before sanctions could become effective.

Whenever a Fitness to Practice Panel makes its determination on a case, brief reasons for the basis of its decisions regarding serious professional misconduct, and for the imposition of any sanction, must be set out, in compliance with the Privy Council's ruling in the appealed cases of *Stefan v. GMC* (1999)[11] and *Selvanathan v. GMC* (2000).[12] However, in the case of *Gupta v. GMC* (2001)[13] the Privy Council later held that there was no similar duty to give reasons for decisions on matters of fact.

The case of Dr. Harold Shipman

The problems with the former leisurely approach to disciplinary matters were well illustrated by the case of Dr. Harold Shipman. He was a family doctor, but also Britain's most prolific serial killer. The police arrested him on September 7, 1998, and he was charged with murder. Following a lengthy period in custody, on January 31, 2000, the criminal courts found him guilty of murdering 15 of his patients, usually in their homes. Most had been fairly healthy. He was sentenced to life imprisonment.

The GMC organized an almost immediate hearing before its Professional Conduct Committee. Dr. Shipman was found guilty of serious professional misconduct on February 11, 2000, and suspended from the Medical Register with immediate effect. However, his name could not be erased from the Medical Register until 28 days later, on March 11, 2000, to allow for appeal. (He did not in fact appeal from the GMC's decision.) Thus, the GMC was powerless but to allow his name to remain on the Medical Register for more than 18 months after he was first charged with multiple murder, and for more than 5 weeks after he had been convicted of multiple murder in the criminal courts. During most of this time (i.e., until his suspension on February 11, 2000) he was legally entitled to practice medicine in prison (including the prescription of drugs), and indeed he did so. Other prisoners consulted with him.

When all criminal and disciplinary hearings were concluded, the Chief Medical Officer commissioned a clinical audit[14] into Dr. Shipman's clinical practice between 1974 and 1988. This conducted a review of the clinical records and cremation forms that were still available, and it concluded that there were in fact 236 deaths about which there was concern. However, the Crown Prosecution Service took the view that the public interest would not be served by investigating the matter any further.

Interim Orders Committee

The Shipman case highlighted the fact that the GMC should be empowered to act swiftly and effectively when a doctor's fitness to practice is called into question, particularly in very serious cases. However, the GMC had been advised by its lawyers that, as the law stood in early 2000, it was unable to suspend a doctor charged with a criminal offense, even in the most serious cases, until the doctor is convicted. During 2000 the government therefore used its powers granted under Section 60 of the Health Act 1999 to promulgate an Order in Council[15] amending the Medical Act 1983. This established an Intermediate Orders Committee, which had the power, *inter alia*, to suspend a doctor, with immediate effect, at any stage of the fitness to practice procedures, if this is in the public interest or the doctor's interest.

If it is to act effectively in this regard, the GMC is clearly dependent on early notification of concerns. But in a small number of police investigation cases, the police may ask the GMC to delay a decision to ask a doctor to appear before the Interim Orders Committee, if it believes that early action could compromise an ongoing police investigation.

Appeals

At the time of writing this chapter, appeals against decisions of the Professional Conduct Committee are to the Privy Council. However, the National Health Service Reform Act 2002 has now charged the High Court with responsibility to hear these. This is an important change in the appeals procedure, and it is likely that it will greatly increase the frequency of appeals against the GMC's disciplinary decisions. At the time of writing there have been no appeals under this new procedure. Nevertheless, the present and extensive case law on appeals to the Privy Council from decisions of the Professional Conduct Committee will apply with binding authority on the new panels. For this reason, such Privy Council cases are referenced in this chapter.

INTERNATIONAL CONSIDERATIONS ON IMPAIRED DOCTORS

There have been notorious cases where doctors were erased from the medical register in another jurisdiction, yet allowed to remain on the UK Medical Register, and so could practice medicine legally in the UK. Dr. Richard Neale is an example.

The case of Dr. Richard Neale

Dr Neale graduated in medicine in England in 1970. In 1977 he emigrated to Canada, where he worked as an obstetrician and gynecologist. In 1978 he was banned from surgery in British Columbia after he had operated on a patient against his chief's advice, and she died. He then moved to Toronto but, after the deaths of two further patients, he was erased from the Canadian Medical Register in 1985. He then returned to the UK where he obtained a consultant post.

A former colleague in Canada telephoned the GMC in London to alert them to the events in Canada. He was told that the GMC had no jurisdiction to take action regarding the events in Canada. But now that Dr. Neale was working in England, further serious problems arose from his clinical practice, particularly his surgery. In 2000, he was called before the GMC's Professional Conduct Committee to answer 37 charges relating to poor standards of treatment, treatment without consent, and false claims about qualifications and experience. He was found guilty of serious professional misconduct, and his name was erased from the UK Medical Register, 15 years after he had first been erased in Canada for similar offenses.

Only when Dr. Neale was found guilty of serious professional misconduct in the UK could his name be erased from the UK Medical Register. Neither in 1985, nor in 2000, did the GMC have any legal authority to take into account, let alone to base any sanctions upon, adverse professional findings that had been made earlier in another jurisdiction. The legal situation in this regard has now changed (see below).

Registration and disciplinary authorities in the EU

Since 1959 the Standing Committee of European Doctors (at www.cpme.be) has led the way in standardizing the recognition of medical degrees within the EU. The competent registration and disciplinary authorities in the EU member states that are equivalent to the UK's General Medical Council are given in Appendix 73-1.

Future restrictions in the UK

In future, by virtue of the Medical Act 1983 (as amended in 2002), any doctor who has been disqualified in an EU member state, for reasons of professional misconduct, health, or criminal conviction, will be ineligible for registration in the UK. Further, any doctor found guilty of a criminal offense, or subject to an adverse determination by a health care regulator, in any other jurisdiction throughout the world, may be refused registration, or refused continuing registration, in the UK.

It may happen that an EU doctor, who is theoretically entitled to UK registration, but who is not in fact so registered, may render medical services reprehensibly, perhaps in an emergency, whilst visiting the UK. In such a case the GMC, if it thinks fit, may impose a prohibition on him practicing medicine in the UK at any time in the future.

Future dangers in the cross-border practice of medicine in Europe

A new European Directive on the Mutual Recognition of Professional Qualifications (2001/19/EC) was promulgated on July 31, 2001 (Section 2.7 relates to doctors). Its principal aim is to liberalize the law relating to the provision of services, including medical services, across all member states of the EU.

This Directive imposes on each EU member state a mandatory obligation to take into consideration the recognition by another member state of non-EU qualifications, irrespective of where those qualifications were obtained. It also puts an obligation on the relevant authorities to determine applications for mutual recognition within a maximum of 4 months. This short time scale will make it difficult when authorities are asked to recognize medical qualifications obtained in remote parts of the world.

Most importantly, the Directive would allow a doctor established in any one of the EU's 15 (soon to be 25) member states to practice medicine in another EU state for up to 16 weeks a year, without being subject to registration requirements in the host state. There is no requirement that he should understand the host state's language. Thus, he could practice medicine legally in England without the GMC being aware of his presence, let alone authorizing him. If found guilty of medical malpractice, the GMC could not erase him from the Medical Register, as his name would not be there.

Clearly there will be dangers to patients if this Directive comes into force as presently drafted. In response, the GMC has linked with other regulatory bodies, in the UK and the EU, in the hope that the draft Directive will be considerably amended, in the direction of safety, before it comes into force in the medical arena. The Alliance of UK Health Regulators on Europe (AURE) has its own website at: www.aure.org.uk.

However, not everyone sees the European Directive on the Mutual Recognition of Professional Qualifications in a negative light. Stephen Whale, who is a leading English human rights lawyer, has recently written that:

Vested interests in the British medical establishment have to appreciate that the legitimate need to maintain standards cannot be used as a convenient cover for frustrating the legal rights of European doctors.[16]

Issues arising from the European Convention on Human Rights

Severity of sanctions. Some have argued that the GMC's Professional Conduct Committee has, on occasion, been too severe in the sanctions that it imposes on doctors who are found guilty of serious professional misconduct. In the appealed cases of *Bijl v. GMC*[17] and of *Hossain v. GMC*,[18] the Privy Council addressed this point. Dr Bijl had removed a kidney stone laparoscopically but he encountered massive hemorrhage. He then left the hospital too soon, when his patient's bleeding was not yet under full control, and the patient died. As for Dr. Hossain, a general practitioner, one Law Lord hearing the case said that he was probably "overworking, overstretched and overtired" when he failed to make adequate assessments or adequate records on four patients he visited at home. The Professional Conduct Committee found both doctors guilty of serious professional misconduct, and erased their names from the Medical Register.

On appeal, the Privy Council reversed both of these decisions. Dr. Bijl was given a year's suspension, and Dr. Hossain was referred back for reconsideration as to whether conditions on clinical practice should be imposed.

In *Bijl*, the Privy Council held that when a surgeon was found guilty of serious professional misconduct involving an error of judgment, rather than any allegation against his practical skills, and it was unlikely that he would repeat the error, it was not appropriate that the maximum sentence available (i.e., erasure) be imposed. The desire to maintain public confidence in the medical profession should not result in sacrificing the careers of otherwise competent and useful doctors who presented no danger to the public, in order to satisfy a demand for blame and punishment.

It may be argued that a sanction too severe may breach Article 3 of the European Convention on Human Rights, which proscribes "degrading treatment or punishment."

Right to a fair trial (in England). In disciplinary hearings before its Professional Conduct Committee, the GMC acts both as prosecuting body and adjudicating body. Furthermore, cases have taken very many years before they come to a hearing. It has been argued that this breaches the fair trial requirements of Article 6.1 of the European Convention, which requires "a fair and public hearing within a reasonable time by an independent and impartial tribunal established by law." The Privy Council considered this point in *Ghosh v. GMC* (2001).[19] But it dismissed it, on the grounds that the processes of the Professional Conduct Committee were subject to control by an appellate body that had full jurisdiction to reverse the initial decision if it saw fit.

"Chinese walls" operate to keep separate the GMC's various functions. In the case of *Nicolaides*, the High Court accepted this arrangement, and it explained it as follows:

. . . the functions of the Professional Conduct Committee as a panel are separate from those of the GMC as a whole; investigation/presentation and adjudication functions are kept entirely separate and are performed by different people.[20]

Right to a fair trial (in Ireland). In 2000 the GMC's Professional Conduct Committee found that Dr. Borges, an Irish gynecologist who worked in England, was guilty of serious professional misconduct for sexually inappropriate behavior with two patients. It erased his name from the Medical Register with immediate effect. An appeal to the Privy Council failed.[21]

He then faced similar disciplinary action before the Irish Medical Council, but the GMC's principal witness in London, England, refused to testify in Dublin, Ireland. The Irish Medical Council then proposed to erase his name from the Irish Medical Register without a full hearing. But his lawyers applied to the Irish High Court for judicial review, arguing that it would contravene his human rights if they erased him, without him being able to cross-examine before the Irish Medical Council those witnesses who had given evidence against him in London. The judicial review in Ireland is still in progress.[22] Furthermore, the European Court of Human Rights in Strasbourg has agreed to hear the case later on appeal, if needs be.

International collaboration in the future

Given that there is a significant international traffic in doctors, it is becoming increasingly important that regulatory authorities should exchange between themselves information concerning deficient doctors who ply their trade internationally. The International Association of Medical Regulatory Authorities (IAMRA) has been set up as a forum to develop new concepts and approaches in medical regulation, and to support regulatory authorities in protecting the public. IAMRA aims to promote international cooperation and collaboration among regulatory authorities, and to facilitate exchange of medical regulatory information. Its website is to be found at membersonly.fsmb.org/IAMRA/IAMRA_text.htm.[23]

ENDNOTES

1. This point was debated in the case of *McAllister v. GMC*. The Privy Council ruled that English law would apply for GMC hearings held in Scotland. [1993] 1 All E.R. 982.

2. Legislation recently passed will soon introduce a "license to practice medicine" in the UK.

3. *A Guide to the Registers 2002* is available from the General Medical Council, 178 Great Portland Street, London W1W 5JE, England (www.gmc-uk.org.uk).

4. *Rao v. GMC*, Privy Council (Appeal 21/2002), judgment given on December 9, 2002. All Privy Council judgments may be freely downloaded from www.Privy-Council.org.uk.

5. *Idenburg v. GMC*, Privy Council (Appeal 62/1999), judgment given on March 23, 2000.

6. *Langdon v. GMC*, PCC determination on January 15, 2003. Copies of determinations of the GMC's disciplinary committees may be obtained by post from the GMC's address above. They are not yet available on the GMC's website.

7. *Whitefield v. GMC*, Privy Council (Appeal 90/2001), judgment on November 14, 2002.

8. *Crabbie v. GMC*, Privy Council (Appeal 7/2002), judgment given on September 23, 2002.

9. *Krippendorf v. GMC*, Privy Council (Appeal 43/1999), judgment on November 24, 2000.

10. *Walker v. GMC*, Privy Council (Appeal 94/2001), judgment given on November 5, 2002.

11. *Stefan v. GMC*, Privy Council (Appeal 16/1998), judgment given on March 8, 1999.

12. *Selvanathan v. GMC*, Privy Council (Appeal 21/2000), judgment given on October 11, 2000.

13. *Gupta v. GMC*, Privy Council (Appeal 44/2001), judgment given on December 21, 2001. The lawyer for Dr. Gupta who led in this case was Cherie Blair, Q.C., the wife of Tony Blair, who was Prime Minister at the time.

14. "Harold Shipman's Clinical Practice: a Clinical Audit Commissioned by the Chief Medical Officer," Department of Health, London (Dec. 2000). This may be downloaded free of charge from www.doh.gov.uk/hshipmanpractice/shipman.pdf.

15. Medical Act 1983 (Amendment) Order 2000 (SI 2000/2052).

16. S. Whale, *Developments in the European Legal Orders: Implications for the Medical Profession*, 70 Medico-Legal Journal 80-86 (2002).

17. *Bijl v. GMC*, Privy Council (Appeal 78/2000), judgment given on October 2, 2001.

18. *Hossain v. GMC*, Privy Council (Appeal 74/2002), judgment given on January 22, 2003.

19. *Ghosh v. GMC*, Privy Council (Appeal 69/2000), judgment given on June 18, 2001.

20. *R. v. General Medical Council, exp. Nicolaides* [2001] Lloyds L.R. Med. 525 s24.

21. *Borges v. GMC*, Privy Council (Appeal 71/2000), judgment given on September 10, 2001.

22. *Borges v. Irish Medical Council*, listed in the High Court of Ireland on December 12, 2002.

23. Tip: do not put 'www' in the address, or you will be connected to the homepage of the Illinois Alaskan Malamute Rescue Association!

APPENDIX 73-1   **Registration and Disciplinary Authorities in the EU**

Austria	Vienna	Österreichische Ärtzekammer www.aek.or.at
Belgium	Brussels	Ordre des Médecins Ministère de la Santé Publique et de l'Environnement www.health.fgov.be and www.socialsecurity.fgov.be
Denmark	Copenhagen	Danish Board of Health www.sst.dk and www.sum.dk
Finland	Helsinki	National Board of Medico-Legal Affairs www.fimnet.fi
France	Paris	Conseil National de l'Ordre des Médecins www.conseil-national.medicin.fr
Germany	Cologne	Bundesärtzekammer www.bundesaertzekammer.de
Greece	Athens	Ministry of Health, Welfare, and Social Security www.ypyp.gr
Ireland	Dublin	Medical Council of Ireland www.rcsi.ie
Italy	Rome	Ministero della Sanità www.sanita.it
Luxembourg	Luxembourg	Ministère de la Santé www.santel.lu
Netherlands	Rijswijk	Ministry of Health www.minvws.nl
Norway	Oslo	Norwegian Board of Health www.legeforeningen.no
Portugal	Lisbon	Ministério de Saude www.ordemdosmedicos.pt
Spain	Madrid	Consejo General de Colegios de Médicos de España www.msc.es
Sweden	Stockholm	Socialstyrelsen www.slf.se
UK	London	General Medical Council www.gmc-uk.org.uk

Privacy

ROY G. BERAN., M.D., F.R.A.C.P., F.R.C.P., F.R.A.C.G.P., F.A.C.L.M., B.Leg.S., M.H.L.

MEDICAL RECORDS
ACCESS TO PATIENT RECORDS
NATIONAL PRIVACY PRINCIPLES (NPPs)
SPECIAL CIRCUMSTANCES
APPLICATION OF PRIVACY RULES TO CLINICAL PRACTICE
CONCLUSION

The Hippocratic oath, which dates to about 460 B.C., recognizes the importance of the confidential nature of information that passes between doctor and patient.[1] The actual wording, which includes " . . . what I may see or hear in the course of treatment . . . I will keep to myself, holding such things shameful to be spoken about . . . ,"[1] enshrines the privacy that is the cornerstone of the doctor-patient relationship.

This concept of confidentiality, which underpins medical care, has withstood the test of time, with the Royal Australasian College of Physicians (RACP), the accreditation body for specialist physicians within the Australasian region, elaborating on it in its code of ethical conduct. The RACP code includes the following:

. . . The principle of confidentiality is fundamental to the relationship between doctor and patient. Respect for confidentiality, as with consent, gives expression to the patient's autonomy by acknowledging that it is the patient who controls any information relating to his or her medical condition or treatment. Medical information should not be divulged by a physician except with consent of the patient. . . .[2]

The RACP code of conduct also acknowledged that there exist circumstances in which this imposed confidentiality or privacy may, or even must, be overridden. The above quotation continued with:

. . . Difficult ethical questions will arise if the physician believes there is an overriding public interest in disclosing confidential patient information to a third party, such as the Government agency responsible for issuing driver's licences. . . . In other cases, there may be statutory provisions that permit or compel the physician to breach patient confidentiality in these circumstances. In other cases, the physician should decide whether the public interest favouring disclosure is sufficiently great to justify breaching the obligations of confidentiality owed to the patient. . . .[2]

One important additional factor was added by the RACP when it wrote: " . . . In all cases, the patient should be told that the physician intends to make the disclosure and the reason for this decision should be explained. . . ."[2]

This addendum to the concept of confidentiality should be self-evident for the doctor who elects to disclose patient information in contravention of the patient's expressed wishes, but it is not always followed.[3] Some doctors will not advise patients that they have disclosed confidential information in the hope of both fulfilling their duty to society while at the same time preserving the doctor-patient relationship.[3] Obviously this approach brings into question the foundation of trust that should provide the basis for the doctor-patient relationship. It highlights the need to review and appraise the fundamental legal medicine issue of privacy in which honesty should still constitute an integral component.

Josefowicz[4] reviewed the history of professional privilege for doctors, in common law, which translates to the concepts of privacy and confidentiality as delineated since the Hippocratic Oath. He noted that such privilege was not part of old English common law and, as such, confidence passing between doctor and patient stood " . . . upon no better legal footing than others. . . ."[4]

Until recently, access to medical records was governed by the doctor rather than the patient.[5,6] This, at least in the Australian context, changed when the amendments to the Privacy Act (Cth) 1988, namely the Privacy Amendment (Private Sector) Act Cth 2000, came into force on December 21, 2001.

It is over one year since the amendments became law and the result has been a 300% increase in calls to the Commonwealth Privacy Commissioner,[7] with access to medical records being the main complaint from patients.[7] The actual workload of the Privacy Commission was anticipated to double after the amendment became law but in fact has quadrupled with a budget overspend of almost one million Australian dollars (equivalent to approximately $U.S. 500,000).[7] To allay doctor concerns, the Privacy Commission sent out pamphlets to local doctors, but this has only fueled antipathy and has caused quite an angry response from recipients.[8]

What follows will be a review of the concepts of privacy and confidentiality on a wider scale plus an examination of changes to privacy in the Australian context. Following a presentation at the 14th World Congress for Medical Law in Maastricht, The Netherlands, in August 2002, it is clear that the Australian situation is not unique and is mirrored in other jurisdictions, such as Canada,[9] thereby reinforcing the concept of a shrinking world stage and greater global relevance of local experience.

MEDICAL RECORDS

Australia was not alone in its perception that medical records were the property of the doctor who created them.[5,10,11] Some countries actually stipulate that the retention of medical records be restricted to a finite period (e.g., 10 years in The Netherlands) so as to protect against material being retained beyond its time frame of relevance.[11]

Preparation of medical records serves vital functions in patient care, namely: database for the individual patient; mapping out the patient's medical history; source data should there be a change of doctor or need to audit patient care; and documentary evidence of what was done or not done with the patient.[10] As stated by McQuoid-Mason:[10]

. . . good medical records are not only indispensable on medical grounds, but are also desirable on legal grounds if a patient's treatment becomes the subject of litigation . . . well kept records give the impression of good medical care, badly kept medical records create the opposite impression . . .[10] (at 500).

While it is generally accepted that information obtained for the development of medical records may be sensitive and will be maintained in confidence, there are definitive areas in which the medical practitioner will have a duty to breach rules of privacy. These include: court order to disclose; statutory provision for disclosure; an overriding legal, moral, or social duty; and in concert with a patient's implied or expressed consent.[10]

As already established by Jozefowicz,[4] there is no absolute privilege in the doctor-patient relationship in the common law jurisdictions. This is in contrast to the civil law doctrine as exists in France where a doctor called to court to give evidence is expected to refuse, " . . . stating that to do so would be to commit a breach of professional confidence. . . ."[12] Even in this jurisdiction there is dispensation " . . . as in the case of cruelty to a minor. . . ."[12] Evidence obtained in France, which has violated professional confidence, is deemed inadmissible.[12]

Greece is also part of the European Union, and Article 371 of the Greek Penal Code provides for:

. . . doctors . . . in whom due to his job or status, patients . . . confide, are punishable on conviction by fine or by imprisonment for up to a year in case of disclosure of what has been learned in the course of professional practice. Similarly, any person who keeps documents or notes after the death of anyone of the aforementioned professionals, is liable to a fine or imprisonment for up to a year on conviction of disclosure . . .[13] (at 452-453).

Again there are grounds for sanctioned disclosure, such as " . . . the preservation of an essential public interest, and the confidential information could not be preserved otherwise . . ."[13] (at 453).

With the development of information technology, patient records are also being developed in electronic format for computer storage and manipulation. The application of modern computer technology has made transfer of data and access to confidential patient information easier.[11] This has led to the expectation that electronic filing of sensitive data will be protected by privacy-enhancing technology complemented by access authorization methods.[11]

As was stated earlier, the actual records remain the property of the doctor, and this has been enshrined in some patients' rights acts.[14] There is cogent argument that this gives the doctor the right to refuse patients access to more sensitive sections of medical records, such as the insight into some of the decision-making processes or psychodynamic theories which underpin final diagnosis and treatment.[14] Such debate, especially in the domain of psychotherapy, can be quite controversial and may require the maintenance of edited records that fail to include all relevant facts and that could, of itself, pose a risk to optimal care, should another doctor later rely on the contents of the records as a basis for future decision-making.

ACCESS TO PATIENT RECORDS

Application of the Privacy Amendment (Private Sector) Act Cth 2000 effectively changed the Australian access to medical records from December 21, 2001. The provisions of the Act rest on the ten National Privacy Principles (NPPs), which include consideration of: data collection; disclosure; quality; security; openness; access and accuracy; identifiers; anonymity; data flow; and sensitivity.[15-18] These ten principles have universal relevance, but it was almost a year after the amendments came into force that doctors received packages to explain their obligations.

The preamble from the Federal Privacy Commission (FPC) encapsulated the ethos of the protection of medical records[15] (at 4):

When deciding how best to protect a person's health information, health service providers may need to consider:
— Who should be allowed to see hospital medical records, records kept in a pharmacy, or computerized records in a medical practice?

— When and how is it appropriate for one health service to transfer information to another?

— What safeguards must apply when information is used for health research?

— Is the person's consent needed for handling health information in each situation? . . .[15]

While the above is from an Australian publication,[15] it holds universal relevance to the management of sensitive medical records. The first question acknowledges that the issues are equally relevant to hospital (public) records, pharmacy data (potentially either public—as in the case of a hospital pharmacy—or private sector), and private clinicians.

The FPC went to lengths to define a health service by the activities conducted rather than the title of those undertaking those activities. These include " . . . assessing, recording, maintaining or improving a person's health; or diagnosing or treating a person's illness or disability; or dispensing a prescription drug or medicinal preparation by a pharmacist . . ."[15] (at 5). To ensure unambiguous interpretation, there was also a proposed list of health services covered, which included " . . . private hospitals and day surgeries, medical practitioners, pharmacists, and allied health professionals, as well as complementary therapists, gyms, weight loss clinics . . ."[15] (at 5).

In conclusion, " . . . all private sector health service providers that hold health information . . ."[15] (at 5) were included by the Act and hence any of their data would have mandated access in accordance with the Act, thereby bringing the private sector into line with the public domain as is provided by various freedom of information laws. Access to these records is no longer dictated by the doctor but is enforceable by the patient unless the doctor can substantiate that such access would " . . . pose a serious risk to a person's life or health . . ."[15] (at 10). Other grounds for refusing such access might be that the records contain sensitive information relating to others and hence the access would violate the privacy of a third party; the request for access is either frivolous or vexatious; or denying access is dictated by law (such as being prejudicial to an ongoing investigation of possible unlawful activity).[17,18] Access is determined by the NPP No. 6.

NPP6 has provided for individuals to have a general right of access to their own health records with the option of correcting them if an inaccuracy is identified or if they are incomplete or out of date. The obligation under the Act is for the health care provider to take all reasonable measures to so amend the information[15] (at 10).

The *Handbook*[18] (at 6) has stipulated that in most circumstances the right to access will be satisfied " . . . by way of an accurate and up to date summary containing all relevant material. . . ."[18] If the patient requests alterations to the records, the doctor should note the " . . . details of the request on the medical record and indicate whether they agree that the request for alteration or correction is appropriate . . ."[18] (at 6).

Good clinical practice would suggest that patient access be provided in a controlled environment in which either the doctor, or a substitute, is present to note and address any areas of concern. While there cannot be an access fee, there may be charges generated to retrieve archived files, cover costs of copying, and, most importantly, cover the costs of salaries involved both in the time taken to provide the material and the supervision of the actual review process.[16-18] These costs should not be excessive and should make allowance for the patient's financial circumstances but at the same time should not result in a financial burden on the doctor.[16-18] Patients should have prior notification of possible costs and be advised of possible alternative arrangements where appropriate.[17]

NATIONAL PRIVACY PRINCIPLES (NPPs)

Recognizing that this review of privacy has been taken from the Australian context, as stated earlier, its dictates and application have global relevance. As such it is appropriate to examine at least one jurisdiction, such as Australia, in depth to allow sufficient consideration to contemplate wider application.

The provisions of the Privacy Amendment (Private Sector) Act Cth 2000 are based on the ten NPPs. It is therefore appropriate to examine these NPPs in some depth before further exploring the legal medical questions of privacy and its relevance to patient care. NPP 1 and 10 relate to the collection of sensitive information.[15-18] There is an implied burden upon the health care provider to ensure that the patient is aware of: what information is being collected; why it is collected; who will be able to access it; how it will be used; where appropriate, the statutory obligations upon disclosure (as with infective diseases); proposed disclosure to third parties; potential for the patient to have access to it; the consequences of not giving full information to the doctor; the potential for computerized storage; where collected in the name of a third party (such as a group practice or health facility), the nature of same and scope of access; and that information collected is strictly for the purpose defined and collected in a lawful, fair, and not unreasonably intrusive manner[18] (at 4). Once the patient understands these criteria, then there exists empowerment to decide to give the information and the provision of it would, under normal circumstances, be deemed to constitute informed consent.[15-18]

Where data are to be collected from third parties, such as other professionals or health care providers, the patient should be made aware of this and consent to it. Similarly, where the information is to be provided to others, patient consent should also be sought.

Use and disclosure of information is the purvey of NPP2.[15-18] This covers both the internal use of information gathered within the practice, and disclosure of same to others. It is accepted that the information collected will only be used for the reasons for which it was collected.[15-18] Deviating from this will require seeking further approval from the patient[18] (at 8).

Disclosure to others has been the subject of much of the preceding material and is the essence of medical privacy. As a blanket statement, patient consent is required for disclosure to a third party. Exceptions exist where:

. . . the medical practitioner reasonably believes the use or disclosure is necessary to lessen or prevent a serious and imminent threat to an individual's life, health or safety, or a serious threat to public health or public safety . . .[18] (at 8).

Other exceptions include: mandated disclosure by law (e.g., infectious diseases or child abuse or subpoena or court order); suspicion of unlawful activity (e.g., social security fraud); incompetent patient where others need to know for compassionate reasons or enhanced patient care; and research approved by a properly constituted Human Research Ethics Committee[18] (at 8).

There are situations where a doctor retires, sells a practice, or there is a new doctor entering what was a sole therapist practice; patients should, where practicable, be advised of such changed circumstances as this will have direct consequences upon who has access to collected information.

Data quality and security constitute NPP3 and NPP4 respectively. It has already been established that the doctor should make all reasonable efforts to ensure that active patient files are up to date, accurate, and complete.[15] Similarly, there should be a commitment to try to protect and secure from loss, misuse, or unauthorized access the information collected. There is an issue of destroying information no longer required.[15-18] As already mentioned, some jurisdictions have stipulated periods after which records should be destroyed.

NPP5 addresses "openness", which means that patients should be aware of how the doctor intends to handle the information gathered.[15-18] Patients have a right to see a policy statement prepared by the doctor/practice that outlines how that practice addresses its obligations to comply with the Act.

Access and correction (NPP6) have been the focus of earlier material and NPP7 examines identifiers used within the practice. There are strict limitations as to where and how Commonwealth Government identifiers (such as Medicare or Veteran's Affairs numbers) may be used or disclosed.[15] Under no circumstances can they be the sole basis for practice patient identification.

Anonymity is the topic of NPP8, which the FPC has summarized to mean " . . . Where lawful and practicable, individuals must be given the option to use health services without identifying themselves . . ."[15] (at 11).

The AMA recognized that this may not always be feasible and wrote, " . . . In the medical context this is not likely to be practicable or possible for Medicare and insurance rebate purposes. It could also be dangerous to the patient's health . . ."[17] (at 11).

The final NPP, namely 9, relates to transborder data flows and requires transfer of information beyond Australian territory to occur only where similar laws (or schemes) protect patient privacy or with patient consent.[15-18]

The *Privacy Resource Handbook*[16] sets out the full detail of the NPPs as well as offering a summary. Like the information prepared by the FPC,[15] the AMA[16,17] offers advice regarding the complaints process. Whereas the FPC, under the rubric of complaints[15] (at 12), invites direct complaints regarding perceived breaches of the NPPs to be directed to the FPC, the AMA first advised mediation. It wrote[16] (at 37): " . . . Patients should feel free to discuss any concerns, questions or complaints about any issues related to the privacy of their personal information with their doctor. If a patient is dissatisfied the Federal Privacy Commissioner . . . handles complaints. . . ."

While this difference may be deemed trivial, the private practitioner, who is already threatened by the impression of bureaucratic intrusion into the doctor-patient relationship, is further alienated by the FPC's failure to first advise patients to try to settle any disagreement regarding the NPPs with the doctor concerned. As was established above, there has been an explosion of work by the office of the FPC, which may be deemed to have been somewhat self-generated by an approach that has ignored the simple remedy of direct negotiation between doctor and patient.

SPECIAL CIRCUMSTANCES

There are circumstances in which normal privacy considerations take on additional dimensions. One such area is the domain of genetic information, where there needs to be established a legal protocol as to: who owns the information and right to determine to whom it is divulged; protection of same regarding possible physical and emotional damage to others; restriction of transfer of information to the stated objectives; and the right to release information important for public safety.[19]

Further controversy arises with the issue of the right to refuse to be given one's own genetic information, thereby protecting one's own privacy, even from information about oneself.[20]

Countries such as Germany, Austria, Switzerland, Sweden, and some Australian states (such as Victoria) have given donor offspring the legal right to know the identity of the gamete donor.[20] In the United States and Spain, the law anticipates that the anonymity of the donor can be abolished when the essential interests of the offspring are jeopardized.[20] It has been recognized that while some patients demand the right to know, others want to preserve their right not to know, and that too must be accommodated.[21]

Another area of concern relates to prisoners and detainees. In the United Kingdom, police surgeons were expected to provide the clinical records irrespective of informed consent from detainees, a subject of Parliamentary concern.[22] The role of the forensic medical examiners (FMEs) is twofold, namely, the collection of forensic evidence and provision of medical care, which may have conflicting concerns.[22] The Criminal Investigation and Protection Act 1996 did address some of these concerns with the Home Office Minister, recognizing that the FME was not part of the "investigating team."[22] There emerged a consent form to bridge the gap between conflicting obligations, but this situation highlights the need for doctors to be " . . . vigilant at all times to protect the best interests of patient care"[22] (at 357).

Clinical research provides yet another fertile ground for controversy with regards to consideration of privacy.[23,24] Good clinical practice,[25] which recognizes a raft of national and international codes of conduct,[26] requires the research to respect the patient's privacy while at the same time advising that external auditors and government agents may access records to confirm source data.[25,26] This necessitates obtaining informed consent prior to inclusion in any study.[24]

An area that may have been overlooked when considering the issue of privacy is the question of managed care. This has the capacity to directly impinge upon the physician-patient relationship, because the U.S. Medicare system deprives patients over the age of 65 years of autonomy and privacy by refusing them the right of others, with private insurance, to contact privately with a physician.[27] Even in Australia, the universal insurance process, also known as Medicare, means that the government knows the date and type of each consultation with a doctor for a rebatable incident and the Pharmaceutical Benefits Scheme (the government-sponsored pharmaceutical formulary) documents all patient therapy, placing this on the public record. The United States system of Medicare Part B aimed to decrease the reimbursement process for seniors and hence Congress also required physicians to submit claims for their patients, thereby creating a similar breach of confidentiality with diagnosis and treatment becoming part of the public record.[27]

APPLICATION OF PRIVACY RULES TO CLINICAL PRACTICE

Within the Australian context a survey was conducted to examine the impact that the new Act had on the delivery of health care and to ascertain what was required after the Act became law. This was conducted approximately 6 months after the Act was enforceable but before some of the above aids to compliance became available.[28,29]

Twenty-one agencies were canvassed and there were responses from only 10, of which neither the FPC nor the Federal Australian Medical Association (AMA) offered useful material. It was later discovered that the AMA structure in Australia meant that the initial approach went to the New South Wales state branch and it was only some time later, following fortuitous contact rather than internal referral, that the Federal AMA became involved. Medical Defence Organizations (MDOs), indemnity insurers, were by far the most prompt and helpful in the advice proffered, thereby suggesting that they should represent the first port of call should there be an area of confusion. The Federal AMA, once it was involved, was likewise of considerable assistance, which suggests that the national medical associations may also be an important reference point to clarify issues of concern when addressing privacy.[9,28] Government agencies were tardy in their responses as were other professional bodies, most of whom appeared to want to deflect responsibility rather than enhance the sharing of information.

Review of the literature, most of which came from the free medical broadsheets in Australia, indicated that application of the legal dictates for privacy identified " . . . many grey areas and there's no doubt the legislation places an increased burden on our doctors. . . ."[29] Parnell wrote that compliance with the Act was " . . . a bit like squeezing a square peg into a round hole. . . ."[29] She described the legislation as " . . . an overarching piece of legislation and not surprisingly [it] doesn't mesh at all well with usual medical practice. . . ."[29]

The Privacy Act was not restricted to the medical profession and a survey of business showed lack of preparedness even in large corporations.[9] That being the case, it would seem reasonable to assume that doctors, especially those in private practice, would be even less equipped to satisfy the dictates of the law. Burdon wrote:

. . . The legislation seeks to address global concerns about security of personal information in the wake of the information technology boom. For health service providers, it goes beyond the existing culture of medical confidentiality by giving privacy safeguards the force of law, encouraging greater openness between providers and their patients and, for the first time, allowing patients access to information held about them. . . .[30]

Since the above survey was conducted, there have been competing laws in Australia regarding privacy and the FPC has acknowledged the potential for "legislature inconsistencies between State and Commonwealth Government privacy legislation. . . ."[31] The FPC has been quoted as raising concerns about the potential confusion as to how doctors should handle patient records, which in turn may threaten the planned national records system, Health Connect.[31] There is little reason to believe that the situation is less confusing in other jurisdictions.

does not negate potential statutory obligation to report those potential drivers who pose risk to the community. At the time of going to press, only one Australian state has mandatory reporting of patients to driving authorities.[10] In Canada, half of the provinces (Ontario, Manitoba, Newfoundland, New Brunswick, and Prince Edward Island) have mandatory reporting by doctors, and McLachlan has described significant negative consequences of this on the doctor-patient relationship.[11] Nevertheless, the doctor has the responsibility to report those patients who pose a risk and who may not comply with their obligations to follow medical advice or notify the authorities themselves.[12,13]

Thus it is clear that the legal requirements of the licensing process have the capacity to directly influence the health care of patients. All three participants—the licensing authority, the driver and the health carer—have prescribed duties that need to be understood and satisfied for the process to function properly. It is imperative to understand that it is the driver who is most likely to act in an unlawful manner to protect his or her license to drive and may bring pressure upon the health carer to also act outside of the defined parameters within any given jurisdiction. Such pressure needs to be withstood, but if the imposition of the rules is deemed unconscionable, the doctor should also voice objection as an advocate for patient rights.

WHICH STANDARDS SHOULD APPLY

It is important to determine the purpose of the license to drive, namely, whether the prospective driver wants to drive for private or commercial reasons. This will be determined by the type of vehicle to be driven and the reason for driving.

So-called heavy vehicles, such as any two-axle rigid vehicle weighing more than 8 tonnes, any rigid vehicle with three or more axles weighing 8 tonnes, prime mover plus single semitrailer or rigid vehicle plus trailer in excess of 9 tonnes and any unladen converter dolly, or any heavy combination vehicle with more that one trailer, will be automatically deemed to require the application of commercial standards[7] (at 12).

Private use guidelines will apply for lighter vehicles, such as motorcycles, cars (defined as less than 4.5 tonnes and seating no more than 12 adults, including the driver), and light rigid vehicles (between 4.5 and 8 tonnes, seating 12-plus adults, weighing no more than 9 tonnes with trailer), if used for private purposes only[7] (at 12). Where the same vehicle will be used to carry public passengers for hire or reward or to carry bulk dangerous goods, then the appropriate standard will dictate commercial criteria.

Some specific extra considerations may apply for disabled drivers, aged drivers or drivers who have conditional licenses. Conditions may specify: periodic medical evaluation; limitations on the distances to be driven; the time of day during which the driver can drive; the location in which driving is permitted (e.g., within a set distance from

home or only to and from employment); or the clear display of an insignia, such as a colored letter "P," to designate that the licensed driver holds a provisional driver's license which of itself imposes well-publicized restrictions such as a reduced allowable maximum speed at which the driver can travel.

As has already been determined, the granting of a license to drive requires both appropriate driving skills and adequate health criteria. This may require the driving authority to reconfirm driving proficiency for special groups, such as the aged, who may have to be reexamined at specified intervals to ensure that subclinical dementia, visual loss or frailty has not impeded their capacity to drive. There is a need for the licensing authority, or even the legislature, to also stipulate such additional considerations as: predetermined maximum speeds for certain classes of vehicles; defined upper limits of alcohol consumption, which may require a medical attendant to take samples for laboratory testing; and modification of the parameters for particular environmental circumstances (such as reduced speeds at times of fog or hampered visibility).

The licensing authority may require demonstrated greater driver proficiency for commercial drivers (such as taxi drivers) and additional competence skills for heavy vehicle drivers. The authority involved in the licensing process, as well as the health professional and driver, all have a defined duty of care, which impacts on the standards to be applied.[14] This may translate into the need to maintain log books regarding driving experience and duration or to validate that the vehicle being driven, for either private or commercial reasons, has satisfied a stipulated standard of roadworthiness as has been designated by the relevant road traffic authority.

CONFIDENTIALITY

With specific focus upon legal medicine, it must be realized that the imposition upon the health professional to report drivers who may fail to comply with health standards has a direct negative impact on the doctor-patient relationship.[11,13,15-18] Kottow[18] acknowledged that if it is anticipated that a doctor would violate the doctor-patient confidence, then patients will be dishonest with that doctor or alternatively may not consult that doctor to avoid imposition of restrictions. This translates into lack of trust and suboptimal medical treatment with consequent greater risk to society.[19]

Mandatory reporting of patients has been codified in many jurisdictions such as Canada,[11] Australia,[10] and also some states of the United States[20] (including California, Delaware, Nevada, New Jersey, Oregon, and Pennsylvania). This creates a conflict both for the patient and the doctor.[11,21] The code of ethics promulgated by the Royal Australasian College of Physicians (the governing body of consultant specialist physicians in Australia) includes the following quotation:

Medical information should not be divulged by a physician except with the consent of the patient.

Difficult ethical questions will arise if the physician believes there is an overriding public interest in disclosing confidential patient information to a third party, such as a Government agency, responsible for issuing driver's licences. . . . In some cases, there may be statutory provisions that permit or compel the physician to breach confidentiality in these circumstances. In other cases, the physician should decide whether the public interest favouring disclosure is sufficiently great to justify breaching the obligation of confidentiality owed to the patient. In all cases, the patient should be told that the physician intends to make the disclosure and the reason for this decision should be explained. . . .[22]

Recognizing the impact that violation of the doctor-patient confidence may have on future patient care, not all physicians are as open and honest with their patients and may elect to conceal the breach of confidentiality.[12,13,21]

A serious consideration in deciding to infringe patient privacy is the possibility of subsequent litigation by the patient for failure of duty of care. Within the Australian context, and presumably elsewhere, legislation has anticipated this possibility and has been enacted to indemnify against action for honest reporting.[23] The problem arises where no such protection is afforded the health professional,[24] as is the case in the Northern Territory legislation. This leaves the doctor vulnerable for doing what is expected as a duty to society.

As with all legal medical issues that raise concerns for the treating physician, it is strongly advised that the health professional maintains complete and unambiguous contemporaneous medical records which document what action was taken, when and why. Where such action is in contradiction to the patient's expressed or implied wishes, the health professional must be aware of the patient's right to access their records under various freedom of information laws.[25]

There is a potential for health care professionals to be too restrictive or to be unsympathetic or even belligerent toward an individual patient and hence, there must be the right to appeal a doctor's recommendation to impose a restriction or refuse to endorse an application. Similar right of appeal must be permissible against decisions from the licensing authority so as to ensure that justice is best served. This necessitates the doctor being able to substantiate any action taken, which further emphasizes the need for comprehensive contemporaneous patient records. Similarly, the driving authority must be able to confirm adherence to set criteria that predetermine set decision-making processes.

MEDICAL CONDITIONS

Each medical condition will carry with it a unique set of circumstances, some of which may impact on the capacity to drive. Some of these have already been alluded to and space obviates the capacity to discuss each condition in depth.

There is unequivocal evidence that alcohol can negatively impact on driving[7] (at 31), with a blood alcohol concentration (BAC) of 0.05 doubling the risk of fatality when compared to the driver devoid of alcohol. This risk climbs to 7 times the risk for a BAC of 0.10 and 25 times the risk for a BAC of 0.15.[7] There may well be pharmacokinetic or pharmacodynamic enhancement of such negative effect when combined with "recreational" drugs such as marijuana[7] (at 32).

Even day-only surgery must be viewed as a potential hazard for driving,[26] and the doctor has a duty of care to ensure that the patient is driven home rather than drives home following such treatment. Cardiovascular diseases pose an obvious risk to drivers, but evidence indicates that the majority of people who have a severe or even fatal coronary attack while driving have sufficient warning to slow down or stop before losing consciousness[7] (at 38).

Figures quoted reveal that collapse from ischemic heart disease (fatal or not) accounts for approximately 15% of sudden illness crashes or about 1 in 1000 reportable crashes[7] (at 38). Within the proposed new guidelines, event-free periods have been stipulated for drivers to resume driving, from as little as 2 weeks for private drivers following acute myocardial infarct (3 months for commercial drivers) and pacemaker insertion (1 month for commercial drivers) to 6 months for private drivers following cardiac arrest (cardiac arrest excludes subsequent commercial driving)[7] (at 39). Strict criteria are defined in the larger document designed to assist the doctor in his or her deliberations for the patient. Such documents need to be prepared and distributed in all jurisdictions where doctors are expected to recommend driving restrictions as a consequence of patients' health standards.

Diabetes has often been used as the control illness in research investigating epilepsy because of its unpredictable nature, defined provocative factors, and potential effects on consciousness.[4] As with all impositions of restrictions to quality of life, there must be an established basis to justify such limitations.[27] With regard to epilepsy, the relative casualty crash risk of drivers with epilepsy compared with other drivers has varied from 1.0 to 1.95,[1,4,28] with the exception of a single study quoting a figure of up to 7.[29] The literature suggests that approximately 11% of crashes that involve drivers with epilepsy are seizure-related[1] with reported prevalence of epilepsy-related crashes.[3,10,30-33] Despite this low rate of cause and effect, Black and Lai[10] found epilepsy to be the single most common medical condition to be reported to the authorities. What this reflects is the influence that emotional connotations and expectations have on the reality of what is experienced.

This should be seen in contrast with sleep disorders, which have a much greater impact on road traffic accidents[34-38] yet are often ignored by driving authorities. The new Australian guidelines have cast much greater attention on sleep disorders[7] (at 81-85) and recognize the greater risk of accident and hence the need to impose restrictions for obstructive sleep apnea and narcolepsy in particular.

The above examples should not be seen as any attempt to be exhaustive. They do reflect the need to appraise each specific illness on its unique merits as established in the scientific literature without regard to the confounding emotive factors that have resulted in past restrictions. As evidenced by the proposed new Australian guidelines,[7] there has emerged an appreciation of the need to be more concise in the affording of specific restrictions to different illnesses which in turn pose different risks to drivers and other road users. It is imperative that conditions for frequent drivers, such as commercial drivers, reflect their enhanced capacity to inflict greater damage.[7]

CONSEQUENCES OF NOT BEING ABLE TO DRIVE

Much has been written about the lack of trust and fractured doctor-patient relationship that emerges consequent to the doctor reporting the patient[12,14,17-22] in contravention to the patient's wishes. This has the capacity to generate great angst and guilt for the doctor, who has a responsibility to both the patient and to society to satisfy a duty of care.

A recent Australian study focusing particularly on the aged has shown that all is not as bleak as the doctor and the patient may have envisaged.[39] This study showed that elderly people who were forced to surrender their driver's licenses did not automatically also relinquish their independence. It was found that they established alternative means of mobility using taxis, public transport such as buses, or enlisted friends who could still drive to offer a lift to or from outings. The study, conducted in the Australian city of Brisbane, found that a considerable proportion of interviewed elderly subjects had voluntarily surrendered their driver's license due to failing vision, an accident, or a frightening event. The respondents acknowledged that this necessitated a period of adjustment after which they evoked strategies to reinstate their independence and capacity to " . . . carry out their regular daily activities without discomfort. . . ."[39]

The findings of this type of study should go some way to appease the conscience of health professionals who have been forced to deny their patients the capacity to drive due to their health standards. Conversely, those same doctors who are concerned about refusing their patients the right to drive should reflect upon the number of innocent others whom they have protected by their actions, let alone the lives of their patients, which they have saved.

CONCLUSION

It is becoming increasingly clear that "Drivers and the Law" is an area in which doctors will be asked to practice legal medicine irrespective of any specific training that they have in the field.

Although this chapter has relied heavily on Australian standards and proposed guidelines, every effort has been made to ensure the content has global relevance. It has established that mandatory reporting of patients to driving authorities is also in force in the United States and, as in South Australia (and the Northern Territory in Australia), has the capacity to impact negatively on the doctor-patient relationship. There is acknowledgment that the doctor has a duty of care both to the patient as well as to society as a whole. Where such a patient poses an unacceptable risk to society, should they drive, then the doctor has an obligation to protect both the patient and society from that potential hazard and must ensure that the patient is refused a license to drive.

As a concluding sobering remark, there is nothing that the doctor can do if the patient continues to drive, even after refusal of a license, other than to report the patient as recalcitrant to the driving authorities. At the same time, patients must recognize that refusal to comply with the driving restrictions may be construed as reckless indifference to human life, which carries with it its own impositions should an unfortunate accident ensue with fatal consequences.[13]

ENDNOTES

1. J.A. Waller, *Chronic Medical Conditions and Traffic Safety*, 273 N. Engl. J. Med. 1413-1420 (1965).
2. S.P. Baker & W.U. Spitz, *An Evaluation of the Hazard Created by Natural Death at the Wheel*, 283 N. Engl. J. Med. 405-409 (1970).
3. P.J.M. Van der Lugt, *Traffic Accidents Caused by Epilepsy*, 16 Epilepsia 747-751 (1975).
4. P. Hansotia & S.K. Broste, *The Effect of Epilepsy or Diabetes Mellitus on the Risk of Automobile Accidents*, 324 N. Engl. J. Med. 22-26 (1991).
5. M. Naughton & R. Pierce, *Sleep Apnoea's Contribution to the Road Toll*, 21 Aust. N.Z. J. Med. 833-834 (1991).
6. T.R. Miller & L.J. Blincoe, *Incidence and Cost of Alcohol-Involved Crashes in the United States*, 26 Accid. Anal. Prev. 583-591 (1994).
7. Austroads, *Assessing Fitness to Drive—For Commercial and Private Vehicle Drivers—Medical Standards for Licensing and Clinical Management Guidelines—A Resource for Health Professionals in Australia—Approved by the Australian Transport Council and Endorsed by All Australian Licensing Authorities*, Draft 3 (Sydney: Austroads, Sept. 2002).
8. Austroads, *Assessing Fitness to Drive: Guidelines and Standards for Health Professionals in Australia* (Sydney: Austroads, 2001).
9. Nation Road Transport Commission (NRTC), *Medical Examinations for Commercial Vehicles Drivers* (Melbourne: NRTC, 1997).
10. A.B. Black & N.Y. Lai, *Epilepsy and Driving in South Australia—An Assessment of Compulsory Society Notification*, 16 Med. Law 253-267 (1997).
11. R.S. McLachlan, *Medical Conditions and Driving: Legal Requirements and Approach of Neurologists*, 16 Med. Law 269-275 (1997).
12. R.G. Beran, *Professional Privilege, Driving and Epilepsy, the Doctor's Responsibility*, 26 Epilepsy Res. 4415-4421 (1997).
13. R.G. Beran, *Confidentiality and the Management of Patients Who Fail to Comply with Doctor's Advice Not to Drive: A Survey of Medico-Legal Opinions in Australia*, 6 Seizure 1-10 (1998).
14. R.G. Beran (ed.), *Epilepsy and Driving* (Tel Aviv: Yozmot, 1999).
15. J. King-Furlow & P. Langham *Confidentiality: Medical Ethics and Professional Morality*, 10 Philosophical Papers 9-15 (1981).

16. A.B. Black, *Reporting Patients to Driver-Licensing Authorities*, 170 Med. J. Aust. 395-396 (1999).

17. B. McSherry, *Epilepsy and Confidentiality: Ethical Considerations*, in R.G. Beran (ed.), *Epilepsy: A Question of Ethics*, 39-52 (Tel Aviv: Yozmot, 2002).

18. M.H. Kottow, *Medical Confidentiality: An Intrasigent and Absolute Obligation*, 12(3) J. Med. Ethics 117-122 (1986).

19. J. Ozuna, *To Tell or Not to Tell: Ethical Dilemmas in People with Epilepsy Who Drive*, 5 Clin. Nurs. Pract. in Epilepsy 7-10 (1998).

20. A.K. Finucane, *Legal Aspects of Epilepsy*, 17 Neurol. Clin. 235-243 (1999).

21. R.G. Beran, *The Doctor/Patient Relationship, Confidentiality and Public Responsibility*, 21 Med. Law 617-637 (2002).

22. Royal Australasian College of Physicians (RACP), *Ethics: A Manual for Consultant Physicians*, 16-17 (Sydney: RACP, 1992).

23. Australian Capital Territory, Road Transport (General) Act 1999, s.230 (3); New South Wales, Road Transport (General) Act 1999, s.49 (3) and (4), Road Transport (Driver Licensing) Act 1998, s.20, Road Transport (Driver Licensing) Regulation 1999 r.31; Queensland, Transport Operations (Road Use Management) Act 1995, s.142; Tasmania, Vehicle and Traffic Act 1999, ss.63 (2) and 56; Victoria, Road Safety Act 1986, s.27 (4); Western Australia, Road Traffic Act 1974, s.42 (4) (currently being revised re Road Traffic Amendment Bill 2002 [being drafted]).

24. Northern Territory of Australia, Motor Vehicles Act 1999, s.11. Indemnity is not specifically covered by the Act, thereby permitting action to be taken, yet there is an obligation stipulated for the health professional to report drivers posing a risk to the public or self.

25. In Australia the Privacy Act 1988 was amended in late 2000 to extend its coverage to the private sector and came into effect on December 21, 2001, with the Privacy Amendment (Private Sector) Act (Cth) 2000.

26. J. Lichtor, R. Alessi & B. Lane, *Sleep Tendency as a Measure of Recovery After Drugs Used for Ambulatory Surgery*, 96 Anaesthesiology 878-883 (2002).

27. K.M. MacLeod, *Diabetes and Driving: Towards Equitable, Evidence-Based Decision-Making*, 16 Diab. Med. 282-290 (1999).

28. J. Taylor & D. Chadwick, *Risk of Accidents in Drivers with Epilepsy*, 60 J. Neurol. Neurosurg. Psychiatry 621-627 (1996).

29. S. Ling, *Increased Driving Accident Frequency in Danish Patients with Epilepsy*, 57 Neurology 435-439 (2001).

30. R.S. Fisher, M. Parsonage, M. Beaussart, et al., *Epilepsy and Driving: An International Perspective*, 35 Epilepsia 675-684 (1994).

31. B. Herner, B. Smedby & L. Ysander, *Sudden Illness as a Cause of Motor Vehicle Accidents*, 23 Br. J. Int. Med. 37-41 (1966).

32. K. Millingen, *Epilepsy and Driving*, 13 Proc. Aust. Assoc. Neurol. 67-72 (1976).

33. A. Krumholz, R.S. Fisher, R.P. Lesser & W.A. Hauser, *Driving and Epilepsy: A Review and Reappraisal*, 365 J.A.M.A. 622-626 (1991).

34. J. Teran-Santos, A. Jimenez-Gomez & J. Cordero-Guevara, *The Association Between Sleep Apnoea and the Risk of Traffic Accidents* (Co-operative Group Burgos-Santander [see comments]), 340 N. Engl. J. Med. 847-51 (1999).

35. M.R. Risser, J.C. Ware & F.G. Freeman, *Driving Simulation with EEG Monitoring in Normal and Obstructive Sleep Apnoea Patients*, 23 Sleep 393-398 (2000).

36. C.F. George, A.C. Boudreau & A. Smiley, *Effects of Nasal CPAP on Simulated Driving Performance in Patients with Obstructive Sleep Apnoea*, 52 Thorax 648-653 (1997).

37. C.F. George, *Reduction in Motor Vehicle Collisions Following Treatment of Sleep Apnoea with Nasal CPAP*, 56 Thorax 508-512 (2001).

38. J.F. Masa, M. Rubio & L.J. Findley, *Habitually Sleep Drivers have a High Frequency of Automobile Crashes Associated with Respiratory Disorders During Sleep*, 162 Am. J. Resp. & Critical Care Med. 1407-1412 (2000).

39. L.R. Buys & L. Carpenter, *Cessation of Driving in Later Life May Not Result in Dependence*, 21 Aust. J. Aging 152-154 (2002).

Glossary: Selected Health Care and Legal Terminology

SAL FISCINA, M.D., J.D., F.C.L.M.
JANET B. SEIFERT, J.D.†

abandonment Termination of a physician-patient relationship by the physician without the patient's consent at a time when the patient requires medical attention, without making adequate arrangements for continued care.

abuse of process Use of legal mechanisms in a manner or for a purpose not supported by law. For example, pursuit of litigation based on little or no legal grounds, intended to harass and cause expense to the defendant. Damages may be recovered for expenses or loss incurred by a defendant as a result of abuse of process.

action Legal action, lawsuit.

affidavit Sworn statement for use in legal process.

affirmative defense An answer to a lawsuit that does not deny the alleged conduct or failure but asserts a legal basis to excuse or foreclose liability. Good Samaritan immunity or a statute of limitations defense are examples.

agent A person authorized by another, the principal, to act for or represent the principal. Agency relationships may include authority to exercise personal judgment.

allegation Asserted fact or circumstance that is expected to be proved by legal process.

allocated loss expense (ALE) See *expenses.*

amortized value See *investments.*

appeal A claim to a superior court of error in process or law by a lower court, asking the higher court to correct or reverse a judgment or decision. An appellate (appeals) court has the power to review decisions made in the trial court or a lower appellate court. An appellate court does not make a new determination of facts but examines the law and legal process as applied in the case.

battery Intentional and unauthorized physical contact with a person, without consent. For example, a surgical procedure performed without express or implied consent constitutes battery. Victims of medical battery may obtain compensation for the touching, even if no negligence occurred. A crime of battery may be defined differently.

bona fide Latin, meaning "good faith," that is, without deceit, fraud, simulation, or pretense.

borrowed servant Agent temporarily under the supervision, direction, and control of another. For example, an operating room nurse technically employed by a hospital may be borrowed by a surgeon in the operating room to perform certain tasks.

breach of contract Failure to perform a legal agreement. If a legally enforceable contract is established, performance of agreed promises may be compelled or adequate compensation for failure to perform may be required.

burden of proof Responsibility of proving certain facts required to support a lawsuit. If the burden of proof is not met, the opposing side prevails on that point, even without a defense or response.

capitation Method of payment in which the provider receives a fixed prospective fee for each plan member serviced during a set period, regardless of the amount or type of services rendered to the member. Rates can be adjusted based on demographics or actuarial cost projections. It also refers to the per capita cost of providing a specific menu of health services to a defined population over a set period. Fee-for-service and prepaid medical groups usually receive in advance a negotiated monthly payment from the HMO, regardless of the amount of service rendered by the group.

captain of the ship doctrine A special agency relationship establishing liability for an employee's or agent's acts. This agency relationship imposes what is called *vicarious liability* on the one employing the agent. Initially used as an analogy in malpractice cases, it asserts that the surgeon in the operating room has total authority and full responsibility for the performance of the operating crew and the welfare of the patient. By this doctrine, the surgeon may be vicariously liable for the negligent act of any member of the surgical team. The doctrine is not accepted in every jurisdiction.

case law Legal principles applied to specific factual situations. Case law is drawn from judicial decisions in similar cases in a jurisdiction. Case law is used to make decisions that are based on precedent, the judicial principle that requires that similar cases be treated alike. Assembled case law principles are also called the *common law.*

case management (large case management) Planned approach to manage service or treatment to a member with a serious medical problem. Goal is to contain costs and promote more effective intervention to meet patient needs. Concurrent evaluation of the necessity, appropriateness, and efficiency of services and drugs provided to patients on a case-by-case basis, usually targeted at potentially high-cost cases.

cause Proximate cause. A reasonable connection between an act or failure alleged as negligence and an injury suffered by the plaintiff. In a suit for negligence, the issue of causation usually requires proof that the negligence of the defendant directly resulted in or was a substantial factor in the plaintiff's harm or injury.

cause of action Facts or circumstances that support a legal right to seek corrective action or compensation.

This glossary was taken in part from S. Fiscina & J.B. Seifert, *Legal Check-up for Medical Practice* (Mosby, St Louis 1997). Insurance and managed care terms contributed by James G. Zimmerly, M.D., J.D., M.P.H.
†Deceased.

chargeback Payment by a pharmaceutical manufacturer to a wholesaler covering the difference between an institution's contract price for a drug and the wholesaler's book price.

civil action Legal proceeding by a party asking for correction or compensation, distinguished from a criminal action, which is brought by the state to punish offenses against public order.

civil liability Legal responsibility to compensate for losses or injuries caused by acts or failures to act. Compensation is awarded as monetary damages paid by the defendant to the injured party. In contrast, criminal liability is the legal responsibility imposed by the state for violation of criminal laws. Consequences of criminal acts may include death, imprisonment, fines, and loss of property or privileges. Civil liability is limited to monetary damages; however, a single act may be both a criminal act and a civil wrong, also called a *tort*.

civil rights Enforceable rights of all citizens guaranteed by several amendments to the U.S. Constitution and laws passed recognizing specific liberties or privileges. Violation of another person's civil rights may result in criminal or civil penalties.

claim A demand to pay. A claim is a demand against a physician or hospital. It may or may not be insured under a policy, depending on the coverage afforded and the nature of the offense.

claims frequency The ratio of the number of claims reported in a period, such as a year, to the number of physicians insured—perhaps "per 100 physicians."

claims-made policy See *coverage.*

class Short for classification; a class is a subdivision of a "universe." To lump all insured persons into the same rate grouping would be to overcharge one subgroup (or class) and to undercharge another. In medical malpractice insurance, approximately 100 classes are based mostly on medical specialties. However, an insurer may have only seven rate groups, so each rate group contains several classes.

class action A legal action instituted by one or more persons on behalf of others in a similar situation. Class actions are used if many plaintiffs must prove the same allegations against the same defendant. An example would be litigation over responsibility for a plane crash with hundreds of victims.

clear and convincing evidence A level of persuasion required to support certain noncriminal legal actions. For example, involuntary civil commitment to mental treatment may require clear and convincing evidence of danger to self or others.

clinical indicator Measurable element in the process or outcome of care, the value of which suggests one or more dimensions of quality of care and is theoretically amenable to change by the provider.

closed panel Managed care plan that contracts with physicians on an exclusive basis to provide health services to members. Nonplan physicians are excluded from participation.

code Collection of laws in a jurisdiction or on a specific topic area arranged and indexed by subject, with revisions added to reflect the law currently in force. Each state's Code of Laws, the U.S. Code, and the Internal Revenue Code are examples.

coinsurance The percentage of a covered medical expense that a member must pay after any required deductible. The percentage of the cost of care paid by the patient as part of insurance coverage.

combined loss ratio The sum of (a) the ratio of losses and loss-adjustment expenses incurred to earning premiums and (b) the ratio of all other underwriting expenses incurred to written premiums.

common law See *case law.*

competitive medical plan (CMP) Health care organization that meets specific government criteria for Medicare risk contracting but that is not necessarily an HMO.

complaint Initial document filed by a plaintiff, also called a *pleading,* which begins a civil lawsuit. The complaint is intended to give the defendant notice of facts alleged in the cause of action on which the plaintiff bases a demand for corrective action or compensation.

confidential communication Medical information given to health care providers in the course of diagnosis and treatment of an illness or injury. Providers are entrusted with the duty to keep the information from disclosure to third parties, subject to existing requirements of statute and case law.

consent Agreement to accept the consequences of an action, such as to allow another person to do something or to take part in some activity. Express consent may be oral or written. Implied consent is agreement shown by signs or actions. An example of conduct showing that consent has been given for an injection or blood test is to roll up a sleeve and extend an arm for vein puncture. Taking part indicates consent to the risks of a game, such as hockey. Where no actual consent or refusal is possible (e.g., in the case of an unconscious person in an emergency situation), consent to others' actions to save life or limb is presumed. Consequences of actions taken without consent remain the burden of the individual acting without consent.

consortium Element of damages generally recoverable by one spouse for loss of company, services, and conjugal relations caused by the spouse's injury. Company, participation, counsel, and affection are consortium losses recoverable by other close family members in some jurisdictions.

consultation Request by an attending physician, generally to a specialist, for information, advice, diagnostic services, or therapy that is indicated or necessary for a patient's condition. A duty to consult may arise when diagnosis is uncertain, therapy is ineffective, or the patient requests a consultation. A consultation that is merely informative does not generally result in a relationship and duties between the consultant and the patient. Other consultations, which require that the consultant examine the patient or records or provide diagnostic or treatment services, may establish a duty to the patient separate from the consulting physician's. A referral is distinguished from a consultation because it involves transfer of responsibility for the care of the patient to the specialist. In many consultations the attending physician also retains some ongoing separate responsibility.

contention Earnest and vigorous assertion of legal significance and interpretation of facts or issues in a dispute.

continuous quality improvement Method seeking to prevent problems from occurring, and if they do occur, to determine the underlying causes of the problem and then fix the process, not just the problem.

contract Agreement by two or more parties to exchange obligations. A contract depends on a similar mutual understanding of the terms of the contract and performance promised. A legally enforceable contract means that compensation for promises not kept can be compelled.

contributory negligence Affirmative defense in which a defendant contends that the plaintiff's negligence wholly or substantially caused the injury complained of by the defendant. The effect of plaintiff's negligence on liability or compensation varies among the states, depending on the timing and circumstances of the plaintiff's and the defendant's acts or failures to act.

copayments Predetermined amount of money a member pays for a specific service. A form of cost sharing in which the HMO member makes a nominal payment to the provider at the time of service, typically for office visits and prescription drugs.

cost-effectiveness analysis Method with underlying premises that, for any given level of resources available, the decision-maker wishes to maximize the aggregate health benefits conferred to the population of concern. Alternatively a given health benefit goal may be set, the objective being to minimize the cost of achieving it. The cost-effectiveness ratio is the ratio of costs to health benefits and is expressed, for example, as the cost per year per life saved or the cost per quality-adjusted year per life saved.

cost shifting Process by which insurers raise prices to some customers to cover discounts granted to other customers. Also, the process by which hospitals and other providers shift the costs of treating indigent patients to paying patients.

counterclaim Defendant's complaint against a plaintiff alleging obligation, failure, and damages for which compensation is demanded. For the counterclaim issues, the defendant is seen as having the burden of a plaintiff.

covenant Specific agreement or promise to act or refrain from acting in exchange for similar promises or payments. For example, a covenant not to sue one defendant may exchange relinquishment of that claim for a payment or a promise not to counterclaim. However, a specific covenant would not release all persons alleged to have a role in causing the injury and does not accept the payment as full satisfaction for the injury. A covenant with one defendant therefore does not bar actions against others.

coverage The insurance afforded by the policy and the endorsements or riders attached to it.
- "Claims-made" insures only those claims that are reported during the term of a policy, regardless of when the incident occurred.
- "Occurrence coverage" insures all incidents that occurred during the term of a policy, no matter when they are first reported.

criminal liability Legal consequence imposed by the government for violation of an offense against the public interest in safety and liberty, and is not directed toward compensating the losses of victims. Consequences of criminal acts may include death, imprisonment, fines, and loss of property or privileges.

damages Money receivable through judicial order by a person sustaining harm, impairment, or loss to person or property as the result of the intentional or negligent act of another. Damages may be compensatory, to reimburse a person for economic losses such as lost income and medical expenses. Other damages recoverable include noneconomic losses, such as pain and suffering or mental anguish, or hedonic damages awarded for the loss of life's enjoyment and aesthetic and other pleasures, such as music, athletics, sunsets, or children. Sometimes, token damages are awarded to demonstrate that a legally recognized error has been committed. So-called nominal damages can be awarded even if no actual economic or noneconomic losses are suffered. Punitive damages are those awarded to inflict economic punishment on defendants who have been found to act maliciously or in reckless disregard of others' rights.

decedent A person who has died and whose interests are involved in a legal proceeding.

deductible A set amount that beneficiaries must pay toward covered charges before insurance coverage can begin. Usually renewed annually.

defamation Intentional communication of false personal or business information that injures the reputation or prospects of another. Spoken defamation is slander; written defamation is libel. Truth is a defense to claims of defamation. Publication of true information may nevertheless violate duties of confidentiality or may be invasion of privacy.

deposition Part of pretrial discovery process in which a sworn out-of-court statement is taken. In a deposition, a witness is asked questions and cross-examined. The statement may be admitted into evidence if it is impossible for a witness to attend in person. Deposition testimony also can be used to cross-question a witness at trial.

diagnosis-related group (DRG) Classification system that groups patients according to diagnosis, age, presence of comorbidity or complications, and other relevant data.

disclaimer Statement before or after disputed events that announces one party's stance and commitment regarding legal aspects of facts and circumstances in question (e.g., a statement that no warranties were intended or offered as part of contract terms or that risks of activities were not assumed by a party). Ordinarily a disclaimer of responsibility

for future negligent conduct is not recognized by the law and would be ineffective as a defense.

discovery Pretrial activities in the litigation process to determine the essential questions and issues in dispute and what evidence each side will present at trial. Discovery is intended to narrow trial questions to allow fair presentation of opposing evidence without surprise during trial. Discovery communications and disclosures may facilitate out-of-court settlement.

drug utilization management Systemic effort to determine the most appropriate drug therapy, based on quality of care, outcomes, and cost.

drug utilization review Systemic review of frequency and usage of prescription drugs, typically on a per-member, per-month basis.

due care Level of reasonable and ordinary observation and awareness owed by one person to another in specific relationship or circumstances, such as a physician's duty of due care in attendance of patients. It anticipates and appropriately manages known, expected, or foreseeable events, especially complications of the patient's disease or treatment.

due process Level of fair method required by the U.S. Constitution in execution of governmental activities. Due process in legal proceedings must reflect both fair substance—the activity is appropriate and constitutional—and fair means—method of proceeding that provides parties involved the opportunity to present appropriate advocacy and evidence in any dispute or legal process.

earned premium See *premium.*

Employee Retirement Income Security Act (ERISA) Comprehensive set of statutes, the provisions of which are found in federal labor codes and the Internal Revenue Code and govern nearly every aspect of operation of most employees' medical and pension plans. It was designed by Congress to supersede state laws that relate to employee benefit plans. This preemption continues to be defined.

evidence beyond reasonable doubt A level of persuasion required to support a judgment of criminal responsibility.

exclusive provider organization (EPO) Organizational arrangements consisting of a group of providers who have a contract with a sponsoring group to exclusively deliver plan benefits. The financial risk is borne largely by the payer and the plan members. There is more restrictive provider selection and credentialing process than with PPOs. Like PPOs, benefits are greater if plan providers are used. Unlike PPOs, the benefits are reduced dramatically or eliminated if plan providers are not used.

expenses (insurance company)
- Loss expense
  —Allocated loss expense (ALE): expense allocated to a specific claim (primarily legal costs)
  —Unallocated loss expense (ULE): primarily claim department cost.

expenses incurred The expenses paid in a period, plus the change in expense reserves. Equal to paid expenses less outstanding expense at the beginning of the period plus outstanding expenses at the end of the year.

experience A matching of premiums, losses, and expenses. May or may not include investment earnings, net profit, or both.
- Calendar year experience: combines the premiums earned in a year and the losses incurred in the year.
- Accident year experience: combines the losses that occurred in a year and the premiums earned on policies in effect during that year. Changes over time. See separate definitions of *premium* and *expenses incurred.*

experience rating A method of determining rates for insurance benefits based on a group's claims history.

expert witness Person invited to testify at a hearing or trial to bring special training, knowledge, skill, or experience to the proceeding where matters in legal dispute are beyond the average person's knowledge. Unlike a fact witness, who is compelled to testify because of involvement in the facts and circumstances of the dispute, an expert witness may be asked for an opinion about specific issues in the case. Fact witnesses are percipient witnesses who testify to what they experienced through their senses. Experts educate the court about the scientific, medical, technical, or other specialized circumstances involved in the dispute.

federally qualified HMO Meets strict standards, including financial solvency and scope of coverage.

fee-for-service System of payment under which a fee is charged for each service provided on a retrospective basis, rather than on a prospective, fixed-rate basis.

fiduciary A person in a position of confidence or trust who undertakes a solemn duty to act for the benefit of another who must trust the good intention and performance of the fiduciary. In a fiduciary relationship, virtually all the power reposes in the trusted fiduciary, and vulnerability lies with the beneficiary of the relationship. This disparity of knowledge and power imposes major duties on the fiduciary. Examples of fiduciary relationships are guardian and ward, parent and child, attorney and client, physician and patient, estate trustee and beneficiary, and other financial relationships. This type of relationship requires that the fiduciary never act to the detriment of the trusting party, certainly not for personal gain or profit.

finder of fact In a trial, the jury, or in trials without juries, the judge. Findings of fact generally are not appealable. Appeals courts review findings of law, admissions of evidence, and application or interpretation of appropriate legal principles and laws.

formulary List of drugs for use by a health institution. An open formulary is a list of preferred drugs, but other drugs can be prescribed. A closed formulary requires permission for prescription of nonlisted drugs.

fraud Intentional misdirection, misinformation, or misrepresentation to another person that causes legal injury or loss to that person. Fraud is an intentional wrong, to be contrasted with negligent conduct causing loss. Examples of fraud in medical practice could be to mislead a patient about indicated procedures or therapies; to misstate diagnoses or treatment codes to falsely maximize reimbursement; or to conspire with patients to misstate injuries to obtain undeserved benefits.

free-standing plan Unbundled or separate health care benefits apart from the basic health care plan, usually dental or vision care. Employees are allowed to select or decline the separate benefit. This choice is often referred to as *cafeteria-type benefits.*

frequency See *claims frequency.*

gatekeeper The primary care physician must authorize all medical services, nonemergency hospitalizations, specialty referrals, and diagnostic workups. The insurer may not pay for services not approved by gatekeepers.

good faith Honest intent to avoid taking unconscionable advantage of another, even if technicalities of law might permit it.

Good Samaritan statute Law enacted by state legislatures to encourage physicians and others to stop and assist emergency victims. Good Samaritan laws grant immunity from liability for negligence to a person who responds and administers care to a person in an emergency situation. Statutes vary among the states regarding persons covered, the scene and type of emergency, and nature of conduct for which immunity is granted.

group-model HMO Contracting with multispecialty medical groups to provide services to plan members. Group is paid a set amount per patient to provide a specified scope of services and determines physician compensation. Physicians are not employees of the HMO but are considered a closed panel and are employed by the group practice. Practice may be in facilities owned by the group or HMO. Physicians generally are paid a fixed capitated amount for each individual enrolled in the HMO. Payments also may be based on costs rather than a set fee. Some groups may be allowed to provide service to patients outside the HMO. A closed panel HMO member may use only physician groups contracted with or employed by the HMO.

group practice without walls Network of physicians who have merged into one legal entity but continue to practice independently in their own office locations.

guardian Person appointed by a court to manage the affairs and to protect the interests of a person who is declared incompetent to manage personal affairs. Incompetence may be due to physical or mental status; guardians may be appointed to manage economic or personal matters, including medical treatment choices.

health maintenance organization (HMO) An organized system of care that provides health care services to a defined population for a fixed, prospective per-person fee. Members are not reimbursed for care not provided or authorized by the HMO. Organization that provides for a wide range of comprehensive health care services for a specified group of enrollees for a fixed, periodic prepayment.

health plan A program established or maintained by an employer for the purpose of providing enrollees or their beneficiaries with health care benefits. An entity that furnishes or arranges for health-related services to entitled individuals for a premium.

health plan employer data and information set (HEDIS) A core set of performance measures developed by the National Committee for Quality Assurance that provides a standardized format for reporting managed care entities' utilization review and quality assurance and cost-containment data. HEDIS enables plans and employers to more accurately evaluate and record the trends in health plan performance and use this information in a comparative manner. Performance measures cover: quality, access, patient satisfaction, membership, utilization, finance, and descriptive information on health plan management and activities.

holding A specific conclusion made by a court in a case, which is used to support the court's final judgment, and may be used to persuade later courts on the same point in similar cases.

IBNR Losses incurred but not reported. See *losses.*

immunity Protection of individuals or entities that shields them from liability for certain acts by establishing as an affirmative defense disallowing prosecution or trial of the dispute. Examples include nonprofit hospitals granted charitable immunity, government agencies' complete or limited sovereign or governmental immunity, or immunity for peer review comment and activities.

in loco parentis A Latin phrase for the status of one assigned by law to stand in the place of parents and exercise their legal rights, duties, and responsibilities toward a minor.

incompetence Legal status of dependence on a natural or appointed guardian to make decisions and manage personal and business affairs. Incompetent persons cannot bind themselves by contract, consent to or refuse medical treatment, or be held to assume consequences of choices made. Parents are the natural guardians of children, who are legally incompetent until the age of majority or until emancipated. Legally recognized incompetent adults have appointed guardians. Medical incompetence is the inability of a person to understand and manage personal affairs or to take responsibility for personal choices. Once this status is legally recognized, a guardian is appointed to act in the person's place.

indemnity Obligation to reimburse someone for specified losses under the terms of an agreement that requires payment under specified conditions. Insurance contracts are examples of indemnity agreements or defense.

indemnity benefit Insurance that pays the individual for medical services after the services are performed, usually on a fee-for-service basis.

independent contractor Person who agrees to perform tasks that are completed without direct supervision or control by the party employing the contractor. Ordinarily this arrangement and relationship shield the employer from liability for negligent acts of the independent contractor that occurred during the performance of the contracted work. Independent contractors are legally distinguished from employees, whose performance is supervised, directed, and controlled by the employer and for whose work the employer is vicariously responsible. Depending on the circumstances, a physician may be either an independent contractor or an employee.

independent practice association (IPA) Organized system of care in which the HMO contracts with independent private practice physicians or an association of such physicians, who provide services to HMO members and other patients in their private offices. Physicians are paid on a negotiated per capita rate, flat retainer fee, or negotiated fee-for-service basis. Most specialty physicians are reimbursed on a discounted fee-for-service basis. When fee-for-service is used, frequently a portion of the payment is withheld as a method of risk sharing. Sometimes, primary care physicians are at financial risk for referral to specialty care and hospital admission.

informed consent A patient's consent to undergo a proposed procedure based on the patient's knowledge of facts needed to choose whether or not to submit it after risks, benefits, alternatives, and consequences have been discussed and weighed.

injunction Court order commanding a person or entity to perform or to refrain from performing a certain act. Failure to obey an injunction may result in a citation of contempt of court and imprisonment until obedience is obtained.

Insurance services office (ISO) An organization that gathers and processes the statistics of most insurance companies and publishes rate manuals for most lines of insurance in the United States.

integrated delivery system (IDS) Combination of a full range of physician and other health services under one corporate entity.

interrogatories Written questions submitted to an opposing party to be answered before and in preparation for trial, the answers to which are signed and affirmed as true by the party in the suit.

invasion of privacy Violation of person's right to be free from unwarranted publicity and intrusions or the unauthorized dissemination of private information about the person, including the disclosure of a medical condition without legal justification or release, which could represent such a violation. It is a tort, for which civil liability damages are awarded to compensate for mental suffering and anguish suffered by the person whose privacy was violated.

joint and several liability Responsibility shared by a number of persons who are found to have contributed to a plaintiff's injury in which each or any one of those liable can be made to satisfy the whole loss to the plaintiff and must then sue the other liable parties for contribution to the payment.

joint venture Enterprise undertaking to carry out limited objectives, entered into by associates under circumstances in which all have an equal voice in directing the conduct of the enterprise. Each is the agent of the others; therefore the act of only one joint venturer is to be charged vicariously against the others. Elements of a joint enterprise include a contract; common purpose; community of interest; and equal right to voice accompanied by an equal right to control.

judgment Official decision of a court about the respective rights and claims of the parties to an action or suit litigated and submitted for determination.

jurisdiction Geographic or subject matter limits to power and authority of courts and other government agencies and officers.

leading case Case decision in a specific jurisdiction dealing with specific facts and circumstances that have decided the same issues involved in a later case. It is determinative of the same issues in subsequent cases unless distinctions from the leading case facts are established.

libel Written defamation by any type of communication or publication, including pictures.

line A general form of insurance, such as workers' compensation or medical malpractice liability.

losses An important insurance statistic profile.
- Losses paid: the losses paid on a body of policies. Calendar year losses paid (see *experience, Calendar year experience*) are the losses paid in a given period, for example, during 1999, on claims whenever occurred or reported but do not include loss adjustment expenses, which are separate. After a claim is paid, it is usually but not always closed. There are partial payments on claims that remain open. Indemnity payments are those made to claimants and do not include payments to defense attorneys (ALEs). Losses paid are indemnity payments only.
- Losses outstanding: losses that are unpaid and are represented by loss reserves.
  —Case reserves: *Case* is a claims department term for "claim" or "file." Technically, a claim number accompanies a case. When a claim is reported and set up, it gets a claim number and a "case estimate"; that is, the claims department estimates the final liability of the claim, that amount goes into reserve, and liability is set up for its ultimate cost. The total of such estimates minus any amount paid thereon becomes the losses outstanding reserve for known cases.
  —Losses incurred but not reported (IBNR): Some claims are not reported promptly; others are reported late because the injury takes a long time to manifest. In any event, provision must be made for such claims, often reported 10 or more years after the event or injury. IBNR reserves, particularly for medical malpractice liability, are substantial and often exceed the reserves for known cases. They are calculated by the actuary and are based on past patterns of claims emergence, trended to the future.
  —Loss adjustment expenses: see *expenses*.
- Losses incurred: the sum of losses paid and losses outstanding, with reserves for both case estimates and losses IBNR. The estimated ultimate cost of a body of claims.

malice The performance of a wrongful act without excuse, with apparent intent to inflict an injury. Under some circumstances of conduct, the law will infer malicious intent from the evidence of the defendant's actions.

malicious prosecution Lawsuit or countersuit seeking damages that have been caused to a defendant by a civil suit filed by a plaintiff in bad faith and without probable cause. Ordinarily the countersuit may not be brought until the initial suit has been found meritless.

malpractice Professional misconduct or failure to properly discharge professional duties by failing to meet the standard of care required of a professional.

managed care Any system that integrates the financing and delivery of appropriate medical care by means of (1) contracts with selected physicians and hospitals that furnish a comprehensive set of health care services to enrolled members, usually for a predetermined monthly premium; (2) utilization and quality controls that contracting providers agree to accept; (3) financial incentives for patients to use providers and facilities associated with the plan; and (4) assumption of some financial risk by physicians. Delivery system approach that brings together different services and technologies simultaneously to affect price, volume, quality, and accountability with the goal of providing cost-effective health care. It is a process, not an end state, depending on the competitive environment and state and federal rules.

managed indemnity insurance Combines fee-for-service coverage with efforts to control hospital admissions, through preadmission certification, concurrent review, second surgical opinion, and mandatory outpatient surgery.

market value See *investments*.

material Influential and necessary. Material facts or issues concern the substance of the matter in dispute as distinguished from form.

maturity See *investments*.

medical foundation Entity that purchases the business and clinical assets of a physician group or services independent physicians, providing all the business and administrative support services needed to support the practice. In certain circumstances this arrangement may represent the prohibited corporate practice of medicine, although a special exemption may be available for medical foundations that accept payment for physician services.

medical risk contract Federal Medicare contract with HMOs or CMPs that pays a prospective monthly capitation payment for each Medicare member in the plan.

Medicare Select Federal program designed to introduce Medicare beneficiaries to managed care systems through prospective payment health insurance.

minor A person who has not yet reached the age determined by law for transactional capacity, that is, a legally incompetent person. Minors generally cannot be held responsible for their contracts or other civil actions; thus minors ordinarily cannot consent to their own medical treatment. An exception exists for emancipated minors, defined as persons substantially independent from their parents, supporting themselves, married, or otherwise on their own, or mature minors, defined as persons who have demonstrated the capacity to make decisions that an adult would be expected to make. A statute also may provide exceptions to legal incapacity to allow minors authority to consent to treatment for drug abuse, venereal disease, birth control, or pregnancy.

misrepresentation Words or conduct amounting to an assertion not in accordance with the existing facts or circumstances. A person who has reasonable grounds for believing that the representation is true makes an "innocent misrepresentation." A "negligent misrepresentation" is made when a person has no reasonable grounds for believing that the representation is true, even if the speaker believes it to be true. A "fraudulent misrepresentation" is made by a person who is aware of the falsity of the representation that causes the other party to enter an arrangement or an agreement or to rely to a detriment on the false representation.

motion Request to a judge for an order or a ruling.

multiple option plan Insurance plan offered by employers, with options, such as an HMO, a PPO, and indemnity coverage. Employees choose coverage annually during an open enrollment period.

multispecialty group practice Independent physicians group that is organized to contract with a managed care plan to provide medical services to enrollees. The physicians are employed by the group practice.

negligence Failure to exercise the degree of diligence and care that a reasonably prudent person would be expected to exercise under the same or similar circumstances. Failure that proximately causes an injury is recognized as a basis for compensation owed to the injured party.

network-model HMO (mixed model) Provider arrangement that contracts with a number of independent practice associations or group practices to provide physician services to HMO members. It can be either an open or closed panel. Physicians work out of their own offices and may see non-HMO patients. Multiple provider arrangement consisting of group, staff, or IPA structures in combination. Sometimes a network model will contract with a number of small primary physician groups and will reimburse them on a capitation basis. These groups are then responsible for providing compensation to member physicians. In other cases the network-model HMO may become more integrated by contracting with primary care groups, specialty care groups, and hospitals to reduce utilization risk to primary care physician groups by spreading the risk to other provider groups. May be either closed or open panels.

no-pay claims Claims closed without indemnity payment. Also known as *closed without payment* (CWOP). There may be some loss adjustment expense paid.

occurrence See *coverage.*

open-end HMO Organized hybrid entity that allows its members to use physicians outside the plan in exchange for additional personal financial liability. It is unique among HMOs in that it allows members to use providers outside the HMO network without referral by gatekeepers. Patients who do so are charged an additional copayment, deductible, or both.

open panel Managed care plan that contracts with private physicians to deliver care in their own offices to plan members. The physicians also may provide services to patients outside the plan.

opinion of the court An appellate court's outline of a case, which states the factual findings and the law applied to the case. It also details the legal reasoning supporting the decision and any issues appealed as error while finally affirming, reversing, or remanding the case appealed.

ordinance A rule established by the authority of the state. Generally this is an enactment by the legislative branch of a municipal corporation, such as a city council or equivalent body.

outcome management Method that seeks to control and improve the quality of care and quality of medical outcomes through a continuous process.

outcome measurement A tool, used to assess a health system's performance, that measures the outcome of a given intervention (e.g., death rates for a given procedure or days needed for recovery).

parens patriae Description of the role of the state as the sovereign guardian of persons under the state's protection. It is the legal basis for the state's power to act to protect the health and welfare of persons who suffer from legal disabilities, such as minority or mental incapacity.

party A more general term than a legal person because it may refer to organizations, groups, and legal entities, such as corporations and partnerships.

peer review Evaluation of the quality and effectiveness of services performed by professionals who have training comparable to those being reviewed.

perjury Willful false testimony under oath and punishable as a crime.

physician hospital organization (PHO) Structures that includes group practice without walls, medical foundation, and integrated delivery system. Common IPA group practice arrangement in which hospitals and physicians organize for purposes of contracting with medical care organizations (MCOs). It is a legal entity formed and owned by one or more hospitals and physician groups to obtain payer contracts and to further mutual interests. The physicians maintain ownership of their practices while agreeing to accept managed care patients. It serves as a negotiating, contracting, and marketing unit. Typically provides for equal physician and hospital ownership and board representation. Includes management service organizations (MSOs), which are legal entities formed to provide administrative and practice management services to individual physicians or group practices.

point of service (POS) plan Combination of HMO and PPO features in which a plan enrollee can opt to use the defined managed care program or can go out-of-plan but pay the difference for nonplan benefits.

police power Authority granted to the state to restrain personal or property rights of persons within the state for the protection of public safety and health but with constitutional limitations.

practice guidelines A specific, professionally agreed-on recommendation for medical practice used within or among health care organizations in an attempt to standardize practice to achieve consistent quality outcomes. Practice guidelines may be instituted when triggered by specific clinical indicators.

practice standard Similar to a practice guideline, but it is stricter and requires specific actions to be taken.

preferred provider organization (PPO) Plan in which members receive a higher level of benefits at a lower cost when they choose physicians in the PPO network. Managed arrangements consist of a group of hospitals, physicians, and other providers who have contracts with an insurer, employer, third-party administrator, or other sponsoring group.

prepaid group practice Fixed, periodic payments made in advance by or on behalf of each plan member.

premium The money a policyholder pays for the policy.

- Written premiums: the sum of all the premiums for all the policies written for a defined period.
- Earned premium: premium representing the expired part of a policy. If a policy has already run for 4 months, then one third of its premium is "earned" and belongs to the insurer and two thirds is "unearned" and refundable to the policyholder if he or she cancels. A proper matching of premiums, losses, and expenses to determine profit includes earned premiums, losses incurred, and expenses incurred.
- Unearned premium: premium representing the unexpired part of a policy. Equals written premium minus earned premium. Can become a substantial item on the balance sheet of an insurer and is carried as a liability because it is theoretically refundable.

preponderance of evidence A level of persuasion required to award judgment in civil actions for damages. Usually a standard of better-than-equal evidence.

presumption An initial rational position of law, which can be challenged unless irrefutable by evidence presented in legal proceedings. An example is the presumption of transactional competence in adult persons.

prima facie case A complaint with supporting evidence that apparently supports all the necessary legal elements for a recognized cause of action if it is sufficient to produce a verdict or judgment for the plaintiff until overcome by evidence in defense of the case.

primary care physician (PCP) Physician who delivers and manages less specialised forms of health care, and is central to controlling costs and utilization.

privilege Exemption or immunity connected to a specific legal situation. For example, the physician-patient privilege is a rule of evidence by which communications made to a physician by a patient in the course of treatment may not be used as evidence in court. It is the patient's privilege to keep such information from disclosure; it is the physician's duty to resist attempts to compel disclosure. This privilege is conditional and usually subject to certain exceptions.

probable cause Evidence that would lead a reasonable person of ordinary intelligence to conclude that a cause of action is supportable in a civil lawsuit.

probate court Court having jurisdiction over wills and supervision of decedents' estates. In some states, probate courts also have jurisdiction over minors, including the appointment of guardians.

reasonable person Hypothetical person used as an objective standard against which a litigant's conduct can be judged. The reasonable person is the figurative standard of care. For example, a standard of care in medical practice could be established by the answer to the question, "What would a reasonably knowledgeable and skilled physician be expected to have done under the circumstances described?"

referral care specialists (RCS) Physicians who provide specialty service on request from primary care physicians.

referral pool Capitation set aside for referrals or inpatient medical services. If utilization targets are met at the end of the year, PCPs may share what is left in the pool.

regulation A rule or order prescribed for the management of specific activities subject to government control. Regulations can be rules or orders issued by executive authority or by an administrative agency of government.

release An agreement to relinquish a right or claim against another person or persons, usually exchanged for a payment or a promise, called *consideration*. A signed release agreement indicates that a claimed injury has been compensated. A release is distinguished from a covenant not to sue by the element of satisfaction of the claim.

res ipsa loquitur (Latin, "the thing speaks for itself.") A legal doctrine sometimes applied in a negligence action when the plaintiff has no direct evidence of negligence but the nature of the injury under the particular circumstances indicates to reasonable persons that such injuries do not occur in the absence of negligence. The doctrine is applicable to cases in which the defendant had exclusive control of what caused the harm to the plaintiff and the plaintiff could not have contributed to the injury. Use of the doctrine does not assure the plaintiff a judgment. After proof of the elements of res ipsa loquitur, the doctrine shifts to the defendant the burden to prove that conduct was reasonable and appropriate or that other mechanisms caused the plaintiff's injury.

rescind To nullify a contract by declaring it void, or never to have existed. Rescission is distinguished from cancellation or termination, which release the parties to a contract from any additional or ongoing responsibilities, even if the contract terms are not fulfilled.

reserve A liability on the balance sheet for future payments of the insurer (see *losses.*) There are reserves for unearned premiums, for losses and loss expenses unpaid, and for other expenses unpaid. The solvency of a company can be determined only after all reserves and other liabilities have been taken into account.

resource-based relative value scale (RBRVS) Method to redistribute physician payments to more adequately encourage the use of primary care physician services.

respondeat superior (Latin, "let the master answer.") A legal doctrine that imposes vicarious liability on the employer for breaches of duties by employees. The duty is the employer's and is imposed if the employer engages others to perform tasks on the employer's behalf, which is work within the scope of employment. For example, a hospital is liable for the negligent acts of a nurse it employs if the acts occurred while the nurse was performing tasks within a nursing job description.

slander Spoken defamation about one person in the presence of another person that harms the slandered person's income, reputation, or character.

speciality HMOs Behavioral health, prescription drugs, and dental services, also known as *carve-outs or single-service entities.*

staff-model HMO Organized system of care in which physicians are salaried employees of the HMO and provide services only to HMO members. Providers are employees of the plan, not outside contractors, and service is provided in plan-owned and plan-operated offices. Tightest control over the practice pattern of physicians.

standard of care The measure of assessment applied to a defendant's conduct for liability determination, comparing what occurred with what an ordinary, reasonable, and prudent person would have done or not done under similar circumstances.

stare decisis (Latin, "let the decision stand.") The principle of case law that requires courts to apply the approach and rationale of previously decided cases to subsequent cases involving similar facts and legal questions. When a point of law has been settled by decision, it forms a precedent that is binding. Later decisions may distinguish their facts or circumstances to come to different results but otherwise must adhere to the rule of precedent. On rare occasion, precedent is rejected, and a new ruling case decision is adopted. Such a case is called a *landmark case.*

statute A written law enacted by the legislature to achieve a specified legislative objective. Statutes apply legislative prescriptions to some of the same factual situations dealt with by case law and administrative law. Generally, former case law governing the situation is no longer operative in situations in which a subsequent statute is applicable.

statute of limitations Laws that specify the permissible time interval between an occurrence giving rise to a civil cause of action and the filing of the lawsuit. Failure to file suit within the prescribed time is an affirmative defense. These time limits for filing suit vary among the states, even for similar legal actions. Most statutes of limitation have exceptions that stop the time from elapsing. Stopping the time is called *tolling the* *statute.* In malpractice actions the time allowed for bringing suit may not begin to run until the party claiming injury first discovers or should reasonably have discovered the injury. Fraudulent concealment of an injury by the defendant tolls the statute.

statutory accounting The system under which insurance companies must report to the state. Unlike generally accepted accounting principles (GAAP) under statutory accounting, an insurer ordinarily may not "discount" its reserves to take into account the investment income they will earn before claims are paid out, and may not be given credit for its "equity" in the unearned premium reserve. This is the prepaid acquisition expense or commission paid to brokers. The unearned premium reserve, which is a liability, may not be reduced to reflect this prepaid expense.

stipulation Acknowledgment by a party of a specific fact or circumstance that will not be disputed in a case. One party may stipulate that a witness is qualified to testify or that a physician had been an employee of a facility at the time of disputed care. Stipulations save time and expense by removing certain issues from trial proceedings.

stop-loss arrangements A type of insurance that provides protection from claims that are greater than a specific dollar amount per covered person. There are many different types of stop-loss arrangements, including:

- Aggregate stop-loss insurance: reimbursement for claims that exceed an aggregate limit within a specified time period. The limit is usually set at a percentage of expected claims and is expressed as a monthly amount multiplied by the number of insureds.
- Specific stop-loss insurance: protection against large individual claims by limiting the buyer's liability for any one insured person during a specified time. The specific stop-loss limit usually is expressed as a dollar amount.

strict liability Liability without the need to prove a negligent act or failure, one form of which is enterprise liability. The proof of damages sustained by the plaintiff in connection with the situation and the involvement of the defendant support the finding of strict liability. Examples could be management by the defendant of inherently dangerous activities, placing a defective and dangerous product into commerce, or assembling hazardous substances.

subpoena A court order requiring a person to appear in court to give testimony or be punished for not appearing.

subpoena duces tecum Subpoena that requires a person to personally present to the court a specified document or property possessed or under the person's control.

tort Civil wrong in which a person has breached a legal duty with harm caused to another. To establish liability for a tort, an injured party must establish that a legal duty was owed to the plaintiff by the defendant, that the defendant breached that duty, and that the plaintiff suffered damage caused by the breach. Torts can be negligent or intentional.

unallocated loss expense (ULE) See *expenses.*

underwriting profit (loss) The amount left over after subtracting from earned insurance premiums in a period the sum of losses and loss expenses incurred in the same period. Investment income is not taken into account; when it is, the result is called *operating profit* or *loss.*

unearned premiums See *premium.*

unrealized capital gains See *investments.*

vicarious liability Derivative responsibility for an agent's or employee's failures based on the defendant's employer-employee or principal-agent relationship. The responsibility is imposed because the ability to supervise, direct, and control hazardous conduct of employees lies with the employer or principal.

waiver Intentional and voluntary agreement to forgo a known claim or right. For example, a patient could waive the privilege of confidential communication, or a defendant could waive the right to challenge certain testimony. Sometimes a right may be unintentionally waived if it is not exercised in time. For example, the right to make or amend allegations and claims not disclosed in pretrial discovery and depositions may be considered waived by the court for failure to assert them in a timely manner.

wanton act Grossly negligent, malicious, or reckless conduct that implies a disregard for the consequences or for the rights or safety of others.

warranty Express or implied commitment or promise undertaken as part of a contract but aside from the central contract purpose. It is to be distinguished from a representation. A warranty is given contemporaneously with the contract agreement as part of the contract. A representation precedes and may be seen as an inducement to enter the contract. For example, a representation would be the disclosed indication for surgery; a warranty would be a promise of a specific result from the procedure.

wrap-around coverage HMO plan that, in some states, was prevented by state law from taking on financial risk for out-of-plan care and therefore joined with insurers to cover the out-of-plan portion of care. Such programs led to development of POS plans.

Case index

Subject index